D1365196

# Magill's Cinema Annual 2002

# Magill's Cinema Annual 2002

## 21st Edition
## A Survey of the Films of 2001

Christine Tomassini, Editor

Carol Schwartz, Contributing Editor

A VideoHound® Reference

GALE®

THOMSON
GALE

Detroit • New York • San Diego • San Francisco • Cleveland • New Haven, Conn. • Waterville, Maine • London • Munich

**THOMSON**

**GALE**

## Magill's Cinema Annual 2002

**Project Editor**
Christine Tomassini

**Editorial**
Carol Schwartz

**Editorial Support Services**
Wayne Fong

**Manufacturing**
Evi Seoud
Rhonda Williams

**Product Design**
Tracey Rowens

ISBN 1-55862-458-9
ISSN: 0739-2141

Printed in the United States of America
10 9 8 7 6 5 4 3 2 1

# Table of Contents

# Preface

*Magill's Cinema Annual 2002* continues the fine film reference tradition that defines the VideoHound series of entertainment industry products published by Gale. The twenty-first annual volume in a series that developed from the 21-volume core set, *Magill's Survey of Cinema*, the *Annual* was formerly published by Salem Press. Gale's eighth volume, as with the previous Salem volumes, contains essay-reviews of significant domestic and foreign films released in the United States during the preceding year.

The *Magill's* editorial staff at Gale, comprising the VideoHound team and a host of *Magill's* contributors, continues to provide the enhancements that were added to the *Annual* when Gale acquired the line. These features include:

- More essay-length reviews of significant films released during the year
- Obituaries and book review sections
- Trivia and "fun facts" about the reviewed movies, their stars, the crew, and production
- Quotes and dialogue "soundbites" from reviewed movies, or from stars and crew about the film
- More complete awards and nominations listings, including the American Academy Awards®, Golden Globe, New York Critics Awards, Los Angeles Film Critics Awards, and others (see the User's Guide for more information on awards coverage)
- Box office grosses, including year-end and other significant totals
- Publicity taglines featured in film reviews and advertisements

In addition to these elements, the *Magill's Cinema Annual 2002* still features:

- An obituaries section profiling major contributors to the film industry who died in 2001
- An annotated list of selected film books published in 2001
- Nine indexes: Directors, Screenwriters, Cinematographers, Editors, Art Directors, Music Directors, Performers, Subject, and Title (now cumulative)

## Compilation Methods

The *Magill's* editorial staff reviews a variety of entertainment industry publications, including trade magazines and newspapers, as well as online sources, on a daily and weekly basis to select significant films for review in *Magill's Cinema Annual*. *Magill's* staff and other contributing reviewers, including film scholars and university faculty, write the reviews included in the *Annual*.

### *Magill's Cinema Annual*: A VideoHound Reference

The *Magill's Survey of Cinema* series, now supplemented by the *Annual*, is the recipient of the Reference Book of the Year Award in Fine Arts by the American Library Association.

Gale, an award-winning publisher of reference products, is proud to offer *Magill's Cinema Annual* as part of its popular VideoHound(R) product line, which includes *VideoHound's Golden Movie Retriever, VideoHound's DVD Guide, and The Video Source Book*. Other Gale film-related products include the *St. James Film Directors Encyclopedia, The St. James Women Filmmakers Encyclopedia* and the *Contemporary Theatre, Film, and Television* series.

## Acknowledgments

Thank you to Judy Hartman, GGS Information Services, for her typesetting expertise, and Wayne Fong for his invaluable technical assistance. The *VideoHound* staff is thanked for its contributions to this project, especially Carol Schwartz for her generosity, hard work, and goodwill, as well as Peter Gareffa for his guidance and direction. Also, the following producers, distributors, and publicists were gracious enough to provide screeners and other materials that helped in the writing of some of the reviews in this edition: Marissa Manne at Sony Pictures Classics; Rebecca Conget and Ron Ramsland of New Yorker Films; Gabriele Carotti at Kino International; Elena Zilberman at Miramax; Jason Leaf at Avatar Films; the Press Office of the New York Film Festival; Tiffany Blair at First Look Media; Leonard Farlinger at New Real Films; Cheryl-Lee Fast at Massey Productions Ltd.; Melanie Hartley at Film Tonic; Damon D'Oliveira at Conquering Lion Pictures; Fidelma McGinn at the Irish Reels Festival; and the Media Offices at Alliance Atlantis, the Seattle International Film Festival, and the Vancouver International Film Festival.

# The Year in Film:
# An Introduction

In the romantic comedy *Someone Like You,* a real estate agent trying to sell an apartment to prospects Greg Kinnear and Ashley Judd comments that from the balcony you could see the twin towers of the World Trade Center. An innocuous line until the momentous events of September 11, 2001, gave it an entirely different meaning. Hollywood was as stunned by the tragedy as anyone else and soon rallied with tributes and telethons to show solidarity and support.

And on the business side of showbiz, there were some delicate decisions to be made. There was no such thing as a flippant remark about airport security, bombs, wars, and terrorists. Films that dealt with such topics, such as Arnold Schwarzenegger's action-drama *Collateral Damage* or the Tim Allen comedy *Big Trouble,* had their release dates postponed while other films that featured the World Trade Center in some fashion were held back for re-tooling. Neither studios nor directors were certain how audiences would react to the sight of the towers still standing on the New York skyline in previously filmed features. (In truth, most found that audiences applauded even the briefest glimpse of the monuments.)

Projects in pre-production with terrorist storylines were canceled and it was a guess as to what America would be in the mood to see. The boxoffice champ the weekends after the disaster turned out to be the inner-city baseball dramedy *Hardball,* starring Keanu Reeves. Some studios took the chance that moviegoers would be in the mood for heroics—so the release date of *Behind Enemy Lines,* a rescue mission military actioner set in Bosnia, was actually pushed up. The film featured Owen Wilson as a pilot shot down behind enemy lines and Gene Hackman as the commander bent on getting him home. It turned out to be standard fare that was neither a boxoffice disaster nor a hit.

Then there was the case of *Black Hawk Down.* Director Ridley Scott ended the year with a horrific re-telling of the true story of American troops caught up in the civil war of Mogadishu, Somalia, in 1993, a seemingly simple assignment that turned into terror and death. This film was also

pushed up from its 2002 release to qualify for Oscar® consideration, and while the film found considerable critical acclaim, it failed to win a Best Picture nomination, though it did garner Scott a nomination for Best Director.

But how did the movie world start out in 2001? Well, the talk in Hollywood was one word—"strike." A word that struck fear into the hearts and wallets of studio heads and caused them to rush into production scores of films with or without adequate scripts, directors, or appropriate stars. And just who was striking? Well, as it turned out, no one. The Writers Guild of America, the Screen Actors Guild, and the AFTRA actors' guild all went past their contract expiration dates but managed to settle with the bosses before the industry collapsed. And after all that *agita* just what happened? Well, the change in Hollywood films that Joe and Jane Moviegoer saw this year hardly seemed different from any other time. Studios had stockpiled so much product that they really didn't know what to do with it all. So they shuffled their schedules and moved expected releases into 2002 instead. With all its chaos, the boxoffice still managed a record-breaking $8.35 billion in domestic ticket sales.

Ridley Scott may have ended the year with *Black Hawk Down* but he started it with the long-anticipated sequel to the 1991 chiller *The Silence of the Lambs.* While that film was blessed by the Oscars, the sequel had no such distinction. Both director Jonathan Demme and actress Jodie Foster turned down the chance to reprise their roles, although Anthony Hopkins returned as everyone's favorite cannibal. Julianne Moore stepped into the character of FBI agent Clarice Starling, but *Hannibal* turned out to be both as gruesome (not unexpected) and problematic as Thomas Harris' book. While the film was no great critical success, it isn't stopping Hopkins from reprising the role of Hannibal Lecter yet again—this time in 2002's *Red Dragon,* which was previously filmed as *Manhunter* (1986).

2001 provided some spring charm with the adaptation of Brit Helen Fielding's novel about life for London "singletons" in *Bridget Jones's Diary.* Petite Texan Renee Zellweger caused howls from the British press when she was chosen for the title role but, with the help of a dialogue coach and some 20 pounds, Zellweger embodied the spirit of the hapless, somewhat plump, romantic. Fellow actors also noticed Zellweger's performance and awarded her a Best Actress Academy Award nomination for her efforts.

Then there was *A. I.* A 20-year unrealized dream of eccentric director Stanley Kubrick, who could never find a precise way to put his vision on the screen before his death, the project became a torch passed to fellow director Steven Spielberg. Except for their love of movies, could any two men's film styles have been more different? The bare bones of the story are actually quite simple—you've got a robot boy who wants to be human (yeah, yeah, it's sci-fi Pinocchio). Kubrick hoped technology would have advanced enough to allow him to use an actual robot for the lead role while Spielberg simply went with the preternatural acting gifts of Haley Joel Osment. The result was an uncomfortable mixture of styles—part Kubrick unease/part Spielberg hope—that left any number of critics and viewers baffled, frustrated, intrigued, and awed. A boxoffice disappointment, *A. I.* could well turn out to be a film that is transformed into a cult curiosity and that undergoes a critical re-evaluation in the future.

*Memento,* on the other hand, was the work of director Christopher Nolan, whose only previous feature was 1998's *Following.* He loosely based his script on a story told him by his brother Jonathan while the two were on a road trip. And what a "trip" the film turned out to be. Its hero, Leonard (Guy Pearce, both vulnerable and irritating), suffers from short-term memory lost—the result of a vicious attack that also caused the death of his wife. Leonard seeks his wife's killer but the only way he can "remember" his immediate past is by tattooing bits of information on his body and through photographs. The film is a continuous loop of scenes told from various perspectives, which all must be put together by the viewer. You actually have to pay attention while watching the movie in order to figure out what's going on. *Memento* was one of the year's few films that was well worth the effort of watching more than once.

The summer blockbuster season made its appearance with the much-hyped Michael Bay–directed *Pearl Harbor.* A long and egregious retelling of the events of December 7, 1941, Bay had the action chops but forgot about plot and character development, which left actors Ben Affleck, Josh Hartnett, and Kate Beckinsale floundering in a clichéd romantic triangle. Summer also witnessed sequelitis with *American Pie 2, Rush Hour 2, Dr. Dolittle 2, Scary Movie 2, Jurassic Park 3, The Mummy Returns,* and Tim Burton's "re-imagined" *Planet of the Apes.* The visuals and makeup may have improved since the 1968 original but the same can't be said of the director's interpretation, which featured astronaut Mark Wahlberg (not in a loin cloth) and Helena Bonham Carter as a very pretty chimp. Tim Roth played the bad monkey and the ending had moviegoers shaking their heads and going, "Huh?!"

Much more appealing to both adults and children alike was the quip-filled animated feature *Shrek,* a loose adaptation of the children's book by William Steig. The title character was a green-skinned, grumpy ogre (voiced by Mike Myers, in a Scottish brogue) who finds his swamp overrun by fairy types (a DreamWorks dig at Disney studios). To get rid of these pests, he must rescue a princess (Cameron Diaz) from a tower guarded by a dragon; Shrek must also endure the accompaniment of his sidekick, a fast-talking donkey (Eddie Murphy in a perfect role). This "happily ever after" turns out to have some unexpected surprises.

Children could also delight in the visual splendor and sweetness of the latest Pixar release, *Monsters, Inc.* It seems monsters have a reason for hiding in children's closets and scaring them at bedtime and this story tells us why, along with showing the buddy relationship of monsters Sully (voiced by John Goodman) and Mike (Billy Crystal), and the havoc caused in their monster world by human toddler Boo. The film was geared to the youngest crowd but parents could sit through repeated viewings without too much suffering.

Another children's release that parents could also easily endure was the adventure of *Spy Kids.* This action comedy by Robert Rodriguez (a director better known for such adult fare as *Desperado* and *From Dusk Till Dawn*) finds a squabbling brother/sister duo discovering their boring parents are actually retired spies who now need rescuing. And these pint-sized adventurers must learn to work together in order to do so. (Hey, no one said that you can't sneak in a moral lesson now and again.) Rodriguez immediately began filming a sequel to his successful film, which is due for release in 2002.

Disney wasn't silent during the year either. *Atlantis: The Lost Empire,* an old-fashioned animated adventure, proved to be a big screen disappointment that will, no doubt, be much more suited to video. Director Garry Marshall did a Cinderella transformation geared towards the tweenie set in the popular *The Princess Diaries,* a film based on the successful young adult fiction series by Meg Cabot. The film told the story of an awkward teenaged girl (the charming Anne Hathaway) who discovers that she is actually the heir to a European kingdom. Royal Grandmama (a regal Julie Andrews) helps transform the dork into princess material.

Lest we forget the part that gossip plays in Hollywood, witness the saga of Tom Cruise and Nicole Kidman. Their 10-year marriage came to an abrupt end early in the year amidst much speculation. Kidman could certainly find some solace in the critical acclaim that followed her acting success in both *Moulin Rouge* and *The Others* (executive-produced by Cruise). The former was an extravagant musical from fellow Aussie Baz Luhrmann (of *Strictly Ballroom* and *William Shakespeare's Romeo + Juliet*) that featured Kidman as a singing/dancing courtesan, the star of the Parisian Moulin Rouge, who falls in love with a penniless writer played by

Ewan McGregor. Both did their own vocals, which consisted of contemporary pop tunes in a turn-of-the-century setting. Audacious, if nothing else, the film earned Kidman many critical accolades, including an Academy Award nomination.

*The Others* turned out to be an old-fashioned ghost story much more popular with the public than the critics. Kidman played a fanatically religious, World War II–era widow who lived with her children in a creepy mansion isolated on an island off the British coast. The children "see" things but the story takes some unexpected twists. Alejandro Amenabar, the director of *The Others*, was also the director of the 1997 Spanish thriller *Open Your Eyes*, the remake of which gave Tom Cruise his one 2001 acting role. Cameron Crowe's re-titled *Vanilla Sky* may have offered some stretching of Cruise's acting muscles, but it left the public either confused or indifferent. Also co-starring in the film was the actor's new romantic interest Penelope Cruz, who re-played her role from the Spanish film and who didn't have any better luck winning over the American public than she had in 2000.

Also finding critical success after much denigration of her acting talents was Halle Berry. Berry displayed her beauty (and her breasts) in the over-the-top actioner *Swordfish* in a prototypical girlfriend role opposite John Travolta. But atypical was the chancy part of a poor, angry single mother in director Marc Forster's *Monster's Ball*. Opposite co-star Billy Bob Thornton, Berry bared soul as well as body in a Southern Gothic saga of hate and redemption. Berry received a nod from Oscar for this role and, for the first time since 1972, was joined by fellow black actors Will Smith and Denzel Washington in receiving Academy notice: Smith for the title role in Michael Mann's boxing bio *Ali* and Washington for his role as a corrupt L.A. cop in the clichéd *Training Day*. The latter film had only Washington to recommend it, although the Oscars felt differently since co-star Ethan Hawke received a Best Supporting Actor nomination as well.

Also up once again for a Best Actor Oscar was Russell Crowe. After last year's win for *Gladiator*, the actor returned in director Ron Howard's *A Beautiful Mind*, a biopic based on the life of mathematical genius and Nobel Prize winner John Forbes Nash Jr., who was lost in the delusions of paranoid schizophrenia for some 30 years. The film drew the usual cavils for playing loose with the "truth," although both Nash and his wife, Alicia, approved the drama. The film also proved to be a personal success for Jennifer Connelly, who played Alicia. Not averse to taking risks (witness 2000's *Requiem for a Dream*), the actress has also suffered from the shortsighted Hollywood "pretty girl" syndrome in previous roles. Connelly received a Best Actress nomination for her efforts after already winning accolades from the British Academy of Film and Television Arts, the Broadcast Film Critics Association, and the Golden Globes.

Perennial Oscar nominee Judi Dench was also back—this time for the title role in *Iris*, another biographical drama, which followed the life of British writer Iris Murdoch, who succumbed to the ravages of Alzheimer's. She shared the role with Kate Winslet (who was nominated for Best Supporting Actress), who played the younger version of the writer. Jim Broadbent (who was also nominated) played Murdoch's caring spouse, a role for which he received earlier attention from the Golden Globes, the National Board of Review, and the Los Angeles Film Critics Association. By the way, Broadbent was also notable as the theatrical manager in *Moulin Rouge*.

Sissy Spacek also made a welcome return to the screen in Todd Field's *In the Bedroom*. This drama turned on the murder of the son (Nick Stahl) of a long-married New England couple played by Spacek and Tom Wilkinson. Their mourning brings out cracks in their relationship that have long been plastered over and takes some unexpected turns towards revenge. Both Wilkinson and co-star Marisa Tomei are well worth watching, and received nominations for their efforts, but it is Spacek who carries the emotional burden, and who was rewarded not only by an Academy Award nomination but by the Broadcast Film Critics, the Golden Globes, and both the Los Angeles and New York Film Critics Associations.

*Magill's* reviewers also saw a number of foreign-made films—some of which turned out to be timely because of the September 11th tragedy. Iranian films were once again prolific, including *Baran* and *Djomeh*, which dealt with the plight of Afghani refugees, and *The Circle*, *The Day I Became a Woman*, and *Khandahar*, all of which focused on the harshness of life for women. *Amores Perros*, from Mexico, also looked at life's tragedies in a series of interconnected plots. Charlotte Rampling gave a mesmerizing performance in the French film *Under the Sun*, about a woman who can't come to grip with her husband's death. Italy's *Ignorant Fairies* also dealt with widowhood and the discovery of a husband's secret life, while *Bread and Tulips* dealt with marriage, but in this case, a neglected wife takes an eventful journey into finding herself. Canada supplied the multi-award-winning *Atanarjuat, the Fast Runner*, the first Inuktikut language feature from the country's far north. Britain's *Sexy Beast* offers the ultimate criminal in Ben Kingsley terrifying psychopath while the Australian *Chopper* is a true-life tale of an unrepentant ex-con played with charisma by Eric Bana.

Not everything was doom and gloom on the screen—there were the disparate lighthearted delights of *Amelie* and *Ocean's Eleven*. *Amelie* was a French romantic comedy by Jean-Pierre Jeunet, with the title gamine winningly played by Audrey Tatou (who does remind one of the film charmers played by Audrey Hepburn). After his award-winning direction of both *Traffic* and *Erin Brockovich* in 2000, Steven Soderbergh turned to a remake of the Frank Sinatra/Rat

Pack heist comedy of 1960 that kept little but the setting of the original flick. Pal George Clooney (who starred in Soderbergh's *Out of Sight*) gathered together a dream cast, which included Brad Pitt, Matt Damon, Don Cheadle, Andy Garcia, Carl Reiner, Elliot Gould, and Julia Roberts, for a twisty Vegas romp.

Pitt and Roberts were paired earlier in the year in the unsuccessful *The Mexican,* a part romance, part road trip, part crime caper that featured James Gandolfini as a gay hit man. (He actually did the best job with his role). A busy boy, Pitt was also featured in the Guy Ritchie–directed ensemble *Snatch* as an unintelligible Irish gypsy boxer and as the spy protégé of Robert Redford in the fall release, *Spy Game.* Redford also starred in a second film, the unsuccessful military prison drama, *The Last Castle* (along with James Gandolfini, who played the blowhard prison warden).

But the busiest actors had to be Cate Blanchett, Gene Hackman, and Josh Hartnett. All three appeared in five releases during the year. Still a newcomer, Hartnett co-starred with varying success in *Black Hawk Down, Pearl Harbor,* a contemporary teen version of Shakespeare's "Othello" called *O,* the long-delayed and disastrous *Town & Country,* and the little British import comedy *Blow Dry.* Besides his role in *Behind Enemy Lines,* veteran actor Hackman made a brief appearance in *The Mexican,* co-starred in the comedy *Heartbreakers* and David Mamet's crime drama *Heist,* and finished up the year with Wes Anderson's *The Royal Tenenbaums.* Hackman starred opposite Anjelica Huston, Ben Stiller, Gwyneth Paltrow, and Owen Wilson as the would-be patriarch in a fractured family saga.

Then there's Cate. The Aussie actress took the title role in the limited release *Charlotte Gray,* as well as roles in *The Man Who Cried, Bandits, The Shipping News,* and in one of 2001's year-end blockbusters, *The Lord of the Rings: The Fellowship of the Ring* as fairy queen Galandriel. New Zealand director Peter Jackson simultaneously filmed three pictures that cover British author J.R.R. Tolkien's fantasy *The Lord of the Rings.* Because the novels have supporters who rival any *Star Wars* adherents in their fanaticism, Jackson had the delicate task of visualizing Tolkien's realm of Middle Earth and all its denizens and making film(s) that would please not only *Rings* fans but those who didn't know a Hobbit from a hole in the ground. Although the large cast all do fine jobs with their respective roles, mention must be made of Ian McKellen, who brings a particular gravity and grace to his role of Gandalf the wizard. Parts 2 and 3 of the quest are expected to be released in 2002 and 2003.

First out of the gate as a special effects blockbuster was also the first of potentially many films drawn from the young adult books by J.K. Rowling: *Harry Potter and the Sorcerer's Stone.* Directed by American Chris Columbus, the British cast featured newcomer Daniel Radcliffe in the role of the boy wizard and such British stalwarts as Richard Harris, Maggie Smith, Alan Rickman, Zoe Wanamaker, Ian Hart, and Robbie Coltrane as Harry's teachers and advisers. Rowling anticipates seven books in her series and, with the success of the first film, it is not unlikely that a potential screen franchise has also been established. Although one wonders what will happen as the youthful cast ages more rapidly than the characters in the books do. (The second book in the series is currently being filmed for release in 2002.)

Last but not least was the more decidedly adult delights offered by 76-year-old master director Robert Altman's *Gosford Park.* Set in the 1930s in the British countryside, it is part social satire and part country house murder mystery, which also looks at the class distinctions between upstairs and downstairs. The large cast featured Helen Mirren, Eileen Atkins, Kristin Scott Thomas, Alan Bates, Derek Jacobi, Michael Gambon, Clive Owen, Richard Grant, James Wilby, Jeremy Northam, Emily Watson, Maggie Smith, and Stephen Fry, with Bob Balaban and Ryan Phillippe as the American interlopers. The film received Best Picture and Best Director Oscar nominations as well as Best Supporting Actress noms for both Mirren and Smith. Altman earlier won awards from the Golden Globes, the National Society of Film Critics, and the New York Film Critics Association.

2001 also saw the deaths of some beloved and respected performers, both in front of and behind the scenes. These included the larger-than-life Anthony Quinn, nervous everyman Jack Lemmon, suave Jean-Pierre Aumont, elegant Nigel Hawthorne, sixties heartthrob Troy Donahue, as well as noir femme fatale Jane Greer, raspy-voiced Eileen Heckart, woman-next-door Dorothy McGuire, gracious star Ann Sothern, and Queen of the Cowgirls Dale Evans. Cinematographers Henri Alekan, Sacha Vierny, Ralf D. Bode, John A. Alonzo, and Piotr Sobocinski, writers Sy Gomberg and Anthony Shaffer, legendary film critic Pauline Kael, directors Budd Boetticher and Herbert Ross, director/producers Roy Boulting, Howard W. Koch, and Jack Haley Jr., and A.I.P. co-founder Samuel Z. Arkoff are also among those profiled in the Obituaries section, located in the back of this book.

As the screen fades upon another year of moviemaking, the *Magill's* staff looks forward to preparing the 2003 *Annual.* We invite your comments. Please direct all questions and suggestions to:

Christine Tomassini
Editor, *Magill's Cinema Annual*
Gale
27500 Drake Rd.
Farmington Hills, MI 48331-3535

Phone: 248-699-4253
Toll-free: 800-347-GALE
Fax: 248-699-8068

# Contributing Reviewers

Michael Adams
*Graduate School, City University of New York*

Vivek Adarkar
*Long Island University*

Michael Betzold
*Freelance Reviewer*

Thomas Block
*Freelance Reviewer*

David L. Boxerbaum
*Freelance Reviewer*

Beverley Bare Buehrer
*Freelance Reviewer*

Peter N. Chumo II
*Freelance Reviewer*

Beth Fhaner
*Freelance Reviewer*

Jill Hamilton
*Freelance Reviewer*

Patty-Lynne Herlevi
*Freelance Reviewer*

Eric Monder
*Freelance Reviewer*

James M. Welsh
*Salisbury State University*

Hilary White
*Freelance Reviewer*

# User's Guide

## Alphabetization

Film titles and reviews are arranged on a word-by-word basis, including articles and prepositions. English leading articles (A, An, The) are ignored, as are foreign leading articles (El, Il, La, Las, Le, Les, Los). Other considerations:

Acronyms appear alphabetically as if regular words.

Common abbreviations in titles file as if they are spelled out, so *Mr. Death* will be found as if it was spelled *Mister Death*.

Proper names in titles are alphabetized beginning with the individual's first name, for instance, *Gloria* will be found under "G."

Titles with numbers, for instance, *200 Cigarettes*, are alphabetized as if the numbers were spelled out, in this case, "Two-Hundred." When numeric titles gather in close proximity to each other, the titles will be arranged in a low-to-high numeric sequence.

## Special Sections

*List of Awards.* An annual list of awards bestowed upon the year's films by the following associations: Academy of Motion Picture Arts and Sciences, Directors Guild of America Award, Golden Globe Awards, Los Angeles Film Critics Awards, National Board of Review Awards, National Society of Film Critics Awards, New York Film Critics Awards, the Screen Actors Guild Awards, and the Writer's Guild Awards.

*Obituaries.* Profiles major contributors to the film industry who died in 2001.

*Selected Film Books of 2001.* An annotated list of selected film books published in 2001.

## Indexes

Film titles and artists are arranged into nine indexes, allowing the reader to effectively approach a film from any one of several directions, including not only its credits but its subject matter.

*Directors, Screenwriters, Cinematographers, Editors, Art Directors, Music Directors,* and *Performers* indexes are arranged according to artists appearing in this volume, followed by a list of the films on which they worked.

*Subject Index.* Films may be categorized under several of the subject terms arranged alphabetically in this section.

*Title Index.* The title index is a cumulative alphabetical list of films covered in the twenty-one volumes of the *Magill's Cinema Annual,* including the 300 films covered in this volume. Films reviewed in past volumes are cited with the year in which the film was originally released; films reviewed in this volume are cited with the film title in bold with a bolded Arabic numeral indicating the page number on which the review begins. Original and alternate titles are cross-referenced to the American release title in the Title Index. Titles of retrospective films are followed by the year, in brackets, of their original release.

## Sample Review

Each *Magill's* review contains up to sixteen items of information. A fictionalized composite sample review containing all the elements of information that may be included in a full-length review follows the outline below. The circled number preceding each element in the sample review designates an item of information that is explained in the outline on the next page.

(1) **Title:** Film title as it was released in the United States.

(2) **Foreign or alternate title (s):** The film's original title or titles as released outside the United States, or alternate film title or titles. Foreign and alternate titles also appear in the Title Index to facilitate user access.

(3) **Taglines:** Up to ten publicity taglines for the film from advertisements or reviews.

(4) **Box office information:** Year-end or other box office domestic revenues for the film.

(5) **Film review:** A signed review of the film, including an analytic overview of the film and its critical reception.

(6) **Reviewer byline:** The name of the reviewer who wrote the full-length review. A complete list of this volume's contributors appears in the "Contributings Reviewers" section which follows the Introduction.

(7) **Principal characters:** Listings of the film's principal characters and the names of the actors who play them in the film.

(8) **Country of origin:** The film's country or countries of origin.

(9) **Release date:** The year of the film's first general release.

(10) **Production information:** This section typically includes the name(s) of the film's producer(s), production company, and distributor; director(s); screenwriter(s); cinematographer(s) (if the film is animated, this will be replaced with Animation or Animation direction, or it will not be listed); editor(s); art director(s); production designer(s); music composer(s); and other credits such as visual effects, sound, costume design, and song(s) and songwriter(s).

(11) **MPAA rating:** The film's rating by the Motion Picture Association of America. If there is no rating given, the line will read, "Unrated."

(12) **Running time:** The film's running time in minutes.

(13) **Reviews:** A list of citations of major newspaper and journal reviews of the film, including publication title, date of review, and page number.

(14) **Film quotes:** Memorable dialogue directly from the film, attributed to the character who spoke it, or comment from cast or crew members or reviewers about the film.

(15) **Film trivia:** Interesting tidbits about the film, its cast, or production crew.

(16) **Awards information:** Awards won by the film, followed by category and name of winning cast or crew member. Listings of the film's nominations follow the wins on a separate line for each award. Awards are arranged alphabetically. Information is listed for films that won or were nominated for the following awards: American Academy Awards®, British Academy of Film and Television Arts, Directors Guild of America, Golden Globe, Los Angeles Critics Association Awards, National Board of Review Awards, National Society of Film Critics Awards, New York Critics Awards, Writers Guild of America, and others.

# ① The Gump Diaries
# ② (Los Diarios del Gump)

③ *Love means never having to say you're stupid.*
—Movie tagline

 **Box Office:** $10 million
④

⑤ In writer/director Robert Zemeckis' *Back to the Future* trilogy (1985, 1989, 1990), Marty McFly (Michael J. Fox) and his scientist sidekick Doc Brown (Christopher Lloyd) journey backward and forward in time, attempting to smooth over some rough spots in their personal histories in order to remain true to their individual destinies. Throughout their time-travel adventures, Doc Brown insists that neither he nor Marty influence any major historical events, believing that to do so would result in catastrophic changes in humankind's ultimate destiny. By the end of the trilogy, however, Doc Brown has revised his thinking and tells marty that, "Your future hasn't been written yet. No one's has. Your future is whatever you make it. So make it a good one."

In *Forrest Gump,* Zemeckis once again explores the theme of personal destiny and how an individual's life affects and is affected by his historical time period. This time, however, Zemeckis and screenwriter Eric Roth chronicle the life af a character who does nothing but meddle in the historical events of his time without even trying to do so. By the film's conclusion, however, it has become apparent that Zemeckis' main concern is something more than merely having fun with four decades of American history. In the process of re-creating significant moments in time, he has captured on celluloid something eternal and timeless—the soul of humanity personified by a nondescript simpleton from the deep South.

The film begins following the flight of a seemingly insignificant feather as it floats down from the sky and brushes against various objects and people before finally coming to rest at the feet of Forrest Gump (Tom Hanks). Forrest, who is sitting on a bus-stop bench, reaches down and picks up the feather, smooths it out, then opens his traveling case and carefully places the feather between the pages of his favorite book, *Curious George.*

In this simple but hauntingly beautiful opening scene, the filmmakers illustrate the film's principal concern: Is life a series of random events over which a person has no control, or is there an underlying order to things that leads to the fulfillment of an individual's destiny? The rest of the film is a humorous and moving attempt to prove that, underlying the random, chaotic events that make up a person's life, there exists a benign and simple order.

Forrest sits on the bench throughout most of the film, talking about various events of his life to others who happen to sit down next to him. It does not take long, however, for the audience to realize that Forrest's seemingly random chatter to a parade of strangers has a perfect chronological order to it. He tells his first story after looking down at the ⑯ feet of his first bench partner and observing, "Mama always said that you can tell a lot about a person by the shoes they wear." Then, in a voice-over narration, Forrest begins the story of his life, first by telling about he first pair of shoes he can remember wearing.

The action shifts to the mid-1950's with Forrest as a young boy (Michael Humphreys) being fitted with leg braces to correct a curvature in his spine. Despite this traumatic handicap, Forrest remains unaffected, thanks to his mother (Sally Field) who reminds him on more than once occasion that he is no different from anyone else. Although this and most of Mrs. Gump's other words of advice are in the form of hackneyed cliches, Forrest whose intelligence quotient is below normal, sincerely believes every one of them, namely because he instinctively knows they are sincere expressions of his mother's love and fierce devotion.

⑥ *—John Byline*

## CREDITS

**Forrest Gump:** Tom Hanks ⑦
**Forrest's Mother:** Sally Field
**Young Forrest:** Michael Humphreys

⑧ **Origin:** United States
**Language:** English, Spanish ⑨
**Released:** 1994
**Production:** Liz Heller, John Manulis; New Line Cinema; released by Island Pictures
**Directed by:** Scott Kalvert ⑩
**Written by:** Bryan Goluboff
**Cinematography by:** David Phillips
**Music by:** Graeme Revell
**Editing:** Dana Congdon
**Production Design:** Danny Nowak
**Sound:** David Sarnoff
**Costumes:** David Robinson
**MPAA rating:** R ⑪
**Running time:** 102 minutes ⑫

## REVIEWS

*Entertainment Weekly.* July 15, 1994, p. 42. ⑬
*The Hollywood Reporter.* June 29, 1994, p. 7.
*Los Angeles Times.* July 6, 1994, p. F1.
*New York Times Online.* July 15, 1994.

## QUOTES

⑭ Forrest Gump (Tom Hanks): "The state of existence may be likened unto a receptacle containing cocoa-based confections, in that one may never predict that which one may receive."

## TRIVIA

Hanks was the first actor since Spencer Tracy to win back-to-back ⑮ Oscars for Best Actor. Hanks received the award in 1993 for his performance in *Philadelphia.* Tracy won Oscars in 1937 for *Captains Courages* and in 1938 for *Boys Town.*

## AWARDS AND NOMINATIONS

⑯ **Academy Awards 1994:** Film, Actor (Hanks), Special Effects, Cinematography
**Nomination:**
**Golden Globes 1994:** Film, Actor (Hanks), Supporting Actress (Field), Music

# A. I.: Artificial Intelligence

*David is 11 years old. He weighs 60 pounds. He is 4 feet, 6 inches tall. He has brown hair. His love is real. But he is not.*
—Movie tagline

*Journey To A World Where Robots Dream And Desire.*
—Movie tagline

*This Is Not A Game.*
—Movie tagline

*This summer, discover the next step in evolution.*
—Movie tagline

 **Box Office:** $78.6 million

In an interview on National Public Radio, Christiane Kubrick, widow of the great director Stanley Kubrick, pointed out that he "liked stories about people who make great plans, and then how they go wrong." Anyone who has seen his *Dr. Strangelove* (1964), *2001: A Space Odyssey* (1968), or *A Clockwork Orange* (1971) will understand ex-

actly what she means. Kubrick had a dark, pessimistic view about human folly, fearing that within our makeup was a fatal flaw—whether foolhardiness, shortsightedness or hubris—which makes us blind to the possible dire consequences of our actions.

During the last two decades of his life, he toyed with the idea of filming what amounted to a futuristic, grim fairy tale based upon the 1969 sci-fi short story "Super-Toys Last All Summer Long" by Brian Aldiss with a healthy dose of the Pinocchio story thrown in. Kubrick endlessly grappled with the project, picking it up and then putting it down, calling in writers and then jettisoning them, picking the brains of cutting-edge special-effects artists and then questioning whether he could ever really get exactly what he wanted onto the screen. By the early 1990s, Kubrick had transformed Aldiss's story into an ominous, complex tale entitled A.I. about an abandoned young robot with the capacity to feel real emotions who goes on a quest to become a real boy in hopes of winning the love of the human "mother" who rejected him. His advanced programming bringing on a painful longing, the poor machine goes through all sorts of travails in yet another Kubrickian "what have we wrought?" story.

However, Kubrick began to feel that another director who had successfully dealt in warmer, more comforting, and even sentimental cinematic tones might be needed to direct a film with the tender feelings of a lost little thing for his mommy at its core. Kubrick approached his friend, Steven Spielberg, asserting that the project would be "closer to your sensibility than mine." To be produced by Kubrick and directed by Spielberg, it would be bleak, cool and cerebral thanks to the former but also warm and heartfelt from the latter, who had already tugged at our heartstrings with tales like *E.T.: The Extra-Terrestrial* (1982). Even though Spielberg ended up politely declining, Kubrick continued to discuss ideas about the film with him through years of countless transatlantic phone calls and secure-line faxes, with Spielberg sworn to secrecy.

After Kubrick's death at the age of 70 in 1999, Christiane and Jan Harlan, her brother and Kubrick's producer, urged Spielberg to take the late director's 90-page treatment and all that had been "downloaded" into him over the years to make the film. As a homage to his much-admired friend, Spielberg agreed, and working much faster than the notoriously slow and painstaking Kubrick, wrote his first screenplay since *Close Encounters of the Third Kind* (1977) and realized Kubrick's dream in the highly-appropriate year of 2001. This Kubrick-Spielberg hybrid is a long, sprawling, highly ambitious, thought-provoking, sometimes disturbing, and always visually masterful fable, which, like many of Kubrick's works, is more likely to inspire fascination and admiration than love.

*A.I.: Artificial Intelligence* begins in the not-so-far-off future, when man's lack of attention to his effect on the environment has caused the polar ice caps to melt, flooding coastal cities. The government controls the birth rate because natural resources are now scarce, and technology has raced forward to provide humans with mechanical helpers of all kinds known as mechas. These sophisticated robots make things easier for humans in many ways, so why not also make them capable of providing love? This is the idea of a futuristic Geppetto named Professor Hobby (William Hurt) of Cybertronics Manufacturing. (Does his name insinuate that he is proceeding with his grand plans too casually?) The new experimental prototype is a child who could not just outwardly express love but actually feel it inside, a problem-free "child substitute" for those without a real one. Questions are raised in this initial scene: if we create something with feelings and emotions, do we then have a responsibility to keep it from getting its heart broken? These godlike scientific people press on with perhaps too little foresight, and David (highly believable Haley Joel Osment) is created.

Cybertronics employee Henry Swinton (Sam Robards) brings David home to assuage the sadness of his wife Monica (Frances O'Connor), as their critically-ill son Martin (Jake Thomas) has been cryogenically frozen awaiting a cure for what ails him. At first she balks at this highly-realistic, ever-pleasant (but creepily-attentive) faux fils, exclaiming in horror that he is no substitute for the real thing. Henry stipulates that she should not go through with the imprinting process until she is certain she will keep him, be-

cause if she changes her mind after that point he will have to be destroyed. Her loneliness for her absent son causes Monica to gradually warm to David, even giving him Martin's favorite supertoy Teddy (voiced by Jack Angel), and goes ahead with the indelible process in a touching scene bathed in glorious light streaming through a window (exhibiting Spielberg's penchant for the use of backlighting).

Things are working out well for all concerned until Martin, all thawed out and the picture of health, returns home, a close-up of David hinting that he wonders where the reappearance of the Swintons' real son leaves him. Monica shifts her focus to Martin, curling up with him in bed and reading Pinocchio to him while David listens alone in his own bed. Monica's actions and the story give David the idea that, if he could somehow become a real boy, Monica would love him the way she loves Martin. To Martin, David is unwanted competition and an expendable toy, and the boy tries his hardest to get David in trouble, including sending him off with a big pair of scissors to cut a lock of Monica's hair in the middle of the night, which startles her to no end. Later, while the mecha is being teased near a pool, he misguidedly hides behind Martin for safety, knocking both into the water and causing the real boy to nearly drown. (After Martin is rescued, Spielberg provides us with effectively-disturbing images of David floating at the bottom of the pool while everyone walks away unconcerned.) Not understanding that David did nothing wrong, Monica tearfully drives him off with Teddy to a dark forest and ditches him in a heartbreaking scene. "I'm sorry I'm not real!" he sobs, devastated.

At this point, the film takes a jolting jump in tone, drawing us into a much darker, frightening setting. We are introduced to smooth-talking Gigolo Joe (effective Jude Law), a "love mecha" designed to sexually satisfy women. Romantic music emanates from him with a quick cock of his plastic-haired head. (This character and his activities were to be much more R-rated in Kubrick's plans, but were toned down by Spielberg.) On the run after one of his clients turns up dead, the innocent mecha meets David and accompanies him on his quest to find the Blue Fairy of the Pinocchio story. The two travel through a dark, bizarre, and nightmarish countryside, hunted by resentful humans who feel they are being supplanted by the proliferation of mechas. After a well-done, exhilarating chase scene, David and Joe are brought to a barbaric Flesh Fair, where robots are horrifically destroyed in front of gleefully-cheering crowds. This reminds us of Kubrick's *Spartacus* (1960), as well as the concentration camps of Spielberg's *Schindler's List* (1993).

They narrowly escape this sickening spectacle and proceed to the Rouge City, which features such Kubrickian items as a milk bar like the one from *A Clockwork Orange*. In the city, they consult the all-knowing Dr. Know (the easily recognized voice of Robin Williams pulling us briefly out of the film). This part is highly reminiscent of 1939's *The*

*Wizard of Oz,* with Joe reminding one of the scarecrow off with Dorothy to see the Wizard in the Emerald City. They are led to a grey, partially-submerged Manhattan and Professor Hobby's factory, where in a tremendously potent scene, David encounters a slew of mechas identical to himself and is unhinged to realize that he is not and can never be special or unique, not one of a kind but merely the first of a kind. Disillusioned and clearly crushed, he sits high up on the ledge of a building, looking utterly empty as he calls out forlornly one last time for his mother and falls into the ocean below. Although Kubrick's treatment did not end here, this would have been a powerful final image to underscore the devastatingly cruel consequences of mankind's misguided innovation.

The remainder of *A.I.* is intriguing but struck many as less successful and, in the end, perhaps too sentimental compared to the material which led up to it. After being rescued by Joe, David and Teddy proceed underwater to a submerged Coney Island site featuring the characters from Pinocchio, including the Blue Fairy. As David practically prays to this smiling, comforting female idol, he is trapped there, remaining for the next 2000 years until an extremely-advanced race of mechas (looking so much like the aliens in *Close Encounters* as to confuse many viewers) find him, still not a real boy but the closest thing to it still in existence, as the human race is now long extinct. These mechas study his memories, and grant his wish of being reunited with his mother and having her want him by using the DNA from the lock of hair he had cut long ago. Monica can only live for one day, but it is a glorious one for a beaming David, alone with her and basking in the love and attention he so desired. As night falls, David curls up in bed and falls asleep (for the first time) with his mother in a last Oedipal moment of bliss as the camera pulls away. It is a sweeter version of the scene Kubrick had envisioned, which consisted of David having the horror of watching Monica fade away from him.

*A.I.* is a challenging film which even Spielberg admits he could not have made earlier in his career, particularly before he entered a more serious vein with films like *Schindler's List, Amistad* (1997), and *Saving Private Ryan* (1998). While Kubrick's next of kin and many critics expressed their approval for *A.I.,* it did not receive overwhelming approval from the public. Some viewers were entranced while others were confounded or merely bored. Made on a budget of $90 million, it grossed a less-than-expected $78.6 million at the box office. Many pointed to the film's advertising campaign as the main reason for the public's tepid response, charging that it set many up for disappointment by focusing initially on the adorable Osment and making the public expect a much lighter, comforting tale a la *E.T.* suitable for even younger moviegoers, which it is not.

Some critics felt that the combined contributions of the two very different men enabled the film to successfully hit a wide variety of notes, while others felt that their differing sensibilities conflict instead of compliment, weakening the film's impact as a whole. There is truth in both points of view. What impact the film does have is due in no small part to Osment, whose character may not be the real deal but he certainly is, giving yet another precociously-skilled performance. Law is also good in a role which substantially landed on the cutting room floor. Kudos also must go to cinematographer Janusz Kaminski, production designer Rick Carter, Industrial Light & Magic, and Stan Winston's robotics. Their work adds brilliance to Spielberg's expert technique in *A.I.,* which might act as a sobering cautionary tale for mankind, a word whose two syllables often qualify as an oxymoron in the oeuvre of Stanley Kubrick.

—*David L. Boxerbaum*

## CREDITS

**David Swinton:** Haley Joel Osment
**Gigolo Joe:** Jude Law
**Monica Swinton:** Frances O'Connor
**Henry Swinton:** Sam Robards
**Lord Johnson-Johnson:** Brendan Gleeson
**Professor Hobby:** William Hurt
**Martin Swinton:** Jake Thomas
**Nanny Mecha:** Clara Bellar
**Murderer:** Enrico Colantoni
**Passenger:** Adrian Grenier
**Sheila:** Emmanuelle Chriqui
**Dr. Know:** Robin Williams (Voice)
**Comedian Mecha:** Chris Rock (Voice)
**Blue Fairy:** Meryl Streep (Voice)
**Teddy:** Jack Angel (Voice)
**Narrator:** Ben Kingsley

**Origin:** USA
**Released:** 2001
**Production:** Kathleen Kennedy, Steven Spielberg, Sylvester Stallone; Amblin Entertainment; released by Warner Bros., Dreamworks Pictures
**Directed by:** Steven Spielberg
**Written by:** Steven Spielberg
**Cinematography by:** Janusz Kaminski
**Music by:** John Williams
**Sound:** Ronald Judkins
**Editing:** Michael Kahn
**Art Direction:** Richard Johnson, Jim Teegarden, Thomas Valentine
**Costumes:** Bob Ringwood
**Production Design:** Rick Carter
**MPAA rating:** PG-13
**Running time:** 145 minutes

## REVIEWS

*Boxoffice.* September, 2001, p. 152.
*Chicago Sun-Times Online.* June 29, 2001.
*Entertainment Weekly.* June 29, 2001, p. 109.
*Hollywood Reporter.* June 19, 2001, p. 16.
*Los Angeles Times Online.* June 29, 2001.
*Nation.* July 23, 2001, p. 44.
*New York Times Online.* June 24, 2001.
*New York Times.* June 29, 2001, p. E1.
*New Yorker.* July 2, 2001, p. 86.
*Newsweek.* June 25, 2001, p. 84.
*People.* July 9, 2001, p. 37.
*Premiere.* July, 2001, p. 88.
*Rolling Stone.* July 19, 2001, p. 54.
*Sight and Sound.* September, 2001, p. 16.
*Sight and Sound.* October, 2001, p. 38.
*Time.* June 25, 2001, p. 60.
*USA Today Online.* June 28, 2001.
*Variety.* June 25, 2001, p. 19.
*Village Voice.* July 3, 2001, p. 117.
*Wall Street Journal.* June 29, 2001, p. W1.
*Washington Post Online.* June 29, 2001.

## QUOTES

Gigolo Joe (Jude Law) to David (Haley Joel Osment): "They hate us, you know, the humans. They made us too smart, too quick, and too many."

## AWARDS AND NOMINATIONS

**Nomination:**
**Oscars 2001:** Visual FX
**British Acad. 2001:** Visual FX
**Golden Globes 2002:** Director (Spielberg), Support. Actor (Law), Score
**Broadcast Film Critics 2001:** Score.

# ABCD

*It's about choices.*
—Movie tagline

As an American film, Krutin Patel's quasi-erotic comedy-drama, *ABCD* (an acronym for "American-Born Confused Desi") falls between two filmic worlds: the Bollywood-inspired grossness of the earlier-released *American Desi* (reviewed in this volume), against which it would seem to be taking itself much too seriously, and the iconoclasm of American independent cinema, in compari-

son to which it cannot help but appear too Brahmanical and orthodox.

Patel, like his ideological cohort, Piyush Pandya, the writer-director of *Desi*, is too hung up on the issue of identity to deliver a dramatically satisfying story. Both writer-directors seem resolved to focus on the "desi in America" ethos to the point of excluding any meaningful interaction with America itself. The term "desi" is a disparaging appellative used by expatriates to refer to everything from the Indian subcontinent. Messrs. Patel and Pandya have adopted the agenda of relocating that term within an American context, thereby hoping to rid it of its less reputable aspects. Patel's desis live in prosperous suburbia and midtown apartments.

Whereas Pandya's film could hide behind its crude frivolity, Patel's effort, with its art-house veneer, remains avowedly serious. It thus emerges all the more disturbing for raising a basic issue about which it keeps us in the dark. If these new immigrants can have everything they want in America, why don't they feel at home at here?

As in the similarly "confused" *Chutney Popcorn* (2000) by Nisha Ganatra, there is the absence of the father figure. Patel's family of three are in America for reasons that have nothing to do with American social, political or cultural values. Raj (Farhan Tahir), the earnest mathematical whiz of a yuppie, more westernized than American, is after financial security. His kid sister, the ravishing Nina (Sheetal Sheth), from all we get to know of her, has built her life around sexual promiscuity, and her career around advertising. Anju (Madhur Jaffrey), their comic virago of a mother, remains bound to the socio-religious values of the Old Country. Recently widowed, she is in America so she can be near Raj and Nina. Patel's obsession with identity keeps his narrative dilemmas grounded in the commonplace. What works in the film's favor though is the compassion he shows to even the most minor of his characters.

Lamentably, the narrative veers towards Raj when Nina is the more interesting of the two. This could be because, like Raj, the film's perspective finds its security in its Indianness. Raj is at that stage in life where his future remains predicated on a promotion to vice-president. This in turn will pave the way for his marrying his fiancée, the beautiful Tejal (Adriane Forlana Erdos). While completely devoted to his work, Raj is in two minds about the marriage Anju seems to be forcing him into. Similarly, Nina revolts when she finds her mother exploiting her recent breakup with her ardent upper-class American suitor, Sam (Rex Young), so as to railroad her into an arranged marriage with Ashok (Aasif Mandvi), who is revealed to be her childhood playmate. Despite his having been in America for only a week, Ashok's crude but jocular ways make him endearing to Nina.

After a joust in bed, however, Ashok falls in love with Nina, but then makes the mistake of bringing up the "m" word. As he pours out his heart, it is more "old world reality" than Nina can handle; she drops him like a hot samosa and takes up where she left off with Sam. Her lovemaking with Sam is intercut with a classical Indian dance recital given by Tejal, thereby bestowing the mantle of Indian tradition upon Nina's new world feminism.

Raj is shattered when he's passed over for the promotion because of, what he perceives as, racial discrimination. When Anju passes away peacefully in her kitchen, it leaves Raj free to not only quit his job, but break off his engagement with Tejal.

Among the film's denouements, it is only Nina's that feels unconvincing. While attending the traditional Indian wedding of a friend, she is so moved by the customary bondage an Indian bride takes upon herself that she promptly turns to Sam and asks him to marry her, but in a church. The film ends with Nina, dressed as a Christian bride, being given away by Raj, an event that would have been a nightmare for their mother had she she been alive. As we take leave of the film, we cannot help but wish it had embraced something of America, like Nina has, instead of remaining aloof from it all, like Raj.

Understandably, critics have compared the film to others preoccupied with the subject of desis in America. In that, Patel's effort seems to have been put in a class by itself. Stephen Holden in the *New York Times* notes that "it doesn't make light of its characters' conflicts, nor does it try to resolve them with feel-good formulaic solutions." In his rave in the *Los Angeles Times*, Kevin Thomas claims that *ABCD* is "not just another culture-clash comedy," and even goes as far as praising its "exceptional depth and perception."

—*Vivek Adarkar*

## CREDITS

**Anju:** Madhur Jaffrey
**Raj:** Faran Tahir
**Nina:** Sheetal Sheth
**Ashok:** Aasif Mandri
**Tejal:** Adriane Forlana Erdos
**Sam:** Rex Young

**Origin:** USA
**Released:** 1999
**Production:** Krutin Patel, Naju Patel; Laxmi Pictures; released by Eros Entertainment
**Directed by:** Krutin Patel
**Written by:** Krutin Patel, James McManus
**Cinematography by:** Milton Kam
**Music by:** Deirdre Broderick
**Sound:** James Espy
**Editing:** Ravi Subramanian

**Art Direction:** Jennifer Galvelis, Rodrigo Guerrero, Robert Serrini
**Costumes:** Naju Patel
**Production Design:** Deborah Schreier
**MPAA rating:** Unrated
**Running time:** 102 minutes

## REVIEWS

*Los Angeles Times Online.* November 30, 2001.
*New York Times Online.* November 30, 2001.
*Village Voice Online.* December 4, 2001.

# About Adam

*He's the most outrageous secret three sisters ever kept . . . from each other.*
—Movie tagline

 **Box Office:** $.2 million

Coming off as a jolly *Hilary and Jackie,* Irish filmmaker Gerard Stembridge also tells a tale about sisters with his cinematic saga *About Adam.* However, the sisters in Stembridge's screenplay unknowingly compete for the affections of the primordial Adam (Stuart Townsend) and not an illustrious music career. *About Adam,* with its multiple-perspective narrative, turns the romantic comedy genre on its head while also highlighting an artsy Dublin few film viewers will have witnessed. Similar to the charismatic Adam, who has a knack for telling people exactly what they want to hear, Stembridge has created a screenplay that portrays a story women want to view.

Stembridge allows us to laugh at Irish quirks without relying on the humor of past Irish comedies such as *Waking Ned Devine.* *About Adam* does not portray stereotypical drunk priests, feisty Irish lasses, or the obligatory pub scene so prevalent in other Irish comedies. Stembridge penned original characters ranging from torch singer Lucy (Kate Hudson), her Victorian heroine-obsessed sister Laura (Frances O'Connor), and the clever "perfect man," Adam. Then, on top of his well-defined characters, Stembridge adds refreshing dialogue and an amusing plot that questions current views of morality. After all, if Adam is able to make all of his lovers happy, does it matter if he's unfaithful?

Stembridge allows us to view Adam from four different perspectives told by siblings, one of whom is a man. First, Lucy tells the story of how she met and fell in love with

Adam ("Adam didn't even come on to me."). After Lucy broke up with her previous lover, she noticed Adam sitting in the restaurant where she doubled as a waitress/singer. Adam appeared shy and let Lucy ask him out; later, he would tell Lucy that she could choose when and where they would first make love. After all, Adam is a sweet and sensitive guy. After Lucy takes Adam home to meet her family, they all decide that he's the perfect guy. One night Lucy invites her entire family to watch her perform and she pops a marriage proposal on Adam, who surprisingly accepts.

However, literary sister Laura ("I think Adam has some deep tragedy lurking beneath the surface.") views Adam as the man who liberates her from her obsession with Victorian authors and literary views of eroticism. Adam seduces Laura by playing on her nurturing sensibilities and revealing his childhood traumas. Laura becomes freed from her erotic inhibitions while in the throes of reciting *Wuthering Heights* and burning up the sheets with Adam. She ends up writing a passionate thesis on the sexuality of Victorian women and she finds that she's perfectly happy pursuing sex with no strings attached.

The eldest sister, Alice (Charlotte Bradley), prefers Adam get down and dirty with her. Unhappily married with a young child, Alice needs approval that she's still sexy. Her alcoholic husband Martin (Brendan Dempsey) proves to be a disappointment in every way possible, but with Adam, Alice experiences sweaty and orgasmic sex. What does it matter if Adam shags her a half an hour before he's to marry her younger sister?

Finally, Adam assists the brother, David (Alan Maher), with a plot to seduce his virginal girlfriend Karen (Cathleen Bradley). In the process, David gets an erection from Adam's soothing words and thinks he's turned queer. Later he overhears an erotic encounter between Karen and Adam. However, the end result is that the impassioned Karen seduces David, leading him towards a renewed respect for Adam.

Stembridge proves his masterful storytelling talents by exposing the human tendency to only see what one wants to see by showing similar scenes played out from different angles. For instance, in a scene where Adam blindfolds Lucy in order to whisk her away to a romantic hideaway, we see a flirtation take place between Adam and Laura, unknown to the dizzy-in-love Lucy who patiently waits in Adam's sporty Jaguar.

Hudson plays the giggly blonde Lucy, who spews out such lines as "I sound like a horse on acid" with aplomb. O'Connor delivers an over-the-top performance as the book-smart Laura, easily swinging from brooding/hysterical to ecstasy in a blink of an eye. Although the ensemble cast bring spunk to Stembridge's zesty characters, O'Connor with her impeccable timing and uninhibited performance, steals the show. When it comes to romance, Stembridge and

Adam both tell us what we want to hear.

*—Patty-Lynne Herlevi*

## CREDITS

**Adam:** Stuart Townsend
**Lucy:** Kate Hudson
**Laura:** Frances O'Connor
**Alice:** Charlotte Bradley
**Peggy Owens:** Rosaleen Linehan
**Martin:** Brendan F. Dempsey
**David:** Alan Maher
**Simon:** Tommy Tiernan
**Karen:** Cathleen Bradley

**Origin:** Ireland, Great Britain
**Released:** 2000
**Production:** Anna Devlin, Marina Hughes; BBC Films, Venus Productions; released by Miramax Films
**Directed by:** Gerard Stembridge
**Written by:** Gerard Stembridge
**Cinematography by:** Bruno de Keyzer
**Music by:** Adrian Johnston
**Sound:** Simon Willis
**Editing:** Mary Finlay
**Art Direction:** Susan Cullen
**Costumes:** Eimer Ni Mhaoldomhnaigh
**Production Design:** Fiona Daly
**MPAA rating:** R
**Running time:** 98 minutes

## REVIEWS

*Entertainment Weekly.* May 11, 2001, p. 52.
*Hollywood Reporter.* December 6, 2000, p. 19.
*Los Angeles Times Online.* May 9, 2001.
*New York Times Online.* May 9, 2001.
*People.* May 14, 2001, p. 40.
*Sight and Sound.* May, 2001, p. 38.
*Variety.* February 21, 2000, p. 43.

## QUOTES

Peggy (Rosaleen Linehan) tells daughter Alice (Charlotte Bradley): "Boring men are the curse of the world and there are so many of them."

# The Adventures of Felix (Drole de Felix)

*Sometimes a little trip can change everything.*
—Movie tagline

Those looking for the animated adventures of Felix the Cat will be disappointed because the Felix in French duo Olivier Ducastel and Jacques Martineau's *The Adventures of Felix* is a French man of Arab descent who's in search of his estranged father. However, even fans of the other Felix can enjoy Ducastel and Martineau's surrealistic road movie, as well as soaking in France's gorgeous countryside. It's a blend of *The Wizard of Oz* and Danish film *Bye Bye Blue Bird* as Felix (Sami Bouajila) also meets unusual characters along the way while realizing that it's easier to create a family from scratch than trying to find one's way back home.

Although *The Adventures of Felix* proves light and breezy for the most part, this isn't a film for children nor is it based on childhood fantasies. Ducastel and Martineau, who are known in the U.S. for their debut feature *Jeanne and the Perfect Guy*, return with another adventure about gay relationships and AIDS. However, they also add issues revolving around racism, deadbeat fathers, and alternative family structure to the mix, while asking the question what is a family? The directors attempt to answer that question by dividing their film into sections such as "My Little Brother," "My Cousin," "My Grandmother," "My Sister," and "My Father." Of course, none of the characters in the segments are related to Felix and his encounters with the characters prove fleeting at best. However, these characters open Felix up to life's possibilities while adding humor to the film.

After losing his job and finding old letters that his estranged father wrote to his mother, Felix decides to travel to Marseille via hitchhiking. With a rucksack in tow, Felix sets out to meet his father for the first time. When Felix meets his "little brother," Jules (Charley Sergue), he shows off by stealing a mini van but pushes away Jules's sexual advances. After all, Felix loves the teenager like a brother and already has a lover, Daniel (Pierre-Loup Rajot), back home in the fishing port of Dieppe. Next, Felix meets the independent and defiant widow Mathilde (Patachou), who mothers Felix after he rearranges her furniture and assists with her household chores. Then, he meets Isabelle (Ariane Ascaride), a mother of three children who all have different fathers. In exchange for a ride and a life lesson about fatherhood Felix changes the flat on Isabelle's van. Later, Felix hitches a ride with a gay man and they have a quickie in the middle of a meadow filled with yellow flowers. Finally, Felix meets an older man fishing in a river. The fisherman tells Felix that perhaps his father doesn't wish to be surprised

by an estranged son, but gives Felix a lift to Marseilles regardless. The directors chose to end the film with Felix reuniting with his lover Daniel in Marseilles and we never see Felix's reunion with his father. This suggests that Felix had found his family within the group of people he already met.

The directors chose to shoot this road movie in sequence as Felix traveled from Dieppe in northern France to Marseilles in southern France. Felix doesn't accumulate the mileage that Jack Keruoac did when he crossed the U.S. via Route 66, but as Felix thumbs his way across France, he collects memorable moments with outrageous individuals. The incidents either cause Felix to question his morality or shed light on his current situation. After all, Felix has been infected by the HIV virus, takes his medicinal cocktail every day while he's on the road, and constantly wonders about the father that abandoned him. But mostly Felix is searching for answers about how a fatherless gay Arab man fits into French society. At one point he breaks down and admits that he's ashamed of being Arab, although Felix is able to deal with his homosexuality and his lack of a father figure.

Bouajila oozes charm while reflecting the vulnerable state of Felix. The French cabaret star Patachou portrays a plucky grandmother—infusing humor into the story, while award-winning actress Ascaride plays a ravishingly liberated earth mother. *The Adventures of Felix* boasts intriguing performances against a backdrop of exquisite photography that proves refreshing.

—*Patty-Lynne Herlevi*

## CREDITS

**Felix:** Sami Bouajila
**Mathilde:** Patachou
**Isabelle:** Ariane Ascaride
**Daniel:** Pierre-Loup Rajot
**Jules:** Charly Sergue
**Laurent:** Clement Reverend
**Fisherman:** Maurice Benichou

**Origin:** France
**Language:** French
**Released:** 1999
**Production:** Philippe Martin; Arte France Cinema, Les Films Pelleas, Pyramide Productions; released by Winstar Cinema
**Directed by:** Olivier Ducastel, Jacques Martineau
**Written by:** Olivier Ducastel, Jacques Martineau
**Cinematography by:** Mathieu Poirot-Delpech
**Sound:** Jean-Jacques Ferran
**Editing:** Sabine Mamou
**Art Direction:** Louis Subrier

**Costumes:** Juliette Chanaud
**MPAA rating:** Unrated
**Running time:** 95 minutes

## REVIEWS

*Boxoffice.* August, 2001, p. 58.
*eye Weekly Online.* June 29, 2000.
*Los Angeles Times Online.* August 10, 2001.
*New York Times Online.* June 15, 2001.
*Sight and Sound.* January, 2001, p. 47.
*Toronto Sun Online.* June 30, 2000.
*Washington Post.* October 26, 2001, p. WE38.

# The Affair of the Necklace

*Her birthright was stolen. Her dignity taken. Her rights denied. Deception was the only option.*
—Movie tagline

**Box Office:** $.3 million

The newspaper advertisements for *The Affair of the Necklace* did their best to make the film look like a lauded prestige picture. "You will not forget this film! It's a gripping, epic drama full of behind-the-curtain intrigue, sex and betrayal," reads one blurb. "I loved this movie! Hilary Swank is perfectly cast in a film that will visually take your breath away," reads another. "I had so much fun I'd see it again," gushes another. In teeny-weeny print under them are the source of the lavish praise. The first is from, uh, Larry King. The second from Bonnie Laufer of Global Network, whatever that might be. And the third is from Joel Siegel of "Good Morning America," a critic who is the savior of all movie publicity people because the man seems to love every movie he's ever seen and is not afraid to use hyperbole—and plenty of it.

The movie marked the first big picture for Hilary Swank after her Oscar®-winning turn as transvestite Brandon Teena in *Boys Don't Cry.* Although she signed on to do *The Affair of the Necklace* before all the *Boys Don't Cry* hoopla, it seems perfectly planned to erase anyone's image that Swank could only look like a boy. With all the lace, bodices and satin on the costumes in *Affair,* even Willie Nelson could probably pass as a lovely young lady of the court.

The film is based on a true episode in French history that's very familiar to the French and those who study the

country, but not especially well known to the rest of the world. There was a nobleman, Darnell de Valois, who had the audacity to be an outspoken protester of King Louis XVI and Marie Antoinette's policies of living a lavish lifestyle at the expense of the large number of poor French people. When his daughter, Jeanne de la Motte-Valois (Swank), is just a young girl, soldiers come to the Valois home, burn all the Valois' possessions and kill Jeanne's father. Soon after, Jeanne's mother dies of a broken heart.

Once the girl becomes a grown woman, she wants nothing more than to authenticate her heritage and then have her home returned to her. She thinks that if she can tell Marie Antoinette (Joely Richardson) about her story, woman-to-woman, the queen will surely grant her wish. She tries all the proper channels, but is refused at every turn because her dress is unfashionable and she's not a part of proper society—despite Jeanne's marriage of convenience to low-level aristocrat, the unfaithful Count Nicolas de la Motte (Adrien Brody).

Jeanne catches the eye of a society gigolo Retaux de Vilette (Simon Baker). Retaux takes an instant liking to Jeanne and sets out to help her attain her goal. He teaches her the various personality quirks of the society figures and tells her that in order to get anywhere, she has to figure out what other people want. The first order of business is to find a wealthy patron and they decide that the man for the job is Cardinal Louis de Rohan (Jonathan Pryce). For years, the Cardinal has been snubbed by Marie Antoinette and he'd like nothing more than to heal that rift. His greatest desire is to be named Prime Minister and without the queen's blessing, he has no chance. Jeanne gets the Cardinal to sponsor her by pretending that she has influence with Marie Antoinette and can help plead the Cardinal's case on his behalf. Jeanne keeps up the fraud by forging letters from the queen to the Cardinal and leading him into a false correspondence with her.

Jeanne's deception escalates when she comes up with a plan to defraud the Cardinal out of quite a bit of money. (As one critic pointed out, it's not entirely clear how this is going to help her case to reclaim her birthright, but it makes sense if you don't think about it too much.) The plan is sort of complicated, so it requires audiences to pay attention (Or not. Most of the fun of this kind of movie is just looking at the costumes and lush settings). The queen has refused to buy a necklace—an incredibly ornate piece with 647 diamonds and 2,800 carats—from the palace jeweler because she knows that it was originally commissioned for Madame DeBarry, mistress to her husband's grandfather, whom the queen considers a "harlot." To make the piece, the jewelers have grossly overextended themselves and are unable to make interest payments on the piece. Jeanne creates an plan whereby the Cardinal will be the guarantor of the jewelry so that Marie Antoinette can buy the necklace in private. Jeanne tells the Cardinal that the deal has to be surreptitious so that the people of France don't find out that the queen is buying such an extravagant piece. Marie, of course, knows nothing about all this.

Enlisting the help of Retaux, her husband, and the Cardinal's trusted, but crooked psychic advisor, Cagliostro (Christopher Walken), Jeanne gets the necklace and proceeds to sell the diamonds one-by-one. The plan unravels, trials are held, people are beaten and heads are removed via guillotine.

This is the kind of film that can benefit from light, playful acting, and there's some of that in here, but only some of the actors seem to get the idea. As the egotistical, lecherous Cardinal, Pryce hams it up, although it would probably have been difficult to do anything but that. He is called upon, for example, to appear in a scene where he's participating in a decadent orgy and many scenes where he's heading to his private chambers to give various young women "private religious instruction"—wink, wink. Also good is Baker as Retaux, who has to go from breezy and flirty to beaten down and ruined. Richardson also has an interesting take on Marie Antoinette. She doesn't play her as a villain but rather as a woman who is half catty and interested in keeping her exalted position among the people and half woman who's just a victim of circumstance.

Swank is overly-sincere in her role. Part of the fun of this film should be about all the various scheming and it should be played lightly. Or, Swank could have gone the other way and played her role as a tragic figure. But she's upstaged in this tactic by director Charles Shyer who insists on playing over and over again the footage of the soldiers burning down Jeanne's family home. Shyer uses the footage as a crutch. Whenever he's trying to gain sympathy for Jeanne or justify her actions, he breaks out that footage again. He doesn't seem to realize that audiences are smart enough to remember that Jeanne has been wronged and don't need to keep being reminded every 15 minutes. Walken seems miscast in his role, not because he can't do it, but because he can do it too well. If he weren't so known for doing this kind of eerie, sinister role, he'd be perfect, but he's done it so much that it's become almost a joke. As good as he is playing this kind of strange heavy, his presence in the movie breaks the spell.

The settings and costumes in the film are appropriately eye-popping. There are plenty of gilded tables, velvet chairs, and gigantic palaces with incredible landscaping. The filmmakers even spent one day filming at the Palace of Versailles. Costumer Milena Canonero clothes the characters in rich satins, bold colors and sumptuous fabrics (all the better to showcase the various heaving bosoms.)

But all the finery didn't help much with the critics. Most of them, besides Joel Siegel, generally weren't impressed. Owen Gleiberman of *Entertainment Weekly* gave the film a C and criticized Swank's performance. "The moment Swank appears," he wrote, "her androgynous rock-star lips framed by an unflattering mass of dollish curls, she looks tentative and uncomfortable, like Alanis Morissette trapped in a bad period-piece video." Jessica Winter of the *Village Voice* wrote that the film was "an endless illustrated Harlequin paperback of mawkish backstory and corset-popping purple prose." A.O. Scott of the *New York Times* wrote, "*The Affair of the Necklace* drags and meanders when it wants clarity and clockwork, and bogs down in hazy, vague emotions."

*—Jill Hamilton*

## CREDITS

**Jeanne St. Remy de Valois:** Hilary Swank
**Cardinal Louis de Rohan:** Jonathan Pryce
**Retaux de Vilette:** Simon Baker
**Nicolas De La Motte:** Adrien Brody
**Minister Breteuil:** Brian Cox
**Marie Antoinette:** Joely Richardson
**Cagliostro:** Christopher Walken
**Monsieur Bohmer:** Paul Brooke
**Monsieur Bassenge:** Peter Eyre
**Minister of Titles:** Simon Kunz
**Young Jeanne:** Hayden Panettiere

**Origin:** USA
**Released:** 2001
**Production:** Charles Shyer, Redmond Morris, Andrew A. Kosove, Broderick Johnson; Alcon Entertainment; released by Warner Bros.
**Directed by:** Charles Shyer
**Written by:** John Sweet
**Cinematography by:** Ashley Rowe
**Music by:** David Newman
**Sound:** Tony Dawe
**Editing:** David Moritz
**Art Direction:** Jean-Michel Hugon
**Costumes:** Milena Canonero
**Production Design:** Alex McDowell
**MPAA rating:** R
**Running time:** 120 minutes

## REVIEWS

*Entertainment Weekly.* December 7, 2001, p. 68.
*Los Angeles Times Online.* November 30, 2001.
*New York Times Online.* November 30, 2001.
*People.* December 10, 2001, p. 37.
*USA Today Online.* November 30, 2001.
*Variety.* November 26, 2001, p. 26.

# Ali

*Forget what you think you know.*
—Movie tagline

 **Box Office:** $58 million

American boxer Muhammad Ali was the 20th century's most famous athlete worldwide. Self-proclaimed as simply "The Greatest," Ali was known around the world for his brash, unapologetic demeanor; his controversial political and spiritual beliefs; and, most of all, for his prowess in the ring. Along with the Rev. Martin Luther King and Malcolm X, he also stood as a symbol of black American pride and racial advancement in the 1960s.

In and out of the boxing ring, he was a loudmouth and a relentless self-promoter, unleashing devastating torrents of crisply rhymed verse about his opponents' ineptitude and his own inevitable triumphs. Obviously, much of this was an act, part of a strategy to humble his rivals and advance his own notoriety. Ali was mesmerizing because he seemed simultaneously a buffoon and a brilliant media strategist, unbeatable and unflappable. He was popular because he combined black militancy with a charming, disarming poetic innocence. Without a doubt, Ali was a model for scores of black athletes who have followed since, and he had a profound influence on global culture; it might be argued that he could be considered the father of rap.

Yet for all his notoriety, Ali's motivations remain an enigma to the casual observer. Unless one has read a detailed biography of the man, questions arise about his persona and his convictions. Was his clowning all an act? How much of his personality was contrived for public consumption? To what extent was he influenced—or controlled—by his various handlers? How firm was his belief in Islam and his opposition to the Vietnam War, and from where did these values arise? One would expect at least some of those questions to be answered in a movie that is titled simply *Ali.* Yet director Michael Mann's sprawling, visually arresting, sloppy, and incoherent film answers none of them.

In an opening montage, Mann intersperses scenes of Will Smith as Ali jogging through the streets of Harlem, pummeling a punching bag in a gym, getting on a segregated bus as a child, and much more—all winding around shots and the sounds of soul singer Sam Cooke in a nightclub. It's a long, simmering, fantastic stew that ends with a crescendo as Ali walks down a tunnel and bursts through the doors into a weigh-in for his fight with Sonny Liston—the bout that would overturn the boxing world. It's a stunning, visually complex, aurally rich opening scene that captures the mood of the times and places Ali in a cultural context as he enters upon the stage of history.

Unfortunately, the entire film consists of such musical montages, one after another, and while some are fascinating, others are clumsy and feel contrived, and they soon become annoying. Mann, who came to prominence in the 1980s producing television's *Miami Vice,* is adept at sound and images, but seems to have lost any touch for exposition. In fact, there is not a shred of exposition in *Ali.* It is in no sense a narrative, and it is not really a biography, but more like a series of dreamy impressions mounted on a large canvas.

Ali emerges from that door into the Liston fight fully formed, with no explanation of how he got there. Why is he a fighter? The movie doesn't tell us; he just is. Where did he come from? Did he grow up in poverty? What was his family like? The answers are only hinted at. And why does he run his mouth? There is no answer.

And so it goes for the entire film. Ali is surrounded by a group of men who serve various functions. None of these men are clearly identified and what they do is undefined. When Ali's second wife tells him they are leeches who have sucked him dry and need to be replaced, the information comes like a bolt from the blue, for Mann hasn't bothered to show what any of them does, and whether it is legitimate or parasitic. Even the man who is his writer, who penned his famous rhymes, isn't identified as such in this film.

Mann's *Ali,* based on material written by Gregory Allen Howard, seems like the product of a director who has been given no access into Ali and has no new information to share about him. Even a viewer with only a casual perception of Ali's life will learn little about him that is not already widely known. There is never an inner dialogue shared with the viewer, so that we do not get insights into Ali's thoughts or motivations. We have few clues as to his driving forces or convictions—other than that we know he wants to be recognized as the best prizefighter in the world.

Mann spent two years and nearly $100 million on this film, which chronicles only the period from 1964 to 1974, during which Ali won the world heavyweight boxing title from Liston, then had it stripped away from him when he refused induction into the Army because of his opposition to the Vietnam War, then lost the crown in the ring, and finally regained it by beating George Foreman in a match in Zaire. Mann and three other screenwriters labored long and hard and produced a stillborn saga. The film is rambling, overlong, and incoherent, and its focus keeps shifting.

For much of the first hour of the film, it is not clear whether the main subject is Ali or Malcolm X (Mario Van Peebles), Ali's friend and fellow Muslim. As Ali and Malcolm are pushed together and pulled apart by the unfathomable dictates of Nation of Islam leader Elijah Muhammad, it remains unclear whether Ali is attracted to Malcolm's politics or simply distracted. In one scene, Ali seems more interested in watching a TV show about termites than in listening to Malcolm discuss his pain about the civil rights struggle. This scene seems to trivialize Ali's mental powers, but its meaning is unclear.

Once Malcolm X is assassinated, Mann seems to be shaken awake and returns to his purported subject—Ali. The champ's refusal to enter military service is also handled in a confusing fashion—without insight or explanation. He seems to take his handlers by surprise. In one interview, Ali blurts out his view that he has no quarrel with the Viet Cong. This is exactly what Ali said, but Mann provides no sense of whether this was a well-thought-out position or simply something that came out of an undisciplined mouth.

And this is the key question—and the key failing—about this movie's take on Ali. To what extent was Ali in charge of Ali? How deeply did this man feel his convictions, and how much of his reactions and statements were calculated? What did he think about his emerging role as a symbol for minority aspirations everywhere? Neither Mann nor Smith has a clue.

Smith puts obvious effort and thoughtfulness into his portrayal of the champ, and it's the best thing the rapper-actor has done to date. But it's not nearly enough. Smith and the film posit Ali as something of a brooding, somber presence. When he shoots off his mouth at a press conference or in a weigh-in, the cockiness and the nervous energy seem to emerge out of nowhere. Smith does not present a sufficiently brash Ali, but neither, strangely enough, does he invest him with sufficient dignity. Smith is stuck in a generational attitude that drips with sarcasm and irony; when he speaks, there is an acidic or laconic tone; and thus he fails to capture the power and the unabashed straightforwardness of Ali's times and attitude.

The standout performance in the film is Jon Voight's as Howard Cosell. Voight completely inhabits the legendary sportscaster/commentator with the unique voice, the un-likely on-air rival and off-air friend of the champ. Voight is so much like Cosell that he disappears, and if you didn't know he was in the film credits, you would never guess it was Voight underneath that makeup and toupee. He has Cosell's accent dead-on without engaging in parody. It is an amazing performance. Yet so slim is this film on substance that, even with Voight's remarkable portrayal, there is no clue as to the genesis or basis of the Ali-Cosell friendship. Similarly, we also discover Ali has a weakness for women, but never learn why. Everything about the characters in this film is a given.

Fortunately, the boxing matches that are the emotional center of the film are executed with impressive gusto and expert filmmaking, even if the actual athletics seem rather slow and clumsy at times. Smith has Ali's trademark floating footwork almost down pat, but falls short in the athletic and charismatic departments. It is asking too much to expect anyone to come close to what Ali did in the ring; there has never been anyone with such flair and flamboyance and strategic intelligence in a boxing match. Few of those

matchless qualities are conveyed, unfortunately; despite the technical competence of the fight scenes, we never really grasp what made Ali so special as a boxer.

For this much effort, at least a few insights into Ali should be expected, but Mann has concocted only a beautiful surface of sight and sound, with nothing underneath. Few movies have ever been made with so little content behind so much sound and fury. This is not a biographical film about Ali; it is a gauzy, murky and intermittently arresting glimpse into a man, an era and a phenomenon about which the director has nothing new to say. It's a long riff on a legend—superficial jazz that sounds no deep chords.

*—Michael Betzold*

## CREDITS

**Muhammad Ali:** Will Smith
**Drew "Bundini" Brown:** Jamie Foxx
**Howard Cosell:** Jon Voight
**Malcolm X:** Mario Van Peebles
**Angelo Dundee:** Ron Silver
**Howard Bingham:** Jeffrey Wright
**Don King:** Mykelti Williamson
**Sonji:** Jada Pinkett Smith
**Veronica:** Michael Michele
**Chancy Eskridge:** Joe Morton
**Dr. Ferdie Pacheco:** Paul Rodriguez
**Belinda:** Nona Gaye
**Bradley:** Bruce McGill
**Herbert Muhammad:** Barry (Shabaka) Henley
**Cassius Clay Sr.:** Giancarlo Esposito
**Luis Sarria:** Laurence Mason
**Martin Luther King Jr.:** LeVar Burton
**Elijah Muhammad:** Albert Hall
**Robert Lipsyte:** David Cubitt
**Joe Smiley:** Ted Levine
**Sam Cooke:** David Elliott
**Sonny Liston:** Michael Bentt
**Joe Frazier:** James N. Toney
**George Foreman:** Charles Shufford

**Origin:** USA
**Released:** 2001
**Production:** Jon Peters, A. Kitman Ho, James Lassiter, Paul Ardaji, Michael Mann; Peters Entertainment, Forward Pass Productions, Overbrook Films; released by Columbia Pictures
**Directed by:** Michael Mann
**Written by:** Michael Mann, Stephen J. Rivele, Christopher Wilkinson, Eric Roth
**Cinematography by:** Emmanuel Lubezki
**Music by:** Lisa Gerrard, Pieter Bourke

**Sound:** Lee Orloff
**Editing:** Stephen E. Rivkin, William Goldenberg,
Lynzee Klingman
**Art Direction:** Bill Rea, Thomas Voth
**Costumes:** Marlene Stewart
**Production Design:** John Myhre
**MPAA rating:** R
**Running time:** 158 minutes

## REVIEWS

*Chicago Sun-Times Online.* December 25, 2001.
*Entertainment Weekly.* January 4, 2002, p. 44.
*Los Angeles Times Online.* December 25, 2001.
*New York Times Online.* September 9, 2001.
*New York Times Online.* December 25, 2001.
*People.* December 24, 2001, p. 31.
*Rolling Stone.* January 17, 2002, p. 56.
*USA Today Online.* December 23, 2001.
*Variety.* December 17, 2001, p. 35.
*Washington Post.* December 25, 2001, p. C1.

## QUOTES

Ali (Will Smith): "I ain't got to be what nobody else want me to be. And I ain't afraid to be what I want to be."

## TRIVIA

Will Smith did not have a stunt double in the film and learned to box himself for the fight scenes.

## AWARDS AND NOMINATIONS

**Nomination:**
**Golden Globes 2002:** Actor—Drama (Smith), Support. Actor (Voight), Score
**Broadcast Film Critics 2001:** Actor (Smith), Film, Support. Actor (Voight).

# Along Came a Spider

*The game is far from over.*
—Movie tagline

 **Box Office:** $74.1 million

Alex Cross, the hero of a series of bestselling novels by James Patterson, is an acclaimed D.C. homicide detective, psychologist, and author. He has a fabulous mind, even able to make sense of what seems to be contradictory, illogical or incredible. Many viewers of *Along Came a Spider* wished they had such abilities when confronted with the film's implausibilities, surprises and loopholes. On too many occasions, one is distracted from what meager suspense this film musters by things which strain credulity, not to mention a gargantuan twist near the end which will make most mutter "Oh, come on!" instead of squeal "Oh, wow!" What is worthwhile in *Spider* and helps distract us from the film's deficits is yet another solid performance by the highly-skilled Morgan Freeman, who previously portrayed Cross in this film's prequel, *Kiss the Girls* (1997).

The most exciting moments in *Along Came a Spider*, directed by Lee Tamahori, are probably in its pulse-pounding opening sequence. Cross and other policemen follow in a helicopter while his partner works a sting next to a vile serial killer in a car riding below. Cross is able to watch and listen to all that goes on in the vehicle with some amazingly sophisticated technology. When the suspect finds the policewoman's earpiece, events—and the car—spin violently out of control. As her car teeters precariously on the edge of a dam, and as Cross calls out reassurance and desperately races to try and save her, she plummets thousands of feet to her death. We get a closeup of his eyes as she falls, clearly reflecting his disbelief and devastation. We then see that, eight months later, he is still sullen and withdrawn, building model ships at home and blaming himself all the while.

He makes a sudden and unexpected return to work when Gary Soneji (suitably-evil Michael Wincott), posing as a teacher at a school for the children of prominent Washington officials, kills another teacher and makes off with Megan Rose (Mika Boorem), the daughter of a little-known U.S. senator. Soneji calls Cross to taunt him back into action. Soneji considers himself to be a criminal genius worthy of recognition and respect, and wants the ultimate challenge of trying to outsmart the illustrious Alex Cross. He compares his crime to the tragic kidnaping of Charles A. Lindbergh's son in 1932. Megan's abduction happened on the watch of Secret Service Agent Jezzie Flannigan (Monica Potter) and her colleague Ben Devine (Billy Burke). When Cross and Jezzie meet, they share a similar gnawing need to somehow make amends for their costly screw ups. They are both clearly, as one of them puts it, "damaged." At first those in charge try to shut Jezzie out of the investigation, but Alex sagely points out that she may have a lot to offer due to her contact with Soneji during her three year's guarding the school. Cross is not ready to have another actual partner, but

Jezzie is eager to find her missing charge and vows to accompany him on his pursuit of the suspect.

Cross and Jezzie head to Soneji's classroom, where nothing escapes the detective's keen, thoughtful gaze. He sits down at Megan's computer and is amazingly able to get to the heart of the matter in just a few clicks of the mouse. (Also questionable is his ability to access a live cam which allows him to read a name off a tiny pill bottle.) He realizes that the psychopath behind the crime had long ago begun carefully constructing his plan, like a spider methodically spinning its web. Meanwhile, while being held captive in a tiny compartment on Soneji's boat, Megan shows herself to be exceedingly resourceful, not to mention gutsy. Somehow she knows to extract the battery pack from the intercom and use it as an incendiary device on a stove, causing an explosion. She dives overboard and screams for help to a fisherman on shore, but Soneji shoots the man and reels Megan back in.

Then, on a cold, rainy evening after not being allowed to speak with Dimitri (Anton Yelchin), Megan's classmate and the son of the Russian president, Cross and Jezzie just happen to have a chance encounter with Soneji. After killing two policemen and nearly getting Dimitri, the madman narrowly escapes because Jezzie fails to get a shot off in time. Then a call comes in to Cross demanding the drop-off of $10 million in diamonds, which sends him racing from payphone to payphone for further instructions before tossing the gems out the window of a crowded subway car. The scene is somehow not nearly as suspenseful as it should have been, and you just start to get tired along with Cross as he jogs from one place to another. Cross, who thought that the kidnapper was in it for fame and not fortune, is baffled by this whole development, and if the great Alex Cross is baffled you know that something is not right.

What also does not seem right is the way Soneji ends up meeting Cross face to face, merely coming to the door, claiming to be a policeman, and having Jezzie open the door to let him waltz on in. Soneji is upset because he has returned to the boat and found that Megan has vanished. The two men have a tense tête-à-tête before Soneji is finally shot by Cross. Jezzie cries that he has just killed the one person who knew where Megan is, but Cross is clearly not so sure. He goes back to review the tapes from the school's security cameras and realizes that someone was onto Soneji before that fateful day, laying in wait to take advantage of his efforts and snatch the fly from this sinister spider.

At this point, an extremely sudden and improbable twist arrives, revealing that Jezzie, aided by her Secret Service partner, is actually the devious and diabolical fiend behind it all, suddenly turning from sweet and forelorn to murderous and steely, slaying Devine before going after Megan, guns blazing. It is a revelation which elicits more groans than gasps. Cross goes to Jezzie's computer and is once again able to simply come up with all the information he needs, includ-

ing gleaning her password in seconds. Jezzie tells Megan, who has barricaded herself behind a door, to open up, but while the girl is initially thrilled that help has arrived, she suddenly gets another flash of amazing shrewdness and balks at letting Jezzie in. Megan even thinks to dash over and break the lightbulb overhead so that Jezzie will find it hard to spot her in the dark. Despite firing endlessly, Jezzie misses every time, but Cross, arriving just in time, does not. As Jezzie's blood leaves her body, Cross leaves with Megan, gently holding her hand.

*Along Came a Spider* was made on a budget of $28 million and succeeded in grossing just over $74 million during its four-month run in theaters. Most critics had nicer things to say about Freeman than the film as a whole. Neither *Kiss the Girls* nor *Spider* measure up to the books upon which they were based. In adapting this film, first-time screenwriter Marc Moss made numerous changes from Patterson's book, one of the most notable being the excision of an affair between Cross and Jezzie. Patterson envisioned his hero as "Muhammad Ali in his prime," but, played by the 64-year-old Freeman, it was thought that the character's credibility would have been undermined by an affair with the 30-year-old Potter. (Why Moss changed the little girl's first name from Maggie to Megan and the spelling of Jezzie's last name from Flanagan to Flannigan is anybody's guess.) Still, Freeman, with his calm authority, commands our respect, and is the main thing the film has going for it. Tamahori gives us numerous closeups of Freeman lost in thought to emphasize his character's cognitive prowess. Boorem, a gifted young actress on a steady rise, succeeds in making us care about her damsel in distress. What is most distressing to us is that what was billed as a heart-pounding thriller with an unbelievably exhilarating twist for an ending turned out to be merely a less-than-thrilling thriller with and unbelievable ending.

*—David L. Boxerbaum*

## CREDITS

**Alex Cross:** Morgan Freeman
**Jezzie Flannigan:** Monica Potter
**Gary Soneji:** Michael Wincott
**Elizabeth Rose:** Penelope Ann Miller
**Senator Hank Rose:** Michael Moriarty
**Ollie McArthur:** Dylan Baker
**Ben Devine:** Billy Burke
**Kyle Craig:** Jay O. Sanders
**Agent Hickley:** Kim Hawthorne
**Megan Rose:** Mika Boorem
**Dimitri Starodubov:** Anton Yelchin

**Origin:** USA

**Released:** 2001
**Production:** David Brown, Joe Wizan; Phase One, Revelations Entertainment; released by Paramount Pictures
**Directed by:** Lee Tamahori
**Written by:** Marc Moss
**Cinematography by:** Matthew F. Leonetti
**Music by:** Jerry Goldsmith
**Sound:** Eric J. Batut
**Editing:** Neil Travis
**Art Direction:** Sandy Cochrane
**Costumes:** Sanja Milkovic Hays
**Production Design:** Ida Random
**MPAA rating:** R
**Running time:** 103 minutes

## REVIEWS

*Boxoffice.* June, 2001, p. 59.
*Chicago Sun-Times Online.* April 6, 2001.
*Entertainment Weekly.* April 13, 2001, p. 48.
*Los Angeles Times Online.* April 6, 2001.
*New York.* April 16, 2001, p. 70.
*New York Times.* April 6, 2001, p. E14.
*People.* April 16, 2001, p. 35.
*Premiere.* April, 2001, p. 107.
*Rolling Stone.* April 26, 2001, p. 67.
*Sight and Sound.* June, 2001, p. 38.
*USA Today Online.* April 6, 2001.
*Variety.* April 2, 2001, p. 17.
*Wall Street Journal.* April 6, 2001, p. W1.

## QUOTES

Gary Soneji (Michael Wincott): "I'm living proof that a mind is a terrible thing."

# Amelie
# (Amelie from Montmartre)
# (The Fabulous Destiny of Amelie Poulain)
# (Le Fabuleux Destin d'Amelie Poulain)

*She'll change your life.*
—Movie tagline

 **Box Office:** $27.9 million

Combining the whimsy of a joyous romantic comedy with the heightened reality of a fairy tale, Jean-Pierre Jeunet's *Amelie* is the rare film that touches the heart while dazzling audiences with its invention and creativity. Set in Montmartre and revolving around the escapades of a sweet woman whose do-gooder instincts transform the lives of the people around her, *Amelie* embraces a hopeful vision that is a stark departure from *Delicatessen* and *The City of Lost Children,* the thematically dark and stylistically dreary films that Jeunet made with Marc Caro. Jeunet may engage in his old visual devices of startling zoom shots and odd close-ups, but the apocalyptic clutter that suffused his old set designs is gone, as is the unrelenting bleakness and pointlessness. In *Amelie,* he and co-screenwriter Guillaume Laurant have created a charmer that embraces the chance encounters and simple joys that make life wonderful and the odd turns of fate that can transform lives.

In an energetic, fast-paced prologue, we are introduced to Amélie Poulain. Raised by her widowed father, who is cold and distant, she has no playmates and must retreat into her imagination to shape her world, a quality that continues to sustain her as an adult (played by Audrey Tautou) when she is a waitress at a café.

Jeunet employs a narrator who introduces the characters and often includes a brief sketch featuring their likes and dislikes. Amélie, for example, enjoys dipping her hands in sacks of grain and skimming stones off the surface of water—having given up on romance, she "cultivates a taste for small pleasures." Even looking at the faces of an audience as they watch a movie brings her joy. This last detail reveals a lot about Amélie—she is a watcher, one who observes life more than she participates in it. Her closest contacts seem to be her acquaintances at the café—Suzanne the owner (Claire Maurier); a hypochondriac tobacconist named Georgette (Isabelle Nanty); a waitress named Gina (Clotilde Mollet); Gina's jealous ex-lover, Joseph (Dominique Pinon); and a struggling writer, Hipolito (Arthus de Penguern).

One night Amélie finds hidden behind one of the tiles in her bathroom an old tin box containing the toys and trinkets of a child from 40 years ago. She decides to seek out the owner of the box, a man named Dominic Bretodeau (Maurice Benichou), who is now in middle age. Apprehensive about Bretodeau's response, she does not face him but comes up with an elaborate scheme. She learns his daily routine and leaves the box in a phone booth that she knows he will pass by. She calls the booth, and he picks up the phone and finds the box waiting for him. This 50-year-old man is overjoyed to see the treasures of childhood before him and yet, saddened to think how one's life can be reduced to a box of toys, resolves to reestablish contact with the daughter he has not seen in many years and spend time with his grandson.

Stunned and moved by the effect she has had, Amélie decides to dedicate her life to helping others. In one of the film's most inspired sequences, she grabs a blind man by the arm and takes him for a quick walk while rattling off what she sees so that he can have some sense of the bustling world around him. It is a fast-paced whirlwind and an energetic piece of filmmaking that captures the unbridled enthusiasm of the heroine while leaving the audience breathless.

Tautou is a pure joy in the title role, embodying two qualities that are difficult to play simultaneously—a sense of innocence and mischief. Amélie is essentially good-hearted and naïve about the world around her, but she is also a true manipulator with a naughty twinkle in her eye and a sly smile that suggests she is not as simple as she may at first appear. Jeunet even has her occasionally look directly at the camera to draw us in to her schemes, a risky trick that works because it is hard not to be enchanted by her.

One role she plays is matchmaker. Seeing that Joseph's jealousy is constantly gnawing away at him and infuriating Gina, Amélie tries to get him together with Georgette, even conspiring to get the pair alone in the same room, where mad, spontaneous lovemaking ensues.

Amélie's schemes for everyone else are just as entertaining and fanciful. In little, devious ways, she makes life miserable for Collignon (Urbain Cancellier), the local grocer, because he publicly humiliates and berates his slow-witted but good-hearted employee, Lucien (Jamel Debbouze). Amélie goes into Collignon's apartment and alters the little things he takes for granted, like swapping the toothpaste and foot cream and changing the handles on his doors. She sets his alarm for four o'clock, and he is so tired that Lucien must run the store that day and ends up shining in his new role.

Amélie's father (Rufus) never fulfilled his dream to travel, so she steals his prized garden gnome and sends it around the world with a friend and has her send back pictures of the gnome in the great cities of the world as a way of inspiring her father's dream.

Madeleine (Yolande Moreau), the concierge of Amélie's apartment building, is still grieving over the husband who was cheating on her when he died years ago in South America. So Amélie cuts and pieces together copies of fragments of his old letters, photocopies the composite, browns it with tea, and sends it to Madeleine as a letter that was lost and went undelivered for many years. In this letter, her husband seems to reaffirm his love for her, turns his back on his philandering ways, and looks forward to the day they will be reunited. Thinking that her husband truly loved her, Madeleine can thus move on with her life

Amélie also develops a friendship with her neighbor, Raymond Dufayel (Serge Merlin), who is known as the Glass Man because his bones are so brittle. He has not left his apartment for 20 years, and everything in his home is padded since the slightest jolt could destroy his frail skeleton. He is the physical counterpart to Amélie, who has developed a psychological barrier to fully engaging with the world. Dufayel passes his time copying Renoir's "Luncheon of the Boating Party," making a new copy each year but always struggling with the expression on one of the girl's faces. She is in the middle of the group and yet somehow detached. What is she thinking? he wonders. The girl becomes a representation of Amélie, and, as they debate the girl's inner life, she becomes a way for them to talk about Amélie's own hesitations to become part of her community as she fixes other people's lives while ignoring her own. Meanwhile, Amélie anonymously drops off videotapes at Dufayel's door that feature odd little snippets of life—a horse joining a bicycle race, a one-legged man dancing—as a lovely way of expanding the boundaries of his own self-enclosed world.

While she is running around doing good deeds, Amélie is becoming fascinated by a strange young man named Nino (Mathieu Kassovitz), whom she sees rooting under photo booths. One day as she is following him, he loses a photo album that Amélie picks up. It contains photos thrown away by people at photo booths all over town. One very serious-looking man pops up many times in the album, and Amélie speculates that he may be dead and taking the pictures so that he will be remembered by the living.

Perhaps Nino is the perfect guy for Amélie. After all, he has constructed a family album of sorts through photos of complete strangers, and, like her, seems to be a lonely observer of humanity. He posts lost-and-found signs asking for the return of his book, and she eventually finds him at the funfair, where he works on the Ghost Train ride. She takes the ride, and Nino, in character as a skeleton, gently caresses her neck. What follows is a game of cat and mouse in which

Amélie and Nino share some close encounters but never quite connect because Amélie is too shy to follow through on her desires.

She leaves a note telling him to meet her at a carousel, where she puts the album in his motor scooter and then calls him at a nearby pay phone to direct him to a certain page of the album, where she asks if he would like to meet her. When he posts signs asking where and when, she responds by leaving pieces of a photo of herself dressed as Zorro (her alter ego in her fantasy life), where he is likely to find them. Sure enough, he pieces the photo together to read her note, which tells him to meet her at the café. He identifies her as the woman in the photo, but, once again too shy to make a connection, she denies it and then has Gina slip a note in Nino's pocket to arrange yet one more meeting at a photo booth. In a great visual moment that expresses her inner regret and longing, Amélie melts into a big splash of water.

Amélie has discovered that the man in so many of the pictures in the photo album is not a ghost trying to gain some kind of immortality on earth but rather the photo booth repairman. And yet learning this mundane fact is not a source of disappointment for Amélie. In the marvelous world of this film, a simple discovery carries as much satisfaction as a supernatural explanation would. Amélie jams a photo booth and calls for repair at the time of her proposed meeting with Nino so that he too can be privy to the big secret. It may seem like such a small gift, but, since both Amélie and Nino take pleasure in life's simple discoveries, she knows that he will appreciate finding out the truth. Unfortunately, while Nino comes face-to-face with the repairman, Amélie once again misses her chance to meet Nino.

Frustrated by all of the missed meetings, Nino finally gets Amélie's address from Gina and comes to Amélie's apartment, but she does not answer the door, yet again sabotaging herself. Then, in a touching yet bittersweet scene, she finds in her apartment a videotape from Dufayel, a video letter in which he implores her not to miss out on love. Spurred on by Dufayel's plea, she runs to her door and finds Nino has returned, and, in the end, Amélie and Nino are together and apparently in love, racing through the streets together on his motor scooter.

*Amelie* is one of the best films of the year—an exhilarating trip to a world in which goodness is magically rewarded with true love. And yet the film is still anchored in some sense of reality. Joseph's incessant jealousy finally destroys his relationship with Georgette, thus implying that Amélie's little schemes are not cure-alls for everyone, and we never learn if Collignon changes his bullying ways. Lucien, however, does gain a sense of confidence by becoming an art student of sorts under Dufayel's tutelage. And Amélie's father finally heads for the airport to fulfill his longings for travel.

Wedded to this sweet story are some dazzling stylistic flourishes—an omniscient narrator who places individual moments in the context of the general flow of life, clever fantasy sequences like Amélie imagining her own lavish state funeral on TV, even photos that talk to Nino about Amélie. Jeunet thus imbues his story with a surreal edge as playful as the unforgettable heroine who celebrates the everyday joys of living.

—*Peter N. Chumo II*

## CREDITS

**Amelie Poulain:** Audrey Tautou
**Nino Quincampoix:** Mathieu Kassovitz
**Raphael Poulain:** Rufus
**Madeleine Wallace:** Yolanda Moreau
**Joseph:** Dominique Pinon
**Bretodeau:** Maurice Benichou
**Hipolito:** Artus Penguern
**Collignon:** Urbain Cancellier
**Georgette:** Isabelle Nanty
**Suzanne:** Claire Maurier
**Eva:** Claude Perron
**Gina:** Clothilde Mollet
**Dufayel:** Serge Merlin
**Lucien:** Jamel Debbouze
**Amelie, age 8:** Flora Guiet
**Narrator:** Andre Dussollier

**Origin:** France, Germany
**Language:** French
**Released:** 2001
**Production:** Claudie Ossard; France 3 Cinema, MMC Independent, Victoires Productions, Tapioca Films; released by Miramax Films
**Directed by:** Jean-Pierre Jeunet
**Written by:** Jean-Pierre Jeunet, Guillaume Laurant
**Cinematography by:** Bruno Delbonnel
**Music by:** Yann Tiersen
**Sound:** Vincent Arnardi, Jean Umansky
**Editing:** Herve Schneid
**Costumes:** Emma Lebail
**Production Design:** ALine Bonetto
**MPAA rating:** R
**Running time:** 120 minutes

## REVIEWS

*Boxoffice.* September, 2001, p. 142.
*Chicago Sun-Times Online.* November 9, 2001.
*Entertainment Weekly.* November 9, 2001, p. 26.

*Hollywood Reporter.* May 8, 2001, p. 15.
*New York Times Online.* October 28, 2001.
*New York Times Online.* November 2, 2001.
*People.* November 19, 2001, p. 45.
*Sight and Sound.* August, 2001, p. 22.
*Sight and Sound.* October, 2001, p. 40.
*USA Today Online.* November 1, 2001.
*Variety.* April 30, 2001, p. 26.
*Washington Post.* November 9, 2001, p. WE38.

## QUOTES

Amelie (Audrey Tatou): "I like noticing the details that no one else does. . . . But I hate it in old movies when drivers don't watch the road."

## AWARDS AND NOMINATIONS

**British Acad. 2001:** Orig. Screenplay
**Cesar 2001:** Art Dir./Set Dec., Director (Jeunet), Film, Score
**Ind. Spirit 2002:** Foreign Film
**Broadcast Film Critics 2001:** Foreign Film
**Nomination:**
**British Acad. 2001:** Actress (Tautou), Director (Jeunet), Film, Film Editing, Foreign Film, Score
**Golden Globes 2002:** Foreign Film.

# American Desi

Piyush Pandya's farcical social comedy, *American Desi,* is a piece of bilingual chauvinism masquerading as a harmless dose of the commercial Hindi film in English for homesick elite Indians. None of the Hindi in the dialogue is translated into subtitles, and neither are the lyrics of the classic Hindi film songs on the soundtrack. This is no oversight; it becomes the film's agenda to exclude non-Indians, who are often the target of its desi (a slang term referring to anyone from India who lives elsewhere) humor.

Pandya's characters, on their part, seem totally unaware of the damage done to their 'Indianness' by the legacy of colonialism; instead we find them revelling in a fresh start on American soil, fabricating a desi, albeit shallow, identity. They scavenge folk and popular entertainment forms from the home country, as and when it suits them, deploying language as a weapon to keep non-Indians away from their newfound haven. In this, they are not very much different from other minorities amongst America's neoimmigrants. The disturbing fact that *American Desi* makes clear is that

the day of the immigrant wanting to be absorbed into the cultural mainstream of American life is long past.

No surprise then that the film's protagonist is meant to be seen as an oddball in the midst of these desis. For Krishna (Deep Katdare), or Kris, as he insists on being called, leaving home for college becomes an occasion for throwing off the yoke of everything Indian that has been foisted on him. Unfortunately, it so happens that on the threshold of his new life, he is stuck with a motley assortment of roommates, all of them Indian. There's Jagjit (Ronobir Lahiri), the wacky turbaned Sikh, who has absorbed all the American lingo, which he spouts forth with an Indian accent. Then there's Ajay (Kal Penn), a jive-talking, hyperactive Afro-centric, whose sensibility reflects what he sees as the historical affinity between India and Africa. On the opposite side of the spectrum is Salim (Rizwan Manji), a soft-spoken, devout Muslim, whose love of curry stinks up the place. One can say in favor of the film's sociological aspirations, evident in its title, that it does portray the changing complexion of the American university. There are very few goras—the desi word for whites—evident in the campus scenes.

Kris' initial response to his unforeseen plight is to keep to himself when in his dorm quarters. An old American friend, Eric (Eric Axen), provides solace at other times. What draws Kris out of his shell, in relation to the desis, is the sight of his classmate, the intelligent and beautiful Nina (Purva Bedi), whom he mistakes for an American. When he finds his preconceptions shattered, he can only gasp: "You don't sound or look like an Indian!" Far more attuned to the roots of her own identity than Kris, she retorts: "don't know whether to take that as a compliment or an insult." Kris thus finds himself learning about popular Indian culture in order to impress Nina. This becomes the plot device intended to carry the picture. It could have, had we come to know Kris' American side, about which the film reveals virtually nothing. Furthermore, Kris doesn't genuinely try to relate to what Nina is so fond of. Instead, he decides to fake it, and is exposed by her each time, resulting in complications that become repetitive. Even his jousts with his rival for Nina's affections, the villainous Rakesh (Anil Kumar) appear hackneyed.

To keep things afloat, Pandya, as writer-director, draws upon a number of subplots, which he milks mostly for their slapstick quotient. Typical is the attempt by Kris' roommates to cook up a traditional Indian meal for Nina. The whole endeavor backfires when things explode and the kitchen is a mess. Similarly, just when Salim decides to visit the campus apartment of Farrah (Sunita Puram), an attractive classmate who has been pursuing him, her parents drop by. Salim gets away, disguised in a black 'chador' draped over his head, and impersonating an orthodox Muslim female. It is Jagjit's tussle with his overbearing father which proves the only relationship to strike a genuine note. The old man wants his son to become a civil engineer, but Jagjit finds his liberation as an artist. For the party finale, he designs huge pop sculptures of Hindu gods.

The film's denouement is nowhere as original. Kris defeats Rakesh and his gang in hand-to-hand combat, then indulges with Nina in a prolonged kiss, still forbidden on the Hindi screen. A punchy hip-hop anthem, "Passage to India," underscores the credits, and ends up being the most original and honest thing in the film.

Clearly, critics of the film haven't forgiven its roots in the milieu of the commercial Hindi film. Typical is Jonathan Foreman's review in the *New York Post*, which finds *American Desi* riddled with "amateurish writing and direction" and "lame slapstick jokes." Michael Atkinson in *The Village Voice* is a bit more receptive when he calls Pandya's effort "pure-hearted." He goes on to note that the film "never forgets about its second-gen issues, but never quite plumbs them, either."

—*Vivek Adarkar*

## CREDITS

**Kris:** Deep Katdare
**Nina:** Purva Bedi
**Jagjit:** Ronobir Lahri
**Salim:** Rizwan Manji
**Ayjay:** Kal Penn
**Rakesh:** Anil Kumar
**Farah:** Sunita Param
**Eric:** Eric Axen

**Origin:** USA
**Released:** 2001
**Production:** Gitesh Pandya; Blue Rock Entertainment; released by Eros Entertainment
**Directed by:** Piyush Dinker Pandya
**Written by:** Piyush Dinker Pandya
**Cinematography by:** Renato Falcao
**Sound:** Robert Tate
**Editing:** Robert Tate
**Production Design:** Len X. Clayton
**MPAA rating:** Unrated
**Running time:** 98 minutes

## REVIEWS

*New York Post Online.* March 16, 2001.
*New York Times Online.* March 16, 2001.
*Variety.* May 7, 2001, p. 55.
*Village Voice Online.* March 20, 2001.

# American Outlaws

*Sometimes the wrong side of the law is the right place to be.*
—Movie tagline
*Bad is good again.*
—Movie tagline
*This much fun can't be legal.*
—Movie tagline

**Box Office:** $13.1 million

"**B**ad is good again," read the tag line on advertisements for *American Outlaws*. In a way, such a bland line that doesn't really mean anything is perfect for this film. The line, like the movie, is just kind of there. It's hard to see why the filmmakers, director Les Mayfield and screenwriters Roderick Taylor and John Rogers, bothered to make the movie at all. It doesn't break any new ground, and many considered it to be just another rehash of movies like *Posse* and *Young Guns* (and *Young Guns 2*, for that matter.) The main reason this film seems to have been released was so that a new crop of hunky guys could end up on the big screen. Besides the good-looking men, the only attempt to make the western seem interesting to the MTV generation was the addition of a few rock and roll tunes here and there. But the music and sexy guys are not enough to revitalize the now-tired genre.

The story is a retelling of the Jesse James myth. Not a whole lot is shown about the specifics of James' life, but it's pretty clear that he was a tough guy. Here James (Colin Farrell of the much more acclaimed film *Tigerland*, also reviewed in this edition) is more like a nice, fresh-faced guy who robs banks only for the most charitable of reasons.

The film starts during a Civil War battle. James and his posse—his intellectual brother Frank (Gabriel Macht), and their cousins Cole Younger (Scott Caan, James Caan's son), Jim (Gregory Smith), and Bob (Will McCormack)—win a battle despite being desperately outnumbered and outarmed. It's the kind of feat that they'll repeat with tiresome regularity. The boys get word that the war is over and head home to Liberty, Missouri, to pick up the pieces of their lives. They plan to do some "corn plantin', corn growin' and corn eatin.'" That wouldn't be the most interesting of movie plots, so of course it's not that easy. Once back home with their beloved, Jesus-obsessed Ma (Kathy Bates), they find out that mean old railroad baron Thaddeaus Rains (Harris Yulin) wants them to sell their property for a mere two dollars an acre so that the rails can go through. They handle this problem by pointing a gun at the men bearing the land sale contract and scaring them off their property.

Rollin Parker (Terry O'Quinn), the kind of doltish, trigger-happy gun who's always the villain's right-hand man, decides to retaliate by burning down the old James farm, killing Ma in the process, and thus getting rid of one of the better actors in the film. The James and Younger boys, who probably were going to have a hard time adjusting to regular non-violent life anyway, take this as a sign that they should declare war on Rains and his company. James is serious about it, too. When his new girlfriend Zee Mimms (Ali Larter) asks him, "When will you stop?", he answers with great gravity, "When I send them to their graves." Now that is some dialogue.

Instead of trying to attack Rains directly, they decide that their best strategy will be to drain his company of money, so they start hitting all the banks in the area. They make sure to share lots of their loot with local charities to gain support of the townspeople. It works—so much so that local bankers are somewhat honored when the James-Younger gang makes an appearance at their bank.

The gang's main adversary is Allen Pinkerton (Timothy Dalton), who is working for Rains to try and capture the notorious James. Pinkerton is obviously a smart guy but he doesn't seem to be doing such a great job of getting his man. He decides he's going to observe the gang for months to figure out the psychology behind their actions. In a time where it probably wouldn't have raised too many eyebrows if he'd just had James hanged, this is an odd approach, but he seems committed to it. Even though Pinkerton and James are mortal enemies, Pinkerton also seems to admire the criminal's daring and gets a slight smile whenever he hears about one of the gang's new exploits. "If I could design the perfect outlaw band, this would be the one," says Pinkerton admiringly. It's like Pinkerton seems to think he's in an elaborate mental chess game with a criminal mastermind when, in actuality, he's just dealing with a young thug who's playing it as it comes. In this film, James seems less like a brilliant criminal than a guy who'd rather be looking for a kegger at the nearest fraternity house.

In between robbin' banks and kissin' wimmen, the guys talk about things like who's wanted poster picture looks the most realistic. Bob Younger is bummed because his picture is generic and he feels that he's not getting enough attention from his public. While their lighthearted patter is more engaging that the Big Important Lines of the rest of the scripts (as in Ma's dying words, "Take care of each other, boys."), it's less interesting than, say, an episode of *The Real World*.

The film has all the superficial elements of a western, but none of the resonance that made films like the John Ford westerns so popular. There is plenty of dust, characters that say things like, "Dad burn, I'll whoop you real good" and "Line 'em up, barkeep," all kinds of scenes involving dyna-mite blowing stuff up and even, yawn, a fight that takes place on top of a moving train. There are so many of the usual elements of a western, they could have just taken a few old movies, spliced them together and saved themselves the trouble of filming anew.

There is no trace of any kind of psychopathic behavior in this Jesse James. This is a modern James, who is less a scary outlaw than a skillful manager who wants to get the best from his people and wants to do the task in the best, most efficient manner. He seems like he'd be equally comfortable in the executive training program at Chrysler. Even when James is put in jail, he makes good use of his time by doing push-ups in his cell (which also, conveniently, provides another chance for Farrell to showcase his muscular frame).

The movie also worships the gang. All the people they get in gun fights with suffer from the hideous aim that all movie bad guys have. There are countless shots of the guys riding their horses toward the camera, which are shot from a low angle, so that they seem to be towering heroically over the audience. In case we don't get the message, they often ride in slow motion to make them seem even more cool.

The acting is as bland as the rest of the film. Farrell, who was lauded for *Tigerland*, does nothing interesting here. He is suitably good-looking and agreeably does all the scenes where he's not wearing a shirt. But he lacks any kind of depth and is one of the least interesting criminals of the year. Caan is the hotheaded member of the Younger gang, but even he isn't too ominous. He's too in awe of James to be any kind of real threat to him. Dalton is almost laughable as the ultra-serious Pinkerton. He's putting way too much effort into his part for a movie of this caliber and it just makes him look silly.

Critics tended not to be blinded by the beefcake and didn't care for the movie. Gary Thompson of the *Philadelphia Daily News* wrote that the movie is "a Jesse James bio so gloriously dumb, so vapidly MTV that when its gunslingers die, they probably go to Bootylicious Hill." David Germain of the *Associated Press* wrote, "May the irascible ghost of John Ford come spit in the filmmakers' trough for the pretension of calling this film a western." Roger Ebert of the *Chicago Sun-Times* wrote, "Farrell here seems less like the leader of a gang than the lead singer in a boy band." And *Entertainment Weekly*'s Lisa Swartzbaum called the film a "puppy-stud Western" and wrote, "About the only way to imagine this genre getting much worse is if they did a remake of *The Wild Bunch* starring Corey Feldman, Corey Haim and the Hanson brothers."

—*Jill Hamilton*

## CREDITS

**Jesse James:** Colin Farrell
**Frank James:** Gabriel Macht
**Cole Younger:** Scott Caan
**Jim Younger:** Gregory Smith
**Bob Younger:** Will McCormack
**Allan Pinkerton:** Timothy Dalton
**Ma James:** Kathy Bates
**Comanche Tom:** Nathaniel Arcand
**Zee Mimms:** Ali Larter
**Doc Mimms:** Ronny Cox
**Thaddeus Rains:** Harris Yulin
**Rollin Parker:** Terry O'Quinn
**Clell Miller:** Ty O'Neal
**Loni Packwood:** Joe Stevens

**Origin:** USA
**Released:** 2001
**Production:** James G. Robinson; Morgan Creek Productions; released by Warner Bros.
**Directed by:** Les Mayfield
**Written by:** John Rogers, Roderick Taylor
**Cinematography by:** Russell Boyd
**Music by:** Trevor Rabin
**Sound:** Pud Cusack
**Music Supervisor:** Maureen Crowe
**Editing:** Michael Tronick
**Art Direction:** John Frick
**Costumes:** Luke Reichle
**MPAA rating:** PG-13
**Running time:** 95 minutes

## REVIEWS

*Boxoffice.* October, 2001, p. 61.
*Chicago Sun-Times Online.* August 17, 2001.
*Entertainment Weekly.* August 24, 2001, p. 103.
*Hollywood Reporter.* September 12, 2000, p. S-12.
*Los Angeles Times Online.* August 17, 2001.
*New York Times Online.* August 17, 2001.
*People.* August 27, 2001, p. 37.
*USA Today Online.* August 17, 2001.
*Variety.* August 20, 2001, p. 23.
*Washington Post.* August 17, 2001, p. WE37.

## QUOTES

Allan Pinkerton (Timothy Dalton) comments on the James gang: "They're disciplined and have a charismatic leader."

## TRIVIA

The real Jesse James was born September 5, 1847 and was killed by a member of his gang on April 3, 1882.

# American Pie 2

*This summer it's all about sticking together.*
—Movie tagline

**Box Office:** $145.1 million

*American Pie 2* is a classic example of a sequel that really had no reason for being made, other than the huge success of the original film. *American Pie* was a surprise hit of the summer of 1999—a cheerful, raunchy teen sex comedy with no stars but with plenty of laughs and some outrageous high jinks. The comedy was decidedly lowbrow, revolving around bodily fluids and sex, but it also had heart and even a kind of innocence. Four best friends—insecure Jim (Jason Biggs), sweet Oz (Chris Klein), nerdy Finch (Eddie Kaye Thomas), and bland Kevin (Thomas Ian Nicholas)—made a pact to lose their virginity by the end of high school, with results that were alternately hilarious, surprising, and even touching. One could leave the theater pleasantly surprised by the script's clever jokes and generous spirit toward its characters.

For the sequel, the original cast has been rounded up, and J.B. Rogers has taken over directing duties from Paul Weitz, but this time, instead of an actual story, the film is composed of a series of gags that are simply not funny. Admittedly, a teen sex comedy does not need a strong narrative, but some semblance of a plot would be welcome in holding the jokes together. The first film had a narrative drive in the boys' quest to find girls they could get to like them and have sex with on prom night. The sequel, however, has no such imperative. The kids, who were getting ready to leave high school in the first film, are now finishing up their first year of college and returning home for the summer. The boys rent a beach house, take a job as housepainters, and of course let their horniness get them in a lot of silly antics.

Perhaps the lack of a plot would be okay in *American Pie 2* if the boys' sexual misadventures were funny, but instead they are rather tiresome, with sequences that drag on a lot longer than they should and that try in desperation to recall or mimic some of the funniest jokes from the original. The film is so thin in terms of plot that it actually resorts to filling screen time with pointless montages set to music.

Another crucial problem with the film is that some of the most charming characters from the original have been diminished in the sequel. One of the cutest stories in the first film revolved around the good-hearted jock, Oz, wooing a cute girl in the school choir named Heather (Mena Suvari). The great thing about their story in the original is that it ends up reversing our expectations—as time goes on, he is less concerned with having sex and more interested in getting to know her as a person. In the sequel, their story is virtually negligible and could have been cut. She is spending the summer in Europe, and the supposed highlight of their relationship is an aborted attempt at phone sex. Their story is a complete waste and an added shame when one considers that Klein and Suvari are two of the most promising actors in the ensemble, having distinguished themselves in two great films the same year *American Pie* was released—Klein in *Election* and Suvari in *American Beauty*.

Natasha Lyonne as Jessica is also given short shrift in *American Pie 2* (Lyonne is also a fine actress, so why the most talented people were downplayed in the sequel is a complete puzzle, unless they were simply smart enough to ask for small roles). In the first film, Jessica is a pivotal confidante for a couple of characters. She advises Vicky (Tara Reid) about whether she should sleep with her boyfriend Kevin, and she helps the intellectual Finch by spreading rumors of his manliness to impress the girls. In the sequel, Jessica becomes a very minor character. Vicky and Kevin have parted ways, even though he pines for her, leaving their story nowhere to go. Meanwhile, Finch spends the whole film doing Tantric exercises so that he will be ready to have sex with Stifler's mom (Jennifer Coolidge), a hot older woman with whom he had sex at the end of *American Pie*. Of course, in the first film, this meeting was hilarious and unexpected—in the sequel, he is counting on another sexual encounter with her, so it simply cannot have the element of surprise anymore. The upshot is that Kevin, Vicky, and Finch are given nothing to do, and poor Jessica, whose deadpan, gently sarcastic persona was a delight in the original, makes very little impression in the sequel.

Not only have the smart, nuanced characters been downplayed in the sequel, but, to make matters worse, the most annoying character in the original has become a major player. Stifler (Seann William Scott) is a loud, boorish jerk who revels in making fun of others and hogging the spotlight. A big, obnoxious bore, he can be tolerable in small doses as a kind of parody of a frat boy type who thinks every woman wants nothing more than to sleep with him. But *American Pie 2* features way too much of him, and he is painful to watch. To make matters worse, Stifler's little brother (Eli Marienthal), essentially a junior version of him, is also given more screen time in the sequel.

This leaves Jim, who is the emotional center of both films. Awkward with girls but essentially a decent person, he is saddled with a dad (Eugene Levy) whose clumsy attempts at being cool and understanding his son's sexual problems are pretty funny—the first time. Now their relationship is just shtick as the ultimate square father constantly tries too hard to be a pal to his son. In the sequel, Jim anxiously awaits a visit from Nadia (Shannon Elizabeth), the sexy Czech exchange student with whom his attempt at sex in the first film was a disaster inadvertently broadcast over the Internet. Nadia was a minor though fun character in *American Pie*, but now she has been elevated to some kind of goddess.

Poor Jim knows that he is sexually inexperienced for a woman like Nadia, so he enlists the help of Michelle (Alyson Hannigan), the only girl with whom he has ever had sex, to train him as a lover. Michelle was the greatest pleasure of *American Pie*—a total geek whose boring stories of her time at band camp masked a sexual dynamo and whose revelation of using her flute as a sex toy was the film's most memorable moment. In the sequel, her role has been expanded, which would seem like a smart move. But, alas, Michelle can no longer be a surprising character. Her interest in the first film derived from her geekiness matched by Hannigan's brilliant deadpan delivery and the way Michelle's dorkiness vanished when she unleashed her sexual power on Jim. Now she has been reduced to the stereotypical plain but good-hearted girl that Jim must come to realize is really the right one for him. Hannigan is the best thing in *American Pie 2*, but, given the rest of the movie, that is not saying much.

Since the stories are either pointless or nonexistent, all the film has to offer are plenty of stupid jokes. For example, Jim is mistaken for a retarded boy at Michelle's band camp and is shoved onto a stage to perform a trombone solo. The sequence drags on forever, and, if the joke were not lame enough the first time, it is reprised at the end when Jim interrupts Michelle's flute solo at a concert to show how much he loves her. Unbelievably, this is how he finally wins her affection. In another unfunny sequence, the boys discover two beautiful women they think are lesbians and try to get them to perform sex acts with each other, but the girls turn the tables by having the boys do sexual things with each other first—an embarrassing, protracted sequence that goes nowhere. The big set piece of *American Pie 2* is Jim watching a porno movie and gluing his hand to his penis when he mistakes a tube of super strong adhesive for lubricant. By the time he glues his other hand to the videotape and is on the roof with a police light shining on him, the joke has already worn thin. It is a transparent attempt to match the hilarity of Jim's close encounter with an apple pie in the original film, and it fails miserably.

The film climaxes with a big party at the beach house, a pale imitation of the prom night that concludes the first film. The prom, after all, has a sense of urgency since it is what the whole film has been leading up to. The party in the sequel means nothing, and nothing of consequence is resolved or discovered. Kevin finally accepts that Vicky and he are no longer a couple, and they remain friends. Heather and Oz are reunited, Jim has Michelle, and Stifler has bedded the two lesbians, who, it turns out, are not really lesbians. In the film's final scene, Finch gets another encounter with Stifler's mom, but the older woman-younger man joke falls flat, just like most of the other jokes that rely on references to the first film.

*American Pie 2* is a crass (in more than one sense) and cynical film—a tired retread whose only purpose is to cash in on the audience's fondness for the original. That film may not have been a masterpiece, but it was funny because screenwriter Adam Herz actually came up with ways to make a fresh, honest teen sex comedy. All he has done in the sequel is throw together some loosely connected, vulgar scenes that attempt to recall the risque humor of the original, but they cannot duplicate its originality or heart. 🎞

—*Peter N. Chumo II*

### CREDITS

**Jim:** Jason Biggs
**Nadia:** Shannon Elizabeth
**Michelle:** Alyson Hannigan
**Oz:** Chris Klein
**Jessica:** Natasha Lyonne
**Kevin:** Thomas Ian Nicholas
**Vicky:** Tara Reid
**Sherman:** Chris Owen
**Stifler:** Seann William Scott
**Heather:** Mena Suvari
**Finch:** Eddie Kaye Thomas
**Jim's Dad:** Eugene Levy
**Stifler's Mom:** Jennifer Coolidge
**Stifler's Dad:** Christopher Penn
**Stifler's Brother:** Eli Marienthal
**Kevin's Brother:** Casey Affleck
**Danielle:** Denise Faye
**Jim's Mom:** Molly Cheek

**Origin:** USA
**Released:** 2001
**Production:** Warren Zide, Chris Moore, Craig Perry; released by Universal Pictures
**Directed by:** James B. Rogers
**Written by:** Adam Herz
**Cinematography by:** Mark Irwin
**Music by:** David Lawrence
**Sound:** Stephen A. Tibbo, Jonathan Earl Stein
**Music Supervisor:** Gary Jones, Dave Jordan
**Editing:** Larry Madaras, Stuart Pappe
**Art Direction:** Kitty Doris-Bates
**Costumes:** Alexandra Welker
**MPAA rating:** R

**Running time:** 105 minutes

### REVIEWS

*Boxoffice.* July, 2001, p. 28.
*Boxoffice.* October, 2001, p. 63.
*Chicago Sun-Times Online.* August 10, 2001.
*Entertainment Weekly.* August 17, 2001, p. 46.
*Los Angeles Times Online.* August 10, 2001.
*New York Times Online.* August 10, 2001.
*People.* August 20, 2001, p. 33.
*USA Today Online.* August 10, 2001.
*Variety.* August 13, 2001, p. 44.
*Washington Post.* August 10, 2001, p. WE33.

### QUOTES

Jim (Jason Biggs) explains on the phone: "I kinda superglued myself—to myself."

# An American Rhapsody

 **Box Office:** $.6 million

Eva Gardos, a Hungarian-born film editor [*Mask* (1985), *Agnes Brown* (1999)] turned writer-director, succinctly titles her debut feature *An American Rhapsody*. True to its title, Gàrdos' memoir blends in equal portions the emotional intensity of a Hungarian rhapsody and the wide-eyed apple pie America of the 1950's. Gàrdos deserves applause for transforming her personal story into a screenplay (not an easy task) and for extracting heart-wrenching performances from both child and adult actors. Of course, Gàrdos was blessed with a cast that includes Scarlett Johansson and Nastassja Kinski, as well as the beautiful backdrop of old-world Hungary.

The performers pace themselves as they endure the film's non-stop emotional riptide that begins with the Russian Communist takeover of Budapest and the evacuation of Hungary's upper-class citizens, then later deals with the process of assimilating into American culture. The heart of the story revolves around Margit (Kinski), who is persuaded to leave her infant Suzy behind while the remainder of her family is smuggled across the Hungarian border. Margit's mother Helen (Agnes Banfalvy) was to arrange for a child smuggler to take the infant across the border but changes her mind after learning that the infant will be drugged and hidden in a potato sack. After Helen is imprisoned by the communists, the baby is sent to live with a rural couple, Jeno (Balazs Galko) and Teri (Zsuzsa Czinkoczi), who lovingly raise Suzy as their own. Suzy adapts to the rustic life with ease, feeding ducks and chickens, cuddling with her adopted parents, and living a simple life.

Meanwhile, Suzy's parents and sister have adapted quiet nicely to the American lifestyle while residing in a Los Angeles neighborhood of matching bungalows, drinking Coca Cola and eating hamburgers. Margit writes to Eleanor Roosevelt pleading for assistance in bringing her daughter safely to America and they finally obtain a visa for Suzy. One day, Suzy's grandmother Helen (who has been released from prison after Stalin's death) shows up to whisk her grand-daughter away to America. The couple believe that Suzy is taking a short trip to Budapest and Suzy also believes that she will return—only to find herself in landing in a new country that confuses her.

The now six-year-old is flaunted to neighboring house-wives and is treated like a victim of communist Russia; one neighbor calls her the "Communist girl from Czechoslova-kia." One night Suzy flees to the park and her father (Tony Goldwyn) makes a promise that he will allow her to return to Hungary when she's older as long as she tries to assimilate into American culture. The cherub-face Suzy transforms into a sullen teen (Scarlett Johansson), who rebels against her parents by drinking and making out with an older boy. Out of frustration, Margit puts bars on Suzy's bedroom window and locks on the bedroom door hoping to keep her daughter safe at home. Only one day, Suzy finds a rifle in her closet and she shoots holes in the door, nearly killing her mother. She pleads with her father to allow her to return to Budapest. So in 1965, the 15-year-old Suzy returns to Budapest and reunites with Jeno and Teri, as well as Helen. She learns about the sacrifices everyone made for her and the truth about communist Hungary. Feeling displaced in Hun-gary, Suzy realizes that her real home is in America with her family. The film ends with Suzy disembarking from a plane as her family waits for her at the airport.

The crux of the story revolves around Margit, who feels guilty for abandoning her daughter in Hungary and fears for Suzy's safety, and Suzy, who feels angry towards her parents for taking her away from her adoptive home. Johansson, who played a high school graduate at odds with adult society in *Ghost World* and an emotionally distraught teen in *The Horse Whisperer*, stretches her talents a bit further here while also learning how to speak Hungarian. Kinski delivers a riveting performance as the overprotective mother, Goldwyn brings warmth and compassion to his role as the overworked father, and the remainder of the cast deliver even performances.

Gàrdos refrains from sentimentality for the most part by building up conflicts scene by scene while showing the characters' problems through smart montages and set deco-

ration. However, the film suffers due to its brevity. After all, life stories, like rhapsodies, need to be savored.

—*Patty-Lynne Herlevi*

## CREDITS

**Margit:** Nastassia Kinski
**Suzanne:** Scarlett Johansson
**Peter:** Tony Goldwyn
**Suzanne, age 6:** Kelly Endresz-Banlaki
**Helen:** Agnes Banfalvy
**Teri:** Zsuzsi Czinkoczi
**Jeno:** Balazs Galko
**George:** Zoltan Seress
**Maria:** Mae Whitman
**Pattie:** Lisa Jane Persky
**Sheila:** Emmy Rossum

**Origin:** USA, Hungary
**Released:** 2001
**Production:** Colleen Camp, Bonnie Timmerman; Fireworks Pictures, Seven Arts Pictures; released by Paramount Classics
**Directed by:** Eva Gardos
**Written by:** Eva Gardos
**Cinematography by:** Elemer Ragalyi
**Music by:** Cliff Eidelman
**Sound:** Peter Kardos
**Editing:** Margaret Goodspeed
**Costumes:** Beatrix Aruna Pasztor, Vanessa Vogel
**Production Design:** Alex Tavoularis
**MPAA rating:** PG-13
**Running time:** 106 minutes

## REVIEWS

*Boxoffice.* September, 2001, p. 141.
*Chicago Sun-Times Online.* August 24, 2001.
*Los Angeles Times Online.* August 10, 2001.
*New York Times Online.* August 10, 2001.
*Seattle Weekly.* August 23, 2001, p. 121.
*USA Today Online.* August 10, 2001.
*Variety.* July 9, 2001, p. 24.

## QUOTES

Helen (Agnes Banfalvy) explains to granddaughter Suzanne (Scar-lett Johansson): "We all make mistakes out of love."

# America's Sweethearts

*A comedy about celebrity, family and other forms of insanity.*
—Movie tagline

 **Box Office:** $93.6 million

Making use of a sparkling and eclectic ensemble cast headed by John Cusack, Catherine Zeta-Jones, Julia Roberts, and Billy Crystal, director Joe Roth's romantic comedy, set against the backdrop of a Hollywood satire, seems to have all the ingredients for success. Indeed, after a decade long hiatus from filmmaking during which the former Disney executive set up his own Revolution Studios, Roth (*Coupe de Ville, Revenge of the Nerds II*) shows he is still quite a connoisseur of funny but is eventually humbled after the film's bright beginning gives way to a more mediocre middle and a drag of an end.

*America's Sweethearts* opens as a promising Tinsel Town send-up with all the usual suspects: a famous on-screen Hollywood couple whose off-screen romance has gone awry, a driven studio boss, an eccentric Kubrick-esque director and a seasoned studio PR pro. An early scene featuring the promo reel for stellar couple Gwen Harrison (Zeta-Jones) and Eddie Thomas's (Cusack) big-budget new time-travel flick, *Time Over Time,* features an especially hilarious montage of their previous nine films together with titles like, *Sasha and the Optometrist* ("Their love opened our eyes") and the legal romance *On the Bench* ("Justice never tasted so sweet"), which pays homage to the PR machine and films of the 30s and 40s from which *Sweethearts* draw its screwball roots.

The set-up is simple: studio boss Dave Kingman (Stanley Tucci) sets his top PR man on the couple's case to stage a reunion for the estranged duo for the benefit of the press in order to ensure the success of the film. There are, of course, a few impediments to his strategy. First, he must lure back his top PR man, Lee Phillips (Crystal), whom he has recently fired. Once that is accomplished, Phillips must get around Gwen's fiery new Latin lover Hector (Hank Azaria) and the fact that the insanely jealous Eddie has tried to kill Gwen and Hector by crashing his motorcycle through the window of a Chinese restaurant where the two were dining. Add to that the fact that the new film's director, Hal Weidmann (Christopher Walken), refuses to hand over the film until the upcoming press junket and Phillips and his young mentor Danny (Seth Green) are forced to come up with a scathingly brilliant plan to ensure that their faux match-making succeeds.

To keep the press off their guard, Phillips carefully stages the scene in a remote desert location, far from cell phone towers and other distractions that could clue the flacks in to the fact that they haven't yet seen the movie they're there to review. Showered with gift baskets and gourmet food, placating the press is an easier task than getting Gwen and Eddie's pampered pusses back together and make nice for the press junket. Phillips manages to lure Eddie away from his anger-management therapy at a remote wellness center to attend the junket, meanwhile calling in Gwen's personal assistant and sister Kiki (Roberts) to work on her stubborn and very spoiled sister. Craftily spinning his story to suit whomever he's working, Phillips show he's the master of the game. And Phillips, further burdened with grooming his dull-witted assistant Danny for future use by the studio, needs all the craft he can muster for this job.

The rest of the film's scenes take place amidst a beautiful desert backdrop in Nevada that is the location for the press junket. Some insightful and slightly zany scenes skewering the press machine are tempered by some hackneyed predictable scenarios. Cusack caught on security cameras in what looks like an uncompromising situation with himself and a cactus while spying on what he thinks is Gwen taking an evening swim plays nicely and is cleverly capped off with Phillips making it pay off for his subplot of subterfuge. The seg which pitches Eddie against Hector in a fist-fight after Gwen's lisping live-in catches the two former flames having dinner (set up, of course, by Phillips) leaves no one a winner, especially the audience. Simultaneously playing confidante to the on-the-verge-of-a-nervous-breakdown Eddie and playing him for all it's worth, Phillips shows he's a showman with an unerring sense of duty, while occasionally revealing he also has a heart. Although uneven in entertainment value, these scenes are worth a look if only for an inside look at the circus-like atmosphere of the junket and its non-stop interviews that fatigue event he most chipper of entertainers.

To make the match-making situation worse, Kiki, Gwen's little brown wren of a sister, has recently shed 60 pounds. That and the fact that she secretly harbors a crush on former brother-in-law Eddie, fueled by the fact the two once shared an innocently intimate encounter years earlier, sets up the film's ensuing turn of events. To screenwriters Crystal and Peter Tolan's credit, Eddie doesn't do the clichéd jaw-drop, eye-pop routine when Kiki suddenly appears at his hotel suite door 60 pounds lighter (or the equivalent of a Backstreet boy as Crystal proclaims in the film and its trailers). It seems he has always seen her as an attractive and compassionate compadre. His romantic inclinations are, natch, stimulated by her new, sleeker package. As the two share an intimate encounter and edge closer to making a real connection, Gwen's hatred of being out of the picture, so to speak, fuels her to tease and tempt Eddie into a sticky situation where he denies that he has any romantic prospects. Overheard by an enraged Kiki, who is ironically in the kitchen cooking Gwen and Eddie breakfast, she is compelled to inject both mega-stars with a mega-dose of reality.

*Sweethearts* loses it's luster from this point on. A rooftop scene involving Eddie doesn't work at all and the films long-awaited denouement—Weidmann helicoptering into the junket proudly brandishing his now-finished masterpiece—is nothing short of a downer. As the film unspools to the eager press and the *Sweethearts* audience, neither gets what it expects, although the press at least have a juicy story to run with. The bad guys—Gwen and the studio boss—get a well-deserved come-uppance but not a satisfactory one. Neither does the fact that Eddie finally comes to his senses and (surprise) makes the more sane choice of life-mates.

Roberts, dutifully kitted out in the latest in latex fat-suit wear for flashbacks from her slightly more expansive years, ably pulls off her part as the only real person in the highly charged world of entertainment inanity. Wisely, Roberts chose Kiki after Roth envisioned her in the part of Gwen, a role closer to her own persona as the big-screen star and America's unofficial sweetheart. Producer Crystal himself was originally slated for Eddie's role, telling *The New York Times'* Rick Lyman, "Initially, I was going to play the actor, and it was something I could do with Meg Ryan." Wisely, he too opted for the less glamorous but ultimately more interesting role as the plate-spinning spin doctor.

Cusack plays Eddie with heart-broken earnestness and a desire to get on with his life but driven to extremes by Gwen's carelessness and vanity. Although he seems to make a connection with Zeta-Jones, there were no big sparks flying around the scenes with Roberts, who seemed more like the good friends they started out as. Zeta-Jones is deliciously bad as the camera-friendly superstar who turns into a super witch once (she thinks) the cameras stop rolling.

Arkin is a standout as the Deepak Chopra-like New Age guru susceptible to more earthly pleasures, as is Walken as reclusive director Weidmann, who buys and then transplants Unabomber Ted Kaczynski's run-down shack onto his lavish estate property to edit his latest film in. Funnyman Azaria takes his mucho macho Latin playboy to the hilt with mixed results and he seems an unlikely match for Zeta-Jones's diva. Though neither had a large role, both Tucci and Green inject as much life and energy into the film as their screen time makes possible.

Had the movie concentrated more on the skewering of the entertainment industry and less on the pre-fabricated and dull romance between its stars, it could have risen to the status of a comic *The Player*. As it stands, it is alternately an entertaining and highly flawed sometimes screwball romantic comedy. Throughout the film, the rich colors, beautiful sets, and striking desert locations are lushly lensed by cinematographer Phedon Papamichael. The film also benefits from superb overall art direction that is unusually good for

this kind of lighter cinematic fare.

—*Hilary White*

## CREDITS

**Kiki Harrison:** Julia Roberts
**Gwen Harrison:** Catherine Zeta-Jones
**Eddie Thomas:** John Cusack
**Lee Phillips:** Billy Crystal
**Hector:** Hank Azaria
**Hal Weidmann:** Christopher Walken
**Danny Wax:** Seth Green
**Dave Kingman:** Stanley Tucci
**Cameo:** Larry King

**Origin:** USA
**Released:** 2001
**Production:** Billy Crystal, Susan Arnold, Donna Roth; Revolution Studios, Face; released by Columbia Pictures
**Directed by:** Joe Roth
**Written by:** Billy Crystal, Peter Tolan
**Cinematography by:** Phedon Papamichael
**Music by:** James Newton Howard
**Sound:** Robert Eber
**Music Supervisor:** Kathy Nelson
**Editing:** Stephen A. Rotter
**Art Direction:** Denise L. Dugally
**Costumes:** Ellen Mirojnick, Jeffrey Kurland
**Production Design:** Gareth Stover
**MPAA rating:** PG-13
**Running time:** 103 minutes

## REVIEWS

*Boxoffice.* September, 2001, p. 149.
*Chicago Sun-Times Online.* July 20, 2001.
*Entertainment Weekly.* July 27, 2001, p. 43.
*Los Angeles Times Online.* July 20, 2001.
*New York Times Online.* May 13, 2001.
*New York Times Online.* July 20, 2001.
*People.* July 30, 2001, p. 31.
*Rolling Stone.* August 16, 2001, p. 111.
*USA Today Online.* July 20, 2001.
*Variety.* July 16, 2001, p. 18.
*Washington Post.* July 20, 2001, p. WE30.

## QUOTES

Publicist Lee Phillips (Billy Crystal) to Kiki (Julia Roberts) about her star sister Gwen (Catherine Zeta-Jones): "You're the only one Gwen'll even pretend to listen to."

# Amores Perros (Love's a Bitch)

*Don't worry if you don't see the picture, you are going to LIVE IT anyway.*
—Movie tagline

**Box Office:** $5.4 million

*Amores Perros* literally bursts at the seams while the first 10 minutes of the film explodes off of the screen leaving little breathing room for its viewers. Translated into *Love's a Bitch* (referring to the dogs in the film), Mexican director Alejandro Gonzàlez Iñàrritu's debut feature begins with a car chase scene that culminates into a catastrophe that destroys several lives from both sides of the tracks.

As hot as the country it comes from, *Amores Perros* has collected awards from a number of film festivals and was also nominated for a Golden Globe and an Oscar® for Best Foreign Language Film. The *New York Times* described the film as "the first classic of a new decade." And *Amores Perros'* brutal and surreal images certainly will stay in viewer's minds as well as turning American eyes south of the border in anticipation of other Mexican releases.

*Amores Perros* has unfairly been compared to Quentin Tarantino's *Pulp Fiction* because of its multiple narrative structure and extreme violence, but Iñàrittu, in an interview that appeared in *Filmmaker,* laughed at the obvious comparison, "The Tarantino thing is funny—I think people have credited Tarantino with the invention of the three-story structure, but what about Faulkner and Garcìa Màrquez? . . . I don't have anything to do with Tarantino, except for maybe the approach to violence more than the structure." The 38-year-old director went on to list Bergman, Fellini, Buñuel and other classic cinema directors as influences and, indeed, *Amores Perros* has a few Buñuelian elements floating through it and certainly Buñuelian humor with an attraction to violent imagery.

Set in Mexico City, one of the most violent, polluted and populated cities in the world, *Amores Perros* takes a blinding look at humanity, while placing the lives of several city inhabitants under a magnifying glass. The wealthy collide with those from the squalid side of the tracks, but all the characters have one thing in common, they all love dogs. However, their love for dogs and their attempts at loving other human beings leads to tragic complications—thus the film's title, *Love's a Bitch.* And the dogs also become a metaphor while presenting the beast side of human beings. The characters participate in dogfights, kill and steal from one another, and in this eye for an eye universe, the characters all careen with dire consequences from a car crash that transforms several lives.

In the first story of the triptych, "Octavio and Susana," rottweiler Cofi's teenage owner Octavio (Gael Garcìa Bernal) enters the brutal world of dog fighting so that he can raise the money that would allow him to escape with his brother's wife Susana (Vanessa Bauch). Cofi's near-fatal injury (he's shot by a dogfight participant) leads to a reckless car chase that ends violently, leading to the demise of Octavio's plans. In "Daniel and Valeria," a middle-age businessman (Guerrero) watches his dream of cohabiting with a Latina super model (Toledo) transform into a nightmare after the car crash physically transforms her. Finally, in "El Chivo and Maru," a former school teacher turned-revolutionary-turned assassin (Echevarria) witnesses the car accident and, after stealing Cofi, is led to an unexpected moral epiphany, which concludes the film.

Screenwriter Guillermo Arriaga skillfully interweaves the character's lives as they pass each other by and, only after the climatic car crash, do we see how unassuming individuals affect the lives of strangers. The car crash is shown from various points of view throughout the film as the lives of the characters intersect. This intricate triptych, with its overlapping narratives, took 36 drafts and three years to write, proving that perseverance pays off in the final analysis.

Emilio Echevarrìa, who plays the assassin who longs to reunite with his estranged daughter, recalls director Jim Jarmusch's character Ghost Dog because he despises cruelty to animals, but who can work as a contract killer. Echevarrìa plays hot and cold equally well. Newcomer Gael Garcìa Bernal, featured in the March/April 2001 issue of *RANT,* proves to be a heartthrob who delivers a heartfelt performance as Octavio. Goya Toledo transforms from a superficial model only concerned about her perfume campaign to a woman suffering intense pain with aplomb and Vanessa Bauche (who plays unhappy wife Susana) could easily compete with her compatriot Salma Hayek in Hollywood.

For viewers who can stomach the violence, *Amores Perros* proves well worth the collision course with life. Echevarrìa's redemptive soliloquy alone is worth the price of admission.

—*Patty-Lynne Herlevi*

## CREDITS

**Susana:** Vanessa Bauche
**El Chivo:** Emilio Echeverria
**Octavio:** Gael Garcia Bernal
**Valeria:** Goya Toledo
**Daniel:** Alvaro Guerrero
**Luis:** Jorge Salinas

**Ramirez:** Marco Perez
**Gustavo:** Rodrigo Murray
**Jorge:** Humberto Busto
**Maurico:** Gerardo Campbell
**Aunt Luisa:** Rosa Maria Bianchi
**Susana's mother:** Dunia Saldivar
**Octavio's mother:** Adriana Barraza

**Origin:** Mexico
**Language:** Spanish
**Released:** 2000
**Production:** Alejandro Gonzalez Inarritu; Altavista, Zeta Films; released by Lion's Gate Films
**Directed by:** Alejandro Gonzalez Inarrita
**Written by:** Guillermo Arriaga
**Cinematography by:** Rodrigo Prieto
**Music by:** Gustavo Santaolalla
**Sound:** Martin Hernandez
**Music Supervisor:** Lynn Fainchtein
**Editing:** Alejandro Gonzalez Inarrita, Luis Carballar, Fernando Perez Unda
**Costumes:** Gabriela Diaque
**Production Design:** Brigitte Broch
**MPAA rating:** R
**Running time:** 150 minutes

## REVIEWS

*Boxoffice.* December, 2000, p. 53.
*Chicago Sun-Times Online.* April 13, 2001.
*Entertainment Weekly.* April 6, 2001, p. 90.
*Los Angeles Times Online.* April 13, 2001.
*New York Times Online.* October 5, 2000.
*People.* April 16, 2001, p. 38.
*RANT.* March/April, 2001, p. 9.
*Rolling Stone.* April 12, 2001, p. 145.
*Sight and Sound.* May, 2001, p. 28.
*Time.* April 16, 2001, p. 78.
*Washington Post Online.* April 20, 2001.

## QUOTES

The director on his film: "We try to show that violence has consequences. When you create violence, it turns against you."

## TRIVIA

The director makes a cameo in the character Daniel's publicity office.

## AWARDS AND NOMINATIONS

**British Acad. 2001:** Foreign Film
**Natl. Bd. of Review 2001:** Foreign Film
**Nomination:**
**Oscars 2000:** Foreign Film
**Golden Globes 2001:** Foreign Film.

# Angel Eyes

*The deeper you look. The more you will find.*
—Movie tagline

 **Box Office:** $24 million

If you look at the trailer, the commercials, even the poster for this movie (which features a soft-focus close-up of Jennifer Lopez's face in misty white and gray), you would be likely to think that there is something supernatural about the story—some otherworldly trauma—maybe a guardian angel. But you would be wrong. Because *Angel Eyes* is a quiet romantic drama about two lost souls who find each other—maybe they are each other's guardian angel. Bad marketing campaign; predictable, but not unworthy movie.

The film (which is set in Chicago but filmed in Toronto) begins with a multi-vehicle accident. A very blonde Lopez is cop Sharon Pogue, who arrives on the scene and offers comfort to an unseen person trapped in a car. We see things from the victim's perspective. Sharon keeps saying: "Look at me. Look at my eyes." Stay with me, hold my hand, don't let me go—until the picture fades out.

A year later, we see a thin guy, unshaven, with haunted very blue eyes, and wearing a long, dark raincoat, wandering the streets. This is Catch (Jim Caviezel). He does random acts of kindness for people but doesn't exactly look crazy or homeless. Sharon, meanwhile, is back in her apartment getting dressed for work, putting on her bullet-proof vest. She goes for coffee at a cop hangout and Catch spots her through the window. Something clicks for him—he flashes back to the scene of a car accident (and, frankly, there should be no surprise to the viewer as to how this twosome are connected).

Sharon stops by a building site to see her brother, Larry (Jeremy Sisto). They are awkward with each other and it's made clear that Sharon is long estranged from her family. He tells her that their parents are having a renewal ceremony of their wedding vows and their mother (Sonia Braga) would like her daughter to be there. They get into a familiar squabble and Sharon leaves things unresolved. It has been shown that she is a tough, no-nonsense cop, given to physical aggression. Perhaps too much so in the eyes of her partner Robby (Terrence Howard), who worries about the level of her anger.

Catch hangs around the coffeeshop, hoping to see Sharon again. This time she notices his staring but then a car pulls up in front and a gun starts blasting away. It's a drive-by, aimed at the cops inside. Neither Sharon nor Robby are injured and they go after the two suspects who have crashed their car and are on foot. Sharon chases a guy down a tunnel but he gets the drop on her, gets her gun, and fires. She's hit twice in the chest (the vest protects her) and is about to be shot in the head, when Catch tackles the guy and saves her.

He's later shown sitting alone in a bar when Sharon comes up. She's invited him for a drink to say thank you but, after asking him numerous questions to which she's received no answers, remarks that "every time I try to talk to people it comes out like an interrogation." Sharon offers to drive Catch home although it's clear that he's uneasy being in a car. Instead she takes him to her apartment. He has told Sharon: "I guess we were supposed to meet" but they are both needy and wary of each other. She is defensive and he refuses to tell her anything personal about himself.

Catch goes home to an empty apartment—literally since about all the furniture he has is a futon and a phone. Sharon calls and invites him to breakfast, then stands him up. Catch shows up at her apartment angry about the slight. She says: "You never said a word about yourself the other night. I need the details." But Catch only replies: "I need to start from here." However, the cop in Sharon can't let it go and she tails him back to his apartment and sees how he lives—or doesn't. But they continue to be drawn to each other.

Sharon responds to a domestic disturbance call at her brother's house. He's hit his wife (Monet Mazur), who makes excuses for his behavior and refuses to press charges. Sharon's heard all this before; she goes ballistic and slugs her brother. She later talks to Catch about her family troubles: her father used to hit her mother and one day Sharon called the cops and her father was arrested. Although she knows she did what was necessary, her actions have caused a rift and Sharon feels that she is being punished for doing what was right.

Meanwhile, Sharon notices Catch seems to be getting more involved in the world. He's gotten some furniture and taken in a stray dog. She even invites him to escort her to her parents' celebration. Sharon may still be uneasy over not knowing anything about Catch's past but they are together—until they visit a blues club and Catch is suddenly drawn to going onstage and playing a trumpet solo (on "Nature Boy"). It's obvious that he's a pro and the club owner (Stephen Thomas Kay) recognizes Catch and calls him "Steve Lambert." He denies knowing who that is and gets into an argument with Sharon. She uses the police

database to check out the name and discovers, of course, that Catch/Steve is the guy from the car accident a year earlier, an accident that killed his wife and young son.

Catch has literally walked out of his previous life—Sharon finds his home abandoned, left exactly as it was on that last day. She confronts Catch with her knowledge and learns that he blames himself for the accident. Sharon tries to get Catch to visit the cemetery where his family is buried but he's angry about her interference. Sharon needs to fix things. She even visits his mother-in-law Elanora (Shirley Knight), whom Catch sees weekly, and who has been supporting him. Elanora tells Sharon to be patient if she wants him in her life—that the wall Catch has built around himself is not about to come down overnight.

Sharon dresses to go to her parents' house. She practices what she will say—some platitude about being happy for them. Meanwhile, a clean-shaven, freshly dressed Catch goes to his family's graveside to apologize for trying to forget the past. He makes peace and, after a tense confrontation with her family, so does Sharon to some small extent. Sharon is surprised to see Catch standing by her car when she leaves the house but he reminds her that she invited him and he keeps his appointments. He tells her he went to the cemetery and Sharon admits that she wants everything to be perfect and knows that life can't be. Both admit their love and drive off (Catch takes the wheel) as the song "Angel Eyes" plays over the closing credits.

Jennifer Lopez is playing a version of her professionally tough-but-personally vulnerable character from 1998's *Out of Sight*. She's decidedly de-glamorized and believable. Sharon is angry and hurt over her family's continuing to blame her for their troubles while still knowing that she did the best she could; she's probably a pretty good cop because she believes that what she does is worthwhile. Jim Caviezel has a rather more thankless task. His character is a passive reactor who has put his life on hold. He's walking wounded and has trouble believing that he even deserves the lifeline that Sharon is so tentatively holding out. Caviezel knows how to show his character's suffering while subduing most of the emotional excess.

The problem with *Angel Eyes* is that you know exactly what's going to happen. You know the two characters have a connection and it's simple (too simple) to figure out what that connection is. And they must be compelling enough to hold the movie together since the rest of the cast is so much window dressing. Unfortunately, the sheer predictability of what occurs lets Lopez and Caviezel down.

—*Christine Tomassini*

**CREDITS**

**Sharon Pogue:** Jennifer Lopez

**Catch:** James Caviezel
**Josephine Pogue:** Sonia Braga
**Robby:** Terrence DaShon Howard
**Larry Pogue:** Jeremy Sisto
**Kathy Pogue:** Monet Mazur
**Carl Pogue:** Victor Argo
**Elanora:** Shirley Knight
**Ray:** Jeremy Ratchford
**Lt. Dennis Sanderman:** Peter MacNeill
**Tony:** Stephen Kay

**Origin:** USA
**Released:** 2001
**Production:** Elie Samaha, Mark Canton; Morgan Creek Productions, Franchise Pictures; released by Warner Bros.
**Directed by:** Luis Mandoki
**Written by:** Gerald Di Pego
**Cinematography by:** Piotr Sobocinski
**Music by:** Marco Beltrami
**Sound:** Owen Langevin
**Editing:** Jerry Greenberg
**Art Direction:** Dennis Davenport
**Costumes:** Marie-Sylvie Deveau
**Production Design:** Dean Tavoularis
**MPAA rating:** R
**Running time:** 104 minutes

## REVIEWS

*Boxoffice.* July, 2001, p. 98.
*Chicago Sun-Times Online.* May 18, 2001.
*Entertainment Weekly.* May 25, 2001, p. 51.
*Los Angeles Times Online.* May 18, 2001.
*New York Times Online.* May 18, 2001.
*People.* May 28, 2001, p. 36.
*San Francisco Chronicle Online.* May 18, 2001.
*Time.* May 28, 2001, p. 84.
*USA Today Online.* May 18, 2001.
*Variety.* May 14, 2001, p. 22.
*Washington Post Online.* May 18, 2001.

## QUOTES

Catch (Jim Caviezel) explains his life to Sharon (Jennifer Lopez): "This is it. I live here. I walk around town. That's all of it, except for how I feel about you."

## TRIVIA

Director Luis Mandoki and screenwriter Gerald DiPego previously worked together on *Message in a Bottle* (1998).

# The Animal

*He wasn't much of a man . . . now he's not much of an animal.*
—Movie tagline

**Box Office:** $55.8 million

More a collection of gags than a full-fledged story, Luke Greenfield's *The Animal* is a sometimes crude, sometimes amusing comedy that is never as clever as it could be but not as bad as one might fear. It is unabashedly lowbrow entertainment probably meant to appeal to teenage boys who enjoy jokes about bodily humor and think that the sight of a grown man acting like a variety of animals is very funny. Nonetheless, while *The Animal* never takes off into great comedic heights, it does offer a few laughs during its brief 83 minutes.

Rob Schneider from TV's *Saturday Night Live* plays Marvin Mange, a sad-sack file clerk in the evidence room of his local police station. He dreams of one day being a policeman like his late father, but his hopes seem rather slim. Little children on a field trip make fun of him and terrorize him when they find out that he is not a real policeman. He fails for the fourth time the obstacle course that he needs to pass to become an officer and even wets himself. (The course itself is an amusing aside that includes outlandish obstacles such as an old lady who attacks each trainee.) Poor Marvin is essentially the laughingstock of his community and struggles to make a good impression on Rianna (Colleen Haskell), an environmentalist and animal lover he admires. To improve himself, he even orders a supply of badger milk, which is sold by infomercial as a miracle energy supplement. (The sight of a badger connected to milking tubes and sexy models endorsing this weird product are inspired throwaway bits.)

One day Marvin gets into a car accident so horrific it would kill anyone almost instantly. Since this is a silly movie, however, Marvin miraculously survives and is put back together with various animal organs by a mysterious scientist named Dr. Wilder (Michael Caton). Dr. Wilder is one of the movie's biggest missed opportunities. He could have been a loony Dr. Frankenstein figure, an inspired spoof of a mad doctor, but he is not particularly crazy or funny, and there does not seem to be any compelling reason why he saved Marvin's life with this bizarre experiment.

At first, Marvin, who is simply deposited back at the scene of the accident, does not realize what has happened to him, but he experiences major changes in his life. The neighbor's dog that used to attack him now backs off. After he takes a shower, he is able to shake himself dry like a dog.

He can run faster than the elderly jogger who used to outrun him and can even race past a horse. Marvin, in short, has a full range of animal instincts and abilities and is even made a police officer when his now acute sense of smell enables him to sniff out some heroin on a smuggler at the airport. However, now that he is a police officer and a celebrity in his town, he invites the jealousy of Sgt. Doug Sisk (John C. McGinley), who suddenly becomes his nemesis.

Many of the early scenes in *The Animal* are entertaining, albeit in an obvious, cornball way, as Marvin, the perpetual loser and underdog in life, comes to discover that he is a kind of superman. While the gags may be dumb, they are often funny, like Marvin practically humping a mailbox and making animal noises when a sexy woman in a tight dress walks by. When he visits Rianna at the animal shelter where she volunteers, he lets a young turkey vulture eat out of his mouth and has a fight with an orangutan, which is so ludicrous and full of slapstick, it cannot help but be amusing.

Soon, however, Marvin has to try to figure out how to control his animal urges. When he finds himself in a butcher shop one morning with his belly bloated, he visits Dr. Wilder to exercise in a human-size hamster wheel. His sexual urges are a more serious problem. When he and Sgt. Sisk go to a farm that has reported a missing tractor, for example, Marvin encounters a goat in heat, which he flirts with and even kisses (as Marvin Gaye's "Let's Get It On" plays on the soundtrack) before the goat rebuffs him. Later, when he goes on a date with Rianna, he urinates to mark his territory and licks her face.

While *The Animal* is often crude in its humor and verges on the disgusting, at least the hero is an innocent we can like and root for. Indeed, this scattershot movie probably would have been unbearable without Schneider's lovable-loser persona. His goofy goodness makes Marvin's antics fun for a while, but unfortunately Marvin basically engages in the same shtick over and over again, the only surprise being what kind of animal he will imitate next. At a lavish outdoor charity event hosted by the mayor, for example, he gets in big trouble when he fights a cat and spits out a hair ball, but then moments later he becomes a hero when he turns dolphin and saves the mayor's son from drowning. He caps off his triumph with some water tricks, as if he were the main attraction at Sea World. After a while, the movie plays as a series of short sketches—some more amusing than others—in which Marvin takes on a variety of animal personae.

While the plot itself is secondary in a film like *The Animal*, one wishes the screenplay, credited to Schneider and Tom Brady, could have been at least a little more engaging and possibly connected Marvin's animal tricks to something resembling a story. The rivalry with Sgt. Sisk feels forced since we never know exactly why he hates Marvin so much, and the romance with Rianna is fairly generic.

If *The Animal* is remembered for anything, it will be for Colleen Haskell's motion-picture debut. A contestant on the first season of the phenomenally popular TV show *Survivor*, she quickly became America's sweetheart of the moment, a winsome, refreshing presence in a show full of backstabbers. The first survivor to land a major movie, Haskell brings her natural charm to the big screen, but she is given relatively little dialogue for a leading part, and her main acting comes in the form of cute smiles and quizzical reactions when Schneider's Marvin does something outrageous. It is not a star-making performance, but, for someone without any real acting experience, she is fine for the role.

The supporting characters are a mixed bag of oddballs. It is sad and embarrassing to see veteran TV actor Edward Asner as the doddering, somewhat nutty police chief who makes random, nonsensical comments every now and then. Louis Lombardi plays Fatty, Marvin's overweight friend, and Guy Torry plays Miles, Marvin's black friend. Miles has a funny running joke in which he tries to prove a theory of reverse racism, the idea that black people are constantly being cut too much slack as a way for whites to assuage their guilt over years of racism. When he flagrantly smokes in an airport, for example, no one stops him.

Marvin becomes the prime suspect when a mysterious beast viciously attacks a farmer's cows one night. Marvin is put on leave, and, when a hunter is also mauled, he is pursued by an angry mob of vigilantes right out of *Frankenstein*. Norm Macdonald (like Schneider, an SNL alum) has a cameo as a townsman who asks a lot of pointed questions about how a mob works and even has the temerity to suggest that the beast be given a fair trial—a genuinely funny moment that spoofs a familiar movie cliché.

Even with the mob chasing after him, Marvin proves his essential goodness when he saves the life of Sgt. Sisk, the man leading the mob, and thus shows that his humanity has prevailed over his animal nature. Sgt. Sisk is determined to kill Marvin anyway, but Rianna suddenly attacks the evil sergeant and rescues Marvin. Rianna, it turns out, is also an experimental animal from Dr. Wilder's lab and is actually the beast who attacked the hunter. Admittedly, *The Animal* is a dopey comedy full of, at best, hit-and-miss humor, but it still should make sense on its own terms, and this twist ending is completely ridiculous. If Rianna is an animal herself, why was she so surprised every time Marvin went nuts? She should have recognized him as one like herself. Also, why does she not display animal tendencies until the very end?

Marvin and Rianna finally escape the mob when Miles claims that he is the beast and the mob quietly disperses because they do not want to lynch a black man, once again proving his theory of reverse racism. A year passes, and Marvin and Rianna are now a couple with children and have turned their home into a wildlife preserve, but Marvin, it seems, still has a wandering eye for a cute goat.

The *Animal* is sporadically amusing but overall fairly thin for a farcical comedy in which the jokes need to come at a rapid-fire pace and possess some spark of originality. Lacking the imagination that could have made it a truly hilarious summertime diversion, *The Animal* still achieves something rare and even strangely refreshing: despite a slew of jokes revolving around urination, flatulence, and bestiality, it manages to maintain a genial, even cheerful tone usually foreign to gross-out comedy in today's Hollywood.

—*Peter N. Chumo II*

## CREDITS

**Marvin:** Rob Schneider
**Miles:** Guy Torry
**Sgt. Sisk:** John C. McGinley
**Rianna:** Colleen Haskell
**Dr. Wilder:** Michael Caton
**Fatty:** Louis Lombardi
**Chief Wilson:** Ed Asner

**Origin:** USA
**Released:** 2001
**Production:** Barry Bernardi, Carr D'Angelo, Todd Garner; Revolution Studios; released by Columbia Pictures
**Directed by:** Luke Greenfield
**Written by:** Rob Schneider, Tom Brady
**Cinematography by:** Peter Collister
**Music by:** Teddy Castellucci
**Sound:** David M. Kelson
**Music Supervisor:** Michael Dilbeck
**Editing:** Jeff Gourson, Peck Prior
**Art Direction:** Domenic Silvestri
**Costumes:** Jim Lapidus
**MPAA rating:** PG-13
**Running time:** 83 minutes

## REVIEWS

*Boxoffice.* August, 2001, p. 61.
*Entertainment Weekly.* June 15, 2001, p. 59.
*Hollywood Reporter.* May 29, 2001, p. 10.
*Los Angeles Times Online.* June 1, 2001.
*New York Times Online.* June 1, 2001.
*USA Today Online.* June 1, 2001.
*Variety.* June 4, 2001, p. 16.
*Washington Post Online.* June 1, 2001.

# The Anniversary Party

*It's not a party until something gets broken.*
—Movie tagline

 **Box Office:** $4 million

At any given moment, it is a safe bet that someone somewhere is dreaming of being a somebody in Hollywood. Their starry-eyed daydreams of the exciting and glamorous life that awaits them almost always fail to recognize that money and fame will neither fill all voids nor heal all wounds nor make one impervious to the pain and insecurities we all face. Watch *The Anniversary Party*, and take it from people who know. The film is written, directed, and produced by actors Alan Cumming and Jennifer Jason Leigh, who also star. With many of their famous friends also playing characters not so far afield from their real selves, the film lets us peek inside the lives of the glitterati and reminds us what we should all know by now: there are ups and downs in the Hollywood Hills, the same as anywhere else. Shot utilizing the ease of digital video in just 19 days, the entire story takes place within a 24-hour period, focusing on the preparations for and repercussions from an anniversary party to celebrate the sixth year of marriage for British author Joe and American actress Sally Therrian (Cumming and Leigh).

It has not been six years of wedded bliss, however, as Joe has strayed for various reasons and with people of various sexual orientations. After being separated for a year, the two are recently reconciled but still on unstable ground. *The Anniversary Party* begins with a closeup of Joe and Sally in bed, with her thoughtfully contemplating his face. Later, while the two receive private yoga instruction on their patio, two calls come in which will lead to much heartache before the next day dawns. One is from Joe's "black sheep sister," a call he avoids taking, and the other, answered by Sally, informs her that she is not pregnant. Apparently the two have been trying to cement their relationship by having a child together, a foolhardy idea to start with which will seem worse and worse as the film progresses. When Sally tells Joe the disappointing news, they quietly agree to keep trying, but there is a faraway look in her eyes.

When the two are alone, they talk about the little shared intimacies they missed during their time apart, and Sally, seemingly needing reassurance, asks Joe if he is really back. "For good," he replies with his smirky smile. Things do not look so good immediately after, however, when another call comes in, disrupting their friskiness and decidedly altering the mood. It seems that Joe will be directing the screen adaptation of his latest novel, the central character of which is a thinly-disguised version of Sally, and he has not only chosen 22-year-old lithe ingenue Skye Davidson (Gwyneth Paltrow) to play the role but has rather thoughtlessly invited her to the anniversary party. Sally is so perturbed that she exits the room, spitting obscenities and insults as she goes. Joe, on the other hand, is obviously tickled pink, and when he tells Skye that he could not even remotely imagine anyone else in the role, we get a shot of Sally's none-too-pleased reaction as she looks at herself in her make-up mirror. We are reminded of Margo Channing and Eve Harrington in the classic *All About Eve* (1950), in which an established actress must deal with the inevitable unpleasantness of being eclipsed by a pretty, young up-and-comer.

Soon the guests begin to arrive for the party, beginning with the couples' managers, Jerry Adams (John Benjamin Hickey) and his wife Judy (indie mainstay Parker Posey). Jerry has gotten the Therrians to invite the "neighbors from Hell," uptight writer Ryan Rose (Denis O'Hare) and his wife Monica (rather touching Mina Badie, Leigh's half-sister) in order to avoid a lawsuit. The Roses are unhappy about the behavior and vociferousness of the Therrians' beloved pooch Otis, and even after being graciously welcomed, Ryan (to his wife and hosts' chagrin) refuses to let sleeping dogs lie and injects his complaints into the already strained small talk. The Roses are like us, outsiders getting a glimpse into the lives of the rich and famous.

More of the guests arrive, including award-winning actor Cal Gold (Kevin Kline), his wife, actress-turned-mother Sophia (actress-turned-mother Phoebe Cates, Kline's wife), and their two children (the Klines' real son and daughter). The director of Sally's latest film, Mac Forsythe (John C. Reilly), brings along the dailies and his basket case wife Clair (Jane Adams), who is unstrung by her duties as new mother and strung out on too many diet pills. Photographer Gina Taylor (Jennifer Beals), best friend/former lover of Joe also shows up (we see Sally's jealous looks), as does Sally's best friend, musician and Peter Sellers look-alike Levi Panes (Michael Panes) and Sanford Jewison (Matt Malloy), who was close to Joe during the recent separation.

*The Anniversary Party* belongs to a familiar genre of films in which a group of characters are gathered together and then blown apart by the eruption of unpleasantness simmering just below the surface, often after an indulgence in alcohol or drugs. (Think 1962's *Long Day's Journey Into Night* or 1960's *Who's Afraid of Virginia Woolf?*) So after a spirited game of charades and a round of often mawkish toasts to the hosts, it is Skye's gift of some Ecstacy that is the catalyst that makes this soiree turn sour. Discretion and inhibitions vanish. Monica, looking to break loose, tries the drug and ends up in a clinch with Joe which Sally sees. Mac ends up humiliating Sally by revealing to various people how unhappy he is with her performance in his current production, and he also nearly drowns while swimming amongst half-naked ladies in the pool. Sophia implores Sally not to

go to London or plan on having a family with Joe: "he'll probably leave you for Skye Davidson anyway!" Cal unsuccessfully fishes for a part in Joe's film, even though the character is roughly half his age. Panes and Skye duck into a bedroom for a quick tryst. Even precious Otis breaks loose and runs away.

This leads to the evening's explosive grand finale, an overplayed histrionic hissy fit between Sally and her rather effeminate hubby (looking ridiculous with his hair gathered into a host of little pigtails). Highlighted by Sally's revelation that she got scared and aborted a recent pregnancy and the resulting slap from Joe, the fight leaves the two emotionally raw and reeling. In a tag-on to the rest of the melodramatics, a call comes in for Joe informing him of his sister's death. While he goes all to pieces in private, Sally shows her claws one more time to a well-meaning Gina, and everyone hangs around as the party turns to something resembling a wake. The film ends with the same closeup of Sally and Joe which began it, their future still uncertain.

Made on a budget of $3.5 million, it received mixed reviews and grossed just over $4 million in limited release. One questions whether things can work out for Joe and Sally, mainly because Joe, especially when portrayed by Cumming, seems a dead-end choice for a woman looking for a man committed to faithfulness and heterosexuality. For all the drama that ensues, nothing that happens in the film is especially unexpected. It reveals little that is new or unique about relationships, in or out of the LA area. More than a few stars in Hollywood think they are a tad more fascinating and witty than they actually are, and Cumming and Leigh apparently felt that way about their script, as well. There is sometimes a washed-out look to *The Anniversary Party* due to the use of video, although cinematographer John Bailey does a good job in minimizing this problem. Still, it is hard not to be intrigued by any glimpse into the lives of those involved in "the business," and perhaps even getting a perverse satisfaction in this reminder that they are grappling with life the same as we are, their uncertain real lives different from their reel ones, where you can simply have someone write you a happy ending.

—*David L. Boxerbaum*

## CREDITS

**Sally Therrian:** Jennifer Jason Leigh
**Joe Therrian:** Alan Cumming
**Skye Davidson:** Gwyneth Paltrow
**Cal Gold:** Kevin Kline
**Sophia Gold:** Phoebe Cates
**Mac Forsyth:** John C. Reilly
**Clair Forsyth:** Jane Adams
**Jerry Adams:** John Benjamin Hickey

**Judy Adams:** Parker Posey
**Ryan Rose:** Denis O'Hare
**Gina Taylor:** Jennifer Beals
**Monica Rose:** Mina (Badiyi) Badie
**Levi Panes:** Michael Panes

**Origin:** USA
**Released:** 2001
**Production:** Jennifer Jason Leigh, Joanne Sellar, Alan Cumming; Pas de Quoi; released by Fine Line Features
**Directed by:** Jennifer Jason Leigh, Alan Cumming
**Written by:** Jennifer Jason Leigh, Alan Cumming
**Cinematography by:** John Bailey
**Music by:** Michael Penn
**Sound:** David MacMillan
**Music Supervisor:** Robin Urdang
**Editing:** Carol Littleton, Suzanne Spangler
**Costumes:** Christopher Lawrence
**MPAA rating:** R
**Running time:** 117 minutes

## REVIEWS

*Boxoffice.* June, 2001, p. 54.
*Chicago Sun-Times Online.* June 22, 2001.
*Entertainment Weekly.* June 15, 2001, p. 59.
*Film Comment.* May, 2001, p. 74.
*Hollywood Reporter.* May 15, 2001, p. 17.
*Los Angeles Times Online.* June 8, 2001.
*New York Times.* June 8, 2001, p. E13.
*People.* June 18, 2001, p. 33.
*Rolling Stone.* July 5, 2001, p. 150.
*Time.* July 23, 2001, p. 70.
*Variety.* May 21, 2001, p. 17.
*Wall Street Journal.* June 8, 2001, p. W13.
*Washington Post.* June 22, 2001, p. C5.

## QUOTES

Clair (Jennifer Jason Leigh) to her guests: "I can't find my husband or my beeper. Have you seen either of them?"

# Antitrust

*Truth can be dangerous. . . . Trust can be deadly.*
—Movie tagline

 **Box Office:** $11.1 million

*Antitrust* is a shameless, preposterous, shallow fantasy about egalitarian computer geeks getting revenge on soulless corporate profiteers. A more balanced, mature script might have made such a story palatable. But *Antitrust* depicts its young heroes and its villainous honchos with all the subtlety of a pornographic web site. It combines glossy images, crude plot points, and empty appeals to emotion. It is cheap and brazen.

Tim Robbins stars as Gary Winston, the enormously rich, exceedingly smart and impossibly vile head of a successful computer software company called Nurv. With small, round, thin-rimmed glasses and modified Prince Valiant haircut, Robbins looks like Bill Gates of Microsoft. What's more, the federal government is investigating Nurv for antitrust violations, just as it did with Microsoft. And Nurv is number one in the business, known for its proprietary attitudes. Clearly, Winston and Nurv are stand-ins for Gates and Microsoft.

When Winston is showing young computer prodigy Milo Hoffman (Ryan Phillippe) around his home office, Milo notices a digital wall painting that changes images to suit the mood it senses in the office's occupants. "Doesn't Bill Gates have something like that?" Milo asks. Gary replies that Gates's digital screen is primitive compared to his. It's a cheap trick in a film loaded with cheap tricks, but it doesn't exonerate the filmmakers of responsibility for the insults they heap on Gates by association.

Soon after, Gary tells Milo that he doesn't mind that people constantly criticize Nurv, because "it's the nature of competitive business" to be attacked when you're on top. But when it gets personal, Gary says, with web sites that portray him as Satan or that put his wife's face on a porn star's body, "I don't like that." You can't help but wonder, then, what Gates thinks of a movie which turns a character obviously based on him into a murderous, lying, thieving hypocrite.

As directed by Peter Howitt (*Sliding Doors*) and written by Howard Franklin (*Someone to Watch Over Me*), *Antitrust* spits out cliches like they were computer code. All its characters are caricatures. Milo and his young partners in a would-be computer startup are brainy, work-obsessed innocents who operate out of a suburban garage. The geeks who work for Nurv are true-believer types who affect nose rings and multicolored hair and work in an office with decorative surfboards hanging on the wall. Winston is an overgrown adolescent who eats potato chips while writing code for a sophisticated satellite-linked all-media transmission system and mouthing loving lines about his computer projects such as "This is the best train set ever." But he has a dark side: a security force of malevolent henchmen who are, as it suits the script, alternately omniscient and clueless.

Winston announces that Nurv is going to launch its new all-in-one system, Synapse, in a matter of months. Milo and his buddies are working on something called "open source;" it's unclear exactly what that is, but they are going to make it available for free to the universe because "human knowledge belongs to the people." While they are watching Winston on a live web broadcast, he calls Milo on the phone and asks him and the other brainiac in the startup, Teddy Chin (Yee Jee Tso), to work for him. But Teddy hates Nurv and all it stands for, so the two friends and partners part ways when Milo takes the job at Nurv.

Before Milo drives up to Portland, where Nurv is based, an agent from the Justice Department drops by to tell him "we could do with a real smart guy on our team" and offers him a Buick and $42,000 a year to work for them. But Milo says no because "It's my time to make my mark." The agent urges Milo that, if he sees anything suspicious at Nurv, he should "do the right thing" and contact the government. The dialogue is just this lame throughout the film.

Of course, Nurv is a cool place to work. The sprawling "campus" has a keyboard-and-mouse sculpture, and Milo works in a space called "The Egg" with all the other hotshots, including a hygiene-challenged guy named Stinky (Jonathon Young) and a brainy, ice-queen brunette named Lisa (Rachael Leigh Cook). Gary drops by occasionally to share new code for the project. He also gives the geeks a classroom pep talk about meeting the Synapse launch date: "There are no constraints. There are no boundaries. Surprise me. Challenge me. Defy me. Defy yourself." Hearing this drivel, the geeks get more geeked.

Life could become complicated for Milo. Lisa approaches him and they go to lunch, and Milo's live-in girlfriend Alice (Claire Forlani) happens to drive by and sees them. It's that kind of movie, with a plot by numbers. Soon, Alice shows up unexpectedly at the office when Lisa and Milo are sharing time in a cubicle. Meaningful glances are exchanged, but Alice seems surprisingly forgiving. Later developments make this subplot come apart at the seams.

All the minor intrigue becomes trivial when, out of the clear blue sky, Teddy is suddenly brutally murdered just as he has unlocked the secret to "open source." It is set up to look like a racist killing. Their mutual friend Larry (Tygh Runyan) tells Milo that Teddy was going to show the rest of the partners the next day what he had discovered but so far had told them only: "The answer's not in the box, it's in the band." When Gary approaches Milo a short time later with another new set of code and tells him: "The answer's not in the box, it's in the band," Milo freaks. We know he freaks because the camera pushes him back, spins him around, and pummels him with pictures and sound bites, just in case anyone with an IQ under 50 in the audience doesn't get the point.

The movie morphs from a cheesy race-against-the-clock saga about getting Synapse launched into an even cheesier suspense film and finally into a youth revenge flick. There is really not much suspense; Howitt prefers false shocks and surprises, such as suspicious people approaching

down hallways in slow motion as the music mounts to an anticlimax.

It's up to Milo to expose Winston, but when he keeps searching for allies, he finds nobody he can trust. He also discovers that the paternalistic Nurv has been spying on and blackmailing its employees. When Milo starts poking around where he shouldn't be, either he is almost caught, or is caught but somehow excuses himself, or we discover that Winston and his henchmen are just leading him on and letting him discover unimportant things. Yet sometimes he discovers crucial information while his surveillance team is napping.

The cat-and-mouse, cloak-and-dagger stuff goes on far too long. Much of it is simply silly. Milo has a potentially fatal allergy to sesame seeds, and there is an unintentionally hilarious scene involving Alice cooking him a Chinese meal and Milo wondering if she's trying to poison him. It's one of many diversionary plot twists; another involves the mystery of what's inside Building 21, which Milo believes to be a surveillance center and spends much time plotting to investigate, only to find there's nothing there.

The logical holes in the plot have plenty of bandwidth. Company spies are tracking Milo's every move, except when it's not convenient to the plot. He and his co-conspirators sometimes take pains to meet outdoors or off the Nurv campus to plot, but at other times they discuss their schemes right at work. One minute Winston is a mastermind and his company surveillance and dirty tricks operations are formidable, and the next minute they completely lose track of what Milo is doing.

The climax is a bracing triumph of the garage geeks over the scurrilous bosses, but what they are exposing is so unbelievably outrageous that it's impossible to take *Antitrust* seriously. The title is a misnomer; the real issues behind computer companies' alleged antitrust violations are much too complex for this film to handle. Instead, there is one simplistic and overwrought scene after another.

The talented Robbins, so adept at playing the kind of soft-spoken, smirking amoral villain that he perfected in *The Player*, is largely wasted here. The script calls for little or no intelligence, as Winston and his opponents are mouthing platitudes half the time. Phillippe seems comfortable with a role that involves little emotional or psychic strain. Cook and Forlani give it their best; Cook is understated but has little to work with, and Forlani seems unable to give her character some needed shadings.

If this were a movie about anything other than computers—say, about nefarious dealings in the tool-and-die industry—it would be easy to unmask its pretensions. Everywhere are ham-handed efforts, including the soundtrack, to make this seem the hippest of topical stories. Everybody who works on the computers seems exhilarated to be writing code. We're supposed to believe that this phony battle is about the future of human rights, climaxed by the total liberation of all the tools needed to make everyone communicate openly. In this sense, *Antitrust* is like a youth exploitation movie of the 1970s, in which past-their-prime writers deliver a counter-culture manifesto using cartoonish hippies—issued years after that train left the station. So it is with this film, whose time came and went in the short-lived dot-com startup frenzy of 1999 and early 2000. After *Antitrust,* we're still awaiting a film that exposes what really goes on inside the top echelons of the computer world; this is only a cartoon version of a Hollywood concept of such a world.

—*Michael Betzold*

## CREDITS

**Milo Hoffman:** Ryan Phillippe
**Gary Winston:** Tim Robbins
**Lisa Calighan:** Rachael Leigh Cook
**Alice Poulson:** Claire Forlani
**Bob Shrot:** Douglas McFerran
**Lyle Barton:** Richard Roundtree
**Teddy Chin:** Yee Jee Tso
**Larry Banks:** Tygh Runyan

**Origin:** USA
**Released:** 2000
**Production:** Nick Wechsler, Keith Addis, David Nicksay; Hyde Park Entertainment, Industry Entertainment; released by Metro-Goldwyn-Mayer
**Directed by:** Peter Howitt
**Written by:** Howard Franklin
**Cinematography by:** John Bailey
**Music by:** Don Davis
**Sound:** Larry Sutton
**Editing:** Zach Staenberg
**Art Direction:** Doug Byggdin
**Costumes:** Maya Mani
**Production Design:** Catherine Hardwicke
**MPAA rating:** PG-13
**Running time:** 120 minutes

## REVIEWS

*Chicago Sun-Times Online.* January 12, 2001.
*New York Times Online.* January 12, 2001.
*People.* January 22, 2001, p. 38.
*USA Today Online.* Janaury 14, 2001.
*Variety.* January 15, 2001, p. 54.
*Washington Post Online.* January 12, 2001.

## QUOTES

Gary Winston (Tim Robbins): "The software business is binary. You're a one or a zero—alive or dead."

# Apocalypse Now Redux

**Box Office:** $4.6 million

Perhaps no film of the last quarter century has received the legendary status of Frances Ford Coppola's Vietnam War epic, *Apocalypse Now,* originally released in 1979. From the madness that enveloped the 15-month shoot; Coppola's battle with a typhoon that temporarily shut down production; a heart attack by the star, Martin Sheen, that left completion of the project in doubt; and cost overruns that forced Coppola to mortgage his own property to complete the picture, *Apocalypse Now* may be one of the most heroic (or foolhardy) undertakings in all of American filmmaking. The movie went on to garner mixed reactions but today is considered by many to be a modern classic. And yet, if it is a masterpiece, it is a problematic one at best. Hobbling from set piece to set piece with dead space in between, the film has no clear narrative line and concludes with an anticlimactic section featuring a bloated, confusing Marlon Brando.

Loosely based on Joseph Conrad's classic novella, *Heart of Darkness,* the film follows Captain Willard (Sheen), a U.S. Army intelligence officer who is given a mission to travel up river into Cambodia to find and "terminate with extreme prejudice" the renegade Colonel Kurtz (Brando), who has abandoned the military and set up his own command, where he rules as a kind of deity over a tribe of natives and a few American expatriates. Willard's journey is, above all, a sensual experience. The film contains relatively little combat for a war picture but strives to give us the feeling and visceral experience of the Vietnam War.

More than two decades after its debut, Coppola and Oscar®-winning sound editor Walter Murch have gone back to the raw footage and created a new version of the film, which contains an additional 49 minutes not used in the initial theatrical release. Employing the Technicolor dye transfer process, they have given the film an exquisite look, bringing out the richness of Vittorio Storaro's Oscar®-winning cinematography. The new cut, called *Apocalypse Now Redux,* is fascinating because the new footage heightens in some cases our appreciation for what Coppola was trying to accomplish but still fails to clarify an already muddled film. What was great in the original work is still great, and what was weak remains so. Add to that the fact that the new edition clocks in at a staggering three hours, 22 minutes, and that makes for a very long and often tedious journey up the river.

The most famous and thrilling sequence in the original film is Willard's encounter with Lt. Colonel Kilgore (Robert Duvall, in an Oscar®-nominated performance), the surfing-obsessed air cavalry commander who serves as Willard's escort part of the way and who secures a beach so that his men can surf. Kilgore's macho posturing, his love of "the smell of napalm in the morning" (the film's most famous line), and his blaring of Wagner as his helicopters attack a Vietnamese village are among the most memorable moments in any film of the '70s (or perhaps ever) and clearly the best sequences in the film. Unfortunately, everything that follows the mesmerizing Kilgore section can only be a letdown. Among the additions in *Redux* is a grand entrance for Kilgore by chopper, a short scene in which he helps a wounded child to safety, and, most important, footage that expands on his passion for surfing. Willard, in a rare joking mood, steals Kilgore's surfboard as he and his crew run back onto the boat. Later, they hear Kilgore's voice booming overhead, demanding the surfboard's return. It is a funny, light scene that helps to heighten the camaraderie among Willard and his four-man crew, but it does not add anything crucial to the story.

The next addition is an extra Playboy Playmates sequence. In the original version, the Playmates appear to entertain the troops in a show that Willard and his men happen to see. In *Redux*, they later come upon the Playmates (Colleen Camp and Cynthia Wood) stranded during a storm, and Willard trades two barrels of fuel for sex with his men. This extra footage is a bit puzzling since it really adds nothing to Willard's journey. In the press notes for the film, Coppola defends the addition: "In their way, the girls are the corresponding characters of those young boys on the boat, except they're being exploited in sexual ways. But it's the same thing, you know how they're being consumed—used up by a society that calls itself moral and yet isn't." This explanation, however, feels like a big stretch. One simply would not glean this parallel from the rather clumsy encounters in which the guys are amazed to have their fantasies fulfilled and the girls become sex objects that the guys do not really listen to. The two kinds of "exploitation" Coppola discusses are so different that one would not link them if he did not suggest the connection. These scenes were shot during the typhoon that halted production on the film and so were never completed. Since they serve no clear narrative purpose and feel rather sloppy, it probably would have been better if they had been left on the cutting room floor.

The bulk of the restored footage is the French plantation sequence, one of the most famous lost scenes in film history. Coppola, in the brilliant 1991 documentary *Hearts of Darkness: A Filmmaker's Apocalypse*, says he ended up

hating the sequence because, while he could not get the French cast he wanted due to budgetary constraints, the set designers did not cut back on their budget, leaving him with an elaborate set that made him angry. In the press notes for *Redux*, however, Coppola claims to have "always loved this scene," which begins with Willard and his crew happening upon a family of French colonials. They allow Willard to give a decent funeral to Clean (Larry Fishburne), the youngest kid of Willard's crew, who was just killed in an encounter with the Vietnamese.

Essentially a journey into the past, the encounter with the family is meant to evoke the French colonial chapter in the history of Vietnam and give a fuller picture of the historical context. The main part of the sequence is a lengthy dinner scene that turns into an extended history lesson on the French experience in Vietnam. The patriarch, Hubert deMarais (Christian Marquand), angrily tells Willard that his family stays there to keep what is theirs but the Americans "are fighting for the biggest nothing in history." The scene is meant to put America's involvement in the war in an historical context, but it has a weird effect. As a set piece, the dinner has an almost hypnotic quality, a sensuous, dreamy trip into a lost world full of human ghosts. But as a political statement, it is obvious, preachy, and boring.

In the final part of the plantation sequence, Willard has a tender encounter with a widow, Roxanne Sarrault (Aurore Clement), who was making eye contact with him throughout the dinner and practically signaling him to come to her. They finally go to bed and smoke opium together in a hazy encounter that lets us see a softer side to Willard's character, but the overall effect of the addition is still questionable. At this point in the film, we are close to Kurtz's compound, and this sequence further delays the big concluding encounter that the audience has been waiting for. The French plantation scenes may be worth seeing for their haunting beauty—Storaro's golden hues are gorgeous—but, on a narrative level, they form one more episode that only serves to slow down the rhythm of an already long journey.

The final piece of new footage is in the Kurtz section of the film—an extra scene focusing on Brando, the only one showing him in daylight. Kurtz reads to Willard a collection of news clippings from *Time* magazine that present an unrealistically positive view of America's involvement in the war while little children gather around him. Given the fact that Brando acts so infrequently, seeing new footage of him may be a welcomed treat, but does this scene add new dimension to his character or the film as a whole? It does suggest that he is not as mad as he otherwise seems, that fleeing the army and setting up his own rogue tribe is bred of a discontent with American hypocrisy.

And yet the scene still feels superfluous. Brando's other scenes, steeped in darkness, are simultaneously enigmatic and maddening—they are filled with the quasi-philosophical ramblings of a madman who has lost touch with reality and were the result of Brando's own often indifferent improvisations. (*Hearts of Darkness* reveals Coppola's struggle with Brando, who seemed to care very little about shaping a character.) In short, this new scene provides more historical context that we already know and a bit of background for a puzzling character whose convoluted mumbling in darkened shadows makes for a frustrating final act. The Kurtz section is the most problematic of the film, and it is an issue that no amount of tinkering will probably ever clear up.

Many critics consider *Apocalypse Now* a classic, and the *Redux* version received exceptional raves, with many critics using it as a barometer of how Hollywood's ambitions have fallen in the years between the two releases. Could a film of such scope and magnitude be attempted in today's Hollywood was a common question underlying many reviews, and the answer was that indeed it could not. And yet it feels like a mistake to use *Apocalypse Now* as a measure of great filmmaking, thus confusing Coppola's grand ambition with a result that is alternately brilliant and tedious. The movie's disjointed episodic structure almost guarantees that some sections will be stronger than others, and the resolution in which Willard kills Kurtz, crosscut with the ritualistic killing of a water buffalo, is viscerally powerful while narratively unsatisfactory. The lack of a firm ending plagued *Apocalypse Now* from the beginning of shooting, and Coppola never found a resolution that would answer the big questions that he was asking about the war, morality, and hypocrisy.

*Apocalypse Now*, in both its original and *Redux* versions, contains some breathtaking filmmaking. Individual sequences have become indelible film moments—the hallucinogenic opening of exploding napalm in the jungle scored to the Doors performing "The End," Kilgore's village assault, the massacre on a Vietnamese boat—while the story itself, always half-baked and bloated at the same time, never gels into a coherent whole. Coppola claims that financial pressure forcing him to produce a hit coupled with the belief that audiences of the era were not able to handle a longer film kept him from cutting and releasing the film he wanted to in 1979. But perhaps those pressures actually forced him to make a film that is, albeit flawed, more economical and accessible than *Redux*. Forty-nine minutes is a lot of footage to add to an already long film, and, in the case of *Apocalypse Now*, is simply too much.

—*Peter N. Chumo II*

## CREDITS

**Capt. Benjamin L. Willard:** Martin Sheen
**Col. Walter E. Kurtz:** Marlon Brando
**Lt. Col. Kilgore:** Robert Duvall
**Chef:** Frederic Forrest
**Lance Johnson:** Sam Bottoms

**Colby:** Scott Glenn
**Chief Phillips:** Albert Hall
**Mr. Clean:** Laurence "Larry" Fishburne
**Col. Lucas:** Harrison Ford
**The General:** G.D. Spradlin
**Photojournalist:** Dennis Hopper
**Hubert deMarais:** Christian Marquand
**Roxanne Serrault:** Aurore Clement
**Playmate of the Year:** Cynthia Wood
**Playmate:** Colleen Camp
**Playmate:** Linda Carpenter
**Narrator:** Michael Herr

**Origin:** USA
**Released:** 2001
**Production:** Francis Ford Coppola, Kim Aubry; American Zoetrope; released by Miramax Films
**Directed by:** Francis Ford Coppola
**Written by:** Francis Ford Coppola, John Milius
**Cinematography by:** Vittorio Storaro
**Music by:** Francis Ford Coppola, Carmine Coppola
**Sound:** Walter Murch
**Editing:** Walter Murch, Richard Marks
**Art Direction:** Angelo Graham
**Production Design:** Dean Tavoularis
**MPAA rating:** R
**Running time:** 202 minutes

## REVIEWS

*Boxoffice*. August, 2001, p. 55.
*Chicago Sun-Times Online*. August 10, 2001.
*Entertainment Weekly*. August 10, 2001, p. 48.
*Entertainment Weekly*. August 17, 2001, p. 18.
*Globe and Mail*. May 5, 2001, p. R1.
*Hollywood Reporter*. May 8, 2001, p. 10.
*Los Angeles Times Online*. July 29, 2001.
*New York Times Online*. May 13, 2001.
*New York Times Online*. May 16, 2001.
*New York Times Online*. August 3, 2001.
*People*. August 13, 2001, p. 35.
*Rolling Stone*. August 16, 2001, p. 114.
*Sight and Sound*. November, 2001, p. 12.
*Time*. August 6, 2001, p. 60.
*USA Today Online*. August 8, 2001.
*Variety*. May 14, 2001, p. 21.
*Washington Post*. August 10, 2001, p. WE33.

## QUOTES

Kurtz (Marlon Brando) to Willard (Martin Sheen) on his mission: "You're an errand boy, sent by grocery clerks, to collect a bill."

# Atanarjuat, the Fast Runner

The winner of the 2001 Cannes Camera d' Or, *Atanarjuat, the Fast Runner* has taken the festival crowd by storm. An Inuit video collective produced the award-winning feature while recalling the legend of the arctic hero Atanarjuat, portraying Inuit culture of a by-gone era (Inuit people no longer live in igloos and have since adopted snow mobiles and video technology in their daily lives) as well as showcasing Inuit talent. The film received a standing ovation at its Toronto International Film Festival screening and was runner up for Best Film at the Vancouver International Film Festival.

*Atanarjuat*, which was adapted by the late Paul Apak Angilirq who died of cancer in 1998, acts as the directorial debut for soap-carver-turned-videomaker Zacharias Kunuk. Both the film and the director have collected kudos from film critics. Mark Freeman for the online site, *Critical Eye* praised the film's composition and use of natural light, ". . .the purity and clarity of light bathes the whole landscape in a kind of pristine, crystalline beauty." And this "crystalline beauty" runs throughout the 165 minute feature. Freeman also commented on the videomaker's cinema verite style that recalls Robert Flaherty's 1922 cinema verite-style documentary *Nanook of the North*. One might add that Flaherty has been criticized for staging scenes in his alleged authentic documentary and the film subjects experienced tragedy. *Atanarjuat* might feel like a documentary, but it is, in fact, a drama that portrays fictitious tragedies.

In an interview that appeared on the online site, *Cinemascope*, producer and cinematographer Norman Cohn responded,: "We aren't filmmakers, but a collection of artists who happen to use this medium to tell a story." Cohn, along with Kunuk, are participants of a video explosion that has come out of Igloolik (the Northern Territories of Canada). Two video workshops, the Inukshuk Video Project and the Women's Video Project, are behind this explosion. While it might look like the masterful *Atanarjuat* came out of nowhere, the film is a culmination of previous projects that includes *Nanvut,* a 13-part docudrama series produced in 1994–95. This indigenous film collective recalls similar Canadian film collectives (Quebec of the 1960s and Toronto during the 1980s) that sparked film industries in Canada. This leaves us to wonder if a rival film industry will develop in the Northern Territories and if other First Nation filmmakers will emerge in the next decade from other Canadian provinces.

As the film opens we are thrown into an arctic setting where a shaman places a curse on a village and upon two families. Twenty years later, we see two brothers, Amaqjuac (Pakkak Innuksuk) and his younger brother Atanarjuat (Natar Ungalaaq), play tricks on their rival Oki (Peter Henry Arnatsiaq), the son of Sauri (Eugene Ipkarnak) and ruler of the community. A new rivalry breaks out between Atanarjuet and Oki when Oki's fiance Atuat (Sylvia Ivalu) takes a fancy for Atanarjuat. The battle between Oki and Atanarjuat is settled during an Inuit custom where the men take turns pounding each over the head until the winner remains standing. Atanarjuat wins the fight and, a few months later, he and his wife Atuat set up a home together. But soon Oki's sister, Puja (Lucy Tulugarjuk), comes sniffing around and she makes a play for Atanarjuat when the two set out to locate caribou. Puja succeeds in her efforts to become Atanarjuat's second wife, leading to a menage a trois that would shame the French.

One day, after Antanarjuat and his brother return from an extensive hunt, Puja deceives the other wives by telling them that they should go for a walk while she puts out the brothers' furs to dry. Then, as the brothers sleep, Oki and his cousins ambush the sleeping brothers and murder Amaqjuac. Atanarjuat escapes and is pursued by Oki and the cousins as he runs naked across the frozen tundra (*Atanarjuat*'s most memorable scene). True to his title, the Fast Runner outruns Oki and practically destroys his feet in the process. He hides out with a distant relative and eventually returns to avenge the death of his brother. The shaman returns and removes the curse that had fallen on the rival families and peace is restored.

Bill Evans for *Cinemascope* best sums up the film as capturing "a very complex community at work" and he cites Kunuk as "a masterful observer of human interaction and a filmmaker worth watching." *Atanarjuat* proves worthy of our attention too. 🎞

—*Patty-Lynne Herlevi*

## CREDITS

**Amaqjuac:** Natar Ungalaaq
**Atanarjuat:** Pakkak Innuksuk
**Oki:** Peter Henry Arnatsiaq
**Atuat:** Sylvia Ivalu
**Puja:** Lucy Tulugarjuk

**Origin:** Canada
**Released:** 2001
**Production:** Paul Apak Angilirq, Norman Cohn, Zacharias Kunuk; National Film Board of Canada, Igloolik Isuma Productions Inc.
**Directed by:** Zacharias Kunuk
**Written by:** Paul Apak Angilirq
**Cinematography by:** Norman Cohn

**Music by:** Chris Crilly
**Sound:** Richard Lavoie
**Editing:** Zacharias Kunuk, Norman Cohn, Marie-Christine Sarda
**Costumes:** Atuat Akkitirq
**Production Design:** James Ungalaaq
**MPAA rating:** Unrated
**Running time:** 165 minutes

## REVIEWS

*Boxoffice.* November, 2001, p. 140.
*Sight and Sound.* February, 2002, p. 22.
*Sight and Sound.* March, 2002, p. 35.

## AWARDS AND NOMINATIONS

**Cannes 2001:** First Feature
**Genie 2001:** Director (Kunuk), Film, Film Editing, Screenplay, Score
**Nomination:**
**Genie 2001:** Costume Des.

# Atlantis: The Lost Empire

*Discover the adventure. The magic. The fun.*
—Movie tagline

  **Box Office:** $84.1 million

In its search for new territory for adventure tales, Disney Pictures in the summer of 2001 took audiences to the famous lost continent of Atlantis for a much-heralded film. *Atlantis: The Lost Empire* was promoted as a breakthrough for Disney in several respects. Unlike the studio's usual animated feature summer releases, *Atlantis* sported a PG, rather than a G, rating, and it had no show-stopping musical numbers. Though there was little apparent reason for the PG rating, the film's story line, characters and dialogue aimed way above the heads of the preschool set. And *Atlantis* employed sophisticated computer graphics (CG) animation to a degree not seen before at Disney (though CG has been used with more impact by other animation studios).

All these ingredients were supposed to accelerate a comeback for Disney, which was facing stiffer competition for dominance of the cartoon feature market from studios like Warner Bros. and Fox. But despite obviously Herculean efforts, *Atlantis: The Lost Empire* was a resounding disappointment. Technically, the film is sound and represents Disney's most extensive and successful foray into CG animation to date, though without any notable breakthroughs in the use of that technology. But its story line is a mishmash, its characters singularly unappealing, and its focus fuzzy and aimless. Worse yet, it borrows from so many other films—and one in particular—that it is highly derivative.

The legend of Atlantis has been a favorite subject for speculative science fiction for more than a century, but, surprisingly, it had never been the source for an animated feature. Screenwriter Tab Murphy scored with a more straightforward script for another legendary story with Disney's *Tarzan* in 1999. This time, however, he turns the hoary tale of the underwater kingdom into a strange hybrid of outer-space, inner-space, and water-logged mysticism.

In a prologue, we witness an advanced civilization being overwhelmed by a huge tsunami as a mysterious ball of light descends, beaming up a queenly figure and taking her away from her child. The film then flashes forward to 1914 and Washington D.C., where a young linguist named Milo Thatch (voiced by Michael J. Fox) is trying to convince his museum employers to sponsor his obsessive quest for discovering the secrets of Atlantis. Following the footsteps of his maligned grandfather—who had the same genius, the same obsession, and a reputation for eccentricity—Milo has learned how to read the language of ancient Atlantian and believes a long-lost guide book written in the obscure tongue can help him find the submerged kingdom. A financier who knew his grandfather summons Milo; it turns out he not only has the guide book but a futuristic submarine, an experienced crew, and the money to finance the expedition.

The submarine is a marvelous computer-generated toy, half leviathan and half battleship, equipped with torpedoes and other weapons. Suitably designed as a period piece, it is one of the film's most alluring concepts, looking like something straight out of Jules Verne. Its auxiliary fleet of fight-worthy submersibles is also very cool and comes in handy when the crew must confront a sea monster which guards the underwater caverns that lead to the lost continent. Inexplicably, the monster turns out to be a machine, a large underwater fighting robot.

Unfortunately, directors Gary Trousdale and Kirk Wise seem more interested in the crew of regrettably conceived characters than in the submarine and expedition itself. Apart from the brief battle with the sea monster, there is no action until the explorers meet up with the inhabitants of Atlantis. Even then, any possible conflict is quickly resolved. But way too much time is spent instead on trying to be too clever with the crew's dialogue and interactions.

Instead of the cute animal sidekicks that typically populate Disney movies, the protagonist of *Atlantis* is surrounded by a gaggle of adult characters who manage to be stereotypical even while embodying the diversity that has become mandatory in all Disney enterprises. In 1914, it would have been unusual for any expedition to have a black doctor and two women—one as the second-in-command and another as the ship's crack mechanic. But in a Disney film, this historical wishful thinking is unremarkable and excusable. Much more grating is that each of the crew members seems calculated, cunning and crudely scripted. They are all caricatures.

Commander Rourke (James Garner) is the square-jawed military leader with a chiseled face, a gruff manner, phony warmth, and a heart of stone. Lieutenant Helga Sinclair (Claudia Christian), drawn in a completely different style than the other characters, looks like a 1930s-style European femme fatale masquerading as a 1990s-style female action hero. Dr. Joshua Sweet (Phil Morris) is a huge, brainy, sensitive doctor who at first glance is eerily reminiscent of the advertising figure Mr. Clean; his mother, we learn, was a Native American, so he covers two ethnic bases at once. The obligatory Hispanic is the teenage mechanic Audrey Ramirez (Jacqueline Obradors). Vinny Santorini (Don Novello) is a heavily accented and heavily stereotyped Italian demolitions expert. Fitting in with this group not at all is a backwoods character out of an old western, a cook named Cookie (the late Jim Varney). This is a very odd group, but it gets odder: The ship's navigator, Mrs. Packard (Florence Stanley), is a spoof of a gum-chewing, hairnet-wearing telephone operator or receptionist. And there's a creature named Mole (Corey Burton), who is fat, French, unshaven, and given to wallowing in the dirt and making crude come-ons toward females.

Idle time is spent as each of these characters tells Milo a background story as they bed down one night during the expedition. Their tales are all heartwarming but stilted. Throughout the film, the scriptwriters work overtime as the characters use sarcasm and quick-witted repartee to verbally jostle. Little of it is funny. In its efforts to be adult and witty, the dialogue falls flat. It's way too wry and calculated. This is a disagreeable pack of mercenaries, and something is wrong with the tone of *Atlantis*. In its efforts to reach an older audience, the film has lost its bearings. Its characters are likely to put off children and insult the intelligence of adults.

Milo Thatch is only marginally more interesting. He is overdrawn as a ridiculously bumbling nerd, with impossibly oversized glasses and a hunched-over, stick-figure body. Fox helps as much as he can but he is saddled with poor lines. The scientist-meets-research-subject romance goes way off the mark, too. Kida (Cree Summer), the young girl of the prologue who has grown into a 2,000-year-old teenage princess, is drawn as the typical Disney babe-heroine—beautiful and brainy and bold. Her attraction to Milo seems forced—there is nothing to pull them together except a very pat and predictable mutual mission. This is familiar Disney territory, but at least this time the romance is kept low-key and tuneless.

In *Shrek* (also reviewed in this edition), animators achieved a new level of realism by using CG animation to sculpt faces that looked authentically human. *Atlantis* uses the CG to do its fantastic landscapes and machines, and many of the images of the watery lost empire are astonishing. But the animators resort to an overly crude cartooning style to draw its characters—more precisely, an annoyingly mismatched mix of traditional techniques. The only intriguingly drawn characters are the Atlantians, especially Kida's father, the old king (voiced by Leonard Nimoy).

The plot is bizarre. The inhabitants of Atlantis are mortal but live thousands of years. They can understand and speak English and other modern languages even though they have been cut off from the rest of the world since before those languages existed. Yet they cannot understand the ancient texts of their own tongue, so they need Milo to decipher them. They are controlled by a mysterious life force contained in a ball of light. This light is capable of being a vengeful god. The king explains this to Milo in a few sentences hurriedly spoken to cover up their lack of logic. The film eventually becomes a mundane and hackneyed battle of money versus spirit, and after another brief battle and a volcanic cataclysm, there is the expected happy ending.

*Atlantis* borrows heavily from many sources, including Verne, Indiana Jones, *Star Wars*, *The Iron Giant*, and World War I fighter pilot flicks. But more than anything, its plot resembles *Titan A.E.*, an inventive animated science-fiction feature that was rejected by major studios and finally made by Don Bluth and his team. In *Titan*, the film opens with an apocalyptic cataclysm (an invasion of Earth by aliens); the young hero loses a parent who flies off into the sky, and he eventually discovers a map to take him to the lost world. *Atlantis* has the cataclysm, the ascending parent, and the map that only the protagonist can decipher. In both films, the hero goes on a mission (in *Titan*, to outer space) with a crew that eventually betrays him for mercenary reasons. Both crews include a heartless, conniving, militaristic commander and similarly conceived and motivated underlings. In both, the mission has to navigate a labyrinth to find the lost world, and in both the hero must battle the turncoat commander to gain control of a power source which can remake an entire civilization. Both films have young princesses whom the hero befriends and then rescues. These are certainly a disturbingly large number of similarities.

*Atlantis* is certainly not groundbreaking. In fact, it covers a lot of old territory, including the usual Disney obsessions with missing parents, betrayal, and romance-and-rescue. And it's all wrapped up in a bunch of metaphysical gobbledygook. Disney needs to first find a strong story with compelling characters and then decide how much it wants to depart from company tradition. *Atlantis* plays like a concept executed by a committee who were instructed by marketers, looking for a lost purpose.

*—Michael Betzold*

**Milo Thatch:** Michael J. Fox (Voice)
**Commander Rourke:** James Garner (Voice)
**Helga Sinclair:** Claudia Christian (Voice)
**Princess Kida:** Cree Summer (Voice)
**Preston B. Whitmore:** John Mahoney (Voice)
**King of Atlantis:** Leonard Nimoy (Voice)
**Fenton Q. Harcourt:** David Ogden Stiers (Voice)
**Cookie:** Jim Varney (Voice)
**Dr. Sweet:** Phil Morris (Voice)
**Vinny Santorini:** Don Novello (Voice)
**Mrs. Packard:** Florence Stanley (Voice)
**Mole:** Corey Burton (Voice)
**Audrey Ramirez:** Jacqueline Obradors (Voice)

**Origin:** USA
**Released:** 2001
**Production:** Don Hahn; Walt Disney Pictures; released by Buena Vista
**Directed by:** Gary Trousdale, Kirk Wise
**Written by:** Tab Murphy
**Music by:** James Newton Howard
**Editing:** Ellen Keneshea
**Art Direction:** David Goetz
**Visual Effects:** Marlon West
**MPAA rating:** PG
**Running time:** 95 minutes

REVIEWS

*Boxoffice.* June, 2001, p. 32.
*Boxoffice.* August, 2001, p. 59.
*Chicago Sun-Times Online.* June 15, 2001.
*Entertainment Weekly.* June 15, 2001, p. 59.
*Hollywood Reporter.* June 8, 2001, p. 10.
*Los Angeles Times Online.* June 8, 2001.
*New York Times Online.* June 8, 2001.
*People.* June 25, 2001, p. 35.
*USA Today Online.* June 15, 2001.
*Variety.* June 11, 2001, p. 17.
*Washington Post Online.* June 15, 2001.

Helga (Claudia Christian) sarcastically tells Milo (Michael J. Fox): "Cartographer, linguist, plumber—it's hard to believe you're still single."

Greek philosopher Plato wrote about Atlantis in 360 B.C. in his dialogues *Timaeus* and *Critias*.

# Baby Boy

*One man's fight to change the game.*
—Movie tagline

**Box Office:** $28.7 million

In his landmark film, *Boyz N the Hood*, writer-director-producer John Singleton trained an unflinching eye and an uncanny ear on the chaos of life among people caught in the cross-fire of a drug-ridden, gunslinging Los Angeles inner city neighborhood. Ten years later, Singleton returns to the same South Central L.A. turf with *Baby Boy*—but the landscape has changed markedly.

The drugs, the guns and the culture of freewheeling sex and violence are still in evidence, but people aren't shooting up and getting shot up left and right—at least not on camera. The threat of an early death on the street looms in the background of the action and figures heavily in the thinking and feelings of Jody (Tyrese Gibson), who at age 20 is at a crossroads in his life, haunted by nightmares of his own demise and unable to take the next step into adulthood.

Jody already has been in jail—for an unspecified period for an unspecified crime. Tellingly, the film makes only passing references to this history, as if it is so typical as to be unremarkable. Jody also has fathered two children by two different women: a daughter with Peanut (Tamara LaSeon Bass) and a son with Yvette (Taraji P. Henson). Yet Jody doesn't have a job and usually lives with his mother Juanita (A.J. Johnson). He also spends a lot of time hanging out with his best friend Sweetpea (Omar Gooding), a similarly situated man who is unemployed and spends his idle moments playing video games or cruising the streets.

In a prologue to the film, Singleton shows Jody curled up in an oversized womb and quotes a psychologist who theorizes that many American black men are victims of arrested development. It notes that in the popular lingo they call their girlfriends "momma," their buddies "my boys," and their home their "crib." *Baby Boy* is explicitly an exploration of this theory, using Jody's relationships with women, men, and the world at large to repeatedly pose questions about his maturity—and, by extension, about the maturity of other such men immersed in his culture of irresponsibility and lack of opportunity.

Jody has the trappings of adulthood, since he already has children, and he is both sexually experienced and active. He talks trash to his girlfriends, his mother, his mother's new boyfriend, and his friends. But beneath the surface bravado, Singleton suggests, Jody is frightened and insecure. And he has good reason to be. His older brother died on the streets after their mother kicked him out of the house because she got a new boyfriend. Jody is afraid the same thing will happen to him, especially when the commanding figure of Marvin (Ving Rhames) becomes his mother's new suitor and, soon after, her live-in lover.

It's not that Jody doesn't have somewhere else to go. He and Yvette are trying in an off-and-on fashion to form a stable family, but Jody's immaturity is a huge impediment. Yvette has a job and a car, which Jody frequently "borrows." Jody thinks keeping the car maintained, paying occasional visits to Yvette and their son Jo-Jo, and driving Yvette to and from her job at a phone company are sufficient evidence that he is doing his part in the relationship. Yvette, of course, sees it differently, and is especially disturbed that Jody won't give up his habit of seeing other women on the side. The two are constantly fighting—and frequently making up.

Seemingly out of the blue, Jody says he is going to take charge of his life and comes up with an entrepreneurial plan—selling women's clothes. That they are stolen dresses and shoes, lifted from a fashion warehouse with the help of some friends he commissions, doesn't seem to matter much to Jody or anyone else. Jody has a knack for convincing customers to buy even the most outrageous outfits. His sales jobs are blatantly seductive; as he lays his hands and merchandise on his customers and sweet-talks them, they succumb to his charms. Jody is a ladies' man and Gibson, a model and vocalist before landing this role, is achingly handsome. Singleton likes his camera to linger on Gibson's face or bare torso and to catch him in various attractive poses. Gibson's naturalistic acting is a tour de force of sensitivity mixed with bravado and this makes the movie far more compelling than the story line warrants.

For all his deficiencies, Jody is kind-hearted. Jody loves Yvette in his own immature way, but his selfishness prevents him from seeing the entire picture. Though he sometimes affects the talk and demeanor of a "gangsta," he is no killer, and even when provoked his response is usually mild. He is terribly afraid of becoming abusive toward women like his father—a despised figure whose beating and abandoning of

Juanita is also referred to mostly in passing, as another inevitable part of life.

It is Marvin's successful courting of his mother than most enrages Jody. Jody fears being evicted but he also seems to cower and rage just at the very presence of this mature black man. As played with mesmerizing self-assurance by the always-excellent Rhames, Marvin, a reformed gangsta, is everything that his women are urging Jody to grow up and become. He owns his own landscaping business and walks unafraid on the streets, strong and self-reliant but under control. Jody, however, believes Marvin is a fraud, a violent and bad man masquerading as a responsible citizen, and he keeps unearthing evidence to prove it.

The interplay between Jody and Marvin is tense and engaging. Marvin is the sage survivor who tells Jody he's seen and done it all—and apparently he has. He could be the father Jody never has had but that's the last thing Jody wants. It turns out that Jody is right about Marvin's dangerous side but Marvin understands more about Jody than any of the women in his life can.

The acting in *Baby Boy* is uniformly first-rate. Rhames is simply magnificent, and Tyrese Gibson is almost iconic—a star in the making. Henson and Johnson are also compelling in more restricted roles. Once again, Singleton succeeds in writing at times hilarious but always trenchant and authentic dialogue, and his crew of stars and supporting actors is uniformly believable.

Singleton shows only occasional flashes of the brilliance that earned him a best director Oscar® nomination for *Boyz*. He keeps Jody's fears looming in the background, except when they emerge in rapid-fire dream sequences. One series of shots in particular is breathtakingly daring—a fight between Yvette and Jody in which Jody breaks his promise not to hit her, a tearful and desperate making up and lovemaking, and flashes of scenes of bliss and tragedy that enter the characters' minds. In *Baby Boy*, the hopes and fears of Jody and Yvette are palpable.

Unfortunately, Singleton lingers much too long over the same material, and for much of the movie the plot seems to be spinning its wheels. Jody and Yvette fight, Jody and Marvin fight, Jody and his mother have heart-to-heart talks, and eventually the interactions take on a soap-opera quality. Singleton doesn't advance his coming-of-age film with anything like alacrity, and the film comes perilously close to stalling out at several points. Some of the transitions between scenes are very awkward, and some of the material seems simply egregious. Do we really need a phone conversation with Yvette's girlfriend in which the girlfriend and a male visitor engage in the crudest interplay? And there are far too many times when someone tells Jody that he hasn't grown up. Singleton is a little too enamored of his man-as-baby concept, and even the listenable mix of background songs are a little too obviously thematic.

When Yvette's ex-boyfriend, Rodney (played by rapper Snoop Dogg), returns from prison, the plot begins to simmer a little, but even then it's a long time before it goes full boil. Finally, Singleton resolves Jody's dilemma in a manner which smacks of scriptwriting convenience and raises serious moral questions about what passes for maturity in the culture he's depicting. But Singleton is studiously non-judgmental, and in the end it's possible to take *Baby Boy* as another of this director's wonderfully balanced slice-of-life sagas. Singleton doesn't take as many risks with this material as he did with *Boyz N the Hood*, though in fact his refusal to immerse the plot in violence is itself a risky move in terms of audience appeal.

It should be obvious that *Baby Boy* demands both maturity and perspective from its potential audiences. It is drenched with profanity, sexual encounters and innuendoes, and is entirely conducted in the gritty, tough language of urban America. For those with the proper appreciation for the art of insult, there is endless amusement in the finely honed, rapid-fire verbal battles between the principles. Following his entertaining detour into the frivolous with *Shaft*, Singleton has returned to a serious and thoughtful dissection of American culture, even though this latest film is short on both action and plot and has strange lapses into near-somnolent sentimentality. As a character study, however, it's both mature and entrancing—and both Gibson and Rhames deserve Oscar® attention.

—*Michael Betzold*

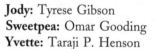

## CREDITS

**Jody:** Tyrese Gibson
**Sweetpea:** Omar Gooding
**Yvette:** Taraji P. Henson
**Juanita:** Adrienne-Joi (AJ) Johnson
**Rodney:** Snoop Dogg
**Peanut:** Tamara La Seon Bass
**Melvin:** Ving Rhames

**Origin:** USA
**Released:** 2001
**Production:** John Singleton; New Deal; released by Columbia Pictures
**Directed by:** John Singleton
**Written by:** John Singleton
**Cinematography by:** Charles Mills
**Music by:** David Arnold
**Sound:** Veda Campbell
**Editing:** Bruce Cannon
**Costumes:** Ruth Carter
**MPAA rating:** R
**Running time:** 129 minutes

## REVIEWS

*Boxoffice.* September, 2001, p. 153.
*Chicago Sun-Times Online.* June 27, 2001.
*Entertainment Weekly.* July 13, 2001, p. 56.
*Los Angeles Times Online.* June 27, 2001.
*New York Tiimes Online.* June 27, 2001.
*People.* July 9, 2001, p. 39.
*USA Today Online.* June 27, 2001.
*Variety.* July 9, 2001, p. 22.
*Washington Post Online.* June 27, 2001.

## QUOTES

When girlfriend Yvette (Taraji P. Henson) complains he lies to her, Jody (Tyrese Gibson) replies: "I'm out in these streets telling these 'hos the truth. I lie to you because I care about you."

## TRIVIA

Omar Gooding is the brother of Cuba Gooding Jr. whom John Singleton cast in his first movie *Boyz N the Hood.*

# Bandits

*Two's company, three's a crime.*
—Movie tagline

 **Box Office:** $41.4 million

**B**andits is a rarity these days—a film that seems like it was made for adults. It's not too much of a surprise that it was the project of director Barry Levinson (*Wag the Dog, Diner*), one of the few directors who aims for an audience older than 13. Ostensibly, it's a movie about bank robbers, but it's really a character study and a laid-back, loopy comedy that just happens to be about criminals.

The story is told in flashback. When we first meet Joe Blake (Bruce Willis) and Terry Collins (Billy Bob Thornton), we know it's all going to end badly. They're in a bank, aptly named the Alamo, and surrounded by Los Angeles police officers. We learn from loud TV announcer Darren Head (Bobby Slayton), host of a tacky *America's Most Wanted*-type show called "Criminals at Large" that the two have been killed. We know it has something to do with a dame. But of course.

Flashback to the two in an Oregon prison. Terry is complaining because the prison is going to ban garlic, the miracle food. Joe seems like he's listening, but part of his mind must be on something else because, all of a sudden, he hijacks the truck of a worker who's on the prison grounds. Terry somehow manages to leap on back and Joe crashes the truck through the prison doors.

Terry, a neurotic guy who is constantly monitoring his body for symptoms of the hideous diseases that he's sure he's coming down with, mentions that they're going to need clothes and money. Joe slams on the breaks in front of a local bank and declares that they're going to get some money by robbing the bank. Joe, who's an action-oriented guy, grabs a highlighter marker, stuffs it in his pocket and proceeds to rob the bank, while Terry's fretting the whole time. "You're gonna rob a bank with a magic marker? What are you gonna do—write on them?" he says. During the robbery itself, Terry vents testily to one of the hostages, "He made no plan whatsoever for this."

The bandits solve their clothes problem by breaking into a house where a teen girl and her boyfriend are staying while the girl's father is away for the weekend. The girl, who thinks the bandits are cool, lends them some of her father's clothes. The next day, when Terry comes downstairs in his new get-up, he complains to Joe about his tacky plaid pants. "I look good in this color but you boned me on the pants," he says.

Joe comes up with a plan for the two. They will rob banks to earn enough money to go to Mexico. In Mexico, they're going to open up a nightclub and restaurant where they'll wear tuxedos and sell margaritas to the tourists. "Tuxedos and margaritas" becomes their mantra. Terry's contribution to the plan is a new method of robbery. Instead of breaking into the bank during business hours, they'll go to the bank manager's house the night before, spend the night at his or her house, then have the manager open the safe for them in the morning. Joe enlists the help of Harvey Pollard (Troy Garity, Jane Fonda's son), his dim cousin who's an aspiring stuntman, to be their lookout guy.

They're successful and soon gain infamy as "The Sleepover Bandits." Their fame makes their jobs much harder. When they arrive at the door of one bank manager, she is delighted to have the bandits from TV robbing her bank, but isn't able to take them seriously. "Everyone knows you wouldn't really hurt a fly, Joe," she says, giggling.

The pair soon hook up with their femme fatale, Kate Wheeler (Cate Blanchett). Kate is a well-to-do housewife who's stuck with a husband who doesn't notice her. When we first meet her, Kate is cooking up a fancy dinner for her husband and singing a bad Bonnie Tyler song at the top of her lungs. Her husband comes home and coldly announces that he's going to the gym and won't be eating dinner. Kate runs out of the house and starts driving madly down the street. She almost hits Terry, who decides to hijack her car.

After spending a few minutes in her car, Terry's sure Kate is insane and tries to get out, but Kate insists that he stay. "I shouldn't be alone right now!" she insists.

Kate ends up coming to Joe and Terry's hideout where she takes an immediate liking to the handsome and brave Joe. Later, after insinuating herself into the gang and getting a charge out of the robbing, she starts liking the smarter, more sensitive Terry, too, making for a love triangle. "I can't decide between you two," she tells them, "Together, you're the perfect man."

But the love triangle isn't the main point of the story, nor is the question of how and why the crime spree will end. The fun part of this film is watching the interaction of the characters. The film has a loose, improvisational feel and it's nice that everything the characters say doesn't have some official plot reason for being there. When Terry and Joe are talking, Joe is just as likely to absently say, "Yes, I think I did chip that tooth," instead of some big proclamation about their next job. It's fun to hear them discussing trivia or bickering over minor issues. In one sequence, Terry is dressed in a disguise with big mutton chop sideburns and sunglasses. Kate suggests that he looks like Neil Young on the "After the Gold Rush" album. Terry corrects her and says he was going for a look on another Young album. In another scene, Kate earnestly describes Tyler's sappy "Total Eclipse of the Heart" as "a haiku to the complexity of love." It's hard to tell if these sort of casual off-kilter moments are the product of some successful improv or the work of screenwriter Harley Peyton.

The various disguises the men don are a running joke in the movie. They wear a wide variety of ridiculous wigs, big ugly mustaches and out-of-date fashions with a certain glee. As one critic put it, the film must have been a hairstylist's dream job. The highlight of *Bandits* is Thornton's Terry. His character is a mess of nerves—"I don't care what that doctor says, I've got symptoms"—and neuroses. When he's driving in his getaway car, he pops in a cassette of the medical book, *The Merck Manual*. He hears about a brain tumor that has the symptom of smelling burning feathers and immediately can smell those burning feathers, too. He's got phobias about everything, including antique furniture (a phobia that Thornton shares with his character). "It gives me the heebie-jeebies," he explains. At one point, he wakes up from a nightmare shouting, "Beavers and ducks!"

The film's biggest flaw is the running length. It's 2 hours and 3 minutes. If it were packed with consistently high-quality content, the length wouldn't have been a problem, but there's a lot of dead spots that could have easily been cut out. Critics varied in their reactions to *Bandits*. Kenneth Turan of the *Los Angeles Times* wrote, "An amusing tale of larceny triumphant, *Bandits* is an entertainment with a rogue's imagination." Roger Ebert of the *Chicago Sun-Times* said, "*Bandits* is a movie so determined to be clever and whimsical that it neglects to be anything else. That decision wouldn't be fatal if the movie had caved in and admitted it was a comedy, but no, it also wants to contain moments of pathos, suspense and insight, and it's too flimsy to support them." *Entertainment Weekly*'s Lisa Schwarzbaum wrote, "While they banter playfully—aiming for Butch and Sundance chemistry, or maybe the Ur-bickering of *The Odd Couple*'s Oscar and Felix—these two happy chappies in snappy serapes nearly crow: Ain't we cute!"

—*Jill Hamilton*

## CREDITS

**Joe Blake:** Bruce Willis
**Terry Collins:** Billy Bob Thornton
**Kate Wheeler:** Cate Blanchett
**Harvey Pollard:** Troy Garity
**Darren Head:** Bobby Slayton
**Darill Miller:** Brian F. O'Byrne
**Cheri:** Azura Skye
**Chloe Miller:** Stacy Travis
**Charles Wheeler:** William Converse-Roberts
**Lawrence Fife:** Richard Riehle
**Sarah Fife:** Micole Mercurio
**Claire:** January Jones

**Origin:** USA
**Released:** 2001
**Production:** Michael Birnbaum, Barry Levinson, Paula Weinstein, Ashok Amritraj, Michele Berk; Baltimore Pictures, Hyde Park Entertainment, Spring Creek Productions, Empire Pictures, Lotus Pictures; released by MGM
**Directed by:** Barry Levinson
**Written by:** Harley Peyton
**Cinematography by:** Dante Spinotti
**Music by:** Christopher Young
**Sound:** Ron Cogswell
**Editing:** Stu Linder
**Art Direction:** Dan Webster
**Costumes:** Gloria Gresham
**Production Design:** Victor Kempster
**MPAA rating:** PG-13
**Running time:** 123 minutes

## REVIEWS

*Boxoffice.* December, 2001, p. 62.
*Chicago Sun-Times Online.* October 12, 2001.
*Entertainment Weekly.* October 19, 2001, p. 53.
*Los Angeles Times Online.* October 12, 2001.
*New York Times Online.* October 12, 2001.
*People.* October 22, 2001, p. 37.
*Rolling Stone.* November 8, 2001, p. 134.
*Sight and Sound.* December, 2001, p. 42.
*USA Today Online.* October 11, 2001.
*Variety Online.* October 4, 2001.
*Washington Post.* October 12, 2001, p. WE43.

## QUOTES

Terry (Billy Bob Thornton) warns partner Joe (Bruce Willis): "Kate's an iceberg, waiting for the Titanic."

## AWARDS AND NOMINATIONS

**Natl. Bd. of Review 2001:** Actor (Thornton)
**Nomination:**
**Golden Globes 2002:** Actor—Mus./Comedy (Thornton), Actress—Mus./Comedy (Blanchett)
**Screen Actors Guild 2001:** Support. Actress (Blanchett).

# Baran (Rain)

Celebrated Iranian filmmaker Majid Majidi's teenage love story, *Baran*, received an uncannily timely showcasing at the 2001 New York Film Festival. Set against the background of downtrodden Afghani illegals in Iran, the film's showing coincided with the U.S. bombardment of Afghanistan. The filmmaker, who could not attend, sent a statement that was read out before the screening in which he claimed that the film's intent was to show that "love crosses all borders."

Latif (Hossein Abedini), the nondescript protagonist in his late teens, is nothing more than an Iranian menial worker for a construction firm in Tehran that is illegally employing Afghani refugees. Yet in the film's scheme of things, he serves to illustrate how the socio-political forces he cannot change become a displacement for a higher will, presumably that of the Almighty.

At the start of the film, all Latif wants is the year's pay owing to him from his ruthless irate boss, Memar (Mohammad Reza Naji). Latif knows better than to push the issue. The work Memar has him do is child's play compared to the back breaking duty of the men to whom he has to keep bringing glasses of tea. The catalyst in Latif's life takes the form of Rahmat (Zahra Bahrami), a sullen, frail new worker.

Rahmat is not only physically unsuited to carry the heavy bags of cement, but he also happens to be an Afghani without a work permit.

Latif realizes that the reason Rahmat has been sent to work there in the first place is because Najaf, Rahmat's father, suffered a crippling accident on the job and, with five mouths to feed, has been forced to send his son. Latif thus becomes morally bound to help Rahmat, and even take his side in every situation.

After Rahmat drops a cement sack, its contents spilling onto a worker below, a fight ensues between the worker and the quick-tempered Latif. For Memar, this is the last straw. Latif is put on heavy duty, while Rahmat is given the task of preparing and serving the tea. Now that he himself has to carry the heavy bags of cement, Latif begins to hate Rahmat. Rancor turns to jealousy when Latif sees Rahmat preparing a feast for the workers, who voice their appreciation unanimously.

Soon Latif is thrown for a loop when he spies on Rahmat, and sees the silhouette of a young woman combing her long hair. Latif's astonishment now turns into desire, but his growing passion has to remain a secret lest Memar come to know. Though Latif doesn't appear to be consciously aware of it, the tables have now been turned on him. Now it is he who is helpless in the light of the overwhelming sociopolitical forces. We are meant to perceive Latif's desire as doomed to remain unrequited since he can never ask for the hand of his beloved in marriage, owing to the fact that she is a Suni Muslim and he is a Shia. The film doesn't make this clear, thereby lessening its dramatic impact for foreign audiences who may be ignorant of this basic divisive force in Islam.

It is here, following Latif's epiphany, that the film's narrative hits a snag. Majidi could have switched viewpoints at this stage. Instead, Rahmat continues to remain a cipher. Even after Latif rescues her from the clutches of the inspectors, he cannot pursue his desire as any healthy young man would, so that expressions of his ardor are confined to the most undramatic of events transpiring within the rigor of his everyday life. For example, Latif finds that his heartthrob has left a glass of tea waiting for him along with a sugar cube broken in half. The gesture is touching, but doesn't spur him to do anything about it.

After a raid by the authorities results in the Afghanis having to flee for good, Latif draws on the pay owing to him so as to help Najaf. When Soltan (Hossein Mahjoub Abbas Rahimi), the intermediary, flees with the amount, Latif takes an advance from Memar, claiming his sister is ill, and even sells his I.D., so as to purchase a set of crutches for Najaf. With Rahmat's ornamented hairpin as a memento, Latif sets out to find the village Najaf and his family are hiding in. It is through this quest that he comes to know that Rahmat's real name is Baran.

When he does track her down, Latif spies Baran working in a group of women near a shrine, helping to lift heavy rocks over a raging forest stream. When he meets Najaf, he is told that the family is returning to Afghanistan the next day. The following morning, Latif does get to behold the sight of his beloved for the beautiful young woman she really is, but only for an instant. No sooner does a faint smile cross her face, than the customary chador drops down. Latif is then left alone as it starts to thunder. Even so, he smiles down at the rain, as if he is seeing his love reflected in it, as part of some inscrutable higher will.

Critics in this country will no doubt be struck by the timeliness of the film's plot elements. A.O. Scott in the *New York Times* goes even further. For him, *Baran* "exemplifies the power of cinema . . . to achieve a paradoxical universality," transmuting its brutal "reality into a lyrical and celebratory vision."

—*Vivek Adarkar*

## CREDITS

**Latif:** Hossein Abedini
**Rahmat/Baran:** Zahra Bahrami
**Memar:** Mohammad Reza Naji
**Soltan:** Hossein Rahimi

**Origin:** Iran
**Language:** Farsi
**Released:** 2001
**Production:** Majid Majidi, Fouad Nahas; released by Miramax Films
**Directed by:** Majid Majidi
**Written by:** Majid Majidi
**Cinematography by:** Mohammad Davudi
**Music by:** Ahmad Pejman
**Sound:** Yadollah Najafi
**Editing:** Hassan Hassandust
**Art Direction:** Behzad Kazzazi
**Costumes:** Malek Jahan Khazai
**MPAA rating:** PG
**Running time:** 94 minutes

## REVIEWS

*Los Angeles Times Online.* December 7, 2001.
*New York Times Online.* October 9, 2001.
*Newsweek Online.* December 6, 2001.
*USA Today Online.* December 6, 2001.
*Variety Online.* February 16, 2001.

Latif (Hossein Abedini) threatens his Afghan coworkers: "I'll ram your nose into your brain."

# Beautiful Creatures

*Dorothy & Petula have a body to die for.*
—Movie tagline

Bill Eagles's *Beautiful Creatures* aspires to be a hip, savvy thriller about two women who attempt to scheme their way to a small fortune and, in the process, turn the tables on a bunch of noxious men determined to make their lives miserable. Set in Glasgow, Scotland, the film features a promising setup for a female buddy picture, but unfortunately the screenplay very quickly degenerates into a disappointing mishmash of unfunny dark comedy and lackluster neo-noir that never finds its own unique rhythm. The basic plot, revolving around a dead body and a fake kidnapping, is riddled with holes and grows increasingly silly, finally leaving the overall film a hollow mess.

When we meet Dorothy (Susan Lynch), she is arguing with her abusive boyfriend, Tony (Iain Glen), over his set of golf clubs, which she has pawned. When she arrives home, she finds her bra cooking on her stove and her dog, Pluto, dyed a garish red—silly acts of revenge courtesy of the loathsome Tony. Petula (Rachel Weisz) also has trouble with her brute of a boyfriend, Brian (Tom Mannion). One night he is beating her in a parking lot when Dorothy, who is hoping to take the bus to London, happens by and comes to the battered woman's defense. She whacks Brian across the head with a huge metal pole, a deed that would normally kill a person instantly. Brian survives the blow, however, so the panicked women are forced to form an alliance and take him back home, where they put him in Dorothy's bathtub. When the hapless Brian suddenly dies, Dorothy and Petula have to figure out what to do with the corpse. At this point, *Beautiful Creatures* looks like it could turn into a film like *Shallow Grave*, a Scottish thriller that took a troublesome corpse as a springboard for some wicked twists and turns, but *Beautiful Creatures* instead sputters off into other, less promising directions.

The opening scenes of *Beautiful Creatures* highlight many of the problems that plague the film as a whole, the most important being the film's uncertain tone. For example, is Brian's death, punctuated by a gruesome shot of blood dripping from his eye, supposed to be darkly funny or genuinely scary? Or is it both? The film seems to be aiming for a kind of self-conscious, black humor where we can cheerfully laugh at death, but the scene is more disgusting than clever.

Moreover, both Tony and Brian are so odious from the outset that they become nothing more than mere stereotypes of bad male behavior. We will see variations on this type when we meet other men throughout the film, including Brian's thuggish brother, Ronnie (Maurice Roeves), for whom Petula works, and George (Alex Norton), a corrupt, leering police inspector. No man possesses a single redeeming feature, not even the clerk at the bus terminal, who is a porn enthusiast. Merely highlighting the worst in men, however, does not a feminist statement make, and yet the film seems to want to be a kind of gutsy female revenge picture, with two plucky women taking on all the creepy men they encounter.

To make the situation more tiresome, the heroines themselves are not very compelling. Dorothy is attractive in a down-to-earth way, while Petula, with her platinum-blonde hair, is exotic and quite stunning, but both are one-dimensional characters, and neither changes much during the course of the adventure. Moreover, as a team, Lynch and Weisz never click and have practically no chemistry. There is the faint suggestion that Dorothy may be attracted to Petula, but not much is made of it. More important, except for the initial rescue that brings them together (a possible homage to *Thelma and Louise*, the classic film about female outlaws), it is never clear why Dorothy and Petula even like each other, let alone why they would become friends.

The nosy policeman, George, appears unexpectedly and starts investigating Brian's disappearance. As he is questioning Petula, a ransom letter from Dorothy happens to arrive, complete with Brian's severed finger. (Pluto has bit off one of the corpse's fingers—a ghoulish running joke that is not very funny.) Petula must then call Dorothy in front of George and act as if she is gathering information from the kidnapper. On the spot, Petula makes up a ransom figure, settling on the high figure of one million pounds. Petula's improvisation of a phony ransom conversation for George's benefit could have been simultaneously funny and suspenseful, but, like many scenes in *Beautiful Creatures*, it never develops any real tension and simply falls flat.

George learns from a pathologist friend that the finger was severed from a dead body, but that does not stop him from going along with Petula's story and telling Ronnie that the ransom for his brother is two million pounds so that he can take a share for himself. A shot of ketchup squirting out of a bottle right after the pathologist sees the finger says everything we need to know about the film's lame attempt at dark humor.

If Dorothy and Petula did not have enough to deal with already, Tony, who is a drug addict, reappears out of nowhere to claim his golf bag, which contains his stash of heroin. He knows about Dorothy and Petula's kidnapping scheme and, like George, wants his own cut of it. The ransom plan itself, however, is not really discussed. Instead, in a grotesque scene that really has nothing to do with the main plot, Tony forces Dorothy to shoot him up and then orders her to do the same to herself. The scene grows more perverse when he has Petula tie Dorothy's hands behind her back and then orders Petula to take off her pants. Just when it looks like he is going to rape Petula, the women fight back and knock him out. In the struggle, however, Pluto is shot. Even though the women triumph over Tony, the episode has a queasy, even sick tone, as if Eagles really enjoyed humiliating his female characters and placing them in the most distasteful of situations.

The film is disjointed and messy. Simon Donald's screenplay is not a tight noir piece but rather a loose collection of scenes that often make no sense, like a bizarre encounter in which George appears in Petula's room, approaches her bed, and ominously slips a rifle under the covers. When he says that he has "wanted one like you all my life," we think that he is going to try to rape her, but, instead of menacing her, he just leaves. Like the encounter with Tony, it is yet another pointless scene that seems to revel in putting the women in danger but does not make sense in the overall plot. After a while, it seems like Donald did not even have a feature-length story to tell; his sluggish script merely staggers along from one odd scene to the next without any focus. Is the film supposed to be a neo-noir, a farce, a dark comedy, a feminist revenge flick? It is hard to tell. Of course, it is possible for a screenplay to do more than one thing effectively, and a select few writers can indeed juggle many genres at once. But that requires a skillful blending of plot elements and moods, and Donald's script does not deliver in even one way, let alone as an imaginative pastiche.

The big climax of the film is the ransom drop and its absurd aftermath. Having obtained the money from Ronnie in two bags, Petula takes one, while George surreptitiously keeps the other in his car. Petula makes her way to the bus station with her bag for the drop, where Pluto, who has very quickly healed from his bullet wounds, is waiting. She fastens the money to the dog, who then runs away. When George arrives and quickly realizes that Petula has pulled a fast one on him, he handcuffs her to a wall. He then runs after the dog in a chase that leads him straight to Dorothy for an over-the-top showdown. Dorothy and George have their guns drawn on each other, but he ultimately forces her to throw hers down.

Then Ronnie, who has been growing suspicious of the whole operation, suddenly appears. Just when it looks like George will kill Ronnie, Tony, who has been hiding in the closet the whole time, emerges and kills George. It is completely ridiculous to think that Tony, who had previously been knocked out and was virtually at death's door, could be strong enough to plan an ambush. Then Ronnie kills Tony, even though he has just saved his life. Just when it looks like Ronnie is going to kill Dorothy, we are treated to yet another surprise from out of the blue when Petula arrives (apparently the handcuffs were not an impediment after all) and shoots

Ronnie, thus saving Dorothy's life. The ending comes across as a contrived, nonsensical way of bringing together all the characters for an obligatory, gun-blazing finale.

Dorothy and Petula finally find the other million pounds in George's car trunk and presumably will be happy now that all the troublesome men in their lives are dead. It would be wonderful to cheer these spirited women, but it really feels like they lucked into the money rather than earning it through superior wit and sharp strategy. Also, since Dorothy and Petula barely seem to connect with each other on an emotional level, it is hard to imagine what kind of friendship they will have in the future.

*Beautiful Creatures* has been compared to *Thelma and Louise* and *Bound* as female outlaw/revenge films. But that brief generic description is where the similarity ends. The idiotic and at times misogynistic *Beautiful Creatures* has neither the smart, witty script and epic sweep and grandeur of *Thelma and Louise* nor the tricky, clever plot of *Bound*. Eagles's film, however, actually seems to be aiming for something different from these films. It more closely resembles a highly stylized caper film marked by dark humor, violent gunplay, and lowlife characters—possibly a distaff version of a Quentin Tarantino or Guy Ritchie film. But Eagles does not have the snappy rhythm or exuberant style needed to prop up Donald's flat screenplay. The characters are thin, the plot is illogical, and the pacing is too slack to make a difference.

—*Peter N. Chumo II*

## CREDITS

**Petula:** Rachel Weisz
**Dorothy:** Susan Lynch
**Det. Insp. George Hepburn:** Alex Norton
**Tony:** Iain Glen
**Ronnie McMinn:** Maurice Roeves
**Brian McMinn:** Tom Mannion

**Origin:** Great Britain
**Released:** 2000
**Production:** Alan J. Wands, Simon Donald; DNA Films Ltd., Snakeman, United Pictures International, Arts Council of England; released by Universal Focus
**Directed by:** Bill Eagles
**Written by:** Simon Donald
**Cinematography by:** James Welland
**Music by:** Murray Gold
**Sound:** Louis Kramer
**Editing:** Jon Gregory
**Art Direction:** Frances Connell
**Costumes:** Trisha Biggar
**Production Design:** Andy Harris

**MPAA rating:** R
**Running time:** 88 minutes

## REVIEWS

*Chicago Sun-Times Online.* April 20, 2001.
*Entertainment Weekly.* April 13, 2001, p. 49.
*Hollywood Reporter.* December 8, 2000, p. 85.
*Los Angeles Times Online.* April 6, 2001.
*New York Times Online.* April 6, 2001.
*People.* April 16, 2001, p. 38.
*Sight and Sound.* February, 2001, p. 25.
*Variety.* September 18, 2000, p. 41.
*Washington Post Online.* April 20, 2001.

# A Beautiful Mind

*He saw the world in a way no one could have imagined.*
—Movie tagline

**Box Office:** $138.9 million

Mathematician John Nash (Russell Crowe) certainly has had an interesting life. Discarded by the academic world after being diagnosed as a schizophrenic, Nash rebounded after receiving a Nobel Prize in 1994. Ron Howard's *A Beautiful Mind*, based on the book by Sylvia Nasar, is a slick recounting of this remarkable story made palatable primarily by yet another remarkable Russell Crowe performance.

The film begins in the late 1940's with Nash's arrival at Princeton University to study for a Ph.D. His fellow graduate students, particularly his chief rival, Martin Hansen (Josh Lucas), regard Nash as an amusing, harmless eccentric good for an occasional laugh, as when he bungles picking up women in bars. Nash's goal is to earn his degree by coming up with one original idea. While searching for the inspiration that will lead to the idea, he does not attend any classes or do any work. Viewers familiar with the way institutions of higher learning operate may be left wondering about the accuracy of all this. The entire film, in fact, is a glowing advertisement for the tolerance and good-heartedness of Princeton.

Nash does eventually stumble upon his idea, which director Howard and screenwriter Akiva Goldsman do their best to dramatize when Nash and some other math students are attracted to the same blonde in a bar. (The idea laid the groundwork for the mathematical concept of game theory.)

Some viewers may actually understand the analogy, but it doesn't really matter. If Nash were simply a genius, *A Beautiful Mind* wouldn't have been made. He has to suffer to earn our interest. And boy does he suffer. After receiving his Ph.D. in 1950, Nash joins a government-sponsored research unit on the campus of the Massachusetts Institute of Technology. The Cold War between the United States and the Soviet Union is growing in intensity, and Nash proves invaluable, at least in the one example shown, as a codebreaker. Soon, federal agent William Parcher (Ed Harris) gives Nash a special assignment on which he spends all his time.

*A Beautiful Mind* is full of wonderful little scenes that delineate Nash's character. One of these occurs when he returns to MIT from a visit to the Pentagon to discover that he must immediately teach a class for which he has done no preparation. Entering the classroom in a tee-shirt because of the heat, Nash promptly tosses the textbook in a trash can and scribbles a problem on the board for the students to spend the semester trying to solve. The only student who gets his attention is Alicia (Jennifer Connelly) who shows the socially inept Nash how to silence noisy construction workers. The aggressive Alicia eventually entices the shy, bungling professor into a date, and they are soon married.

While Alicia is pregnant, she sees the first signs of her husband's instability. It soon becomes obvious that some important people in his life are figments of his imagination. While delivering a public lecture at Harvard, Nash is grabbed, a tad too dramatically, by what he thinks are Soviet agents but who are actually working for Dr. Rosen (Christopher Plummer), a psychiatrist. In Rosen's hospital, Nash is subjected to barbaric insulin-shock treatments. Once released, he vows not to return. The rest of the film focuses on Nash's efforts to avoid, despite Alicia's prompting, recognizing he has a problem and, once he finally acknowledges that he is seeing people who aren't there, his efforts to rebuild his life. Allowed to hang around the Princeton campus and eventually teach again, he is never entirely free of his demons.

*A Beautiful Mind* simplifies the anguish brought on by schizophrenia because Howard and company are, after all, trying to make a mainstream entertainment. Their portrait of Nash is therefore a bit easier to take than the hyperkinetic genius of *Shine* (1996), perhaps a more realistic, less glamorized treatment of schizophrenia.

A craftsman rather than an artist, Howard has ranged from engaging light films such as *Splash* (1984) to overblown epics such as *Far and Away* (1992) to tedious, self-important bores such as *Apollo 13* (1995)—an inexplicable critical and commercial success—to the ridiculous such as the universally reviled *How the Grinch Stole Christmas* (2000). *A Beautiful Mind* is easily Howard's best film.

As always, the director keeps things simple. About the only overtly cinematic touch is a shot, from outside his dorm room, of Nash composing his masterpiece as the seasons change around him while the image of the solitary scholar remains fixed. The cinematography is by one of the modern masters, Roger Deakins: *Homicide* (1991), *The Secret Garden* (1993), *Fargo* (1996), *Kundun* (1997). Sections of the film, especially when Nash is at his worst, are shot in a shadowy film noir style; the early Princeton scenes with a nostalgic autumnal glow; some of Nash's other low points in bright sunlight for ironic contrast.

If Howard's general adeptness is slightly surprising, the quality of Goldsman's screenplay is a genuine shock. This is the man who wrote *Batman and Robin* (1997) and three other equally dreadful Joel Schumacher films as well as *Lost in Space* (1998). Goldsman and Howard seemingly perceived the impossibility of communicating the complex and settled for dramatizing, with plenty of artistic license, the highlights of a turbulent life. While some would, with perhaps some justification, object to the film's superficial treatment of mental disorders, a strained marriage, and the academic life, others might see a well-structured film that achieves its aims.

*A Beautiful Mind* has been attacked for an unrealistic depiction of a serious disease, for giving false hope to those who suffer from schizophrenia and those who care about them, for implying that sick people can cure themselves. But while Nash does learn to deal with his hallucinations, they are still present. The filmmakers clearly show that Nash is an unusual man. What works for him will obviously not be true for most. The film is drama, not documentary.

The same goes for the objections to details of Nash's life as described in Nasar's book but omitted from the film, such as the illegitimate child he fathered before meeting Alicia and his alleged bisexuality. The film has Alicia standing by her man, but the real Mrs. Nash divorced her husband in 1963 only to remarry him in 2001. The most significant departure from reality is having Nash begin experiencing hallucinations upon his arrival at Princeton rather than over a decade later. Experts say that Nash could not have done his groundbreaking work if he was already schizophrenic.

A more adventuresome director than Howard may have been willing to risk losing the audience's sympathy by showing Nash warts and all, but such is not Howard's approach. As an actor growing up on television and in films, Howard, somewhat like Ronald Reagan, is limited by seeing life not as it is but filtered through a Hollywood dreamscape. As he has said it numerous interviews, this is a love story.

Another concern is that many viewers will see the film as saying something about mental illness, genius, the individual in an uncaring society, the effect of America's institutions on the sensitive soul, the need for friends and family to stand by regardless how difficult someone they care for might be, and so on. The film touches on all this but doesn't really say anything substantive about any of these subjects. Like films from *One Flew Over the Cuckoo's Nest* (1975) to *American Beauty* (1999), it seems, for the impressionable, to be much more than it is. It bombards the audience with elements that don't add up to a unified whole beyond love conquering all.

Howard's greatest accomplishment is his careful direction of a very talented cast. With the exception of Harris, who has stiffly played too many such one-note characters, all the actors are excellent. Paul Bettany is magnetic as Nash's unpredictable, supportive Princeton roommate Charles, moving easily from one emotional extreme to another. Connelly is believable as the wife who loves Nash despite his initial eccentricity and who stays with him in the face of much greater problems. Much of her role is simply responding to Nash, but she helps guide the audience in its responses as well. When Connelly ably shows how Alicia sets aside her fears for her safety and sanity and that of her son, she demonstrates how Nash is salvageable.

Just as Connelly's skills have grown since her striking debut as a child performer in *Once Upon a Time in America* (1984), Crowe has more than lived up to the promise he showed in *Proof* (1991) and *Romper Stomper* (1992). With *L.A. Confidential* (1997), *The Insider* (1999), *Gladiator* (2000), and now *A Beautiful Mind*, Crowe has established himself as a truly great film actor, worthy of comparison to the likes of Marlon Brando and Gene Hackman. No one better combines the rugged masculinity of Burt Lancaster and Kirk Douglas in their prime with the sensitivity of Dustin Hoffman or Anthony Hopkins.

Crowe seems a little too mannered at first as his Nash moves his hands involuntarily to his head to convey his insecurity. The actor's point, however, is that Nash did not slide gradually into paranoia. He is a prime candidate for instability from the beginning. Crowe is equally adept at showing Nash's anguish and the self-deprecating humor he employs to deflect his demons. Highlights include Nash's absorption during his first exposure to a television remote control and the graphic pain in Crowe's eyes when a colleague suggests there is more to life than work and Nash plaintively asks what. Ironically, this is a case of the actor being in total control of a character out of control. Nash's aging process from the 1940's to the 1990's is credible not only because of Crowe but the exceptional makeup by Greg Cannom. The Nash of 1994 looks like Crowe should appear as an old man. Connelly's more artificial, almost unrecognizable appearance is less successful.

Nash has superficial similarities to Russell Crowe's tobacco-industry scientist in *The Insider*, an even better performance in a much more substantial film. Yet the characters, one fighting outside enemies and the other battling himself, are finally distinctive thanks to Crowe's chameleon-like abilities. If Nash treads a thin line between inspiration and greatness, Crowe moves beyond inspiration to greatness.

*—Michael Adams*

## CREDITS

**John Nash:** Russell Crowe
**Alicia Nash:** Jennifer Connelly
**William Parcher:** Ed Harris
**Charles:** Paul Bettany
**Dr. Rosen:** Christopher Plummer
**Helinger:** Judd Hirsch
**Sol:** Adam Goldberg
**Hansen:** Joshua Lucas
**Bender:** Anthony Rapp
**Thomas King:** Austin Pendleton
**Marcee:** Vivien Cardone

**Origin:** USA
**Released:** 2001
**Production:** Brian Grazer, Ron Howard; Dreamworks
Pictures, Imagine Entertainment; released by Universal
Pictures
**Directed by:** Ron Howard
**Written by:** Akiva Goldsman
**Cinematography by:** Roger Deakins
**Music by:** James Horner
**Sound:** Allan Byer
**Editing:** Mike Hill, Dan Hanley
**Art Direction:** Robert Guerra
**Costumes:** Rita Ryack
**Production Design:** Wynn Thomas
**MPAA rating:** PG-13
**Running time:** 129 minutes

## REVIEWS

*Boston Globe.* December 21, 2001, p. F10.
*Chicago Sun-Times Online.* December 21, 2001.
*Entertainment Weekly.* January 4, 2002, p. 46.
*Los Angeles Times Online.* December 21, 2001.
*Los Angeles Times Online.* January 22, 2002.
*New York Times Online.* June 3, 2001.
*New York Times.* December 21, 2001, p. E1.
*New Yorker.* January 7, 2002, p. 82.
*Newsweek.* December 24, 2001, p. 41.
*People.* December 24, 2001, p. 32.
*Rolling Stone.* January 17, 2002, p. 56.
*San Francisco Chronicle.* December 21, 2001, p. D1.
*Time.* December 31, 2001, p. 140.
*USA Today.* December 21, 2001, p. W1.
*Variety Online.* December 14, 2001.
*Wall Street Journal.* December 21, 2001, p. W1.
*Washington Post.* December 21, 2001, p. WE43.

## QUOTES

John Nash (Russell Crowe): "That's the only way I'll ever distinguish myself—find a truly original idea."

## TRIVIA

John Nash's doctoral dissertation, "Non-Cooperative Games," is only 27 pages long.

## AWARDS AND NOMINATIONS

**Oscars 2001:** Adapt. Screenplay, Director (Howard), Film, Support. Actress (Connelly)
**British Acad. 2001:** Actor (Crowe), Support. Actress (Connelly)
**Directors Guild 2001:** Director (Howard)
**Golden Globes 2002:** Actor—Drama (Crowe), Film—Drama, Screenplay, Support. Actress (Connelly)
**Screen Actors Guild 2001:** Actor (Crowe)
**Writers Guild 2001:** Adapt. Screenplay
**Broadcast Film Critics 2001:** Actor (Crowe), Director (Howard), Film, Support. Actress (Connelly)
**Nomination:**
**Oscars 2001:** Actor (Crowe), Film Editing, Makeup, Score
**British Acad. 2001:** Adapt. Screenplay, Director (Howard), Film
**Golden Globes 2002:** Director (Howard), Score
**Screen Actors Guild 2001:** Actress (Connelly), Cast.

# Behind Enemy Lines

*In war there are some lines you should never cross.*
—Movie tagline
*Prepare to cross the line.*
—Movie tagline

**Box Office:** $57.8 million

Late in the tragic autumn of 2001, it was less than obvious that filmgoers needed a war movie of any type. It was far from certain that audiences were hungering for a combat flick set in Bosnia. Clearly, it was not a propitious time for the release of *Behind Enemy Lines*. But no time would have been apropos for this dog of war to start barking.

The fifth film in 16 years to be released with this same title—the others were mostly World War II and Vietnam movies—*Behind Enemy Lines* is one long complaint about how frustrating it is for the American military to have its hands tied in complicated foreign conflicts. Its protagonist, Lt. Chris Burnett (Owen Wilson) is a cynical Navy fighter pilot who is itching for real combat and sick to death of flying reconnaissance missions over the Bosnian theater. He's tired of the everyday military routine and disgusted with wishy-washy United States foreign policy. "I'd like to be in a fight I can understand," whines Burnett in an early scene. "It's like a joke to the people back home. It's like, it's Tuesday, now we're helping these people." Burnett soon continues: "Everybody thinks they're going to get a chance to punch some Nazis in the face at Normandy. Those days are long gone."

In December 2001, when this film was released, the sound of military people complaining about a lack of opportunity to pursue bad guys rang rather hollow. So did Burnett's sarcastic comments about the uselessness of U.S. military hardware. When he is sent on a photo mission on Christmas Day, he mocks: "Yet another useless joyride at a cost of millions to the U.S. taxpayer." This sort of dialogue should have sounded silly when it was written and the movie was filmed, and it sounded awful when *Behind Enemy Lines* hit the theaters. Audiences probably were less interested than ever in learning exactly why there have been few Hollywood movies made about the mid-1990s conflict in the former Yugoslavia. For one thing, there are no easily identifiable good guys and bad guys. For another, there is little opportunity for clear-cut combat. The movie solves these problems by making all the inhabitants of the area into swarthy, dour killers and connivers and by milking a preposterous one-American-against-everybody plot for all it's worth.

*Behind Enemy Lines*, in all other respects, is a standard war-movie duet featuring the trigger-happy, cocky, green young soldier (Wilson's Burnett) and the no-nonsense, seen-it-all decorated veteran commander, in this case Admiral Leslie Reigert (Gene Hackman). Hackman, professional and highly nuanced as always, brings some solidity and humanity to the film, though he is reduced through most of the movie to pacing around control rooms. Because of the script's insistence at repeatedly showing how hamstrung the U.S. military is, Hackman's character has little to do but chafe. Hackman makes chafing into an art form, and even in this supremely silly and trifling film, manages to fashion Reigert into a memorable and noble character despite very little to work with in the script.

It's fascinating to note how with one word Hackman can create a complex personality out of what could have been a hackneyed character. When someone knocks at his office door, he issues the quiet, clipped response: "Come." Three times in the film he does this, and each time he conveys a complete picture of a fascinating man with a rough façade who brooks no nonsense yet also invites visitors to enter and speak their mind. He's a man who's too busy to say "Come *in*" but too human to bark or grunt. This is a military man, used to stripping down interactions to their bare essentials. Given Hackman's succinct performance, it is completely unnecessary for his NATO superior (Jaoquim de Almeida) to tell Reigart early on in the film: "You are an uncomplicated man."

But screenwriters Zak Penn and David Veloz don't leave anything to chance. Neither does first-time director John Moore. How Moore came to command the helm of *Behind Enemy Lines* explains everything you need to know about the film: He came to fame directing a television commercial that was broadcast during the 1999 MTV music awards show. And that ad was for a video game system.

No wonder the film looks, and plays, like a video game crossed with a music video. In fact, it would have saved everyone a lot of money and trouble to make this the first direct-to-video-game movie, skipping the theatrical and video releases altogether. Here's the plot of this film-as-video-game: In the first level, you are an American pilot flying over enemy territory. Surface-to-air missiles lock in on your position and are fired. They hunt you down. You try to do evasive spins and loops. Eventually, you are hit. You and your co-pilot eject and parachute down. Next, you must negotiate a tricky parachute landing into a forest. Your co-pilot is injured. You must get to higher ground to radio for help. Meanwhile, the enemy forces surround your comrade, and an assassin shoots him in the head, killing him.

The next level, which lasts for the most of the film, has the assassin and a bunch of other unsavory characters chasing you. The assassin, a dour-looking man wearing a name-brand blue jacket and carrying an assault rifle, shoots at Burnett while the American is resting by the side of a dam, but misses, and Burnett slides down the dam. Next thing we know, Burnett is running in the woods. Regular troops are also chasing him, sweeping the woods, but Burnett manages to make it to high areas where he can transmit messages back to Reigert. Just as in a video game, there is no explanation of how the protagonist gets from one place to another—he just jumps into the next scene.

What else happens? Not much. There is one border crossing in which the hero has to step across trip-wires tied to explosives; there are also land mines in the forest. As in a video game, Burnett seemingly has many lives—endless shots are fired at him, bombs goes off, he even hides in a mass grave, but he escapes unscathed. Eventually, Reigert works up the guts to defy his commanders and send in a helicopter rescue team. If you stay awake long enough to reach the final level, you can pretend to be Burnett and try to grab an incriminating aerial surveillance videotape and board a rescue copter under heavy fire.

This ending—in which Burnett finally discovers a reason for his quest—makes little sense. A shot that played in all the trailers for the films somehow didn't make it to the final cut. It showed Burnett's spy plane snapping photos of mass graves. Somehow, Burnett at the end of the movie knows that he has pictures of the graves, even though he's never shown flying over them. It's a seemingly small problem, easily drowned out in the video game cacophony of loud noises, raging music, and pop-up villains. There are also the "weather technicians" in the credits who can't seem to decide if it's fall or winter, as we shift back and forth between snow-covered, partially-snow covered, and dry bare ground in the course of a few minutes.

The visual effects for *Behind Enemy Lines* are poorly executed *Matrix* knockoffs. While some shots are gripping, most of the razzle-dazzle looks like—well, like a video game. The computer-enhanced effects are too obvious, the backgrounds are overexposed, and the film has a grainy video look. The superannuated editing is obsessed with stuttering zooms, slapdash quick cuts, and grandstanding staccato visuals. The overall effect is stupefying.

Wilson, who co-wrote the canny script for *Rushmore* and also collaborated with director Wes Anderson on *Bottle Rocket* and *The Royal Tenenbaums* (reviewed in this edition), is a lightweight comic actor who is completely unsuited for dramatic heavy lifting. Since he doesn't have to do much but run away from the assassin, the job Wilson performs is passable, but he fails to give the character any much-needed heft. The rest of the flick is filled out with pursuing villains. The forest scenes were shot in the Slovak Republic, though unnecessarily so; they're so repetitive and unimaginative they could have been shot on a sound stage.

*Behind Enemy Lines* has a contrived gritty feel and a triumphant ending in which Americans can finally do some shoot-'em-up in the rescue effort. But even at the end, you have no idea who the bad guys were—apparently they are supposed to be a rebellious group of Serbs bent on breaking a cease-fire arrangement, but who they are working for and what their purpose is in unclear. It doesn't matter. This is a video game, not a movie, and the only thing that's required of the villains is that they chase and shoot, and shoot poorly—and that they certainly do, over and over and over.

—*Michael Betzold*

## CREDITS

**Burnett:** Owen C. Wilson
**Reigart:** Gene Hackman
**Piquat:** Joaquim de Almeida

**O'Malley:** David Keith
**Stackhouse:** Gabriel Macht
**Rodway:** Charles Malik Whitfield
**Likar:** Olek Krupa
**Tracker:** Vladimir Mashkov
**Bazda:** Marko Ogonda

**Origin:** USA
**Released:** 2001
**Production:** John Davis; Davis Entertainment Company; released by 20th Century-Fox
**Directed by:** John Moore
**Written by:** David Veloz, Zak Penn
**Cinematography by:** Brendan Galvin
**Music by:** Don Davis
**Sound:** Ian Voigt
**Editing:** Paul Martin Smith
**Art Direction:** Patrick Lumb
**Costumes:** George L. Little
**Production Design:** Nathan Crawley
**MPAA rating:** PG-13
**Running time:** 106 minutes

## REVIEWS

*Chicago Sun-Times Online.* November 30, 2001.
*Entertainment Weekly.* December 7, 2001, p. 66.
*Los Angeles Times Online.* November 30, 2001.
*New York Times Online.* November 30, 2001.
*People.* December 10, 2001, p. 36.
*USA Today Online.* December 3, 2001.
*Variety.* November 26, 2001, p. 25.
*Washington Post.* November 30, 2001, p. WE49.

## QUOTES

Reigart (Gene Hackman) about Burnett (Owen Wilson): "The American people want their pilot back!"

# Behind the Sun (Abril Despedacado) (Broken April)

Master Brazilian filmmaker Walter Salles' *Behind the Sun* emerges as a filmic ballad steeped in magic realism. As such, it is bound to overturn audience expectations based on his previous film, the uncompromisingly realistic *Central Station* (1998), which was nominated for two Academy Awards®, including Best Actress. What Salles achieves in his latest work is a cinematic blend that feels more organic than many recent such attempts. In both Neil Jordan's *The Butcher Boy* (1998) and Jane Campion's *Holy Smoke* (1999), to name just two, the "magic" comes across as part of a digitalized special-effects horizon, at a clear remove from the gritty realism espoused by the rest of the film. Salles, on the other hand, draws upon his country's tradition of the historical filmic ballad, though he doesn't carry it to the bold, revolutionary extremes of Glauber Rocha in the classic *Antonio Das Mortes* (1968). In *Behind the Sun*, the moving musical score functions as a displacement for the singing we would have expected from a chorus.

Salles has taken his story from an Albanian novel and relocated it amidst the history of family feuds in Brazil. An introductory title tells us the year is 1910. The earthy, elemental plot, into whose midst we are thrown, revolves around a land feud between the currently dominant, and arrogant, Ferreiras, aristocrats who have taken over the land belonging to the humbled Breves who, without slaves, have now been reduced to farming and processing their sugarcane by themselves. Ignacio, the eldest of the Breves, has just been murdered. As dictated by custom, his blood-drenched shirt has been left to hang on a clothesline by itself until the full moon. The stain, sanctified by the hole of a bullet wound, has now turned yellow. At the dinner table, the vengeful Father (Jose Dumont) orders his son Tonio (Rodrigo Santoro) to gun down the eldest son of the Ferreiras. When little Pacu (Ravi Ramos Lacerda), barely 10, objects out of concern for his brother, the Father slaps him hard, bringing his fury down on anything that might come in the way of the family's honor.

Tonio sets off that night. He waits outside the Ferreira house a good part of the next day. Then, at twilight, he follows the eldest son of the Ferreiras to the barn. There, he shoots, but misses. This leads to a prolonged savage chase through the forest, at the end of which Tonio does get his target.

At the funeral, Father Breves offers his sympathies amongst the wailing of the women, and seeks permission for Tonio to pray for the deceased. As Tonio enters the chapel, there is a sudden silence. Before he leaves, Tonio seeks a truce from the Ferreira patriarch, the blind Grandfather (Everaldo De Souza Pontes), who grants him his wish, but only until the next full moon. That is when the bloodstain on the shirt will turn yellow, signifying that that is all the time Tonio has to live. Affirming the power of tradition, the Grandfather ties a black armband around Tonio's upper arm, marking him out for revenge.

From the way we enter into this narrative dilemma at the core of the film, it becomes clear that Salles wants us to sympathize with Tonio, but not identify with him. The master filmmaker that he is, Salles is after a theme grander than that of the vicious circle of revenge.

Salles thus chooses little Pacu, the character most distanced from the film's dark concerns, to serve as his narrator. In fact, from the opening shot, it is made clear that the story of the film to follow is being told by Pacu, or rather being "recalled" by him. As we see Pacu striding through the forest in silhouette on a moonlit night, wearing a funny hat, it is his voiceover that serves as our gateway into the film. The film will return to this shot only at the end, when Pacu has finished telling his story.

Through Pacu, we learn that the Breves live in a place called "Stream-of-Souls," and that it is located in such a forgotten part of the earth that it may as well be "behind the sun." The burden from God that the family has to bear is that of milling the sugarcane from the fields into molasses, a process that is rendered in all its earthy faithfulness, with a musical score underlining its simplicity and sanctity. The film, through this poetic rendition of labor, takes on the form of a ballad, one found in an antique volume, inviting us to step into a lost time.

This ambiance becomes reinforced on a narrative level when, out of nowhere, two circus performers on a motley cart enter Pacu's life. The fiery Salustiano (Luis Carlos Vasconcelos) and his dark, beautiful daughter, Clara (Flavia Marco Antonio), who ironically looks about Tonio's age. She presents Pacu with a storybook of magical tales. Pacu treasures the volume even though he admits to not being able to read. "I can read the pictures!" he says to her. His delight takes the form of imagining the tales from the illustrations, his favorite being the one about the mermaid inviting him to live with her in the sea.

But it is in relation to Tonio's life that the two gypsy-like vagrants prove to be the much-needed catalysts. When Tonio accompanies his father into town to sell the raw sugar, he sees Salustiano and Clara walking on stilts, announcing their show that evening. Tonio is at once smitten by Clara.

That night, Tonio sneaks Pacu out of the house to visit the circus show. On a makeshift stage in town, Tonio watches entranced as Clara exhales a thick plume of fire out of her mouth. The evening proves the occasion for Pacu's informal christening by Salustiano who, as his godfather, gives him the name "Pacu," and blesses him with a liquor bottle. Prior to this, he was known only as "Nini" or "Kid." When the two brothers return home, the father slaps Tonio in a violent rage, claiming that he has shown no respect for the dead.

The next day, the oxen bound to the mill wheel collapse. Tonio helps his Father get them onto their feet. It is a heart-wrenching sight, both man and animal subjected to the same grind. That evening, it is Pacu who witnesses the oxen, though freed of their yoke, going round the vat by themselves. He calls out to Tonio, who begins to see himself in the plight of the oxen.

That night, Pacu finds Tonio's bed empty. We see Tonio in town the next day helping Salustiano and Clara pack their stage onto their cart. He then decides to travel with them to Ventura, their next destination, after which he will return home to face his fate. On their journey, the mountains tower like dark giants in the background. The first stirring of romance between Clara and Tonio is deli-cately rendered with Clara eyeing Tonio, who is sitting up in the front with her as she steers the cart, while Salustiano is lying drunk in the back.

Tonio's running away is seen as a blessing by the Mother (Rita Assemany). "In this house, the dead command the living," she muses aloud, before getting into bed. Her husband tells her that, as poor peasants, they have lost everything. "If Tonio doesn't come back," he adds, "we will lose our honor too!"

In the bustling town of Ventura, as Salustiano runs into an old friend, Tonio and Clara are left to themselves. Away from the crowd, Clara finds a rope swing. She climbs up and gets Tonio to spin it faster and faster. As she swings higher and higher, up against the blue sky, she becomes the embod-iment of profligate liberation. The film cuts to show her coming down only after sunset.

Again, it is the bloodstained shirt, hanging by itself on a clothesline, this time on the Ferreira estate, that sounds the death knell. The Ferreira clan is so bloodthirsty that they lie to their blind Grandfather. They tell him the stain has turned yellow when it is still red. When Tonio returns home in time for the full moon, his fate appears sealed. What turns things around is Clara. When Salustiano tells her that Tonio is already dead, she replies, "But I'm not!"

A windy, rainy night sets the stage for the film's climax. Clara comes to Tonio to tell him that she has run away. In the heat of passion, she tears the black armband off Tonio's arm and throws it on the ground. That night, after they have made love, she leaves a sleeping Tonio with the words, "I'll be waiting!" Then it is Pacu who picks up the black armband and wears it on his arm, and puts on Clara's hat which he finds nearby. The Ferreira brother who has been stalking the

house loses his spectacles, and in the darkness, takes aim at Pacu, shooting him dead.

The Father now urges Tonio to seek vengeance, threat-ening to shoot him if he doesn't do as he's told. Tonio however walks away, and keeps walking into the forest, until he comes to the sea. With a smile of enlightenment, he stands facing the waves rising higher and higher, as if transported to a timeless realm, liberated from tradition, history, and even the constraints of nature.

While comparing the film with the stark neorealism of *Central Station*, critics have accepted Salles' latest effort on its own poetic terms. The filmmaker Anthony Minghella, writing in *The Guardian*, concludes that *Behind the Sun* is "as close to poetry as cinema gets." He finds the film "creates a pungent evocation of a primitive rural landscape" and that it "manages to speak volumes about violence while being almost wordless." Richard Schickel in *Time* believes the film has a message for "a world in which nations, like these families, engage in mindless blood feuds."

*—Vivek Adarkar*

## CREDITS

**Father:** Jose Dumont
**Mother:** Rita Assemany
**Tonho:** Rodrigo Santoro
**Pacu:** Ravi Ramos Lacerda
**Salustiano:** Luiz Carlos Vasconcelos
**Mr. Lourenco:** Othon Bastos
**Clara:** Flavia Marco Antonio

**Origin:** Brazil, France, Switzerland
**Language:** Portuguese
**Released:** 2001
**Production:** Arthur Cohn; Haut et Court, BAC Films Ltd., VideoFilmes, Dan Valley Film; released by Miramax Films
**Directed by:** Walter Salles
**Written by:** Walter Salles, Karim Ainouz, Sergio Machado
**Cinematography by:** Walter Carvalho
**Music by:** Antonio Pinto
**Sound:** Felix Andrew, Francois Groult, Waldir Xavier, Francois Musy
**Editing:** Isabelle Rathery
**Costumes:** Cao Albuquerque
**Production Design:** Cassio Amarante
**MPAA rating:** PG-13
**Running time:** 91 minutes

## REVIEWS

*Boxoffice.* February, 2002, p. 60.
*Entertainment Weekly.* January 11, 2002, p. 50.
*The Guardian Online.* February 16, 2002.
*Los Angeles Times Online.* December 21, 2001.
*New York Times Online.* December 21, 2001.
*Time Online.* January 21, 2002.
*USA Today Online.* December 12, 2002.
*Variety.* September 10, 2001, p. 63.

## QUOTES

Salustiano (Luiz Carlos Vasconcelos) about the blood feud: "They would rather kill than solve their problems; those are the real fanatics."

## TRIVIA

The novel by Ismail Kadare is set in the Balkans in the 1930s.

## AWARDS AND NOMINATIONS

**British Acad. 2001:** Foreign Film.

# Better Than Sex

*3 days in the life of a 1 night stand.*
—Movie tagline

Australian filmmaker Jonathan Teplitzky asks the question "Is there such a thing as a one night stand?" in his debut feature *Better Than Sex*. Can two passionate adults throw themselves into an intimate act and then simply walk away with no regrets? Teplitzky, with the support of actors Susie Porter who plays Cin, a former fashion designer, and David Wenham who plays Josh, a wildlife photographer, answer no to that question. After all, when you put two hot-blooded adults in the same bed for three days they're bound to either fall in love (which they do reluctantly here) or kill each other. And what begins as a playful ploy with no strings attached soon becomes a life-transforming situation that engrosses its intended audience of 20- to 30-year-old singles.

*Better Than Sex* takes a frank look at contemporary views on sex. It might prove too revealing for some viewers since the film focuses on sexual secrets that belong behind closed doors. Shot in a fake documentary style, Teplitzky breaks away from the bedroom now and again by presenting interviews with the characters Cin, Josh, and their candid friends as they discuss their views on sex. Teplitzky knew the danger of trying to keep an audience interested in just two characters relating to each other in a single space. Thankfully, the film's witty dialogue and chemistry between the two lovers keeps viewers interested. Also the freckle-faced Porter's unabashed portrayal of the outgoing Cin proves refreshing in itself. She honestly throws herself into her role while using the vulnerable situation between her lover and herself to its full advantage. She's a vivacious girl-next-door whom you want to root for, and watching her transform into an adult that can commit to a relationship proves satisfying as well.

Of course, Teplitzky doesn't explore any new territory here nor does he take an innovative approach with his film. *Better Than Sex* proves to be a straight forward comedy about sex and relationships. In its own way it takes a few calculated risks with its subject matter by presenting Cin as a sexually liberated woman. She loves orgasms, she hates the idea of marriage, and she keeps a vibrator wrapped up in her fridge. She's also audacious enough to let a complete stranger stay with her in her cramped apartment for three days. They never eat, they hardly ever sleep, and they use the toilet in front of each other. Ironically, Cin and Josh claim to be weary of intimacy even though they have taken each other's bodies hostage.

Cin and Josh meet at a party where they exchange small talk. Neither of them seems interested in each other until they share a taxi ride. In a self-reflexive fashion that recalls Woody Allen's *Annie Hall*, Cin and Josh think out loud to the camera. Cin thinks that Josh is attractive and he'll be returning to London in three days, while Josh also ponders the pros and cons of having a one-night stand with the attractive Cin. So they retreat into Cin's apartment for one night of pleasure. Only Josh can't bring himself to leave the next morning and Cin can't squelch her hunger for sex. Another 24 hours pass by through a blur of laughter and erotic escapades, but Cin and Josh begin to wear on each other's nerves. Josh complains that there's nothing to eat and only finds rotten vegetables and a vibrator in the fridge. Cin wishes out loud that Josh would flush the toilet and would it hurt if he also washed his hands after relieving himself? Meanwhile, Cin must finish her friend Carole's wedding dress before Monday (a chore that she has no desire to perform).

Eventually Cin's friend, Sam (Catherine McClements), shows up at the apartment to meet Josh, but Sam's appearance causes Cin's insecurities to surface. As Sam flirts with Josh, Cin finds that she cannot control her explosive temper, so she kicks Sam out. Later she kicks Josh out too after accusing him of flirting with Sam. So much for an uncomplicated one-night stand. However, after much soul searching, Cin reunites with Josh in London.

*Better Than Sex* sends out a positive message despite its bold gaze at the sexual act. The woman-next-door does enjoy sex and it's about time singles stop playing the field and commit to their lovers. Teplitzky suggests love is better than sex.

—*Patty-Lynne Herlevi*

## CREDITS

**Josh:** David Wenham
**Cin:** Susie Porter
**Sam:** Catherine McClements
**Taxi Driver:** Kris McQuade
**Tim:** Simon Bossell
**Carole:** Imelda Corcoran

**Origin:** Australia, France
**Released:** 2000
**Production:** Frank Cox, Bruno Papandrea; Fireworks Pictures, Samuel Goldwyn Films; released by IDP Films
**Directed by:** Jonathan Teplitzky
**Written by:** Jonathan Teplitzky
**Cinematography by:** Garry Phillips
**Music by:** David Hirschfelder
**Sound:** Andrew Belletty
**Editing:** Shawn Seet
**Costumes:** Kelly May
**Production Design:** Tara Kamath
**MPAA rating:** R
**Running time:** 85 minutes

## REVIEWS

*Boxoffice.* November, 2000, p. 177.
*Los Angeles Times Online.* October 26, 2001.
*New York Times Online.* October 26, 2001.
*People.* November 5, 2001, p. 38.
*Variety.* June 19, 2000, p. 29.

## QUOTES

Josh (David Wenham): "It starts off as a sex thing, and then suddenly there's an emotional energy you can't control."

## AWARDS AND NOMINATIONS

**Australian Film Inst. 2000:** Director, Film, Score (Hirschfelder)

**Nomination:**
**Australian Film Inst. 2000:** Actor (Wenham), Actor (Wenham), Actress (Porter, Porter), Director (Teplitzky), Film, Orig. Screenplay (Teplitzky), Screenplay, Support. Actress (McQuade, McQuade), Score.

# Black Hawk Down

*Leave No Man Behind.*
—Movie tagline

 **Box Office:** $104.6 million

War movies are often heavy on preaching and moralizing, sliding easily into flag-waving, hero-worship, or finger-pointing. Ridley Scott's *Black Hawk Down* is a welcome exception. Though clearly told from the viewpoint of American forces, it doesn't whitewash or pander, and it is remarkably free of rhetoric and contrived melodrama. Scott shows what happened to elite American fighters over a fateful 24-hour period in October 1993 in Mogadishu, Somalia, during a heretofore forgotten and inconsequential battle. His brutally honest, surprising film is the definitive movie about an increasingly familiar kind of post-Cold War conflict—cramped, frustrating, lethal, and full of moral quicksand.

*Black Hawk Down* falls into that small group of "war-is-hell" movies that don't flinch from harrowing, gut-wrenching visual descriptions of combat. It doesn't promote realism for his own sake, however. There are human stories and technical wizardry to keep mainstream audiences entertained. And that's essential to its impact. If Scott's cannonball of a movie serves to awaken naïve Americans to warfare's latest face, it will serve a vital purpose. But it does more. It sets a new standard for frank, forceful yet accessible storytelling about modern conflicts.

Based on a series of articles in the *Philadelphia Inquirer* and a script by Ken Nolan and Steve Zaillian, Scott's film is journalistic in the best sense. It focuses on a sickening turning point in the United States' brief, ill-fated attempt to intervene in Somalia's long-running, gruesome civil war. The United States entered Somalia with a limited agenda and a humanitarian purpose. But it soon became embroiled in a fight among brutal local warlords.

Although Scott stays clear of passing judgment on the U.S. mission, he does allow a few telling comments. Near the film's beginning, a man who runs guns to the warlords tells the Americans' base commander, Major Gen. Wiliam F. Garrison (Sam Shephard), that this is a civil war and the

United States shouldn't interfere. Harrison replies that, with 300,000 casualties and counting, it's really genocide, and preventing further mass slaughter is the United States' obligation. The near-impossibility of that task is the film's lesson. U.S. forces may have high-tech weapons, but those are still far too blunt to be effective in dicey urban street fights against fired-up opponents.

In scenes introducing various members of the U.S. Army Rangers and the elite Delta force, the two squads quartered at the Mogadishu airport, Scott also provides a range of views from the soldiers. Some are gung-ho, itching for a fight and have no qualms about the mission. Others, such as Staff Sgt. Mark Eversmann (Josh Hartnett), are more ambivalent. Some are idealistic and feel they are serving a humanitarian purpose; others are simply soldiers who don't question orders. Most are newcomers to conflict and few have any idea of the baptism by fire that's in store for them.

There's a palpable sense of the hamstrung Americans chomping at the bit. The film shows that the U.S. forces can't act even when they see a warlord's henchmen gunning down Somali civilians looting a truck full of food—humanitarian aid that the warlord has claimed as his own. The rules of engagement dictate that the Americans can't fire unless fired upon. Even in the streets of Mogadishu, the soldiers refuse to shoot as armed men are descending on them—until the other side opens fire.

Eventually, the Americans get a mission. To some, it satisfies their desire for action; to others, it looks horrifying and full of danger. The plan is to capture some of warlord Mohammed Farah Aidad's top lieutenants as they meet in a building in the middle of the Baraka marketplace, the heart of hostile territory. An informant will mark the building, four helicopters will anchor each corner of it as Rangers descend by rope to guard the exits, and the Delta forces will enter, corral the targets, force them into armored Humvees, and carry them back to the base. The mission is audacious and fraught with risks.

Even at the command level, however, the U.S. forces exude an air of naïve confidence, as if nothing can thwart the American military. But everything goes wrong from the start. As the helicopters fly into town, a boy on a hillside makes a call on a cell phone, and militia members mobilize. Fires are set to warn others of the incursion. Crowds rush toward the building before the U.S. forces even enter it. Eversgard sees a man miss the rope and fall to the ground, and he rushes to his aid. Snipers begin to open fire.

The staging of this rapid invasion and response is absolutely gripping. Scott seamlessly employs live shots (executed in two Moroccan cities) along with subtle computer effects to create a nightmarish urban landscape of bombed-out buildings, crowded markets, and lethal weapons. The black helicopters loom above the streets, their whirling blades stirring up dust storms and confusion. For more than 90 minutes of film time, the U.S. men maneuver through a chaotic jumble of rubble, sniper fire, and conflicting orders, and Scott infects every second with palpable lethal danger—stretches of calm and cacophony spiked with dread and uncertainty.

Things go from bad to worse when snipers shoot down one of the helicopters. Forces try to get to the crash site to rescue the wounded or remove the dead. Later, a second chopper goes down. The U.S. men are separated from one another, in small groups, and some are pinned down. Night falls, and the situation gets more desperate. Throughout, Scott spins a steady, concise, disarming course, cutting back and forth between different squads of desperate men, alternating between fierce battles and eerie silences, desperate forays and dispirited waiting for rescue that never comes. Many scenes are confusing, but they mirror the chaos that existed that day and night. After an entire afternoon and night of skirmishing, the fighting resumes with renewed vigor as the final rescue effort is mounted, and Scott brilliantly includes a couple of shots of the spent shell casings clanking against the ground, a telling testament to the endless death-dealing.

If there is anything to criticize about this expertly executed film, it is that Scott seems to grow tired of the endless, confusing firefights, and takes refuge after a time in a few standard war movie tropes, including a wrenching, gruesome effort to save a dying soldier; the overlooked cook (Ewan McGregor) who is called into combat and proves his mettle; Hartnett's green, ambivalent soldier who must pass tests of courage; frightened men who gulp down their terror and return to battle, or simply melt away; others who follow orders stone-faced and go to their deaths; and men looking at family photos as they await death. Yet though many of these characters seem familiar, Scott always stops short of the kind of sappy melodrama which pervaded the bloated *Pearl Harbor.*

The entirety of *Black Hawk Down* hints at, but never speaks, the unspoken questions about this bizarre mission. Some of the orders coming down from the top are foolish and lethal; the men moving the pawns on the chessboard make many wrong moves; but instead of preaching or patronizing, Scott contents himself with a single, beautiful, telling scene—Harrison, the mission leader, trying in vain to wipe blood off the floor of the field hospital where the men he sent to battle are suffering and dying.

Many such small moments go farther than the usual long-winded visual or verbal rhetoric of "message" war movies (whether pro- or anti-war). One man is captured, and brought to Aidad, who interrogates him. The warlord offers the U.S. soldier a cigarette; the man refuses, and Aidad remarks: "None of you Americans smoke any more. You all lead long, dull, uninteresting lives."

In the end, one of the survivors gives a speech that sums up the film's only discernible viewpoint: War is about soldiers looking out for each other, trying to do their job, and help each other get through it all. The Mogadishu battle is so frustrating, costly, chaotic and purposeless that it's the only way Scott and the soldiers he portrays can salvage some heroism out of the sorry affair.

Throughout the battle, it seems as if the overriding American purpose is summed up in the slogan "Leave no man behind." Men continually risk their lives to rescue fallen or wounded comrades. What is lacking in the film is any explicit questioning of that goal. In fact, if the Americans had simply abandoned the fallen Black Hawk helicopter, many lives could have been saved. How many of the 1,000 Somali and 19 American lives lost could have been saved if the U.S. hadn't prolonged the incursion by trying to remove a few wounded men—and a few other corpses?

*Black Hawk Down* is so incisive that it raises these questions perforce. Without telling you what to think, it raises difficult issues. How does one superpower used to long decades of peace and prosperity fight small wars with limited objectives against masses of combatants willing to risk their lives to defend their beliefs? *Black Hawk Down* illustrates all the disparities: The Somalis come in human waves, relentless, willing to risk many lives to triumph over the invaders. The American men fight defensively, protectively, and their overriding purpose is to get in, do their job, and get out. Tellingly, it's not even clear in the film that the American forces captured the right men in their raid, and what difference it made anyway.

Scott shows nearly every one of the 19 American deaths, in gruesome and personal ways. His film also shows hundreds of Somalis being gunned down; most of them are more distant strangers. But he allows room for their pain to pour through as well. In one wrenching scene, a young boy and his father (or older brother) hunt down one American, who escapes by hiding in a schoolroom; the Somali teacher huddles her young children; the soldier escapes out another door, and the boy, trying to shoot the invader, instead kills the older man. Scott fails to show what motivates the Somalis to fight so fiercely, but to his credit he does know that the enemy is not faceless, and that though Americans may not understand them, it does no good to demonize them.

The film is that rare war movie which combines thrilling action and thoughtfulness; which balances an American point of view with a wide-awake appreciation of an inscrutable enemy, whose faces the Americans witness and shoot at but do not comprehend. Aidad says: "You have the power to kill but not to negotiate." And that is exactly the frustration of the soldier, and why war is hell. We grab what meaning we can out of it, and take what solace we can in our own solidarity under fire. *Black Hawk Down* is chilling and brings little comfort. It is unflinching—and very much needed.

—*Michael Betzold*

## CREDITS

**Eversmann:** Josh Hartnett
**Hoot:** Eric Bana
**Grimes:** Ewan McGregor
**McKnight:** Tom Sizemore
**Sanderson:** William Fichtner
**Garrison:** Sam Shepard
**Kurth:** Gabriel Casseus
**Wex:** Kim Coates
**Schmid:** Hugh Dancy
**Durant:** Ron Eldard
**Beales:** Ioan Gruffudd
**Yurek:** Tom Guiry
**Smith:** Charlie Hofheimer
**Pilla:** Danny Hoch
**Steele:** Jason Isaacs
**Harrell:** Zeljko Ivanek
**Matthews:** Glenn Morshower
**Wolcott:** Jeremy Piven
**Kowalewski:** Brendan Sexton III
**Shughart:** Johnny Strong
**Busch:** Richard Tyson
**Struecker:** Brian Van Holt
**Cribbs:** Steven Ford
**Galentine:** Gregory Sporleder
**Goodale:** Carmine D. Giovinazzo
**Joyce:** Chris Beetem
**Atto:** George Harris
**Nelson:** Ewen Bremner
**Goffena:** Boyd Kestner
**Gordon:** Nikolaj Coster-Waldau
**Waddell:** Ian Virgo
**Twombly:** Thomas (Tom) Hardy
**Thomas:** Tac Fitzgerald
**Sizemore:** Matthew Marsden
**Blackburn:** Orlando Bloom
**Othic:** Kent Linville
**Ruiz:** Enrique Murciano
**Maddox:** Michael Roof
**Firimbi:** Treva Etienne
**Wilkinson:** Ty Burrell

**Origin:** USA
**Released:** 2001
**Production:** Jerry Bruckheimer, Ridley Scott; Scott Free, Revolution Studios; released by Columbia Pictures
**Directed by:** Ridley Scott
**Written by:** Ken Nolan
**Cinematography by:** Slawomir Idziak
**Music by:** Hans Zimmer
**Sound:** Tomo Fogec
**Editing:** Pietro Scalia
**Costumes:** Sammy Howarth-Sheldon, David Murphy

**Production Design:** Arthur Max
**MPAA rating:** R
**Running time:** 143 minutes

## REVIEWS

*Chicago Sun-Times Online.* January 18, 2002.
*Entertainment Weekly.* January 18, 2002, p. 38.
*Entertainment Weekly.* January 18, 2002, p. 54.
*Los Angeles Times Online.* December 28, 2001.
*New York Times Online.* December 28, 2001.
*People.* January 28, 2002, p. 33.
*USA Today Online.* December 28, 2001.
*Variety.* December 10, 2001, p. 31.
*Washington Post.* January 18, 2002, p. WE37.

## QUOTES

Lt. Col. Danny McKnight (Tom Sizemore): "It's all about the man next to you. That's all it is."

## TRIVIA

Ridley Scott dedicated the film: For My Mum. Elizabeth Jean Scott 1906–2001.

## AWARDS AND NOMINATIONS

**Oscars 2001:** Film Editing, Sound
**Nomination:**
**British Acad. 2001:** Cinematog., Film Editing, Sound
**Directors Guild 2001:** Director (Scott)
**Writers Guild 2001:** Adapt. Screenplay.

# Black Knight

*He's about to get medieval on you.*
—Movie tagline

*An adventure to the past.*
—Movie tagline

 **Box Office:** $32.6 million

**B**lack Knight is another in the long line of fish-out-of-water stories. It came out within the same year as *The Visitor.* In *The Visitor,* knights from the past show up in modern day times and, presumably, hilarity ensues. *Black Knight* is that story, but flipped. In this film, a guy from the present time shows up in the past.

But in *Black Knight,* the guy's not just any guy. He's Martin Lawrence! Screenwriters Darryl J. Quarles (*Big Momma's House*), Peter Gaulke and Gerry Swallow (both from the wretched Farrelly brothers' pic *Say It Isn't So*) seem to think that that's enough to carry much of the movie. And, in a funny way, it almost is. Lawrence has a big personality and his mugging is almost enough to save a movie with such a dumb and lackluster premise, but in this case, it's only almost. Alas, even Lawrence can't save *Black Knight.*

Jamal Walker (Lawrence) is a goof-off who works at Medieval World, an old, ramshackle theme park in a down-and-out neighborhood in Los Angeles. His boss (Isabell Monk), who's proud that's she's provided fun and quality jobs for the community for 27 years, rounds up her employees and gives them the bad news that a fancy new park, Castle World, is going up nearby. Walker advises her to cash out and head to Florida. Walker is disappointed in him because she just knows he has more potential than that. (And we just know that Walker is somehow going to end up reaching that potential by the end of the film.)

Walker gets sent to clean the filthy moat of its floating garbage, old cups and similar yuckiness and discovers a gold amulet just under the surface. Thinking he could sell it for lots of money, Walker starts to grab for it, falls in, and— insert cheesy, er, we mean, magical special effects here— suddenly ends up in a meadow in England a long, long time ago. Of course he doesn't know that.

He comes upon the once-great knight Knolte (Tom Wilkinson), who's staggering around drunk. Walker sees this behavior and Knolte's primitive outdoor living conditions and assumes he's a homeless man. Sample line from Walker: "What you been eating, spoiled nachos?" Walker gives Knolte a couple of bucks and advises him on how to get into a shelter. (Like many people in the film, Knolte seems to not notice that this guy is saying completely insane things.)

Eventually Walker makes his way to the main castle area where, after he says he's from the streets of Florence and Normandie, he's mistaken for being the Duke's messenger from Normandy. It seems that the Duke is supposed to be arriving to marry King Leo's (Kevin Conway) lusty young daughter, Princess Regina (Jeannette Weegar), and the messenger is supposed to be bringing word of the arrival. At first Walker thinks all of this is some really good acting from the folks at Castle World. He's very impressed by the smells, the costumes and the realism of it all. But sometime after getting his first good look at one of their privies, he starts realizing that this is no Castle World.

Sensing that he's on the verge of being in big trouble, Walker pretends that he is the messenger and, to cover a few gaping plot holes, adds that he's also the court jester. This allows him to explain away such problems as not being able to ride a horse. It also gives the writers an opportunity to stage an unfunny sequence where Walker gets dragged around by a horse in front of everyone. Since Walker's supposedly from France, the townspeople accept his strange dress and speech. (Though, again, sticklers for accuracy will be annoyed that the townspeople would understand Walker's saying things like "That's tight! Boo-yeah!")

To provide a structure for Walker to say stuff like "That's tight! Boo-yeah!", there is a not particularly interesting plot. See, King Leo is a bad man who does things like starve the poor people and behead citizens for stealing a turnip. His evil right hand man, Percival (Vincent Regan), seems even worse than him and has a dark and deep hatred for Walker. There's an underground movement that seeks to return the previous, beloved queen (Helen Carey) back to her throne. One of the members of the movement is Walker's beautiful Nubian chambermaid, Victoria (Marsha Thomason). (It seems so silly that in this day and age, Walker's love interest would have to be the one black person in this old English town.)

In the end, goodness prevails, Walker becomes a better person, blah, blah, blah. But no one cares whether Walker reaches his full potential, do we? The important question is whether it's funny or not, specifically whether Lawrence is funny or not. The answer is, eh, sort of. The film is filled with lots of uninspired jokes. When Walker arrives at the castle, the guards block him with their swords and say, "Who be you?" "I be stompin' on your ass, that's who I be," says Walker. There are also some low physical comedy moments like someone's face landing in manure and someone's foot landing in a groin.

Some things could be funny, but somehow just aren't. The prime example of this is a scene where Walker is called upon to show the fine dancing talents of his homeland. After a failed attempt at imitating the dancing he'd seen the English doing, he gets the band to start playing a thumping bass line which eventually—and improbably—turns into Sly and the Family Stone's "Dance to the Music." Even the choreography by Paula Abdul can't help this scene.

But the film does take some advantage of its time travel aspects. When Walker offers to take her phone number, Victoria exclaims, "You can read and write!" Lawrence replies, "Yeah! Who you been dating?" After Walker sees the primitive privy, he asks his attendant, "Where the Texaco?" And there are a few, very few, understated jokes. In a big climactic sequence where Walker is supposed to be saving the day, he fails to leap on his horse in the grand heroic way that we'd expect. "Fifth time's the charm," he mumbles to himself as he tries and tries. There are also some messages in the film that pacifists might not care for. Knolte has decided

that he doesn't want to fight anymore, and when he does decide to fight again, it's supposed to be a good thing. Also Walker gets his army together and inspires them to violence by having them focus on their anger and desire for revenge.

Lawrence, for his part, certainly tries. The man is an expert at mugging for the camera and there is not a moment in the film when he isn't making one funny face or another. The opening scene is just Lawrence in front of a mirror getting ready for his day. He makes his every gesture count, trying to wring any and all comedy from the scene. He's paid an obscene amount for his films (and probably even more for this one since he's an Executive Producer), but he certainly works for his money. It's a shame so much of his energy was wasted on this lackluster project.

Critics were pretty united in their distaste for Lawrence's latest. Owen Gleiberman of *Entertainment Weekly* wrote, "'Monty Python and the Holy Martin'. . .this ain't," and gave the film a C+. Rob Blackwelder of Spliced Wire wrote, "It's pretty clear that Quarles, Junger and 20th Century-Fox were content with the minimal effort put into this movie's hit-or-miss humor, counting on whatever audience Lawrence draws to have low standards." Stephanie Zacharek of Salon wrote, "Almost every gag in *Black Knight* feels forced and contrived, as if the movie is desperate to squeeze laughs out of us." Kevin Thomas of the *Los Angeles Times* led the minority of those who liked the film. He wrote, "It has more hilarious throwaway lines than most comedies offer up as their best jokes, and it is consistently inspired, energetic and, most important, light on its feet."

—*Jill Hamilton*

## CREDITS

**Jamal Walker:** Martin Lawrence
**Sir Knolte:** Tom Wilkinson
**Sir Percival:** Vincent Regan
**Victoria:** Marsha Thomason
**King Leo:** Kevin Conway
**Steve:** Darryl (Chill) Mitchell
**Princess Regina:** Jeannette Weegar
**Ernie:** Michael Burgess
**Mrs. Bostwick:** Isabell Monk
**The Queen:** Helen Carey

**Origin:** USA
**Released:** 2001
**Production:** Arnon Milchan, Paul Schiff, Darryl J. Quarles, Michael Green; Regency Enterprises, New Regency Pictures, Runteldat Entertainment; released by 20th Century-Fox
**Directed by:** Gil Junger

**Written by:** Darryl Quarles, Peter Gaulke, Gerry Swallow
**Cinematography by:** Ueli Steiger
**Music by:** Randy Edelman
**Sound:** Carl Rudisill
**Editing:** Michael R. Miller
**Costumes:** Marie France
**Production Design:** Les(lie) Dilley
**MPAA rating:** PG-13
**Running time:** 95 minutes

## REVIEWS

*Entertainment Weekly.* November 30, 2001, p. 63.
*Los Angeles Times Online.* November 21, 2001.
*New York Times Online.* November 21, 2001.
*People.* December 3, 2001, p. 34.
*USA Today Online.* November 21, 2001.
*Variety.* November 26, 2001, p. 25.
*Washington Post.* November 23, 2001, p. WE43.

# Blow

**Box Office:** $53 million

B*low*, based on a true story, is about a guy who continually screws up and doesn't learn anything from his mistakes until his life is irreparably damaged. The film starts with scenes of workers picking and processing coca leaves into cocaine over the Rolling Stones song, "Can't You Hear Me Knocking." An overweight, middle-aged George Jung (Johnny Depp) is setting up a cocaine deal that you know will go sour. He flashes back to his days as a Boston kid (Jesse James) in the 1950s, whose hard-working dad Fred (Ray Liotta) has his business go bankrupt despite all his efforts. Fred tries to reassure George that "sometimes you're flush and sometimes you're bust.... But life goes on, remember that. Money isn't real, George, it doesn't matter. It only seems like it does." But George knows that his mom, Ermine (Rachel Griffiths), doesn't believe that. She's a money-hungry nag who constantly walks out and returns to the family. George vows he will never have their kind of life but it's inevitable that he falls into the same pattern.

George first decides to change his life by moving to Manhattan Beach, California, in 1968 with his buddy, Tuna (Ethan Suplee). Neither wants to get a real job and they notice everybody is getting stoned. George gets a stewardess girlfriend, Barbie (Franka Potente), who introduces the boys

to Derek Foreal (Paul Reubens), a hairdresser who sells them pot. They've become big dealers on the local scene when George is surprised by the arrival of a vacationing buddy, Kevin Dulli (Max Perlich), who comes up with the idea to expand the operation to the east coast college campuses. Barbie acts as a drug courier when she flies from California to Boston but soon the demand is too much for such a simple operation. George decides they need a direct source and they head down to Puerto Vallarta, Mexico in 1969 to make a connection, which they successfully do, and George is now flying the pot in using small planes.

He gets a house in Acapulco with Barbie but then gets busted in Chicago in 1970 with 660 pounds of weed. When he learns Barbie has cancer, George skips bail to be with her until she dies. Although a fugitive, George decides to visit his parents and his mom winds up turning him in. George does time at the Federal Correctional Institute in Danbury, Connecticut, where he soon realizes that "Danbury wasn't a prison, it was a crime school." His cellmate, Diego (Jordi Molla), is from Colombia, and they agree to become partners delivering coke when both are released. George meets Diego in Cartagena in 1976 and sends up a delivery with Diego's contact, Cesar (Dan Ferro).

Then Diego sends George to Miami to do him a favor—meet with some suppliers and dispose of 50 kilos of cocaine as quickly as possible. In a panic, George heads back to California and his old friend Derek to persuade him that coke is the new drug of choice. When all the kilos sell in three days, George finds himself in Medellin, Colombia, meeting drug lord Pablo Escobar (Cliff Curtis) and he and Diego are soon partners in a major drug operation, selling some 85 percent of all the cocaine coming into America. As George remarks: "Cocaine exploded upon the American culture like an atomic bomb." In fact, there's so much cash that both Diego and George head to Panama City to deposit their ill-gotten millions where the cartel also banks.

When Diego gets married, George is introduced to his major downfall at the reception. Mirtha (Penelope Cruz) is a babe who likes to party. George also realizes that the Latina could change perceptions in the cartel since, as a gringo, George is still an outsider and she soon becomes his trophy wife. He's also got problems with Diego, who resents the fact that George has never told him the identity of his California middleman contact (Derek). When a deal goes bad, George finally introduces him to Derek but soon learns that Diego has decided to cut George out of the operation altogether.

George is actually not too upset—Mirtha is pregnant and he decides to become a real family man. After dealing with his own drug problem, George quits the business to become a full-time father to daughter Kristina and manages to stay clean for five years. Too bad Mirtha isn't contented; a serious coke addict, she misses the high-living lifestyle and, on George's 38th birthday, throws a party with too many drugs and suspicious guests. George gets busted, cuts a deal, and then skips bail again. But when he goes to Panama to get his drug money, he learns that the bank has been nationalized and the money has been appropriated by the government. Now living in Liberty City, Florida, in 1987, George is broke and Mirtha isn't dealing with the prospect of being poor very well at all. She rants about how useless George is as daughter Kristina (Emma Roberts) listens in a replay of George's own childhood.

George gets picked up in a traffic accident and winds up in prison where, after three years, Mirtha informs him that she's getting a divorce and custody of his daughter who now wants nothing to do with him. When he gets out, George slowly wins Kristina's trust back, promising that they will start a new life together in California. Of course, George has no money and decides to get quick cash but going back into the drug business with Derek yet again. His latest cocaine buy turns out to be a set-up and he winds up sentenced to 60 years. He mournfully intones that "everything I love in my life goes away" and he must tape a message to his dying father when his mother refuses to sanction a furlong that would allow George to see him in person. Eventually, he even fantasizes that a grown-up Kristina (James King) has come to visit him in prison. In fact, the real Kristina has never visited her dad, who will be eligible for release in 2015.

The first time George skips bail and goes to see his parents, he tells his father "I'm really great at what I do, Dad" and he's telling the truth in one regard. George does know how to push product but *Blow* shows him being loyal to the wrong people for too long and never really asserting himself. Still, you can't feel sorry for a drug dealer, especially one who gets repeatedly caught and still goes back to the same line of work. And George seems a patsy for sticking with the bitchy Mirtha—since he was clean, he would have been better off taking Kristina and getting the hell out of Dodge. You never feel any particular attraction between the two of them once the initial passion has died down. Oh, and the '70s and '80s clothes, hairstyles, and décor are positively frightening to the 21st-century eye. There's some flashy camerawork but the film is enervating and gets mawkish as George pines for his lost parental responsibilities. Even the talented Depp can't do much with these later scenes; he (and the viewer) has a lot more fun when George was young and ambitious. It may be a true story but these people seem so removed from the world that the viewer has a hard time investing any interest in them.

—*Christine Tomassini*

## CREDITS

**George Jung:** Johnny Depp
**Mirtha Jung:** Penelope Cruz
**Diego Delgado:** Jordi Molla
**Barbara Buckley:** Franka Potente
**Ermine Jung:** Rachel Griffiths
**Fred Jung:** Ray Liotta
**Tuna:** Ethan Suplee
**Derek Foreal:** Paul (Pee-wee Herman) Reubens
**Kevin Dulli:** Max Perlich
**Pablo Escobar:** Clifford Curtis
**Augusto Oliveras:** Miguel Sandoval
**Leon Minghella:** Kevin Gage
**Young George:** Jesse James
**Cesar Toban:** Dan Ferro
**Young Kristina:** Emma Roberts
**Mr. T:** Bob(cat) Goldthwait
**Kristina:** James King

**Origin:** USA
**Released:** 2001
**Production:** Ted Demme, Joel Stiller, Denis Leary; Apostle Pictures, Spanky Pictures; released by New Line Cinema
**Directed by:** Ted (Edward) Demme
**Written by:** David McKenna, Nick Cassavetes
**Cinematography by:** Ellen Kuras
**Music by:** Graeme Revell
**Sound:** Allan Byer
**Music Supervisor:** Amanda Scheer Demme
**Editing:** Kevin Tent
**Art Direction:** David Ensle, Bernardo Trujillo
**Costumes:** Mark Bridges
**MPAA rating:** R
**Running time:** 124 minutes

## REVIEWS

*Boxoffice.* April, 2001, p. 216.
*Chicago Sun-Times Online.* April 6, 2001.
*Entertainment Weekly.* April 13, 2001, p. 46.
*Hollywood Reporter.* March 20, 2001, p. 17.
*Los Angeles Times Online.* April 6, 2001.
*New York Times Online.* April 6, 2001.
*Newsweek.* April 16, 2001, p. 56.
*People.* April 16, 2001, p. 36.
*Rolling Stone.* April 12, 2001, p. 145.
*Sight and Sound.* June, 2001, p. 40.
*Time.* April 9, 2001, p. 74.
*USA Today Online.* April 6, 2001.
*Variety.* March 19, 2001, p. 29.
*Washington Post Online.* April 6, 2001.

# Blow Dry

*A comedy for anyone who's ever had hair.*
—Movie tagline

*This Spring, Love Is In the Hair.*
—Movie tagline

 **Box Office:** $.6 million

Paddy Breathnach's *Blow Dry* is a sometimes pleasing yet ultimately disappointing British comedy that revolves around a goofy hairstyling competition. It is a subject that seems rife with comic possibilities, and, if executed like last year's *Best In Show*, a hilarious send-up of a dog show and the fanatical owners who love their pets just a little too much, it could have been a gem. Unfortunately, despite a uniformly fine cast, *Blow Dry* is unsure of its comic potential and gets bogged down in subplots that never quite connect emotionally or even seem very important.

The credits tell us that the film is based on a screenplay called *Never Better* by Simon Beaufoy, who also wrote *The Full Monty,* a quirky comedy about unemployed steel workers who turn to stripping to regain their self-respect. *Monty* is amusing but rather slight and ultimately became one of the most overrated films of 1997. Nonetheless, it does have a certain charm and the feel-good premise of ordinary guys finding an improbable moment of redemption.

*Blow Dry* also focuses on a group of underdogs—all of them in the world of hairstyling. Phil (Alan Rickman) was once a star hairstylist who has not been the same since his wife, Shelley (Natasha Richardson), also a hairstylist, left him on the eve of a major competition to be with Sandra (Rachel Griffiths), his hair model. Even though they live in the same small town of Keighley, Shelley and Phil have not spoken for 10 years, and he is presently raising their son,

Brian (Josh Hartnett), who is himself a budding hairdresser. Shelley has been diagnosed with cancer and wears a wig to hide her condition from Sandra, who believes Shelley when she tells her that she is in the clear.

Keighley is hosting the British Hairdressing Championships, which is a great event for the mayor, Tony (Warren Clarke), whose boundless enthusiasm for the competition is one of the best jokes in the film. When he proudly announces the town's honor to the press, the reporters are underwhelmed. Phil's old rival, Ray (Bill Nighy), comes to Keighley to compete and is the favorite to win the coveted trophy. He is the reigning champion, and, in a plot point that is never really explained, it seems that, if he wins again this year, he will get to keep the trophy for good.

Inspired by an elderly friend, Daisy (Rosemary Harris), who regrets "all them little ends I never tied up," Shelley decides to use the competition as a way to reconcile everyone in her life before she dies. And so, since Keighley does not have an entrant, she tries to bring her ex-husband, lover, and son together to form a team. Phil, naturally still bitter over losing his wife to Sandra, declines her offer, but Brian decides to enter the contest with his mother after Ray taunts him about the failure his father has become.

In each round of the competition, a stylist works on a person's hair for a short period of time, and then the judges evaluate the results, which are generally outlandishly styled coifs. Because the notion of a hairstyling competition is funny in itself, the screenplay could have mined the various comic possibilities of such a daffy contest. But the screenplay has other things on its mind that are simply not very compelling. There is, for example, the young-love subplot. Ray has a daughter, Christina (Rachael Leigh Cook), and she and Brian vaguely remember each other from childhood and start seeing each other despite their fathers' bitter rivalry.

Their story, however, never feels fresh—just an excuse to get away from the competition every now and then—and their antics are not particularly funny. Christina is a would-be hair colorist who inadvertently ruins some wigs when she does some tests on them and, for no apparent reason other than to impress Brian, colors some sheep a multitude of colors. Brian works in a mortuary and experiments with his hairstyling techniques and colors on the corpses and, in a rather unfunny bit, gets in trouble when one family does not appreciate the red, spiked hair he has given its deceased relative.

The competition's first round, "Women's Timed Blow Dry," turns into a disaster when Ray's henchman, Louis (Hugh Bonneville), switches the official combs with combs that easily melt—a prank that ensures Ray's victory in the round. In one of the film's many unexplained plot points, it is not clear why Ray, the champion and the favorite to win, feels that he has to cheat. To compound Brian's problems, angry relatives of the red-haired corpse come after him in the middle of the first round and injure his hand, which leads to an argument with his father. To stop their fighting, Shelley removes her wig and reveals her illness to them.

Phil cannot stay away from the competition for long and soon is helping the home team. Having caught on to Ray's little trick in the first round, Phil discovers his plans to cheat in the next round, "Men's Freestyle." Ray is preparing a model the night before the competition and fixing the contest so that he gets that model when in fact the selection of models is supposed to be random. Phil foils the plan and turns the second round into a fair fight. While Brian gets a tough head of hair to cut, he does well anyway.

The weakest aspect of *Blow Dry* is the way it tries to be several different kinds of movies without doing any of them especially well. The film juggles the young-love angle with the adults' conflict and Shelley's cancer and even throws in yet another minor story involving a team called the Kilburn Kutters. They are two brothers engaged in a jealous rivalry over their model, Jasmine (Heidi Klum), who is married to one of them. It is a pointless subplot whose comic high point is supposed to be the shaping and coloring of her pubic hair into a heart. The screenplay lurches clumsily from such silly antics involving the haughty Jasmine to a serious scene in which a distraught and hurt Sandra learns that she is the only person in the "family" who does not know about Shelley's condition.

Meanwhile, the competition itself simply plods along. In the third round, "Hair By Night," Shelley assumes cutting duties for the team and brings Daisy on as her model. Implausibly enough, Shelley gives the old lady a fancy hairdo suitable for a Friday night out and wins the round, putting the home team within striking distance of the championship as they head toward the end.

The film's various conflicts resolve themselves rather neatly but without any real dramatic tension. Christina takes a stand against her father's cheating by cutting her hair so that she cannot be his model in the final round. This moral victory endears her to Brian, who was earlier disenchanted with her when he saw her helping Ray prepare his model for the "Men's Freestyle." Then Phil, who seems to have forgiven Shelley in the wake of her illness, has a heart-to-heart talk with Sandra and basically convinces her that Shelley needs her. Sandra puts aside her anger over not being told the truth about Shelley's condition, and Phil overcomes his anguish over losing his wife in the first place. It is a facile, overly emotional climax that feels simplistic.

As if to seal their newfound friendship, Phil cuts Sandra's hair in the concluding round, "Total Look." In a bizarre finish, Phil wins the round and the competition for his team by shaving Sandra's head and revealing a huge tattoo underneath. In a breathtaking appearance before the judges, Sandra presents herself as an elaborately painted nude body. While she is a stunning model, why a shaved head would be part of the winning look in a hairstyling competition is puzzling, to say the least. Obviously, we are

not meant to consider this absurd ending too closely. The good guys have won, Ray has lost, Christina will stay in Keighley to be with Brian (although how this city girl will be happy in this small town is anybody's guess), and, most important, Shelley has succeeded in uniting all the parts of her unconventional family. The ending is sweet and joyful but, like most of what has preceded it, not very persuasive.

What elevates this clichéd story is the acting. Rickman is perfect as the burnt-out hairdresser looking for redemption, and Richardson is quite sympathetic as the brave heroine trying to remain strong through her illness. They do their best to make the characters believable despite the screenplay's wildly shifting tones. Among the supporting performers, Clarke's Tony is a small joy as the mayor trying to turn the most improbable of events into his town's one shot at fame.

*Blow Dry* really wants to be liked. It has a genial tone and a positive if somewhat unbelievable message about a family's reconciliation after many years apart. Finally, though, it ends up an uneasy mix of maudlin disease drama and eccentric comedy. Worst of all, despite scattered moments of humor, the screenplay is not very funny. The best bit actually comes during the end credits when Tony, who, quite endearingly, loves being the star of his own universe, lip-synchs to Elvis Presley's "I Just Can't Help Believing" to the now empty auditorium where the competition took place. If the rest of the film had matched Tony's flat-out glee and silliness, *Blow Dry* could have been a pure delight.

—*Peter N. Chumo II*

## CREDITS

**Phil:** Alan Rickman
**Shelley:** Natasha Richardson
**Sandra:** Rachel Griffiths
**Christina:** Rachael Leigh Cook
**Brian:** Josh Hartnett
**Ray:** Bill Nighy
**Tony:** Warren Clarke
**Daisy:** Rosemary Harris
**Louis:** Hugh Bonneville
**Vincent:** Peter McDonald
**Jasmine:** Heidi Klum
**Robert:** Michael McElhatton

**Origin:** Great Britain, USA
**Released:** 2000
**Production:** Ruth Jackson, William Horberg, David Rubin; Intermedia Films, Mirage Enterprises, West Eleven Films; released by Miramax Films
**Directed by:** Paddy Breathnach
**Written by:** Simon Beaufoy

Cinematography by: Cian de Buitlear
Music by: Patrick Doyle
Sound: Peter Lindsay
Music Supervisor: Bob Last
Editing: Tony Lawson
Art Direction: Sara Hauldren
Costumes: Rosie Hackett
Production Design: Sophie Becher
MPAA rating: R
Running time: 91 minutes

## REVIEWS

*Boxoffice.* May, 2001, p. 60.
*New York Times Online.* March 7, 2001.
*Sight and Sound.* April, 2001, p. 39.
*Variety.* March 12, 2001, p. 36.
*Washington Post Online.* March 9, 2001.

## TRIVIA

The Redken company supplied the salon products and stylists who trained the actors for their roles.

# The Body

*A lost tomb. An unexpected discovery. Chaos unearthed.*
—Movie tagline

**Box Office:** $.1 million

The Body was in theaters for about two seconds and it's easy to see why. The film doesn't know what it wants to be. It's a thriller with few thrills, an action movie with scant action scenes and a romance between two people who seem to like each other but never go so far as to do anything about it.

Father Matt Gutierrez (Antonio Banderas), a young priest who seems to be on the fast track at the Vatican, is called in by one of his superiors, Cardinal Pesci (John Wood). The Cardinal wants to send Gutierrez to Jerusalem to investigate an interesting phenomenon. It seems that while digging in his basement, a shop keeper (Makhram J. Khoury) has discovered a grave. This grave is odd because the person buried in it was crucified. Archaeologist Sharon

Goldban (Olivia Williams) further discovers that the grave contains coins baring the face of Pontius Pilate as well as other indicators of wealth. At the time when the mystery man was killed, crucifixion was only used on poor people. Could the man in the grave be Jesus? The Cardinal certainly hopes not, as that would ruin Christianity, plus send him to the unemployment line. He tells Father Matt that his duty is to go to Jerusalem and prove that the body is not Christ's. Whether or not the body really is Christ's is irrelevant to the Cardinal.

Once Father Matt arrives at the grave, sparks fly between Sharon and him. They are sparks of disgust mingled with an attraction—that is, the usual kind of sparks in movie romances. Father Matt is angry that Sharon is being so cavalier about what her findings might mean to one of the world's strongest religions. Sharon in turn is annoyed that Father Matt is there in the first place since he's not an archaeologist and seems more interested in covering up the truth than uncovering it. "My findings will contradict with your religious beliefs," says Sharon, at the beginning of the movie, so that all of the viewers can clearly see their conflict spelled out.

As Father Matt becomes more convinced that the grave could well be Christ's and in turn becomes more disillusioned with the church, he and Sharon become closer. It seems pretty obvious that the movie's going to go the typical Hollywood route and have the priest toss his vows aside and start romancing the girl. Everything in the film points to this happening—there's even a montage near the end of the film showing them pining and reading letters from each other. But then they don't have the romance. Even though it's certainly a twist on the usual, in a way, it's sort of disappointing.

But then a lot of people will be disappointed by this movie. Those who were intrigued by the religious premise will be disappointed that *The Body* doesn't explore these issues in any kind of depth. If the body is really Christ's, would that necessarily mean the death of Catholicism? After all, some Catholics believe that the resurrection referred to his spirit rather than his actual body. But the movie doesn't worry about these issues, preferring to stick with more superficial things. Those going for the action sequences will be sorry to see that the biggest action scene is when a group of Orthodox Jews try to break into the grave and Father Matt and Sharon fight them by wielding two by fours. And the thriller aspect is pretty nonexistent. As far as archaeological thrillers go, this is many, many excitement levels below the Indiana Jones movies.

Those who like bad drama, though, will be pleased by several scenes. In one, an archaeologist and priest (Sir Derek Jacobi) is so overcome by the theological implications of this grave that he hurls himself from a roof. Father Matt yells "Nooooo!" in slow motion, which just highlights how silly and movie-like yelling "Nooooo!" is.

Despite that, Banderas generally does a good job. He seems earnest and truly conflicted in his role as the holy man who also wants to find the truth. Williams takes a big step down from her role in *Rushmore*. Her character starts out being a feisty woman who drives like a maniac and is sassy to the Father and ends up being wishy-washy and wimpy. There's no reason for the change, it's more like writer Jonas McCord forgot to keep writing the sassy scenes and settled on letting her be the typical nondescript movie heroine.

Maybe the problem was that McCord was also making his directoral debut. The screenplay is adapted from Richard Ben Sapir's novel and McCord seems unsure of what to do with it. *The Body* is destined to be confined to a dusty shelf at the video store, being exhumed only occasionally by rabid Banderas fans.

—*Jill Hamilton*

**Father Matt Gutierrez:** Antonio Banderas
**Sharon Golban:** Olivia Williams
**Cardinal Pesci:** John Wood
**Moshe Cohen:** John Shrapnel
**Father Lavelle:** Derek Jacobi
**Father Walter Winstead:** Jason Flemyng
**Nasir Hamid:** Makram Khoury
**Monsignor:** Vernon Dobtcheff
**Dr. Sproul:** Ian McNeice

**Origin:** USA
**Released:** 2001
**Production:** Rudy Cohen; Helkon Media AG, Green Moon Productions; released by Avalanche Releasing
**Directed by:** Jonas McCord
**Written by:** Jonas McCord
**Cinematography by:** Vilmos Zsigmond
**Music by:** Serge Colbert
**Sound:** Yohai Moshe
**Editing:** Alain Jakubowicz
**Art Direction:** Nenad Pecur, Giora Porter
**Costumes:** Caroline Harris
**Production Design:** Allan Starski
**MPAA rating:** PG-13
**Running time:** 108 minutes

REVIEWS

*Boxoffice.* June, 2001, p. 56.
*Entertainment Weekly.* May 11, 2001, p. 53.
*Los Angeles Times Online.* April 20, 2001.
*New York Times Online.* April 20, 2001.

*People.* April 30, 2001, p. 33.
*Variety.* April 23, 2001, p. 18.

QUOTES

Father Lavelle (Derek Jacobi): "An unrisen Christ would mean the end of Christianity."

# Born Romantic

*Romance isn't dead . . . it's just not very well.*
—Movie tagline

Has the British film industry fizzled over the past couple of years? What happened to the industry that once brought us such comedy hits as *The Full Monty, Brassed Off,* and *Four Weddings and a Funeral*? 2000 releases such as *East is East* and other comedic smash hits in England performed badly at the U.S. boxoffice. There's an occasional exception such as *Bridget Jone's Diary,* but that film has star power with Renee Zellweger and Hugh Grant cast in lead roles, and it was adapted from a best-selling novel. Although English filmmakers might blame this boxoffice defeat on a market place saturated by Hollywood movies, the real problem lies with filmmakers coasting on past success. Take the latest English romantic comedy *Born Romantic,* which is a delightful film in its own right but nothing out of the ordinary.

Written and directed by David Kane, *Born Romantic* proves similar to the British releases *The Low Down* or *Peaches* in its depiction of scruffy singles searching for romance in London's seedier districts. However, as the title implies, Kane's film portrays romantic elements while the aforementioned films focused on 20-something men dealing with commitment phobias. In that respect, *Born Romantic* feels more like an adult film with its multiple narrative courtship and the driving beat of salsa music. *Born Romantic* comes across as a marriage between *Bossa Nova* and *Strictly Ballroom* in which a dance club and a taxi dispatch office act as the film's core locations in which three couples cross paths.

Liverpudlian musician Fergus (David Morrissey) scours the streets of London in search of the fiancee that he jilted the day of their wedding. Desperate, Fergus confesses his love for Mo (Jane Horrocks) to cabbie Jimmy (Adrian Lester) and the compassionate cabbie steers Fergus towards a Latin music club where party girl Mo dances her nights away. However, Mo rejects Fergus' amorous advances and lashes out at him because he plastered posters of her all over London. What woman wouldn't be upset? However, Fergus slowly worms his way back into Mo's life by impressing her with his dance moves.

Dean Martin wannabe and recently divorced-but-still-living-with-his-ex, Frankie (Craig Ferguson) has a different sort of fish to catch. After spotting the elegant Eleanor (Olivia Williams) sweating it out on the dance floor, he falls in love. But the happily single Eleanor tells Frankie that he's not her type. Her type happens to be tall, dark, handsome, and wealthy. However, Frankie just won't give up his pursuit, so he hires a jazz ensemble to perform "L-o-v-e" for Eleanor which barely chips away at her icy heart. Finally, Frankie gives Eleanor an ultimatum and eventually hooks up with another dancer at the club until cabbie-love expert Jimmy convinces Eleanor to give Frankie a chance.

Small time burglar Eddie (Jimi Mistry) falls head-over-heels for the hypochondriac academic Jocelyn (Catharine McCormack), while he hides out from police at the salsa club. Of course in staying true to the rest of the story, Jocelyn, similar to the other female leads, plays hard to get. She's more interested in decorating gravestones and performing Day of the Dead ceremonies for other people's dead relatives than dating. The unlikely couple of Jocelyn and Eddie offer many comical moments. In a dinner scene Eddie's senile father (a brain-damaged retired boxer) takes a chicken out of the oven, then places it in the freezer. Later, when Eddie serves the dinner he prepared, Jocelyn comments about how frozen chicken is a breeding ground for salmonella. In another scene, Eddie accidentally mugs Jocelyn at an ATM. And yes, Eddie and Jocelyn end up giving romance a chance.

The British press gave *Born Romantic* lukewarm reviews. Liz Beardsworth of *Empire Magazine* compared Kane's film to his debut feature *This Year's Love* as a "lightweight but enjoyable confection. . . ." Jenny Turner of *Sight and Sound* criticized various aspects of the film and commented: "The acting for the most part is undemanding, although it's fun to watch Olivia Williams as the elegant and aloof Eleanor." However, for those looking for light entertainment filled with romance and vibrant salsa tunes *Born Romantic* is the ticket. And is equivalent to dancing the night away, fun but forgettable. 🎬

—*Patty-Lynne Herlevi*

**CREDITS**

**Frankie:** Craig Ferguson
**Jimmy:** Adrian Lester
**Jocelyn:** Catherine McCormack
**Eddie:** Jimi Mistry
**Fergus:** David Morrissey
**Eleanor:** Olivia Williams
**Mo:** Jane Horrocks
**Carolanne:** Hermione Norris
**Second Cab Driver:** Ian Hart
**Barney:** Kenneth Cranham
**First Cab Driver:** John Thompson
**Ray:** Paddy Considine

**Origin:** Great Britain
**Released:** 2000
**Production:** Michele Camarda; BBC Films, Harvest Films, Kismet Film Company; released by United Artists
**Directed by:** David Kane
**Written by:** David Kane
**Cinematography by:** Robert Alazraki
**Music by:** Simon Boswell
**Sound:** Stuart Wilson
**Music Supervisor:** Abi Leland, Dan Rose
**Editing:** Michael Parker
**Art Direction:** Alison Harvey
**Costumes:** Jill Taylor
**Production Design:** Sarah Greenwood
**MPAA rating:** R
**Running time:** 97 minutes

**REVIEWS**

*Boxoffice.* December, 2000, p. 54.
*Empire Magazine Online.* February 23, 2001.
*Entertainment Weekly.* October 12, 2001, p. 63.
*Hollywood Reporter.* January 5, 2001, p. 87.
*Los Angeles Times Online.* September 28, 2001.
*New York Times Online.* September 28, 2001.
*Variety.* October 9, 2000, p. 27.

# Bread and Roses

*The balance of power is about to change.*
—Movie tagline

 **Box Office:** $.5 million

In Y2K tens of thousands of service workers took to the streets in New York, Denver, San Diego, and other U.S. cities as part of the Justice for Janitors campaign and won dramatic raises, health insurance, and full-time work contract negotiations for 100,000 building service workers. And the so-called invisible workers (some illegal immigrants) beat their corporate bosses at a wicked game. English director Ken Loach (best known for docudramas that rake societal ills over the coals) brings us an intimate gaze at the lives of janitorial workers in Los Angeles with *Bread and Roses.*

Written by Paul Laverty, with riveting performances by Mexican newcomer Pilar Padilla and veteran actress Elpidia Carrillo, *Bread and Roses* is a relentless heartbreaker that roots for the downtrodden. The film recalls Jean Renoir's sentiment that people have reasons for doing what they do, so withhold judgment. Such is the case with characters Maya (Padilla) and Rosa (Carrillo), since both cunning women do what they do to survive. Rosa hired smugglers to bring her sister Maya across the U.S. border. Then, without Maya's knowledge, Rosa slept with her sleazy employer so that Maya would be hired for janitorial work. In order to help a fellow worker pay his college tuition after the worker's fired, Maya steals money from a convenience store and her action eventually backfires on her. The tragic choices that the characters make is the glue that holds *Bread and Roses* together and leads to explosive confrontations between the characters.

Spirited young Mexican Maya enters the U.S. via un-scrupulous "coyote" smugglers. When Rosa fails to pay the fee for Maya's liberation, one of the smugglers escorts and locks Maya in his hotel room. Fortunately, the nervy Maya outwits her captor and escapes with his cowboy boots. Rosa, a married woman with an incapacitated husband and two children, finds a janitorial job for Maya. However, Maya's optimism fails after she learns that her treacherous boss (George Lopez) requires a commission of a month's salary and the wages are already laughable. The boss appears to be in charge of the workers' fate, with the exception worker Ruben (Alonso Chavez), who earns enough money to attend law school while everyone else has accepted their dismal fate. That is until disarming union organizer Sam (Adrien Brody) shows up shouting union battle cries for the workers.

However, social change doesn't come about without consequences and Sam opens too many cans of worms. As the boss gets wind of the workers' meetings, he fires employ-ees and threatens the remainder with loss of employment and deportation. Workers bicker among themselves. Ruben decides not to join the demonstrations in order to save his hard-earned entrance into law school, but is fired regardless and owes the remainder his tuition. Rosa accepts a manage-rial position by betraying other employees, who are system-atically fired. But on closer inspection Rosa finally decided to look after herself instead of being a slave to other people's needs. During a tear-drenched showdown, Rosa confesses to Maya how she was forced to prostitute herself in order to support Maya and the rest of her family. Then she delivers the clincher that she prostituted herself so that Maya would be hired.

After Ruben is fired, Maya robs a convenience store to pay the remainder of his tuition. But when Maya is arrested after engaging in a civil disobedience act with her comrades, her charitable act leads to her deportation. However, with her help the workers reach a well-deserved victory against their employer.

*Bread and Roses* premiered at the 2000 Cannes Film Festival and marks Loach's eighth appearance at the Festi-val, where the film garnered a nomination for the Golden Palm award. *Bread and Roses* possesses the right mix of ingredients to win both audiences and critics' affections. First, Loach and writer Laverty provide us with a compelling drama with a sympathetic heroine. Then, Loach presents us with a passionate cause in which we want to witness the downtrodden overcome their unscrupulous employers. We are reminded of child labor in India or perhaps we recall Cesar Chavez farm workers' victory. The Latino workers in *Bread and Roses* remind us that Hispanics are the backbone of America because they baby sit our children, sew our clothing, bus our tables, pick our crops, and clean our offices under harsh conditions. Loach, however, suggests that this type of slavery has expired. Like Chavez's message which rung out decades before, Loach's powerful film ignites a new era for humanity.

—*Patty-Lynne Herlevi*

## CREDITS

**Sam:** Adrien Brody
**Rosa:** Elpidia Carrillo
**Maya:** Pilar Padilla
**Perez:** George Lopez
**Bert:** Jack McGee
**Ruben:** Alonso Chavez

**Origin:** Great Britain
**Language:** Spanish
**Released:** 2000
**Production:** Rebecca O'Brien; Parallax Pictures, Road Movies, Alta Films SA, Tornasol Films SA; released by Lion's Gate Films
**Directed by:** Ken Loach
**Written by:** Paul Laverty
**Cinematography by:** Barry Ackroyd
**Music by:** George Fenton
**Sound:** Ray Beckett
**Editing:** Jonathan Morris
**Costumes:** Michele Michel
**Production Design:** Martin Johnson
**MPAA rating:** R
**Running time:** 106 minutes

## REVIEWS

*Boxoffice.* August, 2000, p. 54.

*Chicago Sun-Times Online.* June 1, 2001.
*Los Angeles Times Online.* May 11, 2001.
*New York Times Online.* June 1, 2001.
*Sight and Sound.* May, 2001, p. 36.
*Washington Post.* July 12, 2001, p. WE38.

# Bread and Tulips (Pane e Tulipani)

*Imagine your life. Now go live it.*
—Movie tagline

**Box Office:** $5.3 million

Italian director Silvio Soldini's *Bread and Tulips* comes across as a succinct version of *Juliet of the Spirits* by Federico Fellini. Soldini's film, written by Soldini and Doriana Leondeff, also focuses on a bored housewife who discovers enchantment in the world around her—only she finds her enchantment in the real world as opposed to a Jungian-based fantasies. Those viewers who recall Giulietta Masina's ethereal performance as the housewife in Fellini's film will also enjoy Licia Maglietta's performance in *Bread and Tulips.* Although Maglietta's face might be new to American viewers it won't be long before she captures our hearts with her sweet, vulnerable performance as Rosalba Bartletta.

While Fellini's exploration of the female psyche portrayed rooms crowded with phantasmagoric characters oftentimes acting in a ribald fashion, Soldini's film focuses on more innocent characters. And while both films deal with a bored housewife with a philandering husband who appears unable to meet his wife's inner needs, Soldini focuses on the sweetness of life rather than the psychological reasons for the housewife's predicament. Perhaps much of this has to do with the era in which we live. More individuals are beginning to take responsibility for their actions as opposed to blaming their current situations on childhood events or at least so cinematically if not in reality. Fellini also made his most outlandish films during the 1960's and 70's when many intellectuals were deep in the process of liberating their subconscious minds through drug use and through the exploration of Jungian principles.

Now that Jungian psychology has moved to a back burner and the women's liberation movement all but passed by, movie audiences seem to be searching for simple stories about characters awakening to life's possibilities and that's exactly what *Bread and Tulips* offers. After 40-something

Rosalba finds herself left behind at a rest stop by a tour bus while on a family vacation, she comes to realize the extent of her invisibility in other people's lives. As her husband Mimmo (Antonio Catania) chews her out on the phone while his mistress Ketty (Vitalba Andrea) fondles him, Rosalba questions her choices. Rosalba decides to in Venice on her way back home and soon forgets her family's needs and finds better uses for her nurturing talents.

After missing her train, Rosalba convinces elderly florist Fermo (Felice Andreasi) to hire her, and a suicidal waiter (originally from Iceland) to give her bed and board. The waiter, Fernando Girasoli (Bruno Ganz), relinquishes his plans to hang himself after he falls under the enchantment of Rosalba's lust for life and slowly he reveals his past to her. Then Rosalba meets her neighbor Grazia (Marina Massironi) after the plumbing in her apartment goes haywire. Grazia happens to be a beautician and a masseuse, who is also in love with life, so Rosalba and Grazia become inseparable soulmates.

Meanwhile, Mimmo and his two sons realize the extent of Rosalba's housewifely talents as their home has fallen into disarray. His mistress complains to Mimmo to bring his wife home since she doesn't clean houses (that's not what mistresses do). Mimmo decides to hire a private detective—only he's too cheap—so he hires a plumber with an obsession for detective novels to sniff out Rosalba's whereabouts. The plumber, Costantino (Guiseppe Battiston), leaves his mother's home with a plan to bring Rosalba back, only it takes him several days to locate the housewife and then she alludes capture. One fateful night when Costantino locates Rosalba, he also meets and seduces Grazia under an assumed identity. When Grazia realizes that Costantino is really a detective out to destroy her friend's life, she goes into a diatribe about her past lovers. But Costantino sincerely loves Grazia so he lets Rosalba off the hook. However, just when Rosalba's life has taken a harmonious turn, Ketty shows up to remind Rosalba of her family duties. Guilt-stricken Rosalba returns to her family but is constantly reminded of the fulfilling life she abandoned. Fortunately, her friends soon lure her back to Venice.

Ganz and Maglietta entice us with their sumptuous romance and it would be best to ignore Fernando's words that "sometimes distractions can prove fatal."

—*Patty-Lynne Herlevi*

## CREDITS

**Rosalba Bartletta:** Licia Maglietta
**Fernando Girasoli:** Bruno Ganz
**Grazia:** Marina Massironi
**Costantino:** Guiseppe Battiston
**Mimmo Bartletta:** Antonio Catania

**Fermo:** Felice Andreasi
**Ketty:** Vitalba Andrea

**Origin:** Italy, Switzerland
**Language:** Italian
**Released:** 2001
**Production:** Daniele Maggioni; RAI, Monogatari SRL, Instituto Luce; released by First Look Pictures
**Directed by:** Silvio Soldini
**Written by:** Silvio Soldini, Doriana Leondeff
**Cinematography by:** Luca Bigazzi
**Music by:** Giovanni Venosta
**Sound:** Maurizio Argentieri
**Editing:** Carlotta Cristiani
**Costumes:** Silvia Nebiolo
**Production Design:** Paola Brizzarri
**MPAA rating:** PG-13
**Running time:** 105 minutes

 REVIEWS

*Boxoffice.* April, 2001, p. 227.
*Chicago Sun-Times Online.* August 31, 2001.
*Hollywood Reporter.* August 8, 2001, p. 18.
*Los Angeles Times Online.* August 10, 2001.
*New York Times Online.* July 27, 2001.
*Washington Post.* August 24, 2001, p. C4.

# Bride of the Wind

 **Box Office:** $.3 million

B*ride of the Wind,* written by Marilyn Levy and directed by Bruce Beresford, happens to be one of the summer's most boring releases and critics agreed that this biopic, portraying one of the 20th century most notorious females, lacks vitality. Catharine Tunnacliffe of *eye Weekly* notes: "Considering the richness of her life, it's hard to believe a biopic about Alma could be lifeless, but *Bride of the Wind* struggles to maintain a faint pulse." A.O. Scott of the *New York Times* criticized Levy's underwritten characters, "Alma's men are reduced to stock figures, and the talents of several fine actors are wasted." The coup de grace came from the *Washington Post* as Desson Howe criticized the script's pretensions: "It's only one level away from becoming an unintentional Monty Python sketch, in which famous characters are made into buffoons." However, Emily Baillargeon Russin of the *Seattle Weekly* praised the artistic merits of the

film by noting, "Fin-de-seicle Vienna never looked so good" and other critics also praised the photography, costumes, and production design.

*Bride of the Wind,* named after one of Oskar Kokoschka's paintings, equates itself with the popular phrase, "she's all dressed up with no place to go." And it's truly a pity that Levy wrote such a stuffy and pretentious screenplay about an artist and woman who once came across as a breath of fresh air. So why is this film about Vienna's elite bohemian circle of artists, which included painters Oskar Kokoschka and Gustav Klimt, Bauhaus architect Walter Gropius, novelist Franz Werfel, and composers Gustav and Alma Mahler so boring? First, Levy fails to send out a clear message of what the film's about. Is the point of the film to reveal that Alma (Sarah Wynter) was a feminist and a headstrong woman ahead of her time? If that's the case, Levy has portrayed just the opposite about her lead, who gives up her own artistic career to please her first husband Gustav (Jonathan Pryce). Later, instead of leaving with one of her lovers, Alma stays on with Gustav even though he fails to show her any affection. Even after Gustav's death, this bride of the wind flies through various lovers' lives while searching for the one man who will allow her to return to her true self. Perhaps this film is a study of the woman behind the artist and how those women give up their own ambitions to please their husbands. Of course, better cinematic debates on this subject exist, Ed Harris' *Pollack* being one of them, and Pat Murphy's *Nora* also reflects on this topic.

The film opens in 1902 Vienna where we meet an outspoken, yet cloistered Alma. Later, at a dinner party, Alma boldly critiques Mahler's compositions in front of the composer and his colleagues. However, Mahler appears to be intrigued with Alma's beauty, commenting "I hope to change your mind about my music, but there's not much we can do about my head." [Alma had also criticized the composer's head.] Gustav and Alma quickly become lovers and Gustav proposes to Alma. Of course, Gustav asks Alma to stop composing music and, instead, support his music. Alma reluctantly complies but she loses her soul in the process. As the years roll by, Alma suffers other losses, including the loss of her eldest daughter and later the death of Gustav. She's also forced to end a love affair that did provide for her emotional sustenance. However, these losses barely register emotionally beyond the few icy tears that actress Wynter sheds. Eventually we see Alma through a succession of famous lovers until she meets her soulmate, novelist Franz Werfel (Gregor Seberg), who reunites Alma with her music. However, unlike Alma's music, which plays to an appreciative audience, *Bride of the Wind* simply disappeared from view.

—*Patty-Lynne Herlevi*

## CREDITS

**Alma Mahler:** Sarah Wynter
**Gustav Mahler:** Jonathan Pryce
**Oskar Kokoschka:** Vincent Perez
**Walter Gropius:** Simon Verhoeven
**Gustav Klimt:** August Schmolzer
**Franz Werfel:** Gregor Seberg
**Anna Moll:** Dagmar Schwarz
**Karl Moll:** Wolfgang Hubsch
**Alexander Zemlinsky:** Johannes Silberschneider

**Origin:** Germany, Great Britain
**Released:** 2001
**Production:** Evzen Kolar, Lawrence Levy; Apollomedia, Firelight Films, Total Film Group; released by Paramount Classics
**Directed by:** Bruce Beresford
**Written by:** Marilyn Levy
**Cinematography by:** Peter James
**Music by:** Stephen Endelman
**Sound:** Petter Fladeby
**Editing:** Tim Wellburn
**Art Direction:** Christian Mann
**Costumes:** Shuna Harwood
**Production Design:** Herbert Pinter
**MPAA rating:** R
**Running time:** 99 minutes

## REVIEWS

*Boxoffice.* August, 2001, p. 60.
*Chicago Sun-Times Online.* June 22, 2001.
*eye Weekly Online.* June 14, 2001.
*Hollywood Reporter.* June 8, 2001, p. 20.
*Los Angeles Times Online.* June 8, 2001.
*New York Times Online.* June 8, 2001.
*New York Times Online.* June 10, 2001.
*San Francisco Chronicle Online.* June 15, 2001.
*Seattle Weekly.* June 28, 2001, p. 94.
*Toronto Sun Online.* June 15, 2001.
*Variety.* June 11, 2001, p. 18.
*Washington Post Online.* June 15, 2001.

## QUOTES

Gustav (Jonathan Pryce) tells Alma (Sarah Wynter): "A symphony should be like the world. It should contain everything."

# Bridget Jones's Diary

*This year's resolutions: Stop smoking. Stop drinking. Find inner poise. Go to gym three times a week. Don't flirt with boss. Reduce thighs. Learn to love thighs. Forget about thighs. Stop making lists.*
—Movie tagline
*Uncensored. Uninhibited. Unmarried.*
—Movie tagline

**Box Office:** $71.5

Renee Zellweger stars as the single, chain-smoking, booze-gulping, calorie-obsessed, anti-heroine title character in *Bridget Jones's Diary,* delightfully adapted from Helen Fielding's 1996 best-selling novel, which was loosely based on *Pride and Prejudice.* This is acclaimed documentary filmmaker Sharon Maguire's first feature and her quick pacing and excellent casting capture all the angst-ridden comedy that surrounds Bridget, who with her band of singleton friends, struggle to join the ranks of the smug-marrieds, while enjoying themselves along the way.

The film plots a year in the life of Miss Jones, from one Christmas to the next, and the quest she meticulously chronicles in her new diary: to quit all her bad habits, stop obsessing, and find a suitable boyfriend. The movie opens with a hilarious segment of a tipsy and maudlin Bridget in flannel pajamas, alone for the holiday in her apartment, belting out "All By Myself" along with the radio. Not long to wallow in self-pity, Bridget grudgingly accepts her mother's invitation to the annual turkey-curry New Year's buffet with family friends. As a thirty-something single, the very hung over Bridget is forced to endure the snide comments of the smug-marrieds and the efforts of her ditsy mother (Gemma Jones) to set her up with the dull-but-eligible Mark Darcy (Colin Firth), a bachelor barrister and the son of a friend. Bridget's nervous babbling seems to annoy the stuffy, arrogant would-be suitor, who's obnoxiously clad in a reindeer sweater. Afterward, Bridget dismisses the disastrous encounter and declares Mark dull and boring, albeit cute and very wealthy. To further deter an unlikely romance, Mark also keeps popping up at events with the sophisticated and svelte Natasha (Embeth Davidtz), also a lawyer.

Things begin to look more rosy in the romance department when Bridget, an assistant in a publishing house, arrives at work one day to find a flirtatious e-mail awaiting from her dashing cad of a boss, Daniel Cleaver (Hugh Grant). After walking by Daniel's office in one of her typical mini-skirted outfits, she returns to her desk to find he had sent the following message, "Message Jones: You appear to have forgotten your skirt." A flurry of hilarious skirt-related messages cement the budding romance: Is the skirt merely off sick? Since skirt is clearly not off sick, does management have a size-ist attitude towards skirt? Mildly shocked but flattered, Bridget, against her better judgment, throws herself wholeheartedly into the daring tryst with the cheeky Cleaver. Some of the movies funniest dialogue occurs while Daniel is wooing his insecure employee—when undressing her in their first intimate encounter, Daniel responds to Bridget's rather over-grown knickers: "Absolutely enormous panties!" Mortified, Bridget struggles to get them back up as he continues, "You have nothing to be embarrassed about. I'm wearing something quite similar myself," to which Bridget can't help but laugh.

Surprisingly, the somewhat elusive Daniel seems almost willing to have an actual relationship with Bridget, who declares him the perfect boyfriend after going away on a "mini-break" to the country. Bridget's bliss is short-lived, however, when she catches Daniel with another, and much thinner, woman. Unable to face him at work, Bridget decides to make a bold move into a whole new career as a television reporter, which she dives into with characteristic naivete and enthusiasm with mixed results. During this time, Mr. Darcy reappears, and is gradually showing himself to be less of a stuffed-shirt and more like a genuinely decent and kind human being. A remorseful Daniel, though, is still waiting in the wings for Bridget and in an interesting plot twist, the love triangle finally culminates at Bridget's 32nd birthday party where the two men actually come to blows. Bridget is then left to choose between the two, whose characters must now be totally re-evaluated, ala *Pride and Prejudice*. The final segment of the film comes off awkwardly after it becomes clear who is going to end up with whom.

If Maguire seems to have a surprisingly good grasp of the material, it may come from the fact that she is a good friend of the author and upon whom the author modeled the character of Bridget's friend Sharon a.k.a. Shazza. Remarking about the aims of the film in the press notes, Maguire says: "We wanted to be independent and strong—but we also wanted to be in love. And that's the contradiction that makes Bridget so brilliant a character. That's what I wanted to get across in the movie: the issues about women and love that are relevant, universal and side-splittingly funny." She records events of the novel faithfully and her onscreen interpretation will leave lovers of the book little to be concerned with.

A large part of the film's success no doubt goes to Zellweger, a native Texan whose controversial casting in the role of a staunchly English cultural icon had some Brit's up in arms. Gaining 20 pounds for the role, along with daily dialogue lessons with renowned coach Barbara Berkery, helped Zellweger on her way to embodying the endearingly

clumsy Jones, winning over even English critics. She slides into Miss Jones's shoes easily and most believably, with the required amount of self-deprecating wit, spot-on comic timing, and plenty of onscreen chemistry with both her leading men. She makes the most of each bewildering event: parading around gamely in a Playboy Bunny costume at a "Tarts and Vicars" party where the theme was changed and everybody is in normal dress, and a well-publicized scene where, as an on-camera reporter, Bridget is forced to slide down a firepole in a miniskirt only to fall prey to a most unfortunate camera angle.

Brits Grant and Firth are also perfectly cast in their roles. Grant, playing against type, seems to relish playing the cad for once instead of the boyishly charming gentleman one would happily bring home to mother. His charm perfectly balances the darker qualities of Cleaver so that even when his flaws are dramatically revealed, you don't necessarily write him off as not having a future with Bridget. Firth as Darcy proves clever casting as well, as he also played Mr. Darcy in the BBC television's adaptation of *Pride and Prejudice*. Firth deftly plays the nuances of his character, who gradually reveals his attractive qualities along with his vulnerability. The role is less glamorous than that of Grant's, but much more difficult to pull off. Jones is wonderful as Bridget's mother who, mirroring her daughter's own love triangle, inexplicably decides to run off with a dubiously-tanned television shopping channel salesman. Jim Broadbent plays Bridget's long-suffering father who stoically and dutifully waits for his wife to return home.

Bridget's fellow singletons are business whiz Jude (Shirley Henderson), extreme feminist Shazza (Sally Phillips), and sarcastic Tom (James Callis), who provide stability for each other in between relationships with witty but sometimes misguided advice. In her hopeless quest to develop "inner poise—complete without boyfriend—as best way to obtain boyfriend" her friends are there to reassure Bridget that they value her own unique appeal. After Bridget hopelessly bungles her own birthday meal, they gamely eat the blue soup she prepared and give her this toast: "To Bridget, who we love just as she is." When Darcy directs a similar statement later in the film at Bridget, "I like you very much. Just as you are," we know she has found her true mate.

Making cameos are some of Britain's leading literary figures, most notably Salman Rushdie, whose praise of the novel was quoted on it's cover. He appears as himself at one of Bridget's publishing parties and, flustered by the famous author, all Bridget can muster is a question about the location of the powder rooms.

The winning script and dialogue come from Fielding, Andrew Davies (scriptor of the BBC's *Pride and Prejudice*), and Richard Curtis (*Four Weddings and a Funeral, Bean* and *Notting Hill*). The writers have captured all the British wit of the novel and translated it perfectly on-screen. They faced the challenge of turning the novel, in diary form, into cinematic, as well as highly comedic, events. The film begins, taking advantage of the diary form, complete with voice-overs, to introduce Bridget's comically tortured inner thoughts, people, and events, but then moves away from it somewhat as the characters establish their own voices and the film its own momentum. Cinematographer Stuart Dryburgh infused London's Notting Hill with a vibrancy that reflects Bridget's own and provides exciting locales for events of the scattered heroine's life.

Utilizing such apt song classics as "Respect," "Have you Met Miss Jones" and "I'm Every Woman," the soundtrack unapologetically mirrors many other emotional moments in Bridget's eminently relatable and exuberant life. The film definitely does justice to the popular novel and one can only hope the same group re-team if there is a movie version of the novel's sequel, *Bridget Jones: The Edge of Reason.*

—*Hilary White*

## CREDITS

**Bridget Jones:** Renee Zellweger
**Daniel Cleaver:** Hugh Grant
**Mark Darcy:** Colin Firth
**Bridget's Mum:** Gemma Jones
**Bridget's Dad:** Jim Broadbent
**Natasha:** Embeth Davidtz
**Jude:** Shirley Henderson
**Tom:** James Callis
**Shazza:** Sally Phillips

**Origin:** USA
**Released:** 2001
**Production:** Tim Bevan, Eric Fellner, Jonathan Cavendish; Working Title Productions, Universal Pictures, Miramax Films, StudioCanal; released by Miramax Films
**Directed by:** Sharon Maguire
**Written by:** Richard Curtis, Andrew Davies, Helen Fielding
**Cinematography by:** Stuart Dryburgh
**Music by:** Patrick Doyle
**Sound:** David Crozier
**Music Supervisor:** Nick Angel
**Editing:** Martin Walsh
**Costumes:** Rachel Fleming
**Production Design:** Gemma Jackson
**MPAA rating:** R
**Running time:** 115 minutes

## REVIEWS

*Boxoffice.* June, 2001, p. 58.
*Chicago Sun-Times Online.* April 13, 2001.
*Entertainment Weekly.* April 20, 2001, p. 42.
*Los Angeles Times Online.* April 13, 2001.
*New York Times Online.* April 13, 2001.
*Newsweek.* April 16, 2001, p. 54.
*People.* April 23, 2001, p. 37.
*Rolling Stone.* April 26, 2001, p. 66.
*Sight and Sound.* April, 2001, p. 36.
*Time.* April 16, 2001, p. 79.
*USA Today Online.* April 13, 2001.
*Variety.* April 2, 2001, p. 17.
*Washington Post Online.* April 13, 2001.

## QUOTES

Bridget (Renee Zellweger): "Unless I changed my life I was destined to die alone and be found three weeks later, half-eaten by Alsatians."

## TRIVIA

Helen Fielding based the character of Mark Darcy on Colin Firth's portrayal of Mr. Darcy in the BBC adaptation of Jane Austen's *Pride and Prejudice.*

## AWARDS AND NOMINATIONS

**Nomination:**
**British Acad. 2001:** Actress (Zellweger), Adapt. Screenplay, Film, Support. Actor (Firth)
**Golden Globes 2002:** Actress—Mus./Comedy (Zellweger), Film—Mus./Comedy
**Screen Actors Guild 2001:** Actress (Zellweger)
**Writers Guild 2001:** Adapt. Screenplay
**Broadcast Film Critics 2001:** Actress (Zellweger).

# The Brothers

*They're ready for some one-on-one.*
—Movie tagline
*Refusing to Exhale.*
—Movie tagline

*After a lifetime of playing the field, four friends have to do something they never thought possible . . . grow up.*
—Movie tagline

 **Box Office:** $27.5 million

The Brothers is the latest in what is becoming somewhat of a mini-genre—movies about African-American men facing commitment. *The Brothers'* kin are films like *The Best Man* and *The Wood.* Writer and director Gary Hardwick reportedly nicknamed his film *Refusing to Exhale,* in a reference to Terry McMillan's *Waiting to Exhale.* Like the women in *Waiting to Exhale,* the guys of *The Brothers* have a penchant for standing around and talking about the opposite sex.

The characters in *The Brothers* have another thing in common with the women of *Waiting to Exhale.* They are well-educated, "good catches" who are just looking for a good relationship. "We're the cream of the crop!" says Brian Palmer (Bill Bellamy), insisting that they should have the pick of the best women available. Brian's a little cocky, but the guys are desirable, with good jobs and a degree of emotional maturity that makes them at least attempt to have straight-forward relationships with women.

Brian is a sassy lawyer who is known for having trouble with women. His fancy sports car is repeatedly mangled by a spurned former lover, but Brian's track record is so bad that he has no idea who could be doing it. Jackson Smith (Morris Chestnut of *The Best Man*) is a handsome pediatrician. (So handsome is he that when he first appeared on the screen bearing some skin, several of the ladies in the audience shrieked with sudden lust.) Jackson is a commitment-phobe and knows it. He suffers from recurring nightmares in which a mysterious bride chases him down pointing a gun at him. But he's an enlightened guy and trying to work on his issues. He sees his psychiatrist who suggests that he should open his heart to the next woman he becomes involved with.

It's unclear what Derrick West's (D.L. Hughley of TV's *The Hughleys*) job is but he seems to be some sort of executive who works in a nice office. He is the only married guy of the bunch but he's having problems of his own. His wife Sheila (Tamala Jones) is a high powered magazine editor, and at home she wants to call all the shots, too. She refuses to give him oral sex and this becomes a major point of contention Terry White (Shemar Moore) is approaching 30 and is getting antsy about making a commitment to someone. He's been a love-'em-and-leave-'em type in the past but he thinks he's getting too old for that kind of behavior.

The four guys have been friends since childhood and meet every week to play basketball, go out to a nightclub and talk about love and life. The balance of this is upset when Terry suddenly announces that he is going to marry his girlfriend. Brian, especially, is against the union. It's hard to tell whether it's because he thinks this girl is wrong for Terry or that he's just sad about the change in his gang. It's probably a little of both.

The impending marriage sends all the guys into a search to solve their own relationship problems. Brian decides that the solution to his problems is to stop dating "sistahs" and to concentrate solely on white women. This is a provocative issue and one that would be interesting to explore in depth but writer Hardwick (who has also been a lawyer, novelist and stand-up comedian) doesn't give Brian enough screen time to give the issue any kind of depth. Brian is also working on an issue about his mother who refuses to hug her son or acknowledge that she loves him. Meanwhile, Derrick and his wife reach a crisis in their marriage and things deteriorate. It gets so bad that Sheila locks Derrick out of the house and asks for a separation. Derrick is shocked. He has always tried to do the right thing—after all, he married Sheila after learning that she was pregnant—and can't believe his marriage is failing.

The most engaging story is Jackson's. Jackson finds his match Denise Johnson (Gabrielle Union) in a park. Although Jackson doesn't seem to realize it, Denise is the one for him. She is beautiful, they are mental equals and she is brave enough to help him face down his commitment issues. But Jackson won't be able to function until he can deal with the pain that his parents' divorce has caused him. His father (Clifton Powell) abandoned the family but after seeing Jackson's still feisty and sexy mother (Jenifer Lewis) at a party many year later, dad starts dating mom again. Jackson is disgusted. His disgust is furthered when he finds out that his father and his new girlfriend had briefly dated in the past. Will Jackson be able to get over this and continue his relationship with Denise, or will he go back to his old pattern of avoiding commitment. In his review of the film, the *Chicago Sun-Times'* Roger Ebert makes the comment that the story works because the two lovers aren't kept apart by false plot-derived obstacles, but by real problems that they will have to deal with (or ignore) in a realistic fashion.

The acting in the film is universally good. The standout performance probably would be Lewis as the salty mother. She's fun to watch because she oozes self-confidence and is the kind of character who creates a party wherever she is. Also good is Chestnut as the confused Jackson. He gives an emotional depth to his character that makes him seem like a real person with real problems. Hughley does a good job at taming his comedic tendencies. He's still funny, but instead of just being a funny character, he's a more realistic character, who's also funny.

There are a lot of good things about *The Brothers.* The film is an easy-going watch and Hardwick is sincere about wanting to explore these issues between men and women. And it's certainly nice to see African-American men in roles that aren't the usual ones that Hollywood doles out. The screen has seen enough African-Americans playing hard-edged ghetto-dwelling criminals or fast-talking, not particularly intelligent, small time crooks.

Hardwick also does a nice job with the women's roles. The women aren't just there to serve the stories of the men, but have their own stories going on. Hardwick even puts a scene in the film with no men and just the women. Jackson's sassy mom dispenses advice about men to the guys' girlfriends like, "It's love if it's late at night and he gives you the last bite of the food." Hardwick has a nice feel for how women really talk when they're together and that's a nice surprise, especially in a film that's supposed to be about men's lives.

Of course all this sensitivity and getting in touch with emotions doesn't sit well with everybody. Renee Lucas Wayne of the *Philadelphia Daily News* wrote that the movie "is a chick flick masquerading as a completely mindless night out with the boys." Another critic suggested that the film might have been more at home on the Lifetime channel. But generally critics enjoyed the chance to review a film that made a stab at intelligent talk. *Entertainment Weekly* called it a "passionate and saucy comedy" and said "the movie digs more vibrantly into issues of trust, fear, pleasure, commitment, and camaraderie than any Hollywood feature in recent memory." The *Los Angeles Times* was similarly impressed saying, "Hardwick pushes his cast beyond their daytime soap perfection and the Terry McMillan-esque tendencies (both good and bad) of his script and toward a consistent emotional truth for their characters." Carrie Rickey of the *Philadelphia Inquirer* said the film "may be the first Freudian urban-commitment comedy not made by Woody Allen or Nora Ephron." Hardwick is a welcome addition to the genre.

—*Jill Hamilton*

## CREDITS

**Jackson Smith:** Morris Chestnut
**Derrick West:** D.L. Hughley
**Brian Palmer:** Bill Bellamy
**Terry White:** Shemar Moore
**Denise Johnson:** Gabrielle Union
**Sheila West:** Tamala Jones
**BebBe Fales:** Susan Dalian
**Judge Carla Williams:** Angelle Brooks
**Louise Smith:** Jenifer Lewis
**Fred Smith:** Clifton Powell
**Mary West:** Marla Gibbs
**Cherie Smith:** Tatyana Ali
**Jesse Caldwell:** Julie Benz

**Origin:** USA
**Released:** 2001
**Production:** Darin Scott, Paddy Cullen; Screen Gems; released by Sony Pictures
**Directed by:** Gary Hardwick
**Written by:** Gary Hardwick
**Cinematography by:** Alexander Grusynski
**Sound:** Willie Burton
**Music Supervisor:** Melodee Sutton
**Editing:** Earl Watson
**Art Direction:** Austin Gorg
**Costumes:** Debrae Little
**Production Design:** Amy Ancona
**MPAA rating:** R
**Running time:** 101 minutes

## REVIEWS

*Boxoffice.* May, 2001, p. 58.
*Entertainment Weekly.* March 30, 2001, p. 44.
*Los Angeles Times Online.* March 23, 2001.
*New York Times Online.* March 23, 2001.
*People.* April 2, 2001, p. 35.
*Variety.* March 19, 2001, p. 30.
*Washington Post Online.* March 23, 2001.

# Bubble Boy

*Life is an adventure. Don't blow it.*
—Movie tagline

 **Box Office:** $5 million

**B**ubble Boy certainly didn't look promising. It's about a boy with an auto-immune deficiency who has to live in a plastic bubble. Trailers for the film showed the boy in his bubble bouncing around in various settings, being hit by buses, etc. It looked like it would be the latest in a season of slapstick-oriented tasteless summer flicks marketed to teen boys.

To make matters worse for the film's pre-release buzz, the Immune Deficiency Foundation protested the film saying it made light of the disorder. One critic, the mother of David Vetter, was particularly vociferous in her condemnation. Vetter became semi-famous for his rare condition that kept him in a protected bubble for his short 12-year life. His nickname was also Bubble Boy.

Between the ad campaign for *Bubble Boy* and the protests against it, the movie wasn't looking like such a good bet. After all, if its premise is already offensive, wouldn't the rest of the film be even worse? But all this bad publicity oddly works in *Bubble Boy*'s favor. The protests and studio's promotional efforts made the movie look so bad, that the movie itself turns out to be a pleasant surprise. It's much more subtle and witty than you'd guess. Was the promotional team horribly misguided? Or were they marketing geniuses, purposefully setting up low expectations for the film so it would, by contrast, seem like a witty romp? Probably the former, but it's fun to think it could be the latter.

Like John Travolta in the 1976 made-for-TV movie *The Boy in the Plastic Bubble*, Jimmy Livingston (Jake Gyllenhaal of *October Sky*) has to live in a plastic bubble to protect himself from germs. If Jimmy is exposed to even one germ, he will die. When he is four years old, he is released from the hospital and sent to live with his parents in their sterile (in many ways) Palmdale, California, home. His parents set up a Habitrail-like environment for him, complete with a plastic bubble room filled with toys and equipped with a pair of rubber arms so that his mom can hug him.

Mrs. Livingston (Swoosie Kurtz) is a religious fanatic who rules her household completely. Having little Jimmy in a bubble sort of works well for her because she can control every aspect of his environment. Since Jimmy has no outside influences, he has no reason to doubt anything she says and is her eager pupil. He happily eats her crucifix-shaped wheat-free, sugar-free cookies and listens to her versions of the fairy tales she reads him which all happen to end with a boy tragically leaving his bubble. "And then Rapunzel came out of her bubble and died," she reads. Or "and Pinocchio came out of his plastic bubble and touched the filthy whore next door and died." She also controls his TV and reading habits. Jimmy thinks the only show on TV is the 1970s dinosaur show *Land of the Lost* and the only magazine is the tame kid's mag *Highlights*. "Gee," he says, wistfully, "I wish they had more than one magazine than *Highlights*." But in general, Jimmy accepts his lot and is a happy kid.

At 16, he gets a "rock music guitar" and starts jamming in his room. What does he play? A rocking version of the *Land of the Lost* theme song. Becoming a teen doesn't change Jimmy's good-natured blind obedience to his parents. When he is shocked to find his body becoming sexually excited, he panics and asks his mother for advice. "Just do what I tell your father to do and say the Pledge of Allegiance until it goes down," she tells him. Jimmy tries it and it works. "Thank you," he sighs gratefully.

But things start changing when Jimmy spies his next door neighbor Chloe (Marley Shelton) washing her car outside of his window. Jimmy starts spending a lot of his time standing by his window, pretending to wash it while he watches Chloe. Chloe is a beautiful girl, who also happens to

be nice, and she and Jimmy strike up a friendship. She visits him every day and they become inseparable friends. They both want more but there's the bubble problem.

Naturally, Mrs. Livingston doesn't like any of this. As she puts it, "Something tells me she's not the kind of girl Jesus would pick for a friend." She seethes over the friendship and is delighted to hear when Chloe decides to give up on Jimmy and marry her longtime on-and-off loser boyfriend Mark (Dave Sheridan). Mark is a would-be rock star who's uncool enough to sport a mullet hairstyle and boorish enough to say "Oh yeah" in place of "I do" at a wedding. Jimmy panics at the idea of losing Chloe and realizes that he loves her. He decides to go to Niagara Falls and break up the wedding. And, for added drama, he only has three days to get there.

Jimmy rigs up a travel bubble that's kind of like a human-sized, clear beach ball. He sets off across the country and the movie shifts to a typical road trip movie. Jimmy meets a group of traveling circus freaks, an Indian man who sells ice cream in order to spread the work about Hinduism and a rough motorcycle guy Slim (Danny Trejo). The best of these road vignettes involves a religious cult/"Up With People" type of group called "Bright and Shiny." Decked out in bright matching t-shirts, the group is absurdly happy. The women are all called Lorraine and the men all called Gil and the whole gang travels around in a bus spreading the word. They are devoted to their charismatic leader, played by real life romance novel cover boy Fabio.

There is plenty in this movie to offend people. Practically everyone is stereotyped. Chinese people, circus freaks, Jews, Christians, are but a few of the groups that get a joke or two leveled at them. But somehow, the film is not nearly as offensive as others of its ilk. The jokes are good-natured and since they're doled out so evenly, it's harder to get really offended. And, thankfully, this is a movie completely free of gross-out and bathroom humor. That a teen movie could be made in 2001 without one horribly gross bathroom scene is an amazing achievement in itself.

Since the movie's not cluttered up with dumb jokes about boogers and the like, there's more room for jokes about other things and this is where *Bubble Boy* shines. It has an offbeat quality, like *Election*, where the jokes are more about attitude and gentle satire, rather than just for shock value. When Chloe is off in Niagara Falls, trying not to think about Jimmy, she turns on the TV and sees an ad for Mr. Bubble, Bubblicious, and Don Ho singing "Tiny Bubbles." This in itself is not that funny, but it's the way that its handled that makes it work. When Jimmy has a nightmare about Chloe, it is done in the style of *Land of the Lost*, complete with the fake-looking backgrounds and dinosaurs made of modeling clay.

A big part of what makes this all work is Jimmy. He's an innocent, but not dumb. This is a marked contrast from similar movies where the lead or leads are stupid guys who do stupid things. Unlike, say, a Rob Schneider character, Jimmy obviously has a lot of intelligence even though he's not particularly street smart. When he meets the Hindu ice cream truck driver, he tells him earnestly, "Your religion is all lies anyway." The first time he sees Chloe, he reports to her eagerly that she is the whore who lives next door. In both cases, he means no harm, he's just reiterating what his mother's taught him. Gyllenhaal has such a sweet quality that he's able to say lines like this without seeming the least bit obnoxious. He comes across as a good guy who just wants to do the right thing. He's an innocent in the nicest possible sense. The movie is also helped by an off-beat soundtrack ranging from songs by modern groups like the Offspring to 70s chestnuts like "Wildfire" and "Sometimes When We Touch."

Critics were divided in their reactions to the film. Philip Wuntch of the *Dallas Morning News* wasn't impressed, saying, "If unfunny isn't enough, this film is also guilty of smugness." Charles Savage of the *Miami Herald* felt more kindly toward the film and wrote, "*Bubble Boy* belongs to that genre of movie that works hard to achieve a certain twisted and demented wit, like a *Citizen Ruth* minus most of the abortion politics." *Newsday*'s Jan Stuart called it "a frenetic whoopee cushion of a road comedy."

—*Jill Hamilton*

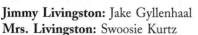

**CREDITS**

**Jimmy Livingston:** Jake Gyllenhaal
**Mrs. Livingston:** Swoosie Kurtz
**Chloe:** Marley Shelton
**Slim:** Danny Trejo
**Mr. Livingston:** John Carroll Lynch
**Chicken Man:** Stephen Spinella
**Dr. Phreak:** Verne Troyer
**Mark:** Dave Sheridan
**Puskpak:** Brian George
**Pappy/Pippy:** Patrick Cranshaw
**Gil:** Fabio

**Origin:** USA
**Released:** 2001
**Production:** Beau Flynn; Bandeira Entertainment; released by Touchstone Pictures
**Directed by:** Blair Hayes
**Written by:** Ken Daurio, Cinco Paul
**Cinematography by:** Jerzy Zielinski
**Music by:** John Ottman
**Sound:** James Thornton
**Music Supervisor:** John Houlihan
**Editing:** Pamela Martin
**Art Direction:** Troy Sizemore, Christa Munro

**Costumes:** Christopher Lawrence
**MPAA rating:** PG-13
**Running time:** 84 minutes

**REVIEWS**

*Boxoffice.* August, 2001, p. 22.
*Boxoffice.* October, 2001, p. 60.
*Entertainment Weekly.* September 7, 2001, p. 135.
*Los Angeles Times Online.* August 24, 2001.
*New York Times Online.* August 24, 2001.
*People.* September 10, 2001, p. 41.
*USA Today Online.* August 24, 2001.
*Variety.* August 27, 2001, p. 32.
*Washington Post.* August 24, 2001, p. C1.

**TRIVIA**

This is director Blair Hayes' first feature film.

# Bully

*It's 4 AM. Do you know where your kids are?*
—Movie tagline

 **Box Office:** $.5 million

**B**ully marks another effort by former photographer Larry Clark to accurately portray the lives of disaffected modern youths, but despite a real-life story basis, the film seems more cartoonish than realistic. Clark's 1995 cause celebre, *Kids*, was just as exploitative as this new film, but the director's debut at least had a measure of authenticity. Actually, Clark's second film, the gangster flick *Another Day In Paradise* (1998), succeeded best of all as a mixture of naturalism and impressionism. Perhaps Clark should reconsider using a neorealistic approach to his violent and sexual material. In any case, *Bully* is the worst of his three films to date.

Zachary Long and Roger Pullis's screenplay, based on a novel by Jim Schutze, takes place in 1993 in the middle-class suburbs of Hollywood, Florida, where Marty Puccio (Brad Renfro) tags along with Bobby Kent (Nick Stahl), despite the fact that Bobby constantly abuses Marty, both verbally and physically. After Bobby rapes Ally (Bijou Phillips), forcing her to watch gay porn during the act, some of Marty's friends, including Marty's girlfriend Lisa (Rachel Miner), finally convince Marty to seek revenge on his so-called best friend.

The teenage slackers hire a "hitman" (Leo Fitzpatrick, from *Kids*) and develop a scheme where they make Bobby think he will be part of a group orgy at a local swamp, but then beat and kill him instead. After some stumbling and fumbling, the execution takes place, with Marty contributing the coup de grace stabbing.

But in the days following the murder, the conspirators begin to crack: some feel they left behind evidence at the swamp and worry about being caught; others, like Lisa, begin bragging to untrustworthy friends. Once their parents find out about the crime, Marty, Lisa, and the others are arrested and put into jail, where they await what promises to be a sensational trial.

*Bully* starts out promisingly, with a pensive if disturbing portrait of the troubled "friendship" between Bobby and Marty. During the first reel, *Bully* makes perceptive points about the dark side of masculinity, how homophobia often masks homosexual feelings, and how class influences sex and power relations.

But just as the plot veers into revenge melodrama, the movie itself goes haywire. In one unintentionally (?) comic scene after another, the self-absorbed teenagers clumsily plan Bobby's murder while they get high on drugs and/or sexually arouse themselves. The climactic murder scene is lengthy and exceedingly violent, yet despite the emphasis on the savagery, the second half of the movie preaches an obvious "Crime Does Not Pay" message. This is bit like Cecil B. DeMille's old gambit of giving the public sex and violence, only to moralize at the end of his pictures.

Larry Clark's photorealist technique should be the right approach to a real-life modern murder case, but Clark pushes his style to an extreme. Clark photographs the half-naked bodies in the style of Calvin Klein underwear commercials, using extreme close-ups of nipples, underarms, and crotches (curiously, with more panning over the boys than the girls). In one particularly comic moment, Clark films the close-up of a dog nose. All this begs the question: what was the intention behind *Bully*? At the time of release, the film was compared unfavorably to Jean-Pierre Ameris's serious study of French youth, *Bad Company*, but *Bully* seems more like a Troma-styled remake of Tim Hunter's *River's Edge*. Could it all be a spoof? One never knows. But it doesn't feel right to be laughing at criminal activities like rape and murder.

The two lead actors—Brad Renfro (*The Client*) and Nick Stahl (*In the Bedroom*)—try hard to redeem some of the sleaze. But their affecting portrayals make it even harder to know where the film is coming from (or going to). Paradoxically, Stahl makes the title character more sympathetic than his foolish victims! This is because the supporting players perform so poorly, Ed Wood amateur-style. The

less said about them the better. Ultimately, *Bully* is just an annoying assault on the senses. Why should we ponder even a moment about its meaning and significance?

*—Eric Monder*

## CREDITS

**Marty Puccio:** Brad Renfro
**Bobby Kent:** Nick Stahl
**Ali Willis:** Bijou Phillips
**Lisa Connelly:** Rachel Miner
**Donny Semenec:** Michael Pitt
**Heather Swaller:** Kelli Garner
**Derek Dzvirko:** Daniel Franzese
**Derek Kaufman, the hitman:** Leo Fitzpatrick
**Cameo:** Larry Clark

**Origin:** USA
**Released:** 2001
**Production:** Chris Hanley, Don Murphy, Fernando Sulichin; Blacklist, Gravity Entertainment; released by Lion's Gate Films
**Directed by:** Larry Clark
**Written by:** Zachary Long, Roger Pullis
**Cinematography by:** Steve Gainer
**Sound:** Rob Freeman
**Editing:** Andrew Hafitz
**Art Direction:** Laura Harper
**Costumes:** Carleen Ileana Rosado
**Production Design:** Linda Burton
**MPAA rating:** Unrated
**Running time:** 113 minutes

## REVIEWS

*Boxoffice.* September, 2001, p. 149.
*Chicago Sun-Times Online.* July 20, 2001.
*Hollywood Reporter.* July 10, 2001, p. 16.
*Los Angeles Times Online.* July 13, 2001.
*New York Times Online.* July 13, 2001.
*Sight and Sound.* March, 2002, p. 24.
*USA Today Online.* July 13, 2001, p. 21.
*Variety.* July 9, 2001, p. 21.

## QUOTES

Lisa (Rachel Miner) about Bobby: "I want him dead."

Director Larry Clark has a cameo as the stepfather of Derek Kaufman (played by Leo Fitzpatrick).

# The Business of Strangers

**Box Office:** $.4 million

Lately American independent filmmakers have been stripping down their screenplays to the bare essentials. Both Richard Linklater's *Tape* and newcomer Patrick Stettner's *The Business of Strangers* feature small casts and the scenarios basically take place in a single location—hotel rooms. Sans camera movement, colorful décor, and lush musical scores, dialogue, plot twists and performances take center stage. But the two independent films share more in common than the hotels rooms in which the characters confront each other. Both films cleverly provide viewers with a Rorschach test while presenting us characters that barely skirt around stereotypes. And both films present us with a mystery surrounding an alleged rape from the past that ignites emotional fireworks as the characters own up to it. We find ourselves in an uncomfortable situation as we consider whether or not the rapes took place. Like the characters, we too get caught up in an intense power struggle.

*The Business of Strangers* exploits the myth behind feminism by showing that women coming from different backgrounds often do not bond into the type of sisterhood explored in films such as *Thelma and Louise*. Women engage in mind games with each other and this manifests itself in the corporate world where women who compete against men for the executive chair often take out their frustration on a younger generation of women. Although the screenplay was written and directed by a male director, the film hits the target when exploring the personal issues that no-nonsense business woman Julie Styron (Stockard Channing) and 20ish upstart Paula Murphy (Julia Stiles) do battle over. Julie finally tastes victory after a long struggle up the corporate ladder, but finds success bittersweet. Paula, who seems to have everything going for her on the surface, boils over with rage. She shouts profanities at people and talks dirty to get a rise out of middle-age businessmen. But it becomes increasingly difficult to fathom whether Paula is a sociopath or a rape victim. And we never find out the truth of her situation. Similar to Julie, we also don't know if we can place

our trust in a cynical brat, especially since Paula plays Julie (and the viewer) like a well-tuned instrument.

In an interview for *RANT,* Channing describes the relationship between the two female characters: "I thought it was very interesting to see a relationship between two women that I've never seen before, not in an American film at least." And it's true that you will find women characters doing battle with each other's egos and vulnerabilities in European films. Claude Chabrol's *La Cèrèmonie* (1995) portrays two women, a disgruntled postal worker (Isabelle Huppert) and young maid (Sandrine Bonnaire), who play off of bourgeois gallery owner (Jacqueline Bissett). Inequality between an upper class family and the working class postal worker and maid, along with issues of trust, surface and reach an extremely violent conclusion. Channing and Stile's characters also find themselves at odds when it comes to age and status. Similar to Chabrol's characters, trust becomes an issue, especially since the younger woman appears to be avenging a past grievance with her superior.

Scott Macaulay (*Filmmaker*) describes *The Business of Strangers* as "*Persona* meets *Straw Dogs.*" Ingmar Bergman's 1966 classic *Persona* features a cast of two women, Liv Ullmann and Bibi Andersson, and takes place in a single location. Ullmann plays an older actress who suffered a nervous breakdown and Andersson plays a younger nurse who betrays the actress in her care. Again, we have a younger woman pitting herself against an older woman in a vulnerable situation, and again, the subservient woman takes out her frustrations on the older woman. Paula in *The Business of Strangers* and the nurse in *Persona* use sex as a weapon and their young flesh as enticing bait. These women have learned to use their sexual allure to bring so-called powerful men to their knees. They have learned to turn male sexual urges against the men. It's a game that only younger women can win and, cinematically, these female characters have won the game countless times and in numerous films.

However, films such as *The Business of Strangers* leave women viewers who were weaned on Hollywood's female bonding films feeling uneasy. The films do not feel warm or fuzzy and they show women in the worse light possible. After all, we would like to believe in sisterhood despite the torment women inflict on each other in the name of competition—both in the work place and the sexual arena. We feel comforted when we see women team up against the male enemy in such films as Mexican director Maria Novaro's *Without a Trace,* and American films *Thelma and Louise* and *Fried Green Tomatoes.* We want to define the enemy as male, but the real enemy is within us and projected on to other women who also feel victimized by the system. When these femmes feel helpless in fighting battles with men they take out their frustrations on other victimized women.

As the film opens, we see a wide shot of a crowd of people gliding through an airport terminal. The camera lens zooms into Julie's (Channing) back as she struts through the terminal on her way to another sale's pitch. She phones her secretary and learns that she has just been fired. She then gives a sales pitch to detached businessmen without the help of her visual aids since her temporary audio-visual technician, Paula (Stiles) shows up 45 minutes late. Consequently, Julie fires Paula, then heads to a meeting with oily headhunter Nick Harris (Frederick Weller) in hopes that she'll land a new position. But moments later when Julie meets with her boss, she learns that she hasn't been fired but promoted to CEO of the company. Stunned, she doesn't know how to respond, so she gets plastered at the hotel bar.

Julie runs into Paula at the bar and offers an apology. The women bond over drinks. The female bonding ritual continues through a workout at the gym and a steam in the sauna. Later, after the women have returned to the bar, Nick shows up. Seemingly upset over Nick's appearance, Paula rushes out of the room. She confesses to Julie that Nick had raped a friend of hers at a fraternity party in Boston, but in actuality, he allegedly raped Paula. Julie goes into a rage and confides that she won't let Nick off the hook. Paula drugs Nick and the women drag Nick's body to a room under construction. Paula and Julie strip Nick's clothing off, then they write obscenities on his body. Julie violently erupts and nearly suffocates Nick. Paula threatens Julie with arrest for their crime, but appears to be bluffing. The women sneak out of the room, leaving Nick in a humiliating state.

The next morning, Paula sneaks out of Julie's room while stealing Julie's cash. As Julie prepares to shower, she finds the word loser written on her stomach. Later, Julie runs into Nick at the airport. When Julie questions Nick, she learns that he never attended a fraternity party in Boston. Julie knows that either Nick or Paula has lied to her. Most important Julie now faces a sense of emptiness instead of victory over her current success and she wonders if the CEO position is worth years of sacrifice and degradation.

Channing meets the challenge of portraying a non-stereotypical menopausal businesswoman head on, while the younger Stiles holds her own against the multiple award-winning Channing. Annlee Ellington of *Boxoffice* says, "Channing and Stiles share appropriately uneasy chemistry together." Frederick Weller, who plays an unconscious man through most of the film, suffers the humiliation of lying on a bed in his boxers while two actresses scratch obscenities on his body. Stettner felt self-conscious about putting the actor through the rigorous role and he warned Weller about the character's unglamorous aspects. Weller proved to be a good sport while allowing the actresses to engage in "a danse macabre of sex, revenge and professional one-upmanship" as cited by the Seattle International Film Festival program guide.

While Channing has played gritty roles in the past, Stiles worried about how film audiences' would react to Paula. Until this point Stiles has played teen queens and has appeared in three Shakespearean adaptations geared at a teen audience, including *10 Things I Hate About You, Hamlet,* and *O.* In the press notes, Stiles confided, "I was worried because I didn't want to be supporting or instigating any sort of Tawana Brawley scenario. If I made this movie and people misinterpreted Paula's actions and made assumptions about those sorts of accusations . . . I would be upset about that." However Stiles slices it, Paula proves recalcitrant. But after all, sophisticated audiences can distinguish between characters and actresses.

—*Patty-Lynne Herlevi*

## CREDITS

**Julie Styron:** Stockard Channing
**Paula Murphy:** Julia Stiles
**Nick Harris:** Frederick Weller
**Robert:** Marcus Giamatti

**Origin:** USA
**Released:** 2001
**Production:** Susan A. Stover, Robert H. Nathan; i5 Picture, Headquarters; released by IFC Films
**Directed by:** Patrick Stettner
**Written by:** Patrick Stettner
**Cinematography by:** Teodoro Maniaci
**Music by:** Alexander Lasarenko
**Sound:** Noah Vivekanand Timan
**Editing:** Keiko Deguchi
**Art Direction:** Richard Burgess
**Costumes:** Kasia Walicka Maimone, Dawn Weisberg
**Production Design:** Dina Goldman
**MPAA rating:** R
**Running time:** 83 minutes

## REVIEWS

*Chicago Sun-Times Online.* December 14, 2001.
*Entertainment Weekly.* December 14, 2001, p. 55.
*Filmmaker Online.* Summer, 2000.
*Los Angeles Times Online.* December 7, 2001.
*New York Times Online.* December 7, 2001.
*People.* December 17, 2001, p. 34.
*RANT.* November/December, 2001, p. 28.
*Rolling Stone.* December 6, 2001, p. 156.
*USA Today Online.* December 6, 2001.
*Variety.* January 29, 2001, p. 49.
*Washington Post.* December 14, 2001, p. WE36.

QUOTES

**QUOTES**

Paula (Julia Stiles): "I hate how the hotel windows never open. They don't want you to breathe real air." Julie (Stockard Channing): "Or jump."

**TRIVIA**

Stockard Channing and Frederick Weller worked together in the Broadway productions of *Six Degrees of Separation* and *The Little Foxes*.

# Calle 54

**Box Office:** $.1 million

Sending shivers of joy and causing festival audiences to leap to their feet at the Toronto International Film Festival, Fernando Trueba's music documentary *Calle 54* portrays celebrated Latin jazz musicians and their sensual music. Obviously a personal film, Trueba sought out his musical heroes, then artfully blended "snapshots" with intimate in-studio live performances of these musical icons. However, highlighting live performances in front of an appreciative audience would have further emphasized the featured musicians' legendary status. In fact, director Wim Wenders's choice to film celebrated Cuban musicians performing for audiences in his Academy Award®-nominated documentary the *Buena Vista Social Club* added warmth and humanity to the musical documentary.

*New York Times* film critic Elvis Mitchell stated that Trueba's documentary was bound to draw comparisons to Wenders's film. However, "This film, set in a variety of locales from New York to Europe, is a completely different take." Reviewer Paul Fontana of the *Seattle Weekly* reached the same conclusion: "The comparison, however, is not one born entirely of laziness; indeed, the divergent takes on a similar subject illustrate choices involved in making a picture about a primarily aural medium." Both documentaries feature aging Latin musicians displaying their expertise and musical chops. Viewers who felt that the *Buena Vista Social Club* spent too much time in conversation and who would have enjoyed seeing additional performance footage will be pleased with Trueba's documentary treatment. However, viewers who enjoy narrative arcs within documentaries or who enjoy witnessing intimate moments in the featured musicians' lives might come away feeling disappointed.

According to Trueba, "I think the only reason I make movies is because I can't write novels, paint or compose music. And making movies is the only activity where I feel like I do a little of each." Trueba's musical heroes have allowed the director countless hours of pleasure. So as a tribute to these diverse musicians who range in age and background, as well as musical styles, Trueba has documented never before seen or heard live recordings of the musicians' work. After necessary globe-trotting, the end result proves to be a captivating music documentary in which the musicians' rapturous performances ignite the screen. Agile fingers race across keyboards, hands pound furiously on congas and timbales while saxes and trumpets herald the musical gods. What ensues is a festivity of rhythm, haunting melodies, and musical innovation.

The barefoot Brazilian pianist Eliane Elias falls into a trance as her fingers race across a keyboard. Late Puerto Rican percussion Tito Puente (who passed away in 2000) can't seem to keep his tongue in his mouth as his hands attack timbales. Father and son, Bebo and Chucho Valdes, reunited after years of estrangement, play a touching duet on duel pianos. Spanish pianist Chano Dominguez successfully blends flamenco rhythms with Latin jazz by including flamenco dancers, clappers, and a gypsy vocalist, while creating aural fireworks. Dominican Michel Camilo, all smiles, wears a blue shirt that is as electric as his virtuoso piano performance. And a host of other musicians blend rhumbas, sambas, tangos, and salsas along with jazz syncopation.

While viewers do not need to be of Latin descent to enjoy this musical journey, it does help. Trueba highlights the Latin culture and family traditions along with the music. Although Latin music seems to be increasing in popularity among people of all backgrounds, Hispanic-Americans also seem to be increasing in numbers thus allowing a larger market for films relating to the Latin experience. One only needs to see the popularity of the *Buena Vista Social Club* soundtrack and all of its offspring. In any case, Trueba noted: "A friend is someone who introduces you to books, films, music and new friends. . . . And the aim of *Calle 54* is primarily to share a musical banquet with anyone who is ready for it."

Anyone who believes that music has lost its panache needs to look no further than this array of musicians. *Calle 54* is a music festival that explodes with mouth watering notations, insightful innovations and musical pyrotechnics. No wonder the festival audience in Toronto leapt to their feet in appreciation. *Calle 54* es caliente.

—*Patty-Lynne Herlevi*

**CREDITS**

**Origin:** USA

**Language:** Spanish
**Released:** 2001
**Production:** Christina Huete, Fabienne Servan Schreiber;
Arte France Cinema, Le Studio Canal Plus, Cineteve,
SGAE; released by Miramax Films
**Directed by:** Fernando Trueba
**Written by:** Fernando Trueba
**Cinematography by:** Jose Luis Lopez-Linares
**Sound:** Martin Gamet, Pierre Gamet
**Editing:** Carmen Frias
**MPAA rating:** G
**Running time:** 105 minutes

 **REVIEWS**

*Boxoffice.* July, 2001, p. 100.
*Entertainment Weekly.* May 25, 2001, p. 51.
*Seattle Weekly.* May 10, 2001, p. 87.
*USA Today Online.* May 11, 2001.
*Washington Post Online.* May 11, 2001.

 **TRIVIA**

The title means 54th Street, the location of Sony's New York
recording studio where Trueba filmed his performers.

# Captain Corelli's Mandolin

 **Box Office:** $25.5 million

A few months after the release of the Hollywood behemoth *Pearl Harbor* (also reviewed in this edition), a less bombastic movie about a World War II love triangle, *Captain Corelli's Mandolin,* debuted. Based on a popular novel by Louis de Bernieres, the film was directed by John Madden, who proved he could handle heartfelt period romances with the acclaimed *Shakespeare in Love.* This new film, shot entirely on the Greek island of Cephallonia where the novel is set, opened first in Great Britain, where it was roasted by critics who were not enchanted by the unusual casting and the indelicate handling of what some considered a precious literary work. In the United States, it was distributed by Miramax, the film company known for its success at promotional campaigns aimed at Academy Awards® voters and for a resultant bundles of Oscars® for its "small" pictures.

*Captain Corelli's Mandolin* certainly has the Miramax feel to it—a gauzy, pseudo-sophisticated blend of easily digestible ideas, picture-postcard settings, a tangy international flavor, and a deeply romantic point of view. Its plot is fairly faithful to the original novel, but it is also uncannily parallel to *Pearl Harbor.* In both films, a woman interested in medicine (Kate Beckinsale's nurse, or Penelope Cruz's Pelagia, who is training under her father to be a doctor) falls in love and gets engaged to a boy-next-door type who is going off to war. She writes tearful, heart-wrenching letters (which she narrates in a voiceover), but communications from her lover stop, and he is missing and presumed dead. Against her better judgment, the woman falls for another warrior, only to find that her original lover has returned— and she must choose between the two. The two men end up fighting side by side, and she fears one or the other will die.

Many other wartime romances have had similar plots, presenting a conflict from the viewpoint of the woman left behind, whose heart is tossed and turned by forces she cannot control. In this story, the beautiful, intelligent young Pelagia is living in an idyllic though sheltered setting with her sagacious father, Dr. Iannis (John Hurt), who fancies himself the village philosopher. Based on what little she knows of men and her heart, Pelagia believes she is in love with Mandras (Christian Bale), an illiterate and foolish but big-hearted fisherman. Her worldly father thinks Mandras is not good enough for her, because he is not as smart as her, and the doctor likes to speculate she would be better matched with a (presumably more enlightened) foreigner— this is the movie's idea of foreshadowing. Even Mandras's mother (Irene Papas) makes fun of her son, who is something of a buffoon. (The film clumsily underlines his ridiculousness by having him get hit in the buttocks by a rock shot out of a cannon during a village festival.) But against her father's advice, Pelagia and Mandras are betrothed just before Mandras goes off to join the Greek Army who are fighting the Italians in Albania. Pelagia writes him a hundred tear-stained letters but hears nothing in return.

Soon, the Germans invade Greece and conquer Athens, and they send contingents of Italians to occupy the islands under German supervision. Captain Corelli (Nicolas Cage) commands one of the units occupying the village. Conveniently for the progress of the love story, he is billeted at Dr. Iannis's home after the doctor negotiates a deal to get precious medical supplies in exchange for hosting the captain.

Corelli is a reluctant occupation chief. His troop is composed of opera singers, and they perform while shaving in the morning or doing maneuvers. Corelli, who constantly carries his mandolin with him, is more enthusiastic about Verdi than about Nazism. He frequently hurls barbed comments at the local German in charge, Captain Weber (David Morrissey), who tries to befriend him. In fact, none of Corelli's men is a big fan of Mussolini; they are simply serving their time in the military, trying to make the best of a bad situation. They have brought their own women with them, and they often drink and party. In one scene the women cavort and bare their breasts on the local beach, which is a neat way to give the film an unthreatening adult cachet.

Still, it is a war, and the Italians are an occupying force, and the two ancient cultures draw upon centuries of mutual resentment. The proud Greeks at first refuse to surrender to the Italians, and they insist on giving up the village's authority to a German. Similarly, Pelagia is at first disdainful of Corelli; she finds him crude and silly, making light of a situation in which her countrymen, including Mandras, are suffering and dying. The obligatory spats between them ensue—always a prelude to a love affair in this type of film. If there is any doubt as to where their relationship is heading, the scene in which Corelli first plays the mandolin should resolve it, because the music has an inexplicable mesmerizing effect on Pelagia. It's the kind of movie where a woman can be swept away by one delicate song. The hackneyed scenes unfold with predictable precision. If you enjoy meaningful glances across tables or dance floors or war scenes, *Captain Corelli's Mandolin* should satiate your appetite for such standard romantic foreplay. If you find such scenes ridiculously trite, however, you will find the long middle of the movie drags on and on until the inevitable occurs.

After the mutual longing is consummated, there is still almost an hour left, and some unanticipated plot developments finally occur. Following one another in an awkward fashion are a battle scene and some war atrocities, and an uneasy postwar epilogue that includes a quick earthquake and a puzzling delay until the fulfillment of the romantic promise.

Until these rather anticlimactic plot twists, nothing is a surprise except the casting choices for the two main roles. In his career, Cage has ranged across comic, action and dramatic roles, usually acquitting himself well, but he would not be the first choice to come to mind to play a devil-may-care "life-is-beautiful" Italian. Penelope Cruz has been a star in Spanish cinema and lends an earthy gravity to her role, but she does not fire up the screen. Both Cage and Cruz are good at looking dumbstruck, as if they were daydreaming their way through the frequent stolen-glances scenes and absurdly overripe situations with which they are burdened.

Madden aims for verisimilitude in shooting on Cephallonia and including many precious scenes of village life. But his is a greeting-card kind of realism, and how he has chosen to handle the language problem illustrates its deficiencies. He has a British actor playing Dr. Iannis, the narrator, and Hurt is insufferable and not remotely believable as a Greek. He has an American playing an Italian, and although Cage has obviously studied hard to perfect his accent, it still sounds forced. Cruz does not look at all Greek.

Bale is also British; the only Greek among the major characters is Papas. The accents hardly matter, though, since all the characters inexplicably speak English. This makes for some strange moments. For example, during the key surrender scene in which Corelli is introduced, he is supposed to serve as a translator between the Greeks, Italians and Germans. Since he is doing all the translation into English, the whole scene founders. Also, characters read newspaper accounts of the war written in Greek and discuss them in English. It's strange to stick with English and then include scenes that puncture the illusion you are trying to create.

But the Miramax treatment demands a sort of fairytale pseudo-realism in which the simple life of a European village is depicted as profound. The film opens and closes with paired scenes about a patient whom Iannis has cured of deafness complaining about how he can now hear his wife's nagging, and an annual holy day ritual in which the town's sick and infirm are prayed over. These are supposed to create philosophical bookends for the story, but they are too precious by half. Iannis the narrator explains the moral and perspective of the movie several times: It's about doing what you can to heal wounds in a world where the Gods and fate control your destiny. Iannis is impossibly (and irritatingly) wise. He's the kind of father who knows everything that is in his daughter's heart, and gives her pompous lectures about the difference between love and lust immediately after she returns from her tryst with Corelli.

Indications of the film's disdain for real authenticity abound amid its endless evocations of trite peasant images and its shameless manipulation of emotions. Pelagia is always carrying about a basket of some flowers or herbs. She or her neighbor's daughter is always staring at the sea at some opportune moment. Village buildings that are reduced to rubble one day emerge miraculously unscathed the next. A character who has been near death awakens from a coma with his skin tanned and healthy looking. And what can you say for the dignity of a film that creates the impression a major character has died in a quake only to have him discovered a few anxious moments later alive and outside the house?

*Captain Corelli's Mandolin* is pretty, and its blend of fatalistic, romantic philosophy can be intoxicating to certain viewers. But few of its scenes or ideas are original or compelling. This is formulaic romance, stuffed with platitudes, and revolving around the vulnerability of a woman in wartime—made no less vulnerable just because she is intelligent and ambitious. As played by Cruz, Pelagia seems passive and reactive, buffeted and bereft, but rarely intriguing. As played by Cage, Corelli is a man whose lust for life seems rather forced and constrained. There is little grandeur in their romance or in the story of Cephallonia that surrounds it—and there is no gritty, slice-of-life honesty in Madden's depiction of the larger issues the film toys with. While *Pearl*

*Harbor* was derided by critics as being obvious and emotionally exploitative, *Captain Corelli's Mandolin* is just a highbrow version of the same tired, outdated story. Despite its more sophisticated trappings, it is just as cheap.

—*Michael Betzold*

## CREDITS

**Capt. Antonio Corelli:** Nicolas Cage
**Pelagia:** Penelope Cruz
**Mandras:** Christian Bale
**Dr. Iannis:** John Hurt
**Capt. Weber:** David Morrissey
**Drosoula:** Irene Papas
**Col. Barge:** Patrick Malahide

**Origin:** Great Britain, USA
**Released:** 2001
**Production:** Tim Bevan, Eric Fellner, Kevin Loader, Mark Huffam; Working Title Productions, Free Range Films; released by Universal Pictures
**Directed by:** John Madden
**Written by:** Shawn Slovo
**Cinematography by:** John Toll
**Music by:** Stephen Warbeck
**Sound:** Peter Lindsay, Adrian Rhodes
**Editing:** Mick Audsley
**Art Direction:** Gary Freeman
**Costumes:** Alexandra Byrne
**Production Design:** Jim Clay
**MPAA rating:** R
**Running time:** 127 minutes

## REVIEWS

*Boxoffice.* October, 2001, p. 62.
*Chicago Sun-Times Online.* August 17, 2001.
*Entertainment Weekly.* August 24, 2001, p. 103.
*Los Angeles Times Online.* August 17, 2001.
*New York Times Online.* August 17, 2001.
*People.* August 27, 2001, p. 35.
*Sight and Sound.* May, 2001, p. 17.
*USA Today Online.* August 17, 2001.
*Variety.* April 30, 2001, p. 25.
*Washington Post.* August 17, 2001, p. WE37.

## QUOTES

Dr. Iannis (John Hurt): "When you fall in love, it is a temporary madness. It erupts like an earthquake, and then it subsides."

## TRIVIA

Louis de Bernieres's novel *Captain Corelli's Mandolin* was published in 1994.

# Cats & Dogs

*Things are gonna get hairy.*
—Movie tagline

 **Box Office:** $93.4 million

From the days of TV's *Mister Ed* and much farther back, talking animals have been a staple of entertainment fantasies. Human beings who grow close to their pets or work animals imagine them speaking and invest them with all kinds of human attributes. In cartoons, animals that talk have always hogged the majority of screen time—it's one of the best uses of animation. Making a live animal talk, however, adds both to the realism and the incongruity of the feat—and thus carries the potential for more humor.

Technical advances now allow filmmakers several choices for talking animal movies—straight animation, mechanical creations, or computer-graphic enhancement of live animals. The problem is, even with these improvements, animals moving their mouths now look only slightly more realistic than Mr. Ed did. The most successful of the modern talking animal movies—such as *Babe*—have strong stories. Others, such as *Dr. Dolittle,* play it strictly for laughs. *Cats and Dogs* is a hybrid—in many ways. At times, this live-action feature is one of the wackiest movies ever conceived. Then, a few minutes later, it's drowning in sentimental goo. It doesn't make much sense, which would be fine if it stuck to its anarchic tone throughout. Unfortunately, it's all over the map.

The premise is that dogs and cats are in a war for worldwide domination. That's hardly a new idea, but *Cats and Dogs* gives each side a formidable arsenal. The dogs—or at least some of them—belong to a worldwide counter-terrorist organization that is obviously modeled on *Mission: Impossible.* Those in the "agency" communicate by audio-video collars, access control panels in their doghouses, and get together by traveling in rockets that connect by tunnels under their doghouses. Their mission is to thwart feline efforts to remove the pups from their rightful place as humans' best friends.

The newest threat to canine hegemony is Mr. Twinkles (voice of Sean P. Hayes), a megalomaniacal white Persian who lives in a mansion owned by a comatose factory owner but actually run by an overbearing maid who likes to bathe the cat and dress him in silly outfits. In between these undignified sojourns, Twinkles is plotting to take over the world. His immediate goal is to steal a formula being developed by Professor Brody (Jeff Goldbum) that would cure human beings who have dog allergies. Twinkles starts by having his minions kidnap Buddy, the beloved pet dog of the Brody family. After a long chase, the dog is decoyed by a cat pretending to lay dead in the street, then whisked away in a van.

When the dog network's local head agent, Butch (voice of Alec Baldwin), learns of the kidnapping, headquarters tells him they will send a replacement to guard the Brody household. But when Carolyn Brody (Elizabeth Perkins) goes to a farm to select a new puppy to cheer up her son Scott (Alexander Pollock), she selects an adventure-seeking young beagle instead of one of the agent dogs (who have dognapped the remaining beagles). But Scott is still mourning the death of Buddy and he calls the beagle "Loser," which mom corrects to Lou (voiced by Tobey Maguire).

Butch soon finds out Lou doesn't have the proper training, but the eager little beagle quickly warms to the task of being a secret agent after meeting Butch's local gang of co-conspirators, which includes a clumsy something named Sam (voiced by Michael Clarke Duncan) and a communications-specialist Pekinese named Peek (voiced by Joe Pantoliano). Lou helps fends off various forays by Mr. Twinkles' forces, including a kamikaze attack by flying Siamese ninjas and a sneaky invasion by a Russian kitten who is an explosives expert and coughs up hairballs that contain deadly weapons and (to get Lou into trouble with the humans) a fresh pile of dog feces.

The various battles between dogs and cats—and the conversations among the members of the two competing armies—are often interrupted by the intrusion of humans, at which point the animals act like humans expect them to do—sniffing each other's behinds or pawing in the dirt. All this ranges from pleasantly wacky to way over the top, but it's plunked down in the middle of a terribly overplayed lonely-boy-meets-dog saga.

Scott, who is cute as a button, doesn't seem to have any friends, can't get his mad-inventor father (who has a laboratory in the basement) to remember to pay attention to him, and is constantly patronized by his real-estate agent mother, who is trying way too hard to be the perfect supermom. To add to his woes, he doesn't do well in the tryouts for the travel soccer team. Lou is increasingly torn between his built-in, boyish desire for adventure and his growing affection for Scott. A homeless former beau of Butch, Ivy (voice of Susan Sarandon), shows up and counsels Lou to cherish his human companionship. However, Butch keeps warning Lou that his first loyalties are to his organization.

Not only does this make for some blatantly sappy moments, including a slow-motion montage of Scott and Lou

playing together that looks like it came out of an old-fashioned TV commercial,it also makes the plot break down. Are we supposed to root for the dogs in their battle against the fiendish cats when the dogs themselves place their own status above that of the families they are supposed to be loyal to? Well, there is certainly more pleasure in rooting for the cats. With a strong assist from Hayes, who combines oozing British classism with a sort of psuedo-fascism, and from Jon Lovitz, perfectly insolent as one of Twinkles' underlings, Calico, the cats are much the more interesting creatures. In comparison, the dogs seem a little slow and clumsy.

The whole thing ends in a confusing mess, with huge and illogical jumps in the action and some awfully awkward editing. John Requa and Glenn Ficarra's very offbeat script succumbs in the end to its own contrary impulses of wanting to be both cuddly and cynically clever. Ivy disappears from the picture without explanation, and director Lawrence Guterman is more intent on milking easy laughs than at tying up many loose ends. Goldblum is not at all funny, while Perkins strives mightily to inject some humor into her stale role.

But as with all talking-animal pictures, the film's impact depends on execution. With Jim Henson's Creature Shop providing some of the fake live animals, and this work melded together with cute and well-trained real dogs and cats whose mouths move through the magic of computer animation, the result could have been a marvel of invention. Instead, it's a pastiche of mismatched shots, with all the seams showing between the various techniques. In a way, it's a relief to find a film that's not afraid to show animals flying through the air, smashing into doors and ceilings, and engaging in brutal combat, but the way in which they turn from obvious live animals to cinematic rag dolls should be obvious even to the youngest tykes. In the most frantic action scenes, the editing is so hectic and the focus so often fuzzy that it's obvious the filmmakers are covering up the tawdry-looking transitions between the various modes of filming the story.

Strange as it may seem, the more high-tech tricks that are employed to make talking animals seem realistic, the more unrealistic they look, and *Cats and Dogs* is inadvertently an argument for traditional animation. At least in that mode, belief can be more easily suspended. In this film the fantasy world of talking animals and the real world as viewed by humans co-exist uncomfortably and then merge inconsistently.

Along the way, there's no doubt that the filmmakers are having fun, paying homage to all manner of movies from westerns to adventures to romances to political documentaries. But it's a herky-jerky, grab-bag effort and it produces something of a soporific effect. The movie's jokes and bizarre conceits register on the brain, which recognizes that they ought to be funny, but they fail to emit laughs. Kids, however, will enjoy the general mayhem and won't care much about the inconsistent tone. It all adds up to a boxoffice hit for Warner Bros. and even more incentive for more talking-animal movies.

—*Michael Betzold*

## CREDITS

**Professor Brody:** Jeff Goldblum
**Mrs. Brody:** Elizabeth Perkins
**Sophie:** Miriam Margolyes
**Scott Brody:** Alexander Pollock
**Russian Kitty:** Glenn Ficarra (Voice)
**Lou:** Tobey Maguire (Voice)
**Mr. Twinkles:** Sean P. Hayes (Voice)
**Butch:** Alec Baldwin (Voice)
**Peek:** Joe Pantoliano (Voice)
**Ivy:** Susan Sarandon (Voice)
**Sam:** Michael Clarke Duncan (Voice)
**Calico:** Jon Lovitz (Voice)
**The Mastiff:** Charlton Heston (Voice)
**Collie:** Salome Jens (Voice)

**Origin:** USA
**Released:** 2001
**Production:** Warren Zide, Andrew Lazar, Christopher DeFaria, Craig Perry; Village Roadshow Pictures, NPV Entertainment, Mad Chance; released by Warner Bros.
**Directed by:** Lawrence (Larry) Guterman
**Written by:** John Requa, Glenn Ficarra
**Cinematography by:** Julio Macat
**Music by:** John Debney
**Sound:** Larry Sutton
**Editing:** Michael A. Stevenson, Rick W. Finney
**Art Direction:** Sandra Tanaka
**Costumes:** Tish Monaghan
**Production Design:** James Bissell
**MPAA rating:** PG
**Running time:** 87 minutes

## REVIEWS

*Boxoffice.* September, 2001, p. 151.
*Chicago Sun-Times Online.* July 4, 2001.
*Entertainment Weekly.* July 13, 2001, p. 56.
*Los Angeles Times Online.* July 4, 2001.
*New York Times Online.* July 4, 2001.
*People.* July 16, 2001, p. 31.
*Sight and Sound.* September, 2001, p. 38.
*USA Today Online.* July 4, 2001.
*Variety.* July 9, 2001, p. 20.
*Washington Post Online.* July 6, 2001.

## QUOTES

Mr. Twinkles (Sean P. Hayes): "Cats rule."

 ## TRIVIA

There are more than 800 visual effects in the movie.

# The Caveman's Valentine

*Romulus Ledbetter lives on the edge. The view is incredible.*
—Movie tagline

**Box Office:** $.6 million

Samuel L. Jackson's multidimensional performance in *The Caveman's Valentine* proves that this prolific, versatile and well-respected actor can do more than just strike the pose of a John Shaft or a Jedi councilor. Jackson invests so much emotion and humanity in his character, a delusional wanderer living in a cave in Central Park, that the preposterous though admirably offbeat story at the heart of this disappointing film almost comes to life.

Characteristically a smooth customer in his many movie roles, Jackson turns into a raving, wild-eyed madman as Romulus Ledbetter. Known as the Caveman, Ledbetter is a paranoid, hallucinating street person who believes an omnipotent businessman named Cornelius Gould Stuyvesant is watching him from the tower of the Chrysler Building. Wearing a huge overcoat, a rectangular fur hat, and very long dreadlocks, the imposing Jackson looks like a formidable urban beast. He raves to passersby about his defiance of the vengeful Stuyvesant, whom he believes to be controlling the city while broadcasting the Caveman's every movement on his own television network.

Jackson not only stars in *Valentine*, he helped to produce the film, just as he did with director Kasi Lemmons's first film, *Eve's Bayou*. In this higher-budgeted effort Lemmons makes frequent and creative use of video segments and a bizarre, hallucinatory soundtrack by Terence Blanchard to display a disconcerting vortex which recreates Caveman's disorienting mental world. Sometimes the Chrysler Building sends out golden "Z-rays" or green "Y-rays" that seek to overpower Ledbetter's mind; in these scenes, Lemmons makes the building seem absolutely menacing. Sometimes the Caveman sees televised images, even though the TV he watches is not plugged in to anything. And that is how he first experiences a murder scene outside his cave, by seeing it on his TV set.

When he discovers the frozen dead body of young homeless Scotty in a tree near his park, Ledbetter feels a compulsion to investigate, especially since he believes Scotty recently left him a scrawled plea for help on a poster on a street. Another homeless drug addict, Matthew (Rodney Eastman), tells the Caveman that Scotty used to be a model for renowned artist David Leppenraub (Colm Feore), who has become a huge success in upper-class art circles for his homoerotic photographs, which trade heavily on images of sadism interspersed with religious icons. Matthew swears to Ledbetter that Leppenraub tortured Scotty, and it was all captured on videotape, and that when Scotty tried to blackmail Leppenraub by threatening to go public with the tape, the artist had him murdered. This all dovetails rather neatly into the Caveman's paranoid fantasies; he immediately figures Leppenraub is a pawn of the dreaded Stuyvesant.

The screenplay for *The Caveman's Valentine* was written by George Dawes Green, based on Green's own novel. In the novel, the multi-layered and fascinating paranoia of the Caveman helps to create a fuzzy dissonance in which art and big business blur the line between reality and delusion. But some of the novel's quirky conceits end up looking a little ridiculous on film, despite the Herculean efforts of Lemmons to keep many pots boiling at once. Many memorable images and scenes, bolstered by Jackson's on-target renderings of a man who slips in and out of rationality, fail to compensate for the considerable weaknesses of the story.

Lemmons chooses wisely when she employs frequent apparitions and clever whispers from Jackson's estranged wife Sheila (the lustrous Tamara Tunie) to provide the Caveman with an inner voice of rationality as he struggles to keep his mind together. The scenes with Sheila are knowing, clever, comic and expertly realized.

But none of the techniques that Lemmons employs makes it any easier to believe in the rather strained plot. It's very hard to swallow that Ledbetter was once a renowned concert pianist who fell apart and turned to living in a cave just because of performance anxiety. And flashback images of a winged dance troupe that keep haunting the Caveman make no sense at all, though they would look stunning in a music video.

The occasionally intriguing quirkiness of the story, music, settings and performances is unraveled by a rather pedestrian murder plot. To try to pin down Scotty's murderer, the Caveman goes to Leppenraub's studio, on an upstate farm, and there becomes attracted to his sister Moira (Ann Magnuson). This leads to the film's most ridiculous scene. After the Caveman spoils his piano performance at a ritzy party by accusing Leppenraub of murder and is thrown out of the farm as a lunatic, a henchman in a white mask tries to run him down with a car and shoot him on a country road.

Ledbetter coolly makes his way back to the farm and spends the night with the accommodating Moira. Talk about grace under fire!

Through his rather unorthodox investigative techniques, the Caveman is trying to prove to his daughter Lulu (Aunjanue Ellis), a New York police officer, that Leppenraub is the murderer. So he keeps skulking around the farm looking for evidence. Solving the murder would redeem himself in the eyes of his daughter. Soon the once-brave movie turns maudlin. Lulu and her father seem to be reconciling as she drives him around New York City and they reminisce about old, saner days. Then she abruptly throws him out of her car just because he again asks her for the autopsy report on Scotty. She acts as if the request were absolute evidence of his madness.

As the murder investigation plot chugs fitfully along, the movie concentrates less and less on the Caveman's hallucinations. Are the Chrysler Building and its evil occupant losing their hold over the Caveman, an indication that he is healing mentally? Or is the film merely growing tired of a going-nowhere device that the script never ties in to the rest of the proceedings? After awhile, you give up on any explanation of who Stuyvesant is or how the Caveman worked up such an elaborate mental force field about this mythical person (his name is a combination of three New York historical figures). A richer plot would have dovetailed the Caveman's delusions about Stuyvesant with his real-life villains; instead, Green comes up embarrassingly empty.

It's never quite clear what the larger point of this film is. Themes about the pretensions of popular art, the poison of artistic conceit, and the control of the wealthy and powerful over the homeless and indigent keep popping up, but they are never allowed to ripen. The metaphysical reasons for the Caveman's madness aren't well developed. The story becomes more and more ordinary, turning up the juice on the rather uninvolving murder plot and the insipid father-daughter reunion theme.

A final series of plot twists leaves the viewer utterly cold. This is the type of movie where everything is explained in a rapid-fire monologue during a showdown scene in a subway car. It's a bad sign when the protagonist has to explain the tables-turning plot developments in a long set speech. And it is most unpleasant when the climax suggests that the Caveman and the film's most odious character are going to end up being good friends.

While *The Caveman's Valentine* is more successful than most Hollywood movies at capturing the dynamics of mental illness, it's not because the script has anything new to say about the contours of what society sees as delusional behavior. Most of the credit for believability should go to Jackson. At one minute his character seems fully in command of his capacities, but then he is overcome by fear and confusion, and he seems to drown emotionally before our eyes. Jackson's performance is by turns exhilarating, frightening, hilarious, and bizarre. His range is incredible, and his physical presence astounding. When he plays piano for an amazingly (and unbelievably) accommodating bankruptcy lawyer (Anthony Michael Hall) and his wife, it's a memorable performance.

Ultimately, though, the welcome inventiveness of the film is dragged down by the contrivances of its pedestrian and often ludicrous murder plot and the inability of the script to connect the Caveman's madness to the events that unfold around him. This is the kind of film in which an award-worthy performance can be scuttled by the mediocrity of the script. Director Lemmons's firm grasp on the weird material slips halfway through the film, as if she has lost confidence in her ability to involve the audience in the world of the main character. Stunning visuals at the start of the film give way to almost a sitcom feeling by film's end.

Despite Jackson's great efforts, Romulus Ledbetter makes less sense at the end of the film than he did at the beginning. At least at the start, his paranoia and madness had the feel of authenticity, but he is beaten down eventually and inexorably by convention. We are left with confusion about his fate: Can the Caveman adapt to society? Does he even want to? Are his demons exorcised? The script is uncomfortably silent on all these points.

*The Caveman's Valentine* did not live up to expectations upon its release, getting a lukewarm reception from critics and audiences. It seemed to lack the energy and guts to make it as a cult film, which was its only real hope for success. But against all odds, Jackson's performance may endure. His wild man riff is irresistible.

—*Michael Betzold*

## CREDITS

**Romulus Ledbetter:** Samuel L. Jackson
**Lulu:** Aunjanue Ellis
**David Leppenraub:** Colm Feore
**Moira:** Ann Magnuson
**Matthew:** Rodney Eastman
**Sheila:** Tamara Tunie
**Bob:** Anthony Michael Hall
**Joey:** Jay Rodan

**Origin:** USA
**Released:** 2001
**Production:** Danny DeVito, Michael Shamberg, Stacey Sher, Elie Samaha, Andrew Stevens; Franchise Pictures, Jersey Shore, Arroyo Films; released by Universal Focus
**Directed by:** Kasi Lemmons
**Written by:** George Dawes Green
**Cinematography by:** Amelia Vincent
**Music by:** Terence Blanchard

**Sound:** Glen Gauthier
**Editing:** Terilyn Shropshire
**Art Direction:** Grant Van Der Slagt
**Costumes:** Denise Cronenberg
**Production Design:** Robin Standefer
**MPAA rating:** R
**Running time:** 105 minutes

## REVIEWS

*Chicago Sun-Times Online.* March 2, 2001.
*Entertainment Weekly.* March 16, 2001, p. 43.
*Hollywood Reporter.* January 19, 2001, p. 20.
*New York Times Online.* March 2, 2001.
*Variety.* January 22, 2001, p. 45.
*Washington Post Online.* March 9, 2001.

## QUOTES

Romulus (Samuel L. Jackson) on his schizophrenia: "I have brain typhoons."

## TRIVIA

Samuel L. Jackson worked with Kasi Lemmons in her directorial debut, *Eve's Bayou.*

# The Center of the World

*Warning. Sex. Come closer. Enter.*
—Movie tagline

*1. No kissing on the mouth. 2. No talking about feelings or emotions. 3. No more than 3 days and 3 nights. 4. No penetration. 5. $10,000 cash, up-front. These are my terms. Florence*
—Movie tagline

 **Box Office:** $1.1 million

A Silicon Valley venture capitalist hires a stripper to spend three days with him in Las Vegas only this isn't a cross between *Pretty Woman* and *Leaving Las Vegas.* Wayne Wang's *The Center of the World* is in fact, a misogynist diatribe that barely tackles the power struggle between the sexes but instead exploits feminine beauty and sensuality by reducing female sexuality to the lowest common denominator. And if Wang's digital video improvised film weren't laughable it would certainly be appalling to at least to some women viewers. Wang's effort follows a trend of Dogme 95-style films that cater to human exploitation and cry out "look we have a lightweight camera that goes anywhere," with the problem being that the camera goes places that should be left only to one's imagination.

Wang might have written and directed a poignant cinematic work had he concentrated less on a detached sexual act, omitted the rape scene, and focused on the characters' personalities outside of the sexual arena. We garner bits and pieces about the characters such as Florence (Molly Parker) worked at Wal-Mart to pay her way through college and majored in physics before she became a stripper at Pandora's Box. But none of this explains why she became a stripper or what motivated her (besides a $10,000 fee) to spend three nights whoring with a computer geek. We understand that Richard (Peter Sarsgaard) is a lonely computer porn-obsessed man looking for love in the wrong places. But he's a difficult character to empathize with because, even though he plays Mr. Nice Guy, he's also manipulates Florence into falling in love with him then, when she acts detached, he rapes her.

The problem with digital or any type of video production is that directors allow for too much improvisation. In the right hands, improvisation can lead to fresh dialogue and a new way for characters to relate to each other. However, Wang's feature comes across as awkward at best. Had Wang and his team of writers focused on the power struggle between Florence and Richard an intriguing story line might have been more fully developed. Wouldn't the film have been more interesting if Richard lost everything due to his sexual demons and manipulative attitude? Or if Richard's attraction to stripper Florence had been fully examined? Is this only about sex?

An article in *Film Comment* states that Artisan Entertainment, "wins the booby prize for the quickest fall from the top of the indies heap" after *Book of Shadows: Blair Witch 2* flopped at the boxoffice. Judging from audience response to *The Center of the World*, Artisan will most likely sink deeper into the red. After the success of *The Blair Witch Project*, the distributor has miscalculated the risks of buying the rights to digital video projects.

Molly Parker, who is known for portraying dangerous characters, rises above Wang's cliché-laced script. But some viewers who have seen Parker in such films as Michael Winterbottom's *Wonderland* might wonder what possessed the actress to take on such a role. At least with Lynne Stopkewich's *Kissed* and *Suspicious River*, sexual acts were mostly implied and the characters' acts led to redemption of one type or another. Here, Florence performs lap dances for

lonely men to support her career as a drummer in a punk band.

*The Center of the World* received mixed reviews. Jeffrey M. Anderson of *The San Francisco Examiner* called the film a "passionate, dark and delicate achievement." However, A. O. Scott of the *New York Times* as well as Richard Horton of *Film.com* panned the film and Scott felt that the performers were worthy of better material.

It's safe to wonder why Wang's fascination with sexuality led him to direct a sexual exploitation film. Why would a director who in the past expertly handled delicate material about the human bond (as in the film *The Joy Luck Club*) waste his sensitivities on a tawdry film that offers nothing new? Every director is entitled to at least one boxoffice failure, but *The Center of the World* also fails its crew, cast and viewers. Wang would have been less self-indulgent had he considered the price of admission.

—*Patty-Lynne Herlevi*

 **CREDITS**

**Richard Longman:** Peter Sarsgaard
**Florence:** Molly Parker
**Jerri:** Carla Gugino
**Brian Pivano:** Balthazar Getty
**Roxane:** Mel Gorham

**Origin:** USA
**Released:** 2001
**Production:** Peter Newman, Wayne Wang; Redeemable Features; released by Artisan Entertainment
**Directed by:** Wayne Wang
**Written by:** Wayne Wang
**Cinematography by:** Mauro Fiore
**Sound:** James Steube
**Music Supervisor:** Deva Anderson, Deva Anderson
**Editing:** Lee Percy
**Art Direction:** Diana Kunce
**Costumes:** Sophie de Rakoff Carbonell
**Production Design:** Donald Graham Burt
**MPAA rating:** Unrated
**Running time:** 86 minutes

**REVIEWS**

*Boxoffice.* May, 2001, p. 58.
*Chicago Sun-Times Online.* May 4, 2001.
*Entertainment Weekly.* April 27, 2001, p. 88.
*Los Angeles Times Online.* April 20, 2001.
*New York Times Online.* April 18, 2001.
*Sight and Sound.* October, 2001, p. 43.
*Variety.* April 23, 2001, p. 17.

*Washington Post Online.* May 11, 2001.

## QUOTES

Florence (Molly Parker) describes her college physics courses: "You know, black holes and big bangs."

## TRIVIA

Wayne Wang wrote the screenplay using the pseudonym Ellen Benjamin Wong.

# Chopper

*"Never let the truth get in the way of a good story."*
—Movie tagline

Andrew Dominik's indulgent and harrowingly violent *Chopper,* while based on a real-life serial killer who achieved notoriety as a best-selling author, and who is currently living on a farm in Australia, comes across as a stag movie that substitutes violence for sex.

Mark Reid, the Chopper, as played by Eric Bana, resembles Rob Reiner of TV's *All in the Family,* and sometimes even looks as congenial. The film takes up Reid's story when he's already serving heavy time in prison for abducting a judge. These prison scenes unfold amidst spotless white settings, against which the blood spreading across bodies and floors stands out even more. Reid's first target is Keithy (David Field), a fellow prisoner whom he bludgeons so as to affirm his own rule over the cell block. Sitting up on a blood-splattered floor, Keithy still has the spunk to curse the Chopper as someone who just craves cheap publicity. Reid, on his part, breaks down after the deed, and even offers his victim a cigarette. We remain in the dark as to what trauma in Reid's past could have led him to such violent behavior. Reid's genuine regret, however, which surfaces repeatedly after his acts of brutality throughout the film, introduces a rare element into the genre of the crime film.

After Keithy succumbs to his injuries, Reid practices the first of his many imaginative deceptions, claiming that no one saw anything. The film makes clear whose side it is on when, as in the killings to follow, we are shown the event recreated in line with Reid's testimony. The prison detectives, like their counterparts in the instances to come, have no proof to charge Reid. To his compatriots, which include Jimmy (Simon Lyndon) and Bluey (Dan Wyllie), Reid maintains that it was a preemptive strike.

Reid's winning personality has the prison guards on his side as well. It is they who tell him that there's a contract out on him. What Reid doesn't suspect is that Jimmy has been chosen to do away with him. In a stylized ritual, Reid allows Jimmy to stab him repeatedly, even embracing him, and refusing to squeal. The attack however brings Reid national publicity. Reid then has parts of his ears "chopped" off so as to convince the authorities to transfer him to another facility.

The film then skips to Reid's release. With his Fu Manchu mustache, and a reputation that has preceded him, Reid is a hero on the local club scene. Lacking any strength of character, he soon falls victim to the wiles of illicit drugs and indiscriminate sex, both provided by Tanya (Kate Beahan), whose walks on the wild side end with the Chopper bludgeoning her in front of her mother, after he suspects her of carrying on with one of his prison chums behind his back.

When his father teases him about the paisley print on the shirt he's wearing, we get something of a clue as to what kind of childhood trauma could have instigated Reid's behavior. Of immediate concern to Reid becomes the contract he suspects has been put out on him by the former inmate, and now wealthy, Neville (Vince Colosimo), who is living the life of the druggy prince.

As Reid picks out his targets, which include Jimmy, who is now settled with a pregnant fiancée and little daughter, there is a level at which he wins the audience's sympathy, since these criminals have no right to be living as well as they are. Reid's most astonishing killing, or so the film would have us believe, is when he blows off the head of Sammy the Turk (Serge Liistro) in the club parking lot in another preemptive move. This time, as he spins his account of the bloody event, the law doesn't believe him, but for the wrong reason; they've apprehended the real culprit. Reid does get slapped with minor time.

Having disclaimed any biographical intent, the film now cuts to a TV interview with Reid, with him watching the telecast from his cell, thrilled to the gills. Reid is glorified as having committed 19 murders, charged with one, and acquitted of that. This final scene does contain a wallop for any viewer prepared to "read" the image: in the background, on a shelf of the cell, beside the color TV is a large boombox, the accoutrements of luxury, which have now become a part of the penal system.

Stephen Holden in the *New York Times* can be taken to represent the consensus of critical opinion when he says that "the most disturbing thing about *Chopper* is the reality factor." He finds Eric Bana's performance "scarily convincing" in portraying "a volatile emotional cycle."

—*Vivek Adarkar*

## CREDITS

**Mark "Chopper" Read:** Eric Bana
**Neville Bartos:** Vince Colosimo
**Jimmy Loughnan:** Simon Lyndon
**Keithy George:** David Field
**Bluey:** Daniel Wyllie
**Detective Downey:** Bill Young
**Kevin Darcy:** Gary Waddell
**Tanya:** Kate Beahan
**Keith Read:** Kenny Graham

**Origin:** Australia
**Released:** 2000
**Production:** Michele Bennett; Australian Film Finance Corp., Mushroom Pictures, Pariah Films; released by First Look Pictures
**Directed by:** Andrew Dominik
**Written by:** Andrew Dominik
**Cinematography by:** Geoffrey Hall
**Music by:** Mick Harvey
**Sound:** Frank Lipson
**Editing:** Ken Sallows
**Art Direction:** Jeff Thorp
**Costumes:** Terry Ryan
**Production Design:** Paddy Reardon
**MPAA rating:** Unrated
**Running time:** 94 minutes

## REVIEWS

*Boxoffice.* November, 2000, p. 176.
*Chicago Sun-Times Online.* June 1, 2001.
*Entertainment Weekly.* April 20, 2001, p. 46.
*Los Angeles Times Calendar.* April 8, 2001, p. 20.
*Los Angeles Times Online.* April 13, 2001.
*New York Times Online.* April 11, 2001.
*Newsweek.* April 23, 2001, p. 58.
*Village Voice.* April 17, 2001, p. 139.
*Washington Post Online.* May 18, 2001.

## TRIVIA

Mark Read has written nine autobiographical bestsellers, including *How to Shoot Friends and Influence People.*

## AWARDS AND NOMINATIONS

**Australian Film Inst. 2000:** Actor (Bana), Director (Dominik), Support. Actor (Lyndon)

**Nomination:**
**Australian Film Inst. 2000:** Adapt. Screenplay, Cinematog., Film, Film Editing, Sound, Score.

# La Cienaga (The Swamp)

*La Cienaga* wasn't the most talked-about movie at the 2001 New York Film Festival, but it unobtrusively made its own profound impact. Former documentarian Lucrecia Martel created this languorous but intriguing tale about two Argentinean families tossed together at the conclusion of a smoldering hot summer. If the plot sounds like something from Luis Bunuel, the mood is more dark than darkly comical. Mecha (Graciela Borges) is a middle-class matron who lives in the country with her self-absorbed husband and a dysfunctional household of slothful grown children and unhappy servants.

Mecha's less prosperous cousin, Tali (Mercedes Moran), lives in the city (called La Cienaga or "The Swamp"), but suddenly needs a place for her family to stay. Tali's husband is more faithful to his wife, and Tali's children are younger and rowdier than Mecha's, but Mecha welcomes them all into her dilapidated estate. As the two families come together under one roof, nerves become frayed. In an atmosphere of insufferable heat, the adults exchange cross words, the youngsters party hedonistically, incestuous crushes end badly, and petty jealousies lead to fighting. Finally, an unexpected tragedy ends the sad and sorry saga.

The Argentinean-born Martel uses a seemingly routine series of episodes, primarily insensitive characters, and a harsh, neorealist style for her first fiction film (Martel's documentaries include *Dead King* [1995] and *Silvina Ocampo* [1998].) By showing the tiresome lives of these families in a ordinary way, Martel risks losing her audience to boredom and frustration, particularly at the start (there are many scenes of people simply laying in bed).

Fortunately, as *La Cienaga* proceeds, the stark depiction of these lost souls becomes increasingly more compelling, with an ending which is as poignant as any melodrama (though not at all melodramatic). Martel's critique of class impudence and its sorrowful effects is never overwhelmingly conspicuous, and the "slice-of-life" style makes the ideological points all the more meaningful. Without making an obvious statement about it, Martel indicts an entire older generation who condoned the Argentinean government's "dirty war" campaign on their own citizenry. Their blindness is symbolized by the literal blindness of Mercedes Moran's arrogant diva character (modeled after the definitive shrew, Harriet Craig).

Martel gets persuasive work from the cast, especially Graciela Borges and Moran as the "city mouse-country mouse" cousins. The production superbly maintains a natural appearance, ever-threatening to become surreal and hallucinatory. One second-order continuity mistake, involving Mecha's disappearing (then re-appearing) bandages, doesn't detract from the overall technical expertise of the production. *La Cienaga* is well worth seeking out, however difficult it may be to find.

—*Eric Monder*

## CREDITS

**Gregorio:** Martin Adjemian
**Joaquin:** Diego Baenas
**Veronica:** Leonora Balcarce
**Mercedes:** Silvia Bayle
**Momi:** Sofia Bertolotto
**Jose:** Juan Cruz Bordeu
**Mecha:** Graciela Borges
**Rafael:** Daniel Valenzuela
**Tali:** Mercedes Moran
**Luciano:** Sebastian Montagna

**Origin:** Argentina
**Language:** Spanish
**Released:** 2001
**Production:** Lita Stantic; Code Red, Orfeo Films International, 4K Films Productions; released by Cowboy Booking International
**Directed by:** Lucretia Martel
**Written by:** Lucretia Martel
**Cinematography by:** Hugo Colace
**Editing:** Santiago Ricci
**Art Direction:** Graciela Oderigo
**MPAA rating:** Unrated
**Running time:** 96 minutes

## REVIEWS

*Boxoffice.* November, 2001, p. 149.
*Chicago Sun-Times Online.* October 19, 2001.
*Entertainment Weekly.* October 19, 2001, p. 55.
*Film Comment Online.* March/April, 2001.
*Los Angeles Times Online.* October 12, 2001.
*New York Times.* September 30, 2001, p. AR15.
*New York Times Online.* October 1, 2001.
*Sight and Sound.* December, 2001, p. 45.
*Variety Online.* March 2, 2001.

# The Circle (Dayereh)

*Her only crime was being a woman.*
—Movie tagline

A circle has no beginning or end, but is continuous as it moves around. In the case of Iranian filmmaker Jafar Panahi's *The Circle*, it begins with the question of why a distressed mother laments her daughter giving birth to a girl and, by the time the film has moved full circle, we know the answer. While many couples around the world would be pleased to give birth to a girl, this particular mother only sees the ruination of her daughter. Panahi (*The White Balloon*, *The Mirror*), who is best known for his films about girl children, found his inspiration from a newspaper article regarding an Iranian mother who killed her two daughters and then committed suicide. Thus the seed for the unimaginable horrors that *The Circle* characters' face had been planted.

As the film opens we see the back of a chador-cloaked woman as she receives news that her daughter just gave birth to a girl. The woman laments that her daughter was told that she was to give birth to a son and now the daughter's husband will divorce her. Next, we meet two young women, Arezou (Mariam Palvin Almani) and Nargess (Nargess Mamizadeh), who have temporarily been released from prison. (We never learn their crimes.) Arezou commits an unspeakable act to raise money for Nargess' bus fare back to her village. Nargess, who fantasizes about weddings and her idealistic village, never does board the bus home since she doesn't have any identification and she isn't permitted to travel alone because she's female.

Instead, Nargess leads us to former inmate Pari (Fereshteh Sadr Orfani), who has been thrown out by her family and seeks an abortion. Her husband had been executed and now the widow faces other horrors if she gives birth to a child. She seeks help from another former inmate turned nurse (Elham Saboktakin) but the nurse won't take the risk of assisting Pari with the abortion because her doctor husband might learn of her prison record. So Pari journeys through the crowded city where she witnesses young mother Nayereh (Fatemeh Naghavi) abandoning her little girl on a busy street. Heartbroken, Nayereh admits that she loves her child but she believes that the girl would be better off with a proper family.

Police eventually pick Nayereh up after she illegally accepts ride from a stranger and is mistaken for a prostitute. Nayereh's steps eventually lead her to a defiant prostitute (Mojhan Faramarzi) who we watch being transported to prison. In the final scene, the prostitute is shoved into a prison cell and the camera slowly pans over the faces of women we saw earlier and who have indirectly answered the question of why giving birth to a girl is considered a curse in their society.

Banned in Iran, *The Circle* miraculously appeared at the Venice Film Festival where it won the Golden Lion award and then made its way to North America. A.O. Scott of the *New York Times* wrote that the film "focuses with unflinching candor on some of the harsher aspects of life in that Islamic republic." *The Circle* pleased audiences with its complex narrative structure and its poignant message. And Panahi has proven his compassion for oppressed women despite his newly tainted reputation as a banned Iranian filmmaker. However, when it comes to controversial Iranian cinema, he's in good company.

—*Patty-Lynne Herlevi*

### CREDITS

**Arezou:** Mariam Palvin Almani
**Nargess:** Nargess Mamizadeh
**Pari:** Fereshteh Sadr Orfani
**Nayereh:** Fatemeh Naghavi
**Ticket Seller:** Monir Arab
**Nurse:** Elham Saboktakin
**Prostitute:** Mojhan Faramarzi

**Origin:** Iran
**Language:** Farsi
**Released:** 2000
**Production:** Jafar Panahi; Mikado/Lumiere & Company; released by Winstar Cinema
**Directed by:** Jafar Panahi
**Written by:** Kambozia Partovi
**Cinematography by:** Bahram Badakhshami
**Sound:** Mehdi Dejbodi
**Editing:** Jafar Panahi
**Art Direction:** Iraj Raminfar
**MPAA rating:** Unrated
**Running time:** 91 minutes

### REVIEWS

*Chicago Sun-Times Online.* June 8, 2001.
*Entertainment Weekly.* April 4, 2001, p. 49.
*Film Comment.* March/April, 2001, p. 22.
*Hollywood Reporter.* September 19, 2000, p. 20.
*International Herald Tribune Online.* September 21, 2000.
*Los Angeles Times Online.* May 18, 2001.
*New York Times Online.* April 15, 2001.
*Newsday Online.* September 26, 2000.
*RANT.* March/April, 2001, p. 14.
*Seattle Weekly.* April 26, 2001, p. 75.
*Variety.* September 11, 2000, p. 25.
*Village Voice.* April 17, 2001, p. 139.
*Washington Post Online.* May 25, 2001.

### QUOTES

Arezou (Mariam Palvin Almani) to Nargess (Nargess Mamizadeh) about not travelling together to her village: "I couldn't handle seeing that your paradise might not exist."

### AWARDS AND NOMINATIONS

**Venice Film Fest. 2000:** Film.

# The Claim

*Everything has a price.*
—Movie tagline

In 1996, British director Michael Winterbottom completed a wonderfully stark adaptation of Thomas Hardy's 1894 novel *Jude the Obscure* titled, simply, *Jude,* but scrupulously faithful to Hardy's plot and characters. *The Claim,* then, is Winterbottom's second Hardy adaptation, but the approach here is considerably different. The setting, for example, is in the gold fields of the American West during the 19th-century, instead of Hardy's "Wessex," and the characters differently imagined. Indeed, even readers familiar with Hardy's *The Mayor of Casterbridge* (1886) will not be immediately reminded of Thomas Hardy while watching this film. It is certainly bleak enough for Hardy, but it is very loosely based on the novel Although the film retains Hardy's central plot device, a man regrettably selling his wife and child for his personal gain, screenwriter Frank Cotrell Boyce has made several significant changes.

The film's story is set in the Sierra Nevadas during the winter of 1867. A railroad surveyor named Daglish (Wes Bentley) arrives with his crew in the mining settlement of Kingdom Come. If the Central Pacific Railroad decides to take this route on the way to joining with another rail line running eastward from California, Kingdom Come will flourish. If not, the town will wither and die. Presiding over the town is Daniel Dillon (Peter Mullan), the town's founder, mayor and chief moral and legal authority, who is understandably anxious to court and flatter Daglish. Also recently arrived are two strangers, Elena (Nastassja Kinski) and her teenaged daughter, Hope (Sarah Polley). Dillon scarcely notices them, until the mother sends Dillon a necklace that seems to have a profoundly disturbing meaning for him.

A series of brief flashbacks then reveals the secret Dillon and Elena have in common. Years before Elena, her new baby, Hope, and her husband, Dillon, sought shelter in a stranger's crude hut. The stranger tempts Dillon by offering to barter his "claim" in exchange for Elena and Hope. Dillon is all too willing to give her up, for Elena and the baby have become burdensome to him. Years pass. Elena and Hope disappear. Dillon's claim prospers meanwhile, and he becomes the patriarch of Kingdom Come. Seriously ill with tuberculosis, Elena has come to Kingdom Come to die, but she has never told Hope that Dillon is her father.

New relationships develop. Dillon decides to marry Elena, even if in the process he has to abandon his long-time mistress, Lucia (Milla Jovovich), giving her the claim to his land down in the valley. Dillon then decides to move his mansion down the mountain (in one of the film's best sequences) in order to be nearer to Elena. Daglish, meanwhile, is attracted to Hope. A major complication comes when the railroad survey concludes that it will have to bypass Kingdom Come and choose the valley as an alternative route. The townspeople decide to follow Daglish and relocate in the valley, choosing the land now owned by Dillon's ex-mistress. Left behind, bereaved by Elena's death and rejected by Hope (to whom he has at last confessed and revealed himself as her father), Dillon, a dispirited, isolated and lonely figure, stalks through his deserted ghost town and sets it ablaze. He then wanders out into the snowy wastes and perishes.

The film ends as the new town of "Lisboa" springs up, where Hope has gone to join Daglish. When the citizens see the smoke billowing from Kingdom Come, they rush back, not to save the town, but to pillage the gold that Dillon has hoarded there, and to lay claim to his claim. The camera lifts up and away, shifting from the new settlement to the charred remains of Kingdom Come, now a kingdom gone.

Thus was Hardy's novel transformed into a chronicle of the forging of the American West. The cinematography by Alwin Kuchler is chillingly spectacular. Against the vast backdrop of snow, mountain passes, and valleys, the human figures appear merely as black dots splattered against the white field. The dominant imagery of the picture is just that, tiny black figures etched against the enormous swells and edged contours of the hostile terrain that will ultimately consume the once powerful Dillon. True in this respect to Thomas Hardy, the landscape is dominant, and the human story pales into insignificance: Dillon's moral struggle and his longing for redemption; Daglish's turmoil over the choice of railway routes, finally determined by the terrain; Hope's weariness over the care of her dying mother; her mother's conflicted attitudes over the reunion with Dillon—all are flattened out and drained of their real emotion.

Individual set pieces stand out—the barter scene in the huddled shack as gold is exchanged for Elena; Dillon's house tugged and hauled by teams of horses and straining men down a mountainside towards the town; the laying of the railbed through the valley; Elena's desperate gasps for breath as she expires (the moment lensed by an overhead camera, her bed-ridden form framed upside down, splayed against the white sheets); Dillon's torching of the town as he smashes the windows of the shops and houses; the frenzied scramble for gold at the end as the camera retreats to a high position above the fray. The film's most explosive moment comes when a wagon carrying nitroglycerin blows up while moving over rocky terrain, with ghastly consequences, as men and horses are blown to bits, with one of the horses, set ablaze, galloping away in terror.

As was also true of *Jude,* there is an emotional disconnect between Winterbottom, his characters, and the audience. Although interesting in a grotesque and depraved way, the film is too grim to be especially entertaining. The plot is shot through with betrayal and rejection. For example, after Dillon gives his mistress three gold ingots after he decides to marry Elena, Lucia goes on to set up a new town and bordello at the new railhead, more than decimating the population of Kingdom Come, and then has a brief fling with Daglish (who has betrayed Dillon by rerouting the rail line through the valley), until Hope rejects her father for Daglish after learning the truth. *The Claim* presumes to reinvent Hardy's novel as a western, but, as such, it still demands a powerful confrontation that is set up to occur when Daglish returns to Kingdom Come with the news that the railroad will be taking an alternative route. Daglish intends to reclaim his railroad supplies, but he has to fight for his claim to these. An armed confrontation, that is rather too briskly ended when Dillon's marshal is shot dead, settles the issue, since no one else cares to challenge Daglish.

The elaborated theme of betrayal is faithful to Thomas Hardy. If Alfred Hitchcock was the Master of Suspense, so in English fiction Thomas Hardy was the Master of Misery, and Winterbottom's script is faithful to the design. As Edward Buscombe noted in his *Sight and Sound* review, Michael Henchard, the character in *The Mayor of Casterbridge* upon whom Dillon was based, "mistakenly believes that his wife's daughter is his own, whereas she's actually the child of the man he sold her to when she was a baby." Consequently, Michael Henchard's fate is "even more calamitous" than Dillon's, "since he loses not only his supposed daughter, but also his house, business and fiancée to a man he had trusted as his assistant." Henchard is crushed in the end by Hardy's fatalistic machinery, whereas Dillon, later eulogized by Daglish as a "king," "goes out in a blaze of glory," literally.

Buscombe remembered, as other reviewers did not, that Nastassja Kinski, who plays the ill-fated Elena, also played Tess of the D'Ubervilles in Roman Polanski's 1979 Hardy adaptation, *Tess,* a far better film and a more faithful rendering of Hardy. Other reviewers, lacking any literary memory, could only cite resemblances with Robert Altman's *McCabe & Mrs. Miller* (1971), another bordello western set in a miserable mining town. For Rita Kempley of the *Washington Post* the picture's major flaw was that "Dillon isn't worthy of redemption." Kempley also dismisses Hardy, whom she describes as "an acquired taste—like Hemlock." David Thomson, discussing the film as an adaptation in the *New York Times,* seemed to agree with Kempley: "how could a movie (that sentimental form) ever make such a man acceptable?" But whereas other American reviewers found the film an unsatisfactory, displaced western, Thomson deemed it "entirely surprising yet wonderous." Although Thomson concedes that Winterbottom has not yet produced an "outright hit," he sees more potential in his work than in the work of such "rowdy novices" as Guy Ritchie.

The Claim makes more sense as a Hardy adaptation than as a western. Such a film is clearly not for everyone. A Hardy adaptation, however loose, loopy, or transformed, has its own demands, a film made for viewers who are also readers, not for the illiterate or the alliterate (those who know how to read but choose not to). And reviewers not grounded in Hardy need not apply for such an assignment. Winterbottom made the film for just over $16 million, itself an amazing achievement. He is a director who takes chances and should be admired for his courage to swim against the tide.

*—James M. Welsh, with John C. Tibbetts*

## CREDITS

**Dillon:** Peter Mullan
**Elena:** Nastassia Kinski
**Hope:** Sarah Polley
**Dalglish:** Wes Bentley
**Lucia:** Milla Jovovich
**Sweetley:** Sean McGinley
**Bellinger:** Julian Richings

**Origin:** Great Britain, Canada
**Released:** 2000
**Production:** Andrew Eaton; Revolution Films, Alliance Atlantis, Arts Council of England, Pathe Pictures; released by United Artists
**Directed by:** Michael Winterbottom
**Written by:** Frank Cottrell-Boyce
**Cinematography by:** Alwin Kuchler
**Music by:** Michael Nyman
**Sound:** George Tarrant
**Editing:** Trevor Waite
**Costumes:** Joanne Hanson

**Production Design:** Mark Tildesley, Ken Rempel
**MPAA rating:** R
**Running time:** 120 minutes

## REVIEWS

*Chicago Sun-Times Online.* April 20, 2001.
*Entertainment Weekly.* April 27, 2001, p. 86.
*Entertainment Weekly.* May 4, 2001, p. 22.
*Movieline.* February, 2001, p. 30.
*New York Times.* January 7, 2001, p. 13.
*New York Times.* April 20, 2001, p. B16.
*People.* April 30, 2001, p. 32.
*Sight and Sound.* March, 2001, p. 44.
*Variety.* December 4, 2000, p. 26.
*Washington Post.* April 20, 2001, p. C12.
*Washington Post Weekend.* April 20, 2001, p. 37.

## TRIVIA

Fortress Mountain in Canada stood in for the California Sierras.

## AWARDS AND NOMINATIONS

**Nomination:**
**Genie 2001:** Support. Actor (Richings).

# The Closet
# (Le Placard)

*He was about to lose his job, until a friend offered to start a rumor. . . . Now he's about to come out of the closet he never went into.*
—Movie tagline

  **Box Office:** $6.7 million

French playwright-filmmaker Francis Veber argued against turning his play *The Dinner Game* into a feature film. However, his long-time producer Alain Poirè (who passed away spring of 2000) convinced the reluctant Veber to bring the raucous comedy to the big screen and *The Dinner Game* was a smash hit in France. Veber has returned with an even funnier film, *The Closet,* about a straight man who comes out of the closet in order to save his job at a condom factory. Starring Daniel Auteuil, Gèrard Depardieu, Thierry Lhermitte, and Michèle Laroque, *The Closet* attracted three million French viewers during its opening week in France. According to Judith Prescott of the *Hollywood Reporter,* the French farce was "the strongest opening of any French film in nearly a year."

Although Veber has resided Stateside for the past 15 years, where he has become acquainted with the Hollywood movie machine, his French farces prove more successful when the films wear subtitles as opposed to American remakes. Veber's 1978 American remake of *La Cage aux Folles* proved to be an exception to the rule. And the verdict is still out on the American remake of *The Dinner Game,* which stars Kevin Kline. Veber commented (press kit interview) on his French temperament "My mother was Russian and I thought of myself as being international. . . . Somewhere in me there lies a French chromosome that is very dominant." That might be the case, but when a French director who resides in America writes French farces starring international actors, it takes a global village to produce a film.

This comedy of errors revolves around Francois Pignon (Auteuil), an accountant who works at a condom factory and who leads an uncomplicated life. Dressed in gray suits and hardly ever speaking above a whisper, Pignon has grown into the invisible and disposable everyday man. His wife divorced him, his son ignores him, and now the company director at the factory plans on firing Pignon. Why? Because Pignon is boring. After Pignon gets wind of his termination he attempts suicide only to be saved by a plain gray kitten and his neighbor Belone (Michel Aumont). Belone comes up with a plan to save Pignon's job by having Pignon come out of a closet he never went into. Of course, the homosexual Belone, who was fired from a job 20 years ago, seeks karmic justice. To cut to the chase, the plan works.

All of a sudden Pignon's coworkers, including his supervisor Mlle. Bertrand (Laroque), but excluding macho personnel director Fèlix Santini (Depardieu), find Pignon fascinating. Of course, Fèlix becomes the victim of an office prank when coworker Guillaume (Lhermitte) lies to Fèlix by telling him if he doesn't cut out his homophobic act he will be sacked. So Fèlix invites Francois to lunch, then confesses that he only plays rugby because he enjoys showering with sweaty male bodies. But soon, Fèlix grows soft and confesses to his wife that Francois doesn't like him and he hasn't worn the pink sweater that Fèlix bought him. Finally, Fèlix has a nervous breakdown as he stumbles out of the closet himself.

Meanwhile, the big boss comes up with a marketing scheme in which Francois would appear on a float promoting condoms in the Gay Pride Parade. In the comical highlight of *The Closet,* Francois does indeed appear on a float wearing a condom on his head while he nonchalantly waves at a crowd. Francois' son has a change of heart after seeing his father's appearance in the parade and his former wife agrees to meet Francois for dinner. Everything seems to be going well until the night when the heterosexual Francois is caught making love to Mlle. Bertrand. However, Francois stays employed and pairs up with Bertrand.

The ensemble cast, led by the versatile Auteuil, transforms a lightweight comedy into a laughathon with each scene building on the momentum of the last. Depardieu, who suffered from a major heart attack before shooting began, performed the double duty of playing a macho rugby coach and a vulnerable (closeted) homosexual. Laroque plays the dignified fellow accountant whose lust for Pignon leads to sexual mayhem, and Lhermitte skillfully plays a prankster bent on humiliating Fèlix.

Veber suggests that the simple man in the crowd can live life to the fullest—if he comes out of the closet. And this crowd-teaser might even provide a politically correct solution for victims of corporate downsizing.

—*Patty-Lynne Herlevi*

## CREDITS

**Francois Pignon:** Daniel Auteuil
**Felix Santini:** Gerard Depardieu
**Guillaume:** Thierry Lhermitte
**Belone:** Michel Aumont
**Miss Bertrand:** Michele Laroque
**Kopel:** Jean Rochefort
**Christine:** Alexandra Vandernoot

**Origin:** France
**Language:** French
**Released:** 2000
**Production:** Alain Poire, Patrice Ledoux; Gaumont, Efve Films, TF-1 Films; released by Miramax Films
**Directed by:** Francis Veber
**Written by:** Francis Veber
**Cinematography by:** Luciano Tovoli
**Music by:** Vladimir Cosma
**Sound:** Bernard Bats
**Editing:** Georges Klotz
**Art Direction:** Hugues Tissandier
**Costumes:** Jacqueline Bouchard
**MPAA rating:** R
**Running time:** 86 minutes

 ## REVIEWS

*Chicago Sun-Times Online.* July 6, 2001.
*Entertainment Weekly.* July 20, 2001, p. 45.
*Los Angeles Times Online.* July 6, 2001.

*New York Times Online.* June 29, 2001.
*People.* July 16, 2001, p. 32.
*Variety.* January 22, 2001, p. 44.
*Washington Post Online.* July 6, 2001.

**TRIVIA**

A character named Francois Pignon (played by Jacques Villeret) also appeared in Veber's 1998 film *The Dinner Game.*

# Come Undone (Presque Rien)

The French-language film *Come Undone* falls into the category of a gay coming of age tale but, probably because it is French, it's very matter-of-fact about its protagonists sexuality. It's frequently melancholy and distant and it's also non-linear. Instead, *Come Undone* is set-up as a series of scenes that the viewer must put together in order to get a not-always clear picture of what happened and when; and not everything that happens to the characters is spelled out. The film opens as a young man, who's maybe in his late teens and who looks lost, waits for a train. The weather is bleak; it looks like winter. You don't know who the young man is or where he is going. While on the train, he starts to make a tape recording—maybe a journal of some kind—but is interrupted by another passenger.

The scenery switches to a crowded beach in summer. The same young man is with a younger girl and they are sunbathing when he catches the eye of a slightly older young man. The viewer doesn't learn the names of the characters yet, but for the sake of clarity, his name is Mathieu (Jeremie Elkaim in his feature film debut), he's 18, and she is his sister, Sarah (Laetitia Legrix). Mathieu and Sarah walk back to their vacation house. They are spending the summer with their mother (Dominique Reymond), who is ill, and their aunt, Annick (Marie Matheron), who's serving as nurse/housekeeper. Back at the beach the next day, Mathieu spots the same young man who later follows them home.

Instead of continuing, the scene switches to Mathieu in a hospital having his stomach pumped after a suicide attempt. He's seen by a psychiatrist (Rejane Kerdaffrec) and refuses to call his parents or let anyone know where he is. A switch back to the summer finds the two young men finally meeting. Cedric (Stephane Rideau) and Mathieu go for a walk and make small talk. While sitting on the beach, Mathieu finds himself attracted and uncertain—unlike Cedric who tells Mathieu he wants to kiss him and then does

so. The next day, the two fight on the beach because Mathieu is wary of them being seen together by his sulky sister and his aunt. He later meets an angry Cedric down at the beach and apologizes for his behavior.

Another switch back to winter and Mathieu is breaking into the family's closed-up summer home and settling in, even taking in a stray cat to care for. The scenes continue to switch from summer to winter. Mathieu and his family come annually to the seaside resort town of Pornichet from Paris but this summer, since his dad can't cope with his wife's depression, he stays in Paris to work and doesn't visit. Cedric and Mathieu grow closer as they go to the beach, a carnival, and a dance club where Cedric gets into a fight with his ex-boyfriend, Pierre (Nils Ohlund). They have sex although Cedric's sexual aggressiveness sometimes disturbs Mathieu.

Cedric is seen talking to Mathieu's hospital psychiatrist. It was he who brought Mathieu to the hospital but all he can tell the doctor is that Mathieu had seemed fine and he thought that things between them were alright although, Cedric casually admits, he was unfaithful. Annick figures out what's going on between the boys and is upset, thinking that the news will distress Mathieu's mom. At a restaurant, Mathieu explains to Cedric that his baby brother has recently died from cancer and his mother hasn't taken an interest in anything since then: "Between my crazy sister and my depressed mom, I've had enough." The boys make love on the beach, which segues into Mathieu waking up alone in the house. Later, he gets a job in a local bar and eventually calls his mother but pretends he and Cedric are still living together in Nantes. When Cedric tracks him down to the house in Pornichet, Mathieu refuses to come to the door.

During a summer lunch, Sarah, who appears jealous, asks Mathieu if he is in love with Cedric but he doesn't answer. Then Cedric winds up in the hospital after an accident and Mathieu meets Cedric's father (Guy Houssier) who asks if Mathieu is his son's boyfriend and he admits that he is. Mathieu tells his mother that he loves Cedric and that he thinks that Cedric loves him, although neither has apparently said it to the other. His mother is accepting of the relationship but worries that his first love will break Mathieu's heart.

Before he leaves the hospital, Mathieu tells his psychiatrist that it's over between him and Cedric—that he needs to be alone. She suggests he keep a journal of what he is feeling and he agrees to make a tape recording. As the summer comes to an end, Cedric wants Mathieu to stay with him. When Mathieu doesn't respond, a hurt Cedric says "So, it didn't mean anything?" and walks away. However, Mathieu tells his mother that Cedric is moving to Nantes to take a computer course and that he has decided to go with him and go to university there, although his family seems to think Mathieu is moving too fast. The boys make up again and Mathieu tells Cedric his decision.

Back in the winter, Mathieu spots Pierre in the bar and decides to track him down at his parents' home. Although surprised, Pierre agrees to go for a walk and it turns out that more than a year has passed. Cedric and Mathieu did live together in Nantes and broke up. Mathieu doesn't want to talk about himself and you never do learn what caused his suicide attempt. They discuss Pierre's volatile relationship with Cedric and Mathieu tells Pierre his romance is over for good and that he is staying in Pornichet for the winter while he decides what to do. The two agree to have dinner together and then continue to walk on the nearly empty winter beach.

The literal translation of the film's French title *Presque Rien* is "almost nothing." In some ways, almost nothing happens during the film and you learn almost nothing about the characters. In other ways, you can piece together a great deal. Cedric's parents divorced when he was one and he hasn't seen his mother in years. He lives with his father, didn't like school and dropped out, and has had a simple summer job for the past three years. Taking a computer course is the first step in making a life for himself that lasts longer than a moment. Cedric is outgoing and at ease with his sexuality but his feelings for Mathieu are deeper than a summer fling, although he's clearly unused to articulating such emotions and tends to express himself either sexually or with anger.

In contrast, Mathieu is bottling everything up. When Cedric remarks that he doesn't seem affected by his young brother's death, Mathieu replies that since the boy spent all his time in the hospital, they never became close. He's resentful of his absent father, although he pretends to be unconcerned. He also resents his mother's illness taking her away emotionally from him and his sister, but he also understands it. He should—it's clear that Mathieu suffers from depression himself. If Mathieu is struggling with his sexuality, he doesn't appear to show it once he gets past his discomfort at Cedric's public displays of affection. His attraction to Cedric is strong although, again, they don't discuss their feelings. Mathieu tells others he loves Cedric but they make decisions separately about their lives together; maybe this lack of communication between them is what eventually drives them apart.

*Come Undone* is a film where you have to pay attention. The jumbled time frame can be frustrating but it's not insurmountable. Director Sebastian Lifshitz also doesn't spoon feed his viewers; you're watching first love from the status of an outsider and, just as in real life, you never discover everything that goes on in private.

—*Christine Tomassini*

## CREDITS

**Mathieu:** Jeremie Elkaim
**Cedric:** Stephane Rideau
**Annick:** Marie Matheron
**Sarah:** Laetitia Legrix
**Mathieu's mother:** Dominique Reymond
**Pierre:** Nils Ohlund
**Psychiatrist:** Rejane Kerdaffrec
**Cedric's father:** Guy Houssier

**Origin:** France
**Language:** French
**Released:** 2000
**Production:** Christian Tison, Marion Hansel; Man's Films, Lancelot Films; released by Picture This! Entertainment
**Directed by:** Sabastian Lifshitz
**Written by:** Sabastian Lifshitz, Stephane Bouquet
**Cinematography by:** Pascal Paoucet
**Music by:** Perry Blake
**Sound:** Quentin Jacques, Cyril Holtz
**Editing:** Yann Dedet
**Art Direction:** Roseanna Sacco
**Costumes:** Elisabeth Mehu
**MPAA rating:** Unrated
**Running time:** 98 minutes

## REVIEWS

*Detroit Free Press Online.* December 7, 2001.
*Los Angeles Times Online.* August 24, 2001.
*New York Times Online.* June 29, 2001.
*San Francisco Chronicle.* August 24, 2001, p. C3.
*Sight and Sound.* October, 2001, p. 56.
*Variety.* July 30, 2001, p. 19.

## QUOTES

Annick (Marie Matheron) scoffs about Mathieu's (Jeremie Elkaim) absent father: "He's like all men. A coward, afraid of illness."

# Company Man

*International intelligence just got dumber.*
—Movie tagline

*A Devious Dictator. A Top Secret Mission. And the Perfect Spies to screw it up.*
—Movie tagline

 **Box Office:** $.1 million

Allen Quimp (Douglas McGrath) is the runt under-achiever in a family of astronauts, inventors, and Nobel Prize winners. As an English instructor at Greenwich Prep and some-time drivers' ed instructor, the highest achievement he can claim is the manuscript for his book, "The Grammar Crises in the English Speaking World," which, in his words, "will blow the lid off one of the greatest scandals known in the free world."

Unfortunately for Allen, his wife, Daisy (Sigourney Weaver) is a social climber par excellence. She wants to be seated at the best tables in restaurants not near the kitchen door which is where she ends up with Allen. She wants a maid and a fur coat and a husband with a six-figure income, and if Allen won't get all this for her she'll call her daddy who'll make sure he does. So, when daddy puts the pressure on Allen he responds with the most preposterous lie: his job as a teacher is just a cover because in reality he works for the CIA. Incredulous at first, Daisy's father is eventually convinced by the logic that "the standard for being right for the CIA is how wrong you are for the CIA." Which as everyone would agree makes Allen perfect for the CIA.

Allen swears Daisy's father to secrecy, but in no time everyone knows about Allen's "secret" primarily thanks to Daisy's fanatical desire to be seen as someone special in the community. So when Daisy and Allen attend their local Arts Center benefit where the Soviet ballet dancer Rudolph Petrov (Ryan Phillippe) is performing, even Petrov finds out about Allen's clandestine identity. Consequently, the next day, Petrov defects to Allen while he is teaching his drivers' ed course.

Of course this is a great coup for the CIA, so instead of censuring Allen for impersonating an agent, the CIA hires him. And what do they do with this untrained agent? They "put him on the payroll and send him to some third-world backwater." And which backwater do they send him to? Cuba. By the way, was it mentioned that the year is 1959? Allen is sent to Cuba to replace Agent Johnson (John Turturro) who is going around claiming there is a mole in the organization, Agent X, who is passing secrets to the Soviet Union and that Cuba is on the verge of a revolution. According to Agent Fry (Denis Leary) and the Chief (Woody Allen) this is absurd and that's why they're getting rid of him. Quimp is now given the job as the head of a dummy corporation called The American Fruit Company which will be his cover for running around Cuba.

The Chief also has a job for Quimp. It seems the Chief used to work in Paris but he left a code book of agents in a Soviet-owned brothel. Because of this 45 agents were hanged and the Chief sent into exile in Cuba, which he hates. He wants to go back to France, and if Quimp can uncover the agency's mole that just might happen. Poor Agent Fry also has a burden. He has to put up with Quimp's obsessive correction of his grammar. His rational is that "there's very little use winning the battle against Communism if we lose the war against double negatives." So they battle over who vs. whom, like vs. as, adjectives vs. adverbs and are totally oblivious to Cuba bursting into flames behind them.

Then one day Quimp's quiet is disturbed when the grasping Daisy walks in the front door and the over-the-edge Agent Johnson comes crashing in the window. And Agent Johnson has brought with him the fey President of Cuba, Batista (Alan Cumming). Batista's government has just been overthrown by the Communist revolutionary Fidel Castro (Anthony La Paglia). Almost immediately Daisy sees the potential for a best-selling book in the drama surrounding her and although Quimp is terrified by all the murder and mayhem and wants to leave, Daisy is already typing up her manuscript on a pink typewriter. Furthermore, she refuses to leave Cuba until Castro is overthrown and she has an ending for her book.

So, Allen tries to come up with a plan to get rid of Castro and since he loathes the idea of assassination, he believes that just by making Castro unpopular he'll be overthrown by his own people. How to accomplish this? How about slipping him a drug—say, LSD—that could alter Castro's speech while engaging him in a debate where he would make a fool of himself. But that plan is foiled when the glass of LSD-laced water meant for Castro ends up in front of Quimp and a toast is proposed that Quimp can't turn down. If there's a fool on the debate podium, it's the American Fruit Company representative, Allen Quimp. If at first you don't succeed.... How about having Marilyn Monroe send Castro a shampoo that will cause all his hair to fall out? But Daisy confuses the bottles and uses it herself, going bald in the process. Back to the drawing board. How about a box of poisoned cigars? Hey, weren't those supposed to be exploding cigars? And what does Quimp have to do with the Bay of Pigs?

Lampooning the Cuban Revolution may have seemed like a good idea—20 years ago—but it falls flat today. And to make matters worse, not only is the topic not necessarily funny to today's audiences, it is given such heavy-handed treatment that it's really not funny at all. The plot comes off like a series of lame jokes with tired and obvious punch lines bracketed by lamer sight gags. While attempting to incorporate all the rumors about CIA activities in Cuba during this time period it fails to do so in any imaginative way other than implying that they were all Allen's doing and all went wrong. This kind of tomfoolery with history was done much more effectively and with a great deal more affection and humor in *Dick*. Scenes that would have been thrown away in the background of funnier films—such as when Woody Allen leans out a window to light a cigarette on a burning effigy of Batista—are the high points of this movie.

It's as if *Company Man* were the product of some high school comedy writer wannabe. One can imagine him and his pals sitting around the lunch table saying "hey, ya know what would be really funny?" What's funny is that this film was written by Douglas McGrath whose previous screenplay for 1996's *Emma*, starring Gwyneth Paltrow, wasn't that bad. In fact, McGrath also co-wrote *Bullets Over Broadway* with Woody Allen and perhaps that's why the "hero" in this film is named Allen and why Woody Allen agreed to appear in the film—although he is unbilled. Wonder why? Perhaps more telling is the fact that in 1980 McGrath worked as a writer for television's *Saturday Night Live*. Wasn't that one of the show's worst years?

As if the amateurish writing for *Company Man* wasn't sad enough, McGrath, also the film's director, manages to get some very talented actors to turn in terrible performances. Perhaps they're just mirroring his own performance for McGrath may have spread himself too thinly when he decided to play the character of Quimp along with all his other duties. The actors end up playing one-dimensional caricatures and every scene comes off like a barely thought through sketch, stagy and stiff. The dialogue is even stiffer and delivered with such dullness that it's as if the actors were thinking about their next gig while saying their lines.

It should be no wonder then that this film was made in 1999 but wasn't released until 2001. But even then the distributor must have decided to cut its losses and run because *Company Man* was only in release for a week before it was relegated to the ranks of those films meant for another life on video as soon as decently possible. 🎞️

*—Beverley Bare Buehrer*

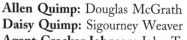

## CREDITS

**Allen Quimp:** Douglas McGrath
**Daisy Quimp:** Sigourney Weaver
**Agent Crocker Johnson:** John Turturro
**Fidel Castro:** Anthony LaPaglia
**Petrov:** Ryan Phillippe
**Officer Fry:** Denis Leary
**Batista:** Alan Cumming
**Chief Lowther:** Woody Allen
**Nora:** Heather Matarazzo
**Senator:** Jeffrey Jones

**Origin:** USA

**Released:** 2000
**Production:** John Penotti, Guy East, Rick Leed, James Scotchpole; Intermedia Films, GreeneStreet Films, Foundry Films, Wind Dancer Films; released by Paramount Classics
**Directed by:** Douglas McGrath, Peter Askin
**Written by:** Douglas McGrath, Peter Askin
**Cinematography by:** Russell Boyd
**Music by:** David Lawrence
**Sound:** Tod A. Maitland
**Editing:** Camilla Toniolo
**Art Direction:** Patricia Woodbridge
**Costumes:** Ruth Meyers
**Production Design:** Jane Musky
**MPAA rating:** PG-13
**Running time:** 81 minutes

 REVIEWS

*Boxoffice.* April, 2001, p. 237.
*Chicago Sun-Times Online.* March 9, 2001.
*Chicago Tribune Online.* March 9, 2001.
*Entertainment Weekly.* March 16, 2001, p. 44.
*Los Angeles Times Online.* March 9, 2001.
*New York Times Online.* March 9, 2001.
*People.* March 19, 2001, p. 36.
*USA Today Online.* March 8, 2001.
*Variety.* May 22, 2000, p. 31.

QUOTES

Agent Crocker Johnson (John Turturro): "Do you think I went into the CIA just because it was easy to spell?"

# Corky Romano

*Who is Corky Romano?*
—Movie tagline

 **Box Office:** $23.6 million

It seems like after starring in the really bad film *A Night At the Roxbury, Saturday Night Live*'s Chris Kattan would have developed some sort of savvy about choosing scripts. It's not like he's an inherently unfunny guy. His impersonation of Olympic gymnast Kerri Strug was note perfect and his character Mango, a cabaret star that is overwhelmingly attractive to each SNL guest star, is inspired. The kindest way to look at his decision to make this movie is that maybe he's not getting many offers and had to take this just to get himself into theaters. Surely he couldn't have looked at the script and thought, "Oh yes, this is my ticket to comedy success."

The film starts out with promise. Corky Romano (Kattan) is driving down the road, cheerfully singing "Take On Me" by 80s group A-ha. He wears a guileless broad smile and we see that his license plate reads "Free Hugs: One Size Fits All." In a couple of seconds, director Rob Pritts has shown a lot about Corky—he's corny, he's an innocent, he's a nerdy guy who doesn't realize it.

But the film takes a nosedive once Corky reaches his place of employment. For one thing, it's a vet's office named, "Poodles and Pussies." Ick. Then, Corky's boss leaves the office to play golf and puts Corky in charge of things. Within a few minutes, Corky has lost control of everything. A cat is chasing an older couples' beloved bird, mice are running all over the floor, and Corky somehow has a snake in his pants. The snake ends up coming out through Corky's fly while an elderly pet owner looks on admiringly. Ick. At one point, Corky is just spinning around the examining room, knocking stuff over. As Roger Ebert of the *Chicago Sun-Times* put it, "I submit as a general principle that it is not funny when a clumsy person knocks over everything in a room. The choreography makes it obvious that the character, in one way or another, is deliberately careening from one collision to another. It always looks deliberate. Indeed, it looks like a deliberate attempt to force laughs instead of building them." Amen to that.

But we know that Corky must wreck his clumsy havoc in a world bigger than the vet's office. That's where his family comes in. Dad is a mob boss, Pops (Peter Falk), who's ailing and about to be prosecuted by the FBI. Taking the advice of his longtime right-hand man Leo Corrigan (Fred Ward), Pops decides that Corky should infiltrate the FBI and steal all the evidence that the agency has against him. It's a strange move since Corky has been estranged from the family for years—at the family's choice. Corky's so naive that he actually thinks that his father's in the landscaping business. His brothers, the thuggish and secretly illiterate Paulie (Peter Berg) and the thuggish and closeted Peter (Chris Penn), aren't very keen on the idea since they think (rightfully so) that Corky is an incompetent wuss, but they have to be loyal to their father.

Corky gets a trumped up resume that boasts such skills as having obscure martial arts prowess, speaking several languages, and holding a degree from Harvard. It seems a little unbelievable that someone could cook up a fake resume, send it to the FBI, and start working on the highest level cases, but then no one is watching this film to get true life inside information on the Bureau. Corky, as Agent Pissant (ha . . . ha), starts working with his boss Howard

Shuster (Richard Roundtree) and uptight senior agent Brick Davis (Matthew Glave, who played similar types in *Rock Star* and *The Wedding Singer*), who may be on to Corky's lies. There's also his co-worker Kate Russo (Vinessa Shaw), who's a shapely blonde who wants to be taken seriously and treated as one of the guys. That the effeminate, so not-hetero Corky starts up a romance with Kate is one of the least believable things in a movie filled with unbelievable things.

While in the FBI, Corky performs supposedly hilarious hijinks. At one point, he accidentally inhales part of a big bag of cocaine and has to speak to a group of school kids. "You had a question?" he screams repeatedly at the bewildered kids. It's difficult to believe that not one of his coworkers would notice that he was acting like a Chihuahua experiencing an electric shock. When Corky's brothers make him wear a wire, they place it in his crotch. Whenever Corky's in trouble, he starts yelling for help to his crotch. This is not funny the first time and it's not funny each of the many times it's repeated. To give the comedy a jolt, the soundtrack frequently resorts to cartoon-like jolly music to give the audience the idea that the unfolding slapstick is indeed funny. Naturally, all of Corky's bumbling somehow works out right so that on case after case, he ends up being a hero. This is even the case when, during a hostage situation, he accidentally shoots off a machine gun, repeatedly showering nearby crowd with stray bullets.

It's not that the movie is completely void of humor. When Corky comes across his first grisly crime scene, he does a huge double take and screams. He takes a closer look at the cadaver in question and squeals "Maggots! That is so gross!" (Of course a vet probably wouldn't be so squeamish, but this movie's so hurting for good jokes that it's worth sacrificing some of the film's continuity.) When Corky tries to impress Russo, he buys her a poster. It reads, "You don't have to be crazy to work here, but it sure helps." When Corky gives it to her, he can scarcely contain his delight at finding such a clever poster. Corky's character is interesting and it would have been nice if screenwriters David Garrett and Jason Ward would have concentrated on Corky's corny tendencies played out in a more realistic setting, like a downtown office, instead of having him embroiled in the ridiculous crime plot.

The film is also strangely traditional. Kattan is a guy who begs for a quirky, strange comedy. Everything that's usual and by the book in this film is a misstep. The writers try to add touching family moments, complete with sappy soundtrack flourishes. They're not developed enough to be truly affecting and are out of place. If the writers wanted to keep them, they should have goosed them up with a bit of humor.

The main thing that can be said for Kattan's performance is that he brings energy to it. He's practically jumping out of his skin trying to impress the audience. His face and body are never at rest and he makes silly faces and strange contortions with his body in his ceaseless attempt to grab the audiences' attention. Other performances are serviceable but nothing more. Falk phones in his performance as the mob boss and Roundtree is bland as an agency bureaucrat. It's sort of funny to cast the burly Penn as the secretly gay brother, but not nearly as funny as the film seems to thing it is.

The critics were not impressed (though, come to think of it, if they were, would they admit it?). Ebert wrote, "*Corky Romano* is like a dead zone of comedy. The concept is exhausted, the ideas are tired, the physical gags are routine, the story is labored, the actors look like they can barely contain their doubts about the project." Kevin Maynard of Mr. Showbiz wrote, "Frankly, there wouldn't have been enough shtick here to warrant an SNL skit. And if the material isn't even up to those standards, then who the hell green-lit it as a feature?" Owen Gleiberman of *Entertainment Weekly* gave the film an F and wrote, "It might be courting hyperbole to call *Corky Romano* the single worst movie ever to feature an SNL cast member (Dan Aykroyd hit some pretty arid valleys), but I'm willing to go out on a critical limb and rank it among the all-time bottom dozen."

*—Jill Hamilton*

## CREDITS

**Corky Romano:** Chris Kattan
**Agent Kate Russo:** Vinessa Shaw
**Pops:** Peter Falk
**Paulie:** Peter Berg
**Peter:** Christopher Penn
**Leo Corrigan:** Fred Ward
**Howard Schuster:** Richard Roundtree
**Agent Brick Davis:** Matthew Glave
**Agent Terence Darnell:** Dave Sheridan
**Agent Bob Cox:** Roger Fan

**Origin:** USA
**Released:** 2001
**Production:** Robert Simonds; released by Touchstone Pictures
**Directed by:** Rob Pritts
**Written by:** David Garrett, Jason Ward
**Cinematography by:** Steven Bernstein
**Music by:** Randy Edelman
**Sound:** Kim Harris Ornitz
**Music Supervisor:** Lisa Brown
**Editing:** Alan Cody
**Art Direction:** Thomas Voth
**Production Design:** Peter Politanoff
**MPAA rating:** PG-13

**Running time:** 85 minutes

## REVIEWS

*Chicago Sun-Times Online.* October 12, 2001.
*Entertainment Weekly.* October 19, 2001, p. 54.
*Los Angeles Times Online.* October 12, 2001.
*New York Times Online.* October 12, 2001.
*People.* October 29, 2001, p. 40.
*USA Today Online.* October 11, 2001.
*Variety.* October 15, 2001, p. 33.
*Washington Post.* October 11, 2001, p. WE44.

# crazy/beautiful

*Break the rules. When it's real. When it's right. Don't let anything stand in your way.*
—Movie tagline

 **Box Office:** $17 million

Kirsten Dunst is no teen pop tart. She displayed an uncanny talent at the age of 12 in her first movie, 1994's *Interview with the Vampire*, and she has had a solid career every since. As she's grown older, Dunst has been heartbreaking in *The Virgin Suicides* (1999), dizzily wacky (along with Michelle Williams) in the satiric *Dick* (1999), preternaturally perky as a cheerleader in *Bring It On* (2000), and, okay, stuck with the rest of the cast in the below-average, wannabe teen comedy *Get Over It* (2001). With *crazy/beautiful*, Dunst takes on a predictable wrong-side-of-the-tracks teen romantic drama that shows she can break hearts (and cry) with the best of them.

"I remember most of 17. I remember the day we met. His smile. His touch. You could be anywhere when your life begins." Nicole (Dunst) just happens to be wearing an ugly orange vest and picking up trash under a California pier as part of her community service for a DUI when she's hustled by some Latino homeboys, including the handsome Carlos (newcomer Jay Hernandez). It turns out they go to the same high school in wealthy Pacific Palisades. Carlos is from East L.A.; he takes a bus two hours to get to a school that can give him a head start in the world. The differences between the two are apparent from the opening scenes. Carlos's mom (Soledad St. Hilaire) wakes him up in their crowded house and feeds him breakfast before he rushes to catch the bus. Wealthy and white Nicole lives in an arty glass box and is awakened by a Latina maid. She gets into an argument with her stepmother Courtney (Lucinda Jenney), and takes prescription drugs along with her juice before getting picked up by her best friend, Maddy (Taryn Manning).

Nicole is a wild child who favors a wardrobe of teeny cropped shirts with no bra, low-rider jeans, a greasy blonde crop haircut, and dark circles under her eyes. She and her equally wasted friends like to skip class and hang out drinking in the parking lot, which is where Carlos spots her again. Nicole manages to immediately get Carlos into trouble, earning the hard-studying student what is probably his first detention, which causes him to be late for football practice and miss the bus home as well. Carlos's mom, who speaks to him in (untranslated) Spanish, is obviously not pleased. Nicole, however, is turned on by the handsome Latino and even persuades Maddy to go to a school football game with her in order to watch him play. They offer to drive Carlos home after the game, though it's obvious that the girls have been drinking, if not drugging, throughout the evening. When they reach his house, his older brother Hector (Rolando Molina) gives Carlos some hard looks and asks where he met the girls. At least the film acknowledges the racial differences between the two—Nicole mockingly remarks "You get assigned a white girl when you go to Pacific," with Maddy chiming in, "And Carlos is so cute, he got two." No matter—his family can recognize trouble when it appears on their doorstep.

Of course, hormones win out for the both of them. They get caught fooling around in the school darkroom—Nicole likes taking pictures—before she takes Carlos home for sex. She's sexually aggressive but Carlos freaks when he realizes that her dad is just outside on the patio and could look into her uncurtained bedroom at anytime. He tells her she's crazy and she replies with, what else, "You're beautiful." Nicole introduces Carlos to her father, Tom Oakley (Bruce Davison), and Carlos discovers not only does Nicole have money but dad is a local liberal congressman, who also happens to have the influence to sponsor Carlos to Annapolis, since the young man's dream is to become a naval pilot. Tom pointedly remarks that it's good to meet someone who has a plan for their life.

Later, Nicole surprises Carlos with a private plane ride and a flying lesson before they go back to her (now-curtained) bedroom. (The nudity is suggested and the sex discreet. The film seems to have been edited to obtain its PG-13 rating.) When Carlos sees a photo of Nicole's mother, she tells him that her mom left when she was 12 and is remarried and living a boring life in Virginia. Carlos tells her that his dad went back to Mexico when the boy was five. His life is planned out and Nicole does not fit into the equation. And the more they hang out, the more apparent that is. Carlos begins to neglect his schoolwork and his friends; he comes home late and worries his mother, which leads to an unpleasant conversation with Hector about the teen's responsibilities. When Nicole goes to Carlos's for a family

celebration, she feels out of place. She can't speak Spanish, she's dressed wrong, and a pretty homegirl is flirting with Carlos, so she leaves. After tracking her down, Carlos is uncomfortable when Nicole tells him she loves him, although she doesn't expect Carlos to say it in return.

Carlos has an eye-opening meeting with Nicole's father. He's willing to sponsor Carlos to the Naval Academy if Carlos will stay away from his daughter—because she will be bad for him. "I know the powerful effect that Nicole can have on people. She's absolutely fabulous at taking a perfectly-oiled train and running it right off the tracks." Carlos learns that Nicole's mother actually killed herself when Nicole was 12 and that the girl found the body. "She's tried to kill herself a number of times. . . . She lies and she drinks—does drugs—she hate me, she hates her stepmother. . . . I want you to listen to my advice. Stay away from my daughter. You hear me? For your own good and for my peace of mind, stay away from Nicole."

Needless to say, Carlos doesn't know how to react, so he does the wrong thing by ignoring Nicole at school. They quarrel and Nicole learns what her father said and that Carlos is worried about his future. She feels betrayed and reverts to her old behavior of getting wasted and partying too hard. Carlos has a change of heart and rescues her from a party, only to get stopped by the cops while driving a passed-out Nicole home in her car (which has expired tags). Both teens are driven by the police to her home and Nicole has an ugly confrontation with her exasperated father, who tells Carlos just to go home while Nicole tearfully makes a scene: "Why do you hate me so much? How can you tell the one person in the world that I love, that I care about so much . . . how could you tell them to stay away from me? Do you think the only thing that I'll do to anyone is screw them up? Do you think that I'm not worth loving?"

Carlos blows off an important test to find Nicole in the school darkroom packing her things. Her father is sending her to a rehab ranch/school in Utah for a dose of tough love. Carlos suggests they run away together after finally saying that he loves Nicole. They spend the night in a motel where they look through one of Nicole's scrapbooks and she admits to what happened to her mother. She fears that her dad thinks she and her mother are alike and that Nicole will end up the same way. Carlos tells her "I think you scare him, you scare me sometime. You get out of control." Carlos wants Nicole to talk to her father about her fears and Nicole decides that she's through running away from her problems.

Carlos drives Nicole home and she admits to her father that she has a pattern of destructive behavior. But she also feels that he's waiting for her to screw up and that he doesn't love her: "I know I'm not easy to love but could you try anyway?" "I do love you. . . . I'm frightened for you every minute, every minute." Carlos has been waiting in the car at the end of the driveway when Nicole and her father make their appearance. It's apparent that father and daughter have made a sort of peace and Tom thanks Carlos for sticking around and believing that Nicole is worth something. Over a series of Nicole's photos, it's apparent that Carlos has gotten into Annapolis and Nicole ends by saying "There are millions of people out there but, in the end, it all comes down to one."

As must be required in any recent teen-oriented film where the soundtrack can be a bestseller even if the film tanks, there's a lot of overly-intrusive music punctuating practically every scene. If you can make out the lyrics, the songs will tell you what you should be feeling at any given moment. Fortunately, when Kirsten Dunst has her cathartic crying scenes, the music stops and she's allowed to just act. Nicole is something of a wounded drama queen but Dunst doesn't allow herself to go over the top. Nicole is more than a poor little rich girl; she may be manipulative and self-destructive but there's also something heartbreakingly fragile about her.

Jay Hernandez has to make do with a close to one-dimensional character. He's ethnic, he's smart, he's athletic, he's his struggling family's hope for the future. Hunky Carlos is also both frightened of and drawn to Nicole's recklessness. He's torn by his obligations and his feelings and his sense of loyalty to everyone, including Nicole. What girl wouldn't want a boyfriend who cares that much? The only other member of the cast who gets any significant screen time is Bruce Davison, who doesn't have to stretch any of his acting muscles playing the role of the worried father. The two teens are the focus and he does what's necessary as the obligatory adult. *crazy/beautiful* might hit all the teen romance clichés but, thanks to the performances of Kirsten Dunst and Jay Hernandez, this is one romance you'll root for.

—*Christine Tomassini*

## CREDITS

**Nicole Oakley:** Kirsten Dunst
**Carlos Nunez:** Jay Hernandez
**Maddy:** Taryn Manning
**Hector:** Rolando Molina
**Tom Oakley:** Bruce Davison
**Courtney:** Lucinda Jenney
**Mrs. Nunez:** Soledad St. Hilaire

**Origin:** USA
**Released:** 2001
**Production:** Harry Ufland, Mary Jane Ufland, Rachel Pfeffer; released by Touchstone Pictures
**Directed by:** John Stockwell
**Written by:** Phil Hay, Matt Manfredi
**Cinematography by:** Shane Hurlbut

**Music by:** Paul Haslinger
**Sound:** Steve Weiss
**Music Supervisor:** Evyen Klean, P.J. Bloom
**Editing:** Melissa Kent
**Art Direction:** Tom Meyer
**Costumes:** Susan Matheson
**Production Design:** Maia Javan
**MPAA rating:** PG-13
**Running time:** 99 minutes

## REVIEWS

*Boxoffice.* September, 2001, p. 153.
*Chicago Sun-Times Online.* June 29, 2001.
*Entertainment Weekly.* July 13, 2001, p. 55.
*Los Angeles Times Online.* June 29, 2001.
*New York Times Online.* June 29, 2001.
*People.* July 9, 2001, p. 38.
*Rolling Stone.* June 19, 2001, p. 55.
*Sight and Sound.* October, 2001, p. 46.
*USA Today Online.* June 28, 2001.
*Variety.* July 9, 2001, p. 23.
*Washington Post Online.* June 29, 2001.

## QUOTES

Carlos (Jay Hernandez) tells Nicole (Kirsten Dunst): "You don't care what people think and, when I'm with you, I don't care what people think."

## TRIVIA

Theatrical feature debut for director John Stockwell.

# Crocodile Dundee in Los Angeles

*He heard there was wildlife in L.A. He didn't know how wild.*
—Movie tagline

 **Box Office:** $25.6 million

It's hard to imagine anything but money being the motivator for *Crocodile Dundee in Los Angeles*. The first *Crocodile Dundee* film came out in 1986 and was a charming, lightweight hit, featuring an Aussie croc hunter navigating the wilds of New York City. It was a fish out of water tale and spawned enough interest in Australia to make Americans aware that "G'day, mate," means "Hey there" and "barbies" are barbecues. It was a mini-phenomenon and making *Crocodile Dundee 2* in 1988 seemed a logical next step—though the film was less charming that time around. But then to make a new one 15 years after the original? Why? Was anyone clamoring for this? Even the title suggests that the film is going to be a rehash of the same old stuff, only this time with the jokes focusing on wacky Los Angeles.

And that's exactly what it is. This time out, Dundee (Paul Hogan) is living with his girlfriend, Sue Carlton (Linda Kozlowski from the first two films and Hogan's real life wife), and their son Mikey (Serge Cockburn) in Australia. Dundee is feeling a bit outmoded since new rules outlaw crocodile hunting and he feels like he's more in the tourism business than the adventure business. So, when Sue gets a chance to move to Los Angeles to take over her dad's newspaper, Dundee is eager to go.

Once in Los Angeles, Sue starts looking through the notes of a reporter who died suddenly. It seems he was investigating a low-level movie studio that has put out a string of unsuccessful action films that they market in Eastern Europe. The reporter was sensing that the sleazy studio heads were involved with something more sinister, but his mysterious death put an end to his investigation. Sue starts interviewing the studio bigwigs and gets suspicious, too. As reviewer Rob Blackwelder of Spliced Wire put it, "Could all these mean-looking toughs in ponytails and shark skin suits be—oh, I don't know—crooked?"

Dundee decides to help out the little lady by taking on a job as an extra on the studio's latest action film so he can nose around and see if he finds anything suspicious. It also provides a chance to him to engage in acts that are supposed to be amusing. A fellow extra (Paul Rodriguez) is a mentor of sorts to Dundee, but Dundee seems to be an incredibly slow study. All he has to do in his scene is walk down the street, but he ruins take after take by doing things like punching out the lead actor as he rushes through the scene. "Reflexes," says the croc hunter. In another take, he can't even seem to walk properly, swinging his arms awkwardly and staring into the camera. Yes, he is from a different land, but how could this man still be such a rube? They have TV and movie production in Australia, plus he's been in New York City for two films, surely he's picked up some cultural literacy after 15 years. And hasn't living with his girlfriend for a decade and a half taught him anything about American ways?

After charming an errant stage monkey, Dundee gets a promotion to substitute animal manager. This is good for the audience because it puts an end to the painful "extra" scenes. But the crime and intrigue is only in the film to provide some sort of forward motivation for the characters. The real purpose of the film is for Dundee to walk around and goof on Los Angeles. This isn't inherently bad. After all, there is a lot to make fun of about the city, but unfortunately, Dundee only covers the most tired and overworked cliches. For example, he makes a joke about how Angelinos are such nice people except when they get behind the wheels of their vehicles. That Angelinos are mean drivers is not exactly a news flash.

In another scene, Dundee runs into George Hamilton who, in a career lowlight, has to extol the virtues of coffee colonics. Another cameo comes from boxer Mike Tyson. Dundee and his son find Tyson meditating in a park and he teaches them how to do it too. The joke is that Dundee, not knowing who Tyson is (they apparently must not have boxing broadcasts in Australia) doesn't know who he is and decides that Tyson is a very gentle man. (Dundee's ignorance isn't just about boxing. He also doesn't know who Picasso or Tom Cruise are and when a woman he meets on the beach asks if he's gay, he says that, yes, he is a rather jolly person.) Other hilarity involves Dundee accidentally walking into a gay bar and accidentally stabbing the fake animal props on the Universal Studio Tour. In another scene, he is flummoxed by the remote control on a fancy whirlpool bathtub and does things like turning on the bubbles and being shocked by them. For someone who's supposed to have such superb hunter's instincts, he seems to be easily thrown.

In between the gently lame jokes, the movie goes to a lot of trouble to show that Dundee, now firmly entrenched in middle age, is still a cool hero who's appealing to the ladies. When he is walking on Venice Beach with his son, a comely roller skater stops and is immediately attracted to him. Even little Mikey's teacher lusts after Dundee. She is so entranced after meeting him that she starts reading a book about crocodiles and darned if she doesn't manage to look lascivious while reading it. After she meets Dundee, she comments quietly to herself, "Nice butt." It's good that the film has so many characters telling us that Dundee is a looker because it's unlikely that anyone in the audience would be having such thoughts on their own.

This *Dundee* also repeats gags from the first movie. Instead of the famous "THIS is a knife" scene from the first film, we get one where Dundee foils a group of would-be muggers by being quick enough to snatch their guns out of their hands. The jokes in *Dundee* aren't particularly good, but they aren't offensive either, which is a bonus for a recent comedy. It almost has the feel of a film made for kids. It's simple, slow-moving and doesn't have any cursing or sex.

The jokes are silly and easy, the kind of set-ups that a child might like.

Hogan is able to get back into his old character as easily as he dons his old Outback costume. He's older, certainly, but his character never relied on youth as part of his appeal. In a way, it's nice to see an older Dundee. He relies on his wits and skill instead of brute strength and is still able to foil criminals half his age. Kozlowski is blandly pretty as Dundee's girlfriend who's happy to jump back into the business world. It's a credit to screenwriters Eric Abrams and Matthew Berry (former story editors on TV's *Married . . . With Children*) that they were able to envision a male hero whose wife works while he stays home and tends to the child. It's also a nice change to see an older couple onscreen who are happily married. Cockburn, as the requisite cute kid, is not at all annoying, which is a great change from usual child actors. The side characters in the film are just cartoonish figures there in service of the jokes.

Critics found the film to be a middling affair. "*Crocodile Dundee* is slow and fairly funny, but works mostly as a pleasant nostalgia trip for fans of Hogan and the first two films. This one lacks punch," wrote Liz Braun of the *Toronto Sun*. Blackwelder of Spliced Wire called the film a "lifeless, asinine, staggeringly inept mess of haggard franchise gags, out-of-date pop culture japes and Hollywood backlot antics that are less realistic than the tour at Universal Studios." And Max Messier from Filmcritic.com mourned, "It's hard to watch your favorite childhood movie characters grow up and try to capitalize on the same, tired dog and pony show."

—*Jill Hamilton*

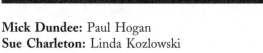

## CREDITS

**Mick Dundee:** Paul Hogan
**Sue Charleton:** Linda Kozlowski
**Arnon Rothman:** Jere Burns
**Milos Drubnik:** Jonathan Banks
**Diego:** Paul Rodriguez
**Jacko:** Alec Wilson
**Mikey:** Serge Cockburn
**Jean Ferraro:** Aida Turturro
**Miss Mathis:** Kaitlin Hopkins
**Cameo:** Mike Tyson

**Origin:** USA
**Released:** 2001
**Production:** Lance Hool, Paul Hogan; Silver Lion, Visionview, Bangalow Films; released by Paramount Pictures
**Directed by:** Simon Wincer
**Written by:** Matthew Berry, Eric Abrams

**Cinematography by:** David Burr
**Music by:** Basil Poledouris
**Sound:** Ben Osmo, Thomas Brandau
**Editing:** Terry Blythe
**Art Direction:** Ben Bauer, Bill Booth, Liz Thomas
**Costumes:** Marion Boyce
**Production Design:** Leslie Binns
**MPAA rating:** PG
**Running time:** 95 minutes

## REVIEWS

*Chicago Sun-Times Online.* April 20, 2001.
*Entertainment Weekly.* April 27, 2001, p. 91.
*Los Angeles Times Online.* April 20, 2001.
*New York Times Online.* April 20, 2001.
*People.* April 30, 2001, p. 31.
*Sight and Sound.* September, 2001, p. 40.
*USA Today Online.* April 29, 2001.
*Variety.* April 16, 2001, p. 28.
*Washington Post Online.* April 20, 2001.

## QUOTES

Mick Dundee (Paul Hogan) about L.A.: "No wonder they call it the city on wheels, they don't even get out of their car to mug you."

# The Curse of the Jade Scorpion

 **Box Office:** $7.5 million

Woody Allen has been making about one film a year for nearly 40 years, so it's not surprising that his work is becoming predictable. Allen's recent movies are almost always set in New York City in the 1930s or 1940s. The soundtrack is jazz from that era. They feature an ensemble of actors: a star or two (including a sexy young Hollywood actress) and an ensemble of reliable, lesser-known supporters. The protagonist is usually played by Allen, or, if not, by an actor who is functioning as a stand-in for Allen. His character is a wisecracking, prickly, neurotic personality who gets in over his head in some shady enterprise and some unlikely romantic entanglements. The closing credits always roll over a black background, there is not even the tiniest of special effects, most of the scenes are interiors, and the film is over in 100 minutes or less.

As a director, Allen is interested only in stories, characters, ideas and dialogue—a fine set of interests, since these remain the central aspects of film and they seem to be in increasingly short supply in an era of bloated star vehicles and expensive special effects. Allen makes his films for a few million dollars, so they can't lose much money even if they're flops. Because he is known as an actors' director, big-name stars work for him for a pittance just for the fun of it. Allen's previous film, *Small-Time Crooks* (2000), was one of his most successful in recent years, both at the boxoffice and among critics. His latest, *Curse of the Jade Scorpion,* is snappy, well-written, and entertaining, but completely uninvolving and inconsequential—an utter trifle.

The days of Allen experimenting with grand themes (as in *Love and Death*) or probing the dark corners of intimacy and truth-telling in relationships (as in *Crimes and Misdemeanors*) are long gone. Like a man who has been playing the same jazz standards for half a century—as Allen in fact has done in his smaller parallel career as a musician—he is doing new riffs on the same old songs. There is nothing ambitious in his latter-day films. Everything is safe and familiar, like the New York of his childhood, which is his only canvas. *Curse of the Jade Scorpion* is pleasant enough, but a year or so after viewing it, it will be hard for one's memory to distinguish its plot from *Manhattan Murder Mystery, Deconstructing Harry,* or other Allen trivialities.

*Curse of the Jade Scorpion* has Allen's signature snappy dialogue and the story line is clever—up to a point. Allen plays C.W. Briggs, an early-1940s insurance investigator who relies on street contacts and intuition to solve difficult cases. He is outraged when his firm hires a new efficiency expert, Betty Ann Fitzgerald (Helen Hunt), who views him as a dinosaur and wants to bring more scientific investigative techniques to the company. Briggs and Fitzgerald quickly develop a nasty mutual antipathy. At a birthday celebration for George (Wallace Shawn), the office's amateur magician, a hypnotist named Voltan (David Ogden Stiers) uses Briggs and Fitzgerald in a stage trick, getting them under his spell and inducing them to profess their love for each other. Later, Voltan calls Briggs on the phone, triggers a hypnotic trance with a voice command, and compels him to steal jewels from mansions whose security systems Briggs himself devised. Of course, Briggs awakens from his trances with no memories of the heists.

Various plot twists keep bringing Briggs and Fitzgerald on collision courses, and they become increasingly entangled in misunderstandings. The new detectives that Fitzgerald has brought into the firm find evidence that points to Briggs, and he comes under heavy suspicion. The plot thickens when Voltan also calls on Fitzgerald to do another heist.

Meanwhile, Briggs discovers that Fitzgerald is having an affair with the firm's boss, Chris Magruder (Dan Aykroyd).

The repartee comes fast and furious but evokes fewer laughs than it should. Briggs is a conceited, though inwardly insecure, man who is adept at barbed comments and double entendres, especially toward women. But because we expect Allen's character to be unceasingly witty, he must say ever more clever and outrageous things to hold our attention. In fact, I get the sense that Allen the writer recognizes that familiarity breeds boredom (if not contempt) and is working too hard to coax laughs. As a result, the dialogue—especially the endless histrionic exchanges of mutual insults between Briggs and Fitzgerald—seems overwrought.

Sadly, Allen's familiar shtick is getting wearisome. Longtime viewers of Allen films are familiar with every acting trick in his repertoire—the shoulder shrugs, the facial twitches, the blank expressions, the stuttering when he is caught in a tight spot. The funniest parts of the film are when the hypnotized Briggs starts speaking in overly polite language—reverting to the kind of stilted dialogue you'd find in the worst films of the era. Otherwise, though, one wants Allen's character to just shut up for a second or say something that is not so belabored in its cleverness.

Problems of believability also dog the plot. When Fitzgerald discovers that the jewels are in Briggs's possession, she threatens to call the police, but inexplicably fails to do so and leaves him with the stolen booty, which he dutifully delivers to a train station locker at Voltan's instructions. Later, when Briggs escapes after being arrested and comes to hide at her apartment, she again decides not to call the authorities. But the biggest credibility gap is the same one that has plagued Allen throughout his career—the problem of explaining why beautiful women in his films are strangely attracted to the nebbish-like character he portrays. In this film, not only does Allen flirt with Elizabeth Berkley (in a small role), he is aggressively seduced by a dolled-up Charlize Theron (playing a naughty, man-eating heiress), and ends up winning the affections of Hunt. Not only is Allen much older than all these women, he is not in their league when it comes to looks. Allen, as he often does, tries to soften the obvious incongruity with a series of self-deprecating remarks by Briggs. Theron is so sexually supercharged and glamorous (she is cast as a prototypical blonde bombshell, and plays it to the hilt) that Allen must expend a lot of dialogue trying in vain to explain her unlikely attentions.

It doesn't help matters to have Aykroyd in a pivotal role with no funny lines. Aykroyd has resurrected his flagging career by playing straight dramatic parts, but he is wooden and unemotional in a role that requires some depth and warmth to help explain why Fitzgerald is attracted to him. Allen, as is often the case with his leading ladies, gives Hunt a lot of lines and scenes, and she performs creditably in a thankless role. Allen gives Briggs all the best lines in their many mutual verbal slugfests; Hunt is reduced to shouting out death wishes. Hunt's part is also thankless because it's difficult to give credence to a bright, attractive young woman whose major problem is that her affections are torn between Allen and Aykroyd, two over-the-hill guys who were never hunks even in their younger days.

The direction that the film is heading is obvious from the beginning, because whenever a man and a woman fight viciously in this type of movie, they end up in love. The whole thing is preposterous, but intermittently enjoyable, thanks to Allen's unflagging skills at writing caustic, period-appropriate dialogue. Allen knows how to dress and pose his characters as send-ups of a bygone era. But the film revolves too much around Briggs, who is an overly familiar Allen character—the smart-ass, slightly defensive, urbane throwback to a simpler era.

Allen also knows how to make a low-budget movie look marvelous; he can adeptly advance even the slightest of plots; and he still can tickle the funny bone. But his films proceed almost as if by rote. When Briggs and Fitzgerald are sent on their hypnotic heists, the same big-band jazz riff plays each time, too loudly, and it's a familiar and annoying Allen convention—using a theme song to illustrate a repeated joke. Another problem with *Curse of the Jade Scorpion* is that the central characters are too buffoonish, shallow, or inconsequential to care about. The characters are not nearly as rich or complex as in some of his best early films. The story line is clever but ultimately pedestrian. And the overarching theme—let's not forget about the heart as we are marching ahead with progress—is trite.

Ironically, the best bit is when Briggs explains to Fitzgerald why she has to believe he is innocent. Frantically, he pleads for her to pay attention to the heart rather than the brain, because the heart is pumping blood that is alive and rich while the brain is just a bunch of relatively lifeless gray cells. Unintentionally, this dialogue serves as a metaphor for Allen—his brain is getting lazy and lifeless and he is falling back, more and more, on the familiar. He is immersed in his fantasy world of bygone New York. He can't resist giving his character a totally incongruous power over beautiful women. His movies, full of that intriguing combination of sarcasm and warmth, have grown stale and unambitious. Woody Allen will always have his fans and critics and a large number of people who just don't care for him. But who would have predicted that this intriguing talent would settle for having such limited horizons?

—*Michael Betzold*

**Chris Magruder:** Dan Aykroyd
**Jill:** Elizabeth Berkley
**Laura Kensington:** Charlize Theron
**George Bond:** Wallace Shawn
**Voltan:** David Ogden Stiers
**Mize:** John Schuck
**Al:** Brian Markinson
**Herb Coopersmith:** Michael Mulheren
**Joe Coopersmith:** Peter Linari
**Charlie:** Prof. Irwin Corey
**Ned:** Peter Gerety

**Origin:** USA
**Released:** 2001
**Production:** Letty Aronson; released by Dreamworks Pictures
**Directed by:** Woody Allen
**Written by:** Woody Allen
**Cinematography by:** Zhao Fei
**Sound:** Gary Alper
**Editing:** Alisa Lepselter
**Art Direction:** Tom Warren
**Costumes:** Suzanne McCabe
**Production Design:** Santo Loquasto
**MPAA rating:** PG-13
**Running time:** 103 minutes

## REVIEWS

*Boxoffice.* October, 2001, p. 58.
*Chicago Sun-Times Online.* August 24, 2001.
*Entertainment Weekly.* August 24, 2001, p. 100.
*Hollywood Reporter.* August 7, 2001, p. 14.
*Los Angeles Times Online.* August 24, 2001.
*New York Times Online.* August 24, 2001.
*People.* September 3, 2001, p. 37.
*USA Today Online.* August 24, 2001.
*Variety.* August 13, 2001, p. 43.
*Washington Post.* August 24, 2001, p. WE34.

## QUOTES

Betty Ann (Helen Hunt) to nemesis C.W. (Woody Allen): "You're a shallow, skirt-chasing egomaniac who's probably more lucky than good!"

## CREDITS

**CW Briggs:** Woody Allen
**Betty Ann Fitzgerald:** Helen Hunt

# Dad On the Run (Cours Toujours)

We often forget how difficult life is for a new father—couple that with pratfalls, mistaken identity, and the traditional Jewish bris and a rambunctious screwball comedy ensues. Dante and Agnes Desarthe's *Dad On the Run*, as the title implies, moves at a staccato pace, punctuated with plenty of chaos and suspense as 23-year-old new father Jonas (Clement Sibony) races against time searching for a place to bury his son's foreskin. The film has also been set against the backdrop of the Pope's August 1997 visit to Paris when tens of thousands of Catholic youth mobilized to promote the love of Jesus.

Jonas, recalling the Jonah and the whale myth, is surrounded by aquatic symbolism. Jonas happens to be a Pisces and instead of ending up in the belly of a whale, he inadvertently ends up in a refrigerated truck filled to the brim with fish where he thinks that he's met his end. Jonas and his best friend Paco (Isaac Sharry) earn a living performing for barmitzvahs and weddings, not exactly satisfying work, but Jonas must support his wife Julie (Marie Desgranges) and their newly born son. After the bris, Jonas learns that he must bury his son's foreskin within three days, only he procrastinates until the last possible moment. Julie phones Jonas while he performs at a bar-mitzvah and demands that he bury the foreskin before dawn.

Reluctant, Jonas' attempts set him off on an unusual journey. When Jonas returns to the bar-mitzvah to borrow Paco's van, his former biology teacher hits on him under the watchful eye of her jealous husband Maurice (Gilbert Levy), leading to further complications for Jonas. As Jonas drives the van onto a motorway, one of the van's tires blows, leading to more misfortunes, including a ride in an ambulance, the loss of shoes and a wallet, and an abduction by a Christian brigade. Later Jonas meets a Romanian woman Nina (Rona Hartner), who's having a nervous breakdown about meeting the Pope because she must steal the religious icon's aura. Wanting to assist the distressed woman, Jonas hands Nina a tissue that may or may not contain his son's foreskin. Needless to say, Jonas won't let Nina out of his sight and later, after Maurice (the jealous husband) and his reluctant thugs pursue Jonas throughout the streets of Paris, Nina believes that the thugs are pursuing her. After the thugs chase Jonas into a warehouse, Jonas hides in a refrigerated truck only to find that he can't escape from the locked truck. Fortunately, Paco rescues Jonas and Jonas manages to bury the foreskin before dawn. Whew!

*Dad On the Run*, with its flaming colors, as well as its screwball characters takes viewers on a fun roller coaster ride through Paris. The film's Jewish traditions do not inhibit the film from reaching a non-Jewish audience and in fact, invite viewers to experience a different culture. *Dad On the Run* presents us with plenty of lighthearted suspense, with questions such as will Jonas retrieve his son's foreskin from Nina's purse and will he bury it in time? The Desarthes built a delightful comedy around the bris tradition while infusing their story with plenty of what-if-this-happened situations. And while the plight of a new father can in itself be daunting, throw in mistaken identity, a Jew being abducted by Christians and later being chased by a gun-wielding jealous husband, and the father has the grounds for a full blown nervous breakdown.

Sibony delivers a flawless performance as a nervous father who will do almost anything to ensure his family's happiness. The young actor oozes innocent charm and immaculate comedic timing and his awkward attempts at burying his son's foreskin or supporting his wife recall Jean-Pierre Leaud's character Antoine Doinel of Truffaut fame. In fact, *Dad On the Run* closely resembles Truffaut's Doinel film cycle sans the chase scenes. Similar to Truffaut, Desarthe possesses a keen visual style and a humanistic approach to comedy. Desgranges portrays exhausted new mother Julie with aplomb. While undergoing a sedate nervous breakdown, Julie attempts to return her baby to the hospital, but is instead sent home. Finally, Hartner brings the right blend of madness, sexuality, and obsessed spirituality to the paranoid Nina as she pursues her quest to capture the Pope's aura.

*Dad On the Run* breaks free of the usual Jewish stereotypes and creates an original comedy that doesn't let up until the last frame.

*—Patty-Lynne Herlevi*

## CREDITS

**Jonas:** Clement Sibony
**Nina:** Rona Hartner
**Paco:** Isaac Sharry
**Julie:** Marie Desgranges
**Sophie:** Emmanuelle Devos
**Maurice:** Gilbert Levy
**Trouillard:** Francois Chattot
**Trouillard's mother:** Francoise Bertin

**Origin:** France
**Language:** French
**Released:** 2000
**Production:** Marin Karmitz, Fabrice Guez; Arte France Cinema, MK2, Les Films du Bois Sacre; released by First Run Features
**Directed by:** Dante Desarthe

**Written by:** Dante Desarthe, Agnes Desarthe, Fabrice Guez
**Cinematography by:** Laurent Machuel
**Music by:** Krishna Levy
**Sound:** Dominique Lacour
**Editing:** Martine Rousseau
**Costumes:** Anne Schotte
**Production Design:** Jean-Hughues de Chatillon
**MPAA rating:** Unrated
**Running time:** 92 minutes

## REVIEWS

*eye Weekly Online.* July 5, 2001.

## QUOTES

Julie (Marie Desgranges) is puzzled by her husband's reaction to their son's birth: "I don't get it. Men usually like to have boys."

# Dark Blue World (Trmavomodry Svet)

Jan Sverak's romantic World War II melodrama, *Dark Blue World,* can be seen as the latest in a line of Czech lyrical sagas extending from the Czech film renaissance that burst upon the world stage in the late '60s. No other film culture has been able to evoke that lyrical blend of tragicomedy and pathos. Sverak's effort harkens back to Jiri Menzel's *Closely Watched Trains* (1966), also set during World War II, which won the Oscar® for the Best Foreign Film. Having won the same award for his *Kolya* (1996), Sverak here seems to take himself much too seriously.

*Dark Blue World* could have used some absurdist slant, especially since the terrain it treads over is all too familiar. Even its juggling of time periods feels derived from Anthony Minghella's *The English Patient* (1996). Sverak's subject matter appears original only in relation to the nationality of his characters and the foreign settings they are thrown into. That said, it should be noted that what redeems the film is its unabashed romanticization of wartime aviation, along with the soft-focus cinematography that suffuses the romantic scenes set on terra firma with a sense of loss experienced by memory.

The film's protagonist, Franta (Ondrej Vetchy) is portrayed as a dashing ace aviator, who has to flee his native Czechoslovakia after the Nazis invade. The film then cuts to his entire squadron in England, where they're being taught English so that they can fly for the RAF. These scenes, which take up the bulk of the film's narrative, are intercut with those showing Franta as a powerless prisoner in a Soviet-run labor camp 10 years after the War has ended.

As a young man, what Franta is forced to leave behind in Czechoslovakia is his heart, which he has promised to the beautiful Hanicka (Linda Rybova). He finds a displacement in the bond of comradeship he develops with Karel (Krystof Hadek), an impulsive junior aviator he takes under his wing.

On their first mission, Franta and his Czech squadron are ambushed and lose two of their planes. Franta ends up being reprimanded by his Wing-Commander (Charles Dance in a cameo role). "What did you expect to find up there?" he remarks, with acerbic British wit. "Flies?" Karel's crash landing, however, proves a blessing in disguise. He finds the pretty Susan (Tara Fitzgerald) living by herself in a house in the country, looking after children rendered homeless by the air raids over London, while she waits for her husband to return from the navy.

In comparison with these pastoral interludes, with their old-fashioned romantic twists, the scenes with Franta in the labor prison are mostly set within a hospital ward, where the only dramatic quotient is provided by a fellow prisoner's half-hearted plan to escape.

Karel, unable to keep his good fortune to himself, introduces Franta to Susan. She in turn breaks off with Karel, and initiates a romance with Franta, who is at first hesitant, but then gives in. The bond between Franta and Karel, however, remains unaffected. When Karel crash lands in France, Franta returns to pick him up.

What provides the reversal is Karel spying on Franta and Susan making love. This leads to his attacking Franta, who is now racked with guilt. In the dark skies, in the midst of an aerial dogfight, Franta suspects Karel of firing upon him. This leads to Franta attacking him when they return. Film footage of the encounter, however, proves Franta wrong, but Karel will not accept his apology. Franta's voiceover muses, "A wounded soul takes longer to heal than a wounded body."

Franta's guilt becomes worse when Karel ends up sacrificing his life in the process of saving his. Franta sobs helplessly as he sees Karel's plane make a nosedive into the sea. That event prefigures the further blows the War has in store for Franta's hopes.

When Franta visits Susan, he finds her husband has returned. As he sees her wheeling him around, Franta pretends to be looking for directions, and vanishes out of her life forever. Similarly, when he returns to Czechoslovakia, he finds that Hanicka, after hearing a rumor of his death, has gotten married to the local station guard.

As an epilogue, of sorts, we see Franta take a breather during his drudgery in the labor prison. In those few moments of rest, he hears Karel's voice, and imagines their two planes flying together in an eternal twilight.

Critical response to the film has found it falling between the art film and the commercial epic. Kevin Thomas in the *Los Angeles Times* admits Sverak's "narrative is unnecessarily protracted and conventional" and that the film's "aerial sequences are not all that exciting by Hollywood standards," but that its "uncompromising bleakness and its Eastern European sense of life's cruel absurdities give it a sophistication" above the multiplex fare.

—*Vivek Adarkar*

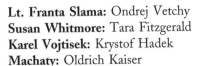

## CREDITS

**Lt. Franta Slama:** Ondrej Vetchy
**Susan Whitmore:** Tara Fitzgerald
**Karel Vojtisek:** Krystof Hadek
**Machaty:** Oldrich Kaiser
**Wing Commander Bentley:** Charles Dance
**Hanicka:** Linda Rybova
**Dr. Blaschke:** Hans-Jorg Assmann
**English teacher:** Anna Massey

**Origin:** Czech Republic, Great Britain
**Language:** English, Czechoslovakian, German
**Released:** 2001
**Production:** Eric Abraham, Jan Sverak; Portobello Pictures, Helkon Media AG, Phoenix Films, Fandango, Czech Television; released by Sony Pictures Classics
**Directed by:** Jan Sverak
**Written by:** Zdenek Sverak
**Cinematography by:** Vladimir Smutny
**Music by:** Ondrej Soukup
**Sound:** Pavel Rejholec
**Editing:** Alois Fisarek
**Art Direction:** Vaclav Novak
**Costumes:** Vera Mirova
**Production Design:** Jan Vlasak
**MPAA rating:** R
**Running time:** 115 minutes

## REVIEWS

*Boxoffice.* December, 2001, p. 57.
*Chicago Sun-Times Online.* January 25, 2002.
*Entertainment Weekly.* January 25, 2001, p. 78.
*Los Angeles Times Online.* December 28, 2001.
*New York Times Online.* December 28, 2001.
*New York Times Online.* January 6, 2002.
*People.* January 14, 2002, p. 32.
*Variety.* June 4, 2001, p. 18.
*Village Voice Online.* January 1, 2002.

*Washington Post.* February 7, 2002, p. WE42.

## QUOTES

Dr. Blaschke (Hans-Jorg Assmann) tells Franta (Ondrej Vetchy) in their prison camp: "The same blows. Nazi interrogations. Communist interrogations. No difference."

## TRIVIA

More than 2,000 Czechs who fled their homeland in 1939 served with the Royal Air Force in England.

# The Day I Became a Woman

**Box Office:** $.1 million

*T*he Day I Became a Woman, a deceptively simple debut feature from Iran, directed by Marzieh Meshkini, and scripted by the renowned Mohsen Makmalbaf, offers a refreshing perspective on contemporary Iranian life, a terrain by now quite familiar to arthouse audiences in the U.S. Meshkini, like recent Iranian filmmakers, exploits the legacy of neo-realism, with its use of nonprofessional actors and on-location shooting, but she also rises above it. The eponymous *Day* is split into three distinct episodes, each introduced by independent titles.

On a sunny morning, in a small seaside town, it is a momentous day for little Havva (Fatemeh Cheragh Akhtar). At noon today, Havva will be nine years old, crossing that border into womanhood, which will require her to cover herself with the dark chador. When her playmate Hassan (Hassan Nabehan) comes around, he is rudely told to leave her alone by the stern Grandmother (Ameneh Passand), who, in addition to the chador, wears a mask of a thick mustache and eyebrows. The Mother (Shahr Banou Sisizadeh) then intervenes, and Havva is allowed out, provided she returns before noon.

When Havva does catch up with Hassan, it is he who is grounded. Even so, through the bars of his window, he gives her money to get some ice cream. She however returns with tamarind candy and a lollipop. Havva, whose performance up to this point has been lackluster and dull, now comes alive, along with the film. To get over the sourness of the candy, Hassan demands a lick from her lollipop. We then see how licking the same lollipop is arousing Hassan in an innately sexual way. As the lollipop is passed back and forth, we are treated to an eroticism so pure and natural as rarely seen in the plethora of films about children.

All too soon, the Mother comes to get Havva and put a chador over her. Despondent, Havva then sits on the beach by herself. Two boys, who are preparing a raft, get her to trade her chador for a plastic toy. The episode's final image shows the raft sailing away, with Havva's chador functioning as its only sail.

The second episode takes us smack into the middle of a long distance bicycle race for women, winding its way along a track by the sea. Ahoo (Shabnam Toloui), clothed in a black chador like everyone else, is not only pedaling with a bad leg, but has to face the ranting of her bigoted Husband (Cyrus Kahouri Nejad), riding on horseback beside her, imploring her to drop out of the race. After Ahoo ignores him, the Husband returns with Mullah Osmaan (Mahram Zeinal Zadeh), a Muslim cleric, also galloping on horseback, who threatens to sanction a divorce on the spot if Ahoo doesn't do as ordered.

Meshkini's camera shows us road signs that signify a new and progressive Iran, but it is a modernity that clearly excludes women like Ahoo. Adamant in her will, she is next confronted by her brothers, also on horseback. They yell at her for bringing humiliation upon their tribe, which frowns on divorce. Ahoo, despite the pain in her leg, manages to surge ahead, but has to forfeit her lead when two riders from the tribe actually block her path. The camera keeps pulling back from the sight of Ahoo, giving up in tears, the sheer might of male power appearing as natural as the waves crashing on the rocks nearby.

The third episode shows us elderly Houra (Azizeh Seddighi), confined to a wheelchair, who has chosen the same day to make her lifetime dream come true, which is to shop for all the consumer goodies she has always wanted to possess. After alighting from a plane, she commands an array of urchin boys. Her shopping spree in the duty-free town soon becomes a procession of giant cartons, containing a refrigerator, a cooking range, and even a bedroom set, complete with a giant bed and two wardrobes. There is however one item she cannot recall to the very end. Through her jaunt, we get a glimpse of the glitzy shopping mall culture that Iran has so readily embraced.

Houra then has the goods unpacked and placed on the beach, where they resemble a surreal tableau, as would be found in a film by Fellini. While waiting for a boat, she is befriended by two young women in chadors, who tell her what happened to Ahoo during the bicycle race. Eventually, Houra's belongings are set up on little rafts, in a line as wide as the horizon. She then sets sail towards a waiting steamer, as little Havva watches from the beach.

Critics have found the film strikingly different from the Iranian cinema they have been exposed to in this country. Stephen Holden in the *New York Times* calls it "a stunner of a film" and "an astonishing directorial debut." He finds that there isn't "a single loose end or extraneous image. What appears on the screen has a starkness that is almost indelible." John Anderson in *Newsday* notes the film's "freshness and audacity," as well as its "anger rooted in basic Iranian womanhood."

—*Vivek Adarkar*

## CREDITS

**Havva:** Fatemeh Cheragh Akhtar
**Hassan:** Hassan Nabehan
**Grandmother:** Ameneh Passand
**Mother:** Sahr Banu Sisizadeh
**Ahoo:** Shabnam Toloui
**Husband:** Cyrus Kahouri Nejad
**Mullah Osmaan:** Mahram Zeinal Zadeh
**Houra:** Azizeh Seddighi
**Young Boy:** Badr Irouni Nejad

**Origin:** Iran
**Language:** Farsi
**Released:** 2001
**Production:** Makhmalbaf Film House; released by Shooting Gallery
**Directed by:** Marzieh Meshkini
**Written by:** Mohsen Makhmalbaf
**Cinematography by:** Ebraheem Ghafouri, Mohammad Ahmadi
**Music by:** Mohammad Reza Darvishi
**Sound:** Behrouz Shahamat, Abbas Rastegar Pour
**Editing:** Shahrzad Pouya, Mayssam Makhamalbaf
**Production Design:** Akbar Meshkini
**MPAA rating:** Unrated
**Running time:** 74 minutes

## REVIEWS

*Boston Globe Online.* April 6, 2001.
*Boxoffice.* June, 2001, p. 60.
*Chicago Sun-Times Online.* April 6, 2001.
*Entertainment Weekly.* April 20, 2001, p. 49.
*Los Angeles Times Online.* April 6, 2001.
*New York Times Online.* March 24, 2001.
*Newsday Online.* April 6, 2001.
*Village Voice.* April 24, 2001, p. 142.
*Washington Post Online.* April 6, 2001.

**TRIVIA**

Debuting director Marzieh Meshkini is the wife of director/writer Mohsen Makhmalbaf.

# The Deep End

*Go deeper.*
—Movie tagline

**Box Office:** $8.8 million

The Deep End might have been written, directed, and produced by two men, David Siegel and Scott McGehee (the team that made *Suture*), but this thriller wears a woman's sensibility. Here is a thriller that focuses on the mother-child bond and shies away from histrionics normally associated with women having a "bad day." And the central character, Margaret Hall (Tilda Swinton), a suburban housewife living in the sticks near Lake Tahoe, endures a string of bad days.

On one bad day Margaret finds the corpse of her son's lover and, fearing the worse, she drags the corpse onto a skiff and then dumps the body into Lake Tahoe. On another day, a blackmailer shows up expecting a large payoff just as Margaret's father-in-law keels over from a heart attack. Fortunately, the blackmailer knows CPR. Meanwhile Margaret protects the illusion of domestic bliss. She picks up her children from school, ala soccer mom, and folds the family laundry while arguing with unhelpful bank managers. But even tigresses lose their composure and eventually fall off the deep end.

*The Deep End* was adapted from a rediscovered 1940's noir novel, *The Blank Wall*, by Elizabeth Sanxay Holding. Once hailed by Raymond Chandler and Alfred Hitchcock, Holding's novels have since fallen into obscurity. That is, until filmmakers McGehee and Siegel discovered a once-celebrated novelist who focuses on women, marriage, and motherhood. McGehee and Siegel took some liberties in updating the story—they replaced the daughter character with a son and, for narrative purposes, added a gay element because they wanted to create an emotional gap between Margaret and her son.

As the film opens Margaret Hall barges into a nightclub in search of her son Beau's (Jonathan Tucker) alleged lover, Darby Reese (Josh Lucas). Darby tells Margaret that he will leave her son alone in exchange for $5,000. Later she confronts Beau about his love affair, but Beau dismisses his overprotective mother. One night Darby shows up at the house and beckons for Beau to join him. The two men fight on the dock. Darby crashes through a railing and dies after being impaled by an anchor. The next morning Margaret finds the body, places the body in a boat, and buries Darby at sea. She returns to the house only to find Darby's Corvette in the driveway, so she returns to Darby's corpse and retrieves the keys to his car. She hides all evidence of a crime, then goes on with her domestic life as if nothing had happened until Alek Spera (Goran Visnjic) shows up with a videotape of her son having sex with Darby and demands $50,000 in exchange for the tape.

Try as she might, Margaret can't come up with the cash. It appears that the bank needs her husband's permission, but Margaret's husband is a naval officer away at sea. Menacing stranger Alek has a change of heart after he shows up at the housewife's house while she's in the throes of performing CPR on her father-in-law (Peter Donat), who just suffered a heart attack. However, Alek's partner Nagle (Raymond Barry) berates Alek for going soft on him and decides that he'll pursue Margaret to complete the transaction—leading to dire consequences.

Similar to Dominique Moll's *With a Friend Like Harry* (also reviewed in this edition), *The Deep End* marks another smart and terse thriller. Yet, despite a couple of fight scenes and sharp objects impaling bodies, *The Deep End* portrays few violent moments. The most remarkable moments in the film come through the irony of contrasting domestic life with the nightmare that only Margaret is aware of. And, in the midst of her terror, Margaret still picks her children up from school and even attends her daughter's ballet recital of *Swan Lake*.

All of the actors deliver strong performances, but Swinton, with seeming effortlessness, carries the burden of the film. She plays a woman who will do anything to protect her family, who loves her son, misses her husband, and is attracted to the blackmailing Spera. Known for taking on complex and outrageous characters in such films as *Orlando* and *Female Perversions*, Swinton seems to also be at home playing the complex housewife Margaret.

McGehee and Siegal indulge too heavily in water motifs and the characters appear to be drowning in a sea of blues and greens. The nightclub, with its watery décor, is called The Deep End and the camera lens often shoots through aquariums. However, *The Deep End* shows that old master of suspense Hitchcock has some new successors.

—*Patty-Lynne Herlevi*

**CREDITS**

**Margaret Hall:** Tilda Swinton
**Alek Spera:** Goran Visnjic
**Beau Hall:** Jonathan Tucker

**Carlie Nagle:** Raymond J. Barry
**Darby Reese:** Joshua Lucas
**Jack Hall:** Peter Donat
**Paige Hall:** Tamara Hope
**Dylan Hall:** Jordan Dorrance

**Origin:** USA
**Released:** 2001
**Production:** Scott McGehee, David Siegel; released by Fox Searchlight
**Directed by:** Scott McGehee, David Siegel
**Written by:** Scott McGehee, David Siegel
**Cinematography by:** Giles Nuttgens
**Music by:** Peter Nashel
**Sound:** Robert Eber
**Editing:** Lauren Zuckerman
**Costumes:** Sabrina Rosen
**Production Design:** Kelly McGehee
**MPAA rating:** R
**Running time:** 99 minutes

## REVIEWS

*Boxoffice.* April, 2001, p. 219.
*Chicago Sun-Times Online.* August 15, 2001.
*Entertainment Weekly.* August 10, 2001, p. 49.
*Filmmaker.* Summer, 2000, p. 22.
*Los Angeles Times Online.* August 8, 2001.
*New York Times Online.* August 8, 2001.
*People.* August 20, 2001, p. 34.
*Rolling Stone.* August 16, 2001, p. 111.
*USA Today Online.* August 8, 2001.
*Variety.* January 29, 2001, p. 46.
*Washington Post.* August 17, 2001, p. WE34.

## QUOTES

Darby (Josh Lucas) to a complaining Beau (Jonathan Tucker): "She's a mother, not a moron."

## TRIVIA

Based on the 1947 novel *The Blank Wall* by Elizabeth Sanxay Holding, which was previously filmed by Max Ophuls as *The Reckless Moment* (1949).

## AWARDS AND NOMINATIONS

**Sundance 2001:** Cinematog. (Nuttgens)
**Nomination:**

**Golden Globes 2002:** Actress—Drama (Swinton).

# The Devil's Backbone (El Espinazo del Diablo)

**Box Office:** $.3 million

An aficionado of the horror genre, Mexican filmmaker Guillermo del Toro (*Cronos*) has fallen prey to the genre's clichés with his latest outing, *The Devil's Backbone*. Co-produced by del Toro and Spain's master of kitsch Pedro Almodòvar, this horror film, while rabidly praised by critics, delivers loads of blood, masochism, and disgusting images, but proves as frightening as Casper, the friendly ghost. In fact, the most frightening aspect of *The Devil's Backbone* is its talented cast, who delivers lukewarm performances, its trite dialogue, see-through plot, and badly-written screenplay. We might ask ourselves while viewing the film if the filmmakers were trying to incite laughter from their viewers or screams. One might actually end up screaming with laughter while watching this absurd film.

And yet, the critics don't agree with the above observation. Star struck by the likes of Almodòvar and del Toro, as well as cast members Marisa Paredes (an Almodòvar favorite), Eduardo Noriega (*Open Your Eyes*) and Federico Luppi (*Cronos*), members of the press fell over themselves when reviewing the film. Ed Scheid of *Boxoffice Magazine* called *The Devil's Backbone* "unabatingly compelling." A. O. Scott of the *New York Times* agreed that the film delivered its intended horror, "Mr. del Toro provokes your screams and shudders, but he also earns your tears." Perhaps he was referring to tears of boredom or laughter. Finally, J. Hoberman of the *Village Voice* cited Buñuelian symbolism, "*The Devil's Backbone* is well furnished with Buñuelian touches." And it's true that the one-legged mistress played by Paredes, anti-clerical gibes, jars of deformed stillborn babies, and a sadomasochistic Oedipal sex triangle that appear in the film could have come straight out of a Buñuel classic. However, Buñuel would have upped the ante by adding a bit of melodrama and black comedic moments. *The Devil's Backbone* proves too subtle for Buñuelian comparisons and feels like a cheap imitation of the master's films.

The setting of the film takes place in an ancient schoolhouse in the middle of an Andalusian desert (southern Spain) during the last days of the Spanish Civil War. The school houses children of deceased Marxists and Republicans, as well as principal Cesares (Luppi) and headmistress

Carmen (Paredes), who support the Republicans, greedy groundskeeper Jacinto (Noriega), and an avenging child ghost. As the story begins the protagonist, the orphaned Carlos (Fernando Tielve), is dropped off at the school to basically fend for himself. On his first day, another student, Jaime (Inigo Garcès), picks a fight with him and he meets a ghost of a boy (Junio Valverde) who was murdered on the same day that Franco's army dropped a bomb on the school. However, as the story ambles along we soon realize that the ghost is in fact harmless even if Franco is not and that the groundskeeper is the evil antagonist.

Although the narrative provides few moments of fright, it provides plenty of disgusting images empowered by composer Javier Navarrete's discordant soundtrack and plenty of creepy special effects. For instance, Cesares lectures Carlos about his bottled, deformed fetuses, telling his young student that the fetuses came from misfortune and have been steeped in rum—therefore drinking from the bottles makes one strong. Then Cesares pours and downs himself a glass of fetus-soaked rum. The filmmakers also serve up plenty of pulp in the form of broken ankles, glass impaled flesh, and ghastly wounds after Jacinto ignites an explosion in the old schoolhouse while killing and maiming its occupants.

The film's narrative is too obvious for astute viewers. The ghost is actually warning Carlos of Jacinto's homicidal tendencies instead of seeking revenge on the school's inhabitants, which adds little tension to the film, and Jacinto's evil role could have been played up a few notches. Unintended comical moments arise when Jacinto finds gold nuggets in his dead mistress's wooden leg or when a blood-soaked Cesares lectures the students and plans his revenge on Jacinto when, in fact, his great blood loss would have disabled him. After all, no one walks around talking when they have lost pints of blood.

To the director's credit, the film begins on a promising somber note and ends in a cinematic fashion as the remaining students hobble away across an empty desert towards an unpredictable fate. And the film's concept of setting a horror film against the backdrop of the Spanish Civil War also proved equally promising. However, the boxoffice returns will prove frightening.

*—Patty-Lynne Herlevi*

## CREDITS

**Carmen:** Marisa Paredes
**Casares:** Federico Luppi
**Jacinto:** Eduardo Noriega
**Carlos:** Fernando Tielve
**Jaime:** Inigo Garces
**Conchita:** Irene Visedo
**Alma:** Berta Ojea

**Origin:** Spain, Mexico
**Language:** Spanish
**Released:** 2001
**Production:** Bertha Navarro, Augustin Almodovar; El Deseo, Tequila Gang, Anhelo Producciones; released by Sony Pictures Classics
**Directed by:** Guillermo del Toro
**Written by:** Guillermo del Toro, Antonio Trashorros, David Munoz
**Cinematography by:** Guillermo Navarro
**Music by:** Javier Navarrete
**Sound:** Miguel Rejas
**Editing:** Luis de la Madrid
**Art Direction:** Cesar Macarron
**Costumes:** Jose Vico
**MPAA rating:** R
**Running time:** 106 minutes

## REVIEWS

*Boxoffice.* December, 2001, p. 58.
*Chicago Sun-Times Online.* December 21, 2001.
*Entertainment Weekly.* December 7, 2001, p. 70.
*Los Angeles Times Online.* December 14, 2001.
*New York Times Online.* November 21, 2001.
*Variety.* April 30, 2001, p. 28.
*Village Voice.* November 27, 2001, p. 101.
*Washington Post.* January 11, 2002, p. WE38.

## QUOTES

Professor Casares (Federico Luppi): "What is a ghost? An emotion, a terrible moment condemned to repeat itself over and over? An instant of pain, perhaps? Something dead which appears at times alive. A sentiment suspended in time . . . like a blurry photograph . . . like an insect trapped in amber."

## TRIVIA

Federico Luppi also worked with director Guillermo del Toro on his 1993 film *Cronos*.

# Dinner Rush

*Revenge is a dish best served cold.*
—Movie tagline

**Box Office:** $.6 million

Veteran adman Bob Giraldi's *Dinner Rush*, billed as "his first independent feature" at age 60, has truth-is-stranger-than-fiction stamped all over it. Almost everything we see in the film takes place during the course of one night at an Italian restaurant in a fashionable part of Lower Manhattan. Sadly, mere authenticity in a fiction film has rarely resulted in engrossing viewing. Giraldi, who owns a number of elite New York restaurants, has no doubt found safety in numbers. With a basically skimpy storyline to work from, he has resorted to a host of subsidiary characters, and punctuated whatever little there is of the main story with the true-to-life frenetic pace of kitchen activity. We are no doubt meant to think of ourselves as amongst the guests at this classy trattoria; instead, we end up feeling like the kitchen help. Thus, despite, its feet being planted in the nitty-gritty of its setting, *Dinner Rush* emerges as exploiting the seamier aspects of Italian-American life for its all-too-pat sensationalistic ends. There is very little here of the epicurean bliss of Italian food evoked in the memorable *Big Night* (1996) by Stanley Tucci and Campbell Scott.

A prologue depicts the cold-blooded murder of Rico, a senior partner in the restaurant, which leaves Louis (Danny Aiello) as sole owner. After 25 years, Louis wants out of the bookmaking operation he has been running on the side. Worse, Duncan (Kirk Acevedo), his favorite cook, is a compulsive gambler, using his connection to Louis to accumulate large debts. Udo (Edoardo Ballerini), Louis' son and the head chef, has allowed the food reviews, and the resulting surge in clientele, to go to his head. He wants Louis to make him a partner. Behind it all, nagging at Louis' mind is the need to avenge Rico's murder. However, as lord of a restaurant where it now takes "three months to get a reservation," Louis can afford to take his time on all fronts, even in relation to the crush he has been harboring for Natalie (Polly Draper), Rico's strikingly beautiful daughter.

In the kitchen, Udo throws his temper tantrums, firing a cook because he cannot get the slicing right, while himself reaching, whenever he can, for Nicole (Vivian Wu), an attractive Asian-American waitress, who is really in love with Duncan. The latter comes in late, half-distracted by the collegiate basketball game, on which he has $13,000 riding, on credit. Even so, with the mastery of his culinary touch, he prepares sausages with peppers specially for Louis, and serves them with pride. Louis conveys his appreciation by smiling up at Duncan, and remarking how simplicity, once a staple of the place, has now been lost to the fancy items masquerading as food.

As the dinner crowd gathers momentum, Gigino's is packed, with a line of devotees with reservations waiting for a table. The underrated center of gravity, appearing to keep egos and tempers in their place, is Marti (Summer Phoenix), a waitress and part-time artist, whose paintings adorn the restaurant walls. The night's guests are varied, but Marti seems to be looking after them all. There's the middle-aged art dealer, Fitzgerald (Mark Margolis), and his guests. There's the senior police detective and his wife. Also, there are the two hit men we have seen gun down Rico: Carmen (Mike McGlone) and his fat, non-English speaking accomplice Paolo (Alex Corrado). They've been invited by Louis ostensibly to take over the bookmaking. Carmen, however, wants to cash in on Duncan's debts in order to acquire the restaurant. The most honored guest of the evening though, fawned over by chef and waitress alike, is Jennifer (Sandra Bernhard), a savage food critic, who is having a secret affair with Udo. For her and her female companion, Udo prepares a monumental delicacy of lobster and fried pasta, which he serves himself.

In this melee, whatever payoff the film offers in terms of character revelation comes through the abbreviated intensity of Danny Aiello's performance. At the end of the evening, Louis does have his day. A customer we could never have imagined as a hit man guns down both Carmen and Paolo in the restaurant rest room. Closure follows in the form of Louis passing on the business to Udo. In the film's final moments, Louis is allowed to put his own spin on an old adage. With a self-satisfied air, he proclaims: "Revenge is a dish best eaten cold!"

If Elvis Mitchell's review in the *New York Times* is any indication, *Dinner Rush* will surely be perceived by critics as a "food film," replete with the appeal that that subgenre holds. Despite the film's melodramatic leaning, Mitchell concludes that it's "light on its feet and will send you out in search of a meal."

—*Vivek Adarkar*

### CREDITS

**Louis Cropa:** Danny Aiello
**Udo Cropa:** Edoardo Ballerini
**Nicole:** Vivian Wu
**Carmen:** Mike McGlone
**Duncan:** Kirk Acevedo
**Jennifer Freeley:** Sandra Bernhard
**Marti:** Summer Phoenix
**Natalie Clemente:** Polly Draper
**Fitzgerald:** Mark Margolis
**Ken:** John Corbett
**Paolo:** Alex Corrado

**Origin:** USA
**Released:** 2000

**Production:** Lou DiGiaimo, Patti Greaney; released by Access Motion Picture Group
**Directed by:** Bob Giraldi
**Written by:** Brian Kalata, Rick Shaughnessy
**Cinematography by:** Tim Ives
**Music by:** Alexander Lasarenko
**Sound:** Gautam K. Choudhury
**Editing:** Allyson C. Johnson
**Costumes:** Constance Parlounis
**Production Design:** Andrew Barnard
**MPAA rating:** Unrated
**Running time:** 98 minutes

 REVIEWS

*Entertainment Weekly.* October 12, 2001, p. 62.
*Hollywood Reporter.* May 29, 2001, p. 21.
*Los Angeles Times Online.* November 2, 2001.
*New York Times Online.* March 31, 2001.
*People.* October 15, 2001, p. 42.
*Variety Online.* November 20, 2000.

# The Dish

*As Neil Armstrong set foot on the moon our only link was a satellite dish in rural Australia with a few bugs. (And a few hundred sheep.)* The Dish. *This is the true story of what we didn't see.*
—Movie tagline

 **Box Office:** $2.2 million

In the summer of 1969 all America was abuzz about the upcoming landing of the first man on the moon. It would be our proudest moment as a nation. A symbol of American expertise, ability and determination. And what many people don't realize is that we never would have seen it happen if it weren't for a bunch of Australians.

Located in the middle of nowhere, actually in the middle of a sheep paddock, stands the radio telescope at Parkes, New South Wales, Australia. It weighs 1000 tons and is larger than a football field. Heck it's big enough to play cricket in, and that's exactly what the crew of the largest radio dish in the southern hemisphere do on their time off. The Parkes' dish is manned by sarcastic technician Ross "Mitch" Mitchell (Kevin Harrington) whose job is to maneuver the dish and shy mathematician Glenn Latham (Tom Long) who is such a calculations wizard that he

actually recalculated NASA's "book" because their figures were for the Northern Hemisphere and as Glenn points out this is the Southern hemisphere. In charge of the crew is the recently widowed team leader Cliff Buxton (Sam Neill) whom they affectionately call "the Dishmaster."

Also on hand at the Dish during the summer of 1969 is NASA's American representative Al Burnett (Patrick Warburton) whose responsibility to NASA sometimes clashes with his growing friendship with the not-so-by-the-book Aussies. Guarding it all is a Barney Fifeish, over-zealous guard by the name of Rudi (Tayler Kane) who can't believe his good luck that NASA has issued him a gun and who loves to play with his walkie talkies. Then, every now and then Rudi's sister Janine (Eliza Szonert) stops by with lunch. Janine has a crush on Glenn who has a crush on Janine, but they're both too shy to do anything about it.

Of course America, being as self-sufficient as it can, has a radio telescope at Gladstone, California which will actually transmit the television signal when the astronauts step out of their landing craft, but just in case, NASA has made arrangements with the Australian dish as a back-up receiver. Also, because Australia is on the other side of the Earth, when Apollo XI is out of touch with the United States, Australia can communicate with it. But as mentioned, since the moon walk is to take place while the U.S. is facing the moon the role of the Parkes dish will be minimal at that time.

Nonetheless, it is a proud moment for the tiny, backwater town of Parkes to have even the smallest role in the Apollo XI mission. The townspeople are obviously excited and make special preparations for the big day. Town Mayor Bob McIntyre (Roy Billing) and his wife May (Genevieve Mooy) entertain the U.S. Ambassador (John McMartin) who has come to town to be near the action. Later the festivities will include the Australian Prime Minister (Bille Brown) who doesn't so much care about the moon landing as he does the press coverage and exposure he can gain from the event.

As Apollo XI launches, everyone in town watches in awe. Even their small contribution gives them a firm connection with the world event. But then, during the party for the American Ambassador, the electricity goes out all over town . . . and at the dish. With no power, the dish is useless and Australia will be shamed in the eyes of the world. And even when the power does come back on there's still trouble, the computer has crashed. They've lost all the calculations . . . and Apollo XI. Cliff covers for his crew with Houston to buy them time to solve the problem, and surprise of surprises, even Al goes along with the coverup.

All through the night the crew works to recalculate where the signal will be coming from the next day. As they ponder and think and fret, the U.S. Ambassador shows up for a tour and he wants to stick around and hear the transmission from the spacecraft. So Al and Mitch create a phony transmission for him to hear. As Al worries that he has committed a felony because he has impersonated an astronaut he is also suddenly struck by an easy way to solve their calculation problem. Since Apollo XI is on it's way to the moon just aim the dish at the moon. Simple and effective. What a relief to get Parkes back on line again.

Then comes word that the astronauts don't want to sleep once they've landed on the moon, they want to take those first steps right away. This last-minute change, however, means that the television pictures won't be received by the dish in California but by Parkes. It will be Australia not America that will be facing the moon at that time. The ante has just been upped for Australia's role in the Apollo XI mission.

On the day of the landing, as the Australian crew prepares for their moment in the sun, the dial on the wind gage begins to shudder. This is very odd since the reason Parkes was chosen as the site for the dish in the first place was its atmospheric stability. The dish is rated to withstand 30 knot winds, but if it goes above 10 they're supposed to lock it down. In reality, though, no one knows exactly what kind of wind the dish can withstand. As the moon walk nears, the wind continues to increase. At exactly 12:56 they have to have that dish pointing at the moon. Wind or no wind, and it's now gusting at 55 miles per hour. Dishmaster Cliff canvasses his crew and decides that even though it might put their lives at risk, they must take the chance. So as the wind blows, the dish is joltingly moved into position and everyone holds their breath to see if the dish holds and if the signal can be received. Because if it's not, six million people won't be able to see Neil Armstrong take one small step for man and one giant leap for mankind.

Can you imagine the jubilation in the town of Parkes when everyone realizes that the pictures of man's first steps on the moon are coming from their own sheep paddock and not from Goldstone, when everyone realizes that Australia played a major part in that monumental event that had us all glued to our televisions that incredible day in July 1969? Who'd have thought that there could be so much suspense left in the telling of a space mission from more than 30 years ago? Of course we know that everything will work out OK, but that doesn't make this delightful movie any less suspenseful, and the fact that it's based on a true story makes it all the more interesting to watch.

Almost the entire film was shot on location at or near where the real events took place and, in fact, the dish still is considered a part of the NASA system—and is still surrounded by a sheep paddock. Even the recreation of the 1969 control room is realistic because the film's art department actually found some of the original equipment which was too heavy for NASA to ship back so they left it in Australia.

The Dish, one of the highest grossing films in the history of Australian cinema, was a favorite at the Sundance Film Festival and a runner up for the People's Choice Award at the Toronto Film Festival. It is also only the second film from the Working Dog production company, but they are the same filmmakers who are responsible for another Australian gem of a movie, The Castle. One of the reasons that both are such delightful films is the superb ensemble of actors—both main and supporting—and the wonderfully entertaining characters they bring to life. At the top of the list has to be Sam Neill in a beautifully understated and confident performance. Most recently seen in Jurassic Park III, his performance here not only holds the film together, he is its heart. It is his strength that allows the other actors to be more eccentric and still be believable.

Also worth a mention is Patrick Warburton. Mostly recognized as Elaine's boyfriend Puddy from television's Seinfeld, here Warburton infuses a character who could have been nothing more than a rigid, jingoistic bureaucrat into a warm but nonetheless serious professional. But one has to admit that it is guard Rudi who provides much of the film's comic relief, for example, asking "who goes there?" even of the passing sheep.

Obviously another reason for the film's success is a script that can weave together a story of teamwork and technology while still keeping the tone light and carefree. Screenwriters Santo Cilauro, Tom Gleisner, Jane Kannedy and writer/director Rob Sitch should be commended for being able to capture the humor in the innocence of the Australia of 1969 while never losing their affection for the people, the place or the time when pretzels in the local pub was an indication of a world event and the playing of the theme from Hawaii 5-0 is confused for the American national anthem.

While The Dish may not be rolling-in-the-aisles funny, its ability to be consistently humorous while also being suspenseful is quite an achievement. Simultaneously the writers also manage to skillfully juggle two main plots—what goes on at the dish and what goes on in town—along with several subplots, especially those involving the love interest of Glenn and Janine and the Mayor's sullen daughter and the "boy scout" next door. The beauty of the film is the way it focuses on the people behind the scenes of this tremendous historical event. By doing this, not only do we get to spend time with some wonderful characters, we also get to re-experience the moon landing from an original point of view, and an Australian point of view at that.

The Dish is an endearing, good-natured celebration. It is filled with plenty of drama and overflows with heart. It is entertaining and yet filled with substance and a sense of wonder. Just as in the end Apollo XI's mission meant more than just technological achievement, this movie too is about more than just technicians and scientists. It's about the human spirit. How lucky we are that it is so well done. 🎞

—Beverley Bare Buehrer

**Cliff Buxton:** Sam Neill
**Al Burnett:** Patrick Warburton
**Glen Latham:** Tom Long
**Ross "Mitch" Mitchell:** Kevin Harrington
**Prime Minister:** Bille Brown
**U.S. Ambassador:** John McMartin
**Rudi:** Tayler Kane
**Janine Kellerman:** Eliza Szonert
**Billy McIntyre:** Carl Snell

**Origin:** Australia
**Released:** 2000
**Production:** Santo Cilauro, Tom Gleisner, Jane Kennedy, Rob Sitch; Working Dog Productions; released by Warner Bros.
**Directed by:** Rob Sitch
**Written by:** Rob Sitch, Santo Cilauro, Tom Gleisner, Jane Kennedy
**Cinematography by:** Graeme Wood
**Music by:** Edmund Choi
**Sound:** Roger Savage
**Editing:** Jill Bilcock
**Art Direction:** Ben Morieson
**Costumes:** Kitty Stuckey
**Production Design:** Carrie Kennedy
**MPAA rating:** PG-13
**Running time:** 104 minutes

## REVIEWS

*Boxoffice.* November, 2000, p. 166.
*Chicago Sun-Times Online.* April 6, 2001.
*Entertainment Weekly.* March 23, 2001, p. 80.
*Los Angeles Times Online.* March 14, 2001.
*New York Post Online.* March 31, 2001.
*New York Times Online.* March 14, 2001.
*People.* April 9, 2001, p. 51.
*Sight and Sound.* May, 2001, p. 48.
*USA Today Online.* March 14, 2001.
*Variety.* October 2, 2000, p. 23.
*Washington Post Online.* April 6, 2001.

## QUOTES

Cliff (Sam Neill): "We're part of a worldwide team; NASA's just a bigger part of us."

## TRIVIA

The film was shot almost entirely on location at or near where the events of 1969 took place.

# Divided We Fall
# (Musime si Pomahat)

*Czechoslovakia, 1943. The Nazis have arrived. An unlikely couple learns what it means to keep a dangerous secret.*
—Movie tagline

 **Box Office:** $1.3 million

When Roberto Benigni won an Oscar® for *Life is Beautiful* some viewers and critics were appalled that someone would have the audacity to write a comedy about the Holocaust. Radu Mihaileanu's *Train of Life* followed Benigni's film and also drew several comparisons due to its comical gaze at the Holocaust. *Divided We Fall*, the Czech Republic's 2001 Oscar® nominee for Best Foreign Language Film, written by Petr Jarchovsky and directed by Jan Hrebejk, pushes the envelope even further. It portrays unlikely heroes, traitors, and cowards against the backdrop of World War II and the Nazi occupation of Czechoslovakia. However, this black comedy has viewers holding their breath as opposed to laughing with its unexpected twists and suspense.

Here is a film with a misleading trailer. First of all married couple Josef (Boleslav Polivka) and Marie (Anna Siskova) hide a single Jewish man as opposed to providing shelter for several Jews fleeing the Nazis as the film's trailer indicated. But in any case, saving the single Jew proves perilous in itself. Add collaborating Nazi neighbor, Horst (Jaroslav Dusek), who is in hot pursuit of the married Marie, an SS officer who befriends Josef, and nosy neighbors, and a comedy of misunderstandings and mistaken identities ensues, keeping viewers on the edge of their seats. And as the director describes the film, it is the "dramatic story of a hero against his will."

Set in a small Nazi-occupied Czech town during the final years of World War II, a childless couple yearns for a baby but Josef learns he's sterile. One fateful day, Jewish David Weiner (Csongor Kassai), their former neighbor who recently escaped a Polish concentration camp, arrives and seeks refuge in the couple's home. On one hand, Josef doesn't want to endanger his wife, his neighbors, or himself, but on the other hand, he can't turn his former employer over to the Nazis, so the couple hides David in a makeshift pantry. Meanwhile Nazi collaborator Horst, who makes a living off of selling goods confiscated from the Jews, keeps showing up at the couple's home uninvited. In order to keep Horst's suspicions at bay, Josef reluctantly seeks employment selling confiscated goods at Horst's request. However, the neighbors take note of Josef's dealings and turn against him.

One day, Josef, Horst, and the Nazi who purchased David Weiner's confiscated home show up at the house without warning. Marie hides David in her bed, then sweats out a scene in which Horst makes a move on her. Fortunately Josef saves the day by engaging Horst and the Nazi in a rousing German song. On another fateful day, Horst insists that Marie go on an outing with him even though this would be improper behavior for both of them since Horst is also married. Horst drives Marie out to the country, then attempts to rape her but Marie escapes. However, Horst seeks revenge on the childless couple and he shows up with the Nazi, asking the couple to hide the soldier in their home. Marie feigns pregnancy, but after she confesses the truth to her sterile husband, Josef realizes that if Horst learns the truth the couple will be executed.

Josef makes the painful choice of asking David to impregnate his wife in order to save all of their lives. But Marie nearly has a nervous breakdown when faced with making love to a man other than her husband. Fortunately, David does impregnate Marie, which culminates with a birth at the exact time the war ends and communist rule takes over. However, our unlikely hero Josef now faces charges of Nazi collaboration under the new leadership. Horst poses as a doctor and delivers Josef and Marie's son into the world and David surfaces just in time to prove that Josef couldn't have possibly been collaborating with the Nazis since he was, in fact, hiding a Jew in his home.

Doe-eyed Anna Siskova displays a range of expressions as well as immaculate comic timing, while actors Boleslav Polivka and Jaroslav Dusek deliver memorable performances too, with Polivka portraying the unlikely hero and Dusek the unassuming villain. While everyone won't be laughing at Hrebejk's black comedy, *Divided We Fall* proves unforgettable and provides much needed comic relief.

—*Patty-Lynne Herlevi*

**Eva:** Simona Stasova
**Albrecht:** Marin Huba
**SS Officer:** Vladimir Marek
**Dr. Fischer:** Jiri Kodet
**Captain:** Richard Tesarik

**Origin:** Czech Republic
**Language:** Czechoslovakian
**Released:** 2000
**Production:** Ondrej Trojan, Pavel Borovan; Total Helpart (T.H.A.) Film Company, Czech Television; released by Sony Pictures Classics
**Directed by:** Jan Hrebejk
**Written by:** Petr Jarchovsky
**Cinematography by:** Jan Malir
**Music by:** Ales Brezina
**Sound:** Karel Jaros
**Editing:** Vladimir Barak
**Art Direction:** Milan Bycek
**Costumes:** Katarina Holla
**MPAA rating:** PG-13
**Running time:** 123 minutes

## REVIEWS

*Boxoffice.* August, 2001, p. 60.
*Entertainment Weekly.* June 22, 2001, p. 63.
*Los Angeles Times Online.* June 8, 2001.
*New York Times Online.* June 8, 2001.
*People.* June 18, 2001, p. 34.

## QUOTES

Josef (Boleslav Polivka): "You wouldn't believe what abnormal times do to normal people."

## AWARDS AND NOMINATIONS

**Nomination:**
**Oscars 2000:** Foreign Film.

# Djomeh

Hassan Yektapanah's low-key debut feature from Iran, *Djomeh*, raises an issue pertaining to many of the films that have come to comprise the much celebrated New

Iranian Cinema. These filmmakers, in eschewing narrative contrivance, could well be using the objectivity of the film medium, along with their self-effacing stance, to conceal their individual powerlessness, as filmmakers, within a repressive political climate. The simplicity which their films espouse could be less a matter of creative choice than expediency to get the film made in the first place. When these films are showcased at film festivals and in art houses in the west, the repression of a filmmaker's individual creativity that they embody remains masked, as it is located within an aesthetic modality. Unfortunately, aesthetics does not easily translate into dramatic involvement.

For most of its duration, *Djomeh,* which was awarded the Golden Camera for best first feature at the 2000 Cannes Film Festival, labors under this curse. It is redeemed, however, by its eponymous protagonist (Jalil Nazari), a "milk boy" in his late teens, a good-natured simpleton, who has fled war-ravaged Afghanistan, and now has the audacity to look for love in Iran. What makes Djomeh endearing is his solipsistic wisdom by which he cheerfully steers himself through his plight as a refugee.

While mistreated by his Afghani boss, Habib (Rashid Akbari), at the barn where he works, Djomeh finds solace in the avuncular Mahmoud (Mahmoud Behraznia), whom he accompanies in his van to collect milk from a nearby village. On their route, Djomeh bares his soul as regards how it was really a foible of his heart that forced him to flee his home country. As he tells it, he fell in love with a widow 12 years older than him, but her family opposed their union. There is no sense of loss in his recollection. It is as if it has left him more convinced than ever of the need and power of love, howsoever shorn of romance.

It is in a village on the slopes of a barren hill that Djomeh first sees Setareh (Mahbobeh Khalili), a shy young woman who works in her father's grocery store, and who, one morning, is standing in line to sell milk to Djomeh. Their first meeting is barely an exchange of glances, yet Djomeh appears smitten. He finds excuses to visit the store on his bike, but cannot approach Setareh in front of her father. Once, he does find her alone, and places a long order of items, which he doesn't intend to buy. As she is measuring and packing, he confesses his attraction to her, but she remains silent, not even responding with a smile.

Djomeh's life is complicated by Habib's wish to return to Afghanistan, and bring Djomeh back with him. As Habib comes to know of Djomeh's interest in Setareh, he sees his own reputation besmirched, and beats Djomeh mercilessly. Yektapanah cuts to an exterior of their cottage as Habib starts to lash at Djomeh.

Yektapanah's decision to treat his audience as a detached witness leads him to adopt prolonged long takes of proscenium-like medium shots for most of his compositions. We find ourselves standing, not in the middle, but at a distance from these scenes. Interestingly, our sense of the filmmaker's presence becomes erased, so that we feel we are seeing the events firsthand, but unfortunately, what we are witnessing is none too dramatic. We cannot identify with Djomeh's desire, because without Setareh's response, it remains mere infatuation.

Even so, we cannot help but be struck by Djomeh's self-empowering wisdom. "Women are for love and tenderness," he says to Mahmoud, as part of one more conversation on the road, "while from men one can expect duty and friendship." He then gets Mahmoud to intercede on his behalf and speak to Setareh's father. Mahmoud is at first hesitant, and repeats what Habib has been telling Djomeh all along, that as an immigrant he shouldn't be thinking of marrying a local woman, but finally relents.

With all his hopes pinned on Mahmoud, Djomeh waits for the answer. Mahmoud arrives the next day with another worker in tow, and not requiring Djomeh's services any longer. When Djomeh inquires about the result of the meeting, Mahmoud postpones telling him. It is, however, clear to Djomeh, and to us, that his rose-colored view of reality has received a jolt. In the last of its prolonged takes, the camera holds in medium shot on the door to the barn. Then Djomeh enters the frame and slams the door shut after him, as if on life itself.

Critics seem to have accepted the film on its own terms, and found an universality in its focus on the aspect of alienation integral to the immigrant experience. Like others who seem to have been won over to the director's style, A.O. Scott in the *New York Times* admires the film's "quiet, contemplative pace," and sees it as the "latest evidence that the spirit of Italian neorealism has taken up residence in Iran."

—*Vivek Adarkar*

## CREDITS

**Djomeh:** Jalil Nazari
**Mr. Mahmoud:** Mahoud Behraznia
**Habib:** Rashid Akbari
**Setareh:** Mahbobeh Kalili

**Origin:** Iran
**Language:** Farsi
**Released:** 2000
**Production:** Ahmad Moussazadeh; Lumen Films, Behnegar Films; released by New Yorker Films
**Directed by:** Hassan Yektapnah
**Written by:** Hassan Yektapnah
**Cinematography by:** Ali Longhmani
**Sound:** Yadollah Najafi
**Editing:** Hassan Yektapnah
**MPAA rating:** Unrated

**Running time:** 94 minutes

## REVIEWS

*Christian Science Monitor Online.* August 31, 2001.
*New Republic Online.* September 17, 2001.
*New York Times Online.* September 5, 2001.
*Variety Online.* May 29, 2000.
*Village Voice Online.* September 11, 2001.

# Dr. Dolittle 2

*The doctor is in again.*
—Movie tagline

**Box Office:** $113 million

For the discerning filmgoer, the words *Dr. Dolittle 2* are not the most promising on earth. The first *Dr. Dolittle*, while not hideous, was certainly not hailed as groundbreaking cinema. And sequels, well, they aren't generally known for their creative spark. But *Dr. Dolittle 2* had a few things going for it, and one of them was that it was a sequel. For many moviegoers, a sequel is like a Good Housekeeping Seal of Approval. The first film was fine enough, they reason, and the second film won't stray too far from the formula. A "2" after Dr. Dolittle guarantees that the film is going to be about Eddie Murphy and some wacky animals instead of, say, a dark gritty crime drama about urban drug wars.

The second thing the film had going for it is Eddie Murphy. Far from being the comic who once made a comedy special called *Raw*, Murphy is now buffed down to family-friendly comedian. Even his more raucous-than-usual turn as a smart-mouthed donkey in *Shrek* would offend few people. Murphy gave the film another kind of seal of approval. His presence meant the film would be funnier than if it starred someone like Bob Saget, formerly of the excretable *Full House*, but not edgy enough to make anyone uncomfortable in their movie seats.

But the biggest factor in *Dolittle*'s favor was that it was a film to take the kids to that wouldn't be completely painful for adults to watch. As Liz Braun of the *Toronto Sun* put it, "That *Dr. Dolittle 2* is not really a movie is sort of moot. Your little kids will like it. You will not mind it. You will take out your wallet at the box office."

Unlike the first Dr. Dolittle film, in this edition everyone already knows that Dr. Dolittle can talk to the animals.

Since the first film got its dramatic conflict from the fact that Dr. Dolittle had this secret talent/curse, writer Larry Levin had to come up with something to keep those kids from squirming in their seats. Levin must have looked in his old Screenwriting 101 textbook to come up with his tired good vs. evil plot for this one.

In the years since the first film, the good doctor has apparently become renowned for his skill in chatting up the animals. This has caused him trouble with his wife (Kristen Wilson) because he's away from home a lot and his daughter, Charisse (Raven-Symone) because she finds his chosen career to be a personal embarrassment. (Never mind that all teens find their parents mere existence to be a personal embarrassment.)

All this means family conflict when the doctor cancels a fun family trip for business reasons. It seems an evil developer (Jeffrey Jones, an actor who never gets to play a sympathetic character) wants to tear down a lovely forest so that he can sell off its lumber. He's aided by an unscrupulous lawyer played by Kevin Pollack. The forest animals appeal to Dr. Dolittle and together they decide that their only hope is a legal loophole involving one of the forest's female bears, Ava (voiced by *Friends* Lisa Kudrow) who is a Pacific Western Bear, which is an endangered species. If Dr. Dolittle can find a male bear of her type to mate with her, then, yay, the forest will be saved.

Unfortunately, the only male bear of this type is Archie (voiced by Steve Zahn and played by a real bear named Tank). Archie was raised by show people in captivity and knows nothing about living in nature. He's like a old-time Vegas performer, always working his tired shtick and full of show tunes and bad puns. When Archie first shows up at the forest, he greets his new animal friends with a rendition of the song "I Will Survive."

But it's not too certain that Archie will survive since he has all the forestry skills of Zsa Zsa Gabor. When Dr. Dolittle shows him how to peel a piece of bark back to reveal the tasty bugs beneath, Archie swoons with nausea. And when Archie first gets to the forest, he is disgusted. "I'm so dirty," he says with horror. "Look at my paws!" The conflict between what Archie is and what he must become make for a few funny moments. To prepare the big bear for his stint in the forest, Dr. Dolittle shows Archie a documentary on bears in the wild. Archie watches with boredom, saying at one point, "What's he doing—digging?!" as though he can't believe the primitive tedium of the wild bears' lives.

Murphy also has some funny moments with his family, especially in the beginning of the film. He plays the dad figure in the style of a Bill Cosby rather than a Ward Cleaver. His dad is loving but a bit smart alecky. When his daughter complains after her father makes her turn down her music, Murphy says, "Do I look like I care?" playing it to the hilt. "No, stop and look at this face," he says making a hilarious expression of non-caring. It's a quick flash of what makes Murphy funny, and it's unfortunate that there aren't more of these. With a few funny moments like these, Murphy's dad character starts out promising—Murphy could really be successful with a sassy dad character—but for some reason, the sass putters out as the film progresses. Murphy becomes more serious, which is just a waste of his talent. For all the sincere and tender family moments that Murphy is forced to participate in by the end of the film, he may as well have been played by Saget.

Since Murphy is so often called upon to play the straight man, the comedy comes courtesy of the talking animals. In the first film, the animal humor was more focused on scatological issues, but in this one, the humor is more gentle (or some could use the work "unfunny" instead). There's a raccoon (voiced by Michael Rapaport), for example, who seems to think he is some sort of mafia godfather. The *Miami Herald*'s Rene Rodriguez made the point that the quality of voice actors in the second film fell quite a bit: "Where the first film boasted the likes of Chris Rock, Albert Brooks, John Leguizamo, and Ellen DeGeneres, the sequel gives you Jamie Kennedy, Andy Dick and Michael Rapaport." Also in there is Norm MacDonald returning as a randy dog, plus Isaac Hayes as an opossum, and Joey Lauren Adams as a squirrel. Cedric the Entertainer, John Witherspoon, and Frankie Muniz also put in some voiceover time, though only a devoted celebrity hound would be able to identify them.

Reviewers were aware that *Dr. Dolittle 2* was mostly a kids' film and reviewed it accordingly, as one parent to another. "*D2* will not turn up on the American Film Institute list of treasured cinema, but so what—Mom, Dad—this baby moves. (I logged it: In at 7 p.m., out in time to see the Phillies lose to some guy named Beimel)," wrote Gary Thompson of the *Philadelphia Daily News.* Braun of the *Toronto Sun* wrote, "*Dr. Dolittle 2* is easy fare for a hot summer afternoon, the sort of film you can leave and reenter three or four times (for those inevitable trips with the kiddies to the bathroom or the concession stand) knowing that you won't have missed anything crucial." *Entertainment Weekly*'s Ty Burr gave the film a C+ and said: "If you're a parent looking to blow 81 minutes on a sequel that painlessly combines cute talking critters, a hug-a-tree message broad enough for a 2 year-old to catch and a few de rigueur poop jokes, here's your cinematic baby sitter."

—*Jill Hamilton*

**Maya Dolittle:** Kyla Pratt
**Lisa Dolittle:** Kristen Wilson
**Eric Wilson:** Zane R. (Lil' Zane) Copeland Jr.
**Lucky:** Norm MacDonald (Voice)
**Ava:** Lisa Kudrow (Voice)
**Archie:** Steve Zahn (Voice)
**Sonny:** Mike Epps (Voice)
**Joey the Raccoon:** Michael Rapaport (Voice)
**Pepito:** Jacob Vargas (Voice)
**Possum:** Isaac Hayes (Voice)
**Lennie the Weasel:** Andy Dick (Voice)
**Squirrel:** Joey Lauren Adams (Voice)
**God Beaver:** Richard Sarafian (Voice)

**Origin:** USA
**Released:** 2001
**Production:** John Davis; Davis Entertainment Company; released by 20th Century-Fox
**Directed by:** Steve Carr
**Written by:** Larry Levin
**Cinematography by:** Daryn Okada
**Music by:** David Newman
**Sound:** David MacMillan
**Music Supervisor:** Spring Aspers
**Editing:** Craig P. Herring
**Art Direction:** Bradford Ricker
**Costumes:** Ruth Carter
**Production Design:** William Sandell
**MPAA rating:** PG
**Running time:** 87 minutes

## REVIEWS

*Boxoffice.* September, 2001, p. 153.
*Chicago Sun-Times Online.* June 22, 2001.
*Entertainment Weekly.* June 29, 2001, p. 114.
*Los Angeles Times Online.* June 22, 2001.
*New York Times Online.* June 22, 2001.
*People.* July 2, 2001, p. 29.
*Sight and Sound.* August, 2001, p. 41.
*USA Today Online.* June 22, 2001.
*Variety.* June 25, 2001, p. 20.
*Washington Post Online.* June 22, 2001.

## CREDITS

**Dr. Dolittle:** Eddie Murphy
**Joseph Potter:** Jeffrey Jones
**Jack Riley:** Kevin Pollak
**Charisse Dolittle:** Raven-Symone

## QUOTES

Ava (Lisa Kudrow) to Dolittle (Eddie Murphy): "I don't talk to bear pimps."

**TRIVIA**

Archie the bear is played by 800-lb. Tank.

# Domestic Disturbance

*He will do anything to protect his family.*
—Movie tagline

**Box Office:** $44.7 million

A few minutes into *Domestic Disturbance,* an utterly incon-sequential film by director Harold Becker, it becomes clear that this is not a movie that is going to demand much of its audience. The opening credits roll through a series of tableaux in the seaside town of Southport, North Carolina—where the movie was shot on location—as menacing music swells. The music cues the audience that something will be very rotten in this little corner of everyday paradise.

Quickly, the characters are introduced and their charac-ters and motivations are immediately made crystal clear. Frank Morrison (John Travolta) is a third-generation wooden shipbuilder who has a soft heart—we know this because his secretary tells him he's undercharged another client. He rushes off to school to see his son's basketball game and meets up with his divorced wife, Susan (Teri Polo). They find out their son, Danny, never showed up for the basketball game. It turns out he stowed away in a stranger's car and went for some kind of joyride. At the police station, Frank and Susan talk over the situation with Sgt. Edgar Stevens (Ruben Santiago-Hudson). The ser-geant recounts Danny's previous brushes with the law: One after Frank and Susan separated, another after they divorced, and now this third incident upon learning that Susan is set to marry Rick Barnes (Vince Vaughn), a wealthy, likeable new-comer to town. No subtleties here: This is a script that tells you exactly what motivates all the characters and immedi-ately explains all their actions. The film wants to make the point that Danny acts up whenever there's a new issue about his parents—so it simply tells you that he does. Neat and clean, with no loose ends. For a movie that wants to be suspenseful, that's a big problem.

The paint-by-numbers emotional landscaping contin-ues. In a car with his dad, Danny asks: "Ever wish things could be like they were?" Frank replies: "Things weren't so great. Your mom and I were arguing all the time." We quickly are told, in no uncertain terms, that Danny and Frank are very close, that Danny is hurt by every step that

takes Frank and his mother further apart, and that Danny hates the idea of Rick as his stepfather.

The next big scene is on Frank's boat. Susan has talked Frank into letting Rick go sailing with Frank and Danny so that Frank can ease Danny into accepting Rick. Rick tells Frank: "I'd never try to take your place with him." After the sailing is over and Frank is alone with Danny, he asks his son: "Are you feeling just a little bit better about mom marrying Rick?" And Danny says yes. Watching this movie is like reading the pages of a book for children who are just learning how to read. Everything is explained in large, bold print, and short, easy words. The culprit is screenwriter Lewis Colick, who did such an admirable job writing *October Sky.* Why he chose to revert to such a simplistic tone here is only one of the many puzzles about *Domestic Disturbance.*

The plot, such as it is, gets into gear when a stranger shows up at the wedding. It's a shady-looking man named Ray Coleman (Steve Buscemi) who has a mysterious con-nection to Rick's past. Frank's suspicious are aroused, espe-cially after he meets Ray in a diner a few weeks later. The two old friends' stories about their past keep changing. Even this unremarkable and obvious discrepancy is telegraphed in the script. This is a movie for adults who can only parse cinema at the first-grade level.

In case we didn't already know it, we find out Rick is a bad guy when he cruelly berates Danny during a game of catch in the yard of Rick's huge mansion. In a scene with Rick and Ray, we discover the big secret: Ray and two other former partners went to prison for a past crime, while Rick kept the money they embezzled and hired a top-notch lawyer who got him acquitted. A movie that didn't want to spell out everything would have skipped this scene and re-vealed the damning information later; but in *Domestic Dis-turbance* absolutely nothing is below the surface.

Vaughn, tall, square-jawed and stoic, has a menacing stare lurking beneath an oily veneer of suave charm. He's like a comic-book version of the good-looking, smooth-talking villain. Travolta attempts to play a long-suffering, misunder-stood, working-class hero, and he does so with his character-istic stuffed-emotions simmering; the role doesn't stretch him, and he relies completely on his ruffled, ain't-I-a-nice-guy bonhomie. Buscemi provides a little zing by looking and acting like a small-time crook out of a 1950s television show. His lips almost look tobacco-stained as he wraps them limply around a cigarette; he wears pale green shirts and sticks out in the upscale town like a sore thumb.

Polo, who got her big break playing Ben Stiller's fiancee in *Meet the Parents,* is the stereotypically underwritten clueless dupe manipulated by a romantic swindler; her char-acter doesn't have much to do except react to events. O'Leary does well in the key role, making a 12-year-old boy's terror seem palpable; he's the emotional center of a film that wears all its emotions openly on its sleeves.

Soon, Danny runs away from home, stowing away in the backseat of Rick's van, and witnesses Rick taking Ray to a brick works, stabbing him to death, and then burning his body in a kiln. No one except Frank believes Danny's story—especially not the police sergeant, who's fed up with the boy's stunts to try to get attention. And when even Frank falters in his support for Danny, Danny has no choice but to knuckle under to Rick's terrifying threats.

Becker does solid, though never subtle, work in the scenes in which Rick is terrorizing Danny. Vaughn's villainy is certainly convincing, as is O'Leary's plight. There are moments of middling suspense, but also, unfortunately, moments of hilarious incredulity. Would a mother and son who are fleeing for their lives stop to answer a cell phone call before opening their garage door and speeding away? Only in *Domestic Disturbance*. In the end, we know that Frank will come to his son's rescue; it's just a matter of waiting around till that happens. When it does, the climactic battle, like everything else in this film, is short, simple, and none too sweet, and then everyone says they are sorry for misunderstanding and misjudging Danny and Frank, and all is well.

The entire film clocks in under 90 minutes—the length of a typical Disney animated feature—and even then there are scenes that could have been excised. To say that *Domestic Disturbance* is a trifle is obvious. It breaks new no ground in terms of plot, style, or technique; it has nothing to say beyond telling a rather trite and simple story. There is absolutely no mystery, and one foot follows the next, as if this were a march rather than a film.

And then there is the title. It sounds like a courtroom movie, or a mannered family parlor drama, and it is neither. Perhaps "Killer Stepdad" would have been appropriate, though it implies a tongue-of-cheek quality that is absolutely missing from this rote exercise. Certainly, no one was going to flock to see something called *Domestic Disturbance* (and virtually no one did). The film is yet another in a long string of poor choices for Travolta, who hasn't done anything that's really challenged him in a long time. And this exercise rather clearly displays his limited emotional range, although to be fair, he doesn't have much material to work with. *Domestic Disturbance* doesn't have the worst script in film history, but it certainly has one of the most predictable and wooden, and Becker's efforts to give the story some zing mostly fail to click.

*Domestic Disturbance* got short shrift, deservedly so, with an early November release and a quick fadeout before the holiday blockbuster rush kicked in. One wonders how movies such as this one keep getting made. With all its financial uncertainties, you'd think Hollywood would be more selective. But this undoubtedly cost little to make, beyond Travolta's salary, and his star appeal may have been enough to guarantee modest profits. But, with its all-around mediocrity, *Domestic Disturbance* has no chance of being memorable, because it doesn't accomplish anything worth remembering.

—*Michael Betzold*

## CREDITS

**Frank Morrison:** John Travolta
**Rick Barnes:** Vince Vaughn
**Susan:** Teri Polo
**Danny Morrison:** Matt O'Leary
**Sgt. Edgar Stevens:** Ruben Santiago-Hudson
**Diane:** Susan Floyd
**Ray Coleman:** Steve Buscemi
**Patty:** Angelica Torn

**Origin:** USA
**Released:** 2001
**Production:** Jonathan D. Krane, Donald De Line; released by Paramount Pictures
**Directed by:** Harold Becker
**Written by:** Lewis Colick
**Cinematography by:** Michael Seresin
**Music by:** Mark Mancina
**Sound:** Douglas B. Arnold
**Editing:** Peter Honess
**Art Direction:** Barry Chusid
**Costumes:** Bobbie Read
**Production Design:** Clay A. Griffith
**MPAA rating:** PG-13
**Running time:** 89 minutes

## REVIEWS

*Chicago Sun-Times Online.* November 2, 2001.
*Entertainment Weekly.* November 9, 2001, p. 81.
*Los Angeles Times Online.* November 2, 2001.
*New York Times Online.* November 2, 2001.
*People.* November 12, 2001, p. 37.
*USA Today Online.* November 2, 2001.
*Variety.* October 29, 2001, p. 25.
*Washington Post.* November 2, 2001, p. WE39.

# Don't Say a Word

*. . .I'll never tell . . .*
—Movie tagline

**Box Office:** $54.9 million

D r. Nathan Conrad (Michael Douglas) is, quite frankly, too good to be true. An upscale New York City child and adolescent psychiatrist, he has it all. He is sensitive, intelligent, and wealthy. He has a beautiful wife, Aggie (Famke Janssen), and a smart and perky eight-year-old daughter, Jessie (Skye McCole Bartusiak). This guy can cure the psychologically sick, give his wife a sexy sponge bath, make French toast for breakfast in bed, and still pick up the turkey for Thanksgiving dinner. Surely sainthood can't be far behind.

Patrick B. Koster (Sean Bean), on the other hand, may be too evil to be true. He has coldly masterminded a robbery, has no second-thoughts about throwing a fellow robber in front of a subway train, and kidnapping an eight-year-old is, well, child's play.

So how will these two opposites find themselves attracting? Koster wants something that, unknown to Conrad, only the psychiatrist may be able to obtain And should Conrad refuse, Koster has an insurance policy, he has Conrad's daughter Jessie.

Here's the set up. Ten years earlier, Koster and his pals robbed a bank, taking only a diamond worth $10 million dollars. However, Koster quickly realizes there is no honor among thieves because one of his pals runs off with the diamond, leaving Koster empty-handed. But the evil Koster hunts him down right into the bowels of a New York city subway station where the double-dealing thief is thrown in front of a train and killed. Watching it all is the thief's eight-year-old daughter and Koster would easily have tortured her for the diamond except the police arrest him and his pals right there in the subway station.

Flash forward 10 years and the thief's traumatized daughter, Elisabeth Burrows (Brittany Murphy), who has spent her childhood in mental institutions, has just been transferred to Bridgeview Psychiatric Hospital after severely cutting up an orderly at her previous "home." Because Elisabeth's mental condition is so puzzling, her doctor, Louis Sachs (Oliver Platt), has called in an old friend and colleague who is an expert in the field, Nathan Conrad. Conrad is intrigued by the case but it is Thanksgiving Eve so the best he can do is a quick consult before returning home for a holiday with his perfect daughter and almost perfect wife—seems she can't ski very well and has broken her leg and is stuck in bed.

The next morning, however, Nathan's perfect world is about to fall apart. Jessie is nowhere to be found. With panic rising in their hearts, they receive a perfectly-timed phone call. It's Koster. "We have your daughter," he tells Aggie and Nathan, and the only way they can get her back is to solve a mystery. Elisabeth Burrows has an six-digit number locked inside her unstable brain and Koster wants it no matter what. Conrad is the key to getting it, and he has until 5 p.m. or Jessie never comes home again.

So while Nathan frantically researches Elisabeth's condition and prepares for one of psychiatry's fastest therapy sessions, and while Aggie is stuck in bed with the bad guys watching her every move via cameras placed in every room of their apartment, Jessie proves she's a chip off the old psychiatrist's block. Trying to befriend the one kidnapper given the job of watching her, she asks Max (ex-NFL player Conrad Goode) his name, asks him about his tattoos, comments on his long hair, asks him if he likes country and western music, and sings to him. Of course she's actually trying to signal her mother who, after peaking out the window, Jessie has just realized is in the apartment below where she is being held.

But did Aggie hear her? And if she did, why didn't she and Nathan hear the incredible racket the bad guys must have made during the night when they crashed into the old lady's apartment above them or when they went through every room of the Conrads' apartment setting up their surveillance system, not to mention kidnapping Jessie who I imagine would not go quietly.

These are just a few of the logic problems that plague a movie that is all gloss and little substance. *Don't Say a Word* is based on the 1991 novel of the same name by Andrew Klavan which won the Mystery Writers of America's "Edgar" award for best mystery novel of the year. The mystery here may be "what happened?" When the novel was turned into a screenplay, it's new authors added characters, gave Aggie a broken leg to immobilize her, had a field day with the film's voyeurism angle, and moved the story to Thanksgiving Day.

Unfortunately, the result is that as coldly as Koster masterminds his evil deeds, we coldly sit and watch them unfold, while the only mystery worth figuring out is what the six-digit number will refer to. Furthermore, since being absorbed in the story isn't a problem, with all that time on our hands, we start to notice the plot inconsistencies and holes like the ones mentioned above.

There's nothing new here. We know what the outcome will be, because this is a very traditional, formula thriller. Anyone who's seen a Hitchcock film has seen this one before. An innocent man, in the wrong place at the wrong time, who suddenly finds himself trapped in situation beyond his control is a central theme to many a Hitchcock film. Add a little *Rear Window* voyeurism and the kidnapping and racing the clock of *The Man Who Knew Too Much* and voila, *Don't Say a Word.*

And talk about formula, haven't we seen Michael Douglas play this character before? A clench-jawed everyman who has everything suddenly finds it stolen by the bad guys whom he must fight to recover it. (And when will these male matinee stars finally have cinema wives/girlfriends who aren't half their age?)

Even the talented Sean Bean is doing yet another reprise of a familiar role. Along with fellow Brit Tim Roth, Bean is one of cinema's most chilling villains, showing his steely-eyed menace in such films as *Patriot Games* (1992), *Ronin* (1998), and as 006 in *Goldeneye* (1995). So here it's just business as usual for Bean. Personally, I find him a much more fascinating hero, such as he played in the British television film series—all of which have his character's name in the title like *Sharpe's Rifles*. There the dark edges seep through to make for an interesting character study.

The center of the film, however, belongs to Brittany Murphy. A veteran of many movies, she may be familiar as the valley girl Tai in *Clueless* (1995) or as the voice of Luanne on Fox's animated television show *King of the Hill*. But undoubtedly it was her role as Winona Ryder's suicidal roommate Daisy in *Girl, Interrupted* (2000) that gave her some basic training for her role here as a woman lost inside her own mind. Unfortunately, even her convincing performance is betrayed by an implausible story. Instead of giving the story life, her character becomes just another one of the story's illogical problems. Is she really mentally ill or is she a sane woman feigning illness to hide away from the villains, or is she really mentally ill but then capable of moments of sanity? She seems to be able to turn her post traumatic stress syndrome on and off at will. How convenient for the story. Nonetheless, Murphy is a talented and versatile young actress—she's set to play Janis Joplin in *Piece of My Heart*, a biopic temporarily sidelined because of a music-rights problem.

As for Famke Janssen's Aggie, she's basically unnecessary as is a character added by the screenwriters, Sandra Cassidy (Jennifer Esposito), a detective who is inexplicably and obsessively investigating murders that could easily wait until after the one-day Thanksgiving vacation. It would seem her characters only purpose is to arrive at just the last minute to save the hero. Surely there could have been a more imaginative way to end the film than employing a character who could easily be left on the cutting room floor.

To be fair, *Don't Say a Word* was released just three weeks after terrorists attacked the Pentagon and the World Trade Center on September 11. And its opening weekend marked the first one since the event in which boxoffice receipts improved—they doubled over the previous weekend with *Don't Say a Word* coming in first with $18 million in grosses. We were all too glued to our television screens before then to go to the movies. Interestingly, this was the best opening for any Michael Douglas film (1998's *A Perfect Murder* only opened with $16.6 million).

This small return to normalcy, however, is no indication of the quality of the movie, which in this case is riddled with inconsistencies and implausibilities. The hero manages to "cure" a patient in eight hours who couldn't be cured in 10 years? The villains get out of jail after 10 years and have no trouble setting up an elaborate surveillance system—

probably using technology not available before their jail terms—virtually overnight? And they must have stashed away a lot of money before being incarcerated, but how did they do that when they don't even take the money when they rob a bank? Not to mention the fact that they all got out at the same time? And 10 years for murder? And why does the all-important diamond look like a ruby?

In short, *Don't Say a Word* offers only superficial tension and few plot surprises, it's an adequate thriller, but breaks no new ground. Mel Gibson did this better in *Ransom* as did Harrison Ford in *Frantic*.

—*Beverley Bare Buehrer*

## CREDITS

**Dr. Nathan Conrad:** Michael Douglas
**Patrick B. Koster:** Sean Bean
**Elisabeth Burrows:** Brittany Murphy
**Jessie Conrad:** Skye McCole Bartusiak
**Aggie Conrad:** Famke Janssen
**Martin J. Dolen:** Guy Torry
**Det. Sandra Cassidy:** Jennifer Esposito
**Russel Maddox:** Shawn Doyle
**Sydney Simon:** Victor Argo
**Dr. Louis Sachs:** Oliver Platt
**Max J. Dunlevy:** Conrad Goode
**Jake:** Paul Schulze
**Arnie Carter:** Lance Reddick

**Origin:** USA
**Released:** 2001
**Production:** Arnon Milchan, Anne Kopelson, Arnold Kopelson; Regency Enterprises, Village Roadshow Pictures, NPV Entertainment; released by 20th Century-Fox
**Directed by:** Gary Fleder
**Written by:** Patrick Smith Kelly, Anthony Peckham
**Cinematography by:** Amir M. Mokri
**Music by:** Mark Isham
**Sound:** Gary Alper, Glen Gautier
**Music Supervisor:** Peter Afterman
**Editing:** William Steinkamp, Armen Minasian
**Art Direction:** Dennis Davenport, Kim Jennings
**Costumes:** Ellen Mirojnick
**Production Design:** Nelson Coates
**MPAA rating:** R
**Running time:** 112 minutes

## REVIEWS

*Boston Globe Online.* September 29, 2001.

*Boxoffice.* November, 2001, p. 149.
*Chicago Sun-Times Online.* September 28, 2001.
*Chicago Tribune Online.* October 1, 2001.
*Entertainment Weekly.* October 5, 2001, p. 110.
*Hollywood Reporter Online.* September 24, 2001.
*Los Angeles Times Online.* September 28, 2001.
*New York Times Online.* September 28, 2001.
*USA Today Online.* September 27, 2001.
*Variety.* September 24, 2001, p. 23.
*Washington Post.* September 28, 2001, p. WE37.

## QUOTES

Patrick Koster (Sean Bean) to Dr. Nathan Conrad (Michael Douglas): "Rule number 1: Don't say a word."

# Double Take

*One big shot. One big mouth. The switch is on.*
—Movie tagline

**Box Office:** $29.8 million

Any whirring noises heard in theaters while watching *Double Take* most likely came from the projection booth, but one cannot rule out the distinct possibility that it was actually the sound of famed author Graham Greene spinning in his grave. The unfortunate decision to turn the admirable 1957 Rod Steiger drama *Across the Bridge,* based upon the Graham Greene short story, into a comedy came to director George Gallo and producer David Permut while watching the film and having the curious reaction of uncontrollable and convulsive laughter. The plot of that fine film concerns a financier who steals a fortune and then, on the run to Mexico, also unfortunately steals a wanted man's identity on his way to a sad end. It does not strike most viewers as a comedy, and neither will *Double Take,* a lame, often grating, and tangled mess of a film.

Also perplexing is its gleeful perpetuation of the racist notion that you cannot tell one black person from another. The two characters in this misfire are poised and polished Daryl Chase (Orlando Jones of *Evolution* and all those goofy 7-Up commercials), a Harvard educated, wealthy New York financier with a beautiful and spacious high-rise office, and Freddy Tiffany (Eddie Griffin of 1999's *Deuce Bigalow*), a boisterous, crude and flashy street hustler. One day, while leaving the offices where Daryl is clearly liked and respected, his briefcase is suddenly snatched by a passerby. As Daryl cries out after the man, Freddy appears and fells the thief

with some well-executed Kung Fu moves. When the police arrive, they see Freddy and the expensive briefcase and jump to the conclusion that he is the culprit, a false impression that Daryl clears up while Freddy spouts off. Daryl offers his thanks and a crisp $100 bill (Freddy tries to extract more out if him with a sob story about a poor, dying mother). Daryl is not quite as grateful, though, when he spots Freddy across the street palling around quite familiarly with the thief.

After this introduction to these two very different people, we learn about the suspicious money transfer of $106 million which Daryl questions and which sets the film's plot in motion. Shortly thereafter, Freddy pops up again, this time perched behind Daryl's desk, using his phone and making suggestive comments about Daryl's sexy supermodel girlfriend, Chloe (stunning model-turned-actress Garcelle Beauvais). She will be appearing at the club where conspicuously-glass-eyed Thomas Chela (Shawn Elliott), the man who made the questionable transfer, will be wined and dined by Daryl and his boss, Charles Allsworth (excellent actor Edward Herrmann, who should know better than to sign on for a film like this). At the club, Daryl is incredulous when Freddy shows up yet again, and the financier is chagrined by the crude comments and embarrassing antics of what he calls the "leprechaun pimp." It seems that things could not get any worse, at least until some mysterious gunmen violently attacked and nearly kill Daryl and Chloe later that night.

They are saved by T.J. McCready (familiar TV face Gary Grubbs), who proclaims himself to be a CIA agent and tells Daryl that Chela's company is a front, laundering money from drug trafficking and responsible for the murder of a Mexican governor. It appears that Daryl is going to be blamed for the suspicious transaction and is wanted by both the authorities and the bad guys. McCready instructs him to lay low while the agent heads south of the border to clear things up. When Shari, Daryl's secretary (Vivica A. Fox in an unbilled appearance), is murdered, the police think he did this as well, McCready tells Daryl to meet him in Mexico. Daryl makes a beeline for Penn Station, shadowed all the way by two men he was warned to watch out for, and once there is greeted by Freddy, whose bombastic badgering gives a desperate Daryl the idea of switching identities to avoid detection. Ducking into a bathroom, the two men who look nothing alike exchange outfits and attitudes, and—voila!— the bad guys and police are instantly baffled. Daryl follows Freddy's advice to "act black," which here means grabbing your crotch, talking trash, inserting a prominent gold tooth in your mouth, and, once on the train, loudly demanding Schlitz Malt Liquor.

Freddy's presence becomes increasingly vexatious to Daryl and to us, especially as the film goes into overdrive with its increasingly fevered attempt to keep us guessing whether this strange character and just about every other character in the film is out to help Daryl or hinder him. Freddy tells Daryl that he is a highly decorated FBI agent sent to protect him and flush out the real crooks. Daryl reacts by pushing Freddy out of the moving train, but soon after the tiny dog Freddy kept hidden in his bag gets Daryl kicked off, as well. Now here is where the ridiculousness and offensiveness kicks into high gear. Driving to the Mexican border, Daryl shows Freddy's passport to the guard, who looks at it, looks at Daryl, and cannot detect that something is not right here. The guard knows the name Freddy Tiffany and the face that goes with it quite well, as they are both prominently displayed on a nearby poster declaring that he is wanted for the murder of Governor Quintana. Clearly, whoever Daryl is, he is not Freddy Tiffany, but the authorities nevertheless are certain that they have got their man and the guns start blazing.

Horrified, Daryl beats a hasty retreat to a used car lot, where he is saved by yet another one of Freddy's out-of-the-blue appearances. Freddy asserts that Agent McCready is tied in with mobster Chela, a.k.a Minty Gutierrez, and so Daryl better start realizing who he can trust. Things seem to warm between the two, but then Daryl abruptly ditches Freddy and takes refuge in a motel permeated with the stench from a nearby emu farm. (This is supposed to be utterly hilarious, one supposes, in a low-brow sort of way, but it just starts one making mental comparisons of which stinks more, the farm or the film.) A redneck there matches the name Freddy Tiffany to the wanted poster, and even though Daryl is obviously not the wanted man, the guy is not fazed in the least by this glaring discrepancy. Meanwhile, Daryl calls McCready and is told that Freddy was, indeed, an FBI agent, but received a mental discharge, is dangerous, and must be avoided at all costs. The fact that Freddy has continued to miraculously reappear (much to our dismay) throughout the film leaves little hope of that. When he materializes yet again, he tries to explain to Daryl about how the drug cartel actually killed Gov. Quintana and framed him for the crime.

Even though Daryl was told earlier that Chela's company was actually a front for drug smuggling and other nefarious activities, it inexplicably comes as a surprise to him when he hears it for the second time. Also baffling is Daryl's seemingly relaxed joshing with Freddy in the midst of his increasingly dire situation. That situation only gets worse—as does *Double Take*—when McCready's men, the authorities, and the aforementioned reward-hungry man descend upon the motel for a scene which, for all its gunfire and explosions, has little dramatic force. Separated once again from Freddy, Daryl makes it back to the border, where he is arrested for being Gov. Quintana's murderer. Clues pertaining to Freddy's nippy dog (which was originally owned by the assassinated official) make Daryl finally realize that Freddy was telling the truth about McCready all along, and he escapes. As Daryl flees, McCready and the two men who sought him back in New York chase after him, but he is once again saved by Freddy's sudden appearance.

All this confusion (and there is even more ridiculousness than is detailed here) leads to the climactic scene in the mansion of Gutierrez, where we see that the mobster with the goofy gaze has not only been in cahoots with McCready and other dirty agents but also with Daryl's esteemed boss. They rehash their convoluted shady dealings and how things went wrong for our benefit, although it never quite makes complete sense, which is okay anyway because few in the audience will have any interest whatsoever at this point in getting it all straight. Daryl and Freddy arrive to get the bad guys and rescue Chloe and Gutierrez's wife, who turns out to actually be Freddy's partner/lover. With still more confusion about who is on whose side, the big scene is ridiculously executed, with elements more cockeyed than Gutierrez. The final revelation that one of the special agents who comes to their rescue is Shari, Daryl's supposedly dead secretary, should be enough to shake loose any in the audience still trying to stay with this endlessly senseless swirl (or is that swill?) as it finally winds down.

*Double Take* received many negative reviews, all of which were richly deserved. Put forward as a comedy/action-thriller, it fails on both counts. It is one of those films in which you can tell that the stars thought they were doing hilarious work, but they enjoy themselves far more than we ever do while watching them. Griffin's irritating character is so off-putting that, as critic Roger Ebert put it, "your heart sinks" whenever he reappears. The filmmakers never make us care who is who or worry much what happens to them, whoever they are. *Double Take*'s reversals and revelations are meant to be clever but are so ceaseless and unconvincing that they merely test your patience instead of your wits. Despite all of the aforementioned shortcomings, the film, made on a budget of $24 million, grossed almost $30 million at the box ffice. Because of those shortcomings, however, *Double Take* was never worth a single look.

—*David L. Boxerbaum*

## CREDITS

**Daryl Chase:** Orlando Jones
**Freddy Tiffany:** Eddie Griffin
**Timothy McCready:** Gary Grubbs
**Agent Norville:** Daniel Roebuck
**Agent Gradney:** Sterling Macer
**Chloe:** Garcelle Beauvais
**Charles Allsworth:** Edward Herrmann
**Martinez:** Benny Nieves
**Thomas Chela/Minty Gutierrez:** Shawn Elliott
**Junior Barnes:** Brent Briscoe
**Captain Garcia:** Carlos Carrasco

**Origin:** USA

**Released:** 2001
**Production:** David Permut, Brett Ratner; Rat Entertainment, Permut Presentations; released by Touchstone Pictures
**Directed by:** George Gallo
**Written by:** George Gallo
**Cinematography by:** Theo van de Sande
**Music by:** Graeme Revell
**Sound:** Kim Harris Ornitz
**Music Supervisor:** Gary Jones, Happy Walters
**Editing:** Malcolm Campbell
**Art Direction:** Virginia Randolph-Weaver, Clayton Hartley
**Costumes:** Sharen Davis
**Production Design:** Steven Lineweaver
**MPAA rating:** PG-13
**Running time:** 88 minutes

 **REVIEWS**

*Chicago Sun-Times Online.* January 12, 2001.
*Hollywood Reporter.* January 12, 2001, p. 10.
*New York Times Online.* January 12, 2001.
*USA Today Online.* January 11, 2001.
*Variety.* January 15, 2001, p. 54.
*Washington Post Online.* January 12, 2001.

# Down to Earth

*A story of premature reincarnation.*
—Movie tagline

 **Box Office:** $64.2 million

Poor Chris Rock. The man can't seem to get himself in a good movie. His oeuvre includes some of the worst movies of recent memory, including the wretched *Pootie Tang*, and *Dogma*. He can't even get good bit parts as was evidenced by his unfunny roles in the late Chris Farley's *Beverly Hills Ninja* and *Jay and Silent Bob Strike Back*. By Chris Rock standards, then, *Down to Earth* is his finest movie work so far. It's a pity that Rock can't score at the movies, because he's quite a funny guy. His stand-up comedy is some of the best around; his HBO sketch comedy series, *The Chris Rock Show*, was quite good; and his book of comedic essays, *Rock This!*, was hilarious.

*Down to Earth* sounded promising. Rock has seen Warren Beatty's *Heaven Can Wait* and decided that the film

had a lot of comedic potential, especially using a black actor in the lead role. (*Heaven Can Wait* itself was a remake of the 1941 film *Here Comes Mr. Jordan*.) Rock was further inspired by meeting Beatty and learning that Beatty has originally pictured Mohammed Ali in the title role. It's not a brilliant starting point for a film, but it seems like something that could yield some good comedy. And *Down to Earth* does have some good comedy. It just doesn't have great comedy. And since Rock is more than capable of great comedy, the film ends up being a disappointment.

Rock, who co-wrote the film with Lance Crouther, Ali LeRoi and Louis C.K., also made himself the leading man. He plays Lance Barton, a stand-up comedian who's funny offstage but just can't seem to work up a good routine onstage. A typical line for him is, "I know a girl so ugly she had to wear make-up on the radio." He lives in fear of being booed off the stage, which happens pretty much every time he does his routine. Despite his bad stage presence, his loyal manager Whitney (Frankie Faison) believes in Lance and sticks by him through bad performance after bad performance.

While working at his day job as a bike messenger, he gawks at a girl, Sontee (Regina King), and promptly gets run over by a truck. An angel named Keyes (Eugene Levy) snatches Lance up and transports him to heaven. Lance is annoyed at being dead and complains to Keyes' boss, King (Chazz Palminteri). As it turns out, Lance is right. Keyes mistakenly yanked Lance from Earth too early—he's not scheduled to die for another 40 years. King offers to rectify the situation by offering Lance the chance to inhabit the body of someone else on Earth. If Lance occupies the body before anyone knows the person is dead, then the trade should work out. Lance is not so happy about the deal, but he's not exactly in a position to bargain.

After rejecting a few unacceptable bodies, Lance finally agrees to occupy the body of Charles Wellington (Brian Rhodes). Although Lance is the same guy on the inside, to everyone else he'll look and sound just like Wellington. Wellington is a rich, old white guy who's just been offed by his cheating trophy wife (Jennifer Coolidge) and her smarmy boyfriend (Greg Germann). They're naturally quite shocked when old Wellington shows up in the drawing room quite alive. They're even more shocked when he tells them he knows that they tried to kill him, but says he forgives them since he knows he's been a jerk. The household help (Martha Chaves and a wonderful Wanda Sykes) are equally surprised when Wellington suddenly wants to watch Black Entertainment Television and offers them big raises. In one of the movie's small, funny moments, the two housekeepers are seen later doing their dusting in new mink coats.

It's a bonus for Lance that Wellington's rich but the real reason he chooses that particular body is because Wellington is acquainted with Sontee, the woman who Lance was (almost) killed by looking at. It doesn't matter much that Sontee hates Wellington. She's an activist for a community hospital that Wellington's company is planning to take over and privatize. Lance as Wellington responds by becoming a somewhat crazed philanthropist. Sontee's impressed, especially since her portly new friend likes rap music and is surprisingly sweet. The two start a romance because, as Sontee puts it more than once, "There's just something about your eyes."

One of the big running jokes in the movie is that Lance is doing all his normal stuff that he likes to do, like sing along to Snoop Dogg, but looks like this old white guy. A few times the movie takes advantage of this, but for some reason, directors Paul and Chris Weitz (*American Pie*) don't use the visual effect of showing Wellington in Wellington's body. Most of the time, the audience sees Wellington as Lance. The few times they do use the effect, it really works. At one point, Lance decides to try his stand-up comedy again. He gets a spot on a show at a primarily black club and starts doing material about the "black" mall in town. "They ain't got nothing in the black mall but sneakers and baby clothes because all we're doing is running and screwing," he says. The line's pretty iffy coming from a black man, but coming from Wellington, it couldn't be more offensive.

Still, a lot of the humor hinges on racial issues. At the beginning of the film, Lance shows up at a building with a doorman and is sent to the back service entrance. "How do you know I'm not here to visit a friend?" says Lance irately. "How do you know I didn't just show up to have a cup of cocoa?" Part of the joke is that he actually is there to make a delivery. Later in the movie, when Lance finds himself back in a black man's body, he tries in vain to catch a cab. "I'm black again!" he yells excitedly.

The center of the film is Rock's performance. He seems believable enough as a leading man, although his character of a stand-up comedian seems a lot like Rock's real life persona as . . . a stand-up comedian. Even though he's playing an angel, Palminteri is doing a same old, same old role as a guy who seems a lot like a mafia don. "I'm a friggin' angel, I can do what I want," he says. Levy is amusingly nervous as the low-level angel who goofs up Lance's case. But the standout supporting performance is Sykes as the spunky maid who hates Wellington and whispers insults under her breath while smiling sweetly at him. It's a reprise of the maid on *The Jeffersons* but Sykes makes it seem fresh and new.

*Down to Earth* landed in theaters with mixed reviews. "Rock has everything it takes to keep the film from bogging down. Let loose, he cruises through the movie with a lightning-speed restlessness: As you're processing one joke, you can see his mind spinning forward to the next two," wrote Stephanie Zacharek of Salon. Rob Blackwelder of Spliced Wire wrote, "The film's bevy of writers overstuff the picture not only with trademarked Rock humor, but with an ample supply of situational comedy." Liz Braun of the *Toronto Sun*

wasn't so fond of the picture. "More than two writers generally indicates a dog's breakfast, and that would be true of *Down to Earth*. The pace is way off for comedy; the story is plot heavy and clumsy whenever it lurches toward a punch line," she wrote. Larry Terenzi of Mr. Showbiz was similarly unimpressed. "For the most part, what passes for energy and agitation onstage translates cinematically to a shrill approximation of his stand-up act." Ernest Hardy of Film.com wrote, "Pandering and tired, *Down to Earth* lurches from one dead gag to the other, in search of both comedic rhythm and a dramatic pulse."

—*Jill Hamilton*

## CREDITS

**Lance Barton:** Chris Rock
**Sontee:** Regina King
**King:** Chazz Palminteri
**Keyes:** Eugene Levy
**Whitney Daniels:** Frankie Faison
**Cisco:** Mark Addy
**Sklar:** Greg Germann
**Mrs. Wellington:** Jennifer Coolidge

**Origin:** USA
**Released:** 2001
**Production:** Sean Daniel, Michael Rotenberg, James Jacks; Village Roadshow Pictures, NPV Entertainment, Alphaville 3 Arts Entertainment; released by Paramount Pictures
**Directed by:** Chris Weitz, Paul Weitz
**Written by:** Chris Rock, Lance Crouther, Ali LeRoi, Louis CK
**Cinematography by:** Richard Crudo
**Music by:** Jamshield Sharifi
**Sound:** Bill Meadows, Douglas Ganton
**Editing:** Priscilla Nedd Friendly
**Art Direction:** Dennis Davenport, John J. Kasarda
**Costumes:** Debrae Little
**Production Design:** Paul Peters
**MPAA rating:** PG-13
**Running time:** 87 minutes

## REVIEWS

*Chicago Sun-Times Online.* February 16, 2001.
*Entertainment Weekly.* March 2, 2001, p. 42.
*New York Times Online.* February 16, 2001.
*People.* March 5, 2001, p. 39.
*Sight and Sound.* July, 2001, p. 42.
*USA Today Online.* Fbruary 16, 2001.
*Variety.* February 19, 2001, p. 37.

# Driven

*Welcome to the human race.*
—Movie tagline

 **Box Office:** $32.6 million

*D*riven manages the impressive feat of being even worse than it sounds like it would be. And it sounds pretty bad. It's written by Sylvester Stallone (not good), is directed by over-the-top action director Renny Harlin (uh-oh) and covers the world of auto racing (see also: *Days of Thunder*). What puts this movie in a category even lower than it would usually be is that even the people who would normally like such a combo didn't like this film. It was a complete bomb at the boxoffice. Even people who know about racing and were presumably interested in a film about the subject were turned off by the fact that the film contained numerous errors and wasn't any true representation of the sport. The sport in this case is racing CART vehicles (Championship Auto Racing Team). Reportedly Stallone studied the subject for years to give his script authenticity. It's too bad he spent so much time researching because for all that his knowledge shows in the final script, he could have just watched a show about it on TV.

The characters, besides the zooming cars, are men who like to face death down in order to win, although that sounds a lot more interesting and dramatic than anything that's actually in the film. Jimmy Bly (Kip Pardue) is the young upstart with talent to burn. We know how great he is because the sports announcers who are annoyingly present throughout the whole film keep telling us this in voiceovers. Actually, these announcers spell everything out in voiceovers, lest we miss any of the few plot points or moments of vague character development. Bly is pushed to succeed by his brother and manager DeMille Bly (Robert Sean Leonard) who can't wait for Jimmy to become a champion so that he can sell him off to any and all endorsement contracts. Bly's also feeling the pressure from his manager, Carl Henry (Burt Reynolds), a mean old coot who yells at his racers from his wheelchair. Bly's big competitor for the championship is the cold German Beau Brandenburg (Til Schweiger).

But Stallone wrote the best part for himself. His Joe Tanto is a once-great racer who threw all his chances away. He's back to mentor Bly and also maybe cheat a little. If he can do things like pull his car in front of Brandenburg's during a race, it gives a little edge to Bly. Tanto is all soulful

glances and wisdom. He helps everyone with their problems and gets the girl. Tanto's lady is Luc (Stacy Edwards), a reporter doing a story on racing. We know it's love when Tanto calls her "wise-ass." Tanto's ex-wife is Cathy (Gina Gershon) who says sharp-tongued things like "Fasten your seatbelt. It's going to be a bumpy ride" to Tanto's new date. She's now married to one of Tanto's competitors and friends Memo Moreno (Christian de la Fuente). And, in perhaps the most thankless role of all, Sophia (model Estella Warren) is first Brandenburg's girlfriend, then Bly's, then Brandenburg's again. She's seems to be as much a trophy of the circuit as the actual win.

There is also a large cast of other female characters, but they are uncredited extras. Before every race, Harlin put in some crowd shots for atmosphere. There we see women's rear ends and women's boobs. Harlin doesn't just try to subtly include these body parts in the shot, he makes them the whole darned show. So, there are actually shots of a woman's butt as the woman makes her way through the crowd and that's all that's in the shot. Even *Three's Company*'s infamous chest close-ups of Joyce DeWitt and Suzanne Sommers would show John Ritter in the shots.

The plot is there, but it really isn't there either. It's impossible to care who wins the race because Stallone never sets any stakes for his character. It's seems like we're supposed to want Bly to win, but there's really no reason for it. He seems like a nice enough guy, but he's not someone that you feel like rooting for. Stallone could have taken the time to throw in a dying grandma or something to give the kid some motivation. The way Harlin filmed the movie makes the viewer detached from what little story there is. He obviously wanted the film to have the feel of a video game and it does but it also has the plot depth of a racing video game. (Non-racing video games have far more intricate plots than this one does.) The races all start out with an aerial view of the course, words superimposed on the screen describing where the course is, then a quick zoom down to the course. Anyone who's ever played a racing video game is familiar with this format. The announcers who repeatedly chatter over the action are as engaging as the announcers on video games. They are talking so much, it's easy to tune then out and make them part of the atmosphere instead of listening to their commentary. After all, if you see a racer's car going off the course, it doesn't offer any additional insight to hear an announcer saying, "His car's going off the course."

But the main factor in the distance between the audience and the action is the editing. Whether the editing style was decided by the editors Stuart Levy and Steve Gilson or was dictated by Harlin himself isn't clear, but it has a huge effect on the film. Shots are barely onscreen for seconds before they flash back off. Instead of seeming exciting, this give the viewer little time to even figure out what's going on. The result is a montage of images that don't add up to a real movie. This seems like it would work well to add excitement to the racing scenes, but it has the opposite effect. There is so much random cutting going on that it's impossible to tell who's ahead in the races or what's even going on. Additionally, the editing is terrible during the few times characters hold conversations with each other. When one actor is emoting, the editors often flash over to a reaction shot of the other actor. It renders the scenes lifeless. Besides, with actors like Schweiger and Stallone, who are barely coherent on the best of days, you need to see their lips moving to figure out what they're talking about.

The acting throughout is laughable. It becomes most apparent when the actors are called upon to give some sort of speech that's longer than a grunt or "Come on!" Pardue, for example, seems merely dull and uncharismatic in his role until he is in a scene where he has to fight with girlfriend Sophia. Then his truly hideous acting becomes immediately apparent. Reynolds, who is not known for being particularly bad, is just as awful as the rest here. And the sight of his strangely taut unlined face is disconcerting. Liz Braun of the *Toronto Sun* described him as "Burt Reynolds, or someone who looks just like him."

But then no one goes to these kinds of films to see the acting (or the plastic surgery, for that matter), it's the action. Does that hold up? Sadly, no. Harlin's short-attention scan camera work ruins any kind of excitement and, to make matters worse, he relies a lot on computer-enhancement. So when a car crashes, we see the beginning of a crash, then an obvious computer simulation of the car swirling through the air. Viewers don't have to be movie buffs to see these fake parts—they'd be obvious to anyone. Movie effects can be frighteningly realistic these days. It's difficult to see why this film would use such chintzy ones. Between all the incessant product placements that bombard the screen, surely they could afford better effects.

Critics, who were willing to give a break to the far superior racing film, *The Fast and the Furious*, weren't cutting any slack to this incoherent mess. Braun of the *Toronto Sun* called it a "technically-wretched movie with a negligible plot, wooden dialogue, indifferent performances and illogical action." Andrew O'Hehir of Salon called it "basically a bad prequel to what might be a pretty good video game." And Rob Blackwelder of Spliced Wire was offended by the "heaps of cliches, stock characters, video game gimmickry, overly elaborate Ginsu editing, moronically contrived filler sequence, inadequate special effects and about four minutes of plot."

—*Jill Hamilton*

**Joe Tanto:** Sylvester Stallone
**Carl Henry:** Burt Reynolds

**Jimmy Bly:** Kip Pardue
**Beau Brandenburg:** Til Schweiger
**Cathy Moreno:** Gina Gershon
**DeMille Bly:** Robert Sean Leonard
**Lucretia Clans:** Stacy Edwards
**Sophia Simone:** Estella Warren
**Memo Heguy:** Christian de la Fuente
**Crusher:** Brent Briscoe

**Origin:** USA
**Released:** 2001
**Production:** Elie Samaha, Renny Harlin, Sylvester Stallone; Franchise Pictures; released by Warner Bros.
**Directed by:** Renny Harlin
**Written by:** Sylvester Stallone
**Cinematography by:** Mauro Fiore
**Music by:** BT (Brian Transeau)
**Sound:** John J. Thomson
**Music Supervisor:** Debra Baum
**Editing:** Stuart Levy, Steve Gilson
**Art Direction:** Chris Comwell
**Costumes:** Mary McLeod
**Production Design:** Charles Wood
**MPAA rating:** PG-13
**Running time:** 117 minutes

 REVIEWS

*Chicago Sun-Times Online.* April 27, 2001.
*Entertainment Weekly.* May 4, 2001, p. 44.
*New York Times Online.* April 27, 2001.
*People.* May 7, 2001, p. 34.
*USA Today Online.* April 27, 2001.
*Variety.* April 23, 2001, p. 17.
*Washington Post Online.* April 27, 2001.

 TRIVIA

The cast includes race car drivers Juan Montoya, Max Papis, Dario Franchitti, and Kenny Brack.

# Enemy at the Gates

*Some men are born to be heroes.*
—Movie tagline
*A single bullet can change history.*
—Movie tagline

*A hero never chooses his destiny. His destiny chooses him.*
—Movie tagline

*A battle between two nations became a conflict between two men.*
—Movie tagline

 **Box Office:** $51.4 million

The battle of Stalingrad, between Hitler's Nazi soldiers and Stalin's Red Army, lasted 180 days from September 1942 to February 1943. Unfortunately, watching Jean-Jacques Annaud's film about a particular episode during the siege feels about that long to the viewer, although it is also based on real personages. (Sniper Vassili Zaitsev was declared a Hero of the Soviet Union for his actions at Stalingrad.)

The film starts with a prologue. A young boy is seen holding a rifle, hunting a wolf in a snowy forest with his grandfather's watchful eye upon him. The old man intones to the boy "I am a stone. . . . I breathe slowly. . . . I aim at the eye." But the boy misses his shot and his grandfather must finish the kill.

Then the action starts, Vassili Zaitsev (Jude Law), the shepherd from the Ural mountains, is seen aboard a troop train eyeing a pretty girl (Rachel Weisz). Before he knows it, he reaches the horrors of Stalingrad where Soviet troops are being led like lambs to the slaughter. The Nazis want to destroy the city so that they can get to the Soviet oil fields in the east but the battle has proved to be more difficult than anticipated. Although the city has been reduced to a pile of burning, smoking rubble, with Nazi planes bombing and strafing the city constantly, Stalin refuses to surrender. The generals throw the untested troops at the superior Nazi forces like so much fodder for their tanks and artillery.

Vassili can't even get a rifle of his own since supplies are so scarce and is forced to take one from a dead soldier during a charge, which is also where he meets the well-educated political officer, Danilov (Joseph Fiennes). When Danilov witnesses Vassili shoot five Nazi officers (one shot each) from long range, a propaganda hero is born. Danilov pipes up to his superior Krushchev (Bob Hoskins), who has been sent by Stalin to the city to "handle" things, that morale is low and "we need our heroes." So Vassili is suddenly front page news on every Soviet paper: the "young shepherd boy from the Urals" who is a master sniper and the Nazi's new bogeyman. In fact, Vassili's exploits have drawn so much attention that the Germans are forced to send their own master marksman, Major Koenig (Ed Koenig), as a counteragent.

Meanwhile, there's always time for a romance. In this case, Tania, the girl from the train, makes a re-appearance as a soldier assigned to the local militia and re-meets Vassili. But Tania's also eyed by Danilov, who wonders why an educated young woman who can speak German should be wasting her time as a foot soldier. So he has her transferred to Soviet headquarters to work near him.

Koenig has also been busy, setting traps for Vassili, trying to lure him into his sights. Danilov has been using a young Russian shoeshine boy, Sacha (Gabriel Marshall-Thomson), as a double-agent. Sacha has been working for the German Major in exchange for supplies, while feeding him misinformation about Vassili's whereabouts. So far neither man can get close to the other, although after Koenig kills several of Vassili's comrades, the young man begins to lose his confidence.

When Tania learns her parents have been rounded up and killed by the Germans (they're Jewish, of course), she asks to be transferred to the sniper division. Vassili tries to discourage her: "It's not like just firing at a distant shape. It's not just a uniform. It's a man's face and those faces don't go away, they come back." Tania insists and begins to accompany Vassili. Koenig has become suspicious of the information that Sacha has been supplying to him, especially after he is wounded by Vassili during a hunt.

Vassili is also tired of Danilov's constant propaganda and protests: "You've built me up and up into someone I'm not. I can't carry that weight anymore." He then misses a chance to get Koenig when he falls asleep after waiting all night for an assault to begin and has his identity papers stolen. The Germans proclaim that Vassili is dead, though Koenig does not believe it. He sets Sacha up to lure Vassili to the train station. Tania follows, and then Danilov follows her—finally realizing that the two have fallen in love, which makes him wild with jealousy.

Koenig knows that Sacha has betrayed him and kills the boy, leaving the body where it will send a message to Vassili. There is to be a final assault on the city and Tania is hit during the bombing. Danilov thinks she is dead and goes to the station to tell Vassili, also admitting that he has sent him on a suicide mission because of his own jealousy. Both know Koenig is lurking somewhere about and Danilov tells his friend: "I want to help you, Vassili. Let me do one last thing. Something useful for a change. Let me show you where the major is." He pops his head out of the rubble and is promptly killed by the German sniper. When Koenig moves out of cover, Vassili is waiting and finally kills his opponent.

Two months later, on February 3, 1943, the Soviets declare victory over the Nazis, and Vassili, who has learned that Tania is alive, is reunited with her in a Soviet hospital. It's very anticlimactic.

The movie is actually at its best during the sniper sequences. The tension mounts as the nobleman from Bavaria faces off against the skills of the peasant from the mountains.

Even a small miscalculation could mean their death. The middle-aged Koenig is a consummate cool professional battling a myth, while the young Vassili becomes increasingly burdened by his propaganda role as a great Soviet hero and has lost confidence in his sharpshooter abilities.

However, *Enemy at the Gates* is surrounded by a predictable romantic triangle, although it certainly takes Danilov a good while to realize what's going on. Maybe Tania's attracted to Vassili because he's played by the grimy-yet-gorgeous Jude Law and poor Joseph Fiennes is stuck with wire-rim glasses and makeup that makes him look ghostly, 'cause there never seems to be any sign of passion between the characters. And did Tania really have to be Jewish and have her family killed in order to have a reason to want to fight an army invading her homeland? Of course, Danilov is also Jewish and they are apparently the only educated Russians in the movie—even Krushchev is depicted as a foul-mouthed, cunning lout.

The rest of the film is standard war issue—lots of rubble, lots of smoke, lots of dirt, lots of slaughter, lots of sappy music—all of it surprisingly unengaging. Which is unfortunate, since the siege of Stalingrad is one of the most powerful stories of World War II. In fact, if you want a feel for what did happen in the bombarded city, watch the 1988 Russian production *Stalingrad* by Iurii Ozerov or Joseph Vilsmaier's 1993 German production *Stalingrad* instead.

—*Christine Tomassini*

## CREDITS

**Vassili Zaitsev:** Jude Law
**Major Koenig:** Ed Harris
**Danilov:** Joseph Fiennes
**Tania:** Rachel Weisz
**Krushchev:** Bob Hoskins
**Sacha:** Gabriel Marshall-Thomson
**Mrs. Filipov:** Eva Mattes
**Kulikov:** Ron Perlman
**General von Paulus:** Matthias Habich

**Origin:** Germany, Great Britain, Ireland, USA
**Released:** 2000
**Production:** John Schofield, Jean-Jacques Annaud; Reperage; released by Paramount Pictures, Mandalay Entertainment
**Directed by:** Jean-Jacques Annaud
**Written by:** Jean-Jacques Annaud, Alain Godard
**Cinematography by:** Robert Fraisse
**Music by:** James Horner
**Sound:** Eddy Joseph, Martin Mueller, Rich Kline, Chris Carpenter

**Editing:** Noell Boisson, Humphrey Dixon
**Art Direction:** Steven Lawrence, Dominic Master
**Costumes:** Janty Yates
**Production Design:** Wolf Kroeger
**MPAA rating:** R
**Running time:** 131 minutes

## REVIEWS

*Boxoffice.* May, 2001, p. 60.
*Chicago Sun-Times Online.* March 16, 2001.
*Entertainment Weekly.* March 23, 2001, p. 73.
*Los Angeles Times Online.* March 16, 2001.
*New York Times Online.* March 16, 2001.
*Rolling Stone.* April 12, 2001, p. 146.
*San Francisco Chronicle.* March 16, 2001, p. C1.
*Sight and Sound.* April, 2001, p. 3.
*USA Today Online.* March 16, 2001.
*Variety.* February 12, 2001, p. 35.
*Washington Post Online.* March 16, 2001.

## QUOTES

Danilov (Joseph Fiennes), referring to Major Koenig, tells Vassili (Jude Law): "If you kill him, you could win the war for us."

## TRIVIA

Vassili Zaitsev wrote his own memoir of his duel with enemy sniper Major Konings, which was published as *Beyond the Volga There Was No Land for Us* in 1971.

# Escanaba in da Moonlight

*A comedy about family, love and the great outdoors.*
—Movie tagline

 **Box Office:** $2.2 million

Michigan native Jeff Daniels has appeared in his share of comic and dramatic hits and misses over his career, including boxoffice smashes such as *Dumb and Dumber* and *101 Dalmatians* and wonderful small films such as *Fly Away Home.* Despite his leading-man looks and impressive acting abilities, Daniels has never become a top-echelon

Hollywood star. Part of the reason may be his commitment to maintaining a home and solid roots in the small town of Chelsea, about 60 miles west of Detroit.

For years, Daniels has been heavily involved in local theater as the founder and chief force behind Chelsea's Purple Rose Theatre. Daniels named the place after Woody Allen's *The Purple Rose of Cairo,* in which Daniels turned in his most compelling and enchanting performance. Over the years, the Purple Rose Theatre has specialized in showcasing Michigan playwrights, including Daniels himself. By far its longest-running and most successful play has been Daniels's own *Escanaba in da Moonlight,* a satire of deer hunting in the state's Upper Peninsula. The play was so popular it had a lengthy second run in Detroit.

The popular local reception convinced Daniels to make *Escanaba* into a movie, but he had trouble pitching it in Hollywood. One Hollywood producer who saw the script suggested that the story be set in Las Vegas. Daniels figured the only way to remain true to his vision was to make the film independently, shoot it in Escanaba, a small city in the Upper Peninsula, and use most of the original cast from the Purple Rose production. And that is how Hollywood, in the person of Daniels, came to "Yooper" territory, Yooper being regional slang for a resident of the U.P. When Daniels was done shooting and editing the film, he had trouble finding a national distributor for the film, and began distributing it independently, an extremely difficult feat. It performed beyond expectations during its initial run in Michigan.

Clearly, *Escanaba in da Moonlight* is a heartfelt gift from Daniels. It is his first movie as a writer-director as well as a star, but there is not a trace of pretension in it. Whereas a Hollywood-based director would have distorted the characters and the story to provide a dose of condescending irony, Daniels displays his crudely drawn characters and homespun fable, warts and all, without a trace of embarrassment. This is the product of a local boy made good, coming back home to bring the benefits of his connections and talents to the economy of small-town "flyover" country.

Don't get the idea, however, that *Escanaba* reeks of authenticity. Despite spending most of his life in Michigan, Daniels had never been to Escanaba when he wrote the play, and his family didn't have a tradition of deer hunting in the north woods. He based the story on an adventure book he read as a child and on one trip to a deer camp near Marquette with his brother-in-law.

*Escanba in da Moonlight* takes the form of a tall tale, narrated by Alvin Soady (Harve Presnell), about a decisive hunting season in the life of his son Reuben (Daniels). Reuben is known throughout town as the "Buckless Yooper," because he has managed to reach the age of 43 without ever bagging a deer, though not for lack of trying. When he drives his truck out of town on the eve of opening day of deer season, kids in a school bus openly deride him,

and ladies, fearing the curse of his proximity, drop their grocery bags and scurry to get away from him.

Reuben has been given a loving send-off by his wife, a Native American spiritualist named Wolf Moon Dance (Kimberly Norris Guerrero), who has bestowed on him all kinds of good luck charms and potions. At the family deer camp are his father Alvin and his brother Remnar (Joseph Albright), a dim-witted, beer-bellied, superstitious Joe Six Pack type. Haunting Reuben are generations of family deer camp traditions and endless bragging by his father and brother about record kills both real and imagined. In the deer camp's logbook, his great-grandfather has recorded the biggest buck ever taken in the state. The skeptical Reuben dares to question its veracity, sending his father into a rage.

Completing the hunting party is a whacked-out, bearded and bushy-haired elf, Jigger Negamanee from nearby Menominee. As played by veteran Michigan comic actor Wayne David Parker, Jigger is a puckish vagabond recently been kidnapped by aliens who have scrambled his speech patterns. Narrator Alvin explains that UFO sightings and alien abductions are common fare in the Upper Peninsula, but what is most remarkable about Jigger is that he now has an unlimited capacity for drinking. That is fortunate, because Reuben, who is supposed to bring the traditional meal of pasties (a meat-and-vegetable pie), instead forces the other hunters to drink his wife's good-luck potion, which includes moose testicles, and to splash porcupine urine on themselves to attract deer.

The introduction of the UFO theme begins the script's unfortunate descent into a stew of spiritual potpourri. Arriving on the scene is Ranger Tom (Randall Godwin), a recent transfer from Detroit, who claims that he just saw God in a blaze of flashing lights up on the ridge. Ranger Tom suddenly launches into a rendition of "Swing Low, Sweet Chariot." As the night wears on, Reuben awakens to his own puzzling transcendental experience, which includes an encounter with his wife, with an image of himself as a child, and with a football stadium full of jeering townspeople.

What began as a promising comedy about a man's inability to execute certain important rituals of small-town American manhood turns into an unappealing mixture of extended flatulence jokes and ridiculous metaphysical happenings. It doesn't help that the film's $1.5 million budget allows for only the cheesiest of special effects—some flashing strobe lights and smoke.

Inconsistencies in tone and execution abound. Daniels's script and the film's soundtrack bounce back and forth between a near-reverential view of Yooper family life, crude potty humor, inconsequential absurdism, and an all-purpose spirituality that conflates and confounds native myths, Christianity, and *X-Files*-style New Age mumbo-jumbo. In the end, the plot holds no big surprises or revelations, which makes it clear that much of the middle was mere filler. Most surprisingly, even though the movie is all about killing a deer, we never see any deer on screen.

Unusually for an independent film, it is the performances, not the story, which carry the day. The slovenly Albright and the pixieish Parker turn in masterful comic efforts, milking Daniels's often silly material for all it's worth and whisking audiences past inconsistencies in their characters. Albright's Remnar is supposed to be dumb as a post, but he occasionally offers complex insights; Parker's Jimmer has an alien-fried brain, but he also lapses into frequent bouts of logic. Presnell provides a steadying veteran influence. But his character seems so emotionally detached that you have to keep reminding yourself he's the father, not the uncle, of Remnar and Reuben.

Daniels the actor seems a little tired and distracted, perhaps from the multiple burdens of starring, writing, directing, and getting the film made. He captures the beleaguered, hangdog expression of a man desperate to keep from failing at manhood's rituals, but the script keeps tripping him up, throwing out crude analogies to sexual performance and murky references to spiritual awakenings. As an actor, he is foiled by his own personas.

There is a generosity of spirit in *Escanaba in da Moonlight,* which stems from Daniels's obvious affection for the locals his story both lampoons and lionizes. The generosity extends to Daniels's bringing fine regional actors like Parker the recognition they deserve, and to refusing to sell out his story to a more marketable setting. But no matter how well-intentioned, the film is an auteur project by a film star who hasn't forgotten his roots, but does seem to have forgotten the essential movie-making ingredient: a strong, cohesive story line. There is plenty of comic promise in *Escanba* about the ridiculousness of modern outdoorsmen, but it is not nearly as well realized as the similar material on Canadian television's syndicated *Red Green Show.* In the end, *Escanaba* is not a brilliant slice-of-life about deer hunting, it's not consistently funny enough to be a rip-roaring comedy, it doesn't delve deeply into the male psyche in any dramatic or comic sense, and it doesn't live up to its metaphysical pretensions. It's quirky but unsatisfying.

After releasing *Escanaba in da Moonlight,* Daniels was ready to shoot another film in Michigan. However, *Escanaba* is not another *Fargo:* by itself, it's not going to put Michigan on the cinematic map. This film is a pleasant diversion and a testament to the powers of persistence. But it looks as if the Hollywood bean-counters may have been right about its potential for more than regional appeal. Daniels should get a trophy for effort, but he hasn't really bagged a big buck yet.

—*Michael Betzold*

## CREDITS

**Reuben Soady:** Jeff Daniels
**Albert Soady:** Harve Presnell
**Remnar Soady:** Joey Albright
**Jimmer Negominee:** Wayne David Parker
**Ranger Tom:** Randall Goodwin
**Wolf Moon Dance Soady:** Kimberly Norris Guerrero

**Origin:** USA
**Released:** 2001
**Production:** Jeff Daniels, Tom Spiroff; Purple Rose Productions; released by Purple Rose Films
**Directed by:** Jeff Daniels
**Written by:** Jeff Daniels
**Cinematography by:** Richard Brawer
**Editing:** Robert L. Tomlinson
**Production Design:** Christopher H. Carothers
**MPAA rating:** PG-13
**Running time:** 90 minutes

## REVIEWS

*Detroit Free Press Online.* January 26, 2001.
*Detroit News Online.* January 26, 2001.

## QUOTES

Remnar (Joey Albright) considers hunting season: "It's like Christmas with guns."

# Eureka

*E*ureka, Shinji Aoyama's three hour and 40 minute, black and white opus from Japan, not only affirms that film can be a serious avant-garde art form, but that the very cultural traditions that such a film emerges out of, as well as a filmmaker's uncompromising faithfulness to them, can render such artistic effort inaccessible to anyone not belonging to an exogamous select elite. This is lamentable because *Eureka* is too honest a film to be forced to carry such elitist baggage.

As the film unfolds at its own lugubrious pace, one gets the unique impression that one is viewing a masterwork that is being irretrievably drawn into the black hole of oblivion as one is viewing it. No 'letterbox' video edition can engulf the viewer in the manner of the vastness of the anamorphic screen that the film demands to be projected upon. In its cinematic form, the film evokes a particular tradition of Japanese nature painting that is intended for contemplation by those who cannot afford the luxury of escaping to nature. As such, the landscapes of contemporary rural Japan, which dominate the second half of the film, function as a lynchpin binding both its form and content around the notion of escape from the technological thrust of our time.

However, what renders the film alienating from a western perspective is that Aoyama, as director and screenwriter, seems inspired by another equally profound aesthetic tradition, that of the Noh theater of medieval Japan. Noh plays are pithy, highly abbreviated dramatic pieces, which fall into four categories, each related to a season. More important, each stage movement within them becomes elongated to an unnatural extent, so that the simple movement of an arm can take up to three minutes. This presumably is intended to raise the consciousness of the audience, weaning them away from the pace of everyday life. Dramatic art, kept within a representational mold in the west, here becomes a direct means of spiritual detachment. For most of its inordinate length, *Eureka*, owing to its timely content, strives for just this effect.

If senseless tragedy, borne out of inhuman terrorist acts, has become so interwoven with the fabric of our existence, no matter who or where we are, then Aoyama's film seems avowed to tackle that problem on the very level it affects us the most, that of the everyday. Aoyama is not so much concerned with the motivation behind such acts of random violence or the liberal socio-political institutions that appear to invite them, but rather with their aftermath, which Aoyama portrays as a kind of emotional and moral vacuum within which those who survive such acts are forced to pick up whatever is left of their shattered lives and attend to the business of living.

The above concern, which forms the narrative backbone of the film, is prefaced by a brief visionary prologue. Kozue (Aoi Miyazaki), a teenage schoolgirl, who has never seen the sea, stands facing a row of hills while experiencing a premonition relayed to us through a voiceover: "A tidal wave is coming. Soon, I am sure, it will sweep us all away." Seemingly wise beyond her years, Kozue accepts this apocalyptic fate with a childlike sense of the inexorable.

The film then begins its narrative proper on a typical summer day in a small town in southwest Japan. Kozue, burdened with her schoolbooks, and her elder brother, Naoki (Miyazaki Masaru), get onto an almost empty public bus and silently take their places in the back row. Naoki is immersed in a volume of the violent Japanese comic strip "Akira" while Kozue stares listlessly out the window. We follow the bus, driven by Makoto (Yakusho Koji), along its quiet rural route, as it picks up a few passengers, and the Main Titles are superimposed.

Suddenly, the film cuts to an extreme close-up of a lifeless bloodstained hand. A dead body lies face down on the cement of a vacant lot, bathed in bright sunshine, near the stationary bus. The silence is broken as a passenger comes running out and is shot dead from inside the bus. In the distance, behind the security of a fence, police can be seen milling about as more police cars arrive with sirens whining. As the men take their positions, Shigeo (Mitsuishi Ken), the local young police captain, takes charge and studies the bus with his binoculars.

Inside, Makoto looks on helplessly from a passenger seat. The Hijacker (Go Riju), who looks a normal young officegoer, has a gun in one hand and with the other uses his cell phone to speak to the authorities. Kozue, petrified, sits with her hands clutched to her ears, her head down. No demands are stated. Instead, the Hijacker, clearly deranged, decides to step out for "some fresh air" and enjoy "the beautiful day," taking Makoto as protection. With their backs joined, the two men rotate as the Hijacker, wearing Makoto's cap, confides, "I'm sick of everything!" Makoto, using a moment of distraction, falls to the ground, thereby allowing the policemen, their rifle sites trained on the Hijacker, to fire at him.

Even so, as if determined to kill as many as possible, the Hijacker clambers back into the bus, and is about to shoot Kozue and Naoki dead at point blank range, when he himself is gunned down by Shigeo. In the immediate aftermath, as Makoto sits shivering under a blanket, his eyes widen in horror, as if unable to make sense of what has happened. By endowing his stunning opening sequence with all the trappings of normalcy, Aoyama is able to then take up its long-term effects on lives that will never again be normal.

As newspapers roll off the press, the incident is related in terms of its deaths: six shot dead, including one policeman, with Makoto, Kozue and Naoki as the only survivors. Just as each element of the busjacking pointed to its basis in the everyday world we take for granted, each non-event that follows, as part of the ensuing trauma in the lives of all three, while rooted in the everyday, points to a hollow at its core. To those not prepared to accept the film's realism on these terms, *Eureka* can prove dreary viewing indeed. The film does not abandon the forward movement in time integral to any narrative axis, but the events that comprise that movement bring the film, its narrative, its three principals, and the viewer back to the circle with meaninglessness at its center.

The film skips two years to show that Makoto is still racked by guilt for having survived. His bouts of melancholia result in his straying for long periods away from home, in response to which his attractive wife, Yumiko (Kokusho Sayuri), leaves him. Through a friend, Shigeo (Ken Mitsuishi), he finds menial work with a construction firm. Kozue, having dropped out of school, has become reticent to the point of dumbness. She remains silent throughout the rest of the film. Naoki too does nothing but loll around the house. Their mother leaves their father, who soon dies in a car crash. The two then continue to live on the insurance money. One day, Shigeo idly points out to Makoto the house where the two are living. This rekindles his guilt.

Seemingly independent of its three principals, the film now takes up the subplot of unsolved serial murders in the small town, one of which is that of Makoto's female colleague. The police captain suspects Makoto but cannot make the charges stick. Harangued by his elder brother, Yoshiyuki (Shiomi Sansei), with whom he shares a roof, Makoto decides to leave and move in with Kozue and Naoki, both of whom accept his avuncular care and affection. Makoto cleans up their place which has become a mess. In so doing, we can see that he's cleaning up his own act, so to speak, in relation to his conscience. The harmony of their lives is soon disrupted by the arrival of Akihiko (Saito Yohichiroh), an unruly cousin in his early twenties.

This does not prevent Makoto from attaining his wish to undo the events of that long-ago morning. He acquires a secondhand bus and equips it with the latest hi-tech devices, and the four, now a makeshift family, set off on a cross-country trip. The film now becomes an elongated road movie, locating their journey against the vistas of a Japan unspoilt by technological change, the objective correlative of the clean start Makoto is seeking.

Makoto soon comes to know with a shock that it is Naoki who has been the serial killer. After turning Naoki in to the police, Makoto, in a fit of rage, throws Akihiko out of the bus. This leaves him and Kozue to find their final deliverance by the sea. She begins to speak again and the film turns into color, an epiphany the viewer is intended to share with its characters.

Critical response to the film has understandably veered to extremes. Stephen Holden in the *New York Times* finds the film goes overboard with its "aesthetic agenda," so much so that it "never comes to life." He finds the cinematography, "in sepia-toned black and white, reduces everything to the same muddy hue." At the opposite end of the spectrum, Gene Seymour in *Newsday* finds the landscapes "breathtaking." For him, the film's length allows you "time to feel the characters' wounds and . . . the tortuous effort of their healing. At the end, you feel a sense of both triumph and melancholy."

—*Vivek Adarkar*

**Origin:** Japan
**Language:** Japanese
**Released:** 2000
**Production:** Takenori Sento; released by Shooting Gallery
**Directed by:** Shinji Aoyama
**Written by:** Shinji Aoyama
**Cinematography by:** Masaki Tamura
**Music by:** Shinji Aoyama, Isao Yamada
**Sound:** Nobuyuki Kikuchi
**Editing:** Shinji Aoyama
**Production Design:** Takeshi Shimizu
**MPAA rating:** Unrated
**Running time:** 218 minutes

## REVIEWS

*Boxoffice.* June, 2001, p. 55.
*Entertainment Weekly.* May 11, 2001, p. 53.
*Los Angeles Times Online.* May 4, 2001.
*New York Times Online.* May 4, 2001.
*Newsday Online.* May 4, 2001.
*Sight and Sound.* November, 2001, p. 20.
*Washington Post Online.* May 4, 2001.

## QUOTES

Kozue (Aoi Miyazaki): "A tidal wave is coming soon; and it will sweep us all away."

# An Everlasting Piece

*Piece on Earth.*
—Movie tagline

One of Baltimore filmmaker Barry Levinson's contributions to the worst movie season of the 1990s was *An Everlasting Piece*, a load of Irish blarney that attempted to make light of the "Troubles" in Northern Ireland. Levinson has proved himself as a bankable director many times over, but not all of his films have been as popular as *The Natural* (1984), his popular adaptation of Bernard Malamud's novel starring Robert Redford, and the Academy Award®-winning *Rain Man* (1988). Much of Levinson's best work has been Baltimore based, from his first semi-autobiographical feature film, *Diner* (1982) to the splendid *Avalon* (1990) to *Liberty Heights*, perhaps the best neglected film of 2000. Even so, Levinson's track record has not been perfect, and he has also directed some marginal films, such as

## CREDITS

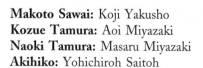

**Makoto Sawai:** Koji Yakusho
**Kozue Tamura:** Aoi Miyazaki
**Naoki Tamura:** Masaru Miyazaki
**Akihiko:** Yohichiroh Saitoh

the eccentric *Toys* (1992) and *Jimmy Hollywood* (1994). Unfortunately, *An Everlasting Piece,* released late in December of 2000 and unable to pull its weight in stronger competition, falls into the latter category, even though it was produced by Oscar®-winner Mark Johnson, who also worked with Levinson on the popular *Rain Man.* After opening to disappointing reviews in January of 2001, the film nearly went straight to video after a limited theatrical release.

The whimsical and eccentric story, set in Belfast and written by the Irish-American actor Barry McEvoy, who is also cast on one of the leading roles, perhaps failed because it was a well-intentioned comedy about the "Troubles" in Northern Ireland. Two barbers, Colm O'Neill (Barry McEvoy), a Catholic hothead and extrovert, and his Protestant friend George (Brian F. O'Byrne), who is Colm's temperamental opposite, have clients at a mental institution, where they discover an inmate known as the "Scalper" (Billy Connolly), who once sold toupees but was imprisoned for scalping people. With some difficulty, they manage to get a list of the Scalper's customers and decide to go into business for themselves. "We're the only hair-piece company in all Northern Ireland," they conclude, as they form a company calling themselves "The Piece People."

Their ambition is to establish a monopoly, but to do so they need an exclusive franchise with a British supplier, Wigs of Wimbledon. They find themselves competing with another operation, called "Toupee or not Toupee" for this franchise, however, so they strike a bargain with the competition: Whoever sells the most hair pieces by Christmas will get the monopoly. As the competition gets underway, the other company seems to have the edge, until "The Piece People" have an opportunity to sell 30 wigs in volume to the Irish Republican Army.

One night Colm and George were stopped on the road by an IRA patrol. Concealing the fact that George is a Protestant, they managed to sell a sample wig to the local IRA leader, who later loses the wig on a terrorist mission. The police find the wig and then set about rounding up all of the bald male Catholics they can locate. This creates a market within the IRA for wigs, and "The Piece People" find themselves in a position to follow through in order to satisfy the demand. Since George is Protestant, however, he naturally has qualms about this arrangement, and Colm reluctantly decides not to work with the IRA for that reason.

Four days before the Christmas deadline, Colm and George are behind in the competition since they refuse to deal with the IRA. But another solution is found by Colm's girlfriend, Bronaugh (Anna Friel), a nurse at the psychiatric hospital, who had sided with George in questioning the ethics of the IRA contract. The young British soldiers on duty in Northern Ireland suffer from a disease called depletia, brought about through stress, which, in turn, causes their hair to fall out in clumps. To improve morale for their

soldiers, the British are willing to offer "The Piece People" a government contract that saves the day for them.

Screenwriter Barry McEvoy's father, it turns out, is an Irish barber who works in downtown Washington, D.C. at a barbershop called the Executive, at Connecticut Avenue and K Street, NW. The elder McEvoy was apparently a technical consultant for the wiggy script: "He claimed that I couldn't properly discuss hairpieces without showing how you anchored them to a customer's head," McEvoy told Gary Arnold of the *Washington Times.* "So I made a big running gag about sticky tape." In fact, the McEvoy family had emigrated to Washington from Ireland when Barry McEvoy was 15 years old. "Belfast didn't seem like such a great place to raise kids when my parents decided to move," McEvoy explained. He described Belfast as dangerous: "Quite apart from the threats of political violence, there were gangs who had begun making a habit of robbing people and stealing cars, feeding off the general breakdown of law and order."

None of that grimness is evident in the film, however, though the O'Neill house is located on the so-called "peace line" in Belfast, separating Catholic and Protestant neighborhoods. Levinson shot the film on location in Belfast for two weeks, then directed interior scene for the movie at a studio in Dublin. Returning to Northern Ireland to make *An Everlasting Piece,* he found Belfast "like an alternate-universe," McEvoy told Gary Arnold: "The same streets and houses, but clean. Far less graffiti on the walls. No smell of smoke. No searches or army presence."

American reviews were simply terrible. Rita Kempley was relatively kind in her *Washington Post* review, which noted that the plot was "a bit thin." As noted, McEvoy credits his father as having inspired the screenplay. "My dad is funnier than I could ever be," he told Gary Arnold. "Dad's stories may have been dandies," Rita Kempley wrote, "but as strung together here they haven't enough dramatic fuel to propel even so modest an undertaking." The screenplay lacks mature vision and is too often a silly exercise, marked by adolescent humor, as when a police inspector accidentally knocks the sample wig he is holding for evidence into a commode he is using, urinates on it, then flushes it away.

After his family settled in Gaithersburg, Maryland, McEvoy wanted to enroll in a good film school, according to Gary Arnold, but "found the costs prohibitive" and had to settle for courses in acting and video production locally at Montgomery College in Rockville, Maryland. He later moved on to New York in 1991 to pursue an acting career off-Broadway. Curiously, the early trajectory of his career paralleled that of director Barry Levinson, who also started in Maryland, but went on to pursue a career in writing for television and film rather than an acting career.

Owen Gleiberman of *Entertainment Weekly* considered the film an utter failure, concluding that "*An Everlasting Piece* doesn't go any deeper than the title's pun." Explaining that "poor films are never in short supply, even from well-known figures," Stanley Kauffmann of the *New Republic* was fascinated by a film he considered "too grotesquely misconceived even to be called tasteless." Recalling earlier Levinson pictures such as *Diner, Rain Man*, and *Wag the Dog* (1997), Kauffmann wrote that "Whatever one's opinion of those films, they do not lead one to expect the sheer stupidity from Levinson that we get here."

Almost any film has its moments, however, and even its supporters. Gary Arnold was charmed by the "exceptional zest" Anna Friel brought to her role as Bronaugh, Colm's nurse-girlfriend, for example. "Although the movie buys somewhat into the long-held premise that the Irish are lovable cartoon characters," Desson Howe wrote in his *Washington Post Weekend* review, the film "has an authentic undertone," as "IRA soldiers and English troops in riot gear menacingly roam" the streets of Belfast.

Reviewing the film for the British film journal *Sight and Sound*, Richard Kelly was far more positive about the project than his American counterparts. He found merit in McEvoy's "appealing" performance. Kelly found the film's best moments "funny, not least because they ring true." Kelly described the patronage of Steven Spielberg and DreamWorks a "mixed blessing." Spielberg, he explained, "has been charged with 'burying' the film so as to curry favour with the Labour government that lately knighted him." He adds, however, that the film's release was hampered because of disagreements between Levinson and Jeffrey Katzenberg "over issues of political context." Regardless, however, the plot was more than a little bit "thin," as Rita Kempley stated, and a wider release would not have made the film better than it turned out to be.

—*James M. Welsh*

## CREDITS

**Colm:** Barry McEvoy
**George:** Brian F. O'Byrne
**Bronagh:** Anna Friel
**Scalper:** Billy Connolly
**Gerty:** Pauline McLynn
**Mickey:** Laurence Kinlan
**Mrs. O'Neil:** Ruth McCabe

**Origin:** USA
**Released:** 2000
**Production:** Barry Levinson, Mark Johnson, Lou DiGiaimo, Paula Weinstein, Jerome O'Connor; Baltimore Pictures, Spring Creek Productions, Bayahibe Films; released by Dreamworks Pictures, Columbia Pictures
**Directed by:** Barry Levinson

**Written by:** Barry McEvoy
**Cinematography by:** Seamus Deasy
**Music by:** Hans Zimmer
**Editing:** Stu Linder
**Art Direction:** Mark Lowry, Padraig O'Neill
**Costumes:** Joan Bergin
**Production Design:** Nathan Crowley
**MPAA rating:** R
**Running time:** 103 minutes

## REVIEWS

*Chicago Sun-Times Online.* December 22, 2001.
*Entertainment Weekly.* January 12, 2001, p. 53.
*Hollywood Reporter.* December 19, 2000, p. 20.
*New Republic.* January 1, 2001, p. 22.
*New York Times Online.* December 25, 2000.
*Sight and Sound.* April, 2001, p. 47.
*Washington Post.* December 25, 2000, p. C4.
*Washington Post Weekend.* December 22, 2000, p. 41.
*Washington Times.* December 29, 2000, p. C5.

# Everybody's Famous! (Iedereen Beroemd!)

*How far would you go to get famous?*
—Movie tagline

A father's show business dream for his daughter is the basis of *Everybody's Famous!*, a cute comedy from Belgium that was a contender for Best Foreign Language Film at the 2000 Academy Awards®. When the frumpy, seemingly talentless daughter tells her mother that "Everybody wants to be famous," it does not feel like a shocking or controversial statement the way it might have been a few years ago. In a world where reality-TV shows are slowly dominating network programming and more and more common folk seem to be grabbing their 15 minutes of fame, it is not so far-fetched that an overweight, plain teenager could imagine herself in the spotlight as a superstar chanteuse.

Back in 1983, Martin Scorsese's *The King of Comedy* told the chilling story of a deranged loser (Robert De Niro) who kidnaps a talk show host (Jerry Lewis) and holds him for ransom so that he can get his big break on TV. *Everybody's Famous!* follows a similar plot line revolving around a showbiz kidnapping but recasts the essential conceit as a fairy tale of sorts. Writer-director Dominique Deruddere has created a world in which fame is attainable in the most unlikely of ways, but the quest for celebrity itself is not a twisted, dark fantasy but rather an expression of a father's devotion for his daughter. In the end, the ugly duckling of a daughter is transformed into a superstar, and everyone lives happily ever after.

Jean (Josse De Pauw) is a downtrodden, 45-year-old factory worker who has put all of his own showbiz dreams into his daughter, Marva (Eva Van Der Gucht), who enters musical competitions where she dresses up like pop stars such as Vanessa Paradis and Madonna and sings their tunes. Unfortunately, she never wins. If her weight problem were not enough of an impediment, her performance style, which is passionless and mechanical, almost guarantees her low scores every time. She seems to shine only when putting on a puppet show for the town's kids when she is not self-conscious about her weight, and we are treated to a touching scene of Jean secretly watching the performance and taking great pride in his daughter.

A man obviously beaten down by life's disappointments and a menial factory job inspecting bottles on an assembly line, Jean himself is a sad figure who composes simple melodies in a tape recorder and hopes that one day they will be turned into full-fledged songs. When the factory goes bankrupt and Jean loses his job, he does not tell his wife, Chantal (Gert Portael), or Marva. He knows that they do not keep up with the news and that he can actually get away with pretending that he still has a job. Such is the charm of this movie that he is able to pull off this most improbable of schemes without even thinking that he might get caught.

Even more improbable is the lucky break that comes his way. One day Jean's car stalls on a deserted road, and the premier pop star in the country, who goes by the single name of Debbie (Thekla Reuten), comes by on her bicycle and offers to help Jean get his car started. Auto mechanics just happens to be her personal hobby. On the spur of the moment, Jean gets the idea to drug her with sleeping pills and kidnap her. He takes her to an out-of-the-way house and enlists the help of Willy (Werner De Smedt), another recently unemployed factory worker, to help guard the superstar. Willy is much younger than Jean but hapless in his own way, supporting a girlfriend who is still in school and going out of town with a handsome colleague for a professional conference. Since Willy is at a low point anyway, he goes along with his friend's plan.

At first Jean hopes to ask for a huge ransom, but then he hits upon a better idea. He contacts Debbie's manager, Michael (Victor Löw), with a strange demand. He has the bare bones of a tune and wants it transformed into a song complete with lyrics that his daughter can sing. Hiding behind a ridiculous Michael Jackson mask for anonymity, Jean has a ransom meeting with Michael and requests that the song be completed in a week. Of course the gentle Jean has no intention of actually killing Debbie if his demand is not met. He is basically making things up as he goes along and is hoping that everything will work out in the end.

Meanwhile, both Chantal and Marva remain oblivious to Jean's scheme.

De Pauw's performance as Jean is the heart of the movie. He is essentially a decent family man who strives to be a good father but does not get love in return from his daughter, who resists his affection. At times she is not even very nice to her father, and, in one sad scene, she refuses to kiss him good night, which leads him to reflect on how much he misses his own father's kisses. Jean may be misguided in thinking that his daughter could be a superstar, or he may see something in her that no one else can, but his motives are pure-hearted—he does not want her to slave away in a factory, as he has done his whole life.

In a subplot, Willy and Debbie start to grow close when she worries about her dog being left alone in her flat without food and Willy offers to go retrieve it. First, however, Debbie requests that he remove her blindfold so that she can see him, and his acquiescence signals that he is willing to take a chance by revealing his identity to her. The punch line to this episode is that, after he gets the dog, the media report that the dog too has been kidnapped, and Debbie's neighbor, who hated her music as well as the dog, appears on TV fretting over Debbie's safety. It is a cute, if rather obvious way of showing the way the media distort the truth in their quest for a sensationalistic story.

When Jean meets Michael again and finally hears his song set to music, he loves it and gives Michael his daughter's name so that he can contact her. Michael is a smooth operator who takes Marva out to a fancy restaurant and even tries to seduce her. It is part of the movie's magic, however, that even the seemingly worst character is not really evil. He may be a typical showbiz hotshot who sports a feathered haircut and verges on being slimy—he releases a new single from Debbie to capitalize on her fans' love during her kidnapping—but he never becomes a true villain. At times he is even likable as he takes Marva under his wing.

Marva casually mentions to Michael that her father makes musical tapes, thus enabling Michael to figure out that the kidnapper is Marva's father. Instead of turning him in to the police, however, he asks Jean to keep Debbie a little longer. To make matters more complicated for poor Jean, Willy and Debbie have fallen in love and fled the hideout, thus leaving him alone and having to pretend that there is still a kidnapping in progress when reporters appear on the night of his daughter's television debut.

What follows is a goofy yet surprisingly affectionate take on a media circus. Marva is scheduled to sing live on the nation's big music program when the show cuts to TV reporters in front of Jean's hideaway. The news is portraying him as a man who has gone crazy from losing his job, and Michael sets out to choreograph the whole incident to his advantage. Decked out in a bandit's costume complete with a mask to conceal her less than photogenic features and dubbed "Lonesome Zorra," Marva is set to go on the air. To pump up the drama, Michael has Jean demand that Lonesome Zorra sing or else Debbie will be killed, and Marva finds herself talking to her father over live TV—a heartbreaking reality-TV moment that Michael is all too eager to milk for all its worth. He is not too happy, however, when Jean urges Marva to remove her mask, but one of the film's lessons is that Marva must learn to be comfortable with herself as a performer and not hide behind a persona. In a weird twist on media chicanery, all the phony manipulation actually produces a poignant moment between father and daughter. With his encouragement, Marva sings a song with conviction for the first time in her life. The song is called "Lucky Manuelo," and its lyrics about a long-suffering man who fought for his happiness becomes a tribute to her dad. Marva gets her moment of glory, and Jean becomes a hero when he finally surrenders to police. It is a completely implausible ending in which Marva is on her way to stardom and Jean is somehow forgiven for his kidnapping. Incidentally, Debbie, having found true love with Willy in Australia, abandons her singing career.

*Everybody's Famous!* may be a slight film, especially given its status as an Academy Award nominee, but it is a refreshing twist on the media obsessions that fuel so many lives. Instead of the usual cynical take on celebrity, Deruddere gives us a lighthearted yet touching story. Here is a film, after all, in which the quest for fame is looked upon fondly, kidnapping leads to romance with a superstar who is actually a decent person, and celebrity itself becomes a cure-all that helps bring a father and daughter together. It is of course the most unbelievable of fantasies, but it is executed with such a light touch that it maintains a buoyant spirit right up to the triumphant ending.

—*Peter N. Chumo II*

## CREDITS

**Jean Vereecken:** Josse De Pauw
**Marva Vereecken:** Eva Van der Gucht
**Willy Van Outreve:** Werner De Smedt
**Debbie:** Thekla Reuten
**Michael Jansen:** Victor Low
**Chantal Vereecken:** Gert Portael

**Origin:** Belgium
**Language:** Dutch, French
**Released:** 2000
**Production:** Loret Meus, Dominique Deruddere; Otomatic, Get Reel Productions, Les Films des Tournelles; released by Miramax Films
**Directed by:** Dominique Deruddere
**Written by:** Dominique Deruddere
**Cinematography by:** Willy Stassen

**Music by:** Raymond van het Groenewoud
**Sound:** Rene Van den Bergh, Bert Koops, Alek Goosse
**Editing:** Ludo Troch
**Costumes:** Loret Meus
**Production Design:** Hubert Pouille
**MPAA rating:** R
**Running time:** 99 minutes

## REVIEWS

*Boxoffice.* August, 2001, p. 58.
*Chicago Sun-Times Online.* July 13, 2001.
*Entertainment Weekly.* July 20, 2001, p. 45.
*Los Angeles Times Online.* July 5, 2001.
*Washington Post.* July 13, 2001, p. C5.

## TRIVIA

Eva Van Der Gucht's makes her film debut as Marva.

## AWARDS AND NOMINATIONS

**Nomination:**
**Oscars 2000:** Foreign Film.

# Evolution

*Have a nice end of the world.*
—Movie tagline
*Coming to wipe that silly smile off your planet.*
—Movie tagline

**Box Office:** $38.3 million

Wayne Green (Seann William Scott) is a fireman wannabe who goes above and beyond the call of studying while practicing for his fireman's exam. In fact he's taken a blow-up doll out into the Arizona dessert, thrown her into a shack, set the shack on fire and goes in to rescue her. Well the doll may have survived, but not Wayne's car. It has just been hit by a meteor which has punched down 80 feet into the caverns below.

This event causes Harry Block (Orlando Jones), a geology professor at Glen Canyon Community College, to spring into action as the official local representative of the

United States Geological Survey. He is going out to investigate the meteor landing and is taking along his pal, Ira Kane (David Duchovny), the college's biology professor.

What Harry and Ira find when they arrive at the landing site—besides a singed Wayne—is a large rock that is infested with a goo that contains single-celled aliens. What a surprise! But that's not all. Just a few hours later, those single-celled organisms are now multi-celled. "It's like they're evolving," declares Harry. "It's evolution," replies Ira, but "it's 200 million years worth in a few hours." Furthermore, on Earth, DNA has four base pairs, but these quickly multiplying aliens have 10 base pairs.

Eighteen hours later, Ira and Harry take their students on a field trip to the cavern to collect samples. Now they find the alien life forms have evolved into flatworms and mushrooms. But the team also discovers that these aliens can't survive outside of the cavern. It seems they can only live while breathing their own special atmosphere which they have created in the cave.

But since the aliens are evolving and multiplying so rapidly, Harry prudently wonders if they shouldn't call in the government. After all, he is their representative. "No! No government!" says Ira. "I know those people." Is this a sly reference to Duchovny's role as the paranoid paranormalist and alien hunter Fox Mulder on television's X Files? No, it seems Ira used to work at the Pentagon. He was a colonel and top researcher from 1994–97 but was dismissed because his experiments with an anthrax vaccine left 140,000 soldiers suffering from "Kane Madness" which includes such symptoms as stomach cramps, diarrhea, memory loss, drooling, bleeding gums, uncontrollable flatulence, facial paralysis and impotence, just to name a few.

Consequently Ira has been in exile in Arizona for the past five years, but this discovery is his ticket out of the boonies. Unfortunately for Ira and Harry, their discovery is about to be purloined by the government. Almost overnight, the meteor site is quarantined, contained and under the control of General Russell Woodman (Ted Levine) who is the head of U.S. Army Research. How did they know about the aliens? They have been monitoring Ira's computer ever since he left the Pentagon. Also working with the army is Allison Reed (Julianne Moore) who is the slightly klutzy but good-looking senior researcher for the Center for Disease Control.

Despite the army's efforts, however, it soon becomes obvious that the aliens are spreading out. Especially after one country club member is sucked out of the sand trap and into the water hazard on the 4th green. While initially it seemed as if the aliens might be containable because they needed their own special environment, it now seems they are adapting. Furthermore, they are using the extensive caves and abandoned mine shafts in Arizona to move around underground and surface in further and further locations. As Ira

now realizes, "we've got to kill these things while we still can."

Of course the army comes up with a plan, but ya' just know that in this kind of movie the army's strategy will not only not kill the monsters it will do something so inept that it will help them to take over the Earth. This means our intrepid heroes not only have to stop the army from following through on their strategy but also come up with an alternate plan of their own. (In this case their alternate plan may be the ultimate movie product placement.)

Director Ivan Reitman has given audiences such laugh-filled hits as *Meatballs, Stripes,* and *Dave,* but may be best known for his 1984 hit *Ghostbusters.* Wanting to take his comic talent into the realm of science fiction, he took an immediate liking to Don Jakoby's script about aliens landing on Earth. Of course, it wasn't a comedy then, but leave it to Reitman and writers David Diamond and David Weissman to fix that. And so Jakoby's serious story became, unfortunately, a weak clone of *Ghostbusters.*

And this clone is also guilty of another syndrome that seems to be plaguing comedies lately: a penchant for any joke that has to do with butts. Why do current filmmakers have such an anal fixation? Why do they think that everything is funnier with flatulence? Did the screenwriters go to the Junior College where Ira teaches and gives virtually everyone A's on papers regardless of their true academic value? Ira may be guilty of grade inflation, but Reitman and his pen pals are guilty of comedy inflation. *Evolution* contains no less than three major butt jokes: Ira moons the army through his car windshield, Harry has to have an alien removed from his body through . . . you guessed it, his butt, and the final destruction of the alien lifeform requires an enema. Even *Ghostbusters'* Sta-Puff marshmallow man fared better in his swan song.

Butt jokes aside, the writing in *Evolution* is uneven with the aliens evolving faster than the pacing of the story. The comedy is more often lame than funny, going for the easy punchline instead of something truly creative. The dialogue is weak and shows little energy or sense of fun on the part of the actors.

Julianne Moore is a fine dramatic actress and seems to have a flair for comedy, but all this script gives her to do is affect an unnecessary clumsiness (it didn't work for Sandra Bullock in *Miss Congeniality* either) and wear a t-shirt that enlightens her male counterparts about how to destroy the aliens. It is a thankless role for so good an actress.

The same is true for Duchovny. Some of the best *X Files* episodes were those where Duchovny's character provided humor instead of suspicion. And like Moore, he, too has a knack for comedy—the drier the better—but *Evolution* is not the vehicle to showcase this.

Even the very funny Orlando Jones is given little more to do than mug at the camera. He is served better by his "Make 7-Up Yours" commercials. As for Seann William

Scott, he strains no acting muscles here. It's just a repeat of his innocent doofus from the earlier *Dude, Where's My Car?* and *American Pie.*

Faring better is special effects supervisor Phil Tippett who was responsible for the dinosaurs in *Jurassic Park* and the giant insects in *Starship Troopers* and who provides a few interesting aliens in *Evolution.* The seemingly sweet, doe-eyed monster that emerges from a suburban closet provides one of the film's few jolts and as the monsters evolve into medieval dragons they do become more interesting and threatening (but how does one lose a 20-foot flying reptile in an enclosed shopping mall?). The alien's final blob form, however, is entirely built for fart-jokes and not for scares or even good comedy.

It's a shame Ivan Reitman's comic talent hasn't evolved more since *Ghostbusters.* Here he just resorts to a tried and true formula and drags a promising premise and a talented cast along with him. Sure, *Evolution* can be mildly diverting in the early summer before the true blockbusters get released and will probably do better when released on video than it is doing in theaters, but that's really no excuse for why the director just goes back and makes yet another movie about everyman-experts overcoming overwhelming odds and destroying a huge menacing monster, because, in the end, that's all one finds in *Ghostbusters,* er, I mean *Evolution.*

—*Beverley Bare Buehrer*

## CREDITS

**Ira Kane:** David Duchovny
**Allison Reed:** Julianne Moore
**Harry Block:** Orlando Jones
**Wayne:** Seann William Scott
**Gen. Woodman:** Ted Levine
**Deke:** Ethan Suplee
**Danny:** Michael Ray Bower
**Nadine:** Katharine Towne
**Governor Lewis:** Dan Aykroyd
**Fire Training Inspector:** Richard Moll
**Cartwright:** Gregory Itzin

**Origin:** USA
**Released:** 2001
**Production:** Ivan Reitman, Daniel Goldberg, Joe Medjuck; Montecito Picture Co.; released by Dreamworks Pictures
**Directed by:** Ivan Reitman
**Written by:** David Diamond, David Weissman, Don Jakoby
**Cinematography by:** Michael Chapman

**Music by:** John Powell
**Sound:** William B. Kaplan
**Editing:** Sheldon Kahn, Wendy Greene Bricmont
**Art Direction:** Richard F. Mays
**Costumes:** Aggie Guerard Rodgers
**Production Design:** J. Michael Riva
**MPAA rating:** PG-13
**Running time:** 101 minutes

## REVIEWS

*Boxoffice.* August, 2001, p. 60.
*Chicago Sun-Times Online.* June 8, 2001.
*Entertainment Weekly.* June 15, 2001, p. 53.
*Hollywood Reporter.* June 8, 2001, p. 10.
*Los Angeles Times Online.* June 8, 2001.
*New York Times Online.* June 8, 2001.
*People.* June 18, 2001, p. 31.
*Sight and Sound.* August, 2001, p. 42.
*USA Today Online.* June 8, 2001.
*Variety.* June 11, 2001, p. 17.
*Washington Post Online.* June 8, 2001.

## QUOTES

Dr. Henry Block (Orlando Jones): "I seen this movie. The black guy dies first."

# Exit Wounds

*What can two men do against a gang of crooked cops? Whatever it takes.*
—Movie tagline

 **Box Office:** $51.8 million

It's hard to believe that people actually categorize Steven Seagal movies as being good or bad, but they do. It would seem that blowing things up, car chases that invariably end in flames, and slow motion fighting would be rather standard in quality. Among students of the Seagal oeuvre—and there are really such people—*Exit Wounds* is not considered to be the finest of his work. That honor would belong to films like *Above the Law* and *Hard to Kill.* And no, those are not the same films. But *Exit Wounds* is not the worst of his movies. The film is considered to be a step up from some of his most recent work, which went straight to video. *Exit Wounds* is somewhat of a comeback for the 1980s star because a) it made it to theaters, b) Seagal lost a few pounds, and c) he finally lost that ridiculous tiny pony tail that had attached itself to the back of his head. Thankfully, these steps weren't enough to single-handedly marshal in a return to 1980s-style action flicks. They might not even be enough to guarantee that Seagal's next movie gets wide-screen release.

One thing that Seagal hasn't changed from the 1980s is the sort of plots he uses. In this one, Seagal plays Orin Boyd (what kind of tough guy name is that?), a cop who doesn't play by the rules. (Come to think of it, that particular plot is borrowed from *Dirty Harry,* circa 1971.) No matter what he is doing, he has a habit of running into big crimes that are in the process of being committed. (Such a habit could make a simple act like picking up the dry cleaning stretch into a three hour job.) Thus, the movie begins, when Boyd happens upon the vice-president who is stuck in a ruckus that involves not only gun fire, but a car chase, too. This, by the way, is immediately after the veep has given a speech decrying the use of guns. The film seems to be trying to make some sort of political point here, but this is one—and probably the only—instance in which it's just too subtle. Is the film saying that it's ironic that a person against guns would be saved by guns? Or is it that the gun fire/car chase is a perfect example of why guns should be outlawed?

It would be nice if the visual cliches in this particular scene were outlawed. We are treated to such sights as multiple people being gunned down by rapid-fire guns, their bodies jerking with each shot as the rat-tat-tat of the bullets fill the soundtrack. If that's not exciting enough, others are run over with a truck, a dead guy is used as a shield and there are explosions galore.

Boyd is a big part of the melee and his bosses don't take kindly to it. He gets a lot of speeches from his superiors where they say things like, "You don't even obey the law!" and "You're a renegade!" But we know that we're supposed to admire Boyd anyway because the movie tells us that it's wise to take the law into your own hands and just start shooting people based on whatever your own sense of justice is. Still, such behavior must be reprimanded by the police department because everyone there is such a stickler for those dumb old rules and procedures. What a drag. Seagal is sent to Detroit where he is first a traffic cop, then he's teamed up with a novice partner, George Clark (Isaiah Washington). Detroit, by the way, doesn't have much of a Detroit feel. As one reviewer, Norman Wilner at the *Toronto Star,* pointed out: "It would seem that Detroit has cornered the American market on Pizza Pizza and Tim Hortons franchises, the result of no one bothering to disguise the Toronto locations."

The Detroit precinct is a strange place. His precinct commander (Jill Hennessy) is a looker and she seems to be somewhat bemused by Boyd's maverick ways. But the rest of the place has a strangely homoerotic vibe. The guys are always working out at the gym and seem to have misplaced their shirts. They also like to be half-naked while they spend their downtime at the station using stun guns on each other. It's difficult to say what the movie's fixation on male nudity and males causing pain to each other is, but it's a definite motif. Actually, besides the homoeroticism and the afore-mentioned gun control messages, there are other half-formed messages that director Andrzej Bartlowiak (*Romeo Must Die*) seems to be trying to convey, but they just don't come across. At one point, Boyd must attend an anger management class. There he becomes a hero because he breaks his desk when he can't get out of it. It would seem that the message is that anger management classes are stupid. (It's much better to blow things up during high speed car chases?) But then later in the film, Seagal returns to the class, apparently ready to give it another, more serious try. There appears to be a comment on such classes somewhere in there, but darned if it's possible to tell what it is.

Boyd, who thankfully leaves his own shirt on, soon gets involved in trying to uncover a drug ring. He enlists the help of a local obnoxious TV personality (Tom Arnold) and starts to gather background information. He starts trailing various suspicious types like Latrell Walker (rapper DMX), a guy who's become incredibly wealthy by cashing in on dot.com stock options. Or maybe Walker is more mysterious than he seems. Or, could it be that Boyd's peers at the police station like Officer Montini (David Vadim) might be involved? Eh, it doesn't matter much. The point is that much butt will have to be kicked and Boyd is just the guy to do it.

Or perhaps, Seagal was the guy to do it. Though not as paunchy as he's been in some of his films, Seagal looks slow and tired. He tries to disguise the spare tire by wearing an oversized shirt over his clothes in every scene, but like wearing vertical stripes, the illusion only goes so far. In all action films, it's improbable how the hero defeats so many strong enemies, but in *Exit Wounds,* it's worse than usual. Seagal looks like he would get winded stepping into the kitchen to get more chips, let alone fighting off an army of mask-wearing, gun-bearing thugs. Bartkowiak tries to handle Seagal's immobility by filming some of his stunts in slow motion, but it doesn't really work. Seeing Seagal's lumbering frame, heaving itself over a car or whatever doesn't disguise that the whole thing is less than graceful.

Since it's none-too exhilarating to watch Seagal as a fighting machine, the movie tries to make up for it by filling itself with many other boy movie elements. There are topless women at a strip bar (though, strangely, less topless women than topless men in the film), scenes filmed in sports bars where the men discuss topics like who was the greatest athlete of all times, and even a car shopping scene. But all of that stuff is just to fill space between the violence, which occurs at regular intervals. Guys are impaled on hooks protruding from the wall, guys are impaled on stakes and chain saws are welded. Seagal beats up a whole truckload of baddies, even though his arms are chained to the sides of the truck. Of course, the drive ends with the truck going up in flames. No wonder car shopping scenes were necessary.

Critics weren't overly impressed, though some gave the film a break. Liz Braun of the *Toronto Sun* wrote, "This is another shoot-'em-up cop undertaking and fairly putrid in both concept and execution. Still, you can't stop looking at it." Anthony Breznican of the *Associated Press* wrote, "Say what you will about Steven Seagal, the man knows how to kill people." Max Messier of filmcritic.com wrote, "By over-extending the violence, the ludicrousness, and the sheer improbability, *Exit Wounds* plays out like a circus of the damned with Tom Arnold working the Tilt-A-Whirl." And Wilner of the *Toronto Star* wrote, "*Exit Wounds* makes no pretense toward realistic depictions of police work—or anything, really. The movie's just an excuse for the entire cast to point guns at each other before engaging in verbal or actual smackery."

—*Jill Hamilton*

## CREDITS

**Orin Boyd:** Steven Seagal
**Latrell Walker:** DMX
**George Clark:** Isaiah Washington
**T.K.:** Anthony Anderson
**Strutt:** Michael Jai White
**Hinges:** Bill Duke
**Mulcahy:** Jill(ian) Hennessey
**Henry Wayne:** Tom Arnold
**Daniels:** Bruce McGill
**Montini:** David Vadim
**Trish:** Eva Mendez

**Origin:** USA
**Released:** 2001
**Production:** Joel Silver, Dan Cracchiolo; Village Roadshow Pictures, NPV Entertainment, Silver Pictures; released by Warner Bros.
**Directed by:** Andrzej Bartkowiak
**Written by:** Ed Horowitz, Richard D'Ovidio
**Cinematography by:** Glen MacPherson
**Music by:** Jeff Rona, Damon Blackman
**Sound:** Greg Chapman
**Music Supervisor:** Barry Hankerson, Jomo Hankerson
**Editing:** Derek G. Brechin
**Art Direction:** T. Arv Grewal
**Costumes:** Jennifer Bryan
**Production Design:** Paul Denham Austerberry
**MPAA rating:** R

**Running time:** 98 minutes

## REVIEWS

*Boxoffice.* March, 2001, p. 60.
*Entertainment Weekly.* March 30, 2001, p. 47.
*Los Angeles Times Online.* March 17, 2001.
*New York Times Online.* March 17, 2001.
*San Francisco Chronicle.* March 17, 2001, p. B3.
*Sight and Sound.* June, 2001, p. 44.
*Variety.* March 19, 2001, p. 29.

# Faithless (Trolosa)

In *Scenes from a Marriage*, the great Swedish director Ingmar Bergman provided a disturbing look at a decaying marriage heading toward divorce. Twenty-eight years later, Liv Ullman's absorbing but morose *Faithless* follows much the same path—though there is more emphasis on the wife's disastrous affair and the divorce than on the marriage.

*Faithless* is haunting in several respects. Written by Bergman (now in his early 80s), it indicates that the writer-director has not shaken his lifelong grappling with the shame, guilt and grief that result, in his rather gloomy view, from the doomed interactions of human beings. Bergman's surrogates are in different roles now, but their influence also hangs heavy over this dour story. Ullman, Bergman's former leading lady as well as one of his real-life lovers and the mother of his daughter, is directing her fourth film, the second written by Bergman (the first focused on the director's parents). Erland Josephson, who played opposite Ullman in *Scenes* and had roles in many other Bergman films, plays a character called Bergman, an aging, lonely movie director living alone on Faro Island off the coast of Sweden—just as the real Bergman does. The fictional Bergman seems to be probing his life's decisive love affair retrospectively, and perhaps so is the real Bergman.

As Bergman often does in his stories, *Faithless* uses a theatrical framework as a metaphor for its characters' interactions. Josephson's character is trying to write a script about infidelity. He summons—from his imagination or from his own past—a ghostly actress, Marianne (Lena Endre), to help him reconstruct what may or may not be an incident from his own life. At the old man's direction, Marianne reluctantly recites a long and puzzling story about her affair with David (Kirster Henriksson). It's a disastrous and doomed relationship that destroys her marriage to Markus

(Thomas Hanzon), a renowned orchestra conductor, and fractures her relationship with their daughter, Isabelle (Michelle Gylemo). The old director explains early on how in "the twilight before death" he has a strange compulsion, an emotional "vortex" pulling at him: "I'm searching for answers to questions I never asked." His technique is to combine therapy and theater, as Bergman always has done.

The introspective, ingrown quality of the film is heightened if you consider that Bergman's own life story is fraught with affairs. Just as Marianne in the film provides the director-character Bergman with the answers he seeks—painful though they may be—as director Ullman may be providing the real Bergman with the same service. Never have an affair and a divorce seemed quite so devastating as in this film. It is as if through this story Bergman were seeking to purge a lifetime of guilt. There is no moral ambiguity in the script. In *Faithless,* being faithless is the ultimate sin, as it sets in motion a tragedy that destroys, in one way or another, all four people involved. An opening quotation asserts that "no form of common failure" is so fatal and afflicting as a divorce, which "with one stab, penetrates as deeply as life can reach."

What's frustrating and compelling at the same time is that, as in most Bergman films, the tragedy is not pinned on some clearly identifiable human trait or failing. Ullman provides a much-needed woman's perspective on Bergman's stern righteousness, and the film plays beautifully with images of light and darkness. Endre is astoundingly good and achingly authentic, as is the entire cast; like many Bergman movies, this is a tour de force of subtle yet powerful acting. Yet neither Ullman nor Endre provide much insight into why Marianne cheats on her husband. It's puzzling why Marianne, who is a beautiful, accomplished actress who admittedly shares a wonderful, lusty marriage with Markus and has a delightful child, would take up with David, a self-loathing creature who too often wallows in his own inadequacies and constantly needs reassurance. The answer, as with most Bergman scripts, is that the motivation is unknown, even to the principals. Marianne is driven to David and the affair against her better judgment, but not by lust or curiosity or boredom but something much less transparent—something like fate. People are like actors playing roles.

At times Marianne's motives seem to include pity—but her willingness to engage in bold-faced lies and take foolish risks seems to betray something deeper. Though she blames herself for all that happens, the script simply presents her as being pulled, almost against her will, into the same sort of "vortex" that has enveloped the old man and is almost a life condition for the hapless David. Love is perhaps one motive—but when the characters speak of love, it is only to talk of how it renders its victims helpless and insensible, so that it seems more like a drug than a many-splendored thing. And none of the three in the love triangle ever says "I love you" or

anything remotely like that to another; there is a curious kind of sterility to the relationships, and very little tenderness.

Despite all this, *Faithless* is utterly absorbing. The first two of its two-and-a-half hours, at least, pass quickly. The fine actors draw us into their emotional maelstrom almost effortlessly. Ullman displays a deft touch for cutting back and forth between narration and exposition, using some of her mentor's simple but powerful directorial methods, though she tends to overuse the overhead shot. Endre is luminous without being glamorous; she has an earthy though refined beauty and a capacity for knowing anguish. Josephson is a treasure trove, his soft and expressive face revealing the impact wrought by Marianne's every painful word, with Ullman's reaction shots showing the woman's words making psychic impacts on Josephson's face as if they were little darts.

The approach to the sexual material is restrained for most of the movie, so much so that it is a startling moment when Ullman suddenly shows both lovers naked on their bed. The wonder is quickly ruined when each takes a bit of sheet and covers up, as if they knew themselves to be caught by a hidden camera. The restraint in language and visuals makes some of the graphic material that later crops up all the more compelling and brutal. The story is especially ruthless in showing the terrible consequences of the messy adult behavior on Isabelle. Once the affair has progressed beyond return and the rift destroys the marriage, Marianne describes tearfully to the old director how she told Isabelle that she was moving in with David and leaving her to live with Isabelle's grandmother while Markus goes on tour. The script and Ullman's camera and editing are acutely open to the emotional wounds of the child, which are brilliantly and mercilessly displayed in this and later, even more disturbing, scenes.

So beautifully is the film written, framed, shot and acted that it is almost pleasurable to watch all this intense self-flagellation. Certainly Ullman and Bergman are not afraid of the depths of the human soul, and the film is blessedly free of the Hollywood conventions by which romances become syrupy mush. But *Faithless* cries out for at least a little levity to provide some perspective. If Bergman the old man has become even harsher in his condemnation of human beings and their insensitive behavior, it can hardly be an unexpected development. His films have contributed a body of work to the cinema that are unmatched in their frankness. The master's characters still are struggling with their own capacity for deceit, pride, and shamefulness, still condemned to the sort of inner hell which Ullman so magnificently helped to portray in *Persona.*

There are echoes of that landmark film in a scene in which Ullman photographs Endre looking in a mirror, mulling over her own culpability and indecision, and the face of her child appears between her two mirror images. In

*Faithless* the specter of the children, and what these failed adults do to them, gets full play as part of the puzzle of self-awareness. This may be the greatest achievement of this extraordinarily uncompromising film. It is hard to argue with its dogged insistence that children are the biggest victims of the inability of adults to come to grips with their own emotions.

The film progresses from being observant to being solemn and then descends into tragedy, and Ullman does not provide the false salve of a neat way out of its moral dilemmas. No one is redeemed at the end. But the central puzzle remains: Is this the old master's last conjuring trick? It appears that the Bergman in the film is the Bergman who wrote the script and that he is also the aged remains of David. But is this really that blatantly autobiographical, or is the film more of an extended meditation on the burden faced by many old people—regret? In letting Ullman and Marianne report and shape the story, is this Bergman's way of revisiting and rounding out a life that has always been rich in understanding the female perspective, yet never fully committed to allowing that female judgment to prevail? Like all compelling films about human failings, *Faithless* raises more questions than it answers.

In the end, the film can be seen as a trenchant coda to the shared cinematic life of Bergman and Ullman. The final frames—showing Josephson walking alone on a beach under dark skies, and then revealing his study to be empty as a music box plays—are undoubtedly Ullman's final tribute to her friend and mentor, and they are surprisingly moving in their simplicity. Ullman is imagining a world without Ingmar Bergman—and, in such a world, how we are left utterly alone.

—*Michael Betzold*

## CREDITS

**Marianne Vogler:** Lena Endre
**Bergman:** Erland Josephson
**Markus:** Thomas Hanzon
**David:** Krister Henriksson
**Martin Goldman:** Philip Zanden
**Anna Berg:** Marie Richardson
**Isabelle:** Michelle Gylemo
**Margareta:** Juni Dahr
**Petra Holst:** Therese Brunnander

**Origin:** Sweden
**Language:** Swedish
**Released:** 2000
**Production:** Kaj Larsen; Svensk Filmindustri; released by Samuel Goldwyn Films, Fireworks Pictures
**Directed by:** Liv Ullmann

**Written by:** Ingmar Bergman
**Cinematography by:** Jorgen Persson
**Sound:** Gabor Pasztor
**Editing:** Sylvia Ingemarsson
**Costumes:** Inger E. Pehrsson
**Production Design:** Goran Wassberg
**MPAA rating:** R
**Running time:** 142 minutes

## REVIEWS

*Boxoffice.* November, 2000, p. 158.
*Chicago Sun-Times Online.* February 16, 2001.
*Entertainment Weekly.* February 16, 2001, p. 73.
*Los Angeles Times Calendar.* February 11, 2001, p. 19.
*New York Times Online.* September 29, 2000.
*Sight and Sound.* February, 2001, p. 41.
*Time.* February 5, 2001, p. 76.
*Variety.* May 22, 2000, p. 19.
*Washington Post Online.* March 2, 2001.

## TRIVIA

Ingmar Bergman retired from screen directing in 1983.

# The Fast and the Furious

*If loyalties must be broken, if lines must be crossed, do it fast, do it furious.*
—Movie tagline

*When the sun goes down, another world comes to life.*
—Movie tagline

 **Box Office:** $144.5 million

When director Rob Cohen was told by his studio, Universal Pictures, that they wanted to move his film from a March to a June release, he was worried. After all that pushed his film right into the middle of summer blockbuster season. His film, *The Fast and the Furious*, didn't have any big stars, and was on a topic—car racing—that had been done over and over for decades. And recent racing films, like the Sylvester Stallone and Renny Harlin project *Driven* (also reviewed in this edition), hadn't exactly caught on at the boxoffice. But in this case the "suits" at the studio had the right idea. Even though *The Fast and the Furious* was let loose against such heavy competition as *Lara Croft: Tomb Raider* and *Pearl Harbor*, it was the number one movie the week it was released.

Part of the reason for its popularity was that the film tapped into a burgeoning youth movement. Cohen, who also directed *The Skulls*, was inspired to do a film on illegal street racing after he attended one such race in Los Angeles' San Fernando Valley. (The film was also based on an article about the underground phenomenon in *Vibe* magazine by Ken Li.) The director was shocked to see the number of teens who showed up and was thrilled by the adrenaline rush as the kids revved up engines, sped down empty streets, then scrambled in different directions as the police showed up. Hundreds to thousands of kids can show up at such events.

Another factor working in *The Fast and the Furious'* favor was the film's multicultural aspect. The street racing world attracts people from a bunch of different races and, oddly, is a place where all kinds of kids can meet on common ground. This certainly didn't hurt the film at the boxoffice since it was able to draw from a wider audience than the more limited group for a white-oriented teen film like *Clueless*.

But the biggest reason for *The Fast and the Furious'* success was adrenaline. The film runs like a video game with the action fast and furious, practically nonstop. To add to the video game flavor, the soundtrack is pumped up with a constant pounding rhythm of fast-paced rock and rap. And there are plenty of video game-like graphics. Whenever a racer engages his car's nitrous oxide, an engine additive that instantly propels a car into super speeds, we see shots of the nitrous pouring through the car's pipes like blood coursing through veins.

Probably no one in the film's large audience base showed up for the film's story, but the story's there nonetheless because the characters have to do something between the races. Brian (Paul Walker) is a blond surfer-looking guy who works for the token cool adult, Harry (Vyto Ruginis), at an auto parts shop and wants to get involved in the world of street racing. He shows up at one of the secret races and immediately gets into the action. He challenges alpha male Dominic (Vin Diesel) to a race. Brian can't compete with the big money bets—races can pay up to $10,000 apiece— so he bets his souped up car. But, because in movies like this, Dominic must remain dominant to uphold his hero status, Brian loses the race and his car.

But the race helps Brian gain access to Dominic's group, and soon he is one of Dominic's favorites, much to the chagrin of Dom's former favorite, Vince (Matt Schulze). Brian also catches the attention of Dom's little sister, Mia (Jordana Brewster). Even though Mia's a racer herself, she's as in awe of her brother as everyone else is. "He's like gravity," she tells Brian with the utmost gravity, in one of the film's many bad lines. "Everything just gets pulled to him."

The twist, though perhaps twist is too strong of a word since this particular plot point is pretty obvious, is that Brian is actually a cop. He's undercover to try to figure out who is behind a spate of truck hijackings of stolen electronic equipment. Could the villain be Dominic's arch rival Johnny Tran (Rick Yune), the head of an Asian gang who seems to be a bit of a loose cannon? Brian's police bosses keep telling him to keep an eye on Dom, but Brian is too blinded by Dom's charm to take him seriously as a suspect. (Or maybe it's that Brian is too in love with Dom to rat him out. More than one reviewer noted a strong homoerotic undercurrent between the two guys. Rene Rodriguez, in her review for the *Miami Herald*, wrote, "The bond between the two buff guys, who are always walking around in tight t-shirts and tank tops and trading brooding glances, makes you wonder if there isn't something else going on. As one audience member at a recent preview screening cried out during one such eyelock, 'Why don't they just get it over with and [expletive]?'")

That particular love story isn't too fleshed out, but then none of the other, more overt ones are either. Dom has a girlfriend, Letty (Michelle Rodriguez of the acclaimed *Girlfight*), but she has little more to do than to scowl and act tough. And even though Mia races, her main function is to wash up the dishes after dinner and to cheer the guys on when they race. Girls in this film exist only to wear skimpy clothing and to offer sexual favors to the guys after the races. In fact, so prevalent is this sexy cheerleading girl image, there seemed to be only one overweight girl in the entire film. And that is including all the extras.

The dialogue in the film veers between the banal and laughable. "I live my life a quarter of a mile at a time," says Dom, with full seriousness. "For those ten seconds, I'm free." Another good/bad line is: "He's got nitrous oxide in his blood and a gas tank for a brain. Don't turn your back on him." But dialogue reaches a B-movie pinnacle when someone says to a guy making out in public with his girl, "Yo Einstein! Take it upstairs. You can't detail a car without a cover."

The acting is equally lackluster. Diesel does the best job possible with a character that's supposed to be deep, but never has a chance to show any depth besides scowling. Walker is decidedly bland as the newcomer Paul. He seems like he'd have been much more comfortable with a role on *Beverly Hills 90210*. The biggest disappointment is Rodriguez who showed true star power in *Girlfight*. Here, she just spends her time glowering on the sidelines.

But that's beside the point, since here, cars, not people, are the stars. This becomes obvious with a long lingering shot of . . . auto parts waiting to be installed. It's like auto parts porn. And the film is very exciting. The hijacking sequences are particularly breathtaking. The bandits approach a speeding truck and while all are barreling down the road, attempt to enter the truck, beat up the driver and take over his rig. In another sequence, Dom and Brian are racing at top speed when they realize they are about to go into the path of a speeding train. Will one or both of them chicken out? Will they risk using the nitrous for a final burst of speed? Yikes. The film realizes that an action film should contain action and lots of it, and that puts it way ahead of a competitor like *Tomb Raider*.

*The Fast and the Furious* seems like a new breed of film, designed to appeal to those overstimulated by violent shows, video games, and full speed ahead music with plenty of, yes, violence, speed, and loud music. The filmmakers have an uncanny sense of the human adrenal gland and how to manipulate it for maximum result.

Perhaps surprisingly, considering the kind of throw-away film *The Fast and the Furious* is, reviewers liked it. "Loud, trashy, implausible and exciting. As a showcase for muscular chests and tattooed biceps, long legs and tight skirts, double overhead nitrous-oxide injectors, I dare say it can't be beat," wrote Andrew O'Hehir in *Salon*. "*The Fast and the Furious* will appeal to the inner juvenile delinquent in all of us," wrote Philip Wuntch in the *Dallas Morning News*. And *Newsday*'s Jan Stuart thought: "*The Fast and the Furious* is guilt-free pleasure, the sort that wears its trashiness on its sleeve and exults in it."

—*Jill Hamilton*

## CREDITS

**Dominic Toretto:** Vin Diesel
**Brian O'Conner:** Paul Walker
**Mia Toretto:** Jordana Brewster
**Letty:** Michelle Rodriguez
**Johnny Tran:** Rick Yune
**Sgt. Tanner:** Ted Levine
**Edwin:** Ja Rule
**Agent Bilkins:** Thom Barry
**Jesse:** Chad Lindberg
**Leon:** Johnny Strong
**Vince:** Matt Schulze
**Harry:** Vyto Ruginis

**Origin:** USA
**Released:** 2001
**Production:** Neal H. Moritz; Mediastream Film; released by Universal Pictures
**Directed by:** Rob Cohen
**Written by:** Gary Scott Thompson, Erik Bergquist, David Ayer
**Cinematography by:** Ericson Core
**Music by:** BT (Brian Transeau)
**Sound:** Felipe Borrero
**Music Supervisor:** Gary Jones, Happy Walters
**Editing:** Peter Honess

**Art Direction:** Kevin Kavanaugh
**Costumes:** Sanja Milkovic Hays
**Production Design:** Waldemar Kalinowski
**MPAA rating:** PG-13
**Running time:** 101 minutes

## REVIEWS

*Boxoffice.* September, 2001, p. 154.
*Chicago Sun-Times Online.* June 22, 2001.
*Entertainment Weekly.* June 29, 2001, p. 112.
*Los Angeles Times Online.* June 22, 2001.
*New York Times Online.* June 22, 2001.
*USA Today Online.* June 22, 2001.
*Variety.* June 25, 2001, p. 19.
*Washington Post Online.* June 22, 2001.

## QUOTES

Dom (Vin Diesel): "There's nothing more addictive than speed."

## TRIVIA

Director Rob Cohen has a cameo as a pizza delivery guy.

# Fast Food, Fast Women

*There are 10 million people in New York City, but only one like Bella.*
—Movie tagline

**Box Office:** $.1 million

A young woman by the name of Bella (Anna Thompson) lies down in the middle of a busy New York City street, nearly being run over by an irate driver. When the driver inquires about Bella's current state of sanity, she replies that she was just trying to start her day with a little bit of excitement. Too bad the same thing couldn't be said for Israeli director Amos Kolleck's comedy *Fast Food, Fast Women*. Kolleck's multiple narrative, which follows the romantic twists and turns of coffee shop patrons and an overworked waitress (Bella), feels too sedate and lacks any real conflicts. In fact, despite the film's title, *Fast Food, Fast Women* plods along at a pedestrian pace while exposing the characters' minor problems in the romantic arena. And although the film's narrative provides some pleasure, viewers might still reply with a "so what?" or "who cares?"

As self-effacing Bella's 35th birthday approaches, Bella's mother (Judith Roberts) decides to fix her daughter up with the son of a friend, against Bella's wishes. After all, Bella is already involved with George (Austin Pendelton), a married theater director and misogynist. However, after much persuasion Bella goes on a date with an irresponsible taxi driver, an Englishman named Bruno (Jamie Harris, the son of Richard Harris). The pair hit it off until Bella mentions that she hates children and this causes conflict because Bruno recently got saddled with his ex-wife's children, only one of whom was actually fathered by him. However, as she teeters on high heels and flaunts her breasts, Bella doesn't realize she uttered the wrong words to Bruno.

Meanwhile, aging coffee shop patron Paul (Robert Modica) answers a personal ad placed by 60-year-old widow, Emily (Louise Lasser). Although Emily and Paul appear nervous on their first date as they sip red wine at the coffee shop, they too seem to hit it off. But Emily becomes increasingly upset as each date passes without Paul putting out sexual overtures. One night Paul invites Emily to his apartment, but even after dancing closely with Emily, Paul decides to end the night without making love to the disappointed Emily. So the distraught Emily ends up spending the night with taxi driver Bruno. To make matters worse Paul shows up at Emily's apartment at the wrong time to apologize for his behavior. Although Paul appears slightly upset over Emily sleeping with a younger man, this scene provides little conflict. Later, Emily shows up at Paul's apartment to confess her sexual indiscretion and the couple finally end up making love.

Meanwhile, Bella saves an elderly lady from muggers and is beaten in the process. A week or so later, Bella receives a call from a corporate attorney's office and later learns that the elderly lady left Bella an inheritance of some $9 million. Bella gives up her apartment and purchases a country estate, complete with wild beasts. She confesses to Bruno that she does loves children, so the couple reunites. And with the remainder of her inheritance, Bella opens a restaurant called Fast Food, Fast Women that features waitresses on roller skates.

Louise Lasser portrays Emily with her usual signature wide-eyed expression and slow careful speech, while Robert Modica delivers a warm performance as the vulnerable widower seeking companionship in his golden years. Jamie Harris plays his contradictory role of a tender father and irresponsible lover with aplomb. And although Anna Thompson seems anorexically thin, she adds another engaging performance to her list of roles. Although *Fast Women* ambles along, Kolleck manages to reveal human frailties that people of all ages can relate to. He suggests to us to slow down and tell the truth if we want to enjoy healthy relationships.

—*Patty-Lynne Herlevi*

## CREDITS

**Bella:** Anna Thompson
**Bruno:** Jamie Harris
**Emily:** Louise Lasser
**Paul:** Robert Modica
**Sherry-Lynn:** Lonette McKee
**Seymour:** Victor Argo
**George:** Austin Pendleton
**Vitka:** Angelica Torn
**Graham:** Mark Margolis
**Bella's mother:** Judith Roberts
**Wanda:** Valerie Geffner
**Mugging victim:** Irma St. Paul

**Origin:** France, USA
**Released:** 2000
**Production:** Hengameh Panahi; Lumen Films; released by Lot 47 Films
**Directed by:** Amos Kollek
**Written by:** Amos Kollek
**Cinematography by:** Jean-Marc Fabre
**Music by:** David Carbonara
**Sound:** Chen Harpaz, David Raphael
**Editing:** Sheri Bylander
**Costumes:** Pascal Gosset
**Production Design:** Stacey Tanner
**MPAA rating:** R
**Running time:** 96 minutes

## REVIEWS

*Chicago Sun-Times Online.* June 8, 2001.
*Los Angeles Times Online.* June 22, 2001.
*New York Times Online.* May 18, 2001.
*Variety.* May 22, 2000, p. 29.

## QUOTES

Bella (Anna Thompson) wonders about Bruno (Jamie Harris): "Why do I get all of the lunatics?"

## TRIVIA

Anna Thompson also starred in the Kolleck films *Sue* and *Fiona*.

AWARDS AND NOMINATIONS

**Nomination:**
**Cannes 2000:** Film.

# Fat Girl
# (A Ma Soeur)
# (For My Sister)

 **Box Office:** $.5 million

While enfant terrible filmmaker Catherine Breillat's 1999 release *Romance* came across as an adolescent gaze at female sexuality, the French director's latest, *Fat Girl*, resembles an erotic, Hitchcockian thriller. *Romance* suffered from its weak plot, voiceover narration, and overt focus on the sexual act (lacking sex appeal) but, fortunately, those tendencies were not repeated with *Fat Girl*. Both films portray young women exploring their sexuality. In *Romance*, the protagonist, a prim schoolteacher with a sexually ambivalent lover, explores various degrading sexual acts with strangers. She is raped in one scene and, in another scene, she experiences a sexual awakening through a degrading S & M session.

The teenage sister protagonists in *Fat Girl* also explore sexual rites through voyeurism as younger sister Anais (Anais Reboux) watches her haughty and ravishing older sister Elena (Roxane Mesquida) lose her virginity to Italian womanizer, Fernando (Libero de Reinzo). Similar to *Romance*, Breillat chose to shoot the scenes in long shots from Anais's POV and we can feel the younger sister's discomfort as Elena painfully experiences a rite of passage. The varied erotic scenes appear equally clinical and disturbing as we watch a sacrificial lamb prepare to be sexually conquered in a loveless act. The scenes are chilling and reek of societal taboos. The naughty curious teen has committed a crime against her younger sister and because she crossed an invisible line, she will be punished.

However, unlike *Romance* or *A Real Young Girl*, sex is not the central focus of *Fat Girl* and the dynamics of the sisters' relationship allows for rich dialogue to develop. We are drawn into the story of the two sisters at the top of the film as they take their daily walk while discussing how they wish to lose their virginity. In a scene that foreshadows future events, Elena confesses that she would have to be in love with her first lover while Anais argues that she would rather not be in love. The teenagers stop for drinks at a local café where Fernando woos Elena. Through a brief conversation we learn that the sisters are on holiday with their parents and have grown bored with their daily routine.

Later, as the teens prepare to sleep, Anais spies Elena putting on lipstick and she learns of Elena's sexual rendezvous, which will take place in the bedroom that the sister's share. Elena commands Anais to go to sleep, but suffering from a case of insomnia and curiosity, Anais watches the deflowering of her sister. Traumatized by her sister's act, Anais stuffs herself (she's bulimic) and plays a game in the swimming pool, pretending that she has two invisible lovers that she swims between. As her sister and Fernando grow into a sexual item, Anais also suffers from her sister's cruel words and deeds. The fat sister often must wait for her slim sister, who treats her like a pawn. Elena blows hot and cold towards Anais. In one scene that resembles a slumber party for two, the sisters engage in pillow talk in a loving fashion, but soon Elena turns vicious towards Anais, which leads to Anais suffering a breakdown on the beach.

On a fateful day Fernando's mother (Laura Betti) shows up and demands to the sister's chainsmoking mother (Arsinee Khanjian) that Elena return the priceless ring that Fernando gave her. Fernando had lied to Elena earlier, telling the naïve teen that his grandmother gave the ring to him when, in fact, he stole the ring from his overbearing mother. Humiliated, the sisters' mother decides to end their holiday abruptly and whisks the girls back to Paris via a grueling drive. At this point, the film transforms into a thriller as the mother drives the long distance from the Basque coast to Paris. Elena confesses to Anais that she wants to murder their mother and kill herself. We watch the mother weave in and out of traffic as she swerves around large trucks, but the film's climatic moment, which includes murder and rape, comes as a complete shock.

Frederic Bonnaud wrote in *Film Comment* that "in *A ma soeur!*, the dominant undercurrent is autobiographical. . . . In France, everyone knows that Catherine Breillat has a big sister named Marie-Helene . . . it's obvious that *A ma soeur!* feeds off the memory of lost familial intimacy." It's a wicked sister act, haunted by the macabre wish fulfillment of lovesick teens.

—*Patty-Lynne Herlevi*

## CREDITS

**Anais:** Anais Reboux
**Elena:** Roxane Mesquida
**Fernando:** Libero De Rienzo
**Mother:** Arsinee Khanjian
**Father:** Romain Goupil

**Fernando's mother:** Laura Betti

**Origin:** France
**Language:** French
**Released:** 2001
**Production:** Jean-Francois Lepetit; Flach Films, Arte France Cinema, CB Films; released by Cowboy Booking International
**Directed by:** Catherine Breillat
**Written by:** Catherine Breillat
**Cinematography by:** Yorgos Arvanitis
**Sound:** Vincent Arnardi
**Editing:** Pascale Chavance
**Costumes:** Anna Dunsford Varenne
**Production Design:** Francois-Renaud Varenne
**MPAA rating:** Unrated
**Running time:** 95 minutes

## REVIEWS

*Boxoffice.* November, 2001, p. 146.
*Entertainment Weekly.* October 19, 2001, p. 56.
*Film Comment.* March/April, 2001, p. 14.
*Los Angeles Times Online.* October 26, 2001.
*New York Times Online.* October 8, 2001.
*People.* October 22, 2001, p. 40.
*Variety.* February 19, 2001, p. 41.
*Village Voice.* October 9, 2001, p. 128.
*Village Voice.* October 16, 2001, p. 131.
*Washington Post.* November 16, 2001, p. WE41.

## QUOTES

Anais (Anais Reboux) tells sister Elena (Roxanne Mesquida) about sex: "The first time should be with a nobody."

## TRIVIA

Anais Reboux was 13 when she filmed *Fat Girl.*

# 15 Minutes

*America likes to watch.*
—Movie tagline

**Box Office:** $24.4 million

*1 5 Minutes* is not the first film from writer-producer-director John Herzfeld dealing with the American media's breathless pursuit of every last titillating detail about questionable characters and lurid crimes. He has, after all, brought to television the sordid, sensational, and over-covered cases of *The Preppie Murder* (1989) and the Joey Buttafuoco-Amy Fisher saga *Casualties of Love: The Long Island Lolita Story* (1993). In his latest film, Herzfeld does not just chronicle a case of this type but attempts to show us the error of our ways. Isn't it amazing what some people will do for their Warholian "15 minutes of fame"? Why do we decry shocking, unsavory or simply unattractive behavior and yet gobble it up with a voracious appetite as fast as it is shoveled to us in print, on television, or in films? Is the media to blame, or are they simply providing us with what we desire? Another good question is whether this film which examines the problem is also part of it.

*15 Minutes* begins with throbbing, dramatic music to get our juices flowing from scene one. People chatting in various foreign tongues are going through customs at the airport. Among them are demonically intense Czech Emil (Karel Rodin) and his traveling companion, loopily breezy and overly brawny Russian Oleg Razgul (Ultimate Fighting champion Oleg Taktarov), the later of whom, enamored with legendary director Frank Capra and making movies, is hoping to document their trip to America, "where anyone can be anything." The two have trouble written all over them.

No sooner have they arrived in New York City itself, Oleg, spellbound by a digital video camera in a store window display, steals it and proceeds with Emil to pay a call at the apartment of some Russians who stiffed them after a bank job in the old country. With a cry of "Action!" Oleg endeavors to record this ominous reunion, getting just the right angles, zooming in for closeups and utilizing the various video effects at his disposal. When this meeting degenerates into bitter, maniacal laughter and horrific, bloody butchering, Oleg keeps the camera rolling much to the consternation of Emil, who barks for his comrade to turn it off. Oleg does not stop, however, and also documents Emil's incineration of the apartment to cover up the murders. If Emil is so concerned about getting rid of any and all evidence of the slayings, it is hard to believe that he does not make sure that Oleg destroys what he has shot. The men's "Bohemian barbecue" completed, they head out to hunt for Daphne (Vera Famiga), who was lucky enough to escape the residence.

In contrast to these two barbarians are homicide detective Eddie Flemming (the great Robert De Niro) and arson investigator Jordy Warsaw (blandly portrayed by Edward Burns). Eddie is a famous, media-savvy veteran, his face often gracing magazine covers and his often sensational cases reported by serious journalists and on sleazy tabloid television shows like Top Story, hosted by shameless, anything-for-ratings anchor Robert Hawkins (Kelsey Grammar). When we first meet Eddie, he is in a men's room trying to mask the signs of a hangover, submerging his face in a sink full of ice water and using drops for his bloodshot eyes. (De Niro talks into a mirror, reminding us of his performance in 1976's *Taxi Driver*.) He holds a ring, planning to propose the following day to his beautiful television reporter girlfriend, Nicolette Karas (Melina Kanakaredes). Jordy is a young, serious straight arrow who, unlike Eddie, has no desire or use for media attention or celebrity, and does not even own a television set.

We first meet Jordy as he heroically races through Central Park on his way to answer a page, leaping over benches and subduing a would-be mugger with ease, handcuffing the man to a tree for safekeeping. Both Eddie and Jordy have been called to the scene of Emil and Oleg's murder/arson, and when the two meet there is some underlying tension and resentment over who is in charge. It is a horrific scene, and Herzfeld makes sure to show us closeups of the charred bodies, and a nauseating finger sweep inside the mouth of one of the victims. The two run into each other again after Emil tries to lure call girl Daphne to a hotel room and gets so angry when another woman comes in her stead that he savagely slaughters her, again enthusiastically lensed by Oleg and potently presented to us. (From early on in the film, Oleg's constant, enthusiastic capturing of it all gets old, and when, for example, he even holds it at arm's length to shoot himself and Emil fleeing the authorities, it eventually becomes ridiculous.) About this time Emil is watching television and learns how some people have been able to beat the system by claiming they were emotionally incapacitated at the time of their crimes and are therefore not legally responsible. When he hears that a murderer Eddie tracked down in a high-profile case was found criminally insane, got psychiatric treatment, and was released back into society to sign multi-million dollar movie and book deals, a lightbulb goes on for Emil. "It pays to be a killer in this country," he is told at a corner newsstands.

As *15 Minutes* ticks by, the relationship between Eddie and Jordy develops along predictable lines. (There is little believable chemistry in the partnership between De Niro and Burns.) It is something seen many times before, and we know that the initial rivalry between the two men—different in personality, age, experience, status, and style—will gradually give way to respect as they work together. Eddie initially toys with Jordy, as if to let him know who is in command here, but as they rush to save Daphne from her pursuers the two come to realize that they both get an invigorating sense of satisfaction from working valorous jobs they always dreamed of having. So when Jordy takes an unwise detour from procedure, Eddie covers for him, skillfully smoothing things over. Attitudes lighten further, and Eddie passes on sage advice about fame and its uses, and jokes that he helped Jody because the younger man reminds

him of a puppy he kept around despite the fact that it urinated on his carpets. To underscore for us that there is a growing connection between the two, Herzfeld has Jordy jump up to light Eddie's cigar.

Eddie provides Jordy with more words of wisdom and a two-headed coin he always carries around before heading off to pop the question to Nicolette. Before she arrives for a candlelight dinner, Emil and Oleg attack Eddie, tie him up in a chair, and torture him. Emil proclaims that killing a celebrity will be their ticket to fame and fortune, and after ordering Oleg to stop his camera, he details a plan to avoid jail by feigning insanity and then, once back on the streets, enjoy immense profits from book and film deals. The scene in which they kill Eddie while Oleg's camera rolls is yet another of the film's excessive, shockingly graphic scenes. When Emil calls Hawkins offering their snuff film for $1 million, the anchor, attending Eddie's wake, reacts only with excited demands for exclusivity. Despite angry objections from Eddie's coworkers on the force in an over-the-top scene, the footage is broadcast as seemingly all of New York pauses to watch in horror. Among those watching in a Planet Hollywood are the cutthroat Czech and his buddy, sitting triumphantly in plain sight and arguing loudly over who deserves credit for their grisly production. How believable this scene is is highly debatable, but it ends with Jordy collaring Emil (Oleg escapes) and then taking the scenic route on the way to the station for a little vigilante justice.

Emil successfully avoids prison thanks to attorney Bruce Cutler (the real life lawyer of high profile clients like the infamous John Gotti), who plays himself and is apparently unaware or unconcerned that he comes off as such a loathsome individual. It all leads up to a climactic scene in which the best and the worst versions of ourselves battle it out under the watchful gaze of the Statue of Liberty. As Emil is carted off to the psych ward on Rikers Island, Nicolette, Hawkins, and other members of the media swarm around. Also there is Jordy (on suspension due to bad publicity about the guy he shackled and forgot about earlier on), and Oleg, who reveals to Hawkins that his camera stayed on when Emil was telling Eddie about the diabolical plan to pretend to be insane. With a dramatic flourish, Hawkins waves the evidence in the air and declares Emil a faker, which causes all hell to break loose. Before we know it, Emil is holding Nicolette hostage, and Jordy, after some hesitation, evens the score for his dear departed partner and shoots the scum full of holes. Oleg also expires in the scene, asking with his last gasp if his film (yes, he is still shooting) was well-done enough. Morally outraged, Jordy gives Hawkins a good wallop. The last word goes to Hawkins, who looks into the camera and files a report, false and detestable as ever.

*15 Minutes*, which was not well liked by critics, was shot on a budget of $42 million, and grossed a disappointing $24 million at the boxoffice. A catch phrase of Hawkins is "Hard to believe. . . . Watch!" and as we watch the film we find more than a few things that are, indeed, rather hard to believe. Many critics felt that the whole premise was too farfetched and contrived, and that the script was wildly unsubtle. What strikes one most is an unavoidable sense that there is hypocrisy here on the part of Herzfeld. Next to the two disturbing and disturbed tourists, *15 Minutes* expends a lot of energy pointing out how smarmy and contemptible the character played by Grammar is. (The actor lays it on thick—and then some.) How shameless and shameful he is, Herzfeld clearly feels, to use shocking images to grab as big an audience as possible. It seems that Herzfeld is doing the same, his own film repeatedly ultra-violent and blood-soaked, careful to capture the butchery in great and ghastly detail. It seems that he is eliciting the public's salivation in a manner which—and for behavior that—he purports to abhor.

—*David L. Boxerbaum*

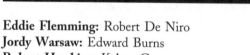
## CREDITS

**Eddie Flemming:** Robert De Niro
**Jordy Warsaw:** Edward Burns
**Robert Hawkins:** Kelsey Grammer
**Leon Jackson:** Avery Brooks
**Nicolette karas:** Melina Kanakaredes
**Daphne Handlova:** Vera Farmiga
**Emil Slovak:** Karel Roden
**Oleg Razgul:** Oleg Taktarov
**Bobby Korfin:** John DiResta
**Captain Duffy:** James Handy
**Tommy Cullen:** Darius McCrary
**Rose Hearn:** Charlize Theron
**Cassandra:** Kim Cattrall
**Mugger:** David Alan Grier

**Origin:** USA
**Released:** 2001
**Production:** Nick Wechsler, Keith Addis, David Blocker, John Herzfeld; Tribeca Productions, Industry Entertainment, New Redemption; released by New Line Cinema
**Directed by:** John Herzfeld
**Written by:** John Herzfeld
**Cinematography by:** Jean-Yves Escoffier
**Music by:** Anthony Marinelli, J. Peter Robinson
**Sound:** Kim Harris Ornitz
**Editing:** Steven Cohen
**Art Direction:** Jess Gonchor
**Costumes:** April Ferry
**Production Design:** Mayne Berke
**MPAA rating:** R
**Running time:** 120 minutes

## REVIEWS

*Boxoffice.* April, 2001, p. 237.
*Chicago Sun-Times Online.* March 9, 2001.
*Entertainment Weekly.* March 16, 2001, p. 41.
*Film Comment.* March, 2001, p. 74.
*New Republic.* April 2, 2001, p. 28.
*New York.* March 19, 2001, p. 60.
*New York Times.* March 9, 2001, p. E22.
*New Yorker.* March 26, 2001, p. 103.
*People.* March 19, 2001, p. 35.
*Sight and Sound.* May, 2001, p. 48.
*USA Today Online.* March 9, 2001.
*Variety.* March 5, 2001, p. 42.
*Wall Street Journal.* March 9, 2001, p. W1.
*Washington Post Online.* March 9, 2001.

## QUOTES

Eddie Flemming (Robert De Niro) to new partner Jordy Warsaw (Edward Burns): "The little bit of fame I have in this city makes my job a whole lot easier."

# Fighter

*Loyalty, the limits of friendship, and fighting back.*
—Movie tagline

Director Milos Forman called Amir Bar-Lev's documentary *Fighter* "robust and beautiful" and one might add the words spirited and insightful. Bar-Lev has proven that one doesn't have to be complex to make a point and, in fact, by stripping away to the essentials, one can create a powerful cinematic work. Bar-Lev chose to focus on two aging men, professor/author Arnost Lustig and former British Royal Air Force soldier Jan Weiner. The two men, both Jewish and former Czech citizens, take a journey together back to Europe to retrace Weiner's escape route from the Nazis. However, this road trip is filled with bitter memories of loss, as well as tension between the two men who see life completely differently.

Bar-Lev employs a cinema verite approach as he follows the men back to the (now) Czech Republic where, as adolescents, Lustig and his family were deported to Auschwitz while Weiner escaped to Slovenia after receiving an exit visa from a deplorable immigration officer. The officer rechecked Weiner's list of belongings, subtracting as he went along. Two suits, no, you only need one, and then he delivered the coup de grace after he saw that Weiner had four pairs of shoes: "Jew, you won't have time to wear out one pair." Humiliated and angry, Weiner decided at that moment that he would survive the Nazis and kill that officer after the war.

Upon arriving in Yugoslavia, Weiner and Lustig visit the former home of Weiner's father and stepmother and he tells the story of how the couple committed suicide when they learned that the Nazis had occupied Belgrade. The father told his son that they were going to die anyway, so it would be more dignified to take one's own life rather than let the Nazis do it for them. While Weiner once thought of his father as cowardly, Lustig interprets the father's action as heroic. He considered that the father must have known that in order to save his son's life, he would have to sacrifice his own. This sequence ends up being the most poignant in the film and also one of the only times that the two men don't do battle with their opposing life philosophies.

Next, the two men travel to Trieste, Italy where Weiner stowed away under a locomotive and spent 18 hours under a toilet hole, clutching an excrement-slicked steel plate just over the train's wheels. Weiner was heading to France where he hoped to join the British Royal Air Force, but instead he was captured by the Italians and thrown into solitary confinement. Of course, at the time, Weiner found this to be a blessing, since instead of being sent back to Czechoslovakia where he would have been executed, he stayed in an Italian prison. Eventually, he was sent to a POW camp in Italy where he and another prisoner escaped—later to enjoy the hospitality of Italian villagers in the area.

While at an Italian restaurant in Paola, Weiner picks a fight with Lustig—then Weiner refuses to complete the film. We watch Weiner tear off his microphone and stomp out of the restaurant while Lustig quietly finishes his meal. Three days later, filming resumes while the two men play a board game on the beach. However, soon the two men pack their belongings and head back to the States. Lustig concludes, "Fighters are important during times of war, but maybe a fighting nature isn't so good during a time of peace." Ironically, the film ends with Weiner and his wife Suzana practicing Tai Chi (a tranquil form of martial arts) in their back yard.

Not only do we get a clear account of the two men's personal Holocaust stories, but a history lesson is also presented to us. Footage is shown of a Nazi propaganda film called *The Fuhr Gives a City to the Jews* in which Jewish prisoners are shown being fed and taken care of by the Nazis, leaving us to wonder how many people actually believed the content of those films. And Lustig and Weiner argue over how Lustig could have joined the Communist party when they also annihilated Jewish populations? Lustig believed that not all Communists were evil and he concluded that despite Weiner's defensive attitude, "Weiner is a hero of a time with millions of cowards."

—*Patty-Lynne Herlevi*

## CREDITS

**Origin:** USA
**Released:** 2000
**Production:** Amir Bar-Lev, Jonathan Crosby, Alex Mamlet; Next Wave Films; released by First Run Features
**Directed by:** Amir Bar-Lev
**Cinematography by:** David Collier, Gary Griffin, Justin Schein, Jay Danner McDonald
**Sound:** Peter Cikhhart
**Editing:** Amir Bar-Lev
**MPAA rating:** Unrated
**Running time:** 86 minutes

## REVIEWS

*Chicago Sun-Times Online.* February 22, 2002.
*Hollywood Reporter Online.* August 1, 2000.
*Los Angeles Times Online.* October 26, 2001.
*Variety Online.* April 24, 2000.

## QUOTES

Jan Weiner recalls his father's suicide after the Nazi invasion: "Tonight I am going to kill myself. That is the only freedom we have left."

# Final Fantasy: The Spirits Within

*Unleash a new reality.*
—Movie tagline
*Open your mind. Unlock the secret. Experience the fantasy.*
—Movie tagline
*Enter a new dimension, beyond all you imagine, where fantasy becomes reality.*
—Movie tagline

**Box Office:** $32.1 million

Unfortunately, *Final Fantasy: The Spirits Within*, a technical triumph with digital cardboard characters, was symptomatic of the state of the cinema at the turn of the new century. Though inventive and innovative, it represented a quantum leap towards gimmickry and nonsense, utilizing a far-fetched futuristic plot stripped of human content in an attempted collaboration between the videogame industry and Hollywood and following the example of *Tomb Raider*, by which Paramount Pictures attempted to create a film franchise out of a successful videogame series. But *Tomb Raider* at least offered Angelina Jolie as Laura Croft, whereas *Final Fantasy* took a more risky approach that offered a lifeless digital creation for its heroine, Aki Ross. As Stephen Holden observed in the *New York Times* on August 31, at the conclusion of a miserable summer movie season, "It's all about technology. In the technoscape of the contemporary event movie, human beings have become part of the machinery, and that machinery is increasingly fake." *New York Times* reviewer Elvis Mitchell called *Final Fantasy* "the first movie to be peopled with non-actors," adding, sardonically, "if you don't count *Pearl Harbor*."

The plot of this lifeless epic is hardly worth summarizing, since one suspects many viewers went to see it out merely out of curiosity and to experience the novelty and the spectacle. In the year 2065 alien beings have conquered planet earth. Those human beings who have survived are fighting to reclaim the planet, even though they do not fully understand the enemy. All of the "characters" are digital creations. The "heroine" is Dr. Aki Ross, voiced by Ming-Na Wen, whose breakthrough role was the character June in Wayne Wang's adaptation of Amy Tan's novel *The Joy Luck Club*, in 1993, followed in 1998 by the Disney animated musical *Mulan*, in which she voiced the eponymous lead. In *Final Fantasy*, Dr. Ross believes "she" is qualified to unlock the alien mystery and save the planet, guided by her spiritual and theoretical mentor, Dr. Sid (voiced by Donald Sutherland), but her time is running out. She has been infected by the alien "phantoms" but has survived the infection because of a containment procedure clever Dr. Sid has developed. She is assisted in her mission by Captain Gray Edwards (voiced by Alec Baldwin). Other actors providing voices for sidekicks are Ving Rhames (for Ryan Whittaker) and Steve Buscemi (for Neil Fleming). The casting and voice director was Jack Fletcher.

Dr. Sid's notions are unpopular with the governing Council, and are strongly opposed by the hateful General Hein (voiced by James Woods), who advocates using a space-mounted weapon, the "Zeus Cannon," to destroy the aliens—though how he intends to do that is unclear, since the phantoms have infested the whole planet. The General is a mad man and a would-be autocrat. Dr. Sid believes the ecological effects of the Zeus Cannon would be disastrous and might even give birth to new aliens. Dr. Sid seeks a scientific rather than a military solution. Aki Ross believes in Sid's "wave theory" and is attempting to locate and collect "spirit waves" that may be used to cure her of her "infection" and may ultimately counteract the alien force. That is her quest.

General Hein has a personal agenda. He wants to destroy the alien invaders who have destroyed his family. He stages a coup that places Aki and Dr. Sid in prison, then breaches security for the New York biosphere in order to convince the Council that the Zeus Cannon must be used. His plan backfires, however, and the biosphere must then be evacuated. The aliens traveled to earth on a meteor. Aki has isolated all but one of the spirits needed to cure her. She and Dr. Sid and Captain Gray and his loyal squadron to the meteor crater in the Caspian Mountains, as General Hein makes his way into space to the Zeus Cannon, which he intends to use, with the crater as his target. Overall, the plot is not entirely coherent, and the characters are pretty flat, metaphorically and literally.

The film was written, designed, and directed by Hironobu Sakaguchi of the Japanese videogame operation Square, who developed the "Final Fantasy" series of interactive, role-playing videogames, the first of which was introduced in 1987. Final Fantasy VIII was released in 1999 by Sony Play Stations. The most popular film of the summer of 2001 was *Shrek*, which involved a total illusion created by digital animation. The digital fabrication of *Final Fantasy* simply represents the next logical step in challenging the reality-based assumptions of Sigfried Kracauer and other theoreticians whose cinematic ideal was "the redemption of physical reality." But the so-called "hyper-Realistic" style of *Final Fantasy* is a far cry from that ideal. Disney's *Tron* (1982) was a benchmark in its time in the way it attempted to combine live action with computer effects, but in that film, though the plot was not sufficient to carry the film, at least Jeff Bridges was on camera to provide some human interest. The goal of Sakaguchi's CGI-animation technique was to replicate "photo-real" human characters.

The British journal *Sight and Sound* reported that the film represented an investment of four years and "a rumored cost of $100 million." While expressing reservations that it was "unlikely *The Spirits Within* will redefine the art of cinematic narrative or extend the boundaries of filmic vocabulary," reporter David McCarthy questioned the quality of the script composed by *Apollo 13* screenwriter Al Reinert, but was impressed by the technical accomplishment of the CGI animation: "The final result may not be quite as convincing as the real thing, but motion-capture technology has been married with handcrafted animation skills to convey impressive results." To recover the production costs *Final Fantasy* had to be a blockbuster hit, but it fell far short of that goal, thankfully for those who may prefer humanistic-centered films.

Critical reception was mixed. Seduced by the techno-logical achievements of the picture, Lisa Schwarzbaum of *Entertainment Weekly* considered the film a "gorgeous curi-osity," though she conceded that the story "is merely average by sci-fi standards." *Variety* reviewer Todd McCarthy saw the film as a "secret weapon" for the studios in future negotiations with the Screen Actors Guild, after the threat-ened walk-out earlier in the year, since it potentially raises the question of "how replaceable actors may be—and how soon—in dramatic material." McCarthy found the "acting" in this picture "no worse than that found in the majority of sci-fi films," and even claimed (debatably) that the virtual figures drawn for the film "are sufficiently real-looking to evoke virtually emotional (and virtually erotic) responses." Moreover, McCarthy believed, "as computer game-derived features go, it surely beats *Laura Croft: Tomb Raider.*" But McCarthy found flaws as well. The "phantoms," for exam-ple, were not "particularly effective villains," in his opinion, "so there is a fundamental lack of visceral engagement in the central conflict."

The main problem, then, is the inhuman vacuity that is at the center of the plot. How can one possibly evaluate "acting" if there are no real "actors" in such a movie? Can a non-human image project "personality" or charisma if there is no real person involved beyond the voice-print? One might argue that the best Disney animation came closest to achieving that goal, perhaps, but this new technology comes up short. The "characters" of *Final Fantasy* often seem to float. They are dead behind the eyes, like pixel zombies. The story cannot be character-driven if the characters are devoid of human content. Finally, this "fantasy" is merely a game, and not a very convincing one at that. "Is the clock ticking for traditionally animated movies?" as Jeff Fensen and Steve Daly speculated in *Entertainment Weekly.* Well, perhaps, for novelty seekers, but there is truly no "spirit" within this "final fantasy." Though the videogame may enjoy continued popu-larity, continued movie potential for the enterprise seems decidedly limited.

—*James M. Welsh*

## CREDITS

**Dr. Aki Ross:** Ming Na (Voice)
**Captain Gray Edwards:** Alec Baldwin (Voice)
**Neil:** Steve Buscemi (Voice)
**Jane:** Peri Gilpin (Voice)
**Ryan:** Ving Rhames (Voice)
**Dr. Sid:** Donald Sutherland (Voice)
**General Hein:** James Woods (Voice)
**Council Member #1:** Keith David (Voice)
**Council Member #2:** Jean Simmons (Voice)
**Major Elliot:** Matt McKenzie (Voice)

**Origin:** USA
**Released:** 2001
**Production:** Hironobu Sakaguchi, Jun Aida, Chris Lee; Square Pictures; released by Columbia Pictures
**Directed by:** Hironobu Sakaguchi
**Written by:** Al Reinert, Jeff Vintar
**Music by:** Elliot Goldenthal
**Sound:** Randy Thom
**Music Supervisor:** Richard Rudolph
**Editing:** Christopher S. Capp
**MPAA rating:** PG-13
**Running time:** 104 minutes

## REVIEWS

*Boxoffice.* September, 2001, p. 149.
*Chicago Sun-Times Online.* July 11, 2001.
*Entertainment Weekly.* July 20, 2001, p. 42.
*Los Angeles Times Online.* July 11, 2001.
*New York Times Online.* July 11, 2001.
*People.* July 23, 2001, p. 34.
*Sight and Sound.* September, 2001, p. 42.
*USA Today Online.* July 11, 2001.
*Variety.* July 9, 2001, p. 20.
*Washington Post Weekend.* July 13, 2001, p. WE36.
*Washington Times.* July 13, 2001, p. C6.

## QUOTES

Dr. Sid (voiced by Donald Sutherland): "It is not a fairy tale. It is true."

# The Forsaken

*The night . . . has an appetite.*
—Movie tagline

 **Box Office:** $6.7 million

*T*he Forsaken, is, to say the least, a disturbing movie, a schlock, shock horror film that is also something of a perverse road movie. It begins with a literal bloodbath as the credits roll, showing a young blonde, later seen freaking out in a local roadhouse when the plot is set in motion, in the shower and covered with blood, which she carefully washes off of her right breast. So there it is, in one opening, iconic image, sex and violence, with a psycho in the shower. What is to follow should come as no surprise, but the gross-out violence is so extreme that it surprises, none the less. This movie is neither for the faint of heart nor the sound of mind. It is also not for mature adults, who will find it merely disgusting.

The story proper begins with a young man named Sean (played by Kerr Smith of television's *Dawson's Creek*), who needs to get from Los Angeles to Miami in order to attend his sister's wedding. He works as an editor for a low-profile film production company and has to negotiate with his boss for a week off to make the trip. He has arranged to drive a car to Florida to deliver it to a woman who is entitled to it as part of a divorce settlement. It turns out to be a vintage Mercedes convertible worth $50,000. At first Sean seems to be sitting on top of the world, but his world will begin to tremble and shake as soon as his journey gets underway. There he is, driving across the desert with the top down, basking in glorious sunshine. Two girls in another convertible pass him and flirt with him, inviting him to attend a rally and party they are headed for in the desert. One of them flashes him, putting her top down as they drive past, offering the promise of sex in the desert. The violence is sure to follow.

When the Mercedes has a flat tire, while attempting to fix it Sean encounters Nick (Brendan Fehr), a hitchhiker who needs a ride and offers to pay for the gas. At first Sean has reservations, but since he has lost his wallet (which, it turns out, Nick has stolen), Sean agrees. Next they encounter a marauding tribe of vampires in a beat-up old car that needs a jump-start. After the car has been started, one of the vampires remarks, "The one riding shotgun [i.e., Nick] is a hunter." Nick later explains his "mission" as a "hunter" of vampires, useful exposition since *The Forsaken* concocts its own vampire "legend."

Nick tells Sean his own version of how vampires came into the world, which has nothing to do with Bram Stoker's classic novel. The film invents its own medieval legend dating back to the crusades, when a group of doomed knights made a pact with the devil during the siege of Antioch. The Turks slaughtered 200 French knights in the 11th century. An angel from hell, Abaddon, offered nine survivors eternal life. Eight of them accepted and sealed their pact by murdering the one knight who refused and then drinking his blood. Known thereafter as "The Forsaken," their fate was to roam the earth at night, seeking victims. One of the cursed knights was executed during the Spanish Inquisition. Three more were dispatched during later centuries. Four still survived, two of them in the United States. How Nick the hunter came by this arcane information is never explained.

Nick and Sean are joined by Megan (Izabella Miko), the infected blonde seen in the opening credits. They notice her in a restaurant. Disturbed and hungry, she cannot pay her bill, which Nick offers to pick up, remarking "I know what I'm doing, Sean." After the three of them check into a motel room, Nick explains that she has a blood disease, and later

explains further that she is in danger of turning into a vampire, after she has had a nasty seizure in the bathtub of the motel where they are staying that night. During that seizure, she bites Sean, putting him at risk. But Nick offers Sean a "cocktail" of medications that will delay his own "turning." Megan is not given this cocktail, however, because Nick intends to use her as bait. The vampires thought she died, but since she is still alive, she represents "unfinished business" for them. So long as she is not under medication, the vampires can track her, bringing them to Nick, who intends to kill them. Only by killing the host vampire (one of the original "Forsaken") can the victims be cured.

And so the vampires are slain, one by one. They run in a pack with a male leader, Kit (Johnathon Schaech), the 900-year-old vampire who is Nick's main prey, two female vampires, one white and one black (no doubt for the sake of diversity), and a retarded driver (Simon Rex), who keeps them on the move during the day, when exposure to sunlight would destroy them. Why the driver chooses to run with the vampires is a mystery, other than the fact that he is retarded. Here, as elsewhere, plot logic is seriously flawed. Their night adventures involve crashing a teen party held in the desert. When one party guy insults them, Kit rips his heart out, which keeps the blood flowing. Meanwhile, back at the sleazy motel, naked Megan in the bathtub freaks out, as if she is telepathically linked to the murderous band of blood-sucking, flesh-eating vampires, who eventually end up at the same motel.

The next morning, Teddy (Alexis Thorpe), the white female vampire is killed when Nick opens up the trunk of the vampire car, where she is hidden under a tarp. Why she is in the trunk of the car while the others are in the darkened motel room is another unexplained mystery. When she is exposed to the sunlight, she explodes in another irrational bloody spectacle. The plot soon turns into a chase, with the vampires in pursuit of Nick and Sean, who outsmart them at every turn. The retarded driver dies when he crashes a van he has stolen, so at the end there are only two vampires left, who attack Sean, Nick, and Megan at the home of an older woman named Ina (Carrie Snodgress, the brightest star this film has to offer), who has let them in out of pity for the Megan's sickness. Sean turns out to be the most effective hunter. Using the old woman's shotgun, he blows the head off the remaining subordinate female vampire (played by Phina Oruche) in one unpleasant climax, then tricks Kit, the vampire leader, into being exposed to the rising sun, which causes him to explode, unpleasantly. Nick, Sean, and Megan all end up in a hospital. Nick and Megan are released first. She intends to return home to Arizona, while Nick heads for Denver to fine another "host" vampire. After his stay in the hospital Sean returns to the west, locates Nick hitchhiking towards Denver and joins in the hunt to protect humankind as the film ends.

This demented sexy-dude vampire-road movie was written and directed by J.S. Cardone, a Los Angeles native who was educated at Northern Arizona University, where he studied political science, an odd preparation for gothic mysticism and his higher purpose in life, writing and directing exploitation films. *Shadow Hunter* (1992) attempted to be a metaphysical thriller and chase film in the desert (similar in design to *The Forsaken*). *Shadowzone* (1989) was a low-budget science fiction thriller. In 1991 *A Climate for Killing* was judged the Best Independent Feature Film at the Houston International Film Festival. Producer Carol Kottenbrook, also a graduate of Northern Arizona University, worked with Cardone on all of these pictures.

*Sight and Sound* reviewer Kim Newman pointed out that Cardone's "new" vampire legend is in fact derivative of *John Carpenter's Vampires* (1998), which was in turn "derivative of Kathryn Bigelow's *Near Dark* (1986)." Other "borrowings" are noteworthy, as Newman explains: "Like Joel Schumacher's *The Lost Boys* (1986), *The Forsaken* deploys a get-out clause that allows those bitten by vampires to regain their normality if the master vampire at the head of their bloodline is destroyed." But unlike Schumacher's vampires, these bloodsuckers are not "remotely appealing." The vampires themselves lack dimension and definition, except, perhaps, for the retarded driver Pen, a "Renfield-type minion," in the words of Kim Newman, but he is still more caricature than character. The film's open conclusion, with Sean and Nick on the road again, in search of another host vampire, begs for a sequel, but one imagines it will keep on begging. Badly structured and misdirected, *The Forsaken* hardly deserves a sequel. Had the film "exhibited a modicum of restraint, *The Forsaken* could have been twice as scary," A.O. Scott wrote in the *New York Times*, but, instead, "it trots out its full arsenal of shock tactics far too early in the game and squanders the suspense it has accumulated." Thereafter all it can do is lay on its ghoulish, bloody spectacle.

—*James M. Welsh*

## CREDITS

**Sean:** Kerr Smith
**Megan:** Izabella Miko
**Kit:** Johnathon Schaech
**Nick:** Brendan Fehr
**Pen:** Simon Rex
**Ina:** Carrie Snodgress
**Cym:** Phina Oruche

**Origin:** USA
**Released:** 2001
**Production:** Carol Kottenbrook, Scott Einbinder; Screen Gems, Sandstone Pictures; released by Sony Pictures

**Directed by:** J.S. Cardone
**Written by:** J.S. Cardone
**Cinematography by:** Steven Bernstein
**Music by:** Johnny Lee Schell, Tim Jones
**Sound:** George Burton Goen II
**Music Supervisor:** Alex Patsavas
**Editing:** Norman Buckley
**Costumes:** Ernesto Martinez
**Production Design:** Martina Buckley
**MPAA rating:** R
**Running time:** 90 minutes

## REVIEWS

*Boxoffice.* July, 2001, p. 106.
*Chicago Tribune Online.* April 28, 2001.
*Entertainment Weekly.* May 11, 2001, p. 50.
*Houston Chronicle Online.* April 28, 2001.
*Los Angeles Times Online.* April 28, 2001.
*New York Times Online.* April 28, 2001.
*San Francisco Chronicle.* April 28, 2001, p. B1.
*Sight and Sound.* October, 2001, p. 48.
*Variety.* April 30, 2001, p. 26.

## QUOTES

Vampire Cym (Phina Oruche): "Time to die, cowboy."

# Freddy Got Fingered

*This time you can't change the channel.*
—Movie tagline

 **Box Office:** $14.2 million

Watching Tom Green in *Freddy Got Fingered* is like watching a toddler eat a spaghetti dinner. Some of the food gets in the mouth, but most of it drops onto the tray or the floor or gets smeared on fingers and cheeks. It's a mess, and so is this movie. But this analogy is unfair—to the toddler. At least the toddler is *trying* to eat the food and using whatever physical abilities are available for that task. The toddler is authentically incompetent at eating and his failures possess an innocence and charm. But though Green acts childish, he completely lacks childlike innocence. His work is a too-obviously cunning and calculated effort to be juvenile. It's a pose.

Green is a television comic who made his mark with a series of shows and specials for MTV. His comic technique is to trash the bounds of good taste and decency by going, literally, for the jugular. His main delight is to ignore audience squeamishness about things like bodily functions, deadly diseases, death and birth, children and violence, sexual perversion and even child abuse. With the glee of the sort of adolescent who tortures cats and finds it funny, Green rubs the audience's noses in feces, blood and guts, masturbation and sadism and other taboos. Such an approach to humor might have merit if Green had some overriding moral imperative in smashing taboos, or if these excursions into the messier parts of human existence were part of some general anarchic philosophy or simply madcap mayhem. But Green is not railing against conventional morals. And for all its veneer of rebellion, his work is actually very controlled. He rubs our faces in excrement, over and over again, just for the sheer pointlessness of it and because it's an act that he thinks will shock and succeed.

*Freddy Got Fingered* is ample testimony to what is required to make a Hollywood movie these days. And that is merely one thing: celebrity. For being the darling of the arrested-development set, Green was able to write, direct and star in his own feature-length film. It plays like a series of skits, which is often the case when a TV comic makes the transition to the big screen. Green plays Gord Brody, an unemployed 28-year-old still living at home with his parents Jim and Julie (Rip Torn and Julie Hagerty). He and his friend are building a skateboard ramp near the garage. Gord's other pursuit is cartooning. He has developed a character called "X-Ray Cat" who can see through wood but not other materials. As the movie opens, Gord is leaving to go to Los Angeles to sell his cartoons to an animation studio. Gullible dad presents his son with a new convertible and they gush over how he's finally going to make his father proud.

In Los Angeles, Gord takes a job at a cheese sandwich factory for no apparent reason. He decides to barge in on one of Hollywood's chief animation moguls, Dave Davidson (Anthony Michael Hall). He finds that Davidson is at lunch, but he scams the receptionist (Drew Barrymore) by telling her that Dave's wife has died and he has to go to the restaurant where he is lunching to tell him. Eventually, Davidson is forced to look at Gord's drawings but tells him they are stupid. "There has to be something happening that's actually funny," Davidson tells Gord. It's good advice; too bad Green didn't heed it when he made this movie.

The story of the nobody-who-goes-to-Hollywood then takes a U-turn. Gord returns to Portland and his parents' basement and constant ugly fights with his father. In a rare chance to do over-the-top comedy, Torn upstages Green in every one of their scenes together. Jim is a long-suffering millworker who is fed up with his son's shenanigans. The younger of the two Brody sons, Freddy (Eddie Kaye Thomas), is the "good" son who has a job at a bank. After a series of tiresome family scenes, Gord and the parents go to see a therapist. Gord says that his father has sexually assaulted Freddy. Despite his protests, Freddy is taken to a home for children who are abuse victims. Julie leaves Jim. Somehow Jim escapes being jailed, and this charming little plot device is left in the dust. That Green would trivialize sexual abuse by lampooning the idea of a false accusation is monstrous enough. That he would take this plot point and make it the title of the film says all you need to know about his infantilism.

The target audience for *Freddy* is pretty obvious: It's all those 20-something (or 30-something) slackers still living with their parents and unable to commit to the responsibilities of adulthood, and all the teenage boys who aspire to be slackers. Tellingly, masturbation is one of the repeated preoccupations of the movie. At the cheese factory, Gord climbs on the assembly line and makes obscene gestures with a sausage. On his drives to and from Hollywood, he repeatedly visiting a stud farm and tries to join in the action. At the end of the film, he has his way with an elephant. Green is absolutely fascinated with the male anatomy, fixated in a phase that most teenage boys—and certainly most adult filmmakers—outgrow.

In addition, Gord becomes involved with a paraplegic doctor named Betty (Marisa Coughlan) whose two fetishes are having her paralyzed legs whipped and (conveniently enough) sharing Gord's phallic obsessions. Green attempts to satirize romantic movie conventions by substituting Betty's obscene urges for the usual lines about undying love. This is about as good as the movie gets, thanks largely to Coughlan's noticeable comic gifts. Incongruously, though, Green's plot occasionally lapses into hackneyed melodrama itself, or a poorly conceived satire of it. His father's approbation somehow finally gets to Gord, and he throws his drawings in a trash can as the camera shows his face set against a hard rain while a throbbing rock song wails on the soundtrack. Betty's success at inventing a rocket-powered wheelchair inspires Gord to believe in himself, and he returns to Hollywood to try to wow Davidson again.

Though Green's antics sometimes approximate mayhem, the entire film has a controlled, phony feeling to it. Despite all the plot detours and gutter-comedy distractions, it is a very conventional rags-to-riches story, complete with a running conflict between father and son and a seemingly doomed romance. And while Green sometimes has clever ideas, his comic talents don't even approach those of a Jim Carrey. His repertoire is limited, consisting mostly of a singsong, childish repetition of words and phrases. As is his custom, Green also repeatedly combines blood and guts with mouths and faces in various repulsive combinations. He likes to show reaction shots of crowds spattered with blood, as in a particularly repugnant scene where Gord delivers a baby and then gets it to breathe by swinging it around by the umbilical cord. This brand of "comedy" used to be known as "sick" humor but all the shock value has gone out of it. It's no more outrageous than a Marilyn Manson concert, and just as affected.

In fact, Green's humor is hardly as cutting-edge as he appears to think it is. It's merely overblown "performance art" of a type that went out of style in the 1980s, an empty-headed look-how-outrageous-I-am posing that serves no purpose and has no meaning. Worst of all, it violates Dave Davidson's cardinal rule: It's not funny. A lot of what's in *Freddy Got Fingered* seems forced and tired, and the entire movie is driven by the writer-director-star's obvious fondness for himself. In short, it's masturbatory. As a minor pop-culture icon, Green has more significance as an illustration of the dumbing-down and grossing-out of entertainment than as a memorable comedian in his own right. Green is something of a live-action *South park*, but without nearly that cartoon's comic genius. The only thing Green appears to be a genius at is self-promotion. What other film director would have the conceitedness to end the film's trailers with a gratuitous outtake of himself kissing his then-fiancee (Barrymore)?

Green may have a future as a cameo movie comic. He was fine in *Charlie's Angels,* where he played Barrymore's tugboat-captain lover. But more than 10 minutes of Tom Green is enervating. His repeated attempts to shock and grandstand are boring, and in this 87-minute film he continually repeats the same routines. Only Torn's wondrous rages save *Freddy* from being totally unwatchable. Maybe if everyone stops paying attention, little Tommy will actually eat his spaghetti instead of smearing it on his face—and our movie screens.

—*Michael Betzold*

## CREDITS

**Gord Brody:** Tom Green
**Jim Brody:** Rip Torn
**Darren:** Harland Williams
**Freddy Brody:** Eddie Kaye Thomas
**Julie Brody:** Julie Hagerty
**Mr. Davidson:** Anthony Michael Hall
**Betty:** Marisa Coughlan

**Origin:** USA
**Released:** 2001
**Production:** Larry Brezner, Lauren Lloyd, Howard Lapides; Regency Enterprises, New Regency Pictures, Epsilon Motion Pictures, MBST; released by 20th Century-Fox
**Directed by:** Tom Green
**Written by:** Tom Green, Derek Harvie

**Cinematography by:** Mark Irwin
**Music by:** Mike Simpson
**Sound:** Darren Brisker
**Editing:** Jacqueline Cambas
**Art Direction:** Katterina Keith-Szalay
**Costumes:** Glenne E. Campbell
**Production Design:** Bob Ziembicki
**MPAA rating:** R
**Running time:** 88 minutes

## REVIEWS

*Boxoffice.* June, 2001, p. 56.
*Chicago Sun-Times Online.* April 20, 2001.
*Entertainment Weekly.* May 27, 2001, p. 83.
*Los Angeles Times Online.* April 20, 2001.
*New York Times Online.* April 29, 2001.
*USA Today Online.* April 19, 2001.
*Variety.* April 23, 2001, p. 17.
*Washington Post Online.* April 20, 2001.

# From Hell

*Only the legend will survive.*
—**Movie tagline**

 **Box Office:** $31.5 million

Do we really need any more films about Jack the Ripper? Yes, it's one of history's most notorious unsolved crimes—but it happened in 1888 and has been overly sensationalized ever since. *From Hell,* the latest and perhaps most overheated movie about the infamous London slasher, opens with a quote allegedly attributed to the Ripper: "One day men will look back and say I gave birth to the Twentieth Century." True, but that century is over, and maybe it's time to move on.

Based on an ambitious and speculative historical "graphic novel" by Alan Moore and Eddie Campbell, *From Hell* brews up a heady concoction of gore, dream fantasies, political conspiracy theories, and populist rhetoric. It's both visually arresting and tawdry, and its ideas are both fascinating and ridiculous. Albert and Allen Hughes, makers of such gritty urban American underworld films as *Menace to Society, Dead Presidents,* and *American Pimp,* bring a similar dressing-down to Victorian London and its Whitechapel District. They spin out a vision of an oppressive society ruled by a ruthless clique of privileged white men—prominent doctors and lawyers, royal advisers and police officials, and organized crime syndicates—who use various hypocritical poses and interlocking loyalties to impose their iron will on the underclass.

The hero of the film, Scotland Yard Inspector Fred Abberline (Johnny Depp), is a courageous, principled rebel working within the establishment—an American-style individualist. An opium addict, he solves cases by picking out clues from his drug-induced dream states, though it must be said that his psychic powers don't help much in the Ripper case. It seems he is always to be one step behind the criminals. Depp inhabits this bizarre character as if he's lived in this milieu all his life. His brooding, heavy eyes with drooping eyelids and slightly slurred, careless speech suggest a simmering intelligence barely able to cope with living in such a stupid, hopeless world. He has no tolerance for the hypocrisy all around him but demolishes pretense quietly and with a certain barely restrained desperation.

The Hughes brothers fairly wallow in violence and threats of violence, especially in the first half-hour of the film. The circle of five prostitutes targeted by the killer live a life of constant danger. Men are always jumping out from the shadows to grab them from behind or poking knives at their bosoms, eyes, or faces. These assailants include not only the Ripper but a group of local gang members, police authorities, and, in one scene, even Abberline's partner, Sergeant Peter Godley (Robbie Coltrane), who jumps out from an alley to throttle Mary Kelly (Heather Graham) and pull her into a carriage for a talk.

Gruesomely, these scenes paint a devastating portrait of life as an "unfortunate" in Victorian England—the euphemism for prostitutes, since British society didn't admit London had any. Everyday life for Mary's circle of friends seems to include the constant threat of random, surprise violence. In such a society, it's not the deaths of the prostitutes that excite the public imagination, fueled by a sensationalist media—it's the methodical and outrageous gruesomeness of the killing. The killer mutilates and disembowels his victims or cuts out various organs.

With cinematographer Peter Deming capturing iconic scenes and some tight, incisive editing by Dan Lebenthal, the Hughes brothers make the horror of the Ripper's murders almost unbearable. Slashing knives, spurting blood, and body parts are everywhere—the film allows viewers no escape from the mayhem. As with other films in which women are menacingly threatened and graphically dismembered, there surfaces the troubling question of whether the filmmakers are a little too enthusiastic about these scenes. Does From Hell really need to get so graphic in order to underscore the inexcusable brutality of the victims' plight, or is there some effort being made to titillate certain segments of the audience?

Without a doubt, the film's plot and dialogue make it clear where fingers are being pointed—straight into the heart of a corrupt, patriarchal monarchy. Various powerful figures in the film are quick to cast blame on foreigners or Jews because, they all say, no English gentleman could do something so dastardly. Abberline—who with a change of time and venue could easily stand in for a hip American street cop—dismisses all this racist speculation with shrugs of the shoulders and witherings look of disdain.

From Hell takes pains to present what passes for modern scientific authority in Victorian England as just bizarre variations on the ritual mutilations of the Ripper. In a series of scenes in mental hospitals, prisons, and medical school classes and hospitals, the Hughes brothers show authorities crowing about strange forms of human experimentation. The scenes have learned madmen driving nails into the skull of mentally unfit members of the underprivileged classes, for example, or displaying the notorious Elephant Man as a medical specimen. It's an intriguing view of the cultural milieu in which Jack the Ripper prospered—no doubt overdone and sometimes beside the point, but still a worthwhile side trip. Unfortunately, by the film's end, the Hughes go way overboard, dabbling in cult theories of Freemasonry to explain what might best have been left alone to be a more subtle dissection of the Victorian power structure.

Amid all the political and visual histrionics, the story of Abberline's investigation unfolds as a fairly standard detective story, with various twists and turns that sometimes strain credulity. The tension stops and starts between violent spasms and spurts of blood and dull stretches of routine police work, punctuated by Abberline's occasional forays into his opium dream world. From Hell is undeniably stylish, and it strains for authenticity. Its London is a dark, grimy corner of hell on earth. But the computer-painted red and orange skies are a little much even for a Gothic fantasy. It's a nightmare world, much like the American ghettoes of earlier Hughes films, but more stylized than it needs to be to achieve complete believability.

One of the other major problems of this ambitious film is plunking down sunny, apple-cheeked Heather Graham into the most crucial role other than Depp's. The rest of the circle of prostitutes look the part—cheap, vulgar, worn and desperate. Graham looks like Graham in a period dress and corset—the same fresh, cute, American-girl-next-door-turned-sexpot that she is in all her movies. She doesn't have the acting depth to give her character much weight. When she tells off Abberline in one key scene, she can muster only a flimsy imitation of anger. Her Irish accent is intermittent and approximate and she is only vaguely believable. Why Depp's character would fall for her seems preposterous. She is incongruously angelic in a film that is devilishly exact in its depiction of hellish people and bedraggled victims in a hopelessly degraded society.

The rest of the cast—including a slew of good British character actors like Ian Holm, Ian Richardson, Jason Flemyng, Terence Harvey, and Coltrane—is magnificent, including the rest of the women (Katrin Cartlidge, Susan

Lynch, Lesley Sharp, and Annabelle Apsion), who are as authentic as Graham is not. The sets are stunning, and the Hughes Brothers perform some intriguing directorial flourishes. Helped by a lavish orchestral soundtrack, *From Hell* is a sumptuous sensual feast, even though what is being served up is gruesome and disturbing in the extreme.

In the end, the targets are too easy and the conclusion too facile. If Jack the Ripper was in fact a perpetrator sanctioned and spawned by the highest authorities in England, why was—and is—the case so endlessly intriguing to the popular mind? Psychologically, *From Hell* is a case of an overactive imagination descending into unsupported mumbo-jumbo. It's an interesting fantasy, nonetheless, but the film has the hothouse air of an overwrought political melodrama. If connections such as those this film makes obvious were merely suggested, if the Ripper's affinities to the pseudo-scientific "advances" and the not-so-subtle racism of the era were left in a more speculative state rather than bludgeoned home with underlines and exclamation points, then *From Hell* might have been masterful. As it is, it is merely arresting, disturbing, painful to watch yet mesmerizing, tragic and thought-provoking—and ultimately, unfortunately, an intellectual and artistic letdown.

—*Michael Betzold*

 **CREDITS**

**Inspector Fred Abberline:** Johnny Depp
**Mary Kelly:** Heather Graham
**Shir William Gull:** Ian Holm
**Sgt. Peter Godley:** Robbie Coltrane
**Sir Charles Warren:** Ian Richardson
**Netley:** Jason Flemyng
**Dark Annie Chapman:** Katrin Cartlidge
**Ben Kidney:** Terence Harvey
**Liz Stride:** Susan Lynch
**Kate Eddowes:** Leslie Sharp
**Polly:** Annabelle Apsion

**Origin:** USA
**Released:** 2001
**Production:** Don Murphy, Jane Hamsher; Underworld Pictures; released by 20th Century-Fox
**Directed by:** Albert Hughes, Allen Hughes
**Written by:** Terry Hayes, Rafael Yglesias
**Cinematography by:** Peter Deming
**Music by:** Trevor Jones
**Sound:** Steven D. Williams, Franklin D. Stettner
**Editing:** George Bowers, Dan Lebental
**Art Direction:** Mark Ragget
**Costumes:** Kym Barrett

**Production Design:** Martin Childs
**MPAA rating:** R
**Running time:** 121 minutes

 **REVIEWS**

*Boxoffice.* November, 2001, p. 146.
*Chicago Sun-Times Online.* October 19, 2001.
*Entertainment Weekly.* October 26, 2001, p. 87.
*Hollywood Reporter.* November 28, 2000.
*Hollywood Reporter.* September 11, 2001, p. 16.
*Los Angeles Times Online.* October 19, 2001.
*New York Times Online.* October 14, 2001.
*New York Times Online.* October 19, 2001.
*People.* October 29, 2001, p. 40.
*USA Today Online.* October 18, 2001.
*Variety.* September 17, 2001, p. 19.
*Washington Post.* October 19, 2001, p. WE37.

**TRIVIA**

19th-century London was recreated outside the village of Orech, near Prague, Czech Republic.

# Gaudi Afternoon

Imagine Susan Seidelman's *Desperately Seeking Susan* set in Barcelona, with a few minor character changes, themes that revolve around sexual identity, and an alternative family structure. Of course, the minor character changes would involve Oscar®-winning actress Marcia Gay Harden (*Pollack*) playing a male transsexual, as well as Lili Taylor playing a "butch" lesbian (they're an estranged couple). And the only crime committed here is the alleged kidnapping of Frankie (Harden) and Ben's (Taylor) daughter Delilah (Courtney Jines). Rounding off the collection of odd characters are Cassandra (Judy Davis), a globe-trotting American translator who gets caught up in Frankie and Ben's melodrama, and April (Juliette Lewis) as Ben's sprout-eating current lover.

Based on a novel by Barbara Wilson, *Gaudi Afternoon* proves to be more than a zany comedy set on Barcelona's winding streets. After Seidelman became a mother 10 years ago, she took an interest in contemporary family values. In a press kit interview Seidelman related "There are now so many different structures and different ways of being a family and this film deals with a new kind of family." The mystery presented here, which revolves around discovering Frankie and Ben's true identities, also reflects on contemporary female and male roles since the line that defined the two sexes has become increasingly blurred. But even if the film's viewers do not care to delve into the film's overt themes, they can enjoy watching these actresses juggle their complex comedic roles.

Cassandra has secluded herself in a crumbling flat in the older section of Barcelona, where she attempts to quit smoking and finish translating a Latin American novel into English. However, landlady Carmen's (Maria Barranco of *Women on the Verge of a Nervous Breakdown*) children, who live upstairs, cause a huge racket, making it increasingly difficult for Cassandra to complete her work. One day, Cassandra receives a mysterious phone call from femme fatale Frankie, who asks Cassandra to find her ex. At first, Cassandra turns down the offer, but later reconsiders. After all, $3000 is a lot of money for such a small task. However, there are a few minor complications. Frankie doesn't want Ben to know that she is searching for him because he's volatile and she can only provide Cassandra with a phone number and not an address.

Cassandra proves her cleverness by locating Ben's address, but when she asks Frankie for a description of Ben, she is only told that he's average-looking. So with camera in hand, Cassandra photographs every single man that emerges from Ben's apartment building (Antonio Gaudi's famous La Pedrera). She finally photographs a couple who are obviously American and, although she photographs the right couple, a huge shock awaits Cassandra. First, she learns that Frankie is a transsexual and later that Ben is female. On one hand, Cassandra wishes to wash her hands of this motley crew, but on the other, she's intrigued by their melodrama.

However, Cassandra doesn't know who to believe. Is Frankie trying to kidnap Delilah from Ben or is it the other way around? And what are hippie chick April and her friend, the magician Hamilton (Christopher Bowen), up to? At this point the film's narrative loses momentum and also its humor as it delves too deeply into family values territory and causes Cassandra to examine her relationship with her mother. Because after all, the film suggests that motherhood is sacred and depending on a viewer's personal values, the film either ends on a cloying or satisfying note.

Harden's fans will be happily surprised to view the actress's range as she plays a man transformed into a woman and Davis, who plays the American translator hiding behind her glasses, also stretches her wings here. Taylor doesn't offer any surprises and Lewis's hippie chick provides some uncomfortable laughs. Sadly, Barranco's talents are underused since the Spanish actress has a special gift for comedic melodrama. *Gaudi Afternoon* could be labeled an American *Women on the Verge of a Nervous Breakdown* due to the films' similarities. If viewers can get past the family value theme *Gaudi Afternoon* proves a pleasurable romp.

—*Patty-Lynne Herlevi*

## CREDITS

**Cassandra:** Judy Davis
**Frankie:** Marcia Gay Harden
**Ben:** Lili Taylor
**April:** Juliette Lewis
**Carmen:** Maria Barranco
**Hamilton:** Christopher Bowen
**Delilah:** Courtney Jines

**Origin:** Spain
**Released:** 2001
**Production:** Andres Vicente Gomes; Lola Films, Via Digital, Antena 3
**Directed by:** Susan Seidelman
**Written by:** James Mhyre
**Cinematography by:** Josep Civit
**Music by:** Bernardo Bonezzi
**Editing:** Deidre Slevin
**Costumes:** Yvonne Blake, Antonia Marques
**Production Design:** Antxon Gomez
**MPAA rating:** Unrated
**Running time:** 88 minutes

## REVIEWS

*Variety.* June 4, 2001, p. 20.

## QUOTES

Cassandra (Judy Davis): "Home is where I plug in my laptop."

## TRIVIA

Antonio Gaudi (1852–1926) was most famous for his whimsical architecture, including the Palau Guell, La Pedrera, and the Sagrada Familia church.

# Get Over It!

*Get Dumped. Get Pumped. Get Even!*
—Movie tagline
*Split happens . . .*
—Movie tagline

**Box Office:** $11.5 million

Was *Get Over It* an unusually witty take on the teen romance flick or a tired retreat that was void of humor? Depends on who you ask. *Entertainment Weekly* was in the latter camp, calling it "mostly an amateur-hour fiasco." The magazine said, "Between bouts of rancid slapstick that make *Saving Silverman* look competent, the film delivers a pastel version of a fifth-rate John Hughes love triangle." In case the words didn't hammer the point in enough, the magazine branded the film with a D grade. Other critics were charmed by the film—or at least somewhat charmed. The critic for the *Toronto Star* said that it was "a teen movie that for once delivers brains along with babes and buffoons," adding that the film had "real humour and bite." The *Los Angeles Times* called it a "blithe-spirited comedy" with a script that is "deft and amusing."

Berke Landers (Ben Foster) is the person who the title is exhorting to get over it. He was in high school heaven in his relationship with his girlfriend Allison (Melissa Sagemiller). The two had been childhood friends until Allison's family moved away, breaking Berke's heart. When Allison suddenly shows up at Berke's school, he is shocked to see that she's turned beautiful. He's even more shocked when she agrees to start dating him. Berke's blissful until one day when Allison has a talk with him and explains that she wants to break up because their relationship has grown boring.

As high school students are wont to do, Berke does not take the break-up well and can't seem to get on with his life. He does a lot of dumb things to express his love like getting really drunk and serenading his ex with a bad rooftop rendition of Elvis Costello's "Allison." Despite such alluring moves, Allison remains uninterested. And worse, she starts dating a new student Striker (Shane West). Striker is an overly cute guy, who not only has an English accent, but was once the member of an 'N Sync-like boy pop group. Sigh! West as Berke's competition for Allison is appropriately cute and conniving. He has that perfect mixture of feminine looks and studied wardrobe that mark a member of a boy band.

The fierce competition makes Berke even more determined to win back his Allison. His biggest plan is to get a part in the school musical, *A Midsummer Night's Rockin' Dream*, which is a new version of Shakespeare's "A Midsummer Night's Dream." Berke's big handicap is that he can neither sing nor dance. He enlists the help of Kelly (Kirsten Dunst), who is the younger sister of his best friend, Felix (Colin Hanks, Tom Hanks's son). Kelly tries to teach Berke the finer points of acting and singing, but he is a distracted student. She is equally unsuccessful trying to show him that it is her, not Allison, who is truly his dream girl. The plot provides a sort of a show within a show. The romantic

intrigues of the character are mirrored in the action of the play. When the climax of the movie's plot finally hits, it's reflected in what happens in the play. Some critics found this twist clever, others were nonplused.

But it's not plot that a teen romantic comedy relies upon, it's chemistry; and on that score, *Get Over It* is a washout. Foster is supposed to be a sympathetic regular-guy type, like John Cusack. But what the casting direction seems to have forgotten is that although Cusack's characters aren't terribly handsome, they work because they are charming or witty or both. Foster's got the not-handsome thing down, but he is witless and void of charm. *Entertainment Weekly* described his character as a "glum, charmless, sub-Jon Cryer putz." (Cryer, for those not well-versed in teen movie factoids, was a staple of 1980s teen romantic comedies like *Pretty in Pink.*) It's hard to believe this character got one cool girl to date him, let alone the fact that he has another one panting after him.

There are also problems with the other half of the chemistry, or lack thereof. Dunst tries her darndest to be sweet and lovelorn, but it doesn't make up for the couple's utter lack of chemistry. Whether or not she actually is in real life or not, she comes across as being much older than Foster—maybe 25 to his 18. It's even harder to believe that she's supposed to be someone's little sister. It seems like she should be buying beer for Foster or something instead of lusting after him.

It's too bad that the central chemistry in the film is wrong because the acting around it is often quite good. Especially good in small roles are Swoosie Kurtz and Ed Begley Jr. as Berke's parents who are trying to stay hip with the kids. Berke's dad likes to pepper his speech with supposedly cool lingo like, "Word!" The two host a sex advice TV show and bring their understanding and liberated sexual attitudes into their lives at home, much to Berke's dismay. After Berke ends up getting busted for being at a strip club (don't ask), his parents drive him home, telling him they are proud that he is getting over Allison and jumping back into the sexual arena. They suggest going out to get ice cream to celebrate, but then Berke's mom, ever sensitive to her child, says, "Oh, but he might want to go home and polish the rocket."

Also making the most of a small role is Martin Short. Short plays Dr. Desmond Forrest Oakes, the director of *A Midsummer Night's Rockin' Dream*. Oakes is a man who is untalented enough to have turned Shakespeare's play into some sort of terrible rock opera that he wrote himself. He's pompous enough not to realize that the songs are all hideous. Oakes is high-strung, pretentious and treats the school play like it's going to be opening on Broadway. He's fond of starting stories with, "As Bobby De Niro once said . . .," but the closest he's ever gotten to any celebs is in *People* magazine. The overly dramatic high school drama teacher is a cliche but what makes this role special are the throwaway lines Short has. When one student gives a particularly bad line reading, Short says loudly, "You'd tell me if you'd had a stroke, right?"

It's interesting to watch the young Hanks playing Berke's best friend, but the role doesn't offer much in the way of acting opportunities. He pretty much just has to say stuff like "Get over Allison" and "Stop hanging around with my sister so much." Music star Sisqo, who plays Berke's other friend, Dennis, has an even tinier role, but still manages to be bad. His main job is to stand next to the two other guys and nod in agreement (or frown, depending on the occasion) when one of them says something. Somehow, he manages to look unnatural even doing that. It seems like it would be difficult to look like you're acting when you're just nodding but Sisqo does it every time. Despite his acting, Sisqo is part of one of the best moments in the film. As the end credits roll, we see a video of Sisqo and the cast members belting out Earth Wind and Fire's "September." Sisqo throws his soul into the performance and makes the song seem new, vibrant and exciting again. He's completely different singing than acting—he's alive, entertaining and in control.

The other best moment in the film, oddly enough, is also a musical number. After Allison dumps Berke, he leaves her house and walks dejectedly down the street. Pop singer Vitamin C pops out of nowhere and starts gyrating along to the Captain and Tennille's "Love Will Keep Us Together." The song parade keeps picking up members until it's turned into a full-scale song and dance number. It's a fun, exuberant moment. Actually, all the music in the film is well chosen. There's a nice eclectic mix of background songs from older acts like Elvis Costello to newer talents like Badly Drawn Boy.

Besides the music, the film does have a few nice touches, courtesy of the script by R. Lee Fleming Jr., who also wrote *She's All That*. It's filled with fresh pop culture references and bouncy dialogue. When Striker first arrives at the high school and starts speaking, a girl whispers to her friend, "What's up with that accent. He sounds like Madonna." The best long running joke is the school musical itself. When we finally see the finished production, it's shocking to see just how bad those songs really are. It's made all the more funny by how the students sing their little hearts out like they're in "Grease" or something. Unfortunately the script's good ideas are generally balanced out with bad ideas like a dog that likes to have sex with anything or a girl who is so klutzy that she sets a restaurant on fire. *Get Over It* is a romantic teen comedy that fails on two out of three of its missions. It is indeed for teens but it's not romantic or comedic enough to become a teen classic.

—*Jill Hamilton*

## CREDITS

**Kelly:** Kirsten Dunst
**Berke Landers:** Ben Foster
**Felix:** Colin Hanks
**Allison McAllister:** Melissa Sagemiller
**Dennis:** Sisqo
**Bentley "Striker" Scrumfeld:** Shane West
**Dr. Desmond Forrest-Oates:** Martin Short
**Beverly Landers:** Swoosie Kurtz
**Frank Landers:** Ed Begley Jr.
**Maggie:** Zoe Saldana
**Basin:** Mila Kunis
**Mistress Moira:** Carmen Electra
**Cameo:** Coolio

**Origin:** USA
**Released:** 2001
**Production:** Michael Burns, Paul Feldsher, Marc Butan; Ignite Entertainment, Morpheus; released by Miramax Films
**Directed by:** Tommy O'Haver
**Written by:** R. Lee Fleming Jr.
**Cinematography by:** Maryse Alberti
**Music by:** Steve Bartek
**Music Supervisor:** Elliot Lurie, Randy Spendlove
**Art Direction:** Andrew Hull
**Costumes:** Mary Jane Fort
**Production Design:** Robin Standefer
**MPAA rating:** PG-13
**Running time:** 90 minutes

## REVIEWS

*Boxoffice.* May, 2001, p. 60.
*Entertainment Weekly.* March 23, 2001, p. 79.
*New York Times Online.* March 10, 2001.
*Sight and Sound.* June, 2001, p. 45.
*Variety.* March 12, 2001, p. 34.

## QUOTES

Felix (Colin Hanks) to Berke (Ben Foster): "Hey grabby hands—step away from the sister!"

# Ghost World

*Accentuate the negative.*
—Movie tagline

 **Box Office:** $6.1 million

Most coming-of-age films feature awkward teenagers who face emotional crises and, with the aid of well-meaning adults and peers and timely life lessons, learn to tap inner resources to meet the challenges of adulthood. *Ghost World* is not at all like that. This adaptation of the Daniel Clowes comic book of the same name centers on an awkward teenager who thinks the world is full of phonies and whose emotional problems are compounded by her adults and peers and by strange plot twists.

In its dogged refusal to superimpose rosy hues on the difficulties of growing up as a misfit adolescent girl, *Ghost World* most resembles Todd Solondz's brutally honest and depressing *Welcome to the Dollhouse*. But director Terry Zwigoff, making his first film since 1994's offbeat *Crumb*, makes *Ghost World* funnier, more entertaining, and not nearly as bleak as *Dollhouse*. His protagonist, recent high school graduate Enid (Thora Birch), is much older than the 12-year-old heroine of *Dollhouse*—and much wiser in the ways of the world. And Enid's wide-ranging misanthropy is redeemed by her sense of humor. She likes to play pranks on people and get a laugh or a rise out of them, but she doesn't really intend to hurt anyone. She's wickedly playful, not malicious.

We first meet Enid and her caustic friend Rebecca (Scarlett Johansson) at their high school graduation, as they cynically ridicule a wheelchair-bound classmate who tells the assembled students that high school was "like the training wheels for the bicycle of life." "She gets in one car wreck and suddenly she's Little Miss Perfect," Enid grouses. Their disgust is ubiquitous. "What a bunch of retards!" is their summary judgment of their classmates.

It soon becomes clear that dismissive reactions to their town and its inhabitants—and to the world in general—constitute the defense of Enid and Rebecca to any possibility that life will surprise or entertain them. In their jaded cynicism, they are typical of many American teenagers around the turn of the 21st century, who have learned sarcasm at any early age. To their minds, there is plenty to view with disdain—peers who are perky about community theater or sports or mainstream popular music; people who troll for dates in personals ads; fake 1950s-style retro-diners.

Enid and Becky are latter-day Holden Caulfields, fascinated at the manifestations of hypocrisy that they see every-

where. But, like Robert Crumb and some other comic strip artists, they are also abnormally attracted to the perverse underbelly of American culture. Enid, in particular, loves to laugh at the seriousness with which Americans pursue sex—and both girls are dying to have a male escort them into the local adult book and video store. When Enid gets her wish, she cackles out loud at the ridiculous paraphernalia she finds there. It's a remarkable scene.

For emotional reasons left unexplained, the two girls have deliberately set themselves apart from their peers to constitute a tiny committee of superior moral and aesthetic tastes. Johansson's Becky looks fairly normal; she is blonde and middling attractive, dresses casually and carelessly, and has an air of diffidence and resignation. Reluctant to enter the adult world but resigned to her fate, she takes a job and pushes Enid to act on their long dream of getting an apartment together. Johansson, who played Kristin Scott-Thomas's daughter in *The Horse Whisperer*, handles her part with understated effectiveness; she has a raspy voice, cloudy eyes, and a sometimes fixed stare, as if being only a step away from a coma or a nap. Life just isn't very interesting for Becky, but she will manage somehow.

Enid is the live wire of the two. As played by the marvelously talented Birch (who warmed up for the part by playing the repressed misfit daughter of Kevin Stacey in *American Beauty*), Enid is an outrageously flamboyant iconoclast. She dresses in strange combinations of punk and retro fashions, has several pairs of nerdish-looking eyeglasses, wears her hair dyed jet-black with severe bangs, and alternates between various bizarre shades of lipstick. Birch has put on weight for the part, making her legs and cheeks chubbier, and aiming for a defiant, take-me-as-I-am look. Enid is an expert at both put-ons and put-downs. She and Becky take delight in tormenting Josh (Brad Renfro), who works at a convenience store called the Sidewinder and seems annoyed by their attentions, as if somehow, despite his apparent normality, he can't shake off these pesky misfits.

After several throwaway scenes that define their characters, the movie gets its offbeat plot in gear when Enid decides to play a trick on a guy who has placed a newspaper personals ad hoping to arrange to meet a blonde with whom he traded meaningful glances. Enid calls and pretends to be the woman and tells him she'll meet him at Wowsville, the 1950s diner. She, Becky and Josh wait for him to show up and then watch him dolefully down a milk shake as he waits in vain for his mystery date. Enid is drawn to his rather muted despair—"He must have this kind of thing happen to him all the time!" she exclaims.

At first, she just feels sorry for him, but soon enough, Enid becomes infatuated with the guy. His name is Seymour (Steve Buscemi) and he works as an assistant manager for a fast-food corporation, but his consuming passion is collecting old blues, jazz and folk recordings. Enid buys a record Seymour suggests and falls in love with one old blues song on it; she has a soft spot for offbeat music, such as 1960s Indian rock-and-roll. Seymour is an orthodontically challenged, insufferably priggish, down-on-himself nerd who has given up on relationships after many failures. Twice Enid's age, he is oblivious to her amorous intent, which she masks very well, and they form a friendship based on their mutual antipathy to popular culture and clueless, middle-of-the-road people. Enid, whose intentions are unclear, tries to set up Seymour with women his age, to no avail. But then the real blonde from the personals ad calls, and she and Seymour strike up a relationship.

Up until this point, *Ghost World* adamantly avoids maudlin entanglements, content to take a sardonic comic strip approach to its material. The attitude is epitomized in sequences involving a summer school art class that Enid is forced to take in order to complete her graduation requirements. The teacher (Illeana Douglas) is an ardent feminist and promoter of political art, and she praises a student who brings in a sculpture of twisted coat hangers as a statement about abortion, while dismissing Enid's twisted and ironic cartoons as "lesser" works. Enid eventually decides to test her teacher's tolerance by borrowing a poster of an old racist company logo from Seymour and submitting it, saying it's an exploration of racism. The teacher praises the work—a touch of absurdism that is not quite so absurd if you stop to think that Spike Lee has made an entire movie based on the same premise (*Bamboozled*).

Then the film starts heaping disappointments on Enid's shoulders, and her pose disintegrates. Seymour and Becky both cool towards her, her mousy father (Bob Balaban) resumes a relationship with a hated would-be stepmother (Teri Garr), and her art class prank ruins her chance at a college scholarship. When Enid eventually breaks down, it's a gamble. Instead of continuing to view the world through Enid's sardonic gaze, the film asks audience to sympathize with her plight. Not only is it a radical change in tone, it may be difficult for many to feel much empathy with Enid, since she has seemed like such a spiteful and intolerant person. The film gets away completely from Zwigoff in the end; he doesn't seem to know whether to resolve things in tragedy, comedy, or uplifting moral resolution, and the zigs and zags in Enid's relationships and the plot don't make much sense.

Fortunately, Birch redeems many of these faults. A lesser actress would have made Enid an object of pity or scorn, but Birch fully fleshes out a character whose defiant pose is equal measures self-protection and self-promotion. Other than his lapse into a kind of formulaic crisis that shows Enid is all too human, Zwigoff seems content to let Birch construct a believable, caustic misfit, a protagonist who can make audiences laugh and squirm at the same time. Birch is simmering both with barely repressed sexuality and with equally repressed intellect. Her Enid is about to burst at the seams with disgust at the lousy options adulthood has in

wait for her, but it seems equally possible she could turn her considerable talents and knack for black humor into something transcendent. Buscemi plays well off her by making Seymour a sad, understated character who nevertheless has heart and passion, even if he doesn't always connect with people.

It's hard to make a film about people who don't relate easily to other people without making it into some sort of freak show. Zwigoff carries off this task with considerable grace, with Birch, Buscemi, and Johansson all turning in performances that humanize their misanthropic characters. Like few other directors besides Solondz and perhaps Atom Egoyan, Zwigoff is totally at ease with awkward moments, awkward dialogue, and socially clumsy characters. Zwigoff revels a bit too much in the perversity of their sensibilities and makes several missteps with bringing his tale to a resolution, but *Ghost World* nonetheless remains valuable and entertaining—an object lesson in how to make a teen movie that really has teeth.

*—Michael Betzold*

## CREDITS

**Enid:** Thora Birch
**Rebecca:** Scarlett Johansson
**Seymour:** Steve Buscemi
**Josh:** Brad Renfro
**Roberta:** Illeana Douglas
**Dad:** Bob Balaban
**Maxine:** Teri Garr
**Dana:** Stacy Travis
**Doug:** Dave Sheridan
**Sidewinder Boss:** Brian George

**Origin:** USA
**Released:** 2001
**Production:** Lianne Halfon, Russell Smith, John Malkovich; United Artists, Granada Film Productions, Jersey Shore; released by MGM
**Directed by:** Terry Zwigoff
**Written by:** Daniel Clowes, Terry Zwigoff
**Cinematography by:** Alfonso Beato
**Music by:** David Kitay
**Sound:** Marc Weingarten
**Editing:** Carole Kravetz
**Art Direction:** Alan E. Muraoka
**Costumes:** Mary Zophres
**Production Design:** Edward T. McAvoy
**MPAA rating:** R
**Running time:** 111 minutes

## REVIEWS

*Boxoffice.* August, 2001, p. 54.
*Chicago Sun-Times Online.* August 3, 2001.
*Entertainment Weekly.* July 27, 2001, p. 45.
*Los Angeles Times Online.* July 20, 2001.
*New York Times Online.* July 20, 2001.
*People.* August 6, 2001, p. 38.
*Rolling Stone.* August 2, 2001, p. 70.
*USA Today Online.* July 20, 2001.
*Variety.* June 25, 2001, p. 22.
*Washington Post.* August 3, 2001, p. WE34.

## QUOTES

Seymour (Steve Buscemi): "I don't want to meet someone who shares my interests. I hate my interests."

## AWARDS AND NOMINATIONS

**Ind. Spirit 2002:** Support. Actor (Buscemi)
**N.Y. Film Critics 2001:** Support. Actor (Buscemi)
**Natl. Soc. Film Critics 2001:** Support. Actor (Buscemi)
**Nomination:**
**Golden Globes 2002:** Actress—Mus./Comedy (Birch), Support. Actor (Buscemi)
**Writers Guild 2001:** Adapt. Screenplay.

# Ginger Snaps

*Hungry like the wolf.*
—Movie tagline
*They don't call it the curse for nothing.*
—Movie tagline

Canadian low-budget thriller *Ginger Snaps*, which revolves around menstruation and werewolves, has stirred up its share of controversy. Based on a screenplay by Karen Walton and directed by John Fawcett, the history of the film's production proves more horrific than the film itself. First there was the nightmare of actually funding the project when a major distributor fell out, and then finding a casting agency that wasn't offended by the screenplay's content became another problem. Pre-production of the thriller took place around the time of the Columbine tragedy when teen slasher films were the hottest topic of the day. To make matters worse, the *Toronto Star* made inaccurate claims that *Ginger Snaps* was a teen slasher film while alluding to recent tragic events involving teen violence. Eventually, funding

did come through and actors enthusiastic with the screenplay came on board.

Many coincidences surround the making of *Ginger Snaps:* the two lead actresses, Emily Perkins (Brigitte) and Katharine Isabelle (Ginger), both auditioned for their roles in Vancouver, B.C. on the same day. Later, Perkins commented about the screenplay, "Before I read the script, when I'd only read a couple of scenes for the audition, I thought what is this? This is some kind of semi-pornographic movie geared towards 15-year-old boys." But later, after the actress read the entire script, she commented on its merits. Walton also commented on the synchronistic events that led to Perkins and Isabelle being chosen for their roles: "This is eerie how perfect they are; it gives me goose-bumps. Because they are exactly, as individuals, how I'd hoped the performers who accepted the roles would be."

Once the two lead roles were cast, Mimi Rogers accepted the role of the girls' overly cheerful mother and Kris Lemche (Sam) accepted the other supporting lead. Jesse Moss and Danielle Hampton play the popular kids at the high school where the sisters remain outcasts and Nick Nolan portrays the Creature and Gingerwolf. Special effects expert Paul Jones (*Bride of Chucky*), cinematographer Thom Best (*Queer as Folk*), production designer Todd Cherniawsky (*Sphere*), and editor Brett Sullivan all pitched in their creative talents that fostered this cut-above werewolf flick. And the combination of staccato edits, special effects, eerie music, and dynamo performances by the two leads created one of the best teen movies to date, which teens will not get a chance to witness due to its R rating. Of course, a video release would reach the film's intended market.

The core of *Ginger Snaps* revolves around teenage sisters, the older sexy Ginger and the introverted Brigitte. The sisters despise the Toronto 'burbs where they reside and they stage their own deaths for a macabre slide show to be screened in class. Their father is a patriarchal bore not interested in the workings of the female body while their perky mother's hormones seem to be in overdrive. At 16, Ginger finally gets her first period to the delight of her mother, who celebrates this rite of passage with a bundt cake dressed in strawberry syrup. However, Ginger finds that she's been doubly cursed after being attacked by a mysterious creature the same night she experiences her first moon cycle. Ginger falls under the spell of denial even after she sprouts a tail and white dog hair. She also bleeds profusely and falls over from menstrual cramps, telling Brigitte that the words "just" and "cramps" do not belong in the same sentence.

As her illness progresses, Ginger grows more aggressive and sexual. She starts smoking pot with the popular boys and, after high school stud Jason (Moss) falls under the spell of Ginger's animal magnetism, Ginger ravages him while also passing on the werewolf virus to another victim. She later tells her concerned sister: "I've got this ache, and I thought it was for sex, but it's to tear things to . . . pieces."

Desperate to save her sister and others that might fall victim to Ginger's ferocity, Brigitte hooks up with pot grower and amateur botanist Sam (Lemche), who believes that a certain perennial flower could save Ginger's life. So Brigitte and Sam race against time and circumstances to save Ginger, as well as themselves, from Ginger's fury.

While some audiences might just dismiss *Ginger Snaps* as another teen werewolf flick, independent film magazines such as *Sight and Sound,* as well as *Film Comment* and *Filmmaker,* have taken the film quite seriously. *Filmmaker's* Steve Gallagher commented: "Clearly influenced by the work of David Cronenberg, Fawcett is more of a humanist. Despite the film's gothic horror, biological metaphors and often biting humor, *Ginger Snaps* is essentially a tender, albeit tragic, coming of age story." Gallagher also recalled the negative media frenzy that the *Toronto Star's* front page article on *Ginger Snaps* provoked, saying "it was the most talked about production in Canada before a frame of film had even been shot."

Assistant editor Nicole Armour of *Film Comment* labeled *Ginger Snaps* "a whip-smart, darkly funny teen horror film." Armour went on to praise screenwriter Walton and director Fawcett's work: "*Ginger Snaps* is a model of economy and inventiveness and a good example of a kind of sharp low-budget film being produced in Canada by a number of bright young talents who navigate between television and movies."

And when it comes to talent and inventiveness, the team that put *Ginger Snaps* together proves to be no exception. Thirty-two-year-old Fawcett graduated from the Canadian Film Center and, after directing episodes of TV shows such as *Xena: Warrior Princess* and *La Femme Nikita,* went on to direct his first feature film *The Boy's Club.* Screenwriter Walton also graduated from the Canadian Film Center and has written episodes for television shows on real teen issues, so it comes as no surprise that she would enlist those same talents for *Ginger Snaps.* And it should also come as no surprise that Walton walked away with the Special Jury Citation award at the prestigious Toronto International Film Festival (2000) for her screenplay.

At 22, Vancouver-based actress Perkins has already won awards for her performances. She has appeared in the Canadian detective drama *DaVinci's Inquest* and an array of other TV shows. Among her film credits are appearances in *In Cold Blood* and *Small Sacrifices.* Eighteen-year-old Isabelle (who ironically plays the older sister Ginger) boasts a list of film credits, including *Disturbing Behavior* and *Spooky House,* as well as appearing in several movies of the week. We will most likely be seeing more of this feisty redhead, and in more sophisticated features, as she matures into adulthood. But for the time being, she will be remembered as the Canadian gothic transformed into a werewolf amidst rabid sexuality and adolescent metamorphoses.

While *Ginger Snaps* might be labeled a gore fest by some viewers and critics, this thriller does portray a meaningful drama of a turbulent relationship between two sisters. And the relationship dynamics between the siblings might seem all-too-familiar to female viewers. The younger sister, Brigitte, lives in the shadows of her older more-extroverted sister. Ginger portrays a sense of wild abandonment while taking a brazen stance towards her cookie-cutter classmates long before the creature's virus transforms her. Her defiant attitude leads her to take charge of the macabre slide project of fake deaths that she and Brigitte produce for a psychology class. And it is Ginger that decides to seek revenge on high school dream girl Trina (Danielle Hampton), which leads to both Ginger and Trina's ultimate demise.

Brigitte, on the other hand, proves her level-headed sensibility by researching the topic of werewolves and even comes off as the younger nerdy sister. She hides in the shadows of Ginger's newfound sexuality and seeks out the school's bad boy, Sam, in order to rescue Ginger from her rabid prowls. But Brigitte's failure to live her own life and instead live through her older sister proves tragic, in the end, for all concerned. While Ginger might warn Brigitte to save herself, Brigitte would rather go down with the sinking ship if Ginger were on board.

*Ginger Snaps,* with its sophisticated themes, attracts an adult audience but also delivers a positive message to teens that young women can explore their sexual identity without becoming a media cutout. While this thriller recalls the film *Carrie,* in which an outcast gets revenge on her inconsiderate classmates, echoes of John Hugh's teenage dramas also come into play. But mostly *Ginger Snaps* explores the changes brought on through adolescence involving issues surrounding menstruation, aggression, and budding sexuality. It also reflects on school violence and AIDS. It's not far-fetched to blend werewolf mythology with the female rite of passage of spilling one's own blood and the result proves refreshing.

—*Patty-Lynne Herlevi*

## CREDITS

**Henry:** John Bourgeois
**Mr. Wayne:** Peter Keleghan
**Brigitte:** Emily Perkins
**Ginger:** Katharine Isabelle
**Sam:** Kris Lemche
**Pamela:** Mimi Rogers
**Jason:** Jesse Moss
**Trina:** Danielle Hampton

**Origin:** Canada
**Released:** 2001

**Directed by:** John Fawcett
**Written by:** Karen Walton
**Cinematography by:** Thom Best
**Music by:** Michael Shields
**Sound:** Robert Fletcher, Lou Solokofsky, Orest Sushko
**Editing:** Brett Sullivan
**Art Direction:** Mary Wilkinson
**Costumes:** Lea Carlson
**Production Design:** Todd Cherniawsky
**MPAA rating:** R
**Running time:** 107 minutes

## REVIEWS

*Boxoffice.* December, 2000, p. 53.
*eye Weekly Online.* May 10, 2001.
*Film Comment.* November/December, 2000, p. 16.
*Filmmaker.* Fall, 2000, p. 36.
*Sight and Sound.* June, 2001, p. 36.
*Toronto Sun Online.* May 11, 2001.
*Variety.* December 9, 2000, p. 27.

## QUOTES

Ginger (Katharine Isabelle) to sister Brigitte (Emily Perkins): "If you don't like your ideas, stop having them."

## TRIVIA

Other names for werewolf include wendigo, kelpie, botu, and lycanthrope.

## AWARDS AND NOMINATIONS

**Nomination:**
**Genie 2001:** Cinematog., Film Editing.

# Glamour

According to Hungarian filmmaker Frigyes Godros his film *Glamour* "is an album of destinies and excerpts of fates." However, this story, which embraces 100 years of history and chronicles the fate of a single Jewish Hungarian family, is frustratingly told in fragments in which characters float in and out of the story ghost-like. No one would argue against the fact that Godros' *Glamour* has hauntingly beautiful images, inspired performances, and a gorgeous soundtrack, but the film plods along in a detached manner, disallowing viewers to feel the emotions presented by the film's characters. Viewing *Glamour* takes a lot of patience and focus. Fortunately, those viewers who possess these attributes will be rewarded with wry comical moments and surrealistic scenes that recall Luis Buñuel and Salvador Dali's *The Golden Age.*

The film opens with a narrator poetically explaining a scene in which an aging Jewish father blesses his two sons before partaking in a Passover feast. The boys prove to be gifted with wild imaginations as they envision a plague of toads taking over the dinner table during a raging storm. Next, we see a grown man meeting with a matchmaker. Apparently time has passed and the boys in the first scene have grown into adults. Imre (Karoly Eperjes) chooses to marry a German woman named Gerda (Eszter Onodi), but is told by a family lawyer that the only way a Semite can marry an Aryan is if she had already divorced her first husband. So Imre stages a false marriage between Gerda and one of his employees. But Imre doesn't trust the fake husband to keep his hands off of Gerda so the group travels in a threesome until Gerda divorces her fake husband, then marries her real husband three months later. However, Imre's father disapproves of his son's marriage to an Aryan (an enemy of the Jewish race) so he disowns his son and grandson, temporarily.

As time passes the family evades Nazi occupation and the Communist regime, but does suffer through familial tragedies. Imre's brother commits a heroic suicide and Gerda's brother, who briefly appears, also dies a tragic death. The local priest suffers humiliation and torture and the hanging judge who executed the torture becomes a masochist years later, adhering to self-flagellation. The son grows into manhood and Gerda dies, leaving her husband and son to fend for themselves. And so the family legacy continues on as a surrealistic merry-go-round appears with young versions of the characters' ghosts. Godros suggests that as long as we can remember our loved ones and our history, they will never disappear.

While Hungarian films with Jewish themes such as Istvan Szabo's *Sunshine* have surfaced over the last couple of years, the films usually acquire critical acclaim while being largely ignored by American film audiences. It's hard enough attracting audiences to films with subtitles but American audiences also demand a compelling story to which they can relate. While arthouse audiences enjoy poetic films filled with symbolism and humanistic history lessons, they can also lose their patience with films that plod through dynasties of unrecognizable characters.

After all a film's substance is of more interest than its packaging, especially when that film comes with subtitles. And American audiences can discern between a film that is dressed up in breathtaking photography and haunting melodies with nowhere to go and a dressed down film full of passion and gusto. Godros' *Glamour* portrays plenty of allure but the film lacks gusto. However, the luminescent Eszter Onodi delivers a heart-warming performance as a young German woman falling in love with a Hungarian Jew, who leaves her homeland in order to wed her Jewish suitor. Karoly Eperjes, who resembles actor John Turturro, portrays a vulnerable lover with finesse, especially in the scenes where he watches his future bride dance with her false husband.

According to director Godros, "*Glamour* is not just a kind of light, it is also a style. It is Hollywood's gloss paint on the face of great heroes, the good or the really evil ones. It is a fallible halo that sheds light onto the face of the characters of our film." *Glamour* is also the veneer that obscures the humanity that lies beneath, which is the case with Godros' beautifully wrapped film.

—*Patty-Lynne Herlevi*

## CREDITS

**Imre:** Karoly Eperies
**Gerda:** Eszter Onodi
**Grandfather:** Gyorgy Barko
**Young son:** Jonas Togay
**Adult son:** Miklos Lang

**Origin:** Hungary
**Language:** Hungarian
**Released:** 2000
**Production:** Kornel Sipos; Focusfilm kft; released by Sony Pictures Classics
**Directed by:** Frigyes Godros
**Written by:** Frigyes Godros
**Cinematography by:** Sandor Kardos
**Music by:** Laszlo Melis
**Editing:** Maria Rigo
**Costumes:** Janos Breckl
**Production Design:** Gyvla Pauer
**MPAA rating:** Unrated
**Running time:** 115 minutes

## REVIEWS

*Los Angeles Times Online.* January 26, 2001.

# The Glass House

*Be careful who you trust.*
—Movie tagline

**Box Office:** $18 million

According to *The Fiction Dictionary*, foreshadowing is "the technique of giving the reader a subtle hint of some important event that will occur later in the story—especially a surprising or shocking event." In *The Glass House*, TV director Daniel Sackheim (in his feature film debut) and screenwriter Wesley Strick are anything but subtle in the heavy-handed way they telegraph everything to the audience.

The story here involves a newly-orphaned brother and sister (Leelee Sobieski and Trevor Morgan) who are taken in by a couple they have known all their lives. A worthwhile film would have it slowly dawn on the viewer that perhaps these new guardians are more concerned with the children's wealth (they've just inherited $4 million) than their welfare. It is so easy to see through *The Glass House* from early on that you are left to plod along with the supposed thriller from one scene to another as the kids go through the expected turmoil and come out the other end. Near the film's finale a car careens all over a winding coastal highway before finally plunging over a cliff, which is much the same way *The Glass House* ultimately veers out of control into risible ridiculousness.

It begins with a cheap attempt to startle us from the start: we see young people being terrorized by a knife-wielding fiend, only to learn that we are actually viewing a teen slasher film along with Ruby (Sobieski) and her popcorn-munching pals at the local cineplex. (It should be noted that *The Glass House*'s producer, Neal H. Moritz, has also brought us films like 1997's *I Know What You Did Last Summer* and 2000's *The Skulls*.) Ruby enjoys drawing, as well as painting the town with her friends. Like most teens, she thinks that she is oh-so-clever and in command, riding in fast cars, smoking and partying, while her parents remain "adorably clueless."

Upon returning home one night, Ruby sees police cars in front of her house and braces for what she assumes will be hell to pay for her late night of teenage revelry. Instead, she must face a totally different and unexpected form of hell: her parents, out for a 20th wedding anniversary celebration, have been killed in a car accident. At the funeral, she and her brother are comforted by ever-so-caring Terry and Erin Glass (Diane Lane and Stellan Skarsgard), who succeed in making us vaguely uneasy about them from the start. Also at the mournful ceremony is the children's Uncle Jack (Chris Noth) who, unlike the Glasses, has been a total stranger to the children, and he gets a fairly chilly response from Ruby.

With the reassuring news from her parents' estate lawyer, Alvin Begleiter (skilled vet Bruce Dern) that her and Rhett's (Morgan) inheritance will at least keep them from ever having to worry about finances, the children are driven to the Glasses' Malibu home, a huge, coldly-modern structure perched high above the pounding surf of the Pacific and featuring an incredible overuse of glass. (That the people who live in the glass house just happen to be named Glass is a warning sign of the nonsense to follow.) The dwelling is incredibly spacious, including a gym and a theater, and so it is hard to understand why the film has the brother and sister put in the same cramped and dimly-lit room. Ruby does not even have a place to change, and must do so in the hallway after telling her brother not to peek. As she does, she hears a noise and has an eerie feeling that somewhere eyes are lingering on her fetching form. This is the first hint of the element of sleaze which slinks through the film.

Soon our sneaking suspicions about the Glasses begin to be confirmed when Ruby finds that Erin has "accidently" listened in on one of her phone calls. Then, as a bikini-clad Ruby takes a 3 a.m. dip in the Glasses' pool, Terry startles her with his sudden appearance and looks her up and down but good before finally handing her a towel. When Ruby goes looking for something in the Glasses' unusually well-stocked medicine cabinet, Erin pops out of nowhere to ask her what she is looking for. While Rhett contentedly enjoys his endless supply of expensive video games, Ruby overhears the Glasses having a fight, which Terry explains away and states with palpable creepiness and a leering look in his eyes that it is time to "get you to bed." He makes Ruby even more uneasy when he leans across her in the car, explaining, upon seeing her discomfiture, that he was merely reaching to help her with her shoulder belt.

Even if Ruby is financially secure, her sense of personal safety in the Glasses' home is being shattered. Ruby decides to go to back to Mr. Begleiter, but instead of immediately offering help he oddly puts a scare into her about the possibility that she and Rhett could end up as wards of the state. As Sackheim often does in *The Glass House*, we get a close-up full of import, this time of Dern, pointing out much too clearly that sinister things lurk behind the facades. For those in the audience who might be slow on the uptake that Ruby and Rhett are in trouble, Sackheim has her class repeatedly discussing Shakespeare's "Hamlet" and how the title character came to sense that "something was wrong right under his nose." (This follows a comment early on by Ruby's mom (Rita Wilson) about how sometimes it is "hardest to see what's right in front of you," and precedes a comment Ruby makes later on that she now sees "what's right in front of me.")

Even after the Glasses try to ease Ruby's concerns with flimsy explanations such as that Erin is a diabetic and was actually giving herself an insulin injection, Ruby's suspicions remain. They strengthen further when she stops by Glass Transit Inc. and overhears Terry being roughed-up by some thugs who clearly want repayment of a loan. (With all the times Ruby is in the right place at the right time to overhear key pieces of information, not to mention her ability to take cover with lightning speed, you can almost hear the job offers being typed up at FBI and CIA headquarters.) For some reason, she makes her way to the garage, and what she sees leads her to look up articles about her parents' accident. Ruby comes to the horrific realization that the Glasses supplied the car which took her parents to their deaths.

More travails follow until Ruby has had enough, packs a disbelieving Rhett into a car, and speeds away towards safety. We have repeatedly been shown in the film that Ruby is struggling to get through her Drivers Ed. classes, and so of course she has to desperately attempt to negotiate all the twists and turns in the dark and surrounded by rain, thunder and lightning. Unfortunately, police flag them down because a mudslide across the road makes it impossible to proceed, and as Ruby grapples with what to do, who should immediately pull up but the Glasses. Ruby could have shown her smarts and screamed her head off until the policemen listened to her, but obviously the film is not done putting her through the wringer yet. Back at the house, a livid Ruby lets accusations fly, and after a brutal struggle between her and Terry, he drags her inside so that Erin can sedate her.

At this point, the film, like Ruby on the road, is clearly having problems retaining control. While Ruby is in a perpetual, drug-induced slumber, people finally start seeing through the Glasses. Terry's use of the children's millions to pay off his debts begins to be detected, and Erin's career in the medical field ends when her suspiciously large drug orders lead to revocation of her licence. Terry vows to kill Ruby before she can tell tales to the authorities, something which Erin cannot bear, and so the despondent woman opts to shoot up, lie next to Ruby, and die, which does Ruby no favors upon awakening. Once Ruby is up she finds herself thrown down in the basement with Rhett.

An all-too-easy escape allows the two to see the mobsters kill Begleiter and depart with a terrified Terry in a car he had rigged to kill the children. (He could not take the other, perfectly good, car because the tires have been slashed all of a sudden, and apparently still thinking we are dense, Sackheim once again heavy-handedly underlines things with a close up of Ruby's hand holding the knife.) After Ruby and Rhett, walking hand-in-hand down the highway, are picked up by a policeman, they look down a steep embankment and observe the aftermath of Terry's crash. *The Glass House* reaches its height of ridiculousness when the cop, seeing no signs of life below, turns from the guardrail and is about to call in the accident when Terry leaps wildly up onto the highway and kills him. Raising the policeman's gun to shoot Ruby and Rhett, the two kids simply hop into the squad car and neatly run him down. As Terry fails to scrape himself up off the pavement to try again (in this film, that could easily have happened), the kids are now free to walk into a sunlit future, sheltered by their kindly Uncle Jack.

It is hard for a suspense film to succeed when everything becomes clear so soon after the opening credits. In *The Glass House*, we can see where it is headed thanks to a script, direction and music which provide blinding neon signs pointing unmistakably to what lies ahead. (The trailer used to advertise the film did not help matters either.) There certainly is mood here—pounding rain, cold and eerie blue lighting—and there are fine actors trying their best, but the film is clearly second-rate and, finally, laughable. Sobieski received a career-high $1 million for *The Glass House*, which had its release date pushed back four times before opening within a couple weeks of her *Joy Ride* and *My First Mister*. The film was not well-received by critics, and grossed about $4 million less than the $22 million it took to make it, mainly because it is all too easy to see what is going on in *The Glass House*. 🎞

—David L. Boxerbaum

## CREDITS

**Ruby:** Leelee Sobieski
**Terry:** Stellan Skarsgard
**Erin:** Diane Lane
**Rhett:** Trevor Morgan
**Begleiter:** Bruce Dern
**Nancy Ryan:** Kathy Baker
**Uncle Jack:** Christopher Noth
**Grace Baker:** Rita Wilson
**Dave Baker:** Michael O'Keefe
**Whitey:** Vyto Ruginis

**Origin:** USA
**Released:** 2001
**Production:** Neal H. Moritz; Original Film; released by Columbia Pictures
**Directed by:** Daniel Sackheim
**Written by:** Wesley Strick
**Cinematography by:** Alar Kivilo
**Music by:** Christopher Young
**Sound:** Mark McNabb
**Editing:** Howard E. Smith
**Art Direction:** Sarah Knowles
**Costumes:** Chrisi Karvonides Dushenko
**Production Design:** Jon Gary Steele
**MPAA rating:** PG-13
**Running time:** 111 minutes

## REVIEWS

*Chicago Sun-Times Online.* September 14, 2001.
*Entertainment Weekly.* September 28, 2001, p. 52.
*Los Angeles Times Online.* September 14, 2001.
*New York Times Online.* September 15, 2001.
*USA Today Oline.* September 13, 2001.
*Variety.* September 17, 2001, p. 20.
*Wall Street Journal.* September 14, 2001, p. W1.

# The Gleaners and I (Les Glaneurs et la Glaneuse)

You see them sorting through wheat and produce in the agricultural fields of France or perhaps you see them sorting through the rubbish bins of an outdoor market. Whether we call these individuals gleaners, salvagers, or retrievers, all of us exhibit this desire to recycle material goods or receive a free gift from the environment. With her documentary *The Gleaners and I* Agnes Varda, known as the Grandmother of French New Wave cinema, explores the history and the act of gleaning by exposing us to various individuals who employ some form of gleaning in their lives. Varda portrays a humanistic spirit while interviewing impoverished and dispossessed individuals who glean the potato fields or the orchards in order to feed their families. However, *The Gleaners* also shows Varda's tough-minded and whimsical qualities, never allowing us to feel pity for the film's subjects. And in fact, viewers learn resourcefulness and compassion from these individuals, as well as gleaning inspiration from the subjects' intriguing stories.

Varda introduces us to an array of colorful characters ranging from salvager/gleaner Francois, who claims "I have eaten 100% trash for 10 years, I've never been ill." to the unemployed Claude, who's not afraid to get his hands dirty digging through trash. But not all gleaners are impoverished or desperate. Some rural gleaners believe that it's a mistake to let tons of crops rot in the fields while people go hungry and so they glean. Francois eats food from the trash because he believes he's fighting the values of a disposable society. Varda locates another gleaner at an outdoor market who sells newspapers despite having earned a Masters degree. But this same man also teaches English free of charge to African immigrants at a shelter where he resides. Painter Louis Pons salvages discarded furniture and other trash to produce recycled art, while artist VR 2000 feels rewarded by the discarded treasures he locates on the streets of Paris, "it's like

Christmas, these leftovers." After all, Varda suggests that someone else's trash is another's treasure.

Varda's *The Gleaners and I* blends an on-the-road adventure with poignant stories as her lens captures the impressionistic landscape of northern France's countryside and small villages. The film turns up treasures at every corner in the form of insightful individuals or a history lesson. Throw in Varda's off-beat narration and what comes off is a refreshing documentary that recalls the spirit of the New Wave director's early feature films. Varda's philosophy claims that a woman isn't born a woman, she becomes one, can be transferred over into humans aren't born human but become human through life circumstances that shape their character. Through watching Varda's documentary about the disposable society in which we all partake, we can glean compassion for the natural world and also learn to be more resourceful in our daily lives. After all resourcefulness is just a form of creativity and the subjects in this film do not fall short on imagination.

The *New York Times'* A.O. Scott praised Varda and the film's subjects writing, "Ms. Varda's gleaners retain a resilient, generous humanity that is clearly brought to the surface by her own tough spirit." Andrea Meyer of *RANT* cited "the film's unusual melange of vivid, unsentimental portraits and Varda's poetic personal commentary brought tears to my eyes." Finally, Harlan Jacobson of *Film Comment* noted "This is one persistent old lady, and in the cinema of persistent old ladies, she will run you to the ground in *Gleaners*. . .and lift you up until you say yes."

Over the course of her illustrious career, Varda has displayed her persistence and versatility as a filmmaker without ever allowing us to forget the ills of society. In her 1961 release, *Cleo, From 5 to 7* we glimpse two hours in the life of a chanteuse as she awaits the results of a medical test. We watch Cleo transform from a spoiled girl to a woman who learns to enjoy the world. Through her own suffering, she develops compassion for humanity. Now with *The Gleaners*, we see various individuals transforming the world by showing us the discarded treasures of our disposable society and only a truly hardheaded individual will miss the point of Varda's film. With so many films being released and so many themes being recycled, Varda's simple documentary acts as an oasis from films of lesser quality. As A.O. Scott observed, "She's (Varda) a treasure." And the ultimate gleaner.

*—Patty-Lynne Herlevi*

**Released:** 2001
**Production:** Cine-Tamaris Productions; released by Zeitgeist Films
**Directed by:** Agnes Varda
**Written by:** Agnes Varda
**Cinematography by:** Stephane Krausz, Didier Rouget, Didier Doussin, Pascal Sautelet
**Music by:** Joanne Bruzdowicz
**Editing:** Agnes Varda, Laurent Pineau
**MPAA rating:** Unrated
**Running time:** 82 minutes

## REVIEWS

*Film Comment.* March/April, 2001, p. 76.
*Los Angeles Times Online.* April 6, 2001.
*New York Times Online.* September 30, 2000.
*New York Times.* March 11, 2001, p. AR15.
*RANT.* March/April, 2001, p. 31.

## QUOTES

Claude, an unemployed gleaner: "We are not afraid to get our hands dirty. We can always wash our hands."

## TRIVIA

The film took its title and inspiration from Jean-Francois Millet's 1867 painting entitled *Les Glaneuses/Women Gleaning.*

## AWARDS AND NOMINATIONS

**L.A. Film Critics 2001:** Feature Doc.
**N.Y. Film Critics 2001:** Feature Doc.
**Natl. Soc. Film Critics 2001:** Feature Doc.

## CREDITS

**Narrator:** Agnes Varda

**Origin:** France
**Language:** French

# Glitter

*In music she found her dream, her love, herself.*
—Movie tagline

**Box Office:** $4.3 million

litter, the star vehicle starring singer Mariah Carey, didn't get off to a promising start. Months before it was released, word leaked out that it was a stinker. Then, Carey had a very public nervous breakdown that pushed back the release of the film and inhibited her from doing a lot of publicity for it. And finally, the film was released shortly after the World Trade Center bombings, a time when many people were reluctant to go out and enjoy frivolous pursuits.

But all this wasn't so bad for the film. For one thing, the fact that people were talking about the film months before it was released, even though it wasn't flattering talk, was still a form of hype for the film. Carey's breakdown, which was of course tragic, still managed to get the name of the film in the paper more than it would have otherwise. And despite being released on an unfortunate weekend, *Glitter* was the only major release that weekend, meaning it had a good chance of hitting the box office charts. But it wasn't enough for *Glitter*. Despite having no new competition, in its first week out, the film didn't even manage to crack the top ten. (The total box office for all films that weekend was notably poor.)

Although *Glitter* is certainly no masterpiece, it didn't seem worthy of the critical scorn that was heaped upon it. Critics didn't just dislike this film, they hated it. Many even made crude references in their reviews to Carey's breakdown along the lines of "Seeing this movie could give you a breakdown too." It seemed awfully harsh for a film that's really quite benign. *Glitter* doesn't try to be anything more than a new, lighter version of *A Star Is Born* or *Mahogany*. The idea behind it is that fame is not all it's cracked up to be, fame can ruin relationships, and similar messages. Sure, we've heard it all before, but it's a good theme and always at least a little interesting to see.

When we meet Billie Frank (Carey), she's a little girl in the 1970s watching her mother Lillian Frank (Valarie Pettiford) perform jazz standards in a small nightclub. Although her mother is obviously very talented, she loses track of the words to one of her songs and appears to have some sort of problem with drugs and/or alcohol. After forgetting her lyrics, the mother calls young Billie (Isabel Gomes) to hop up on stage to help her finish her song. The shy Billie has quite a set of pipes and starts belting out the rest of the song in a duet with mom. It's one of their last happy memories together. The mother is soon fired and turns to Billie's absentee father for some money. The father gives them a few dollars but makes it clear that he doesn't want them in his life. Billie's mom spirals downward and has to give her daughter up to an orphanage. There, Billie meets two girls Louise (Da Brat) and Roxanne (Tia Texada) and becomes fast friends with them.

The film jumps ahead to 1983 and the trio is still hanging out together. They are club kids who spend their time dancing in New York discos. They get their first big break when a record producer, Timothy Walker (Terrence

Howard), signs them up as back-up singers for his highly untalented girlfriend Sylk (Padma Lakshmi). In the studio, Timothy realizes that Billie is singing the song a whole lot better than Sylk and brings Billie's voice way up in the mix so that she's basically singing the song.

The catchy song quickly snags the attention of the resident cool DJ Julian "Dice" Black, aka The Diceman (Max Beesley). He recognizes that Billie's the real singer and offers Timothy $100,000 to take over the back-up singers' contracts. Timothy accepts and Billie is on her sharp climb to fame. Dice is a smooth wheeler dealer and soon has Billie signed to a good contract with a record label. From there her fame skyrockets. She gets a number one hit and is asked to perform at a big music awards show. But all, of course, is not well. As Billie starts getting more famous, the record company starts trying to cut Dice out of the action. This makes Dice mad, and completely out of character from how he's behaved the rest of the film, he starts acting like a big jerk. For some reason, he decides he doesn't want to pay Timothy his money, he starts yelling at Billie's friends, and begins to treat Billie poorly.

The relationship between Billie and Dice is one of the parts of the movie that doesn't work. It's hard to tell what director Vondie Curtis-Hall is trying to show with their relationship. It's weird that Dice turns into such a cad all of a sudden but Billie's reaction to him is even stranger. She moves out of his apartment, much to her own relief (as well as her friends) but later in the movie starts mooning over him. There's even a post-breakup scene where the two, in their separate apartments, are composing a song that unbeknownst to the other is note for note the same. Are we to take this as a sign that the two are soul mates? If so, isn't it kind of a rip-off for Billie that her soul mate is an abusive jerk?

Critics found fault with other oddities in the film, too. In one scene, the record company insists that Billie wear a skimpy bikini in a video shoot. Billie is offended because she's much too modest for such a thing. But in subsequent scenes when she picks out her own clothes, she's wearing skin-tight dresses and the like. Another wardrobe groaner was that when Billie goes to the country to visit someone, she wears a floor-length sequined gown. Part of the unintended appeal of the film must have been to search for prebreakdown signs in Carey. Another part was that the film resembled Carey's own story in a lot of ways, especially the idea of her being controlled by a Svengali-like mentor.

Critics were loathe to give her any kudos, but for a first time starring in a film, Carey did a fine job. Her character was meant mainly to belt out songs and smile modestly, but Carey seems natural on the screen and her performance rings true. In performance, she often seems overwrought, but on film she comes across as more relaxed and likable. Beesley, a Brit by birth, adopts an only occasionally successful New York accent and seems to be trying to imitate Mark

Wahlberg. He does the best he can with a character that's not especially sketched out. In her brief time on screen, Pettiford is good as Billie's talented, yet doomed mother. Eric Benet, the singer and husband of Halle Berry, shows up as a soulful singer who's interested in doing a duet (and maybe more) with Billie.

Critics were in no mood for a new *A Star Is Born* and raked the film over the coals. Rene Rodriguez of the *Miami Herald* called it "the kind of movie only 11-year-old girls who dot their i's with hearts would find bearable" and said it was "filled with unintentionally humorous moments that tower over any comedy released this year." John Anderson of *Newsday* said it had "all the makings of an interactive camp classic." David Kronke of the *Long Beach Press-Telegram* wrote, "It's too dispiriting to even qualify as inadvertent camp fun." And Kevin Maynard of Mr. Showbiz wrote, "Only diehard Mariah fans, 11-year-old girls, or anyone truly desperate to escape last week's terror might find some reason to sit through this bland, bloated, self-addressed valentine."

—*Jill Hamilton*

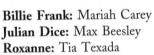
## CREDITS

**Billie Frank:** Mariah Carey
**Julian Dice:** Max Beesley
**Roxanne:** Tia Texada
**Louise:** Da Brat
**Lilian Frank:** Valarie Pettiford
**Kelly:** Ann Magnuson
**Timothy Walker:** Terrence DaShon Howard
**Guy Richardson:** Dorian Harewood
**Jack Bridges:** Grant Nickalls
**Rafael:** Eric Benet
**Sylk:** Padma Lakshmi
**Young Billie:** Isabel Gomes

**Origin:** USA
**Released:** 2001
**Production:** Laurence Mark; Maroon Entertainment; released by 20th Century-Fox
**Directed by:** Vondie Curtis-Hall
**Written by:** Kate Lanier
**Cinematography by:** Geoffrey Simpson
**Music by:** Terence Blanchard
**Sound:** Thomas K. Hidderley
**Music Supervisor:** Robin Urdang
**Editing:** Jeff Freeman
**Art Direction:** Peter Grundy
**Costumes:** Joseph G. Aulisi
**Production Design:** Dan Bishop
**MPAA rating:** PG-13

**Running time:** 104 minutes

## REVIEWS

*Boxoffice.* November, 2001, p. 151.
*Chicago Sun-Times Online.* September 23, 2001.
*Entertainment Weekly.* October 5, 2001, p. 112.
*Globe and Mail.* September 22, 2001, p. R4.
*Los Angeles Times Online.* September 20, 2001.
*New York Times Online.* September 21, 2001.
*USA Today Online.* September 20, 2001.
*Variety.* September 24, 2001, p. 23.

# The Golden Bowl

**Box Office:** $3 million

A handsome prince has a lusty affair with a vibrant woman, but both are poor and must reluctantly break things off to marry money. He ends up with the beautiful and virtuous daughter of an illustrious billionaire, and she with the billionaire himself, but neither marriage ends their passionate connection. Let the melodrama begin! With such a plot, it would seem like we are in for a great deal of bodice-ripping romance and wailing accusations of betrayal. *The Golden Bowl,* however, is based upon the 1904 novel by the much subtler Henry James, and it is brought to the screen by those masters of repressed emotion, director James Ivory and producer Ismail Merchant. While the great author considered the book to be his best, the rich but tortuously complex prose of his last and longest novel are considered by most to be a difficult read. Even Ivory told *Vanity Fair* that he gave up after the first one hundred pages.

Written by Merchant-Ivory screenwriting vet Ruth Prawer Jhabvala in their third collaboration based upon a work by James (the previous being 1979's *The Europeans* and 1984's *The Bostonians*), it is basically what we have come to expect from this team: a slowly unfolding literary adaptation, muted emotions, and a mise-en-scene brimming with high production values. The hard part of this adaptation was to take the lengthy, intricately-written, enigmatic tome with its detailed character analysis and unspoken inner complexity and convey enough of it through images and dialogue to make an involving, potently-dramatic film. The simplified, literal, and sometimes heavy-handed script succeeds to some extent, but too much of what has made it to the screen fails to stir us.

*The Golden Bowl* begins with a scene of purposeful foreshadowing, which is from Jhabvala and not James, in which an Italian Renaissance Duke discovers his current wife having an affair with his son, and guards with sharp weapons put an end to the sordid adulterous affair. Jump ahead to 1903, where the Duke's descendent Prince Amerigo (Jeremy Northam) continues the fine family tradition of lustful behavior in a relationship with European-schooled American expatriate Charlotte Stant (Uma Thurman). While ardor has been passed down in Amerigo's line, affluence has not. We cannot say whether he has been involved in any adultery up to this point, but it seems clear that is in the cards when he breaks up with Charlotte to marry her old school friend Maggie Verver (Kate Beckinsale), an American living in England whose virtue is as prodigious as her wealth. Charlotte asks Amerigo not to do it, but his future requires money and Charlotte has none to offer.

Amerigo and Maggie have been introduced by matron Fanny Assingham (excellent Anjelica Huston), who knows everyone and everything in this expanding, increasingly-complex web. As Maggie does not know that her fiancee and friend were lovers, she is thrilled when the latter comes for their nuptials, unaware that the woman is still hoping for at least one last crack at him. While Amerigo and Charlotte are out walking, they stop in a shop and observe a gilded crystal bowl that Charlotte thinks would be a fine wedding present. The shopkeeper states that it is flawless, but Amerigo insists that, while it appears so, it actually contains a crack and is damaged goods. This is, of course, a metaphor for the less-than-perfect wedded life which awaits him and Maggie.

We then jump ahead again to 1905 and the English castle rented by Maggie's widowed father Adam Verver (Nick Nolte, who appeared in Merchant-Ivory's less than successful *Jefferson in Paris*), America's first billionaire who made his money in bituminous coal. He is currently collecting objects de art throughout Europe to put in an American museum he is designing. Maggie and her father have an unusually close, emotionally incestuous relationship, spending as much time together since her marriage as before. Apparently she has broken away for at least some time with Amerigo, as we see that they now have a baby boy. Having felt as if she ditched her father to take a husband, Maggie is all atwitter when she gets news that Charlotte has agreed to marry Adam. A closeup of Amerigo shows that he knows a troubling development when he hears one.

The film then moves to London three years later, and we see that Maggie and Adam are still so joined at the hip that Amerigo and Charlotte have begun to feel similarly left out. At a lavish party, we see Charlotte in an ostentatious costume complete with feathers, eyeing the crowd for Amerigo like a hungry bird of prey. As the two enjoy themselves, Fanny lets her disapproval be known (to no avail), but she later tells her husband (James Fox) that shattering poor,

innocent Maggie with news of this extracurricular coziness is out of the question. Charlotte and Amerigo rationalize that they are doing their absent spouses a favor by keeping them happily ignorant. During a boisterous weekend away, which Adam and Maggie choose not to attend, Charlotte and Amerigo finally allow their simmering passions to boil over.

When he arrives home later than expected, there is James's heroine Maggie, dressed in white and, significantly, sitting in the dark. She senses that something is up, but does not pointedly confront her husband. Maggie would also sooner die than do anything that might end up causing her father any grief. Amerigo starts to worry that the Ververs are on to them, but Charlotte is less concerned, stating that it is the Ververs' fault that she and Amerigo have sought comfort with each other.

What makes it all come to a head is when Maggie and Fanny happen to buy the golden bowl as a present for Adam's birthday, and the young woman is shocked when the shopkeeper informs her that a chummy Charlotte and Amerigo had almost purchased it five years before, revealing that the two had known each other before their supposed introduction before Maggie and Amerigo's wedding. Maggie shows a new sense of strength and maturity in the scene where amorous Amerigo learns that the jig is up. "I want a happiness without a hole in it," she cries. "I want a bowl without a crack!" Amerigo sides with Maggie over Charlotte, lying to the latter when she fears that Maggie knows all. When Charlotte realizes that it is over between her and Amerigo, she gives him a good slap, her hair askew and her face wet with tears.

Cut loose and crushed, Charlotte is further unhinged by Adam's plans for the two of them to move to America to set up his museum, responding to the news with what resembles a desperate, sick bark. (It is an idea Maggie has given to Adam, who clearly senses the danger to his beloved daughter's happiness.) Trying to preserve her pride, Charlotte pretends to Maggie (who is kind as ever, despite what she knows) that it was actually her own idea to go far away, and then, sobbing, turns to Adam for comfort, clinging tightly to him like a drowning woman who feels about to be swept under. The film's final images reveal that the always stylish Charlotte has generated admiration in America at her husband's side, although her true happiness remains in question.

*The Golden Bowl* was originally to be distributed by Miramax, but the company complained about the film's length before finally dropping it entirely. The film premiered at the 2000 Cannes Film Festival, where it reportedly was met with a lack of enthusiasm. Most critics thought it to be one of the lesser Merchant Ivory productions. Made on a budget of $15 million, the film grossed merely a fifth of that in limited release. Perhaps because so much between the characters is kept in reserve, the film is only modestly involving and lacks potency throughout. There is never a sense of mounting tension while awaiting the film's climax. It seems to simply seep towards its ending rather than building to any sort of satisfying conclusion.

*The Golden Bowl* is often enjoyable to look at: lovely gardens, homes with striking exteriors and lavish, beautifully-decorated interiors, and women in long dresses with hat, gloves and parasol. These visuals come off as more vivid than the characters. It is hard to warm up to, or be especially concerned about how things work out for, these people, with the possible exception of Maggie. Huston is especially good, and Beckinsale is quite believable as pristine Maggie. Nolte and his wan characterization make little impact. Northam seems miscast as the Italian prince, failing to come across as someone these ladies would get so tied up in knots over. (It might be noted that those who pay great attention to the authenticity of accents will, at times, be disappointed during this film.) The complexity needed for Thurman's role may have been a little beyond her range. All the characters are less complex and interesting than in James' book, as is the film in general. Like the golden bowl of its title, the film is eye-catching enough but also has flaws which decrease its value.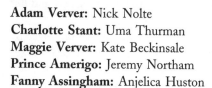

—*David L. Boxerbaum*

### CREDITS

**Adam Verver:** Nick Nolte
**Charlotte Stant:** Uma Thurman
**Maggie Verver:** Kate Beckinsale
**Prince Amerigo:** Jeremy Northam
**Fanny Assingham:** Anjelica Huston
**Bob Assingham:** James Fox
**Lady Castledan:** Madeleine Potter
**Jarvis:** Peter Eyre

**Origin:** France, Great Britain, USA
**Released:** 2000
**Production:** Ismail Merchant; Merchant-Ivory Productions, TF-1 Films; released by Lion's Gate Films
**Directed by:** James Ivory
**Written by:** Ruth Prawer Jhabvala
**Cinematography by:** Tony Pierce-Roberts
**Music by:** Richard Robbins
**Sound:** David Stephenson
**Editing:** John David Allen
**Art Direction:** Lucy Richardson, Gianni Giovagnoni
**Costumes:** John Bright
**Production Design:** Andrew Sanders
**MPAA rating:** R
**Running time:** 130 minutes

### REVIEWS

*Boxoffice.* August, 2000, p. 63.
*Chicago Sun-Times Online.* May 18, 2001.
*Entertainment Weekly.* May 4, 2001, p. 43.
*Los Angeles Times Online.* April 27, 2001.
*New Republic.* May 7, 2001, p. 30.
*New York.* May 7, 2001, p. 58.
*New York Times.* April 27, 2001, p. E10.
*New Yorker.* May 7, 2001, p. 101.
*People.* May 7, 2001, p. 35.
*Premiere.* May, 2001, p. 88.
*Rolling Stone.* May 10, 2001, p. 94.
*USA Today Online.* April 27, 2001.
*Variety.* May 22, 2000, p. 24.
*Washington Post Online.* May 18, 2001.

### TRIVIA

*The Golden Bowl* was previously filmed in 1972 as a six-part British miniseries.

# Gosford Park

*Tea at four. Dinner at eight. Murder at midnight.*
—Movie tagline

 **Box Office:** $31 million

Director Robert Altman has called *Gosford Park* a "who-cares-whodunit film," and it's a description that's right on the money. Julian Fellowes' script, from an idea by Altman and actor Bob Balaban, fuses Agatha Christie's drawing room murder mysteries and Jean Renoir's *Rules of the Game* into the supreme hyphenated movie: a drama-comedy-mystery-musical with documentary overtones. That so many genres have been welded into a unified exploration of England's class structure is impressive enough, but *Gosford Park* is a triumph of direction that shows off America's greatest filmmaker at the top of his game. The result may well be Altman's best work since his dazzling string of pictures in the early 1970s.

*Gosford Park* takes place over the course of a long, rainy weekend in 1932, as a party of aristocrats gathers for a pheasant hunt at the country estate of Sir William McCordle (Michael Gambon) and his wife Lady Sylvia (Kristin Scott Thomas). Some of the visitors have arrived with more than mere socializing on their minds. Constance Trentham (Maggie Smith), for instance, hopes to secure a lifetime allowance from Sir William, while the conscienceless Freddie Nesbitt (James Wilby) splits his time between trying to cajole money from the McCordles' malleable daughter Isobel (Camilla Rutherford) and exploiting his homely but perceptive wife Mabel (Claudie Blakely). Morris Weissman (Balaban), an American producer doing research for his new Charlie Chan film, has insinuated himself into the household through his friend Ivor Novello (Jeremy Northam), a movie star and a distant cousin of the McCordles. (Novello, an actual film star of the era, starred in Hitchcock's first great success *The Lodger,* and the tunes Northam sings in the film are actual Novello compositions.)

The mansion is looked after by a small army of servants who are never farther away than a half-closed door, and who in some cases do more than witness their masters' foibles, but actively abet them. The regular household staff is supervised by an eagle-eyed triumvirate: the head butler Jennings (Alan Bates), the ascetic housekeeper Mrs. Wilson (Helen Mirren), and Mrs. Croft (Eileen Atkins), the formidable head of the kitchen corps. Their staff includes the housemaid Elsie (Emily Watson), who's discreetly sharing Sir William's bed, the satyr-in-tails first footman George (Richard E. Grant), and Sir William's loyal valet Mr. Probst (Derek Jacobi). The weekend introduces several newcomers into this mix, most notably Weissman's valet Henry Denton (Ryan Phillippe), whose dicey Scottish accent arouses suspicion in the other servants, the saturnine valet Robert Parks (Clive Owen), and Mary Macreachran (Kelly Macdonald), the young maid who serves as our eyes and ears in certain crucial passages.

If all this sounds more like a corporation's organizational flowchart than a movie's plot synopsis, it should be pointed out that *Gosford Park* is more about the relationships between its characters than any of the events they participate in. Things *do* happen in the course of the weekend: the hunting party shoots a great many birds out of the sky, a timorous little man suffers financial ruin, an adulterous affair receives a very public exposure, and there's even a murder on the second night of the gathering, when someone sneaks into Sir William's library and sends him to meet his Maker. But *Gosford Park* is more concerned with giving shape to the unspoken tensions that tweak its characters' personalities, and it does so not by the familiar method of building to a climax through a series of increasingly heated scenes, but through a gentle centrifugal motion in which scores of disparate details settle into a pattern of larger meanings. By the time the movie ends, and the guests have returned to their cars and dispersed along England's country lanes, it's reached a plane of emotional resolution that feels whole and mysteriously right.

For more than three decades Robert Altman's most abiding interest has been in the ways human beings—especially combinations of men and women—dote and grate on each other when they're thrown into close quarters.

Altman fixes his people in concrete milieus—a military triage unit, a filthy Western mining town, the L.A. suburbs—so deeply that they seem to have sprung organically from their settings. And though he rarely uses film to make social statements, he's one of the great democrats in the history of the cinema: everyone in his world, down to the town drunk, gets a hearing and a place at the table.

Technically *Gosford Park* represents one of the highest peaks in Altman's career for he and his collaborators have so completely thought their way into their environment that there's no reason to believe this *isn't* what a 1930s gathering of gentry and servants would've looked like. It isn't just the details of costume and set décor that are so convincing, but the actors' very postures and attitudes, for in *Gosford Park* character is conveyed as much by the way people hold their cigarettes or hand-feed their dogs as by anything they say. The story's energy refuses to be tied down by any single protagonist or crisis, but instead is evenly distributed throughout its large cast. The heart of the movie lies not in any heated confrontation, but in the long, fragrant sequence in which the servants are seen enjoying Novello's musical repertoire from a series of shadowy vantage points just out of sight from their masters. Altman maintains a respectful touch throughout, recording what goes on in distanced medium shots that allow the actors to fully inhabit the skin of their characters. His style is as silky as ever, his camera sliding in subtle rhythms along the outskirts of his group compositions, or discreetly trailing the characters through the manor's labyrinthine corridors, allowing us to pick out for ourselves the points of interest within the action.

In this way we're guided through the intricacies of their relationships, including the pecking orders that exist both between and within the two classes. Novello, whose fame carries no cachet with this hardhearted crowd, is treated by his relatives like a performing seal, while his friend Weissman is handicapped by his nationality, occupation, and religion. The servants don't care about any of that (they notice Weissman only when his vegetarianism wreaks havoc with their menu), yet their lives are just as bound by ironclad traditions that ostensibly "avoid confusion." When Weissman points out that Novello is providing the group with a lot of free entertainment, Novello replies with wry resignation, "Morris, I'm *used* to it." The appalling thing is that *all* these people are "used to it." The masters are too deadened by complacency to sense anything wrong with the situation, and while the servants forever daydream of a better existence, at the end of the day they're still resigned to their life sentences.

One of cinema's most enduring myths holds that Robert Altman despises genre movies. It's an absurd accusation, and in its implication that he wrecks people's fun just for the hell of it it's only slightly less galling than the charges of misogyny that occasionally get leveled against him. Like the rest of us, Altman grew up on genre movies, but in his lifetime he's seen their conventions ossify into clichés, and watched them turn into mass-produced entertainments with all the conviction of a crossword puzzle. In *McCabe & Mrs. Miller* and *The Long Goodbye,* he recycled their genres' frayed and shabby threads and used them to embroider some lively new patterns. If he really meant to destroy the western in *McCabe,* he wouldn't have injected such elemental force into that old chestnut, a cowpoke getting murdered after he's tricked into touching his gun. *The Long Goodbye* is studded with powerful moments—a nighttime suicide in the Malibu surf, a hoodlum's act of unthinkable sadism—that Altman plays entirely straight, augmenting the detective picture in ways that the glib, emotionally vapid *Murder on the Orient Express* doesn't dream of doing.

In *Gosford Park* Altman's credo is spelled out in Morris Weissman's phone call to his Hollywood confederates: "We can't keep doing the same shit over and over again." These words are spoken just as the pipe-smoking, trench-coated Inspector Thompson (Stephen Fry), come to investigate the murder, is seen alighting from his roadster. This would-be Poirot is actually the bastard child of Tom Stoppard and Monty Python, a dash-it-all clue-destroying bumbler and fumbler whose presence puts us on notice that we shouldn't start worrying about such irrelevancies as legal culpability. After a million tedious mysteries whose solutions hinge on meaningless MacGuffins, Altman and Fellowes have relocated the emphasis from *who* committed the crime to *why* it was committed, and tied the motive to one of the most enduring human drives.

In his long and prolific career Altman has worked with scores of talented actors, but he's never had an ensemble like this team of British professionals, each of whom selflessly calibrate their performance to fit the movie's schema. Maggie Smith, who could have pleased her fans by simply showing up in the role of a penniless countess, instead works to make us feel how Constance's trenchant snobbery is tied to her desperation. Emily Watson and Clive Owen turn in bookend performances as people of shrouded intentions: where Owen's deeply wronged valet, book in hand and sprawled carelessly across his bed, is a model of measured casualness, Watson's Elsie is his opposite number. Blunt and unsentimental for most of the way, her pragmatism flowers into the film's most resilient perspective, a far cry from the cynicism that checkered women are usually rewarded with in films. Gambon's Sir William is a multi-hued creation, by turns bilious, avuncular, and offhandedly villainous, yet his tender relationship with Elsie constantly checks our condemnation of him. (Gambon, who delivered the Jupiter Symphony of televised performances in the 1986 miniseries *The Singing Detective,* is a specialist in complex, outsized animals.) And throughout the proceedings Helen Mirren takes a cue from her character, giving her all while laboring deep in the background. Her taut face, constrained movements, and drab costumes make Mrs. Wilson look like a

woman driven mad by Lutheranism, but these are only expressions of the rue she wears like punishment for her past naivete. Mirren delivers a speech near the end that sounds tailored to her voice, and her enunciation of such phrases as "the gift of anticipation" is enough to send a thrill charging through the nervous system.

Late in *Gosford Park* the butler played by Alan Bates, having been forced to confront a past disgrace, looks into a mirror and gives himself a starchy salute. It's the one time that the filmmakers tug at our emotions in the boxy, stage-bound manner of regular dramas, the one flaw in an otherwise impeccable surface. The many instances in which Altman's fragile aesthetic has failed to take flight can never detract from his successes, but so many of those successes occurred so long ago that today they seem miraculous, the product of alchemy or a once-in-a-lifetime astral alignment. Altman was 76 years old when he made *Gosford Park,* a time of life in which Ford, Hawks, and Wilder were content to rehash old material. Altman, though, has stepped up to the plate and knocked one clean out of the park, and no less admirable than the accomplishment itself is the way he's stayed true to his art. He refuses to ever get "used to it."

—Tom Block

### CREDITS

**Sir William McCordle:** Michael Gambon
**Lady Sylvia McCordle:** Kristin Scott Thomas
**Constance, Countess of Trentham:** Maggie Smith
**Mrs. Wilson:** Helen Mirren
**Mrs. Croft:** Eileen Atkins
**Jennings:** Alan Bates
**Morris Weissman:** Bob Balaban
**Henry Denton:** Ryan Phillippe
**Mary Maceachran:** Kelly Macdonald
**Robert Parks:** Clive Owen
**Ivor Novello:** Jeremy Northam
**Elsie:** Emily Watson
**George:** Richard E. Grant
**Raymond, Lord Stockbridge:** Charles Dance
**Louisa, Lady Stockbridge:** Geraldine Somerville
**Lt. Commander Anthony Meredith:** Tom Hollander
**Freddie Nesbitt:** James Wilby
**Dorothy:** Sophie Thompson
**Inspector Thompson:** Stephen Fry
**Constable Dexter:** Ron Webster
**Isobel McCordle:** Camilla Rutherford
**Mabel Nesbitt:** Claudie Blakley
**Lady Livinia Meredith:** Natasha Wrightman
**Arthur:** Jeremy Swift
**Bertha:** Teresa Churcher

**Origin:** Great Britain
**Released:** 2001
**Production:** Robert Altman, Bob Balaban, David Levy; Sandcastle 5 Productions, Medusa Film, Chicagofilms; released by USA Films
**Directed by:** Robert Altman
**Written by:** Julian Fellowes
**Cinematography by:** Andrew Dunn
**Music by:** Patrick Doyle
**Sound:** Peter Glossop
**Editing:** Tim Squyres
**Art Direction:** John Frankish
**Costumes:** Jenny Beavan
**Production Design:** Stephen Altman
**MPAA rating:** R
**Running time:** 137 minutes

## REVIEWS

*Boxoffice.* January, 2001, p. 36.
*Chicago Sun-Times Online.* January 4, 2002.
*Detroit Free Press Online.* January 11, 2002.
*Entertainment Weekly.* January 18, 2002, p. 52.
*Globe and Mail.* December 29, 2001, p. R5.
*GQ.* January, 2002, p. 30.
*Los Angeles Times Online.* December 26, 2001.
*New York Times Online.* September 9, 2001.
*New York Times Online.* December 26, 2001.
*Newsweek.* January 14, 2002, p. 60.
*People.* January 14, 2002, p. 30.
*Rolling Stone.* January 17, 2002, p. 56.
*Sight and Sound.* June, 2001, p. 5.
*Sight and Sound.* January, 2002, p. 15.
*USA Today Online.* December 16, 2001.
*Variety.* November 12, 2001, p. 27.
*Washington Post.* January 4, 2002, p. WE34.

## QUOTES

Housekeeper Mrs. Wilson (Helen Mirren): "I am the perfect servant. I have no life."

## TRIVIA

Jeremy Northam plays the only nonfictional character: actor/composer Ivor Novello, a British matinee idol of the 1920s.

## AWARDS AND NOMINATIONS

**Oscars 2001:** Orig. Screenplay
**British Acad. 2001:** Costume Des., Film

**Golden Globes 2002:** Director (Altman)
**N.Y. Film Critics 2001:** Director (Altman), Screenplay, Support. Actress (Mirren)
**Natl. Soc. Film Critics 2001:** Director (Altman), Screenplay, Support. Actress (Mirren)
**Screen Actors Guild 2001:** Support. Actress (Mirren)
**Screen Actors Guild 2003:** Cast
**Writers Guild 2001:** Orig. Screenplay
**Broadcast Film Critics 2001:** Cast
**Nomination:**
**British Acad. 2001:** Director (Altman), Orig. Screenplay, Support. Actress (Mirren, Smith)
**Golden Globes 2002:** Film—Mus./Comedy, Screenplay, Support. Actress (Mirren, Smith).

# Greenfingers

*A bloomin' comedy.*
—Movie tagline

 **Box Office:** $1.4 million

Critics were divided on *Greenfingers*, probably a lot more so than audiences. Since a lot of critics had to see the film as part of their jobs, many of them had to sit through a movie that they had no interest in. For some of them, a quaint Brit movie about gardening probably sounded about as appealing as the latest *Saturday Night Live* skit-turned-movie. The *Greenfingers* audience, on the other hand was largely comprised of people—and the people who love them—who thought, "A quaint Brit movie about gardening—sounds wonderful."

*Greenfingers* is along the same lines as gently humorous fare from overseas like *Saving Ned Devine, The Full Monty* and *Brassed Off.* It's the kind of film that's populated with characters, meaning eccentric types, who do colorful things. This film was inspired by the *New York Times* article "Free to Grow Bluebells in England," written by Pam Deitz in 1998. The article detailed the story of a group of prisoners at Her Majesty's Prison Leyhill who won two gold medals at the Hampton Court Palace Flower show, which is a big-deal, invite-only contest given by the Royal Horticultural Society. The British take their gardening very seriously—Americans use the term "green thumb," while the British include the whole hand for their term, "greenfingers."

The tale centers around Colin Briggs (Clive Owen of *Croupier*), a prisoner who has just been moved from a regular high-security prison to a new experimental one for low-risk inmates. As the new warden, Governor Hodge (Warren

Clarke), explains, there are no fences because prisoners are on the honor system. The prisoners are to choose a work assignment that they enjoy so that they can become skilled at it and get a job in that field more easily once they are released.

But even these nurturing and cushy circumstances don't affect Colin much, who is a classic movie loner. He eats by himself and talks to no one, preferring to squint intently off into the horizon, like a 1950's strong silent type. He refuses to choose a work assignment and is given the chore of cleaning the bathrooms, which he does in a strong and silent manner. He isn't even interested in his charmingly full-of-life elderly roommate, Fergus Wilks (David Kelly, best known as the highly thin, occasionally naked old guy from *Waking Ned Devine*). Though beset by cancer and a host of other ills, and faced with the certainty of dying in prison, Fergus keeps a hopeful buoyant outlook. He makes Colin his personal project. After lively conversation and invitations to dance don't work, he gets Colin a packet of seeds. Colin dutifully dumps the seeds in the cold, unforgiving ground and promptly forgets about them.

But that spring, when he and Fergus notice that, against all odds, those fragile little flowers have come up, Colin has an epiphany. Before he could only see himself as a man capable of taking life. Now he has found a way that he can give life. (This would be the type of epiphany that many critics found to be overdone and as overly sentimental as a Hallmark card.)

The gruff, yet kindly governor, immediately creates a new work program for Colin. Colin is to plant the prison's first garden. He recruits fellow inmates Fergus; Raw (Adam Fogerty), who is a big bald lug; Tony (Danny Dyer), a cocky youngster looking to score with a pretty member of the prison staff; and Jimmy (Paterson Joseph), a man, who despite his claims of being innocent of his crime, is rejected by his young son. Predictably, the ragtag team becomes obsessed with their garden and, Colin, particularly, seems to be quite talented at it. The gardeners ignore the teasing of their disgusted fellow prisoners and get more involved with activities like reading seed catalogs.

Eventually, the men's work comes to the attention of Georgina Woodhouse (Helen Mirren), who's roughly the British gardening equivalent of Martha Stewart. Georgina is taken by Colin's skill and, while lauding herself for doing such a good deed, becomes something of a mentor to him. She gets the prisoners a job on the outside doing landscaping for a wealthy couple and encourages the men to consider entering the Hampton Court Palace Flower Show.

She is not so benevolent, however, when her shy, sweet daughter Primrose (Natasha Little) starts taking more than a botanical interest in the handsome Colin. We suspect that the affair might not have such smooth sailing since the film tips us off early that Colin's headed for a little trouble. The first few minutes of the movie shows us a flash forward into Colin's future. We see him breaking into a flower show, stealing a bouquet and presenting it at Primrose's door. His prison may have been lenient, but this would be a pretty solid example of "parole violation."

Since the story is not especially compelling, what holds a film like this together are the characters. Owen does a fine job as Colin. He has the ability to convey a lot without speaking like '50s actors Robert Mitchum and Burt Lancaster. His quiet strength makes it more palatable when he is called upon to give faintly yucky speeches about the joys of gardening like the one he gives to his parole board about the delights he has gotten in discovering the power of giving life to plants. Kelly is also good as the feisty Fergus. From the beginning, it looks as though his character is on the way out, but Kelly manages to wrestle his role away from pathos and sappy sentimentality. Instead Kelly plays him as a man full of zest and fun, like Ruth Gordon's Maude in *Harold and Maude*. Also good is Mirren as the full-of-herself master gardener. In her grand hats, she sweeps into scenes, ready to take charge and start ordering the others around. In an instant, we see her go from cranky to amped up and perky once the TV cameras are on her. She likes all the attention but holds a faint disdain for the fans who love her. The rest of the cast play their rather limited roles well. As the tough prisoner turned softie, for example, Fogerty does a good job though he doesn't get to go beyond those confines.

The writer and director of the film is Joel Hershman, who did the much edgier *Hold Me, Thrill Me, Kiss Me*. Here, Hershman is in a mellower mood, letting the camera linger on a clump of violets or letting characters get by with lines like "Adversity is your ally." He captures the quiet joy of creation that gardening gives, though anyone who thinks gardening is a boring subject matter would probably not be convinced otherwise by this movie. The movie is a feel-good comedy so things are idealized in it. The gardens grow as expected, the warden is an old softie and the prisoners are more interested in peony beds than in gouging each other with gardening implements.

Critics who prefer their cinematic fare edgier and less sweet than *Greenfingers* gave the film pans. "If . . . your allergies to comedies bred from British-style mugging crossed with Disney-style prancing has, like mine flared up in recent years, this hybrid . . . will make you wheeze," wrote Lisa Schwartzbaum of *Entertainment Weekly*, who gave the film at D+. "Heart-tuggers don't come much more shameless than *Greenfingers*," wrote Kevin Thomas in the *Los Angeles Times*, though he does concede that the film "offers the genuine pleasure of watching real pros doing their stuff." Pam Grady at Reel.com felt more kindly toward the picture: "In a summer replete with animatronic dinosaurs, bellowing apes and android boys, *Greenfingers* offers the gentle, humanist humor of a tiptoe through the tulips." Charles Taylor of Salon.com was less impressed, offering,

"*Greenfingers* is certainly pleasant enough, and if you can put the preachiness out of mind, it's entertaining in its square, conventional way"

—*Jill Hamilton*

## CREDITS

**Colin Briggs:** Clive Owen
**Georgina Woodhouse:** Helen Mirren
**Fergus Wilkes:** David Kelly
**Governor Hodge:** Warren Clarke
**Tony:** Danny Dyer
**Jimmy:** Paterson Joseph
**Primrose Woodhouse:** Natasha Little
**Raw:** Adam Fogerty

**Origin:** Great Britain, USA
**Released:** 2000
**Production:** Travis Swords, Daniel J. Victor; Boneyard Film Company, Overseas Film Group; released by IDP Films
**Directed by:** Joel Hershman
**Written by:** Joel Hershman
**Cinematography by:** John Daly
**Music by:** Guy Dagul
**Sound:** Derek Norman
**Editing:** Justin Krish
**Art Direction:** Neesh Ruben
**Costumes:** Frances Tempest
**Production Design:** Tim Hutchinson
**MPAA rating:** R
**Running time:** 90 minutes

## REVIEWS

*Boxoffice.* December, 2000, p. 54.
*Chicago Sun-Times Online.* August 3, 2001.
*Entertainment Weekly.* August 3, 2001, p. 41.
*Los Angeles Times Online.* July 27, 2001.
*New York Times Online.* July 22, 2001.
*New York Times Online.* July 27, 2001.
*People.* August 5, 2001, p. 40.
*Sight and Sound.* September, 2001, p. 43.
*USA Today Online.* July 27, 2001.
*Variety.* October 16, 2000, p. 28.
*Washington Post.* August 3, 2001, p. WE34.

## QUOTES

Fergus (David Kelly) to Colin (Clive Owen): "Sometimes it takes very little to put things right."

## TRIVIA

The prisoners at Leyhill have been exhibiting their gardens at the Hampton Court and the Chelsea Flower Show for the past 10 years.

# Hannibal

*Break the Silence.*
—Movie tagline
*Never Forget Who He Is.*
—Movie tagline
*The world's most deliciously evil gentleman is back!*
—Movie tagline
*How long can a man stay silent before he returns to the thing he does best?*
—Movie tagline

 **Box Office:** $165.1 million

One of the most anticipated movies of the year, *Hannibal* boasted major talent across the board when it arrived in theaters almost 10 years to the day that its Oscar®-winning predecessor, *The Silence of the Lambs*, was released. Anthony Hopkins returned to reprise his award-winning role of Dr. Hannibal "The Cannibal" Lecter, a character who quickly became a cultural touchstone. Julianne Moore stepped into the shoes of Special Agent Clarice Starling when Jodie Foster, who also won an Oscar® for *Silence*, declined to do the sequel. The script, an adaptation of Thomas Harris's gorefest of a novel, is credited to Pulitzer Prize–winning playwright David Mamet and Oscar®-winning screenwriter Steven Zaillian. Ridley Scott, who, coincidentally, lost the Best Director award for *Thelma and Louise* to Jonathan Demme when *Silence* swept the Academy Award®s in 1992, signed on as director. Yet, despite all of these giants, *Hannibal* cannot be considered anything less than a major disappointment, a meandering, disjointed thriller with few thrills, whose main claim to fame is its perverse celebration of the grotesque, with bodily disfigurement a central motif.

*Silence* remains a classic of the horror genre—a psychological thriller whose central cat-and-mouse game between Lecter and Clarice is absolutely riveting. *Hannibal*, on the other hand, does not revolve around a compelling story or take the characters into an exciting or fresh direction. On the contrary, nothing about the film feels necessary, other than the desire to make a load of money off the fans who loved Demme's masterpiece.

Based on Harris's novel but altered, as we shall see, in significant ways, the film picks up the story 10 years after Dr. Lecter's escape from custody. The notorious psychiatrist who ate his patients is now looking after a library in Florence, Italy, where, surprisingly enough, no one recognizes him. (The novel explains his anonymity through the fact that Lecter has altered his face, but the film offers no reasonable explanation why he can move around unnoticed.) Meanwhile, Clarice, whose graduation from the FBI Academy marks the ending of *Silence*, is facing problems of her own. An FBI raid at the outset of the film goes awry, leaving five dead by Clarice's hand and putting her at odds with her superiors. Her battle within the government, particularly with a Justice Department official named Paul Krendler (Ray Liotta), is the essence of her story.

The main plot of *Hannibal*, however, is the quest for revenge by one of Lecter's former patients and his one surviving victim, a pedophile named Mason Verger (an uncredited Gary Oldman). Years ago, Lecter drugged him and persuaded him to cut off his face and feed it to his dogs. The makeup on Oldman is excellent. He is virtually unrecognizable but so hideous that looking at his non-face is hard to stomach. Now the horribly disfigured but wealthy Verger is coming forward with new information about Lecter, and Clarice is sent to interview him. Verger, however, does not really want to help the FBI find Lecter; instead, he is hatching a diabolical plan to capture his old nemesis and feed him alive to a pack of hungry pigs.

Lecter's sophistication and refinement make him the perfect lecturer on Italian art, and Hopkins is excellent in a role that he clearly relishes. The problem is that Lecter has lost his sense of mystery. Lecter in the first film is a mesmerizing presence, from his first appearance confronting the neophyte Clarice to his long walk to have "an old friend for dinner." Hopkins's eerie stillness and his haunting facial expressions in close-up make Lecter almost a force of nature, a primal, nightmarish figure who has joined the pantheon of great screen villains—at once frightening, charismatic, and even oddly sympathetic. In the sequel, however, the mystique is gone. He is now just another serial killer on the loose, albeit one who is cultured and educated.

Lecter's antagonist in Italy is a police inspector named Pazzi (Giancarlo Giannini), who is investigating the mysterious disappearance of Lecter's predecessor at the library. Pazzi and Lecter play their own game of cat and mouse— Lecter even gently taunts him about his dismissal from a bigger case and pronounces his name "patsy." Yet Pazzi never comes off as a real threat to Lecter, which makes their scenes together rather dull, whereas, in *Silence*, Lecter is truly engaged and intellectually challenged by Clarice.

Another problem with the Italian section of the film is that there really is no logical place for Clarice. She simply disappears from this part of Harris's novel, but the filmmakers, probably aware that moviegoers want to see this character, give her meaningless things to do. So we are treated to pointless scenes of her doing research and reflecting on her relationship with Lecter, even listening to tape recordings of her old interviews with him. This is a risky ploy since hearing Moore's voice on these interviews only reminds us of Foster's absence and makes these scenes, which should invoke our memories of the Lecter-Clarice relationship, more jarring than resonant.

Clarice receives a letter from Lecter, in which he sympathizes with her for her humiliation at the hands of the FBI while taunting her with her white-trash upbringing. Setting in motion a series of improbable plot turns, she tries to track down the origin of Lecter's letter by its scent and seeks out perfume stores throughout the world. Amazingly enough, Pazzi happens to see the Italian perfume store's security tape that Clarice has ordered, recognizes Lecter, does some research on the Internet (where he learns of Verger's reward for Lecter's capture), and proceeds to try to win Lecter's trust so that he can hand him over to Verger. Clarice even tries, to no avail, to warn Pazzi of the danger he is in when she figures out via the Internet that he is trying to catch Lecter on his own. These convoluted links between Clarice, Pazzi, and Verger are so forced and unbelievable and built on such a coincidental chain of events that one can only assume the filmmakers were desperate for a way to keep Clarice in the story.

Verger's minions are no match for Lecter in Italy. Lecter stabs and kills a henchman of Pazzi's when he bumps into Lecter to get his fingerprint (getting Lecter's fingerprint to verify that he has been found is the first requirement in claiming the reward). Later, Lecter subdues Pazzi and proceeds to hang and disembowel him. In the wake of the murder, Lecter returns to America, and the film virtually starts over. Where *Silence* is intricately plotted and Clarice's relationship to Lecter is developed beautifully in a series of quasi-therapy sessions that become the context for the pursuit of another serial killer, *Hannibal* merely plods along in a lackluster revenge plot.

Moore, usually one of our boldest actresses, is simply adequate as Clarice, but the role itself is very thin and does not give her much to explore. Clarice in *Silence* is a scrappy, poor kid battling her own demons as she gains Lecter's trust and saves a girl from a serial killer. Clarice in *Hannibal* is almost ancillary to the Verger-Lecter contest and a reactive character. Even her struggle with her superiors is not very interesting.

Verger thinks that putting Clarice in distress will draw out Lecter, so Verger enlists Krendler to ruin Clarice's career (the source of Krendler's hatred is not completely clear, although it seems to stem from Clarice rebuffing his sexual advances years ago). Verger manufactures a postcard supposedly sent by Lecter to Clarice to demonstrate that she is withholding evidence, and she is suspended from the Bureau. Lecter makes contact with Clarice, and they engage in a kind of impromptu therapy session via cell phone (making her confront all of her insecurities about her place in the FBI) as he leads her on a rambling trip through D.C.—a pointless, quasi-chase scene that goes nowhere. He is finally captured by Verger's henchmen and whisked away as Clarice watches helplessly.

Just when it seems that Verger may triumph in turning Lecter into pig food, Clarice appears at Verger's estate and rescues Lecter. Before they can get away, however, Clarice is shot and wounded, and Lecter must now rescue her. Lecter is miraculously able to walk among the wild pigs and not be eaten, and, before he departs, he even persuades Verger's doctor, Cordell (Zeljko Ivanek), to push Verger into the pig pen, where he is devoured. This is a completely farfetched climax. Does Lecter all of a sudden have superhuman mental powers as well as an immunity to pigs? It is ludicrous, after all, to think that Lecter is so persuasive that he can simply tell a loyal employee to kill his boss and he will obey. Moreover, since Verger is set up as a supposed match for Lecter, his easy demise is particularly disappointing. In the novel, Verger's death at the hands of his twisted lesbian sister, Margot, and a hungry eel is more grotesque, but at least it has a sick grandeur befitting the overall story. In fact, Margot's absence from the film version robs Verger's world of the internal intrigue that spices up the long, rambling novel.

What does not make sense in Harris's novel is the ending, which was roundly and justly criticized. In the novel, after Lecter rescues Clarice, they develop a genuine relationship in which he exorcises her memories of her dead father and she becomes a kind of replacement for Mischa, the sister he lost at an early age. (This back story, meant to explain Lecter's cannibalism, does not figure in the film.) Then Lecter holds a banquet for Clarice in which Krendler is the unwilling guest of honor; Lecter removes part of Krendler's brain, cooks it, and feeds it to him. The novel's ending is not only sickening in detailing the slow torture of a man forced to eat his own brain before being killed but also a complete betrayal of Clarice, who willingly and gleefully joins Lecter in partaking of the ghastly meal. Lecter and Clarice, improbably enough, become a couple and are last seen living the high life in Buenos Aires.

The film wisely discards this ludicrous twist in the Lecter-Clarice relationship, but the macabre dinner is still in the story. Krendler eats a piece of his brain (seeing a befuddled Ray Liotta with the top of his head removed and his brain exposed is an utterly ghoulish sight), but, instead of being darkly comic or scary, Lecter's culinary horror show is merely a disgusting, nonsensical ending for a film that never finds a compelling angle or engrossing story for its characters. At least Clarice does not turn cannibal, as in the novel. Although Lecter has drugged her, she valiantly tries to fight back. She is able to alert the authorities by telephone and traps Lecter, even handcuffing his wrist to hers (a fairly unlikely act given her drugged-out state), but he escapes before the police arrive. He even cuts off his own hand to free himself, apparently sparing hers because he loves her so much.

Considering the source material, not much could be done to improve the ending of Hannibal. At least the filmmakers wisely maintained the integrity of Clarice—the idea of her becoming both a cannibal and Lecter's lover was ridiculous in the novel and would have been a disaster on film. And yet the film's ending really takes us nowhere. It just brings us back to the beginning. Lecter is once again on the loose—in the last scene he is introducing a little boy to the pleasure of eating brains—and Clarice's position in the FBI is still in question.

Hannibal is a major travesty that not only wastes the talents of so many gifted people but also comes close to damaging the reputation of The Silence of the Lambs. The only winners in this disaster are Jonathan Demme and Jodie Foster, who wisely knew to stay away from this mess. Perhaps most disconcerting of all, however, is Ridley Scott's direction. He is responsible for some of the most visionary films in contemporary cinema, most notably Alien, Blade Runner, and Thelma and Louise. Even his lesser films usually exhibit his trademark visual splendor, which is sorely lacking in Hannibal. Scott has had the biggest financial successes of his career in the last two years with back-to-back blockbusters—Gladiator and Hannibal—but he seems to have lost his visual flair. While Gladiator is a solid, rousing update of Hollywood's old-fashioned Roman epics, it is not among Scott's most distinctive or innovative works, and Hannibal is clearly among his worst. One can only hope that Scott will soon return to the visually sumptuous, daring filmmaking that once defined him as a unique talent.

—Peter N. Chumo II

## CREDITS

**Hannibal Lecter:** Anthony Hopkins
**Clarice Sterling:** Julianne Moore
**Mason Verger:** Gary Oldman
**Paul Krendler:** Ray Liotta
**Barney:** Frankie Faison
**Pazzi:** Giancarlo Giannini
**Allegra Pazzi:** Francesca Neri
**Dr. Cordell Doemling:** Zeljko Ivanek
**Eveida Drumgo:** Hazelle Goodman
**FBI Agnet Pearsall:** David Andrews
**FBI Director Noonan:** Francis Guinan
**Gnocco:** Enrico Lo Verso

**Origin:** USA
**Released:** 2001
**Production:** Dino De Laurentiis, Martha De Laurentiis,
Ridley Scott; Scott Free; released by MGM
**Directed by:** Ridley Scott
**Written by:** David Mamet, Steven Zaillian
**Cinematography by:** John Mathieson
**Music by:** Hans Zimmer
**Sound:** Danny Michael
**Editing:** Pietro Scalia
**Art Direction:** David Crank
**Costumes:** Janty Yates
**Production Design:** Norris Spencer
**MPAA rating:** R
**Running time:** 131 minutes

## REVIEWS

*Boxoffice.* April, 2001, p. 239.
*Chicago Sun-Times Online.* February 9, 2001.
*Entertainment Weekly.* February 16, 2001, p. 67.
*New York Times Online.* February 9, 2001.
*Newsweek.* January 29, 2001, p. 62.
*Newsweek.* February 12, 2001, p. 56.
*Rolling Stone.* March 1, 2001, p. 56.
*Time.* February 12, 2001, p. 84.
*USA Today Online.* February 9, 2001.
*Variety.* February 5, 2001, p. 37.
*Washington Post Online.* February 9, 2001.

## QUOTES

Hannibal (Anthony Hopkins) to Clarice (Julianne Moore): "Is this coincidence, or are you back on the case? If so, goody goody."

# Happenstance (The Beating of the Butterfly's Wings) (Le Battement d'Ailes du Papillon)

*Chance, chaos, destiny, fusion, liaisons.* Merde
*happens.*
—Movie tagline

A bald, gnomic figure, who walks into the middle of Laurent Firode's romantic comedy from France,
*Happenstance*, expounds, "The most insignificant gesture can change the world. The batting of a butterfly's wings
over the Atlantic can cause a hurricane over the Pacific."
Firode, for his debut feature, doesn't pursue such a chain of
causality to any kind of grand geophysical finale. Instead, he
calls it quits somewhere in between, settling instead for
romantic irony.

The film gets under way with Irene (Audrey Tatou,
France's latest boxoffice sensation), a pretty shopgirl, being
harangued on a Paris subway by an inquisitive middle-aged
woman with a questionnaire, who tells her that today, under
the light of the full moon, she will meet her soul mate.
Younes (Faudel), a young, Algerian immigrant, also sitting
across from Irene, perks up when he hears Irene's birthdate.
After Irene gets down at her stop, he tells the woman that he
too was born on the same day. From this point on, all the
wayward coincidences that comprise the film serve to reunite
Irene and Younes at the end.

Irene, we come to learn, is an example of someone who
needs romance to be thrust upon her. When approached by a
fortune-teller in a café, she admits flat out that she doesn't
believe she's going to be finding any love. Audrey Tatou's
star quality, along with an affecting chamber music score,
bolster the film's romantic leanings. If Firode, as writer-
director, were to have abandoned his philosophical
cleverness and kept his sights on just Irene, his film would
have had far more universal appeal. Instead, he juxtaposes
Irene's fate with that of Richard (Eric Savin), who is trying
to juggle his responsibility to his devoted wife, Marie
(Nathalie Besancon), with the demands of his consuming
mistress, Elsa (Lysaine Meis). No doubt Richard is meant to
represent those who pursue romance at all costs. In his first
scene, when he's jolted out of bed by the message Marie has
left on his answering machine, the film shows him in full

frontal nudity. This sudden frankness finds its correlative in our being allowed access to his neurotic thoughts. Even so, Richard emerges a mere curiosity in relation to Irene. When he's reunited with Marie, also in the film's last scene, there's little dramatic payoff.

Viewers able to recall Jean-Pierre Jeunet and Marc Caro's *City of Lost Children* (1995) will find nothing new in Firode's narrative hijinks. Those earlier explorers of this terrain showed in their "children's film" for adults how a flea could cause a steamer to run aground within the laws of a crazy fantasy universe. Firode has toned down that very same approach, and given it a romantic twist.

Irene's life is affected by the intersection of two other independent lines of cause-and-effect. Luc (Eric Feldman), a ritzy but unemployed twenty-something, is taken by his mother (Lily Boulogne) to visit his Granny (Francoise Bertin) in the country. His Granny presents him with a coffee-maker, which fails to work. This sets into motion one chain of coincidences. Granny sets out to return the coffee-maker to the department store where Irene works. Her plight elicits the sympathy of the scruffy Bobby (Frederique Bouraly), who steals a new appliance for her under Irene's nose. This gets Irene fired from her job.

Granny has also presented Luc with a box of macaroons she has baked herself, which gives rise to an even more incredible chain of events. Luc's mother is so disgusted with their taste that she throws one out the car window while driving back. A pigeon nibbles at its remnants, then flies towards the city, only to relieve itself over a couple who have just collected a set of prints from a photo store, where Irene's roommate, the plain-looking Stephanie (Irene Ismailoff), works. As Stephanie wipes off the offensive dripping, she recognizes the face of her long lost lover, Franck (Mathieu Ducrez), now a paramedic, whom we have earlier seen being snapped by the couple after an incident on a subway platform. When Irene returns home in a depressed mood, her roommate tells her that she will be meeting Franck that night. Irene senses she is not wanted, and storms out with her things.

Unemployed and homeless, Irene, on her way to her mother's in a cab, hits her nose against the window pane at a sudden stop. This requires stitches at a hospital. It is here, once she is discharged with strips of bandage across her face, that she is reunited under the full moon with her soul mate, Younes, similarly bandaged, who has been led there by a quite different, but equally fortuitous, set of circumstances.

Critics here have excused the film falling short of its philosophical aspirations. Elizabeth Weitzman in the *Daily News* finds its coincidences "contrived," but is willing to accept it as "breezy escapist fare." A.O. Scott in the *New York Times* calls Audrey Tatou a "cross between Audrey Hepburn and Giulietta Masina," and adds that, in conjunc-

tion with *Amelie*, released at the same time, she may turn out to be "the queen of art-house serendipity."

—*Vivek Adarkar*

## CREDITS

**Irene:** Audrey Tautou
**Younes:** Faudel
**Richard:** Eric Savin
**Luc:** Eric Feldman
**Marie:** Nathalie Besancon
**Elsa:** Lysaine Meis
**Luc's mother:** Lily Boulogne
**Granny:** Francoise Bertin
**Bobby:** Frederique Bouraly
**Stephanie:** Irene Ismailoff

**Origin:** France
**Language:** French
**Released:** 2000
**Production:** Anne-Dominique Toussaint, Pascal Judelwicz; Les Films des Tournelles, Les Films en Hiver; released by Lot 47 Films
**Directed by:** Laurent Firode
**Written by:** Laurent Firode
**Cinematography by:** Jean-Rene Duveau
**Music by:** Peter Chase
**Editing:** Didier Ranz
**Art Direction:** Laurent Firode
**Costumes:** Najat Kas
**MPAA rating:** R
**Running time:** 97 minutes

## REVIEWS

*Boxoffice.* December, 2001, p. 59.
*Entertainment Weekly.* November 23, 2001, p. 55.
*Los Angeles Times Online.* December 21, 2001.
*New York Daily News Online.* November 2, 2001.
*New York Post Online.* November 2, 2001.
*New York Times Online.* November 2, 2001.
*Village Voice Online.* November 6, 2001.
*Washington Post.* February 15, 2002, p. WE45.

# Happy Accidents

*Sometimes the future is better than it used to be.*
—Movie tagline

**Box Office:** $.5 million

Brad Anderson, the writer, director and editor of *Happy Accidents*, was also behind the 1998 indie hit, *Next Stop Wonderland*. This time out, he wanted to do another love story, but didn't want to do one for a major studio. "I didn't want to get on this course where I was going to be doing just big, goofy romantic comedies with the latest cast of *Dawson's Creek*," he said in an interview with the *Los Angeles Times*.

By doing his film as another indie, he did avoid using *Dawson's Creek* actors, but he'd probably be hard pressed to come up with an argument that *Happy Accidents* isn't at least a little goofy. For one thing, one of the love interests in his film claims to be a time traveler. "The initial premise was what would be the most absurd thing that in the course of a relationship between two people would throw the whole relationship into a tailspin or freak it out and how that relationship would proceed from that time," Anderson also said. Time travel did indeed fit the bill for absurdity. What he ends up with is sort of a sci fi/romantic comedy. If nothing else, it would be one of the few films in the section of the local video store for that particular genre.

Ruby Weaver (Marisa Tomei) is a single girl living in New York. Her life isn't so great. She's just been fired from her job as a telephone operator after being a little flirty with a caller. And her love life stinks, too. She and her friends, including the requisite sidekick Gretchen (Nadia Dajani), are so unlucky in love that they periodically gather to put new photos in their "ex-files." The box is filled with photos of rejected boyfriends, including "the artist," "the Jew for Jesus," and "the fetishist." Ruby's problem is that she's a "fixer." She finds wholly inappropriate guys, tries to fix them up and when that doesn't work, she dumps them. Ruby knows she has a problem and talks about it often with her therapist (Holland Taylor). The therapist gives her daily affirmations to repeat in front of the mirror, like "I am willing to find a balance between my own needs and my concern for others."

When she meets Sam Deed (Vincent D'Onofrio), she briefly thinks that she might have found someone normal. He seems nice, he works for a hospice and he's kind of fun. She is so desperate for a good relationship that she sleeps with him the first night and lets him move into her apartment a few days later.

There are red flags all over the place with this guy, but Ruby doesn't seem to notice them. He is deathly afraid of little dogs, he is prone to staring off into space in a trance, and he doesn't seem to know some basic things about living on Earth. He is flummoxed by a turntable and doesn't know how to "court" a lady. Ruby doesn't think to much about all this because he claims to be a small town guy from Dubuque,

Iowa, and she thinks it might be due to his upbringing. But his idiosyncrasies get harder to ignore.

Finally one day, Sam shares a secret: he is a back-traveler from the year 2439. He says that in the future, most people are clones called Gene Dupes made by corporations. He claims to be from a family of anarchists, those who believed in reproducing the old-fashioned way. He says he back-traveled to find Ruby after seeing a picture of her in a curio shop. He was so entranced by the picture that he had to come back and find her. (He guessed she was in New York because people in the photo were wearing so much black.)

You'd think this would be the point that Ruby tosses Sam out into the street, but instead of thinking that he's crazy, she decides that he is doing a fun role-playing game. "He's a freak, but he sure tells a good story!" she says. Sam also has some ominous undertones in his story. Ruby finds a notebook full of drawings of a woman and a name written over and over, obsessively. He says his little sister drowned after being at the beach alone, but later changes his story so that he is there at the beach, too. He also tells Ruby that she is going to die the following Friday. Is he the one who's going to kill her? Did he kill his sister, too?

On the other hand, some of the stranger things Sam says seem like they could really be true. He is full of tales—including the information that the Dubuque of the future borders the Atlantic Ocean, all plants and animals died after the Great Infestation and there was a great Petroleum War of 2011—and the amount of details he has about these events signal that he either lived through them, or he is highly demented.

The thing that doesn't work about this story is that it seems like Ruby, no matter how bad her past dating life was, would not want to get involved with Sam. Even when they first meet, he is pretty weird. He shows up unannounced at her door to return a book he found that she'd left in the park. After giving her the book, he follows her to her new job as a teacher of English as a second language. Instead of being romantic, it seems a little creepy, but Ruby doesn't seem to notice. Also, Sam's behavior is beyond eccentric, it's bizarre. He seems to have an obvious mental illness and Ruby's refusal to examine that is disingenuous at the least.

But then, Ruby doesn't seem to have a lot of gumption. When she's making a decision in the film, her argument for going the course that she's going to take is, "I have a therapist to answer to!" The film explains away Ruby's lack of judgment as being a somewhat astute decision, considering the other love options she could be having. Her girlfriend Gretchen, for example, is putting up with a boyfriend, Mark (Sean Gullette) who likes to pretend that he is *Sixteen Candles'* Anthony Michael Hall in bed.

With such a flaky character to play, Tomei has her work cut out for her. She does a good job being a vulnerable romantic, but it's very difficult to see why she would be attracted to such a psycho. She seems moderately smart, she's attractive, and doesn't have to be nearly as needy as she is. D'Onofrio puts in an enjoyably weird performance. He is childlike and will stop to marvel at a smell he encounters on the street. At the same time, he is vaguely menacing and walks with a strange lurch in his step (maybe it's leftover from his role in *Men In Black*). At times he seems smart, like when he exhibits his knowledge of several languages including ancient Greek, but other times, he blurts out embarrassing tales of time travel in inappropriate situations. D'Onofrio plays his character too quirky to be romantic in any traditional sense. He might be fine as an amusing houseguest, but having him as boyfriend material is kind of stretching it. Taylor is excellent as the therapist who appears cool and calm no matter what kind of bizarre story Ruby is telling her. Also good is Dajani as the sassy best friend (are there any other kind in romantic comedies?) As Lillian, Ruby's mother, Tovah Feldshuh, has a poignant scene where she describes how she finally got her husband to stop drinking after years of alcohol abuse, only to find that his sobriety made their marriage lose its spark. Anthony Michael Hall is game in a cameo that's not particularly flattering to him.

Critics generally liked the film. Roger Ebert of the *Chicago Sun-Times* wrote, "*Happy Accidents* is essentially silliness crossed with science fiction. The actors make it fun to watch." Pam Grady of Reel.com said: "It's warm-hearted (and) funny. If you should happen to stumble upon it by chance at the local multiplex, give it a shot." Jane Sumner of the *Dallas Morning News* wrote, "It's a meet-cute Twilight Zone with a kiss blown to the shade of Rod Serling." Jan Stuart in the *Los Angeles Times* wasn't as enamored and wrote, "Any picture about a guy tattooed with a bar code seems more like an Orwellian horror story than a dewy romantic comedy."

—*Jill Hamilton*

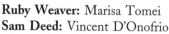

## CREDITS

**Ruby Weaver:** Marisa Tomei
**Sam Deed:** Vincent D'Onofrio
**Lilian:** Tovah Feldshuh
**Gretchen:** Nadia Dajani
**Therapist:** Holland Taylor
**Trip:** Richard Portnow
**Mark:** Sean Gullette
**Betty:** Cara Buono
**Claire:** Liana Pai
**Robin:** Tamara Jenkins
**Jose:** Jose Zuniga
**Actor:** Anthony Michael Hall (Cameo)

**Origin:** USA

**Released:** 2000
**Production:** Susan A. Stover; released by Independent Film Channel (IFC)
**Directed by:** Brad Anderson
**Written by:** Brad Anderson
**Cinematography by:** Terry Stacy
**Music by:** Evan Lurie
**Sound:** Noah Vivekanand Timan
**Music Supervisor:** Linda Cohen
**Editing:** Brad Anderson
**Art Direction:** Lucio Seixas
**Costumes:** Victoria Farrell
**Production Design:** Susan Black
**MPAA rating:** R
**Running time:** 110 minutes

## REVIEWS

*Boxoffice.* April, 2000, p. 223.
*Chicago Sun-Times Online.* September 14, 2001.
*Los Angeles Times Online.* September 14, 2001.
*New York Times Online.* August 24, 2001.
*Variety.* February 7, 2000, p. 55.
*Washington Post.* September 14, 2001, p. C5.

## QUOTES

Sam (Vincent D'Onofrio) to Ruby (Marisa Tomei): "Don't bad things take longer than good ones, but good things seem to fly by?"

# Hardball

*The most important thing in life is showing up.*
—Movie tagline

 **Box Office:** $40.1 million

It's difficult to imagine that any movie critic was really all that geared up to see *Hardball*. After all, as one put it, it looked more than a little like "The Bad News Bears N the Hood." It was about a grouchy guy who had to coach a down and out baseball team. It threatened to be uplifting. And perhaps most unforgivable of all, it starred Keanu Reeves, an actor who has been described as "historically vacuous." But *Hardball* had enough going for it that it won over more than a few critics. Of course they all had to point out that they were quite aware that the film was formulaic and that they were cynics who were not usually fooled, but that the movie just may have gotten to them anyway.

Audiences were less wary than critics to go to the theater to see Reeves in a *Bad News Bears*-type film. The weekend it came out, it was the number one movie. It did quite well in comparison to the same weekend in other years, too, despite being released the weekend after the World Trade Center bombings, when many Americans were sticking close to home.

It's odd that the film was so often considered to be formulaic, since it was based on a true story. Daniel Coyle, a self-proclaimed yuppie, detailed his experiences coaching a little league team from the infamous Chicago housing projects Cabrini Green in his book *Hardball: A Season in the Projects.* Roger Ebert of the *Chicago Sun-Times,* who didn't read the book, speculated that the formulaic structure of the film was not the fault of the book but rather that the "screenplay shows signs of having been tilted in the direction of the basic Hollywood workshop story structure in which we get a crisis because it's time for one."

The film starts out markedly different from the book. For one thing, the hero, Conor O'Neill (Reeves), is about the furthest thing there is from a yuppie. In the opening scenes, he's in jail and we learn that he owes several thousand dollars to various nefarious types. O'Neill is a compulsive gambler and his technique of continuing to gamble with different bookies in order to pay off the bookies he already owes just isn't working out as a smart financial plan. At least two of his bookies have sent off their goons to threaten O'Neill and he has to do something fast.

He goes to the banking firm where his old buddy, Jimmy (Mike McClone), is a successful investment banker. Jimmy, who is wise to O'Neill's usual tricks, won't give him any money but does offer him a deal: if O'Neill will agree to coach a little league team in Cabrini Green, Jimmy will pay him $500 a week. Jimmy is partly being generous but partly being a jerk, too. Although Jimmy loves the idea that he's "giving back to the community," he's not so interested in actually doing the dirty work himself. O'Neill is not very hot on the idea, but he has to do it because his back-up plan—betting $12,000 with a new bookie on a Bulls game—won't give him the money he needs in time.

O'Neill is taken aback by the kids when he meets them. Even though they're just little ones, they've already done some hard living and act and talk tough. "What position do you play?" O'Neill asks one kid. The kid points to his crotch and says, "Big willie." Director Brian Robbins (*Varsity Blues* and *Ready to Rumble*) edited out some of the rawer language so that the film could get a PG-13 rating, but these kids don't say stuff like "heck" and "darn." They call everyone "bitch" and are so foul-mouthed it makes one wonder what these kids were saying before the edit job.

At the outset, it looks like we can guess where this is going. The team is filled with the usual "types." There's

Jefferson (Julian Griffith), a chubby kid who can't play that well because of his asthma; G-Baby (DeWayne Warren), the one that's too small to play but desperately wants to fit in; and the requisite sullen older kid, Miles (A. Delon Ellis Jr.) O'Neill also encounters Elizabeth Wilkes (Diane Lane), the kids' fetching teacher at the Catholic school. We can guess that romance is in the works when O'Neill meets her and discovers that she is not a nun, like he'd assumed. "Thank God!" he enthuses. We can also guess that these kids will win O'Neill over and he'll grow from the experience, maybe even give up gambling. And it doesn't seem like too much of a stretch to imagine that this rag-tag team might end up vying for—and possibly winning—the Big Game.

All of this does indeed happen, but it's not all as awful as it sounds like it would be. Although the film touches all the usual bases, it doesn't linger on them like a similar film would. O'Neill does romance the teacher, but it's made to be just part of the story and not that big of a deal. The team does go from a bunch of kids who don't know what they're doing on the field to a group of champions, but we're spared seeing the nitty-gritty details of how all that transpires.

In fact, for a film about baseball, *Hardball* focuses surprisingly little on the actually game. O'Neill is the team's coach, but he never appears to give them any advice about how to play or anything like that. Director Robbins shows plenty of scenes on the field, but the scenes don't concentrate on specific plays, but rather a more impressionist feeling of how the game is going in general. The scenes are just as notable for showing the bad condition that the old, weed-filled field is in as it is for who made what catch when.

Instead of hitting the big obvious emotional checkpoints, Robbins does a good job of hitting subtler ones. He shows the poor conditions that the boys have to live in, but doesn't hammer it in in a preachy manner. When O'Neill casually keeps the kids on the field longer than the 6:00 p.m. deadline, we see that the deadline's there because after that hour, neighborhood gang bangers start blocking the doors to the apartments. O'Neill drops one of the boys off at home and sees all the tenants sitting on the floor. The boy explains that the people are staying low to avoid stray bullets. Without pointing it out so bluntly, Robbins let the audience realize how shocking it is to see how the teen gangs make living in the projects a scary hell.

To be sure, *Hardball* is not a masterwork. The fact that it's better than one would guess counts for something, but doesn't make it great. There are a lot of clunker lines, an overwrought soundtrack and the aforementioned predictability.

Reeves does a good job here, but he's limited by his abilities. On the other hand, no one but a master actor could make lines like, "I swear, I was lifted to a better place. He made me a better person, even if for just that moment," sound like a real thing a real person would say. The best acting is by the kids, many of whom had never acted before.

It's too bad that the movie mostly treats them like one big lump of kids instead of individuals because these small actors would have been up to the task. When they do get to act, they are sassy and fun. "Coach, you ain't trying to get Ms. Wilkes, are ya?" says Jefferson. "No," answers O'Neill. "Good, 'cause I already tried and she ain't having it," answers Jefferson.

"Cynics may roll their eyes at *Hardball*'s earnestness, but the movie proves even the most conventional stories can move and engage you, provided they're told well," wrote the *Miami Herald*'s Rene Rodriguez. Kevin Thomas of the *Los Angeles Times* called the film "a surefire heart-tugger made with skill and judgment." *Entertainment Weekly*'s Lisa Schwartzbaum was less enthralled. "The movie is so littered with cliches of genre, as well as cliches of artifice in Reeves' pained performance, that any semblance of social reality goes foul," she wrote, giving the film a D.

—*Jill Hamilton*

**Conor O'Neill:** Keanu Reeves
**Elizabeth Wilkes:** Diane Lane
**Ticky Tobin:** John Hawkes
**Andre Ray Peetes:** Bryan C. Hearne
**Jefferson Albert Tibbs:** Julian Griffith
**Miles Pennfield II:** A. Delon Ellis Jr.
**Jarius "G-Baby" Evans:** DeWayne Warren
**Jamal:** Michael Jordan
**Matt Hyland:** D.B. Sweeney
**Jimmy Fleming:** Mike McGlone
**Duffy:** Graham Beckel
**Fink:** Mark Margolis

**Origin:** USA
**Released:** 2001
**Production:** Mike Tollin, Brian Robbins, Tina Nides; Fireworks Pictures; released by Paramount Pictures
**Directed by:** Brian Robbins
**Written by:** John Gatins
**Cinematography by:** Tom Richmond
**Music by:** Mark Isham
**Sound:** David Obermeyer
**Music Supervisor:** Michael McQuarn
**Editing:** Ned Bastille
**Costumes:** Francine Jamison-Tanchuck
**Production Design:** Jaymes Hinkle
**MPAA rating:** PG-13
**Running time:** 106 minutes

*Chicago Sun-Times Online.* September 14, 2001.
*Entertainment Weekly.* September 21, 2001, p. 56.
*Los Angeles Times Online.* September 14, 2001.
*New York Times Online.* September 15, 2001.
*USA Today Online.* September 14, 2001.
*Variety.* September 10, 2001, p. 57.
*Washington Post.* September 14, 2001, p. WE39.

# Harry Potter and the Sorcerer's Stone (Harry Potter and the Philosopher's Stone)

*Let the magic begin.*
—Movie tagline
*A journey beyond your imagination.*
—Movie tagline

 **Box Office:** $291.6 million

In the opening minutes of the film *Harry Potter and the Sorcerer's Stone*, Professor Dumbledore (Richard Harris) tells Hagrid (Robbie Coltrane) after he drops the infant Harry on the doorstep of his aunt and uncle: "This child will be famous. There won't be a child alive who doesn't know his name."

Certainly, that prophecy has come true. Harry Potter is the most famous child on the planet, as a result of an unprecedented and still largely unexplained publishing phenomenon. How did a children's book by a previously unknown author, J.K. Rowling, concerning a British schoolchild who is a wizard, become a worldwide sensation, spawning sequels that generate lengthy queues at bookstores when they are released?

Substantial children's books that achieve mass sales have been infrequent in recent decades. Most best selling books for children have been thin or exploitative; the most recent juvenile publishing phenomenon prior to Harry Potter was the cheap-fright "Goosebumps" series. Parents and educators have been excited about Harry Potter, the books have gotten high praise from critics, and the series has been hailed as one of the rare examples of something kids like also being edifying.

With the release of what is sure to be only the first among many Harry Potter movies, this incredibly popular saga has become an overarching commercial franchise. AOL Time Warner, the enormous media giant, launched an all-out, multi-platform publicity and merchandising campaign for Potter paraphernalia prior to the movie's release on the weekend before Thanksgiving 2001. It was guaranteed to capitalize on the existing mountain of Harry Potter interest and to make good on Dumbledore's prediction that no child alive would be ignorant of the little British 11-year-old with the bangs and round glasses.

The payoff was immediate. *Harry Potter* broke the all-time U.S. single-day box office record on its opening day (eclipsing that set by *Star Wars Episode 1: Phantom Menace* in 1999), raking in close to $30 million on November 16, 2001. (It debuted in England under the title *Harry Potter and the Philosopher's Stone* 12 days earlier, smashing records there too.) Parents and their children endured long lines to buy advance tickets. Before the movie even began, the spin-off advertising was in full gear. A slick animated commercial advertisement hawking a new Harry Potter video game appeared with the trailers before the feature. In fact, the toy industry was counting heavily on Harry Potter merchandise to bring cheer to an otherwise gloomy 2001 holiday season.

With all this good will and high expectations going for it, it was certain *Harry Potter* would not only be a blockbuster, but that it would delight millions of Potter fans. And it appears it has done exactly that. But for those looking to find a plausible explanation of the Potter phenomenon, the movie is a vast disappointment. Whatever it is that "clicked" about Rowling's book can't easily be discerned in this bloated, episodic, cheesy, and frustrating fantasy film.

Director Chris Columbus—who certainly knows how to make crowd-pleasing hits such as *Gremlins, Mrs. Doubtfire, Home Alone,* and *Jingle All the Way*—shared screenwriting credits with Steve Kloves (*Wonders Boys*) and two others. They approach the material with the obvious goal of not offending any of the legions of Potter faithful by leaving any character or chapter out of the original 300-page novel. This play-it-safe approach makes for a badly bungled movie that has everything but the kitchen sink. The Potter books have succeeded, as did the *Lord of the Ring* trilogy and other famous fantasies, by creating and detailing an entire world of make-believe. They are page-turners because they string together a series of episodes and scenes while keeping the elements of an epic saga. Columbus has no idea how to make this work on the screen. Instead, he keeps all the important scenes, characters, and references, but none of the tension. Plot points play out by being announced in the dialogue; tension is almost nonexistent, and scene follows scene with little connection or overall buildup.

Even at an attention-challenging 142 minutes, the story of Potter's first year at the Hogwarts School of Witchcraft and Wizardry doesn't fit on the screen. Approaching this gold mine with caution, no one in the project was brave enough to zero in on a certain part of the story, to lop off unnecessary characters, or to stop the meandering exposition and get to the point. Much of the first 100 minutes or so is simply a long introduction to what happens at the school and why Potter is so famous. Characters and scenes are completely transparent. And—fatally for a film of this kind—nothing is left to the imagination.

Books that delve in the supernatural have their own kinds of logic and their own techniques for creating magic. They weave a literary spell. Moviemaking magic can't use a linear format to succeed. Columbus confuses technical trickery with magic. "Magic" things happen so frequently in this film—ghosts of past graduates moving through the school, figures in paintings on the wall moving, staircases rearranging themselves, candles suspended—that they become routine, mere parts of the scenery. Scenes are presented that depend on the audience's familiarity with the book; thus, when the giant Hagrid takes Harry to get his school supplies, he moves some bricks in the wall and announces "Diacon Alley"—a sort of alternative universe of London sorcery shops. Merely to announce the name of the place seems to require no other explanation. Those few people coming to the film with no prior knowledge of the story line will find themselves alternately scratching their heads in confusion and wondering what all the fuss was about.

The movie makes it all too clear that Rowling has borrowed heavily from pre-existing material to weave her stories. One obvious source is the *Star Wars* canon. The story features a wayward Hogwarts graduate, Voldemort, who has gone over to the "dark side" and murdered Harry's parents. His powers are sapped and he needs the sorcerer's stone and its energy to regenerate himself; can anyone say "the force"? When he is finally revealed in the film's climactic showdown, Voldemort talks with a kind of gasping wheeze, just like Darth Vader.

The sequence where Harry's Gryffindor housemates are playing the game of "quidditch" against the rival house of Slytherin is very reminiscent of the pod race in *The Phantom Menace,* complete with crowds in towers cheering, and the evil opponents cheating and jostling Harry and his teammates as they all ride around on broomsticks chasing various balls. The biggest difference is that the special effects are quite ordinary in comparison with *Star Wars.* The gigantic troll who terrorizes Harry's friends on Halloween is a rather awesome creature, though he looks more like an ogre than a troll. However, a three-headed dog guarding the entrance to the stone's hiding place is not too convincing a computer creation. The deadly chess game that Harry and his friends must play to get to the stone is well done, with plenty of slashing metal as the conquering piece draws a sword and smashes the captured piece to bits. There's also an enchanted mirror that can bewitch its admirers, a newly hatched dragon that is superfluous to the plot, and a very handsomely executed centaur who saves Harry but whose place in the fantasy world isn't clearly defined.

No fewer than eight separate special effects companies, including George Lucas's Industrial Light and Magic, were enlisted in the film—certainly a record. That may account for the unevenness of the technical achievements here since they range from quite ordinary to intermittently spectacular. Why the special effects couldn't be entrusted to one outfit is unclear, but one thing that is clear is that Warner Brothers and producer David Heyman spared no expense, and why not? It was a guaranteed blockbuster from the get-go, with no doubt the brightest "green light" in Hollywood history. The film is certainly handsomely mounted and lushly photographed, yet the editing is far from seamless and the story has a herky-jerky quality as it lurches from one chapter's events to the next in a disconnected, rambling fashion.

John Williams's characteristically grandiose score is overdone, obvious, and often dreadful. Too many reaction shots show the director is trying to cue in the audience to the sense of wonder in Harry and his classmates. It's a poor substitute for really awe-inspiring moviemaking. If the movie is weaving a spell, we don't need to see the characters in the film with their mouths agape, over and over, just as we don't need to hear the music swell or tinkle as every new scene unfolds.

The acting is similarly uneven. Coltrane plays Hagrid as a typically absent-minded, not-too-bright giant. His effectiveness as a believable character is continually compromised because he has to say repeatedly "I shouldn't have told you that" when he reveals the next significant plot point by blurting out a secret to the kids. No need for anyone to think too hard in this film. Maggie Smith, the venerable British actress, looks a little befuddled playing the stern but kind headmistress Professor McGonagall. It's been a long time since Richard Harris had as significant a role as the iconic Dumbledore, and while he's sufficient, he fails to give the enigmatic character much memorable authority. John Cleese has rather high billing for an extremely small cameo part as a ghost named Nearly Headless Nick. Alan Rickman goes way over the top with a villain's piercing-eyed, slow-talking demeanor as the misunderstood Professor Snape.

Among the child actors, four have significant parts. Newcomer Daniel Radcliffe landed the plum part of Potter; it's sort of like winning the lottery, and he does a credible job of inhabiting the cartoonish face that the books' illustrator has bestowed on the protagonist. Radcliffe manages to stay calm and understated while flying about on brooms; otherwise, he seems unremarkable. Even less successful is Emma Watson as Hermione Granger. While the know-it-all Hermione is supposed to be annoying, it's rather distracting to see an actress move her mouth quite so broadly while enunciating; Watson looks like a student in an acting class trying to please her instructor. Tom Felton as Draco Malfoy is a rather too-obvious annoying rich-kid bully. Most suc-

cessful is Rupert Grint as Ron Weasley, Harry's luckless but plucky best friend. With his genuinely childlike expressions of exasperation and puzzlement, Grint steals nearly every scene he's in, and he makes a far more compelling emotional center to the movie than Radcliffe's Potter.

With the lay-in-on-thick, everything-must-be-included approach of director Columbus, this *Harry Potter* has the dreary feel of a merchandising vehicle rather than a film that takes true delight in its material. Most of the quirkiness and tongue-in-cheek humor that redeems Rowling's highly derivative fantasy is missing from this ponderous compendium of Potter moments. It's more like a "greatest hits" album than a movie. Worse yet, there's no emotional heart to the proceedings. Talking about the mirror, Dumbledore tells Potter to be wary of following his dreams. Later, he talks in passing of love and courage. But Potter's quest doesn't have mythic qualities; it's unclear what he is all about, why he is destined to be great, and what his true purpose is in life. Without some grander themes, Potter seems destined to have a rather pedestrian sort of fame, and in the real world his powers are quickly becoming dedicated solely to rampant merchandising. Immediately after the film's release, Rowling bought an expensive Scottish mansion and went into semi-seclusion, refusing to say much about what she thought of the phenomenon she had unleashed upon the world. No wonder.

—*Michael Betzold*

## CREDITS

**Harry Potter:** Daniel Radcliffe
**Ron Weasley:** Rupert Grint
**Hermione Granger:** Emma Watson
**Hagrid:** Robbie Coltrane
**Albus Dumbledore:** Richard Harris
**Professor McGonagall:** Maggie Smith
**Madame Hooch:** Zoe Wanamaker
**Professor Snape:** Alan Rickman
**Prof. Quirrell/Voldemort:** Ian Hart
**Mr. Ollivander:** John Hurt
**Draco Malfoy:** Tom Felton
**Dudley Dursley:** Harry Melling
**Uncle Vernon Dursley:** Richard Griffiths
**Aunt Petunia Dursley:** Fiona Shaw
**Nearly Headless Nick:** John Cleese
**Professor Flitwick:** Warwick Davis
**Mrs. Weasley:** Julie Walters
**Oliver Wood:** Sean Biggerstaff
**Mr. Filch:** David Bradley
**Neville Longbottom:** Matthew Lewis

**Origin:** USA

**Released:** 2001
**Production:** David Heyman; 1492 Films, Heyday Films; released by Warner Bros.
**Directed by:** Chris Columbus
**Written by:** Steven Kloves
**Cinematography by:** John Seale
**Music by:** John Williams
**Sound:** John Midgley
**Editing:** Richard Francis-Bruce
**Art Direction:** Neil Lamont, John King
**Costumes:** Judianna Makovsky
**Production Design:** Stuart Craig
**MPAA rating:** PG
**Running time:** 152 minutes

## REVIEWS

*Chicago Sun-Times Online.* November 16, 2001.
*Entertainment Weekly.* November 23, 2001, p. 52.
*Los Angeles Times Online.* November 16, 2001.
*New York Times Online.* November 16, 2001.
*People.* November 26, 2001, p. 39.
*USA Today Online.* November 16, 2001.
*Variety.* November 12, 2001, p. 27.
*Washington Post.* November 16, 2001, p. WE41.

## QUOTES

Mr. Ollivander (John Hurt) to Harry (Daniel Radcliffe): "I think we can expect great things from you."

## TRIVIA

The Harry Potter series (thus far) have sold more than 100 million copies in over 46 languages.

## AWARDS AND NOMINATIONS

**Nomination:**
**Oscars 2001:** Art Dir./Set Dec., Costume Des., Score
**British Acad. 2001:** Costume Des., Film, Sound, Support. Actor (Coltrane), Visual FX
**Broadcast Film Critics 2001:** Score.

# Head Over Heels

*Unleash your inner model.*
—Movie tagline

*Four supermodel roommates. One regular girl. The guy next door doesn't stand a chance.*
—Movie tagline

 **Box Office:** $10.4 million

The "story by" credit for *Head Over Heels* lists four people, the screenwriters Ron Burch and David Kidd, plus two producers John J. Strauss and Ed Decter. Judging by what they came up with, it seems like each one of those guys had a completely different vision of what the movie should be like. Either the four were all unwilling to compromise their vision or else they were too willing to cede to the other ones' ideas because their final product is a giant mismatch. It's like some sort of Frankenstein's monster with parts taken from here or there with no thought given to the whole.

The main tone of the film is that it's a romantic comedy, the kind with cute lead characters who wear cute clothes and live in cute apartments. But then there's also some sort of cockamamie plot involving a possible killing, a smuggling ring, and some nefarious characters. Then there is lots of immature and gross-out humor. And intermixed with that mishmash, there are parts, woefully small, unfortunately, of sharp, smart, biting humor. In only the filmmakers could have stuck with one or two of these ideas—we'd vote for the romantic comedy/smart humor combo—they would have had something, but they went for the more-is-better approach and ended up with a very mediocre film.

Our heroine is the perky, wholesome, and pretty bland Amanda (Monica Potter). As she tells us in a voiceover, she is a woman who constantly chooses the wrong men. To prove the point, at the beginning of the film, she walks in on her boyfriend while he's having sex with a model. "This isn't what it looks like," he says weakly. Amanda throws herself into her work at the Metropolitan Museum of Art where she restores paintings. Whenever a new work of art comes in, she is so overcome that she goes weak in the knees. Her co-worker advises her that she should look for a man who makes her react in the same way. So when Amanda meets Jim, (Freddie Prinze Jr. the It boy of teen movies like *She's All That* and its numerous offspring), we know it is going to be true love when she goes weak in the knees upon seeing him. This weak-in-the-knees joke is repeated several times, by the way, to diminishing funniness. As Kevin Thomas at the *Los Angeles Times* put it, the routine happens so many times that it gets "to the point that you start saying to yourself, 'Surely the Met offers health insurance.'"

After leaving her errant boyfriend, Amanda takes a closet-sized room in an apartment with four models—all played by real life models—Candi (Sarah O'Hare), Jade (Shalom Harlow), Roxana (Ivana Milicevic), and Holly (Tomiko Fraser). The models happen to know that Jim is a top fashion executive and encourage Amanda to pursue him. Also, their high-rise apartment, conveniently, overlooks Jim's apartment and they don't seem to think that Amanda is a weirdo when she constantly spies on him. (Jim is not a man to use curtains, apparently).

This would be when the movie tries to turn into a lame version of *Rear Window*. While doing her frequent stalking, oops, spying on Jim, she thinks she sees him killing one of his female coworkers. It's "thinks" because this is the one time Jim has drawn his shades. This sets off a whole wacky plot of Amanda and the models trying to figure out if Jim is really the killer or not. There's not much drama at all in this because we're pretty certain that Jim is not a killer. After all, Amanda went weak in the knees over him, and there's just no way that a movie this corny is going to stray into territory where Amanda is in love with a killer. Plus, Jim is played by Prinze, the most innocent-looking young actor around. He conveys such low levels of ominousness that it's impossible to take him seriously as a suspect. When this part of the plot ends up having to do with undercover cops and an international smuggling ring, it's difficult to believe that anyone in the audience is still caring. Anyone who likes movies about smuggling rings and like will have left the movie long before, probably during one of those cheesy weak in the knees bits.

Awkwardly coexisting in there like a boorish uncle making inappropriate comments at a Thanksgiving dinner are a smattering of jokes that range from tired slapstick to shockingly graphic bathroom jokes. In one sequence, Amanda and the four models have broken into Jim's apartment to look for "evidence." Jim makes a surprise visit to his house and the four models duck into the shower to hide from him (why is the shower the number one hiding place for sneaks in movies?) This movie's twist on the cliche, though, is that Jim comes into the bathroom, sits down on the toilet and makes use of it. He must have a some sort of stomach illness because the episode is long, loud and gross. Not only is this a squirmingly embarrassing scene, this is supposed to be the hero. Does anyone really want to see a romantic lead performing such a graphic act? This is why we never saw Cary Grant tending to his bunions or Robert Redford picking at a boil. In another excrement-related scene, the models all get covered in excrement. As Roger Ebert in the *Chicago Sun-Times* put it, "The scene betrays a basic ignorance of a fundamental principle of humor: It isn't funny when innocent bystanders are humiliated. It's funny when they humiliate themselves."

These sudden shifts into graphic territory are shocking and weird. When Amanda meets Jim, for example, she gets so flustered that she keeps goofing up what she's trying to say and making Freudian slips. But her slips involve making direct references to his genitalia. That this kind of racy humor would be coupled with dumb slapstick jokes about Jim's klutzy dog knocking Amanda down is a strange juxtaposition, to say the least. Then, to throw us off even more, there is smart humor. The jokes about the models are especially sharp. The four women who play the models are game to make fun of themselves and make good use of their material. When trying on a new outfit, one of the models pouts, "This shirt makes me look like a heroin addict. And not in a good way." But just when the movie seems like it might start being clever and funny, then a character will slip and fall on the stairs or knock over a stack of cans or something.

Like the models, Prinze makes a good try with the material. As in his other films, he has a gentle, likable presence. He comes across as a solid guy—not a dashing type, but a nice enough guy. During that bathroom scene, it's difficult not to admire his work ethic and his good sportsmanship to participate in such a dumb and humiliating scene. Potter, who is mainly known for looking a lot like a blonder and blander Julia Roberts, isn't as good. She's a bad enough actor that during some scenes she looks like she forgot to stay in character. And when she is in character, she plays Amanda as a kind of innocent goody-goody who's difficult to root for.

It's difficult to believe that the film came from some folks with some good pedigrees. Writer/producers Decter and Strauss also wrote *There's Something About Mary* and director Mark Waters helmed *The House of Yes*. Critics did not go weak in the knees for the film. Steven Rea of the *Philadelphia Inquirer* called it "a bubble-brained comedy with as much bearing on the real world as a Pokemon cartoon." Sara Wildberger of the *Miami Herald* said, "The shifts in tone are as irritating as the grate of bad gears." Liz Braun at the *Toronto Sun* wrote, "This thing is all over the place. Somewhere under the mess of stuff piled on to divert your attention from the plotlessness is a potential story. Well, we thought we caught a fleeting glimpse anyway." And Roger Ebert wrote, "It's as if the production were a fight to the death between bright people with a sense of humor, and cretins who think the audience is as stupid as they are."

—*Jill Hamilton*

**CREDITS**

**Amanda Pierce:** Monica Potter
**Jim Winston:** Freddie Prinze Jr.

**Jade:** Shalom Harlow
**Roxana:** Ivana Milicevic
**Lisa:** China Chow
**Halloran/Strukov:** Jay Brazeau
**Candi:** Sarah O'Hare
**Holly:** Tomiko Fraser
**Alfredo:** Stanley DeSantis

**Origin:** USA
**Released:** 2001
**Production:** Robert Simonds; released by Universal Pictures
**Directed by:** Mark Waters
**Written by:** Ron Burch, David Kidd
**Cinematography by:** Mark Plummer
**Music by:** Randy Edelman, Steve Porcaro
**Sound:** Michael McGee
**Music Supervisor:** Gary Jones, Happy Walters
**Editing:** Cara Silverman
**Art Direction:** Lance King
**Costumes:** Valerie Halverson
**Production Design:** Perry Andelin Blake
**MPAA rating:** PG-13
**Running time:** 86 minutes

 **REVIEWS**

*Boxoffice.* April, 2001, p. 240.
*Chicago Sun-Times Online.* February 2, 2001.
*New York Times Online.* February 2, 2001.
*USA Today Online.* February 1, 2001.
*Variety.* February 5, 2001, p. 38.
*Washington Post Online.* February 2, 2001.

# Heartbreakers

*Caution: Dangerous Curves Ahead.*
—Movie tagline
*They will love you for richer. And leave you for poorer.*
—Movie tagline

 **Box Office:** $40.3 million

**H**eartbreakers is a cynical romantic comedy with a farcical center involving a mother-daughter team of con artists, Max Conners (Sigourney Weaver) and her daughter Page (Jennifer Love Hewitt). The film starts with one wed-

ding con involving the mother and ends with another involving the daughter, who thinks she is tough enough and skilled enough to work con games on her own, but she is not as tough as she thinks, and her mother is more sentimentally attached than she knows. Max considers Page immature and likely to let romance get in the way of her ability to con male dupes ruthlessly. The story unfolds later to prove her right.

The first wedding and reception is shown while the opening credits are still rolling. Using the assumed name of Angela Nardino, the mother gets married to Dean Cabanno (Ray Liotta), a New Jersey gangster who runs a chop shop, and a certain romantic dupe. At the reception the bride dances with everyone, including the busboy, before being carried to her room down a comically long hotel hallway, that seems to have no end, the best sight gag in the film. After finally arriving at the room, Dean is aroused and amorous, but the bride falls asleep immediately, or pretends to. So Dean checks in at his office and is promptly seduced by his secretary, Wendy, who is really Page Conners. By prior arrangement, the wronged bride turns up just in time to see Dean involved with the secretary, but, of course, it's all a set up, leading to a divorce settlement of $300,000, plus a Mercedes.

Max tells Page they only took Dean for $80,000 and the car, but she sets up another con with her friend Barbara (Anne Bancroft) to make Page think that they have lost all of their money to the IRS. After the con is completed and not quite penniless, the team of gold-diggers strikes out for Palm Beach. Once there, the mother sets her sights on wheezing tobacco tycoon William B. Tensy (Gene Hackman with a bad cough and a W.C. Fields nose), who seems to have one foot in the grave. She meets him at an auction by outbidding him on a nude male statue with an erection. The statue and its erection is used for a second, less than hilarious, sight gag, as the erection is broken off as workers move the statue through a doorway. Meanwhile, the daughter has set her sights on a pleasant young man named Jack (Jason Lee), who first seems to be a bartender but later turns out to be the owner of a night spot worth three million dollars. They fall in love; she feels guilty about conning him, but still wants to make a point with her mother.

Pretending to be a Russian named Ulga Yevanova and forced to sing in a language she really doesn't know in a Russian restaurant ("Back in the U.S.S.R." is what she comes up with as a solution, as balalaikas strum the Lennon-McCartney melody in wonderfully fast tempo), the mother lures the tobacco tycoon to her hotel. He proposes marriage, then has a coughing fit and dies, almost allowing Hackman to escape from an embarrassing role. Meanwhile, Dean turns up from New Jersey after having had "Angela" traced to Palm Beach. Then he sees Page, known to him as "Wendy," and he knows that he has been had. He demands his money back and the Mercedes. The women agree, but only if Dean will help them dispose of Tensy's body. By this point in the movie some viewers may be asking themselves if they are still having fun.

Max is willing to pay Dean back, but she discovers her friend Barbara has emptied out her bank account, since she gave Barbara her bank account numbers to work the con on her daughter. So much for loyalty and trust. Page comes to the rescue by working the wedding con on Jack, the man she loves. They get married. Page pretends to fall asleep. The mother finds an excuse to invite Jack to her room and attempts to seduce him, but he is not at all interested. So she drugs his drink to make him look guilty. Later she gets to feeling guilty herself and confesses her skullduggery to Page. By this time the divorce con has been completed. Jack has been taken to court and to the cleaners, having been forced to sell the restaurant he inherited from his father in order to pay the divorce settlement. But—surprise!—there is honor among thieves. At the last minute Max gives Page the money, and Page uses it to buy back the restaurant for Jack, with whom she is reunited at the end. He had known her as Jane Halstrom. She tells him at the end her real name is Page. Meanwhile, at the very end Dean is seen seducing Barbara, working a scam with Max to recover his money. But at least Page seems to be totally reformed at the end.

Though amusing and funny in places (but not many), this is not exactly a two-thumbs-up movie because of its cynicism and vulgarity. As *Washington Post* reviewer Rita Kempley wrote, the movie "makes the men look like nincompoops," and that is certainly true of Dean, Jack, and Tensly. One begins to feel sorry for Gene Hackman, who is trapped in a terribly stupid, stereotypical role as the good-natured tobacco tycoon. Hackman is seen wearing chartreuse socks and boxer shorts for his boudoir death scene. The indignities are compounded when, by accident, his body is then knocked off a hotel balcony in another sequence that fails to be funny and is merely grotesque. This was not Hackman's biggest role in 2001, nor was it by any stretch of the imagination his best. One doubts that he would take much pride in having played a wealthy slob, an addict, and, finally, a corpse. Ray Liotta's "antic incredibility," on the other hand, and his "colorful non-sequiturs," in the words of *New York Times* reviewer A.O. Scott, sustained the film's comic momentum and kept it running until the end. Too bad Liotta has to disappear during the film's middle portion.

And yet the reviewers were fooled. A.O. Scott of the *New York Times* claimed that the "marks very nearly steal the movie," and described Hackman as "gleefully repulsive." Rita Kempley claimed that Hackman "all but saves the picture," but, then, she had nothing favorable to say about Sigourney Weaver: "Hewitt and Weaver," she wrote, "with their strained rapport, are hardly convincing as disgruntled daughter and overly protective mother." A.O. Scott was far more positive about Weaver and her ability to parody a "certain movie-star sexiness," whereas Kempley criticized her for acting too much like a bimbo "to be mistaken for a

shrewd" con artist. Scott claimed that Weaver "has an underappreciated gift for comedy," which is unlikely, considering her outstanding "bimbo" performance in last year's *Galaxy Quest*. Nora Dunn as Miss Madress and Anne Bancroft as the double-dealing con artist Barbara were deemed praiseworthy, especially Anne Bancroft: "In only three scenes as Weaver's mentor," Kempley wrote, "Anne Bancroft demonstrates the timeless appeal of brains, class and knowing when to give up on the garter belts." For Kempley, Sigourney Weaver is "clueless when it comes to portraying women, mature or otherwise, who are confident in their sensuality."

The clunky screenplay was written by a committee of "talents" (as they say in the Industry), "Robert Dunn and Paul Guay & Stephen Mazur." In the coding of the Writers Guild, each conjunction and ampersand had significance for writers eager to take credit. A.O. Scott praised the "sharp script" for its "satiny opulence," giving the movie "a shine as pleasing as the chrome on that Mercedes." Scott believed the film perpetrates "an honest and sophisticated con," and it would appear the reviewer himself was conned. Not so Rita Kempley, who dismissed *Heartbreakers* as "a sporadically amusing romp modeled on *Dirty Rotten Scoundrels*." Scott considered the film "elegantly directed," apparently confusing mere competence for elegance. It would be more accurate to say that the film was directed with middling results by David Mirkin. That it went fairly quickly to video is hardly surprising.

—*James M. Welsh*

## CREDITS

**Max Conners:** Sigourney Weaver
**Page Conners:** Jennifer Love Hewitt
**William B. Tensy:** Gene Hackman
**Dean Cumanno:** Ray Liotta
**Jack Withrowe:** Jason Lee
**Gloria Vogal:** Anne Bancroft
**Mr. Appel:** Jeffrey Jones
**Miss Madress:** Nora Dunn
**Leo:** Julio Mechoso
**Dawson's Auctioneer:** Ricky Jay

**Origin:** USA
**Released:** 2001
**Production:** John Davis, Irving Ong; released by MGM
**Directed by:** David Mirkin
**Written by:** Paul Guay, Robert Dunn, Steve Mazur
**Cinematography by:** Dean Semler
**Music by:** John Debney
**Sound:** David Ronne
**Music Supervisor:** Maureen Crowe

**Editing:** William Steinkamp
**Art Direction:** John Warnke
**Costumes:** Gary Jones
**Production Design:** Lily Kilvert
**MPAA rating:** PG-13
**Running time:** 123 minutes

## REVIEWS

*Boxoffice.* May, 2001, p. 59.
*Chicago Sun-Times Online.* March 23, 2001.
*Entertainment Weekly.* March 30, 2001, p. 46.
*Los Angeles Times Online.* March 23, 2001.
*New York Times Online.* March 23, 2001.
*People.* April 2, 2001, p. 33.
*Sight and Sound.* September, 2001, p. 44.
*USA Today Online.* March 23, 2001.
*Variety.* March 14, 2001, p. 34.
*Washington Post Online.* March 23, 2001.

## QUOTES

Maxine (Sigourney Weaver): "The older, the better. With luck they die right after the wedding."

# Hearts in Atlantis

*What if one of life's great mysteries moved in upstairs?*
—Movie tagline

 **Box Office:** $24.2 million

Gentle, sweet, and poignant, *Hearts in Atlantis* is a small story with a lot of big names behind it. It is based upon two stories from a book of the same name by the wildly-popular author Stephen King, directed by Oscar®-nominated Scott Hicks (1995's *Shine*) from a script by Oscar-winning vet William Goldman, and stars Oscar-winner Anthony Hopkins. It is a well-acted elegy for innocence lost, holding even greater resonance for moviegoers who felt that things would never be quite the same after the stunning terrorist attacks of September 11 just days before the film opened. (It's big U.S. premiere was cancelled amidst the uncertainty and sadness.)

The film harks back along with middle-aged photographer Bobby Garfield (David Morse, who appeared in 1999's King-based *The Green Mile*) to a simpler time in his life and American life, as well, namely the waning, halcyon days of a childhood in small town U.S.A. between the staid 1950's and the turbulent 1960's. Hicks gives us warm, sunlit, nostalgic images through the excellent work of cinematographer Piotr Sobocinski, who tragically died at the age of 43 immediately after shooting this film. Recalled are summers which passed at a languorous pace, highlighted by boisterous adventures with best friends, as well as a restless yearning for something truly remarkable to happen, even just once, in your neck of the woods.

For Bobby, that happened during the summer in which he turned 11, when a seemingly ordinary man with extraordinary abilities came to board one floor up from him. Bobby's recollections are triggered by a trip back home for the funeral of Sully, one of his closest boyhood friends. At that somber ceremony, Bobby is shaken even more deeply to learn that Carol Gerber, the golden girl with whom he shared his first chaste kiss and the other member of their inseparable childhood triad, is also dead. Bobby makes his way through the cold and snow for a bittersweet visit to the house, now condemned, where he grew up. Gazing out the window which faced towards where Carol used to live, he is transported back to that last summer of his childhood.

Back then, cherubic, curly-haired Bobby (Anton Yelchin) lived with his edgy and bitter widowed mother Liz (Hope Davis), who focused almost all of her time and spent most of her money on succeeding at the real estate office. She also put a lot of effort into disparaging Bobby's late father, dismissing the man Bobby is curious about as a worthless gambler responsible for their current financial woes. It is not hard to sense (or understand) the discontent she feels for her present situation: 35 and single for five years now, struggling to start a career and a social life while taking care of a son. She is so self-absorbed, eagerly buying pretty dresses to make a good impression at work, that she merely gives her son a library card for his birthday instead of the bicycle he has been coveting. Bobby's anticipation and subsequent deflation upon receiving such an underwhelming present is clear. Even a birthday dinner does not go off as planned.

He is starved for an adult who will take the time to listen and pay attention to him until Ted Brautigan (Hopkins), an elderly, soft-spoken gentleman, arrives. Ted becomes a sort of mentor/father figure for Bobby. Conversations between the two consist of everything from sage advice to the making of farting noises on your hand. Bobby is fascinated by Ted, and appreciates feeling appreciated. Both delight in this comfortable and comforting give and take. Ted offers Bobby the job of reading the daily newspaper to him for a dollar, as the older man's sight is failing. He tells Bobby that the money could go toward the bike he wants, a statement which baffles the boy because there had been no mention of it in their previous conversations. This is the first sign of Ted's psychic abilities. Ted begins to seem even more intriguing and mysterious when he also asks Bobby to keep his eyes open for "low men," dangerous figures who might show up looking for the boarder for reasons which he declines to fully explain. He tells Bobby to look for reward posters around town purporting to be searching for lost animals. Bobby, wary but curious, offers his help on all counts. Liz is suspicious of Ted, and Bobby feels insulted when she wonders why the man would want to be spending time with him. Bobby begs her not to spoil things for him.

The bonding between Bobby and Ted is cemented in a fine scene in which the latter vividly relates that he saw legendary Bronco Nagurski play football in a memorable game the boy's father also attended. Bobby is enraptured with this story about an older man who showed up, changed things for the better, and then was gone again. Bobby gently asks if Ted will also have to leave if the low men start coming around, and the boy winces at the unhappy answer. Bobby is also upset upon finding Ted in a sort of trance on the day of the fair, hugging the man and fearing that he might die. After this encounter, the closeness between the two seems to have caused some of Ted's intuitive abilities to rub off on Bobby, empowering him to outwit a card shark at the fair. Perched on the Ferris wheel on the same night, Bobby shares a sweet first kiss with Carol (Mika Boorem), a milestone which Ted had predicted, saying that no other kiss would ever be quite as magical. "Sometimes when you're young," says Ted, "you have moments of such happiness, you think you're living in someplace magical, like Atlantis must have been. Then we grow up and our hearts break in two."

Ted plays a vital role in both youngsters' lives when Liz reluctantly leaves her son in his care as she goes off to a seminar with her solicitous boss. Ted, feeling that the people who are hunting him (apparently to harness his psychic abilities for the government, although this is never made clear) are drawing nearer, takes Bobby with him to a pool hall in a shadier part of town to win enough money to travel. (Bobby has, indeed, seen the warning signs of the low men around town, but has kept the information to himself for fear of losing his valued friend.) This trip with Ted to the hall enables Bobby to meet people who give him another perspective on his father, a positive picture untainted by his mother's bitterness. He is thrilled to learn that his father is fondly remembered as a generous, enjoyable man who won as well as lost.

Ted and his powers of perception are also helpful in interrupting and briefly silencing the local bullies' taunting of Bobby and Carol, as well as enabling Bobby to rescue her after the angriest of the young punks assaults the girl in the woods with a baseball bat. This distressing scene is intercut with views of an apparent sexual assault on Liz by her boss. Bobby uses Ted's story of Nagurski's strength and courage against daunting odds to carry Carol up a steep hill to get help. (Along with swelling music, we hear a crowd cheering as Bobby performs his own heroics.) While Ted is successfully tending to her, an unhinged Liz arrives, sees the girl's blouse disarranged, and angrily accuses him of being a molester. Her distrust of people heightened by her assault, Liz wants this strange stranger gone, and quietly calls those looking for him.

Bobby bravely sneaks out to pick up Ted's winnings for him so that the man can skip town, but the faceless low men get to Ted first. "I wouldn't have missed a minute," Ted yells as Bobby looks on helplessly. "Not for the world." In another touching scene, Bobby also must say goodbye to Carol, whose family is moving away. The boy's growth through his experiences with Ted enables him to stand up to his mother, telling her off for her hurtful misrepresentations of both Ted and Bobby's father, which leads to dialogue and, finally, healing. The only somewhat false note in the film comes at the end, when the adult Bobby walks out of his old house and runs into a young girl who just happens to be Carol's daughter. Their meaningful meeting may seem a tad too contrived for some. In the end, Ted's parting words are echoed by Bobby as his reminiscing comes to a close.

In light of the physic powers Hopkins character possesses, the way in which he became involved in *Hearts in Atlantis* is interesting. While in Italy making this year's *Hannibal*, he was reading Goldman's book *What Lie Did I Tell?* and came to the part about the screenwriter's adaptation of King's *Misery* (1990). Hopkins thought to himself how great it would be to appear someday in a Goldman adaptation of a King work, at which point his agent called with the offer for *Hearts*. Made on a budget of $31 million, the film grossed just over $24 million at the boxoffice. Although it received praise, overall critical reaction was mixed. It belongs in the subcategory of films based upon King's works in which the focus is more human than horrific. Like 1986's *Stand by Me*, it takes an intelligent and somewhat sentimental look back at defining moments of youth on the verge of adulthood.

*Hearts in Atlantis* succeeds through the utterly believable rapport between Hopkins and the immensely winning Yelchin (like Boorem, a noteworthy young star on the rise), as well as between the actors (including Will Rothhaar as Sully) portraying the childhood friends. Some familiar with what King wrote in almost 700 pages complained about what had been excised here, including the toning-down of a greater supernatural element in the original material which, with the low men apparently being from another realm, added more tension. While what Goldman has chosen to bring to the screen does not illicit intense dread, it does successfully bring back memories of things in our own past which happened long ago but which shaped us and stay with us to this day.

—*David L. Boxerbaum*

**Ted Brautigan:** Anthony Hopkins
**Bobby Garfield:** Anton Yelchin
**Liz Garfield:** Hope Davis
**Carol Gerber:** Mika Boorem
**Bobby Garfield (adult):** David Morse
**Monte Man:** Alan Tudyk
**Len Files:** Tom Bower
**Alana Files:** Celia Weston
**Donald Biderman:** Adam LeFevre
**Harry Doolin:** Timothy Reifsnyder
**Mrs. Gerber:** Deirdre O'Connell
**Sully:** Will Rothhaar

**Origin:** USA
**Released:** 2001
**Production:** Kerry Heysen; Castle Rock Entertainment, Village Roadshow Pictures, NPV Entertainment; released by Warner Bros.
**Directed by:** Scott Hicks
**Written by:** William Goldman
**Cinematography by:** Piotr Sobocinski
**Music by:** Mychael Danna
**Sound:** Tod A. Maitland
**Music Supervisor:** John Bissell
**Editing:** Pip Karmel
**Art Direction:** Mark Worthington
**Costumes:** Julie Weiss
**Production Design:** Barbara C. Ling
**MPAA rating:** PG-13
**Running time:** 101 minutes

*Boxoffice.* November, 2001, p. 149.
*Chicago Sun-Times Online.* September 28, 2001.
*Entertainment Weekly.* October 5, 2001, p. 111.
*Los Angeles Times Online.* September 28, 2001.
*New York Times.* September 28, 2001, p. E16.
*People.* October 8, 2001, p. 43.
*Premiere.* October, 2001, p. 94.
*USA Today Online.* September 28, 2001.
*Variety.* September 10, 2001, p. 61.
*Wall Street Journal.* September 28, 2001, p. W8.
*Washington Post.* September 28, 2001, p. C1.

Liz (Hope Davis) about Ted Brautigan (Anthony Hopkins): "I never trust a man who carries his possessions in grocery bags."

The Stephen King stories adapted for the film are "Low Men in Yellow Coats" and "Heavenly Shades of Night Are Falling" from the *Hearts in Atlantis* collection.

# Hedwig and the Angry Inch

*An anatomically incorrect rock odyssey.*
—Movie tagline

**Box Office:** $3 million

Hedwig and the Angry Inch was one of the break-out indie hits of 2001. Even though the film was such a crowd-pleaser, it's easy to see why it had to come out as an independent film rather than otherwise. It's difficult to imagine, say, Steven Spielberg directing a film that has at its core a drag queen wearing a Farrah Fawcett wig and a botched sex change operation. *Hedwig* is an adaptation of a long-running Off-Broadway play written by John Cameron Mitchell with music and lyrics by Stephen Trask. With its trailer park glam and powerful music, the rock opera became a cult hit.

We first met Hedwig (Mitchell) under pretty pitiable circumstances, although judging by her behavior, we'd never guess. Hedwig and her band, the Angry Inch have been booked by their mother hen manager, Phyllis Stein (Andrea Martin), on a U.S. tour of Bilgewater's restaurants, a seafood chain that's like a down-and-out Red Lobster's. As Hedwig sings her heart-wrenching, overly personal songs while wearing her blonde wig, Tammy Faye make-up and Cher castoffs, the audience of bland retirees looks on with varying reactions of boredom to utter horror. The movie follows Hedwig and the band through the various stops on their tour. The cities may change, but the set-up remains the same. Hedwig pours her heart out in song to tiny audiences in bibs eating fried shrimp. Each song reveals part of Hedwig's story and, in flashbacks, we begin to see how she got where she is today.

Hedwig was born Hansel in East Berlin, Germany. With an absent father and inattentive mother (Alberta Watson), Hansel retreated to American pop culture for solace. He listened to the sounds of American Armed Forces radio and, with equal seriousness, he studied the works of Debby Boone and Lou Reed. One day, while sunning himself,

Hansel is spotted by an American Army sergeant, Luther Robinson (Maurice Dean Wint). At first, Luther thinks that Hansel is a girl. After Hansel turns over and proves that theory wrong, Luther is still interested and becomes Hansel's sugar daddy. The two decide that they will marry and Hansel will be able to escape East Berlin for West Berlin. The one catch is that Luther, as well as Hansel's mother, decide that the only way that the plan will work is if Hansel gets a sex change operation. Hansel's mother, with a strange sort of enthusiasm, says that she knows just the person. Unfortunately, the doctor botches the job and Hansel, now Hedwig, ends up with only a nub of flesh in his genital area (that would be the "angry inch" of the title). To make matters worse, soon after, the Berlin Wall comes down, making the operation seem even more pointless and cruel.

Hedwig ends up in a trailer in Kansas, disillusioned and, after Luther leaves her, alone. She decides that the only thing to do is to become very glamourous and start a band. Her idea of glamour makes her look more like Dee Snyder than Farrah, but she is undeterred and puts her whole energy into becoming a grand diva. Her first band is a ragtag affair with several Asian women from the base serving as her back-up.

She earns extra money babysitting for the General and it is at his house that she meets her next true love, the General's teenage, Jesus-loving son, Tommy (Michael Pitt). Tommy and Hedwig soon begin a hot and heavy affair where they write an album's worth of songs together. But Hedwig, as she so often is, is unlucky in this love affair, too. Tommy leaves Hedwig and becomes a famous rock star. Worse, he also takes several things Hedwig gave him, including his new name—Tommy Gnosis, to signify knowledge—and the album's worth of songs.

This, then, is the reason for the Bilgewater's tour. Every stop on Hedwig's tour is set in the same town as a stop on Tommy's tour because she thinks that stalking him is the best way to resolve their differences. Now, with a new band, including her lover Yitzhak (Miriam Shor, who is a woman playing a man)—and, incidentally songwriter Trask (as Skszp)—Hedwig is in full diva mode. She treats everyone poorly, especially Yitzhak, and she goes into tirades about things like bras that have been thrown in the dryer.

Between the flashbacks showing crucial points in Hedwig's life and the songs that explain what she's been through, the film also effectively uses animation done by Emily Hubley, the daughter of noted experimental animators John and Faith Hubley. The stage show didn't have the animation and only explained through the songs, rather than showed, the early sequences from Hedwig's life. Both additions are welcome to the screen adaptation.

Overall, Mitchell, who directed the film, did a fine job of translating his work to the screen. In the live version, he made good use of strengths of being on stage, like the intimacy with the audience, to help tell the story. In the film version, he shows the same savvy of his medium. A lot of film adaptations of stage shows are basically filmed versions of the show, and the characters seem confined, but this film goes way beyond that. Mitchell uses the animation as well as clever camera shots and editing to take advantage of the fast-paced brashness of film.

For a film like this to work, the main character has to be appealing and Hedwig is. Mitchell's character is not exactly likable—at one point she rips up Yitzhak's passport so that he will not be able to leave her—but she is charismatic. Mitchell plays the stereotypical drag queen role to the hilt and he does a good job of it. In the musical numbers, Hedwig sings her heart out, no matter how small the audience. She breaks instruments, throws herself into the audience and is every inch the performer. He revels in his bitchy glory, tossing aside vaguely stale one-liners like "The audience threw tomatoes at me and after the show, I had a nice salad." Ba-da-bum.

Everyone else in the film is, by necessity, merely a bit player in Hedwig's world but a few do manage to eke out a little love from the camera. Martin has a barely hidden jittery nervousness as the band's not-particularly good manager. The character seems like the type of woman who starts her day off with some affirmations in front of the mirror. Shor is understated as Hedwig's long suffering beau with aspirations of his own. And Pitt is appropriately pouty and beautiful as Hedwig's boy toy who betrays her.

Critics know a good drag queen when they see one, as Boy George once put it, and gave the film high marks. Kevin Thomas of the *Los Angeles Times* wrote, "For all its serious subtext, the movingly affirmative *Hedwig* is raucous, racy and full of hilarious, lowdown survivor's wit." *Entertainment Weekly*'s Lisa Schwartzbaum gave the film an A- and said, "Mitchell has done the damn difficult thing of giving a staged work a look that honors the original medium while recognizing that movies are a whole other shebang." Stephanie Zacharek of Salon.com wrote, "*Hedwig* is aggressively, winkingly glam. It helps to have a taste for T-Rex, Iggy and the like, but you should feel free to check reverence at the door: Trask's songs are enjoyable as both sendup and tribute." And Geoff Pevere of the *Toronto Star* thought, "It's a glam fantasy for trailer trash intellectuals, the kind of camp experience that revels in the contradiction between the grand romantic fantasies of rock and the salad bar cheesiness of Hedwig's reality."

—*Jill Hamilton*

**CREDITS**

**Hedwig/Hansel:** John Cameron Mitchell
**Tommy Gnosis:** Michael Pitt

**Phyllis Stein:** Andrea Martin
**Yitzhak:** Miriam Shor
**Hansel's Mom:** Alberta Watson
**Sgt. Luther Robinson:** Maurice Dean Wint
**Krzysztof:** Rob Campbell
**Skszp:** Stephen Trask
**Jacek:** Theodore Liscinski
**Schlatko:** Michael Aranov

**Origin:** USA
**Released:** 2000
**Production:** Christine Vachon, Katie Roumel, Pamela Koffler; Killer Films, New Line Cinema; released by Fine Line Features
**Directed by:** John Cameron Mitchell
**Written by:** John Cameron Mitchell
**Cinematography by:** Frank DeMarco
**Music by:** Stephen Trask
**Editing:** Andrew Marcus
**Art Direction:** Nancy Pankiw
**Costumes:** Arianne Phillips
**Production Design:** Therese DuPrez
**MPAA rating:** R
**Running time:** 95 minutes

## REVIEWS

*Chicago Sun-Times Online.* August 3, 2001.
*Entertainment Weekly.* July 27, 2001, p. 45.
*Los Angeles Times Online.* July 20, 2001.
*New York Times Online.* May 13, 2001.
*New York Times Online.* July 20, 2001.
*People.* August 6, 2001, p. 39.
*Rolling Stone.* August 2, 2001, p. 69.
*Sight and Sound.* September, 2001, p. 44.
*Time.* January 15, 2001, p. 126.
*USA Today Online.* July 20, 2001.
*Variety.* January 29, 2001, p. 48.
*Washington Post.* August 3, 2001, p. WE34.

## QUOTES

Hedwig (John Cameron Mitchell): "How did some slip of a girly/ boy from communist East Berlin become the internationally ig- nored song stylist barely standing before you?"

## TRIVIA

*Hedwig and the Angry Inch* began Off Broadway in 1998.

**Nomination:**
**Golden Globes 2002:** Actor—Mus./Comedy (Mitchell).

# The Heist

*It isn't love that makes the world go round.*
—Movie tagline
*Love makes the world go round. Love of Gold.*
—Movie tagline

**Box Office:** $23.5 million

Taut is the operative word for David Mamet's approach in *Heist*—a tight, polished, hardworking and professional piece of very satisfying filmmaking. Mamet has some- what restrained his habitual impulse to have his characters talk constantly in too-brilliant tough-guy aphorisms. The former playwright's precious bon mots often tend to sound like they were ripped off the printed page and stuffed awk- wardly into his characters' mouths. Mamet, who has always been adept with plot, timing, and intricate gamesmanship, has finally realized that believable characters are the key to great moviemaking—and this film is full of them.

Yes, they still talk cute from time to time in Mamet's trademark clipped phrases, ripping off slang metaphors that are too precious to believe. A grand heist plan is "cute as a Chinese baby." One of the gang of thieves could "talk her way out of a sunburn." An apprentice reassures an experi- enced thief that he will be "as quiet as an ant pissing on cotton." But the other tells him he wants him to be "as quiet as an ant not even thinking about pissing on cotton." The man's sidekick reassurances the apprentice that his man is "so cool that when he goes to bed, sheep count him." They rip off such phrases while in the thick of close work, under pressure from the cops, and smack in the middle of tough fixes. As usual with Mamet, some of the language is delight- ful, some is hilarious, and some sounds awfully out of place.

But Mamet keeps the smartass talking to a tolerable level—the sum of the dialogue in *Heist* probably totals half of most of his previous films. And the fine ensemble he has enlisted for *Heist* is able to make most of these phrases go down easily. Start with Gene Hackman. A hardworking, prolific veteran who has done fine jobs in scores of bad, mediocre, and brilliant movies, Hackman here is at the top of his game. His character, Joe Moore, is a smart but aging thief looking to finally score enough dough so he can get out of debt and retire to sunnier climes on his boat with his young wife Fran (Rebecca Pidgeon). It's a familiar crime-movie character, and it easily could have been a stereotype, but Hackman (with Mamet's help) makes Joe into a complicated, fascinating man. Under pressure, he is just as cool as his partner Bobby (Delroy Lindo) describes him in the sheep metaphor, but he's also volatile, has a quick temper, and betrays his tension when he gets in a tight spot. Lindo's just as good. His Bobby is a man who's calm and smooth as silk, but all too human in a pinch. Hackman and Lindo work together like they've been lifelong partners—and their parting scene in a café at the film's end is nothing short of brilliant, packing incredible pathos into a few simple sentences of dialogue.

The other gang members—Mamet stalwarts Ricky Jay as Pinky and Pidgeon as Hackman's tough-as-nails, sultry wife—have fewer dimensions. Pidgeon, brilliant at playing the brainy, sassy flirt in recent Mamet films such as *The Spanish Prisoner* and *State and Main*—here seems badly miscast and underwritten. Nevertheless, Hackman's great charm is sufficient to make the older-man, younger-vixen pairing with Pidgeon plausible. Jay, who goes back a long way with Mamet (to *House of Games*) always makes the best of the slim sidekick's hand that's dealt him.

But that's not all that's cooking in this dream of an actors' movie. Mamet coaxes an edgy, unnerving, twitchy performance out of Danny DeVito as Bergman, a fur-store-owning fence jerking Joe Moore around, and it's one of the best of DeVito's career. Bergman is a tightly wound, explosive, jive-talking villain—oily but with a see-through veneer of cheap charm. Sam Rockwell, as his lame nephew Jimmy Silk, is the cast member who seems most out of sync with the Mamet rhythms and language, but he's the stooge, and in Mamet films stooges are supposed to look lame. In fact, Jimmy is so lame the other thieves use "lame" as a noun to talk about him.

As the film opens, Joe Moore's crew pulls off a clever, audacious jewelry store robbery. Distraction is their main tool—staging a nearby traffic accident to divert the attention of the police. Fran, working as a waitress in a nearby coffee shop, has put sedatives in the store employees' coffee. One thing goes wrong, though: one woman hasn't drunk the coffee and Joe must approach her, mask off. In Mamet films, crimes closely resemble theater performances (and probably intentionally so)—they're well scripted and rehearsed, but there's inevitably a false step and the criminals must improvise on the go. In this case, Joe's face is caught on the surveillance tape, and so he's now a marked man. It's a handy excuse: Joe's hankering to retire anyway. But when Bergman refuses to pay the money from the heist unless Joe and his crew help him with another big score, Joe is caught in a trap. Worse yet, Bergman insists that Jimmy Silk be part of the next heist.

Joe doesn't like that idea at all. Testing Jimmy, the gang finds out he's a trigger-happy, impulsive, stupid young crook who can't be trusted and doesn't fit into the gang's well-honed modus operandi, which includes plenty of experienced double-talk, stage presence and role playing when authorities get too close and ask questions. The group stages a scene where they pretend they have blown their cover and ruined the heist in order to get rid of Jimmy, but it doesn't work—he comes back. Those viewers familiar with the con artist schemes of other Mamet movies will quickly cotton on to the chicanery. The plot of *Heist* isn't nearly as intricate as his previous con-artist films but the score that the group plans is much more audacious. It involves robbing an airplane that is carrying a gold shipment to Switzerland—on the runway, before it takes off. An explosion as a diversion, a well-tuned plan that involves posing as security personnel, and an elaborate escape all add up to many moments of sublime tension.

But the real plotting is just beginning. Joe has determined to double-cross Silk and Bergman, and it is a risky venture. In the end, it leads to bloodshed and some severe tests of Joe's friends and their loyalties—with a surprising result. Uncharacteristically, Mamet's plot leads into something of a dead-end and the ending is both a little too cute and conventional to believe. But along the way, the ride is mightily enjoyable, packed with the kind of intelligent suspense that few directors other than Mamet know how to script and to carry off. Mamet is becoming masterful at shooting his characters' professional work, using a lot more close-ups than he once did and frequently employing the camera as a sort of surveillance tool.

And he makes us care about the characters without resorting to sentiment. Joe Moore, Bobby, Pinky, and Fran seem to be honorable thieves with clear though not sentimental motivations. They're after the score, they work hard, and they're smart—they think on their feet. But they are not romanticized. They have tempers and they do nasty things. Fran will use her body to advance the group's plans—at Joe's command. He tells her to "suit up" when he wants her to seduce Jimmy and Bergman into seeing things his way and we next see her in a slinky evening dress courting the two men. And while the gang is audacious and cunning, they sometimes get into fixes they can't get out of. These are not invincible crooks, evil henchmen, nor incredibly cool characters—they are believable working stiffs with elaborate plans and experience, so watching them work is entertaining. Mamet doesn't need to resort to cheap emotional tricks to keep us interested in what happens to them and among them. Even Bergman and Jimmy, the villains of the piece, seem like guys who are just trying to get along, in their own way.

Mamet has proven he can handle other material, including historical drama (*The Winslow Boy*) and comedy-satire (*State and Main*), but *Heist* is a return to the kind of work Mamet is best at—the elucidation of con games. The films he makes about expert thieves and hustlers are finely detailed and intricately plotted, like chess on a grand scale, but also completely frank, straightforward, and honest. And the good guys don't always win. Mamet's never going to play to the cheap seats in the audience. But he knows how to make actors playing hustlers elucidate what theater—and film—depend on: The maintenance of illusion, distraction, and brilliant manipulation in the service of higher arts. In other words, a little bit of old-fashioned magic. *Heist* has that beautiful chicanery.

—*Michael Betzold*

## CREDITS

**Joe Moore:** Gene Hackman
**Mickey Bergman:** Danny DeVito
**Bobby Blane:** Delroy Lindo
**Jimmy Silk:** Sam Rockwell
**Fran:** Rebecca Pidgeon
**Pinky Pincus:** Ricky Jay
**Betty Croft:** Patti LuPone
**D.A. Freccia:** Jim Frangione

**Origin:** USA
**Released:** 2001
**Production:** Art Linson, Elie Samaha, Andrew Stevens; Morgan Creek Productions, Franchise Pictures, Indelible Pictures; released by Warner Bros.
**Directed by:** David Mamet
**Written by:** David Mamet
**Cinematography by:** Robert Elswit
**Music by:** Theodore Shapiro
**Sound:** Patrick Rousseau
**Editing:** Barbara Tulliver
**Art Direction:** Isabelle Guay
**Costumes:** Renee April
**Production Design:** David Wasco
**MPAA rating:** R
**Running time:** 107 minutes

## REVIEWS

*Boxoffice.* November, 2001, p. 145.
*Chicago Sun-Times Online.* November 9, 2001.
*Entertainment Weekly.* November 16, 2001, p. 144.
*Los Angeles Times Online.* November 9, 2001.
*New York Times Online.* November 9, 2001.
*People.* November 19, 2001, p. 43.
*Rolling Stone.* November 8, 2001, p. 134.
*USA Today Online.* November 8, 2001.
*Variety.* September 10, 2001, p. 62.

*Washington Post.* November 9, 2001, p. WE38.

## QUOTES

Joe Moore (Gene Hackman): "Anybody can get the goods. The hard part is getting away."

## TRIVIA

Gene Hackman, Danny DeVito, and Delroy Lindo previously worked together in the film *Get Shorty.*

# Here's to Life

When filmmaker Arne Olsen sought a Hollywood producer for his screenplay about a group of elders who wanted to set out for a final hooray before they expired, Hollywood producers rejected the well-written screenplay because it wouldn't appeal to the typical moviegoer. While it's true that the largest movie-going audience falls between the ages of 18-25, a catch-22 situation has also presented itself since the type of movies released by Hollywood studios would only appeal to that age group. However, statistics also show that the baby boomer generation is fast approaching their golden years and the generation before them is still lively enough to attend a screening for a film they could relate to if given the chance. So why hasn't Hollywood figured that out?

Fortunately for Olsen, he found a supportive Canadian producer, William Vince, to ensure that *Here's to Life* manifested into a touching film about passing the torch from one generation to the next. According to Olsen, "The real spark of the story came when I decided to take the elderly characters out of a retirement home and put them on the road where they could take their rich life experiences and transfer them onto the character Owen who is lost in the world." And *Here's to Life*, with its panoramic scenery of Victoria, British Columbia, its rambunctious elderly folk, and the transformation of the 30-something Owen acts as a tribute to life, recalling the sentiments found in Louis Armstrong's *What a Wonderful World*. *Here's to Life* might appear light and breezy on the surface but heavier issues surface in the film regarding life and death, as well as the sacrifices those before us made without our knowledge.

When faced with jail for tax fraud or granting the wish of three blackmailing retirement home residents, 35-year-old Owen Rinard (Eric McCormack) grants the rambunctious elderly folk their final wishes. Their leader, Gus Corley (James Whitmore), desires to catch a King Salmon in Victoria, BC; Nelly Ormand (Kim Hunter) desires to hear a symphony play a Mozart concerto; and former boxing coach Duncan Cox (Ossie Davis) desires to see a champion boxing match one last time. And the anal-retentive and fastidious Owen must figure out how to manifest those wishes or go to prison.

*Here's to Life* acts as a road flick and as a study of how others can plant the seeds for another person's transformation. As a road movie, we see the reluctant Owen drive the others to Victoria where (against Owen's wishes) the group stay at a hotel that costs around $2,000 a night. Along the way, they stop at a fast food restaurant where they gorge on an array of deep fried food only to down a bottle of antacid after their excursion. But mainly they listen to classic forties music as they ride in a classic '50s convertible while enjoying every moment of their last hoorah.

One by one, the elders sacrifice their last wishes to assists the lonely Owen. Nelly decides to teach Owen how to relate to women and then she fixes Owen up with local waitress Carley (Marya Delver). Duncan decides not to attend a championship fight in Vancouver and instead gives Owen boxing lessons, and after Owen confronts the surly Gus and reveals his painful past to him, Gus allows Owen to catch his King Salmon. At the beginning of the film, we see Owen furiously wash his hands after a dying man has touched him and later we see him alone in a posh hotel piecing together a puzzle of the great outdoors when the real great outdoors beckons to him. By the end of the film, Owen has bonded to Carley the waitress and the residents of the retirement home.

*Here's to Life* is a small film with a universal story and its breathtaking photography saves it from becoming another movie of the week. The ravishing Hunter proves that an aging actresses can deliver a mesmerizing performance and Whitmore, with his gritting teeth and periodic outbursts, plays a man who demands respect from those younger than himself. McCormack and Davis round off the other actors' strong performances.

—*Patty-Lynne Herlevi*

## CREDITS

**Owen Rinarad:** Eric McCormack
**Gus Corley:** James Whitmore
**Nelly Ormand:** Kim Hunter
**Duncan Cox:** Ossie Davis
**Carley:** Marya Delver

**Origin:** Canada
**Released:** 2000

**Production:** William Vince; Rock Up a Hill Productions; released by Overseas Film Group
**Directed by:** Arne Olsen
**Written by:** Arne Olsen
**Cinematography by:** David Geddes
**Music by:** Patric Caird
**Editing:** Lisa Binkley
**Art Direction:** Ray Lai
**Costumes:** Patricia Hargreaves
**Production Design:** Don MacAulay
**MPAA rating:** Unrated
**Running time:** 94 minutes

## REVIEWS

*eye Weekly Online.* August 23, 2001.

## AWARDS AND NOMINATIONS

**Genie 2000:** Score
**Nomination:**
**Genie 2000:** Actor (Whitmore), Actress (Hunter), Costume Des., Song ("Dumb ol' Heart", "I've Never Been in Love Before").

# High Heels and Low Lifes

*Crime has never been so attractive.*
—Movie tagline

**Box Office:** $.1 million

The *Los Angeles Times* didn't minced words when describing the performance of *High Heels and Low Lifes* on its opening weekend. The paper reported that the film "bombed," taking in a "dismal" $648 average per screen. Contrast this to *Life as a House*, a film with a similarly limited release that came out the same weekend. That film took in $10,138 per theater. There was really nothing wrong with the film, it just didn't seem to capture the attention of moviegoers. And while *High Heels and Low Lifes* was a perfectly acceptable little film, it wasn't good enough to spark the kind of word of mouth advertising that might perk up its box office receipts the following weekend.

The film, an import from the U.K., is a crime comedy with its twist being that its main characters are women. In

2001, that's not really much of a twist, but then the film was written by Kim Fuller, whose previous career high point was *Spice World*, the Spice Girls' movie. To be fair, *High Heels* is nothing like the random, senseless *Spice World*. Thankfully, the only thing the two films share is female heroines.

Shannon (Minnie Driver) is a British nurse who comes home from work ready to celebrate her birthday with her boyfriend (Darren Boyd). The boyfriend is a snobby fellow who fancies himself an avant-garde artist. He uses a scanner to pick up other people's phone conversations, then mixes then together into what he calls an "urban noise symphony." He's so involved with his work that he can't drag himself away to celebrate Shannon's birthday. When she protests, he complains that she doesn't understand his work. Dejected and realizing that she's going to have to break up with him, Shannon turns to her only other friend, Frances (Mary McCormack), an actress. Frances isn't very successful at her work. She can't even get a job doing a voiceover for an cartoon alien tomato.

The two girls go out drinking and celebrating and when they return, drunk, to Shannon's apartment, they start listening to Shannon's boyfriend's scanner and overhear a nighttime bank robbery being committed. They go to the police to report what they know but aren't taken seriously. As no reasonable real person would do, but any person in a movie would do, they decide to take matters into their own hands. Frances, affecting the voice of a thuggish British guy, calls the cell phone of one of the criminals and threatens to turn him in to the police, unless he hands over part of the money. At first Shannon isn't very eager about this plan, but when Frances explains that she could use her part of the haul to buy equipment for the hospital, Shannon relents. This is one of those plot points that doesn't seem very realistic but that we must just accept.

The criminals, Mason (Kevin McNally) and his boss, Kerrigan (Michael Gambon), are tough guys and aren't about to just hand over any money. At a planned money drop in a city park garbage can, the women watch as one of the criminals leaves a sack in the can. As they get ready to retrieve it, they notice a homeless person getting there first. They're shocked when some of Mason and Kerrigan's men rush back to the scene and start shooting the poor guy, nearing killing him.

You'd think that this would clue the women in to the idea that maybe they're in over their heads, but no, they decide to get even more involved. Of course, it would not be much of a movie if the two just stopped there and went back to their everyday jobs, but still, it would have been nice if the plot didn't force the characters to make such ridiculous decisions. So instead of giving it all up and saving their hides, Frances calls the criminals back and ups the ante.

So continues the somewhat forced wackiness. There is shooting, the blowing up of cars, and heartless killing. Ha ha ha! To make sure that we realize that it's different that it's

women who are involved with all these activities, director Mel Smith (who also directed *Bean* and the much more subtle and funny *The Tall Guy*) makes sure the Annie Lennox and Aretha Franklin hit, "Sisters Are Doing It For Themselves" is playing. Smith does have a few brief moments of inspiration during the film. The best is a montage where the women are gearing up for a face-off with the bad guys that's done with a multiple split screen. It's all very mod and 1960s and fun to watch. Especially good is that on some of the screens, the characters are shown doing not particularly interesting things.

The movie takes much of its humor from the idea that these women don't really know what they're doing and their lack of slickness. When they're making a threatening call to the criminals, for example, Shannon complains, "Hurry up! This phone booth smells of pee." When Frances is using a cell phone to give complicated instructions about yet another money drop (don't these women learn that these hardened criminals aren't just going to hand over money?), her slick plan is hindered by the fact that her cell phone keeps cutting out. *High Heels* makes good use of the idea of everyday nuisances cropping up in these big, high stakes criminal activities. In one funny recurring joke, Shannon just happens to be the nurse for each of the series of victims that result from their shenanigans. The humor isn't that even. At one point a character explains that something is "child's play." "That should be easy for you then," retorts the other. It's okay humor for the fifth grade playground, but not exactly the stuff of witty Brit crime capers.

And the movie is stuck with the same dumb plot moments that most crime movies seem to have. At one point Mason doesn't kill one of the girls, even though according to his behavior throughout the rest of the film, he should have no problem doing so. "You're lucky to be alive—for the moment!" he says ominously. Why do they not teach this on the first day of criminal school—when you finally catch your enemy after a long and arduous chase, THAT would be the time to kill them.

The performers seem to be having a good time with their roles. Driver uses her usually tart tongue and comic timing to tweak some of the lines into sounding better than they are. Especially good is Gambon as big boss Kerrigan. He has an essentially silly role—his character lives in a giant mansion and has a handsome servant boy who caters to his every whim—but he manages to convey that Kerrigan is both ultra-powerful, yet vulnerable and out of touch. As Mason, McNally plays a standard tough-guy role and, indeed, appears appropriately tough. McCormack isn't up to par. When she calls the bad guys and pretends to be a guy herself, she doesn't sound anything like a guy. Or maybe that's the point. It's difficult to tell if she's supposed to be showing that her character is a bad actress or if she is actually a bad actress herself.

Critics had a decidedly mixed reaction to the film. Kevin Thomas of the *Los Angeles Times* hated it and wrote, "It's essentially a numskull business in which everyone suffers from varying degrees of stupidity, and it depends on violence for much of its humor, which these days is less amusing than ever." Mark Adams of the *Hollywood Reporter* loved the film and wrote, "There is a lot of subversive fun to be had in the comedy-thriller *High Heels and Low Lifes,* a refreshingly engaging British movie that isn't afraid to go all out for laughs and thrills, leaving its social conscience behind." Kevin Maynard of Mr. Showbiz wrote, "At its best, *High Heels* is an enjoyable female buddy caper—more *Outrageous Fortune* than *Thelma and Louise*—worth cheering if for no other reason than because its screwball protagonists get the dough and save the day without the slightest assistance from the opposite sex." And Rob Blackwelder of Spliced Wire had a mixed response in his own review, writing "Despite the fact that I'm about to rip into this picture for its non-stop, intelligence-insulting assault to idiotic cliches, plot holes, predictability and common sense chasms, *High Heels* has such an infectious, lively spirit that I wish it could have been better."

—*Jill Hamilton*

**Shannon:** Minnie Driver
**Frances:** Mary McCormack
**Mason:** Kevin McNally
**Tremaine:** Mark Williams
**Danny:** Danny Dyer
**Kerrigan:** Michael Gambon
**McGill:** Kevin Eldon
**Barry:** Len Collin
**Ray:** Darren Boyd
**Rogers:** Julian Wadham

**Origin:** Great Britain, USA
**Released:** 2001
**Production:** Barnaby Thompson, Uri Fructmann; Fragile Films; released by Touchstone Pictures
**Directed by:** Mel Smith
**Written by:** Kim Fuller
**Cinematography by:** Steven Chivers
**Music by:** Charlie Mole
**Sound:** Colin Nicolson
**Editing:** Christopher Blunden
**Art Direction:** Roger A. Bowles
**Costumes:** Jany Temime
**Production Design:** Mike Pickwood
**MPAA rating:** R
**Running time:** 85 minutes

## REVIEWS

*Los Angeles Times Online.* October 26, 2001.
*Sight and Sound.* July, 2001, p. 43.
*Variety.* July 23, 2001, p. 17.

# Hit and Runway

Those individuals considering a career as a screenwriter would benefit from watching independent director/screenwriter Christopher Livingston's *Hit and Runway,* for this small film not only explores the agonizing process of writing a screenplay but also shows a possible end result. Based on co-writers Livingston and Jaffe Cohen's premise "what if the next Matt Damon and Ben Affleck had nothing in common? In fact, what if one of them was a working-class stiff with more determination than talent and the other was gay and gifted, but so full of cynicism that he could never see actually accomplishing anything," this independent release comes across as a contemporary *Odd Couple.* And this screenplay about writing a screenplay also warns that two guys being forced together to write a screenplay is like a marriage in which the couple needs to communicate with one another.

At times *Hit and Runway* buries itself in a sea of corny situations or one-liners and barely takes off. It's hard to tell if the writers were laughing at the corny scenes they created or if those scenes were created in earnest. For instance, in a bar scene aspiring screenwriter Alex (Michael Parducci) laments to the bookish Gwen (Judy Prescott), a fellow screenwriter, about how playwright Elliot Springer (Peter Jacobson) wanted the female lead to be a bookworm that wore glasses. Alex concluded that a bookworm wouldn't be sexy enough until, of course, Gwen takes off her glasses and proves Alex wrong. In fact, most of the scenes with Gwen prove to be rife with clichès. Fortunately, she's not the female lead but a supporting character and most of the film revolves around partnership tension between gay, Jewish Elliot and testosterone-driven Alex. And even some of those scenes lack a fresh take on the art of screenwriting.

The premise of the film revolves around stale material and most of the humor derives from what would happen if a stereotypical Italian working-class aspiring writer came together with a Jewish gay man. Basically these men are complete opposites. Alex is the macho, ambitious optimist while Elliot appears to be a gay version of Woody Allen, whining about his pathetic life and afraid of almost everything. Although the Elliot character adds much-needed humor to the film with his cynical one-liners, especially his put downs of Alex's small vocabulary, this character relies too heavily on the Allen comparison, but his gayness does add a bit extra to the character and actually saves the film.

Alex's uncle asks Alex to write a screenplay for action movie star Jagger Stevens (Hoyt Richards), which is the chance of a lifetime. However, Alex can't write, so he makes a deal with Elliott, who appears to be overly cynical of Hollywood and afraid of success. Elliott agrees to assists Alex with his screenplay *Hit and Runway* if Alex fixes him up with gay waiter Joey (Kerr Smith), who works at Alex's family's café. At first things go smoothly. Elliott and Joey hit it off since Joey has a fetish for Jewish men, especially when they speak in Yiddish. But then problems arise after Elliott takes Joey to his synagogue and Joey lusts after Elliot's rabbi (Stephen Singer).

The film's narrative falls apart at this point because there's little tension to sustain the plot further. Writers Livingston and Cohen throw in a few disasters, such as the script being destroyed a few hours before its deadline, a moral issue about Alex turning in one of Elliot's plays as his writing sample, and the disastrous effect the Hollywood treatment would have on the screenplay. Perhaps if the writing team had endured a few more drafts of their screenplay, *Hit and Runway* would have given us a fresh take on the creative process between two opposing personalities instead of an episodic soap opera.

Independent films expose us to new faces or allow television personalities to hit their mark on the big screen. Jacobson in particular possesses wonderful comedic timing—blurting out cynical one-liners as in the case where Joey says he'd like to hang something neutral on his apartment walls and Elliott tells him to hang a poster of Switzerland. Jacobson renders Elliott as one of the funniest gay characters to come along in the past few years. His exploits would be worth exploring further but *Hit and Runway* lacks the ability to entertain.

—*Patty-Lynne Herlevi*

**Alex Andero:** Michael Parducci
**Elliot Springer:** Peter Jacobson
**Joey Worcieukowski:** Kerr Smith
**Gwen Colton:** Judy Prescott
**Ray Tillman:** J.K. Simmons
**Lana:** Teresa De Priest
**Jagger Stevens:** Hoyt Richards
**Frank Andero:** John Fiore
**Rabbi Pinchas:** Stephen Singer

**Origin:** USA
**Released:** 2001

**Production:** Andrew Charas, Chris D'Annibale, Christopher Livingston; released by Lot 47 Films
**Directed by:** Christopher Livingston
**Written by:** Christopher Livingston, Jaffe Cohen
**Cinematography by:** David Tumblety
**Music by:** Frank Piazza
**Editing:** Christopher Livingston, Rhonda Mitrani
**Costumes:** Jory Adam
**Production Design:** Mark Helmuth
**MPAA rating:** R
**Running time:** 90 minutes

REVIEWS

*New York Times Online.* March 9, 2001.

QUOTES

Elliot (Peter Jacobson): "Joey is gorgeous. I'm funny looking. In the gay world we have a caste system no less rigid than the Hindus. It would be like a Brahmin dating an untouchable."

# The Holy Tongue (La Lingua del Santo)

Starring accomplished actors Antonio Albanese (Antonio) and Fabrizio Bentivoglio (Willy), Italian director Carlo Mazzacurati's *The Holy Tongue* recalls Federico Fellini's *La Strada* and *Variety of Lights* with its tragicomedy approach. In fact, *The Holy Tongue*, with its absurd narrative and disenfranchised characters, portrays the range of humanity found in Fellini's first few outings. David Rooney of *Variety* wrote ". . .Albanese and Bentivoglio bounce off each other with effortless affinity. Their contrasting personalities and physical types—the former chubby and jovial with a volatile and sometimes surly streak; the latter dejected and lost-looking, incapable of reacting against the sadness that weighs him down—provide the comedy with a lively dynamic that recalls any number of classic comic screen pairings. . . ." Rooney goes on to praise cinematographer Alessandro Pesci's handy work calling it "handsome," then adding that his "customary use of deep, robust colors has never been sharper. . . ." And yes, *The Holy Tongue* proves to be all of that without the usual melodramatics found in Italian cinema.

As the film opens, an English narrator provides the voice for Italian character Willy, who recently lost his wife and his job but who also embarked on an amazing friendship with Antonio, a former rugby champion. The English narrator, with his distinct upper-class accent, feels out of place representing an Italian working-class man who never learned English or how to use a computer, limiting his job prospects. The director should have cast an Italian actor who spoke English instead, because this flaw detracts from the narrative throughout the film.

One fateful night Antonio and Willy decide to steal computers from the same elementary school and so begins an unusual friendship between petty thieves. Willy proves to be the rational-minded one when he isn't scheming ways to get his ex-wife back from the wealthy doctor that she married. Antonio plays opposite to Willy's calm and self-contained demeanor since he is indulgent (cigarettes, booze and food), lacks any self-control, and has a knack for getting himself into uncomfortable situations. The first collision of personalities appears when the men rob a church and Antonio steals a holy relic, the tongue of Saint Anthony. A former altar boy, Willy demands that Antonio return the tongue, but the reluctant Antonio would rather cash in on fame and fortune. Although guilt-ridden, Willy caves in when he thinks how proud his former wife will be if he suddenly became wealthy, so the two men cook up plan to collect a ransom for the relic.

However, the plan goes awry when leaders of the Catholic church admit on the TV news that they have plenty of holy relics and, although they feel upset over the missing tongue, they won't spend any time searching for it. However, a local mayor, who wishes to be a hero, puts a call out for the kidnappers to return the tongue for a ransom. This causes the thieves to set up camp in Willy's ex-wife's country home. But paranoia almost destroys the two men. After a couple of attempts to collect the ransom, they finally succeed, but the ending proves bittersweet since Willy stays behind to reunite with his former wife while Antonio leaves Italy never able to return.

In many ways, *The Holy Tongue* recalls Jim Jarmusch's *Down by Law* because both films concern the unlikely friendships of people who are forced together by life circumstances. Antonio is the brainless former athlete who is ruled by his lust for life, while the unemployed Willy still wears a suit and tie while relentlessly stalking his ex. Antonio substitutes vices for his former glory, while Willy rejects fleeting pleasures. He is as single-minded as Antonio is absent-minded, leading to some wonderful comic moments.

*—Patty-Lynne Herlevi*

## REVIEWS

*Variety.* September 18, 2000, p. 35.

# House of Mirth

*When a woman has the beauty men admire and women envy . . . it is wise to tread carefully.*
—Movie tagline

**Box Office:** $2.9 million

Mirth is noticeably absent in Terence Davies's soporific film adaptation of the Edith Wharton nove *The House of Mirth*. The story follows the downward spiral of an early 20th century New York City socialite, Lucy Bart (Gillian Anderson), who refuses to follow the social conventions of the day but is unable to break free from their hold on her life and fortunes.

The film is unusual in several respects. Davies is best known for chronicling the troubles of the British working class in films such as 1988's *Distant Voices, Still Lives.* But Wharton's novel begs audiences to sympathize with various paltry problems of the upper classes, having mostly to do with matrimonial and sexual scruples. Although *The House of Mirth* is one of Wharton's most acclaimed novels, prior to this effort it had not been filmed since 1918, and for good reason. The decision to remake it was no doubt due to the relative success of two 1990s adaptations of other Wharton novels, *Ethan Frome* and *The Age of Innocence,* as well as a spate of other recent artsy films about mores in Victorian society.

The casting of this version of *Mirth* is problematic. The first non-*X-Files* starring vehicle for television and Internet cult goddess Gillian Anderson, the film puts its leading lady on excruciatingly close-up display for long stretches of time, demanding far more than most actresses can sustain. Anderson is surrounded by a hit-and-miss supporting group. The film makes good use of the underappreciated Eric Stoltz and character actor Anthony LaPaglia. Laura Linney brilliantly steals her few scenes, playing Lucy's most formidable nemesis. On the other hand, comic Dan Aykroyd is ridiculously miscast in a crucial role as Lucy's meddlesome benefactor. Veteran Eleanor Bron, playing Lucy's stern aunt, looks like she is mimicking Margaret Hamilton's Wicked Witch of the West in *The Wizard of Oz..* Largely wasted is rarely seen former teenage star Elizabeth McGovern, playing an unexplained friend of Lucy's who pops out of nowhere two-thirds of the way through the movie and then disappears.

Davies, who wrote this extremely faithful screen adaptation of Wharton's dense book, deserves credit for authentic period detail both in the look and dialogue of the film. Cinematographer Remi Adarafasin and costume designer Monica Howe also deserve plaudits for the striking realism of *The House of Mirth.* In many quiet moments in which Lucy is contemplating her fate, Davies focuses with great subtlety on small objects in the room, or his star's reflection in a train window, or some minor but revealing feature of apparel or furnishing. Only on a few occasions does Davies go overboard, resorting to gauzy, sepia-toned shots which try too obviously to invoke the feelings of a bygone era.

When we first meet Lucy, she is a sassy though self-doubting eligible young woman of scandalous independence. She is brazen enough to accept an invitation from Lawrence Selden (Stoltz) to spend an idle afternoon hour in his Manhattan flat and share a few cigarettes and some daring conversation. Already, though, she is wondering aloud whether her reputation for being on the prowl for a well-to-do husband is damaging her worth on the marital commodities market.

In this early going, Davies trains a gently satiric focus on the foibles of the idle classes. Selden and Lucy engage in an elaborate form of verbal and social gamesmanship, trading witty thrusts of their linguistic sabers while disguising the depths of their true mutual affection. Selden teases Lucy for wanting a richer man than him to marry; Lucy strikes back at Selden's own hypocrisy while toying with his affections. But it is Selden's refusal to risk his own cause that dooms Lucy to keep looking elsewhere.

This story is full of such thwarted romantic ambitions and frustrating blind alleys. Wharton is expert at delineating the various elaborate traps by which Victorian society kept women dependent. Lucy is modern but not quite freethinking enough to throw off conventions; she is doomed by her own financial restraints and never seems to have a full deck of cards to play in her social quests.

The film moves at a glacial pace as it unfolds the key plot elements and outlines the increasing desperateness of Lucy's dilemma. Linney's Bertha Dorset is Lucy's slyly scheming friend, providing her with husband-hunting opportunities at soirees on a country estate while laying her own plans to cheat on her husband George (Terry Kinney). Aykroyd's Gus Trenor helps Lucy with investments, using the services of brilliant Wall Street financier Sim Rosedale (LaPaglia), but it turns out that both men are seeking something back from Lucy in return for their help. Despite never transgressing seriously against Victorian society's strict mores, Lucy skates on thin ice as her behavior increasingly inspires gossip. The talk unnerves her aunt, Mrs. Peniston (Bron), who provides Lucy with room and board and some regular income, but who ends up favoring her other niece Grace Stepney (Jodhi May).

Eventually, Bertha unfolds her most dastardly plot during a Mediterranean vacation, taking her own liberties with a local Frenchman at Monte Carlo while setting up Lucy to take the fall for their marital troubles. Unjustly accused and disgraced, Lucy stubbornly refuses to salvage her hopes for marriage and respectability out of loyalty to Selden. Letters from Bertha to Selden, which Lucy has acquired, would give Lucy several avenues to rehabilitate herself, but instead she sinks into poverty, wage labor, and despair.

The most glaring flaw in this muddled film is its lack of explanation for Lucy's reluctance to use the letters. One interpretation is that Lucy, for all her minor transgressions against the social code, is actually the most ethical person in her social set; this would make the story a devastating critique of Victorian hypocrisy. But Lucy has already revealed herself to be shallow and selfish, and perhaps she is doomed because she clings to her own pride. Clearly, the only man who interests her is Selden, but he keeps withholding his declarations of true love until it is too late.

Lucy's motivations are somewhat opaque partly because it is difficult to appreciate fully the nuances of Victorian strictures. Davies refuses to help clarify things, and Anderson's performance fails to make Lucy's feelings come alive. Brilliantly cunning in her flirtatious mode, Anderson has both the intelligence and the quirky, porcelain beauty to portray a free spirit straining at and toying with the boundaries of acceptable behavior. Yet she is quickly used up as the camera plays with the upturned corners of her mouth, lingers too long on her face, makes her into too much of an icon. Few actresses could bear this scrutiny, and Anderson doesn't hold up well. Her performance takes on a rote, stagy quality as her character descends further into desperation. Could a woman this resourceful and intelligent also be so clueless about how to manipulate situations to her advantage? The problem with Lucy Bart is making her intelligible to modern audiences, and Anderson does not find the key to this difficult portrayal.

In contrast is the extremely talented Linney, an absolute marvel of repugnant self-assurance. It is true that Bertha Dorset is an easier part than Lucy Bart, but Linney is so compelling that one can be forgiven for wondering what she might accomplish if she had been given Anderson's role. Stoltz is eminently watchable in an even more forgiving role.

In the end, most of the blame for how badly *The House of Mirth* goes astray must go to Davies. The plot turns to mush in places where new characters such as McGovern's Carry Fisher are introduced as if they should be well known to audiences. Davies does not solve the screenwriter-adapter's key dilemma in approaching a long, complicated novel: cutting to the chase. Indecisive about minor characters, Davies lets them hang around on the fringes, cluttering up the landscape. The same is true with some of the more minor plot points. This lack of focus is both fatal and inexcusable, because Wharton's story is at bottom not all that complicated. It just takes her—and Davies—a long time to get it resolved.

A film in which you know a half-hour before the climax exactly what the end is going to be cannot be called a success. One should not be kept waiting for the inevitable. And for someone with a demonstrated authority about matters of social class, Davies treads much too lightly on the moral vicissitudes of his upper-class protagonists.

But Davies has at least made a defensible choice in his approach. To many latter-day revisionists, it would be tempting to make Lucy Bart into a courageous though doomed pre-feminist heroine. *The House of Mirth* prefers a frustrating realism. Combined with Anderson's sometimes flat performance, that choice makes Lucy Bart into an unsympathetic, hard-to-grasp protagonist. We are distanced from her plight in so many ways that it becomes as antique and uninvolving as a room full of Victorian furniture. In both the best and the worst senses, *Mirth* is a period piece—stodgy, refusing to take risks, but uncompromising in its devotion to its source material.

—*Michael Betzold*

## CREDITS

**Lily Bart:** Gillian Anderson
**Lawrence Selden:** Eric Stoltz
**Gus Trenor:** Dan Aykroyd
**Mrs. Peniston:** Eleanor Bron
**George Dorset:** Terry Kinney
**Sim Rosedale:** Anthony LaPaglia
**Bertha Dorset:** Laura Linney
**Grace Stepney:** Jodhi May
**Carry Fisher:** Elizabeth McGovern

**Origin:** Great Britain, USA
**Released:** 2000
**Production:** Olivia Stewart; Showtime Networks, Granada, Arts Council of England, FilmFour, Glasgow Film Fund; released by Sony Pictures Classics
**Directed by:** Terence Davies
**Written by:** Terence Davies
**Cinematography by:** Remi Adefarasin
**Sound:** Paul Hamblin
**Editing:** Michael Parker
**Costumes:** Monica Howe
**Production Design:** Don Taylor
**MPAA rating:** PG-13
**Running time:** 140 minutes

## REVIEWS

*Boxoffice.* November, 2000, p. 153.
*Chicago Sun-Times Online.* December 22, 2000.
*Entertainment Weekly.* December 15, 2000, p. 44.
*Los Angeles Times Online.* December 22, 2000.
*New York Times Online.* September 23, 2000.
*Rolling Stone.* December 14, 2000, p. 178.
*Variety.* August 14, 2000, p. 20.
*Washington Post Online.* January 19, 2001.

## QUOTES

Lily Bart (Gillian Anderson): "I have been about too long. People are tired of me."

# Human Resources (Ressources Humaines)

French director Laurent Cantet's debut feature, *Human Resources,* is a provocative, yet bleak, film that unveils the social upheaval between labor and management. Cantet blends hyper-realism, recalling Roberto Rossellini and Vittorio De Sica's films with an explosive father and son drama (the father representing labor and the son representing management). While the writer-director reveals both sides equally, he leans heavily towards the workers' side. In the end, Cantet paints a grim picture of the future of the work force, but he refuses to write a happy ending, thus leaving viewers with a provocative topic to discuss after viewing the film. The actors who portrayed the factory workers in *Human Resources* were actual factory workers. The film was also shot inside a factory, leaving viewers with an authentic setting based on real life circumstances and yet, the film is fictional and not a fly-on-the-wall documentary.

Cantet's film begins with the arrival of the college-educated Franck (Jalil Lespert) returning to his home town to intern in the human resources department of the factory where his father (Jean-Claude Vallod) has toiled as a laborer for 30 years. The enthusiastic yet cocky Franck wins the admiration of the executives in his department, but he also falls into the trap of management's deception by accepting his boss's false flattery. As management give Franck a tour of the factory, his father glows with pride for his son, who strides by dressed in a borrowed business suit. The father, who sacrificed to send Franck to university, now lives out his own unrealized ambitions through his son, but he displays unease when seeing Franck mingling with the executives and, similar to the other laborers, the father also fears his son's newly acquired power.

Franck impresses his boss with his proposal, which would allow the workers to give their opinion about a 35-hour workweek. While the executives jump at the opportunity to question the workers behind the union organizer's back, organizer Danielle Arnoux (Danielle Melador) dukes it out verbally with the naïve Franck. However, Arnoux loses the battle and she resigns as the factory's union rep. While Franck celebrates his victory with the duplicitous executives, the executives deal the final coup de grace after they use the workers' opinions as an excuse to fire the 12 eldest workers, including Franck's father. After Franck finds a secret letter on the computer that mentions the termination of the workers, he switches sides and posts the confidential letter on the factory window to incite the workers, which eventually culminates in a strike in which the workers shut down production at the factory.

The final showdown between the father and son takes place at the factory as the loyal factory laborer refuses to stop working while his son berates him in front of a crowd of his colleagues and the union representative. The crest-fallen father loses the battle with Franck and reluctantly joins the workers on strike. However, no one wins the war between management and labor and film's open ending leaves viewers with a question and not a solution.

Film critics praised the realistic portrayal of the plight of factory workers by the non-professional actors. Stephen Holden of the *New York Times* wrote: "It is so beautifully acted that the cast, especially the non-professional actors playing the embattled factory workers, seems plucked from the streets of a provincial French town." And *Village Voice* critic Amy Taubin thought "The father is played with remarkable nuance and vulnerability by Jean-Claude Vallod."

—*Patty-Lynne Herlevi*

## CREDITS

**Franck:** Jalil Lespert
**Father:** Jean-Claude Vallod
**Mother:** Chantal Barre
**Sylvie:** Veronique de Pandelaere
**Olivier:** Michel Begnez
**Mrs. Amoux:** Danielle Melador
**Alain:** Didier Emile-Woldermard
**The Boss:** Lucien Longueville

**Origin:** France
**Language:** French
**Released:** 1999
**Production:** Carole Scotta; Haut et Court; released by Shooting Gallery
**Directed by:** Laurent Cantet
**Written by:** Gilles Marchand, Laurent Cantet
**Cinematography by:** Mathieu Poirot-Delpech, Claire Caroff
**Sound:** Antoine Ouvrier
**Editing:** Robin Campillo
**Art Direction:** Romain Denis
**Costumes:** Marie Cessari
**MPAA rating:** Unrated
**Running time:** 100 minutes

## REVIEWS

*Boxoffice.* November, 2000, p. 182.
*Chicago Sun-Times Online.* September 15, 2000.
*Entertainment Weekly.* September 29, 2000, p. 104.

*Seattle Post Intelligencer Online.* September 15, 2000.
*Seattle Times Online.* September 14, 2000.
*Seattle Weekly.* September 14, 2000, p. 96.
*Variety.* October 4, 1999, p. 87.
*Village Voice Online.* September 13, 2000.

# I Am Sam

*love is all you need*
—Movie tagline

 **Box Office:** $35.4 million

In Jessie Nelson's *I Am Sam,* Sean Penn gives a tender, sympathetic performance as Sam Dawson, a mentally retarded man fighting for custody of his daughter when the state tries to take her from him. It is a potentially melodramatic situation, but the film largely succeeds because it earns its emotions with the well-drawn relationships among the principal characters. While the script is full of holes and odd lapses, especially in the legal aspects of the story, the brave performance by Penn as well as the performances of Michelle Pfeiffer as Sam's hard-bitten lawyer and Dakota Fanning as his seven-year-old daughter make up for the often clumsy storytelling.

No sooner does Sam become a father at the film's opening than he is on his own. The mother, a homeless woman to whom Sam had given shelter, deserts him immediately after giving birth, leaving the helpless Sam to fend for himself. His early attempts at caring for a baby, however, are pretty awkward—even pinning diapers seems out of his grasp—but his kind neighbor, Annie (Dianne Wiest), an agoraphobic pianist, provides help along the way. As a huge fan of the Beatles, Sam names his daughter Lucy after "Lucy in the Sky with Diamonds." She has a wonderful rapport with her father, who adores her, plays with her, and, when she grows up, even reads to her from Dr. Seuss.

Around the time Lucy is seven, the situation starts to get complicated. Lucy is on the verge of surpassing her father's mental capacity and is so uncomfortable that she starts holding herself back in school, even resisting reading a book assigned for class because her father cannot read it. In a heartbreaking scene, Sam struggles with the words, and Penn, through the subtlest facial gestures, brilliantly communicates Sam's pain at not being able to read a simple book to his daughter. At about the same time, in a huge plot contrivance, Sam is arrested on the charge of soliciting a prostitute—any policeman with just an ounce of common sense would be able to see that Sam was not propositioning the woman.

The film, however, needs a pretext for the Department of Child and Family Services to get involved, and, even though Sam is quickly released from jail, a social worker, Margaret Calgrove (Loretta Devine), begins investigating Sam. It is more than a little perplexing why Sam's suitability as a parent has never been questioned before by anyone—Lucy's teachers, for example. In yet another plot contrivance, Margaret sees him get mad at a little boy at Lucy's surprise birthday party and, concluding that Lucy needs a so-called normal home, has her taken from Sam pending a custody hearing.

Sam has a group of mentally challenged friends like himself who help him find a lawyer, and they settle on one from the Yellow Pages because the ad looks so good. Soon Sam is at the office of Rita Harrison (Pfeiffer), a high-powered, workaholic attorney who lives a fast-paced life and cannot connect with her own son. At first, she tries to give Sam the brush-off, but he persistently keeps coming to her office, and she is embarrassed in front of her colleagues into taking the case pro bono.

It is of course a tough case since none of Sam's retarded pals would make persuasive witnesses. Rita does, however, get the upper hand on a court-appointed psychologist testifying against Sam by questioning her about her own failures as a parent, namely her own son's death by a drug overdose. Unfortunately, this feels like a diversion from the real issue, which is Sam's abilities as a parent.

Much of the testimony, in fact, feels scattershot, as if screenwriters Nelson and Kristine Johnson were unsure how each witness fit into the overall case. Mary Steenburgen pops up out of nowhere as a successful doctor whose own personal story illustrates that a person raised by a mother of less than normal intelligence can succeed, but we never find out where Rita found her, and she never appears again.

Worried that she will be separated from her father forever, Lucy escapes from custody and persuades Sam to run off with her, whereupon they take a long bus trip and spend the night in a park only to be caught by authorities and brought back. A "kidnapping" charge is the last thing Sam needs, and, while it is alluded to at the hearing, it is not really given much weight. Annie finally testifies on Sam's behalf, but, under cross-examination, the mean opposing attorney, Turner (Richard Schiff), drills her about her agoraphobia and her own strained relationship with her father, which, like so much of the courtroom testimony, feels like a nonissue.

Thus, the courtroom scenes, which should form the heart of the debate of what makes a good parent, are pretty flimsy, but the central relationship between Sam and Lucy makes up for the film's flaws. Fanning projects an intelligence and maturity as Lucy without becoming a stereotypical precocious movie child. And Penn envelops his character completely—struggling to put thoughts together and express himself coherently or simply reacting spontaneously in the moment, throwing his arms around someone to show his unbridled affection or shouting to his friends when they support him in the courtroom. While it hearkens back to Dustin Hoffman's role in *Rain Man,* Sam is not a savant. Negotiating his way in a supermarket, making simple purchases, and keeping track of bus schedules are chores, and the movie shines when it presents us with the little moments that show how Sam struggles each day to get through life. It also shows the funny, happy moments—the joy he takes in his work as a busboy at Starbucks as he cheerfully interacts with customers and the camaraderie he feels with his friends.

The script, however, contrives to make Sam the biggest underdog possible. On the day of his courtroom testimony, he wears to work the expensive clothes that Rita picked out for him from her husband's wardrobe. It just so happens that on this day he has been promoted at Starbucks to making coffee for the first time. He does fine for a while, but, when the pace gets to be too much for him, he ends up getting coffee all over himself and then comes to the courthouse late and must give his testimony looking like a mess. This is unbelievable—no lawyer as savvy as Rita, who spent the previous night rehearsing with him, would let him go to work in his dress clothes and then not make sure that he arrived in court on time. To make matters worse, once he is on the stand, Sam lapses into Dustin Hoffman's monologue on the witness stand in *Kramer vs. Kramer* and completely embarrasses himself. (One of his friends is a big fan of the movie.) Sam loses the case, but we do not hear the judge's decree, which is frustrating since this is supposed to be what all the courtroom scenes have been leading up to.

Lucy is assigned to a foster family that would like to adopt her. Sam, it seems, has certain visitation rights, but, when he approaches the home of Lucy and her foster mother, Randy (Laura Dern), he grows intimidated and turns away. Instead of visiting Lucy, he sulks in his apartment, where Rita finally finds him and tries to rouse him from his depression and urge him not to give up. Although the legal details are, once again, not made clear, Rita seems to suggest that he can still win Lucy back if he makes more money. Pfeiffer remains one of the most stunningly beautiful actresses in movies, and this scene in which she breaks down to Sam and cries about how she is not perfect like he thinks and even feels ugly strains believability. But it is a credit to Pfeiffer's skill that Rita's overall transformation under Sam's influence is subtle and feels natural as she slowly lets her guard down and opens herself up to others, especially her son.

As Sam is walking dogs to supplement his income, he finally sees Lucy, who is upset that he has not contacted her, but he quickly wins her over. He even moves to a new apartment to be near her—the screenplay, in yet another odd lapse, never makes it clear how Sam is able to live alone in nice apartments on his low wages, first at Starbucks and then at Pizza Hut. In a cute montage, Lucy keeps running

away at night to be with him, and he dutifully brings her back each time. Randy seems to have the best intentions and really loves Lucy, but she soon sees how much Lucy loves her father. So she brings Lucy to him and implies that she will side with him in the upcoming custody hearing.

The ending of the film is very murky. Once again, we do not hear the judge's decision, but, in the last scene, Sam is happily refereeing Lucy's soccer game. Randy and her husband watch from the stands, as do Rita and her son and all of Sam's old buddies. Under Sam's influence, Rita has gotten closer to her son, is less of a workaholic, and is now separated from her husband, who had been cheating on her. But despite the general feeling of goodwill in the last scene, it is a letdown that the film fudges on its resolution. We do not learn specifically what kind of deal or arrangement has been made regarding Lucy's future, although it seems that Sam, with a vast network of support behind him, has won custody.

The soundtrack features some great covers of classic Beatles songs by contemporary artists to punctuate certain emotional moments. For example, the idyllic "Strawberry Fields Forever" plays when Sam and Lucy run away, and "You've Got to Hide Your Love Away" expresses Sam's feelings when he first sees Lucy with Randy and turns away. Sam also uses his vast knowledge of Beatles trivia to express himself when all other ways fail him. When Lucy asks if her mom will return, for example, he tells her that John and Paul lost their mothers at an early age. There is even a cute moment when Sam, Lucy, and his pals walk across a street in imitation of the Abbey Road album cover.

Nelson and Johnson's screenplay spends a lot of time having characters debate what it means to be a good parent and then ends up consistently avoiding making a definitive statement on the legal issues involving Lucy's future and how Sam overcomes the opposition's concerns about his parenting abilities. While these plot holes prevent *I Am Sam* from becoming a great film of its genre, like *Kramer vs. Kramer,* which it liberally references, the heartfelt, moving relationships ground the film in an emotional reality that overcomes the screenplay's narrative shortcomings.

*—Peter N. Chumo II*

## CREDITS

**Sam Dawson:** Sean Penn
**Rita:** Michelle Pfeiffer
**Lucy:** Dakota Fanning
**Annie:** Dianne Wiest
**Margaret Calgrove:** Loretta Devine
**Turner:** Richard Schiff
**Randy Carpenter:** Laura Dern
**Brad:** Brad Allan Silverman
**Robert:** Stanley DeSantis

**Ifty:** Doug Hutchison
**Joe:** Joseph Rosenberg
**Dr. Blake:** Mary Steenburgen

**Origin:** USA
**Released:** 2001
**Production:** Richard Soloman, Marshall Herskovitz, Edward Zwick, Jessie Nelson; Bedford Falls, Red Fish, Blue Fish Films; released by New Line Cinema
**Directed by:** Jessie Nelson
**Written by:** Jessie Nelson, Kristine Johnson
**Cinematography by:** Elliot Davis
**Music by:** John Powell
**Sound:** Douglas Axtell
**Editing:** Richard Chew
**Art Direction:** Erin Cochran
**Costumes:** Suzie DeSanto
**Production Design:** Aaron Osborne
**MPAA rating:** PG-13
**Running time:** 93 minutes

 **REVIEWS**

*Chicago Sun-Times Online.* January 25, 2002.
*Entertainment Weekly.* January 18, 2002, p. 55.
*Los Angeles Times Online.* December 28, 2001.
*New York Times Online.* December 28, 2001.
*People.* January 21, 2002, p. 29.
*USA Today Online.* December 28, 2001.
*Variety.* December 24, 2001, p. 21.
*Washington Post.* January 25, 2002, p. WE39.

**QUOTES**

Lucy (Dakota Fanning): "Daddy, did God mean for you to be like this, or was it an accident?"

**AWARDS AND NOMINATIONS**

**Nomination:**
**Screen Actors Guild 2001:** Actor (Penn), Support. Actress (Fanning)
**Broadcast Film Critics 2001:** Actor (Penn).

# Ignorant Fairies (Fate Ignoranti) (Blind Fairies)

In a style similar to Pedro Almodovar's audacious cinema, Turkish-born director Ferzan Ozpetek's film *Ignorant Fairies* also seems to understand the machinations of a woman's heart. Ozpetek contrasts a conservative upper middle-class housewife's life with that of an Italian gay community in Rome. In many ways *Ignorant Fairies* resembles Almodovar's *All About My Mother* and the resemblance between the two films proves striking. Although both films portray a "camp" atmosphere, they also reflect on deeper issues revolving around love, family, community, and diversity. Ozpetek describes his film in the press kit: "The conventional single-nucleus family—that of the original couple in the film, Massimo and Antonia—is changing into an increasingly extended family, which to the superficial eye may seem alternative and revolutionary."

With his first film *Steam: A Turkish Bath* (1998), Ozpetek attempted to rediscover his Turkish roots through Italian eyes. His second film, 1999's *The Last Harem/Harem Square,* was an investigation into why the director broke away from his Turkish roots while immersing himself within the culture of his adopted country, Italy. *Ignorant Fairies* succinctly represents the contemporary times in which we live and the alternative lifestyles of urban communities. But even more, *Ignorant Fairies* reflects on how newly-widowed Antonia (Margherita Buy) mothers a diverse extended family.

After her husband Massimo (Andrea Renzi) is killed in a car accident, a painting (which gives the film its title), with an inscription from a mystery lover, arrives at Antonia's home. Grief-stricken Antonia decides to investigate Massimo's affair. Her investigation leads her to an artist community in the working-class Ostiense district and to one apartment in particular, which belongs to Michele (Stefano Accorsi). Here she learns that Massimo was having a long-term affair with a man and belonged to a community of gay men, transsexuals, and their women friends. A dramatic conflict arises between Michele and Antonia, leaving Michele feeling pangs of guilt for the distraught widow. But soon an unlikely friendship develops between the two and they realize that they have more in common with each other than they ever had in common with Massimo.

In one poignant scene Michele relates the story of how he met Massimo to Antonia—at a bookstore where both men fought over an out-of-print poetry book. Michele said that he fell in love with Massimo because of their love for the same poet. After Michele finishes his touching story, Antonia quotes one of the poet's poems, surprising Michele. Then she drops the bomb that Massimo bought the book for her and never knew the poet. And the film is peppered throughout with similar revelations about the characters' relationships with one another.

Meanwhile, Antonia's mother Veronica (Erica Blanc) intrudes upon her daughter's life. She tells everyone she knows that her daughter's deceased husband had an affair. She reflects on how hard it is to be the mistress and asks her daughter to befriend her former husband's lover, not realizing that the mistress was actually a mister. Later, after the maid Nora spies on Antonia and Michele, the mother thinks that her daughter is engaging in a new relationship. And in a way, she's right because Antonia has fallen for the gay Michele. However, Antonia also senses that her life has gotten out of hand, so she decides to take a vacation away from the madding crowd, but in actuality she has discovered a new life with a wonderful extended family.

Buy has the ability to capture one's heart with her expressive gaze while Accorsi blends vulnerability with intense sex appeal. Serra Yilmaz, who plays overweight neighbor Serra, who has a horrific past, adds the right blend of pathos to the mix, while Erica Blanc's Veronica brings much needed comic relief to the story and the remainder of the cast fill in the gaps by providing intense subplots and by creating a diverse community of people we learn to love.

—*Patty-Lynne Herlevi*

### CREDITS

**Antonia:** Margherita Buy
**Michele:** Stefano Accorsi
**Serra:** Serra Yilmaz
**Massimo:** Andrea Renzi
**Veronica:** Erika Blanc
**Ernesto:** Gabriel Garko
**Luisella:** Rosario De Cicco
**Mara:** Lucrezia Valia
**Emir:** Koray Candemir

**Origin:** France, Italy
**Language:** Italian
**Released:** 2001
**Directed by:** Ferzan Ozpetek
**Written by:** Ferzan Ozpetek, Gianni Romoli
**Cinematography by:** Pasquale Mari
**Music by:** Andrea Guerra
**Sound:** Marco Grillo
**Editing:** Patrizio Marone
**Costumes:** Catia Dottori

**Production Design:** Bruno Cesari
**MPAA rating:** Unrated
**Running time:** 105 minutes

### REVIEWS

*New York Times Online.* June 3, 2001.
*Variety.* February 26, 2001, p. 43.

### QUOTES

Antonia (Margherita Buy) to Michele (Stefano Accorsi): "I don't mind anything anymore."

### AWARDS AND NOMINATIONS

**Nomination:**
**Berlin Intl. Film Fest. 2001:** Film.

# In the Bedroom

*A young man. An older woman. Her ex-husband. Things are about to explode . . .*
—Movie tagline

 **Box Office:** $28.6 million

*I*n the Bedroom was to domestic drama what *Lord of the Rings* was to fantasy, an astonishing release that came as if from nowhere, directed by a novice director, Todd Field, a still photographer, sometime actor, and jazz musician, who earned critical accolades for his debut feature film, adapted with screenwriter Rob Festinger from the story "Killings" written by the late Andre Dubus in 1980. A native of Oregon trained by the American Film Institute, Field played piano player Nick Nightingale in Stanley Kubrick's last film, *Eyes Wide Shut* (1999). Field made the film for less than $2 million, but, he told David Ansen of *Newsweek,* "If I had $20 million it would look exactly the same." Anson considered Field a contender for Best Director and Best Adapted Screenplay. The cast was also considered Oscar®-worthy by other reviewers. This was a remarkable achievement for a novice director.

The story concerns a summer romance between a working-class married woman and mother, Natalie (Marisa Tomei), who intends to divorce her abusive husband, Richard Strout (William Mopother), and college-bound Frank Fowler (Nick Stahl), the son of local physician Matt Fowler (Tom Wilkinson) and Ruth Fowler (Sissy Spacek), a choral instructor who has specialized in the folk music of the Balkans (Croatia, Macedonia, and Bulgaria). The music, sung by her students, provides an eerie and primal aural background for the disturbing violence that results when the Richard attempts to return to the wife who has rejected him. Frank comes between Richard and Natalie when an armed Richard attempts to break into "his" house and shoots Frank in the face, killing him. The rest of the film concerns the consequences of this shooting.

From that point forward, the film finds its true subject as the Fowlers attempt to come to grips with what has happened to their family. Frank had told his mother and father about Richard's violent tendencies and Ruth had urged Matt to advise the police; but Frank did not want to involve the police, and his father remains neutral on this point. Had the police been advised, and had the courts placed a restraining order on Richard, the tragedy might have been averted.

Richard, the murderer, is the son of a wealthy and powerful family that owns the local canning factory in the Maine coastal town (Camden) where the action is set. When he is brought to trial, his lawyer establishes that Natalie heard the shot (she was upstairs at the time with her children) but did not witness the shooting. Richard claims that Frank had got physical with him and in the scuffle that developed he had shot Frank in self-defense. So instead of being charged with murder, Richard faces a manslaughter charge that would only carry a prison sentence of from five to fifteen years. The fact that justice will not be served exacerbates the Fowlers' rage, frustration, and grief. To make matters worse, the young murderer is released on bail.

At that point, halfway through the film, the plot takes a different direction that explains the title of the story, "Killings." The violence has not ended with Frank's death, as the story is then transformed into a revenge vehicle. Transfixed by rage, the parents lose their basic decency and become conspirators, as the doctor plots to murder the man who had murdered his son. His motive is effectively foreshadowed. He knows his wife holds him in part responsible because he refused to report Richard's wife-beatings to the police. Ruth is so consumed by her hatred that she cannot concentrate on her teaching. Likewise, he begins to neglect his practice, as witnessed when he refuses to see a sick child brought to his office. It soon becomes apparent that the father is so preoccupied because he is plotting with a close friend vigilante action to avenge his son's murder.

Released on bail, Richard is working as a bartender. One night after work, Richard is taken hostage by the father, armed with a pistol, and forced to drive home to pack his bags. Richard is led to believe that the father is going to force him to jump bail in order to extend his prison sentence. This puts Richard momentarily at ease, but when the doctor drives him north of the airport to an isolated wooded area, he realizes what the father really has in mind. The killer is murdered in cold blood and then buried. The airline ticket was planted at Richard's apartment merely to make it appear that Strout had jumped bail.

In the way both "killings" are treated, the viewers are lulled into what seems to be a calm normality and then surprised by the eruptions of violence. As David Denby perceptively explained in *The New Yorker*, "one feels the same disbelief" when violence breaks out in this film "that one feels when it breaks out in life." The nearest equivalent in American films to the way this film treats unexpected violence and profound grief was in Robert Redford's *Ordinary People* (1980), which offered moving performances by Mary Tyler Moore and Donald Sutherland as parents grieving the unexpected loss of their son in a sailing accident. *Ordinary People* won Academy Awards® for Best Picture, Best Director, and Best Screenplay, and *In the Bedroom* seemed positioned to follow Redford's success, though it would be odd for a novice director to have a nomination for Best Director.

When the film was first released, it was hailed as a paradigm for the grief the nation was experiencing after the September 11th terrorist destruction of the twin towers of the World Trade Center in New York City and the damage done to the Pentagon in Washington, D.C. The national response to that tragedy was to bomb the Taliban out of power in Afghanistan. The film works out its own reprisal for Frank's father and mother, who seems to know what her husband is up to and calmly wants to know when he returns home after a night of ritual murder if the deed has been done. David Ansen noted that in the 18-page story from which the film was adapted, the father was a merchant who sells women's clothes rather than a doctor who had taken an oath to preserve life rather than to take it. The film has an open-ended conclusion that leaves the father "in the bedroom" to ponder the consequences of what he has done, with a look of utter desolation. Now a murderer, he can no longer be the kindly village doctor he once was. The film's ending is not very hopeful, but it is powerful.

Reviewer Joe Morgenstern of the *Wall Street Journal* not only called *In the Bedroom* the "sleeper of the year," described as "a seriously beautiful, deliberately paced drama that meanders for a while at the pace of a summer romance, then explodes with phenomenal force." Morgenstern concluded his review by asserting that this was "the best American film I've seen so far this year." Since reviewers praised Sissy Spacek's anguished portrayal of a mother burned out by grief and hatred, and since Hollywood loves actresses who come out of semi-retirement to demonstrate that their talents are still luminescent, it hardly came as a surprise that Spacek won a Golden Globe for her performance, positioning her also for a possible Academy Award® nomination. The film was given a platform release, initially to be seen only at a limited number of screens in urban areas as its Oscar® "buzz" began to develop. Marisa Tomei was also being mentioned as the Best Supporting Actress. Tom Wilkinson's performance as the avenging father, however, might have been considered the film's most powerful.

Reviews were nearly consistently and impressively favorable. Desson Howe of the *Washington Post* called the film "the most riveting movie of the Christmas season." His colleague Stephen Hunter demurred, however, writing that the film was "short of good, better than awful, it opens brilliantly, then just goes on, toward self-negating absurdity." The story is clearly more tragic than absurd, however, and its plot line is credible enough. Hunter considered the issue of repression the "intellectual core" of the film: "between Matt and Ruth," he wrote, "lies a frozen chunk of emotion that not even tragedy can melt." Since "neither husband not wife has felt love for the other for a long time," they cannot confront the reality of what has happened, turning instead toward denial, expressed "by taut, curt, shallow, clipped conversation." Just as Ruth blames Natalie for involving her son in events that led to his murder, she also blames Matt for encouraging Frank's romance with Natalie "because he himself was attracted to the young woman but never had the guts to cheat or divorce." There is enough discomfort in that accusation to make Matt feel guilty for having used his son "as a weapon in his passive-aggressive war against Ruth."

*New Yorker* critic David Denby was certainly impressed by Todd Field's "terrific talent" for capturing "moments, silently observed, saturated with an emotion not quite specified but ready to spill." Field's drama, Denby claimed, "unfolds with a logic that borders on the Sophoclean." Denby was more charitable toward the father than Hunter, claiming only that Matt may feel "a slight envy" as he seems to "enjoy" his son's affair vicariously without using it to taunt Ruth. Spacek provides a chilling performance of Ruth without pity, who blames Natalie for her son's death and lusts for revenge as she is transformed into a bitter, cold, and unforgiving woman. As Denby also observed, this is new territory for Spacek, intelligently and effectively explored by a gifted and mature actress.

—*James M. Welsh*

## CREDITS

**Ruth Fowler:** Sissy Spacek
**Matt Fowler:** Tom Wilkinson
**Frank Fowler:** Nick Stahl

**Natalie Strout:** Marisa Tomei
**Richard Strout:** William Mapother
**Willis Grinnel:** William Wise
**Katie Grinnel:** Celia Weston
**Marla Keyes:** Karen Allen

**Origin:** USA
**Released:** 2001
**Production:** Graham Leader, Ross Katz, Todd Field; Good Machine, GreeneStreet Films; released by Miramax Films
**Directed by:** Todd Field
**Written by:** Todd Field, Rob Festinger
**Cinematography by:** Antonio Calvache
**Music by:** Thomas Newman
**Sound:** Edward Tise
**Editing:** Frank Reynolds
**Art Direction:** Shannon Hart
**Costumes:** Melissaa Economy
**MPAA rating:** R
**Running time:** 131 minutes

## REVIEWS

*Boxoffice.* September, 2001, p. 18.
*Boxoffice.* November, 2001, p. 128.
*Chicago Sun-Times Online.* December 25, 2001.
*Entertainment Weekly.* November 30, 2001, p. 60.
*Los Angeles Times Online.* November 23, 2001.
*Nation.* December 24, 2001, p. 44.
*New Republic.* December 17, 2001, p. 28.
*New York Times Online.* November 23, 2001.
*New Yorker.* November 26, 2001, p. 121.
*Newsweek.* January 21, 2002, p. 52.
*People.* December 3, 2001, p. 35.
*Rolling Stone.* December 6, 2001, p. 155.
*San Francisco Chronicle.* December 25, 2001, p. D1.
*USA Today.* November 23, 2001, p. E5.
*Variety Online.* January 23, 2001.
*Wall Street Journal.* November 23, 2001, p. W9.
*Washington Post.* December 24, 2001, p. C1.
*Washington Post.* December 25, 2001, p. C1.
*Washington Post Weekend.* December 28, 2001, p. 36.

## QUOTES

Matt (Tom Wilkinson) holds up a lobster that's lost a claw: "You know the old saying: Two's company, three's a crowd. More than two of these in the bedroom, chances are something like this will happen."

The film is based on the short story "Killings" by Andre Dubus, who died in 1999.

AWARDS AND NOMINATIONS

**Golden Globes 2002:** Actress—Drama (Spacek)
**Ind. Spirit 2002:** Actor (Wilkinson), Actress (Spacek), First Feature
**L.A. Film Critics 2001:** Actress (Spacek), Film
**Natl. Bd. of Review 2001:** Director (Field), Screenplay
**N.Y. Film Critics 2001:** Actor (Wilkinson), Actress (Spacek), First Feature
**Broadcast Film Critics 2001:** Actress (Spacek)
**Nomination:**
**British Acad. 2001:** Actor (Wilkinson), Actress (Spacek)
**Golden Globes 2002:** Film—Drama, Support. Actress (Tomei)
**Screen Actors Guild 2001:** Actor (Wilkinson), Actress (Spacek), Cast
**Broadcast Film Critics 2001:** Film, Support. Actress (Tomei).

# In the Mood for Love

 **Box Office:** $2.7 million

*I*n *the Mood for Love* tells a familiar tale in an unfamiliar way. The story of a two people brought together because of the erring ways of their spouses has a unexpectedly poetic quality in Wong Kar-wai's hands. Wong Kar-wai takes a simple melodrama formula from the past and transforms it into something special. The plot itself seems less than intriguing—at least at first. In 1962 Hong Kong, Chow (Tony Leung) and his wife move into an apartment next door to Su (Maggie Cheung) and her husband. Before long, Su, a secretary, suspects that her husband is having an affair. Eventually, she realizes it is with Chow's wife! Likewise, Chow, a reporter, slowly comes around to admit that he is a cuckold.

At first, Chow and Su exchange pleasantries. Only much later do they become closer and tell each other their suspicions. They also begin to play the part of each other's spouses, confessing things they never would to their real spouses. Chow and Su begin to feel guilty about their own relationship and try to hide it from Mrs. Suen (Rebecca

Pan), the superintendent. To cover their feelings, Chow invites Su to his newspaper to collaborate on a story. Sadly, the burgeoning friendship and potential love affair ends abruptly, leaving Chow and Su only memories of each other.

Like its title suggests, *In the Mood for Love* has more to do with old Hollywood melodrama than new Chinese cinema, but Wong Kar-wai has a way of informing his stylish soap opera with the essence of Eastern sensibility. It is as though Douglas Sirk and Kenji Mizoguchi had collaborated upon the ultra soaper. The plot, as described, is even more classical than something Sirk or Mizoguchi would have normally used—a *Brief Encounter* of symmetrical partners. As Andrew Sarris put it in his *New York Observer* review, ". . .the problem for me is with a plot that has become overly familiar in the West. . . . Two triangles equal a hexagon with only four participants."

But, with style to spare, Wong Kar-wai turns it all into his own velvety package. From the use of Nat King Cole's singing on the soundtrack to the rich color design by William Chang Suk-ping, *In the Mood for Love* indeed creates a mood for love, and the repressed sexual longing of the two protagonists is beautifully played out by Tony Leung and Maggie Cheung (William Chang Suk-ping deserves additional mention for contributing the memorable period costumes and the supple cinematography, including the series of slow-motion sequences in which the unrequited lovers pass each other in the hallway). Wong Kar-wai's best stylistic decision was to cut out a love seen between the leads. In this movie, less is more, much more.

Yet, in the end, an affecting end, the film may leave some modern viewers feeling cheated. What is not at all revisionist about *In the Mood for Love* is the way the would-be love affair concludes: Chow tells Su to "keep a closer eye on your husband," as if Mr. Chan's affair was Su's fault! After all the pain Su has expressed to Chow, the statement seems stunningly insensitive. Still, Su takes the advice and reunites with her husband (the other spouses are never seen, which is an interesting technique, borrowed from *Brief Encounter*, David Lean's 1945 film about marital infidelity. *In the Mood for Love* isn't just a time trip back to 1962, but to something earlier as well.

*—Eric Monder*

CREDITS

**Chow:** Tony Leung Chiu-Wai
**Li-zhen:** Maggie Cheung
**Mrs. Suen:** Rebecca Pan
**Mr. Ho:** Lai Chen
**Ah-ping:** Siu Ping-Lam

**Origin:** Hong Kong

**Language:** Chinese
**Released:** 2000
**Production:** Wong Kar-Wai; Paradis Film, Jet Tone Productions, Block 2 Pictures Inc.; released by USA Films
**Directed by:** Wong Kar-Wai
**Written by:** Wong Kar-Wai
**Cinematography by:** Christopher Doyle, Mark Lee Ping-Bin
**Music by:** Michael Galasso, Umebayashi Shigeru
**Sound:** Kuo Li-chi
**Editing:** William Chang Suk-ping
**Art Direction:** Man Lim-chung, Alfred Yau Wai-ming
**Production Design:** William Chang Suk-ping
**MPAA rating:** PG
**Running time:** 97 minutes

## REVIEWS

*Boxoffice.* November, 2000, p. 153.
*Boxoffice.* December, 2000, p. 32.
*Chicago Sun-Times Online.* February 16, 2001.
*Entertainment Weekly.* February 16, 2001, p. 71.
*New York Observer Online.* January 29, 2001.
*New York Times Online.* January 28, 2001.
*Rolling Stone.* February 15, 2001, p. 84.
*Sight and Sound.* August, 2000, p. 14.
*Variety.* May 29, 2000, p. 23.
*Washington Post Online.* February 23, 2001.

## TRIVIA

The director spent 15 months shooting the film, which was filmed in Bangkok, Thailand.

## AWARDS AND NOMINATIONS

**Cannes 2000:** Actor (Leung Chiu-Wai)
**N.Y. Film Critics 2001:** Cinematog., Foreign Film
**Nomination:**
**Ind. Spirit 2001:** Foreign Film
**Natl. Soc. Film Critics 2001:** Cinematog., Foreign Film
**Broadcast Film Critics 2001:** Foreign Film.

# Intimacy

**Box Office:** $.4 million

Patrice Chèreau's *Intimacy* almost defies description. Although the film portrays explicit sex, it can not be labeled pornographic since come-hither looks, glossy lips, buxom bimbos, and muscular studs are absent. In fact, the sex in this film shows itself as furtive, primal, and depressing while focusing on two pasty strangers doing the deed in a squalid basement. So while *Intimacy* highlights explicit sex, it's hardly erotic and it is a cinematic downer to say the least. And yet, Chèreau and co-writer Anne-Louise Trividic almost succeed in their character study of a man who abandoned his wife and who has anonymous sex with a woman every Wednesday. The end result proves to be a grittier version of Frederic Fonteyne's *An Affair of Love.*

*Intimacy* is based on two stories, *Intimacy* and *Night Light,* by Hanif Kureishi. By blending the two stories, Chèreau and Trividic manage to create a broader canvas in which the characters Jay (Mark Rylance) and Claire (Kerry Fox) explore the boundaries of marriage, anonymous sex, and the politics of intimate relationships. Their weekly coupling involves sex punctuated by silence as the partners disengage from their feelings by dressing quickly after the completion of the act. We also get a peek into Jay's dismal life as we watch him manage a seedy bar for a living, reside in a grotty basement, and lament over having left his wife and two sons. Although Claire lives in a nicer flat, complete with husband and son, she's obviously searching for someone to rescue her from a boring life in which she teaches drama to amateurs and performs second-rate theatrical productions in the basement of a pub.

The film opens with Jay waking up just in time for the arrival of his nameless lover. The partners ravage each other, tear off each other's clothing, then participate in wordless and rushed sex while Eric Gautier's lens travels over thighs, breasts, hands, and contorted faces. After they complete the act, Claire quickly dresses and exits the flat as if nothing had taken place. Later, when Jay arrives at the bar he manages, he takes his frustrations out on other employees—saying he's had it with arty types.

Soon Claire piques Jay's and our curiosity. Who is she? Where does she live? Jay follows Claire and slowly uncovers clues about her life. Jay learns that Claire appears as a regular theatrical performer at a pub. By accident Jay also learns that Claire happens to be married and a mother of a son. Although the news upsets Jay, he befriends Claire's husband Andy (Timothy Spall) at the pub where Claire performs. But he also takes out his anger on Claire as he engages in rough sex that nearly leads her to a nervous breakdown. Eventually Andy learns that Jay has been engaging in sex with his wife but even so, Claire chooses the domestic life that Jay hastily abandoned.

Fox mentioned in the press notes that she didn't want to repeat herself in roles, so she chooses ones "that will give me a bit of a fright and make me go places that I haven't been." True to her word, Fox has played diverse roles in such films as *The Hanging Garden, An Angel At My Table*, and *Welcome to Sarajevo*. In *Intimacy*, Fox bares her body and soul while rendering a precarious role. At ease on both the stage and the screen, Rylance blends vulnerability and violence while portraying the emotionally impoverished Jay. Yet despite the roomful of talent, *Intimacy* never rises beyond its bleak narrative. In fact, the film only manages to show the seedier side of London and the irony of sex between strangers as they crash and burn due to their primal instincts. Their behavior and unfulfilled desires remain an unsolved mystery.

—*Patty-Lynne Herlevi*

## CREDITS

**Jay:** Mark Rylance
**Claire:** Kerry Fox
**Andy:** Timothy Spall
**Victor:** Alastair Galbraith
**Betty:** Marianne Faithfull
**Susan:** Susannah Harker
**Ian:** Philippe Calvario
**Pam:** Rebecca Palmer
**Dave:** Fraser Ayres

**Origin:** France, Great Britain
**Released:** 2000
**Production:** Jacques Hinstin, Patrick Cassavetti; Le Studio Canal, Arte France Cinema, France 2 Cinema; released by Empire Pictures
**Directed by:** Patrice Chereau
**Written by:** Patrice Chereau, Anne-Louise Trividic
**Cinematography by:** Eric Gautier
**Music by:** Eric Neveux
**Sound:** Guillaume Sciama, Jean-Pierre Laforce
**Editing:** Francois Gedigier
**Costumes:** Caroline De Vivaise
**Production Design:** Hayden Griffin
**MPAA rating:** Unrated
**Running time:** 119 minutes

## REVIEWS

*Chicago Sun-Times Online.* October 26, 2001.
*Entertainment Weekly.* November 2, 2001, p. 51.
*Los Angeles Times Online.* October 19, 2001.
*New York Times Online.* October 11, 2001.
*Sight and Sound.* July, 2001, p. 20.
*Sight and Sound.* August, 2001, p. 47.
*Variety.* January 29, 2001, p. 51.

## TRIVIA

This is French director Patrice Chereau's English-language debut.

# Invisible Circus

*All they wanted was to change the world . . . instead they changed each other.*
—Movie tagline
*The journey is the destination.*
—Movie tagline

**Box Office:** $.1 million

When speaking about actress Cameron Diaz, director Adam Brooks sums up her talents, "there's just Something About Cameron." And while Diaz only plays a supporting role in Brook's adapted-from-a-novel *The Invisible Circus* her on-screen presence has the ability to captivate audiences that will never see the film. *The Invisible Circus*, with its surrealistic ride through the 1970s, its intriguing mystery that surrounds a suicide, and tense narrative only played to a limited audience. One can only guess why the distributor chose a limited release for the film with the exception that critics panned it. But, there's something about the American film industry that doesn't allow audiences to decide the fate of a film. After all, critics are paid to analyze films whereas the film-going public only wants to be entertained. While *The Invisible Circus* isn't a cinematic masterpiece, it still possesses entertaining qualities.

Similar to *Hideous Kinky*, *The Invisible Circus* takes a ride back through the liberal landscape of the 1970s. As the film opens, the camera lovingly focuses on a young woman (Diaz) dancing on the edge of a cliff. The slightly blurred image reminds us that we are witnessing images from the past and the mesmerizing image of the woman dancing draws us into her personal story. Cut to San Francisco where 18-year-old Phoebe (Jordana Brewster) tries to piece together her sister's mysterious suicide that took place seven years prior. She recalls a time before her father and sister's deaths when the family frolicked on the beach and in the forest. But after her father's untimely death, Faith took her father's advice to heart about changing the world—leading to her fearless behavior and her mysterious death.

Phoebe also sees the world through rose-colored glasses. She moves into Faith's old room, which she has made a shrine. However, a memory of a person is hardly the same thing as living with the person on a daily basis. The dead become martyrs who can do no wrong and in Phoebe's case, the ghosts of her father and sister hold her back from living a fulfilling life. When Phoebe notices her mother kissing a man, she berates her for replacing her dead father. Later, when Phoebe arrives at Faith's former lover Wolf's (Christopher Eccleston) flat in Paris, she can't accept that Wolf has become engaged to a French woman, Claire (Isabelle Pasco).

With postcards in hand, Phoebe retraces Faith's journey in Europe, hoping to find an answer for her sister's suicide. She begins her journey in Amsterdam where she feels uninspired, then she quickly makes her way to Paris where she reunites with Wolf in hopes that he will solve Faith's mystery. Wolf, who had once promised Faith that he would never reveal her terrorist activities to her family, easily succumbs to Phoebe's unrelenting inquisition. Phoebe resists seeing her sister's dark side since she remembers her sister as a happy, fearless free spirit

Phoebe and Wolf visit the ledge in Portugal where Faith jumped to her death, but only after an erotic pit stop in which the older Wolf becomes sexually involved with teenaged Phoebe. On one hand, this sexual interlude adds an unnecessary baggage to the film but on the other, it adds a lyrical quality that contributes to the film's sensuality. In the end, Phoebe comes to the painful realization that Faith did not act in a saintly fashion and in fact, she committed suicide because she accidentally killed a man who had a family. And Wolf can also finally unburden himself of Faith's ghost.

Although critics zeroed in on Brewster's acting and Brook's unsuccessful attempt at telling a story in flashbacks, *The Invisible Circus* is not without merits. Director of Photography Henry Braham lovingly captures the actors' faces as well as the luscious European locales, while composer Nick Laird-Clowes further emphasizes the film's lyrical landscape with a blend of sitar music and a tingle of reggae. However, as noted by critic Carla Meyer of the *San Francisco Chronicle*, Brewster didn't resemble her blonde, blue-eyed family members and the young actress delivered a flat performance. So it became a bit of a clichè to cast a dark-haired actress to bask in the shadows of her sunny blonde sister. Bubbly blondes kill themselves while clear-headed brunettes suffer. Do we actually believe this?

—*Patty-Lynne Herlevi*

## CREDITS

**Faith:** Cameron Diaz
**Phoebe:** Jordana Brewster
**Wolf:** Christopher Eccleston
**Gail:** Blythe Danner
**Gene:** Patrick Bergin
**Eric:** Moritz Bleibtreu
**Claire:** Isabelle Pasco

**Origin:** USA
**Released:** 2000
**Production:** Julia Chasman, Nick Wechsler; Industry Entertainment; released by Fine Line Features
**Directed by:** Adam Brooks
**Written by:** Adam Brooks
**Cinematography by:** Henry Braham
**Music by:** Nick Laird-Clowes
**Sound:** Jean-Paul Mugel
**Editing:** Elizabeth Kling
**Art Direction:** Stephen Alesch
**Costumes:** Donna Zakowska
**Production Design:** Robin Standefer
**MPAA rating:** R
**Running time:** 98 minutes

## REVIEWS

*Chicago Sun-Times Online.* February 2, 2001.
*New York Times Online.* February 2, 2001.
*People.* February 19, 2001, p. 36.
*San Francisco Chronicle Online.* February 8, 2001.
*San Francisco Examiner Online.* February 8, 2001.
*Seattle Weekly.* February 1, 2001, p. 32.
*Sight and Sound.* April, 2001, p. 50.
*Variety.* January 29, 2001, p. 52.
*Village Voice Online.* January 24, 2001.

# Iris

*Her greatest talent was for life.*
—Movie tagline

 **Box Office:** $1.6 million

According to British author/lecturer Dame Iris Murdoch "the writer's duty is to produce the best literary work of which he is capable, and he must find out how this must be done." Writing is never an easy task, especially in the case of Dame Murdoch whose brilliant mind dimmed under the attack of Alzheimer's disease as she completed her 26th and last novel, *Jackson's Dilemma*. She died four years later, no longer capable of thinking philosophical thoughts. Her husband and academic John Bayley described Iris as "a very nice three-year-old." Bayley is also credited for writing the memoir, *Elegy for Iris,* which director Richard Eyre and screenwriter Charles Wood adapted for the film version of Iris's life.

The film, simply titled, *Iris* operates on various levels and in itself portrays a complicated narrative structure reflecting Murdoch's 26 novels. On one level, the film reflects on memory by shifting back and forth between the young iconoclastic Iris (Kate Winslet) swimming nude in ponds, making love to lesbians, as well as shocking stuffy academics, and the older Dame Murdoch (Judi Dench) as her mind deteriorates. On another level, the film responds to the author's penchant for liberation of the mind and heart. Believing that education won't lead to happiness but to freedom, Murdoch and her characters struck battles with famous philosophers, religion, metaphysical concepts, and political ideologies in a restless fashion. After all, we live in a chaotic world in which you can go mad trying to pin down the truth or experience liberation in its fullest capacity. Finally, *Iris* acts as a biopic that also educates the public about Alzheimer's disease (a disease that afflicts 2.5 million Americans and according to a 1989 report in a British medical journal has risen 50% in areas in Britain).

Similar to the British film, *Hilary and Jackie, Iris's* dramatic arc revolves around a tragic character a fighting degenerative disease with a thimble full of hope. Both Jacqueline Du Pre and Iris Murdoch thought that they would win over their respective diseases and reclaim their lives, but instead these great artists were eaten alive by diseases in which we still know little. We can also compare *Iris* with its crosscuts between a young version of a couple and an older version of the same couple to Paul Cox's *Innocence. Iris* is also a love story, but one that depicts a 40 year marriage between two academics and not a story of two people who rediscover each other in their twilight years. *Iris* is also an unflinching gaze at mortality and an Oscar®-caliber screenplay that actors worth their salt dream about.

As the film credits roll, a naked young Iris swims underwater with her lover John Bayley (Hugh Bonneville). It's a whimsical image that is replaced by the older version of the couple played by Judi Dench and Jim Broadbent, thankfully clothed. This scene sets up the crosscuts between the two couples that continue throughout the film. We see Dame Murdoch performing a lecture in which she forgets her speech and breaks out with an Irish tune. Then the film cuts to 1953 when Iris meets John and publishes her first novel, *Under the Net.* The first narrative takes us through Iris and John's journey with the debilitating disease, beginning with Iris repeating herself, forgetting phrases and words, and ending with Iris's death in 1999. The second narrative focuses on Iris' friendships with academics and artists and her courtship with John that culminates in the couple's marriage. The first narrative proves to be bold and shocking while the second narrative focuses on a mature but co-dependent relationship between the aging academics. And it is the second narrative, with its powerful performances by Dench and Broadbent, that provides award-winning material.

Watching the film feels similar to reading Murdoch's novels, especially the novel, *A Message to the Planet* since that novel portrays characters on the verge of madness and the character Marcus's daughter commits Marcus to a posh mental home. In the film, John commits Iris to a similar establishment after she became a danger to herself. In the same novel, the characters Alison and Jack swim naked in a pond and are spied on by a friend who happens to be passing by. In the film, Iris is also caught unawares by a schoolteacher and students as she steps naked out of a pond. This leaves us to wonder how much of Iris's personal life ended up in her novels and in her husband's memoir.

*Iris* skirts around the disease-of-the-week genre due to the film's arty narrative structure, but even so, viewers will not escape an in-depth gaze at Alzheimer disease. Dench thoroughly entrenches herself in her role while also identifying with the disease. It is a frightening experience to watch Dench portray a woman who is transformed from a formidable scholar pontificating about various philosophers to a woman mesmerized by *Teletubbies.* Because Dench resembles the late author we believe that she has become stricken with the disease. As she ambles through traffic on the motor way or swims in a pond we imagine the worse possible nightmare. *Iris* is fueled by this sort of tension. We as viewers know that Iris needs professional care, yet her husband refuses to allow anyone to help him with his burden. This, too, is quiet common with individuals whose spouse or family member suffers from Alzheimer disease. After all, blood is thicker than water, marriage is for better or worse, and in England no one is allowed to see you suffer.

American filmgoers have become acquainted with Dench since she has appeared in such diverse films as *Mrs. Brown,* for which she received a best actress Academy Award® nomination, *Shakespeare in Love,* (Dench won a best supporting actress Oscar®), *Chocolat* (in which she played another character suffering from disabilities and received a best supporting actress nomination), and *The Shipping News.*

Kate Winslet, who plays the restless and quick-witted young Iris, has also built up a following. Many viewers will recall Winslet playing opposite Leonardo DiCaprio in *Titanic* for which she took home an Oscar® nomination for her leading role. Jane Austin fans will recall Winslet's performance in *Sense and Sensibility* (she received an Academy Award® nomination for her supporting role), and her feisty roles in Jane Campion's *Holy Smoke*, in which she played a headstrong cult fanatic, and *Quills*, where she rendered the role of the Marque de Sade's object of desire.

Those who would argue that playing the young Iris doesn't qualify as a challenging role would be mistaken. Winslet portrays the crass iconoclast with aplomb. She is a woman who desperately needs to be anchored but can not find the wherewithal to stop racing through life. She's the type of person so full of passion (while burning her candle at both ends) that even her earthy husband suffers from Iris' need for freedom. Winslet plays harsh to Dench's soft and yet, the two actresses are able to create a seamless continuity between the young Iris and the invalid scholar Iris. This in itself is an accomplishment.

Actors Hugh Bonneville (*Mansfield Park, Blow Dry*) and Jim Broadbent (*Moulin Rouge, Bridget Jones's Diary*) also create a seamless transition between the young John Bayley and the mature Bayley. Bonneville plays the nervous 29-year-old virgin who stammers his way into the young Iris' heart while delivering a self-conscious performance. Broadbent plays a man so hopelessly in love with his ailing wife that he begins to lose his own mind in the process. As Iris' mind deteriorates she gets lost in her past while dragging John along with her. In the past, Iris had many affairs and friendships that excluded John from her life and as Iris' mind turns to the past, John is forced to deal with his anguish of losing Iris once again.

In the end, *Iris*, similar to *Hilary and Jackie*, proves to be a chilling biography about mortality. While the film does portray our capacity to love others, it also reminds us that even the most brilliant minds, like flames, can be blown out.

—*Patty-Lynne Herlevi*

 **CREDITS**

**Iris Murdoch:** Judi Dench
**John Bayley:** Jim Broadbent
**Young Iris:** Kate Winslet
**Young John:** Hugh Bonneville
**Janet Stone:** Penelope Wilton
**Young Janet:** Juliet Aubrey
**Maurice:** Timothy West
**Young Maurice:** Samuel West
**College Principal:** Eleanor Bron

**Origin:** Great Britain, USA
**Released:** 2001

**Production:** Robert Fox, Scott Rudin; BBC Films, Intermedia Films, Mirage Enterprises; released by Miramax Films
**Directed by:** Richard Eyre
**Written by:** Richard Eyre, Charles Wood
**Cinematography by:** Roger Pratt
**Music by:** James Horner
**Sound:** Jim Greenhorn
**Editing:** Martin Walsh
**Art Direction:** David Warren
**Costumes:** Ruth Myers
**Production Design:** Gemma Jackson
**MPAA rating:** R
**Running time:** 90 minutes

**REVIEWS**

*Entertainment Weekly.* December 14, 2001, p. 52.
*Los Angeles Times Online.* December 14, 2001.
*New York Times Online.* December 9, 2001.
*New York Times Online.* December 14, 2001.
*USA Today Online.* December 13, 2001.
*Variety.* December 10, 2001, p. 32.

**QUOTES**

Young Iris (Kate Winslet): "There is only one freedom of any consequence: that of the mind."

**AWARDS AND NOMINATIONS**

**Oscars 2001:** Support. Actor (Broadbent)
**British Acad. 2001:** Actress (Dench)
**Golden Globes 2002:** Support. Actor (Broadbent)
**L.A. Film Critics 2001:** Support. Actor (Broadbent), Support. Actress (Winslet)
**Natl. Bd. of Review 2001:** Support. Actor (Broadbent)
**Nomination:**
**Oscars 2001:** Actress (Dench), Support. Actress (Winslet)
**British Acad. 2001:** Actor (Broadbent), Adapt. Screenplay, Film, Support. Actor (Bonneville), Support. Actress (Winslet)
**Golden Globes 2002:** Actress—Drama (Dench), Support. Actress (Winslet)
**Screen Actors Guild 2001:** Actress (Dench), Support. Actor (Broadbent)
**Broadcast Film Critics 2001:** Support. Actor (Broadbent).

# Italian for Beginners (Italiensk for Begyndere)

*To speak the language of love, first you have to feel it.*
—Movie tagline

Italian for Beginners. *Attendance Optional. Passion Required.*
—Movie tagline

 **Box Office:** $1.6 million

No charm is spared in *Italian for Beginners*, a film made in the Danish "Dogma" movement style, but without the tortured Sturm und Drang. On the surface, writer-director Lone Scherfig's third film resembles many of the other Dogma productions, but its effect is much lighter and more enjoyable. On the other hand, *Italian for Beginners* is also *too* lightweight at times, really a bit of a creampuff.

The story takes place in a small Copenhagen town where a young, widowed minister Andreas (Anders W. Berthelsen) arrives to fill in for an elderly pastor. While adjusting to his new environment, Andreas befriends Olympia (Anette Stovelbaek), a pastry chef who cares for her ailing, disagreeable father. Andreas takes up residence at a hotel managed by the bashful Jorgen Mortensen (Peter Gantzler), who secretly loves the Italian cook Guila (Sara Indrio Jensen). What Jorgen doesn't realize is that Guila secretly loves him back.

Both Jorgen Mortensen and Andreas have their haircut by the local hairdresser, Karen (Ann Eleonora Jorgensen), who turns out (in an unexpected plot twist) to be Olympia's sister. Karen, who takes care of her sick mother, is attracted to the handsome but egotistical restaurant manager, Hal-Finn (Lars Kaalund). When Hal-Finn replaces the professor of a local Italian-language studies class, Karen, Olympia, Andreas, Jorgen, and Guila all sign up for the course, as much to learn Italian as to get to know one another better. After Karen and Olympia's parents die (coincidentally around the same time), the sisters decide to use their inheritance money to finance a class trip to Italy. While in Venice, the romantic feelings amongst the group members are finally evident and everyone ends up with a loving partner.

*Italian for Beginners* arrived as the 2001 Dogma film at the New York Film Festival, but unlike more controversial past entries (from *Julien Donkey-Boy* to the underrated *The Idiots*), Lone Scherfig's fluffy tale aims solely to please. Like the other Dogma films, *Italian* adheres to the Dogme 95 doctrine: the cinematography mimics cinema verité, the production values are minimal, and there is no off-screen source music; but in most other ways, the film is a romantic comedy in the mode of *If It's Tuesday, It Must Be Belgium* or *French Kiss* (one could even imagine Meg Ryan appearing in the Hollywood remake).

Fortunately, Scherfig keeps the cutesy sitcom moments to a minimum and allows the wry Nordic humor to dominate over the classical contrivances (one such latter bit finds the sisters unreservedly donating their inheritance to sponsor the group's trip). The cast makes the roundelay likeable, even though Hal-Finn's evolution from sexist rake to romantic hero seems less than convincing (and we still don't want the lovely Karen to end up with him). But to the film's credit, Olympia's clumsiness is played out for real pathos rather than easy slapstick laughs. *Italian for Beginners* may end not please hard-core Dogma fans, but it is an engaging trifle for everyone else.

—*Eric Monder*

## CREDITS

**Andreas:** Anders W. Berthelsen
**Jorgen:** Peter Gantzler
**Olympia:** Anette Stovelbaek
**Karen:** Ann Eleonora Jorgensen
**Hal-Finn:** Lars Kaalund
**Giulia:** Sara Indrio Jensen

**Origin:** Denmark
**Language:** Danish
**Released:** 2001
**Production:** Ib Tardini; released by Miramax Films
**Directed by:** Lone Scherfig
**Written by:** Lone Scherfig
**Cinematography by:** Jorgen Johansson
**Sound:** Rune Palving
**Editing:** Gerd Tjur
**MPAA rating:** R
**Running time:** 112 minutes

 ## REVIEWS

*Boxoffice.* December, 2001, p. 57.
*Chicago Sun-Times Online.* February 1, 2002.
*Entertainment Weekly.* January 25, 2002, p. 77.
*Los Angeles Times Online.* January 18, 2002.
*New York Times Online.* October 2, 2001.
*New York Times Online.* January 13, 2002.
*People.* February 4, 2002, p. 36.
*Variety.* February 19, 2001, p. 40.
*Washington Post.* February 22, 2002, p. WE46.

TRIVIA

The press kit offers "Special Thanks to Maeve Binchy" whose 1997 novel, *Evening Class*, is about a group of Dubliners taking Italian-language classes.

# Jackpot

Written and directed by the extraordinary filmmaking duo of Michael and Mark Polish, *Jackpot* feels like a dispatch from the heartland of America. Shorn of the euphoria of bluegrass and the glitter of Nashville, the film finds its heart amidst the smoky, plodding, secondhand ambiance of karaoke. In their unforgettable debut feature, *Twin Falls Idaho* (1999), in which they also starred, the Polish Brothers juxtaposed the grotesque workings of nature against the conformity of smalltown American life that would prefer to sweep it under the rug. Here, they pit the dogged repetition at the heart of country-and-western music against the promise of the unending American highway, which seems to lead nowhere. Their title does not refer to a gambler's dream but to the town of Jackpot, Nevada, the supposed mecca of karaoke artists, which the principal characters never reach.

Sunny Holiday (Jon Gries) is the all-American loser, exhuding pride and aplomb as the substratum of his life and career is slipping from under his feet. As an urban cowboy, if he falls off his steel bronco, he's convinced he can pick himself up again. Closest to him in his quest to become a recording star is his longtime black manager and source of spiritual sustenance, Les (Garrett Morris). The undertow to Sunny's self-confidence recurs in the form of the ravishing wife he has had to leave behind, Bobbi (Daryl Hannah). She is like a refrain, repeated ad nauseum throughout the film, reminding him that his escapades on the road, at the expense of her and their little daughter, comprise a no-win situation. Sunny dutifully mails her a lottery ticket every week, which is his form of child support.

All this could have led to a "buddy movie" as sprightly as *Easy Rider* (1969) or as emotionally affecting as *Scarecrow* (1973) if the filmmakers had shed their detachment and objective stance towards their characters and milieu. Instead, they seem resolved to present us with repetitive scenes of life on the karaoke circuit that keep us from identifying with Sunny and the precise nature of his ambition. We never get to know what exactly Sunny or Les hope to contribute musically to a scene dominated by such stalwarts as Garth Brooks and Shania Twain. We thus begin to see Sunny as a clown, so that the emotional and sexual connections he tries to make with the women he meets up with leave us cold.

For example, we never see Bobbi except in the one scene that keeps repeating itself, as if the filmmakers could only obtain the services of Daryl Hannah for just one afternoon. Similarly, Janice (Peggy Lipton), an aging but still beautiful waitress, who takes Sunny to her trailer home for a one-night fling, is discarded by the wayside after Sunny leaves her disappointed in bed. Sunny also rejects the advances of Cheryl (Crystal Bernard), a roadhouse goodtimer, and her sexually precocious teenage daughter, Tangy (Camillia Clouse).

Sunny's adventures on the road are brought to an abrupt end when the police stop him for having stolen the car that belongs to Bobbi. Les bails him out of jail, but at the expense of exhausting what little income his tour has generated. This leads to the two men coming to blows outside a diner. Even here, the filmmakers resort to a stylized depiction using stop-motion techniques so that even though the fight is real, we are prevented from seeing it as such.

Down on his luck and broke, Sunny turns to his brother, Tracy (Anthony Edwards), who is a motel owner. Availing himself of a bathtub in which to slash his wrists, Sunny is saved at the last minute by Les. The two unite and hit the road again, to what end remains unclear.

The film does have some redeeming features. The cinema of the Polish Brothers is a cinema of gestures, and it is on that level that it works the best. A customer at a table raising his drink to an absent Patsy Cline proves haunting. Also, a few crumbs for thought are thrown our way in the form of wisdom from an incongruous self-help tape that Sunny keeps listening to. For all its lofty insights about silence and the music ensuing therefrom, it doesn't seem to bring Sunny any inner peace. Despite its visual flair, *Jackpot* leaves us with the feeling that the directors just weren't up to revealing the raw, neurotic, and even frightening, potential of their downhome American protagonist.

Critics have found the film a letdown after the filmmakers' striking debut feature. Kevin Thomas in *Newsday* finds Sunny and Les "endearing" but the narrative "predictable and stretched-out." Elvis Mitchell in the *New York Times* concludes that "the movie is smart in small ways" and that it may have a future on the small screen. In a similar vein, Desson Howe in the *Washington Post* points out the "quietly assured flourishes" in the direction, as well as the film's "entertainingly eclectic cast."

—*Vivek Adarkar*

CREDITS

**Sunny Holiday:** Jonathan (Jon Francis) Gries
**Lester Irving:** Garrett Morris
**Bobbi:** Daryl Hannah
**Janice:** Peggy Lipton

**Mel James:** Adam Baldwin
**Sammy Bones:** Mac Davis
**Cheryl:** Crystal Bernard
**Tracy:** Anthony Edwards

**Origin:** USA
**Released:** 2001
**Production:** Mark Polish, Michael Polish; released by Sony Pictures Classics
**Directed by:** Michael Polish
**Written by:** Michael Polish, Mark Polish
**Cinematography by:** M. David Mullen
**Music by:** Stuart Matthewman
**Sound:** Brian Best
**Music Supervisor:** Jonathan Daniel
**Editing:** Shawna Callahan
**Art Direction:** David Cannizzarro
**Costumes:** Bic Owen
**Production Design:** Michele Montague
**MPAA rating:** R
**Running time:** 100 minutes

## REVIEWS

*Boxoffice.* July, 2001, p. 97.
*Buffalo News Online.* September 28, 2001.
*Chicago Sun-Times Online.* August 24, 2001.
*Entertainment Weekly.* August 8, 2001, p. 43.
*Hollywood Reporter.* June 26, 2001, p. 18.
*Los Angeles Times Online.* July 27, 2001.
*New York Times Online.* July 27, 2001.
*Newsday Online.* July 27, 2001.
*USA Today Online.* July 27, 2001.
*Variety.* July 9, 2001, p. 24.
*Washington Post Online.* August 31, 2001.

## TRIVIA

Patrick Bauchau, whose voice is heard on the motivational tapes Sunny listens to, worked with Jon Gries on the TV series, *The Pretender.*

# Jay and Silent Bob Strike Back

*Hollywood Had It Coming.*
—Movie tagline

**Box Office:** $30.1 million

Kevin Smith bids adieu to his "New Jersey Chronicles" characters in *Jay and Silent Bob Strike Back,* but some in the audience will simply say good riddance! Generation X "auteur" Smith promises this is the fifth and last time we will see Jay (Jason Mewes) and Silent Bob (Smith), a mean-spirited slacker duo modeled after Laurel & Hardy (well, sort of). Even some Smith fans may rejoice at the departure of this comedy team, since these characters represent the lowliest aspects of Smith's previous films (*Clerks, Mallrats, Chasing Amy, Dogma*). But for fans of Jay and Silent Bob, *Jay and Silent Bob Strike Back* celebrates Smith's juvenile side in all its spectacular splendor.

Smith's plot begins when the two Jersey-born dudes, Jay and Silent Bob, find out that a friend, local cartoonist Brodie (Jason Lee), has sold his "Jay and Silent Bob" story to Miramax studios. Fearing that the movie version of their lives will only contribute to the Internet slander against them already on the World Wide Web, Jay and Silent Bob begin a road trip to Hollywood in order to stop the filming from getting under way.

Along their cross-country trek, Jay and Silent Bob meet many other oddballs, including a hitchhiker (George Carlin), a nun (Carrie Fisher), a federal marshal (Will Ferrell), a sheriff (Judd Nelson), and a gang of thieves posing as animal rights activists who give them a ride in exchange for helping them steal a monkey from a test lab. What Jay and Silent Bob fail to realize is that the monkey theft provides the activists (Eliza Dushku, Shannon Elizabeth, Ali Carter, Jennifer Schwalbach) with cover while they steal some precious diamonds next door. Jay and Silent Bob take the monkey with them on the rest of their journey, as Jay mourns the death of Justice (Shannon Elizabeth), one of the phony activists killed during the robbery.

Once they reach their destination, Jay and Silent Bob sneak onto the Miramax lot, and somehow replace the leading actors (James Van Der Beek and Jason Biggs) playing Bluntman and Chronic, the characters based on their lives. On the set, Jay and Silent Bob end up as part of the production, battling with the film's villain, Cocknocker (Mark Hamill). The film, *Bluntman & Chronic,* is eventually completed, but thanks to Silent Bob's wheeling and dealing, at least he and Jay get paid their fair share of the profits. Jay also reunites with Justice when she reveals that she wasn't killed after all, although she turns in herself and her accomplices to the authorities for stealing the diamonds.

From the title sequence onward, *Jay and Silent Bob Strike Back* displays a parade of Kevin Smith preoccupations: science fiction movies (e.g. *Star Wars*), sexy women, comic strips, homoeroticism in everyday male bonding, the worth of his own talent, and pop culture in general. Smith's work is as uneven as ever but unlike in the past the director merrily surrenders any pretense toward making a "legitimate" film, and the effect is curiously emancipating. Not surprisingly, the mainstream reviews were pretty harsh on *Jay and Silent Bob,* but at least no one could complain that Smith spoiled a potentially great work (such as he did in *Chasing Amy*) with amateurish immaturity.

The best moments of this big screen cartoon include a vaudeville-styled routine between Jamie Kennedy's sad sack production assistant and Chris Rock's racially-touchy film director. During the Hollywood satire, Ben Affleck and Matt Damon also pop up as themselves in an inspired parody of a *Good Will Hunting*-turned-action-movie-sequel. Morris Day and The Time provide the musical highlight, reprising their hit from *Purple Rain,* though the number is somewhat lost under the closing titles.

Unfortunately, most of the other guest stars aren't as well used: Mark Hamill plays the silly villain in the film-within-the-film; Judd Nelson and Will Ferrell play typical redneck law enforcement figures; Gus Van Sant and Shannon Doherty play themselves very badly; and so on. Other lesser moments include homages to *Charlie's Angels, The Fugitive,* and *Scooby-Doo.*

Despite some sharp bits, one has to question whether Smith is pulling his punches at times. Ben Affleck refers to all his flop films at one point, but there is no mention of that summer 2001 disappointment, *Pearl Harbor.* Could it be that the man who stood up to the Catholic church in his earlier work (particularly with *Dogma*) was forced to scuttle mentioning Miramax's corporate parent, Disney, and its products? Miramax is gently kidded, by the way, but where is Gwyneth Paltrow or Tina Brown or Harvey Weinstein? Aren't they ripe enough for satire? Since most of the humor is crassly sexual, deriving from nervous homophobia, *Jay and Silent Bob Strike Back* is basically the cinematic counterpart to an Eminem song, for good or bad, with expletives to match. Parents beware!

—*Eric Monder*

## CREDITS

**Silent Bob:** Kevin Smith
**Jay:** Jason Mewes
**Brodie:** Jason Lee
**Holden:** Ben Affleck
**Justice:** Shannon Elizabeth
**Sissy:** Eliza Dushku
**Chrissy:** Ali Larter
**Missy:** Jennifer Schwalbach
**Chaka:** Chris Rock
**Willenholly:** Will Ferrell
**Dante:** Brian O'Halloran

**Brent:** Seann William Scott
**Hitchhiker:** George Carlin
**Nun:** Carrie Fisher
**Sheriff:** Judd Nelson
**Reg Hartner:** Jon Stewart
**Cocknocker:** Mark Hamill
**Security guard:** Diedrich Bader
**Cameo:** Wes Craven
**Cameo:** Gus Van Sant
**Cameo:** Matt Damon
**Cameo:** Shannen Doherty
**Cameo:** Jason Biggs
**Cameo:** James Van Der Beek
**Cameo:** Joey Lauren Adams
**Cameo:** Alanis Morissette
**Cameo:** Renee Humphrey

**Origin:** USA
**Released:** 2001
**Production:** Scott Mosier; View Askew, Dimension Films; released by Miramax Films
**Directed by:** Kevin Smith
**Written by:** Kevin Smith
**Cinematography by:** Jamie Anderson
**Music by:** James L. Venable
**Sound:** Whit Norris
**Editing:** Kevin Smith, Scott Mosier
**Art Direction:** Elise Viola
**Costumes:** Isis Mussenden
**Production Design:** Robert Holtzman
**MPAA rating:** R
**Running time:** 95 minutes

## REVIEWS

*Boxoffice.* July, 2001, p. 34.
*Boxoffice.* September, 2001, p. 147.
*Chicago Sun-Times Online.* August 24, 2001.
*Entertainment Weekly.* August 24, 2001, p. 104.
*Entertainment Weekly.* September 7, 2001, p. 134.
*Los Angeles Times Online.* August 24, 2001.
*New York Times Online.* August 24, 2001.
*People.* September 3, 2001, p. 38.
*Sight and Sound.* January, 2002, p. 45.
*USA Today Online.* August 23, 2001.
*Variety.* August 20, 2001, p. 23.
*Washington Post.* August 24, 2001, p. WE34.

## QUOTES

Holden (Ben Affleck) explains the Internet: "It's a place used the world over where people can come together to bitch about movies and share pornography together."

# Jeepers Creepers

*What's eating you?*
—Movie tagline

 **Box Office:** $38 million

*J*eepers Creepers came out at a time when it was hard for a scary movie to be scary. Films like *Scary Movie* and *Scream* mixed their thrills with self-referential jokes and commentary on the conventions of horror films. In 2001, a horror film that did not acknowledge some of the inherent silliness of fright films risked looking silly and old-fashioned. Audience members, trained to be ironic about such things, would never let, say, a woman go back into a house that has a killer in it, without heckling the character on the screen.

So, even though *Jeepers Creepers* tries its darnedest to be a really scary movie in the old sense, it still has to bow to the new conventions of the genre. After all, characters in a scary movie have to do stupid things, otherwise, instead of being in close proximity with a killer/monster/escaped lunatic, they'd be back at home watching *Who Wants to Be a Millionaire?* and drinking hot chocolate. *Jeepers Creepers* is forced to acknowledge that its characters, like all horror movie characters, often have to abandon reasonable decisions for the sake of keeping the plot moving along. That means when Darius Jenner (Justin Long) decides to look deep into a scary pipe protruding from the ground, his sister Trish (Gina Philips) is compelled to say, "You know that part in scary movies when somebody does something really stupid and everyone hates them for it? Well, this is it." Plot problem solved. The audience gets to feel smart and hip and writer/director Victor Salva gets his characters down that pipe.

The best of the film is the first part. Salva does a wonderful job of creating an ominous atmosphere. Darius and Trish are taking the back way home from college break in Trish's old car. Trish has broken up with her boyfriend and her semi-nerdish brother is needling her about it. The two bicker good-naturedly about whatever they can think of, but somehow something seems off. Salva has the soundtrack cranked up so even something as innocuous as Trish clicking through the stations on the radio has a jarring, foreboding sound to it. The weird mood isn't lightened when the siblings have the inevitable conversation about the teen guy and girl who mysteriously disappeared on this very road. "They never found her head," reports Darius, though he adds lightly, "I think every generation has their cautionary tale of drinking and driving on prom night." Trish adds

oddly, "I always had the feeling I would die on this highway."

In the midst of such talk, out of nowhere comes an old, weirdly painted truck with blacked-out windows. The unseen driver seems to be in an awful hurry and starts banging into the back of their old car, leaning on the truck's ancient and creepy sounding horn. "Go around" yells Darius, who's trying desperately to get out of the truck's way. It's a scene reminiscent of Steven Spielberg's early film *Duel.* The two vehicles jockey for space on the road and the siblings' car gets more and more beat up. Finally, Darius pulls into a field and the truck roars off. Whew, they're safe. For now.

But later, they spot the mysterious truck parked at an old boarded-up church. They see the driver who is wearing a strange hat and looks very weird and suspicious. But it's not his attire that's bothering Trish and Darius. It's the fact that the man is dumping what seems to be bodies wrapped in bloody sheets down a big pipe coming diagonally out of the ground. This is the part where Darius does something stupid. After he and his sister are down the road, safely out of harm's way, he decides that they should go back and look down that pipe. After all, someone could be in there who is alive and needs to be rescued. He decides that going back is somehow more logical and smart than to just call the police and let them handle it.

Once back at the site, Darius peers into the pipe while his sister holds onto his ankles. Of course, she ends up letting go of his feet and, of course, he ends up sliding down the tube. He discovers a macabre lair of some sort with the ceiling decorated with the bodies of hundreds of dead people. It's really quite eerie and later he describes it as "a psycho version of the Sistine Chapel."

This is the point in which the tone of the movie changes for the worse. It's when the monster stops being some mysterious creature and becomes just a regular old movie demon. Once Darius and Trish make their way into a creepy diner, they get a phone call from Jezelle Gay Hartman (Patricia Belcher), a woman who claims to be a psychic. She explains that she knows something of this monster: "I don't know if it's a demon or a devil or a dark, hungry thing." Helpfully, she does say he needs to eat humans to gain the strength from their body parts and that once he smells someone with a body part he wants he trails them until he can eat them. She tells Darius that he will know when the monster is coming because he will hear the oldie "Jeepers Creepers" being played. That means "something so terrible you can't even dream of it." Despite her ominous words, Jezelle's character doesn't add an extra layer of creepiness because it's a little too obvious that her role in the film is to help explain the plot.

But the film's main flaw is that it shows the monster, now called The Creeper (Jonathan Breck), too frequently and with too much detail. Darius and Trish just happen to be around when The Creeper decides to suck one body part or another out of someone. As The Creeper indulges, he's standing in front of a billboard that says "Tastes Darn Good!" Moments like these can be funny or they can be scary but they can't be both. And the scariness loses out.

Once the audience has seen The Creeper, the film loses most of its oomph. When the creature is mysterious, he's terrifying. What is he and what is he doing? Imaginations can create all kinds of various scary scenarios. But once he's out in the open, he becomes less frightening. After all, how scary can a guy in a rubber suit be? It's much more effective, for example, when The Creeper is an angry unseen entity ramming his truck into Darius and Trish's car, than when he's engaged in hand to hand combat with them. After all, you can see the latter in a *Godzilla* movie.

The acting is fairly good for a horror film. The fact that Philips can act in a scene with a monster and say lines like "You want me! Drop him and take me!" without sounding completely ridiculous should count for something. And Long does a good job of playing a smart, regular guy caught up in some bad, bad circumstances. Eileen Brennan shows up as The Cat Lady, though that probably won't be the top entry on her resume.

Critics, who don't often agree on much, were almost universally in agreement that the film lost its punch in the later sections. "(Salva) goes over the top, injecting a note of pitch-dark humor that turns *Jeepers Creepers* into yet another amusing horror-comedy, spooky and jolting but too literally preposterous to regain its initial aura of suspense," wrote Kevin Thomas of the *Los Angeles Times*. *Entertainment Weekly*'s Owen Gleiberman praised the first half hour of the film but said that later: "*Jeepers Creepers* forfeits any pretense to suggestive horror; it turns into a grab-bag freak show as desperate as it is arbitrary." Rene Rodriguez of the *Miami Herald* called the first 30 minutes of the film "an eerie, grandly effective creepfest." She said of the later part, "Salva isn't shy about doling out every cliche imaginable, like characters who behave in profoundly stupid ways in order to advance the plot; cars that don't start when you really, really need them; (and) cops that are skeptical and dismissive until it's, you know, too late." Nonetheless, *Jeepers Creepers* was the number one movie the week it debuted, breaking the previous record for a movie opening on Labor Day.

—*Jill Hamilton*

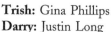
## CREDITS

**Trish:** Gina Phillips
**Darry:** Justin Long
**The Creeper:** Jonathan Breck
**Jezelle Gay Hartman:** Patricia Belcher
**Sgt. Davis Tubbs:** Brandon Smith

**The Cat Lady:** Eileen Brennan

**Origin:** USA
**Released:** 2001
**Production:** Barry Opper, Tom Luse; American Zoetrope, Cinerenta-Cinebeta; released by United Artists
**Directed by:** Victor Salva
**Written by:** Victor Salva
**Cinematography by:** Don E. Fauntleroy
**Music by:** Bennett Salvay
**Sound:** Joe Foglia
**Editing:** Ed Marx
**Art Direction:** Kevin Egeland
**Costumes:** Emae Villalobos
**Production Design:** Steven Legler
**MPAA rating:** R
**Running time:** 89 minutes

## REVIEWS

*Entertainment Weekly*. September 7, 2001, p. 135.
*Los Angeles Times Online*. August 31, 2001.
*New York Times Online*. August 31, 2001.
*People*. September 10, 2001, p. 40.
*USA Today Online*. August 31, 2001.
*Variety*. August 27, 2001, p. 31.
*Washington Post*. August 31, 2001, p. C5.

## QUOTES

Darry (Justin Long): "I'm being chased by a guy who likes to pull the tongues out of severed heads with his teeth."

# Jimmy Neutron: Boy Genius

*I can fix that . . .*
—Movie tagline

 **Box Office:** $49.5 million

When kids imagine how cool it would be to be a scientist, they think of somebody like Jimmy Neutron. Jimmy (voiced by Debi Derryberry) is the school's brainiac—so big is his brain that he has an oversized, Big

Boy-like head to contain it. Little Jimmy likes to use his powers for the goofy sorts of things that kids would use prodigious scientific knowledge for. He builds a machine that can shrink people, a bubble so that he can bounce to school instead of taking a bus, and a robot dog, Goddard (in the movie's lone poo poo joke, when Goddard uses the restroom, he leaves behind a pile of nuts and bolts). But Jimmy hasn't found his great invention yet. Everything he creates seems to have a little problem with it. His shrinking machine accidentally shrinks his teacher, Miss Fowl (Andrea Martin) causing her to be terrorized by a worm from an apple on her desk. His bubble transportation works for a while, until his journey ends abruptly with Jimmy in a big heap on the road, covered in broken bubble. Even Goddard has his quirks. When Jimmy tells him to play dead, he takes the command very seriously and blows himself up into a thousand pieces.

*Jimmy Neutron* is the spawn of the Nickelodeon network, the kinetic kids' network where bright colors, zippy action and wacky kids rule. (Excessive marketing rules there, too. Coming this fall is a series "The Adventures of Jimmy Neutron: Boy Genius" to go with the Jimmy video game, greeting cards, books, toys, and a Jimmy feature Nick magazine.) Jimmy Neutron did quite well in theaters. Besides getting heaps of hype from Nickelodeon, the movie was the only G-rated film to come out during the busy Christmas season. Of course big marketing pushes can only take a film so far (disturbingly far, but only so far). What gave *Jimmy* a second push is that it's also a light, bubbly, fun film. It looks great, too.

When we first meet Jimmy, he's taking a joy ride in his spaceship with his hapless friend, Carl Weezer (Rob Paulsen). Poor old Carl is a chubby, asthmatic fellow, who is often pretty scared by Jimmy's plans but isn't assertive enough to complain. When the ride ends with Jimmy crashing into the house, his parents, Judy (Megan Cavanagh) and Hugh (Mark DeCarlo), are angry, but they're used to this kind of thing. When he tells his mother that he's contacted alien life forms, his mother says blandly, "Jimmy, how many times have I told you not to talk to strangers?" He protests but she insists, "I don't care how advanced they are. If your father and I haven't met them, they're strangers."

The other kids in Jimmy's universe include the lollipop-eating, cool kid Nick (Candi Milo), Jimmy's nerdy comic book worshiping pal, Sheen (Jeff Garcia) and Cindy (Carolyn Lawrence), the girl who would be the smartest kid in school if not for Jimmy. Whenever Jimmy screws up with one of his inventions, Cindy is the first in line to start the taunting. Despite this, Jimmy might have a little crush on her. After an encounter with Cindy, Carl asks, "We don't like girls yet, do we, Jimmy?" Jimmy answers, "No, no, not yet. But hormones over which we have no control will overpower our better judgment." And anyway, Jimmy feels like he's no catch. "What kind of girl wants to dance with a

guy who looks like he's still in Gymboree," he says, bemoaning his short stature.

One night when Jimmy uncharacteristically sneaks out with Sheen and Carl, the aliens he's contacted swoop down and take away his parents, as well as all the parents in town. The aliens intend to eat the parents, although like all good movie villains, they wait to do their villainy until there's been ample time to thwart their plans. When the kids wake up the next morning, they are thrilled. They overdose on coffee, take over the school and run around like maniacs. One kid leaves the refrigerator door open, chanting "I'm letting out the coooold." Another pees in the shower. The next day, though, they're feeling lonely. Some have boo-boos that they need kissed by mommy, some want to hear bedtimes stories and others just want . . . their . . . mommies!

It's up to Jimmy to save the day. Using his vast skills, he fashions space ships out of the rides at the local amusement parks. The sight of these jimmy-rigged spaceships flying through the air ends up being the best visual in a film filled with good visuals. Tumbling through the vast darkness of space are surreally colorful rides like a ferris wheel, a big, goofy octopus ride, and a roller coaster. During a pit stop on an asteroid, the queasy kids on the octopus ride offer to trade places with the others.

The brave band of kids finally make it to the alien planet which is inhabited by the Yokians, gooey egg-like creatures who live in a plastic shell. Their king is King Goobot (Patrick Stewart), who's aided by his obsequious sidekick, Ooblar (Martin Short). It turns out that their plan is not to eat the parents themselves, but to sacrifice them to their god, Poltra, a big chicken-looking kind of creature. (Note to parents: Poltra is scary enough to serve his movie purpose, but not so scary that he's going to scare the bejesus out of most little kids.) Will Jimmy be able to save the day, get the girl and be home in time for dinner? Well, sure.

Part of the charm of *Jimmy* is the way it looks. It was digitally animated by director John A. Davis and his DNA Productions and they do a fine job. They used software that anyone could pick up at the local computer store and it's amazing what they came up with. Every frame bursts with vibrancy. Jimmy inhabits a town called Retroville and everything there has a stylistic 1950's flair. Jimmy's spaceship has huge tail fins and the furniture in his house is brightly colored with wild, curvy angles.

The other half of *Jimmy*'s charm are the jokes sprinkled throughout. The film had several writers, including the director Davis and Steve Oedekerk, who wrote both *Ace Ventura* movies. Especially good are lines from Jimmy's nerdy friend, Sheen, who likes to pretend he is a comic book character. "I do so relish these times of peril," he says during a scary meteor shower. Later when someone makes fun of his comic book doll, he shrieks, "It's not a doll! It's an action figure!" The film is filled with funny tweaks on pop culture. When the kids arrive on the alien planet, they are shown a cheery infomercial designed for those whose "friends or relatives are about to be sacrificed to Poltra." There are lots of quick visual gags, too. One of the rides at the amusement park is called "Bat Outta Heck." The book that Jimmy's mother reads is "Unwrapping Your Gifted Child." The film has a more sophisticated humor, too. At one point, Jimmy bemoans, "In times of crisis, the intellectuals are always the first to go."

The film was a big hit with kids and a semi-hit with critics. Gary Dowell of the *Dallas Morning News* wrote, "Jimmy's creators obviously remember what it was like to be a kid, and they've channeled those memories into a charming movie." Rob Blackwelder of Spliced Wire wrote that the film is "absolutely popping with personality and prodigious production design." Others took issue with the low-cost animation. "There's no mistaking that the relatively flat, motion-limited animation *Neutron* operates on comes from a different, cheaper dimension," wrote Bob Strauss at the *Long Beach Press-Telegram.* "There's barely more invention in the animation than in the concept," sniffed Gene Seymour in the *Los Angeles Times,* though he conceded that the film "has so many bright colors and whirring parts that you wish it were either on your Christmas tree or beneath it." And Roger Ebert of the *Chicago Sun-Times* was just happy there were no fart jokes. "All movies for kids currently pay intense attention to bodily functions, and it is progress of a sort, I suppose, that *Jimmy Neutron*'s rude noise of choice is merely the belch."

—*Jill Hamilton*

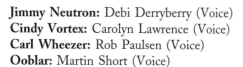

**CREDITS**

**Jimmy Neutron:** Debi Derryberry (Voice)
**Cindy Vortex:** Carolyn Lawrence (Voice)
**Carl Wheezer:** Rob Paulsen (Voice)
**Ooblar:** Martin Short (Voice)
**King Goobot:** Patrick Stewart (Voice)
**Mom/Vox:** Megan Cavanagh (Voice)
**Dad/Pilot:** Mark DeCarlo (Voice)
**Sheen:** Jeff Garcia (Voice)
**Nick Dean:** Candi Milo (Voice)
**Miss Fowl:** Andrea Martin (Voice)

**Origin:** USA
**Released:** 2001
**Production:** Steve Oedekerk, John A. Davis, Albie Hecht; Nickelodeon, O Entertainment; released by Paramount Pictures
**Directed by:** John A. Davis
**Written by:** David N. Weiss, J. David Stem, Steve Oedekerk, John A. Davis
**Music by:** John Debney

**Sound:** Christopher T. Welch
**Music Supervisor:** Jeff Carson, Frankie Pine
**Editing:** Jon Michael Price, Gregory Perler
**Art Direction:** James Beihold
**Production Design:** Fred Cline
**MPAA rating:** G
**Running time:** 90 minutes

**REVIEWS**

*Chicago Sun-Times Online.* December 21, 2001.
*Entertainment Weekly.* January 4, 2002, p. 48.
*Los Angeles Times Online.* December 21, 2001.
*New York Times Online.* December 21, 2001.
*USA Today Online.* December 21, 2001.
*Variety.* December 24, 2001, p. 20.
*Washington Post.* December 21, 2001, p. WE48.

**QUOTES**

Jimmy (voiced by Debi Derryberry): "What good is it to be a genius if you can't even go out on a school night?"

# Joe Dirt

*His Name's Not Mud, But It's Close.*
—Movie tagline

 **Box Office:** $27.1 million

One of the original titles for *Joe Dirt* was *The Adventures of Joe Dirt.* A few weeks before the movie arrived in theaters, the title was chopped down. It was probably decided that it was too long and complicated for the target audience because, after all, "adventures" is kind of a big word to sound out. The last minute title switcheroo didn't seem to hurt the movie much. In its first week it opened in the top 10 grossing movies. That's not bad considering that its big star was David Spade who hadn't yet proven himself at the boxoffice. Although he scored big results in movies like *Tommy Boy,* his hits were in pictures that teamed him with the late Chris Farley. His previous solo movie outing was *Lost and Found,* a film that justifiably did little at the boxoffice.

Spade is best known for playing the smart-alecky little guy—a role he perfected on several seasons of *Saturday Night Live,* and on the TV sitcom, *Just Shoot Me.* This time out he tries a different character. His Joe Dirt is what the movie calls "white trash"—a mullet wearin', AC/DC t-shirt-havin', *Auto Trader*-readin' kind of guy.

The character is supposed to be a lovable loser—the kind of character that Adam Sandler has made a fortune playing. Lawrence Toppman of the *Charlotte Observer* calls such a character a "Sandlerism," describing the type as "idiotic goober becomes not only a hero but attractive to beautiful women and lovable to all." The "Sandlerism" shouldn't come as much of a surprise—the film was produced by Sandler and Robert Simonds, the guy who produced Sandler's' last several films. (The team is also responsible for *Deuce Bigalow: Male Gigolo.*) The film was directed by Dennie Gordon, who is making her film directing debut. Her previous other gigs were TV shows like *The Practice* and *Ally McBeal.* The script was written—yes, someone does have to sit down and script out fart jokes—by Spade and Fred Wolf, who wrote for SNL. All those people with TV backgrounds has an effect on the movie. The movie plays like a TV show by moving briskly from one episode to the next.

The movie is told in a flashback. Joe Dirt is working as a janitor at a Los Angeles talk radio station when one of the DJs, Zander Kelly (Dennis Miller), takes an interest in him. It's not a kindly interest, mind you. Kelly simply cannot believe that such a guy who is, as he puts it, "ingrained in white-trash DNA" walks the Earth. Initially, Kelly puts Joe on the air to make fun of his bad hairstyle and pitiful life, but as Joe starts telling his story, the host, as well as a large part of the Los Angeles listening audience, becomes engrossed in Joe's history.

Joe was abandoned by his parents at the Grand Canyon when he was only 8 years old. The young Joe (Erik Per Sullivan of TV's *Malcolm in the Middle*) is left to fend for himself. The poor boy never gets a break. He is placed with a series of evil foster parents, including one who uses him as a hunting dog to retrieve downed ducks and one who lets her dog hump Joe's leg ("Just wait 'til he's done," she admonishes Joe.) As he gets older and is out on his own, Joe has but one goal—to find his lost parents. As he searches, he has all kinds of adventures, and needless to say, they are all wacky.

He runs into a very interesting supporting cast, including a Native American fireworks salesman (Adam Beach) who is unsuccessful because he only sells unexciting sparklers and snakes. Clem (Christopher Walken) is a mob boss who's participating in a government witness relocation program and working as a janitor in an elementary school. Joe works a short stint as an alligator trainer at a roadside stand run by a embittered trainer (Rosanna Arquette, sporting a really awful accent). The one bright spot in his life is Brandy (Brittany Daniel), a beautiful girl who loves Joe but who Joe considers to be too much out of his league. Their would-be romance is further thwarted by Brandy's mean drunken fa-

ther (Joe Don Baker) and Robbie (Kid Rock), a surly redneck who has designs on Brandy.

There is also a rather large supporting cast of gross jokes. Not just once, but at two different times in the film, objects fall from the sky that Joe thinks are valuable but turn out to be some sort of excrement. Once he finds what he thinks is a meteor, but it turns out to be some frozen space poop flushed from a plane. The other time he thinks he's found an atomic bomb, but it turns out to be a septic tank filled with, yes, more human waste. Of course it is necessary that at some point in the film the tank will burst and Joe will get covered with its contents. But the film is more that poop jokes, there are also fart jokes, including one about lighting a cow's fart on fire. If that's not enough comedy for you, there are also jokes about missing chunks of skull and the resulting exposed brain, having sex with one's sister (or supposed sister), and a scene involving a lengthy and graphic close-up of a dog's genitalia. Suffice it to say, eat that popcorn quickly during the opening previews.

Joe is also held back on his quest by the fact that people seem to like to beat him up. He spends large parts of the film getting made fun of or beaten up by various mean packs of teens, co-workers and the like. Despite his setbacks, Joe remains eternally optimistic and follows his homey life philosophies like "Keep on keepin' on," and "Life's a garden—dig it." When things get really bad, Joe will allow himself a "dang."

The acting in the film is pretty good, especially considering that it really didn't have to be. The actors seem like they're having a good time, which goes a long way in making the movie seem enjoyable to the audience. Spade manages to shed any bit of his usual sarcastic character and comes off as really being a sweet, though woefully unfashionable guy. In an interview with the *Arizona Republic,* Spade admitted to having an affinity for the character and said, "I am Joe Dirt. I go to 7-Eleven. I have walked with a gas can. I've had my sleeves cut off my flannel shirts. And I buy *Auto Trader* every time I'm in Phoenix, looking for a Grand National or '68 Roadrunner." Kid Rock is surprisingly good as Joe's surly, not-so-smart romantic rival. Walken is his usual strangely off character. And Miller is his usual caustic self, perhaps even more so, as the cruel radio host.

Also adding a lot to the movie is the soundtrack, which sounds like it's tuned into a classic rock station. The action is marked by what Joe would call "kick-ass" songs by Lynyrd Skynyrd, Bob Seger, and Eddie Money. Joe takes his music seriously and boasts that his coolness credentials are that he likes "Skynyrd and Van Halen, not Van HAGar."

The movie, predictably, was not a critic's favorite, but it wasn't as loathed as Spade's *Lost and Found* or a usual Sandler movie. *People* magazine said, "Sure, this is another of those extra-crude comedies—and a good, silly one, at that—but Joe, as played by Spade, is a genuine comic inspiration." The *Charlotte Observer* says that Spade "proves he really can act: He's endearing without straining to win us over, and he makes Joe silly enough to mock yet real enough to like after a while." Others weren't as taken with the film. *Newsday* said, "The jokes tend to drift toward that territory below the belt favored by people who would boast of their sexual prowess on their T-shirts" and the *Philadelphia Daily News* said, "Unfortunately, the audience is left saying, 'Just Shoot Me.'" 🎞

—*Jill Hamilton*

## CREDITS

**Joe Dirt:** David Spade
**Zander Kelly:** Dennis Miller
**Kicking Wing:** Adam Beach
**Clem:** Christopher Walken
**Jill:** Jaime Pressly
**Joe's Mom:** Caroline Aaron
**Joe's Dad:** Fred Ward
**Robby:** Bob (Kid Rock) Ritchie
**Little Joe Dirt:** Erik Per Sullivan
**Joe's little sister:** Megan Taylor Harvey

**Origin:** USA
**Released:** 2001
**Production:** Robert Simonds; Happy Madison Productions; released by Columbia Pictures
**Directed by:** Dennie Gordon
**Written by:** David Spade, Fred Wolf
**Cinematography by:** John R. Leonetti
**Music by:** Waddy Wachtel
**Sound:** David M. Kelson, Richard Lightstone
**Music Supervisor:** Michael Dilbeck
**Editing:** Peck Prior
**Art Direction:** Alan Au
**Costumes:** Alexandra Welker
**Production Design:** Perry Andelin Blake
**MPAA rating:** PG-13
**Running time:** 91 minutes

## REVIEWS

*Boxoffice.* June, 2001, p. 58.
*Chicago Sun-Times Online.* April 11, 2001.
*Entertainment Weekly.* April 20, 2001, p. 44.
*Los Angeles Times Online.* April 11, 2001.
*New York Times Online.* April 11, 2001.
*People.* April 23, 2001, p. 40.
*Variety.* April 16, 2001, p. 28.
*Washington Post Online.* April 13, 2001.

# Joe Somebody

*A comedy about somebody everybody can believe in.*
—Movie tagline
*Someone just picked on the wrong nobody.*
—Movie tagline

 **Box Office:** $22.7 million

Joe Scheffer (Tim Allen) is a nobody. A divorced father of a 12-year-old underachieving daughter, Natalie (Hayden Panettiere), Joe is the invisible man walking the halls of Starke Pharmaceuticals where he works. Although Joe excels at his job as a video communication specialist, no one respects him. When his co-workers aren't ignoring him, they're walking all over him. All, that is, except Meg Harper (Julie Bowen), the coordinator of the company's wellness program. Joe may be socially inept, but he's still a nice guy. When he tries to help Meg hang a banner in the cafeteria, he ends up stapling his sleeve to the bulletin board. The two make a brief connection, but the awkward, recently-wounded-by-divorce Joe and the permanently perky Meg do nothing about it.

But Joe's life is about to take a serious turn. It's "take your daughter to work" day, and Joe is bringing Natalie to his cubicle. Unfortunately, trying to find a place to park ends up cutting the day short. Joe, a 10-year employee, finds himself cut off in the 10-year employee parking lot by seven-year employee and office bully Mark McKinney (Patrick Warburton). When Joe stands up to Mark's obvious breach of company etiquette, McKinney ends up slapping him in the face not once but twice . . . and to make the humiliation complete, Joe's daughter sees it all. This sends Joe into a deep funk and he refuses to leave his home or speak to anyone for days. This worries his daughter Natalie who point-blank asks him, "What are you scared of?" After thinking about it Joe answers, "disappearing, I think." This is a man totally unaware of his own worth.

But why should Joe think he's worth anything. As one company executive put it, "He's a schmuck: his wife left him, he was passed over for promotion and was bitch-slapped in the parking lot." That last act took Joe's last shred of self-respect and even though Mark has been suspended and will have to take Meg's anger diffusion workshop when he returns, it does nothing to save Joe. However, even Joe's insensitive company begins to worry about his behavior—actually they're worried about being sued since the incident took place in their parking lot—so Meg is sent to Joe's house to get him to come back to work. The depressed Joe—who takes out his depression in fits of cleaning and drinking—refuses to return, but is struck by one question Meg asks, "What do you want?" This brings on a panic attack for Joe, but it will also bring about his redemption. Joe's answer to Meg's question turns out to be simple, "I am gonna kick Mark McKinney's ass." Joe will regain his self-respect through a rematch. With this announcement, Joe returns to work. But he returns a hero. Everyone hated Mark and they eagerly want vicarious retribution against the company bully. They can't wait for the "thrilla in vanilla" as one employee calls it and this makes Joe the man of the hour and everyone's friend.

Suddenly everything turns around for Joe. Everyone says hi to him in the company corridors. He's invited to the exclusive company gym, Club 13, and asked to partner a company executive for a squash match . . . which he ends up winning. He's invited to a karaoke party where he is a singing sensation and given corporate front row tickets to the Minnesota Timberwolves basketball game where he meets Governor Ventura. Joe changes his hairdo and buys expensive clothes, and even gets his promotion. Joe the nobody is now Joe somebody. As Meg says, "it looks like you're hanging with the cool kids now." But in Joe's defense he points out, "I wasn't getting a lot of positive feedback with who I was."

There's just one catch. In three weeks it will all end when Joe is once again trounced by the bigger and badder Mark McKinney. Then one day Joe passes by a strip mall and sees just what he needs: Scarett's Martial Arts. Perhaps Joe can buff up, learn a few moves and actually pull off a victory for the little guy. Then again, maybe not. This martial arts studio is run by a beer-swilling, overweight, has-been martial arts actor, Chuck Scarett (Jim Belushi). But could it be that Joe's redemption will also rescue Chuck . . . and Meg . . . and Natalie. Of course it will. Why? Because *Joe Somebody* is just that kind of feel-good movie.

*Joe Somebody* should never have been released during the holiday hustle of big-budget blockbusters like *Lord of the Rings* and *Harry Potter*. It should not have to compete with art films making their end-of-the-year Oscar® bid like *Vanilla Sky*, *A Beautiful Mind*, *The Shipping News*, and *Gosford Park*. Like it's unprepossessing romantic counterpart, *Kate & Leopold*, this little comedy can't compete with the big boys, and that's a shame. It's not that *Joe Somebody* is a great movie, or even a really good movie for that matter, it's just a nice, little movie. A fairly predictable story with a few laughs, some congenial performances, an uplifting message, and a lot of heart. It's one of those family films everyone keeps moaning they want to see Hollywood produce, but then don't bother to see in the theater.

*Joe Somebody* is the third film collaboration between director John Pasquin and Tim Allen (*The Santa Clause* in 1994 and *Jungle2Jungle* in 1997 are the other two) not to mention the fact that Pasquin also worked with Allen on his highly popular television show *Home Improvement*. There's

not much new here in *Joe Somebody*, but the final product is consistent with the family fare the two have produced in the past. It's interesting to see how beautifully the twin cities of Minneapolis and St. Paul are filmed and this Midwest setting further links the film with family fare instead of the usual Hollywood product. But while the use of the Minnesota cities is nicely original, most of the characters in the film are strictly from stereotype city.

Starting with Tim Allen's Joe, the characters seem more suited to an "After School Special" than an adult film, but maybe that simplicity and clarity is what helps to make it an attractive family film. Allen often plays characters caught in circumstances beyond their control, but Allen's usual reaction is humor couched in cantankerousness. Here, however, the fact that he is put upon is teamed with a self-consciousness and shyness that is typical of a Milquetoast, not exactly what we have come to associate with Allen. However, to his credit, he does manage to imbue his Joe with enough vulnerability that we gladly root for him.

Similarly, the shy hero must have a sweet, basically innocent, love interest and that is amply provided by Julie Bowen (best known from TV's *Ed*). Both Julie's Meg and Allen's Joe are fish out of water in the shark-eat-shark world of corporate America. Of course a man this inept usually has a daughter who is wise beyond her years and Hayden Panettiere has done this role before in *Remember the Titans*. Along with Meg, it is Natalie who has to help her father learn the after school lesson that being yourself is more important than being cool.

While perhaps not belonging in the after school special, even Jim Belushi's washed up martial arts actor is typical of the man who still has something to teach others even while learning lessons himself. His hapless character embodies a sense of honor hidden within a sense of humor. His Chuck Scarett is more Steven Seagal than Seagal is, offering our hero a path to discovering his own self worth while regaining his own sense of balance.

Perhaps the most underwritten character, however is that of the school . . . er, company bully, Mark McKinney. In typical pop-psych style, we know that bullies are misunderstood, but poor Patrick Warburton's Mark is given no depth. We can only guess as to what makes him tick—shaking hands on the day of the rematch and a solitary father-son photo at his bedside are our only hints. It would have been more interesting if the filmmakers had told us more about his character. (We would gladly trade the lame subplot involving Allen's wife Kelly Lynch for more Warburton screen time.)

The film is at its best, however, not when it is offering us uplifting inter-personal relationships, but when it is lampooning America's corporate culture. Starke Pharmaceuticals just begs to be skewered and there are hints that the filmmakers are capable of doing just that. Besides the hypocritical way the employees treat Joe, the film also points out the hypocritical way the corporation treats its employees. This is wonderfully illustrated when Meg's boss Jeremy (Greg Germann) callously points out that the purpose of Meg's job is not to take care of the well-being of the employees, but just to make the employees "believe" the company cares. Funnier still are the commercials for the company's products that can often be heard in the background. These drugs promise to make us "better than we really are" and then offer a prolonged list of side-effects that would make very few drugs worth taking . . . especially when we don't know what they're really for.

These jabs at corporate culture are a bit fainthearted but then again, that is not the film's purpose. Some may have wished *Joe Somebody* had had less schmaltz and more black humor. That it had traded some of its wholesomeness for a little more sly wickedness or at least just not been so bland, but then it wouldn't have been one of those nice movies parents are always demanding. Let's see if all those people bemoaning the lack of family fare actually put their dollars where their demands are. Somehow I doubt it. It's more fun to complain than to support the films which offer exactly what they want.

—*Beverley Bare Buehrer*

### CREDITS

**Joe Scheffer:** Tim Allen
**Meg Harper:** Julie Bowen
**Natalie Scheffer:** Hayden Panettiere
**Callie Scheffer:** Kelly Lynch
**Chuck Scarett:** James Belushi
**Mark McKinney:** Patrick Warburton
**Jeremy:** Greg Germann
**Pat Chilcutt:** Robert Joy
**Rick Raglow:** Ken Marino

**Origin:** USA
**Released:** 2001
**Production:** Anne Kopelson, Arnold Kopelson, Brian Reilly, Matthew Gross, Ken Atchity; Fox 2000 Pictures, Kopelson Entertainment, Regency Enterprises; released by 20th Century-Fox
**Directed by:** John Pasquin
**Written by:** John Scott Shepherd
**Cinematography by:** Daryn Okada
**Music by:** George S. Clinton
**Sound:** Marc Weingarten
**Editing:** David Finfer
**Costumes:** Lou Eyrich, Kathy O'Rear
**Production Design:** Jackson De Govia
**MPAA rating:** PG
**Running time:** 97 minutes

### REVIEWS

*Boston Globe Online.* December 21, 2001.
*Chicago Sun-Times Online.* December 21, 2001.
*Chicago Tribune Online.* December 23, 2001.
*Entertainment Weekly.* January 4, 2002, p. 48.
*Hollywood Reporter Online.* December 17, 2001.
*Los Angeles Times Online.* December 21, 2001.
*New York Times Online.* December 21, 2001.
*USA Today Online.* December 21, 2001.
*Variety.* December 17, 2001, p. 36.
*Washington Post.* December 21, 2001, p. WE48.

### QUOTES

Joe (Tim Allen) to Chuck (Jim Belushi): "I didn't come here to get my angst reviewed by a has-been movie star."

# John Carpenter's Ghosts of Mars (Ghosts of Mars)

*Terror is the same on any planet.*
—Movie tagline

**Box Office:** $8.4 million

On Mars in the year 2176, grumbling men work in dusty red mines, wear breathing masks, and submit reluctantly to the commands of a matriarchal society. People ride trains with trapezoid-shaped rusty red cars, though occasionally they command some sort of mechanized hot-air balloons. Mars looks like a dusty, dirty, God-forsaken place, and it's apparently run by some nameless, mysterious mining cartel. This is the dreary landscape that director John Carpenter concocts for his latest sci-fi horror film, ominously titled *John Carpenter's Ghosts of Mars* to distinguish it from any other potential *Ghosts of Mars* movies other directors might make in the future.

The man responsible for the original *Halloween*, as well as *The Fog, The Thing,* and other 1970s and 1980s horror flicks, was less productive in the 1990s. If Carpenter's large cult following was crying for blood by the year 2001, the director seemed in a mood to give it to them with a film that's so laughably lame and formulaic that it's almost a guilty pleasure. Carpenter doesn't bother to jazz up *Ghosts of*

*Mars* with any high-tech special effects or grand ideas; it's unapologetically cheesy and derivative.

Having the film set in Mars adds nothing to the plot, because the film is not really science fiction. The same events might transpire anywhere in the realm of horror filmdom. But the other-worldly setting does give Carpenter the chance to blow a lot of red dust around. Not surprisingly, none of it ever gets on the alabaster face of model-turned-actress Natasha Henstridge, who barely breaks a sweat or raises an eyebrow as the stoic Lt. Melanie Ballard. Ballard is a bad-ass but mostly by-the-book cop who tells her story to a panel of officials after returning, handcuffed and alone, on a train coming back on autopilot to Mars Central from an outpost known as Shining Canyon.

Ballard was sent to the mining camp town to pick up a notorious prisoner, James "Desolation" Williams (Ice Cube), who is being held there in a jail cell on charges of murdering five miners in another outpost. With her are her no-nonsense commanding officer, Helena Braddock (Pam Greer); hot-to-trot locksmith and mechanic Jericho Butler (Jason Statham), who speaks with a thick Australian-type accent; and two rookies, Bashira Kincaid (the intriguing, up-and-coming Clea Duvall) and Descanso (Liam White), who don't get many lines and who you suspect will eventually meet with a bad end.

The corny and B-grade lines come thick and fast right from the start. When Braddock catches Ballard getting high by taking some mysterious aspirin-like pill she keeps in an amulet, the commander tells the lieutenant the job will be tough and insists: "I need you straight." Ballard replies: "I'm as straight as they come," and Braddock, leering, replies: "That's too bad." When they get to the mining town, it at first appears to be deserted and one officer asks: "Where is everybody?" The other remarks that on a Friday night, it should be crowded with "money to spend, whores to fuck, and drugs to take." Jericho makes the first of many outrageous plays for Ballard, who replies in a deadpan: "Maybe I'd sleep with you if you were the last man on Earth. But we're not on Earth."

It takes awhile—and many detours back and forth through what should be a simple bit of filming, except Carpenter insists on much backtracking—for the officers to learn the truth. People in the mining town have been invaded by strange, evil, formless creatures who turn them into self-mutilating and sometimes murderous zombies. Much later we learn in yet another flashback that archaeologist Professor Whitlock (Joanna Cassidy) is to blame for this sorry state of affairs. At a nearby desert site, she and her team blasted open an ancient tunnel, and when she pushed on a wall, she released a huge cloud of red dust, which contains (or is) the native Martians, who are intent on taking their planet back from the Earthling invaders.

Martians over the years have so often been depicted as little green men that perhaps Carpenter despaired of creating anything that would not be laughable, but it is a big disappointment that the master monsters of this film are nothing but a cloud of red dust that blows on the wind. The dust apparently carries camera equipment, however; Carpenter's way of letting you know the Martian ghosts are about to take possession of another human is to shoot from the Martians' perspective. This technique consists of putting a red filter on the camera, blurring the focus a little bit, and moving it about in creepy hand-held amateurish horror-movie fashion while vague grunting and breathing noises play on the soundtrack. (Carpenter is responsible for the score, too, which alternates standard creepy special effects with gleeful pounding rock and roll during the many fight scenes).

When someone who has been possessed by the Martian ghosts dies, the ghostly spirit goes looking for another body to inhabit. However, this doesn't happen all the time. Braddock is killed off surprisingly early, leaving the film without a commanding Pam Greer with lesbian proclivities. Then Ballard and the rookies join up with Williams and his gang, and after some skirmishing they agree to a temporary truce in order to fight their common enemy. Holed up in one of the clunky, industrial-age buildings, they kill off enough ghoulish figures and possessed Earthlings to free up ten times the spirits needed to take possession of them. But only Ballard is taken over, and surprisingly, her drugs provide an antidote and free her from possession after a minute or so of really murky and strange dream-time in which she sees things from a Martian perspective. That perspective is vaguely Nazi-like.

The possessed beings who are trying to kill off the cops and criminals look and behave exactly like a bunch of 1950s-style zombies from a cheap horror flick. Their leader is a bellowing beast who resembles a refugee from the band Kiss. They sometimes chant something that sounds like: "Oooh—ahh!" They favor cutting instruments of all varieties, including flying blades that can—and do—decapitate some of the heroes. Other than that, they make good punching bags for the Earthlings, as well as good targets for guns, grenades, and karate kicks (Ballard, as is all female action heroines, is adept at a well-placed heel to the groin). As science fiction villains, however, these beasts are hardly inventive.

Ice Cube, as Williams, brings some needed levity to the film with his doggedly tongue-in-cheek portrayal of the fearless, uncompromising, cop-hating, yet kindhearted street criminal. He has most of the best lines, too, because he gets to swear profusely and he's hip. "Let's party!" is his rallying cry when the Earthlings go out to battle the possessed zombies. "I never give my word," he says to Ballard when she tries to get him to promise to behave during a truce. "That's OK, I never make deals with criminals," the steely, sassy Henstridge replies. After Williams saves Ballard a second time and points that out—in the midst of an all-out melee—Ballard comments; "Run me a tab." It's that kind of flick.

When Ballard summons the troops back for a return engagement, Williams complains: "I don't give a damn about saving this planet." But it turns out he likes working with Ballard so well—what a surprise!—that he returns in the end to mow down some more Martians. It's that kind of movie too.

It's hard to say what Carpenter had in mind beyond some mindless good fun. The film is pleasantly predictable, easy on the brain, and intermittently entertaining, if you appreciate imitations of B movies. It's not quite cheesy enough to match what once passed for science fiction, but it has no grand ambitions or pretensions, and that's almost a pleasant diversions in these days of overblown epics. The movie leaves a viewer feeling completely unburdened and anticipating what might be next—maybe some blue liquid ghosts in *John Carpenter's Ghosts of Venus* or some ring wraiths in *John Carpenter's Ghosts of Saturn*. For the moment, we must be content with this horror sci-fi laugher that is neither scary nor intelligent but provides plenty of old-fashioned us-against-the-zombies—er—Martians—action. It's a throwback to the days when scary movies were simple and entirely brainless.

—*Michael Betzold*

## CREDITS

**Melanie Ballard:** Natasha Henstridge
**James "Desolation" Williams:** Ice Cube
**Bashira Kincaid:** Clea DuVall
**Helena Braddock:** Pam Grier
**Jericho Butler:** Jason Statham
**Whitlock:** Joanna Cassidy
**Inquisitor:** Rosemary Forsyth
**Michael Descanso:** Liam Waite
**Big Daddy Mars:** Richard Cetrone

**Origin:** USA
**Released:** 2001
**Production:** Sandy King; Storm King; released by Screen Gems
**Directed by:** John Carpenter
**Written by:** John Carpenter, Larry Sulkis
**Cinematography by:** Gary B. Kibbe
**Music by:** John Carpenter
**Sound:** Willie Burton
**Editing:** Paul Warschilka
**Art Direction:** William Hiney, Mark Mansbridge
**Costumes:** Robin Michel Bush
**Production Design:** William Elliott
**MPAA rating:** R

**Running time:** 98 minutes

## REVIEWS

*Boxoffice.* July, 2001, p. 32.
*Boxoffice.* October, 2001, p. 59.
*Chicago Sun-Times Online.* August 24, 2001.
*Entertainment Weekly.* September 7, 2001, p. 135.
*Hollywood Reporter.* August 21, 2001, p. 24.
*Los Angeles Times Online.* August 24, 2001.
*New York Times Online.* August 24, 2001.
*Variety.* August 27, 2001, p. 31.
*Washington Post.* August 24, 2001, p. C5.

# Josie and the Pussycats

*Here kitty, kitty, kitty . . .*
—Movie tagline

**Box Office:** $14.2 million

First it was a spin-off comic book from the "Archie" series, then it became an animated cartoon. Now it's in its third incarnation as a film. Strange, since the original comic wasn't really that interesting in the first place. But the one thing the comic has going for it is name recognition, which counts for a lot in selling stuff to the American public. Just ask George W. Bush.

The original "Josie," while certainly "groovy," to use the parlance of the time, were never particularly smart or funny. If you looked beyond the giant flared pants and peace sign adorned shirts, it was all really quite square. This "Josie" aims to be everything the originals weren't. It tries to be ironic, smart and sassy.

*Josie and the Pussycats* purports to be skewering consumer culture, but there's a little conflict of interest. The movie is filled with product placements and references to consumer goods, not to mention that there's a soundtrack for purchase. Even though the film's message is that such marketing is bad, the film itself is an ad. After all, whether or not a shot of a big billboard for Coca-Cola on screen is intended ironically or not doesn't really matter, it's still a big ad that everyone who watches the movie will see.

The film begins with a take on the omnipresent late 1990's/early 2000's phenomenon, boy bands. DuJour (ha-ha) is a cute boy band riding on top of the music charts. (The band's single is called "Back Door Lover," which is the kind of risqué humor that the movie sometimes sneaks in.) Everything is going fine with their career until they notice that there's an odd backing track on the mix of their new single. Upon the band's questioning, manager Wyatt Frame (Alan Cumming) becomes alarmed and plots for the plane that the group is riding to have a sudden crash. Frame, who parachutes out to safety, is the only one to survive the accident. In one of the many commentaries on crash consumer cultures, we see on an MTV News update (featuring real VJ Serena Ahctull) that the record company is waiting to release a statement, but is rushing to put out a DuJour commemorative boxed set.

Frame's boss Fiona (Parker Posey), who is the head of MegaRecords, is not happy to hear that Frame has killed off her top act. It's not because she's against killing rock stars who know too much, after all that's what happened to Elvis, Buddy Holly, etc., she's just mad because she needs a new band to market. She demands that Frame find a new band by morning.

Frame happens to be right outside of Riverdale, home of Josie and the Pussycats. Josie (Rachel Leigh Cook) and her bandmates, Melody Valentine (Tara Reid) and Valerie Brown (Rosario Dawson), are trying to make it big, but having little success. They play gigs at places like bowling alleys and are happy to earn $20. They have no fans, since all the local teens are into DuJour. After making a vow that they are going to start being more aggressive about the band's career, the three meet up with Frame. Frame immediately offers the band a contract, even though he hasn't even heard them play. Josie and the gang are a little wary of this, but they do want to be famous and get their big break, so they sign up.

Things start happening fast for the band, really fast. In the space of a week, the band poses for a bunch of photo shoots, puts out a record and watches it climb from eightysomething on the charts to number one. Josie and co. are thrilled about all this until they, too, start getting wise to the evil plans of MegaRecords. It seems that the label, which is in cahoots with the federal government, is putting these subliminal tracks on hit records in order to get the economy going by controlling the spending habits of teens. The messages on the songs are things like, "Orange is the new red," "Gatorade is the new Snapple" and "Heath Ledger is the new Matt Damon." (In a funny touch, the messages are done by the same guy who does the "Mr. Moviefone" recordings.) Impressionable teens, upon hearing the song, immediately rush zombie-like to the nearest store to purchase the song plus whatever is suggested to them. (How this is different from teens' responses to regular advertising is kind of negligible.)

To hammer in its point about the omnipresence of advertising (or perhaps to score some advertising bucks to fund the movie), *Josie and the Pussycats* is crammed with product placements. DuJour's private plane, for example, is decked out with logo's from Target and has products like Bounce fabric softener sitting randomly about. Melody's

bathroom at the hotel she's staying in is decorated with a McDonald's theme. Even the washcloth is shaped like a pack of fries. Whenever a character has any kind of lengthy speech to give, they're invariably standing in front of a huge billboard. Even the water at the aquarium where Josie and her love interest Alan M (Gabriel Mann) go to have a quiet talk is an ad for Evian water.

Deborah Kaplan and Harry Elfont, who wrote and directed the film, are wise to the silliness of making a movie based on a cartoon and have a couple of jokes that poke fun at the comic. (Since the original comic has so little personality, they don't really have a whole lot to go on.) When minor characters Alexandria and her brother Alexander end up coming along on Josie and the Pussycats' big adventure, Alexander, the Pussycats manager says to his sister, "I still don't understand why you're here." Alexandria replies, apropos of nothing in the film, "I was in the comic book." Frame mocks Alan M with "What's with the initial? It didn't work for Shelia E, it doesn't work for you." The in-humor even applies to the filmmakers' own work. One of the subliminal messages in the film is "*Can't Hardly Wait* was underrated." (*Can't Hardly Wait* was their previous film.)

The film is also filmed with the kind of references that would appeal to pop culture fans. When one of the guys in DuJour is complaining that his bandmate has stolen the face he always makes for publicity shots, Frame says patiently, "I will call the choreographer and she will give you a new face." There's also a cameo from Carson Daly, MTV personality and host of the teenybopper fave *TRL*, who is game to take on his image. He calls himself "a key player in this conspiracy to brainwash the young of America with pop music."

Critics liked the cheeky humor of the film and gave it generally favorable reviews. "It's Rock Satire 101, a good starting point for kids who will hopefully want to move up to such big-time pop-cult assassinations as *This is Spinal Tap* and *High Fidelity*," wrote Peter Howell of the *Toronto Star*. "Here's (an) irony," wrote David Edelstein of Slate, "Even if you find the satire in *Josie and the Pussycats* self-serving, you might still love the movie, buy the soundtrack, and surrender to the hype. That's what happened to me." Kenneth Turan of the *Los Angeles Times* took a darker view of the film. "You could argue that a film that's supposed to mock commercialism in modern life needs to have corporate logos on every vacant space, but it's unnerving how cleverly *Josie* manages to profit from the very thing it's supposedly skewering," he wrote. "It's a potent reminder that no matter how innocent a film may seem, there's a Hollywood cash register behind almost every frame." ☉

—*Jill Hamilton*

## CREDITS

**Josie McCoy:** Rachael Leigh Cook
**Melody Valentine:** Tara Reid
**Valerie Brown:** Rosario Dawson
**Fiona:** Parker Posey
**Wyatt Frame:** Alan Cumming
**Alan M.:** Gabriel Mann
**Alexander Cabot:** Paulo Costanzo
**Agent Kelly:** Tom Butler
**Alexandra Cabot:** Missi Pyle
**Himself:** Carson Daly
**Cameo:** Seth Green
**Cameo:** Breckin Meyer
**Cameo:** Donald Adeosun Faison

**Origin:** USA
**Released:** 2001
**Production:** Marc Platt, Tracey E. Edmonds, Chuck Grimes, Tony DeRosa-Grund; Riverdale; released by Universal Pictures, Metro-Goldwyn-Mayer
**Directed by:** Deborah Kaplan, Harry Elfont
**Written by:** Deborah Kaplan, Harry Elfont
**Cinematography by:** Matthew Libatique
**Music by:** John (Gianni) Frizzell
**Sound:** Eric J. Batut
**Editing:** Peter Teschner
**Art Direction:** Kevin Humenny
**Costumes:** Leesa Evans
**Production Design:** Jasna Stefanovich
**MPAA rating:** PG-13
**Running time:** 99 minutes

## REVIEWS

*Boxoffice.* June, 2001, p. 59.
*Chicago Sun-Times Online.* April 11, 2001.
*Entertainment Weekly.* April 20, 2001, p. 48.
*Los Angeles Times Online.* April 11, 2001.
*New York Times Online.* April 11, 2001.
*People.* April 23, 2001, p. 38.
*Sight and Sound.* September, 2001, p. 46.
*TV Guide.* March 31, 2001, p. 20.
*USA Today Online.* April 13, 2001.
*Variety.* April 9, 2001, p. 17.
*Washington Post Online.* April 13, 2001.

## QUOTES

Josie (Rachael Leigh Cook): "Oh my god. I'm a trend pimp!"

## TRIVIA

Rachael Leigh Cook's vocals are sung by Letters to Cleo singer Kay Hanley.

# Joy Ride

*It started as a joke. Now the joke is on them.*
—Movie tagline

**Box Office:** $22 million

*J*oy Ride is an entertaining suspense yarn in the great tradition of B-movie film noir. Directed by John Dahl, whose *Red Rock West* and *The Last Seduction* were two of the most successful entries in the neo-noir cycle of the '90s, *Joy Ride* represents a return to form after his mediocre foray into the mainstream with the poker film, *Rounders.* More specifically, *Joy Ride* is a return for Dahl to the noir terrain he seems to know best—the dark, desolate highways of the American Midwest where hapless, decent folk get ensnared by a relentless evil that threatens to swallow them up. True to its B-movie forebears, *Joy Ride* has a simple plot and fairly two-dimensional characters; it is not wholly original, but it is rich in atmosphere and gradually builds a sense of dread that intensifies right up through the nerve-racking climax.

Paul Walker, who made a splash in the summer car-racing flick, *The Fast and the Furious,* is once again behind the wheel. He plays Lewis, a young college student about to return home from Berkeley. When he learns that Venna (Leelee Sobieski), a friend of his, has just broken up with her boyfriend, he realizes that he may have a chance to become more than friends and offers to pick her up in Boulder and give her a ride home. He trades in his plane ticket, buys a 1971 Chrysler Newport, and hits the road. On his way to meet Venna, however, he makes a detour in Salt Lake City to spring his wayward brother, Fuller (Steve Zahn), on a drunk-and-disorderly charge, even though he has not seen him in some time. Fuller is the classic ne'er-do-well and perpetual loser who loves acting on the anarchic impulses that his more straitlaced, younger brother represses.

No sooner have they gotten started than Fuller has a CB radio installed in the car and gives himself the handle Black Sheep and his brother, Mama's Boy, which tells us everything we need to know about their family relationships. As Fuller is goofing off with his new toy, he encourages Lewis to adopt a woman's voice and tease a lonely trucker as a practical joke. Lewis spontaneously makes up the name of Candy Cane and does a seductive come-hither purr that grabs the attention of the trucker, who goes by the ominous handle Rusty Nail. They plan to toy with him for a while and then tell him it is all a joke, but they lose Rusty Nail on their CB before Lewis can confess to their shenanigans.

When they arrive at a motel for the evening, Fuller encounters a rude traveler named Ellinghouse (Kenneth White) in the lobby, and, when Rusty Nail's voice comes back on the CB, Fuller gets the idea to play a joke. Coaxing Lewis to do the voice again, Fuller has him suggest a rendezvous with Rusty Nail in Room 17, which is Ellinghouse's room. Hoping to get a big laugh, the brothers instead are startled when they hear trouble next door and, thinking that the trucker has been attacked, report the incident to the manager. Everything seems fine until the next morning when the boys are questioned by authorities—it turns out that Ellinghouse was found facedown on the highway median with his jaw torn off and is now in a coma.

Once they hit the road, Rusty Nail's voice again comes in on the radio seeking out Candy Cane. Lewis confesses that he is a man playing the dream girl, but, when Rusty Nail demands an apology for the joke, Fuller instead antagonizes him further by telling him how sick he is. The demented trucker, making it clear that he is stalking them, counters that they should fix their taillight. Thus begins a series of scary cat-and-mouse encounters in which Lewis and Fuller are terrorized by the unseen Rusty Nail, who seems to know their every move.

Dahl is expert at building tension in a scene and then defusing it with a comic payoff. For example, after the boys buy gas, they are pursued by a trucker, who, it turns out, is just trying to be a good Samaritan returning the credit card that the frazzled Lewis had left in the convenience store. But then Dahl very quickly ramps up the terror when Rusty Nail's truck barrels right through the helpful driver's ice truck and starts chasing the boys. The pursuit ends on a deserted road when the brothers' car hits a tree and stalls, and Rusty Nail pushes right up against it and lifts it up, smashing the windows. Now scared to death, Fuller frantically apologizes, and Rusty Nail finally backs off.

Getting a respite from their fright, Lewis gets the taillight fixed and decides not to tell Venna what they have been through, while Fuller throws the CB out the car window, as if he were swearing off his mischievous ways. When the boys reach Venna, a new wrinkle is introduced as Fuller takes an interest in her. Unfortunately, not much is made of this potential conflict between the brothers. Dahl, it seems, is more interested in cranking up the suspense than in developing complex characters—no sooner does Fuller try to make a move on Venna in her room than Rusty Nail calls Lewis to inquire about the girl now traveling with them, and the chase is back on. As the panicked trio race away from the motel, they discover a message from Rusty Nail scrawled on the road signs telling them to look in their trunk, where they find the old CB radio. At this point, one could easily call the

whole plot utterly implausible; how could Rusty Nail so doggedly watch every move the kids make and know precisely where they are and which roads they will take?

Indeed, the most questionable aspect of *Joy Ride* is the villain. We never see Rusty Nail's face, and he comes across not so much as a character as a kind of omniscient force of evil that is always one step ahead of the unsuspecting kids. Moreover, since he has no motivation other than to be an instrument of vengeance, the conflict works only on the most basic of levels. *Red Rock West* and *The Last Seduction* are memorable for their finely drawn characters, especially the villains, but *Joy Ride* falls short in this area.

Rusty Nail is so far ahead of these kids, in fact, that he even kidnaps Venna's friend from school, Charlotte (Jessica Bowman), and threatens to dismember her if they do not follow his orders. How he finds Venna's friend is another odd plot turn that cannot be explained, but somehow it does not matter. Rusty Nail's mission is simply to toy with his victims with requests that are alternately funny and scary, but they feel a bit disconnected and random, as if screenwriters Clay Tarver and J.J. Abrams were unsure how to proceed but needed to fill time before the thrilling ending. Rusty Nail has the brothers go into a restaurant naked to order food (a plot point that goes nowhere) and then has them drive to a cornfield so that he can chase them. The result of the cornfield chase is that Rusty Nail captures Venna and orders the boys to meet him in Room 17 in a motel in the next town.

Dahl delivers a suspenseful, skillfully edited climax in which the boys first must find the right motel and then the right room (Rusty Nail actually has Venna in Room 18), which is not an easy task. What Fuller and Lewis do not know is that Rusty Nail has tied and gagged Venna and booby-trapped the door with a shotgun so that, when they open it, she will be killed. Once they get to the right motel, Fuller goes around the back of the building, sees that the door is rigged, and, despite the fact that Rusty Nail attacks him, is still able to shout a warning to Lewis not to open it. Rusty Nail disappears, and his truck is soon heading straight toward Fuller, who has been pinned to a fence with a pipe jammed in his leg.

Meanwhile, sheriff's men (called by Rusty Nail) are kicking down motel room doors and getting close to Venna's, leaving Lewis to try to rescue two people. He saves Venna at the last possible moment just as the gun-rigged door is opened and then frees his brother while getting the sheriff's men to fire on the speeding truck, which ends up crashing into the motel. They find Charlotte tied and gagged in the truck and the dead body of a trucker, who drove for an ice company, which suggests that it is the trucker who returned Lewis's credit card to him. In the final twist, however, we hear Rusty Nail's voice on the ambulance CB. He merely substituted the other trucker's body for his own and has escaped, leaving the conclusion open-ended.

*Joy Ride* has a fairly straightforward, episodic plot, but Dahl's snappy direction and pacing keep the action compelling, even as the logic of the story becomes increasingly farfetched. Dahl stays on safe ground and does not rework the familiar noir formulas in fresh ways, but his sense of style makes the movie a fun, creepy trip. There are some beautiful, eerie shots of the darkened highways and lonely roads, as well as the characters' faces reflected in the red glow of their car's lights. Dahl also elicits fine performances from his cast, especially Zahn. While Walker plays the typical straight arrow, and Sobieski's main purpose is to play the beautiful girl in distress in the final act, Zahn's Fuller is the wild card who can get everyone around him in loads of trouble and yet still be sympathetic. Zahn gives him a wild streak and a sardonic outlook on life that are appealing and dangerous and that jumpstart the thin plot with the extra kick it needs.

—*Peter N. Chumo II*

---

## CREDITS

**Lewis Thomas:** Paul Walker
**Fuller Thomas:** Steve Zahn
**Venna:** Leelee Sobieski
**Charlotte:** Jessica Bowman
**Danny:** Stuart Stone
**Car Salesman:** Basil Wallace
**Officer Keeney:** Brian Leckner
**Rusty Nail:** Ted Levine (Voice)

**Origin:** USA
**Released:** 2001
**Production:** Chris Moore, J.J. Abrams; Regency Enterprises, New Regency Pictures, Bad Robot, Liveplanet; released by 20th Century-Fox
**Directed by:** John Dahl
**Written by:** J.J. Abrams, Clay Tarver
**Cinematography by:** Jeffrey Jur
**Music by:** Marco Beltrami
**Sound:** Tim Cooney
**Music Supervisor:** John Bissell
**Editing:** Glen Scantlebury, Eric L. Beason, Scott Chestnut, Todd E. Miller
**Art Direction:** Michael Rizzo
**Costumes:** Terry Dresbach
**Production Design:** Rob Pearson
**MPAA rating:** R
**Running time:** 96 minutes

---

## REVIEWS

*Boxoffice.* October, 2001, p. 60.
*Chicago Sun-Times Online.* October 5, 2001.
*Entertainment Weekly.* October 12, 2001, p. 63.
*Los Angeles Times Online.* October 5, 2001.
*New York Times Online.* October 5, 2001.
*People.* October 15, 2001, p. 43.
*USA Today Online.* October 4, 2001.
*Variety.* September 10, 2001, p. 60.
*Washington Post.* October 5, 2001, p. WE37.

---

## QUOTES

Venna (Leelee Sobieski): "How scared am I supposed to be?" Fuller (Steve Zahn) replies: "Much more than usual."

---

# Jump Tomorrow

**Box Office:** $.1 million

Londoner Joel Hopkins, who studied film at New York University, received a grant to expand his 1999 short *Jorge* to feature length, again starring fellow NYU grad, Tunde Adebimpe. *Jump Tomorrow* is a romantic comedy for the alternative film crowd, who will appreciate Hopkins' non-formulaic approach and multicultural characters since the film presents a microcosmic global village with its Nigerian, American, Spanish, English, and French characters. Throw in some Spanish lessons, a few key French phrases, flamenco dancing, a traditional arranged marriage, and a smart comedy is born.

The film opens on George's (Adebimpe) face as a ladybug lands on him (ladybugs represent romantic encounters). A group of coworkers approach George and congratulate him on his upcoming marriage. They glibly tell George, "Smile, George, you're getting married," but George can barely drag his lips across into a smile. Next we see a quick montage of George visiting the tailor and picking up a wedding ring while the sentiment "smile, you're getting married" is repeated, adding to George's agitated state. George arrives at the airport to pick up his fiancee—24-hours too late as she has already left for the wedding's destination of Niagra Falls. While his Nigerian uncle (Isiah Whitlock Jr.) is chewing out George, a vivacious Hispanic woman, Alicia (Natalia Verbeke), appears at the adjacent phone booth and George finally finds a reason to smile. She invites George to a party.

Meanwhile, lovelorn Frenchman Gèrard (Hippolyte Girardot) has been dumped after proposing to his girlfriend at the airport. Gèrard and George's paths cross in a bathroom where Gerard laments to George about his shattered romance. Soon the unlikely pair show up at Alicia's "leaving" party since Alicia has decided to move to Canada with her English boyfriend Nathan (James Wilby). While George flirts with Alicia, Gerard heads to the roof of the building where he prepares to jump. However, George stops Gerard from committing suicide by telling him, "jump tomorrow because you'll regret it if you jump today." The next morning Gerard thanks George by insisting that he drive George to his wedding. George reluctantly accepts.

A road trip that should only take a few hours extends for a couple of days. During that time George and Gerard wind up staying at the same love lodge as Alicia and Nathan. But sparks don't begin flying until Gerard and George pick up the couple, who are hitchhiking to Canada. Gerard offers to drop Alicia and Nathan off at her mother's home, only to be invited to stay the night. Nathan becomes ill after eating hot peppers and once he's out of the picture, Alicia and George spend a few quiet moments together as they cement their bond. The next day, Gerard drives George to the church where his wedding to his childhood friend Sophie (Abiola Wendy Abrams) awaits him, while Alicia and Nathan head to the Canadian border. Director Hopkins keeps us guessing the film's climatic ending as to whether or not true love will run its course.

Similar to the title of the film, Hopkins employs a series of jump cuts as he quickly enters and exits all the scenes in the film. His use of bright colors and 1960's pop classics such as John Lennon's *Instant Karma* add a playful quality. In fact, *Jump Tomorrow* recalls such English 1960's classics as *To Sir With Love* and Richard Lester's films. Adebimpe has a detached and droll humor that plays well off of French actor Hippolyte's Chaplinesque demeanor. Wilby plays the pretentious Englishman that we all love to hate, while Spaniard Verbeke creates a new definition for vivacious and performs a hot flamenco number. This delightful road flick with its unforgettable characters proves to be the perfect escape and filled with guilty pleasures.

—*Patty-Lynne Herlevi*

**George:** Tunde Adebimpe
**Gerard:** Hippolyte Girardot
**Alicia:** Natalia Verbeke
**Nathan:** James Wilby
**Consuela:** Patricia Mauceri
**Sophie:** Abiola Wendy Abrams
**Old Man:** Gene Ruffini

**George's Uncle:** Isiah Whitlock Jr.
**Heather Leather:** Kaili Vernoff

**Origin:** Great Britain, USA
**Released:** 2001
**Production:** Nicola Usborne; FilmFour, Eureka Pictures; released by IFC Films
**Directed by:** Joel Hopkins
**Written by:** Joel Hopkins
**Cinematography by:** Patrick Cady
**Music by:** John Kimbough
**Sound:** Judy Karp
**Editing:** Susan Littenberg
**Art Direction:** Gonzalo Cordoba
**Costumes:** Sarah J. Holden
**Production Design:** John Paino
**MPAA rating:** PG
**Running time:** 96 minutes

## REVIEWS

*Boxoffice.* July, 2001, p. 88.
*Chicago Sun-Times Online.* July 27, 2001.
*Entertainment Weekly.* July 27, 2001, p. 47.
*Los Angeles Times Online.* July 6, 2001.
*New York Times Online.* July 6, 2001.
*RANT.* July/August, 2001, p. 10.
*San Francisco Chronicle Online.* July 6, 2001.
*Sight and Sound.* October, 2001, p. 50.
*Variety.* February 12, 2001, p. 40.

## QUOTES

George (Tunde Adebimpe) advises his suicidal friend: "Jump tomorrow."

# Jurassic Park 3

*This time it's not just a walk in the park!*
—Movie tagline
*Something unexpected has evolved.*
—Movie tagline
*Dream . . . Fantasy . . . Destruction . . . Evolution of Adventure.*
—Movie tagline

 **Box Office:** $181.2 million

sla Sorna is a picturesque island 200 miles west of Costa Rica. It would be the perfect location for a tropical vacation if it weren't for the fact that it was InGen's site B during their dinosaur cloning heyday. Because there are still dinosaurs there, it is highly restricted, but where there's a buck to be made there's a way.

Consequently, a few entrepreneurs with a boat and a parasail offer people the chance to hover over Isla Sorna and possibly glimpse the forbidden dinosaurs. So, flying in tandem, the adult Ben (Mark Harelik) and a young boy, Eric (Trevor Morgan), sail high above the island, videocamera at the ready, looking for traces of dinosaurs. It's an exciting adventure that is about to get even more exciting and more dangerous when their tow boat disappears into a mist only to reappear battered and without its crew. The parasailing duo has no choice but to cut loose and attempt to land on the forbidden island.

Isla Sorna and its InGen sister island, Isla Nebula, are places Dr. Alan Grant (Sam Neill) would just as soon forget. He still has nightmares about his experience at Jurassic Park eight years ago, and although he still loves theorizing about dinosaurs, he'd just as soon do it from their bones imbedded in rocks as from the possibility of their teeth imbedded in his flesh. The famed archeologist, however, is finding it more and more difficult to get funding for his work and is frustrated that people are only interested in his experiences on Isla Nebula or want to know about the dino that escaped in San Diego—which he had nothing to do with—than his current theories on raptor intelligence. These are the woes he pours out to his colleague Ellie (Laura Dern) whom he visits in her suburban home, complete with two kids and a State department working husband.

Back at Fort Peck Lake in Montana, site of Alan's current dig, Alan's assistant Billy Brennan (Alessandro Nivola) has a surprise for Alan. He has purchased a machine that can take computer images and turn them into physical three-dimensional recreations. He has just made a raptor nasal cavity for Alan which, when blown through, creates different sounds which might possibly confirm Alan's theory that the predatory dinosaurs actually communicated with each other. This would make them much smarter and more socialized than Alan would have believed—before he was at their mercy years earlier, that is.

At this point Alan and Billy find themselves faced with an unusual proposition. Paul Kirby (William H. Macy) and his wife Amanda (Tea Leoni) are a wealthy couple who enjoy adventure vacations. They have a special anniversary coming up and want more than anything else to fly over Isla Sorna with Dr. Grant as their guide. Billy leaps at the possibility to see dinosaurs up close and personal, but Alan pales at even the thought of being that close to them again. It's only when Kirby assures them that he has the permission of the Costa Rican government (because of his import-

export business connections) and offers them a blank check to finance their research that Dr. Grant eventually relents.

The expedition to fly over the restricted island is headed by a man named Udesky (Michael Jeter) and also includes two other mysterious men, Cooper (John Diehl) and Nash (Bruce A. Young). This adventure vacation, however, takes an ominous turn when the plane, instead of just circling the island, actually lands on it. This was not in Dr. Grant's plans. Why is the plane landing in such a dangerous location? Because the Kirby's are not who they say they are. In reality, they are the divorced parents of 12-year-old Eric who parasailed onto the island eight weeks earlier. They're here to rescue him. After their plane is wrecked by a dinosaur, however, the new question is who will rescue the rescuers?

It's a simple question, making for a simple plot and culminating in a simplistic ending. This is probably the major objection most critics have had to this third installment in the *Jurassic Park* franchise. (That and the fact that the original author, Michael Crichton, and the original director, Steven Spielberg, have virtually nothing to do with this tame installment.) *Jurassic Park III* has no secondary plot lines; it is a simple survive and rescue story with an abrupt ending that smacks more of desperation than ingenuity.

It has been said that the script for *JP III* was begun in 1999 and then featured half a dozen teenagers getting marooned on the island. That idea was scrapped and was followed by two other complete versions that were written and storyboarded—and thrown away. Then, five weeks before shooting began, all scripts were scrapped and the whole process was begun again which meant that there was a lot of writing and rewriting going on while the film was actually shooting.

As a consequence, the plot is thin and predictable and doesn't have much of a dramatic arc, just going from one dinosaur scare/fight to another. Similarly slighted are the characters who are only perfunctorily written, more like stock personalities than anything three-dimensional. Plus, most of them are stupid. They're always splitting up and walking and yelling where and when they shouldn't. Sure, that ensures dino-action will follow, but at the expense of these people as believable characters. In fact, so predictable are they that we even know who will be the first two characters to die. They're just like those unknown crewmen on the old *Star Trek* TV series who beam down to a hostile planet. We've never seen them before so they're expendable and are not going to live to beam back up.

However, the most obvious casualty of the film's uncertain script process is the film's ending. In fact, according to two actors, there was no ending at all when filming began. Without giving anything away, the ending comes suddenly and totally out of the blue. Furthermore, the nonplussed reactions of the survivors to see some dinosaurs escaping from the restricted area at the end is very jarring. After all they've been through, the only comment they make is the equivalent of "I don't care where they're going as long as it's not my hometown."

Another problem for *Jurassic Park III* is its cinematography. Although the Hawaiian islands of Oahu, Molokai and Kauai make for good substitute Isla Sornas, when the action on them is filmed it is claustrophobic. During the first encounter between the huge, menacing dinosaurs, it is filmed in such close ups that it's very difficult to tell one from the other. The final battle between humans and dinosaurs is similarly muddled because it is shot in the dark and in the rain. It is very hard to follow. And the quick cutting within the airplane as it is tumbling and being squashed is just as perplexing.

This isn't to say there aren't things to like about *JP III*, especially as a summer escape film. There's one particularly funny plot point involving a cell phone and the inspired off-beat casting of Michael Jeter as a mercenary, but they are minor amusements. Obviously, the fascination here is the dinosaurs themselves. It's mesmerizing to watch them move on the screen, and the special effects even have gotten better since the first two installments. For the close ups that show a dinosaurs' subtle expressions, credit must be given to Stan Winston; for those dinosaurs that are featured in physical actions, compliments should go to Industrial Light and Magic. Even current research on dinosaurs has not been overlooked and has caused subtle changes to the dinosaurs: more bird-like moves and features have been added. Their colors are more vibrant than the old lizard grays, their noses have been elongated like bird bills, and the raptors now sport feathery crowns.

The raptors, like the T-Rex, are veterans of the first two movies and therefore familiar to audiences. Although this time the raptors obviously communicate and seem smarter than before, which gives them the appearance of a bunch of street punks. There are, though, two new dinosaurs in this installment. There is the massive Spinosaurus who can hunt on both land and in water, has a long, tooth-lined jaw and a sail on his back. According to scientists he was "the biggest meat-eating dinosaur that ever lived," which means he easily outclasses the other *Jurassic Park* movie villains, including the T-Rex. Guess which one will win when the two have their inevitable showdown? (FYI: There has been only one Spinosaurus skeleton ever found and is was bombed out of existence during World War II.)

The second new dinosaur is the Pteranodon who can not only peck you to death on land but also can fly around and pluck you right off your feet and into the mouths of its nest of babies. However, according to dino expert Jack Horner, who is also the film's paleontology consultant, the Pteranodon's are fictitious but based somewhat on Pterosaurs. Why not just use Pterosaurs and at least keep the film's credibility in tact?

However, all these interesting new dinosaurs and even the old ones are often lost in the murkiness of the film's cinematography. When we finally do lighten up and slow down on a boat ride past a herd of more benign dinosaurs and get a chance to watch in wonder at their massiveness, their movements, their marvelousness—it's over all too briefly.

One has to wonder why director Joe Johnston, whose earlier film credits are founded in visual effects, would short change them so badly here. It's easy to see why Spielberg would turn the reigns of the series over to Johnston with whom he first worked in 1981 when Johnston was the visual effects art director on *Raiders of the Lost Ark*, which won Johnston an Oscar® for his efforts. But it's not so easy to see why the director of *Honey, I Shrunk the Kids; The Rocketeer; Jumanji;* and *October Sky* wouldn't lavish his attention on the visually amazing dinosaurs—especially if he's going to have a minimalist plot.

*Jurasic Park III* is the first in the series not to be adapted from a Michael Crichton novel, although the ending is more like the one Crichton wrote in the original novel than was the one Spielberg put on his film. Without the inspiration of both Steven Spielberg and Michael Crichton, however, even bigger and better dinosaurs can't compensate for a weak story, cardboard characters and muddy filming.

Although it has been said that Spielberg has an idea for *Jurassic Park IV* that has nothing to do with the Pteranodon sequel implied in the ending of this film, one has to wonder if the series has run its course. If he does have something new and interesting to tell, let's hope he gets back on board as the director, too. Otherwise the *Jurassic Park* series itself may become extinct.

—*Beverley Bare Buehrer*

## CREDITS

**Dr. Alan Grant:** Sam Neill
**Paul Kirby:** William H. Macy
**Amanda Kirby:** Tea Leoni
**Billy Brennan:** Alessandro Nivola
**Udesky:** Michael Jeter
**Eric Kirby:** Trevor Morgan
**Cooper:** John Diehl
**Nash:** Bruce A. Young
**Mark:** Taylor Nichols
**Ben:** Mark Harelik
**Enrique:** Julio Mechoso
**Ellie:** Laura Dern

**Origin:** USA
**Released:** 2001

**Production:** Kathleen Kennedy, Larry J. Franco; Amblin Entertainment; released by Universal Pictures
**Directed by:** Joe Johnston
**Written by:** Peter Buchman, Alexander Payne, Jim Taylor
**Cinematography by:** Shelly Johnson
**Music by:** Don Davis
**Sound:** Thomas Causey, Gary Summers, Christopher Boyes
**Editing:** Robert Dalva
**Art Direction:** Doug Meerdink
**Costumes:** Betsy Cox
**Production Design:** Ed Verreaux
**Visual Effects:** Jim Mitchell
**MPAA rating:** PG-13
**Running time:** 90 minutes

## REVIEWS

*Boxoffice.* September, 2001, p. 149.
*Chicago Sun-Times Online.* July 18, 2001.
*Entertainment Weekly.* July 27, 2001, p. 46.
*Los Angeles Times Online.* July 18, 2001.
*New York Times Online.* July 18, 2001.
*People.* July 30, 2001, p. 32.
*Sight and Sound.* September, 2001, p. 47.
*USA Today Online.* July 18, 2001.
*Variety.* July 23, 2001, p. 17.
*Washington Post.* July 18, 2001, p. C1.

## QUOTES

Amanda (Tea Leoni): "Is this how you make dinosaurs?" Grant (Sam Neill): "No, this is how you play God."

# Just Looking (Cherry Pink)

*A voyeuristic coming-of-age comedy.*
—Movie tagline

Despite what else went on in the film *Just Looking*, it was probably destined to be known as Jason Alexander's big stab at film directing. The first, smaller stab, was a little seen film called *For Better or Worse* that came out in 1996 and ended up on Showtime. Alexander, for those who save their brain cells for things other than TV sitcom trivia, played the crass George Costanza on the long running TV series *Seinfeld.* Even though it would be better to accept the film based solely on its own merits, it's hard not to watch the film without thinking at least a little bit about the George character. As Gene Seymour noted in the *Los Angeles Times,* at a preview screening of the film someone remarked, "That's just the kind of creepy story you'd expect from George."

Not that this has anything to do with Alexander having played George—after all, the film was written by an entirely different guy, a TV writer Marshall Karp—but there is a certain inappropriateness to the story that is kind of George-like. As Robert Horton of film.com put it, "(The movie) occupies an uncomfortable place between *Stand by Me* and the Penthouse Forum." If that doesn't sound like the greatest cross-breeding to you, you would be right.

The story takes place in the mid-1950s in the Bronx and Queens. Lenny (Ryan Merriman) is a 14-year-old boy who is having a bad time. His beloved father is dead and his mother has remarried a sweaty overweight butcher (Richard V. Licata). Lenny, who protests his new stepfather by becoming a vegetarian, doesn't like hanging around the house with this new dad, but he's shocked when his mother, Sylvia (Patti LuPone), insists that he spend the summer with her pregnant sister and husband in Queens. Lenny feels like he's being exiled—especially since he knows that his mother doesn't like her brother in law (Peter Onorati) because he's Italian. (Or as Sylvia puts it, she doesn't hate him because he's Italian, but because he's a non-Jew.)

All of this has a very sepia-toned, *Brighton Beach Memoirs* feel. That's why it's shocking when suddenly Lenny will give voice to one of his more sexual thoughts. It's not that it's odd that the kid would have sexual thoughts—after all, he is 14. Lenny is so obsessed with sex that even the sight of a record being impaled by the record player is hot stuff to him. But what's weird is the combo of the sexual thoughts with the 1950s family setting, which we've been trained to associate with more innocent times. For example, when Lenny gets the idea that he wants to watch his mother and stepfather having sex so he can get a good look at a couple doing the deed, it doesn't seem like light-hearted hijinks, it just seems kind of weird. In any film, having a character who actually wants to see their parents having sex would cross some sort of imaginary boundary of taste, but in this malt shoppe 'n' crew cut setting, it's even more jarring. It would be akin to something like Barney the lovable purple dinosaur suddenly letting loose with a string of curse words.

When Lenny arrives in Queens, he thinks that his summer goal of seeing two people "engaged in an act of love" will be thwarted. But he quickly meets a new best friend John (Joseph Franquinha) who informs him that he and a couple of the local Catholic girls have formed a "sex club." Hubba-hubba. There is no actual sex involved, but plenty of talking about it. The girls are, to Lenny, very worldly in matters of sex and he listens intently to all their instruction.

(As well he should. Despite his vast interest in the subject, poor young Lenny barely has any idea of the nuts and bolts of "acts of love." You see, back in those days, they didn't have the USA Network.)

But all of Lenny's sexual feelings eventually wind up focused on Hedy (Gretchen Mol), the girl who most of the men in town fixate upon. Hedy is beautiful, nice and once earned money modeling brassieres. It's almost too good to be true. As Lenny puts it, excitedly, "She's a bra model and she lives on my block!" He makes it his immediate goal to see her engaged in an act of love. This is where it enters creepy territory again. Binoculars and peeping are involved.

Lenny's plan gets confused when he starts getting to know Hedy and realizes that he likes her as a person. The two bond over watered down beer and talk about how they both lost a beloved father at an early age. The bonding makes Lenny wonder about his plan to spy on her. Would it be right, now that he likes her? Horton, in his film.com review wrote, "In a way, I suppose, Lenny's friendship with nurse Hedy epitomizes the eternal dilemma of the American male: how to build a relationship with a woman you like while being distracted by the desire to see her naked."

What's good about the story is the leisurely pace of the storytelling. So many films coming out of Hollywood these days are obviously the work of screenwriters who have studied too many screenwriting books and have faithfully followed such dictums as "end act 2 on a crisis that will be resolved in act 3." With his background in TV, writer Karp obviously knows the rules of writing a screenplay, but he also knows enough to disguise the fact that he is following a formula. The action in the film is gentle. Lenny has a goal—that sex-peeping thing—but it's not the sole focus of the film. Whether he meets his goal or doesn't doesn't really matter. It's not the kind of film where there is a ticking bomb, and if Lenny doesn't succeed, the world will blow up. And that is a nice thing.

The acting in the film is uneven. Merriman is good at conveying how Lenny is on the border between boyhood and manhood. He doesn't know a lot about how the world works, but he knows enough to pretend like he has a clue as to what is going on. LuPone is also good as Lenny's mother who is dealing with her grief, a sullen boy, and a new husband who is far from a dashing romantic figure. Also turning in a nice performance is Onorati as Lenny's uncle. He's a surrogate father figure to Lenny and has to find the tact to teach him about one of the gray areas about being a man. Mol is also good as the kind of girl that always seems to show up in these kinds of films. She's a lovely woman, but has somehow gained a vaguely racy reputation in town which will be difficult to overcome. Other performances in the film kick in for awhile, then sputter. Sometimes characters sound like they are delivering monologues rather that having real conversations.

Critics were divided in their responses to the film. The *Associated Press* panned the film saying, "All these pre-pubescent high jinks feel contrived and the characters two-dimensional. When the film takes a serious turn toward the end, it's hard to care." The *Los Angeles Times* liked it more, and said that "Alexander displays . . . a finely tuned approach to the movie's period setting and an ability to coax bright, sassy performances from his actors." The *Austin Chronicle* also liked the film, saying, "*Just Looking* won't become a mainstay of the prolific coming-of-age drama, but, as its title indicates, it may be worth a perusal—especially if you're tired of the way teen sexuality is portrayed in movies from the post-*Porky's* generation."

—*Jill Hamilton*

## CREDITS

**Lenny:** Ryan Merriman
**Hedy:** Gretchen Mol
**Sylvia:** Patti LuPone
**Phil:** Peter Onorati
**Norma:** Ilana Levine
**Polinsky:** Richard V. Licata
**Dr. Flynn:** John Bolger
**John:** Joey Franquinha

**Origin:** USA
**Released:** 1999
**Production:** Jean Doumanian; Camellia Productions; released by Sony Pictures Classics
**Directed by:** Jason Alexander
**Written by:** Marshall Karp
**Cinematography by:** Fred Schuler
**Music by:** Michael Skloff
**Editing:** Norman Hollyn
**Art Direction:** Mark Ricker
**Costumes:** Karen Perry
**Production Design:** Michael Johnston
**MPAA rating:** R
**Running time:** 97 minutes

## REVIEWS

*Los Angeles Times Online.* October 13, 2000.
*New York Times Online.* October 13, 2000.
*San Francisco Chronicle Online.* October 20, 2000.
*Village Voice.* October 11, 2000.

# Just One Time

*Three's not always a crowd.*
—Movie tagline

Just One Time was director, writer and actor Lane Janger's fifth film and his biggest success to date. It was a low-level indie type success, but, hey, he was probably happy with it. *Just One Time* started its life as a highly acclaimed low-budget short film and turned into a longer (92 minutes), less acclaimed, low-budget feature-length film. The one big thing that the film has going for it is an intriguing concept: sex. Sex as in very adult topics such as threesomes, the fluidity of sexual identity, and whether or not fantasies should be explored or left as fantasies.

Anthony (Janger) is a fireman who's engaged to a sweet lawyer, Amy (Joelle Carter). The two are set to be married in a big traditional Catholic ceremony. All would be well in their cute life, involving a cute apartment in the East Village and their cute puppy dog-like flirting, but for one thing: Anthony has a fantasy to be with Amy and another woman. He insists that he would just want to try it just one time, hence the title. As their wedding date approaches, Anthony starts pressing Amy to help fulfill his fantasy—as a religious guy, he feels that it would be a-ok to be in the threesome if he just manages to do it before his wedding (after which he will presumably just engage in for procreation-only sex—preferably in the missionary position).

Unfortunately for Anthony, Amy doesn't share his fantasy. In fact, the more he presses her to help him fulfill it, the more she feels unloved and like she's not enough to satisfy him on her own. Finally, she comes up with a plan that she thinks will divert her beau's attention from his obsession. Amy suggests that if she is to fulfill his fantasy by being with another woman, then he should do the same in return for her. In other words, Anthony needs to agree to be with another man.

Conveniently, there happens to be one such agreeable man right there in the neighborhood. Victor (Guillermo Diaz) is a young virgin who looks like Antonio Banderas and is nursing a strong crush on Anthony. Anthony, as most American men in sitcoms would be, is horrified by the idea and tries to get out of it. But due to plot constraints, as well as his very strong desire to do the two women thing, he decides to go through with the plan. He and Amy decide to proceed slowly. They will date their future bed partners in order to get to know them before the big events. Amy starts a flirtation with her neighbor Michelle (Jennifer Esposito), a furniture maker and conveniently-located lesbian.

Meanwhile, Anthony agrees to go on a date with Victor, reasoning that if he starts going through with the deal, Amy will get nervous and back out. He enlists the help of his handsome firefighter buddies (Vincent Laresca, Domenick Lombardozzi, and David Lee Russek) to go on the date with him. The quintet end up hitting a gay bar, where they make sure they are exhibiting the utmost in heterosexual behavior. Soon, Anthony's macho buddies start relaxing and having fun. They dance, accept some drinks from some cute guys, and agree to return for a special night where patrons get in free if they wear a wig. Only Anthony remains steadfastly repulsed by the scene. His insistence on being such a uber-heterosexual seems to betray some issues that he may have of his own, but this film isn't going anywhere near that idea.

The film does goes to extraordinary lengths to make sure that Anthony has no other option than to continue to explore a homosexual relationship with Victor. For example, Anthony goes to his priest (Mickey Cottrell) for some counsel on the issue, but doesn't actually state what the issue is. The priest tells Anthony that he can't imagine him doing anything wrong and that he should pursue whatever it is that he's pursuing. Not only is everything in the plot pushing Anthony and Victor together, the relationship even gets the inadvertent blessing of the church.

It is interesting how the male characters are "forced" to explore gay culture. It's reminiscent of how the sexual fantasies of women earlier in history, when female sexuality wasn't as accepted, often involved being taken by force. A woman couldn't just enjoy the sexual act, but if it were somehow forced upon her, then maybe that would be acceptable. The same goes for these guys. The firefighters wouldn't dream of going to a gay bar on their own accord, but since they are forced—and certainly Anthony makes it darned clear that he has no other choice than to attend gay functions, date a man, etc.—it is somehow more okay.

The film, while being tolerant of gay life, doesn't exactly break any new ground in upending stereotypes. Resident lesbian Michelle is very aggressive and in-your-face. Victor is a cute little boy toy who chooses his outfits carefully. He's not out to his parents but Michelle thinks they probably know anyway: "You wear pink shoes—do you think they're stupid?" "They're fuschia," says Victor, in the kind of dialogue that wouldn't be out of place in an episode of *Will and Grace*. It retains its indie feel, though it's hard to pin down what, exactly, are the elements that make one film seem like an indie and another not. Maybe it's the uneven acting performances. Maybe it's the slightly-off rhythm. Maybe it's the fact that there is nary a car chase, gun fight or gratuitous boob shot.

The weakest link in the acting department is Janger himself. He's not very good, but he was the boss of the film. Who among his cast and crew was going to be the one to tell him that his line readings were wooden? And, though supporting the unhandsome in films is an admirable cause, maybe Janger isn't really handsome enough to have this role. His character is supposed to be a macho fireman, so desirable that someone like Victor would lust after him and call him "totally hot." A critic from *Matinee Magazine,* Chuck Rudolph, wrote that Janger was "perhaps the most obnoxious and repulsive presence to grace the screen in a decade. Droopy-eyed and tousle-haired, he's like a mutated Mongoloid cousin of Tony Manero, or maybe a burned-out junkie who took one too many downers after shooting up speed and then decided to act in a movie." Although to be fair, this critic seemed to have a particularly virulent reaction to poor Janger, even taking issue with his "inappropriately straight teeth."

Also weak is Carter as girlfriend, Amy. Amy is supposed to be a "nice" girl, but Carter makes her so bland, it's difficult to see why Anthony would be so in love with her. The script actually has other characters saying things to Amy like, "Anthony is so in love with you," so it will be spelled out for us. And, although Amy is a lawyer, she never exhibits any signs that would indicate that she has an active intellect of any sort. Jennifer Esposito is okay but she brings the same kind of strange glassy-eyed intensity that she's brought to other roles. It's like she doesn't know how to act, so she overcompensates by staring deeply into the other characters' eyes. Many critics, particularly male ones, don't seem to notice this trait. For example, Kevin Thomas of the *Los Angeles Times* called her "stunning" and "sultry." Diaz maintains his bouncy good humor throughout the film while managing to convey the poignancy of situation. He is so eager to go to bed with Anthony that he allows himself to be subjected to Anthony's crass and disrespectful behavior. It's a nice performance.

Critics ranged in their reactions to *Just One Time.* Kevin Thomas was a fan of the film, saying, "wisdom and humor, some of it broad and boisterous, dovetail in this modestly budgeted venture." Christopher Null at filmcritic.com was more tepid in his approval: "It's not a bad way to spend 90 minutes, but not fantastic cinema either." Rudolph of *Matinee Magazine* is a good representative of the contingent that didn't care for the film: "Just like *The Contender, Just One Time* doesn't have the guts to back up its premise. All the dirty talk reveals motives that are unfashionably—dishonestly—square."

*—Jill Hamilton*

**Anthony:** Lane Janger
**Amy:** Joelle Carter
**Victor:** Guillermo Diaz
**Michelle:** Jennifer Esposito
**Nick:** Vincent Laresca
**Dom:** David Lee Russek
**Cyrill:** Domenick Lombardozzi

**Origin:** USA
**Released:** 2000
**Production:** Lane Janger, Jasmine Kosovic, Exile Ramirez; Danger Filmworks; released by Cowboy Booking International, Alliance Atlantis
**Directed by:** Lane Janger
**Written by:** Jennifer Vandever, Lane Janger
**Cinematography by:** Michael St. Hilaire
**Music by:** Edward Bilous
**Editing:** Michael Stanley
**Art Direction:** Andy Biscontini
**Costumes:** Melissa Bruning
**Production Design:** Stephen Beatrice
**MPAA rating:** R
**Running time:** 94 minutes

REVIEWS

*Los Angeles Times Online.* March 23, 2001.
*New York Times Online.* October 19, 2000.

# Just Visiting

*They're not just from another time, they're from France.*
—Movie tagline

 **Box Office:** $4.7 million

Just Visiting is a remake of a French film called *Les Visiteurs* (that's *The Visitors* for those who like their French thoroughly translated). The 1993 film was a huge hit—the highest grossing comedy in French history. Because it seems as though most Americans don't want to suffer through the tyranny of subtitles, the filmmakers felt that for the film to make it in America, they would have to remake it in English. Not only that, but they would have to completely Americanize the story, lest any viewer be made to feel uncomfortable by anything that seemed even vaguely European.

To that end, the filmmakers got one of the most American writers around: John Hughes, who is responsible for *Home Alone, Trains, Planes and Automobiles,* as well as 1980s teen films like *The Breakfast Club* and *Sixteen Candles*—to help out on a rewrite. Not only that, but the studio who released the film is one of the most American around—Buena Vista Pictures, aka Disney. The director of the original, Jean-Marie Gaubert, stayed on, and the two main actors, Jean Reno and Christian Clavier, reprise their roles. The story is a tired fish-out-of-water tale. It's hard to imagine that the French would be so charmed by it. Have they never seen *Crocodile Dundee* or even time traveling episodes of *Bewitched* or *The Flintstones*? But the players play the story like it's the newest thing around.

Count Thibault of Malfete (Reno) is a rich French nobleman from the 12th century who is about to get married to the loveliest woman in all of England, Rosalind (Christina Applegate). All would be going well for him but, unbeknownst to the Count, a romantic rival has enlisted the help of a witch to break up the marriage. The witch makes up an evil potion, as witches in these sorts of films are wont to do. The potion will make Rosalind see her beloved Count as an ugly evil monster and refuse to marry him. The witch puts the potion in the bride-to-be's wine glass at a big celebratory engagement dinner. At the dinner, the couple decides to drink out of each other's wine glass, and oops. The Count drinks the bad wine and goes on somewhat of a bad trip. He sees all the assembled guests as various sorts of hideous creatures. He looks at Rosalind and sees that she has somehow turned into a monster, so he stabs her to death.

Naturally, everyone is horrified and the stabbing pretty much ends the party. The Count is thrown in jail to await execution. He's accompanied by his faithful manservant, Andre (Clavier, who also co-wrote both the original script and the rewrite), an Igor-like, goofy sidekick. Just before he's to be put to death, the Count enlists the help of an English wizard (Malcolm McDowell). The wizard cooks up a potion that will allow Andre and the Count to travel back in time to the moments just before the stabbing. This time, the Count will not stab his bride, which should be quite a bit more conducive to his wedding plans. Unfortunately, the wizard, being English and all, screws up the potion and accidentally sends the Count and Andre forward in time to present-day Chicago.

The two land in a medieval display at a museum where they conveniently meet Julia (Applegate, again) who looks just like the Count's beloved Rosalind. Julia thinks that the Count is a distant cousin of hers and decides to take him in. Julia lives with her evil, money-grubbing boyfriend, Hunter (Matthew Ross), who just wants to get his hands on the Count's money. Meanwhile, Hunter is having a fling with his tarty secretary, Amber (Bridgette Wilson-Sampras).

This would be the part where all the shenanagins start happening. The Count and Andre see all kinds of modern-day inventions and don't know how to respond to them. They encounter an SUV, think it's a dragon and beat it up with their swords. They destroy a TV with their swords, thinking that they need to rescue the tiny people inside. They see a toilet, think it's a bathing sink and toss the water all over themselves. Most of the humor of the film tends to hover near the bathroom. Andre, who is about as smart as a

wedge of cheese, finds an air freshening cake in the bottom of the urinal, decides it's a mint and eats it. The fact that he's not in his own time would explain why he takes the first bite from the cake. It's hard to see why he would ever take that second (and third and fourth) bite, but he does.

A lot of the film is centered around Andre's "comedy." See Andre at the fancy restaurant, sitting on the floor, hoping for table scraps. Watch Andre pouring a bottle of toilet cleaner in the tub, thinking it's fancy bath oil. Look at Andre belching and farting loudly at the dinner table. To be fair, the film is aimed at a older kid/young teen audience and this sort of thing may be just up their alley, but for the accompanying adult tagalongs, it's a bit dreary. This goes for the verbal wordplay, too. After the wizard somehow ends up with his body in several pieces, he says—as, of course he would—"Best I pull myself together."

To give the gross-out humor some balance, the writers also threw in a little romance, too. At first it looks like Julia and the Count are going to have some sort of romance, but after they figure out that Julia is one of the Count's descendants, it kind of puts the kibbosh on that plan. (How the Count is supposed to have descendants when he killed his bride isn't even explained.) Even weird Andre gets to have a fling with the dim gardener who works next door, Angelique (Tara Reid). Even though Angelique is supposed to be a simple gal, it's hard to see how she could be attracted to Andre. After all, it's been well established by the script that he smells really bad, he's got an awful haircut and he says things like "Sire, I have to make pee pee" at the dinner table.

One area that the film does excel in is special effects. With such a cheesy premise, it seems like there should be equally cheesy effects, but that's not the case. The scene in medieval times where the people at the wedding banquet turn into various hideous monsters is quite well done. They mutate into strange and imaginative creatures—all of which are amusing and real-looking. The time travel sequences are also done well. Whoever tries one of the wizard's potions undergoes a variety of interesting transformations, including shrinking into a tiny speck. The acting in the film is fine, though it's hard to judge acting when said involves, say, Clavier playing an idiot servant who plays with an ice cube dispenser on a refrigerator and spills ice all over the floor. Reno, who doesn't have the bland handsomeness of an American leading man, lends a dignified presence to the film.

Critics wrote tepid reviews about the film, mostly dismissing the story, but offering faint praise for Reno and Clavier's performances. The critic for the *Charlotte Observer* said, "With his shrewd, sad eyes and hooked nose, Monsieur Reno walks through the film with the dignity of an elderly owl." The critic for the *Philadelphia Inquirer* said that the film caused him to nod off. The *Los Angeles Times* placed the blame for the film's badness on John Hughes saying he "drains the original story of its satire and juices up its shtick schmaltz and special effects." The *Scripps Howard News Service* review said, "Unless I miss my guess, the title will describe its stay in theaters."

—*Jill Hamilton*

## CREDITS

**Count Thibault:** Jean Reno
**Andre:** Christian Clavier
**Rosalind/Julia:** Christina Applegate
**Angelique:** Tara Reid
**Hunter:** Matt Ross
**Amber:** Bridgette Wilson
**Byron:** John Aylward
**Dr. Brady:** George Plimpton
**Wizard:** Malcolm McDowell
**Queen:** Sarah Badel
**King Henry:** Richard Bremmer
**Earl of Warwick:** Robert Glenister

**Origin:** USA
**Released:** 2001
**Production:** Patrice Ledoux, Ricardo Mestres; Gaumont; released by Hollywood Pictures
**Directed by:** Jean-Marie Poire
**Written by:** Christian Clavier, Jean-Marie Poire, John Hughes
**Cinematography by:** Ueli Steiger
**Music by:** John Powell
**Sound:** Ray Cymoszinski
**Editing:** Michael A. Stevenson
**Art Direction:** Stephen Cooper
**Costumes:** Penny Rose
**Production Design:** Doug Kraner
**MPAA rating:** PG-13
**Running time:** 88 minutes

## REVIEWS

*Boxoffice.* June, 2001, p. 60.
*Chicago Sun-Times Online.* April 6, 2001.
*Entertainment Weekly.* April 20, 2001, p. 46.
*Los Angeles Times Online.* April 6, 2001.
*New York Times Online.* April 6, 2001.
*Variety.* April 9, 2001, p. 17.
*Washington Post Online.* April 6, 2001.

# K-PAX

*Change the way you look at the world.*
—Movie tagline
*Celebrate the possibilities.*
—Movie tagline
*Open your mind and admit the possibility.*
—Movie tagline

 **Box Office:** $50.3 million

K-PAX, a friendly alien visitation picture, deserved better reviews than it got. It was a pleasing and amusing fantasy about human decency and understanding, potentially a healing fable after the terrorist attacks on the World Trade Center in New York and the Pentagon in Washington, D.C., on September 11th. The main character (Kevin Spacey), who says his name is Prot (rimes with "emote," as one reviewer noted), appears out of nowhere in New York's Grand Central Station. Moments later, a woman is knocked to the ground by a mugger. Prot approaches to help her, but is quickly apprehended by the police. When he explains that he is from a planet named K-PAX in a galaxy far away, he is, of course, taken to a mental hospital for observation, under the care of Dr. Mark Powell (Jeff Bridges).

As expected, Dr. Powell concludes his patient is delusional. Prot claims to be a visitor from a superior civilization, sent to study our planet and its inhabitants. He claims to be 175 years old by Earth standards. When asked how he has managed to travel through space, he explains that he is able to travel by light rays, but at several times the speed of light, since his planet is 1000 light years away. His fact-finding mission on Earth was to last five years, and he is scheduled to return to K-PAX in less than a month, on July 27th. Dr. Powell believes that he has to bring his patient back to "reality" before the time of Prot's scheduled return, for if he fails to do so, he may lose the patient. The clock is running, and Dr. Powell seems to be short of his goal of curing his patient.

On the other hand, Powell is open-minded enough to at least consider that his patient may be telling the truth. Prot has a phenomenal knowledge of astronomy, and when asked by physicists and astronomers to give the coordinates of his planet, one of nine in a solar system with twin suns, he is successfully able to do so. The stars exist, but their existence is not common knowledge, and their discovery has not yet been published in scientific literature. Consequently, the scientists are confused and dazzled by his knowledge. He is a "man" sure of himself, confident of his knowledge, wonderfully articulate and gentle, and obviously brilliant. He refuses to disclose his knowledge about space travel and the power of light rays, however, because, he claims, humanity is not sufficiently developed to cope with such power. Prot claims that he has to "travel north" to Greenland, Iceland, Labrador, and Newfoundland and in fact disappears from the hospital for three days, until, one morning Dr. Powell finds him mysteriously returned, perched in a tree with his notebook.

Prot is also able to reach other patients on the mental ward in a way that specialists like Dr. Powell cannot. He helps them to overcome long-standing phobias—one mental patient named Bess (Melanee Murray) who has never spoken begins to speak, for example. Another patient with a phobia concerning germs is cured when Prot helps him to overcome his fear of death. Prot has the power to cure patients considered hopeless by giving them "tasks." Irritated by this interference, Dr. Powell tells Prot that it is his own responsibility to deal with his patients, but Prot shoots back: "Then why don't you?" Although Dr. Powell cannot ignore Prot's obvious gifts, he continues to search for a "logical" explanation for his patient's presumed "delusions," and eventually finds the sort of solution that would satisfy his colleagues by examining Prot under hypnotic regression therapy.

Under hypnosis, Prot reverts to the personality of Robert Porter of Guelph, New Mexico, who works as a "knocker" at a slaughter house. But Robert Porter is not really Prot. Five years earlier, at exactly the time Prot claims to have come to Earth, Porter went through a traumatic event that would have killed him, had not Prot taken over his body and identity. Going back in time under hypnosis, Porter remembers Sarah (his wife) and Rebecca (his daughter), but Dr. Powell can only access the memory of Robert Porter, not the memory of Prot, which is quite beyond his reach. Prot is, after all, a superior being with powers that border on the supernatural.

Powell makes Porter remember coming home one night and killing a drifter who had raped, then murdered his wife and daughter. Porter killed the drifter, breaking his neck "like a twig," as the local sheriff in New Mexico recalls when Dr. Powell goes to him to investigate. Porter then turned off a water sprinkler that was left running, and, severely depressed, waded into a river that ran by his house, presumably intending to commit suicide. His head is submerged as he wades into deep water, and, apparently, Prot took over his body at that point. After Prot leaves at the designated time he told Dr. Powell he would, at 5:20 a.m., he leaves Porter's catatonic body behind, but the night before he had told Dr. Powell to "take care of Robert Porter." At the end of the film, Dr. Powell is seen pushing Porter in a wheelchair; when he speaks softly to Porter, what seems to be a smile of recognition crosses Porter's face.

The Robert Porter identity provided an escape hatch for literal minded reviewers, such as Arch Campbell, who reviews for the NBC television affiliate in Washington, D.C. Refusing to acknowledge the metaphysical implications of the plot, Campbell degraded the film in his two-minute "review" by claiming that Prot turns out to be "a homeless guy." In fact (or in fiction), however, Prot is a mystery, not merely a homeless street person, but literal-minded critics do not like to be mystified. Even so, the film leaves the circumstances purposefully ambiguous. As A.O. Scott wrote, "the story is cleverly structured and allows us to entertain two contradictory possibilities without seeming egregiously illogical."

The story was adapted by Charles Leavitt from a novel by Gene Brewer published in 1995 but the project was in development for six years before Kevin Spacey read the script and agreed to play the character of Prot. "I fell in love with Prot," Spacey explained, because "the character is just beautiful. He's placed in the world of this mental institution, and the story is, on some level, about what happens when you encounter a stranger who has some rather extraordinary effect on all the people around him." Although he had strong support from Jeff Bridges as Dr. Powell, the film succeeds mainly because of Spacey's distinctive talent and the eccentric charisma he brings to the role. He impersonates two characters, Prot the alien, and Robert Porter, the human being whose body he inhabits, but his acting presents them as two separate entities. "What's important about Prot was not just what he says, but how he says it," Spacey explained. "He has a calming presence and an odd ability to bring out honesty in people." The voice Spacey finds for the Robert Proctor character has a regional dialectical inflection and is discernibly not the voice of Prot.

But Spacey's performance involves more than just diction and delivery, though the deadpan delivery is certainly amusingly distinctive. "Your produce alone made the trip worthwhile," Prot says as he devours a whole banana, skin and all. Prot's bearing is also distinctive, especially the way he cocks his head. He finds the sun's rays too bright, so he usually wears sunglasses to protect his eyes, which are able to see ultraviolet extremes of the visual spectrum. Director Iain Softley claimed that "What makes Prot a strange character is his very normality," but Prot is not entirely normal in the way he speaks, moves, and behaves. In fact, he is more compassionate than the people around him, but he seems to recognize that quality in Dr. Powell, and he advises Powell to spend more time with his family and to be less consumed by his work. Sure enough, after Prot's departure, we see Dr. Powell meeting his rebellious son, from whom he has been alienated. It apparently takes an alien to promote family values on this planet.

CBS television critic John Leonard described the formula of K-PAX as "Close Encounters meets Cuckoo's Nest," a snide but fair comparison. The fact that the patients of the mental hospital, under the guidance of Prot, seem to be more sane than the doctors who run it (with the possible exception of Dr. Powell) certainly recalls Ken Kesey's novel and play. Reviewing the film for the *New York Times*, A.O. Scott also found the film derivative and clichéd. What is the message this brother from another planet has to deliver? "Get it right this time. This time is all you have." Director Iain Softley, fresh off the success of his Henry James adaptation, *The Wings of a Dove* (2000), told Dave Kehr of the *New York Times* that he did intend for the film "to be hopeful and uplifting. The plan was that the realism and the research would ground it and we could go from there." Perhaps he tried too hard to achieve that "uplifting" goal. "The problem with *K-PAX*," for *Washington Times* reviewer Gary Arnold, "is that Prot's sanctimonious tendencies approach the insufferable when confined to a would-be-realistic setting."

At any rate, the film did not have the desired effect with cynical reviewers. In his *Washington Post Weekend* review Desson Howe called the film "a disappointing journey." First-string *Post* review Rita Kempley was less disappointed, describing the film as "a provocative if simplistic parable on the familiar foibles of humankind." At least Kempley had the good sense to praise the casting of "the splendid Kevin Spacey" and to conclude that this picture "never quite reaches the stars, but it definitely rises above much of what passes for entertainment today." While this was not unqualified praise, it was about as favorable as American reviewers were willing to be. This eccentric film deserved better than it got.

*—James M. Welsh*

## CREDITS

**Prot:** Kevin Spacey
**Dr. Mark Powell:** Jeff Bridges
**Rachel Powell:** Mary McCormack
**Claudia Villars:** Alfre Woodard
**Howie:** David Patrick Kelly
**Ernie:** Saul Williams
**Sal:** Peter Gerety
**Mrs. Archer:** Celia Weston
**Dr. Chakraborty:** Ajay Naidu
**Russell:** John Toles-Bey
**Joyce Trexler:** Kimberly Scott
**Abby:** Mary Mara
**Michael Powell:** Aaron Paul
**Sheriff:** William Lucking

**Origin:** USA
**Released:** 2001

**Production:** Lawrence Gordon, Lloyd Levin, Robert F. Colesberry; Intermedia Films; released by Universal Pictures
**Directed by:** Iain Softley
**Written by:** Charles Leavitt
**Cinematography by:** John Mathieson
**Music by:** Ed Shearmur
**Sound:** Marc Weingarten
**Editing:** Craig McKay
**Art Direction:** Alexander Hammond
**Costumes:** Louise Mingenbach
**Production Design:** John Beard
**MPAA rating:** PG-13
**Running time:** 120 minutes

## REVIEWS

*Baltimore Sun.* October 26, 2001, p. E1.
*Chicago Sun-Times Online.* October 26, 2001.
*Entertainment Weekly.* November 2, 2001, p. 45.
*Los Angeles Times Online.* October 26, 2001.
*New York Times.* October 25, 2001, p. E27.
*New York Times.* October 26, 2001, p. E8.
*People.* November 5, 2001, p. 38.
*USA Today.* October 26, 2001, p. C1.
*Variety.* October 29, 2001, p. 25.
*Washington Post.* October 26, 2001, p. C1.
*Washington Post Weekend.* October 26, 2001, p. 37.
*Washington Times.* October 26, 2001, p. B6.

## QUOTES

Prot (Kevin Spacey) to Dr. Powell (Jeff Bridges): "Be prepared for anything."

# Kandahar

*Journey into the heart of Afghanistan.*
—Movie tagline

 **Box Office:** $1.1 million

Renowned Iranian filmmaker Mohsen Makhmalbaf reveals the underbelly of a contemporary political tragedy in *Kandahar*, proving that jolts of documentary reality can have twice the impact when we have been lulled into accepting a fiction. The film's story concerns the travails of Nafas (Nelofer Pazira), a beautiful Afghani émigré, settled in Canada, who sets off on a noble mission to save her sister in Afghanistan from committing suicide. Ironically, it is the everyday suffering of a people ravaged by war, from within and without, that continues to haunt the viewer. Makhmalbaf's style allows him to render their pain through moments when it fills the screen. Thus, even though we know that the political climate has changed in Afghanistan since the film was made, we remain convinced that nothing can alleviate the pain we are witnessing. Makhmalbaf's cinema of moments, for want of a better term, transcends the fabrications spun by the forward thrust of time, so integral to the global media.

We learn that Nafas' family was forced to leave her sister, who was crippled by a land mine, behind when they emigrated. That sister, under the virulently anti-feminist Taliban regime, has now abandoned all hope and threatened to end it all during the next solar eclipse. At the start of the film, Nafas, who has managed to make her way to the border between Iran and Afghanistan, has three days to reach her.

We come to know how much this journey means to Nafas through her thoughts, which she dictates into a tape recorder, and which serve as a voiceover commentary, interpreting everything she sees of the real life plight of Afghani refugee women. An Afghani male has a tribal identity, she muses, whereas a woman is considered a nonentity. Nafas is living out a hope beyond hope that, in some way, on some intangible level, she is communicating with her sister, and thereby transmitting hope. Her voiceover, rendered in a listless monotone, is also her means of assuring herself, as is the untranslated Sanskrit chant on the soundtrack, which no doubt is meant to evoke the path of the eclipse extending to the Indian subcontinent.

Makhmalbaf's austere approach to narrative, devoted as he remains to the least amount of dramatic contrivance, prevents him from rendering the plight of the sister, whose suffering we are meant to imagine from the subjugation of the women we do see. But here is where the film hits a snag. Nafas' torment, and presumably that of her sister, stems from a western view of the societal role of women. The Afghani women we see, both young and adult, have accepted the role a repressive political regime has assigned to them, but at the same time have clung to their femininity.

For example, the opening section of the film shows schoolgirls who have been studying in Iran, since the Taliban have banned women's education, preparing to return home for the holidays. As Makhmalbaf's camera tracks along rows and rows of excited faces, the element of repression is evoked by Nafas' voiceover, and not by their smiles. Similarly, Nafas, who is disguised in a head-to-toe burqa and is traveling as the wife of a peasant on the back of a makeshift van propelled by a motorcycle, notices a woman beside her applying lipstick underneath her burqa. Nafas can only smile at this gesture of defiance, but has no comment to make.

What shatters our composure though is the extent of pain and insecurity that makes its way into the life of the everyday under such political circumstances. The schoolgirls are offered instruction on how to detect land mines by throwing their dolls on the ground. Then, when the group Nafas is traveling with is stopped by brigands on a desert road, we begin to understand what western news commentators have long maintained, of how for a people living in a lawless domain, the Taliban, for all their repression, provided a welcome alternative. As we see the brigands snatch the meager bundles of possessions the schoolgirls are carrying, leaving them crying, and driving off with the peasant's vehicle, we realize that at this level of existence the shift in the distribution of political power now taking place in Afghanistan can change very little.

Nafas and her "family" are thus forced to traverse the desert on foot, till they get to the nearest town. At this point, Makhmalbaf cuts to what must surely be the most frightening of his digressions for western audiences. We find ourselves in the middle of a class for young boys at a "madrasa," a school where the only teaching is that of the Koran. But it is not learning, as we have come to think of the process. Here, young boys, barely in their teens, all dressed in uniform white, are sitting cross-legged on the floor, bowing back and forth, forced to memorize Koranic text. The "mullah," or the religious figure of authority, who is their instructor, questions them on the use of the weapons they have beside them, from swords to Kalashnikov semi-automatics. The ideological correlation becomes readily apparent. Whether in the context of Afghanistan, or Pakistan, or any other country with a traditional Muslim faction, this is an entire generation being brainwashed by religious dictates, and then set loose, not so much to preach but to kill.

Amongst these boys is Khak, who is expelled by the mullah for not being able to recite the text like the others. Khak thus becomes Nafas' guide and agrees to take her to Kandahar, charging her an exorbitant 50 U.S. dollars. As the two are traversing a barren landscape, Nafas falls sick from drinking well water. Here, the film makes its second digression to introduce the enigmatic figure of Tabib (Hassan Tantai), the town doctor, whom we first see speaking in the vernaculat but muttering to himself in English. In accordance with religious custom, he cannot speak directly to a woman patient. We thus see him looking into her mouth through a hole in a curtain, while a little girl serves as an intermediary. When it is Nafas' turn, he does the same, except that after the examination, he volunteers advice in English. He tells her to get rid of Khak, since such boys cannot be trusted, and offers to take her to Kandahar himself.

On the road, Tabib reveals his true identity as a black American, who left the U.S. "to search for God." His false beard, he remarks, is the burqa that men need to wear. While steering his mule-driven cart, he explains that he came to Afghanistan to fight the Russians, then stayed on to fight for God on the side of the Taliban against the local tribesmen.

A stark revelation emerges from his story. The warfare between Afghani tribes has not been over land or economic benefits, but over whose path to God is real, a truth mostly ignored in news reports, along with its disturbing implication. Even after the liberation of Afghanistan from the repressive Taliban regime, and despite the contribution of western powers to raise the living conditions of the Afghani people, especially its women, peace will remain a distant prospect since the forces dividing the country are not economic or political, but religious.

Tabib, for his part, finally came to the conclusion, as he puts it, that the search for God means to heal the pain of others. He then explains that he did not need medical training to serve as a doctor, since the people around him were dying from "simple diseases."

The lift that Tabib gives to a peasant on crutches takes the film to its next digression, a Red Cross camp for amputee victims of land mines. When Nafas' journey resumes on Tabib's cart, another peasant stops them, one with plaster legs to sell, and eventually agrees to take Nafas to Kandahar, after Tabib decides to turn back. Here again, it is money that talks. The peasant goes off, saying he will return, after he is promised 200 U.S. dollars, a small fortune in that region.

As Nafas and Tabib wait, she gets him to record a message for her sister. He waxes eloquent on the nature of hope. "For the thirsty, it is water," he begins. "For the lonely, it is love." He concludes, "For the woman in a burqa, it is the day she will be seen." Ironically, his words foreshadow the twist of fate about to befall Nafas. Soon, a group of women approach covered in multicolored burqas on their way to attend a wedding. One of the burqas hides the peasant they have been waiting for. He and Nafas join the women as they make their way across the barren land, chanting in unison.

In comparison to these women bound by centuries of repression and tradition, Nafas' western sensibility lacks the bulwark needed to combat the overwhelming odds stacked against her. The futility of her effort in trying to reach her sister becomes clear when the Taliban guards discover her identity and take her captive. The film chooses to leave her in that state.

While being struck by the film's timeliness, critics have noted that Makhmalbaf's offering doesn't make for uniformly compelling viewing. Eric Harrison in the *Houston Chronicle* finds "the film lingers too long on side stories, allowing the narrative tension to dissipate." Loren King in the *Boston Globe* concurs that Nafas' plight results in "a bleak road movie that often ambles." Steven Rosen in the *Denver Post* maintains that "we never really get caught up in her journey." Even so, what has been admired is the film's "gritty realism" (King) and its evocation of "a land out of time, all but abandoned by modernity . . ." (Kent Jones in *Film Com-*

*ment*). David Ansen in *Newsweek* notes that the film's "lunar landscapes and grotesque visions are as strange and haunting as a science-fiction fantasy. Would that it were."

—*Vivek Adarkar*

## CREDITS

**Nafas:** Nelofer Pazira
**Tabib Sahid:** Hassan Tantai
**Khak:** Sadou Teymouri

**Origin:** Iran
**Language:** English, Farsi
**Released:** 2001
**Production:** Mohsen Makhmalbaf; BAC Films Ltd., Makhmalbaf Film House; released by Avatar Film Corporation
**Directed by:** Mohsen Makhmalbaf
**Written by:** Mohsen Makhmalbaf
**Cinematography by:** Ebraheem Ghafouri
**Music by:** Mohammad Reza Darvishi
**Editing:** Mohsen Makhmalbaf
**MPAA rating:** Unrated
**Running time:** 85 minutes

## REVIEWS

*Boston Globe Online.* January 11, 2002.
*Chicago Sun-Times Online.* February 15, 2002.
*Entertainment Weekly.* December 14, 2001, p. 55.
*Film Comment Online.* January/February, 2002.
*Houston Chronicle Online.* February 15, 2002.
*Los Angeles Times Online.* January 11, 2002.
*New York Times Online.* November 5, 2001.
*New York Times Online.* December 14, 2001.
*Newsweek Online.* December 24, 2001.
*Premiere.* January, 2002, p. 29.
*Sight and Sound.* July, 2001, p. 12.
*Sight and Sound.* January, 2002, p. 46.
*Time Online.* December 19, 2001.
*USA Today Online.* December 13, 2001.
*Washington Post.* January 4, 2002, p. WE34.

## TRIVIA

Upon the film's release, American authorities identified Hassan Tantai as American David Belfield, who fled in 1980 to Iran after a murder indictment.

# Kate & Leopold

*If they lived in the same century they'd be perfect for each other.*
—Movie tagline

 **Box Office:** $22.1 million

Kate & Leopold is a time-travel romantic fantasy starring smiley Meg Ryan, who could do these parts in her sleep (but fortunately she chooses not to sleepwalk through this version), and handsome Aussie Hugh Jackman as her dream guy. Meg is a cynical, 21st century New York career gal and Hugh is a chivalric British duke who happens to be from the 19th century. Bummer. But love will find a way—plot holes be damned.

In New York City in 1876, Leopold (Jackman), Duke of Albany, has joined the crowd watching the dedication of the unfinished Brooklyn Bridge when he spots a strange man who just happens to be taking pictures of the proceedings with a modern camera and writing with a ballpoint pen. He gets away before an intrigued Leopold has a chance to question him and Leopold returns to his uncle's home. Leopold might have good looks, good breeding, and a title but what he doesn't have is hard cash and his Uncle Millard (Paxton Whitehead) insists Leopold stop his dilettante pursuits (he's working on a prototype for an elevator) and marry an heiress. The party being given that evening is intended to announce Leopold's engagement but when Leopold spots the stranger from the bridge among the dancers, he chases him out into the streets and back to the Brooklyn Bridge. They climb higher and higher and Leopold thinks the man is going to commit suicide and tries to prevent him from jumping off, instead they both fall—and wind up in present-day Manhattan. Oh, and suddenly all the elevators stop working.

Stuart (Liev Schreiber) is a mad scientist type who has been working to find "a crack in the fabric of time" (shouldn't it be a tear in the fabric?) and his discovery of a portal has allowed him to visit 1876. Now he's stuck with Leopold, who just happens to be Stuart's great-great grandfather (or will be if he gets back to the right time period) and who cannot return to his own time until the portal opens again, which won't be for a week. Not only does Stuart have to deal with a disbelieving Leopold, who thinks he's been kidnapped, he has to explain things to his downstairs neighbor, and ex-girlfriend, Kate McKay (Ryan) who doesn't want to hear anything more of Stuart's crazy ideas. Stuart warns Leopold before he meets Kate that "women have become dangerous since your time" while Kate, who sees Leopold in all his princely evening finery, thinks he's some sort of Sgt. Pepper wannabe.

Unfortunately, Stuart isn't around to tutor Leopold in the nuances of modern life. He takes a tumble down the apartment building's empty elevator shaft and winds up in the hospital. Meanwhile, Leopold has gone for a little walk and is amazed to see the Brooklyn Bridge completed and still standing 125 years later. He might be astounded by the city's changes and all the modern conveniences, but even walking around New York in a gold-braided tailcoat doesn't earn Leopold much of a second look from jaded New Yorkers who are used to ignoring eccentrics.

Kate is a hotshot at a market research firm where she's up for a big promotion to vice president from her smarmy boss J.J. (Bradley Whitford) who regards it as a compliment when he tells Kate that "you skew male" and "you understand them [women] but you're not really one of them." This still doesn't prevent him from arranging a cozy "business" dinner for two. Kate also has to deal with the return of her amiable younger brother, Charlie (Brecklin Meyer), a struggling actor who meets Leopold and thinks he's a fellow thespian staying in character. But Leopold being mistaken for an actor and Kate's job turns out to be the factor that gets the twosome back into each other's company. Kate must find a male spokesman for a commercial for a diet spread that is supposed to taste like butter. At Kate's request, Leopold reads for the part and is offered the job because the test audience (all women) find Leopold handsome, honest, and courteous. Leopold, who has met J.J., thinks that Kate needs a chaperon on her dinner date.

When Kate tries to flag down a taxi near Central Park, her purse is grabbed and she starts chasing the thief into the park. Before she knows what's happening, Leopold (who has borrowed a carriage horse) swoops her up and rides after the miscreant who, naturally, doesn't want some crazy guy on a horse coming after him and drops Kate's purse. Kate still doesn't believe that Leopold is a 19th-century prince but she is willing to believe that he's different from the usual losers in her life. And Charlie is pleased when Leopold's advice on wooing a woman results in Charlie's getting a date; in fact, Charlie thinks Leopold should take his own advice and use it on Kate.

However, when the duo horn in on Kate's dinner with J.J. it turns into a disaster since Leopold makes his distrust and disdain of the other man all too clear and Kate is forced into making apologies in order to save her career. In turn, Leopold writes Kate an abject letter of apology and invites her to a private candlelight dinner on the apartment's rooftop. Kate, who dresses in pantsuits with high-collared, long-sleeved blouses, actually finds a slinky dress to dazzle Leopold. The two have a heart-to-heart about love, which Kate regards as the grown-up version of Santa Claus, and she tells Leopold that you can't live in a fairytale. She says she can't leap into love, but she will of course, quite literally.

Still, they grow closer and spend the day wandering the city together, when Leopold discovers his uncle's mansion is still standing and is being used as some kind of local community center/rental hall. He goes up to his old room and finds a box he had hidden that contains his mother's engagement ring. Even though they spend another romantic evening together, Leopold hesitates before asking Kate to marry him. The next day, Leopold is shooting the commercial for the fake butter and has to taste it for the first time. He proclaims it to be saddle soap and stalks out, followed by an angry Kate. He castigates her for peddling "pond scum" and she replies that she's had to work too hard to have the luxury of integrity and that she's paid her dues, is tired, needs some rest, and doesn't need advice from a man who has never had to work in his life. Leopold also realizes that Kate still doesn't believe that "I'm the man I say I am."

Poor Stuart, whose babblings about the space/time continuum have gotten him locked in the loony ward, finally manages to get out of the hospital and back to Leopold just in time to tell the Duke that he must return home and that he will return the same day and approximate time that he left. Kate has gotten her promotion and leaves a message for Leopold that after the business party she must attend that evening she wants to talk to him. But he is gone (the elevators are all functioning again) and only Stuart hears the message. When Charlie comes to Stuart's apartment to look for Leopold, he sees the pictures that Stuart took of his day in 1876 and also realizes something Stuart missed—something very important.

In 1876, a disheartened Leopold assures his uncle that he will marry whatever heiress his uncle thinks best and the engagement announcement will be made at midnight. In the present, Stuart and Charlie crash Kate's business party, which is also being held at the mansion, and show her the photographs. Kate is clearly seen among the guests at the Duke's party—Stuart figures that everything that happened was meant to be—Leopold had to come to the future, meet Kate and go back, and she is supposed to follow him. However, the only way for Kate to get to Leopold is through the portal, which means she has to jump off the Brooklyn Bridge at midnight when it next opens. Does Kate make it in time? Well, what kind of romance would it be if she didn't: just as Leopold is about to announce his bridal choice, he spots Kate in the crowd, names her as his intended, and the two literally waltz off into happily ever after.

Not that you should think of these things but Kate is giving up her independence, her career, and most modern conveniences for the restricted life of a Victorian aristocrat—and Leopold still needs money. Oh, well, maybe one of his inventions will make them rich. (It won't be the elevator since the first safety elevator was invented by Elisha Graves Otis in 1852 and the first passenger elevator was actually installed in New York in 1857.)

There's a saying that "manners maketh man" and it's certainly true in Leopold's case. He's polite and noble—not just because he's been well taught but because it's part of his character. When Kate asks him if he misses where he came from, Leopold replies that he misses the slower pace of life, the chance to savor it. Of course, as Kate has pointed out, it's easy when you don't have to work for your living and someone else takes care of the drudgeries of everyday life. Leopold actually does quite well for someone who must be used to being waited on and catered to at every opportunity. He also doesn't believe in taking advantage of a lady, besides a couple of kisses, he doesn't seem to make any sexual moves on Kate (they cuddle fully clothed). Kate's character is more problematical because it's so trite—a stressed-out career woman who seems to live for her job and admits to having problems with men. Leopold literally sweeps her off her feet (more than once) but he is like a prince from a fairytale. The tall, handsome Jackman has no problem filling this role.

Ryan has laughingly suggested in interviews that now that she's turned 40, she should be stopped from doing these patented romantic comedy parts but she is good at them and the last thing you can say about the character of Kate is that she's perky, which is a change from the "Meg Ryan" oeuvre. But about Meg's hair—ugh. It's an ironed straight choppy shag of blondish hue that is only attractive when it's pulled away from her face—not one of the actress's better looks. Let's face it, *Kate & Leopold* is a chick flick and we women viewers notice these things. Of course, with Hugh Jackman in the picture, Meg isn't the only one giving a romantic sigh.

—*Christine Tomassini*

## CREDITS

**Kay McKay:** Meg Ryan
**Leopold, Duke of Albany:** Hugh Jackman
**Stuart Bessler:** Liev Schreiber
**Charlie McKay:** Breckin Meyer
**Darci:** Natasha Lyonne
**J.J. Camden:** Bradley Whitford
**Uncle Millard:** Paxton Whitehead
**Dr. Geisler:** Spalding Gray
**Otis:** Philip Bosco

**Origin:** USA
**Released:** 2001
**Production:** Cathy Konrad; Konrad Pictures; released by Miramax Films
**Directed by:** James Mangold
**Written by:** James Mangold, Steven Rogers
**Cinematography by:** Stuart Dryburgh
**Music by:** Rolfe Kent

**Sound:** Matthew Price
**Editing:** David Brenner
**Art Direction:** Jess Gonchor
**Costumes:** Donna Zakowska
**Production Design:** Mark Friedberg
**MPAA rating:** PG-13
**Running time:** 121 minutes

## REVIEWS

*Boston Globe Online.* December 25, 2001.
*Chicago Sun-Times Online.* December 25, 2001.
*Detroit News.* December 25, 2001, p. E1.
*Entertainment Weekly.* January 4, 2002, p. 47.
*Los Angeles Times Online.* December 25, 2001.
*New York Times Online.* December 25, 2001.
*People.* December 24, 2001, p. 32.
*US Weekly.* December 24, 2001, p. 67.
*USA Today Online.* December 23, 2001.
*Variety.* December 17, 2001, p. 36.
*Washington Post.* December 25, 2001, p. C10.

## QUOTES

Leopold (Hugh Jackman): "Marriage is a promise of eternal love. As a man of honor, I cannot promise eternally what I have never felt momentarily."

## TRIVIA

The real Prince Leopold, Duke of Albany (1853–1884), was the eighth child and fourth son of Queen Victoria and Prince Albert. He was a hemophiliac and died from a burst blood vessel.

## AWARDS AND NOMINATIONS

**Golden Globes 2002:** Song ("Until")
**Nomination:**
**Oscars 2001:** Song ("Until")
**Golden Globes 2002:** Actor—Mus./Comedy (Jackman)
**Broadcast Film Critics 2001:** Song ("Until").

# Keep the River On Your Right: A Modern Cannibal Tale

*In 1955, Tobias Schneebaum disappeared in the Peruvian Amazon. One year later he walked out of the jungle . . . naked. It took him 45 years to go back.*
—Movie tagline

**K**eep the River On Your Right: A Modern Cannibal Tale by the brother/sister directing team of David Shapiro and Laurie Gwen Shapiro juxtaposes the contemporary and primitive to occasional scintillating effect. This documentary, inexplicably shot on video, falls somewhere between the "shockumentary," best exemplified by *Mondo Cane* (1963) and earnest ethnographic excursions such as *The Sky Above the Mud Below* (1961).

Unlike those two, this film lures its audience with the promise in its title, but then turns the tables. The *Tale* is really a portrait in retrospect of the explorer and author Tobias Schneebaum, an octogenarian New Yorker. Schneebaum continues to make a living by lecturing on the ways and artifacts of the headhunters of New Guinea and Peru. Unfortunately, the filmmakers remain determined to carve out a feature-length theatrical attraction not so much out of his work, but out of his life, and that too, from the perspective of what he is today. We thus get the feeling that they're not looking where he wants them to, but instead choose to remain fixated on the old codger himself.

Schneebaum's travels in the film's present tense are more in the way of a return to his life amongst the primitives decades ago. This pulls the rug out from any sense of immediacy this *Tale* might have possessed. Thus, while promising the dope on cannibalism, the Shapiros keep their captive audience waiting. And waiting. The film opens with the overriding passion in Schneebaum's life: his love of drawing. His voiceover tells us that his visit to Peru, at age 55, was the turning point in his life, one that made his New York-centered world appear hollow. Drawing then became a means of coming to terms with this change.

The film, however, first takes us to Indonesia where, as a tourist guide on a cruise ship, Schneebaum leads his party to witness the mass circumcision of 30 little boys. Before we're told what that ritual means, and before we can absorb any of the local color, we're on a jungle waterway in New Guinea. Like excited tourists just returned from a vacation, the Shapiros intercut footage of Schneebaum amongst the headhunters with comments from experts in the field. There are also bits from TV talk shows hosted by Mike Douglas and Charlie Rose. What surfaces to grab our interest does so, despite this filmic hopscotch.

Typical are the tracking shots of riverside life, possessing all the technical quality of a home movie, which are underscored by Schneebaum's musings. His immersion in tribal ways, he says, led him to accept "being alone." In rejecting the advances of civilization, he found "a more civilized world," a world where the social institution of the family didn't exist, nor any conception of private ownership. Consequently, he argues, there was no theft or crime.

As Schneebaum introduces us to the modern-day Asmat savage, Aipit, he admits to having shared a long and loving friendship with him, which was also sexual. When Charlie Rose sounds taken aback by Schneebaum's admission of homosexuality, the latter explains his behavior as a need to "partake in their ways" in order to acquire information, and adds that the Asmat way of greeting was "to hold the testicles." Rose promptly cuts to a station break. The film hits dull stretches when "the lifelong New Yorker" is shown with his relatives at a ritual seder. This is followed by memories of his mother on Coney Island. Clearly, this is not what the audience for the film has paid to see.

Things do pick up when we see Schneebaum with the Amerikaire in Peru. It was with them that he participated in the massacre of a neighboring tribe, which ended with him eating human flesh. It was a single piece, he recalls. He was unable to tell from which part of the body, and it tasted "like pork." Presumably, the filmmakers felt it justified to keep us waiting all this while to tell us just this.

Even so, the film does offer flashes of insight as we are shown examples of what an expert calls "neo-primitivism" in contemporary urban settings: the body piercing and tattooing that has now become a part of American shopping mall culture. Also, it must be said in the film's favor that the aged, near-infirm figure of Schneebaum, as interlocutor in front of the camera, does exhibit one winning grace. At 80, approaching the end of his mortal coil, he exhudes the perpetually jovial, though unspoken, stance that he may have been wrong about everything, after all.

Critics on the whole have found this documentary one of a kind. They seem to have taken to, what Jay Carr in the *Boston Globe*, calls Schneebaum's "engaging nature." Amy Taubin in the *Village Voice* is quick to point out that the film "looks like a home movie, but Schneebaum's charming, thoughtful narration compensates for the lack of visual sophistication." Edward Guthmann in the *San Francisco Chronicle* finds that "Schneebaum makes for a fascinating subject," but that the film "doesn't answer the question of how or why . . . (he) took the route that he did."

—*Vivek Adarkar*

## CREDITS

**Origin:** USA
**Released:** 2001
**Production:** David Shapiro, Laurie Gwen Shapiro; Next Wave Films; released by IFC Films
**Directed by:** David Shapiro, Laurie Gwen Shapiro
**Cinematography by:** Jonathan Kovel
**Music by:** Steve Bernstein, Paul O'Leary
**Editing:** Tula Goenka
**MPAA rating:** R
**Running time:** 93 minutes

## REVIEWS

*Boston Globe Online.* May 25, 2001.
*Chicago Sun-Times Online.* May 4, 2001.
*Entertainment Weekly.* April 6, 2001, p. 90.
*Houston Chronicle Online.* August 10, 2001.
*Los Angeles Times Online.* April 20, 2001.
*New York Times Online.* March 30, 2001.
*St. Louis Post-Dispatch Online.* June 15, 2001.
*San Francisco Chronicle Online.* May 6, 2001.
*Village Voice Online.* April 3, 2001.
*Washington Post Online.* May 4, 2001.

## QUOTES

Tobias Schneebaum: "I like to put myself into positions where I become part of the landscape."

# Kill Me Later

*Not every hostage wants to be saved.*
—Movie tagline

The movie script of a man taking a female hostage and, over the course of the movie, having the two start to fall in love is not a new one. So it's difficult to see why Dana Lustig and Annette Goliti Gutierrez (who also worked together on *Wedding Bell Blues*) would decide to revisit the tired old topic in their *Kill Me Later*. They were apparently inspired by a short film on the same topic made by Maria Ripoli (who directed *Tortilla Soup*), but judging by what they came up with, they weren't inspired enough. It's too bad because there are some inklings of interesting things in their film, but not enough to justify taking on such a tired old topic.

The hostage this time out (besides, of course, the audience) is Shawn (Selma Blair). Before she becomes an actual hostage, she is merely a hostage of what she perceives to be her miserable life. She wakes up one morning and her married lover and boss, Matthew (D.W. Moffett), informs her that he is backing out of a weekend trip they'd planned together. It's obvious this is not the first time this has happened. She also discovers that her goldfish is floating on top of his bowl. But things get even worse when she shows up at her boss's office at the bank to break up with him and return all his belongings. His wife barges in and Shawn is shocked to discover that the wife is pregnant. Or as her boss puts it, with a big fake smile at his wife, "Yes, we're pregnant!" It makes it even more clear than ever that Matthew has no intention of leaving his wife.

Shawn takes her fury out on a young couple who come in to see her about their home loan application. "Technically you qualify," she tells them meanly, before launching into a tirade about all the bad things that could happen to them that would make them unable to afford to buy a house. But even taking her wrath out on an innocent couple doesn't cheer Shawn up and she heads up to the top of her high-rise building, clutching a bottle of vodka and intending to jump.

While she is pondering her leap, a man in a building across the street notices her and calls the police. At the same moment that the police arrive, Charlie (Max Beesley) and his accomplice Billy (Brendan Fehr) happen to be robbing the bank. The police blunder onto the crime and shoot Billy, who flees. Charlie runs up to the roof and grabs Shawn just as she is making her big leap. He takes her hostage but finds himself with a problem when she declares that she wants him to kill her. A hostage that wants to be killed is not going to help him so he makes a deal with Shawn: if she will play along at being a hostage, he will be happy to kill her later.

This is but the first unrealistic plot point the film uses to keep these two people together so they can see the light and realize that they're mad for each other. After the danger is over and Charlie is unable to kill Shawn, there's another such plot point. Shawn demands $41,327 from Charlie so that she will not turn him in. He agrees, but for some reason the two keep hanging around together. It would have worked just as well if he had agreed to pay her, say, the following Thursday, but that doesn't have quite the dramatic tension.

While the two are together, Shawn starts getting charmed by Charlie's scruffy British ways. He seems to care about her and tries to charm her out of her permanently dour mood. Shawn is a hard case though. She can't seem to let go of her gloom and need to kill herself, despite Charlie's cheery antics and gentle prodding. "You need to put on some of that white make-up and listen to Black Sabbath for a couple of weeks," he teases her.

They start talking about their lives and begin bonding. Charlie learns that Shawn is the product of a bitter divorce,

with a father that remarried and no longer has time for her. Shawn learns that Charlie was once with a girl who said she'd wait for him while he was in prison but who left him six months later. His girlfriend quickly married and gave birth to Charlie's daughter, who thinks that the new husband is her real father. You know that once a couple starts sharing their traumas, love must be in the making.

To give them something to do on this first date, they're busy being on the lam. They have adventures like stealing a getaway car from a valet that's a stick shift, but—uh-oh—Shawn doesn't know how to drive a stick shift. The two are on the run from a couple of cops who seem to have no other case than this one: Reed (Lochlyn Monroe) is the eager young go-getter, armed with facts and ideas and seemingly obsessed with the psychology of suicide, while McGinley (O'Neal Compton) is the scruffy older boss who's annoyed by constant phone calls from his wife and Reed's overeager behavior. "Will you stop chomping at the bit? I'm still breathing," he tells Reed.

Other side stories include Charlie's sidekick Billy trying to woo a money-hungry exotic dancer and their third accomplice, the feisty old Jason (Tom Heaton), who gets caught while in the hospital recuperating. The best of these side stories by far is the one between Reed and his continually annoyed superior. "How many cups of coffee have you had?" gripes McGinley, when Reed rushes into his office yet again with some exciting new update on the case.

The central story is not so compelling. Charlie and Shawn make an attractive couple, but Shawn is so stuck in her gloom that it doesn't seem that appealing to be around her. Even when it is obvious that she could have a good thing going with Charlie (well, besides that bank robber job and all), she refuses to give up her quest of trying to kill herself. Her fascination with her own misery comes across as more self-indulgent than intriguing.

Still, Blair does a great job portraying someone mired in misery. She is a beautiful woman with striking features and a strong presence, but her eyes are lined with a permanent darkness and sullenness. She is one of the few actress who could make dark undereye circles look appealing. Beesley also does his best as the man who loves his grumpy woman. Despite being a criminal who carries a gun, he's really a sweet guy, darn it, who wouldn't hurt a fly. He's never even used his gun and doesn't really intend to. Beesley has a fine high energy, which is especially notable since Blair's dark presence threatens to drag down every scene.

To juice up things a bit, Lustig likes to fool around with some film techniques. She overlaps scenes of characters having a conversation, but puts the characters in different backgrounds as they continue to talk. This plays with time and place and adds a little of that indie artiness to the film but it often comes across as weakened Steven Soderberg instead of anything bold and original. More interesting is the soundtrack, filled with college indie faves like Luna, Blue Flannel and The Geraldine Fibbers.

Critics were not terribly enthusiastic about the film, though some did like it. Kevin Thomas of the *Los Angeles Times* wrote, "*Kill Me Later* is a gem, even if a little rough around the edges." Stephen Holden of the *New York Times* said "*Kill Me Later* wants to be a kind of screwball caper movie with Mr. Beesley's Charlie a cheeky rogue descendant of Cary Grant or Chevy Chase. But the screenplay never begins to find a workable balance between wit and adventure." The *Hollywood Reporter*'s Kirk Honeycutt felt "Lustig struggles at times to keep a consistent tone, but she does create the kind of quirky film the movie world could use more of in these days of cookie-cutter studio pictures."

—*Jill Hamilton*

## CREDITS

**Shawn:** Selma Blair
**Charlie:** Max Beesley
**Reed:** Lochlyn Munro
**McGinley:** O'Neal Compton
**Billy:** Brendan Fehr
**Mathew, the boss:** D.W. Moffett

**Origin:** USA
**Released:** 2001
**Production:** Ram Bergman, Dana Lustig, Mike Curb, Carole Curb Nemoy; Curb Entertainment, Amazon Film Productions; released by Seventh Art Productions
**Directed by:** Dana Lustig
**Written by:** Annette Goliti Gutierrez
**Cinematography by:** David Ferrara
**Music by:** Tal Bergman, Renato Nero
**Sound:** John Boyle
**Music Supervisor:** Mike Morrison
**Editing:** Gabriel Wyre
**Costumes:** Katrina McCarthy
**Production Design:** Tony Devenyi
**MPAA rating:** R
**Running time:** 89 minutes

## REVIEWS

*Boxoffice*. August, 2001, p. 56.
*Los Angeles Times Online*. September 14, 2001.
*New York Times Online*. September 14, 2001.
*Variety*. March 26, 2001, p. 47.

# The King Is Alive

*As the sand shifts . . . madness near.*
—Movie tagline

An impressive cast, an intriguing idea, and the Dogma 95 style lends spark to *The King Is Alive*, a modern-day version of Shakespeare's *King Lear*. Danish director Kristian Levring (who co-wrote the story with Anders Thomas) updates the story by taking a motley group of travelers on a trip through the Zimbabwean desert. When the bus driver (Vusi Kunene) runs out of gas, the group is stranded. With few options and little food, one of the men (Miles Anderson) goes off to get help. Those staying behind include an American couple (Bruce Davison and Janet McTeer), a British couple (Chris Walker and Lia Williams), a French woman (Romane Bohringer), an ill businessman (Brion James), a single American (Jennifer Jason Leigh), an older Briton (David Calder), and a Shakespearean actor (David Bradley).

To keep the others from thinking about their doomed fate, the actor, Henry, encourages everyone to rehearse for a production of *King Lear*. As odd as it sounds, the idea works and, despite the dire circumstances, performing in the play brings out jealousy and vanity, which at least distracts the players from starvation. Odd alliances form, including a tortured relationship between the young American and the snide Briton. The unhappy married couples only seem to stay unhappy, but try to find meaning in the play. Finally, an unexpected ending shakes the group to their core.

*The King Is Alive* may sound like an Elvis Presley tribute, and it wouldn't be so surprising to see "the King" show up as a mirage, but this film takes only so many chances. The stranded passenger idea is almost always a winner, even if it's not terribly original. The twist this time is the absurd notion of having the starving tourists play out their last days as Shakespearean actors in the Bard's bitterest play. Somehow, through understated humor, Levring makes it work.

The Dogma 95 style (a rejection of cinematic artifice) may not appeal to many tastes, but it fits both the desert setting and idea behind the story of stripping to the bare essentials. *The King Is Alive* also seems to be informed by the existential despair of Jean-Paul Sartre, Paul Bowles, and Albert Camus. Most of the performances are first-rate, from the well-known (Bohringer, Leigh), to the lesser-known actors (Bradley, Calder). Updating Shakespeare is no longer so radical a notion. So it's a tribute to *The King Is Alive* that the film surprises and entertains beyond this conceit.

—*Eric Monder*

## CREDITS

**Jack:** Miles Anderson
**Catherine:** Romane Bohringer
**Henry:** David Bradley
**Charles:** David Calder
**Ray:** Bruce Davison
**Ashley:** Brion James
**Moses:** Vusi Kunene
**Kanana:** Peter Kubheka
**Gina:** Jennifer Jason Leigh
**Liz:** Janet McTeer
**Amanda:** Lia Williams
**Paul:** Chris Walker

**Origin:** Denmark
**Released:** 2000
**Production:** Vibeke Windelov, Patricia Kruijer; Newmarket, Good Machine, Zentropa Entertainment, Danish Broadcasting Corporation, SVT Drama; released by IFC Films
**Directed by:** Kristian Levring
**Written by:** Anders Thomas Jensen, Kristian Levring
**Cinematography by:** Jens Schlosser
**Sound:** Jan Juhler
**Editing:** Nicholas Wayman-Harris
**MPAA rating:** R
**Running time:** 118 minutes

## REVIEWS

*Boxoffice.* November, 2000, p. 154.
*Chicago Sun-Times Online.* May 18, 2001.
*Entertainment Weekly.* May 25, 2001, p. 51.
*Los Angeles Times Online.* May 11, 2001.
*New York Times Online.* April 22, 2001.
*New York Times Online.* May 11, 2001.
*People.* May 21, 2001, p. 44.
*Sight and Sound.* May, 2001, p. 52.
*Variety.* May 22, 2000, p. 29.
*Washington Post Online.* July 20, 2001, p. WE31.

## QUOTES

Liz (Janet McTeer) tells husband Ray (Bruce Davison) about *King Lear:* "You don't have to worry, you know. Nobody has to fall in love and everybody gets to die in the end."

## TRIVIA

The locale is the abandoned diamond mining town of Kolmanskop, Namibia.

# The King Is Dancing (Le Roi Danse)

Part social commentary, part soap opera, and part music history lesson, director Gèrard Corbiau's *The King Is Dancing* might be called a French *Amadeus*. In any case, Corbiau and his fellow screenwriters thoroughly examine the intense relationship between Sun King Louis XIV (who often referred to himself as Apollo) and his court musician, Jean-Baptiste Lully, an Italian exile. The end result becomes a historical epic celebration filled with intrigue, deception, and lavish music, which some viewers might find too talky (the French love to gab), while others will find it to be a passionate history lesson complete with frilly costumes and plenty of choreographed festivities.

Inspired by Philippe Beaussant's book *Lully, the Sun Musician, The King Is Dancing* might be called a youth rebellion within the French monarchy. Long before Princess Diana, accomplished dancer and social reformer Louis XIV thought that performing artists could literally run a kingdom. Donning golden costumes while performing intricate ballets, Louis was to 17th-century France what Madonna was to American 1980's pop music, an iconoclastic superstar. Equally arrogant and shy, young Louis thought that he only needed an accomplished court composer (Lully) and a playwright (Moliere) to successfully rule his kingdom. Of course his conservative mother and church leaders fought Louis every step of the way.

Corbiau focuses on the 15 years of Louis XIV's rule, with the writers packing the screenplay with ballet performances, lavish parties, talk sessions between Moliere (Tcheky Karyo) and Lully (Boris Terral), fights between the queen (Colette Emmanuelle) and Louis (Benoit Magimel), and plenty of melodramatic moments. We see Moliere die from consumption while giving a performance of his play *The Miser*, we see young Louis almost succumb to a fever until Lully serenades him with court violins, and we see the king, now in his thirties, attempt to dance on a broken ankle—only to realize that his reign as a dancer had ended, which helps transforms him into a conservative ruler who disposes of his artisans, including a crestfallen Lully.

While *The King Is Dancing*'s narrative and key performances are impressive in their own right, the picture's soundtrack, based on Lully's original musical scores, deserves a mention. According to the film's press kit, the soundtrack, which "tells the story of the musical career of the dancer king and his favorite composer, Lully . . . is itself a discovery, often using unknown works, pieces that have rarely or never before been performed in concert." The soundtrack includes Lully's ballets and operas, as well as musical compositions by Lully's rival Robert Cambert. Musical director Reinhold Goebel, who specializes in 17th-century music, prepared an orchestration that was played on period instruments and the end result imbeds itself in the fabric of the film.

Tcheky Karyo, whose appearances include Eric Rohmer's *Moon Over Paris*, Jean-Jacques Annaud's *The Bear*, and Nigel Cole's *Saving Grace*, delivers a sedate yet iconoclastic Moliere. Newcomer Boris Terral oozes vulnerability as the libertine court composer Lully. Terral's passionate performance proves volcanic in its intensity. Finally, Benoit Magimel plays the contradictory role of the shy but arrogant Louis with finesse. He transforms from an innocent artist who believes one only needs a star composer to rule his kingdom into a monarch who betrays his colleagues.

Toronto-based *eye Weekly* critic Gemma Files called the film "a vibrant portrait of an unstable, passionate world . . ." and Liz Braun of the *Toronto Sun* praised the film's leading man, "Benoit Magimel is regal and willful as Louis." Viewers will walk away with a French history lesson and humming Lully's sweet melodies as this visually stunning musical epic leaves a lasting impression of the Sun King.

—*Patty-Lynne Herlevi*

CREDITS

**Louis XIV:** Benoit Magimel
**Jean-Baptiste Lully:** Boris Terral
**Moliere:** Tcheky Karyo
**Anne of Austria:** Colette Emmanuelle
**Cambert:** Johan Leysen
**Prince de Conti:** Idwig Stephane
**Madeline:** Cecile Bois
**Julie:** Claire Keim
**Young Louis:** Emil Tarding

**Origin:** France, Great Britain, Belgium
**Language:** French
**Released:** 2001
**Production:** Dominique Janne; Le Studio Canal Plus, France 2 Cinema, MMC Independent, K-Star
**Directed by:** Gerard Corbiau
**Written by:** Gerard Corbiau, Andree Corbiau, Didier Decoin, Eve de Castro

**Cinematography by:** Gerard Simon
**Sound:** Henri Morelle, Nigel Holland, Dominique Dalmasso
**Editing:** Ludo Troch, Philippe Ravoet
**Costumes:** Olivier Beriot
**Production Design:** Hubert Pouille
**MPAA rating:** Unrated
**Running time:** 108 minutes

 REVIEWS

*Boxoffice.* July, 2001, p. 92.
*Variety.* January 22, 2001, p. 44.

# Kingdom Come

*They're not perfect, but they are family.*
—Movie tagline

**Box Office:** $23.2 million

On a hot summer's day in the town of Lula, Raynelle Slocumb (Whoopi Goldberg) sits at her kitchen table reading a letter to her husband from his sister Marguerite (Loretta Devine). Marguerite is very religious and is chastising her brother for not going to church. She even threatens to show up at his house next Sunday and sermonize and sing hymns to him until he capitulates and gets himself to a house of God. He may have wished he had gone more often, for just as Raynelle finishes reading the letter, her husband keels over in his chair and falls dead on the floor.

Now Raynelle's family converges on Lula for the funeral. Marguerite is being driven by her good-for-nothing son Royce (Darius McCrary) whose dream is to marry, have a few kids and go on welfare. They fight over his future, his prisoner brother, and even over what radio station to listen to in the car. Even when the car runs out of gas, the fighting continues on the side of the road.

Meanwhile, in another car heading for Lula, Raynelle's son Junior (Anthony Anderson), who is 33-years-old, broke, unemployed, and saddled with three kids, is having his own battles with his shrewish, self-centered wife, Charisse (Jada Pinkett Smith). While the hellion kids loudly argue and throw shoes in the back seat, Charisse and Junior almost come to blows in the front seat. When Junior pulls a pistol on Charisse and Charisse finds another woman's earring in the car, you just know this is a marriage that would be more at home on the Jerry Springer Show.

Raynell's other son, Ray Bud (LL Cool J), lives in Lula, works hard as a mechanic and is married to the family peacemaker Lucille (Vivica A. Fox). Nonetheless, even Ray Bud is typical of the dysfunctionalness of this family because he is fighting an alcohol problem and a lot of repressed anger at his now dead father. So it should be no surprise that while everyone is trying to decide about the funeral service and the headstone, brothers Ray Bud and Junior break out into a brawl in the living room. This family needs a referee not a minister.

Poor Raynelle, or so one would think. Sons who don't get along and a daughter named Delightful (Masasa) who still lives at home, says little, and has a crush on Reverend Hooker (Cedric the Entertainer) but in her own father's words, "is in love with the refrigerator." Not to mention the fact that Raynelle's husband of more than 20 years has just died. Well, there probably is one good thing in Raynelle's life—her husband is dead. Seems they hadn't had sexual relations in more than 20 years and the only thing she wants chiseled in his tombstone are 12 letters: "Mean and surly."

As if this explosive mix of people weren't enough, also attending the funeral are cousin Juanita (Toni Braxton) the wife of Bud's rich nephew who the impoverished, bitchy Charisse bitterly believes she could have married if she hadn't married the worthless Junior. And then there's Clyde (Richard Gant), Ray Bud's employer who makes passes at both Marguerite and Raynelle and drinks beer at the back of the church during the funeral service. Needless to say, the family patriarch's funeral quickly becomes a family reunion with all the old family problems dredged up, souls searched and more than the corpse laid to rest. The wake is marked by Charisse throwing herself on the corpse, while the funeral is notable for a thrown drink and noisy declarations of love in the pews, a minister who has to excuse himself because of an attack of flatulence, a son's reconciliation with his father and his anger, and another son's finding his path out of a mis- spent life.

*Kingdom Come* was written by David Dean Bottrell and Jessie Jones who also wrote the play it is based on, *Dearly Departed* a popular traveling stage show aimed at black audiences. And while things may have to be "writ large" to be appreciated on live stage, they often seem overdone on the already larger-than-life movie screen. Such is the case for many of the aspects of this translation from stage to screen.

For one thing you need a map to keep track not only of family relationships but also to follow the hairpin turns of emotions the story puts us through. To minimize the first problem each character is painted with incredibly broad brushstrokes. They are often over the top, one-dimensional and stereotypical: the harridan, the adulterer, the town slut, the slacker, the matriarch, etc. Thankfully, with an incredi- bly talented cast, one may be able to overlook all that. The

second problem, however, may be more jarring. Within a running time of just over 90 minutes we're asked to shift between bawdy and sentimental, between slapstick and ten- derness, between farts and tears, between the broad and the intimate, between yelling and forgiveness. That's a lot of emotional rollercoastering for such a short period of time.

Typical of this genre of family-gathering film, it may also succeed or fail depending on the cast assembled to do the job. Luckily *Kingdom Come* sports some top-notch tal- ent. Although the fighting and yelling and hugging and soul-searching are often set against a lot of scenery chewing and mugging, the talented actors still manage to lend this frenzied vehicle a level of believability.

Perhaps the most over-the-top and maybe the most grating of the characters is Jada Pinkett Smith's Charisse, the loud-mouth harpy, followed closely by Loretta Devine's Marguerite, the loud-mouthed evangelist. They may have been fun characters on the stage but their cinema histrionics are overpowering. Seemingly in another movie entirely is Whoopi Goldberg whose Raynelle is the only one whose emotions are entirely in check. Perhaps as the matriarch she has to be the calm center to the family storm raging around her. But if any actor really shines in the film it is LL Cool J whose acting talents improve with every acting job he takes on. His is a subtle performance in a sea or anarchy. And he is especially good when he takes over the minister's duties and pulls his family together at the funeral.

*Kingdom Come* may not be as polished a work as that other, far better, African American family-coming-together saga, *Soul Food*, but it is still far, far better than so many other genre films black actors are often relegated to such as those centering on sexist and lame booty calls or those glorifying the illegal activities of the boys in the 'hood. *Kingdom Come* at least has its uplifting moments at the top of the emotional rollercoaster hills and some wonderful talent to take us on that ride.

—*Beverley Bare Buehrer*

## CREDITS

**Ray Bud Slocumb:** L.L. Cool J.
**Charise Slocumb:** Jada Pinkett Smith
**Lucille Slocumb:** Vivica A. Fox
**Marguerite:** Loretta Devine
**Junior Slocumb:** Anthony Anderson
**Reverend Hooker:** Cedric the Entertainer
**Royce:** Darius McCrary
**Raynelle Slocumb:** Whoopi Goldberg
**Juanita Slocumb:** Toni Braxton
**Delightful:** Masasa
**Charles Winslow:** Clifton Davis
**Clyde:** Richard Gant

**Origin:** USA
**Released:** 2001
**Production:** John Morrissey, Edward Bates; released by Fox Searchlight
**Directed by:** Doug McHenry
**Written by:** Jessie Jones, David Bottrell
**Cinematography by:** Francis Kenny
**Music by:** Tyler Bates
**Sound:** Russell Williams II
**Editing:** Richard Halsey
**Art Direction:** Burton E. Jones Jr.
**Costumes:** Francine Jamison-Tanchuck
**Production Design:** Simon Dobbin
**MPAA rating:** PG
**Running time:** 89 minutes

 **REVIEWS**

*Boxoffice.* May, 2001, p. 58.
*Chicago Sun-Times Online.* April 11, 2001.
*Entertainment Weekly.* April 20, 2001, p. 44.
*Los Angeles Times Online.* April 11, 2001.
*New York Times Online.* April 11, 2001.
*People.* April 23, 2001, p. 39.
*USA Today Online.* April 13, 2001.
*Variety.* April 16, 2001, p. 29.
*Washington Post Online.* April 13, 2001.

**QUOTES**

Rev. Hooker (Cedric the Entertainer): "It's best to remember the happier times." Raynelle Slocumb (Whoopi Goldberg): "Well, they were few and far between."

# Kiss of the Dragon

*Kiss Fear Goodbye.*
—Movie tagline

 **Box Office:** $36.8 million

After hearing from a fan who was looking forward to taking his child to see *Kiss of the Dragon*, Jet Li, star of the film, put up a special notice on his web site warning parents of small children of the film's "very realistic, hard-core, action-packed fight sequences." Maybe that's what the film's publicists should have used in PR materials for the film

because "very realistic, hard-core, action-packed fight sequences" are a big part of the reason people go to martial arts films in the first place. No one's going to a martial arts film for the subtle character nuances and piquant dialogue.

And if they were, they would be sorely disappointed by *Kiss of the Dragon.* Not that the film is a bad one. In fact, it's very watchable. It's just that the characterizations and dialogue combined probably took up about a fifth of the script, with fight choreography taking up the rest of the pages. Or to put it another way, the story, invented by Li himself and written up by Luc Besson and Robert Mark Kamen, was written in only three weeks. In that kind of time, you can be sure that they weren't sweating over the dialogue. Perhaps this is the reason that resident baddie Richard (Tcheky Karyo) says lines to his henchmen like, "Bring him to me. I want him alive. I'll kill him myself." If any consideration had been given to his lines, then maybe they'd have come up the realization that any time a bad guy delays killing the hero, the hero is just going to escape. Attention movie villains: the time to kill the hero is when you have the chance. Just do it and get it over with. Of course, that doesn't deal with the scenario where the hero seems to be dead, then comes alive again, but it's a good start.

The hero in this case is Liu Jiuan (Li), a highly trained and respected Chinese agent. He's summoned to Paris to help a French police inspector, the aforementioned Richard, with a drug case. Even when Jiuan and Richard are on the same side, they don't have the best of relationships. Richard decides he can't pronounce Jiuan's name and decides to call him Johnny Boy instead. Plus he doesn't seem like an especially kind man. When Jiuan first meets him, he is in a hotel kitchen, beating a guy's face into a bloody mess. Richard loses even more first impression points as he and Jiuan work together on the surveillance of a drug dealer. The dealer decides to take on a pair of prostitutes, one of them Jessica (Bridget Fonda). The other prostitute and drug dealer cavort in his hotel room while Jessica is in the restroom throwing up because she is an innocent North Dakota girl and doesn't care for such things. Suddenly, there is chaos. The prostitute kills the dealer and Jiuan rushes in. While he tries to resuscitate the dealer, Richard charges in and shoots the man, then the prostitute. He uses a gun that he'd confiscated from Jiuan so he can blame him for the crime.

Jiuan is forced into hiding in this strange city. In a twist of movie fate, the prostitute posted outside the door of the Chinese cracker shop that he's hiding out in happens to be Jessica. Jessica, a gabby girl, insists on befriending the quiet Jiuan. She tells him how she's just a farm girl from North Dakota who was forced into junkiedom and prostitution by the evil Richard. She feels powerless to escape since Richard has kidnapped her daughter.

Jiuan isn't particularly sympathetic to her plight until he realizes that since she was at the hotel room, she is his only hope for being exonerated for his supposed crime. They make a deal: he gets her daughter back and she will testify on his behalf. To achieve those results, you can be sure that a lot of fighting will have to happen. The task won't be easy since Richard is an especially mean man. He's the kind of guy who shoots one of his sidekicks just for saying, "Boss, I think . . ."

And so the fighting begins. There is killing and danger in all kinds of new and different fashions. Jiuan gets trapped in a flaming laundry shoot. A man gets his legs and lower torso ripped from his body and countless innocent onlookers get gunned down, run over, etc. The movie enjoys these moments, and the camera lingers over them lovingly. At one point, Jiuan kills someone by administering a special acupuncture needle in the back of the neck (acupuncture is his speciality.) This so-called "kiss of the dragon" makes the victim's blood rush to their head, where it never leaves. This causes such unpleasant side effects as blood leaking from various facial orifices. The audience sees all this in real time, living color.

What makes one martial arts film better than another is partly a visceral thing and partly a formula. The more popular martial arts films have something extra going for them, like humor (as in many of Jackie Chan's films), especially graceful choreography (like *Crouching Tiger, Hidden Dragon*) or the fighters having particularly inventive ways of hurting each other. This film's strength is in the last category. Li's persona is a tiny, mild-mannered guy who is able to kick the butts of anyone around him. He is so cool that he never even seems to break a sweat, regardless of who his competitor (and more often, competitors) are. *Kiss of the Dragon* makes light of this several times throughout the film. At one point, Li stumbles onto a large class of martial arts students and has to battle them all. He leaves them all in a writhing, groaning pile. (It's never explained why the class starts fighting with him, but then, why ruin a good gag?) Li is also able to defeat his enemies even when he is hopelessly under-armed. Li defeats one guy brandishing a huge machine gun with a graceful poke in the throat with two chopsticks. Another gun-brandishing crazy is neatly dispatched with one billiard ball.

As in his American breakout film, *Romeo Must Die*, Li is less successful in relationships with the female gender. Here, he is supposed to have some sort of unspoken bond with Fonda's prostitute. But the bond is not only unspoken, it's practically nonexistent. *Los Angeles Times* film critic Kenneth Turan wrote: "*Kiss*, insists against the evidence of our senses that there's a powerful attraction between the nosy, chatty Jessica and the monosyllabic Johnny Boy. In reality there's more physical chemistry between Ariel Sharon and Yasser Arafat than between these two."

It doesn't help that neither Fonda nor Li do a particularly good job of acting. Of the two, Li gives by far the better performance, but his character is ill-defined at best. We know that he's a highly trained agent, but beyond that there's nothing. He's very quiet and soft-spoken and doesn't give

much clue as to what he might be thinking about. Even though he's a dangerous fighting machine, the diminutive Li comes across as more cute than threatening. There's a boyishness to him that belies the fact that he's 38. Fonda is annoyingly whiny as the innocent farm girl. Her character is a hokey one, but it seems like Fonda could have done something to make her more appealing. (Although she should be given some extra credit for running long distances in stiletto heels.) *Entertainment Weekly*'s Lisa Schwarzbaum wrote: "Fonda doesn't know what to do with her. Too wan to play her as a really unstrung skank, the actress makes the faces and gestures of degradation without letting herself get dirty enough."

Critics had a tepid response to the film. Schwarzbaum called Li "a fleet performer with a highly appealing demeanor of patient, quizzical intelligence." Leah Rozen of *People* magazine wrote: "If action counts more than words, *Kiss of the Dragon* is a heck of a film. . . . If, however, one measures a movie by character development, depth of story and sprightliness of dialogue, *Dragon* is belching pure ash." David Germain of the *Associated Press* wrote: "Li has conscientiously warned parents to keep the youngsters out of his latest martial-arts thriller because its extreme violence is not 'appropriate for children.' In the interests of inclusion, let's expand that injunction: Everyone should stay away from *Kiss of Dragon*."

—*Jill Hamilton*

## CREDITS

**Liu Jiuan:** Jet Li
**Jessica:** Bridget Fonda
**Jean-Pierre Richard:** Tcheky Karyo
**Uncle Tai:** Burt Kwouk

**Origin:** France, USA
**Released:** 2001
**Production:** Luc Besson, Jet Li, Steve Chasman, Happy Walters; Europa, Quality Growth International Ltd., Current & Immortal Entertainment, Canal Plus; released by 20th Century-Fox
**Directed by:** Chris Nahon
**Written by:** Luc Besson, Robert Mark Kamen
**Cinematography by:** Thierry Arbogast
**Music by:** Craig Armstrong
**Sound:** Vincent Tulli
**Editing:** Marco Cave
**Costumes:** Pierre Bechir, Annie Thiellement
**Production Design:** Jacques Bufnoir
**MPAA rating:** R
**Running time:** 98 minutes

## REVIEWS

*Boxoffice.* September, 2001, p. 150.
*Chicago Sun-Times Online.* July 6, 2001.
*Entertainment Weekly.* July 13, 2001, p. 53.
*Los Angeles Times Online.* July 5, 2001.
*New York Times Online.* July 6, 2001.
*People.* July 16, 2001, p. 32.
*USA Today Online.* July 5, 2001.
*Variety.* July 9, 2001, p. 19.
*Washington Post Online.* July 6, 2001.

## QUOTES

Richard (Tcheky Karyo): "There is a time for diplomacy and a time for action. Diplomacy is dead."

## TRIVIA

The action choreography director is Corey Yuen, who has worked with Jet Li (who supplied the film's story) on *Fist of Legend, Lethal Weapon 4,* and other films.

# A Knight's Tale

*He Will Rock You.*
—Movie tagline
*He didn't make the rules. He was born to break them.*
—Movie tagline

**Box Office:** $56.1 million

Let's get this out of the way right at the top. *A Knight's Tale* ain't history. What is it? Well how about MTV does Spring Break in the Middle Ages? Or how about the WJF, the World Jousting Federation? Or how about just plain goofy fun? I mean, just look at how this movie starts: with an historical inaccuracy and a sing-along rock song. First the error: peasants weren't pages or squires. These were positions for children of nobility who were training to be a knight not positions for indentured labor, serfdom or slavery. A young aristocratic lad would start as a page at the age of seven or so, then, after about seven years he became a squire. When the squire won his spurs, he became a knight. So there's very little chance a thatcher's son would ever be given to a nobleman as his page. Period.

But perhaps we quibble. Instead, relax and watch the merriment as the crowd gathered for a jousting tournament stomps and claps and does the wave while belting out Queen's rock and roll anthem, "We will, we will rock you!" Could the filmmakers get any more anachronistic? Absolutely, and they do. Could an audience have more fun? Well maybe, but didn't we agree not to nitpick? Here's the setup. A young peasant lad, William Thatcher (Leagh Conwell) is given to Sir Ector to be his page. William wants nothing more than to "change his stars" and become a knight, but peasants don't become knights. It just isn't done. (See, I told you!)

The years pass and Sir Ector (Nick Brinble) and his band of merrie men have fallen on hard times. They haven't eaten in three days, but a payday is in sight because Ector has won two contests out of three in a jousting match. If he can just win number three there will be food on the table. Unfortunately, Sir Ector has also just died. Rushing in to take his place is a now older William (Heath Ledger). Although his comrades, Roland (Mark Addy) and Wat (Alan Tudyk) don't think this is a good idea, starving men are easily convinced . . . especially since they aren't going to be the ones taking the opponent's lance in the chest.

Well William may be of peasant stock, but he has learned well from Sir Ector and what he lacks in pedigree he makes up for in fearlessness. He wins the tournament and immediately sets his sights on competing in another one. As his companions point out, however, no one will let him, a low-born peasant, take part in a tournament meant for nobility. The result? The spontaneous birth of Ulrich von Lichtenstein of Gelderland. Now all he needs is a month of training before the next tournament in Rouen . . . and proof of his phony pedigree.

Luckily, on their way to Rouen, our three intrepid heroes encounter a naked man "trudging" down the road. He turns out to be Geoffrey Chaucer (Paul Bettany). Facile with language but an inveterate gambler, the down-on-his-luck writer (yes, he's supposed to be THAT Geoffrey Chaucer during his pre-*Canterbury Tales* days) exchanges his talents for clothes and joins William's band. Chaucer it turns out is an expert at forging patents of nobility—there's a big call for this sort of thing?—which he promptly does for William. Chaucer also takes on the job as the counterfeit knight's herald whom he now introduces at the matches with phrases like "The lance that thrilled France, the man who gave them hell at New Rochelle . . ." and all in a style reminiscent of "let's get ready to rummmmmbllllle."

At the tournament in Rouen Will/Ulrich not only wins a few contests, but his heart is also won by a beautiful and head-strong young woman, Jocelyn (Shanynn Sossamon). Jocelyn, however, has another suitor who will not only compete with Will for her heart but also on the jousting field for honors, Count Adhemar (Rufus Sewell). Adhemar is the unethical, unlikable, and ignoble leader of the free companies in France. (Actually, free companies—bands of unpaid soldiers—freely roamed 14th-century France during the Hundred Years War against which this story is set, but they were often no better than roving groups of bandits raping and pillaging until the war broke out again. Their having a noble leader is unlikely.)

Also in Rouen, Will discovers a female smithee whose talents he seriously doubts, but with no money to pay a male blacksmith he eventually hires her to replace his antique armor with a lighter, stronger version, which she engraves with "her mark" which looks suspiciously like two Nike trademark swooshes. Her armor, though, wins her a place on Will's "team," and they're off to the next tournament . . . then the next . . . then the next . . . etc. And that "etc." may be part of the problem with *A Knight's Tale*. All of the tournaments eventually blur together and take entirely too long. There's only so many ways to tell one knight and one jousting match from another. And for how light-hearted most of the movie is, the jousting matches seem to take themselves much too seriously.

And speaking of serious, nobody seethes like Rufus Sewell. Dark and brooding, we don't trust him right from the start, but we're still hypnotized by him when he's on screen. He's a good but subtle villain. On the good guys' side, Mark Addy plays Roland like the level-headed heart of the group while Alan Tudyk's Wat always seems in need of a serious dose of Ritalin. But it is Paul Bettany who makes an auspicious film debut here as an irrepressible Chaucer who steals all his scenes, naked or clothed.

Shannyn Sossamon who is undoubtedly beautiful is a bit puzzling in this, her first acting job. Sossamon evidently was spotted by a casting director at a birthday party for Gwyneth Paltrow's brother. She was there with a friend who was working as a disc jockey. (Shades of Lana Turner at Schwab's Drug Store?) Sossamon's Jocelyn is a very modern woman in many respects: self-assured and independent. But then she turns around and does stupid things like demand that Will prove his love by losing a tournament . . . and then changes her mind mid-tournament. In fact, the love scenes between Will and Jocelyn aren't really all that romantic. On the other hand Laura Fraser's feisty blacksmith Kate may have been the most underused character in the film and might even have made a more interesting love interest for our intrepid hero. She's certainly more like him in spirit than is the flighty Jocelyn.

In the end though, any success for *A Knight's Tale* rests with the likability of Heath Ledger. So winning as the good badboy in the Gen X version of "The Taming of the Shrew," *Ten Things I Hate About You* and equally heart-stealing as Mel Gibson's son in *The Patriot*, Ledger lends the film just the right balance of sincerity and light-heartedness to pull of the jousts and the rock and roll.

*A Knight's Tale* does an interesting, if not authentic, job of recreating the feel of Medieval France and England—the computer generated overview of London is quite fascinating—even though it was filmed in Prague in the Czech Republic. This, however, is not the only time the filmmakers cheated a little bit. Over 1,000 weapons were produced for the film, most of them the lances used in the jousting matches. However to protect the actors, they were made of easily breakable balsa wood though most "wood" splinters flying around after a hit are really nothing more than various bits of pasta and spaghetti.

And it's odd, but while on the one hand the filmmakers were serious about accuracy (they evidently scoured eastern Europe looking for the giant Kladruby horses used in the film. Many of them had their own "patent's of nobility" with lineage going back more than 700 years) but then they turn around and allow costumer Caroline Harris to create outfits that are as jarring as the rock and roll score. Several of Shannyn Sossamon's outfits look as if they'd be more at home on a Parisian catwalk than on a castle rampart. And Harris even admits that the clothing worn by Will's band of merrie men was inspired by the clothing worn by the Rolling Stones on their 1972 tour.

Modernization is supposed to make history more accessible, to help modern audiences relate to ancient times, but when the history is as warped as it is in *A Knight's Tale* one has to question just what people are getting access to. I mean it's nice to know people are being exposed to concepts like free companies or events like the battle of Poitiers and people like the Edward, the Black Prince, but where's the black plague and the famine common for the time or even a reference to the sheer destruction and death of the Hundred Years War? In fact, if William had wanted to win his spurs anywhere during this time, it would have been on a battlefield not a jousting field! This is history sanitized for your enjoyment. But, if you're willing to skip the history and go right to the good-natured fun of the film, if you're willing to accept catwalk fashions and rock and roll anachronisms, if you're willing to believe a time as dire as the dark ages could be playfully innocent, then go ahead and enjoy yourself.

—*Beverley Bare Buehrer*

## CREDITS

**William Thatcher:** Heath Ledger
**Roland:** Mark Addy
**Count Adhemar:** Rufus Sewell
**Jocelyn:** Shannyn Sossamon
**Chaucer:** Paul Bettany
**Kate:** Laura Fraser
**John Thatcher:** Christopher Cazenove
**Wat:** Alan Tudyk
**Colville:** James Purefoy

**Origin:** USA
**Released:** 2001
**Production:** Tim Van Rellim, Todd Black, Brian Helgeland; Escape Artists, Finestkind; released by Columbia Pictures
**Directed by:** Brian Helgeland
**Written by:** Brian Helgeland
**Cinematography by:** Richard Greatrex
**Music by:** Carter Burwell
**Sound:** Mark Holding
**Editing:** Kevin Stitt
**Art Direction:** John Hill
**Costumes:** Caroline Harris
**Production Design:** Tony Burrough
**MPAA rating:** PG-13
**Running time:** 132 minutes

## REVIEWS

*Boxoffice.* May, 2001, p. 28.
*Boxoffice.* June, 2001, p. 55.
*Chicago Sun-Times Online.* May 11, 2001.
*Entertainment Weekly.* May 18, 2001, p. 57.
*Los Angeles Times Online.* May 11, 2001.
*New York Times Online.* May 11, 2001.
*People.* May 21, 2001, p. 42.
*Sight and Sound.* September, 2001, p. 48.
*USA Today Online.* May 11, 2001.
*Variety.* April 23, 2001, p. 16.
*Washington Post Online.* May 11, 2001.

## QUOTES

Roland (Mark Addy) to William (Heath Ledger): "You're a knight in your heart but not on paper and paper is all that matters to them."

# L.I.E.

*On the Long Island Expressway there are lanes going east, lanes going west, and lanes going straight to hell.*
—Movie tagline

 **Box Office:** $1.1 million

Beneath its grandiose title, Michael Cuesta's debut feature, *L.I.E.*, is yet another young male coming-of-age story. Cuesta does cut repeatedly to the cars on the eponymous thoroughfare whizzing past the camera, but the leitmotif is not allowed to alter his narrative focus. *L.I.E.* remains doggedly centered on its introspective protagonist, the unassuming, 14-year-old Howie (Paul Franklin Dano), traumatized by the recent loss of his mother in a car crash on the Long Island Expressway. Unfortunately, Dano's facial expressions remain as opaque as the shots of the vehicular traffic. The film though is redeemed by the twists of fate that Cuesta dreams up for his characters.

Howie's life revolves around the easy cash and booty he and his chin-pierced pal, Gary (Billy Kay), are able to burgle from the upper middle class houses in their neighborhood. The L.I.E. runs like a fishbone through their world. Its initials also stand for the lies that surround them. The catalyst who is to overturn their world comes in the form of Big John Harridan (Brian Cox), an amiable retired Marine, who vows revenge when he finds a set of two handguns stolen from his basement. Gary is caught by Big John after he sells one of the guns, and in turn squeals on Howie. Unbeknownst to Howie, his father, Marty (Bruce Altman), is under investigation for a construction fraud. Marty himself couldn't care less about this, or his son, as is evident in the manner he has brute sex with the mistress he has moved into their home.

When Harridan catches up with Howie, he threatens to go to the police unless Howie reimburses him to the tune of three thousand dollars. There then follows a parallel montage in which Howie burgles Gary's miserable dwelling, and finds the other gun under the bed; while Gary breaks into Howie's plush house and stumbles onto the hot cash that Marty has hidden in a bedroom drawer. This allows Gary to realize his dream of running off to California, leaving his friend to face the music. It is when Howie returns the gun to Big John that the latter offers him the option of working off the cost of the other gun through a homosexual favor, but not in so many words. Big John first shows him a porn video, and remarks how fellatio is better than intercourse. Howie is initially repelled, and storms out.

His eventual readiness to give in to Big John's urges remains the film's problematic aspect. Through the verve with which Brian Cox plays his role, Big John's behavior emerges as convincing, though the film doesn't take his side. The film does however try to explain Howie's sexual deviance by the sudden loss of his mother, to whom he was very close, owing to his dysfunctional family life. This presumably has made him unable to look at girls directly, and at women indirectly, in a sexual light. Had the film dramatized this, Howie's sexual yearning for Big John would have appeared as believable as that of Big John for him. Instead, what emerges is Cuesta tapping into sensational subject matter, and at the same time, playing it safe by keeping it under wraps. On a beach outing, Big John allows Howie to drive his snazzy sports car, and even gets him to recite poetry. This lyricism slams right into the demolition of Howie's home life, or what is left of it. While Howie is away, Marty finds that the cash he had hidden has been stolen, just as his house is raided by the FBI, who cart him off in handcuffs.

Not finding anyone at home, and not knowing what has happened, Howie climbs onto the ledge of an overpass above the L.I.E., but just as he raises one foot, his mother appears to him and, with a loving smile, gently feels his face. We then see Howie being held at the police station, along with others in his gang, charged with burglary. Soon however, Big John literally comes waltzing in to collect him. At his new home, Howie drives a wedge between Big John and Scott (Walter Masterson), Big John's live-in boy lover, who's in his late teens. When Howie learns that Marty is being held in a federal prison, he breaks down weeping, then starts to kiss Big John's arm. Playing the kindly father figure, Big John merely tucks him into bed.

When Howie visits Marty, the father tells him of a secret ATM account by which he can support himself. Big John, now hunting for other prey near the shoulder of the L.I.E. where he found Gary, is about to pick up a teenage youth, when Scott drives up and shoots him dead at point blank range, no doubt with the gun returned by Howie.

As can be foreseen from A.O. Scott's review in the *New York Times*, critics are bound to find Big John's character, through Brian Cox's performance, as more interesting than that of Howie. Scott even goes to the extent of saying that "Cox has every charming nook and repellent cranny of his character's psyche so precisely mapped" that we "almost begin to identify with him." For Scott, *L.I.E.* "offers a rich, dark, bitter slice of contemporary life," but one that is compromised by the film's "arty embellishments."

—*Vivek Adarkar*

## CREDITS

**Big John Harrigan:** Brian Cox
**Howie Blitzer:** Paul Franklin Dano
**Gary Terrio:** Billy Kay
**Marty Blitzer:** Bruce Altman
**Kevin Cole:** James Costa
**Brian:** Tony Donnelly
**Scott:** Walter Masterson
**Guidance Counselor:** Marcia DeBonis
**Marty's Lawyer:** Adam LeFevre

**Origin:** USA
**Released:** 2001

**Production:** Rene Bastian, Linda Moran, Michael Cuesta; Alter Ego, Belladonna; released by Lot 47 Films
**Directed by:** Michael Cuesta
**Written by:** Michael Cuesta, Stephen M. Ryder, Gerald Cuesta
**Cinematography by:** Romeo Tirone
**Music by:** Pierre Foldes
**Sound:** David Alvarez
**Editing:** Eric Carlson, Kane Platt
**Costumes:** Daniel Glicker
**Production Design:** Elise Bennett
**MPAA rating:** NC-17
**Running time:** 97 minutes

## REVIEWS

*Boxoffice.* September, 2001, p. 140.
*Chicago Sun-Times Online.* September 21, 2001.
*Entertainment Weekly.* September 28, 2001, p. 52.
*Los Angeles Times Online.* September 28, 2001.
*New York Times Online.* April 6, 2001.
*New York Times Online.* September 16, 2001.
*Variety.* January 29, 2001, p. 52.
*Washington Post.* October 5, 2001, p. C5.

## QUOTES

Howie (Paul Franklin Dano) about the L.I.E.: "It's taken a lot of people and I hope it doesn't get me."

## TRIVIA

Debut director Michael Cuesta grew up in Dix Hills, which is located off Exit 52 on the Long Island Expressway.

## AWARDS AND NOMINATIONS

**Ind. Spirit 2002:** Debut Perf. (Dano).

# Lantana

*Love is the greatest mystery.*
—Movie tagline
*Sometimes love isn't enough.*
—Movie tagline

**Box Office:** $.3 million

Maybe there's something in Australia's water that's made the Down Under continent the setting for some of the most ominous, and truly mysterious, movies made in the last few decades. Films such as *Walkabout, Outback, Picnic at Hanging Rock,* and *A Cry in the Dark* all seemed to draw from the same well of brooding fatalism and creeping internal rot. The trend continues with Ray Lawrence's sinister *Lantana,* a multi-charactered Rubik's cube that switches the members of four marriages into various unhappy combinations before snapping into a final, but still far from settled, position.

The laugh-lines are turning into crow's feet on the faces of *Lantana*'s characters, a group of 40-somethings who are each drowning in their marriages. Fittingly, the movie opens with a bout of lovemaking between two people who don't really know each other: Leon Zat (Anthony LaPaglia), a detective with the Sydney police, and Jane (Rachael Blake), a student in the salsa dance class that Leon and his wife are enrolled in. Jane is looking for someone to fill the void created by her recent separation from her husband, but for Leon the fling is only a sad-hearted attempt to distract himself from his own marooned marriage. His wife Sonja (Kerry Armstrong) is herself trying to cope by seeing a psychiatrist on the sly, while the therapist she's seeing has her own problems. Dr. Valerie Somers (Barbara Hershey) is still recovering from the murder of her 11-year-old daughter two years earlier. She's written a book to help the process along, but the murder has all but dissolved her ties to her husband John (Geoffrey Rush), a law professor who's been emotionally flattened by the killing. Finally, as if in counterpoint to these three troubled unions, there exists a fourth, happier coupling that's about to be severely tested. Nik (Vince Colisomo) and Paula (Daniella Farinacci), Jane's next door neighbors, lead low-rent lives—Nik is unemployed, while Paula works as a nurse—but they share an earthy, genuine love for each other and their three small children.

*Lantana* comes at us like a lazy-Susan, offering up glances into the characters' domestic and professional lives in alternating scenes, and letting us watch as they intersect at their patchwork seams. But the couples are linked in ways that go beyond the mere circumstance of who knows whom. The relationships have all reached such a state that they reflect each other in subtle, indirect ways, so that when one character confides in another, the listener winces as if it's his own situation that's under discussion. Valerie, the therapist, has it worst of all. Not only must she sit still as Sonja pours out doubts about her loveless marriage, but she's also treating a gay patient named Patrick (Peter Phelps) whose main topic of conversation is the affair he's having with a married

man. The details fit Valerie's situation just well enough to plant the uneasy suspicion that John's dwindling sexual interest in her may be due to his having an affair, perhaps with another man—perhaps even with this fellow Patrick.

The first half of the movie belongs to Leon, if only because Anthony LaPaglia's quiet ferocity makes him the dominant figure. Leon's emotional quandary is chipping the patina of civilization from him, making him distant and hidebound in his private life and racist and violent in his professional one. In places Leon skirts dangerously close to being more of a playwright's conceit than a living human being. As conceived by Andrew Bovell (who adapted his own play for the screen), he's so starchy and stifled that he won't even remove his suit-jacket for the salsa class. It's an utterly false note whose wrongness is compounded by the fact that none of the other characters—not his wife, not his lover, not the dance instructor who's trying to get him to loosen up—ever take notice of it. Leon's also been saddled with a bad heart, a hackneyed symbol for what's ailing the story's characters. Such stale literary flourishes feel out of place in *Lantana*'s otherwise understated world, and in other hands they might've sunk both Leon and the film. But LaPaglia's stolid beefiness and pent-up acting style perfectly express the layers of Leon's agonized reserve; one can see the saner man trying to emerge from a countenance that's half blubber and half brick.

*Lantana*'s precipitating action doesn't occur until its halfway point, after we've been thoroughly immersed in the rhythms of its characters' lives. One night Valerie Somers takes a mysterious drive into the countryside—and simply vanishes from the face of the earth. The only clues are her stalled-out car and a cryptic emotion-laden message she leaves on her husband's answering machine. But a canny bit of sound-editing lets us know that at least one other character knows what happened that night, and when Leon is put in charge of the case, all of *Lantana*'s ironies begin percolating towards the surface. Bovell and Lawrence are content to let the four relationships strike resonant sparks off each other; the movie's one explicable theme might be that A.A. mantra of tentative hope, "One Day At A Time." The lantana bush, whose garish flowers hide a spiky, shadowy undergrowth (and a key piece of evidence), is an apt metaphor for the only half-acknowledged internal drives lying just beneath our outwardly placid surfaces.

*Lantana* is a true ensemble piece in which the players scale their performances to each other, and the evenness of the film's conception makes credible a plainly incredible world. It's a treacherous environment, rife with misunderstandings, shrouded motives, wild coincidences, desperately guarded secrets, and unsettling shocks to the system. A stranger whom one encounters in a bar turns out to be your lover's spouse, a casual invitation to coffee seems like an act of friendship one moment and a cold-hearted betrayal the next, a morning's jog is dramatically terminated by an out-of-the-blue collision. Intensely observed, with a melancholy ache that's all its own, *Lantana* explores the harsh surprises, unfulfilled yearnings, and unexpected rewards that come with being in love.

—*Tom Block*

## CREDITS

**Leon Zat:** Anthony LaPaglia
**Sonja Zat:** Kerry Armstrong
**John Knox:** Geoffrey Rush
**Dr. Valerie Somers:** Barbara Hershey
**Jane O'May:** Rachael Blake
**Nik D'Amato:** Vince Colosimo
**Patrick Phelan:** Peter Phelps
**Paula D'Amato:** Daniela Farinacci
**Claudia Weis:** Leah Purcell
**Pete O'May:** Glenn Robbins

**Origin:** Australia
**Released:** 2001
**Production:** Jan Chapman; Australian Film Finance Corp.; released by Lion's Gate Films
**Directed by:** Ray Lawrence
**Written by:** Andrew Bovell
**Cinematography by:** Mandy Walker
**Music by:** Paul Kelly
**Sound:** Andrew Plain
**Editing:** Karl Soderstein
**Art Direction:** Tony Campbell
**Costumes:** Margot Wilson
**Production Design:** Kim Buddee
**MPAA rating:** R
**Running time:** 120 minutes

## REVIEWS

*Boxoffice.* November, 2001, p. 131.
*Chicago Sun-Times Online.* January 18, 2002.
*Entertainment Weekly.* January 11, 2002, p. 47.
*Hollywood Reporter.* August 28, 2001, p. 18.
*Los Angeles Times Online.* December 14, 2001.
*New York Times Online.* November 4, 2001.
*New York Times Online.* December 14, 2001.
*Premiere.* January, 2002, p. 42.
*Variety.* June 18, 2001, p. 17.
*Washington Post.* January 25, 2002, p. WE38.

## TRIVIA

Andrew Bovell expanded his play *Speaking in Tongues* for his screenplay adaptation.

## AWARDS AND NOMINATIONS

**Australian Film Inst. 2001:** Actor (LaPaglia), Actress (Armstrong), Adapt. Screenplay, Director (Lawrence), Film, Support. Actor (Colosimo), Support. Actress (Blake).

# Lara Croft: Tomb Raider (Tomb Raider)

*Who Is Lara Croft?*
—Movie tagline
*Born into wealth. Groomed by the elite. Trained for combat.*
—Movie tagline

 **Box Office:** $131.2 million

One of the most hotly anticipated movies of the summer of 2001 was *Lara Croft: Tomb Raider*. So great was the anticipation, even the fact that the movie wasn't particularly good was not enough to kill the movie at the boxoffice. Why was *Tomb Raider* such a hot commodity? It had several marketing pluses. For one thing, it had a built-in audience. This audience consisted primarily of teenage boys, the same demographic group that movie makers and marketers fall all over themselves to impress. These hormonally-charged up guys knew of the Lara Croft character from the "Tomb Raider" video game that came out on Playstation in the early 1990s. The title quickly became one of Sony's top-selling games. Since a new edition of the comes out almost every year, Croft has become the favorite virtual babe in video land. It doesn't hurt that Ms. Croft has impossibly large mammaries and full, soulful lips.

In a nice bit of luck for the filmmakers, Angelina Jolie happens to look shockingly like Croft, right down to the ability to wear skin tight leather shorts without looking like a discard from the Village People. (Jolie has since admitted that a lot of her curvaceousness is due to a miraculously engineered padded bra.) In another nice touch, Jolie also happens to be an excellent actress, one of the top in her generation. That doesn't end up coming into play in *Tomb Raider*, but it's good to know that if the script had called for it, Jolie could have done some acting.

The "real" Croft, that is the one in the game, was a girl raised in luxury. Her father was a Lord who sent his beloved daughter to the most exclusive schools in the world. Her hobby is looking for adventure. In the film, the elements of wealth and love of adventure are still there, mostly at the same time. When the film begins, Croft is running around her eighty-plus room mansion (now, that is a mansion) shooting guns at scary mechanical monsters. The monsters are operated by Bryce (Noah Taylor) whose job seems to be as Croft's resident nerd. He lives in a trailer on her property (his choice, since Croft certainly has the room to put him up) and spends his time fiddling with mechanical doodads. The other main man in Croft's life is her butler, Hillary (Chris Barrie), who does stuff like try to get her to act more feminine. After Croft comes out of the shower buck naked, he says, "A lady should be modest." "Yes," purrs Croft. "A LADY should be modest," then throws her towel to the floor.

Because the idea of Croft staying at home shooting up robots all the time would be too plotless, even for an action movie based on a video game, there is indeed a story and it is quite a doozy. Doozy, in this case, is not a good thing. The story is somewhat incomprehensible, but we'll make a stab at it.

Croft's quest begins one night when she hears a strange ticking noise coming from under the stairs. (Besides a lack of modesty, Croft seems to have bionic hearing.) She, naturally, starts ripping apart the stairs with her bare hands to see what's inside. It turns out to be an old clock that her now-dead father, Lord Croft (Jon Voight, Jolie's real life father) had planted for her years before. Why he hid such a big secret in the staircase instead of just giving it to her must be some family tradition or something. The clock contains a quote that leads to a note from dad. It seems that the planets are all going to line up to create an eclipse (never mind that planets don't need to be involved with eclipses), an event that only happens once every 5000 years. At that time, there will be the opportunity for humans to control time. Whoever is able to find two pieces of an ancient all-seeing eye artifact and put them together at exactly the moment that the eclipse happens will be the master, or mistress, or time.

Naturally someone bad wants this power. In this case it's the Illuminati, a group of corporate overlords headed by Manfred Powell (Iain Glen), who already run just about everything else in the country. The fact that they also need to control time is just plain greedy, but then that's how these overlord types operate.

Since the artifacts are spread out in two places, it gives director Simon West a chance to shoot some exotic settings, from the rain forests of Cambodia's Angkor Wat to the icy fields of Siberia (although Iceland is Siberia's stand-in). With the exotic settings, the feisty heroine and the time deadline, this all seems like it would be very exciting, but it isn't. West doesn't seem to have any idea of how to build dramatic tension. For example, once Croft breaks into an ancient tomb in the rain forest, she has to battle giant rock statues that have come to life. It's an exciting premise, to be sure. But these creatures crumple up with one or two shots from Croft's gun. Sure there's a lot of these guys trying to attack Croft and her rival tomb raiders, but no one ever seems in any real peril.

The rest of the action in the film suffers from the same malaise. Lara beats up a bunch of masked assassins who break into her house while she is suspended in her grand entrance hallway on a bungee cord (bungee cord hanging is the kind of thing Croft does to wind down at night). Bach's "Concerto in F Minor" plays while Croft twists and turns, knocking off the bad guys one by one. With tedious regularity, the bad guys attack her one by one, instead of charging in as a group. (Perhaps they could have benefitted from an organizer who could have orchestrated a better plan of attack.)

It's a shame that West couldn't come through with the action sequences because he had all the elements at his fingertips. Jolie is certainly game to be an action hero, the story was workable enough, and West had the budget for some cool special effects, but West didn't have the ability to make it all come together.

The casting of the film is similar to the film itself—all promise, no payoff. Jolie doesn't get to use any of her daunting acting skills. She's believable as a cocky adventuress, but the movie doesn't have any fun with her character or let her have any personality traits beyond the aforementioned cockiness and adventurousness. In fact, Croft seems kind of weird. What person would spend most of their time in their creepy mansion, swinging alone from the ceiling on a bungee cord? She does, however, get the chance to sport a nifty English accent. As Croft's nerd, Taylor, who was in *Shine*, wastes his talent on a character that's more of a sketch than a person. Voight brings a sense of heavy drama to his role as the late father, but it's all very heavy-handed with lines like, "You were not ready to hear such things."

*Tomb Raider* had so much jiggling cleavage, that it looked like the 1970s on *Three's Company*. Consequently, many reviewers focused on this aspect. One reviewer even complained because the gawking wasn't good enough for him—apparently, he wanted to see some uncovered cleavage. Others managed to focus on other thing besides the D-cups. Roger Ebert of the *Chicago Sun-Times* wrote: "Since I had no idea what was going to happen, should happen, shouldn't happen, or what it meant if it did happen, I could hardly be expected to care. But did I grin with delight at the absurdity of it all? You betcha." The *Toronto Star*'s

Peter Howell said: "*Tomb Raider*'s preoccupation with time is puzzling, given the movie's leisurely pace. It only serves to make us check our watches, or to reach out for invisible game controllers to see if we can speed up the action a little." Cary Darling of the *Miami Herald* wrote: "In the end, Croft loses to the most dangerous villain of them all: mediocrity."

—*Jill Hamilton*

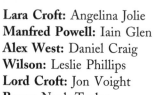

## CREDITS

**Lara Croft:** Angelina Jolie
**Manfred Powell:** Iain Glen
**Alex West:** Daniel Craig
**Wilson:** Leslie Phillips
**Lord Croft:** Jon Voight
**Bryce:** Noah Taylor
**Distinguished Gentleman:** Richard Johnson
**Mr. Pimms:** Julian Rhind-Tutt
**Hillary:** Chris (Christopher) Barrie

**Origin:** USA
**Released:** 2001
**Production:** Lawrence Gordon, Lloyd Levin, Colin Wilson; Mutual Film Corporation; released by Paramount Pictures
**Directed by:** Simon West
**Written by:** Patrick Massett, John Zinman
**Cinematography by:** Peter Menzies Jr.
**Music by:** Graeme Revell
**Sound:** Chris Munro
**Music Supervisor:** Peter Afterman
**Editing:** Dallas S. Puett, Glen Scantlebury
**Costumes:** Lindy Hemming
**Production Design:** Kirk M. Petruccelli
**MPAA rating:** PG-13
**Running time:** 96 minutes

## REVIEWS

*Boxoffice.* May, 2001, p. 27.
*Boxoffice.* August, 2001, p. 59.
*Chicago Sun-Times Online.* June 15, 2001.
*Entertainment Weekly.* June 29, 2001, p. 114.
*Los Angeles Times Online.* June 15, 2001.
*New York Times Online.* June 15, 2001.
*People.* July 2, 2001, p. 30.
*Rolling Stone.* June 19, 2001, p. 55.
*Sight and Sound.* August, 2001, p. 50.
*USA Today Online.* June 15, 2001.
*Variety.* June 18, 2001, p. 17.
*Washington Post Online.* June 15, 2001.

## QUOTES

Lara Croft (Angelina Jolie): "But you might try to kill me." Manfred Powell (Iain Glen): "I'm not going to kill you." Lara: "I said you'd try."

## TRIVIA

Lara Croft is the first female character to star in her own action videogame series, which debuted in 1996 and currently consists of five *Tomb Raider* games.

# The Last Castle

*No castle can have two kings.*
—Movie tagline

**Box Office:** $18.2 million

According to General Irwin (Robert Redford), there are four things a castle must have: location (high ground), protection (big walls), a garrison (men trained to kill), and a flag. The military correction facility to which General Irwin suddenly finds himself confined has all four. But as he goes on, "the only difference between this castle and the rest is that they were built to keep people out and this one was built to keep people in."

This intelligent analysis is the first clue the viewer has that perhaps General Irwin is not a typical military miscreant. In fact, when the prison's commander, Colonel Winter (James Gandolfini), is told of Irwin's imminent arrival, he becomes a bit flustered and not so subtly indicates that the army should be naming a base after the three star general not throwing him in prison. "At the war college his very name was spoken with reverence," says Winter.

Irwin's sudden arrival is due to the fact that he has just pled guilty to his crime and has been sentenced to 10 years in prison. As to what exactly that crime is, audiences will have to wait until the middle of the movie to find out, but right from the start we just know it must actually be a noble deed that went wrong.

On the other hand, Colonel Winter has probably never seen a day of combat in his life. He is a tin soldier ensconced in a cushy position of command where he surrounds himself with old guns and bullets and other souvenirs of past wars which he constantly cleans and polishes to the strains of classical music. His is a sterile "war" in which his enemy, the prisoners, are totally surrounded by his marksmen guards who, although they can shoot only rubber bullets at the men, nonetheless conveniently manage to hit particularly problematic prisoners in the head and kill them. One suspects this is on Winter's orders.

Consequently the meeting between the heroic Irwin and the empty Winter does not go smoothly. Especially when Winter overhears Irwin's condemning remarks over Winter's prized collection of military artifacts, "Any man with a collection like this has never set foot on a battlefield." It is not a good idea to get on Winter's bad side, but then again, what can Winter do to a three star General who everyone still believes is a hero?

No sooner does Irwin find himself in the prison's general population than he is set upon by the men who want him to help them get better treatment from Winter. They tell him about the substandard services . . . and the rubber bullets, but Irwin is a man who just wants to serve his time and go home and get to know the grandson and daughter he barely knows. "Gentlemen, I'm done. I'm not fighting anyone any more," he tells them, but one just knows that something will eventually change his mind.

At first Irwin just watches. He sees things like Winter purposely inciting fights between the men by putting out only one basket ball just so he can watch the "battle" from the picture window of his office high above the courtyard. He sees punishments that far exceed what is allowed by the military code such as when the slow Aguilar (Clifton Collins, Jr.), who insisted on saluting Irwin even though saluting is strictly forbidden in prison, is forced to stand at attention and saluting day and night in the rain. Then, when one guard is about to beat Aguilar, Irwin restrains him and says, "you're better than that." However, touching a guard wins Irwin his own form of Winter punishment.

In the prison courtyard is a wall from the original 1870 prison that stood on the site. Winter is forcing the men to rebuild the wall with original stones. Irwin must move the 25 pound rocks from one pile to another and when he's done, move them back. It is during this punishment that we see Irwin's scarred back, electrical burns from his six years as a POW in Hanoi. And when Irwin successfully completes Winter's punishment, Winter's goal of humiliating the general is turned on its head because he has become even more of a hero to his fellow prisoners.

Winter tries to reason with Irwin, pointing out how evil the men under his charge are, telling him about how Aguilar took a claw hammer to his platoon leader and how seeing the worst in his men makes his job easier, but Irwin refuses to succumb to this sophistry. He, instead, views the prisoners as military men and tries to see the best in them. Even Winter's sees the effects of this but sums up his own view with, "He's offering them self-respect. He can have their hearts and minds as long as we have them by the balls."

Now Winter tries to rid himself of the annoying Irwin by requesting his transfer to a psychiatric facility. He appeals to a higher authority, General Wheeler (Delroy Lindo), who is a friend of Irwin's. But while Wheeler is investigating, Winter receives a note indicating that Wheeler will be taken prisoner at 12:10. It isn't true, but when Winter overreacts at precisely that moment, Wheeler is disgusted and tells him that if one more prisoner is killed under his command then he is through. Winter's entire career is now on the line because of Irwin and we have basically been telegraphed what will have to happen before the movie is over.

What happens next is a rousing, fast-paced, exciting and suspenseful finale as Irwin marshals his "army" to take control of the prison away from Winter. Audiences cheer as rocks are thrown through Winter's window, they applaud as a helicopter is brought down and gasp when they see the captured flag flying at the end. But after all this emotional involvement, after we've left the theater, we begin to have doubts. Where on earth did that trebuchet (a form of catapult) come from that throws those rocks through Winter's window? Hey, weren't the soldiers in that helicopter basically innocent people? Just who is the good guy here and who's the bad guy? Isn't Irwin just as manipulative as Winter?

Suddenly a movie that had been completely engrossing as it was being experienced begins to unravel as it is analyzed after the fact. Suddenly a movie that had seemed clearly black and white is now shades of ambiguous grey. And suddenly we're a bit more ambivalent about how we felt about who we perceived as the good guys. What had been a dramatic and involving story dissolves into one where we begin to speculate about what it was we really experienced. Whether or not screenwriter Graham Yost, who is currently winning acclaim for his writing on HBO's 10-part series *Band of Brothers,* did this on purpose is questionable. Did he want to manipulate the audience, appealing to our emotions over our sense of logic? And this is a question that should also be asked of director Rod Lurie wrote who also and directed and wrote last year's *The Contender.* A West Point graduate himself Lurie has shown that he has a talent for dramatic confrontations between interesting and opposite characters, but did he have to hit us over the head with the symbolism?

It begins innocently enough, the second-rate Winter is listening to the second-rate Salieri on his phonograph while we all await the arrival of the Mozart/Irwin character. Salutes are about respect, therefore salutes cannot be allowed, therefore the men invent a pseudo-salute as they regain their self-respect. There are two walls built in the prison courtyard, a tettering, slipshod one that belongs to Colonel Winter which will be torn down and rebuilt better than ever by the men who take possession of and claim it along with their own self respect. Of course when it is completed, Winter has no choice but to bulldoze it. Then there is the fact that the entire plot is an elaborate chess game with each side trying to negate the other side's king and claim the castle as their own, so obviously we have to see Irwin playing an excellent game of chess while in prison. And finally there is the flag. Capturing the other side's flag is the final sign of victory. Irwin plans on taking over the prison and sending Winter's prized flag up the flagpole upside down, the international sign of distress, but how distressed are the prisoners at the end when they have successfully redeemed themselves and captured the castle?

If it weren't for some sharp performances, one might also wonder if the main characters, too, aren't a little too transparent. Redford, obviously, is always Redford. He brings his own persona to any character and it works in good stead here. His own charisma and his natural, commanding presence instantly establish Irwin's character. No, Irwin has not been unjustly imprisoned—that is never an issue—but we know Irwin was a leader and a hero because that's how we have come to perceive Redford.

James Gandolfini, on the other hand, comes to most viewers solely as the incarnation of Tony Soprano. Here his performance is much more nuanced. His slightly lisping Winter lies coiled like a rattlesnake, and at first we're not sure if he's been defanged or not. There is no doubt that he is the villain of the movie, but as played by Gandolfini, we are also hit by hints of pity for the man who can only dream of being a hero. That nervous smile that flits across his face lets us know that here is a man who is struggling to maintain what little power and dignity he has managed to carve out of his drab military career.

In the end, *The Last Castle* ends up being *Cool Hand Luke* meets *Patton* with a little bit of *Brubaker* thrown in for good measure. It is not a typical prison movie centering on an escape plot, *The Last Castle* is about control. Control of power and control over one's own life. It is a film about honor and leadership and courage and mostly about redemption as each character, except Winter, rises to the occasion and performs his own special act of courage or heroism that will lead them to personal salvation.

What's odd is that all these high goals come off as some kind of distorted patriotism as is evidenced by the boldly colorful flag flying over the gray prison at the end of the film. However, upon thinking about the whole story one may end up feeling morally of two minds about the movie. Because when one thinks about it, we end up cheering for redeemed men who are basically criminals who are fighting against the military establishment who in the wake of September 11th are the good guys but who in this particular case just happen to be personified by one unjust man. And where in the heck DID that trebuchet come from?

—*Beverley Bare Buehrer*

## CREDITS

**General Irwin:** Robert Redford
**Colonel Winter:** James Gandolfini
**Yates:** Mark Ruffalo
**General Wheeler:** Delroy Lindo
**Captain Peretz:** Steve (Stephen) Burton
**Dellwo:** Paul Calderon
**Duffy:** Samuel Ball
**Aguilar:** Clifton (Gonzalez) Collins Jr.
**Doc:** Frank Military
**Thumper:** George W. Scott
**Beaupre:** Brian Goodman
**Enrique:** Michael Irby
**Sgt. McLaren:** Maurice Bullard
**Cutbush:** Jeremy Childs

**Origin:** USA
**Released:** 2001
**Production:** Robert Lawrence; released by Dreamworks Pictures
**Directed by:** Rod Lurie
**Written by:** Graham Yost, David Scarpa
**Cinematography by:** Shelly Johnson
**Music by:** Jerry Goldsmith
**Editing:** Michael Jablow, Kevin Stitt
**Art Direction:** Lawrence A. Hubbs
**Costumes:** Ha Nguyen
**Production Design:** Kirk M. Petruccelli
**MPAA rating:** R
**Running time:** 133 minutes

## REVIEWS

*Boxoffice.* December, 2001, p. 60.
*Chicago Sun-Times Online.* October 19, 2001.
*Chicago Tribune Online.* October 19, 2001.
*Detroit Free Press.* October 14, 2001, p. 8G.
*Entertainment Weekly.* October 26, 2001, p. 92.
*Hollywood Reporter Online.* October 19, 2001.
*Los Angeles Times Online.* October 19, 2001.
*New York Post Online.* October 19, 2001.
*New York Times Online.* October 19, 2001.
*People.* October 29, 2001, p. 42.
*USA Today Online.* October 18, 2001.
*Washington Post.* October 19, 2001, p. C1.

## QUOTES

Col. Winter (James Gandolfini): "Do you see how easy it is to manipulate men? Someone should write a paper on it."

The prison used in the film is the historic Tennessee State Penitentiary, which operated from 1898 to 1992.

# Last Resort

Many films have been produced without a standard screenplay and some films, such as the infamous *La Dolce Vita,* were written literally on the set. While in the hands of a masterful director and a troupe of professional actors, cinema verite style features can engage viewers with stark realism and authentic characters. One only needs to look at the oeuvre of American filmmaker John Cassavetes or to the Iranian filmmaker Abbas Kiarostami's body of cinematic work. But if the proper elements aren't in place, actors wax clichès and viewers' enthusiasm sours because the story they're watching appears to be too close to reality. Imagine sitting on a bus listening to various riders' cell phone conversations—boring at best.

Russian émigré Pawel Pavlikovski successfully blended documentary-type filmmaking with a fictional love story, thus avoiding the pitfalls of both approaches. Of course, Pavlikovski has written both documentary and fictional features prior to shooting his latest release *Last Resort.* Even the film's subject matter—revolving around young Russian Tanya (Dina Korzun) who drags her 10-year-old son Artiom (Artiom Strelnikov) to England so that she can marry her English fiancee—comes close to home for the director. According to the director, the story itself has autobiographical roots but, "The other element, which helped me imagine the story, was the notion of a dead-end seaside resort, a dumping ground for unwanted people (foreign and native) from which there is no escape."

Tanya appears to be a dreamer which, like three generations of women before her, has led her to make a series of mistakes, including two divorces. Upon arriving in England, she learns that her English fiancee has jilted her. Out of desperation, Tanya applies for refugee status, leading to a type of internment where she and her son are stripped of their passports and forced to live in a filthy apartment block with other refugees. When they try to escape and head to London where the fiancee allegedly awaits, immigration officials capture Tanya and Artiom and return them to the apartment building where they're told they'll have to reside for the next 18 months or until their paperwork is processed. The second time mother and son try to escape, they are given a warning that if they're caught escaping again, they will end up in a prison cell.

Although Tanya finds her bleak seaside surroundings unbearable, her level-headed son and newly found friend Alfie (Paddy Considine) do their best to add cheer to the distraught Tanya's life. Alfie and Artiom paint the apartment and add homey touches. Alfie also acts as Tanya's protector and confidant while he pines for her. But Artiom has his own demons with which to deal and he has joined a gang of kids that drink, smoke, and steal for a living. Meanwhile, Tanya spins her wheels trying to earn much-needed cash for plane tickets. She fails to sell dead foxes to a clothier; lacking a work permit, she cannot work at the local café; then, she donates blood in exchange for a few dollars. Finally, out of desperation, Tanya ends up agreeing to perform a cheesy sexual act for Internet pornographer Les (played by the real-life pornographer Lindsey Honey) because he promises Tanya that the work is easy and pays $200 to $350 pounds a night. But in the end, she just can't go through with the naughty school-girl act.

The pornographer returns to taunt Tanya and Alfie is enraged by what she's done, as is Artiom, who runs away. While Tanya searches for her son, Alfie visits the pornographer and badly beats him, thus leading to Tanya, Artiom, and Alfie escaping by a stolen boat. However, when given the choice to stay in England with Alfie or returning to Russia, Tanya chooses the latter and accepts full responsibility for past mistakes. Again, we return to the airport where Tanya and Artiom embark on their return trip to Russia, leaving their nightmare behind them.

Pavlikovski creates a noir setting emphasizing a gray, drizzly English seaside complete with a semi-abandoned carnival setting. Composer Max de Wardner's adds discordant carnival music while embellishing a hollow atmosphere. Viewers are immersed in a drama with no means of escape and feel the characters' confinement. Korzun blends a touch of naiveté with verve in her portrayal of Tanya, which compliments Considine's misfit Alfie. But as the camera studies Korzun's face, we realize it's her film and viewers will remember her story for a long time.

—*Patty-Lynne Herlevi*

**Tanya:** Dina Korzun
**Artiom:** Artiom Strelnikov
**Alfie:** Paddy Considine
**Les:** Lindsey Honey
**Immigration officer:** Perry Benson
**Katie:** Katie Drinkwater

**Origin:** Great Britain
**Released:** 2000

**Production:** Ruth Caleb; BBC Films; released by
Shooting Gallery
**Directed by:** Pawel Pawlikowski
**Written by:** Pawel Pawlikowski, Rowan Joffe
**Cinematography by:** Ryszard Lenczewski
**Music by:** Max de Wardener, Rowan Oliver
**Sound:** John Pearson
**Editing:** David Charap
**Costumes:** Julian Day
**Production Design:** Tom Bowyer
**MPAA rating:** Unrated
**Running time:** 76 minutes

## REVIEWS

*Boxoffice.* April, 2001, p. 237.
*Chicago Sun-Times Online.* February 23, 2001.
*Entertainment Weekly.* March 9, 2001, p. 55.
*New York Times Online.* February 23, 2001.
*People.* March 5, 2001, p. 39.
*Sight and Sound.* March, 2001, p. 16.
*Washington Post Online.* February 23, 2001.

## QUOTES

Tanya (Dina Korzun): "I have to stop dreaming. I've been dreaming all my life."

## TRIVIA

Filmed on location in Margate, England.

# The Law of Enclosures

Set in the bleak oil fields of Sarnia, Ontario as images of scud missiles from the Gulf War ironically appear on Canadian television sets, John Greyson's *The Law of Enclosures* explores the disintegration of human relations. Lamenting violins further emphasize the characters' bleak surroundings and utter hopelessness while two parallel stories, the first involving a youthful love and the second involving an older couple burdened with years of bitterness, emerge. Greyson's screenplay, adapted from Dale Peck's novel, lands somewhere close to Atom Egoyan's cinema of everyday stoics, but doesn't provide the cathartic conclusion of an Egoyan film. Greyson's film provides us with an intriguing narrative structure by showing the characters'

present and future situations side by side, but unfortunately *The Law of Enclosures* proves to be a sleeper.

As the film opens we see a blonde girl snapping a photograph of a red deer that later appears in the town's newspaper. Next, we see a blonde woman burying herself in the sand and counting down numbers and a montage of several haunting images. Then, we see a young Beatrice (Sarah Polley) waiting for a prescription at a local pharmacy as she sits next to the older Bea (Diane Ladd), who also waits for a prescription. After the young Beatrice picks up her prescription, she notices a young man (Brendan Fletcher) with a strange bump on the back of his head. A friend mentions to Beatrice that the young man is gay and dying of AIDS. Intrigued by this sad story, Beatrice stalks Henry.

Meanwhile, the older versions of Henry, who's now called Hank (Sean McCann), and Beatrice quarrel as they drive to visit friends who live in the woods. Hank and Bea both seem to be suffering from physical illnesses and also from the grief they caused each other in the past as they bicker over a cup of coffee that Hank refuses to drink because he would rather just hold the warmth in his hands. Cut back to the younger Beatrice as she confides to Henry that she knows that he's gay and dying of AIDS. Rebuffed and insulted, Henry lashes out at Beatrice and explains to her that he's not gay and he's not dying of AIDS. Henry is awaiting surgery for a brain tumor, which he might not survive, and in a sense, Henry is bitterly preparing for his death.

However, Henry does survive the surgery, then marries the co-dependent Beatrice. Given a new lease on life, Henry begins drinking, carousing, and he has an affair behind Beatrice's back. Beatrice, in turn, learns that she's pregnant—only to miscarry the same night that Henry and his drunken buddies hit a red deer with their truck. And yes, the red deer is significant because the young girl shown at the film's opening sequence was Beatrice as a child. So the deterioration of a marriage begins, which later leads to an estranged marriage between two bitter foes who are building a retirement home in the woods. However, Greyson does allow us a glimmer of hope since the duo rekindle their love for each other. That is, until Hank is shot and killed by a hunter who was pursuing a red deer.

Greyson could take the prize of creating truly depressing cinema away from Ingmar Bergman with *The Law of Enclosures.* Even though his adapted story portrays several human lives, the story lacks humanity and it becomes increasingly difficult to relate to a simpering woman who's turned on by a man who's dying of cancer. We never learn why she has this obsession as we watch her sniffing a bandanna that Henry dropped on a parking lot while she masturbates. In fact, we never learn anything about any of the characters' motivations as if they all live in a vacuum-sealed compartment of the present.

For the most part, *The Law of Enclosures* boasts a talented cast, with the strongest performances coming from Diane Ladd and Sean McCann. Polley comes across as annoying with her girlish whispers and sad doe-eyed expression and Fletcher appears uncomfortable as he renders his clichèd character. While *The Law of Enclosures* won't break Greyson's film career neither will it bring him success. Greyson has works well with an alternative narrative structure, but his humorless film begs to be ignored. 🎬

—*Patty-Lynne Herlevi*

# The Left Hand Side of the Fridge (La Moitie Gauche du Frigo)

## CREDITS

**Beatrice:** Sarah Polley
**Henry:** Brendan Fletcher
**Bea:** Diane Ladd
**Hank:** Sean McCann
**Myra:** Shirley Douglas
**Stan:** Victor Cowie
**Myrah:** Kristen Thompson
**Stanley:** Rob Stefaniuk

**Origin:** Canada
**Released:** 2001
**Production:** John Greyson, Damon D'Oliveira, Phyllis Laing; Pluck Inc., Buffalo Gals Pictures; released by Alliance Atlantis
**Directed by:** John Greyson
**Written by:** John Greyson
**Cinematography by:** Kim Derko
**Music by:** Don Pyle, Andrew Zealley
**Sound:** Jane Tattersall
**Editing:** Michael Munn
**Costumes:** Charlotte Penner
**Production Design:** Rejean Labrie
**MPAA rating:** Unrated
**Running time:** 105 minutes

## REVIEWS

*Exclaim! Online.* September 29, 2000.
*eye Weely Online.* March 22, 2001.
*Variety.* October 2, 2000, p. 25.
*Winnipeg Sun Online.* March 3, 2001.

## AWARDS AND NOMINATIONS

**Genie 2001:** Actor (Fletcher)
**Nomination:**
**Genie 2001:** Actress (Polley), Score.

When renowned Quebecois auteur Robert Lepage handed emerging filmmaker Philippe Falardeau the Claude Jutra Award (which recognizes the special achievement of a Canadian director for their first theatrical feature) at the 2000 Genie Awards, he described Falardeau as "a member of the new wave of Quebecois directors shaking up Quebec cinema." Lepage also described Falardeau's film about a socially conscious filmmaker documenting his apartment mate's job search as a "fresh take on the fake documentary." However, coming at a time of mass globalization, NAFTA policies, and the fear felt by the disenfranchised labor force, Falardeau's faux documentary takes a revealing gaze at current events.

Although Falardeau claims that when he started his film project he was on a mission to portray the economic nonsense that provoked exclusion and unemployment, he soon had to lower his sights after the unemployment rate descended in Quebec. "Through the unemployment and social responsibility themes, I then wanted to talk about our relation with work. Each one of the characters portrays a way to approach work, as a means of subsistence but, most of all, as a self-expression medium. . . . How many among us really like their work?" With the threat of future unemployment related to FTAA policies and protested by millions of North Americans in Quebec City, people might learn to love the jobs they hate or love unemployment.

In an April, 2001 poll of Canadian citizens 4.4 million said that they would attend the FTAA protest in Quebec City if possible. Many of those polled feared that they would lose their jobs due to corporations moving their factories to third world countries that fall into the expanded free trade zone. While Falardeau's *The Left Hand Side of the Fridge* focuses on the problems of globalization and social consciousness that come with choosing politically correct employment, anyone familiar with free trade agreements will make the connection between the film's message of politics as usual.

After mechanical engineer Christophe (Paul Ahmarani) voluntarily leaves his job due to management problems, his apartment mate, theatrical director Stèphane (Stèphane Demers), decides to produce a documentary which revolves around Christophe's job search. But soon Stèphane's political agenda conflicts with Christophe's desire to find a job that matches his skill level and interests. Soon Christophe wonders why he ever agreed to star in his friend's documentary. Stèphane proves to be a thorough filmmaker, filming every second of Christophe's life, including Christophe's battles with his bank, selling his possessions, career counseling sessions, and an appeal session with the employment office. And of course, Stèphane shows up with his camera and sound recordist at Christophe's interviews, thus assuring that the annoyed employers won't hire Christophe.

As Christophe's job search stretches to four months, his hopes of finding suitable employment diminish and he grows anxious. He adopts a diet of carrot and apple juice along with curried popcorn while Stèphane lives lavishly off of his film grant funds. The depressed Christophe tells Stèphane "I feel like I'm in *The Truman Show*" as the camera follows him every step of the way. Finally, when Christophe does accept a temporary assignment that would allow him to work his way out of debt, his social activist apartment mate sabotages his opportunity. Christophe finally ends the documentary and moves to British Columbia where he joins a jazz group.

Recalling Michael Moore's films and "reality" television, *The Left Hand Side of the Fridge* has garnered praise from Quebec film critics. *Hour Magazine* described Falardeau's film as "A small wonder . . . wry and incisive." *The Montreal Gazette* called Philippe Falardeau "one of the most promising young Quebec film-makers." Similar to Shaya Mercer's documentary *Trade Off* or Ken Loach's *Bread and Roses*, *The Left Hand Side of the Fridge* reminds us of our current status quo and machinations behind the economy.

—*Patty-Lynne Herlevi*

## CREDITS

**Christophe:** Paul Ahmarani
**Stephane:** Stephane Demers
**Odile:** Genevieve Neron
**Philippe:** Jules Philippe
**Christine:** Alexandrine Agostini
**Marie-Helene:** Marie-Andree Corneille

**Origin:** Canada
**Language:** French
**Released:** 2000
**Production:** Luc Dery, Josee Roberge; Telefilm Canada, Quatre Par Quatre Films Inc.; released by Film Tonic
**Directed by:** Philippe Falardeau
**Written by:** Philippe Falardeau
**Cinematography by:** Josee Deshaies
**Sound:** Sylvain Bellemare

**Editing:** Sophie Leblond
**Production Design:** Andre-Line Beauparlant
**MPAA rating:** PG
**Running time:** 90 minutes

## REVIEWS

*Toronto Sun Online.* March 2, 2001.

## QUOTES

Christophe (Paul Ahmarani): "Integrity has its limits."

# Legally Blonde

*This summer go blonde!*
—Movie tagline

 **Box Office:** $96.5 million

In the biting satire *Election*, Reese Witherspoon was devastating as Tracy Flick, an overachieving, self-promoting candidate for student-body president—a relentlessly perky popularity queen destined to succeed in life not on merit, but on sheer will power. In *Legally Blonde*, Witherspoon plays Elle Woods, a pampered sorority queen and southern California *Cosmo* girl who also seems destined for big things—until her rich, highly pedigreed East Coast boyfriend, Warner (Matthew Davis), who has political ambitions, dumps her for a more serious, classier model, a "Jackie, not a Marilyn."

Witherspoon, a prodigious comic and dramatic talent who richly deserves the star boost the heavily promoted *Legally Blonde* gave her, is not the problem with this loopy boxoffice hit. Witherspoon showed her mettle playing smart white trash in the unheralded *Freeway* and a sex-crazed teenager in *Pleasantville*. Witherspoon has a wide range, but of late she keeps landing in roles that spotlight her hilarious send-up of various kinds of traditional femininity. The problem with *Blonde* is that the Australian director Robert Luketic doesn't know what to do with Witherspoon's well-sculpted comic character. In addition, Luketic is saddled with a sometimes witty but often ridiculous script by Karen McCullah Lutz and Kirsten Smith, based on a book by Amanda Brown. The script is both preposterous and pompous.

Like her character in *Election*, Witherspoon's Elle Woods has ambition and personality to spare—and sees the world as easily conquered with a smile. But whereas Tracy Flick was portrayed as a pompous snit undeserving of the rewards that society will keep sending her way, Woods is scripted as the victim of society's prejudice against blondes as brainless bimbos. When her boyfriend dumps her, we're supposed to feel her sense of outrage, because she expects marriage as part of her entitlement.

At first, *Legally Blonde* is merely outrageous. Elle inhabits a fluffy fantasy world filled with breast-augmented, manicure-addicted, air-headed throwbacks to a type of femininity that was supposed to have collapsed long ago from its own weightlessness. She and her sorority sisters are heavy into pink outfits, lip liner and glamour magazines, and look forward to a life of shopping, sipping drinks by the pool, and attaching themselves to the arms of rich, handsome husbands. The movie has some easy fun at their expense, not a difficult task since these women are flimsy caricatures.

*Legally Blonde*, however, wants to have it both ways. While making fun of dumb blondes, it's out to demonstrate that blondes aren't really empty vessels—as if anyone still thought so. The movie has a wafer-thin premise that proceeds to crumble as its pretensions grow. It's asking a lot to sympathize with Elle as a victim—to believe that it's society's low expectations that have forced her to become brainless, and that, given half a chance, she can overcome her beauty handicap and tap a wellspring of hidden intelligence.

Luketic doesn't handle the material deftly; he telegraphs every new plot development, so that it is patently obvious where everything is headed. Witherspoon does her best to salvage a corny, clumsy and only occasionally witty script. She gets a little bit of help from Jennifer Coolidge, who plays her new lower-class friend Paulette, but not much from anyone else in a cast that is mostly window-dressing.

When Warner Huntington III cruelly dumps her on the night that Elle expected him to propose marriage to her, Elle goes into the typical junk-food-eating, TV-watching funk that such movies offer for their spurned female characters. Then a light bulb goes off in her head and she decides to become the kind of woman Warner wants by applying to Harvard Law School. On the strength of her 4.0 grade point average in college (major: fashion merchandising), an inexplicably high score on the law school admissions test, and an hilarious video resume (which features her spouting legalistic platitudes in a bikini), Elle is admitted by a panel of overwhelmed and flabbergasted admissions officers; we can assume their motives are partly prurient. (The video is the film's funniest sequence; to demonstrate her ability to employ legal terms, Elle tells a wolf-whistling passer-by: "I object!")

This major plot hurdle clumsily overcome, Elle arrives at Harvard, where the film's tongue-in-cheek attitude turns droopy. She is humiliated by teachers, ridiculed by her classmates, and deflated when she discovers Warner is already engaged to his prep school beau, Vivian Kensington (Selma Blair), a dark-haired, mean-spirited, and smug paragon of privilege and brains. Heartbroken, Elle pours out her sorrows to her manicurist, Paulette, who has also been dumped by her beau, a trailer-trash jerk. Paulette becomes her friend and they buck each other up. Encouraged by Paulette's faith in her, Elle regains her determination and sets out to demonstrate that not only can she compete intellectually but that her real-world knowledge sets her apart from the sheltered upper-crust students and teachers around her.

While the first half of the movie has some mildly amusing lines and situations (including a scene in which Elle's shallow parents tell her not to throw away her life by going to law school), things get much too serious in the second part. After proving her talents in the classroom, Elle joins a law firm as an intern (along with Warner and Vivian) and gets her crack at helping to defend an exercise video maven (Ali Larter) accused of murdering her husband. The contrivance of the plot is all too apparent: The case just happens to be one in which Elle can draw upon her limited expertise (her in-depth knowledge of aerobics). In terms of believability, *Legally Blonde* is also a bust in the courtroom. It's the kind of movie where witnesses break down on the stand and blurt out exactly what the attorneys want them to do, and where we are asked to believe that Harvard-trained lawyers are totally bereft of common sense.

The anti-intellectual strain that *Blonde* wallows in is dangerous water, but plays perfectly well to a mass audience. Elle is a sort of bubble-brained pop culture's answer to East Coast "snobbery" (with Harvard symbolizing the nodal point of intellectual presumptuousness), and the movie ends up embracing her as a common woman's superhero. Knowing about hair and makeup turns out to be important, after all. Blondes are as brainy as anyone else, even though they have been kept down by men who see them as nothing more than little toys. Elle even turns out to be a victim of sexual harassment. The movie also posits that it's not really all that tough to get into Harvard and be a top-notch lawyer, that it's mainly a matter of class privilege and not merit.

In a sort of protean feminist fantasy for the *Cosmo* set, Elle fixes everything. Using her quick wits and social skills, she gets a date for the class nerd, helps Paulette get her dog back from her estranged husband, teaches a whole beauty parlor full of women how to attract a man's attention, gets Paulette hooked up with a dreamy package deliverer, wins the murder case for the wrongly accused exercise video queen, becomes Vivian's best friend, surpasses Warner in intellectual and social achievement, graduates at the head of her class, becomes a top attorney, and even earns the respect of her (highly caricatured) feminist lesbian classmate. And she does it all without ruining her makeup.

In the right hands and with the right tone, this could have been an outrageous screwball comedy. But it's all done wrong. The movie abandons its initial sardonic tenor, and the mood goes everywhere at once. We're supposed to keep laughing at Elle's ridiculously overwrought femininity but at the same time cheer for her to triumph over the bad men who are running things. In the end, we're asked to love her for believing in her own true, pink and pampered self.

Strip away the glossy veneer and *Legally Blonde* is remarkably like other tales about members of the underclass who triumph over a society that has stifled them. Make Elle into a poor black man from the South in the 1950s, and the plot would play out exactly the same. It's a movie about defying expectations. One problem is that sorority members, blondes, and beautiful women are not really doomed by society to a life of underachievement. And the film fails to sustain its punch and its viewpoint. Its central character goes from an object of ridicule and condescension to a hero. The movie doesn't have a consistent attitude about its protagonist. If it had continued to make fun of Elle, we could enjoy some easy laughs. Instead, it seems to suggest that Elle's view of the world was right all along, and everyone else was ignoring her talents and abilities. This makes little sense. How can the same character be so stupefyingly inane and so impossibly brilliant?

Despite its lame plot twists, Witherspoon holds the film together with another tour-de-force performance. This is definitely an actress who deserves better material (of the type provided her in *Election*) and some parts that challenge her. She has a wonderfully pliant and expressive comic face, and a gift for mimicking the extremes of feminine behavior. But, as with her character Elle, there is much more lurking beneath the surface.

*—Michael Betzold*

 CREDITS

**Elle Woods:** Reese Witherspoon
**Warner:** Matthew Davis
**Vivian Kensington:** Selma Blair
**Emmett Richmond:** Luke Wilson
**Brooke Taylor Windham:** Ali Larter
**Prof. Stromwell:** Holland Taylor
**Prof. Callahan:** Victor Garber
**Margot:** Jessica Cauffiel
**Paulette:** Jennifer Coolidge
**Dorky Dave:** Osgood Perkins II
**Serena:** Alanna Ubach
**Mrs. Windham Vandermark:** Raquel Welch
**Chutney:** Linda Cardellini
**Enid:** Meredith Scott Lynn

**Origin:** USA
**Released:** 2001
**Production:** Ric Kidney, Marc Platt; released by MGM
**Directed by:** Robert Luketic
**Written by:** Karen McCullah Lutz, Kirsten Smith
**Cinematography by:** Anthony B. Richmond
**Music by:** Rolfe Kent
**Sound:** Ed White
**Music Supervisor:** Anita Camarata
**Editing:** Anita Brant Burgoyne, Garth Craven
**Art Direction:** Daniel Bradford
**Costumes:** Sophie de Rakoff Carbonell
**Production Design:** Melissa Stewart
**MPAA rating:** PG-13
**Running time:** 95 minutes

REVIEWS

*Boxoffice.* July, 2001, p. 28.
*Boxoffice.* September, 2001, p. 150.
*Chicago Sun-Times Online.* July 13, 2001.
*Entertainment Weekly.* July 20, 2001, p. 43.
*Los Angeles Times Online.* July 13, 2001.
*New York Times Online.* July 13, 2001.
*People.* July 23, 2001, p. 34.
*Rolling Stone.* August 2, 2001, p. 70.
*USA Today Online.* July 13, 2001.
*Variety.* July 9, 2001, p. 19.
*Washington Post.* July 13, 2001, p. C1.

QUOTES

Walter (Matthew Davis) justifies dumping Elle (Reese Witherspoon): "If I'm going to be a senator by the time I'm 30, I need to marry a Jackie, not a Marilyn."

AWARDS AND NOMINATIONS

**Nomination:**
**Golden Globes 2002:** Actress—Mus./Comedy (Witherspoon), Film—Mus./Comedy.

# The Legend of Rita (Die Stille Nach Dem Schuss) (The Silence After the Shot)

Celebrated German filmmaker Volker Schlondorff, who achieved international renown with the advent of the New German Cinema in the late '60s, presents a work of consummate skill in *The Legend of Rita*. Famous for the "realistic fantasy," *The Tin Drum* (1979), which won the Oscar® for the Best Foreign Language Film, Schlondorff in this latest offering seems to be drawing upon a quite different strain in his career.

His eponymous central character has no qualms about killing, since she is an ideologically-driven terrorist. What makes the film gripping is that it doesn't purport to look at her life from an objective moral standpoint, but rather tells its story as Rita would have told it herself using the film medium. This seems perfectly logical as a welding of form and content, since her character can be assumed to have absorbed so much cinema as to be able to at least visualize a film about herself. Thus, self-effacingly, Schlondorff allows the film's narrative axis to be structured like an unwritten diary, dwelling at length on phases of her life, howsoever undramatic, that Rita herself would have been attached to, while condensing scenes, albeit with emotional impact, that she would have deemed insignificant. This does not translate into uniformly engrossing viewing, but it does present a multi-faceted portrait of that most feared and enigmatic nihilistic entity of our time, the state-sponsored international terrorist.

A pre-credit sequence takes us slam bang into a bank robbery executed by Rita (Bibiana Beglau), Andi (Harald Schrott), and their gang in a German city. Wearing dark glasses and a rhinestone jacket, Rita storms into the premises, brandishing a pistol. Her commands to the meek bank clerks are mixed with leftist rhetoric: "We're giving the economy a shot in the arm!" A gang member shouts out: "Ownership is theft! We're nationalizing finance!" Another exclaims, "Down with capitalism!." Then, outside, to the tune of a police siren, Rita and Andi throw their jackets into a garbage can, kiss, and part ways. As she rushes past a drunken tramp, who asks her if she has a mark to spare, Rita empties a bag of coins into his upturned hat with a smile.

Rita's voiceover spells out her intent:"We wanted to abolish injustice and the state along with it!"

The film then links Rita's fervor to the radical politics of the time by having the Rolling Stones' anthem "Street Fighting Man" underscore the main titles, as we see Rita striding down the walkway of the airport in East Berlin, on her way back from Beirut. The distillation of ideology into popular culture becomes evident in the lyrics calling for "palace revolution" instead of "compromise solution." This heady mix absolves the film of the responsibility of justifying just how this sloganeering translates into the taking of innocent human lives, of 10 of those merely doing their job.

It is the mid-'70s. Rita is stopped by the East Berlin authorities when they find a loaded gun in her hand baggage. The crafty intelligence expert, Hull (Martin Wuttke), releases her on condition that she keeps him informed about all operations she and her gang are planning in the West. She is told that they can count on the East for refuge.

This offer is put to the test when Rita and the quiet and attractive Fredericke (Jenny Schilly) practice a deception to spring Andi out of prison, but not without Fredericke shooting a guard. True to his word, Hull welcomes the gang at a congenial barbecue and provides them with a base of operations, supporting their "liberation from the class operation enemy." In her personal life, however, Rita remains racked by doubt. After their love play, she remarks to Andi that maybe they should "abandon it all." To which, he rants, "And let imperialism dig its own grave? Will injustice just wither and go away?" All Rita can answer is, "I just want to be with you."

The levels of ideological commitment surface in the bickering amongst the gang, despite the success of their work in Beirut, which we are not shown, and their being able to hide out in Paris. Andi accuses Rita of "fraternizing with pigs" and throws Fredericke's upper class origins back in her face. As wanted international terrorists in the West, their modus operandi becomes to shoot their way out of any situation, then head back to the cover provided by Hull in the East. A Parisian traffic cop stopping Rita and Fredericke for not wearing helmets while on a scooter, leads to a wild chase, at the end of which Rita shoots him dead. This time, Hull suggests a more lasting solution, at least for Rita, which she accepts despite the heartbreak it causes her to be separated from Andi.

Rita agrees to become Susanne, an employee in the textile printing department of a large factory deep inside East Germany. Here she forms an intimate relationship with Tatjana (Nadja Uhl), an attractive blond co-worker with a drinking problem. Tatjana is as cynical about the East as Rita is about the West. Rita has to use physical force to prevent her newfound friend from sliding deeper into an alcoholic hell. On a Sunday visit to Tatjana's folks in the country, Rita comes to know from the news on TV, relayed from West Germany, that Andi has been shot dead while trying to evade a roadblock. The report also mentions her as one of the terrorists wanted, and cites a scar on her left elbow. In the factory changing room, when a co-worker remarks on the scar, Rita fears it is time to quit.

Again, it is a heart-wrenching affair. At the moment of parting, we see the physical bond between the two women. Rita realizes the pain she is causing Tatjana, who has come to believe the gossip about Rita's past as a terrorist. Yet Rita has no option but to continue to lie. The film reaches its emotional apex at this point, as we see the two forced to separate, and weeping soon after.

Rita is then shunted into yet another life: as Sabine, a supervisor in the child care center of a steel factory. While keeping an eye on the kids at a summer camp on the beach, she comes to know Jochen (Alexander Beyer), a young lifeguard. Rita is quick to allow him to fill the emotional vacuum in her life. The two go swimming nude in the moonlight, and we can see that for Rita, the merging of the political and the personal has taken place; this time without any rough edges.

Then, a near visionary encounter brings back the past. On a holiday at a Baltic resort with Jochen, she sees Fredericke singing in a choir by the sea, looking and sounding angelic. She is now married, and with a little son. Rita smiles at her enviously during the few moments they share, and says, "Glad you're happy!" Fredericke answers, "Where'd you get that idea?" Even so, we can sense a wistful longing on Rita's face. Fredericke has been able to reconcile her ideology with her bourgeois roots, as Rita has still been unable to do.

When Jochen proposes to Rita, promising her a move to Moscow, she is noncommittal. When she consults with Hull, telling him that she's pregnant, he still vetos the idea. While Rita sees it as a personal matter, he points out its international ramifications. It is not just Rita who stands to be exposed, but East German intelligence. When she turns down Jochen, she reveals her true identity. A shocked Jochen can only respond, "But terrorists kill innocent people!" Rita answers, "I did that."

A changing political reality quickly renders Rita's revolutionary beliefs obsolete. With the fall of the Berlin Wall in 1989, Rita can no longer feel secure in the East. Her first shock comes when she learns from a tabloid in the factory cafeteria that Fredericke has been arrested. Her co-workers are of course happy that they can now afford Levis. "This country was a revolution!" Rita declaims at them, referring to East Germany. "We had our sights set on values other than money!" From their silence, it is clear that her views are out of place and out of date.

Even the once suave and confident Hull is now forthright with her. "We can't help you anymore," he admits. Whether she runs Eastward or to the West, he explains, it will just be a matter of time before she's picked up. As a last favor, she asks for Tatjana, with whom she has been corre-

sponding, and who has been locked up for knowing her, to be released. A freed Tatjana comes knocking on Rita's door, but is promptly seized by undercover agents.

In a last ditch effort, Rita steals a scooter from a young West German kind enough to give her a lift. Then, in the midst of a snow flurry, as she approaches a roadblock where papers are being checked, she stops. Her face shows she is opting for the only freedom open to the true revolutionary. All her lives come crashing to an end when she charges through, and is gunned down.

Critics have found Rita's plight believable and representative of the politically confused time in which the film is set. A.O. Scott in the New York Times credits Schlondorff and his co-scenarist for bringing their fictitious character to life as someone "sometimes ridiculous and occasionally frightening, but . . . also thoroughly human and at times convincingly heroic." Critical praise has also been lavished on Beglau's award-winning performance. Scott calls her an "intuitive and charismatic" actress, while David Denby in the New Yorker refers to her "challenging stare" and "ferocious will" that result in her appearing "not beautiful, exactly, but radiant and sympathetic."

—Vivek Adarkar

**CREDITS**

**Rita Vogt:** Bibiana Beglau
**Erwin Hull:** Martin Wuttke
**Tatjana:** Nadja Uhl
**Andreas (Andi) Klein:** Harald Schrott
**Jochen:** Alexander Beyer
**Fredericke:** Jenny Schily

**Origin:** Germany
**Language:** German
**Released:** 1999
**Production:** Arthur Hofer, Emmo Lempert; Babelsberg Film Produktion; released by Kino International
**Directed by:** Volker Schlondorff
**Written by:** Volker Schlondorff, Wolfgang Kohlhaase
**Cinematography by:** Andreas Hofer
**Sound:** Manfred Arbter, Detlev Fichtner
**Editing:** Peter Przygodda
**Art Direction:** Susanne Hopf
**Costumes:** Anne-Gret Oehme
**MPAA rating:** Unrated
**Running time:** 101 minutes

 **REVIEWS**

*Los Angeles Times Online.* March 16, 2001.

*New York Times Online.* January 24, 2001.
*New Yorker Online.* February 5, 2001.
*Newsday Online.* January 24, 2001.
*Village Voice Online.* January 30, 2001.

## QUOTES

Rita (Bibiana Beglau): "Reality is a drag."

# Liam

 **Box Office:** $1 million

Stephen Frears' latest film *Liam.* written by Jimmy McGovern and based on Joseph McKeown's novel *The Black Crack Boys,* portrays pride as man's downfall and poses the question of what makes a man a man. If a husband's job is to provide for his family, then is it right for him to spend the family's meager funds on a pint of ale while his wife and children pawn the family's belongings? Is it right to let his pride get in the way of accepting charity that would feed his family or to blame his shortcomings on another race? McGovern suggests that when a man becomes so self-absorbed in his own problems to the point of turning others into scapegoats, it can only lead to tragic consequences. McGovern takes the equation further by showing both ends of the spectrum. On one end is seven-year-old Liam (Anthony Borrows), a stuttering schoolboy who has been thrown into a hostile world where religion only adds to his torment. And on the other end is Liam's unemployed father (Ian Hart), who blames the Jews for his misfortune and joins the fascist party.

*Liam* supplies large themes that revolve around poverty, desperation, and the distribution of wealth. The film's story is set during the Depression when factories closed and laborers found themselves grappling with immense poverty while the Jewish community ran successful businesses and seemingly lived in palaces in comparison to the poverty that surrounded them. Liam's older brother Con (David Hart) toys with joining the Communist party while Liam's father joins the Fascist party because it's easier to blame someone else for one's misery than to face one's own insecurities. And while this film focuses on one family the problems the family faces prove universal.

Set in Liverpool's Irish Catholic community, *Liam*'s narrative focuses on the struggle of a family and how each family member handles their circumstances. Teresa (Megan Burns) finds works as a maid in a Jewish household. She lies about her religious background in order to land the job and is later compromised when she hides the affair between her employer and a young man from her employer's husband. Liam's father loses his job, hangs out in bars, and refuses to accept charity from the church to support his family. Later, after seeing a fascist demonstration in which the Jews are blamed for the loss of the Irish workers' jobs, the dad joins the party. Liam's mom (Claire Hackett) fights like a tigress to save every shred of the family's dignity and it's unclear what Con does because his character barely registers.

Liam grapples with his childhood yearnings for the opposite sex against the backdrop of his strict Catholic school education. While his teacher Mrs. Abernathy (Anne Reid) and the local priest (Russell Dixon) extol the virtues of clean souls and claim that every time a person sins they drive the nails further into Jesus' hands, Liam undergoes the pangs of torment over having seen his mother naked. Once in the confession box, the stuttering Liam finds that he's unable to confess his sins to the priest. Meanwhile, Liam's dad spouts anti-Jewish sentiments and causes confrontations between various family members. Liam is exposed to opposing political idealism, the tragic consequences of his father's actions, and the hypocrisy of the Catholic Church with his innocence remaining barely intact.

*Liam* is not without flaws. The character Con remains a complete mystery and we never learn anything about him, nor does his presence greatly affect the other characters. Also the question arises as to why Con is able to find employment when his father remains unemployed. The film's ending fails to bring any sort of resolution after an explosive climax in which the dad, along with other fascists, throw a torch into the Jewish household where Teresa is working, thus causing her horrible injuries.

Although Ian Hart gets top billing, the young actor Anthony Borrows steals the show portraying the fragile Liam. Borrows' sad brown eyes tug at viewers' heartstrings as he delivers a heartfelt performance. Megan Burns plays the responsible breadwinner faced with a crisis of conscience, while allowing us to feel the weight of her burden. Claire Hackett brings humor, warmth and a fighting spirit to her maternal role especially in the tender scenes between Liam and herself. Despite the film's flaws *Liam* aims straight for the heart, then never lets go.

—*Patty-Lynne Herlevi*

## CREDITS

**Dad:** Ian Hart
**Mam:** Claire Hackett
**Con:** David Hart
**Liam:** Anthony Borrows
**Teresa:** Megan Burns

**Mrs. Abernathy:** Anne Reid
**Father Ryan:** Russell Dixon
**Auntie Aggie:** Julia Deakin
**Uncle Tom:** Andrew Schofield
**Lizzie:** Bernadette Shortt
**Lizzie's husband:** David Corey

**Origin:** Germany, Great Britain
**Released:** 2000
**Production:** Colin McKeown, Martin Tempia; BBC Films, Road Movies; released by Lion's Gate Films
**Directed by:** Stephen Frears
**Written by:** Jimmy McGovern
**Cinematography by:** Andrew Dunn
**Music by:** John Murphy
**Sound:** Chris Atkinson
**Editing:** Kristina Hetherington
**Art Direction:** Hannah Moseley
**Costumes:** Alexandra Caulfield
**Production Design:** Stephen Fineren
**MPAA rating:** R
**Running time:** 90 minutes

## REVIEWS

*Boxoffice.* November, 2000, p. 167.
*Chicago Sun-Times Online.* October 5, 2001.
*Entertainment Weekly.* October 12, 2001, p. 63.
*Los Angeles Times Online.* September 21, 2001.
*New York Times Online.* September 21, 2001.
*USA Today Online.* September 20, 2001.
*Variety.* September 18, 2000, p. 36.
*Washington Post.* October 5, 2001, p. WE37.

# Life After Love
# (La Vie Apres l'Amour)

After *Jaws* was released back in the 1970's, viewers felt that it wasn't safe to swim in the ocean and when Alfred Hitchcock's *Psycho* hit the screens, baths became preferable to showers. Now with the Quebecois comedy, *Life After Love,* many of the film's viewers will put off that much-needed root canal indefinitely since a trip to the dentist could be compared to a Spanish Inquisition torture session. Well, that's only if your dentist's wife just left him for an inferior male specimen and that inferior male happens to be handing

your dentist divorce papers to sign during your routine dental session. And well, compared to the dentist visit, marriage (Quebecois-style) proves to be no picnic either.

Produced by Roger Frappier and Luc Vandal, directed by Gabriel Pelletier, and written by Ken Scott, *Life After Love* demonstrates that French comedy loses its edge when exported to another culture. While *Life After Love* portrays various comical circumstances, none of the scenes could be called hilarious, but only slightly amusing. The film feels like a marriage between a television soap opera and a Quebecois version of *Friends.* Its narrative appears too outrageous at times and the characters' circumstances prove unrealistic at best. It's possible that men as stupid as the film's protagonist Gilles Gervais exists, but his misadventures ask us to go beyond suspending belief. We are asked to believe that a man whose wife just left him will become addicted to anti-depressants (he pops more than enough pills to kill himself), meets and gets involved with a woman that resembles his former wife and bears his wife's name, and completely destroy his life in a matter of weeks. Add Gilles ending up in the hospital twice, in jail once, where he befriends a gay man (Patrick Huard) posing as a heterosexual (who also just happens to be a dental hygienist), and after all of this, his wife Sophie returns to him.

Perhaps the Quebecois enjoy this over-the-top style of comedy. With the recent Canadian success of Denise Filiatrault's *Laura Cadieux* series, it has become evident that French-Canadians prefer to indulge themselves in the absurdities of life turned up a few notches. Even with the right ingredients, which include a bit of slapstick and cautionary humor, something appears to be amiss in *Life After Love.* The scenes follow a logical path of cause and effect, but the characters are weakly defined and their personality flaws do not rub off each other in the right way. It feels as if writer Ken Scott whipped his script out without considering the characters opposing motivations or considering the characters at all. Instead, Scott focused on circumstances, but not the characters' relationship to those circumstances. In short, this could have been a film full of raucous humor had Scott paid more attention to his characters driving needs.

The beginning of the film flashes back to a 1970's wedding in which the groom and his best man are dressed in maroon leisure suits among a sea of polyester-clad relatives. This scene cuts to someone swinging a golf club at a series of wedding photographs. Then the story moves ahead a few years, showing Sophie (Sylvie Leonard) pretending to have an affair with Gilles' (Michel Cote) colleague when, in fact, she's throwing a surprise birthday party for her husband. Then we are shown a series of practical jokes Sophie plays on Gilles over the years until we see that she's the one smashing the photographs with a golf club. Her reason for this deranged behavior is that she's been married to the same man for 20 years and even though she still loves him, she's bored. So in a dramatic fashion, Sophie exits her marriage, speeding off in a sports car with the more exciting Philippe (Denis Mercier). This sequence proves to be strong film-making, but after Gilles misadventures of a jilted husband begin, the film falls apart until its surprise ending, which almost saves the film from its reckless 60-minute episodic excursion.

The film's actors delivered unabashed performances but were defeated by the script. Perhaps *Life After Love* will be appreciated as a video release by viewers who recently suffered a breakup or divorce. It might prove cathartic.

*—Patty-Lynne Herlevi*

## CREDITS

**Gilles Gervais:** Michel Cote
**Sophie Lavergne:** Sylvie Leonard
**Sunsey:** Patrick Huard
**Docteur Bilodeau:** Yves Jacques
**Sophie Taillon:** Guylaine Tremblay
**Philippe Paradis:** Denis Mercier
**Robert Florent:** Norman Helms
**Cure Trepanier:** Dominique Levesque

**Origin:** Canada
**Language:** French
**Released:** 2000
**Production:** Roger Frappier, Luc Vandal; Max Films; released by Alliance Atlantis
**Directed by:** Gabriel Pelletier
**Written by:** Ken Scott
**Cinematography by:** Eric Cayla
**Music by:** Benoit Charest
**Sound:** Yvon Benoit, Mathieu Beaudin
**Editing:** Alain Baril
**Costumes:** Denis Sperdouklis
**Production Design:** Serge Bureau
**MPAA rating:** Unrated
**Running time:** 104 minutes

## REVIEWS

*Variety.* July 17, 2000, p. 26.

# Life as a House

*Seen from a distance it's perfect.*
—Movie tagline

**Box Office:** $15.6 million

George (Kevin Kline) is in pretty bad shape. As we learn during the bizarre opening montage of *Life as a House,* accompanied by an up-to-date rock song, George lives in a dilapidated shack in a tony California seaside community, surrounded by neighbors who despise him. His dog urinates on one neighbor's car; George himself urinates off the cliff into the ocean, arousing the interest and feigned wrath of a neighbor, Coleen (Mary Steenburgen), with whom he once had a romantic fling, and her sunnily sexy 16-year-old daughter Alyssa (Jena Malone), who is following in her mom's free-love footsteps. George is long divorced from Robin (Kristin Scott Thomas), and they have a son Sam (Hayden Christensen) who, during the opening song, tries to hang himself from the clothes bar in his bedroom closet. His mother, upon discovering this, throws up her hands. She doesn't appear to take it seriously as a suicide attempt; apparently it's part of his habit of self-abuse.

This is a lot to throw at audiences in an opening sequence—a mixed bag of silly scenes and overly poignant drama, and it betrays the film's essential sit-com approach: small, uncomplicated, intercutting scenes and patently transparent scriptwriting. It's the fourth directorial effort from longtime Hollywood producer Irwin Winkler, the man who brought us the original *Rocky* and who directed 1995's *The Net.* Complicated plotting is not Winkler's custom, and *Life as a House* proceeds as a paint-by-numbers exercise in maudlin, contrived emotional set-ups. Screenwriter Mark Andrus (*As Good As It Gets*) indulges in melodramatic excesses disguised as heartfelt, knowing speeches. The film has pretensions to deep familial insights, but stumbles over its own pedestrian plotting and dialogue.

Sam is very troubled. We know this because he wears blue eye makeup, has multiple piercings (including a chin stud), has both a "People Suck" *and* a Marilyn Manson poster on his wall, and has a yen for huffing (inhaling aerosols and chemicals) and associated asphyxiation experiences (the pseudo-hanging). Worse yet, he doesn't even seem to be aware that he's only one *Star Wars* episode away from becoming Darth Vader (Christensen stars as Anakin Skywaker in the 2002 release *Attack of the Clones*). Sam is egregiously rude to his mother, father and stepfather, is frequently stretched out on his bed listening to very loud and bad rock music on headphones, and turns occasional homosexual tricks to get money from his best friend, who is a pimp. So what's the root of his problems? *Life as a House* doesn't beat around the bush; Andrus lets us know right away, simply and unabashedly. "He needs a man," Robin tells her new, remarkably unsympathetic husband Peter (Jamey Sheridan). "His father's a man," Peter shoots back. "He needs a man he respects," Robin replies, shooting her ex-husband in the back. A few seconds later, Sam's step-father and two little stepbrothers call him a "queer" to his face. Robin herself confesses: "What kind of a mother can't stand her own son?"

The characters in *Life as a House* have severe and obvious deficiencies—but fortunately they're all of the kind that can be cured by the rediscovered love of a father and son. The characters might as well be wearing little cards around their necks with their emotional problems written in black marker—their personalities are that transparent. Unhappiness abounds. Robin is married to a man who is so obsessed with work, money, and material things that his own kids won't hug him—and worse yet, he doesn't see this as a problem. We don't know the other reasons for Robin's deep unhappiness—she puts up a solid front—but we never see her working, so apparently she's a frustrated, underachieving stay-at-home mom who doesn't even have any household chores to keep her busy, because she has a live-in maid.

Things quickly go from bad to much worse for George. His neighbors not only keep threatening to call the police or their attorneys on him, but he's behind the times at the architectural firm where he's worked for 25 years. He refuses to use a computer to make models of expensive custom-made houses, and instead meticulously builds them by hand. George is a throwback, it seems, a real misfit in the modern world, but we're never clear why. His boss fires him, and he goes into a rage, smashing all the models he built. Then he collapses on the sidewalk after leaving the firm, is rushed to the hospital, and awakens to learn he has terminal cancer.

There is so much middle-aged yuppie anxiety in this plot that it's surprising it doesn't have a special rating to warn away 40- or 50-somethings easily unnerved by life's tragic midlife turns. As a character, George is woefully underwritten. We never learn why he is a misanthropic hermit, refusing to go along with society. He seems to have been sleepwalking through his own life. His life is certainly a mess. Divorce, an addict for a teenage son, job loss, neighbors with lawyers, and terminal illness—it's enough to make an unhappy man want to reclaim his life by spending its last few weeks reconciling with his son and exorcising all his demons.

The set-up is loaded, with a highly stacked deck, and the plot doesn't bother to make sense even on its own terms. If Sam has been spending weekends with his father for the past 10 years, why does the film act like they haven't been together in a decade? If Peter is such an emotionally stunted jerk, why has the sensitive Robin cast her lot with him—is it just for material comfort? Apparently so, since Peter has a huge mansion and George lives in a shack. That's the film's subtle way of conveying that Peter is much more of a success in his life than George.

George changes into a willful, take-charge guy, though no one can figure out why. It goes without saying that he doesn't tell anyone he's dying; this withholding gives the film its only minimal moments of tension. Once George commandeers Sam, who was hoping to spend the summer getting high in Las Vegas, all the pieces fall together in predictable fashion. It doesn't take long for Sam to realize that staying in a garage with his dad all summer while they tear down the shack and rebuild a real seaside house on the site might have some side benefits. Almost on cue, sweetly sexy girl-next-door Alyssa shows up to rub some suntan lotion on Sam's back. She even offers to let him shower at her house, and then blithely lets herself into the shower, posing continual challenges to Sam's uncertain sexual identity. She's that kind of girl—a godsend for a plot that needs a device to explain why Sam doesn't run away and resume his life of hustling and inhaling.

What happens in the rest of the film is crystal clear well in advance. You know that George is eventually going to get Sam to take the stud out of his chin and the rings out of his ears, wash off the makeup, forget about TV, music, the Internet, and huffing, and find the joys of hammering and nailing boards with his dad. It's as inevitable as Alyssa turning Sam away from his flirtations with homosexuality and onto the straight path. Even so, Christensen undergoes quite a transformation from bad boy to straight arrow—there isn't even a mark left on his chin where the stud used to be.

Along the way, George tells Sam that he has always hated living in the house because his father gave it to him. His father was an abusive alcoholic who ended up killing himself, his mother and another woman, and crippling a young girl, by driving drunk. Tearing down the house is George's way of resolving his anger at his father, and getting Sam to help reconciles Sam and George. Both neat and shameless, as is the inevitable reunion between Sam's estranged parents. Robin and George have stormy conversations and, as the sparks fly, the sunsets go more crimson and you know reconciliation is just a kiss away.

The movie is relentlessly manipulative but it inexplicably keeps stopping to interrupt the melodrama with incongruous moments of sit-com comedy involving the dog and the neighbors. Characters who haven't been introduced show up to work on the house. *Life* has one of the most tastelessly egregious subplots ever involving two peripheral characters, Sam's pimp friend Josh (Ian Somerhalder) and Steenburgen's Coleen, hitting the sack together. Why? For no apparent reason other than some diversion in this overlong movie that's otherwise basically a one-note melody. There's also a confusing and ridiculous scene in which Alyssa climbs into bed with George to see if he's as good a kisser as her mom says.

Despite all this folderol, there are genuinely moving scenes involving Kline, Scott Thomas and Christensen—all of them good actors in search of some decent dialogue. Instead, they too often get lines like "Hindsight is just foresight without a future." Kline's George is the familiar cinematic dying hero who rediscovers the joys of living every day and throws off his lifelong unhappiness, gloom, and screwed-up relationships. It's not really a stretch for Kline, but he inhabits George so thoroughly that he becomes a comfortable screen presence despite all the contrivances. Scott Thomas tries to make something out of the typical female "empty shell" character, and Christensen shows his budding range, pulling off the film's only notable transformation.

In the hands of a more unconventional director, *Life as a House* had the potential to be something more substantial, but it's derailed at all points by its stilted dialogue and plotting, its rambling subplots and clots of unnecessary scenes and characters. You might say it lacks the courage of its own melodramatic convictions.

—Michael Betzold

## CREDITS

**George:** Kevin Kline
**Sam:** Hayden Christensen
**Robin:** Kristin Scott Thomas
**Alyssa:** Jena Malone
**Coleen:** Mary Steenburgen
**Peter:** Jamey Sheridan
**Kurt Walker:** Scott Bakula
**David Dokos:** Sam Robards
**Adam:** Mike Weinberg
**Ryan:** Scotty Leavenworth
**Josh:** Ian Somerhalder
**Nurse:** Sandra Nelson

**Origin:** USA
**Released:** 2001
**Production:** Irwin Winkler, Rob Cowan; released by New Line Cinema
**Directed by:** Irwin Winkler
**Written by:** Mark Andrus
**Cinematography by:** Vilmos Zsigmond
**Music by:** Mark Isham
**Sound:** Richard Lightstone
**Editing:** Julie Monroe
**Art Direction:** Tom Taylor
**Costumes:** Molly Maginnis
**Production Design:** Dennis Washington
**MPAA rating:** R
**Running time:** 124 minutes

## REVIEWS

*Boxoffice.* November, 2001, p. 145.
*Chicago Sun-Times Online.* October 26, 2001.
*Entertainment Weekly.* November 2, 2001, p. 48.
*Los Angeles Times Online.* October 26, 2001.
*New York Times Online.* September 9, 2001.
*New York Times Online.* October 26, 2001.
*People.* November 5, 2001, p. 37.
*Variety.* September 9, 2001, p. 60.
*Washington Post.* October 26, 2001, p. WE40.

## QUOTES

George (Kevin Kline) to Sam (Hayden Christensen): "I want you to be happy, and you're not."

## AWARDS AND NOMINATIONS

**Natl. Bd. of Review 2001:** Breakthrough Perf. (Christensen)
**Nomination:**
**Golden Globes 2002:** Support. Actor (Christensen)
**Screen Actors Guild 2001:** Actor (Kline), Support. Actor (Christensen).

# Lift

While living in a capitalist country certainly provides its citizens with more liberties than a citizen of a Third World or Communist country, citizens can also choke on their freedom. Capitalist countries don't provide equality for their citizens but one can rise above their lowly circumstances by working hard or fooling the infrastructure by committing various crimes to acquire wealth. Such is the case with the characters in African-American filmmakers DeMane Davis and Khari Streeter's *Lift*. As the film's title implies, the characters lift their self-esteem through stealing from wealthy establishments via shoplifting (called boosting). However, are the characters here victims of a capitalist economy that promotes materialism over spirituality and family bonds or are they victims of inner-city poverty (or are they simply thieves)?

According to the film's Boston-based writers/directors, the inspiration for *Lift* came from their individual experiences. Khari Streeter had an obsession with top-of-the-line sneakers during his formative years and recalls (in a press kit interview): "My guidance counselor nick-named me "label" because of the attention I paid to sneaker brands rather than school." At 21, Streeter landed a job at an advertising agency where he handled the sneaker accounts. DeMane Davis recalls staying over at a girl's house in the projects where the family worshiped designer clothes and purchased their clothing from a "booster." Later, when Davis decided to pursue a job at an advertising agency, she recalls, "My brother's wife was a booster and encouraged me to borrow clothes for work. The attention I received was overwhelming and I was immediately caught up." Now Streeter and Davis team up to make a film about self-love and about the experience of black women but drew their inspiration from such films as *East of Eden* and *The Little Thief*.

Their stylistic drama was developed at the Sundance Director's and Writer's Lab and garnered a nomination at the Sundance Festival 2001 for the Grand Jury Prize. Since that time, *Lift* has screened at other festivals, including New York's New Directors/New Films Festival and the Seattle International Film Festival. But the film's true test will be with the general public. Will *Lift* attract the same audience as the gritty 2000 independent release *Girlfight*? *Lift* is similar to *Girlfight* in its portrayal of a young inner-city woman attempting to rise out of her birth circumstances despite her dysfunctional family leanings. However, while *Girlfight* resembled *Rocky* with its underdog athlete succeeds theme, *Lift* resembles a somber *High Heels* with an unloved child willing to do anything to win her detached mother's approval. In the case of *Lift*'s Niecy (Washington) that includes stealing and imprisonment.

By day, Niecy works at the elegant Kennedy's department store where she keeps up appearances and up on the latest fashion trends. However, on her time off, the poised Niecy waltzes through high-priced boutiques where she hides clothing underneath her bra and pays for designer label purchases with stolen credit cards. Niecy sells the clothing to her grateful customers but has been unable to please her perfectionist mother Elaine (Lonette McKee). So Niecy decides, with the help of a gang of thieves, to steal a diamond necklace for her mother. The heist gets out of hand and tragedy forces Niecy to finally confront her mother and for both of them to take responsibility for their actions, instead of blaming all of their problems on the abuse Elaine suffered as a child.

Several subplots emerge, creating a more complex situation for Niecy. Niecy learns that her lover, a reformed booster named Angelo (Eugene Byrd), has impregnated her but she thinks that Angelo lacks the maturity to raise a child. Another subplot revolves around Elaine, her sister Lily (Jacqui Parker), their mother (Barbara Montgomery), and the domestic abuse they suffered in the past. An uncomfortable birthday party brings this family tragedy to a head when Elaine refuses to stay at her mother's house because of her memories of abuse. Fortunately all of these subplots are woven successfully into the film and echo a later confrontation between Niecy and Elaine.

Streeter and DeMane present us with a compelling story about a social issue that few of us are aware of within a stylized format of opulent visuals and operatic music. Although *Lift* portrays women grappling with their dire circumstances, the story focuses on redemption of spirit while staying clear of sentimentality and stereotypes.

—*Patty-Lynne Herlevi*

## CREDITS

**Niecy:** Kerry Washington
**Elaine:** Lonette McKee
**Angelo:** Eugene Byrd
**Christian:** Todd Williams
**Camille:** Samantha Brown
**Quik:** Sticky Fingaz
**Dent:** Braun Philip
**France:** Barbara Montgomery
**Miss Kearns:** Annette Miller
**Aunt Lily:** Jacqui Parker
**Uncle Michael:** Naheem Allah
**Shelly:** Susan Alger

**Origin:** USA
**Released:** 2001
**Production:** John Hart, Jeffrey Shary, Robert Kessel, Mark Hankey; True Film Fund, Hart Sharp Entertainment
**Directed by:** DeMane Davis, Khari Streeter
**Written by:** DeMane Davis
**Cinematography by:** David Phillips
**Music by:** Ryan Shore
**Sound:** G. John Garrett
**Music Supervisor:** Sue Jacobs, Ed Gerrard
**Editing:** Lee Percy, Peter Barstif
**Art Direction:** Mark Lane-Davies
**Costumes:** Jacki Roach
**Production Design:** James Chinlund
**MPAA rating:** Unrated
**Running time:** 85 minutes

## REVIEWS

*Film Comment.* March/April, 2001, p. 6.
*New York Times Online.* March 29, 2001.
*RANT.* May/June, 2001, p. 11.
*Variety.* February 5, 2001, p. 41.

QUOTES

Aunt Lily (Jacqui Parker): "Black people need therapy too."

# Lord of the Rings 1: The Fellowship of the Rings

*The legend comes to life.*
—Movie tagline

*Power can be held in the smallest of things.*
—Movie tagline

*Fate has chosen him. A fellowship will protect him. Evil will hunt them.*
—Movie tagline

*One ring to rule them all, one ring to find them, one ring to bring them all and in the darkness bind them.*
—Movie tagline

*Even the smallest person can change the course of the future.*
—Movie tagline

**Box Office:** $175 million

J.R.R. Tolkien's *Lord of the Rings* saga (originally published in three volumes from July 1954 to October 1955) was bound to be adapted eventually to the cinema, but the task of visualizing Tolkien's imaginary world was daunting, and the project awaited a director bold enough and inventive enough to take it on. (Ralph Bakshi had done a partial animated adaptation in 1978 that *Variety* considered "unsuccessful.") New Zealand director Peter Jackson was apparently up to the challenge, one would surmise, on the evidence of the *Rings* trilogy's first installment, *The Fellowship of the Rings*. The film was a huge, sprawling spectacle, astonishing in its grand achievement. Not many Hollywood analogues come to mind, but the nearest one might be *The Wizard of Oz* (1939), though Tolkien's vision is far darker than that of L. Frank Baum. Although the casting of *Oz* would be impossible to match, of course, the casting of *Rings* also impresses. No less impressive is the scope of the tale, elegant, mythic, and fantastic in the truest sense of the word.

In a fairy-tale setting conjured up by a kindly Oxford University specialist in medieval literature, the story involves a mythic quest to destroy a magical ring forged by the wicked Sauron, the Dark Lord of Mordor, in a volcano. The ring is evil and seductive for anyone who wears it. It is a touchstone that can endow its wearer with the power of world domination, but the ring itself is evil and must be destroyed. Once lost for centuries, the ring is found by Bilbo Baggins (Ian Holm), a good-natured Hobbit, a gentle race of furry-footed diminutive creatures who are perfectly happy to live in their sheltered little world, called The Shire, amusing themselves with rustic entertainments, and generally unconcerned and unaware of the larger world or ordinary mortals.

Biblo, a paradigm of decency, has never worn the ring and has therefore avoided being seduced by its evil powers. It has given him a long life, and when the film begins, he is celebrating his 111th birthday. His friend, Gandalf the Grey (Ian McKellen), a good wizard, visits The Shire to celebrate Bilbo's birthday. Feeling old and tired, Bilbo decides to leave The Shire and live out his days in the elfin kingdom, ruled by Galadriel, Queen of the Elves (Cate Blanchett). Following Gandalf's advice, he leaves the ring in the keeping of his young cousin, Frodo Baggins (Elijah Wood), who then becomes the bearer of the ring. Gandalf also advises that the ring be destroyed, but it can only be destroyed by the molten fire in the volcano of Mount Doom in Mordor, where it was forged.

Gandalf goes to seek the advice of a wise wizard, Saruman the White (played by Christopher Lee, himself a veteran of 255 horror films and television productions, and an ideal actor to cast as the villain of the piece), who has gone over to the dark side and seeks the ring for himself. He is in command of an army of fearful spirit creatures that he sets loose to find Frodo. Fortunately, Gandalf escapes and goes to the aid of young Frodo. Catching up with Frodo in the Golden Wood of Lothlorien, Gandalf establishes a protective cadre known as "The Fellowship of the Rings," consisting of Frodo, Gandalf, Frodo's Hobbit friends, Samwise Gamgee (Sean Austin), Peregrin Took (Billy Boyd), and Meriadoc Brandybuck (Dominic Monaghan), Gimli the dwarf (John Rhys-Davies), Legolas the elf (Orlando Bloom), Boromir, a human warrior of Gondor (Sean Bean), and Aragorn (Viggo Mortensen), also known as Strider, Gondor's future King. Aragorn is loved by Arwen (Liv Tyler), the elf princess who saves Frodo's life after he has been wounded by the Nazgul, black spirit warriors on horseback. (The film substitutes Arwen for the elf lord Glorfindel, who saves Frodo in the novel, presumably to introduce her earlier in the story.) Once the Fellowship has been established, pursuit sequences follow fast and furious, as the Fellowship travels from dilemma to dilemma, on their way to Mordor, pausing only to rest a while in the tranquility of the elfin kingdom of Rivendell. Their passage over a snow-capped mountain range is complicated by avalanches conjured by the wizard Saruman from afar, so they are forced to take a dangerous passage through the haunted Mines of Moria, where Gandalf is apparently lost, falling into a chasm while protecting the others from an ancient evil spirit,

Balrog. At the end, Frodo lives, but he is still short of his destination, and audiences are left to await the sequels.

The sequels will of course be forthcoming, since the whole Rings trilogy was shot at the same time, at a risk of perhaps $400 million (the cost estimated by *Variety*, including production and projected marketing expenses). The responsibility must have been tremendous for Peter Jackson, who not only had to direct the whole saga, but also wrote the screenplay, with Fran Walsh and Philippa Boyens. *Sight and Sound* reviewer Andrew O'Hehir noted that although the screenplay "significantly reordered and reshaped Tolkien's narrative, which widens its focus and quickens its pace gradually," the writers had "tremendous respect for the linguistic and mythic density" of Tolkien's story.

Both of the hugely popular fantasies adapted from novels in 2001 were haunted by a monster, the fidelity goblin, let's call it, that threatened to hamstring both films made from two widely read books. But if, as just noted, Jackson took some liberties (one character, the nature spirit Tom Bombadil, is removed from the story, for example), he nonetheless attempted to remain true to the mythic essence. *Harry Potter and the Sorcerer's Stone* was the first out of the gate, designed more to please the young fans of J.K. Rowling than viewers looking for an inventive movie. By the end of the year *Harry* had grossed over $290 million and was braced for the challenge of *The Fellowship of the Ring*, released just before Christmas and topping $174 million after only two weeks of business. The problem is hardly new. David O. Selznick knew he had to keep readers happy when he produced the film adaptation of Margaret Mitchell's *Gone With the Wind* (1939), which was also a huge success on screen. Like *Fellowship of the Ring*, which clocks in at two hours and 58 minutes, *Gone With the Wind* needed two hours and 33 minutes to do "justice" to the book. The challenge of adapting it was somewhat simplified by the repetitious nature of Mitchell's epic yarn. But *The Lord of the Rings*? "Forget translating the entire story to the screen," Neil Golden advised readers of *Film Comment*: "can the books even be summarized in nine hours?" Regardless, Tolkien fans are legion, and they would of course be curious to see what happened to their favorite cult epic.

The year ended with competing fantasies for audiences seeking escapist fare. In a *Wall Street Journal* essay published on November 30th, Brian M. Carney asserted that in this "Battle of the Books" Tolkien should "run rings around Potter," because although *Harry Potter* "may be entertaining, imaginative, and wry," it is not morally challenging. Tolkien's epic fable questions humankind's "ability to resist the temptation of absolute power." Moral complexity of this order, Carney believed, cannot compete with Harry Potter's philosopher's stone (called the "sorcerer's stone" for American readers ignorant of alchemy): "In Tolkien's world the temptation of evil is one that all, or nearly all, of his characters must confront." Bespectacled Harry is beyond such temptation. Tolkien's argument, according to Carney, "is that, while intentions matter, the WAY we act is far more important than WHY we act," and "presents a serious rebuttal to the idea that good ends justify using evil means." Tolkien had a wider and wiser perspective than Rowling. Writing in the context of a world of emerging Nazism in Germany and Stalinism in the Soviet Union, Tolkien's trilogy implied that "by compromising with Stalin in Europe and using the atomic bomb against the Japanese, the Allies had failed to live up to the standards set by his best fictional characters." Jackson's film "makes Harry Potter and Luke Skywalker look like the feeble wraiths they are," according to Andrew O'Hehir of *Sight and Sound*.

Reviews of *The Fellowship of the Ring* were mixed, as digested in *Film Comment* in January 2002, and some reviewers were unable to make distinctions such as Carney had offered. David Ansen of *Newsweek* thought it was "excellent" (4 stars) in comparison to *Harry Potter*, which Ansen considered "mediocre" (1 star), but Roger Ebert of the *Chicago Sun-Times*, on the other hand, thought *Harry* was "excellent" and *The Fellowship* merely "good." Dave Kehr of the *New York Times* agreed that it was "good," while *Harry* was merely "of interest." J. Hoberman of the *Village Voice* thought *Fellowship* was "of interest," but considered *Harry* simply "mediocre." No point in looking for a consensus there, but Jackson's film was both foolproof and critic-proof, and film audiences were bound to queue up to see it, regardless of the reviews. *Variety*'s Todd McCarthy was absolutely on target when he predicted that Tolkien's trilogy was "likely to grab the brass *Ring*."

Neil Golden reported in *Film Comment* the Tolkien Internet chat rooms had become "a war zone" among frantic Tolkien fans upset over the casting of Liv Tyler and debating whether or not director Peter Jackson should "give the Balrog wings, or not," and whether the elves should have pointy ears. ("Diehard fans say no" to that.) Golden forgave Jackson's film for running two minutes shy of three hours after "14 continuous months in production" but criticized the first installment because it "reads more like a visual Cliffs Notes than a full-blown movie adaptation." Although New Zealand looks like Middle-earth, "just as Tolkien described it," Jackson races the characters "through the plot, relying on them to look the part, since they aren't afforded the opportunity to BE the part," except for Frodo (Elijah Wood), Gandalf (Ian McKellen), and Aragorn (Viggo Mortensen). Whereas Tolkien "tells his story as history, Jackson's film is purely fantastic." Tolkien tells his story "slowly and organically," whereas Jackson "takes a gorgeous snapshot of it." But the "film ignites" in the action sequences, which will more than justify the price of admission. The spectacle was truly enchanting, and even visionary, a remarkable cinematic achievement.

—*James M. Welsh*

## CREDITS

**Frodo Baggins:** Elijah Wood
**Gandalf:** Ian McKellen
**Arwen:** Liv Tyler
**Aragorn:** Viggo Mortensen
**Sam:** Sean Astin
**Galandriel:** Cate Blanchett
**Gimli:** John Rhys-Davies
**Merry:** Dominic Monaghan
**Pippin:** Billy Boyd
**Legolas:** Orlando Bloom
**Saruman:** Christopher Lee
**Elrond:** Hugo Weaving
**Boromir:** Sean Bean
**Bilbo Baggins:** Ian Holm
**Gollum:** Andy Serkis
**Celeborn:** Marton Csokas

**Origin:** USA
**Released:** 2001
**Production:** Barrie M. Osborne, Peter Jackson, Fran Walsh, Tim Sanders; Wingnut Films; released by New Line Cinema
**Directed by:** Peter Jackson
**Written by:** Peter Jackson, Fran Walsh, Philippa Boyens
**Cinematography by:** Andrew Lesnie
**Music by:** Howard Shore
**Sound:** Hammond Peek, Ken Saville, Malcolm Cromie
**Editing:** John Gilbert
**Art Direction:** (Peter) Joe Bleakley, Rob Otterside, Phil Ivey, Mark Robins
**Costumes:** Ngila Dickson, Richard Taylor
**Production Design:** Grant Major
**Visual Effects:** Jim Rygiel
**MPAA rating:** PG-13
**Running time:** 178 minutes

## REVIEWS

*Boxoffice.* November, 2001, p. 40.
*Chicago Sun-Times Online.* December 19, 2001.
*Entertainment Weekly.* November 16, 2001, p. 36.
*Entertainment Weekly.* December 14, 2001, p. 50.
*Film Comment.* January/February, 2002, p. 73.
*Hollywood Reporter.* December 4, 2001, p. 8.
*Los Angeles Times Online.* December 19, 2001.
*New York Times.* December 16, 2001, p. 13.
*New York Times.* December 19, 2001, p. E1.
*New York Times.* December 21, 2001, p. E19.
*New Yorker.* December 24, 2001, p. 124.
*Newsweek.* January 29, 2001, p. 60.
*Newsweek.* December 10, 2001, p. 72.
*Premiere.* September, 2001, p. 48.
*Rolling Stone.* January 17, 2002, p. 55.
*Sight and Sound.* February, 2002, p. 51.
*USA Today.* December 14, 2001, p. E1.
*Variety.* December 10, 2001, p. 31.
*Wall Street Journal.* December 21, 2001, p. W1.
*Washington Post.* December 19, 2001, p. C1.
*Washington Post.* December 22, 2001, p. C1.
*Washington Times.* December 19, 2001, p. B5.

## QUOTES

Gandalf (Ian McKellen): "The dark lord needs only this ring to enslave the world."

## AWARDS AND NOMINATIONS

**Oscars 2001:** Cinematog., Makeup, Visual FX, Score
**British Acad. 2001:** Director (Jackson), Film, Visual FX
**L.A. Film Critics 2001:** Score
**Natl. Bd. of Review 2001:** Support. Actress (Blanchett)
**Screen Actors Guild 2001:** Support. Actor (McKellen)
**Broadcast Film Critics 2001:** Song ("May It Be"), Score
**Nomination:**
**Oscars 2001:** Adapt. Screenplay, Art Dir./Set Dec., Costume Des., Director (Jackson), Film, Film Editing, Song ("May It Be"), Sound, Support. Actor (McKellen)
**British Acad. 2001:** Actor (McKellen), Adapt. Screenplay, Cinematog., Costume Des., Film Editing, Sound, Score
**Directors Guild 2001:** Director (Jackson)
**Golden Globes 2002:** Director (Jackson), Film—Drama, Song ("May It Be"), Score
**Screen Actors Guild 2001:** Cast
**Writers Guild 2001:** Adapt. Screenplay
**Broadcast Film Critics 2001:** Director (Jackson), Film.

# Lost and Delirious

**Box Office:** $.2 million

The character Mary Bradford (Mischa Barton) comments, "I felt like a tiny gray mouse heading straight for the mouth of a cat," which also describes the experience of Lèa Pool's first English-language film release into the international market. According to an article on Canada's *Info Culture* regarding Quebecois Pool's feature *Lost and Delirious* screening at the Sundance Film Festival, the director hoped to finally secure commercial success at the age of

50. With an adapted screenplay written by Judith Thompson and based on Susan Swan's novel, *The Wives of Bath*, *Lost* portrays the controversial subject of adolescent homosexuality. A wider release outside the festival circuit might still bring Pool the boxoffice success she deserves.

Annalee Ellingson of *Boxoffice* magazine commented that the "...girls' complicated relationships with their mothers, and adolescent self-hate ring true." And Ron Wells of *Film Threat* praised Piper Perabo's powerful performance and announced that "Mischa Barton is quite a find." *Lost and Delirious* is not without faults, but its faults, which include extremely poetic dialogue as opposed to contemporary adolescent dialogue and dreamy photography, add an other worldly quality to the film. And while some viewers might be distracted by the film's dreamy atmosphere, a passionate story about first love, self-hatred, and the shame associated with teenage homosexuality comes through loud and clear.

*Lost and Delirious*, similar to Pool's last French-language release *Emporte Moi (Set Me Free)*, portrays young women coming to terms with their sexuality. In *Emporte Moi*'s unflinching gaze at adolescent sexuality, 13-year-old Hannah's (Karine Vanasse) descent into adolescent hell begins with the onset of her period. Hannah falls in love with the actress Anna Karina while watching the 1962 film *Vivre Sa Vie* and then transfers her affections to her teacher who resembles Karina. Eventually, Hannah hooks up with a bisexual lover that she reluctantly shares with her brother. *Lost and Delirious* focuses on young women grappling with family and sexuality issues in the confines of a boarding school as they deal with their non-present mothers.

And they also grapple with their individual sexuality. Mary, who goes by the nickname "Mouse," claims that she "felt like a wooden doll down there" until the day she witnessed Tory (Jessica Parè) and her lover Jake (Luke Kirby) doing the deed against a tree. The bisexual and family pleasing Tory tells Mary and dejected ex-lover Paulie (Piper Perabo) that what had previously taken place was just a phase. Paulie, however, denies to Mary that she's a lesbian, but a girl in love with a girl. After all, Paulie and Tory are soul mates, right? Pool has claimed that *Lost and Delirious* isn't about lesbianism, but about love. However, while there is some truth to the director's statement, the complications of homosexuality against the backdrop of the conservative private school reverberates throughout the film. Lesbian themes show up in the film's music soundtrack and an erotic lovemaking scene that recalls scenes from Patricia Rozema's *When Night is Falling*.

*Lost and Delirious* is not the usual coming-of-age drama where a rich girl falls for a boy from the wrong side of the tracks and lands in a doomed love affair. But it is a coming-of-age story where a rich girl falls for a "bad girl" from the wrong side of the tracks then, to avoid complications and future humiliation, settles into a relationship with upperclass male student, Jake. But her easy transition into the hetero-

sexual world brings up a few questions. Did Tory actually love Paulie or was she just experimenting with her sexuality? Will she break ties with her conservative family in the future, similar to the protagonists in Jamie Babbit's homosexual farce *But I'm a Cheerleader*? Or will she come out of the closet similar to the protagonist in Anne Wheeler's *Better Than Chocolate*?

In any case, some lesbian viewers might find *Lost and Delirious*'s ending disappointing since Tory chooses to return to the closet and Paulie commits suicide after a passionate rampage where she injures Jake and devastates Mary. Unlike the films *Better Than Chocolate* and *When Night is Falling*, *Lost and Delirious* proves to be heavy-handed. And the film is reminiscent of *The Children's Hour*, a film in which two teachers are wrongly accused of lesbian behavior. Heterosexual viewers walk away from the film equally confused due to the film's mixed message about homosexuality. After all, they might ask, is it really that easy to deny one's sexuality and to conform to what is considered proper behavior? And if so, then what kind of message does *Lost and Delirious* send out to homosexual teens? Or was the film intended for an adult market and individuals struggling with their political correctness?

Despite its lesbian themes, Pool performs a stellar job directing her first English-language screenplay while striking out in new territory. While Pool has received acclaim in Europe and across Canada, she's yet to break open the American boxoffice for two reasons: Her French-language imports for the most part haven't been released in the U.S., with the exception of *Emporte Moi* and *Straight From the Heart*; and American viewers appear to be phobic of subtitles. Following in the footsteps of Quebecois filmmakers Denys Arcand (*Stardom*) and Robert Lepage (*Possible Worlds*), Pool has given up her status of a big fish in a small pond to become, as one Quebecois filmmaker put it, "a grain of sand on a beach." French-language films are assured a certain success in Europe and in Quebec, but English-language films are forced to compete with Hollywood releases. It's a gamble that did not pay off for Arcand, whose film failed miserably at the American boxoffice, and Lepage, whose film hasn't been released stateside.

As *Lost and Delirious* opens, Mouse's father and stepmother drop her off at the Perkins Girl's College. Mouse, who fits her name to a T, is quickly taken in by her rambunctious roommates—athletic Tory and rebellious "rage on" Paulie. The three bond over the loss of their mothers. Mouse's mother died recently, Paulie was given up for adoption at birth, and Tory has lost her identity by trying to fit her parents' expectations of the perfect conservative rich girl. Tory and Mouse encourage Paulie to write to her birth mother, which in the end proves futile. The women also bond over their rebellious behavior and over a song by the Violent Femmes with the lyrics "I just want to make love to you." and soon this song becomes their teenage anthem with its themes of angst and lust.

One morning Mouse catches Tory naked in bed with Paulie and, though she's appropriately shocked, she knows how to keep a secret. However, on another fateful morning, Tory's sister and her cohorts barge into the room—catching Tory and Paulie sleeping entwined and naked. In order to save her reputation as a good girl, Tory breaks it off with Paulie and begins dating Jake, a student from the nearby boy's private school. Paulie catches Tory and Jake in the middle of the sexual act and goes ballistic. Then, after receiving a rejection letter from her birth mother, Paulie desperately tries to lure Tory back into her life, but Tory refuses to return to her lesbian love affair. Paulie strikes out at Tory, but also at a society that would create the pain she suffers, leading to catastrophic circumstances.

The three leads deliver mesmerizing performances, while Parè and Perabo also play out sensitive and vulnerable erotic scenes. The actresses' performance become even more impressive when one realizes how little film experience each actress possesses. Parè starred in Arcand's English-language *Stardom* and appeared in Lepage's *Possible Worlds*. Perabo is best-known for her role as the naive bartender in *Coyote Ugly* and for her appearance in *The Adventures of Rocky and Bullwinkle*. Barton, on the other hand, brings the most experience to the film. Some viewers might recall her precocious performance opposite Sam Rockwell in *Lawn Dogs* or have seen her in *Notting Hill* or *The Sixth Sense*.

Despite Pool's stellar cast and experienced crew, critics have not warmed to *Lost and Delirious*. The film's U.S. boxoffice performance will determine whether trading subtitles for commercial success is worth the bother. The question remains is it better to be a big fish in a small pond or drown in a sea of mediocrity?

—*Patty-Lynne Herlevi*

## CREDITS

**Mary "Mouse" Bradford:** Mischa Barton
**Pauline "Paulie" Oster:** Piper Perabo
**Victoria "Tory" Moller:** Jessica Pare
**Fay Vaughn:** Jackie Burroughs
**Joe Menzies:** Graham Greene
**Eleanor Bannet:** Mimi Kuzyk
**Jake:** Luke Kirby

**Origin:** Canada
**Released:** 2001
**Production:** Lorraine Richard, Greg Dummett, Louis-Philippe Rochon; Cite-Amerique; released by Lion's Gate Films
**Directed by:** Lea Pool

**Written by:** Judith Thompson
**Cinematography by:** Pierre Gill
**Music by:** Yves Chamberland
**Sound:** Claude Beaugrand, Yvon Benoit, Hans Peter Strobl
**Editing:** Gaetan Huot
**Costumes:** Aline Gilmore
**Production Design:** Serge Bureau
**MPAA rating:** Unrated
**Running time:** 100 minutes

## REVIEWS

*Chicago Sun-Times Online.* July 13, 2001.
*Entertainment Weekly.* July 27, 2001, p. 45.
*Globe and Mail.* July 7, 2001, p. R1.
*Los Angeles Times Online.* July 6, 2001.
*New York Times Online.* July 6, 2001.
*Variety.* January 29, 2001, p. 52.
*Washington Post.* July 20, 2001, p. WE31.

## QUOTES

Mouse (Mischa Barton): "You're a girl in love with a girl, aren't you?" Paulie (Piper Perabo) replies: "No, I'm Paulie in love with Tory."

## AWARDS AND NOMINATIONS

**Genie 2001:** Cinematog
**Nomination:**
**Genie 2001:** Screenplay, Support. Actress (Kuzyk).

# Love Come Down

*Are you down with it?*
—Movie tagline

Canadian director Clement Virgo has proven that the various facets of love can be portrayed without revealing the marks of sentimentalism. His powerful film *Love Come Down* shoots Cupid's arrows towards God, family, friendship, and lovers without flinching. *Love Come Down* even explores all too familiar themes of drug addiction, dysfunctional family relations, and redemption without losing its authenticity and Virgo proves that with enough ingenuity worn-out themes experience a form of rebirth. *Love Come Down* drains the tear ducts while bringing viewers to the core of humanity.

Virgo focuses on two brothers, professional boxer Matthew (Martin Cummins) and his black half-brother Neville (Larenz Tate), and how a childhood trauma influenced the choices they made as adults. Virgo tells his stories in fragments while bouncing between childhood incidents and current events. This parallel narrative allows viewers to gain subtle clues to the brothers' current behavior and tense bond. However, viewers might become confused as to why various joyous familial moments would lead to murder. Otherwise, this slightly flawed narrative doesn't distract from the film's timely message of seeking out love despite one's dark circumstances.

As the film opens, Neville, a drug addict turned stand-up comic, narrates the story of growing up in a biracial home. The film cuts to a rave/dance club where Neville flings himself around the dance floor while his brother Matthew reclines on a couch watching him. Neville sneaks into a toilet where he shoots up. Matthew pursues Neville and would have killed him if family friend Julian (Rainbow Sun Francks) hadn't torn Matthew away. The next day, Neville checks into a rehabilitation center run by nuns where he meets former addict Sister Sarah (Sarah Polley). Sister Sarah tells Neville that the ecstasy he seeks can be found through God's love and pales in comparison to a drug-induced high.

One night, after Neville has cleaned up his act, he meets a beautiful vocalist Niko (R & B sensation Deborah Cox). Niko tells Neville that he must win her love and wait outside the stage door with Sicilian ice cream. Neville soon learns that Niko was adopted and raised by Jewish parents and has chosen to seek out her birth parents—only to learn that she is also the child of biracial circumstances. However, just as Neville begins to fall in love with Niko, he returns to the club and watches her leave with another suitor. Heartbroken, Neville quits his job, returns to drugs, and ends up back at the rehab center. Eventually, Neville and Niko reunite and decide to seek out Niko's birth father.

Neville must also deal with the demons of his own traumatic past and an incident tears Neville away from Matthew. Piece by piece (and shown in flashbacks), the night of the murder of Neville's father reveals itself. The father, Leon (Peter Williams), encourages Neville to smoke weed and becomes violent towards Matthew, who refuses to take a puff. The boys' mother Olive (Barbara Williams) returns and is outraged after she learns that Leon allowed his son to smoke dope. Leon beats Olive, and later Olive attempts to kill Leon with a machete. However, we learn that Olive wasn't the one who murdered her husband but pleaded guilty to protect the child who did.

As Matthew and Neville attempt to purge their past through drug addiction or violent outbursts, a final confron-

tation takes place between the brothers. Neville sits at the kitchen table poised and ready to shoot up again while Matthew hangs over his brother with a machete in hand, ready to end Neville's misery. Essentially the brothers are reliving a traumatic event that took place in the same spot during their formative years. This time their mutual friend Julian intervenes and the brothers choose against their usual destructive patterns. They seek love and through redemption the brothers find that love.

*Love Come Down* takes a refreshing look at societal and familial ills while blending metaphysics and rave culture with the characters' meaningful circumstances. Tate sheds all inhibitions as he portrays Neville's vulnerability and desperate search for love, while Cox delivers a stellar debut performance as Niko and Cummins plays the stoic-yet-violent boxer Matthew with aplomb. Bruce Kirkland of the *Toronto Sun* claims, "*Love Come Down* is an important film that deserves an audience." And he's right in his assessment.

—*Patty-Lynne Herlevi*

## CREDITS

**Neville:** Larenz Tate
**Matthew:** Martin Cummins
**Sister Sarah:** Sarah Polley
**Niko:** Deborah Cox
**Young Neville:** Travis Davis
**Young Matthew:** Jake Le Doux
**Julian:** Rainbow Sun Francks
**Olive:** Barbara Williams
**Leon:** Peter Williams
**Dean:** Clark Johnson
**Ira Rosen:** Kenneth Welsh
**Bea Rosen:** Jennifer Dale
**Ceana:** Naomi Gaskin

**Origin:** Canada
**Released:** 2000
**Production:** Eric Jordan, Clement Virgo, Damon D'Oliveira; Conquering Lion Productions; released by Unapix
**Directed by:** Clement Virgo
**Written by:** Clement Virgo
**Cinematography by:** Dylan Mcleod
**Music by:** Aaron Davis, John Lang
**Sound:** Garrett Kerr
**Editing:** Susan Maggi
**Costumes:** Debra Hanson
**Production Design:** Jennifer Carroll
**MPAA rating:** Unrated
**Running time:** 101 minutes

**REVIEWS**

*Boxoffice.* December, 2000, p. 53.
*eye Weekly Online.* March 8, 2001.
*Toronto Sun Online.* March 9, 2001.

**QUOTES**

Neville (Larenz Tate) opens his stand-up routine with: "I got a story to tell ya all, a fable about brothers—fire and ice."

**TRIVIA**

The film is an expanded version of the director's 1993 short, *Save My Lost Nigga Soul.*

**AWARDS AND NOMINATIONS**

**Genie 2001:** Sound, Support. Actor (Cummins) **Nomination:**
**Genie 2001:** Film, Screenplay, Support. Actress (Williams), Score.

# The Low Down

The Low Down . . . *on life, love and other four-letter words.*
—Movie tagline

The jolly old England of filmmaker Jamie Thraves' *The Low Down* is chemically induced and, judging from the discontent twenty-somethings who appear in the film, jolly old England doesn't live up to its title. Thraves' narrative revolving around a university graduate-turned-malcontent Frank (Aidan Gillen) and his fear of adulthood doesn't offer us anything new. We've already seen the upscale model of the English university graduate turned party animal in *Bridget Jones's Diary* and Whit Stillman has covered a similar American territory with his series of films, including *Metropolitan.* It might appear too hasty to label *The Low Down* a British *Reality Bites,* but with its MTV-style edits and cinema verite approach, the comparison doesn't seem too far off.

*The Low Down* proved edgy enough for the Shooting Gallery Film Series, although the British film doesn't possess the same merits of other films in the series, including *The Last Resort, Croupier,* or the screwball comedy *When*

*Brendan Met Trudy.* The ultra hip *The Low Down* appears to be missing a compelling story with a dramatic arc and the director's approach of showing characters in life's smaller moments just comes across as boring. So what if we know people like the characters in the film? Do we actually want to spend 96 minutes staring at a screen in which characters resembling our friends sit around boozing and smoking cigarettes while talking complete nonsense? Producer Sally Llewellyn thinks that we do and in a press kit interview she raved, "this film is a character study so it had to be small and intimate with a breezy energy . . ."

*The Low Down* isn't a complete loss with its gaze of the gritty side of London and charismatic performances by Kate Ashfield and Aidan Gillen. The film's dialogue also appears fresh and clever as well as informing us of the characters' hidden motivations. In a scene when Ruby (Ashfield) and Frank become acquainted Frank tells Ruby, "Mortgage, I mean mort is a French word for death." Frank's quote not only informs viewers that Frank fears his transformation into adulthood, but many viewers can relate to Frank's sentiment. And equally compelling to the film's dialogue is the viewers' gaze at the rise and fall of relationship between a commitment-phobe and a woman optimist who stays in the relationship against her gut instincts.

Although this is Frank's story, he doesn't live in a vacuum and for the most part his friends prove to be more than wallpaper or mirrors for Frank to project his insecurities. His work colleague Mike (Dean Lennox Kelly) for the most part plays the role of Mr. Responsible and has been in a committed relationship with Lisa (Samantha Power), a bubbly blonde whose main ambition is to obtain a haircut like Sharon Stone. By the film's ending, Mike and Lisa get engaged and prepare to embark on a new life. The character John (Tobias Menzies) graduated with a degree in fine art but would rather live a slacker's life, sleeping all day, showing up late for work, and criticizing his colleagues. His negative attitude eventually rubs Frank the wrong way, leading the two men to a violent confrontation.

At first glance, Frank's apartment mate Terry (Rupert Proctor) comes across as a lush who drifts aimlessly through life; eventually, through Ruby's eyes, we learn that Terry hides his more sensitive side behind booze. Ruby recently broke away from a long-term relationship since her lover let her down too many times. She suffers from job-related boredom but has considered obtaining a degree in English literature. In a revealing conversation with Frank, who confides that when he sees airplanes he thinks of crashes, Ruby instead claims that she thinks of holidays—eventually, this rubs off on Frank.

Thraves' influences Cassavetes and Godard show up in *The Low Down,* but tentatively. For instance, Thraves employs a cinema verite style here, but lacks Cassavetes ability to tell a fluid story. Thraves also recalls Godard's loosely structured films, his roving camera eye, and even achieves the Godard's level of pretentiousness. With his influences intact, Thraves has proven that he also can direct a left-of-center art film, which may, in time, build him a cult following.

*The Low Down* portrays a some smart moments, clever dialogue, and believable performances, but the film lacks a compelling story. Thraves recycled cinematic approach to filmmaking and portrayal of too familiar characters doesn't spell success. We've seen it all before and we've seen it done better.

—*Patty-Lynne Herlevi*

## CREDITS

**Frank:** Aidan Gillen
**Ruby:** Kate Ashfield
**Mike:** Dean Lennox Kelly
**John:** Tobias Menzies
**Terry:** Rupert Proctor
**Lisa:** Samantha Powers

**Origin:** Great Britain
**Released:** 2000
**Production:** Sally Llewellyn, John Stewart; FilmFour, British Screen, Oil Factory, Sleeper Films, Bozie; released by Shooting Gallery
**Directed by:** Jamie Thraves
**Written by:** Jamie Thraves
**Cinematography by:** Igor Jadue-Lillo
**Music by:** Nick Currie, Fred Thomas
**Sound:** Sam Diamond
**Editing:** Lucia Zucchetti
**Costumes:** Julie Jones
**Production Design:** Lucy Reeves
**MPAA rating:** Unrated
**Running time:** 96 minutes

## REVIEWS

*Boxoffice.* November, 2000, p. 157.
*Chicago Sun-Times Online.* April 20, 2001.
*Entertainment Weekly.* April 27, 2001, p. 88.
*Los Angeles Times Online.* April 20, 2001.
*New York Times Online.* April 20, 2001.
*Seattle Weekly.* April 19, 2001, p. 74.
*Sight and Sound.* February, 2001, p. 43.
*Variety.* September 4, 2000, p. 28.
*Washington Post Online.* April 20, 2001.

# Lumumba

 **Box Office:** $.4 million

A political thriller about a real-life hero, *Lumumba* should grip students of history as well as casual moviegoers. Appropriately, the film appeared at the 2001 Lincoln Center Human Rights Watch film festival in New York. *Lumumba* is based on the story of doomed African politician Patrice Emery Lumumba, who was called both the Congo's George Washington and "the Elvis Presley of African politics." Haitian director/co-writer Raoul Peck focuses on the European and American plot to undermine the idealistic leader's attempt at uniting the disparate nations of Africa. With trouble still brewing in the Congo today, the film is both topical and compelling.

Unlike traditional biopics, *Lumumba* concerns itself less with the protagonist's personal history and more with the principal socio-political events of which Patrice Lumumba was part. *Lumumba* even shows the hero's corpse being cut up and burned by soldiers at the beginning of the film, a scene which removes some of the narrative suspense but draws uninitiated viewers into the horrific action. Thus, the story begins in flashback, after riots and protests force the Belgium government to concede the Congo's independence in June, 1960. A self-taught beer company worker, Lumumba (Eriq Ebouaney), rises within his party (the Congolese National Movement) to become—at age 36—the country's new prime minister and defense minister. Meanwhile, the party leader, Joseph Kasa Vubu (Maka Kotto), is elected president, and forges a power-sharing arrangement with Lumumba.

Throughout his short tenure in office, Lumumba fights with several factions, including the Belgian bureaucrats who still crave to control their former colony's course, and the CIA, which works to force out Lumumba and install his adversary, Joseph Mobutu (Alex Descas), as a way to protect U.S. business interests. Once several territories attempt secession, Lumumba beseeches the United Nations to help him, but Mobutu mounts a coup, so Lumumba and his "Lumumbists" must seek refuge. In the end, Kasa Vubu turns against Lumumba by colluding with the Belgians, and Lumumba almost escapes the country, but Kasa Vubu's army catches, arrests and tortures him, then assassinates Lumumba in January, 1961.

Director Raoul Peck had already made the documentary, *Lumumba—Death of a Prophet*, in 1991, and this new feature contains documentary-like elements. The attention to period detail is striking and presumably precise. Obviously, the film is also newsworthy by how it explores the untold facts behind Lumumba's execution. For those distressed over the beleaguered state of the Congo today, following the assassination of Laurent Kabila, *Lumumba* is a reminder of how the past can easily repeat itself. While Kabila was a supporter of Lumumba, many believe that the Congo's new president, Kabila's son, Joseph, is more an ally of the West than of the Congolese people.

Even those unacquainted with African history (and current events) will find *Lumumba* occasionally riveting, although they might get lost in the story details or find some of the acts of political maneuvering a bit dry. Except for a moment or two of bitter irony, there is no comic relief (a notable scene shows John F. Kennedy's representative side against democratic interests). There is also short shrift given to Lumumba's home life (Mariam Kaba plays Lumumba's wife, Pauline, but it's a thowaway role). Still, the last section of the film, where Lumumba is captured, abused and executed, creates a disturbing and powerful impression. As Lumumba, Eriq Ebouaney is especially moving in these disturbing scenes. *Lumumba* may not seem like the kind of film you'll want to rush out to see, but you won't regret it if you do.

—*Eric Monder*

**Patrice Lumumba:** Eriq Ebouaney
**Joseph Mobutu:** Alex Descas
**Maurice Mpolo:** Theophile Moussa Sowie
**Joseph Kasa Vubu:** Maka Kotto
**Godefroid Munungo:** Dieudonne Kabongo
**Moise Tshombe:** Pascal Nzonzi
**Pauline Lumumba:** Mariam Kaba

**Origin:** France, Belgium, Germany
**Released:** 2001
**Production:** Jacques Bidou; released by Zeitgeist Films
**Directed by:** Raoul Peck
**Written by:** Raoul Peck, Pascal Bonitzer
**Cinematography by:** Bernard Lutic
**Music by:** Jean-Claude Petit
**Editing:** Jacques Comets
**Costumes:** Charlotte David
**Production Design:** Denis Renault
**MPAA rating:** Unrated
**Running time:** 115 minutes

 REVIEWS

*Boxoffice.* July, 2001, p. 98.
*Chicago Sun-Times Online.* July 27, 2001.
*Entertainment Weekly.* July 20, 2001, p. 44.
*Hollywood Reporter.* January 19, 2001, p. 123.
*Los Angeles Times Online.* July 20, 2001.
*New York Times Online.* June 24, 2001.
*New York Times Online.* June 27, 2001.
*People.* July 16, 2001, p. 33.
*Washington Post Online.* July 13, 2001.

QUOTES

Patrice Lumumba (Eriq Ebouaney): "I came 50 years too soon. History will have its say someday."

 TRIVIA

The Congo was renamed Zaire until 1997 when Joseph Mobutu's rule was overthrown.

# The Luzhin Defence

 **Box Office:** $1 million

English actress Emily Watson possesses the uncanny ability of giving life to one-dimensional characters and this talent came in handy while rendering the role of Natalia in Dutch director Marleen Gorris' *Luzhin Defence*. While it's true that any actress can garner accolades playing dynamic individuals, for example Julia Roberts won an Oscar® playing the iconoclastic character Erin Brockovich, an actress that can resuscitate life into a cardboard cutout is a thespian rarity. When Watson aims her baby blues at the camera lens, viewers suspend belief that an aristocratic woman who just met an idiot savant would sacrifice everything for love. But the glaring fault of screenwriter Peter Berry's adaptation of Vladimir Nabokov's *Luzhin Defence* can not hide behind passionate performances or stunning photography.

Brian Miller of *Seattle Weekly* wrote: "As for the performers, Watson shines her usual intelligence through an underwritten part, while Turturro starts out refreshingly tic-free, then descends into *Rain Man*-style freak/savant mannerism." When Miller asked the film's director why Natalia would fall for Luzhin the director responded: "She wants the unknown, because the unknown is always far more attractive to some people than what they know."

Neither actor appears out of their depth here. Turturro, who often plays freaks, fits neatly into his role and at times recalls Charlie Chaplin's wobbly gait and pained gestures. Watson plays a world-weary bachelorette and, unlike the virtuoso she played in *Hilary and Jackie*, this time she plays the normal person in pursuit of a virtuoso. So we believe the actors' performances but get lost in the film's narrative, which pleads for our patience as it bounces back and forth between Luzhin's childhood and his current circumstances. We learn many things about the young Alexander and his passion for chess, but this approach doesn't explain why Natalia would fall in love with Luzhin and this is where the film loses its dramatic punch. And why would anyone fall in love with a chess champion unless they were in love with the game itself? Chess doesn't have the same allure as the arts or athletics and although masters of the game of chess are considered geniuses, they hardly offer anything useful to the rest of humanity in the way that the arts offer solace and science advances our way of life.

In 1929, Alexander Luzhin (Turturro), an eccentric chess Grand Master, and Russian aristocrat Natalia (Watson) arrive by train at an Italian lakeside resort. Luzhin has come to play the match of his career, while Natalia has been sent to the resort by her parents to meet and marry an eligible bachelor. Only the independent Natalia doesn't share her parents' taste in men and instead appears to possess a bleeding heart that takes in strays and hobo-like geniuses. After a brief encounter with Luzhin, Natalie becomes intrigued by the unusual man and the game of chess. She's also enamored with Luzhin's clumsy attempt at flirtation (he allows personal items to fall out of his pockets so that Natalie will rush to pick them up for him).

After a few encounters, Luzhin proposes to Natalia against her parent's wishes. However, the main obstacle that the lovers face is the arrival of the Luzhin's former manager Valentinov (Stuart Wilson). Valentinov abandoned Luzhin several years ago, telling the young chess player that he had no future in the game, but upon hearing of Luzhin's success, Valentinov returns to insure Luzhin's failure. The former manager hires a driver to dump Luzhin in the middle of nowhere, causing Luzhin to suffer a complete nervous breakdown. Then, after a doctor warns Natalia that Luzhin must never play chess again in order to live a healthy life, Valentinov lures Luzhin back into the game—leading to tragic consequences. However, Natalia finds Luzhin's strategic notes, takes her lover's place, and wins the championship game for him.

Despite the lack of a compelling drama, the *Luzhin Defence*, with its lush environment, intrigue, and rich performances still possesses entertainment value. The film might be an old-fashioned costume drama filled with discreet and forgettable characters, but some viewers found that they were swept away regardless. Gorris, who is best known for her Oscar®-winning *Antonia's Line*, brings us another pretty film, only the *Luzhin Defence* appears to be lacking a strong

presence. And while the character of Natalia does survive with her fiancee's legacy intact, the film itself won't be a keeper.

—*Patty-Lynne Herlevi*

## CREDITS

**Alexander Luzhin:** John Turturro
**Natalia:** Emily Watson
**Vera:** Geraldine James
**Valentinov:** Stuart Wilson
**Jean de Stassard:** Christopher Thompson
**Ilya:** Peter Blythe
**Anna:** Orla Brady
**Turati:** Fabio Sartor

**Origin:** France, Great Britain
**Released:** 2000
**Production:** Caroline Wood, Stephen Evan, Louis Becker, Philippe Guez; Renaissance Films, Clear Blue Sky Productions; released by Sony Pictures Classics
**Directed by:** Marleen Gorris
**Written by:** Peter Berry
**Cinematography by:** Bernard Lutic
**Music by:** Alexandre Desplat
**Sound:** Peter Glossop, Craig Irving
**Editing:** Michael Reichwein
**Costumes:** Jany Temime
**Production Design:** Tony Burrough
**MPAA rating:** PG-13
**Running time:** 106 minutes

## REVIEWS

*Boxoffice.* November, 2000, p. 153.
*Chicago Sun-Times Online.* May 4, 2001.
*Entertainment Weekly.* April 27, 2001, p. 91.
*Los Angeles Times Online.* April 20, 2001.
*New York Times Online.* April 20, 2001.
*People.* April 30, 2001, p. 32.
*Seattle Weekly.* May 3, 2001, p. 115.
*Variety.* August 28, 2000, p. 30.
*Washington Post Online.* May 4, 2001.

## QUOTES

Luzhin (John Turturro): "There is a pattern emerging! I must keep track—every second!"

# Made

*The easy part is surviving the mob. The hard part is surviving the friendship.*
—Movie tagline

 **Box Office:** $5.3 million

*M*ade re-teams *Swingers* co-stars and real-life friends Jon Favreau and Vince Vaughn in an original gangster comedy that relies more on snappy banter and quirky characters than on a plot that simply recycles all the familiar clichés. The comic emphasis is on the teamwork of the two leads and especially on Vaughn's hilarious turn as a guy trying desperately to be a part of the underworld but always making a mess of every situation he finds himself in. Written and directed by Favreau, *Made* recalls Martin Scorsese's classic *Mean Streets*, and specifically its volatile relationship between Charlie and Johnny Boy, but filters it through a hip, wisecracking sensibility.

Bobby (Favreau) is a hard-luck case trying to establish himself as a boxer while working odd jobs for small-time crime boss Max (Peter Falk, who manages to be both avuncular and quietly menacing at the same time). Bobby does construction during the day and chauffeurs his stripper girlfriend, Jessica (Famke Janssen), to bachelor parties at night. His best friend going back to childhood is Ricky (Vaughn), a loose cannon whose erratic behavior often verges on the psychotic. Their friendship is defined by Ricky's big mouth getting them into tough situations and Bobby quietly growing frustrated with his wild friend, and yet the long history between them suggests a deep and lasting bond.

One night at a bachelor party, Bobby sees a man getting too friendly with Jessica during a lap dance and punches him out, which gets Bobby in hot water with Max. To make amends for the trouble he has caused—$8,000 in dental work—Bobby is given a special assignment, which he accepts when he realizes that it could ultimately free Jessica from her job and give the two of them, as well as Jessica's little daughter Chloe (the adorable Makenzie Vega), a fresh start in life.

Ever loyal to his friend, Bobby persuades Max to let Ricky take part, and their meeting with Max sets the tone for the adventures that will follow. Ricky is unable to sit still and simply follow instructions. He opens up his envelope of expense money before he should, talks when it would be wise for him to be quiet, and generally irritates Max, who is only giving him the job as a goodwill gesture to Bobby. The assignment itself is fairly vague. Bobby and Ricky will be flying from Los Angeles to New York, where they will receive further instructions about a money drop.

The plot itself, however, is a relatively minor concern. The film is largely composed of a series of episodes in which Ricky does or says something stupid and gradually gets on the nerves of Bobby, whose patience with his friend is sometimes hard to believe. Bobby's only concern is to represent Max in a professional manner, but Ricky, who has never been anybody important, relishes the opportunity to impress people and play the big shot everywhere he goes. He annoys the flight attendant in first class to the point where she is about to file a harassment complaint against him, and he tries to play the cool, sophisticated, big tipper with the hotel bellhop but lacks the class to pull it off. While Ricky is a major embarrassment, there is something quite poignant at his core. He has probably watched too many gangster movies and wants to turn the assignment into a high-living mobster's vacation, but he repeatedly misses the mark and comes across as a boorish lout. Vaughn's performance is quite amazing in the way he takes a character who is off-putting and obnoxious and yet makes him likeable. Ricky is basically an overgrown boy out of his depth and yet blithely trying to be a hipster no matter how disastrous the results. Favreau generously takes a back seat to Vaughn's big performance but can easily communicate with the simplest deadpan glower Bobby's growing frustration every time Ricky opens his mouth.

The boys meet a variety of gangster types on their trip—from their stoic limo driver, Jimmy (Vincent Pastore), who looks like a typical Italian mobster, to Ruiz (rapper Sean Combs), their New York contact, who has no patience for Ricky's lame attempts at coolness. Combs is perfect in a small performance as the foul-mouthed gangster who cannot believe what amateurs he is dealing with. His right-hand man, the burly Horrace (Faizon Love), comes to distrust the inept Ricky and treats him like a fool.

With its sketchy narrative, *Made* could have become a one-joke movie about two would-be mobsters who bumble their way into one scrape after another. But Vaughn and Favreau play so well off of each other that the basic premise stays fresh, even if Favreau's storytelling is a bit thin and some scenes do not have much of a payoff. For example, when the trip seems to be going well for Ricky and he impresses some sexy gals during a night out on the town and gets them to come back to his hotel room, the episode ends badly and rather abruptly when the women leave before Ricky gets any action. But why the girls suddenly take off is not really made clear. More important, when the guys' big assignment is revealed to be a simple $200,000 delivery to a mild-mannered gangster named Tom (David Patrick O'Hara), no one explains why such an easy task requires so many men and so much planning. One is left to conclude that the plot details are not a big concern for Favreau, who seems more interested in the contentious friendship between Ricky and Bobby.

The guys finally get instructions from Ruiz regarding the meeting with Tom, who, inexplicably, is known as the Welshman even though he is from Scotland, and they make arrangements for the $200,000 drop. Ricky, however, does not accompany Bobby, leaving him and Horrace to deliver the money to Tom in a bar. At the rendezvous, Tom's own henchmen betray him, and, just when it looks like they are going to kill Bobby and Horrace and take the money themselves, Ricky surprises everyone when he emerges from a back room with a gun to rescue his friends. Earlier, Ricky had been ranting, over Bobby's objections, that they should have a gun for the job, and now his foresight, incredibly enough, seems to have paid off. Unfortunately, one of the thugs can see that he is brandishing a starter pistol, and Ricky is in trouble once again when a brawl breaks out. Finally, Jimmy comes in unexpectedly and saves Tom, Bobby, Ricky, and Horrace and presumably executes all the traitors.

Bobby and Ricky return to California and receive congratulations from Max for a job well-done. To Ricky's disappointment, however, he does not get any money since Max expects to be compensated for a carpet cleaning van that went missing on a previous job (Ricky had actually sold it), but Bobby is paid and looks to have a bright future in the mob. When he takes a stand by quitting and telling Max that Jessica is through working for him, Max surprises him with the revelation that he basically owns her since he has paid her rent for the last eight months. The principled Bobby gives back his payment and walks out.

Back home, Bobby is stunned to find Jessica in their bedroom snorting cocaine with another man. Apparently, Bobby believed in her fidelity and is devastated—even telling Jessica that he has bought her freedom from Max does not move her. When he mentions her little girl, Jessica simply tells him that he can take her, which he does. Six months pass, and, in the film's coda, Bobby and Ricky are having a birthday party for Chloe at Chuck E. Cheese's. Ricky, clueless to the end, is still trying to play the part of a big shot by actually tipping the employee wearing the Chuck E. Cheese costume. The big surprise, though, is that these guys, who once aspired to be mobsters, now appear to be raising a little girl on their own. This sweet, domestic ending really comes out of nowhere and, admittedly, seems at odds with the violent gangster world that Bobby and Ricky have been navigating. And yet, since they act like a bickering married couple throughout much of the film, the ending somehow feels right despite its sentimentality.

*Made* is Favreau's directorial debut, and he demonstrates a facility with actors as he utilizes their improvisational abilities as well as the distinctive rhythms of his own writing. The tough-guy patter spoken by wannabe wiseguys is very funny, but, underneath it all, there is a genuine

affection between Ricky and Bobby. Given the fact that the plot itself is pretty slight, the interplay between the leads is crucial, and their edgy rapport makes *Made* very entertaining. One would think that the last thing we need is yet another mob comedy, but Favreau's entry has enough wit and a beautifully off-kilter performance from Vaughn to make it an original effort.

—*Peter N. Chumo II*

## CREDITS

**Bobby:** Jon Favreau
**Ricky:** Vince Vaughn
**Jessica:** Famke Janssen
**Horrace:** Faizon Love
**Welshman:** David O'Hara
**Jimmy:** Vincent Pastore
**Max:** Peter Falk
**Ruiz:** Sean (Puffy, Puff Daddy, P. Diddy) Combs

**Origin:** USA
**Released:** 2001
**Production:** Vince Vaughn, Jon Favreau; released by Artisan Entertainment
**Directed by:** Jon Favreau
**Written by:** Jon Favreau
**Cinematography by:** Christopher Doyle
**Music by:** John O'Brien, Lyle Workman
**Sound:** Tom Nelson
**Editing:** Curtiss Clayton
**Art Direction:** Roswell Hamrick
**Costumes:** Laura Jean Shannon
**Production Design:** Anne Stuhler
**MPAA rating:** R
**Running time:** 94 minutes

## REVIEWS

*Boxoffice.* September, 2001, p. 150.
*Chicago Sun-Times Online.* July 20, 2001.
*Entertainment Weekly.* July 20, 2001, p. 45.
*Los Angeles Times Online.* July 13, 2001.
*New York Times Online.* July 13, 2001.
*People.* July 23, 2001, p. 36.
*USA Today Online.* July 13, 2001.
*Variety.* July 16, 2001, p. 19.
*Washington Post.* July 19, 2001, p. WE31.

# The Majestic

*Sometimes your life comes into focus one frame at a time.*
—Movie tagline

 **Box Office:** $18.9 million

After the fall of Communism in 1989 in Eastern Europe, after a period of runaway inflation as countries of the Soviet bloc desperately attempted to adjust to the realities of a new economy, some people who believed they were better off under the old system developed a nostalgia for Communism. Frank Darabont's film *The Majestic* also trades foolishly in nostalgia for Communism, putting an unbelievably positive spin on anti-Communist paranoia during the 1950s in America by telling the story of a Hollywood screenwriter named Peter Appleton (Jim Carrey), who, upon the release of his first motion picture, falls victim to the witch-hunt of the House Un-American Activities Committee because he had once attended a political meeting while in romantic pursuit of a young woman.

So far director Frank Darabont has been very lucky. His first two movies—*The Shawshank Redemption* (1994) and *The Green Mile* (1999)—were nominated for Best Picture Academy Awards®, and Darabont, who adapted both films from works by Stephen King, was also nominated for Best Adapted Screenplay. With *The Majestic,* however, Darabont delegated the screenwriting to his Hollywood High School pal Michael Sloane, who apparently understood movie nostalgia better than the historical period in which the story is set. Apparently Darabont wanted to reinvent himself as Frank Capra, regarding *The Majestic* as "the Capra film I've always wanted to make," though it falls far short of that goal. "It rang the Frank Capra bell for me," Darabont said of Sloane's screenplay in a promotional documentary that aired on Home Box Office. If Frank Capra was the inspiration for this confection, the film falls short of being truly Capraesque, though it works overtime to achieve that goal. Capra was fortunate enough to have Robert Riskin writing his best screenplays; Darabont only has Michael Sloane, attempting to write a manipulative screenplay that is all too transparent, clichéd, and mediocre.

In the plot, hack screenwriter Peter Appleton has written a goofy screenplay for a "B" feature entitled *Sand Pirates of the Sahara,* which attempts to parody a genre that is beyond parody. Targeted by HUAC immediately after the film's completion, Peter Appleton therefore loses his job and is forced to clean out his desk. That night he takes his toy monkey into a bar and gets roaring drunk. Then he gets into

his spiffy Mercedes (far too elegant for the achievement level of its owner) and tells his monkey, drunkenly: "How about you and me take a ride up the coast and change our name?" As he is driving across a bridge, a possum crosses the road in front of him. He swerves and loses control of the car and goes off the bridge. Thank goodness the monkey does not survive, at least removing the excuse for any additional monkey-business. On the other hand, Carrey's drunken episode is the only one in the film that gives a glimmer of the comedian's natural talent.

Somehow Peter does manage to survive his plunge into the river below, but when he recovers consciousness, he is suffering from amnesia. He doesn't know where he is or who he is. Rescued by a kindly old geezer (James Whitmore), Peter is then taken into the town of Lawson, California, and given breakfast at the local diner, run (of course!) by a friendly woman named Mabel (Catherine Dent), who tells him he looks familiar. Everyone in town seems to recognize him because he resembles a dead war hero named Luke Trimble. When Luke's father, Harry Trimble (Martin Landau) sees Appleton, he is convinced that he has recovered his son and takes the young man in. "His name was Albert Lucas Trimble," Harry tells Peter, giving him his new but mistaken identity.

Harry Trimble was the owner-operator of a movie house called "The Majestic" that has fallen into disrepair. Believing himself to be reunited with his son and his spirits therefore revived, Harry soon decides to reopen the theatre, and the whole town pitches in to help with the renovation. Lawson is one of those mythic American towns where neighbors help one another just out of rural goodness, the sort of town everyone thinks must have existed at one time. Convincingly transformed into Luke, Peter begins to feel right at home and is soon courting Luke's heartthrob, Adele Stanton (Laurie Holden), the daughter of the respected town doctor (David Ogden Stiers). They talk about movies, since that is apparently all that Peter knows. Peter can quote Paul Muni from *The Life of Emil Zola* (1937) and lines from other movies as well. "You remember movies, but you don't remember your own life?" Adele wonders. That is a telling comment, since the screenwriter obviously knows more about movies than he does about life, and that is ultimately what's wrong with the picture. Of course Appleton is living a lie, and of course his true identity will eventually catch up with him, an inevitable consequence of plot logic.

Peter Appleton is a nobody even before he loses his memory. His only achievement is to have scripted a minor movie that is unbelievably silly, but since Peter himself is silly, he is proud of it. For some peculiar (or convenient) reason Congressman Doyle (Hal Holbrook) and Majority Counsel Elvin Clyde (Bob Balaban) are determined to track Appleton down, and eventually they do. The Majestic theatre is reopened as an amazingly spiffy movie palace, a monument of neon and glitz, an appropriate icon for Darabont's film. Harry Trimble is proud of his helpful adopted son and proud of his renovated theatre. He dies a happy man while running his projectors. But then Peter's world collapses when two Federal Agents (Daniel Von Bargen and Shawn Doyle) roll into town and arrest him, just as he is beginning to recover his memory after seeing *Sand Pirates of the Sahara*, remembering his silly dialogue, and seeing Peter Appleton's name on the movie poster in the lobby. Apprehended oh-so dramatically on Main Street with an audience of astonished locals who turn against him, Peter is then taken away to appear before the Congressional hearings.

Peter is politically naïve and appears to be willing to cooperate as a "friendly" witness, with the understanding that he will therefore escape the blacklist and be able to return to work and have another bad movie made from his second script, "Ashes to Ashes." But Luke's sweetheart Adele Stanton, a trained lawyer, gives him a pep talk about what is right and wrong and also gives him a copy of the Constitution. At the hearing he stands up to the congressional bullies and asserts his constitutional rights. In real life those who were "unfriendly" champions of liberty like John Howard Lawson and the Hollywood Ten were simply shouted down and packed off to prison. But since this is only a movie, let's say things go considerably better for Peter Appleton. He speaks his mind to a televised hearing (so the folks back in Lawson can watch), no less, and all that anti-Communist paranoia that plagued the era seems conveniently to evaporate. He then goes "home" to Lawson, where Adele is waiting for him and where the whole town gives him a hero's welcome. In the film's conclusion, sentimentality is laid on with a trowel as Peter recovers everything—his memory, his self-respect, his girl, and his job. That is his reward for being momentarily courageous and thoughtful.

Reviewers were needlessly outraged by the film's fabrications. Some of the Hollywood Ten were in fact sincere Socialists or Communists who believed their rights as Americans would be protected by the system. The film is set in 1951, about the time of the Korean conflict. The era of McCarthyism did not exactly end that year; the televised Army-McCarthy hearings that were still to come would finally expose McCarthy for the demagogue bully he was. Michael Sloane had no right to rewrite history in such a facile way. As Claudia Puig wrote, witheringly, in *USA Today*, "The McCarthy era has been depicted more convincingly in other films." Moreover, Appleton's "banal work would have been unlikely to call attention it itself, much less inspire the scrutiny of commie-baiting witch hunters."

Stephen Hunter wrote in the *Washington Post* that Darabont's film "doesn't have a single believable second. Every word of it is a lie." Hunter protested, reasonably enough, that amnesia was an unworkable and far-fetched plot gimmick for 1951, when fingerprinting could establish identity in a matter of hours: "So the movie is built on the insistence that we take on faith that which could not and

would not exist." It celebrates the goodness of small-town America in contrast to the political corruption rampant in Hollywood and Washington. Hunter criticized the film for being "mis-wired to politically correct specifications, made absurd by the ludicrous pictorialism of Frank Darabont's style of directing and his insistence that a film increases in excellence in proportion to its length."

What is there to like in this movie that does not allow Jim Carrey to do what Jim Carrey does best, manic comedy rather than droll melodrama and existential angst? Veteran trooper Martin Landau provides a soulful turn as old Harry Trimble and newcomer Laurie Holden provides an appealing presence as sweetheart Adele Stanton who inspires Peter to take his stand heroically, if not very convincingly. Darabont's troupe of gifted character actors provides an American gothic patina to Lawson, a sanitized town that might have been lifted out of a portfolio of Norman Rockwell Americana. Outstanding in Darabont's supporting gallery of coots and geezers are James Whitmore as Stan Keller, the kindly old fella who finds Peter after the accident and brings him into Larson, and Gerry Black as Emmett Smith, the African-American World War I veteran who has been waiting rather too long for the rundown movie theatre to reopen. Both Hal Holbrook and Bob Balaban stand out in the film's rogue's gallery of hissable villains. "I have played some wonderful terrible people," Bob Balaban told Richard Leiby of the *Washington Post*, and Counsel Clyde certainly fits that description. Balaban is probably best known for the five-episode run he did for *Seinfeld* on television, but his film career covers several memorable roles in pictures directed by Steven Spielberg, Woody Allen, and, most recently, Robert Altman in *Gosford Park* (2001).

*The Majestic*, then, attempts to be a postcard from the past, with Jim Carrey playing Jimmy Stewart in a picture more manipulative than anything conjured up by Frank Capra, right down to the flag-waving patriotic spectacle celebrating the sacrifice of war veterans, a riff that might actually help sell the picture in an era of renewed patriotism. It's also about love and conviction and personal integrity, a confection that utterly distorts the politics and the atmosphere of the 1950s it attempts to reconstruct. By and large the picture is distorted and utterly false. But of course Frank Darabont knows what he is doing. He is attempting to make a feel-good movie based upon nostalgia and noble sentiments, a cross between *Mr. Smith Goes to Washington* (1939) and *Cinema Paradiso* (1989), with a touch of Preston Sturges's *Hail the Conquering Hero* (1944) thrown in for good measure, though unlike Darabont or Sloane, Sturges was a master of irony and satire. Darabont, a sentimentalist at heart, has shown talent and has enjoyed a measure of popular success, but *The Majestic* was a disappointment to all of those who reviewed it. Of course it could still find an audience of sentimental suckers and the fans of Jim Carrey, who gives a sincere performance and who is, after all, a likable actor, trapped here in a limited and less than majestic role, diminished to what one reviewer described as a "likable blank."

—*James M. Welsh*

## CREDITS

**Peter Appleton:** Jim Carrey
**Harry Trimble:** Martin Landau
**Adele Stanton:** Laurie Holden
**Doc Stanton:** David Ogden Stiers
**Stan Keller:** James Whitmore
**Ernie Cole:** Jeffrey DeMunn
**Kevin Bannerman:** Ron Rifkin
**Congressman Doyle:** Hal Holbrook
**Majority Counsel Elvin Clyde:** Bob Balaban
**Sheriff Cecil Coleman:** Brent Briscoe
**Emmett Smith:** Gerry Black
**Irene Terwilliger:** Susan Willis
**Mabel:** Catherine Dent
**Avery Wyatt:** Chelcie Ross
**Sandra Sinclair:** Amanda Detmer
**Leo Kubelsky:** Allen (Goorwitz) Garfield
**Federal Agent Ellerby:** Daniel von Bargen
**Federal Agent Saunders:** Shawn Doyle
**Roland the Intrepid Explorer:** Bruce Campbell
**Evil Prince Khalid:** Clifford Curtis

**Origin:** USA
**Released:** 2001
**Production:** Frank Darabont; Castle Rock Entertainment, Village Roadshow Pictures, NPV Entertainment, Darkwoods; released by Warner Bros.
**Directed by:** Frank Darabont
**Written by:** Michael Sloane
**Cinematography by:** David Tattersall
**Music by:** Mark Isham
**Sound:** Mark Ulano
**Editing:** Jim Page
**Art Direction:** Tom Walsh
**Costumes:** Karyn Wagner
**Production Design:** Gregory Melton
**MPAA rating:** PG
**Running time:** 152 minutes

## REVIEWS

*Baltimore Sun.* December 21, 2001, p. E1.
*Boxoffice.* December, 2001, p. 24.
*Chicago Sun-Times Online.* December 21, 2001.
*Entertainment Weekly.* January 4, 2002, p. 47.
*Los Angeles Times Online.* December 21, 2001.
*New York Times Online.* November 4, 2001.
*New York Times.* December 21, 2001, p. E1.
*People.* December 24, 2001, p. 31.
*Variety.* December 17, 2001, p. 36.
*Washington Post.* December 21, 2001, p. C5.
*Washington Post.* January 3, 2002, p. C1.
*Washington Post Weekend.* December 21, 2001, p. 45.
*Washington Times.* December 21, 2001, p. B6.

## TRIVIA

Voice cameos include Garry Marshall, Paul Mazursky, Sydney Pollack, Carl Reiner, Rob Reiner, and Matt Damon.

# Making Love (Canone Inverso)

If movies could have cousins then Italian director Tognazzi's *Making Love* would be the cousin to Quebecois Francois Girard's *The Red Violin*. The films both have similar cinematic DNA: moody temperament, a passion for classical music, heirloom violins, and an international flair. However, if one takes the comparisons further, both films begin with a musical instrument auction in which attendees related to the violin start a bidding war, and end with a mystery regarding a violin's ownership. Women die giving birth, young virtuosos fall in love with muses, and the musical soundtracks by John Corigliano and Ennio Morricone become the language of the films. After all cinema and music are their own languages, which communicate universally over time and space.

A canone inverso is a score with two melodies that can be played in reverse order. Tognazzi structures his adapted screenplay in the style of a canone inverso by starting at both the beginning and the end of the same story. What unravels is a mystery that travels back to the early 1900's and works its way to the late 1930's when a Nazi occupation of Prague proved inevitable. Then the story neatly progresses to the Communist takeover of Prague during the quiet revolution of 1968. However, unlike *The Red Violin*, *Making Love* stays in one location, with its dialogue in English, and the film is based on a novel by Paolo Maurensig as opposed to an original idea. Whereas *The Red Violin* followed the path of a rare violin, Tognazzi's film spends more time exploring the lives of the owner of the violin. While music plays a major role, this film explores the humans behind the music in depth.

In 1970 Prague, young Costanza (Nia Roberts) and older businessman Baron Blau (Peter Vaughn) attempt to outbid each other at an auction of musical instruments. After the Baron wins the bidding war, the distraught Costanza follows him, saying that he will regret taking the violin away from her. Flustered, the Baron agrees to listen to her story about the heirloom violin, which was told to her by a mysterious violinist two years earlier, whom Costanza believes to have been her father. But what unravels is more than a mystery about the father she never knew. At this point, the story travels back to the early 1900's where we meet the child Jeno Varga, who discovers his long-vanished father's violin. As the years fly by, Jeno grows obsessed with the violin and his musical talent is obvious. However, Jeno is poor and illegitimate, living on a farm with his Jewish mother and stepfather, where he works hard by day and plays his violin most of each night.

As time passes, Jeno grows into a man (Hans Matheson) and develops a crush on virtuoso pianist Sophie Levi (Mèlanie Thierry), whom he encounters by chance on a trip to the city. Sophie, who's married and at the peak of her professional career, appears intrigued by Jeno's amorous attention, but she rebuffs the country boy until one day when he plays her one of his compositions. Realizing his talents, Sophie insists that Jeno study at the music conservatory. While at the conservatory, Jeno meets another virtuoso violinist, David Blau (Lee Williams), and soon the two become inseparable. However, the Holocaust, which cast a shadow all over Europe, finally arrives in Prague and Jewish students and professors are expelled from the conservatory.

Jeno stays at David's family home where he accidentally discovers that he and David share the same father. Soon David and Jeno become rivals in music and in life. Jeno is chosen to perform with Sophie, but because of her Jewish status, the Nazis interrupt the concert and send Sophie and Jeno to a concentration camp where Sophie gives birth to a daughter. Then, in 1968, a violinist (Gabriel Byrne) approaches Costanza and plays her a song she remembers from her childhood, a song that was written by Baron Blau and eventually passed down to her. We soon learn the family connection between Costanza, the violinist, and the Baron.

In this film, making love becomes equivalent with making music, and immersing oneself in Ennio Morricone's lush score might just surpass sex. Tognazzi's *Making Love* eloquently captures its viewers' souls.

—*Patty-Lynne Herlevi*

## CREDITS

**Jeno Varga:** Hans Matheson
**Sophie Levi:** Melanie Thierry
**David Blau:** Lee Williams

**The Violinist:** Gabriel Byrne
**Baron Blau:** Ricky Tognazzi
**Old Baron Blau:** Peter Vaughn
**Costanza:** Nia Roberts
**Mother:** Rachel Shelley
**Wolf:** Andriano Pappalardo

**Origin:** Italy
**Released:** 2000
**Production:** Vittorio Cecchi Gori; Cecchi Gori Group
**Directed by:** Ricky Tognazzi
**Written by:** Ricky Tognazzi, Simona Izzo, Graziano Diana
**Cinematography by:** Fabio Cianchetti
**Music by:** Ennio Morricone
**Sound:** Tullio Morganti
**Editing:** Carla Simoncelli
**Costumes:** Alfonsina Lettieri
**Production Design:** Francesco Bronzi
**MPAA rating:** Unrated
**Running time:** 107 minutes

 REVIEWS

*Boxoffice.* November, 2000, p. 171.
*Hollywood Reporter.* January 17, 2001, p. 78.
*Variety.* June 12, 2000, p. 17.

# The Man Who Cried

**Box Office:** $.6 million

In an early scene of *The Man Who Cried*, a little girl, separated from her family and homeland, sits forlornly in the bright and cheerful bedroom provided for her by her foster family. Despite her pretty surroundings, it all seems empty to the child. The film is much the same, with its pleasing (and sometimes even beautiful) visuals prettying up a narrative which lacks expressiveness. This is strange for a story which sounded like it would be charged with emotion and gripping intensity: a tiny Russian Jewish tot with a golden voice is torn from the only people and surroundings she has ever known, grows up to be a chorus girl in glittering pre-WWII Paris, is introduced to love and sex by a smoldering gypsy who rides a powerful white steed, and escapes from Europe a step ahead of the Nazis to search for her long-lost and beloved father in America. Instead, the manner in which this film tells its tale has surprisingly little impact on the viewer.

*The Man Who Cried* begins promisingly, however, amidst Bizet's tender, highly romantic aria "Je Crois Entendre," focusing on the girl (captivating Claudia Lander-Duke) and her father (played well by respected vet Oleg Yankovsky) in 1927 Russia. He is a cantor with a beautiful voice who exudes warmth and possesses the kindliest face you could imagine. That face lights up whenever he looks at the daughter he calls Fegele, meaning little bird. She romps with him in the woods, sometimes perched happily upon her father's shoulders and other times gleefully initiating a game of hide-and-go-seek. We get a number of telling shots which make it abundantly clear that they adore each other. One night, when she overhears talk of his going to America, he comforts her with a kiss and a soothing lullaby. The scene in which she clings to her father, her adorable face dominated by huge, questioning, mournful eyes is both affecting and effective.

Soon afterward, she is packed off by her grandmother seconds before soldiers destroy their little village in a brutal and fiery pogrom, a photograph of her father clutched tightly in her hands. After an arduous and frightening journey to a seaport, Fegele is separated from her fellow travelers and ends up in England instead of America. There, she is renamed Suzie before being taken in by a prim Christian couple, and looks utterly lost and miserable. Unable to speak English, she can express herself through her lovely singing voice, although when the choirmaster hears her singing in Yiddish he reminds her that she must conform to her new situation, wacking her on the hand to emphasize his point. This method evidently works, as we see her singing in English to her classmates in a scene which jumps us ahead to Suzie as a young woman (now played by Christina Ricci) who is auditioning for a job which will earn her enough money to get to America. She ends up in a dance troupe in Paris where the performers wiggle their behinds and wink at the audience while wearing skimpy costumes with sequins and feathers.

It is at this fairly early stage that the audience's emotional involvement in the heretofore rather compelling film begins to wane. A large part of this is due to both the way the central character of Suzie has been written, as well as Ricci's performance. Ricci has spoken of conveying inner thoughts and feelings through facial expressions and gesture rather than through explicit dialogue, but so many of the closeups we get of her all-too-silent Suzie (and we get plenty) are merely blank and lifeless. There is no spark to what is a generally sketchy and colorless characterization. She is overshadowed by Cate Blanchett, who plays her role of roommate and fellow showgirl Lola, a vivacious Russian gold digger, to the hilt with a throaty, thick-accented voice coming forth from bright red, overripe lips. Lola sets her sights on egotistical Italian opera singer Dante Dominio (John Turturro), who sympathizes with Mussolini and the rising wave of Fascism. While Blanchett's performance may lay it on a tad too thickly, it is still enjoyable, but Turturro outdoes her and is sometimes unintentionally comical.

These unrestrained vibrant performances are far different from Ricci's Suzie and the equally mute Cesar (Johnny Depp, who also appeared with Ricci in *Sleepy Hollow*), the gypsy upon the white horse, symbolizing ever young girl's Prince Charming. She keeps looking at him. He keeps looking at her. Nothing is said. If there is supposed to be passion brewing here, it more closely resembles the early stages of catatonia. He gently goes to touch her face. She backs off. She looks at him. He looks at her with a faint smile before galloping away. Compared to these two, the horse is brimming with personality and is an absolute chatterbox. Finally Suzie and Cesar discover speech, and she is introduced to his fellow gypsies who have set up camp in a courtyard. She feels a kinship with these other rootless people, and breaks out into song to their musical accompaniment. (The dubbing of singing voices in this film is not always convincing.) Of course we are to understand here that Suzie is regaining her "voice," finding once again a comfortable niche in the world in which to express herself.

But who is she, and where does she really belong? She feels a connection to Cesar and the gypsies but is not one of them, and she lives in France as a Christian from Britain but is actually a Russian Jew. Only Lola knows her real background, until the woman inadvertently leaks it to Dante, who in turn ends up spitefully informing the Nazis when they occupy Paris, branding her a "gypsy lover" to boot. Suzie has indeed lost her virginity to Cesar in a thoroughly unromantic scene, an experience which barely registers on her poker-face. If we are supposed to sense that their relationship is something wonderful, romantic, and dreamy, there is little here on the screen to make it palpable so we can believe it. We are able to connect more with Lola, whose declining relationship with Dante is well-told in a variety of expressive shots: Lola killing time reading a magazine in the bathtub; Lola leaning listlessly in a doorway in Dante's luxurious house, surrounded by the riches she sought and utterly alone; and a close up of the deflated look on her face when she makes eyes at him and he is too busy enjoying the attentions of another woman to notice. When Dante alerts the Nazis that Suzie is a Jew, it is all there on Blanchett's face that Lola's position at the man's side is no longer tenable. She warns Suzie that she is in danger, and the two women make plans to sail for America. The goodbye scene between Suzie and Cesar is particularly poor, featuring bad and—in a marked change for these two—overwritten dialogue. (This is not the only place in the film where the dialogue is unnatural and stilted.)

While crossing the Atlantic, Lola makes an abrupt exit from the story when a bomb rips directly into the ship's pool where she is swimming, and Suzie, rescued from the dark, frigid waters, must proceed alone once again in her long-deferred quest to rejoin her father. It turns out that he has left his religion behind and gone to Hollywood, where he has nearly worked himself to death on musicals, much to the concern of his new family. When his little Fegele, whom he thought had been killed years before in the pogroms, sits upon his bed and comforts him the way he used to comfort her by singing in Yiddish, it somehow does not quite generate the lump in the throat that the filmmakers were surely hoping for. It does make us realize how much more this warm character drew us to him during his brief screen time than his daughter, once she was portrayed by Ricci, ever did.

*The Man Who Cried* was written and directed by Sally Potter (1992's *Orlando* and 1997's *The Tango Lesson*), who felt it was necessary to keep her Suzie quiet: "Her silence propels her through the film," she asserted to *Entertainment Weekly*. "It's a journey towards somebody refinding her own voice." It is hard to make a film compelling, however, when the heroine at its core hardly speaks and looks as if she is in need of a good multivitamin. Couple that with a lover who is equally mute and muted, and the story merely unfolds without succeeding in being involving. There are numerous scenes which are visually striking, thanks to justly-acclaimed cinematographer Sacha Vierny, whose long career has included films by Buñuel and Resnais. Those who enjoy classical music and opera will appreciate performances by such talents as the famed Kronos Quartet. Potter's film, made on a relatively small budget, grossed under $740, 000 in limited release, and received more negative than positive reviews. "Always look forward," advises the character of Lola, which is probably the best thing to do now for all those involved with the disappointing *The Man Who Cried*.

—*David L. Boxerbaum*

**Music by:** Osvaldo Golijoy
**Editing:** Herve Schneid
**Art Direction:** Carlos Conti
**Costumes:** Lindy Hemming
**MPAA rating:** R
**Running time:** 97 minutes

 **REVIEWS**

*Boxoffice.* April, 2001, p. 227.
*Chicago Sun-Times Online.* June 22, 2001.
*Entertainment Weekly.* June 8, 2001, p. 48.
*Los Angeles Times Online.* May 25, 2001.
*New York Times Online.* May 25, 2001.
*People.* June 11, 2001, p. 35.
*Sight and Sound.* January, 2001, p. 53.
*Variety.* September 18, 2000, p. 37.
*Washington Post.* July 20, 2001, p. WE36.

**AWARDS AND NOMINATIONS**

**Natl. Bd. of Review 2001:** Support. Actress (Blanchett).

# The Man Who Wasn't There

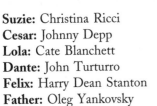 **Box Office:** $6.8 million

Evoking the atmosphere of post-war, small-town life but imbuing it with a fatalistic air, the Coen brothers' *The Man Who Wasn't There* is an odd pastiche of dark comedy and crime drama with a fair smattering of existential musings thrown in for good measure. Beautifully rendered in black-and-white by cinematographer Roger Deakins to imitate stylistically the noir classics it invokes, the film chronicles the downward spiral of a down-on-his-luck schmo, Ed Crane (Billy Bob Thornton), whose every attempt to make something of his life turns into a disaster. His sad story recalls the trajectory of the beleaguered Jerry Lundegaard of the Coens' masterpiece, *Fargo*, but, whereas Jerry was a fidgety, motormouth car salesman, Ed is a passive, nearly silent barber whose main form of expression is his lengthy voice-over narration.

Writer-director Joel and writer-producer Ethan Coen set their story in 1949 Santa Rosa (a clear nod to Hitchcock's *Shadow of a Doubt*) and paint a bleak picture of Ed, who lives

**CREDITS**

**Suzie:** Christina Ricci
**Cesar:** Johnny Depp
**Lola:** Cate Blanchett
**Dante:** John Turturro
**Felix:** Harry Dean Stanton
**Father:** Oleg Yankovsky

**Origin:** Great Britain, France
**Released:** 2000
**Production:** Christopher Sheppard; Working Title Productions, Adventure Films, Studio Canal Plus; released by Universal Focus
**Directed by:** Sally Potter
**Written by:** Sally Potter
**Cinematography by:** Sacha Vierny

a simple, boring existence. Seeming to have accepted his mundane lot in life occupying the second chair in his brother-in-law Frank's (Michael Badalucco) barbershop, Ed nonetheless yearns for something more. His wife, Doris (Frances McDormand), keeps the books at Nirdlingers Department Store, where she works for Big Dave (James Gandolfini), with whom Ed suspects Doris of having an affair.

One day a shifty businessman named Creighton Tolliver (Jon Polito) comes into the barbershop talking about a great business opportunity—dry cleaning, which he thinks is the wave of the future. A potential investor has backed out, leaving him with no one to be his partner. Ed sees this as his chance to establish himself in his own business, but he is lacking the requisite $10,000. However, pretty certain that Doris is cheating on him with Dave, Ed sends an anonymous blackmail note to Dave to try to get the money for the business. Giving up the $10,000 would be a huge loss for Dave, who needs the money to open up an annex to the department store, which he would manage. Since Dave was the one who turned down Creighton's business proposition and the blackmail request just happens to be for $10,000, poor Dave thinks that Creighton is his blackmailer. Dave confides in Ed about the blackmail note but of course does not reveal that he is cheating with Doris.

Feeling that he has no choice, Dave has Doris cook the books at Nirdlingers and embezzles the money to pay the blackmailer, which enables Ed to buy a stake in the dry-cleaning enterprise. He will be Creighton's "silent partner" in the business, which seems to be a pun on Ed's personality. But Dave beats the truth out of Creighton, learns that Ed is his blackmailer, and calls Ed to his office late at night to confront him. "What kind of man are you?" he asks in disbelief of the sullen Ed. Even though he has done wrong by Ed, Dave cannot understand how Ed could destroy him by taking his money. He attacks Ed, and, in the ensuing scuffle, Ed kills his rival, who is left on the floor in a pool of blood. In an ironic twist, Doris is charged with embezzlement and murder. The books she cooked for Dave make her look like the one responsible for his demise.

The hardboiled plot of adultery and murder puts us squarely in James M. Cain territory, but the Coens, never content simply to redo a genre, tweak it with idiosyncratic characters and eccentric plot turns, some of which work better than others. Ed's deadpan voice-over is darkly comic and almost always compelling, providing strange, philosophical asides on such subjects as how hair keeps growing on a person's head. The film's most farcical element is references to flying saucers. Ann (Katherine Borowitz), Dave's widow, claims that he was once abducted by aliens and thinks that his death is part of a conspiracy to shut him up. The alien-abduction angle comes straight out of postwar popular culture but feels underdeveloped and never fully

integrated into the rest of the story—it dangles as a loose plot thread that the Coens perhaps could have cut.

The most entertaining character among the assorted oddballs is Freddy Riedenschneider (Tony Shalhoub), the best defense lawyer money can buy. Shalhoub gives one of the great supporting performances of the year as the arrogant, loquacious lawyer who tries to spin an elaborate defense to win Doris's freedom. The essence of Freddy's charm is that he is a weird breath of fresh air in this dark tale. Ed is so laconic that we can never fully understand his internal workings, which is the film's biggest flaw; it is hard to become emotionally involved with such a cipher, even one who is narrating his own story. Freddy, on the other hand, is all surface and a sheer delight to watch. He struggles valiantly to concoct a believable defense for Doris, but, even when the hapless Ed admits that he killed Dave, Freddy dismisses the story as unbelievable.

Then, in one of the great scenes in any Coen brothers film, Freddy delivers a riveting speech on the Uncertainty Principle, the idea that, "the more you look, the less you know." He builds a whole defense grounded in this idea that really has nothing to do with the case. What makes the scene a classic, though (beyond Freddy's wonderfully tortuous reasoning), is Deakins's gorgeous cinematography. The scene takes place in a prison meeting room, and light from a window above fills the center of the room, where Freddy walks back and forth expounding on his elaborate defense scheme. It is almost as if he is the one in jail, as the vertical shafts of light look like bars that he is walking behind, making him a kind of prisoner of his crackpot theory.

The case, however, never goes to trial. In a shocking twist, Doris hangs herself, apparently because she was pregnant and Ed was not the father, and the narrative loses its tight focus and begins to drag a little. With the trial no longer an issue and the tragic loss hanging over him, Ed becomes more of a nonperson. While people pass him indifferently on the street, he tells us that "I was a ghost," but, still longing for something to make his life worthwhile, he decides to help jumpstart the piano career of Birdy Abundas (Scarlett Johansson), the teenage daughter of one of his friends. In light of Doris's death, Birdy becomes Ed's cause—the one pure thing that he thinks will make everything right. Unfortunately, he has deluded himself into thinking that she has talent (or else he is simply attracted to her but cannot admit his feelings to himself).

When Ed takes Birdy to a renowned music teacher, he is emphatic about her lack of talent, and Ed is devastated at having his last shot at redemption taken from him. To make matters worse, the grateful Birdy makes a sexual advance on him as they are driving home, which, incidentally, feels out of character for this girl. As Ed resists her, he crashes the car and ends up in the hospital, where he has a bizarre vision of a tar salesman visiting his house and Doris sending him away. It is the oddest scene in the film and perhaps one absurdity too many since it comes out of nowhere and seems to relate to nothing else. The Coen brothers have a tendency to indulge in such tangents in many of their films, and this is one of their most nonsensical.

While Ed is in the hospital, everything really unravels for him. The dead body of Creighton is found, along with the partnership papers that Ed signed, making it appear that Ed killed him. So Ed is charged with the murder that Big Dave committed when he beat up Creighton. Freddy takes the case and delivers an impassioned defense using not only the Uncertainty Principle but also a representation of Ed as Modern Man. How, Freddy asks, could a common barber who wanted only to be a dry cleaner actually be a criminal mastermind? But, alas, the case never goes to the jury. Frank barges into the courtroom and knocks out Ed. He gets a mistrial, but, with everything having been mortgaged to pay Freddy, Ed can no longer afford Freddy's services, and so Ed throws himself on the mercy of the court. The judge gives Ed the death penalty, and, in the final scene, he walks to the death chamber and is strapped down for execution. He is still philosophical to the end, pondering how hair continues to grow for a while after death and speculating on the possibility of eternal life and a reunion with Doris.

*The Man Who Wasn't There* presents a stark picture of a society in which no one is able to fulfill his dream of getting somewhere in the world. All the principals are punished but, in cruelly ironic twists, never specifically for what they did wrong. The Coens have thus created an elegant entry in the neo-noir canon but have also spiked it with their usual absurdities, which yield mixed results. Ed's philosophical voice-overs are very funny but sometimes a bit too intellectual for a barber, and too much time is spent on throwaway references to flying saucers. The narrative is thus clever in the way it weaves together the fates of all the characters but at times comes to a standstill for off-the-wall diversions that do not quite add up. While the story may have its flaws, however, the style is perfect. The real star of the film, in fact, is the stunning cinematography and rich period detail, which make *The Man Who Wasn't There* a visual triumph.

—*Peter N. Chumo II*

## CREDITS

Ed Crane: Billy Bob Thornton
Doris Crane: Frances McDormand
Frank: Michael Badalucco
Big Dave: James Gandolfini
Ann Nirdlinger: Katherine Borowitz
Creighton Tolliver: Jon Polito
Birdy Abundas: Scarlett Johansson
Walter Abundas: Richard Jenkins
Freddy Riedenschneider: Tony Shalhoub

**Origin:** USA
**Released:** 2001
**Production:** Ethan Coen; Working Title Productions; released by USA Films
**Directed by:** Joel Coen
**Written by:** Joel Coen, Ethan Coen
**Cinematography by:** Roger Deakins
**Music by:** Carter Burwell
**Sound:** Peter Kurland
**Editing:** Joel Coen, Ethan Coen, Tricia Cooke
**Art Direction:** Chris Gorak
**Costumes:** Mary Zophres
**Production Design:** Dennis Gassner
**MPAA rating:** R
**Running time:** 116 minutes

## REVIEWS

*Boxoffice.* September, 2001, p. 143.
*Boxoffice.* October, 2001, p. 18.
*Chicago Sun-Times Online.* November 2, 2001.
*Entertainment Weekly.* November 9, 2001, p. 79.
*Los Angeles Times Online.* October 31, 2001.
*New York Times Online.* October 31, 2001.
*People.* November 12, 2001, p. 36.
*Sight and Sound.* October, 2001, p. 12.
*Sight and Sound.* November, 2001, p. 50.
*USA Today Online.* October 31, 2001.
*Variety.* May 21, 2001, p. 15.
*Washington Post.* November 2, 2001, p. WE36.

## QUOTES

Defense attorney Freddy Riedenschneider (Tony Shalhoub): "I litigate, I don't capitulate."

## AWARDS AND NOMINATIONS

**L.A. Film Critics 2001:** Cinematog
**Nomination:**
**Golden Globes 2002:** Actor—Drama (Thornton), Film—Drama, Screenplay
**Writers Guild 2001:** Orig. Screenplay
**Broadcast Film Critics 2001:** Film, Screenplay.

# A Matter of Taste (Un Affaire de Gout)

*Seduction comes in many forms . . .*
—Movie tagline

French cinema has received a makeover in the past few years while importing a variety of genres ranging from thrillers to romantic comedies to the States. French television-turned-film director, Bernard Rapp's thriller *A Matter of Taste* follows close on the heels of Dominic Moll's *With a Friend Like Harry*. Both films deal with obsessive sadomasochistic relationships between a wealthy man and a man struggling to pay the bills. However, *A Matter of Taste*, written by Gilles Taurand and Rapp and adapted from Philippe Balland's novel *Affaire de Gout*, also revolves around a master-servant relationship that recalls a similar relationship found in Joseph Losey's *The Servant*. Eventually the tables are turned with disastrous results.

*A Matter of Taste* was nominated for several Cèsar Awards (French Oscars) in 2001, including Film, Actor (Bernard Giraudeau), Screenplay (Bernard Rapp and Gilles Taurand), Supporting Actress (Florence Thomassin) and Most Promising Young Actor (Jean-Pierre Lorit). The *Los Angeles Times* praised the actors' performances, "Remarkable performances!" and *Detour* agreed with the observation, "Splendidly acted! *A Matter of Taste* is one to be savored." While the film revolves around the two lead actors, newcomer Lorit and veteran Bernard Giraudeau, performances by Thomassin, Jean-Pierre Lèaud (of Truffaut fame), and Charles Berling also splash more color on to the film's vast canvas. The performances range from deceptively subtle and melancholic to raging and psychotic. The *San Francisco Examiner* wrote: "If one could imagine Hannibal Lector as a cannibal of souls rather than flesh, he might resemble Delamont."

Viewers realize they are in for a bumpy ride when a sharpening of a knife reverberates during the opening credits. Next, we see a bevy of chefs slicing away at animal flesh, then the film cuts to the character Nicolas Rivière (Lorit) languishing in a prison cell. The next scene involves the aftereffects of a murder. Nicolas' lover Bèatrice (Thomassin) disposes of Nicolas' soiled clothing. Then the story flashes back to incidents leading up to the murder of Nicolas' sadistic boss, Frèdéric Delmont (Giraudeau). Nicolas and Frèderic cross paths at a restaurant where Nicolas has been hired as a temporary waiter. Eccentric multimillionaire Frèdèric asks Nicolas to taste his food for him since he claims to be allergic to cheese and fish. Nicolas reluctantly complies, then later confides in his employer that the prestigious Frèdèric is a "nut case." However, when the nut case phones Nicolas and offers him a lucrative position as a personal taste tester, Nicolas excepts the offer.

A sadomasochistic relationship soon develops between the two men. Frèderic places Nicolas on-call and several times Nicolas is called away from his warm bed to the disdain of his lover. Nicolas is forced to give up smoking and loses his personal freedoms in exchange for an absurd sum of money. Frèdèric also forces Nicolas to endure a week long fast while tucked away in the family mansion. After the fast, Nicolas enjoys a large banquet of seafood, which leads to a poisoning incident that causes Nicolas to endure vomiting episodes for three days. Frèdéric later confesses to Nicolas that he poisoned him so that he would lose his love of seafood and cheese. Now, the men will share the same distaste and taste for food. Most people would have left an employer after such an act, but Nicolas stays to test his level of endurance.

As time goes on, Nicolas loses his lover, endures a week alone in the African desert where he nearly loses his sanity, and then, after breaking his leg on purpose to please his ailing employer, Nicolas is abandoned. Nicolas lands in a mental hospital where he is drugged for weeks, then he avenges himself on Frèdèric upon his release from the hospital. Needless to say the film's cautionary message warns us not to accept a job from a sadistic psychopath—no matter how lucrative the deal or prestigious the employer.

While *A Matter of Taste* is not the perfect thriller by any means, the film does provide viewers with delicious eye candy and solid performances. The film also acts as a canvas on which viewers can project their interpretations. For instance, some viewers might find the relationship between the men to portray overtones of homosexuality while others see it as an unequal relationship between a sadistic boss (predator) and a desperate employee (prey). With such French thrillers as *A Matter of Taste* and *With a Friend Like Harry*, it looks like Claude Chabrol, France's master of suspense, has competition.

—*Patty-Lynne Herlevi*

## CREDITS

**Frederic Delamont:** Bernard Giraudeau
**Nicolas Riviere:** Jean-Pierre Lorit
**Beatrice:** Florence Thomassin
**Rene Rousset:** Charles Berling
**Magistrate:** Jean-Pierre Leaud
**Dr. Rossignon:** Laurent Spielvogel
**Flavert:** Artus de Penguern
**Dr. Ferrieres:** Anne-Marie Philipe

**Origin:** France
**Language:** French

**Released:** 2000
**Production:** Catherine Dussart, Chantal Perrin; France 3 Cinema, Le Studio Canal Plus, Centre National de la Cinematographie, Rhone Alps Cinema; released by Attitude Films
**Directed by:** Barnard Rapp
**Written by:** Gilles Taurand, Barnard Rapp
**Cinematography by:** Gerard de Battista
**Music by:** Jean-Philippe Goude
**Editing:** Juliette Welfing
**Costumes:** Martine Rapin
**Production Design:** Francois Comtet
**MPAA rating:** Unrated
**Running time:** 95 minutes

## REVIEWS

*Los Angeles Times Online.* November 9, 2001.
*New York Times Online.* September 7, 2001.
*San Francisco Chronicle Online.* August 31, 2001.
*Village Voice Online.* September 9, 2001.

## QUOTES

Frederic (Bernard Giraudeau) informs Nicolas (Jean-Pierre Lorit): "Your job is to test, not to consume."

## AWARDS AND NOMINATIONS

**Nomination:**
**Cesar 2001:** Actor (Giraudeau), Film, Screenplay, Support. Actress (Thomassin).

# Max Keeble's Big Move

*Max rules!*
—Movie tagline

**Box Office:** $17 million

M ax Keeble's Big Move starts out with 12-year-old Max Keeble's (Alex D. Linz of *Home Alone 3*) dream of how his life could be great. He's on his paper route and encounters the Evil Ice Cream Man (Jamie Kennedy of *Scream*). The ice cream man starts chasing Max but Max

foils him by doing some cool martial arts moves on him. After vanquishing his enemy, he strolls by the house of his neighborhood's cool blonde ninth grader/dream girl, Jenna (Brooke Anne Smith), and basks in his victory.

Max has got a rude awakening in store for himself. In his non-dream life, he's starting junior high and he's under the common misconception that junior high life will be somehow better than elementary school. He's planning to reinvent himself, changing from overlooked nerd to cool guy with "phatitude." His plan is quickly dashed when he arrives at school for his first day. Not only does no one seem to notice his newfound phatitude, and he sits on the bus with his usual fellow nerds, Megan (Zena Grey), a smart clarinet player who has a small crush on Max, and Robe (Josh Peck, a rotund fellow so named because he wears his robe everywhere.

Max quickly finds himself the target of two bullies. Troy McGinty (Noel Fisher) is a former childhood friend turned sadistic bully who wears a different t-shirt each day featuring the name of the kid who will be the day's victim. On day one of junior high, McGinty's t-shirt reads "Max Keeble." Uh-oh. McGinty dunks Max into a garbage bin, leaving Max covered with smelly goo. As if this weren't enough humiliation, Max is forced to attend the mandatory school assembly covered in garbage. The evil principal Jindraike (Larry Miller, who seems to be making a career out of playing evil principals) unfairly decides that Max is a troublemaker. Max is also the victim of the school's other bully, Dobbs (Orlando Brown). Dobbs, a former stock market millionaire, now is trying to regain his fortune by stealing his classmates' lunch money. He calls the thefts "investments."

Max also has to deal with that Evil Ice Cream Man. The guy was once turned into the health department by Max's mother (Nora Dunn) and has had it in for Max ever since. Finally, the mean principal Jindraike, besides being corrupt enough to be diverting all the school's money into a fund to build a football stadium, has a plan to bulldoze Max's beloved animal shelter to build the stadium. Boo! Hiss! It looks like Max is going to subject to a year of victimhood until his dad (Robert Carradine) tells Max that the whole family is moving to Chicago—by Friday. Max is aghast, until he sees the move as an opportunity. If he doesn't have to worry about repercussions, then maybe, just maybe, he can set up some schemes to foil his various enemies.

Max, showing the kind of planning ability and strategic thinking that only kids in movies show, quickly forms the perfect revenge scenarios for each of his tormentors. The best is the one he chooses for McGinty. Max remembers that as a little boy, McGinty was driven to tears at a birthday party featuring a big Scottish frog character named Mc-Google. Max rigs up McGinty's locker to play McGoogle's silly theme song whenever he opens the door. McGoogle is so harmless seeming and the song so innocuous that it's a funny gag to see the big goofy frog's very appearance making this once proud bully reduced to cowering under a bench, sobbing, "He's gonna eat me!"

Max's devil-may-care attitude makes him suddenly popular. Cool girl Jenna invites him to hang out at the local ice cream place and Max is given entrance into the upper echelon's of middle school society. In his eagerness to appeal to Jenna and her friends, Max skips a going away party given him by his old buddies Megan and Robe.

You probably don't have to be one of the adults in the audience to realize, at the last minute, Max's family is going to decide not to move and Max is going to have to face the consequences of his actions. He's hurt his best friends' feelings, angered two bullies, one Evil Ice Cream Man and one corrupt principal. Will Max be able to triumph over his many enemies? Oh, yes. As Jan Stuart of *Newsday* put it, "We know that Max will rise triumphant, since Disney would be run out of town forever if it foisted a nihilist family picture on unsuspecting children."

To appease its junior high and younger target audience, *Max Keeble's Big Move* loads on the gross-out sequences. It's not the crass gross out humor that's in recent comedies aimed at an older set, but one that's more yucky than actually gross. Besides Max's run in with the gooey trash dumpster, there's a scene where some characters are covered with—ick—melted ice cream and, of course, the requisite big food fight scene. It's all stuff that's common fodder on Nickelodeon. The movie is also peppered with jokes that, while they aren't really that original, are amusing enough. In Max's dream sequence when he fights the Evil Ice Cream Man, the scene is done to look like a poorly dubbed martial arts movie. Sure, it was done first and better in *Wayne's World* but *Max's* intended audience probably hasn't seen that film. There's also a lot of kid friendly puns. The school's newspaper reporter tells a frightened newcomer about the school's history of bullies, including one known for his penchant for giving wedgies who was called the "World Wide Wedge." There are also some welcome jokes for parents. When someone is trying to get Dobbs to get out of the way, they say, "Step off, capitalist tool." When Robe is talking to Max about Chicago, he explains soberly, "They call it the Motor City."

The filmmakers, including director Tim Hill of *Muppets in Space* and writers Jonathan Bernstein, Mark Blackwell, and James Greer, seem like they've gone to the trouble to make the film better than others of its ilk. for example, the bullies' characters are more developed and amusing than usual preteen movie bullies. The financial bully Dobbs, for example, has developed a system of charging his victims to use the restroom. Spitting is one cost, throwing up is another and giving Max a swirlie (that is, pushing a victim's head in the toilet bowl) is on the house.

Even though the plot is predictable, it's fairly complex. Max has so many enemies that just following the various schemes for all of them makes this screenplay a lot more complicated that many movies that have come out recently for older folks. And there are some good lessons hidden in the movie, too. When Max finds himself with a second chance to do exactly to the bullies what they've done to him, he has the realization that bullying the bullies just makes him as bad as them. The lessons are handled lightly and kids shouldn't feel like they're being lectured.

As Max, Linz is thankfully not overly cute and mugging. He's a likable character who uses brains instead of brawn. Also good is Peck as Robe, who comes across as having a certain wry dignity, even though he's apt to eat food that he finds on the ground. Also, despite the fact that he's played the role many times, Miller seems to be especially good in this turn as the kid-hating principal. His character is full of quirks that make him an interesting villain. He has a tenuous grasp on the English language and says things like "You may be under the impression that I encourage horseplay and malarkey. In fact, I excourage it." The film also has a couple of cameos, including pint-sized rapper L'il Romeo playing himself and model Amber Valetta playing a science teacher.

Critics had mixed opinions on the film. Rob Blackwelder of Spliced Wire wrote, "Sure, *Max Keeble* is a giggle-fest for the grade school set, but 90 percent of its laughs are from jokes and cliches that weren't even fresh when the East Side Kids peddled them." Christine Dolen of the *Miami Herald* wrote, "Realistic it's not. But *Max Keeble's Big Move,* predictable though it may be, makes most of the right moves for the older elementary/younger middle school market." Chris Hewitt of the *St. Paul Pioneer Press* said that the film was "a transparent rip-off of *Ferris Bueller's Day Off,* but I'll be darned if it isn't almost as much fun."

—*Jill Hamilton*

**CREDITS**

**Max Keeble:** Alex D. Linz
**Principal Jindraike:** Larry Miller
**Evil Ice Cream Man:** Jamie Kennedy
**Megan:** Zena Grey
**Robe:** Josh Peck
**Dobbs:** Orlando Brown
**Troy McGinty:** Noel Fisher
**Lily:** Nora Dunn
**Don:** Robert Carradine
**Superinendent Knebworth:** Clifton Davis
**Mrs. Rangoon:** Amy Hill
**Mrs. Dingman:** Amber Valletta
**Caption Writer:** Justin Berfield

**Origin:** USA
**Released:** 2001

**Production:** Mike Karz; released by Buena Vista
**Directed by:** Timothy Hill
**Written by:** Jon Bernstein, Mark Blackwell, James Greer
**Cinematography by:** Arthur Albert
**Music by:** Michael Wandmacher
**Sound:** Todd Toon
**Editing:** Tony Lombardo, Peck Prior
**Art Direction:** Kelly Hannafin
**Costumes:** Susan Matheson
**Production Design:** Vincent Jefferds
**MPAA rating:** PG
**Running time:** 101 minutes

## REVIEWS

*Boxoffice.* December, 2001, p. 62.
*Chicago Sun-Times Online.* October 5, 2001.
*Entertainment Weekly.* October 12, 2001, p. 64.
*Los Angeles Times Online.* October 5, 2001.
*New York Times Online.* October 5, 2001.
*USA Today Online.* October 4, 2001.
*Washington Post.* October 5, 2001, p. WE41.

# Maybe Baby

*When it comes to having children, everyone has a position.*
—Movie tagline
*It's a matter of life and sex.*
—Movie tagline

 **Box Office:** $.1 million

A couple wants to have a baby and it seems that they might be infertile. Ha. Ha. That's the premise behind *Maybe Baby*, which despite the rather unfunny subject matter, is a comedy. But then the Brits always did seem to have a better handle on dark comedy than Americans. The film was written and directed by Ben Elton, a British comic and writer who was behind cult BBC favorites, *The Young Ones* and *Blackadder*. Elton made the film as an adaptation of his book called *Inconceivable* and this is his cinematic debut.

The story follows the traumas—the light, happy traumas, that is—of a youngish couple, Sam (Hugh Laurie) and Lucy Bell (Joely Richardson of the Redgrave acting dynasty). [The couple was first teamed up in the live-action *101 Dalmatians* remake, though here they only have one non-dalmatian dog.] They are a yuppie-type couple who

seem to have everything that one imagines people in catalogs have. Their house is immaculate, furnished with tastefully simple patterns and natural fiber. Sam has a good job at the BBC where he is a writer/producer and Lucy has a glamourous job working for an actors' agent. Even their dog looks like he was ordered from page 39 of the Pottery Barn catalog.

But of course all is not well. The two have been trying for quite a while to get pregnant and it's just not taking. They try having sex in especially romantic places and make sure to time the encounters with Lucy's ovulations. Sam is agreeable enough about all this to leave business meetings at work to rush home and do the deed when his wife calls telling him the time is right. But despite their generally upbeat can-do attitude, it's beginning to strike them that they may have some sort of problem. Thus, they enter into the increasingly invasive (and some would say unfunny) techniques used to treat infertility. The news that neither of them seem to have any medical problem cheers them and makes them more eager to suffer such indignities of having to have their sperm count measured (that would be Sam) or being injected with daily doses of hormones (that's Lucy).

The sense of failure hanging over the couple begins to affect their marriage. Sam is suffering from a wicked case of writer's block and Lucy starts taking an untoward interest in a handsome young actor, Carl Phipps (James Purefoy) that her firm represents. Then Sam gets the idea that the couple's struggles would make . . . the perfect script, but Lucy vetoes the idea, saying that she doesn't want their personal life made into entertainment for others. Sam, who is generally an obedient type (see above about skipping meetings to take advantage of ovulation), reluctantly agrees.

But Sam's situation at work gets more desperate. He is demoted to a position in the kid's programming department where he suffers such indignities as having to talk to unruly kids in focus groups to ask for their guidance on programming. Supervising shows that involve actors dressed in giant fur suits finally gets to Sam and he starts secretly writing his infertility screenplay. He passes it around to the folks at work who think it's brilliant. The success gets to Sam and he starts acting more and more like a cad. He feigns an interest in Lucy's infertility treatments and whenever Lucy says something he makes notes, chuckling quietly to himself, "That's quite funny." He reaches a personal nadir when he decides to read Lucy's private infertility diary so that he can get a better handle on "the woman's voice" in his script. Eventually all hell breaks loose.

The main problem with the story is that it seems too self-referential. When Sam gets the idea that the story of a couple dealing with infertility would make a great screenplay, it's difficult not to think of the real writer, Elton, thinking the same thing. So whenever Sam is taking notes and saying that certain scenes would be so hilarious, it makes the audience look at the movie scene with a more critical eye.

Plus, saying that something is going to be funny sort of ruins the possibility that it will be. Also, since Elton was both the writer and the director, it seems that no one was around to tell him to stop praising his own ideas so much. Elton's great enthusiasm for his own ideas and writing means that we have not one but several characters repeatedly telling Sam how brilliant and wonderful his screenplay is. If it's so great, we don't need the other characters hammering that into us all the time. And if it isn't, they can say it a hundred times and it won't make any difference. The script is cute, but hilarious? Brilliant? Not really.

Despite that, the film moves along at a generally fast and witty pace. Elton does manage to do the difficult task of making the whole infertility treatment process seem as funny as possible. He has a talent for putting good quips in his character's mouths and it's a welcome respite from such topics as fertilized embryos that don't survive. When, after yet another session between the sheets, Lucy asks, "Must you go back to work?" Sam replies with mock pride, "I am one of the BBC's senior lunch eaters." Sam applies his dry, put upon wit to any situation, no matter how humiliating. When he learns that he will have to provide a sperm sample on premises at a hospital, he grumbles, "They want me to masturbate inside a municipal building."

A lot of what makes the story work is Sam's character. Lurie, who resembles an offspring of Hugh Grant crossed with Herman Munster, plays Sam as a Grant-like character, a charming but self-depricating chap. It's much funnier that he, for example, would have to suffer these indignities around his private parts than someone less uptight and repressed. Richardson's Lucy, on the other hand, is less interesting because she's more of a cipher. Her obsession with conceiving and her quiet sense of failure isn't exactly ripe for comic exploitation. She does, however, do an admirable job of making what is essentially a one-note character into someone less tiresome than she could have been.

The other characters help to perk up the proceedings. When Sam tells a buddy (Adrian Lester) at work, "Did I tell you I have to have a sperm test?" his friend replies, "No, but I would prefer that you didn't." Another friend, Druscilla (Emma Thompson), has an array of new age therapies/conspiracy theories that she dramatically shares with the couple. The supporting cast is strong and adds some needed bulk to the story. Joanna Lumley is good as Lucy's hard-driving boss, Shelia. When young actor Carl does a sexy reading of a Shakespeare monologue, she quips, "You're in perilous danger of turning me back into a heterosexual." Best of all is Rowan Atkinson, the cartoon-faced British comic best known as Mr. Bean, who plays Lucy's strange gynecologist. Stephanie Zacharek of Salon.com described his work as "nothing short of brilliant" and noted scenes where Atkinson was "squirting a sploodge of lubricating jelly onto a speculum as if it were toothpaste (and) rooting around in Lucy's nether regions with the intense concentration of Indiana Jones on an archaeological dig."

Critics had a tepid response to the film. Zacharek wrote: "The worst of it is that *Maybe Baby* feels very much like an Englishman's attempt to make a Nora Ephron movie, all warm and squishy in a decidedly American way." Jan Stuart of *Newsday* said "This new romantic comedy from the U.K. lands on an emotional gold mine only to spin it into synthetic straw." And the *Village Voice*'s Ed Park felt that "Equipped with its own recursive system, *Maybe Baby* courts structural rather than temporal vertigo and proves infertile in more ways than one."

*—Jill Hamilton*

## CREDITS

**Sam Bell:** Hugh Laurie
**Lucy Bell:** Joely Richardson
**George:** Adrian Lester
**Carl Phipps:** James Purefoy
**Ewan Proclaimer:** Tom Hollander
**Sheila:** Joanna Lumley
**Mr. James:** Rowan Atkinson
**Charlene:** Dawn French
**Druscilla:** Emma Thompson
**Joanna:** Rachael Stirling

**Origin:** Great Britain, France
**Released:** 1999
**Production:** Phil McIntyre; Pandora Film, BBC Films; released by USA Films
**Directed by:** Ben Elton
**Written by:** Ben Elton
**Cinematography by:** Roger Lanser
**Music by:** Colin Towns
**Sound:** John Hayes, Mike Dowson, Mark Taylor
**Editing:** Peter Hollywood
**Art Direction:** Chris Seagers
**Costumes:** Anne Sheppard
**Production Design:** Jim Clay
**MPAA rating:** R
**Running time:** 104 minutes

## REVIEWS

*Boxoffice.* October, 2001, p. 61.
*Los Angeles Times Online.* August 24, 2001.
*New York Times Online.* August 24, 2001.
*People.* September 10, 2001, p. 42.
*Sight and Sound.* July, 2000, p. 50.
*Variety.* June 12, 2000, p. 16.

# Me You Them (Eu Tu Eles)

*It takes three husbands to make the perfect marriage.*
—Movie tagline

*One woman. Four sons. Three fathers.*
—Movie tagline

Earth goddesses appear to be back in fashion, so suggests Brazilian screenwriter Elena Soarez's *Me You Them*, directed by Andrucha Waddington and based on a real life story. The Aphrodite in question, Darlene, rendered by Brazilian television star Regina Casè, doesn't fall in the lines of a conventional beauty (she doesn't possess a lithe figure), but men are magnetically drawn to her voluptuous sensuality nonetheless. Soarez also suggests that women do not have to look like super models to acquire the gift of true sexual pleasure, they just have to love themselves, life, and everyone around them. And so the earthy Darlene loves her three husbands and her children, who all live under one roof.

However, *Me You Them* doesn't ask us to judge Darlene's behavior. In contrast to the Ingmar Bergman screenplay *Faithless*, in which Marianne Vogler is punished for her unfaithfulness towards her husband, the characters in *Me You Them* display a sense of humor tinged with a nondestructive jealousy towards the philandering Darlene. The children (four sons by four different fathers) appear to be content and happily explore the life that surrounds their extended family unlike Bergman's child character Isabelle who suffers psychological damage due to her mother's indiscretions. According to A.O. Scott in the *New York Times* "...if Darlene is promiscuous, she's also faithful. Rather than move from one man to the next, she collects them into an unlikely but surprisingly practical menage a quartre."

At the film's beginning, a pregnant Darlene, dressed in a wedding gown, rides a donkey across a desert ala the Virgin Mary. She arrives at a church hoping to marry the father of her child but is jilted, so she heads to the nearest city. Three years later, Darlene returns to her backwater hometown, only to learn that her mother has passed away. She finds a use for her wedding gown when middle-aged neighbor Osias (Lima Duarte) asks for her hand in marriage. However, Osias is a misogynist stick in the mud who expects his wife to take care of all of his needs and also work the sugar cane fields while he lies on his hammock listening to his portable radio. Although Osias provides a home for Darlene and her son, he's not the complete man, so Darlene has a fling with a black field hand—later giving birth to a son that is clearly not Osias's.

Darlene falls for Osias's cousin Zezinho (Stenio Garcia) after they attend a local event and soon they're shagging each other near the river where Darlene washes her clothing. Unaware of Darlene's involvement with Zezinho, Osias invites his cousin to live under the same roof and soon Darlene gives birth to a son that sports his father Zezinho's blue eyes. But alas, Zezinho is also not a complete man and next Darlene meets the virile curly-haired Ciro (Luìs Carlos Vasconcelos) and Osias invites Ciro to live under the same roof as well. Then Darlene gives birth to a fourth son that resembles Ciro and not Osias. And they all live happily ever after under one roof in the Bahia region of Brazil.

*Me You Them* comes across as a contemporary fairy tale rather than a morality play. Set against a backdrop of leafless trees, parched soil and shadows cast by an overbearing sun, the film also resembles Iranian cinema with sex appeal. In fact, among the countless awards the Brazilian film has received, cinematographer Breno Silveira was awarded a Cinema Brazil Grand Prize for Best Cinematography in 2001. And Silveira's stunning photography, along with strong performances by Casè and Garcia, garnered several prestigious awards for the director Waddington and the film.

According to critic Bob Graham of the *San Francisco Chronicle*, "*Me You Them* needs to be seen and savored. What Casè and director Andrucha Waddington have brought off is a neat combination of healthy sensuality, psychological subtlety and an unapologetic grasp of how the world turns." The film forces us to examine sexual and psychological dynamics between a husband (in this case, husbands) and a wife with an open mind, as well as an open heart. And Casè (whom A.O. Scott compares to the seductive Sophia Loren and Anna Magnani) conveys a remarkable feisty woman that we can't help but adore and so we gladly allow her to live her polygamous life. Darlene proves that an independent woman can thrive in this world as long as she has enough husbands to assist her.

—*Patty-Lynne Herlevi*

**Darlene:** Regina Case
**Osias:** Lima Duarte
**Zezinho:** Stenio Garcia
**Ciro:** Luiz Carlos Vasconcelos
**Raquel:** Nilda Spencer

**Origin:** Brazil, Portugal
**Language:** Portuguese
**Released:** 2000
**Production:** Flavio R. Tambellini; Columbia TriStar
Filmes do Brasil, Conspiracao Filmes; released by Sony
Pictures Classics
**Directed by:** Andrucha Waddington
**Written by:** Elena Soarez
**Cinematography by:** Breno Silveira
**Music by:** Gilberto Gil
**Sound:** Mark Berger, Mark A. Van Der Willigen
**Editing:** Vicente Kubrusly
**Art Direction:** Toni Vanzolini
**Costumes:** Claudia Kopke
**MPAA rating:** PG-13
**Running time:** 107 minutes

 **REVIEWS**

*Chicago Sun-Times Online.* March 23, 2001.
*Entertainment Weekly.* March 9, 2001, p. 57.
*New York Times Online.* March 2, 2001.
*Sight and Sound.* August, 2001, p. 52.
*Washington Post Online.* March 16, 2001.

**QUOTES**

Ciro (Luis Carlos Vasconcelos) to Darlene (Regina Case): "I never
imagined getting in a line this long just because of a woman."

# Memento

*Some memories are best forgotten.*
—Movie tagline

 **Box Office:** $25.5 million

Since Quentin Tarantino fractured the traditional narrative approach to film noir by presenting *Pulp Fiction*
(1994), far and away the most influential film of the past
decade, as three separate but overlapping stories, filmmakers
have been trying, with mostly moderate success, to out-
Tarantino Tarantino. Writer-director Christopher Nolan
succeeds brilliantly with *Memento*. Nolan tells his story
backward not just for novelty, not for easy irony, not for a
trick ending, not just to explore the conventions of the genre,
but to make a philosophical statement about the nature of

truth. Although it bears superficial characteristics of Harold
Pinter's *Betrayal* (another backward tale filmed in 1983),
*Memento* is highly original in its treatment of time.

Leonard Shelby (Guy Pearce) is a former insurance
investigator trying to find the man who raped and murdered
his wife (Jorja Fox). The problem—and what a problem—
is that he has no short-term memory after being struck in
the head by his wife's assailant. Leonard can recall everything about his life up to his wife's death, but since then, he
can remember only what occurred a few minutes earlier. He
does not even know how long ago his quest began. To keep
track of the evidence he has accumulated, he has the clues
tattooed on his body. "John G. raped and murdered your
wife" is written backward across his chest so that he can read
it in a mirror—a backward clue in a backward tale. Leonard's "facts" include that he is pursuing someone named John
or James whose last name begins with *G*. and who is a drug
dealer. He also carries an annotated version of the police
report of the murder and Polaroid photographs of things and
people he wants to make certain he does not forget with
messages on each.

*Memento* begins with Leonard killing the man he believes is his prey. The rest of the film delineates the events
leading up to this execution as Leonard travels about the
seamier side of Los Angeles. Scenes that do not seem in any
way ironic gain irony after what came before is revealed.
Nolan's method is to end each scene with the beginning of
the previous one. There are also flashbacks to the wife's
murder and to fragments of the couple's life together and
black-and-white flashbacks to Leonard talking on the telephone to an unknown—to the audience—listener about an
insurance case he investigated.

Including the story of Sammy Jankis (Stephen
Tobolowsky) takes *Memento* to another level, making it
more than just a talented writer-director showing off his
style. Jankis also suffers short-term memory loss following
an accident. Leonard's job was to decide, after medical and
psychological examinations, whether Sammy was faking his
condition to collect on his disability policy. Leonard decides
that while Sammy is not faking, his condition is psychological, not medical, and therefore not the responsibility of the
insurance company. His decision has tragic consequences for
Sammy's desperate wife (Harriet Sansom Harris). Sammy's
plight parallels Leonard's on several layers. One of the tattoos reads, "Remember Sammy Jankis," but Leonard
chooses to ignore the lesson of Sammy's story for reasons not
revealed until the end of the film. He has earned his living
from determining whether people were lying but finds himself in a situation where the truth is considerably murkier.

The other central characters are Teddy (Joe
Pantoliano), who claims to be Leonard's friend, and Natalie
(Carrie-Anne Moss). The message on Teddy's photograph
reads, "Don't believe his lies." Is Teddy his wife's killer, is he
a policeman, is he a drug dealer, is he trying to prevent

Leonard from discovering the truth, is he using Leonard for his own purposes, or is all this true? Because Teddy is the man executed at the beginning, the audience hopes for Leonard's sake that he turns out to deserve it.

Then there is Natalie, a bartender who has something to do with drug dealers. Her photograph reads, "She has also lost someone. She will help you out of pity." But can Leonard really trust her? He suspects that someone is using his condition to direct his attentions toward someone other than his wife's killer, and Natalie does set Leonard and a drug dealer named Dodd (Callum Keith Rennie) against each other. Is Teddy or Natalie manipulating Leonard, or is he simply paranoid?

Discovering the answers to these and related questions keeps the audience enthralled, of course, but *Memento* is much more than a stylish mystery. Leonard's search and his uncertainties about everything he has not written on his body make the film a metaphor for the need for truth and the often extreme difficulty of attaining it. And what if his clues are not all they seem? Nolan's repetitive technique of showing bits of scenes more than once emphasizes the contemplative nature of the film. Just as Leonard gathers evidence and tries to interpret it, so does the audience. Just as Leonard is handicapped by not remembering what just happened, the audience is at a disadvantage by not seeing the events in a linear fashion. Traditional mysteries build up the clues, but *Memento* starts with the clues—and an apparent resolution—but denies them the context in which they would add up logically.

Nolan's postmodern thriller forces the viewer to think in a different way than does the typical mystery. Hundreds of films, novels, and stories have trick endings that change the way all that has come before has been seen. Each scene of *Memento* changes the way the audience perceives the previous scene. It is obvious Nolan is leading up to an ironic conclusion, but it turns out to be ironic in an unexpected way. While hundreds of novels have employed unreliable narrators, the technique is extremely rare in films. Because of his condition, Leonard is not even aware of the possibility of his unreliability.

In an Independent Film Channel interview with Elvis Mitchell of the *New York Times,* Nolan declined to acknowledge the direct influence of any film-noir precursors, admitting only a debt to the unconventional narratives of Nicolas Roeg. *Memento* does, however, fit comfortably into the genre's tradition. *Black Angel* (1946), in which an alcoholic tries to solve his wife's murder only to discover he is the killer, is one of several films noir built around amnesia-related plots. *Memento* strongly resembles the best revenge film noir, John Boorman's *Point Blank* (1967) not only in its plot and setting but in staging most of its scenes in bright sunlight, providing ironic counterpoint to the dark goings-on.

The casting is also film noir inspired. Pearce starred in *L.A. Confidential* (1997), one of the best recent films noir; Moss is in *The Matrix* (1999), which has strong noir overtones; and Pantoliano appears in *The Matrix* and *Bound* (1996), another highly original, offbeat film noir. Tobolowsky may have been cast because of his role in *Groundhog Day* (1993), a non-film noir which *Memento* resembles through its repetitions of scenes and its tackled-in-a-time-warp plot.

Nolan, whose first film, *Following* (1998), also had an unusual approach to film noir, directs like a confident veteran. The film begins with a hand shaking a Polaroid photograph which, instead of becoming clearer, fades into blankness, deliberately making the viewer unsettled and in the filmmaker's control. The numerous comic touches include a cruel gag with a tankard of beer and the consequence of Leonard's misreading a number on one of his notes.

Nolan is aided by Wally Pfister's atmospheric cinematography and Dody Dorn's precise editing, especially with the brief flashes of Leonard's past life which often interrupt his thoughts. Dorn and Pfister make the film move smoothly from the present—that is, the past—to a different past and from color to black-and-white.

Pearce is nothing like his straight-arrow policeman in *L.A. Confidential.* Many actors might have presented Leonard as a gloomy, pitiful soul, but Pearce makes him reconciled to his condition and resolute, almost at times cheerfully so, about fulfilling his quest. Pearce narrates some of the film in a dry, deadpan voice and is particularly good when, in the middle of a chase, Leonard cannot remember if he is chasing the man with the gun or is being chased. He also looks and talks like a young, slightly nerdy Clint Eastwood.

Moss's appearance and acting style in *The Matrix* and *Chocolat* (2000) resemble Rachel Griffiths', but here she seems more distinctive, especially when Natalie loses her temper and tells Leonard what she truly thinks. Pantoliano, one of the best character actors around, makes Teddy delightfully ambiguous. Is his friendly but sarcastic surface the real Teddy or just a masquerade? Pantoliano is at his best when Teddy insists upon calling the hero Lenny and claiming to forget that Leonard hates being called that and when Teddy rolls his head when Leonard asks if he has told Teddy about his condition or about Sammy. The tender despair Harris conveys as Mrs. Jankis provides the film with a few poignant moments. Mark Boone Junior is amusing as a sympathetic but sly motel manager who rents Leonard two rooms because he won't recall paying for either.

Reviewing *Memento* in *National Review,* John Simon claimed that anyone claiming to understand the film is a liar. The film does not explain how Leonard knows the name of the killer, but otherwise it is relatively easy to follow for anyone willing to pay attention, a quality too few films in recent years have called for. *Memento* is superbly entertaining and rewarding because Nolan forces the viewer to work almost as hard as Leonard.

—*Michael Adams*

## CREDITS

**Leonard Shelby:** Guy Pearce
**Natalie:** Carrie-Anne Moss
**Teddy:** Joe Pantoliano
**Burt:** Mark Boone Jr.
**Sammy Jankis:** Stephen Tobolowsky
**Dodd:** Callum Keith Rennie
**Mrs. Jankis:** Harriet Harris
**Leonard's wife:** Jorja Fox

**Origin:** USA
**Released:** 2000
**Production:** Jennifer Todd, Suzanne Todd; Summit Entertainment, Team Todd; released by Newmarket
**Directed by:** Christopher Nolan
**Written by:** Christopher Nolan
**Cinematography by:** Wally Pfister
**Music by:** David Julyan
**Sound:** William Fiege
**Editing:** Dody Dorn
**Costumes:** Cindy Evans
**Production Design:** Patti Podesta
**MPAA rating:** R
**Running time:** 116 minutes

## REVIEWS

*Boxoffice.* November, 2000, p. 166.
*Chicago Sun-Times Online.* April 13, 2001.
*Christian Science Monitor.* March 16, 2001, p. F2.
*Entertainment Weekly.* March 23, 2001, p. 77.
*Entertainment Weekly.* March 30, 2001, p. 20.
*GQ.* March, 2001, p. 122.
*Hollywood Reporter.* September 12, 2000, p. 86.
*Los Angeles Times.* March 16, 2001, p. F2.
*Maclean's.* April 2, 2001, p. 68.
*National Review.* April 16, 2001, p. 59.
*New Republic.* April 9, 2001, p. 30.
*New Statesman.* October 23, 2000, p. 47.
*New York.* March 26, 2001, p. 112.
*New York Times.* March 16, 2001, p. B21.
*New Yorker.* March 19, 2001, p. 155.
*Newsweek.* March 19, 2001, p. 60.
*People.* March 19, 2001, p. 36.
*Sight and Sound.* November, 2000, p. 42.
*USA Today.* March 16, 2001, p. E3.
*Variety.* September 18, 2000, p. 31.

## QUOTES

Leonard (Guy Pearce): "Uh, what were we talking about? I'm sorry, have I told you about my condition? I can't make new memories. I can't even remember to forget you."

## TRIVIA

The low-budget film was shot over 25 1/2 days.

## AWARDS AND NOMINATIONS

**Ind. Spirit 2002:** Director (Nolan), Film, Screenplay, Support. Actress (Moss)
**L.A. Film Critics 2001:** Screenplay
**Broadcast Film Critics 2001:** Screenplay
**Nomination:**
**Oscars 2001:** Film Editing, Orig. Screenplay
**Directors Guild 2001:** Director (Nolan)
**Golden Globes 2002:** Screenplay
**Broadcast Film Critics 2001:** Film.

# The Mexican

*Love with the safety off.*
—Movie tagline

 **Box Office:** $66.8 million

Unlike most recent quirky crime comedies with unusual structures, *The Mexican* makes only a tentative nod toward the almost inescapable influence of Quentin Tarantino. Instead, the film, written by J. H. Wyman and directed by Gore Verbinski, strives for offbeat romance combined with an old-fashioned thriller plot full of unexpected twists and turns. The most unusual aspect of *The Mexican* is that despite the romantic angle its stars share screen time only at the beginning and end of the film.

Jerry Welbach (Brad Pitt) is indebted to Margolis (Gene Hackman), a Southern California gangster soon to be released from prison, because a traffic accident between the two led to the criminal's incarceration. Jerry's qualifications for a life of crime and what he did before rear-ending the gangster are never stated. Bernie Nayman (Bob Balaban), whom Margolis has left in charge, demands that Jerry go to Mexico to retrieve an antique pistol with a colorful past.

Again, why would the not-too-bright Jerry, who bungled his last assignment, be entrusted with such a job? Why wouldn't the person holding the gun in Mexico simply bring it to the United States? And how is Jerry supposed to get it through customs? *The Mexican* is a star-driven film that constantly ignores logic.

Jerry's other problem is his long-suffering girlfriend, Samantha Barzel (Julia Roberts). Jerry has promised to accompany Samantha to Las Vegas for a new start—she wants to be a croupier—and she accuses him of selfishness because he must go to Mexico instead. That Nayman has threatened to kill Jerry if he fails means nothing to her. So he flies to Mexico, and she sets out for Las Vegas alone in her lime Volkswagen Beetle, a car meant to underscore her wackiness.

In Mexico, Jerry finds, loses, regains, and loses the gun once more. The major flaw in the film's plot is that the criminals who first steal the pistol end up with it anyway. So what's the point of Jerry's turmoil? What's the point of sending him to begin with? Such deficiencies led Stanley Kauffmann in the *New Republic* to term the script the worst ever for a major studio release. These flaws stick out more in retrospect than while viewing the film. Verbenski, whose first film, *Mouse Hunt* (1997), was also a seriously flawed quirky comedy, provides considerable energy, and seeing how Jerry reacts to losing the gun constantly is amusing, as is his relationship with a frightening-looking dog he picks up along the way.

More central to the pleasures of *The Mexican*, however, is Samantha's half of the tale. Her trip to Las Vegas is interrupted by her abduction by Leroy (James Gandolfini), a hit man supposedly sent to make sure Jerry does his job. Leroy is introduced to Samantha by saving her from another would-be abductor who, of course, shows up again later. On the road both to and from trouble, Samantha and Leroy develop an odd relationship as he sympathizes with her conflicted feelings about Jerry. Leroy becomes a kind of father confessor for Samantha, especially after she discovers he is gay. (Is the film implying that the only sensitive males are homosexuals?)

*The Mexican* interweaves the Jerry and Samantha strands of the story with flashbacks to the origins of the pistol in a small Mexican village a hundred or so years earlier. (The film's title refers to the gun.) That story features a pair of doomed lovers, suggesting that a similar bad end may await Samantha and Jerry. And if Leroy is not exactly what he seems to be, who knows?

The film is moderately entertaining, especially to anyone predisposed to liking Roberts, Pitt, or Gandolfini, but its flaws are annoying. The film's timing, comic and otherwise, seems a bit off. Some scenes or shots linger a bit longer than necessary, and smoother transitions could have been possible. And as with too many Tarantino-influenced films of late, there are jarring shifts in tone from the comic to the

serious. (Lawrence Bender, one of the film's producers, also produced Tarantino's 1994 masterpiece *Pulp Fiction*.) Reviewing it in the *New York Times*, Stephen Holden accused *The Mexican* of being too easygoing, but it is much more violent than its advertisements suggest. The fate of a man (Michael Cerveris) Leroy picks up en route is especially at odds with the film's goofier moments. At its best, Alan Silvestri's score resembles a combination of Henry Mancini's music for Orson Welles' Mexico-flavored *Touch of Evil* (1958) with the style of Ennio Morricone during his spaghetti Western phase, but the music occasionally seems too severe to be accompanying a comedy.

When *The Mexican* does succeed, it is primarily because of the performances. Simmons, best known as a racist convict on *Oz* and as a rather humorless psychiatrist on *Law and Order*, plays Jerry's only ally in the Margolis camp as an unusually nerdy gangster in a bad toupee and Hawaiian shirts. The diminutive Balaban is an even more unusual choice to play a vicious thug. (Denise Chamian's casting is excellent even down to the smallest roles.) Balaban plays Nayman almost as he has done television or film executives on *Seinfeld* and *The West Wing* and in *The Late Shift* (1996). He does not look dangerous but conveys a threatening sense of authority—backed up by men with guns. In an unbilled cameo at the end of the film, Hackman is impressive as the world-weary Margolis.

While Pitt has become a star primarily by playing serious parts, he has shown his silly side in such films as *Johnny Suede* (1991) and *Twelve Monkeys* (1995). He displays good comic timing whenever things go wrong for Jerry—which is often. Pitt works well with Roberts in their few, mostly combative, scenes together, but her Samantha would seem too strident—and unlike the typical Roberts character—if she did not have Leroy to play off. Especially compared to her appearance in *Erin Brockovich* (2000), Roberts appears gaunt and tired, and her wardrobe is even more tacky than in her Oscar®-winning film. Both Roberts and costume designer Colleen Atwood may be trying too hard to make Samantha unlike the actress herself.

Though Samantha is initially terrified of Leroy, she softens considerably once they get to know each other. The highlight of *The Mexican* comes in its quietest scene as Leroy and Samantha share a quiet moment in a diner as she guesses his sexual identity, only one of his secrets. In this scene, Roberts allows herself to be the smiling Julia we all know and love.

Even before gaining fame for his magnificent work in *The Sopranos*, Gandolfini was a solid character actor in films, especially with his bumbling strong-arm man in *Get Shorty* (1995). He plays Leroy as a variation on Tony Soprano. While Soprano is a vicious brute capable of occasional human touches, Leroy is an all-too-human creature who just happens to kill people for hire. Even working with two of the biggest stars in the business, Gandolfini arrests the screen with his quiet authority. He alone makes this messy film worth watching.

—*Michael Adams*

**Jerry Welbach:** Brad Pitt
**Samantha Barzel:** Julia Roberts
**Leroy:** James Gandolfini
**Bernie Nayman:** Bob Balaban
**Margolis:** Gene Hackman
**Ted:** J.K. Simmons
**Beck:** David Krumholtz
**Frank:** Michael Ceveris

**Origin:** USA
**Released:** 2001
**Production:** Lawrence Bender, John Baldecchi; Newmarket; released by Dreamworks Pictures
**Directed by:** Gore Verbinski
**Written by:** J.H. Wyman
**Cinematography by:** Darius Wolski
**Music by:** Alan Silvestri
**Sound:** Lee Orloff
**Editing:** Craig Wood
**Art Direction:** Michael Atwell, Diego Sandoval
**Costumes:** Colleen Atwood
**Production Design:** Cecilia Montiel
**MPAA rating:** R
**Running time:** 123 minutes

*Boxoffice.* May, 2001, p. 61.
*Chicago Sun-Times Online.* March 2, 2001.
*Entertainment Weekly.* March 9, 2001, p. 52.
*Maclean's.* March 12, 2001, p. 56.
*National Review.* April 2, 2001, p. 59.
*New Republic.* March 26, 2001, p. 26.
*New York.* March 5, 2001, p. 76.
*New York Times.* March 2, 2001, p. E1.
*New Yorker.* March 12, 2001, p. 108.
*Newsweek.* March 12, 2001, p. 74.
*People.* March 12, 2001, p. 31.
*Sight and Sound.* May, 2001, p. 53.
*Time.* March 12, 2001, p. 93.
*USA Today.* March 2, 2001, p. E7.
*Variety.* March 5, 2001, p. 39.
*Wall Street Journal.* March 2, 2001, p. W1.
*Washington Post Online.* March 2, 2001.

Samantha (Julia Roberts) to Leroy (James Gandolfini): "You know, you're a very sensitive person for a cold-blooded killer."

James Gandolfini also played a hit man opposite Brad Pitt in 1993's *True Romance.*

# The Million Dollar Hotel

*Everyone has something to hide.*
—Movie tagline

"My life only really started about two weeks ago," says Tom Tom (Jeremy Davies), the goofy narrator of *The Million Dollar Hotel,* a decidedly quirky German art film transplanted to Los Angeles by director Wim Wenders. "That's when I lost my best friend Izzy and met Eloise." One problem is that Tom Tom is not exactly a reliable narrator: "I should tell you at the time I was kind of slow in the head," he explains. Therefore, the story as narrated may not seem very coherent.

The film is a Postmodern mystery that brings FBI agent J.D. Skinner (Mel Gibson, looking stiffer than usual in a neck-brace) to the Million Dollar Hotel to investigate an apparent suicide that might have been a murder. Tom's friend Izzy (Israel Goldkiss, played by Tim Roth), the son of an important tycoon, took a header off the top of the hotel building. Media mogul Stanley Goldkiss (Harris Yulin), Izzy's father, wants Agent Skinner to find out if foul play was involved. Tom Tom is impressed and eager to help: "The day he arrived from Washington, I had never seen anyone from Washington." The rest of the tenants of the hotel seem to be a sorry bunch of losers and lay-abouts.

The film begins with Tom Tom on the roof of the hotel, first reflecting, then running and leaping off the roof, in what is either imagined action, a flash-forward, or a framing flashback. It proves to be the latter, as Tom Tom narrates the film while he is falling to the street below. The context is not clearly established for this shot until the end, however, so it is impossible at first to explain this apparently suicidal action. That's part of the mystery, and director Wenders makes no concessions to make this picture viewer-friendly in the way that mainstream American cinema usually is. Caught off guard in an interview, even Mel Gibson called the film "boring," but if so, it is only "boring" by American standards.

Wenders can be the master of enigma, as witnessed in a whole career menu of pictures, from *Lisbon Story* (1995) to *The Goalie's Anxiety at the Penalty Kick* (1971), his first German feature film. In the case of *Wings of Desire* (1988) the director's signature enigmatic style broke through to find a larger popular and critical audience, but even that "classic" was remade and dumbed down for American audiences as the remake *City of Angels* (1998), with Nicolas Cage, Dennis Franz, and Meg Ryan. Interestingly, both *Wings* and the sentimental *City* involved a "fall" from a high building to the streets below.

*Million Dollar Hotel* can be seen as a sort of parody of the European art film. Something is decidedly fishy here as the plot—or what there is of it—is strewn with red herrings. This artsy crew of misfits seems to be involved in not only art fraud but art theft, as a missing Julian Schnabel canvass seems to function as what Hitchcock called a "McGuffin" in a mystery that refuses to take itself too seriously. Izzy's roommate was a Mexican, posing as an American Indian artist named Geronimo (Jimmy Smits), who calls himself a painter and works in the medium of tar. Television reporter Jean Swift (Charlayne Woodard), sent out to cover the death of the "golden boy," reports by mistake that Izzy was the painter and goes on air speaking of "The legacy of Izzy Goldkiss, the man now known as the painter saint." Izzy's friends figure that if Izzy is dead, the paintings supposed to be his will necessarily increase in value.

One of the best sequences of the film is when the friends of Izzy seek help from an art dealer. "You understand," he tells them, "that celebrities depend entirely on my judgment because the line between art and garbage can be thin. Sometimes even artists cannot see it, and sometimes it is my decision that makes it what it is." He tells them that the artist is "merely the painter, and the dealer is actually the artist." Luckily, in this case, "the painter is dead, so I can speak freely. This is, of course, garbage, but important garbage, social, psychotic, elegant, dark, very dark . . . garbage." He concludes in this send-up of the art world, "As art, I like it." More importantly, "I can sell it." Tom Tom is delighted. "To see our plan actually working—amazing!" he says.

The story is told by the "retarded" Tom Tom. This unreliable narrator is excited to think that Izzy's death might provide a sense of community for his friends: "The world was spinning faster then," he says. "I just hoped I could be a part of it. So the plan was put into action. We made a decision. My part was to stay out of the way." In fact, "Izzy hated even the smell of those tar paintings," he adds. On the other hand, Vivian (Amanda Plummer) tells the television reporter that Izzy's "paintings were a love song to me." But then the plot "thickens," as they say. Skinner is investigating a suspected murder. If the suicide turns out to be a murder, then the death of the artist becomes a high-profile media event that will hype interest in the art show that is orches-

trated. Tom Tom volunteers to tape a confession for television that will make him out to be the murderer. In fact, Tom Tom confesses to Eloise (Milla Jovovich, in one of her better roles) that he allowed the suicidal Izzy to fall from the roof after Izzy had told him he raped Eloise in order to prove "she was nothing." To Tom Tom she is everything.

Besides being a mystery, *Million Dollar Hotel* shows some potential for being a tragic love story as well, though there is not much tragic material here. Tom Tom is pathetic. He is desperately in love with Eloise, a Madonna-whore archetype, but he is too shy to make a pass at her. "Izzy and me, we were engaged," Vivian says, "until the Virgin Mary," i.e. Eloise, came along. Talking to Tom Tom in his police car, Skinner tells him that if he will cooperate with the investigation, Skinner will get Eloise to come to his room. "I suppose Skinner was playing dumb," Tom Tom remarks, "but he was out of his league." Indeed! Skinner rescues Eloise from being raped by street thugs, then tells her "Use you brain or at least use your ass to save your neck," then adds: "Do you know what just one night with you would mean to him?" It later turns out that Eloise falls in love with Tom Tom, but that happens rather too late.

Overall, this is one peculiar movie, but a potentially amusing one for those who may have the patience to stay with it. The main mystery, perhaps, is why Wenders chose to test the limits of mainstream American cinema with this slow, atmospheric German arthouse movie that just happens to be set in the "City of Angels." This is not the sort of movie that Americans, who like their entertainments as easily digestible as fast food, could be expected to embrace. Yes, it's got Mel Gibson as an FBI guy wearing a neck-brace, but he looks like a cosmetic spook transplanted from the *X-Files*, and he even has the name of Fox Mulder's superior. The movie is packed with in-jokes like this.

The film also features a talented cast playing the eccentric patrons of the Million Dollar Hotel, though some, like Bud Cort, playing a bewigged, opportunist drunk, tend to blend into the woodwork. Peter Stormare is especially amusing as a musician named Dixie, who seems to consider himself a sort of fifth Beatle. "All he needed was a little help from his friends," Dixie says of Izzy. Elsewhere, Dixie noodles out melodies that unexpectedly turn into Beatles classics. One of these is Beethoven's "Für Elise," as Wenders works in his own obsession with rock'n'roll. The music for the film was provided by Jon Hassell, Bono, Daniel Lanois, and Brian Eno.

Mainstream reviews were not favorable. Lisa Schwarzbaum of *Entertainment Weekly* quickly dismissed the film as a "dawdling tableaux," for example, describing the Jeremy Davies character as a "half-witted skate punk" and the Gloria Stuart character as a "foul-mouthed old lady." Elvis Mitchell of the *New York Times* described the score as "a music-lover's jackpot," adding that "the music has been available on CD for so long that the movie [completed in 1999] seems an afterthought." The film, he wrote, "lacks the decisive logic and Point A to Point B payoff that is normally associated with Mel Gibson movies." In this eccentric picture Gibson merely "observes the chaos instead of churning it up."

Elvis Mitchell pointed out in his *New York Times* review that screenwriter Nicholas Klein "seems to have put together passages that echo the ebb and flow vocal styling of U2's Bono, who shares a story credit and was a co-producer of the film." The cinematography by Phedeon Papamichael offers some striking visual effects, as when, after Tom Tom's initial leap, the camera tracks down the building in a shot that recalls Hitchcock's *Rear Window* (1954), moving from night to day and from the present into the past.

The film was a long time coming to America, though it was made in Los Angeles in 1999. It was released in Britain in 2000 and reviewed by Richard Falcon for *Sight and Sound*, Britain's most influential film magazine. Falcon questioned the film's character development, claiming that the characters were not fully developed, but merely abstract stereotypes. Ironically, the bizarre story was set in 2001, the year it was finally distributed to American markets. Wenders has always appealed to arthouse audiences, if not to mainstream reviewers.

*Million Dollar Hotel* was reviewed respectfully and enthusiastically by Howard Hampton for *Film Comment*, who described the oddball characters as "fallen angels at play—or [at] loose ends—in the ruins of Utopia," as Wenders brings "the euphoric, time-standing-still melancholia of *Wings of Desire* to Los Angeles." He cited Tom Tom's remarks while he was falling, "After I jumped, it occurred to me, life is perfect." Hampton found merit in the film's "mode" of "matter-of-fact reverie: dispossessed romanticism, telepathic facial close-ups, psych-ward humor, the tightrope act of borderline cases trying to snatch a little meaning from the jaws of defeat." In his dissenting opinion, Hampton advised: "Beware the riptides of fashion and pack-mentality scorn for *The Million Dollar Hotel* [which] turns out to be something of a quixotic marvel." The camera style and editing (by Tatiana S. Riegel) recall the Dogma 95 style pleasingly. But all of this, plus the talent of Mel Gibson, was not sufficient to save the film from going almost straight to video. And that is rather a shame.

—*James M. Welsh*

## CREDITS

**Stix:** Conrad Roberts
**Detective Skinner:** Mel Gibson
**Tom Tom:** Jeremy Davies
**Eloise:** Milla Jovovich
**Geronimo:** Jimmy Smits

**Dixie:** Peter Stormare
**Vivien:** Amanda Plummer
**Jessica:** Gloria Stuart
**Hector:** Tom Bower
**Charley Best:** Donal Logue
**Shorty:** Bud Cort
**Terence Scopey:** Julian Sands
**Izzy Goldkiss:** Tim Roth
**Joe:** Richard Edson
**Stanley Goldkiss:** Harris Yulin
**Jean Swift:** Charlaine Woodard

**Origin:** USA
**Released:** 1999
**Production:** Bruce Davey, Deepak Nayar; Icon Productions, Road Movies, Kintop Pictures; released by Lion's Gate Films
**Directed by:** Wim Wenders
**Written by:** Nicholas Klein
**Cinematography by:** Phedon Papamichael
**Music by:** Brian Eno, Bono, Daniel Lanois, John Hassell
**Editing:** Tatiana S. Riegel
**Art Direction:** Bella Serrell
**Costumes:** Nancy Steiner
**Production Design:** Robbie Freed
**MPAA rating:** R
**Running time:** 122 minutes

## REVIEWS

*Entertainment Weekly.* February 16, 2001, p. 73.
*Film Comment.* March/April, 2001, p. 75.
*Los Angeles Times Online.* February 2, 2001.
*New York Times.* February 2, 2001, p. B10.
*Rolling Stone.* March 1, 2001, p. 57.
*Sight and Sound.* May, 2000, p. 53.

## TRIVIA

The tar art objects were made by artist/director Julian Schnabel for the film.

# Monkeybone

*If it yells, if it swings, it's got to be Monkeybone!*
—Movie tagline

*Bone 2 B Bad.*
—Movie tagline

**Box Office:** $5.4 million

*Monkeybone* may begin with one of the world's least funny cartoons. "Show Me the Monkey" tells of a young lad's humiliating sexual experience in the 3rd grade when the wattles under his teacher's arms made him sexually excited. After his erection draws his classmates' attention, he attempts to cover it up by placing his backpack on his lap and blaming the whole thing on a stuffed animal inside it named Monkeybone. The end. Audience applause, and so, inexplicably, takes off the new Comedy Channel cartoon series and the career of subdued cartoonist, Stu Miley (Brendan Fraser). Obviously, the young boy in the cartoon is Stu, and just as obviously Monkeybone is Stu's penis. Even more obviously, from 3rd grade on, Stu is going to distance himself from the obnoxious Monkeybone/penis and the rest of the film will revolve around the cartoonist trying to reintegrate his libidinous id into his bland persona.

Initially Stu is aided in his efforts by his savior/sleep psychiatrist/girlfriend Julie McElroy (Bridget Fonda). Julie helps him to refocus his subconscious problems and sleepless nights into the cartoon character Monkeybone. Monkeybone quickly becomes a successful comic book and is now on the verge of becoming a successful cartoon series complete with all the attendant merchandising. Stu is about to become rich and famous, but one senses it is that last thing he wants. He is especially discomforted by all the merchandising and selling out his manager Herb (Dave Foley) wants him to do. And for some reason he is most distressed by the annoying Monkeybone itself, the character given birth to in his own imagination.

All this is about to take an unusual turn when, on the night of the premier of Stu's cartoon pilot, a freak accident involving a huge Monkeybone balloon inflating in Stu's small car sends it careening out of control and eventually sends Stu to the hospital in a coma. While in this state, Stu's consciousness descends via roller coaster to another realm called Downtown—a kind of limbo between life and death. Downtown is a combination amusement park and surreal prison where the main pastime is watching other people's nightmares at the Morpheum theater and slugging back drinks at the Coma Bar. Downtown is presided over by the half man/half goat Hypnos (Giancarlo Esposito) and is populated with every type of mythological and monstrous character. And for Stu, the most heinous character he meets Downtown is a "real life" Monkeybone (voice by John Turturro).

The souls trapped in downtown just bide their time waiting. Waiting either to be claimed by Death (Whoopi Goldberg) or to obtain a golden exit pass that will return them to life and awaken them from their coma. For Stu, however, there's a time limit on his coma. In three months,

his sister Kimmy (Megan Mullally) will pull the plug despite Julie's bedside vigil. Luckily for Stu, his watchful girlfriend comes to believe that while in his coma, Stu is having nightmares. So, if she can inject him with the nightmare juice she has developed in her sleep lab, maybe she can shock him awake. Unluckily for Stu, it works just as the exit pass they have stolen from Death is purloined by Monkeybone who exits Downtown just in time to inhabit Stu's no-longer-comatose body.

It doesn't take long for Julie to realize that the Stu that has awakened is not the same Stu who was about to propose to her. And it doesn't take long before Stu is back in Thantatopolis pleading with Death to let him return to reality if for no other reason than to tell Julie he loves her. Well, Death, being a soft touch (!?), returns him to life, but in a borrowed body. Stu awakens as a gymnast (Chris Kattan) who broke his neck, has died, and is now on the operating table as an organ donor. Suddenly brought back to life, the organ donor/gymnast Stu jumps off the operating table—head flopping, organs spilling out—and races off to find Julie with the avaricious doctors in hot pursuit for his profitable organs. What follows is a lot of physical shtick involving organ-dropping, head flopping organ donor/Stu chasing after the totally uninhibited Monkeybone/Stu as plots are hatched and foiled and love is lost and regained.

*Monkeybone* is the first combination live action-animation feature from director Henry Selick who previously did the animated films *Nightmare Before Christmas* (1993) and *James and the Giant Peach* (1996). Selick has proven his mastery over stop-action animation in those earlier films, and even though the more sophisticated computer generated graphics seems to make this genre of animation archaic, it still has it's fans and can be done with a high degree of sophistication as last summer's highly successful and entertaining *Chicken Run* proves. And while Selick does, technically, do a good job combining the two elements in this film, there is a bigger problem he didn't or couldn't fix. The story.

The script is thin, flat, unimaginative and worst of all, mostly unfunny. Based on Kaja Blackley's 1995 graphic novel *Dark Town* (illustrated by Vanessa Chong), *Monkeybone* screenwriter Sam Hamm (*Batman* and *Batman Returns*) has resorted to the puerile over the original and flatulence over funny. For example, one would think that the unfettered mind of the title character would have a world of one-liner zingers to hurl throughout this movie, but the only thing he seems to be able to do is be obnoxious, sex-obsessed and foul-mouthed. In fact there are really only two funny things about *Monkeybone*. One is a very brief but funny nightmare experienced by Stu's dog, and the other involves actor Chris Kattan's laughably loose portrayal of an animated corpse with more than a few physical "limitations." It's an inspired bit of lunacy that has Kattan first in line to do the next sequel to *Weekend at Bernie's*.

The rest of the characters and acting in *Monkeybone* are serviceable at best, underdeveloped at worst. Amongst the under-used actors are Whoopi Goldberg as Whoopi Goldberg—er, as Death. As you can see, she has little to do beside be herself . . . with an unexplained eye patch. Similarly, Rose McGowan seems only to have been put in the picture so the animated monkey has some breasts he can ogle, and Dave Foley's only reason for inclusion is to run butt-naked through a room full of posh partygoers wearing nothing but purple on his face. Even Megan Mullally, who plays Stu's sister, just ends up doing a paler version of her Karen character from television's *Will and Grace*.

As for the main characters and actors, well, Bridget Fonda exudes sweetness and patience, but it's basically a thankless role. And Brendan Fraser here turns in yet one more turn as an actor adept at physical comedy and playing multiple personalities in one movie. Think *Blast Off* meets *Encino Man* and you have the two aspects of Stu's personality with and without his id, or just think of *Bedazzled*. Yes, he's a good actor (see *Gods and Monsters*). Yes, he is a good physical comedian (see *George of the Jungle*). Yes, he has an easy-going likability working for him (see *The Mummy*), but it all wears thin in this manifestation. The monkey-love dance he performs for Julie as Monkeybone/Stu isn't erotic, it isn't even funny, it's embarrassing.

About the only thing that will hold a viewer's interest in *Monkeybone* is the Hieronymus Bosch-like Downtown. Although we've been in this territory before (*What Dreams May Come* and *Beetlejuice*), the ambience and the inhabitants at least give the viewer something to distract them from the thin storyline for they are the movie's only true asset. We've also seen before a combination of live action and animation. Most famous is probably *Who Framed Roger Rabbit]* with Ralph Bakshi's *Cool World* coming in a distant second followed even further away by last year's fiasco *Rocky and Bullwinkle*. One of the problems with any film containing animated characters is who is its target audience? *Roger Rabbit* and even *Rocky* were meant for families, but like *Cool World*, *Monkeybone* is too adult-themed to be for kids, yet too dumb to be for adults. A vulgar stuffed toy/animated character may seem to appeal to pre-teen boys, but beyond the special effects, this is a movie steeped in Freudian analysis. Do you think these kids would sit through a story about psychological baggage, sublimation, sexual repression and personality reintegration? Do you think they'd even notice? And if they don't, what's left? Monkey farts.

—*Beverley Bare Buehrer*

**Death:** Whoopi Goldberg
**Organ Donor Stu:** Chris Kattan
**Herb:** Dave Foley
**Hypnos:** Giancarlo Esposito
**Kitty:** Rose McGowan
**Kimmy:** Megan Mullally
**Medusa:** Lisa Zane
**Monkeybone:** John Turturro (Voice)

**Origin:** USA
**Released:** 2001
**Production:** Michael Barnathan, Mark Radcliffe; 1492 Films; released by 20th Century-Fox
**Directed by:** Henry Selick
**Written by:** Sam Hamm
**Cinematography by:** Andrew Dunn
**Music by:** Anne Dudley
**Sound:** Geoffrey Patterson
**Music Supervisor:** Dawn Soler
**Editing:** Mark Warner, Jon Poll, Nicholas C. Smith
**Art Direction:** John Chichester, Bruce Robert Hill
**Costumes:** Beatrix Aruna Pasztor
**Production Design:** Bill Boes
**MPAA rating:** PG-13
**Running time:** 92 minutes

## REVIEWS

*Boxoffice.* May, 2001, p. 61.
*Chicago Sun-Times Online.* February 23, 2001.
*Chicago Tribune Online.* February 23, 2001.
*Entertainment Weekly.* March 9, 2001, p. 55.
*Los Angeles Times Online.* February 23, 2001.
*New York Post Online.* February 23, 2001.
*New York Times Online.* February 23, 2001.
*USA Today Online.* February 23, 2001.
*Variety.* February 26, 2001, p. 39.
*Washington Post Online.* February 23, 2001.

## QUOTES

Death (Whoopi Goldberg) on Stu's personality: "I didn't want to hurt your feelings, but you're a tad vanilla."

## CREDITS

**Stu Miley:** Brendan Fraser
**Julie McElroy:** Bridget Fonda

## TRIVIA

Stephen King has a cameo as himself in a Downtown prison scene.

# Monster's Ball

*A lifetime of change can happen in a single moment.*
—Movie tagline

 **Box Office:** $13.1 million

Halle Berry has had an uneven acting career. Her various movie characterizations have divided critics and audiences. From gripping portrayals of emotionally wounded women in movies like *Isaiah,* to her landmark role in the made-for-cable movie *Introducing Dorothy Dandridge,* to her unfortunate performance in the disastrous *Swordfish,* Berry has had a penchant for overacting and for taking risky roles. When the role is right, the result is often mesmerizing, but too often Berry seems like a fish out of water.

With her portrayal of Leticia Musgrove in *Monster's Ball* however, Berry found a role that she could inhabit with a stunningly unvarnished realism. The part of a Southern black woman buffeted by misfortune—and driven into the arms of a white man who has played a large role in her life's tragedies—gives Berry enough room for emotion but also provides many effective quiet moments. For a change, Berry conveys more in some scenes by not speaking than by raging.

There is a tendency in portrayals of working-class Southern women—no matter their race—to make them either trashy or romanticized and angelic. Berry's Leticia Musgrove avoids these pitfalls; she's a believable, unaffected person. She is crude and weak at times, but occasionally musters up moments of moxie and dignity. Berry seems perfectly at ease wearing the scarves, shorts, and cheap tops of this woman who is too common to be glamorous. In her sex scenes she growls and pounces with a clumsy animal hunger and a somewhat unbecoming desperation not usually exhibited by Hollywood actresses.

Berry's is a magnificent, authentic and never overcooked performance that well deserves the Academy Award® nomination she received. It comes opposite another of Billy Bob Thornton's more typical portrayals of a quiet, traditional man with pent-up rage and an inability to express himself clearly. The film itself, however, is disappointing and frustrating. Director Marc Forster cooks up unsympathetic characters, multiple tragedies, and a simmering stew of leftover racism, but then manages to turn this mess into a rather ridiculous love story with a happy-ever-after Hollywood ending.

The climax of the film comes quickly and so clumsily that it may be one of the most ridiculous endings in movie history. You expect more violence ahead—or at least some

confrontation—but the whole plot dissolves into mush without a clear explanation of how Leticia's character resolves what seems to be a terrible emotional dilemma.

It's a shame, because Forster handles the first hour of the movie with an intriguing style halfway between film noir and Southern melodrama. Based on a script by Milo Addica and Will Rokos, the story concocts a dangerous mix of hatred, anger, and retribution. Thornton plays a federal prison guard, Colonel Hank Grotowski, who is set to preside over the execution of inmate Lawrence Musgrove (Sean Combs). Grotowski's only child, Sonny (Heath Ledger), works under his father at the prison and is part of the execution team.

One wonderful early scene shows Lawrence visiting with his wife and son for the last time. Calmly, Lawrence lectures his son Tyrell (Coronji Calhoun), telling him he has all his good qualities and none of his bad ones. His wife, Leticia, turns away from her doomed husband's attempts to embrace her, saying she has been coming to visit him for 11 years and is sick of the entire thing.

Forster's deft handling of the lead-up to the execution and the electrocution itself promises a much better movie than he is able to deliver. There is power in the details of how Hank and Sonny oversee Lawrence's last hours, with all three men trying to get through the ordeal with as little emotion as possible, Lawrence by drawing sketches of his two guards. Combs steals all these scenes; he is fascinating. Forster focus on the straps and screws of the electric chair, the rhythms of Lawrence's breath, and the stoic expressions of the audience, cutting away to Leticia and Tyrell sitting at home watching TV and stealing whiskey and candy for comfort.

Hank is enraged because Sonny, overcome with so much pent-up emotion, vomits during Sonny's walk to the electric chair. He calls his son weak, and tells him he is like his mother and lacks guts. In response, Sonny grabs a gun, terrorizes his father, and then asks him to confirm that he hates him. Hank replies that he has always hated Sonny, and Sonny says he has always loved him, then turns the gun on himself. Hank and his own father, Buck (Peter Boyle), seem little moved by Sonny's death, but Hank soon resigns from his job at the penitentiary. Buck, a vituperative, openly racist and sadistic man—a typically crazed role for Boyle—tells Hank he's weak for quitting his job and that he reminds him of Hank's mother, who committed suicide rather than continue to take Buck's abuse.

Meanwhile, we discover Leticia is also abusive, prone to slapping around Tyrell, who is grossly overweight, whenever she catches him sneaking candy bars. Conveniently for the plot, Leticia starts working at the restaurant Hank likes to frequent for his nightly bowl of chocolate ice cream. Then, in a highly contrived piece of plotting, Hank happens to be driving by after Tyrell is hit by a car on a rainy night; he takes them to the hospital, but Tyrell dies. Now both of these single parents, who have recently become childless, are thrown together out of desparation and with the aid of frequent coincidental encounters.

Suddenly, Hank, who up to this point has seemed like a heartless cur, unburdens himself to Leticia and turns into a sweet if clumsy courtier. They fumble and flop into breathless sex. For Hank, this is a welcome change from motel-room encounters with the local whore—the same one his son frequented for quick and emotionless sex. A little romance makes Hank into a new man—he is friendly to his black neighbors, buys a gas station and names it after Leticia, and ships his father to a nursing home after he scares off Leticia with his rough talk. These lame plot developments are all the more disappointing because of the film's previous flashes of quiet brilliance.

In addition, *Monster's Ball* is cryptic—and not in a good way. The title, it is explained, refers to a party British executioners throw for the condemned the night before an execution, but it makes little sense to attach that name to this story. We never find out some key things that would make the characters' motivations and behaviors more understandable. Musgrove's crime is never mentioned, and the assumption is that he is justly convicted, but given the film's other gratuitous references to racial injustice, one might wonder. It's not clear why Hank hates Sonny so much, other than that he considers him weak like his mother. It's also not clear where Sonny's mother is or how she died. One might invest Leticia's remark, in looking at a photograph of Sonny, that Sonny doesn't look like his father, with more significance than it should have. And why is Sonny friends with a neighbor's two twin black children who are half his age? It's not clear, other than it helps to enrage his father and grandfather.

Apparently, this film wants to say something about racism and its ugly consequences, but if there is a message, it's muddled. Ultimately it's a film about emotionally flawed people who are weak and get enraged when others close to them show weakness. The plot gets rid of all the characters until no one is left but Hank and Leticia. And when Leticia discovers Hank's connection to her husband's murder, it would seem there should be an emotional explosion. But the script has run out of ideas.

Perhaps this is a film about a black woman's capitulation, out of helplessness, to the primary agent of pain and racism in her life. In some ways, Hank is connected to all the deaths in the film, though he is never directly responsible. Hank has proved to be abusive and uncaring to family members; the idea that Leticia is willing to settle down with him should be unsettling. But *Monster's Ball* lacks the courage to follow through on its plot developments, and settles for a second-rate resolution that will leave most viewers scratching their heads.

Wasted are Berry's fine performance, Thornton's predictable but effective turn, and scene-stealing acting from the rapper Combs and the old veteran of lunatic roles, Boyle. Forster shows promise as a director with a quiet, observant manner. But the film cheats in terms of plot developments and emotional shortcuts, and it shifts its tone and apparent purpose several times. It falls far short of making any cogent statements about race and gender, and settles for being a curiosity piece, a kind of multiple character sketch of some strange people. Worst of all, it's hard to feel any emotional connection to these characters. *Monster's Ball* is condemned to irrelevance.

—*Michael Betzold*

## CREDITS

**Hank Grotowski:** Billy Bob Thornton
**Leticia Musgrove:** Halle Berry
**Sonny Grotowski:** Heath Ledger
**Buck Grotowski:** Peter Boyle
**Lawrence Musgrove:** Sean (Puffy, Puff Daddy, P. Diddy) Combs
**Tyrell Musgrove:** Coronji Calhoun
**Ryrus Cooper:** Dante Beze
**Warden Velasco:** Will Rokos
**Tommy Roulaine:** Milo Addica

**Origin:** USA
**Released:** 2001
**Production:** Lee Daniels; released by Lion's Gate Films
**Directed by:** Marc Forster
**Written by:** Will Rokos, Milo Addica
**Cinematography by:** Roberto Schaefer
**Sound:** Jeff Pullman
**Music Supervisor:** Joel High
**Editing:** Matt Chesse
**Art Direction:** Leonard Spears
**Costumes:** Frank Fleming
**Production Design:** Monroe Kelly
**MPAA rating:** R
**Running time:** 111 minutes

## REVIEWS

*Boxoffice.* January, 2002, p. 57.
*Chicago Sun-Times Online.* Feburary 1, 2002.
*Entertainment Weekly.* January 25, 2001, p. 73.
*Hollywood Reporter.* November 13, 2001, p. 85.
*Los Angeles Times.* August 12, 2001, p. 20.
*Los Angeles Times Online.* December 26, 2001.
*New York Times Online.* December 23, 2001.
*New York Times Online.* December 26, 2001.

*People.* January 14, 2002, p. 29.
*Rolling Stone.* January 17, 2002, p. 56.
*USA Today Online.* December 26, 2001.
*Variety.* November 19, 2001, p. 39.
*Washington Post.* February 8, 2002, p. WE37.

## QUOTES

Hank (Billy Bob Thornton) to Leticia (Halle Berry): "You sure suck that whiskey down. Lord have mercy."

## TRIVIA

First-time screenwriters Milo Addica and Will Rokos completed the script for *Monster's Ball* in 1995.

## AWARDS AND NOMINATIONS

**Oscars 2001:** Actress (Berry)
**Natl. Bd. of Review 2001:** Actor (Thornton), Actress (Berry)
**Screen Actors Guild 2001:** Actress (Berry)
**Nomination:**
**Golden Globes 2002:** Actress—Drama (Berry)
**Writers Guild 2001:** Orig. Screenplay.

# Monsters, Inc.

*We scare because we care.*
—Movie tagline
*You won't believe your eye.*
—Movie tagline

**Box Office:** $239.2

W alt Disney's Pixar Animation Studios made the first computer-generated full-length feature with the tremendous hit *Toy Story,* which opened new ground for Disney and animated films in general. Pixar followed that up with *Toy Story 2* and *A Bug's Life.* All these films displayed the new, more fanciful yet at the same time more realistic imagery that computer animation makes possible. Pixar's latest work in the fall of 2001 was *Monsters, Inc.*

In technical terms, the new film is a slight improvement over the *Toy Story* films. Animation software has gotten more and more sophisticated, and the protagonist of *Monsters, Inc.,* a bear-like critter named John P. "Sully" Sullivan, has realistic fur, with individual strands of hair that react in a lifelike fashion. In one scene, the Abominable Snowman throws lemon-colored snow cones at Sully's back, and they stick and clog to the hair in tremendously believable fashion.

In terms of how computer animation techniques portray human beings, however, Pixar hasn't come quite so far in the six years between *Toy Story* and *Monsters, Inc.* The humans still look too much like dolls. That's why there aren't many humans in any of these pictures—they don't work as well as toys, insects, or monsters. Cartoon figures, being less complicated, require less meticulous computer techniques.

In the meantime, however, Warner Brothers' Dream Works has made *Antz* and *Shrek.* Both these films were far more ambitious and daring than Pixar's recent releases—and technically far superior. In particular, *Shrek* made huge strides in present human and human-like creatures that were capable of portraying complex facial emotions and expressions, and whose bodies moved in realistic fashion. *Monsters, Inc.* presents only one human character, the toddler nicknamed Boo, and she has few pretensions to realism.

*Monsters, Inc.* in contrast to *Shrek,* has put computer animation technology to work to make a very traditional kind of cartoon. While *Shrek* executed a much more sophisticated and groundbreaking type of animation in form and in content, Pixar is content to dabble with rather tame concepts in its creations and its plot.

In fact, *Monsters* is a fairly routine Disney venture dressed up in computer animation wizardry. Tellingly, its opening and closing credits celebrate animation tradition by using a 1950s-type drawing style. The film also makes a nod to animation history when it sets a scene in a place called the Harryhausen Café—a tribute to stop-motion animation pioneer Ray Harryhausen, who directed a lot of science-fiction special effects extravaganzas in the 1950s and 1960s.

The film is guaranteed to go down easily for the tykes, while tossing a few bones of humor in the direction of adults. Screenwriter Andrew Stanton, who worked on both *Toy Story* pictures and *A Bug's Life,* has concocted a simple, silly but interesting movie idea. Starting from the traditional notion that little children are afraid of monsters in their bedroom closets, it imagines a parallel universe inhabited by these monsters. They live in a city whose energy needs are served by harnessing the screams of children. The monsters work for a utilities company named Monsters Inc., which sends designated "scarers" into production when nighttime in each time zone of the world.

The idea is a nifty one but the execution proves to be a little clumsy. Directors David Silverman (a sequence director on *The Road to El Dorado*) and Peter Docter, who rose in the ranks from animator and screenwriter in *Toy Story* to writing the original story for *Toy Story 2,* imagine the scream factory as an old-fashioned assembly line. Each monster is assigned to a particular closet door, which is lowered into place. A bell rings, and the monsters go through the doors and enter kids' bedrooms. Their scream output is measured, bottled, and sent on its way.

The movie at some points strives for realism in its plot by giving us a world map with time zones and showing bedrooms and children getting monster intruders all over the globe—but the factory also inexplicably closes up when it's nighttime in "Monsteropolis," rather than going round-the-clock. Sully is competing for top honors in the scream competition with the villainous Randall Boggs (Steve Buscemi) but it's not clear why each of them can rack up several screams in one visit. Coming out of one door, Sully explains his high count by saying "slumber party"; but in fact, the monsters are getting multiple screams out of single visits throughout their work day.

This sloppiness can be expected in a movie that is clearly aimed at a young audience. The film's monsters are fairly safe and non-threatening. All the creatures are animated in safe, warm, toddler colors; Sully is teal with spots of lavender. These aren't very fantastic monsters—in fact, they are more like Barney-type dinosaurs. The range of what the filmmakers believe a childish imagination might conjure up as a monster seems awfully limited. The only concepts employed by animators are different numbers of eyes, heads, or appendages, but especially eyes; various types of reptilian or insect-like forms; and a few big, hairy beast-like creatures like Sully. Even Randall, whose ability to disappear completely and reappear is slightly unnerving, is more like the Cheshire Cat than a genuinely alarming nightmare creation.

This approach is probably appropriate in a film that complains that the Monsters, Inc. company is experiencing a downturn—and Monsteropolis a resultant energy shortage—because kids just don't scare as easily anymore. Certainly, few modern kids would be scared by monsters this tame. You wonder, however, why Monsters, Inc.'s chief executive, Henry J. Waternoose (James Coburn), is concerned about his company's fate. Is there a competing energy generator in Monsteropolis? None that the plot reveals. And what other source of energy is possible? It isn't clear.

Sully accidentally stumbles upon a sinister plot by Randall to kidnap little children and hook them up to a permanent scream-extracting machine—rather than just depending on frightening them with occasional visits. He also accidentally discovers children's laughter is even more potent and can be harnessed for more reliable energy. But this, too, is rather clumsily explained. Boo, the tyke Randall is after as his first guinea pig, but who accidentally becomes Sully's problem and then his friend, emits laughs on two occasions, and they cause the power to go *out*. How children in the audience are supposed to figure out that the laughter has produced too much power and fried the circuits rather than sucking out the power is beyond imagining.

The plot doesn't ever get too complicated, even though it sometimes gets confusing, and the final climax has to maneuver around several dicey moments concerning the monsters' rather flexible abilities to go in and out of the closet doors. Along the way, much time is filled with the repartee of Sully's sidekick, a wisecracking one-eyed green slimeball with legs named Mike Wazowski (Billy Crystal). Mike tends to get himself into trouble, especially with his girlfriend, a receptionist named Celia (Jennifer Tilly) whose hair is full of little snakelike strands.

While Goodman's talents for being a believable goodhearted, clumsy, well-meaning straight man are being put to good use in animation (both here and in *The Emperor's New Groove*), the idea of putting Billy Crystal into a cartoon feature is fraught with danger. While *Shrek* rung genuine adult humor out of parodying fairy tales and Disney movies and lacing its plot with film and cultural references, *Monsters, Inc.* depends too heavily on Crystal's over-the-top shtick. And depending too much on Crystal jokes—including a few actual stand-up-type routines—is a sign of how lazy and trifling the story line is. It's a gamble that flops. Crystal's Mike is more bothersome than funny. Crystal joins the ranks of popular comics who have just about ruined animated features by making sidekick characters annoying (see Rosie O'Donnell in *Tarzan*).

The film does have an interimittent wackiness to it, and it is an interesting departure to have its main human character be a toddler. Usually precocious kindergarteners or grade-schoolers are at the center of family films; here, little Boo can't even talk yet, and the filmmakers occasionally exploit her age for some good laughs. The computer animation is almost breathtaking during the final long chase sequences where the characters are hopping among hundreds of doors moving along conveyor belts in the massive back rooms of the scream factory. Other than that, though, the animation is a tad disappointing—safe and tame like the movie.

*Monsters, Inc.* was geared to be a crowd-pleaser—it's got the demographics down pat, and enough of a multi-colored visual palette to keep even the smallest of tykes enthralled. And most adults who accompany the children will be mildly amused. But at a time when other animation production studios are doing things as innovative, wacky, and daring as *Chicken Run* and *Shrek*, Disney once again seems a little bit out of step and out of date, even though Pixar is doing Disney's best work. The competition is just getting tougher and tougher. *Monsters, Inc.* goes down easy but doesn't break any new ground. It's content to be cute and charming. 🎞

—*Michael Betzold*

# The Most Fertile Man in Ireland

## CREDITS

**James P. (Sulley) Sullivan:** John Goodman (Voice)
**Mike Wazowski:** Billy Crystal (Voice)
**Randall Boggs:** Steve Buscemi (Voice)
**Boo:** Mary Gibbs (Voice)
**Henry J. Waternoose:** James Coburn (Voice)
**Celia:** Jennifer Tilly (Voice)
**Yeti:** John Ratzenberger (Voice)
**Fungus:** Frank Oz (Voice)
**Roz:** Bob Peterson (Voice)
**Flint:** Bonnie Hunt (Voice)

**Origin:** USA
**Released:** 2001
**Production:** Darla K. Anderson; Pixar, Walt Disney Pictures; released by Buena Vista
**Directed by:** Pete Docter
**Written by:** Andrew Stanton, Daniel Gerson
**Music by:** Randy Newman
**Sound:** Gary Rydstrom
**Editing:** Jim Stewart
**Production Design:** Harley Jessup, Bob Pauley
**MPAA rating:** G
**Running time:** 92 minutes

## REVIEWS

*Chicago Sun-Times Online.* November 2, 2001.
*Entertainment Weekly.* November 9, 2001, p. 82.
*Los Angeles Times Online.* November 2, 2001.
*New York Times Online.* November 2, 2001.
*Newsweek.* November 5, 2001, p. 66.
*People.* November 12, 2001, p. 35.
*USA Today Online.* November 2, 2001.
*Variety.* November 5, 2001, p. 23.
*Washington Post.* November 2, 2001, p. WE36.

## QUOTES

Henry J. Waternoose (James Coburn): "There's nothing more toxic or deadly than a human child. A single touch could kill you!"

## AWARDS AND NOMINATIONS

**Oscars 2001:** Song ("If I Didn't Have You")
**Nomination:**
**Oscars 2001:** Animated Film, Score.

Irish lasses rule Ireland or at least they do in films. The Irish women in such films as *About Adam, When Brendan Met Trudy,* and other contemporary Irish flicks call the shots. They pursue sexual relationships with men of their choice and the Irish men just lie down and take it. Whether this reflects on fact or fiction doesn't matter since narratives revolving around sassy women and pushover men possess a certain entertainment value that female audiences enjoy.

*The Most Fertile Man in Ireland* revolves around shy and seemingly ineffectual carrot-top Eamonn (Kris Marshall), who accidentally learns of a special gift that he possesses. While Irish television news anchors lament the shortage of sperm in Ireland, the unassuming 24-year-old Belfast virgin works at a dating agency called Amore and pines for Rosie (Kathy Kiera Clarke), a dark-haired beauty who works at a funeral parlor across the street from the dating agency. Each day Eamonn wakes up at his mother's (Oliva Nash) house where he still resides and each day Eamonn buys flowers for the lovely Rosie that he never delivers. Meanwhile, Eamonn's Ma lectures him, "Sexual intercourse is the most beautiful thing on God's earth," not knowing that soon her son would take that advice a bit too far.

One night Eamonn meets up with vivacious bimbo Mary Mallory (Tara Lynn O'Neill), who assists Eamonn in gaining his manhood in a wild night of passion. However, Mary learns that she's pregnant despite the overabundance of contraceptives she employed and after word gets out that Eamonn is a baby-making machine, mayhem ensues in Belfast, leading to political chaos between Protestants and Catholics and moral issues revolving around fatherhood. Meanwhile, as Eamonn secretly populates Ireland with red-headed, blue-eyed tykes, he pursues a relationship with Rosie. But in order not to give the film's story away, for every action on Eamonn's part, a counteraction exists that eventually leads to a satisfying ending.

Keeble's screwball comedy screenplay has all the right elements in place from pushy females and unassuming males who range from brainless thugs to shy mama's boy-turned-stud, Eamonn. Many comic moments revolve around brash statements spoken by parental figures or professionals such as Dr. Johnson (Toyah Wilcox) involving sex, reproduction, and sperm counts. However, Keeble's narrative is far from perfect and a subplot involving tension between Protestants and Catholics seems out of place, even if the story does take place in Belfast. Some of the film's comedic edge is also lost when Eamonn starts wondering about the true nature of paternity. After all, he might have earned a decent income selling his sperm and prostituting his body to married women but later, after the same women refuse to let Eamonn see his offspring, he questions the morality of the choice that he made.

Marshall proves to be a natural comedian—playing straight man to the bevy of hysterical women who surround him. The tall and gawky actor transforms into a sexy father of twins over the course of the movie and Marshall employs a believable transformation of character. The not-quite-Goth Clarke contrasts the other hysterical women with her calm almost sullen demeanor. She quietly waits for romance to enter into her lonely life while she works at a funeral parlor and spends the rest of her time watching tropical fish swim around an aquarium. As the title implies, this Irish film provides quirky entertainment and it appears that Irish luck is smiling upon Irish cinema—at least for awhile.

—*Patty-Lynne Herlevi*

## CREDITS

**Eamonn:** Kris Marshall
**Rosie:** Kathy Kiera Clarke
**Mad Dog Billy Wilson:** James Nesbitt
**Millicent:** Bronagh Gallagher
**Da:** Kenneth Cranham
**Maeve:** Pauline McLynn
**Dr. Johnston:** Toyah Wilcox
**Ma:** Olivia Nash
**Mary Mallory:** Tara Lynn O'Neill

**Origin:** Ireland
**Released:** 2001
**Production:** David Collins; Sky Pictures, Samson Film, Hot Film; released by Alibi Films International
**Directed by:** Dudi Appleton
**Written by:** Jim Keeble
**Cinematography by:** Ronan Fox
**Music by:** James Johnston
**Sound:** Mark Berger, Doug Murray
**Music Supervisor:** Maggie Bazin
**Editing:** Emer Reynolds
**Art Direction:** Lesley Oakley
**Costumes:** Eimer Ni Mhaoldomhnaigh
**Production Design:** Tom Conroy
**MPAA rating:** Unrated
**Running time:** 91 minutes

## REVIEWS

*San Francisco Chronicle.* March 15, 2002, p. D3.
*Variety.* May 7, 2001, p. 66.

# Moulin Rouge

*No laws. No limits. One rule. Never fall in love.*
—Movie tagline
*Truth—Beauty—Freedom—Love.*
—Movie tagline

 **Box Office:** $57 million

From its very first image, Baz Luhrmann's *Moulin Rouge* announces that it has something different in store for its audience. A conductor stands before a giant proscenium, lifts up his baton, and strikes up the band. The curtains part to reveal the 20th Century-Fox logo behind him as an unseen orchestra plays the recognizable Fox fanfare. The curtains close and open again for the title sequence, during which the conductor leads a mini-overture of some of the music we will hear through the movie. It is an inspired beginning and a way for Luhrmann to declare, in a creative way, that he will be presenting the familiar in a radically new way. For *Moulin Rouge* is nothing less than an astonishing postmodern collision between old and new—the Moulin Rouge of 1899 Paris giving birth to some of the most famous pop songs of the 20th century, an old-fashioned musical employing accelerated MTV-style editing and over-the-top camera tricks. It is a dizzying, heady experience—a feverish fantasia that throws all the old conventions together to create something breathtakingly original.

With his writing partner, Craig Pearce, Luhrmann has fashioned a story grounded in the Orphic myth. According to Greek mythology, Orpheus was a great musician who descended into the underworld to try to save Eurydice, the love of his life. In *Moulin Rouge,* the young writer, Christian (Ewan McGregor), is an Orphic figure who descends into the underworld of the Moulin Rouge to try to save the doomed showgirl and courtesan, Satine (Nicole Kidman). In flashback he tells the story of how he came from London to the Montmartre district of Paris, home of the infamous Moulin Rouge, a nightclub/dance hall/bordello where the elite of society mingle with the dancing girls and the bohemian artists, dubbed, in the film's wittily anachronistic way, "the children of the revolution." Christian falls in with the diminutive Toulouse-Lautrec (John Leguizamo), who, with a group of fellow artists, is working on a musical to perform at the Moulin Rouge, which is owned by the consummate showman, Harold Zidler (Jim Broadbent). The bohemians are having difficulty with the lyrics when the neophyte Christian reveals a certain knack with words. Anticipating the work of Rodgers and Hammerstein, he spontaneously sings, "The hills are alive with the sound of music" when they are stuck for a line, and he is instantly hailed as a genius.

Soon Christian is joining his new friends in a visit to the Moulin Rouge, a wild and decadent pleasure palace full of sexy dancing girls and seemingly nonstop music set to a driving beat. The songs are essentially eclectic medleys of late-20th century hits: for example, cancan girls perform LaBelle's "Lady Marmalade," while rich, dapper gentlemen sing the chorus of Nirvana's "Smells like Teen Spirit." The visual style is wild and gaudy and accentuated by zoom shots, fast-paced cutting, and an explosion of color in virtually every shot.

Indeed, Luhrmann presents a riot of motion with a frenetic camera style that seems to divide audiences. The camera whirls through throngs of people, smashes through doors, and almost seems drunk on trying to capture everything at once. The widescreen frame is filled with such colorful, exotic sets and an array of dancers in the fanciest turn-of-the-century costumes, courtesy of designers Catherine Martin and Angus Strathie, that it is easy to miss much of the detail. Some viewers find all that Luhrmann offers hard to digest, especially in the scenes introducing us to the Moulin Rouge, but his overheated style is a fitting visual counterpoint to his exuberant postmodern mixing of the 20th century's musical influences.

The star of the Moulin Rouge is Satine, who makes a grand entrance and performs a showstopping rendition of Marilyn Monroe's "Diamonds Are a Girl's Best Friend" mixed with Madonna's "Material Girl." Satine immediately bewitches Christian, and it becomes his task to make her fall in love with the bohemians' musical. For the same evening, however, Zidler has arranged a meeting between Satine and the wealthy Duke (Richard Roxburgh), the film's effete stock villain, who has the money needed to finance the bohemians' new show. The screenplay employs the classic device of mistaken identity as Christian meets with Satine, who thinks that he is the Duke. In a very funny episode, she practically throws herself at him, rolling around on the floor while Christian, the poor innocent, thinks that he is there to share his work on the show.

Christian starts reciting his poetry to Satine, which is recognizable to us as Elton John's "Your Song." Perhaps we have heard this song dozens of times on the radio, but, in this context, we are invited to imagine it being sung for the first time, and what is for us a possibly stale pop standard becomes fresh in a new context. It is as if Christian is writing the song on the spot and the familiar words are meant specifically for Satine. The song seduces her, and, as she finds herself overcome by Christian's soaring, romantic vision, they take flight in a rapturous, transcendent moment in which they seemingly dance on air against the Paris skyline.

Soon Satine, Christian, Zidler and the bohemians are doing an impromptu presentation of their proposed musical, called "Spectacular Spectacular," for the unctuous Duke.

The musical's story, made up by Christian, mirrors the story of Moulin Rouge but is set in India—a penniless sitar player falls in love with a beautiful courtesan but has to overcome a powerful maharaja, who also covets the girl. The simpering Duke agrees to back the show, but, in exchange for his financial investment, he also expects the exclusive services of Satine, who is falling in love with Christian. To make matters more complicated, Satine is dying of consumption, although she herself does not yet know the severity of her condition.

Moulin Rouge combines two traditional story lines of movie musicals—the love story in which the young hero sings to win the girl of his dreams and the backstage musical in which we witness the birth and execution of a stage show. But more important, the film's details pay homage to the history of musical performances. Satine's entrance, for example, not only references Marilyn Monroe and Madonna but also hints at Marlene Dietrich in The Blue Angel and possibly Rita Hayworth in Gilda. Zidler's garish makeup and the way he leads the dancing girls onstage recall the Master of Ceremonies in Cabaret, and Christian's fancy move with an umbrella during "Your Song" evokes Gene Kelly in Singin' in the Rain, with the Eiffel Tower filling in for Kelly's lamppost.

Moulin Rouge is thus filled with playful postmodern riffs, which reach their apex in the "Elephant Love Medley," so-called because it takes place on a large papier-mâché elephant in the Moulin Rouge's courtyard. Christian returns to Satine to find out if she was sincere when she said that she loved him, and she tries to resist him, telling him that it was all an act. Being a woman who sells herself to many men, she cannot fall in love with one in particular. But this is anathema to Christian, whose whole philosophy of life is about love, so he starts singing about love in our pop vernacular. He references lyrics from a variety of songs, including the Beatles' "All You Need Is Love," Phil Collins's "One More Night," and U2's "Pride (In the Name of Love)," all emphasizing the wonder of love, while Satine counters with lyrics that cast a more cynical take on romance. They trade verses on Paul McCartney's "Silly Love Songs," and, when she has finally been won over, they are singing together David Bowie's "Heroes" and concluding with Dolly Parton's "I Will Always Love You" and a short reprise of "Your Song." The familiar fragments of our pop culture are thus magically transformed into the medium of the lovers' courtship.

The challenge for McGregor and Kidman is that they are essentially playing character types—the youthful innocent and the hooker with the heart of gold—in a film that emphasizes style over character development. And yet, even with these potential obstacles, they make us care about their characters. McGregor's wide-eyed boyishness is very appealing, and his ultimate descent into jealousy is quite painful, while Kidman's icy beauty slowly thaws to reveal the humanity and romantic yearning underneath her cool exterior.

More important than the characters or plot, which is, after all, a familiar love triangle, is *Moulin Rouge*'s eclectic musical numbers, which cover a wide range of emotions and styles. When it looks like Satine is being cold to the Duke—she and Christian constantly claim to be rehearsing the show so that she can avoid the Duke's company—Zidler tries to reassure the Duke of Satine's love by telling him that he makes her feel like a virgin. The men then engage in a campy duet of Madonna's "Like a Virgin" with Zidler, improbably enough, playing the virginal bride. Satine is conflicted about Christian because of the Duke's expectations, but Christian keeps pulling her closer to him through the original song "Come What May," which becomes their secret love song. The Duke, however, eventually learns of Satine's duplicity and wants the ending of "Spectacular Spectacular" rewritten so that the courtesan in the show chooses the maharaja, which he correctly sees as corresponding to him. When Christian, defending his original ending that celebrates true love, lets slip that Satine does not love the Duke, Satine must go to him to patch things up. Christian is at his low point when the musical company re-imagines the Police's "Roxanne," the story of a man's obsession with a prostitute, as a dark and foreboding tango of jealousy. Intercut with the number is Satine's rendezvous with the Duke and his attack on her when she finally rebuffs him. Ultimately, she could not bring herself to sleep with him, and she commits herself to Christian. They decide to flee the Moulin Rouge, but then the Duke tells Zidler that he will have Christian killed if he does not get the ending he wants as well as Satine. So Zidler urges Satine to reject Christian in order to save him and also tells her that she is dying.

Even though Satine has rejected Christian, he feels that something is wrong and that she still loves him. So he makes one last trip to the Moulin Rouge to rescue her on the opening night of the musical. A tormented Christian confronts Satine backstage as the Duke's manservant sets out to kill him, and eventually Christian makes his way onstage and becomes part of the show's triumphant climax, the two worlds merging for a splendid moment in which the lovers are united. The musical gets the ending Christian wants, the Duke is ultimately foiled, but Satine succumbs to her illness and dies in Christian's arms as she begs him to write their story. It is a tender sequence in which the movie's tempo slows down so that we can feel the heartbreak and loss that Christian faces at the end of his journey.

*Moulin Rouge* is such an entertaining, surprising whirlwind of a movie that it becomes easy to accept and even embrace its stylistic excesses as integral to Luhrmann's unique vision. But there is something deeper at the heart of the movie. For behind the overpowering glitz, beautiful sets, and manic editing lurks a bold idea—the songs we take for granted as the fabric of our world can also express the emotions of a love story set in a completely different time and place. Perhaps the real genius of *Moulin Rouge* lies not in

the way it dazzles us with gorgeous musical numbers and stylistic flourishes, the likes of which we have never seen before, but rather in the way it invites us to appreciate familiar pop songs as if we were hearing them for the very first time.

—*Peter N. Chumo II*

## CREDITS

**Satine:** Nicole Kidman
**Christian:** Ewan McGregor
**Toulouse-Lautrec:** John Leguizamo
**Zidler:** Jim Broadbent
**The Doctor:** Garry McDonald
**Green Fairy:** Kylie Minogue
**Duke of Worcester:** Richard Roxburgh
**Audrey:** David Wenham
**China Doll:** Natalie Mendoza

**Origin:** Australia, USA
**Released:** 2001
**Production:** Baz Luhrmann, Martin Brown, Fred Baron; Bazmark; released by 20th Century-Fox
**Directed by:** Baz Luhrmann
**Written by:** Baz Luhrmann, Craig Pearce
**Cinematography by:** Donald McAlpine
**Music by:** Craig Armstrong
**Sound:** Guntis Sics
**Music Supervisor:** Anton Monsted
**Editing:** Jill Bilcock
**Art Direction:** Ann Marie Beauchamp
**Costumes:** Catherine Martin, Angus Strathie
**Production Design:** Catherine Martin
**MPAA rating:** PG-13
**Running time:** 126 minutes

## REVIEWS

*Boxoffice.* July, 2001, p. 99.
*Chicago Sun-Times Online.* June 1, 2001.
*Entertainment Weekly.* May 25, 2001, p. 48.
*Hollywood Reporter.* April 24, 2001, p. S-9.
*Los Angeles Times Online.* May 18, 2001.
*New York Times Online.* May 6, 2001.
*New York Times Online.* May 18, 2001.
*Newsweek.* May 28, 2001, p. 61.
*People.* May 28, 2001, p. 35.
*Sight and Sound.* June, 2001, p. 34.
*Sight and Sound.* September, 2001, p. 50.
*USA Today Online.* May 18, 2001.
*Variety.* May 14, 2001, p. 21.
*Washington Post Online.* June 1, 2001.

## QUOTES

Christian (Ewan McGregor): "This story is about truth, beauty, freedom; but above all things, this story is about love."

## TRIVIA

All the lead actors sing with their own voices.

## AWARDS AND NOMINATIONS

**Oscars 2001:** Art Dir./Set Dec., Costume Des.
**Australian Film Inst. 2001:** Cinematog., Costume Des., Film Editing, Sound
**British Acad. 2001:** Sound, Support. Actor (Broadbent), Score
**Golden Globes 2002:** Actor—Mus./Comedy, Actress—Mus./Comedy (Kidman), Score
**L.A. Film Critics 2001:** Support. Actor (Broadbent)
**Natl. Bd. of Review 2001:** Film, Support. Actor (Broadbent)
**Nomination:**
**Oscars 2001:** Actress (Kidman), Cinematog., Film, Film Editing, Makeup, Sound
**British Acad. 2001:** Cinematog., Costume Des., Director (Luhrmann), Film, Film Editing, Orig. Screenplay, Visual FX
**Directors Guild 2001:** Director (Luhrmann)
**Golden Globes 2002:** Actor—Mus./Comedy (McGregor), Director (Luhrmann), Song ("Come What May")
**Screen Actors Guild 2001:** Cast
**Writers Guild 2001:** Orig. Screenplay
**Broadcast Film Critics 2001:** Actress (Kidman), Director (Luhrmann), Film.

# Mulholland Drive

*A Love Story In The City of Dreams.*
—Movie tagline

**Box Office:** $5.6 million

In David Lynch's *Mulholland Drive*, wide-eyed, aspiring actress Betty Elms (Naomi Watts) cannot believe that she has made it to Hollywood from Deep River, Ontario, and exclaims at the wonder of being "in this dream place," a phrase that is not only a commentary on Hollywood itself but also a clue to unlocking the puzzle at the heart of this strange yet beautiful movie. Hollywood of course is commonly known as the dream factory or the City of Dreams, and Lynch's films, reaching back to his debut feature, *Eraserhead*, are filled with stylized dreamscapes, worlds that resemble ours and yet have the surreal edges of our deepest desires and fears. So it is perhaps fitting that Lynch should make a film set in the dream capital itself and explore the many facets of Hollywood dreaming. *Mulholland Drive* features familiar Lynchian tropes—oddball, often freakish characters; bizarre, even confusing plot turns; and gorgeous yet nightmarish set pieces. And yet, despite the familiarity, the film does not feel like a retread but rather a maturation of Lynch's preoccupations wedded to a tragic Hollywood story.

The narrative begins with a car accident on the eponymous street. An elegant, voluptuous brunette (Laura Elena Harring) in the backseat of a Cadillac is about to be killed execution-style when a car full of joyriding kids crashes into the Cadillac, leaving her the only survivor. She staggers from the wreck and eventually takes shelter in an apartment whose occupant is going on a trip.

Meanwhile, fresh-faced, blond-haired Betty arrives in Southern California and takes up residence in her aunt's apartment, which happens to be where the mysterious brunette is hiding. Betty meets the kind yet tough manager of the apartment complex, Coco (Ann Miller), who has the air of someone who has seen it all, and then comes upon the alluring mystery woman. Still reeling from the accident, she suffers from amnesia and assumes the name Rita when she glimpses a movie poster of Rita Hayworth in *Gilda* (a nod, of course, to one of the movies' most famous femme fatales). Betty is very accommodating to Rita and tries to help her discover her identity. They find stacks of hundred-dollar bills in Rita's purse along with a mysterious blue key, but none of these items helps Rita to remember who she is.

In a seemingly separate story line, hotshot director Adam Kesher (Justin Theroux) is having difficulty getting his current movie made. He is in the midst of casting his female lead when he finds himself at a meeting where two mobsters (played by character actor Dan Hedaya and Lynch's long-time composer, Angelo Badalamenti) attempt to intimidate him into casting a particular actress, a cute blond named Camilla Rhodes (Melissa George), for the lead. Adam balks at having creative control wrested from him, but one of the mobsters simply repeats, "This is the girl" like a mantra that will not be denied. More bad news awaits Adam when he gets home. He catches his wife in bed with the pool man, who ends up throwing him out of his own house.

His production having been shut down and his line of credit cancelled, Adam learns that a man known as the Cowboy (Lafayette Montgomery) wants to meet with him in a corral at the top of Beachwood Canyon. The meeting is a pure Lynchian sequence—from the industrial sound of the electric light at the top of the corral sputtering to life to the menacing little man in full Western regalia dressing Adam down for being a smart aleck and then making it clear that he must go back to work and cast Camilla or else face the consequences.

Meanwhile, a waitress's name tag at Winkie's Diner jogs Rita's memory, and she recalls the name Diane Selwyn. When Rita and Betty look her up in the phone book and call her, Rita does not recognize the voice, but they decide to pay her a visit anyway. First, however, Betty has an audition at a movie studio. In the audition, Betty is playing a young woman having an affair with an older man who happens to be her father's friend. When she practices the scene at home opposite Rita, Betty does a standard, melodramatic reading befitting the soap opera material. In the audition itself, however, she astonishes everyone, including the lecherous has-been opposite her, Woody Katz (Chad Everett), by giving a performance that is seductive, sexy, and slightly menacing. In the beginning, Woody takes the upper hand, holding her close and using the audition as an excuse to make out with the pretty, young ingenue. But Betty plays along, intensifying the heat and ultimately taking command of the scene. It is not only a great audition for Betty but also a great scene for Watts, who shows a side of her character that we could never have imagined and hints at the full range of emotions she will exhibit by the end of the film.

Betty is such a standout that an impressed casting agent takes her to see Adam, who is holding auditions for his film, which seems to be a doo-wop film set in the '50s (a favorite era for Lynch). As in *Blue Velvet,* Lynch has the uncanny ability to set a story in the present day and yet layer it with a '50s sheen, giving it the feel of being suspended across time. Betty and Adam do not actually meet, but their eyes lock from a distance. They are transfixed by each other, but, for Adam, there is something more. His eyes seem to suggest that he desperately wants to audition Betty on the spot, but Camilla soon appears, and, knowing what is good for him, he casts her immediately. Before Adam can even talk to Betty, she flees to meet Rita so that they can seek out Diane Selwyn. No one answers at her apartment, but the spunky Betty climbs through a window, and the two women discover Diane's rotting corpse on her bed.

From this point forward, the film takes some very unexpected turns. The frightened Rita dons a blond wig, probably because she thinks that she needs a disguise to avoid Diane's fate. To make her feel protected, Betty invites Rita to sleep with her, and the two friends become lovers in a surprising encounter that is steamy yet tender. Lynch also adds just a touch of humor to leaven the intense eroticism—

when Betty asks Rita if she has done this before, she confesses, "I don't know," because of course she cannot remember.

The situation grows stranger, even surreal. In the middle of the night, Rita suddenly gets the impulse to go to a nightclub called Silencio, an eerie after-hours spot where the women watch a suave master of ceremonies reveal that there is no band, so all the music at the club comes from a tape. The main attraction at Silencio is Rebekah Del Rio, who takes the stage for a Spanish-language a cappella rendition of Roy Orbison's "Crying," whose lyrics about the torment of lost love foreshadow the conflict of the last part of the film. Dolled up in red and yellow eye shadow with a fake teardrop on her cheek and wearing a tight skirt, Del Rio is nothing short of mesmerizing in one of the oddest yet most breathtakingly beautiful scenes of the year. Betty and Rita are moved to tears by the song, as if there were some kind of direct pipeline from Del Rio's consciousness to theirs. The emotion of the song becomes too much for the singer, who collapses on the stage, and yet, because the song is canned, it hauntingly continues as Del Rio is carried away.

In a plot twist that comes out of nowhere, Betty opens her purse and finds a mysterious blue box. It looks like Rita's key will fit it, so they go home, but suddenly Betty disappears, leaving Rita to open the box alone. The camera zooms into the box, and we suddenly enter an alternate reality where identities have changed. The Cowboy appears and wakes Diane from death, but now the woman we have known as Betty is Diane. The woman we have known as Rita is now the young ingenue, Camilla. In this world, Diane and Camilla have a history as lovers, but Camilla is rebuffing Diane's advances because she is in now in love with Adam. Moreover, she is starring in his new movie. A supporting player, Diane seethes with jealousy when she watches Adam demonstrate to an actor how to perform a love scene with Camilla. Naomi Watts is astounding in this second role, playing a burnt-out failure and emotional wreck who, while still young, is a long way from the sweet-tempered, perky optimism of Betty. Watts demonstrates an extraordinary range and power in her dual role, making us believe in both Betty's sunniness and Diane's raging bitterness. It is a career-making performance.

In a scene that echoes the film's opening, Diane takes a ride in a limo that makes an abrupt stop along Mulholland Drive. But instead of having a gun pointed at her as Rita did, Camilla appears out of nowhere and leads Diane up to Adam's house. (It is a beautifully scored, hypnotic walk through a wooded area that plays like a brief fairytale moment for the otherwise beleaguered Diane.)

A party is taking place at Adam's house, where characters from the first part of the film appear but in different forms. Coco is Adam's mother, one of the mobsters is a guest, as is the blond Camilla (we are treated to an odd moment of one Camilla kissing the other passionately on the lips), and even the Cowboy can be glimpsed sauntering in the background. At dinner, we learn the history of the Diane/Camilla relationship. They were both actresses who met on an audition, but Camilla became a star, while Diane garnered only supporting roles, often with Camilla's help. It is obvious that Diane is jealous of Camilla's success and especially of her relationship with Adam. Just as it seems that Adam and Camilla are going to announce their engagement, the film cuts to Winkie's Diner, where a desperate Diane is hiring a hit man to kill Camilla. When the deed is finally committed, Diane becomes so overcome with guilt that she puts a gun to her head and kills herself, her corpse ending up in bed where Betty found Diane's body in the film's first scenario.

How do we reconcile the two sections of *Mulholland Drive*, the change in identities that is at the heart of Lynch's puzzle? Lynch's work is often open to many interpretations, and *Drive* is a complex film whose details could probably be read several ways. But a reading of the overall film suggests that the final section (after the opening of the box) is reality and the lengthy first section is Diane's dream or fantasy of her idealized Hollywood odyssey. Overcome with guilt for killing her lover, Diane constructs in her mind an elaborate fantasy at the moment of her death in which Camilla, stripped of her memory, survives the hit and becomes friends with Betty, who represents Diane's idealized self—an up-and-comer who nails her first audition and is on her way to the stardom that eluded Diane in real life. In this dreamland, the arrogant Adam does not get the beautiful starlet—instead, he is menaced by mobsters and cuckolded by his wife—while Betty and Rita fall in love.

Lynch has brilliantly melded his interest in the surreal with a poignant character study of a disturbed actress seeking relief from despair and guilt by reconfiguring the world around her into her idealized Hollywood life. *Mulholland Drive* thus transcends its roots as a noir puzzle to become a complex exploration of innocence lost (also a theme of *Blue Velvet*), obsession, and, in a strange way, the power of the imagination.

This stunning film is all the more amazing when one realizes that it would not exist in this form if Lynch's original plan had worked out. *Mulholland Drive* began its life as a TV pilot for ABC, but, when the network ultimately rejected it, Lynch rethought the whole structure and secured financing to shoot new scenes so that he could release it as a feature film. Incidentally, this probably explains why certain characters, a detective (Robert Forster), a mysterious movie mogul (Michael J. Anderson), and a psychic (Lee Grant), among others, appear briefly in roles that probably would have figured more prominently in a weekly series.

An older woman, a seeming relic of Hollywood's past who sits alone during the performance at Club Silencio, is revisited at the very end as she utters the film's last word, "Silencio." She bears a passing resemblance to Norma Desmond, the iconic Hollywood has-been from Billy Wilder's *Sunset Boulevard*, another noir classic named for a famous Hollywood street that also explores the underside of the Hollywood dream. But where Norma is an actress past her prime whose sense of rejection drives her to murder, Diane is at the opposite end of the age spectrum—an ingenue whose failure to penetrate the showbiz machine sends her into her own delusions and finally murder and suicide. Like Wilder, Lynch shows great affection for the Hollywood milieu, the narrative conventions that he makes his own, and the talented actors who are able to create magic, but he knows the dark side of Hollywood as well. For all its touches of humor and seductive beauty, *Mulholland Drive* is finally a very melancholy ode to shattered dreams. When we see Betty and Rita together at the end superimposed over the Los Angeles skyline and bathed in white light, the image has a haunting effect, becoming a visual wish fulfillment of all that Diane has lost.

*—Peter N. Chumo II*

## CREDITS

**Betty Elms/Diane Selwyn:** Naomi Watts
**Rita/Camilla Rhodes:** Laura Harring
**Adam Kesher:** Justin Theroux
**Coco Lenoix:** Ann Miller
**Vincenzo Castigliane:** Dan Hedaya
**Cowboy:** Lafayette Montgomery
**Mr. Roque:** Michael J. Anderson
**Wilkins:** Scott Coffey
**Jimmy Katz:** Chad Everett
**Camilla Rhodes:** Melissa George
**Wally Brown:** James Karen
**Cynthia:** Katharine Towne
**Gene:** Billy Ray Cyrus
**Luigi Castigliane:** Angelo Badalamenti
**Joe:** Mark Pellegrino
**Louise Bonner:** Lee Grant
**Martha Johnson:** Kathrine (Kate) Forster
**Diane/Betty the waitress:** Missy (Melissa) Crider
**Detective Domgaard:** Brent Briscoe
**Mr. Darby:** Marcus Graham
**Ed:** Vincent Castellanos
**Billy:** Michael Des Barres
**Detective Harry McKnight:** Robert Forster

**Origin:** USA
**Released:** 2001
**Production:** Mary Sweeney, Alain Sarde, Neal Edelstein, Michael Polaire, Tony Krantz; StudioCanal, Asymmetrical Productions; released by Universal Pictures
**Directed by:** David Lynch

**Written by:** David Lynch
**Cinematography by:** Peter Deming
**Music by:** Angelo Badalamenti
**Sound:** Susumo Tokonow, Edward Novick
**Editing:** Mary Sweeney
**Art Direction:** Peter Jamison
**Costumes:** Amy Stofsky
**Production Design:** Jack Fisk
**MPAA rating:** R
**Running time:** 146 minutes

## REVIEWS

*Boxoffice.* September, 2001, p. 143.
*Chicago Sun-Times Online.* October 12, 2001.
*Entertainment Weekly.* October 19, 2001, p. 51.
*Los Angeles Times Online.* October 12, 2001.
*New York Times Online.* October 6, 2001.
*People.* October 22, 2001, p. 38.
*Rolling Stone.* November 8, 2001, p. 133.
*Variety.* May 21, 2001, p. 15.
*Washington Post.* October 12, 2001, p. WE43.

## AWARDS AND NOMINATIONS

**Cesar 2001:** Foreign Film
**Ind. Spirit 2002:** Cinematog.
**L.A. Film Critics 2001:** Director (Lynch)
**Natl. Bd. of Review 2001:** Breakthrough Perf. (Watts)
**N.Y. Film Critics 2001:** Film
**Natl. Soc. Film Critics 2001:** Actress (Watts), Film
**Nomination:**
**Oscars 2001:** Director (Lynch)
**British Acad. 2001:** Score
**Golden Globes 2002:** Director (Lynch), Film—Drama, Screenplay, Score
**Broadcast Film Critics 2001:** Film.

# The Mummy Returns

*Adventure Is Reborn.*
—Movie tagline
*The most terrifying power on earth is about to be reborn.*
—Movie tagline

*The most powerful force on earth is about to be unleashed by the two people who should know better.*
—Movie tagline

 **Box Office:** $202 million

In 3067 BC, The Scorpion King (The Rock) is determined to conquer the known world. After seven years of campaigning, however, his enemies have defeated him and driven his army into the Ahm Shere desert where his army dies, one by one, until only the Scorpion King survives. With his last efforts, the Scorpion King offers up a trade to the Egyptian god who is the protector of the dead, the jackal-headed Anubis: his soul in return for an army to defeat his enemies. Suddenly, like a swarm of ants emerging from the desert sands, the Scorpion King finds himself in command of thousands of dog soldiers which he takes into battle. When the battle is over, though, the army returns to the sand from which it came, and the Scorpion King's soul must serve Anubis for all time.

In 1933, Rick (Brendan Fraser) and Evelyn (Rachel Weisz) O'Connell are on an archeological dig in Egypt. What's unusual for Evelyn is that she has a very strong feeling that she has been in these buildings before . . . only they weren't ruins then. In fact so strong is her sense of deja vu, that she always seems to know where she's going and how to open secret doors. How can that be? Of course Evelyn also has been having strange dreams recently. They began at the start of the Egyptian New Year, the Year of the Scorpion. What a coincidence!

Elsewhere in Egypt, at Hamanaptara, the City of the Dead, Meela (Patricia Velasquez) and the Curator of the British Museum (Alun Armstrong) are on a dig of their own. They are looking for the remains of the mummy Imhotep (Arnold Vosloo). For Meela, you see, is really a reincarnation of Anck-Su-Namun, Imhotep's lover from ancient times. Eventually both expeditions are successful, with the O'Connell's bringing back to London the bracelet of Anubis and Meela and the curator bringing back Imhotep's remains.

Back in their London home, while Rick and Evelyn are preoccupied smooching, their precocious eight-year-old son Alex (Freddie Boath) opens the box containing Anubis' bracelet and slips it onto his arm. Suddenly panoramas of Egypt are projected into his parents' study, but when they're finished, Alex cannot remove the bracelet. Attempting to cover up his actions, Alex stuffs something heavy into the bracelet's box and pulls his sleeve down over his arm. What Alex doesn't realize is that by activating the bracelet, there are now only seven days before the Scorpion King is awakened and Anubis' army is released upon the world again. The questions become, can the army be stopped, or who will command them?

Of course the good guys, Rick and Evelyn, now joined by Evelyn's brother Jonathan (John Hannah), want to stop they army and they are helped in this by their old friend Ardeth Bey (Oded Fehr). Bey is one of the several leaders of a group called the Medjai all of whom are sworn to be protectors of mankind. And it should be no surprise to discover that the bad guys, Meela, the museum curator, and the newly brought-to-life mummy, Imhotep, plan on controlling Anubis' army to conquer the world. But to do either one, that group must be in possession of the bracelet . . . which eventually means having possession of Alex. And, to make matters worse, if Alex can't get inside the fabled diamond-topped pyramid at Ahm Shere before dawn on the seventh day, all life will be sucked out of him. Unfortunately, no one knows where Ahm Shere is. It has always been considered a myth. Furthermore, it is said that "no one who has seen it has ever returned alive."

Now, you've got to be asking yourself, "if no one who has seen it has ever returned alive, how does anyone know about it?" Well, that's just one of the logical problems with *The Mummy Returns.*. The biggest logical dilemma, however, may be how come Imhotep wants the bracelet to control the Scorpion King and Anubis' army while Rick wants it to destroy them both. So, which does the bracelet do? And somebody ought to teach the bad guys how to shoot. Even with machine guns they can't hit anything! Especially not a good guy standing out in the open. Another leap of logic? How about a boat attached to a hot air balloon that can fly faster than a tidal wave.

Beyond the logic flaws, *The Mummy Returns* also constantly brings to mind other movies: The murdering pygmies marauding through the underbrush of the Ahm Shere oasis act just like velociraptors from *Jurassic Park,* a romantic scene on the prow of the dirigible just barely escapes a "king of the world" *Titanic* reference, the fight between Anck-Su-Namun and Evelyn could have come right out of *Crouching Tiger, Hidden Dragon,* and more than one battle scene brings back memories of *Gladiator.* (And speaking of fight scenes, several of the ones in *Returns* are shot in such close-up that who is doing what to whom is totally lost, and did they have to add all that slow-motion stuff to the final fight between Imhotep and Rick? The kung-fu look of it is quite distracting. Even the fight scene between Evelyn and Anck-Su-Namun is overly choreographed, but hey, at least Evie's not stupid in this movie and she can really kick butt.)

All these negatives aside, however, the public is eating up the sequel. When *The Mummy* opened on Mummy's Day weekend in 1999, it generated a record-breaking $43.36 million. It went on to earn more than $414 million worldwide, was the top-selling live-action video title of 1999 and ranked 31st on the list of all-time box office grossers. Ac-

cording to its writer-director Stephen Sommers, the movie opened on a Friday night, and by 6 a.m. Saturday morning the studio was clamoring for not just one sequel but two. The result, almost two year's later to the day, *The Mummy Returns* opened one week before Mummy's Day 2001. It grossed a whopping $70 million it's opening weekend, making it the biggest non-holiday opening ever. History repeats itself, only this times not only are the box office receipts pumped up, so too are the stunts, the effects, the action and the budget. But that's sequelitis for you.

So why are people plunking down the bucks to see a sequel? Well, there are several likable things about the film. First of all, there's the cast. All the majors have returned from the original and are now surer of their characters. The chemistry between Evie and Rick is solid with more than one reviewer referring to them as the Nick and Nora Charles of Egyptology. The main newcomer, their son Alex, is wonderfully played by Freddie Boath as part Tom Swift and part Bart Simpson.

Another reason for the film's success is its sheer energy in a spring devoid of any movies that can get a viewer's adrenaline going. If you don't allow yourself to be distracted by the plot holes and logical leaps of faith, the movie can really keep the action churning, which makes it a perfect summer blockbuster action ride. And the fact that it's the first one of the summer didn't hurt.

That powerful summer movie formula, however, also insists on combining all that action with more than a dollop of humor. Fortunately, like its predecessor, *The Mummy Returns* has its share of comedy. Personal favorites: all the mummies in the British museum rising up when the resurrection ceremony is chanted in the basement, Rick's effective use of the patented Three Stooges Eye Poke to foil a nemesis, the escape through the London streets in a double decker bus, and Alex tormenting his kidnaper Lock-Nah (Adewale Akinnuoye-Agbaje) with an incessant "are we there yet?". Thank goodness the filmmakers never mistake dramatic momentum for seriousness.

Of course action and humor in summer blockbusters nowadays usually also have to be accompanied by special effects. Although some special effects in *The Mummy Returns* are spectacular—especially the recreations of ancient Egypt—some of them seem less than extraordinary. The army of Anubis is almost too overwhelming to be believable but one has to admit that animating jackals as soldiers walking on two feet must have been tricky. The skeletal pygmies were interesting, but as mentioned before, they just seemed like more humanized velociraptors. The disappearance of the Ahm Shere oasis was good, but the Scorpion/Rock end monster looked pretty cheesy. It might have passed as some kind of camp tribute to Ray Harryhausen's stop-action monsters, but with all the hype about the film's spfx, it was a disappointment.

And speaking of The Rock, some viewers, expecting the wrestler to be a major villain in the movie, will be disappointed to find that their hero makes his theatrical debut as a cameo. He is only in the movie a few minutes, and most of it is as that bargain-basement scorpion-human hybrid that really looks more like a pissed off lobster. However, Rock fans can take heart. The next movie in the Mummy franchise is really a prequel/spinoff, *The Scorpion King*. It's scheduled for a summer 2002 release. Guess who stars. 🎬

—*Beverley Bare Buehrer*

## CREDITS

**Rick O'Connell:** Brendan Fraser
**Evelyn:** Rachel Weisz
**Ardeth Bey:** Oded Fehr
**Jonathan:** John Hannah
**Anck-Su-Namun:** Patricia Velasquez
**The Scorpion King:** Dwayne "The Rock" Johnson
**Imhotep:** Arnold Vosloo
**Alex O'Connell:** Freddie Boath
**Lock-Nah:** Adewale Akinnuoye-Agbaje
**Izzy:** Shaun Parkes
**Curator:** Alun Armstrong

**Origin:** USA
**Released:** 2001
**Production:** James Jacks, Sean Daniel; Alphaville; released by Universal Pictures
**Directed by:** Stephen Sommers
**Written by:** Stephen Sommers
**Cinematography by:** Adrian Biddle
**Music by:** Alan Silvestri
**Sound:** Peter Glossop
**Editing:** Bob Ducsay, Kelly Matsumoto
**Art Direction:** Anthony Reading, Giles Masters
**Costumes:** John Bloomfield
**Production Design:** Allan Cameron
**MPAA rating:** PG-13
**Running time:** 129 minutes

## REVIEWS

*Boxoffice.* April, 2001, p. 22.
*Boxoffice.* May, 2001, p. 23.
*Chicago Sun-Times Online.* May 4, 2001.
*Entertainment Weekly.* May 11, 2001, p. 48.
*Los Angeles Times Online.* May 4, 2001.
*New York Times Online.* May 4, 2001.
*People.* May 14, 2001, p. 39.
*Sight and Sound.* July, 2001, p. 45.
*USA Today Online.* May 4, 2001.
*Variety.* May 7, 2001, p. 49.
*Washington Post Online.* May 4, 2001.

## QUOTES

Rick (Brendan Fraser): "Oh, I hate mummies."

# The Musketeer

**Box Office:** $27.1 million

Seventeenth-century France is ruled by the feeble and ineffectual King Louis XIII (Daniel Mesguich), and a weak king is a sitting invitation for someone else to seek his power. In this case, the opportunist is a churchman, Cardinal Richelieu (Stephen Rea). In his attempt to wrest power from the king, Richelieu is sewing the seeds of discontent amongst the people of France so they will throw off Louis and his meddling queen (Catherine Deneuve). However, Richelieu must be careful not to provoke war with France's powerful neighbors, Spain and England. What he wants is power for himself not a foreign war.

However, Richelieu's henchman, Febre (Tim Roth), couldn't care less about foreign relations. He kills the emissary from Spain and kidnaps the English Lord Buckingham. Where Richelieu had just wanted to embarrass Louis, Febre just enjoys murder and mayhem. Now supposedly the King has an army to protect him, the Musketeers, but when they conveniently are blamed for the Spanish emissary's murder, Richelieu orders their ranks to disband. France is now left wide open for the cardinal's army and the cardinal's maneuverings.

At just this juncture, into Paris comes a young man, D'Artagnan (Justin Chambers), and his teacher/friend Planchet (Jean-Pierre Castaldi). D'Artagnan's father had been a Musketeer, but 14 years earlier he was killed by Febre while the young D'Artagnan watched. Even then D'Artagnan showed great promise as a swordsman and now, after further training by Planchet, he has come to Paris to claim his place in the king's guard. Unfortunately, they don't exist anymore thanks to Richelieu. Their leader, Traville (Michael Byrne) has been thrown in jail and the Musketeers themselves are demoralized and, more often than not, drunk.

This doesn't sit well with D'Artagnan so his first plan of action is to free Traville from prison. Then he plans on saving the King and Queen and the visiting English representative, Lord Buckingham (Jeremy Clyde), from attack by an unruly mob paid for by Febre and peppered with his own troops. D'Artagnan does this by gaining access to the palace through its sewers. By the way, was it mentioned he had a little assistance with all this? Three Musketeers, Aramis (Nick Moran), Porthos (Steve Speirs), and Athos (Jan Gregor Kremp), help but they seem to go along more for the heck of it than out of any sense of commitment.

As can be imagined, this really gets the Cardinal mad so instead of just disbanding the Musketeers, he now has them rounded up and arrested. But when Aramis, Porthos and Athos ask D'Artagnan to help them to break their brothers in arms out of prison, he refuses. So much for "one for all and all for one." But then he has a more important mission. He has been asked to escort the Queen on a mission to undermine Richelieu's plans. And since he was asked to do this by the landlord's pretty niece and friend of the Queen, Francesca (Mena Suvari), how can he refuse?

Naturally Febre gets wind of the Queen's plan and soon she and Francesca are his prisoners and D'Artagnan has to race all the way back to Paris to enlist the help of the Musketeers he has just refused to help. Will they back him? One guess.

There have been many adaptations of Alexandre Dumas' 1844 classic *The Three Musketeers*. They range from the silent version featuring Douglas Fairbanks Jr. to the 1974 Richard Lester spectacle starring Michael York and spawning two sequels (*The Four Musketeers* and *The Return of the Musketeers*). One would think a remake, especially after the 1993 version with Charlie Sheen, Chris O'Donnell, Keifer Sutherland, and Oliver Platt, is totally unnecessary. What could yet another version of this tale possibly contribute to cinema history? Why bother? What could the filmmakers possibly do to infuse new interest in an old story?

One can just imagine *The Musketeer*'s director/ cinematographer Peter Hyams thinking just that. The answer he comes up with is to mix the old-fashioned swordplay action of the 17th century with the recent penchant of Hollywood films, after the incredible success of *Crouching Tiger, Hidden Dragon,* to incorporate the gravity-defying choreography pioneered in the Hong Kong film industry. Witness *The Matrix.*

Hyams is known as an action director: *End of Days, The Presidio, Time Cop.* According to the press notes, Hyams' inspiration for this film happened as he was watching the Australian 2000 Millennium celebration and saw acrobats performing wire work on the walls of the Sidney Opera House. From that we end up with the utterly preposterous penultimate battle in *The Musketeer,* which is fought on ropes dangling down the side of the castle tower where the Queen and Francesca are held captive like two Rapunzels.

It is not the only fight sequence done in a totally unbelievable fashion and making use of whatever is available on the set. D'Artagnan's first skirmish includes fighting while pressed between ceiling beams and then atop wine barrels—but oddly enough instead of making one think of, say, Jackie Chan, it makes one think of Xena, Warrior Princess. While some of the fight sequences are groanably laughable—such as the battle where D'Artagnan jumps from horse to horse—one has to give a nod to the action choreographer, Xin-Xin Xiong who is probably most noted for his choreography of the famous gun-battle scene in Tsui Harks' *Time and Tide.* (Xin-Xin Xiong was also the stunt double for Roth.)

The problem here is that it is a jarring mix of old and new, of trying to recapture the past and infuse it with modern traits. This might work if one completely succumbed to the ludicrousness of this, as was done more successfully earlier this year in *A Knight's Tale* (also reviewed in this edition), which totally refused to take itself seriously, but in *The Musketeer* it just comes off like a mutant hybrid.

This is not to say there aren't some good things about the film. For example, Hyams, who does double duty as the film's cinematographer, does a very good job of capturing the feel of 17th-century France. The actors have the look of men of that period, right down to their often dirty faces. Sets and costumes also work well to give the film the feel of the 1600s as does the way Hyams has placed all this against a dark but lustrous canvass. Hyams has indicated he wanted the film to look like a Rembrandt painting, and indeed it does, reflecting a world lit only by candlelight. But this works both for the film—giving it an authentic look—and against it by betraying the action.

Too often action scenes are filmed too darkly making things difficult to make out. Adding to the confusion is choppy editing and the use of too many closeups. When Febre finally catches his comeuppance, it's filmed so tightly and happens so abruptly that one may be left not knowing how it happened and not even sure he is dead.

The darkness also effects the actors. Justin Chambers is doubly cursed by this because not only is he filmed in minimal light, his D'Artagnan wears a floppy, brimmed hat throughout the film that usually obscures his face. Because of this we often see no facial reaction from D'Artagnan and this gives the impression that Chambers has limited range as an actor and questionable presence on screen. Mena Suvari comes off little better. Although always filmed in bright light, her characterization of Francesca is perhaps a bit too feisty and a bit too contemporary to fit the story. She provides another piece of jarring juxtaposition between old and new.

Stephen Rea does the best he can playing one of literature's if not history's greatest political villains Cardinal Richelieu, but his evilness is eventually undermined in the movie when we witness his ineffectualness in controlling Febre. Hardly a fitting position for a bad guy. And speaking of bad guys, nobody does it better than Tim Roth, but must he play them so often? He did it wonderfully in *Rob Roy* and *Reservoir Dogs* and reprised it in *Planet of the Apes,* which was released less than two months prior to *The Musketeer*, and now he's doing it again.

But pity the actors who play the original three musketeers, Nick Moran's Aramis, Steve Speirs' Porthos, and Jan Gregor Kremp's Athos are here relegated to little more than supporting characters. At least Catherine Deneuve looks as if she's having fun. Regal yet earthy, practical yet caring, and as beautiful as ever, she's a queen in everything but title. However, aficionados of the true Dumas story probably miss the evil Milady who here is replaced by Febre.

The missing Milady obviously is not the only change made to Dumas' story. Perhaps the most jolting is the way D'Artagnan is here portrayed as being more motivated by revenge than idealism as originally written by Dumas. Of course filmmakers are allowed to make changes to stories. They do it all the time in the name of artistic license, and if it's well done we applaud and reward them, but if they can't pull it off their movies flop. Unfortunately, while Hyams' adaptation of Dumas isn't terrible, it's also not that great. It has its good points, especially the way it recreates 17th-century France—and one good use of a modern urban legend about alligators in the sewers that is especially amusing when offered as a throwaway line by Catherine Deneuve—but on the whole it is just jarring. I don't think Dumas envisioned his tale ever being told as Crouching Cardinal, Hidden Musketeer.

—*Beverley Bare Buehrer*

## CREDITS

**D'Artagnan:** Justin Chambers
**Francesca:** Mena Suvari
**Febre:** Tim Roth
**The Queen:** Catherine Deneuve
**Cardinal Richelieu:** Stephen Rea
**King Louis XIII:** Daniel Mesguich
**Rochefort:** David Schofield
**Aramis:** Nick Moran
**Lord Buckingham:** Jeremy Clyde
**Treville:** Michael Byrne
**Porthos:** Steve Spiers
**Athos:** Jan Gregor Kremp
**Planchet:** Jean-Pierre Castaldi

**Origin:** USA
**Released:** 2001
**Production:** Moshe Diamant; Apollomedia, Miramax Films, Q&Q Media, Carousel Picture Co.; released by Universal Pictures
**Directed by:** Peter Hyams
**Written by:** Gene Quintano
**Cinematography by:** Peter Hyams

**Music by:** David Arnold
**Sound:** Detlev Fichtner
**Editing:** Terry Rawlings
**Art Direction:** Keith Slote, Adele Marolf, Petra Weber
**Costumes:** Raymond Hughes, Cynthia Dumont
**Production Design:** Philip Harrison
**MPAA rating:** PG-13
**Running time:** 105 minutes

## REVIEWS

*Chicago Sun-Times Online.* September 7, 2001.
*Chicago Tribune Online.* September 8, 2001.
*Entertainment Weekly.* September 14, 2001, p. 67.
*Hollywood Reporter Online.* September 8, 2001.
*Los Angeles Times Online.* September 7, 2001.
*New York Times Online.* September 7, 2001.
*USA Today Online.* September 7, 2001.
*Variety.* September 10, 2001, p. 58.

## QUOTES

The Queen (Catherine Deneuve): "You have no mercy in your heart." Febre (Tim Roth): "No mercy. No heart."

## TRIVIA

Sarlat in southwest France doubles as 17th-century Paris.

# My Father's Angel

My Father's Angel, Bosnian director Davor Marjanovic and screenwriter Frank Borg's Genie Award–winning film, opens with disturbing footage of the war in Bosnia. War victims cry out in anguish against a backdrop of their city's debris while gunfire and bullets take more victims. It's a scene of total devastation that acts as a psychological backdrop for the emigrant family we are about to meet. We first meet a young Bosnian Muslim, Enes (Tygh Runyan), who laments, "Every night I sleep in Sarajevo and wake up in Vancouver." He pounds on the bathroom door where his father Ahmed (Tony Nardi) prays for an angel to intervene in his life. Meanwhile, his traumatized and mute mother Sayma (Asja Pavlovic) retreats into her inner hell. We later learn that she had been kidnapped by Serbs and detained for six months with other Muslim women who were repeatedly raped every night. But Enes is seemingly unaffected by the war crimes impinged upon his family and he appears interested only in masturbation. Enes labels his parents crazy and he admits that he wouldn't mind returning to Bosnia.

Next, we meet a Serb Bosnian family who arrived in Vancouver before the war. Former soccer champion Djordje (Timothy Webber) teaches his son Vlada (Brendan Fletcher) how to play soccer while he works as a taxi driver. His wife Zlata (Lynda Boyd) throws away a pile of newspapers every day since she doesn't want people in her building to read lies against the Serbs. Denial wouldn't be a strong enough to describe Zlata's emotional state. On a fateful night, the Serb and Muslim families lives collide in the form of a car accident in which Djordje hits the spaced-out Ahmed who has just discovered his angel. Only this angel happens to be one of the regular lunatics that hang out on downtown Vancouver streets dressed as Jesus and proclaiming the end of the world.

Ahmed refuses Djordje's help and spits in the Serb's face while his son Vlada looks on. But Djordje's persistence pays off and he returns the injured Ahmed to his home— only to discover a family completely torn apart by war crimes committed by the Serbs. Ahmed's wife hides under the table, trembling after seeing Djordje. She rips off her clothing anticipating a rape. When Ahmed gains consciousness, he attacks Djordje thinking that the Serb had in fact attacked his wife. While Djordje's eyes are open and he develops compassion for the Muslim family, his son develops bitter hatred towards the family. This is further enhanced after Enes torments him at a school restroom.

Meanwhile, Enes attacks a man that harasses a dog belonging to street kid Laura (Vanessa King), who resembles an anime character with her purple hair and large green eyes. Enes and Laura hit it off, smoke dope together, and act like typical juvenile delinquents. After a cop harasses Laura while she sells dope on the streets, Enes takes the rap, and when he gets into a brawl with Vlada, both young men end up in jail. Vlada's mother gets him released from jail but Enes remains, waiting for someone to pay his bail. Ahmed finally makes amends with the well-meaning Djordje, who sells his taxi to pay Enes's bail and Ahmed discovers that his real angel came in the form of a Serb, although further tragedy still finds his family.

*My Father's Angel* doesn't tie up loose ends but allows viewers to examine the consequences of war. It's not for the faint of heart.

—*Patty-Lynne Herlevi*

## CREDITS

**Ahmed Kadic:** Tony Nardi
**Djordge Vujic:** Timothy Webber
**Enes Kadic:** Tygh Runyan
**Vlada Vujic:** Brendan Fletcher
**Sayma Kadic:** Asja Pavlovic
**Zlata Vujic:** Lynda Boyd
**Laura:** Vanessa King

**Origin:** Canada
**Released:** 2000
**Production:** Mort Ransen, David Bouck; Ranfilm Productions
**Directed by:** Davor Marjanovic
**Written by:** Frank Borg
**Cinematography by:** Bruce Worrall
**Music by:** Shaun Tozer
**Sound:** Rick Bal
**Editing:** Lenka Svab
**Art Direction:** Samantha Travers
**Costumes:** Brad Gough
**Production Design:** Troy Hansen
**MPAA rating:** Unrated
**Running time:** 86 minutes

## REVIEWS

*eye Weekly Online.* November 30, 2000.
*Toronto Sun Online.* December 1, 2000.

## QUOTES

Enes (Tygh Runyan): "My father loves me most when I'm not at home."

## AWARDS AND NOMINATIONS

**Genie 2000:** Actor (Nardi)
**Nomination:**
**Genie 2000:** Actor (Webber), Screenplay.

# My First Mister

*Meet the new odd couple.*
—Movie tagline

**Box Office:** $.6 million

*My First Mister*, directed by actress Christine Lahti and written by first-time feature screenwriter Jill Franklyn, comes off as an unintended remake of Hal Ashby's cult classic *Harold and Maude*. While differences do exist between the two films—Franklyn's script features a young woman protagonist who doesn't embark on a sexual relationship with her older friend—many other similarities beg for comparisons. An older individual befriends a youthful character who obsesses about death and fears life. The virginal protagonists of both films wear black clothing, hang out in cemeteries, and drive black cars. The problem is that *Harold and Maude* delivered extremely memorable performances by Ruth Gordon and Bud Cort, quirky scenes that are difficult to match, and a lilting soundtrack compliments of Cat Stevens, whereas *My First Mister* barely registers on the cinematic gem scale.

*My First Mister* possesses some raw comical moments, as well as heartfelt performances by its young star Leelee Sobieski and comedian Albert Brooks. However, the film proves problematic because of its lack of plausibility. Most of the film's humor revolves around goth character Jennifer's (Sobieski) outlandish attire, tattoos, and body piercings, and how her image contrasts with the conservative world. But only a viewer far removed from an urban setting will truly be shocked by Jennifer's appearance. Still it's hard for viewers to wait patiently for Jennifer to be transformed into a more presentable woman, which includes a change of attitude along with a change of clothing. And this transformation proves refreshing since no one wants to be hammered over the head by a nihilistic middle-class brat who writes eulogies as a form of entertainment. Of course, goth viewers watching this film might find this transformation unnecessary and will find the film disappointing, as will adult viewers recalling *Harold and Maude*, who will desire a more compelling story than what is being offered here.

As the film opens, Jennifer narrates a diatribe of why she hates her life while she reclines in her goth environment. Images of skeletons and death surround her, copies of Anne Rice's books along with Sylvia Path's *The Bell Jar* rest on a night stand while goth music plays in the background. Cut to Jennifer complaining about her creative writing class where she clearly doesn't fit in with "the Ashleys" and their nose jobs. Next we meet Jennifer's over-exuberant mother (Carol Kane) who hides her pain over a divorce with a cheery demeanor resembling Mrs. Brady.

After being fired from a job at a goth clothing store, Jennifer, dressed in the wrong attire, ventures to Center City where she hopes to land a retailing job in a posh establishment. Although she gets booted out of most stores, she intrigues Randall (Brooks), a middle-aged conservative salesman. He tells Jennifer that if she loses her face jewelry, then he'll consider hiring her to work in the stockroom. So an unlikely friendship begins between a 49-year-old loner and a 17-year-old oddity. Jennifer stops torturing herself and

dons other colors besides black and Randall updates his musical taste and his wardrobe, but stops at acquiring a tattoo. However, conflict arises after Jennifer decides to pursue a sexual relationship with the reluctant Randall, who would never take advantage because of their age difference.

All of a sudden Randall collapses while jogging. Jennifer learns about a dark secret that Randall has hidden from her and the film's viewers. Hospitalized Randall suffers from an acute case of leukemia from which he won't recover. After Jennifer discovers the whereabouts of Randall's ex-wife, she sets out to see her, only to discover that the woman died six months earlier, leaving behind another secret. Jennifer meets Randy (Desmond Harrington), Randall's son. Randall meets Randy for the first time at a family gathering, then Randall passes away, leaving Jennifer and Randy to embark on a romantic future.

Director Lahti summed up her film thusly: "The movie is about the end of anonymity. Without Randall, Jennifer might well have become a victim of the self-destruction she toys with. Without Jennifer, Randall might have just faded away." And the film does work as a story about anonymity while barely resisting sentimentality. In the end Lahti and Franklyn uncover humanity in an unlikely relationship. But some viewers have already seen a better version of this story.

*—Patty-Lynne Herlevi*

## CREDITS

**Randall:** Albert Brooks
**Jennifer:** Leelee Sobieski
**Randy:** Desmond Harrington
**Mrs. Benson:** Carol Kane
**Bob:** Michael McKean
**Patty:** Mary Kay Place
**Ben:** John Goodman
**Sheila:** Lisa Jane Persky

**Origin:** USA
**Released:** 2001
**Production:** Carol Baum, Mitchell Solomon, Jane Goldenring, Sukee Chew, Anne Kurtzman; Total Film Group, Firelight Films, Apollomedia, Film Roman; released by Paramount Classics
**Directed by:** Christine Lahti
**Written by:** Jill Franklyn
**Cinematography by:** Jeffrey Jur
**Music by:** Steve Porcaro
**Sound:** Douglas Tourtelot
**Music Supervisor:** Andy Hill
**Editing:** Wendy Greene Bricmont
**Art Direction:** Gary Kosko

**Costumes:** Kimberly Tillman
**Production Design:** Dan Bishop
**MPAA rating:** R
**Running time:** 109 minutes

## REVIEWS

*Boxoffice.* April, 2001, p. 217.
*Chicago Sun-Times Online.* October 12, 2001.
*Entertainment Weekly.* October 19, 2001, p. 55.
*Hollywood Reporter.* January 23, 2001, p. 26.
*Los Angeles Times Online.* October 12, 2001.
*New York Times Online.* October 12, 2001.
*People.* October 22, 2001, p. 39.
*USA Today Online.* October 12, 2001.
*Variety.* January 22, 2001, p. 52.
*Washington Post.* October 12, 2001, p. WE45.

## QUOTES

Jennifer (Leelee Sobieski): "My clothes are not all black. Some of them are blue. Sometimes I wear them together so I look like a bruise."

## TRIVIA

Christine Lahti won a 1996 Oscar® for her short film *Lieberman in Love.*

# Nico and Dani (Krampack)

*Two boys . . . and the summer that would change everything.*
—Movie tagline

Depending on which reviews are read, Cesc Gay's *Nico and Dani* is either "sweet and harmless" according to Edward Guthmann of the *San Francisco Chronicle* or "overall too repellent" according Jeffrey M. Anderson of the *San Francisco Examiner.* It depends on how viewers of the film interpret the character Dani (Fernando Ramallo). Is the adolescent boy just being a boy as in the saying "boys will be boys" when he drugs a girl and then rapes her while she sleeps? One critic merely said that Dani molested a girl. And of course, he did molest his childhood friend Nico (Jordi

Vilches) while Nico slept. It becomes apparent through Dani's actions that he's queer, but he also might be a late-blooming psychopath and in any case, he's a spoiled brat complete with household cook and tutor.

*Nico and Dani* pleased festival crowds, garnering the film the Prix de Jeunesse award from the Cannes Film Festival as well as awards from the Bogota Film Festival, the Stockholm Film Festival, and the Chicago International Film Festival. Stephen Holden of the *New York Times* described Gay's film as "captivating and sustaining the fragile emotional climate of curiosity, fear, innocence and prurience that surrounds adolescent sexual experimentation." And despite molestation scenes that did nothing more than cast a shadow over Dani's psyche, the film portrays a sunny vacation atmosphere where anything goes, including sex, until one grows tired.

As the film's opening credits grace the screen, we see Nico flirting with an older French woman on a train. This pipsqueak has a long way to go before he grows into a man, but he possesses boyish charm and a naïve attitude that causes us to chuckle. Nico is on the cusp of 17 and he wants to get laid. He plans on meeting a willing female while he camps out at Dani's parents' house for a brief holiday. However, Dani has fallen in lust with Nico, putting a huge damper on Nico's summer plans. While Nico brags about how large his Adam's apple is, because he believes that women are turned on by men with a large Adam's apple, Dani appears to be interested in another part of Nico's anatomy.

Upon arriving in town, Nico and Dani run into two vivacious young women, Berta (Esther Nubiola) and Elena (Marieta Orozco), who also desire to lose their virginity during their summer break. Nico quickly pairs off with Elena, hoping that Dani will couple with Berta, but Dani only pretends to be interested in women. Dani and Nico practice mutual masturbation (which they call Kràmpack) but eventually Dani takes it too far as he convinces Nico to have sex with him. However, Nico thinks it's just a game of sexual experimentation since he's unaware of the romantic feelings that Dani has for him. Nico would rather fix a motor bike and hang out with the girls than be trapped in the villa with Dani, but they're friends, right?

One night, Dani goes overboard by convincing Nico to place Valium in the sangria because his father had told him that the drug stimulates sex drives (in women). Drugged, Berta grows ill and falls asleep and then Dani, who's experimenting, rapes her. After he grows bored with Berta, he interrupts Nico and Elena while they make out on the couch and he suggests a threesome. Elena is concerned for Berta, who complains of nausea and the pain that she feels "down there," so she begs off and takes Berta home.

Elena and Nico eventually have sex and, on the same night, the sullen Dani consoles himself by getting drunk with older gay writer Julian (Chisco Amado) and his friends.

Elena jilts Nico afterwards, telling him that her boyfriend will soon be home on leave from the service. Dani spends a day with Julian and even makes a pass at the middle-aged man, but then he flees from the writer's apartment after he gets a case of nerves. After Nico's train departs for Barcelona, Dani lies on a beach while casually checking out two women, then a man, only to decide to go for a swim instead. Clearly he's had enough. So have we.

Recalling Eric Rohmer's *Pauline on a Beach, Nico and Dani* explores sex and limits on friendship. Nico and Dani separate, hopefully learning from their mistakes. Hopefully, Dani learns that rape isn't a normal part of the teenage experience and it's never casual for women.

—*Patty-Lynne Herlevi*

## CREDITS

**Dani:** Fernando Ramallo
**Nico:** Jordi Vilches
**Elena:** Marieta Orozco
**Berta:** Esther Nubiola
**Julian:** Chisco Amado
**Sonia:** Ana Gracia

**Origin:** Spain
**Language:** Spanish
**Released:** 2000
**Production:** Marta Esteban, Gerardo Herrero; Messidor Films; released by Avatar Film Corporation
**Directed by:** Cesc Gay
**Written by:** Cesc Gay, Tomas Aragay
**Cinematography by:** Andreu Rebes
**Music by:** Riqui Sabates, Joan Diaz, Jordi Prats
**Sound:** Juan Quilis
**Editing:** Frank Gutierrez
**Art Direction:** Llorence Miguel
**MPAA rating:** Unrated
**Running time:** 90 minutes

## REVIEWS

*Chicago Sun-Times Online.* June 15, 2001.
*New York Times Online.* February 2, 2001.
*San Francisco Chronicle Online.* February 27, 2001.
*San Francisco Examiner Onlne.* February 27, 2001.
*Washington Post Online.* April 27, 2001.

# No Man's Land

 **Box Office:** $.2 million

Writer-director Danis Tanovic served in the Bosnian army as a film archivist and shot hundreds of hours of footage on the front lines of Sarajevo during the Bosnian war in the early 1990s. He has experienced war and suffering firsthand in his troubled homeland and, in his debut as a writer, has created a darkly comic antiwar parable called *No Man's Land*. It begins promisingly enough with the clever conceit of a warring Bosnian and Serb stranded together in a trench between enemy lines but unfortunately ends up saying nothing new about war in general or the Balkan crisis in particular. While the film has many smart jokes and some strong moments, it lacks an original vision that would make it deserving of the nearly unanimous praise heaped upon it by the nation's critics.

The film, which won the Best Screenplay award at this year's Cannes Film Festival, opens with a small Bosnian relief squad unable to see its way safely in a dense fog, a fitting metaphor for the moral fog of war and international politics. The soldiers decide to wait until the fog lifts to move on, but, when morning breaks, they are suddenly confronted by a Serb tank. Most of the Bosnian soldiers are instantly killed, but two are wounded and survive, only to find themselves stranded in a trench. The Serbs send a couple of soldiers to search the trench, and one of them plants a bouncing mine under the body of one of the Bosnians, Cera (Filip Sovagovic), who appears to be dead. This mine is a particularly insidious explosive that will detonate when the body is moved and destroy everything within a 50-yard radius. The other Bosnian, Ciki (Branko Djuric), who has been hiding from the two Serbs, is able to snatch a stray rifle and kill one of them while wounding the other, a neophyte named Nino (Rene Bitorajac). The situation is soon complicated when Cera regains consciousness only to learn that he will be killed the moment he attempts to make a move.

The setup is intriguing, but the script quickly devolves into petty squabbling between the enemies, which, while funny, is not very insightful. Ciki and Nino bide their time together bickering over who started the war. When Ciki has his rifle aimed at Nino, Ciki forces Nino to admit that the Serbs started the war, but, when Nino later turns the tables on Ciki and aims his rifle at him, Ciki must admit that his side is guilty. Tanovic seems to be presenting the old cliché that the side in power is able to write the history books. The enemies find little common ground, other than a girl they both knew back home. It is a cute exchange that underscores the fact that, if life were different, they could have been friends. The stinging end to the story, though, is that the girl was smart enough to have left the country. The only other thing the men have in common is their desperation to be rescued. In a funny scene, they are both running wildly around the top of the trench and waving white pieces of cloth to signal for help.

Soon a U.N. tank comes rolling through trying to make its way safely to the trench, but the tank commander, a Frenchman named Sergeant Marchand (Georges Siatidis), has a hard time finding soldiers on either side who speak English or French. Language barriers become a running joke and a metaphor for the larger issue of people's inability to communicate with each other. Marchand is the film's most sympathetic character, a sincere, decent officer who wants to do some good despite superiors who would rather he did nothing. For example, Colonel Soft (Simon Callow), the head man at UNPROFOR (the military force of the U.N.), is a stereotypical pompous Englishman who is more interested in his sexy, miniskirted secretary than in getting involved in the conflict. No sooner does Sergeant Marchand arrive at the trench than his superior wants him to pull out. Ciki is committed to staying with Cera, but Nino tries to leave with Marchand. Figuring that Nino's presence is the only thing preventing the Serbs from attacking him, Ciki shoots Nino in the leg to keep him in the trench.

While we may feel for the plight of Ciki and Nino and especially for Cera, whose situation is unrelentingly grim, the central characters do not come across as three-dimensional creations. They may be pawns in the Balkan chess match, but they also feel like pawns in Tanovic's screenplay. He seems to be manipulating them as mouthpieces for their respective sides in order to make some obvious points about the futility of war in a land where hatreds run so deep that two enemies cannot put aside their mutual animosities to survive. Tanovic's screenplay, however, does have some rich ironic moments, as when a soldier looking at a newspaper exclaims, "What a mess in Rwanda!" while apparently unable to see the mess in his own country. Perhaps it is easier for him to acknowledge a tragedy far away than the bloodshed all around him.

Soon the press gets involved, adding yet another layer to the confusion surrounding the trench. A spunky English TV reporter named Jane Livingston (Katrin Cartlidge) has been eavesdropping on U.N. communications on her radio and forces Marchand to speak with her. Realizing that maybe he can use her influence to get something done, he cooperates, and soon Marchand has her talking to his superior, who tries to appease her by spouting lies about negotiations taking place between the warring sides. As dark as the film's take may be on the Serbs and Bosnians, Tanovic seems to have the most contempt for the U.N. authorities, who are depicted as spineless and ineffective. They could intervene but instead allow mass murder to take place all around them while they remain neutral and guard their own reputation.

Once everyone converges on no man's land, the proceedings become a kind of circus, but they never reach the delirious heights of a truly inspired antiwar comedy. Just as Nino attacks Ciki with a knife, the U.N. tank returns to the trench and breaks up the altercation, and the bomb disposal expert finally arrives to try to defuse the explosive. Up to this point, the press has been depicted as smug but still a possible force for good. After all, Jane's efforts to make the situation public could embarrass the U.N. into finding a resolution. Now, however, Jane's colleague calls to tell her to be sure to get a close-up of Cera as the U.N. clears the mine. In its quest for a sensationalistic story to run around the clock on TV, the press, it seems, is just as selfish as everyone else and even willing to put Jane's life at risk for the story. At the same time, however, the behavior of Jane's Global News Channel actually seems fairly tame for an age when many media outlets would have a huge field day with the story of the trench. (Think of Billy Wilder's treatment of the press in a similar situation in 1951's *The Big Carnival*.)

The story comes to a shattering but unsurprising conclusion. When the German bomb expert finally discovers what kind of mine he is dealing with, he realizes that there is nothing he can do to defuse it. Ciki gets hold of a gun to take one final stand against Nino, whom he hates more than ever for attacking him with his own knife. When Nino tries to grab a gun to defend himself, Ciki shoots and kills Nino, and one of the U.N. soldiers shoots and kills Ciki in return. While it is a tragic finish, it feels rather inevitable and not as emotionally devastating as it should be since neither character is especially likeable. Soft abruptly clears the press out of the area, and, in the end, everyone drives away, leaving Cera alone in the film's last shot, lying on the mine and awaiting a certain death. This final, absurdist image of a man resting on an explosive set to go off the next time he moves is an unforgettable, existentialist ending and an apt metaphor for much of the history of the troubled Balkans, always a powder keg ready to explode.

Unfortunately, the film as a whole ends up more a giant metaphor than a drama, with each character representing a certain group to illustrate the bleakness of the crisis. Of course the Serbs and Bosnians hate each other, and no amount of time stuck together in a trench is likely to change that reality for two soldiers. The U.N. is unable and even unwilling to save anyone's life, which suggests that the whole international community is impotent in the face of mass slaughter, and the press, while at times well-intentioned, is also self-serving. Despite its entertaining bursts of gallows humor, *No Man's Land* too often feels like a familiar diatribe about the madness and folly of war when it could have dug deeper to offer fresh insights into the Balkan conflict or make an original statement about war and human nature.

—*Peter N. Chumo II*

**Ciki:** Branko Djuric
**Nino:** Rene Bitorajac
**Cera:** Filip Sovagovic
**Sgt. Marchand:** Georges Siatidis
**Dubois:** Serge-Henri Valcke
**Col. Soft:** Simon Callow
**Jane Livingstone:** Katrin Cartlidge

**Origin:** France, Italy, Belgium, Great Britain
**Language:** Bosnian
**Released:** 2001
**Production:** Cedomir Kolar, Frederique Dumas-Zajdela, Marc Baschet; Noe Productions, Casablanca Productions, Fabrica Cinema, Counihan Villiers Productions, Studio Maj; released by United Artists
**Directed by:** Danis Tanovic
**Written by:** Danis Tanovic
**Cinematography by:** Walther Vanden Ende
**Music by:** Danis Tanovic
**Sound:** Henri Morelle
**Editing:** Francesca Calvelli
**Costumes:** Zvenka Makuc
**Production Design:** Dusko Milavec
**MPAA rating:** R
**Running time:** 98 minutes

## REVIEWS

*Chicago Sun-Times Online.* December 21, 2001.
*Entertainment Weekly.* November 16, 2001, p. 110.
*Entertainment Weekly.* December 14, 2001, p. 55.
*Los Angeles Times Online.* December 14, 2001.
*New York Times Online.* November 4, 2001.
*New York Times Online.* December 7, 2001.
*People.* December 17, 2001, p. 34.
*Rolling Stone.* December 6, 2001, p. 156.
*Variety Online.* May 12, 2001.
*Washington Post.* December 21, 2001, p. WE45.

## QUOTES

Ciki (Branko Djuric): "Who started this war?"

## AWARDS AND NOMINATIONS

**Oscars 2001:** Foreign Film
**Cannes 2001:** Screenplay
**L.A. Film Critics 2001:** Foreign Film
**Nomination:**
**Broadcast Film Critics 2001:** Foreign Film.

# Nora

*She gave a voice to his words and fire to his passion.*
—Movie tagline

Usually writers and directors focus on the lives of artists with biographical features, while relegating spouses and colleagues to the background. However, Irish director Pat Murphy, with her adaptation of Brenda Maddox's biography on the common-law wife of James Joyce, hones in on the life of one of those background characters in her film *Nora.* Then again, as we quickly get to know the fiery Nora, we realize that the strong-willed woman demands our attention and, as she was the central force in Joyce's existence, she's also the driving force behind Murphy's passionate feature.

Of course, artists do not live their lives in a vacuum and they often derive their inspiration from the people in their lives. Yoko Ono played John Lennon's muse and as we recently have seen with Ed Harris' *Pollack,* the compassionate yet overbearing Lee Krasner acted as the driving force behind Jackson Pollock. However, the artists' colleagues spat on those earthy women and Nora was no exception. In Nora's case, she not only had to deal with her husband's intense bouts of paranoia and drunken behavior, but she had to exorcize the demons from her own dysfunctional past.

As we see Nora Barnacle (Susan Lynch) arriving in Dublin by train, we get a glimpse of her abusive familial past through flashbacks to a scene where Nora's uncle beat her because she was caught fooling around with a suitor. Nora escapes to Dublin in 1904 and finds work as a hotel maid, soon encountering a young James Joyce (Ewan McGregor), whom she is passionately drawn to—both by his talent and his insecurities. Nora ignites a volatile but orgasmic relationship with Joyce, but later he questions Nora's whorish behavior, leading to marital complications further down the road. After all, how could she have known how to make love to a man had she not practiced on several men before him, asks his colleague Cosgrave (Darragh Kelly)?

James and Nora have many things in common, one being their need to escape the confines of Ireland. Nora wishes to exorcize her connections to Ireland while Joyce desires to find a publisher that believes in his talent instead of censoring his stories, so the couple relocates to Trieste, Italy. However, this is where the battle of wills takes over. While Joyce spends most of his time drinking and writing, Nora complains about boredom and poverty while giving birth to two children, Georgio and Lucia. Eventually, Joyce can no longer control his paranoid thoughts and possessive streak.

When Joyces sees Nora flirting with Roberto Prezioso (Roberto Citran) at a small gathering, he pries answers out of Nora while they make love. Do you think about Roberto? Do you want to make love to him? Nora appears to think Joyce is just teasing her, but in fact, he's trying to push Roberto on Nora so that Nora will outright reject him. It's a twisted device that eventually leads to a separation between Nora and Joyce. In an earlier scene, Joyce's level-headed brother, Stanislaus (Peter McDonald), warns Nora that Joyce is used to receiving rejection from publishers so he expects Nora to reject him too and will go as far as to set up a scenario in which she has no choice but to reject him. Nora returns to Ireland with the children and is followed by Joyce, the couple eventually reunite and return to Italy. And Joyce's *Dubliners* is published.

*Nora* can be viewed in several ways—as a post-feminist study of women during the Victorian era, as the muse behind the artist, or as an erotic romance with a female gaze. Lynch blends earthiness and fire while appearing as the force behind Joyce's masterpieces while McGregor trembles with fear while stumbling through paranoia and drunken genius behavior. The couple live out a lusty life filled with erotic correspondence that leads us to understand the magnetism and the lure of artistic temperament and the couple's passion. McDonald delivers a sedate yet endearing performance as Joyce's brother. He exudes maturity while acting as the mediator between his paranoid brother and feisty Nora. Murphy's *Nora* is a visual gem that explores the voracious coupling of Joyce and Barnacle and is worth viewing more than once.

—*Patty-Lynne Herlevi*

## CREDITS

**James Joyce:** Ewan McGregor
**Nora Barnacle:** Susan Lynch
**Stanislaus Joyce:** Peter McDonald
**Roberto Prezioso:** Roberto Citran
**Micheal Bodkin:** Andrew Scott
**Uncle Tommy:** Vincent McCabe
**Annie Barnacle:** Veronica Duffy
**Eva Joyce:** Aedin Moloney
**Cosgrave:** Darragh Kelly

**Origin:** Ireland, Great Britain, Germany
**Released:** 2000
**Production:** Bradley Adams, Tracey Seaward, Damon Bryant; Natural Nylon Entertainment; released by Andora Pictures International
**Directed by:** Pat Murphy
**Written by:** Gerard Stembridge, Pat Murphy
**Cinematography by:** Jean-Francois Robin
**Music by:** Stanislas Syrewicz
**Editing:** Pia Di Ciaula
**Costumes:** Consolata Boyle
**Production Design:** Alan Macdonald
**MPAA rating:** R
**Running time:** 106 minutes

## REVIEWS

*Boxoffice.* November, 2000, p. 168.
*Los Angeles Times Online.* May 4, 2001.
*Sight and Sound.* June, 2000, p. 49.
*Variety.* May 8, 2000, p. 64.

## QUOTES

James (Ewan McGregor) to Nora (Susan Lynch): "Why is it that you can touch me and you won't let me touch you?" Nora replies: "Because I'm better at it than you are."

## TRIVIA

The character of Molly Bloom from the James Joyce novel *Ulysses* was inspired by Nora Barnacle.

# Not Another Teen Movie

*They served you* Breakfast. *They gave you* Pie. *Now we're gonna stuff your face.*
—Movie tagline

**Box Office:** $38 million

With the success of spoof films like *Scary Movie*, it's amazing that it took so long to get a big budget satire of teen movies into theaters. (*Wet Hot American Summer*, a viciously witty parody of 1970s preteen films like *Meatballs* only made it to limited release and, as a result, was sadly underattended). It's true that most teen movies are so formulaic that they're almost a satire of themselves, but it's more fun if a movie's intentionally trying to be funny.

*Not Another Teen Movie* follows in the footsteps of films like *Airplane!* It's the kind of film that throws in one joke after another, hoping that with such an onslaught of humor possibilities, audience members will find some of the stuff worth laughing about. There were five writers on the film, Michael G. Bender, Adam Jay Epstein, Andrew Jacobson, Phil Beauman and Buddy Johnson, which is a situation that usual means that a film will be bad and disjointed. In *NATM*, the disjointedness is not necessarily a bad thing. Humor relies on the unexpected, and the frequent non sequiturs and shifts in tone just add to the general raucousness of the proceedings. The writers all bring a different tone to the film which means that fans of the poo joke (you out there, maybe it's time to grow up) will get some jokes of a baser nature, whereas serious students of teen films will enjoy all the in jokes. The TV and stereo repair shop, for example, is called Spicoli's, which is the name of Sean Penn's character in the seminal teen flick, *Fast Times at Ridgemont High*. It's easy to imagine that the more obscure references were written in by Beauman and Johnson, who wrote both *Scary Movie* films. The movie gets extra hip points for being directed by Joel Gallen, who directed parody shorts for the MTV Movie Awards, like "Being Tom Cruise" and "Sex and the Matrix."

The plot of *Not Another Teen Movie* is based heavily on the Freddie Prinze film *She's All That*. Here, the popular student council president Jake (Chris Evans, who looks like a missing Baldwin brother) is smarting after being ditched by his popular cheerleader girlfriend, Priscilla (Jaime Pressly). His pals, including token black guy Malik (Deon Richmond), offer him a bet: can he take a hopelessly ugly, unpopular girl and make her into a prom queen? Jake agrees and the friends start scoping out the possibilities. Instead of picking a girl who's truly hopeless, they—like the guys in every teen flick—pick a girl that they think is hopeless, but is obviously a drop dead gorgeous girl wearing glasses and bad clothes. In this case, it's Janey Briggs (Chyler Leigh), a girl who's from the wrong part of town and is, uh-oh, artsy. As she puts it, "I'm a unique rebel. I read Sylvia Plath, listen to Bikini Kill and I eat tofu." Jake is concerned. "Guys! She's got glasses and a ponytail and paint on her overalls! She'll never be prom queen."

Janey is suspicious of Jake's sudden attention, but he's so darn cute, she just has to give him a chance. She doesn't give in so easily, though. Along the way there's ample time for the film makers to parody every teen movie cliche they can dig up. Not only do they throw in every reference to teen films they can squeeze in, bu there are also a few non-teen film homages. In one scene, a character appears that looks an awful like the videotaping next door neighbor in *American Beauty*. When Jake tries to woo Janey, he takes a tip from *10 Things I Hate About You* and sings Janey a song with her name in it in front of the whole school. His choice of Aerosmith's "Janie's Got A Gun," is probably not the best choice, since it causes Janey to be immediately thrown to the ground and frisked by school policemen. In a scene lifted from *She's All That*, he visits Janey in her basement studio where they bond when Janey confesses her secret urge to go to Paris to art school. Janey lets Jake see her "art" which is filled with ridiculous stick figures. Other films that get tweaked are *Bring It On*, *The Breakfast Club*, *Varsity Blues*, and *Cruel Intentions*.

Other parodies are fun to spot. In one scene borrowed from *Porky's*, Janey's little brother Mitch (Cody McMains), who's one of a pack of young, perennially sex-seeking virgin guys, decides to spy on the girls locker room. Instead of getting the eyeful they're hoping for, they're just a little bit late. "That's a once in a lifetime thing that will never happen again," says one of the girls, after an obvious locker room tryst with a few female classmates.

The movie is populated with favorite teen movie cliche characters. Besides the aforementioned token black guy and the mean cheerleader, there's a busty foreign exchange student who eschews shirts, an overeager virgin from a foreign land and the dumb fat jock. The coach is dead-on perfect, a crusty old guy who peppers his every sentiment with a string of curse words. When a player is accidentally sliced in half, the coach yells out some obscenities, then shouts, "Walk it off!"

The logic of the film is often and happily interrupted in the service of one joke or another. When Janey gets all cleaned up and reveals her made over self to Jake by walking in slow motion down the steps of her house while he gawks in appreciation, he says, "Congratulations, you just got your first slow motion entrance." During the obligatory prom sequence, a onlooker comments, "It's funny. You would never expect that everyone at this school is a professional dancer."

And there are sight gags galore. The football jersey of one of the players reads "Extra." The school is John Hughes High School and their team name is the WASPS. In one scene, Janey's spotted reading "How to Get the Popular Boy Without Compromising Your Unique Rebelliousness." Meanwhile, her dorky friend (Eric Jungman, playing the old Jon Cryer role), who wishes he was something more, reads, "How to Get the Uniquely Rebellious Girl Who's in Love With the Popular Boy." There's even a musical segment. During the montage where the couple is apart, each of the characters in the film breaks into song, describing their predicament. It ends up with a big production number outside of the doors of the prom.

The cameos in the film are fun, too. Former teen queen Molly Ringwald shows up as a jaded flight attendant who interrupts Janey and Jake's big scene at the airport (You know the one. The girl is going to leave the county. The boy, realizing she is the one for him, rushes to the airport to make it for the photo finish to beg her to stay.) Mr. T, of all people, is great as "the wise janitor who guides kids and occasionally changes the urinal cakes." And the music is dead on. There are covers of songs by 80s stalwarts like Spandau Ballet, Jackson Brown, and Simple Minds.

Critics varied in their responses, probably depending on their feelings about teen films in the first place. Owen Gleiberman of *Entertainment Weekly* gave it a B and called it, "a big, fat, juicy spitball lobbed, with mostly dead-on aim, at the teen-smarm cliches that have accumulated like so much earwax over the last three years." Annette Cardwell of Filmcritic.com wrote, "Fitting spoofs of at least 16 teen movies into one questionable parody film is like trying to fit 10 pounds of sausage into a five pound bag. You just end up with a groan-inducing mess." And Robin Rauzi of the *Los Angeles Times* wrote, "*Not Another Teen Movie* makes John Hughes look like Oscar Wilde. It makes *American Pie* seem quaint."

—*Jill Hamilton*

## CREDITS

**Janey Briggs:** Chyler Leigh
**Jake Wyler:** Chris Evans
**Ricky:** Eric Jungmann
**Austin:** Eric Christian Olsen
**Mitch Briggs:** Cody McMains
**Ox:** Sam Huntington
**Reggie Ray:** Ron Lester
**Bruce:** Samm Levine
**Malik:** Deon Richmond
**Priscilla:** Jaime Pressly
**Catherine Wyler:** Mia Kirshner
**Les:** Riley Smith
**Amanda Becker:** Lacey Chabert
**Areola:** Cerina Vincent
**Sadie:** Beverly Polcyn
**Sandy Sue:** Joanna Garcia
**Mr. Briggs:** Randy Quaid
**Coach:** Ed Lauter
**Wise Janitor:** Mr. T
**Richard Vernon:** Paul Gleason
**Flight Attendant:** Molly Ringwald

**Origin:** USA

**Released:** 2001
**Production:** Neal H. Moritz; Original Film; released by Columbia Pictures
**Directed by:** Joel Gallen
**Written by:** Michael G. Bender, Adam Jay Epstein, Andrew Jacobson, Phil Beauman, Buddy Johnson
**Cinematography by:** Reynaldo Villalobos
**Music by:** Theodore Shapiro
**Sound:** Stacy Hill
**Editing:** Steven Welch
**Art Direction:** Jay Pelissier
**Costumes:** Florence-Isabelle Megginson
**Production Design:** Joseph T. Garrity
**MPAA rating:** R
**Running time:** 82 minutes

## REVIEWS

*Chicago Sun-Times Online.* December 14, 2001.
*Entertainment Weekly.* January 4, 2002, p. 48.
*Los Angeles Times Online.* December 14, 2001.
*New York Times Online.* December 14, 2001.
*Variety.* December 17, 2001, p. 38.
*Washington Post.* December 14, 2001, p. WE38.

## QUOTES

Janey Briggs (Chyler Leigh): "I read Sylvia Plath, I listen to Bikini Kill, and I eat tofu—I'm a unique rebel."

## TRIVIA

Director Joel Gallen was Vice President of Production for MTV and still produces the MTV Movie Awards.

# Novocaine

*Crime is not only done by criminals.*
—Movie tagline
*Getting to the root of the problem is like pulling teeth.*
—Movie tagline

 **Box Office:** $2 million

A darkly comic twist on film noir conventions, *Novocaine* stars Steve Martin as Dr. Frank Sangster, a successful dentist who seems to have a perfect life. He has a busy, lucrative practice and an adoring fiancée, Jean Noble (Laura Dern), who also happens to be his hygienist. Frank's life, however, may not really be so perfect after all. It is boring and predictable and perhaps needs to be shaken up a bit. Enter Susan Ivey (Helena Bonham Carter), a dangerous, flirtatious vixen who proves irresistible to the normally staid dentist.

Swinging wildly from traditional crime thriller to absurd black comedy, *Novocaine* sometimes struggles to maintain a consistent tone throughout its relatively brief, 95-minute running time, but it still manages to produce its share of amusing moments. Written and directed by David Atkins, the film begins with the familiar noir setup of the femme fatale who draws the unsuspecting hero into a dangerous web of crime, drugs, and murder. Susan is a new patient for Frank and is obviously trouble, but Frank cannot help himself from surrendering to her trashy, low-rent sex appeal (echoes of Bonham Carter's role in *Fight Club*). No sooner is Susan seeing him for root canal when everyone else in the office has gone home than he is having sex with her in the dental chair—something that Jean would not do. Indeed, Frank welcomes the danger and spontaneity that Susan brings to his humdrum life.

The situation really spirals out of control the next day when Frank finds his supply of narcotics has been stolen and a DEA agent is snooping around, thinking that Frank is selling drugs. Frank immediately suspects Susan since she has already altered a prescription of his for five Demerol to read 50. It turns out that Susan is in cahoots with her bully of a brother, Duane (Scott Caan)—a tough drug dealer with incestuous desires for her. Instead of simply reporting Susan to the police, Frank demands the return of his narcotics vials, which he needs back to prove to the DEA that he did not sell the drugs. Obviously, Frank is resisting turning Susan in because he is attracted to her.

The seductive Susan is not the only strange character in Frank's life. He also has a ne'er-do-well brother, Harlan (Elias Koteas), who is clearly jealous of Frank's success and just happens to show up out of nowhere one evening painting Frank's cabinets for him. Even the seemingly perfect Jean is a bit odd—a control freak and fierce tae kwon do student who exhibits a wildness that verges on the maniacal when she is practicing her martial arts. But the thuggish Duane may be the scariest, albeit the least interesting. He confronts Frank at work, demanding that he stay away from his sister and threatening him if he runs in to him again. Frank, in short, comes across as the one normal person surrounded by a bunch of oddballs, the one sane man in a seemingly absurd world.

The noir hero's undoing generally stems from his falling for the femme fatale. But *Novocaine* tweaks the formula by suggesting that, in some weird way, Frank and Susan are actually perfect for each other and that, in a twist akin to screwball comedy, she has come into Frank's world to wake him from his doldrums. She has the wild streak to make his life exciting, and he perhaps represents a world of sanity and an escape from her lowlife brother.

In a confrontation with Duane, Frank ends up stabbing him in the hand with a pair of scissors as he is defending himself, and later Duane's dead body suspiciously appears in Frank's home. Just when the film looks like it is following a familiar crime formula, however, some comic bit spikes the story. Kevin Bacon, for example, pops up in a funny, uncredited cameo as a Hollywood actor who is following the police around to research a role and even gets to play detective by interrogating Frank.

Susan soon confesses to Frank that she met Harlan in Detroit and he tipped her off about Frank's supply of narcotics. At this point, the police consider Frank a prime suspect in the killing of Duane—Frank's face is all over the television news—and he flees across the roof of the motel where Susan is staying before he crashes onto a police car in a funny slapstick sequence. It seems that Frank's teeth marks were found on Duane's body, which explains why a forensics investigator had previously asked for an impression of his teeth. Frank knows that someone is trying to set him up, and, like a Hitchcockian wrong man, he must try to solve the case to clear his name. Frank eventually makes his escape from the police and is later shielded from authorities by Susan, who, against all evidence, somehow believes in his innocence.

Martin played a dentist before, in the musical horror spoof, *Little Shop of Horrors* (1986), but this time he is not doing a parody of a dentist but rather playing an Everyman figure who is suffocating from everyday normalcy. There is also a philosophical side to Frank that is well suited to Martin's dry wit. In voice-over, Frank expresses his outlook on life through the language of dentistry, commenting, for example, on the way lying is like tooth decay. Martin is also supported well by Dern and Bonham Carter, who seem to be having fun playing women who can pass for normal but who really harbor deep secrets.

*Novocaine* balances its crime thriller plot with loopy bits of comedy, but, as the story progresses, it loses some of its energy when the script takes some arbitrary turns that do not make much sense. From out of the blue, seeing a denture commercial on TV reminds Frank that Jean was interested in learning how to make dentures and made a set of his teeth. So he suddenly suspects Jean and investigates her house. Sure enough, he and Susan find a notebook full of his signatures—Jean was obviously practicing forging his name. They also find his dentures hidden in one of her treasured stuffed animals, which must have been used to make the marks on Duane's body. While it is supposed to be a provocative twist that Jean—not Susan—is the real criminal mastermind, it is not completely persuasive. Only at the end, after all, do we learn that Jean made dentures and, more important, that she made an arrangement in Frank's corporation that she would be a partner, thus making her the beneficiary if he were to be convicted of a felony.

Jean's villainy is very far-reaching. She was in cahoots with Harlan the whole time and was mad that he brought Duane into the plot when he was only supposed to bring Susan. So she had to kill Duane and frame Frank for the murder. A perfectionist, she is also a psychopath fed up with Harlan not doing things right. At the end, she meets him at Frank's office and kills him.

When Frank discovers his brother's dead body, with his teeth marks all over it, he knows that Jean is trying to set him up for another murder, and he hits on a twisted, grotesque way to outsmart her by faking his own death. Using a bottle of novocaine to deaden his senses, he proceeds to pull out each of his teeth. He plants them in Harlan's mouth and then sets the whole place on fire so that, when only the teeth are found, it will look like he has died. It is a macabre ending that feels too extreme, even for a film that is gleefully all over the map. A videotape, which just happens to be protected in a flame-retardant box, shows Jean shooting someone, but since it is not evident in the tape that the victim was really Harlan, it is assumed that it is Frank. In the end, Jean is reduced to a complete madwoman compulsively arranging her stuffed animal collection in her jail cell. Meanwhile, Frank is able to slip out of the country and start a new life with Susan in the French countryside, his dream place, where they are about to have a child. It may be unbelievable that a druggie like Susan could start a seemingly normal life overnight, but the story is so crazy that anything seems possible.

Mixing a film noir plot with dashes of screwball comedy and lacing the whole concoction with a darkly comic sensibility anchored by Martin's deadpan dentist, *Novocaine* is a generally satisfying, albeit somewhat uneven, thriller. It also features clever stylistic flourishes—quick glimpses of skulls shown in X-ray at key moments, which complement the film's theme of looking below surfaces to get to the truth. *Novocaine* may have its share of plot clichés and implausibilities, but it also offers its own eccentric spin on a familiar plot.

—*Peter N. Chumo II*

**Dr. Frank Sangster:** Steve Martin
**Susan Ivey:** Helena Bonham Carter
**Jean Noble:** Laura Dern
**Harlan Sangster:** Elias Koteas
**Duane:** Scott Caan

**Detective Lunt:** Keith David
**Pat:** Lynne Thigpen
**Actor:** Kevin Bacon

**Origin:** USA
**Released:** 2001
**Production:** Paul Mones, Daniel M. Rosenberg; released by Artisan Entertainment
**Directed by:** David Atkins
**Written by:** David Atkins
**Cinematography by:** Vilko Filac
**Music by:** Steve Bartek
**Sound:** David Obermeyer
**Editing:** Melody London
**Art Direction:** Craig Jackson
**Costumes:** Denise Wingate
**Production Design:** Sharon Seymour
**MPAA rating:** R
**Running time:** 95 minutes

 **REVIEWS**

*Boxoffice.* November, 2001, p. 145.
*Chicago Sun-Times Online.* November 16, 2001.
*Entertainment Weekly.* November 23, 2001, p. 54.
*Los Angeles Times Online.* November 16, 2001.
*New York Times Online.* November 16, 2001.
*People.* November 26, 2001, p. 40.
*Rolling Stone.* December 6, 2001, p. 156.
*USA Today Online.* November 16, 2001.
*Variety.* September 17, 2001, p. 21.
*Washington Post.* November 16, 2001, p. WE43.

 **QUOTES**

Dentist Frank Sangster (Steve Martin): "A man can lose his soul. He can lose his life. But the worst thing he can lose is his teeth."

0

*Trust. Seduction. Betrayal. . . . Everything comes full circle.*
—Movie tagline

 **Box Office:** $16 million

A modern retelling of Shakespeare's *Othello*, Tim Blake Nelson's *O* is a risky adaptation that sets the classic tragedy at a Charleston, South Carolina, boarding school and transforms the Moorish general into the school's star basketball player. Admittedly, the premise of *Othello* in high school sounds rather silly, and Shakespearean purists could easily accuse screenwriter Brad Kaaya of pandering to the youth market in some wrongheaded attempt to make the Bard accessible and relevant for today's teenagers. But the great shock of *O* is that the filmmakers are true to so much of the original's essential plot and have created a surprisingly effective and poignant drama. The Elizabethan language has been replaced by the teen vernacular, and the play's rich characters have been somewhat simplified, but the timeless themes of jealousy and betrayal seem wholly fitting for the contentious world of high school rivalries.

The villainous Iago can easily take center stage in any production of *Othello*, but this becomes especially true in *O*—the Iago figure, here called Hugo (Josh Hartnett), is the focus from the very beginning. He is even given an opening and closing voice-over narration, in which he dreams of the ability to fly, to soar above everyone else, which suggests some essential longing in his character. Unfortunately, the motif of birds and flight, prevalent throughout the film, is not handled very artfully—in some heavy-handed symbolism, the high school mascot is a hawk that Hugo ultimately steals, presumably because he identifies with its predatory nature.

The character of Iago is one of the great dilemmas of Shakespearean criticism. What motivates his unadulterated hatred for Othello and his plot to destroy him? It is true that Othello passes him over for his lieutenant in favor of the less experienced Cassio, but scholars still debate the question. It prompted Coleridge to coin the phrase "motiveless malignity" to describe the all-consuming evil at Iago's core. Kaaya's script, however, attempts to explain Hugo's hatred of Odin James (Mekhi Phifer), the film's Othello, as a response to parental rejection.

At Palmetto Grove Academy, Hugo's father, Duke Goulding (Martin Sheen), is the basketball coach and favors Odin as his star player. Odin, the only black student at the exclusive prep school, was recruited to give the school a winning team and is leading the school to a championship season. The coach selects Odin as the team's MVP and publicly declares, "I love him like my own son," which stings Hugo, while the gracious Odin shares the honor with another player, Michael Casio (Andrew Keegan), thus angering Hugo, who now feels doubly passed over. Hugo is thus much less of an enigma than Iago in the play, and, while his back story robs the film of the play's rich ambiguity, it actually makes sense in an adolescent context in which parental approval is so important.

The play's Desdemona becomes Desi (Julia Stiles) in the film, a strong-willed, passionate, and forthright girl.

(This is Stiles's third Shakespearean film, following *10 Things I Hate About You*, based on *The Taming of the Shrew*, and Michael Almereyda's version of *Hamlet*.) When Roger (Elden Henson), the movie's Roderigo figure, at Hugo's urging, falsely accuses Odin of forcing himself on Desi, she stands up to her father (John Heard), the dean of the school. Following the play, Roger is the gullible dupe whom Hugo manipulates for his own evil plan by promising that he can get Desi for him. Later, Hugo eggs him on to provoke a fight with Michael. As a result, Michael is suspended from the basketball team for at least two games (in the play, Cassio is stripped of his lieutenancy) and is now considered a disgrace to the MVP award that he shared with Odin.

Of course, these events are just the beginnings of Hugo's bigger plot to destroy Odin. Hugo urges Michael to have Desi be his intermediary with Odin to get him back on the team, but Hugo knows that this will make Odin suspect Desi of being in love with Michael. Sure enough, just seeing Desi and Michael together in the stands during a big game is enough to plant the seeds of doubt in Odin's mind about Desi's fidelity. Furthermore, Hugo raises questions about Desi's loyalty and even plays the race card, telling Odin that "white girls are snaky," which exploits Odin's insecurity as an outsider at the school, even though he is revered as a great athlete. All the while, Hugo is cagey in the way he pretends to resist telling Odin what he thinks of Desi, as if he did not want to meddle in other people's business because he is not absolutely certain about the matter.

Hartnett's approach is fascinating in the way it plays with our preconceptions of Iago, who is generally thought of as a confident villain who takes such glee in the destruction he wreaks. But Hartnett's Hugo, even when his evil plans are working, maintains the brooding, wounded quality of the son who cannot win his father's love. At the same time, there is, admittedly, something a bit farfetched about the whole notion that a high school student could be so psychologically adept that he could manipulate not only his best friend but also everyone else in his orbit. And yet Hartnett's performance is so self-assured that he makes this unlikely situation seem plausible.

Moreover, many of the translations from play to film are surprisingly smooth, even the potentially clunky matter of the stolen handkerchief, which provides Othello the "ocular proof" of Desdemona's infidelity. In *O*, the handkerchief becomes a treasured family scarf that Odin gives Desi as a sign of his devotion. When Desi accidentally drops it, her roommate and Hugo's girlfriend, Emily (Rain Phoenix), picks it up and gives it to Hugo, who claims that he wants it for a prank. Hugo in turn gives it to Michael and then tells Odin that he saw Michael giving it to another girl, which plunges Odin into a jealous tailspin.

Perhaps the most disturbing aspect of *O* and the greatest departure from Shakespeare is the way that Hugo's scheme reduces Odin, the athletic star seemingly loved by virtually everyone, to white society's worst stereotype of a dangerous black man. In one particularly grim scene, Odin turns violent on Desi as they are making love when he looks in the mirror and sees Michael's reflection staring back at him. Odin essentially becomes a rapist pouring out all of his violent sexual energy on the girl he supposedly loves, even as she pleads with him to stop. Odin also turns to drugs in his despair, a habit, it is suggested, that he quit long ago. Then at a slam dunk contest, he shatters the backboard in his fury and acts like an untamed animal. In short, the film seems to suggest that a young black man, no matter how well respected by his peers, needs just a gentle push to cross the line into rage and criminality. Phifer's raw portrayal of Odin's breakdown is heartbreaking and scary, but Shakespeare's grand, tragic figure of Othello is lost as Odin becomes a walking cliché of urban street life.

Hugo continues to insinuate himself as Odin's confidant as matters get worse and, once Hugo has his complete trust, simply lies about Michael and Desi being together. Then Hugo hatches an elaborate plan in which Odin can kill Desi and frame Michael for the murder. But the plan goes awry when Roger fouls up the killing of Michael so that his death does not look like a suicide. To cover Roger's ineptitude, Hugo has to kill Roger as well. Meanwhile, Odin strangles Desi in a climactic scene that is unflinchingly brutal and tragic. When Emily, having figured out what Hugo has done, reveals the truth about the scarf to Odin, Hugo shoots and kills her. Odin, knowing that he will be arrested for Desi's murder, finally kills himself but first denounces Hugo as his destroyer.

O does not shy away from the multiple tragedies that conclude the play—indeed, the film is more violent than the play, with dead bodies seemingly strewn everywhere as Hugo, the mastermind behind the carnage, is taken away by police. Moreover, given the high school setting, the deaths are more disturbing than in the play—so disturbing, in fact, that the sudden outburst of violence actually caused delay of the movie's release. Scheduled for release in late 1999, O was shelved by Miramax's Dimension Films, the movie's original distributor, after the shootings at Colorado's Columbine High School in April 1999, probably for fear that the climactic slaughter would remind audiences of the real-life teen shootings. The film's opening was postponed several times until Lions Gate picked up the film and released it at the end of summer 2001 to mixed reviews and generally lackluster business.

Stripped of Shakespeare's magnificent poetry, any modern version of his work is bound to fall short of the original's grandeur; indeed, without the Bard's elevated language, O sometimes feels like a high school melodrama. And yet, in cleverly invoking the plot machinations of Othello and in faithfully capturing the dark emotions at the heart of the story, O becomes one of the more thoughtful and original Shakespearean adaptations to appear in some time.

—Peter N. Chumo II

## CREDITS

**Odin James:** Mekhi Phifer
**Hugo Goulding:** Josh Hartnett
**Desi Brable:** Julia Stiles
**Roger Rodriguez:** Elden (Ratliff) Henson
**Michael Casio:** Andrew Keegan
**Emily:** Rain Phoenix
**Dean Brable:** John Heard
**Dell:** A.J. (Anthony) Johnson
**Coach Duke Goulding:** Martin Sheen

**Origin:** USA
**Released:** 2001
**Production:** Eric Gitter, Daniel Fried, Anthony Rhulen; Chickie the Cop; released by Lion's Gate Films
**Directed by:** Tim Blake Nelson
**Written by:** Brad Kaaya
**Cinematography by:** Russell Fine
**Music by:** Jeff Danna
**Sound:** Robert Maxfield
**Music Supervisor:** Barry Cole
**Editing:** Kate Sanford
**Art Direction:** Jack Ballance
**Costumes:** Jill Ohanneson
**Production Design:** Dina Goldman
**MPAA rating:** R
**Running time:** 94 minutes

## REVIEWS

*Boxoffice.* August, 2001, p. 57.
*Chicago Sun-Times Online.* August 31, 2001.
*Entertainment Weekly.* September 7, 2001, p. 132.
*Hollywood Reporter.* July 3, 2001, p. 13.
*Los Angeles Times Online.* August 31, 2001.
*New York Times Online.* August 31, 2001.
*People.* Septebmer 10, 2001, p. 39.
*USA Today Online.* August 31, 2001.
*Variety.* June 11, 2001, p. 18.
*Washington Post.* August 31, 2001, p. C1.

## QUOTES

Hugo (Josh Hartnett) to Odin (Mekhi Phifer) about Desi (Julia Stiles): "White girls are snakes, bro."

The story was filmed in Charleston, South Carolina.

# Ocean's Eleven

*Are you in or out?*
—Movie tagline

**Box Office:** $137 million

Despite mostly tepid reviews, *Ocean's Eleven* was a hit at the boxoffice, thanks to its star-studded cast, Ted Griffin's clever script, and Steven Soderbergh's slick direction. A mindless diversion it may be, but *Ocean's Eleven* is an extremely well-oiled entertainment, vastly superior to the original 1960 Rat Pack film.

Upon his release from a New Jersey prison, Danny Ocean (George Clooney) immediately begins planning to steal $150 million from the vault housing the proceeds from three Las Vegas casinos: the Bellagio, the Mirage, and the MGM Grand. To bring off the heist, Danny enlists master poker player Rusty Ryan (Brad Pitt), pickpocket Linus Caldwell (Matt Damon), explosives expert Basher Tarr (Don Cheadle), casino dealer Frank Catton (Bernie Mac), computer geek Livingston Dell (Edward Jemison), drivers Virgil Malloy (Casey Affleck) and Turk Malloy (Scott Caan), veteran con man Saul Bloom (Carl Reiner), Chinese acrobat Yen (Shaobo Qin), and former casino owner Reuben Tishkoff (Elliott Gould). One of the pleasures of the film is not knowing exactly how the diverse skills of the players will come into play. The audience is kept in the dark about most of the process of the theft until it takes place.

There are always, of course, complications in such films. The Bellagio is owned by Terry Benedict (Andy Garcia), a smooth operator who has forced Reuben out of the business. Reuben must look on with a sick smile while a casino he once owned is demolished by Benedict to make way for a new project. More significantly, however, is Benedict's romance with Tess Ocean (Julia Roberts), the curator of his hotel's art museum and Danny's ex-wife. Rusty is livid when he discovers Danny has been withholding this information but gives in when Danny assures him that revenge is only a secondary motivation for pulling the job. But, of course, it isn't. Danny's jealousy and his need to get Tess back help give a bit of heft to his character while all the others remain mostly one-dimensional. The lack of depth in the characters is highly unusual for Soderbergh since all his previous films focus on character and mood rather than plot.

The robbery itself is the film's highlight as Yen is sneaked into the vault, Livingston uses technology to disguise the robbery, and Linus, Frank, and Saul distract Benedict. Rusty has the presence of mind to bring extra batteries for their vault-busting tools. Most amusing is how Virgil and Turk assume numerous identities simply by changing their clothing.

There are also some delightful moments leading up to the robbery. Rusty is willing to go along with Danny's scheme because he has been reduced to teaching the basics of poker playing to young television actors. Topher Grace of *That '70s Show* Joshua Jackson of *Dawson's Creek,* Holly Marie Combs of *Charmed,* Barry Watson of *7TH Heaven,* and Shane West of *Once and Again* play themselves and allow their lack of gambling sophistication to be made fun of. Danny joins their game to prove that Rusty's techniques do not always win.

The clean, well-pressed tuxedo Danny wears whenever he is released from prison is another good touch. Also impressive is Danny's first meeting with Tess in a hotel restaurant, a scene resembling a similar meeting between Clooney and Jennifer Lopez in Soderbergh's *Out of Sight* (1998). A more obvious self-homage for the director occurs when no one can understand Basher's Cockney rantings, as with Terence Stamp in Soderbergh's best film, *The Limey* (1999).

The restaurant scene is Roberts' best, as she conveys Tess's dismay at seeing Danny again, her fear of what will happen should Danny not leave before Benedict arrives, and a hint of pleasure, despite herself, in her ex-husband's presence. Overall, however, Roberts is simply along for the ride and given little to do. Wearing her hair drawn behind her head most of the time, she looks tired and, as several reviewers observed, almost haggard. Clooney almost saved the Coen brothers' dismal *O Brother, Where Art Thou?* with his goofy charm. Here, his charm is smoother, more polished, more like the suavity of stars of earlier eras. He is the brightest star in the all-star cast.

The best performances in *Ocean's Eleven,* though, are by two actors from those earlier eras. Disheveled, paunchy, wearing oversized glasses and his patented puzzled gaze, Gould is a hoot, giving his best performance since *The Silent Partner* (1978). Although he was good as the egotistical television star in *The Dick Van Dyke Show* (1961–66), Reiner has never really had a good part in a film, including those he wrote and directed. His Saul Bloom is an old man who has seen it all but still wants to savor once again the high of pulling off a fast one. Reiner's best moments come when Saul poses as an Eastern European entrepreneur to bully his way into Benedict's vault.

The original *Ocean's Eleven* was notable for presenting the Rat Pack of Frank Sinatra, Dean Martin, Sammy Davis, Jr., Peter Lawford, and Joey Bishop cavorting together in their prime. The performers spent evenings performing in various casinos and supposedly showed up on the set at their leisure. Director Lewis Milestone, best known for *All Quiet On the Western Front* (1930), said the experience was his worst ever. The stars seem to be having a good time, nevertheless, but their pleasure is not conveyed to the audience, for the film is a sluggish bore. The actual robbery of five casinos is amazingly easy because the casinos have almost no security. The film's highlight is the bright orange alpaca sweater worn by Sinatra in his first scene.

Except for the idea of robbing Las Vegas casinos, Soderbergh's highly professional remake has little in common with its predecessor. The actors, who also seem to be having a good time, work well together, especially Clooney and Pitt who seem the essence of contemporary cool, much cooler than the labored, sexist banter of Sinatra and Martin. In interviews, Clooney and Soderbergh have said that Griffin's script came to them when they formed a production company, Section Eight, and that they were surprised at how much they liked it. If this story is true, it is only a serendipitous coincidence that Martin's "Ain't That a Kick in the Head?" from the original film is heard in the background of *Out of Sight*.

Many reviewers were puzzled that after being nominated for Academy Awards® for *Erin Brockovich* (2000) and *Traffic* (2000) and winning for the latter Soderbergh would turn to something as superficial as *Ocean's Eleven*. Many good directors, however, have become bogged down by a need to make "important" films. While Soderbergh's two 2000 films, especially *Traffic*, have many virtues, both are essentially well-made civics lessons. The director may have seen the task of making a fast-moving entertainment with nothing on its mind as a challenge, and he has met that challenge quite well, even if the film evaporates minutes after seeing it. Soderbergh is to be applauded for accomplishing what he set out to do, for refusing to be pigeon-holed.

Some reviewers were also puzzled by the ending of *Ocean's Eleven* which they said seemed to point toward the possibility of a sequel. Viewers of the original film knew that the thieves could not get away with the robbery because the Motion Picture Code of the time demanded that crime did not pay. Sinatra's gang hides its loot in the coffin of a cohort who has a heart attack only to see the casket cremated. In the post-Code age, the success of thieves is just as predictable as their failures were previously. As played forcefully by Garcia, Benedict is not a man who would let Danny get away with stealing his money and his woman. Hence, the final shots suggest that trouble may be on the way for Danny and Tess. It is admirable of Griffin and Soderbergh to recognize the necessity of undercutting the conventions of heist films.

—*Michael Adams*

## CREDITS

**Danny Ocean:** George Clooney
**Rusty Ryan:** Brad Pitt
**Terry Benedict:** Andy Garcia
**Linus Caldwell:** Matt Damon
**Tess Ocean:** Julia Roberts
**Basher Tarr:** Don Cheadle
**Virgil Malloy:** Casey Affleck
**Turk Malloy:** Scott Caan
**Reuben Tischkoff:** Elliott Gould
**Frank Catton:** Bernie Mac
**Saul Bloom:** Carl Reiner
**Livingston Dell:** Edward Jemison
**Yen:** Shaobo Qin
**Cameo:** Henry Silva
**Cameo:** Angie Dickinson
**Cameo:** Holly Marie Combs
**Cameo:** Joshua Jackson
**Cameo:** Topher Grace
**Cameo:** Steve Lawrence
**Cameo:** Eydie Gorme
**Cameo:** Wayne Newton

**Origin:** USA
**Released:** 2001
**Production:** Jerry Weintraub; Village Roadshow Pictures, NPV Entertainment, Section Eight; released by Warner Bros.
**Directed by:** Steven Soderbergh
**Written by:** Ted Griffin
**Cinematography by:** Steven Soderbergh
**Music by:** David Holmes
**Sound:** Paul Ledford
**Editing:** Stephen Mirrione
**Art Direction:** Keith Cunningham
**Costumes:** Jeffrey Kurland
**Production Design:** Philip Messina
**MPAA rating:** PG-13
**Running time:** 116 minutes

## REVIEWS

*Boston Globe.* December 7, 2001, p. D1.
*Chicago Sun-Times Online.* December 7, 2001.
*Entertainment Weekly.* December 14, 2001, p. 48.
*The Guardian.* December 10, 2001, p. 12.
*Los Angeles Times Online.* December 7, 2001.
*New York.* December 10, 2001, p. 82.
*New York Times.* December 7, 2001, p. E1.
*New Yorker.* December 10, 2001, p. 110.
*Newsweek.* December 17, 2001, p. 113.

46

*People.* December 10, 2001, p. 35.
*Premiere.* January, 2002, p. 19.
*San Francisco Chronicle.* December 7, 2001, p. D1.
*Time.* December 10, 2001, p. E7.
*USA Today.* December 7, 2001, p. E7.
*Variety.* December 3, 2001, p. 36.
*Washington Post.* December 7, 2001, p. C1.

## QUOTES

Rusty (Brad Pitt) to Danny (George Clooney): "Here's the problem. Now we're stealing two things. And when push comes to shove, if you can't have both, which are you gonna choose? Remember, Tess does not split 11 ways."

## TRIVIA

Angie Dickinson and Henry Silva, who appeared in the 1960 film, make cameos in the boxing match sequence.

## AWARDS AND NOMINATIONS

**Nomination:**
**Broadcast Film Critics 2001:** Cast.

# On the Line

*Have you ever met the perfect girl? (and let her get away).*
—Movie tagline
*She's one in a million. His chances of finding her again are a million to one.*
—Movie tagline

**Box Office:** $4.3 million

Critics reviewed *On the Line* like they were expecting quite a bit from it. What they didn't realize is that a movie for preteens, starring members of a trendy pop group, doesn't need the same kind of critical scrutiny that they apply to the rest of their films. (Actually, few Hollywood films are really appropriate for the academic-style analysis that most film critics give them. Do we really need to know about the sub-themes in *The Animal*?) *On the Line* is romantic comedy lite, for teen girls (mostly) who want to see a cute,

nice boy looking for a nice girlfriend. The idea is that they can start to figure out how it all works between the sexes, plus they can imagine themselves being the nice girlfriend in the story. They don't need richly imagined characters, shockingly clever plot twists and sparkling dialogue. Those things would be nice, of course, but with Lance Bass of huge pop group 'N Sync in the starring role, this film barely even needs a plot.

Bass, a blonde with green eyes, is the member of the band who, as Chris Hewitt of the *St. Paul Pioneer Press*, described him, has "the perplexed look, like he's not sure where the camera is." If you're not a teen girl, it's hard to see how Bass is considered dreamy, but he is, so we'll just have to accept that. Bass plays Kevin, a nice guy who lives in Chicago and works as an ad man at a big agency. It's hard to believe that Kevin would be on the creative team since he never says anything even vaguely witty or sharp, but again, this is something we must accept. Kevin wants romance but isn't a "closer." Whenever he meets a girl he likes, he tenses up and can't ask for her phone number. This earns him much ribbing from his roommates, Rod (fellow 'N Sync guy Joey Fatone, the one who looks like a middle-aged man); goofy, dumb guy Eric (GQ); and the smart one, Randy (James Bulliard).

One day while riding on the train, Kevin meets the girl of his dreams, Abbey (Emmanuelle Chriqui). He knows she is the one for him because they are both huge Cubs fans, love Al Green and can recite the names of the presidents in chronological order. (Finally, there's hope for nerd kids! Who knew recitation of historical information was the ticket to winning the heart of a famous musician?) When the time comes for the pair to separate, alas, Kevin chokes again. He wants to ask her for her phone number but just can't seem to get the words out. And, as Roger Ebert of the *Chicago Sun-Times* puts it, "Despite decades of feminist advances, all Abbey can do is smile helplessly and leave the future in his hands."

Kevin moons over Abbey while various pointless subplots are developed. We learn that Abbey has a jerky yuppie boyfriend who doesn't appreciate her. We know this because he talks on his cell phone during their dates and refers to her studies in archaeology as her "fossil hobby." We learn more about Rod, who plays in a hard rockin' cover band that plays hideous hair metal songs from the 1980s. But it's Rod's secret dream to make his own music (that might just sound like the syrupy pop tunes of 'N Sync?) We meet Kevin's work mates, like his wheatgrass-drinking boss, Higgins (Dave Foley, acting like he's in the worst *Kids in the Hall* sketch ever) and the old timer who fixes the copy machines, Nathan (Jerry Stiller). Poor Stiller, again, plays a character that says lines like, "I have cataracts the size of cantaloupes!" Enough!

Once writer Eric Aronson feels like he's padded his script enough, it's back to the main story. Kevin decides he's going to take matters into his own hands and is going to find that girl. He puts up posters all over town, advertising, "Are you her?" He gets an onslaught of calls from the lovelorn. His roommates decide that they will help Kevin out by dating some of the girls who call. The posters catch the eye of an editor of the local paper who has his columnist (Dan Montgomery) write a human interest story on Kevin. This makes Kevin into a city hero, because women, for some reason, find his quest to be romantic instead of pitiful. Inexplicably, the columnist keeps writing follow-up stories on Kevin, even though there are no new developments in his story. It's hard to imagine what all these follow-ups might be saying. It's also inexplicable how Abbey seems to be the only woman in the city who isn't aware of Kevin's quest. In the meantime, Kevin and Abbey have a series of near-misses of running into each other, then misunderstandings, and various other silly plot twists designed to stretch the movie to a respectable length.

The movie reaches one of its many heights of absurdity when Kevin decides to take matters further by plastering the town with huge billboards to find Abbey. Many small companies can't afford such media saturation and this low-level ad guy can? The same guy who shares his apartment with three roommates? The apartment, as are most movie apartments, is decorated way beyond the means and cleverness of the occupants. If set decorators ever saw real guys' apartments, they would probably faint over their IKEA catalogs.

For such a goofy little movie, the performances really aren't that bad. Well, Bass is bad, but that's what's supposedly charming about him. What's bad is that he's really really bland, and in this case, that's good. No teen girl wants to project all her burgeoning fantasies on someone who's too threatening. Bass smiles spacily and makes pleasant expressions. He is as asexual as a Ken doll. Chriqui has a thankless role as the dream girl, but she manages to use her sparse amount of time onscreen wisely. She makes it seems believable that a girl with so much to offer would find Kevin appealing and that's quite a feat. Of the friends, Fatone stands out the most. He is kind of good as the jolly guy's guy, although he is called on to have flatulence as a comic effect one too many times. This kind of real life guy behavior doesn't seem like it would go over too well with the film's intended audience. It's also kind of weird that with dyed hair, painted fingernails and rock and roll banter like, "We were all about the hardcore," Fatone is supposed to be the "punk" one. What punk would ever dream of making the sappy kind of pop that Fatone's character comes up with?

Besides Dave Foley and Jerry Stiller, there are also a couple of cameos. Al Green does a very embarrassing job of lip-synching to his own song and Richie Sambora of Bon Jovi shows up as a famous rocker called The Mick. Stay on after the credits and you'll see other 'N Syncers Justin and Chris doing some very non-PC, but actually sort of funny characters.

Critics who panned the movie delighted in the chance to incorporate the title of 'N Sync's hit "Bye Bye Bye" into their review. "Lance Bass, say 'Bye Bye Bye' to your dreams of stardom," wrote Chris Hewitt. Christy Lemire of the Associated Press wrote, "Lance and Joey should stick to singing and dancing, because unless they get some better material, they'll have to say 'Bye Bye Bye' to their acting careers." Owen Gleiberman of *Entertainment Weekly* wrote, "*On The Line* would like to be *Serendipity* for the Oxy-and-Skechers set, but it feels more like the worst movie Michael J. Fox ever made." Gene Seymour of the *Los Angeles Times* wrote, "*On the Line* is sophisticated romantic comedy for people who think *Corky Romano* is trenchant political satire." And Roger Ebert is tired with this whole particular genre of film: "If this genre ever inspires a satire, it will end with the boy and girl sitting next to each other on an airplane—still not realizing they are together again, because by then they will be 80, having spent 60 years missing each other by seconds."

—*Jill Hamilton*

---

**CREDITS**

**Kevin:** Lance Bass
**Rod:** Joey Fatone
**Abbey:** Emmanuelle Chriqui
**Eric:** GQ
**Himself:** Al Green
**Jackie:** Tamala Jones
**Higgins:** Dave Foley
**Brady:** Dan Montgomery Jr.
**Nathan:** Jerry Stiller

**Origin:** USA
**Released:** 2001
**Production:** Peter Abrams, Robert Levy, Wendy Thorlakson, Rich Hull; Tapestry Films, Happy Place; released by Miramax Films
**Directed by:** Eric Bross
**Written by:** Paul Stanton, Eric Aronson
**Cinematography by:** Michael Bernard
**Music by:** Stewart Copeland
**Editing:** Eric A. Sears
**Art Direction:** Brandt Gordon
**Costumes:** Margaret Mohr
**Production Design:** Andrew Jackness
**MPAA rating:** PG
**Running time:** 90 minutes

**REVIEWS**

*Chicago Sun-Times Online.* October 26, 2001.
*Entertainment Weekly.* November 2, 2001, p. 51.
*Los Angeles Times Online.* October 26, 2001.
*New York Times Online.* October 26, 2001.
*People.* November 5, 2001, p. 39.
*USA Today.* October 25, 2001.
*Washington Post.* October 26, 2001, p. WE40.

# The One

*Stealing the power of the universes one by one.*
—Movie tagline

**Box Office:** $43.9 million

What if the universe we experience is not the only universe? What if instead of one universe there were, say, 125 universes that all existed simultaneously as a multiverse? What if in each of those universes within the multiverse there were duplicates of each one of us? Oh, there may be slight differences, but basically they're all us. And what if each of the "us's" in the multiverse were connected by a chord of energy? What if each time one of the doppelganger "us's" that existed died his/her energy was distributed among those remaining in the multiverse? And what if Hollywood took this very intriguing premise, lobotomized it and turned it into a sci-fi film that emphasized action instead of thought? Well, I guess that last proposition isn't so hard to imagine after all. And it's unfortunate that the makers of the film *The One* didn't stick to the cerebral instead of concentrating on chases, car crashes, explosions and fights. Oh, what might have been.

In *The One*, martial arts expert and acting novice Jet Li exists in a world that has figured out how to travel between the worlds of the multiverse through wormholes that open up at regular intervals. Of course travel through the multiverse is restricted to the point of having a multiverse police force that goes after those who travel without permission. Yulaw (Jet Li) is one of those policemen who has turned into a rogue cop when he discovered that the death of one of his dopelgangers made him stronger, smarter and faster. Now he is jumping through wormholes killing his alter egos throughout the multiverse until he has become the strongest smartest and fastest human to exist . . . with one exception. Yulaw has killed "himself" in 123 of the other universes which means there is still one more "him" out there, and that "him" is also strong, smart and fast. He's also clueless as to why he is so.

No one knows what will happen if the balance of the multiverse is compromised by the completion of Yulaw's plan. When he becomes the only "him" left in the multiverse, becomes The One, will the cosmic balance be so upset that everything will explode? Implode? Or will Yulaw become the equivalent of a god? The uncertainty means that Yulaw must be stopped, and that job falls to multiverse cops Roedecker (Delroy Lindo) and Funsch (Jason Statham).

The last duplicate that Yulaw wants to eradicate is a Los Angeles cop by the name of Gabe (also Jet Li). And, just as Yulaw is aided in his efforts by his girlfriend Massie (Carla Gugino) who has a way with white mice, in Gabe's universe he is married to T.K (also Carla Gugino), a veterinarian. Obviously, most of the plot of *The One* revolves around the problem of if Gabe will wise up to what's happening to him and if he or the mutiverse cops will stop Yulaw before Yulaw exterminates Gabe. Unfortunately, instead of making this a subtle, psychological sci-fi thriller, it instead is played out as a massive action adventure with not a brain in its head once the original and intriguing premise is explained.

Screenwriters James Wong and Steven Chasman, two *X-Files* veterans and the creative team behind the sly sleeper hit *Final Destination*, are capable of so much more, one wonders why they submitted to the easy way and let action overcome their ideas. One could lay the blame for this right at the doorstep of actor Jet Li whose command of English is problematic at best and whose acting abilities run the range from impenetrable to bland. Of course he is best known for his martial arts moves (*Romeo Must Die*) and that could be why the movie stresses motion over reason, but that conclusion is subverted by the knowledge that the actor who was originally set to play the film's lead was wrestling superhero and *The Mummy Returns* co-star, The Rock. *The One* probably would not have fared any better under his leadership. It has also been reported that Li turned down a $3 million payday to appear in the *Matrix* sequels but decided to take this picture instead. One can only wonder.

Although there is no doubt that it is intriguing to watch Li seamlessly fight himself in the final battle between Gabe and Yulaw, in a way it cheats Li's one true skill. (Perhaps only the true martial arts aficionado will even notice that Li uses two different fighting styles in his combat with himself: Ba Qua which employs a circular motion for good Gabe and Shin Yi a more straightforward punching style for bad Yulaw.) However, by making us constantly aware that the only way this superhuman fighter can fight himself is through special effects where all actions are hyped beyond believable, we do end up with a martial arts feast, but it is all artificial. In fact, from the wire work to the slow-motion dodging of bullets, one will probably constantly be making comparisons to *The Matrix*, while the idea of traveling between parallel universes may remind others of the television show *Sliders*.

*The One* does, however, have its good points and its moments of amusement. Two of the four alternate universes we experience in the movie are shown to be different realities only through the device of the ubiquitous television set. The first is obviously not our reality because it shows President Gore on the tube, but the other, showing President Bush, still may not be our reality because it indicates Bush is introducing his comprehensive health care plan! What are the odds of that happening in our universe? Subtle and amusing. Another high point has to do with Roedecker's doppelganger in Gabe's universe unexpectedly, briefly and humorously showing up, but why spoil the fun by telling you how.

Similarly, the two end sets as envisioned by David L. Snyder are by turns striking and interesting and there's no doubt that Trevor Rabin's techno-music keeps one's pulse pounding. Even watching bodies enter the Quantum Tunneler—the wormholes used to traverse universes—is an eye-catching special effect, although it may not be for the squeamish because it looks as if Star Trek's transporter system has suffered a serious nervous breakdown.

*The One* would have made an infinitely better summer release than a fall one. In the summer we want to put our brains on hold, we want to just flow with the action, we want to have our souls dance with exciting choreography and pulsating music. *The One* does have a fast pace and, as mentioned before, an interesting premise, but as it is, it is under-written, under-acted, under-thought and under-plotted.

—*Beverley Bare Buehrer*

## CREDITS

**Gabe/Yulaw/Lawless:** Jet Li
**Roedecker/Attendant:** Delroy Lindo
**T.K./Massie Walsh:** Carla Gugino
**Funsch:** Jason Statham
**Yates:** Dylan Bruno
**D'Antoni:** Richard Steinmetz
**Aldrich:** James Morrison

**Origin:** USA
**Released:** 2001
**Production:** Steve Chasman, Glen Morgan; Revolution Studios, Hard Eight Pictures; released by Columbia Pictures
**Directed by:** James Wong
**Written by:** Glen Morgan, James Wong
**Cinematography by:** Robert McLachlan
**Music by:** Trevor Rabin
**Sound:** Geoffrey Patterson
**Editing:** James Coblentz

**Art Direction:** Paul Sonski
**Costumes:** Chris Karvonides-Dushenko
**Production Design:** David L. Snyder
**MPAA rating:** PG-13
**Running time:** 80 minutes

## REVIEWS

*Chicago Sun-Times Online.* November 2, 2001.
*Chicago Tribune Online.* November 3, 2001.
*Entertainment Weekly.* November 9, 2001, p. 83.
*Hollywood Reporter.* October 23, 2001, p. 18.
*Los Angeles Times Online.* November 2, 2001.
*New York Times Online.* November 2, 2001.
*People.* November 12, 2001, p. 38.
*USA Today Online.* November 2, 2001.
*Variety.* October 29, 2001, p. 27.

## QUOTES

Yulaw (Jet Li): "There's never been anything like what I have become."

# 101 Reykjavik

Spanish bombshell Victoria Abril (best-known for her work with Pedro Almodovar) lacks inhibition. In Almodovar's *Tie Me Up, Tie Me Down* she played a porn star and in *Kika* she portrayed a cruel reality-TV talk show host complete with dominatrix attire; then she portrayed a housewife-turned-lesbian in Josiane Balasko's *French Twish*. Now the 44-year-old diva has returned to the screen, this time donning the role of a lesbian flamenco dance instructor in Icelandic director Baltasar Kormakur's black comedy *101 Reykjavik*. Abril's performance certainly enhances Kormakur's sexy film about a bizarre love triangle, but fortunately she doesn't overshadow the performances of her co-stars or deflect from Kormakur's screenplay, which is adapted from a novel by Hallgrimar Helgason.

The two things viewers need to remember when watching this quirky Icelandic sexcapade are that Scandinavians lack sexual inhibitions (sort of like the Spaniards, but without the Catholic guilt) and unusual individuals, ie: clones of Bjork, populate Iceland. Despite the fact that Icelanders find themselves buried under snow for a good portion of each year, it hasn't stopped them from developing a strong film industry. Thanks to the Icelandic Film Fund (with the ironic postal code of Reykjavik 101), Icelandic cinema has begun to pick up speed.

Theatrical director and actor Kormakur debuts as a feature film director with *101 Reykjavik,* which garnered critical praise. Derek Elley of *Variety* called Kormakur's film an "off-the-wall relationer that's one of the freshest directing debuts in world cinema this year." A critic from the *Independent* remarked "Kormakur's remarkably assured superbly shot first feature portrays a Freudian nightmare." And that's just for starters since this hot little Icelandic number combines Almodovar's sexual frankness with the absurd humor of the American cinema classic *The Graduate.* In fact, actor Hilmir Snaer Gudnason's awkward sexual portrayal of Hlynur recalls Dustin Hoffman's portrayal of the anxious Benjamin Braddock.

As the film opens, Hylnur, a slacker who lives with his mother Berglind (Hanna Maria Karlsdottir) and obsesses about death, climbs up a snowy ridge while claiming that he dies each day and that life is what happens between deaths. Next we see Hlynur hanging out at a bar with other slackers while Hofi (Pruour Vilhjalmsdottir), a wannabe girlfriend, throws herself at Hlynur, even though he acts like a cad towards her. But she has sex with him anyway, knowing that he won't sleep over at her apartment. Hlynur wakes up at home the next morning, masturbates to an aerobics TV program (because there's no porno on TV in the morning), and then eats a bowl of cereal while taking a bath in the kitchen. This is Hlynur's typical routine until his mother throws him a curve ball in the form of her lesbian Spanish friend Lola (Abril), who has come to teach flamenco dance to the natives.

When Berglind goes out of town to celebrate New Year's with her relatives, Hlynur manages to seduce the vivacious Lola but fails to realize that the sex meant nothing special to her. Later, Berglind drops a bomb on Hlynur by telling him that she's a lesbian and has fallen in love with Lola—not only that, but Lola is pregnant. Hlynur, who thinks he's the father, freaks out because his life has grown increasingly complicated. Then Hofi confesses to the reluctant Hlynur that she's also pregnant with his child. It turns out later that Hlynur's best friend impregnated Hofi and she had an abortion, but that doesn't stop Hofi's overprotective brother from attacking Hlynur at a bar. Eventually, Hlynur provokes a confrontation with Lola over her relationship with Berglind and Lola argues that Hlynur needs to grow up. By the film's ending Hlynur has taken her advice and gotten a job checking parking meters.

Kormakur's *101 Reykjavik* calls attention to vibrant Icelandic culture with its musical soundtrack composed by Damon Albarn (Blur) and former Sugarcubes' vocalist Einar Orn Benediktsson and through Abril's alluring performance as Lola.

—*Patty-Lynne Herlevi*

## CREDITS

**Hylnur:** Hilmir Snaer Guonason
**Lola:** Victoria Abril
**Throstur:** Baltasar Kormakur
**Berglind:** Hanna Maria Karlsdottir
**Marri:** Olafur Darri Olafsson
**Hofi:** Pruour Vilhjalmsdottir

**Origin:** Iceland, Denmark, France, Norway
**Language:** Icelandic
**Released:** 2000
**Production:** Baltasar Kormakur, Ingvar Thordarson; Zentropa Entertainment, Icelandic Film Corp., Liberator Productions, Filmhuset
**Directed by:** Baltasar Kormakur
**Written by:** Baltasar Kormakur
**Cinematography by:** Peter Stueger
**Music by:** Damon Albarn, Einar Orn Benediktsson
**Sound:** Kjartan Kjartansson
**Editing:** Skule Eriksen, Sijvaldi J. Karason
**MPAA rating:** Unrated
**Running time:** 100 minutes

## REVIEWS

*Boxoffice.* October, 2001, p. 61.
*Los Angeles Times Online.* August 24, 2001.
*RANT.* March/April, 2001, p. 14.
*Sight and Sound.* June, 2001, p. 51.
*Variety.* August 21, 2000, p. 17.

## QUOTES

Lola (Victoria Abril) to Hlynur (Hilmir Snaer Gudnason): "You're sleepwalking through life and you're too dumb to realize it."

# One Night at McCool's

*A story about finding the perfect woman . . . and trying desperately to give her back.*
—**Movie tagline**

**Box Office:** $6.2 million

It's a pity *One Night at McCool's* doesn't quite hold together. It's from Michael Douglas' new production company, Further Films, and in the scenes Douglas is in, it has an off-beat, funny sensibility. Maybe if Douglas had had more input in the creative process, the film could have been a bit more than it is. The idea for the film sounds pretty intriguing. Basically it's a film noir told in Roshomon-style. The short version is that three different guys go nuts with lust for the same woman and end up doing bad things. The necessary femme fatale in the story—or should we say dame—is Jewel (Liv Tyler).

The first victim is Randy (Matt Dillon), a hapless bartender at a dive named McCool's. He's inherited a dumpy house from his mother, but other than that he's not doing too well on the path to materialism. He's got nothing, not even a car, and nothing other than tap water (no ice) to offer guests. He first sees Jewel while taking out the garbage at the bar at the end of the night. He sees her getting into a fight with her abusive muscle-bound boyfriend, Utah (Andrew Silverstein, aka Andrew "Dice" Clay). He rescues her and takes her back to his dumpy place. She is mighty grateful. After he gives her a glass of tap water, she says "Mmmm, my second favorite thing." (With the salacious tone this movie likes to have, you can guess what her first favorite is.) After the two end up in bed, Jewel confesses that she and Utah have set Randy up. The usual plan is that she will call Utah and he will come and rob the victim. She says she's not going to call since she likes Randy so much. Actually, it's his house and the potential she sees in it, but there's no use telling him that. Utah ends up finding Randy's house anyway and since Randy has nothing good to steal, the three head back to McCool's. As Randy's emptying the safe, Jewel suddenly shoots Utah in the head.

There victim number two comes into the picture. Detective Dehling (John Goodman) is the person assigned to investigate the case. Like Jewel's other two lovelorn guys, when he first sees her, he imagines her walking in sultry slo mo. Dehling, who is a widower, immediately decides that Jewel in the spitting image of his dear departed wife. The detective is a staunch Catholic and instead of seeing his feelings as lust, he images that Jewel is a pure, gentle spirit needing to be rescued by someone just like him. Jewel's third suitor is Carl (Paul Reiser), Randy's cousin who is a high-powered lawyer with a wife and kids. Like the detective, Carl's first image of Jewel is in slo mo and he immediately decides that she's just the girl he needs. In his case, he thinks she's a powerful dominatrix who's just looking to indulge his fetishes for whips and leather. "It's like having a porn star in my house," he says when Randy and Jewel come over for dinner.

All three men tell their stories via their various confessors. Carl hires a shrink, Dr. Green (Reba McEntire), though he seems to be more interesting in bragging than in actually solving his problem. The detective talks to a priest,

Father Jimmy (Richard Jenkins), who seems a little too interested in all the specific sexual details. Randy tells his story to Mr. Burmeister (Douglas), an old guy who still sports the pompadour he wore in his glory days. (Douglas seems game to spoof his old *Streets of San Francisco* look.) Mr. Burmeister is playing bingo, he says, because it's too early to chase women, though he uses coarser language to say this. At first we don't know his relationship to Randy, but we soon find out that Randy's offering him $10,000 to kill Jewel.

How did it come to this? Within a short time, Jewel has brought each man close to ruin. She moves in with Randy and starts fixing up his house. Soon, she wants more things to help make the house the house she's been dreaming of her whole life. Her solution is that Randy should start robbing other people. She finds nothing immoral with this. "Don't you want to live in a home with a first-rate home entertainment center?" she says when Randy refuses to take a DVD player from a guy they've accidentally killed during a robbery.

When the detective starts snooping around the house, she sees an opportunity to better her position. She leads the detective to believe that Randy is abusive and that she needs help. The detective is more than happy to believe this and over-exaggerates evidence so that Randy is kicked out of his house. Jewel uses Carl for free legal advice. He's happy to oblige since he's so taken with Jewel that he's perfectly willing to sacrifice his relationships with his wife and family for a chance with her.

Part of what makes *McCool's* interesting is the differences in how the men's stories differ. Dehling's stories are particularly funny in this respect. In his recollections, Randy is an idiotic drunk, always saying boorish things and taking advantage of Jewel. And of course, the detective is always the saintly hero. In Carl's recollections of events, Jewel comes on to him in an obvious way, until he is helpless to resist. In other peoples' recollections, Carl is an overbearing, obvious lech who drinks too much. The creative team on the film help to set the moods of the various recollection. Director of photography Karl Walter Lindenlaub, production designer Jon Gary Steele, and costume designer Ellen Mironjnick, all help shape the different stories. In Dehling's tales, Jewel is a nice innocent girl, prone to wearing virginal flowing dresses and cooking wholesome pasta dinners. She seems to inhabit a gauzy world of soft fresh colors.

If the performances in the film could have been as inspired as these folks were, maybe *McCool's* could have been more interesting. Even though his part is small, Douglas is the highlight of the film. He seems to be having a ball playing a character so lecherous and not seeming to realize he's past his prime. As Douglas himself has aged, his willingness to play warts and all types has made him one of the more interesting actors working. Goodman, who is quite a fine actor himself, doesn't give his character any kind of spark. He plays it well, but doesn't go beyond that. Dillon is believable as an affable loser, though he's done this kind of role once too often. Tyler's character is ill-defined. She drives men to their ruin and likes to decorate, but other than that, there's not much there. Although, it should be said that Tyler should get some sort of points for being in a cliched scene where she washes a car in a manner more suitable for soft porn than how the rest of us schmucks wash our own cars. (On the other hand, maybe she should have points subtracted for raising the bar on how we should look washing our cars.)

Critics had a tepid response to the film. "*One Night at McCool's* should have been a quick and dirty pulp tall tale. But it pokes along instead of accelerating, and though it isn't exactly smug, it's rather too pleased with its own manufactured outrageousness," wrote Charles Taylor of Salon. Rob Blackwelder of Spliced Wire wrote, "But while *McCool's* is as ripe as can be for wicked laughs, first-time director Harald Zwart seems a little too green to fully harvest the humor." Daniel Eagan of *Film Journal International* wrote, "Those who can't get enough jokes about rape, murder, tight-fitting dresses, and straight men mistaken for homosexuals will find *One Night at McCool's* manna from above." Presciently, he added, "Despite its generally game supporting cast, the film is destined for a quick trip to discount video bins." Kirk Honeycutt of the *Hollywood Reporter* was less accurate in his predictions, guessing that "the film is positioned for a solid theatrical run." "Here is a small, dark comedy with mischievous wit and the goofy charm one associates more with British comedies than American ones," he wrote.

*—Jill Hamilton*

### CREDITS

**Jewel:** Liv Tyler
**Randy:** Matt Dillon
**Carl:** Paul Reiser
**Detective Dehling:** John Goodman
**Mr. Burmeister:** Michael Douglas
**Dr. Green:** Reba McEntire
**Father Jimmy:** Richard Jenkins
**Utah:** Andrew (Dice Clay) Silverstein
**Joey Dinardo:** Leo Rossi
**Greg Spradling:** Eric Schaeffer

**Origin:** USA
**Released:** 2001
**Production:** Michael Douglas, Alison Lyon Segan; October Films, Further Films; released by USA Films
**Directed by:** Harald Zwart
**Written by:** Stan Seidel
**Cinematography by:** Karl Walter Lindenlaub
**Music by:** Marc Shaiman
**Sound:** Kim Harris Ornitz
**Music Supervisor:** Peter Afterman
**Editing:** Bruce Cannon
**Art Direction:** David Lazan
**Costumes:** Ellen Mirojnick
**Production Design:** Jon Gary Steele
**MPAA rating:** R
**Running time:** 93 minutes

### REVIEWS

*Chicago Sun-Times Online.* April 27, 2001.
*Entertainment Weekly.* May 4, 2001, p. 45.
*Los Angeles Times Online.* April 27, 2001.
*New York Times Online.* April 27, 2001.
*People.* May 7, 2001, p. 33.
*Rolling Stone.* April 26, 2001, p. 67.
*Sight and Sound.* April, 2001, p. 54.
*Time.* May 7, 2001, p. 67.
*USA Today Online.* April 27, 2001.
*Variety.* April 23, 2001, p. 18.
*Washington Post Online.* April 27, 2001.

### QUOTES

Randy (Matt Dillon) to Jewel (Liv Tyler): "Everywhere you go there's a dead guy!"

# Original Sin

*Love's a killer.*
—Movie tagline
*Lead us into temptation.*
—Movie tagline

 **Box Office:** $16.5 million

*Original Sin*, written and directed by Michael Cristofer for MGM and released domestically in August of 2002, was not especially "original." In fact, it was a remake of *Mississippi Mermaid*, a commercial flop filmed by the French New Wave director François Truffaut in 1969, adapted from the Cornell Woolrich novel *Waltz Into Darkness*, a dodgy story of love, obsession, deceit and betrayal. Truffaut's film was beautifully photographed, setting a very high standard for Cristofer's cinematographer, Rodrigo Pietro, to match, a challenge that *Variety* review Lisa Nesselson seemed to suggest was met, though in other ways Cristofer's film falls short of Truffaut's treatment because of its steamy, excessively melodramatic treatment edging towards a seamy bodice-ripping spectacle. Owen Gleiberman of *Entertainment Weekly* called it "a textbook case of a movie that would have been better had it been worse."

The story concerns an aristocratic Cuban coffee merchant (the character was a tobacco planter in Truffaut's film) named Luis Antonio Vargas (Antonio Banderas in the role played by Jean-Paul Belmondo in Truffaut's version), who places an ad in a Baltimore newspaper for a mail-order bride. Julia Russell (impersonated by femme fatale Angelina Jolie in the role played previously by Catherine Deneuve) responds to the Vargas offer, but the woman claiming to be Julia Russell is not really who she seems to be. She is in fact a con artist named Bonny Castle, who intends to manipulate Vargas out of his considerable fortune in an complicated scheme orchestrated by Walter Downs (Thomas Jane), who appears to be a private investigator hired by Julia's sister, Emily Russell (Cordelia Richards) to find out what happened to Julia, who has gone missing.

Vargas is impressed by the imposter, who seems at first to be a pure-hearted find, but he also is a bit devious, in that he does not tell her initially about his wealth. But it turns out he does not have to, because this Julia and her partner in crime have carefully researched the situation. When her ship arrives in Cuba, instead of the pious woman Vargas expected, he finds Jolie's sexy vamp, who seeks him out (since he is carrying a photograph of the "wrong" person) and explains that she has deceived him by sending a photograph of less attractive woman because she did not want to be desired merely on the basis of her good looks. But Vargas can hardly hold that against her, since he had not revealed to her how wealthy he was, for he did not want someone to marry him simply because of his money. He is not merely a clerk in a coffee exporting operation, as he had led Julia to believe; in fact, he owns the firm, and he was seeking a good woman to bear him an heir. In her flashback narrative, Julia tells the audience, "This is not a love story, but a story about love." Not a very helpful distinction, that, since the story has more to do with obsessive lust.

Once these disclosures have been made, they get married immediately upon her arrival, and after spending the expected time in their nuptial bedroom, Vargas falls deeply in love, finally infected by l'amour fou. Therefore, his comely bride easily gets access to his personal and business bank accounts and has cleaned them out by the time the film is half over. His obsessive love then is transformed into obsessive hatred, and he hires detective Downs to find Julia, intending to avenge himself by murdering her. But when he catches up to her, he is still enchanted by her wiles. A murder is faked, and the faux Julia turns up in prison. She

narrates the story to a naïve priest, as the film imitates the flashback framework of Milos Forman's *Amadeus* (1984), with mad Antonio Salieri narrating and confessing his wrongdoings to a shocked young cleric. The plot of *Original Sin* is terribly convoluted, a maze of twists, turns, and snares. Both the narrator and the characters are unreliable, and viewers are frequently misled. Therefore, *Sin* is rather more demanding than the usual American movie. The contrived structure could be elegant, but the smoke and mirrors here are too often transparent rather than artfully opaque.

It would take some degree of courage for a director to presume to match, let alone improve upon, the achievement of François Truffaut. Michael Cristofer, an actor-playwright turned screenwriter-director, seemed undaunted when interviewed by Rick Lyman of the *New York Times*. He first read the Cornell Woolrich novel in 1992, but it took him eight years to get the financial backing for his film, which fell into place after Antonio Banderas and Angelina Jolie agreed to star in the film. Cristofer's first film as screenwriter was *Falling in Love* (1984) and as director he had already worked with Angelina Jolie in *Gia* (1998, produced for HBO-TV) followed by *Body Shots* (1999), a boxoffice flop starring no one in particular, described by *Cosmopolitan* magazine as "sexy and sinful," a goal that *Original Sin* also shot for and achieved, since reviews tended to focus on the steamy sex scenes. The film was rated R, even though Cristofer had wanted to make a more explicit NC-17 version. "Nobody does those kind of love-making scenes anymore," Cristofer told the *New York Times*.

Lyman's *New York Times* piece on Cristofer was not innocent of hype, since it described the film in favorable terms as "a character-driven piece amid all the popcorn behemoths." In his *Washington Post Weekend* review, however, Desson Howe dismissed the film as "stupid." Howe found the "narrative pretzel structure . . . more annoying than alluring" and concluded: "It would have taken intelligence and artistry far beyond the reach of writer-director Michael Cristofer to make this mystery-romance successful." Elvis Mitchell's *New York Times* review was tinged with sarcasm and ridicule and dismissed the film as "soft-core nonsense," concluding that "everything in this film is forgettable." Describing the film as an "overheated costume melodrama" and a "corny potboiler" in the *Washington Post*, Rita Kempley supposed that Michael Cristofer could not "decide whether he [was] making a Gothic romance or a film noir" and ended up "with a goofy combination of the two," but in fact the film was more noirish than not.

The criticism tended to get personal, as when Kempley quipped that *Original Sin* "exalts the lips that launched a thousand quips." She claimed that Angelina Jolie's "pulpy, puckered pursed or pouting" lips "can steal any scene." *Variety* questioned Jolie's "careening display of overripe poutiness," considering this "a step backward" for the actress. On the other hand, *Variety* thought that Banderas was able to command "enough gravitas to put across his role as a pragmatic businessman torn between lust and revenge." Describing Jolie as "real-life caricature as drawn by *Mad* magazine's Mort Drucker," Elvis Mitchell wickedly described Antonio Banderas as "the campiest heterosexual left in show business." Even with the stronger talent of Jean-Paul Belmondo and Catherine Deneuve, Truffaut's adaptation of this story was not commercially successful; so by what logic could the less experienced Cristofer presume to succeed where Truffaut had not?

In short, then, the newspaper reviewers were pretty hostile. Owen Glieberman of *Entertainment Weekly* was hardly more encouraging: "It's somber and tasteful trash," he wrote, "and that's exactly what's wrong with it." *Variety* noted that the film opened in France on July 11 to "tepid" reviews but still "performed credibly" at the boxoffice abroad. *Variety* described the film as being "compulsively watchable," thanks to the performances of Jolie and Banderas, so "lavish and florid" that the picture "falls into so-bad-it's-good territory." *Variety* optimistically (and wrongly) predicted that the picture seemed "destined to draw viewers." But to do so, the film would have to overcome negative reviews, and, perhaps because of Cristofer's overheated treatment, reviewers were unwilling to take this picture seriously. The film might reasonably have been expected to do better in a summer of uninspired, lackluster releases when the market was weak.

—*James M. Welsh*

**Luis Antonio Vargas:** Antonio Banderas
**Julia Russell/Bonny Castle:** Angelina Jolie
**Walter Downs:** Thomas Jane
**Alan Jordan:** Jack Thompson
**Colonel Worth:** Gregory Itzin
**Sara:** Joan Pringle
**Augusta Jordan:** Allison Mackie
**Emily Russell:** Cordelia Richards
**Jorge Cortes:** Pedro Armendariz Jr.

**Origin:** USA
**Released:** 2001
**Production:** Denise DiNovi, Kate Guinzburg, Carol Lees; Via Rosa Productions, Hyde Park Entertainment; released by Metro-Goldwyn-Mayer
**Directed by:** Michael Cristofer
**Written by:** Michael Cristofer
**Cinematography by:** Rodrigo Prieto
**Music by:** Terence Blanchard
**Sound:** Antonio Betancourt
**Editing:** Eric A. Sears

**Art Direction:** Jorge Sainz
**Costumes:** Donna Zakowska
**Production Design:** David J. Bomba
**MPAA rating:** R
**Running time:** 112 minutes

**REVIEWS**

*Baltimore Sun.* August 3, 2001, p. E5.
*Boxoffice.* October, 2001, p. 63.
*Chicago Sun-Times Online.* August 3, 2001.
*Entertainment Weekly.* August 17, 2001, p. 46.
*Los Angeles Times Online.* August 3, 2001.
*New York Times.* August 3, 2001, p. B18.
*Rolling Stone.* August 16, 2001, p. 113.
*USA Today Online.* August 3, 2001.
*Variety.* July 30, 2001, p. 18.
*Washington Post.* August 3, 2001, p. C1.
*Washington Post Weekend.* August 3, 2001, p. 39.

**QUOTES**

Luis (Antonio Banderas) on his requirements for a bride: "She is not meant to be beautiful. She is meant to be kind, true and young enough to bear children."

**TRIVIA**

Michael Cristofer won the Pulitzer Prize for his play *The Shadow Box.*

# The Orphan Muses (Les Muses Orphelines)

Quebecois filmmaker Robert Favreau's *The Orphan Muses* threw its viewers into a whirlpool of dysfunctional family life. The year proved to be a stellar one for Canadian-produced family dramas with such films as *New Waterford Girl, The Perfect Son, My Father's Angel,* and *Love Come Down.* Drug abuse, family abandonment, and domestic violence is usually the stuff of movies of the week but when placed in the hands of talented directors, they can transcend the usual lethargy. Dysfunctional families certainly make for good drama but that's only half the story; cinema has the power to heal what is broken and contemporary family life certainly fits into that category.

The beginning sequence of *The Orphan Muses* shows viewers the story's protagonist, who stands on the edge of a dam while the camera lens tilts and zooms around her. Isabelle (Fanny Mallette in a riveting performance) is the youngest of four children abandoned by their mother. Although she's 25, emotionally she resembles an 11-year-old child. She recently uncovered a family secret, one of many lies that surface throughout the film, and in a violent rage she seeks revenge on her authoritarian schoolteacher sister Catharine (Marina Orsini).

Isabelle rampages through the dam's control center, demanding that the dam's engineer, Remi (Patrick Labbe), who is also her lover, turn the dam on full blast and flood her sister's home. Instead, the deranged Isabelle is escorted home by a police officer. However, this event only marks the beginning of Isabelle's plotting. She tricks her arty brother Luke (Stèphane Demers) into coming home by telling him that Catharine had just died in a car accident. Later, she tricks her lesbian soldier sister Martine (Cèline Bonnier) by telling her that Luke had just died. Isabelle, who has been labeled "the village idiot," proves in the end to be rather cunning even if we never fully sympathize with her.

Their mother (played by Louise Portal in flashbacks) abandoned her children, allegedly to move to Spain with her lover Federico, when Isabelle was five. The older siblings lied to Isabelle by telling her that their mother had died. Although at the time they hoped to spare Isabelle grief, their lie comes back to destroy the family 20 years later. At around the same time, the father of the children did actually die while heroically trying to put out a forest fire.

After the orphan muses reluctantly reunite, Isabelle drops one of many bombs by revealing that she knows that their mother didn't die and that she is finally returning to her family. Meanwhile, the village has planned a commemorative event to celebrate the 20th anniversary of the heroic death of the siblings' father. We also learn that Luke had suffered a nervous breakdown years ago while writing a book about his mother and violently lashed out and crippled a village woman. Having received word of Luke's arrival in town, the woman's sons seek revenge, leading to a climatic scene in which Luke is beaten to a pulp at the town hall.

All four siblings have axes to grind with each other and with members of their small community. But the demon they have in common is the mother who abandoned them right after their father's untimely death. While each sibling partakes in subterfuge and acts of denial, we are mostly drawn into Isabelle's claustrophobic and vertiginous world. As she revenges herself on her siblings, while dressed in her mother's clothes, she tells them, "The beautiful thing about family is leaving it behind." Then, in a sheer act of defiance, Isabelle seeks deliverance from her family's psychodrama.

Favreau superbly directs Gilles Desjardin's screenplay, which is adapted from a play by Michel Marc Bouchard. Favreau throws us into the characters' frantic world by cross-cutting flashbacks, a seemingly innocent town celebration, and the siblings' revelations. With staccato edits and shaky camera, Favreau creates a visceral effect likened to a family drama we'll not soon forget.

—*Patty-Lynne Herlevi*

## CREDITS

**Isabelle Tanguay:** Fanny Mallette
**Martine Tanguay:** Celine Bonnier
**Catharine Tanguay:** Marina Orsini
**Luke Tanguay:** Stephane Demers
**Jacqueline Tanguay:** Louise Portal
**Remi:** Patrick Labbe

**Origin:** Canada
**Language:** French
**Released:** 2000
**Production:** Lyse Lafontaine, Pierre Latour; Lyla Films; released by Film Tonic
**Directed by:** Robert Favreau
**Written by:** Gilles Desjardins
**Cinematography by:** Pierre Mignot
**Music by:** Michel Donato, James Gelfand
**Sound:** Serge Beauchemin
**Editing:** Helene Girard
**Art Direction:** Louise Jobin
**Costumes:** Francois Leplanne
**MPAA rating:** Unrated
**Running time:** 107 minutes

## REVIEWS

*eye Weekly Online.* March 8, 2001.
*Montreal Gazette.* November 3, 2000, p. D6.

## QUOTES

Isabelle (Fanny Mallette) to her siblings: "Do we repeat what has been done to us?"

## AWARDS AND NOMINATIONS

**Nomination:**

**Genie 2000:** Director (Favreau), Film Editing, Screenplay, Support. Actress (Bonnier).

# Osmosis Jones

*He's one cell of a guy, and his partner's a real pill.*
—Movie tagline
*Every Body Needs a Hero.*
—Movie tagline

 **Box Office:** $13.5 million

It's strange that the interior of the human body hasn't been explored as the location for more films, but *Osmosis Jones* more than makes up for the lack of previous cinematic attention to inner space. One of a raft of smarter, more adult-oriented "family" films that have popped up in recent years, *Osmosis Jones* combines live action and animation in an absorbing, entertaining fashion. With the able assistance of animators from the wonderful 2000 feature *The Iron Giant*, this film takes viewers on a wisecracking, fanciful adventure into the body of Frank (Bill Murray), an unrepentant fast-food junkie who has frequent dangerous encounters with food-borne bacteria.

The *Magic School Bus* series of books and TV spin-offs did venture inside the human body in a playful though somewhat pedantic way, but *Osmosis Jones* wisely avoids too scientific an approach. Instead, the interior of Frank's anatomy is imagined as its own city, with a smug mayor (voice of William Shatner) supervising in the office-like brain; a police force full of white blood cells, including the well-intentioned but bumbling title character (Chris Rock), and various criminal viruses lurking around unsavory areas like the armpit. Under the direction of Piet Kroon and Tom Sito and with the help of screenwriter Marc Hyman, the body of Frank is a fantastic realm, filled with hilarious signs (such as a poster for "Peace in the Middle Ear"), familiar movie characters and settings, and imaginative scenes.

The Farrelly brothers, Bobby and Peter, are credited as the directors of *Osmosis Jones*, which seems a little unfair, since they directly supervised only the live-action sequences. Those comprise less than half the movie and far less than half the enjoyment. The Farrellys are known as the kings of gross-out movies, having achieved a sort of legendary stature among adolescents with *There's Something About Mary*. Here, their contributions include a booger, vomit, an exploding pimple, and a fart—all emanating from Murray's body in live-action scenes. But they don't contaminate the

movie so much as provide a little diversion between the mesmerizing animated sequences.

The plot is thin and trades heavily on overwrought fears of bacteria. Unfortunately, it also traffics in that staple of children's films (as epitomized by most Disney productions)—the fear of a parent's death. Shane (Elena Franklin), Frank's daughter, is trying to adjust to the recent death of her mother. The script implies that Frank's wife died from eating the wrong type of food—exactly how or what isn't clear. Shane is anxious because Frank won't break his bad eating habits either. When Frank, who works as a zoo-keeper, eats a hard-boiled egg that he has wrestled away from the hands of a chimpanzee and dropped on the ground, he introduces a potential killer virus into his body. It's an unlikely scenario, and it may leave younger viewers with an overly alarmist view of the dangers of eating.

In fact, in some ways *Osmosis Jones* is like a retrograde commercial about antiseptic living—of the kind with which baby boomers were bombarded in the 1950s and 1960s. Interestingly enough, in this film it's the child of a boomer who is still trying to get her parent, who seems to be an egregious example of arrested development, to wash his hands (not to mention his food) before eating. Murray makes Frank into a sadly comic, hard-to-believe, walking hygienic disaster area. He'll put virtually anything into his mouth.

Inside his body, though, the "citizens" of Frank—the cells who have continued to "vote" for the Mayor—have grown fat and contented with Frank's unhealthy lifestyle. A reformist candidate, Tom Colonic (Ron Howard), wants to clean things up in Frank's intestinal tract, and there's a hilarious campaign advertisement which shows Tom as a rolled-up-sleeves, clean-cut do-gooder walking amid the grunge of Frank's bowels, which looks like a grimy industrial wasteland. The Mayor, however, is determined to stay the course, and, since he has a direct pipeline into Frank's conscious thoughts, he is happy to promote the idea that Frank should spend the upcoming weekend at a chicken wings festival in Buffalo, New York. Shane, however, wants desperately to have her father join her on a class hiking expedition. Besides Frank's aversion to exercise and affinity for chicken wings, there is another reason, eventually revealed, that is keeping Frank from pleasing his beloved daughter: her teacher, Ms. Boyd (Molly Shannon), will be on the trip, and she has a restraining order against Frank.

The court order followed a highly embarrassing and preposterous incident during a school science fair, in which Frank ate an oyster from a student's project and ended up vomiting all over Ms. Boyd. Inside the body, it was Osmosis Jones who made the decision to hit the panic button and compel the regurgitation; for acting in what he thought was Frank's best interests (expelling a potential poison), Jones was nearly kicked off the police force. Banished to Frank's mouth, Jones sees a chance to redeem his reputation and do something good for the citizenry of Frank when he spots the incoming bacteria associated with Frank's dirty egg. Despite the efforts of the white blood cells, Frank does get a sore throat, and he decides to take a cold pill. Enter Drix (David Hyde Pierce), a mean, lean, cold-fighting machine who speaks in a commercial monotone and seems to be a real pill. But after a few rides with Jones around the trouble spots in Frank's body, Drix loosens up a little.

Together, the cold pill and the white blood cell try to sound the alarm about a particularly nasty virus that has hidden out in Frank's body and harbors lethal intentions. Thrax (Laurence Fishburne) looks like a ghetto hoodlum crossed with a dapper devil, with his slicked-back red hair and evil grin. Fishburne and the animators make Thrax into a fascinating villain, oozing with repulsive ideas and dreaming of fatal conquests.

What really sets *Osmosis Jones* apart from run-of-the-mill cartoon fantasies is its delightful scenes imagining various parts of Frank's body. An armpit is a Mafia sauna commanded by a Godfather-type germ. Frank's ingrown toenail is an empty warehouse district at the end of the road, where Thrax can hide and plot. The stomach is an airport, with scheduled arrivals of meals and unscheduled flights of snacks, along with departures of digested food. The brain is a downtown of sterile office towers containing switchboard operators, the mayor and his entourage, and members of the press. There is even an in-body all-news television station, which broadcasts reports of alarming or happy developments in Frank's body. Most delightful of all these fantastic inner spaces is the pimple on Frank's face, which is imagined as the Zit, a wild after-hours nightclub where Thrax's mobsters meet to seal their plans. Various sleazy and snazzy characters dance and shake to the throbbing beat of a rock band.

The animation is delightful and nicely understated. Resisting the temptation to depict the human anatomy as some kind of vast, complex science-fiction locale, the creators of *Osmosis Jones* hew closely to the comic-strip approach, and Frank's body becomes a series of places familiar to any viewer of movies or TV shows. The blood stream is portrayed as a vast network of freeways, and the cells like Osmosis rush around in snappy little cars.

What doesn't work is how this pleasantly tongue-in-cheek interior world co-exists uneasily with a very moralistic live-action outer world where bad eating habits can kill you. A teary, preposterous dramatic ending doesn't follow from a movie whose previous animation and live-action scenes stick to a decidedly cartoonish tone. There's that overly simplistic view of health and hygiene that threatens to make the entire effort seem ridiculous. A lot of the live-action scenes are neither comic nor necessary, and every time the cameras take us back inside the cartoon city of Frank, we respond with anticipation of the next clever locale, character or line of dialogue. Rock, freed from his body, is able to tone down his shtick just enough to make his character likeable and funny;

Pierce is deadpan hilarious and his stiff pill character compelling; and Fishburne is outstanding as a menacing, shadowy figure.

Murray, however he tries to make his disgusting character seem real, doesn't seem to have thought deeply about Frank's motivations, and as a result he is entirely one-dimensional. That's almost a dimension more than the unappealing and overrated Elliot and Shannon inhabit in their small and inconsequential roles. Franklin makes a promising debut in a thankless part as Shane.

In the end, *Osmosis Jones* succeeds because its animators are willing to be wacky and unorthodox, taking pleasure in puns and anomalies and in a distorted though familiar view of the human body as something of a collective repository of B-movie locations. Most memorable of all is a quick trip through Frank's unconscious, where film clips of memories and life scenes are constantly playing in loops. It's the only place where the film makes a real grab at getting to the heart. The rest of the film is content to aim for the funny bone and, when it is not moralizing, it mostly hits its mark

—*Michael Betzold*

## CREDITS

**Frank:** Bill Murray
**Mrs. Boyd:** Molly Shannon
**Bob:** Chris Elliott
**Shane:** Elena Franklin
**Osmosis Jones:** Chris Rock (Voice)
**Thrax:** Laurence "Larry" Fishburne (Voice)
**Drix:** David Hyde Pierce (Voice)
**Leah:** Brandy Norwood (Voice)
**The Mayor:** William Shatner (Voice)
**Tom Colonic:** Ron Howard (Voice)

**Origin:** USA
**Released:** 2001
**Production:** Bradley Thomas, Bobby Farrelly, Peter Farrelly, Zak Penn, Dennis Edwards; Conundrum Entertainment; released by Warner Bros.
**Directed by:** Bobby Farrelly, Peter Farrelly, Piet Kroon, Tom Sito
**Written by:** Marc Hyman
**Cinematography by:** Mark Irwin
**Music by:** Randy Edelman
**Sound:** Jonathan Stein
**Music Supervisor:** Ken Ross
**Editing:** Lois Freeman-Fox, Stephen R. Schaffer, Sam Seig
**Art Direction:** Arlan Jay Vetter
**Costumes:** Pamela Ball Withers
**MPAA rating:** PG-13

**Running time:** 95 minutes

## REVIEWS

*Chicago Sun-Times Online.* August 10, 2001.
*Entertainment Weekly.* August 17, 2001, p. 47.
*Los Angeles Times Online.* August 10, 2001.
*New York Times Online.* August 10, 2001.
*USA Today Online.* August 10, 2001.
*Variety.* August 6, 2001, p. 17.
*Washington Post.* August 10, 2001, p. WE34.

## QUOTES

Frank's (Bill Murray) food rule: "If food hits the ground and you pick it up within 10 seconds, you can eat it."

# The Others

*Sooner or later they will find you.*
—Movie tagline

**Box Office:** $96.5 million

It's a foggy day at the manor house on the Isle of Jersey, one of the Channel Islands between Britain and France, where Grace (Nicole Kidman) lives with her two young children Anne (Alakina Mann) and Nicholas (James Bently). But then it's always foggy around her house. The year is 1945 and World War II has just ended, but it seems to have taken with it Grace's husband who is reported missing in action.

As mysterious as the perpetual gloom that surrounds Grace's manor house outside is the perpetual darkness that must exist inside the house because Grace's children are fatally allergic to sunlight. All windows must be securely curtained to prevent the lethal rays from leaking into the house and all doors securely locked so that no child may accidentally wander into a room where sunlight runs rampant. As Grace obsessively insists, "No door is to be opened before the previous one is closed."

Of course a huge manor house such as that in which Grace and her children live requires more upkeep than the husbandless Grace is capable of, and, for a reason unknown to Grace, her previous help vanished a week ago without even taking their final wages. Luckily, one day Grace suddenly finds on her doorstep housekeeper Bertha Mills (Fionnula Flanagan), groundskeeper Edmund Tuttle (Eric Sykes) and the mute maid Lydia (Elaine Cassidy) who are supposedly answering an advertisement Grace had placed in the paper for more help. After showing them around, explaining her children's needs for darkness and her own need for quiet and order, the new help is hired on. Grace never inquires further when the three indicate that they are quite familiar with the house since they used to live and work there during one of the happiest periods of their lives. And Grace is easily put off when she realizes her advertisement never made it to the newspaper so the three could not have known of her need for help that way. The mystery thickens.

Paradoxically, Grace is a demanding, stern, high-strung, deeply religious and yet loving mother. For example, she schools her children at home making them read religious texts and terrorizing them with stories about the Children's Hell and when they become typically annoying in a childish way, she splits them up to force them to study. When she suddenly hears Nicholas crying, however, she can't get through all the locked doors fast enough to run to his side. The only puzzlement is, Nicholas wasn't crying. Neither was Anne. So who was?

Anne claims it was a young boy she has seen in the house named Victor, but there's no Victor residing there. Anne not only claims there is an intruder boy in the house named Victor but that he lives there with his father, a pianist, and his mother. And then there's that mysterious old lady with the very odd eyes which she has seen at least 14 times!

Well, for making up tales like this which terrorize her younger brother, Grace punishes Anne. For three days she has to sit on the stairs and read from the Bible. Then more odd things begin to happen. The children awaken in the morning to find their curtains thrown wide open and toxic sunlight streaming in. A locked piano suddenly begins emanating music. Loud footsteps and dragged furniture boom out of the ceiling over Grace's head, but the locked room on the second floor is empty. Grace wants to blame the new help, claiming it is the silent Lydia who is making all the noise and leaving drapes open, but how can she when she can plainly see Lydia outside, far from the source of the noise. And then there's that ever-so-knowing smile that lightly flits over Anne's face every now and then.

Is Grace going mad? After all, as Mrs. Mill's tells Grace, "Grief over the death of a loved one can lead people to do the strangest things." But then again, it sure does seem that the new servants up to something. What's on those tombstones Mr. Tuttle is very purposely covering with dead leaves? Is the house haunted? An obvious deduction after Grace finds Anne sitting on the floor in her new communion dress only to discover the face of the old lady with the odd eyes under Anne's veil. And speaking of Anne, just what exactly—if anything—does she know? She is, after all, the only one who can "see" the intruders.

The Others is a story with many possible solutions, all seeming to be the obvious choice, but none standing out as the most conspicuous until the very end. In that respect this is a good mystery. Writer/director Alejandro Amenabar subtly draws us into his eerie world in this, his first English-language film. Amenabar allows us to ponder several possible answers to the mystery he so stylishly presents to us, then provides a road or two we may never even have considered.

But then Alejandro Amenabar, the 29-year-old Spanish director of the 1997 cult hit *Open Your Eyes,* is no stranger to twist endings. In fact, one could say that surprise endings are his trademark. The one for the Spanish *Open Your Eyes* was so interesting that, naturally, Hollywood is remaking the film. It is now called *Vanilla Sky,* however, and stars Penelope Cruz, who was in Amenabar's original Spanish version and who is now dating co-star Tom Cruise whose divorce from *The Others* star Nicole Kidman became final the day of this film's premier. Go figure. (As an aside, Amenabar's first film, *Tesis* [*Thesis*], is also getting the Hollywood makeover.)

In some aspects *The Others* may seem to be similar to 1961's *The Innocents,* based on Henry James' *The Turn of the Screw,* with a woman trying to save two children from invaders who threaten them. But that's about as far as the parallel can be drawn. Unlike many movies of the summer of 2001, this is no remake or sequel. Similarly, some critics have been comparing *The Others* to *The Sixth Sense,* but that's only because they are both atmospheric films that build slowly to their surprise conclusions.

To say that *The Others* is a ghost story or a horror story would do it a terrible disservice. This is a story of the hidden ghosts in family relations couched in fascinating metaphors. Grace, by being both obsessively controlling and loving, embodies the inconsistencies that exist within many families. The way Grace is preoccupied keeping her children from sunlight actually reflects the protective way she keeps knowledge from them—keeping them in the dark, if you will. The rooms are purposely dark, and when all their corners are illuminated during a search for the intruders, startling details (information) is revealed. Grace's religious mania, as often happens in fiction, also masks repressed events and feelings.

There is no doubt that this is as much Nicole Kidman's movie as it is Amenabar's. Her hardly suppressed hysteria, her tightly-wound mannerisms, her barely restrained rage (or is it madness) and even her vulnerability are convincingly registered in a wonderfully nuanced performance. Kidman's porcelain face, which many critics compare to Grace Kelly's in the heyday of the glamour films, subtly registers a wide range of emotions while successfully keeping us believing all possibilities as to where the story is going.

*The Others* is not typical of modern ghost/horror films such as the remakes of *The Haunting* or *The House on Haunted Hill.* Instead it harkens back to a more classic genre of horror film. It is atmospheric and beautifully filmed by cinematographer Javier Aguirresarobe. It is sophisticatedly suspenseful with twists not only in the plot but also in the genre. It's a film where fear isn't encapsulated in phony shocks or personified in computer generated images and special effects. It is a film whose quiet eeriness, intelligence and imagination are all that is needed to hold one's interest and make the hair stand up on the back of one's neck. By today's standards, that's one heck of an achievement.

—*Beverley Bare Buehrer*

## CREDITS

**Grace:** Nicole Kidman
**Mrs. Mills:** Fionnula Flanagan
**Anne:** Alakina Mann
**Nicholas:** James Bentley
**Charles:** Christopher Eccleston
**Lydia:** Elaine Cassidy
**Mr. Tuttle:** Eric Sykes
**Old Lady:** Renee Asherson

**Origin:** USA
**Released:** 2001
**Production:** Fernando Bovaira, Jose Luis Cuerda, Park Sunmin; Miramax Films, Cruise-Wagner Productions, Sogecine, Producciones del Escorpion; released by Dimension Films
**Directed by:** Alejandro Amenabar
**Written by:** Alejandro Amenabar
**Cinematography by:** Javier Aguirresarobe
**Music by:** Alejandro Amenabar
**Editing:** Nacho Ruiz Capillas
**Art Direction:** Benjamin Fernandez
**Costumes:** Sonia Grande
**MPAA rating:** PG-13
**Running time:** 101 minutes

## REVIEWS

*Boxoffice.* August, 2001, p. 56.
*Chicago Sun-Times Online.* August 10, 2001.
*Entertainment Weekly.* August 17, 2001, p. 44.
*Los Angeles Times Online.* August 10, 2001.
*New York Times Online.* August 10, 2001.
*New York Times Online.* August 12, 2001.
*People.* August 20, 2001, p. 33.
*USA Today Online.* August 12, 2001.
*Variety.* August 13, 2001, p. 43.
*Washington Post.* August 10, 2001, p. WE34.

Housekeeper Mrs. Mills (Fionnula Flanagan): "Sometimes the world of the dead gets mixed up with the world of the living."

## TRIVIA

The exterior of the English-style mansion is actually located in Cantabrie, a city on the Atlantic Coast of Spain.

## AWARDS AND NOMINATIONS

**Nomination:**
**British Acad. 2001:** Actress (Kidman), Orig. Screenplay
**Golden Globes 2002:** Actress—Drama (Kidman).

# Our Lady of the Assassins (La Virgen de los Sicarios)

 **Box Office:** $.4 million

*Our Lady of the Assassins* is a film that portrays hell on earth. Based on a novel by Fernando Vallejo (the protagonist has the same name), the narrative showcases a real-life Hades (the city of Medellin) where a drug lord sets off fireworks every time a shipment of cocaine makes it onto U.S. soil. Pregnant women witness the murder of the their loved ones, teenage boys blow each other's brains out at the slightest provocation, and it is the world to which jaded author Fernando (German Jaramillo) returns after 30 years, ready to die. Only he ends up witnessing the deaths of two young lovers instead.

As the story opens Fernando attends a party where a longtime friend introduces Fernando to 16-year-old street kid, Alexis (Anderson Ballesteros). Alexis and Fernando hit it off immediately and Alexis moves into the flat that Fernando inherited from his last remaining relative. Alexis complains about the empty apartment and insists that Fernando buy him a stereo and TV. Fernando complies with his adolescent lover's wishes and endures having to listen to heavy metal music or watch the country's much despised president recite speeches for TV. Of course, like everything else in the film, the TV set and stereo are eventually trashed along with a neighbor who constantly pounds on his drums.

At first Fernando doesn't approve of his lover carrying a gun or his trigger-happy madness. He makes many attempts to persuade Alexis to rid of the gun. Eventually, Fernando comes to the realization that the gun is Alexis' only means of protection against rival gang members. However, Alexis finally meets his demise when he loses his gun in a river after Fernando shoots an injured dog to end its misery. Ironically, Alexis' miserable life ends shortly after that incident when his rival Wilmar (Juan David Restrepos) shoots him.

Fernando visits a tango bar where he mourns the loss of his lover. Eventually, without knowing his true identity, Fernando becomes sexually involved with Alexis' murderer Wilmar, who proves to be just as deranged as Alexis but with a more expensive appetite for designer clothing. After learning about Wilmar's true identity from one of Alexis' pals, Fernando tries to murder Wilmar, but changes his mind after Wilmar confesses his love for him. Fernando and Wilmar decide to leave Medellin, but the teen is murdered when he goes to visit his mother before leaving the country.

*Our Lady* proves to be packed with irony all too common in the Latin world. Good Catholic boys who worship their mothers and love animals commit murder without a second thought. Churches become havens for prostitutes and addicts—in one scene a young street urchin resembles a priest placing communion wafers in the mouths of street people as he feeds them pastries from a box. The largest irony revolves around the sixtyish writer who returns home to die and instead outlives his young lovers.

*Our Lady* lacks the humanity present in the Mexican film *Amores Perros* but can compete with its violent images. The film carries an anti-drug message in the same vein as *Traffic*, but the drug theme isn't the film's main focus. It is the dog-eat-dog environment of the cocaine capital and the shattered lives of its inhabitants.

*—Patty-Lynne Herlevi*

## CREDITS

**Fernando:** German Jaramillo
**Alexis:** Anderson Ballesteros
**Wilmar:** Juan David Restrepo
**Alfonso:** Manuel Busquets

**Origin:** Colombia, France
**Language:** Spanish
**Released:** 2001
**Production:** Barbet Schroeder, Margaret Menegoz, Jaime Osorio Gomez; Les Films du Losange, Le Studio Canal Plus, Vertigo Films, Tucan Producciones Cinematograficas; released by Paramount Classics
**Directed by:** Barbet Schroeder
**Written by:** Fernando Vallejo

**Cinematography by:** Rodrigo Lalinde
**Music by:** Jorge Arrigagda
**Sound:** Jean Goudier
**Editing:** Elsa Vasquez
**Costumes:** Monica Marulanda
**Production Design:** Monica Marulanda
**MPAA rating:** R
**Running time:** 98 minutes

## REVIEWS

*Chicago Sun-Times Online.* October 26, 2001.
*Entertainment Weekly.* October 5, 2001, p. 112.
*Los Angeles Times Online.* September 3, 2001.
*Los Angeles Times Online.* September 7, 2001.
*New York Times Online.* September 2, 2001.
*New York Times Online.* September 7, 2001.
*San Francisco Chronicle Online.* September 7, 2001.
*USA Today Online.* September 6, 2001.
*Variety.* September 18, 2000, p. 35.
*Village Voice Online.* September 5, 2001.

## QUOTES

Fernando (German Jaramillo) asks his trigger-happy lover Alexis (Anderson Ballesteros): "Can't you separate thought from action?"

## TRIVIA

Barbet Schroeder shot high-definition video on the streets without permits and cast non-professionals as Alexis and Wilmar.

# Our Song

*Lift every voice.*
—Movie tagline

Jim McKay is a different kind of film maker. For one thing, after the usual credit, "A Film By," he doesn't just list his own name, but the names of the entire cast and crew. But the lack of egoism isn't the only thing that makes McKay an odd duck in Hollywood. He's made a film that's not like the adrenaline- and drama-heavy films that are hot summer sellers. And it's not like he didn't know what he was doing—his film is obviously a deliberate attempt not to be bigger-than-life and exciting. This guy actually wanted to make a film that was slow, off-kilter and not organized into a neat little story arc—like real life. And perhaps even more

amazingly, he got national distribution for it. (It certainly helped that he is a partner with R.E.M.'s singer Michael Stipe in the production company C-Hundred Film Corp.)

McKay, who was also the director of *Girlstown* (1996) is a semi-youngish (30s) white male who's made a movie about African-American and multiethnic teen girls. Not only that, it's a sensitive movie that doesn't involve the girls picking out cool outfits and getting a popular date for the prom. Why him and why this subject matter? "The easy answer is that there's no one else out there doing it," he said in an interview with the *Los Angeles Times.* "I don't think that because I'm a white guy I should not make it, because there will be zero films instead of one."

The story follows the lives of a group of three girls one summer in the Crown Heights area of Brooklyn, New York. Normally the three would be preparing to enter their sophomore year together, but their school's been closed because it has asbestos and they're going to have to face going to separate schools. The three girls know each other because they're all part of the high-energy, high-stepping marching band. (The band is played by real-life band the Jackie Robinson Steppers. McKay was reportedly so blown away after seeing a performance by the band that he changed the direction of his screenplay so that he could include them in the film.)

Joycelyn Clifton (Anna Simpson) is a vivacious glamour girl who works in a semi-nice department store. Her job has given her a bit more confidence than she's had before and she's enthralled by some new friends she's made at the store, seeing them as more sophisticated than her usual friends. She picks up new slang and new ideas about what things are cool from them, then returns to her old friends to flaunt her new knowledge. She's in transition. It seems pretty clear that she will be ditching her old friends and moving on to this new group, but in the film, neither she nor her friends have quite realized it yet. Her career goal is to become a famous singer, but she doesn't seem to be making any efforts in that direction.

Lanisha, or Lani, Brown (Kerry Washington) is a good girl who seems the most likely to have success. She's a good student and seems to be a sensible, level-headed girl, but not in a driven or holier-than-thou way. Her parents, who are divorced, are nevertheless the closest thing to a traditional two-parent family. Her mother, Pilar (Marlene Forte) is a Latina woman who tries to shelter her daughter from the fact that her African-American father, Carl (Ray Anthony Thomas) is more talk than action when it comes to keeping his promises. Still, he's one of the best male role models in the film. For one thing, he's there, which gives him a lot of points over the other absentee dads. And he obviously loves his daughter and makes a point of showing up for her birthday and other celebrations.

Maria Hernandez (Melissa Martinez) has the biggest dilemma facing her. She's gotten pregnant after a one-night stand and is fairly certain she wants to have the baby. The father, Terell (D'Monroe), is not close enough to Maria to qualify as a boyfriend and is only marginally interested in the baby. He says he'll be there, but doesn't look at Maria when he tells her this, preferring to concentrate on the music he's listening to on his Walkman. Maria's mother is against the idea of Maria having the baby, especially since she relies on Maria's afterschool earnings to supplement the family income. Maria doesn't have any plan once the baby is born, but goes forward with her idea to have the baby, becoming agitated if anyone brings up the subject of her future.

McKay strives for a loose, realistic feeling to the film and he achieves it. The film has the look and pace of a documentary. *Our Song* has lots of drama, but at the same time, it's not overly dramatic. The film is filled with dramatic events—there's the unplanned pregnancy, the news that Lani once had an abortion, and casual afterschool shoplifting. But instead of gearing the film around these events like a hysterical soap opera—what will Maria's mother do when she finds out her 15-year-old darling is pregnant?—the film lets these events unfold with the more awkward, slow pace of real life. Maria may be pregnant, but she also cares about finding a cool shirt to wear and eating a frozen drink after school.

McKay focuses on the "off" moments. The girls talk about boys, clothes and whatever happens to cross their minds at the moment. "I just threw up in my own mouth!" says one. "You are so nasty!" says another. Unlike teens from a usual Hollywood movie, the girls don't have the kind of conversations where every sentence is supposed to be funny or dramatic or a device to push the plot along. Where *Our Song* really succeeds is in capturing how it really is to be a young teen. McKay has an eye for the subtleties of teen interactions and the way that teens are hyper-aware of nuances of proper behavior, attire and speech. For example, Maria uses a slang word incorrectly and Joycelyn is quick to point out that she's using the wrong slang. Maria mumbles that she doesn't care, but it's obvious that she does. She won't use the word incorrectly again. Other times someone will say something that's wrong, like "My mother says I was born in the caesarean section of the hospital," but the other girls are not sophisticated enough to realize it.

The girls, especially Maria, have the kind of constant exasperation with others that girls of that age have. When Maria is in a session with a pregnancy counselor, she is quiet and sullen, even though the counselor is being very non-judgmental and supportive. Whenever the counselor says something, you can see Maria rolling her eyes as part of her permanent "whatever" demeanor. The girls' behavior would be mean if it weren't so apparent that they are even more hypercritical of themselves. The acting throughout the film never breaks the documentary feel. The three girls, as well as their supporting players, give natural, unaffected performances. McKay picked the actresses for their real, un-

Hollywood looks and it was a good choice. All are beautiful, but not beautiful in the blond, white Caucasian way that we're usually shown.

Critics, who most likely have sat through more than one too many *Clueless* ripoffs, embraced the film. The *Wall Street Journal* called the film "a small miracle of an independent feature (that is) clearly and wisely based on the faith that quiet revelations could speak louder than conventional action." Kenneth Turan of the *Los Angeles Times* wrote, "Like the quiet stranger who turns out to have something to say, this modest film has virtues that come out of nowhere. It takes familiar material and develops it with such tact and skill that we find ourselves moved and sort of amazed at the same time."

—*Jill Hamilton*

## CREDITS

**Lanisha Brown:** Kerry Washington
**Jocelyn Clifton:** Anna Simpson
**Maria Hernandez:** Melissa Martinez
**Pilar Brown:** Marlene Forte
**Dawn Clifton:** Rosalyn Coleman
**Carl Brown:** Ray Anthony Thomas
**Terell:** D'Monroe
**Eleanor:** Kim Howard
**Rita Hernandez:** Carmen Lopez

**Origin:** USA
**Released:** 2001
**Production:** Jim McKay, Paul Mezey, Diana E. Williams; C-Hundred Film Corporation, Beech Hill Films, Journeyman Pictures; released by IFC Films
**Directed by:** Jim McKay
**Written by:** Jim McKay
**Cinematography by:** Jim Denault
**Sound:** Jan McLaughlin
**Music Supervisor:** Julie Panebianco
**Editing:** Alex Hall
**Costumes:** Tiel Roman
**MPAA rating:** R
**Running time:** 96 minutes

 ## REVIEWS

*Chicago Sun-Times Online.* July 6, 2001.
*Los Angeles Times Online.* June 15, 2001.
*People.* June 4, 2001, p. 32.
*Variety.* February 7, 2000, p. 56.

# Pavilion of Women

**Box Office:** $.1 million

The difference between movies and cinema is that movies are constructed in the office of studio executives and artists create cinema from inspiration. We can only imagine the "high concept" that drifted through the executive offices at Universal Studios when the studio decided to join forces with Beijing Film Studios (China) to produce *Pavilion of Women*. Written by screenwriters Yan Luo and Paul Collins and based on novel written by Pearl S. Buck, A. O. Scott of the *New York Times* cited the film as falling "somewhere between *Thorn Birds* and *The King and I*." Scott also described the film as "half-baked operatic kitsch." Kevin Thomas of the *Los Angeles Times* gave the film a kinder review: "This Chinese production does have scope, passion and energy, but it lacks a distinctive style and the fact that it's an English-language film seriously undercuts its impact."

In any case, *Pavilion of Women* received lukewarm reviews at best and only screened in selected theatres, not quite earning back its $5 million price tag and quickly ending up on video. The film itself suffered a similar fate to Chinese filmmaker Ann Hu's Sony Pictures Classic release, *Shadow Magic*, in that it quickly moved from the big screen to a video release. In all fairness to Hu though, *Shadow Magic*, which starred English actor Jared Harris, proved to be superior to *Pavilion of Women*, which surprisingly stars Willem Dafoe in a role that recalls Peter O'Toole's role in Bernardo Bertolucci's *The Last Emperor*. Consequently, it also comes as a surprise that reviewers did not mention Dafoe's powerful presence in *Pavilion of Women*.

Besides Dafoe's mesmerizing screen presence, *Pavilion of Women* features gorgeous photography (eye candy), gorgeous costumes, a gaze at aristocratic Chinese culture of the 1930's as well as a tense war scene in which the Japanese army attack Manchuria. However, in the hands of screenwriters Collins and Luo, Pearl S. Buck's novel fails to incite romance or excitement on the big screen. The dialogue is written in elementary school English and the Chinese actors deliver stiff performances as they recite the ESL-type dialogue. The scenes feel episodic and do not flow seamlessly into one another and at times, the film does resembles a television miniseries such as the *Thorn Birds*. Discriminating audiences would be better off watching Zhang Yimou's *Raise the Red Lantern*, which features similar themes to *Pavilion of Women* but suffers from none of the above problems.

The crux of the film revolves around Madame Wu Ailan (Luo who also produced and wrote the film) and her decision to find a second wife (read: concubine) for her sexually demanding husband (Shek Sau). At 40 years of age, Madame Wu has already produced three sons for her husband and has grown tired of his sex on demand attitude. So Madame Wu locates orphan peasant girl Chiuning (Ding Yi) and marries the shy girl off to her husband hoping to be relieved from her wifely duties. Problems arise when her husband rejects his young bride and seeks pleasure with local flower girls at a popular brothel. Meanwhile, eldest son Fengmo (John Cho), who's already engaged to a woman chosen by his family, falls in love with his father's rejected bride and she shyly reciprocates this forbidden love.

To complicate matters even further the lonely Madame Wu befriends a missionary/doctor Father Andre (Willem Dafoe). Their relationship is cemented after Father Andre's orphanage burns down and Madame Wu saves Father Andre and his orphans from burning in the fire and later offers part of her home as a temporary orphanage. The film wades through more episodic drama as the son is thrown in jail for hanging up Communist Party posters; later, he joins the Communist Party in rebellion to his parents' sexual promiscuity. The matriarch of the family (Anita Loo) dies, leaving the family in disarray and then the Japanese attack on the day Madame Wu decides to leave her husband. She hides out with the orphans and is nearly killed by Japanese soldiers until Father Andre sacrifices his life to save her. The film ends with Madame Wu running the orphanage that Father Andre left in his wake.

*Pavilion of Women* does present us with passionate and romantic moments, but even those moments do not add up to a movie. Father Andre is wrong when he tells Madame Wu "All love stories have the same ending." A true classic would leave us with at least one memorable moment, whereas *Pavilion of Women* quickly fades to black in our memories.

*—Patty-Lynne Herlevi*

## CREDITS

**Madame Wu:** Luo Yan
**Father Andre:** Willem Dafoe
**Fengmo:** John Cho
**Chiuming:** Yi Ding
**Mr. Wu:** Shek Sau
**Madame Kang:** Amy Hill
**Old Lady:** Anita Loo
**Sister Shirley:** Kate McGregor-Stewart

**Origin:** USA
**Released:** 2001
**Production:** Luo Yan; Beijing Film Studio, China Film Coproduction Corp.; released by Universal Focus

**Written by:** Luo Yan, Paul R. Collins
**Cinematography by:** Poon Hang-Seng
**Music by:** Conrad Pope
**Sound:** John Dunn
**Editing:** Claudia Finkle, Duncan Burns
**Costumes:** Wendy Law
**Production Design:** James Leung
**MPAA rating:** R
**Running time:** 120 minutes

## REVIEWS

*Boxoffice.* July, 2001, p. 102.
*Los Angeles Times Online.* May 4, 2001.
*New York Times Online.* May 4, 2001.
*San Francisco Chronicle Online.* May 4, 2001.
*USA Today Online.* May 4, 2001.
*Variety.* May 7, 2001, p. 50.
*Washington Post Online.* May 4, 2001.

## QUOTES

Father Andre (Willem Dafoe) to Fengmo (John Cho): "Saying and doing are two different things."

# Pearl Harbor

*Courage. Honor. Glory.*
—Movie tagline

*It was the end of innocence . . . and the dawn of a nation's glory.*
—Movie tagline

**Box Office:** $198.5 million

Since the new millennium was only ushered in six months before *Pearl Harbor* was released by Touchstone Pictures, it is safe to say that the film was the most ridiculously over-hyped picture of the millennium. Audiences could have wished for better than they got to memorialize the 60th anniversary of the Japanese surprise attack on Pearl Harbor on December 7th, 1941. Veterans of the attack were still alive, after all, and expectations were high for this picture. But, sadly, *Pearl Harbor* did not do for the Pacific Theatre what *Saving Private Ryan* (1998) had done for the war in Europe. The attack comes as expected—or unexpec-

ted, if you were there—and goes on long enough to evoke the horror of the remembered disaster, but World War II was something more than an over-budgeted disaster movie, one that would run for nearly three hours, leading up to and following the eye-popping, bomb-dropping spectacle.

The awesome advance spin created a buzz that assured hefty boxoffice returns on the opening Memorial Day weekend, but to cover its obscene costs, the film would have to continue to rule the summer market. To be sure, it earned $75 million during the four-day weekend it opened and $30 million the following weekend, but for most reviewers it was a disappointment, if not a critical bomb, and speculation that it could match the second-time return business record of James Cameron's *Titanic* in 1997 seemed doubtful.

For most reviewers, *Pearl Harbor* was a load of sentimental crap. Expensive crap, spectacular crap, to be sure, but crap none the less, and utterly derivative crap. James Cameron lacked the courage to sell *Titanic* as simply a disaster story, so he hedged his bet, successfully, by turning it into a love story. And that is exactly what Michael Bay and his screenwriter Randall Wallace also attempted to do with *Pearl Harbor.* So you were expecting maybe a history lesson? If so, then turn to PBS or the History Channel. Remember the awful floating bodies in Cameron's *Titanic*? Well, you'll also see sinking ships and floating bodies after the smoke clears in *Pearl Harbor.*

Consequently, *Pearl Harbor* was based on *Titanic* as much as on the Japanese sneak attack on December 7th, 1941. CBS television reviewer John Leonard dryly remarked that the film was not interesting enough to "live in infamy," but perhaps he sold it short. So why did the Japanese attack? The movie tells us that they planned the attack because there was an expected shortage of oil, but, then, the movie also tells us that President Franklin Delano Roosevelt (Jon Voight) was able to stand on his own two feet to demonstrate dramatically to his Cabinet that America had the will to win this war. We know that this must be FDR because 1) he is in a wheelchair, and 2) he is seen earlier on with his "little dog Falla." This movie may impress history buffs, but not historians.

The "story" begins in 1923 on Tennessee farmland. Two little boys are pretending to be World War I flying aces. How would they know about such things? Certainly not from the movies. William Wellman's *Wings* was not made until 1927, and Hollywood did not begin to exploit the Great War until the mid-1920s. Then these daredevil kids manage to crank up a crop-dusting plane and almost get it airborne. Next time we see them, they are in the army, trying to earn their wings and getting "poked" in the butt by flirty nurses.

Since the boys are from Tennessee, they are, naturally, "Volunteers," as any football fan from Tennessee will know. After all, it's a state tradition. Rafe McCawley (Ben Affleck) is the alpha male of this twosome, an inspiration to his shy friend Danny Walker (Josh Hartnett, destined to die, eventually, because he is the Less Important Star) and no doubt the best pilot in the Army Air Corps. So alpha Rafe sweeps nurse Evelyn Johnson (Kate Beckinsale) off her feet. Rafe is dyslexic and cannot read the eye chart, but, boy, can he fly. Evelyn is so impressed by his sincerity and gallantry that she approves him anyway. So what does Rafe do to demonstrate his gratitude? Because he is from Tennessee, he volunteers to fly missions over France with the British Eagle Squadron, then gets shot down over the English Channel.

Back in the Pacific, Evelyn thinks he is dead, but, no, as luck would have it, he is conveniently rescued by a French fishing boat after his plane ditches and he somehow manages to escape from the cockpit underwater. Evelyn remains faithful for all of three months before jumping into bed with Danny Walker and promptly getting pregnant. Then, unexpectedly, Rafe returns and nobly gives Evelyn to his friend Danny, after some bickering and fisticuffs. This corny love triangle is mainly what the movie is "about," as the Japanese fleet chugs through the Pacific on its way to Pearl Harbor.

The Japanese eventually get into position for the surprise attack at 7:55 a.m. Sunday, then all hell breaks loose. Not without heroic difficulty, Rafe and Danny manage to get their planes aloft and shoot down seven Japanese Zeroes. In fact, other pilots also got airborne, but only two, Kenneth Taylor and George Welch, managed to destroy six (not seven) of the attacking airplanes. This is the historical core of the film, at the center of screenwriter Randall Wallace's soap-opera plot.

*Pearl Harbor* is not about to end on a note of defeat, however, and before you know it, it's payback time. Within five months Lieutenant Colonel Jimmy Doolittle (Alec Baldwin) has organized an air attack on Tokyo for April 18, 1942, and, of course, Rafe and Danny both volunteer to fly Doolittle's bombers, though, according to Gillian Flynn of *Entertainment Weekly*, no pilots from Pearl Harbor flew with Doolittle's raiders. Motioning toward Rafe and Danny in the distance before the raid, Doolittle says, "There's nothing stronger than the heart of a volunteer." After the raid and running short of gas, Rafe and Danny get to the mainland of China. Out of gas, Rafe has to land in a rice paddy and is immediately under fire by a Japanese patrol; but Danny brings his plane in for a strafing attack to save Rafe's life before landing his own bomber. Danny survives, only to be shot by a Japanese soldier, so Rafe returns and gets the girl, as well as a medal from FDR.

The film ends with the impression that Doolittle's raid turned the tide of the war with Japan, but it was merely a symbolic, Pyrrhic victory. The turning point more likely was the Battle of Midway in June of 1942, as Gillian Flynn noted, but, of course, the war would not end until President Truman ordered the atomic bombing of Hiroshima and Nagosaki in August of 1945, the ultimate payback, after too many lives had been sacrificed on both sides. The movie glosses over all of this in order to leave the audience feeling real good about America. It also celebrates the heroism of Dorrie Miller (Cuba Gooding, Jr.), who took over the anti-aircraft cannon on the USS West Virginia and became the first African-American to earn the Navy Cross. Gooding plays Miller heroically, but not much is seen of him since his character has nothing to do with the sappy love story, and this subplot therefore smacks of tokenism. As A.O. Scott noted in his *New York Times* review, after *Men of Honor* (2000), Gooding's role in *Pearl Harbor* "feels like a step backward into a tokenism one might have thought obsolete."

The media started beating promotional drums weeks ahead of the film's release. John Gregory Dunne wrote an eight-page piece for *The New Yorker* on May 7, a month ahead of Anthony Lane's regular review. *Newsweek* devoted a whole issue and a cover story to the event, the anniversary, and the film on May 14. *Movieline* ran an interview with director Michael Bay in May and another with writer Randall Wallace in June. Pieces appeared in *The New York Times* on May 18 and May 20 before A.O. Scott's review on May 25. Stephen Hunter wrote two pieces for *The Washington Post* (May 22 and May 25), and *USA Today* ran two pieces, one a cover story, on May 25. *Entertainment Weekly* ran five pieces—one on May 11, two on June 1 and two more on June 8. The presses ran non-stop during May and June to create a mighty "buzz" for this picture.

Anyone who read magazines or newspapers therefore had to be aware of *Pearl Harbor* because of this print "Blitzkrieg," as *Variety* called it on April 30. And, still, Jerry Bruckheimer told *Variety:* "Our aim is to appeal to the broadest audience," claiming further that "It is an emotional campaign that we are being careful not to overdo." The book trade also got very busy, preparing coffeetable books, movie tie-ins, and Pearl Harbor memoirs. Other books, such as Tom Brokaw's *The Greatest Generation*, were sure to be boosted by the film's promotion, as will happen, as John Bing reported in *Variety*, "when a major film primes the sales pump by generating widespread interest in a particular subject or title."

The reviews were mixed, though generally lackluster. Stephen Hunter of the *Washington Post* called the film "the best piece of popular entertainment to come along in years" until its "disappointing tailspin in the last hour." Unlike other reviewers, Hunter actually found merit in the concocted love story, which Mike Clark of *USA Today* described more accurately as "lethargic and directionless." Owen Gleiberman of *Entertainment Weekly* noted that the audience sits through the first 85 minutes "knowing that the film, in essence, is killing time," since the coming disaster "dwarfs the lives of the people around it."

Carrie Rickey of the *Philadelphia Inquirer* criticized the film for its "hollow" characters and patriotism and found it "uncomfortably close" to being jingoistic. Michael Sragow of the *Baltimore Sun* dismissed the film as a "brain-dead buddy movie tearjerker with semi-tasteful romance and tasteful gore mixed in with derring-do," concluding that veterans "should be offended" to see "their service reduced to a sentimental fable." *Entertainment Weekly*'s Jeff Jenson watched the film with his grandfather, veteran William Chew, who considered *Tora! Tora! Tora!* (1970) "a better version of what happened," though he also thought the battle scenes captured "the essence of what it was like to be there."

*Tora! Tora! Tora!* was ornamented with Oscar®-winning special effects and did a better job of covering the attack from both American and Japanese perspectives, though Michael Bay does pay some attention to the Japanese planning. The Oscar®-winning *From Here to Eternity* (1953) concluded with the attack on Pearl Harbor but director Fred Zinnemann never disguised the fact that he was selling a love story in a wartime setting. This would also more accurately describe the Bruckheimer blockbuster, but Zinnemann's picture, adapted from a great war novel by James Jones, had far more interesting characters, brilliantly portrayed and scripted by screenwriter Daniel Taradash. And that's where the Bay-Bruckheimer epic comes up short. Reflecting on the superficial characters of *Pearl Harbor*, Todd McCarthy of *Variety* advised readers to remember the complex characters in *From Here to Eternity*, for then "what's missing here becomes terribly clear." Reviewers with shorter memories and no sense of Hollywood traditions could only think of *Titanic* as a model. *Pearl Harbor* would have done better to imitate *Eternity*, but that, too, would have fallen short, lacking the talents of Zinnemann and Taradash. *Pearl Harbor* is just another reminder that movies are certainly not better than ever.

—*James M. Welsh*

**Danny's Father:** William Fichtner
**Red:** Ewen Bremner
**Maj. Jackson:** Leland Orser
**Adm. Nimitz:** Graham Beckel
**Vice Adm. Fletcher:** Tomas Arana
**Seaman Mayfield:** Guy Torry
**Capt. Connor:** Brian Haley
**Ian MacFarlane:** Tony Curran
**Lt. Jack Richards:** Kim Coates
**Rear Adm. William Halsey:** Glenn Morshower
**Cmdr. Nishikura:** John Fujioka
**Navy doctor:** Tim Choate
**Senior doctor:** John Diehl
**Army Corps Major:** Ted McGinley
**Kimmel's aide:** Raphael Sbarge

**Origin:** USA
**Released:** 2001
**Production:** Jerry Bruckheimer, Michael Bay; released by Touchstone Pictures
**Directed by:** Michael Bay
**Written by:** Randall Wallace
**Cinematography by:** John Schwartzman
**Music by:** Hans Zimmer
**Sound:** Peter J. Devlin
**Music Supervisor:** Bob Badami, Kathy Nelson
**Editing:** Chris Lebenzon, Steven Rosenblum, Mark Goldblatt, Roger Barton
**Art Direction:** Jon Billington, William Ladd Skinner
**Costumes:** Michael Kaplan
**Production Design:** Nigel Phelps
**MPAA rating:** PG-13
**Running time:** 183 minutes

## CREDITS

**Rafe McCawley:** Ben Affleck
**Danny Walker:** Josh Hartnett
**Evelyn Johnson:** Kate Beckinsale
**Jimmy Doolittle:** Alec Baldwin
**Doris "Dorie" Miller:** Cuba Gooding Jr.
**Captain Thurman:** Dan Aykroyd
**Admiral Yamamoto:** Mako
**Earl:** Tom Sizemore
**Pres. Roosevelt:** Jon Voight
**Billy:** William Lee Scott
**Admiral Kimmel:** Colm Feore
**Gooz:** Michael Shannon
**Capt. of the West Virginia:** Peter Firth
**Sandra:** Jennifer Garner
**Barbara:** Catherine Kellner
**Betty:** James King
**General Marshall:** Scott Wilson

## REVIEWS

*Baltimore Sun.* May 25, 2001, p. E1.
*Boxoffice.* April, 2001, p. 50.
*Boxoffice.* August, 2001, p. 62.
*Chicago Sun-Times Online.* May 25, 2001.
*Entertainment Weekly.* May 11, 2001, p. 10.
*Entertainment Weekly.* June 1, 2001, p. 59.
*Entertainment Weekly.* June 8, 2001, p. 10.
*Los Angeles Times Online.* May 25, 2001.
*Movieline.* May, 2001, p. 48.
*Movieline.* June, 2001, p. 90.
*New York Times.* May 18, 2001, p. B1.
*New York Times.* May 25, 2001, p. B22.
*New Yorker.* May 7, 2001, p. 46.
*New Yorker.* June 4, 2001, p. 82.
*Newsweek.* May 14, 2001, p. 44.
*People.* June 4, 2001, p. 31.
*Philadelphia Inquirer Weekend.* May 25, 2001, p. W3.
*Premiere.* May, 2001, p. 46.
*Sight and Sound.* July, 2001, p. 47.
*Time.* May 28, 2001, p. 84.

*USA Today.* May 25, 2001, p. E1.
*Washington Post.* May 25, 2001, p. C1.
*Washington Times.* May 25, 2001, p. C5.

## QUOTES

Doolittle (Alec Baldwin): "Do you know what 'top-secret' is?" Rafe (Ben Affleck): "The kind of mission where you get medals. But they send them to your relatives."

## AWARDS AND NOMINATIONS

**Nomination:**
**Oscars 2001:** Song ("There You'll Be"), Sound, Visual FX
**Golden Globes 2002:** Song ("There You'll Be"), Score
**Broadcast Film Critics 2001:** Song ("There You'll Be").

# The Perfect Son

Hopefully newcomer Leonard Farlinger and his debut feature *The Perfect Son* will attract a deserving audience. Starring Colm Feore (*32 Short Films About Glenn Gould*) and Canadian TV hunk David Cubitt, *The Perfect Son* proves to be a compelling drama. Although audiences might be turned off by another film about AIDS and drug dependency, *The Perfect Son* focuses more on the brotherly bond and their respective transformations while facing the grim realities of life.

When their father dies, Theo (Cubitt) and Ryan (Feore) reunite after many years of estrangement. Theo has returned from rehab wanting to start fresh and also reunite with his estranged lover Sara (Chandra West), while respected lawyer Ryan wants to maintain his image as the "the perfect son," although he happens to be gay and dying of AIDS. As you can imagine, both brothers are entangled in stale dysfunctional patterns in which Ryan acts out the role of the overly-responsible and successful brother while Theo, a drug addict and writer, plays the role of the black sheep of the family. But as the story unfolds, Theo learns to be responsible, offering to marry Sara after she finds out she's pregnant with his child, and also becoming Ryan's caretaker during his remaining days. Ryan, on the other hand, lets his guard down while allowing his vulnerabilities to break through his arrogant exterior. Theo sees his brother at his worse—vomiting on the floor of the bathroom, hooking himself up to a set of IV's or wasting away in a drab hospital bed. But despite the ugly reality the brothers face and their

ancient rivalry, they learn to love each other while accepting themselves.

A critic for *eye Weekly* panned *The Perfect Son* by citing that the film didn't offer any new information about people currently dealing with AIDS. Bruce Kirkland, of the *Toronto Sun,* noticed cliches in the film's script, but also noted, "the film is exceptionally well-acted, a credit to Farlinger and his cast." Farlinger shows promise, proving that he can write condensed scenes and move his story along in a fashion free of any narrative obstructions. He expertly weaves the subplot between Sara and Theo in with the story about the brothers. And this becomes important when dealing with a narrative-driven film, especially when the story takes precedence.

Similar to the emotional restraint displayed by the film's performers, cinematographer Barry Stone also practices restraint while photographing the scenes. Although a few scenes display memorable images (such as the church scene at the film's beginning and Ryan's walk on the beach after he learns he's dying), you'll find little camera movement here. In fact, *The Perfect Son* proves economical and conservative in many respects, but this is to the film's credit for it leaves plenty of room for the actors to perform.

Both Feore and Cubitt received Genie nominations for Best Actor for their performances in *The Perfect Son* but lost to Toni Nardi for *My Father's Angel.* Cubitt brings sensuality and pathos to Theo as the character wins his battle over addiction, releases his familial bitterness, and becomes Ryan's caretaker. Feore surrenders himself to his role without ever relying on gay stereotypical behavior and oozes both arrogance and insecurity.

—*Patty-Lynne Herlevi*

## CREDITS

**Theo:** David Cubitt
**Ryan:** Colm Feore

**Origin:** Canada
**Released:** 2000
**Production:** Jennifer Jonas; New Real Films; released by Equinox Entertainment Inc.
**Directed by:** Leonard Farlinger
**Written by:** Leonard Farlinger
**Cinematography by:** Barry Stone
**Music by:** Ron Sures
**Editing:** Glenn Berman
**Costumes:** Chandra West, Linda Muir
**Production Design:** Graeme Morphy
**MPAA rating:** Unrated
**Running time:** 93 minutes

---

## REVIEWS

*eye Weekly Online.* February 1, 2001.
*Toronto Sun Online.* February 2, 2001.
*Variety.* October 2, 2000, p. 27.

## QUOTES

Ryan (Colm Feore) tells his brother Theo (David Cubitt) that he has AIDS: "I know it's dreadfully passe, but there you have it. I was diagnosed 10 years ago and I'm way past my expiration date."

## AWARDS AND NOMINATIONS

**Nomination:**
**Genie 2001:** Actor (Feore), Actor (Cubitt).

# Pinero

**Box Office:** $.2 million

Viewers might get the impression that all Latino writers live tragic lives after watching director Julian Schnabel's *Before Night Falls* (2000) and Leon Ichaso's *Piñero*, a film that chronicles the rise and fall of Puerto Rican poet, Miguel Piñero. And the cliché that New York artists create "real art" because they live hopelessly on the edge of society rings of pretentiousness in itself. After all, art can be created from pleasure or pain and one's suffering doesn't necessarily make one a great artist. While, at times, street art acts as a breath of fresh air in a stuffy artistic environment, there's not much pleasure in watching an artist shoot up drugs, string vulgarities together like a beaded necklace, or play the role of victim-of-the-week. Yet, directors, writers, and actors are drawn to the lives of iconoclastic artists since the drama of the artists' lives already play out like an intriguing screenplay.

However, the life of poet/playwright/actor Miguel Piñero plays out similar to gun-splatter in Ichaso's feature film. With a film structure similar to *Before Night Falls*, Ichaso leaps back and forth through time while punctuating his film with Piñero's rabid spoken word performances and the strong Latin groove of salsa and mambo. The end result recalls the lives of the infamous Beat poets who also lived on the edge of society even if for different reasons than the Puerto Rican ex-cons-turned artists who appear in *Piñero*. After all, Jack Kerouac and company did not grow up in the projects and they didn't have to learn how to survive on the violent and bloodthirsty streets of NYC's Lower East Side.

Piñero began writing poetry and completed his first play, *Short Eyes*, while in the infamous Sing Sing prison. Upon his release, *Short Eyes* ran at New York's Public Theatre and Piñero garnered a Tony Award nomination. However, the young poet (channeled by actor Benjamin Bratt) could only fuel his creativity through drug use and living a life of crime—leading him to live a dualistic life. On one hand, he enjoyed much artistic success with his plays, poetry, and acting career, and on the other hand, he would devour the hand that fed him—even stealing from his close friend Miguel Algarin (Giancarlo Esposito).

No one would argue that Piñero lived a tragic life. His father abandoned the family and he watched his mother try to raise five children on her own. Later, the poet spent time in prison for theft. Even after he found artistic success, Miguel watched his close friends die while he himself suffered from cirrhosis. In one scene, Miguel threatens a transsexual by telling her that he will steal her liver while she sleeps. Even the love of his actress girlfriend Sugar (Talisa Soto) added little solace to Miguel's wretched life. Miguel died a poet's death in a hospital bed at the age of 41 and his ashes were scattered around the Lower East Side. In *The Lower East Side Poem*, Miguel asked to have his remains left, "near the stabbing shooting gambling fighting & unnatural dying & new birth crying . . ."

The clean-cut Bratt, mostly known for his role in the TV series *Law & Order*, becomes Piñero as opposed to just playing a role. He vibrates with intensity as he carries a loaded chip on his shoulder. Jeffrey M. Anderson in the *San Francisco Examiner* poetically described Bratt's performance, "Local nice-guy actor Benjamin Bratt occupies Piñero's persona with gusto, strutting, bowing, stealing the center of the room, wallowing his own destruction."

Rita Moreno radiates in her small role as Miguel's mother. In a scene where she visits Miguel in prison, she asks her incarcerated son whatever happened to the boy who once brought her flowers and read poetry to her. Miguel responds by telling her he remembered a different sort of childhood. Soto also delivers a compelling performance as the girlfriend and struggling actress and Esposito adds warmth to the role of Piñero's most-trusted friend and a co-founder of the Nuyorican Café, Algarin.

It is easy to grow bored from the vulgarity and artist clichès that punctuate Ichaso's biopic even when beauty seeps through the cracks. If viewers can stomach watching characters shoot up drugs for the film's duration they are awarded with a powerful ending in which Piñero's *The Lower East Side Poem* is recited by friends at his funeral.

—*Patty-Lynne Herlevi*

**Miguel Pinero:** Benjamin Bratt
**Sugar:** Talisa Soto
**Miguel Algarin:** Giancarlo Esposito
**Mother:** Rita Moreno
**Joseph Papp:** Mandy Patinkin
**Reinaldo Povod:** Michael Irby
**Edgar:** Michael Wright
**Tito:** Nelson Vasquez
**Father:** Jaime Sanchez
**Jake:** Rome Neal

**Origin:** USA
**Released:** 2001
**Production:** John Penotti, Fisher Stevens, Tim Williams; GreeneStreet Films, Lower East Side Films; released by Miramax Films
**Directed by:** Leon Ichaso
**Written by:** Leon Ichaso
**Cinematography by:** Claudio Chea
**Sound:** Andy Edelman
**Music Supervisor:** Kenny Vance, Ken Weiss
**Editing:** David Tedeschi
**Art Direction:** Timothy Whidbee
**Costumes:** Sandra Hernandez
**Production Design:** Sharon Lomofsky
**MPAA rating:** R
**Running time:** 103 minutes

REVIEWS

*Boxoffice.* December, 2001, p. 50.
*Entertainment Weekly.* January 11, 2002, p. 47.
*Los Angeles Times Online.* December 13, 2001.
*New York Times Online.* December 2, 2001.
*New York Times Online.* December 13, 2001.
*USA Today Online.* December 13, 2001.
*Variety.* September 10, 2001, p. 65.
*Village Voice.* December 8, 2001, p. 130.
*Washington Post.* January 25, 2002, p. WE39.

QUOTES

Miguel Pinero (Benjamin Bratt): "I have to keep doing bad to keep the writing good."

# Planet of the Apes

**Box Office:** $179.8 million

In the year 2029, on the United States Air Force's research station Oberon, Captain Leo Davidson (Mark Wahlberg) is training the monkey Pericles to handle the controls of a small space ship. Pericles is just one of many gene-spliced and chromosome-enhanced apes on the Oberon who are being trained to probe space on behalf of their human masters. Space after all is like a dangerous coal mine, and these monkeys are the canaries.

When an unusual electro-magnetic storm suddenly hits the research station and causes a power problem, Pericles is put in his space ship and sent to investigate. This infuriates Captain Davidson because he, being a typical headstrong, macho-pilot type, insists that Pericles is not ready and besides you should never send a monkey to do a man's job. So, when Pericles' ship disappears, Davidson ignores his commander's orders and boards another ship to chase after him.

It doesn't take long, however, for Davidson to become as lost as Pericles whose ship he only briefly glimpses before it disappears in the storm. His ship out of control, his chronometer racing forward, Leo quickly finds himself crashing on an alien planet and sinking into a small lake. Just barely escaping drowning, Davidson soon realizes that he is not alone—and that all the other people racing past him are running for their lives. He doesn't know why, but he figures he'd better run too.

It turns out that everyone is running away from slave traders who are out hunting humans to sell. One can only imagine Davidson's surprise when he discovers that the slavers are all apes. In fact, the apes on this planet are much more culturally sophisticated than the loin-cloth garbed humans they use as slaves. The slavers, headed by Limbo (Paul Giamatti), capture Leo along with some others and take them back to Ape City to be cleaned up and put on the market.

Leo finds himself and another young woman, Daena (Estella Warren) sold to Ari (Helena Bonham Carter) who is outraged at the way apes treat humans but also senses something special about Leo. He is put to work in the kitchen of Ari's father, Senator Sandar (David Warner), and made to wait on a group of ape dignitaries who are at the Senator's house that evening for dinner. Among the guests is a particularly evil ape, General Thade (Tim Roth), who delights in tripping Leo and prying his mouth open to look for his soul.

Thade is a highly ambitious chimp who is just looking for his chance to take over. He hates humans and chafes at his government's controlling of his actions against them. But when Ari helps Leo escape and goes along with him, Thade sees his door of opportunity opening. "Untie my hands," he says to her father the Senator, "Declare martial law. Give me absolute power to rid this planet of humans." Worried about his daughter, Sandar agrees.

Thade is helped in his extreme efforts by the gorilla general Attar (Michael Clark Duncan) who was the best pupil of the former General Krull (Cary-Hiroyuki Tagawa) whose career was ruined by Thade and who is now employed in the service of the Senator and is Ari's prime protector. In fact Krull has even accompanied Ari as she is sucked into Leo's escape.

Leo and his ape and human entourage now head for the only area where he believes they may be safe, Calima, the forbidden area which holds the secrets to the ape society's true beginnings.

Director Tim Burton insists his 2001 version of the 1968 *Planet of the Apes* is a "reimagining not a remake," and in a way that's good and in a way that's too bad. Reviews of the 2001 version of *Apes* have been mixed, but it does have three things going for it: striking visuals, a great villain, and primitive and pounding music.

The impact of the film's music is evident right from the beginning where Danny Elfman's dark, heavy African/military melodies provide the perfect background mood. Elfman, who won a Grammy for his previous work for Burton on *Batman*, describes the music as extremely muscular, aggressive, a little old fashioned and with a powerful percussive edge. What an understatement. To achieve this effect Elfman not only used a full orchestra, but also laid down his own percussive tracks using 76 different percussive instruments including miner's pans, large West African xylophones, huge trash cans and upside-down Schlitz beer cans played with tiny mallets.

It is against this heavily beating music that the *Planet of the Apes'* actors must do their work—even though some of them have little to do or fail to do it with much conviction. Mark Wahlberg turns in a physical but blankly stoic performance. He never seems to care much about the humans he finds himself amongst even though they see him as their hero and deliverer. He would prefer they light the Batman lamp and leave him alone.

Kris Kristofferson is in the film for only minutes as the hunted human who gives his life early in the film so the others can escape. Estella Warren is blandly beautiful as Kristofferson's scantily-clad daughter with the mandatory crush on "hero" Wahlberg. She has little to do in the film other than look wistfully at Leo and little to recommend her other than a role in this year's *Driven* and the fact that she was a Canadian national synchronized swimmer and world bronze medalist.

As an interesting casting note, Lisa Marie, director Burton's longtime girlfriend and actress, can be found in many of his movies. Here she plays the trophy wife of an orangutan senator. Paul Giamatti provides the film's comic relief as the orangutan slave trader and resident Ape City opportunist tossing off such lines as "Make sure you get rid of [the child pet] by puberty. If there's one thing you don't want in your house it's a human teenager."

Michael Clark Duncan as Attar and Cary-Hiroyuki Tagawa as Krull are suitably tall, dark and menacing as the two lead gorillas. Unfortunately sometimes it's difficult to tell some of the Apes apart, especially the gorillas. Most look and sound just like Attar and it may take awhile to realize that he's the only one dressed in black and silver instead of red, and eventually we figure out the Krull is the one with the grey hairs showing.

Helena Bonham Carter is the most human of all the characters, human or ape, as the human-rights advocate Ari. Her ape mannerisms are convincing and her character's warmth and even her facial expressions are easily evoked even through all the prosthetics.

At least in the 2001 version of *Planet* we don't have apes acting like stiff humans, but humans acting very ape-like. This is thanks to the fact that all ape actors were sent to "ape school" to teach them how to move. Chimps, gorillas, and orangutans all walk differently according to Terry Notary, a former Cirque du Soleil performer and stunt double for Tim Roth. And here Notary has the actors pound their chest, hang upside down, and walk bow-legged in a wonderfully kinetic way.

Nowhere is this more obvious than in the performance of Tim Roth as Thade. Roth, who turned down the plum role of Professor Snape in the *Harry Potter* film that was being shot at the same time, is an actor who knows how to be a villain right from his Academy Award®–nominated role as the bane of Liam Neeson's existence in *Rob Roy*. Thade is cut from that same cloth and given plenty of room to push his villainy to its utmost—even to literally bouncing off the walls. Interestingly, Thade was originally written as a gorilla until special makeup effects designer Rick Baker told Burton that chimps are more sinister and unpredictable, nice one minute, ready to attack you the next. And that perfectly describes Roth's Thade.

It should be no surprise that the creative genius behind all the convincing ape makeup in *Planet of the Apes* is none other than master ape makeup man Rick Baker. A veteran of many ape films (the 1976 version of *King Kong*; *Greystoke: The Legend of Tarzan*; *Mighty Joe Young* and especially *Gorillas in the Mist*) and other films, Baker was a natural choice. In his own words, *Apes* is "a film I was born to do." The fit of film and artist was perfect not only because of Baker's previous work creating movie apes but also because of his previous work with Burton: he won the third of his six Oscars® for turning Martin Landau into Bela Lugosi in Burton's 1994 *Ed Wood*. While Baker did a masterful job of turning Helena Bonham Carter into a real chimp babe, he does admit he never could get her "hairstyle" to meet Burton's expectations. It's still a bit of a sore point to Baker that Burton called in an Italian hairdresser from New York to create a wig for her character.

Baker's makeup is just part of the incredible visuals that are a hallmark of this film. Although other directors were at one time attached to the 2001 version of *Planet,* Oliver Stone, Chris Columbus and James Cameron among them, one can't imagine the film without the visual stylings of Tim Burton. (Especially in collaboration with production designer Rick Heinrichs who has known Burton since college and worked on all his friend's films.) From the red army tent camps to the lines of marching apes, and the Mont St. Michel-like ape city, Burton's attention to detail, his use of colors and light, his surreal sets give his visual style depth and distinctiveness.

This visual distinctiveness is also aided by the choice of shooting locations: Hawaii's lava fields on Mt. Kilauea, the unique geological formations of California's Trona Pinnacles near Death Valley, and even Independence Bay at Lake Powell. This last location is especially interesting because it is only a few miles from sites used in the original 1968 movie. It is not the only homage to the earlier film Burton has slipped into the movie. For example, Linda Harrison, the former wife of producer Richard D. Zanuck, originally played the mute Nova in the first two *Planet* films. Here she is seen briefly in the cart of humans being brought into Ape City, but she still doesn't say a word. (And her name, Nova, is now given to Lisa Marie's character.)

The most blatant homage, however, may be the fact that Thade's father is played by an unbilled Charleton Heston, the human hero of the original film. According to Baker, he'd always wanted to make a Monkey out of Heston, you might notice that Heston refused to wear the prosthetic teeth necessary to complete the make up. One also can't help noticing that Heston's character is the one who reintroduces the apes to guns by giving one to his son Thade and telling him as he dies that they are the source of human power. Considering Heston's fervent NRA stand the irony does not go unappreciated.

In that same seen, Heston then utters with his last breath, "Damn them! Damn them all to hell!" In the original film, upon seeing what humans have done to their own civilization he yells, "Damn you! Damn you all to hell!" Similarly, "Take your stinking paws off me, you damn dirty ape!" are the famous first words Heston's hero speaks to the apes in the 1968 version. In this year's version, "Take your stinking hands off me, you damn dirty human!" is growled by Duncan's Attar.

One tribute the filmmakers unfortunately overlooked is the fact that the original screenplay for the 1968 film was co-written by *The Twilight Zone*'s Rod Serling. He was the one who gave the first film its intensity, its irony, and its social commentary. Although based on the 1963 novel by French author Pierre Boulle, it was Serling who gave the original movie its punch-in-the-gut ending. Burton's film, on the other hand, has no subtle Serling touch. In fact, many audience members find the ending of this year's version of the film confusing, if not downright unacceptable. Burton's ending certainly won't be producing the same kind of iconographic film image as will the Statue of Liberty's arm sticking out of the beach's sand. (However, unlike Matt Drudge who spoiled the ending for many viewers by disclosing it before the movie even came out, no word of revelation will be told here.)

In the end though, one may feel that Tim Burton's 2001 version missed it's chance plotwise. That it could have been more; that it could have had more edge. It is said the screenplay continued to be rewritten throughout the shoot and that Burton himself continued to tinker with the film up to one week before it was to be released, but outside of the three things mentioned earlier, there is still a slight feeling of being let down by the film. That didn't stop it from grossing an estimated $69.6 million its opening weekend, making it the biggest opener of the summer of 2001 and the second biggest opening weekend of all time after *The Lost World: Jurassic Park.* It took in $25 million alone on its opening day, giving it the biggest Friday grosses every.

The producer on Burton's *Planet* is Richard D. Zanuck who was also the production chief at Fox in 1968 and gave the go ahead for original film. That original *Planet of the Apes* gave birth to four sequels and two television shows, one of which was animated. Do you think there will be a sequel to this "reimagining"? Well according to Fox's chief of distribution no sequel has been approved yet, but Mark Wahlberg is already signed up to be in it if there is. Wish Rod Serling were still around.

*—Beverley Bare Buehrer*

## CREDITS

**Capt. Leo Davidson:** Mark Wahlberg
**Thade:** Tim Roth
**Ari:** Helena Bonham Carter
**Attar:** Michael Clarke Duncan
**Limbo:** Paul Giamatti
**Daena:** Estella Warren
**Krull:** Cary-Hiroyuki Tagawa
**Sandar:** David Warner
**Karubi:** Kris Kristofferson
**Tival:** Erik Avari
**Birn:** Luke Eberl
**Thade's father:** Charlton Heston

**Origin:** USA
**Released:** 2001

**Production:** Richard D. Zanuck; Zanuck Company; released by 20th Century-Fox
**Directed by:** Tim Burton
**Written by:** William Broyles Jr., Larry Konner, Mark Rosenthal
**Cinematography by:** Philippe Rousselot
**Music by:** Danny Elfman
**Sound:** Petur Hliddal
**Editing:** Chris Lebenzon
**Art Direction:** Sean Haworth, Philip Toolin
**Costumes:** Colleen Atwood
**Production Design:** Rick Heinrichs
**Special Effects:** Rick Baker
**Visual Effects:** Bill George
**MPAA rating:** PG-13
**Running time:** 125 minutes

## REVIEWS

*Boxoffice.* September, 2001, p. 48.
*Chicago Sun-Times Online.* July 27, 2001.
*Entertainment Weekly.* August 3, 2001, p. 39.
*Los Angeles Times Online.* July 27, 2001.
*New York Times Online.* May 13, 2001.
*New York Times Online.* July 27, 2001.
*People.* August 6, 2001, p. 37.
*Newsweek.* August 6, 2001, p. 58.
*Sight and Sound.* September, 2001, p. 12.
*Time.* August 6, 2001, p. 62.
*USA Today Online.* July 30, 2001.
*Variety.* July 30, 2001, p. 17.
*Washington Post.* July 27, 2001, p. WE32.

## QUOTES

Leo (Mark Wahlberg): "Never send a monkey to do a man's job."

## TRIVIA

The 1968 film spawned four sequels and two television shows.

## AWARDS AND NOMINATIONS

**Nomination:**
**British Acad. 2001:** Costume Des.

# The Pledge

*A detective grappling with retirement. A tragic crime. A life-changing promise.*
—Movie tagline

 **Box Office:** $19.7 million

After *The Silence of the Lambs* (1991) the serial-killer police-procedural became a genre unto itself. The focus is upon the psychology of the killer, not so much what makes him tick (for that would take viewers into the unknowable territory of insanity) but his modus operandi, his habits of stalking his victims, the imminent danger he poses to the innocent and, in the case of Jonathan Demme's film to the novice FBI agent, Clarice Starling (Jodie Foster), who is tracking him down. The focus, in other words, is on the criminal mind. Sean Penn's *The Pledge* takes a wholly different approach. A serial killer is out there in rural Nevada, but the viewer is not entirely certain who he may be. Instead of focusing upon the killer and showing him at work, *The Pledge* focuses instead on the psychology of the police officer, Jerry Black (Jack Nicholson, in one of the best roles of his career), who is obsessed with bringing him to justice.

The film begins with overhead shots of Jerry Black, befuddled and isolated in what seems to be a wilderness. The camera circles him, showing close-ups of his face, marked by a dumbfounded expression that is impossible to interpret, for there is no context that has so far been established. The film ends with the same shots, but by then the viewer understands exactly what is troubling him. He has gone through a difficult transition, from active duty to retirement. He has kept his word and solved a mystery, although he does not realize exactly what he has accomplished. He has ruined a relationship with a woman he probably loved and alienated himself from the woman and her daughter, whom he seems fond of. As far as he knows, he has been an utter failure, nothing more than a drunk and a clown, as one of his police colleagues describes him at the end. However, he has probably saved the little girl's life, but only the viewer knows this because of Penn's masterstroke of camera irony.

This film is utterly focused on the psychology of a dedicated police officer who sacrifices everything to keep his word. He is a fisherman, and the credit montage also shows him ice-fishing. Then as the film's main action begins, Jerry is attending his own retirement party in Reno, Nevada. Crosscut with the party are shots of an adolescent boy in the woods on a snowmobile that breaks down. In the distance a pickup truck is parked. The boy watches as an American Indian runs through the snow to the truck, throws his beaver traps into the truck bed, and takes off in a big hurry, his tires spinning in the snow. The boy walks in the direction from which the man had come and discovers the body of a murdered and mutilated eight-year-old girl named Ginny Larson.

News of the reported murder reaches the retirement party in Reno. Jerry decides to accompany his friend Stan Krolak (Aaron Eckhart) to investigate, even though Jerry is within six hours of retiring. At the scene of the crime local police officers lack the courage to tell the dead girl's parents what has happened, so Jerry drives to the turkey farm they operate, finds them in a breeder house, and tells them. The parents are understandably distraught, and the mother (Patricia Clarkson) asks Jerry to find the killer, "Do you swear by your soul salvation on this cross, made by the hands of my daughter?" Jerry makes this pledge, then devotes the next two years of his life and his retirement to fulfilling it.

Later on, the police have a suspect, a mentally challenged Native American named Toby (Benicio Del Toro), who had a prior rape conviction. Toby has psychological problems of his own, so Jerry does not take his confession seriously, then, as Toby is being led to a jail cell, he grabs the gun of the police officer who is leading him and kills himself. The coroner reports that chocolate was found in the girl's stomach, and chocolate wrappers were "all over" Toby's truck. Case closed, as far as the police are concerned, but Jerry is not at all convinced.

At the retirement party, Jerry had been given an airplane ticket to Mexico to go marlin fishing. He gets as far as the airport, but at the last minute decides not to board the plane. Instead, he goes to visit the dead girl's grandmother, Annalise Hansen (Vanessa Redgrave), who was also her piano teacher and the last person to see her alive. She tells him that the girl's favorite story was Hans Christian Andersson's "The Angel," which claims that whenever a child dies, an angel comes and takes her to the places she loved. "How could God be so greedy?" the grandmother wants to know. Later on one of the girl's classmates tells Jerry about a secret Ginny had shared with her, a "wizard" she identified as the "porcupine giant," whom she trusted. Ginny had drawn a picture of the giant that Jerry finds tacked up on the wall at her school.

"I thought you were supposed to be fishing in Mexico," his friend Stan tells Jerry. "You're retired. You don't work here anymore," but Stan none the less agrees to run a check of other crimes involving dead or missing young blondes. Jerry discovers a pattern, that convinces him he is looking for a serial killer. Another young girl wearing a red dress was murdered eight years before, and five years after that still another young blonde turned up missing and was never found. Jerry attempts to interview James Oldstand (Mickey Rourke), the father of the girl who went missing, who works as a custodian at a retirement home. The film is marked here and elsewhere with images of old and disabled people,

signaling the future that Jerry faces. Authorities in Moorehead, Nevada, tell Jerry that Kathy Oldstand was last seen wearing a red dress when she went missing. Jerry also learns that when the other murder occurred eight years before, Toby was serving time in prison and could not have been the killer. Moreover, Jerry knows that the "porcupine giant" drove a black station wagon or minivan, not a pickup truck.

Eric Pollack (Sam Shepard), Jerry's superior at homicide, concerned about Jerry's obsession, suggests therapy. Jerry's response is "I made a promise to find Ginny Larson's murderer. I intend to keep it." Jerry does visit a psychiatrist (Helen Mirren) for advice. She confirms his suspicion that the intervals between the murders seem to be getting shorter and that the killer may be expected to strike again within the next two years. But the psychiatrist then says: "You came to me for help. Do you mind if I ask you some questions? How long have you been a chain smoker? Are you still sexually active? Do you hear voices?" The thrust of these questions suggests that she suspects that Jerry is not entirely "normal." The viewers are so much in sympathy with Jerry, however, that his behavior does not seem abnormal, until later.

The depth of his disturbance begins to surface when Jerry gives himself a vacation at Thompson's Sugar Bush Fishing Resort, but while fishing, Jerry is really staking out the terrain between the towns of Monash and Moorehead and has triangulated an area where the killer might surface next. After gassing up at a nearby filling station, he talks to the owner, Floyd Cage (Harry Dean Stanton) and offers to buy it. "You'll never be able to sell this place for what you paid for it," the lady realtor tells him, but his purpose in buying it was to keep his eye out for black station wagons.

Jerry then gets friendly with a waitress who works at a nearby bar, Lori (Robin Wright Penn), whose daughter, Chrissy (Pauline Roberts), fits the profile of the victims of the "porcupine giant." After Lori gets beat up by her abusive ex-husband, Jerry suggests that she and her daughter move in with him at the filling station. He then buys a swing set and sets it up by the road outside the station. He is setting a trap and using Lori's daughter for bait. Fishing imagery runs throughout the film, and the screenplay offers many red herrings to be caught. Jerry goes with Lori and her daughter to a local flea market and Chrissy goes missing. Someone has given her a little porcupine. Jerry investigates the store where they are sold and the home of the woman who makes them. Both the woman who makes them and the woman who sells them have sons. The trail seems to be getting warmer, but neither Jerry nor the viewer can say exactly who the killer may be.

The woman who makes the porcupines has a son, Mr. Jackson, who is an evangelical Christian and works for the Department of Roads. One winter day he stops to talk to Chrissy, who is making a snowman and asks her "Has your mom told you about the Word?" Jackson stops a second time and gives the girl a plastic cross and invites her to his church. Jerry returns from a fishing trip to learn that Chrissy has cone to church "with the Jacksons." He freaks out, packs a gun, and drives like a madman to the church, but he finds a service in progress there, with Chrissy attending, unharmed.

Soon thereafter, however, the real deal comes along. "I met the wizard today," Chrissy tells Jerry. The "wizard" had told her not to tell her mother, but she concluded she could tell Jerry. "Jerry, can I go see the wizard tomorrow at the picnic grounds?" she asks Jerry. "I don't see why not," Jerry says, "but let's keep it a secret." The next day Jerry convinces his city friends to send out a SWAT team to set a trap at the picnic grounds. The audience is given privileged information. The Indian woman who owns the shop where the porcupines are sold is seen at home. She notices that candy is missing and calls for her son, Oliver. Oliver is in his black Volvo driving to the picnic grounds, apparently the "porcupine giant," but the viewer never gets a clear look at him, only the back of his head while he drives. On the way, however, he is involved in a terrible accident with a logging truck; the Volvo catches fire, and he is burned to death.

That is as close as Jerry comes to getting his man, but there is no way he can tell what has happened. After waiting in vain at the picnic grounds, Jerry's friend Stan finally stops the operation, and tells Jerry that he has to tell Lori what has transpired, which turns her against Jerry forever. Stan writes Jerry off as a drunk and a clown, adding "he was a great cop once." The film's final image shows Jerry as Stan has described him—lost, drunk, befuddled, standing in front of the now closed filling station, a ruined man.

*The Pledge* was adapted from a story by the German-Swiss novelist Friedrich Dürrenmatt entitled *Das Verspechen* (1958), that, according to critic Roger A. Crockett, was intended to perform "the funeral of the detective novel." A fictional character named Dürrenmatt gives a lecture on "the art of writing detective novels," explaining that the genre is based on logic, a false premise: "You build your plots up logically, like a chess game; here the criminal, here the victim, here the accomplice, here the mastermind. The detective need only know the rules and play the game, and he has the criminal trapped, has won a victory for justice. This fiction infuriates me," he says, because in the real world, chance plays a much larger role than probability. The novel introduces a drunken, feeble-minded gas-station attendant and a slovenly 16-year-old girl named Annemarie in a ramshackle roadside cafe. His name is Matthäi, "once one of the best men in the Zürich Cantonal Police Department." This character in the film first seems to be the one played by Harry Dean Stanton, Floyd, the original owner of the filling station who has a "slovenly" daughter, but finally turns out to be the Nicholson character.

Like Matthäi, Jerry sets an elaborate trap for the murderer, identified by the victim's friend in the novel as the "hedgehog giant." But, as in the film, in the novel the serial killer is killed in a car wreck while on his way to meet his next victim. Matthäi, defeated by this ironic reversal, loses emotional control and slips into drunkenness and madness. Nicholson's character at both ends of the film reflects Matthäi's fate, but the film's only explanation is given by Jerry's friend, who says, in a throwaway line, "He was a great cop once but is now just a drunk and a clown." The action in the film is not so carefully mediated as in the novel, but Penn does an amazingly good job of transferring the story to an American setting.

There are some loose ends, however, that make this film a bit of a puzzler. At the picnic grounds, for example, Chrissy is having a tea party with her dolly, when she tells the dolly that she'll be back and goes down by the river. Did the "giant" set this up as a meeting place? Jerry freaks out when he realizes Chrissy has left the picnic table and the SWAT team is therefore out of position. He has a point, but why doesn't Stan see his point? Jerry snaps when Stan then cancels the SWAT operation and goes into a kind of trance, just as he also does when Lori confronts him about daring to use her daughter as bait for his trap.

The film is shot through with ambiguity as it approximates the haphazardness of real life. The viewer cannot be sure of Jerry's true feelings for Lori or Chrissy. He treats the girl as if she were his daughter; he reads bedtime stories to her. Is his real motive that he is simply building her confidence in him so she will confide in him? When Chrissy wants to buy a red dress, he does not object. When she tells him she wants to see the wizard the next day, he not only agrees, but tells her to keep it a secret from her mother. Is Jerry operating only out of his obsession to satisfy his "pledge"? Is he crazy? There is no way of being entirely sure about this. Surely part of the credit—or blame—here goes to the husband-and-wife writing team of Jerzy Kromolowski and Mary Olson-Kromolowski, who adapted Dürrenmatt's novel. *Baltimore Sun* critic Chris Kaltenbach objected that the movie "owes its audience something by way of explanation."

Michael O'Sullivan was on target in his *Washington Post Weekend* review when he pointed out how unconventional the film was: "Its point is not knowledge or discovery but the assertion that knowledge and discovery are ultimately impossible. The story tracks not the unraveling arc of clues but Jerry's emotional and moral tailspin as he fashions himself into a kind of avenging angel." This is not a film that provides answers. The usual tendency of Hollywood films is not to leave the viewer puzzled, but this film relishes in puzzlement and ambiguity.

Owen Gleiberman of *Entertainment Weekly* and others praised the film for "its haunting and ravaged performance by Jack Nicholson and for Sean Penn's flair for visual suspense, for landscape, [and] for holding his actors in the throes of slow-motion breakdown." Stephen Hunter of the

*Washington Post* found *The Pledge* "far easier to admire" than to enjoy, but praised Sean Penn's "integrity" and Nicholson's "great performance." The film features fine performances and is excellently photographed by Chris Menges. Its ambiguity is to be praised, not excoriated. The film was refreshingly experimental and challenging. How many Hollywood films leave viewers with the impression that they have experienced something new and different? This one does.

—*James M. Welsh*

## CREDITS

**Jerry Black:** Jack Nicholson
**Lori:** Robin Wright Penn
**Stan Krolak:** Aaron Eckhart
**Annalise Hansen:** Vanessa Redgrave
**Margaret Larsen:** Patricia Clarkson
**Toby Jay Wadeneh:** Benicio Del Toro
**Monash deputy:** Costas Mandylor
**Doctor:** Helen Mirren
**Gary Jackson:** Tom Noonan
**Duane Larsen:** Michael O'Keefe
**Jim Olstand:** Mickey Rourke
**Eric Pollack:** Sam Shepard
**Helen Jackson:** Lois Smith
**Floyd Cage:** Harry Dean Stanton
**Strom:** Dale Dickey
**Chrissy:** Pauline Roberts

**Origin:** USA
**Released:** 2000
**Production:** Michael Fitzgerald, Sean Penn, Elie Samaha; Morgan Creek Productions, Franchise Pictures, Clyde is Hungry Films; released by Warner Bros.
**Directed by:** Sean Penn
**Written by:** Jerzy Kromolowski, Mary Olson-Kromolowski
**Cinematography by:** Chris Menges
**Music by:** Hans Zimmer
**Sound:** Rob Young
**Editing:** Jay Cassidy
**Art Direction:** Helen Jarvis
**Production Design:** Bill Groom
**MPAA rating:** R
**Running time:** 124 minutes

## REVIEWS

*Baltimore Sun.* January 19, 2000, p. F1.
*Boxoffice.* April, 2001, p. 241.

*Chicago Sun-Times Online.* January 19, 2001.
*Entertainment Weekly.* January 27, 2001, p. 75.
*Hollywood Reporter.* January 5, 2001, p. 12.
*New York Times Online.* January 19, 2001.
*People.* January 29, 2001, p. 34.
*Rolling Stone.* February 15, 2001, p. 84.
*Sight and Sound.* November, 2001, p. 36.
*Time.* January 22, 2001, p. 78.
*USA Today.* January 6, 2001, p. E6.
*Variety.* January 8, 2001, p. 40.
*Washington Post.* January 19, 2001, p. C1.
*Washington Post Weekend.* January 19, 2001, p. 42.
*Washington Times.* January 19, 2001, p. C5.

## QUOTES

Jerry (Jack Nicholson) to former boss Eric Pollack (Sam Shepard): "I made a promise. You're old enough to remember when that meant something."

# Pootie Tang

*Too cool for words.*
—Movie tagline

 **Box Office:** $3.3 million

Poor old Chris Rock. The man can't seem to make a good movie. It's a shame since Rock is one of the most sharp, intelligent and hilarious comedians of his generation. His HBO sketch comedy show, *The Chris Rock Show,* earned critical kudos, his book *Rock This!* was a success, and his stand-up has earned him legions of fans. But despite his successes, Rock doesn't seem to get the whole movie thing. His movie career has been marked by tepid roles in other people's films like playing a naked religious figure in Kevin Smith's *Dogma* and, in possibly his worst role of all times, a kowtowing bellhop in the hideous Chris Farley vehicle *Beverly Hills Ninja.*

But it's not like Rock is in all these bad movies due to the poor judgment of other people who just don't get his comedy. When Rock has had the chance to make his own movies, he gives himself equally bad material. *Down to Earth* was an unsuccessful (and generally unfunny) remake of Warren Beatty's *Heaven Can Wait. Down* was co-written with Lance Crouther. Unfortunately, the two didn't seem to get the message that the absent audiences for that film were sending them and decided to team up again on *Pootie Tang.*

*Pootie Tang* is based on a character played by Crouther that was a cultish favorite on Chris Rock's HBO show. It's hard to believe that Rock would be short-sighted enough to look towards *Saturday Night Live*'s tradition of stretching short skits into overly long feature films as a model to emulate, but unfortunately that's just what happened. Like 98% of those SNL spinoffs, Pootie Tang should have remain confined to the boundaries of his skits—that way no one would have had to suffer.

Pootie Tang is one cool dude. In the film we learn that even when he was a little boy with a skinny little frame and big dorky glasses, he had a way with the ladies. His father (Rock, in one of many roles in the film) is a strict dad who keeps his boy in line with a belt that he smacks Pootie's hands with whenever the child tries to do something bad. Pootie's early life is marked by tragedy. His mother dies when he is a boy and soon afterwards, his dad dies too, after being mauled by a gorilla in a steel mill. "It was the third time," comments the narrator dryly. On his deathbed, Pootie's father hands him his belt and tells Pootie that the belt has magic powers and will give him the strength to do whatever he wants.

Pootie takes these words to heart and finds his strength in the belt. He grows up to be a rock star, ladies' man, movie star, and crime fighter. When villains try to beat him up, Pootie whips off his belt with the grace of a ninja master and starts taking out the bad guys. He also has the ability to dodge bullets in a slow-motion fashion ala *The Matrix*. Pootie spends his off hours hanging out with his friends, Trucky (JB Smoove), Lacey (Mario Joyner), and JB (Rock, again), who, like everyone else in the movie, don't seem to care that Pootie's speech is all but incomprehensible. "I'm gonna sine your pitty on the runny kine! Sipi-tai!" Pootie says in his trademark catchphrase. But he says it with such feeling that everyone feels like they know what he means.

Pootie's do-gooder tendencies and all around popularity earn him some enemies. One rival, Dirty D. (Reg E. Cathey) is a real dirty guy—dirty, as in messy, soiled, and unclean. He drives a car covered with garbage and has a posse of ladies wearing torn and soiled clothing. (This would be a fine example of that humor in the film that just doesn't work.) Pootie has messed with Dirty D's crime plans one too many times and D. is sent to jail. He vows that when he gets out, he will get revenge on Pootie.

But a more vicious enemy is Dick Lecter (Robert Vaughn), Chief Executive of the mega-conglomerate, LecterCorp. LecterCorp is filled with a bunch of evil guys who like to market stuff like cigarettes, malt liquor, and weapons to kids. Pootie is so popular that, after he makes a series of public service announcements urging kids to shun drinking and smoking and to eat their vegetables, LecterCorp sees a corresponding drop in their sales. "The public service announcements are actually working?" said a Lecter henchman in disbelief.

Lecter tries to offer Pootie a big money deal to endorse some of his products like Pork Chunk Cereal, but Pootie is too responsible to be bought. One of Lecter's underlings says to Pootie disdainfully, "To you, they're children, to me, they're dollars." Lecter breaks out his secret weapon, his girlfriend Ireenie (Jennifer Coolidge). She has some sort of weird charm that puts Pootie in a trance and while he is under her spell, she makes him sign a contract giving full power over his image and likeness to LecterCorp. In a final humiliation, she takes Pootie's belt, and with it, his superpowers.

A weak and bedraggled Pootie wanders dazedly around the streets until Biggie Shorty (Wanda Sykes), a sassy local girl who's always had a big crush on Pootie, offers him the chance to use a country home she has down south. There, in a part of the plot that goes nowhere, Pootie learns to love the land and ends up almost getting hitched in a shotgun wedding to the daughter of the local sheriff. Will Pootie get out of the wedding? Will he ever return to Chicago? Is his belt gone forever? It's not too mysterious since Pootie is Pootie and this is not the best-written film.

Although the writing is weak, *Pootie Tang* does have its moments. In one sequence, Pootie makes a record that consists of nothing but silence. In the studio, Pootie records the record while making a variety of soulful, passionate expressions. The man is so cool that his passion translates on the record and all of his fans call it his best song yet. The film also has an inventive look. There are 1970's-style groovy titles and graphics reminiscent of blaxploitation films. The soundtrack is heavy with retro R & B songs like Zapp and Rogers' "I Want To Be Your Man."

And the actors, bless them, are certainly trying. Rock, in his many roles, hams it up. As a DJ who plays Pootie's song of silence, Rock sways, rocks and rolls in utter abandon as he's swept away by the power of the mute music. It seems like Rock is trying to make the material work just by the sheer force of his energy and enthusiasm. If anyone could do that, it would be Rock, but this material is just too dead to be saved.

Sykes as Biggie Shorty also brings a lot of energy to her role. She's a maternal/lover figure to Pootie and has decided that he is her man and she's going to get him no matter how long it takes. Most of the time when we see Biggie, she is standing on a street corner, dolled up in outfits like a miniskirt with a light blue boa and sky high heels, and dancing to music. When a drooling older man pulls up beside her and thinks she's a prostitute, Biggie says with indignation, "Just 'cause a lady likes to dress up fancy and stand on a street corner with some whores, you think that she's hooking?!" Crouther's Pootie is a weak link. His character is supposed to be so cool, but Crouther doesn't pull it off. The only way we know that Pootie is so charismatic is that the movie tells us he is.

Critics, who are normally Rock's best friends, turned on him with this film. "Each and every shot is agonizing in its own ways—not just in one way, in many ways—the fanatical actors appear disjointed, the painful scene transitions feel awkward, the terrible dialogue reeks of desperation, the poorly written screenplay seems unfinished, the soundtrack gives us a headache. *Pootie Tang* stinks as badly as possible," wrote Blake French of filmcritic.com. Roger Ebert of the *Chicago Sun-Times* wrote, "*Pootie Tang* is not bad so much as inexplicable. You watch in puzzlement: How did this train wreck happen?" Miles Beller of the *Los Angeles Times* said, "*Pootie Tang* too often is as garbled as Pootie's own jargon."

—*Jill Hamilton*

## CREDITS

**Pootie Tang:** Lance Crouther
**Ireenie:** Jennifer Coolidge
**Dick Lecter:** Robert Vaughn
**JB:** Chris Rock
**Dirty Dee:** Reg E. Cathey
**Biggie Shorty:** Wanda Sykes
**Frank:** Dave Attell
**Lacey:** Mario Joyner
**Trucky:** JB Smoove
**Stacy:** Cathy Trien
**Cameo:** Bob Costas

**Origin:** USA
**Released:** 2001
**Production:** David Gale, Chris Rock, Ali LeRoi, Cotty Chubb; MTV, Alphaville, 3 Arts Productions; released by Paramount Pictures
**Directed by:** Louis CK
**Written by:** Louis CK
**Cinematography by:** Willy Kurant
**Sound:** Peter Schneider
**Music Supervisor:** Michael McQuarn
**Editing:** Doug Abel, David Lewis Smith
**Art Direction:** Andrea Stanley
**Costumes:** Amanda Sanders
**Production Design:** Amy Silver
**MPAA rating:** PG-13
**Running time:** 81 minutes

## REVIEWS

*Boxoffice.* September, 2001, p. 153.
*Los Angeles Times Online.* June 29, 2001.
*New York Times Online.* June 29, 2001.
*Variety.* July 9, 2001, p. 22.
*Washington Post Online.* June 29, 2001.

# The Price of Milk

*A man, a woman and 117 cows.*
—Movie tagline

In the imaginary New Zealand created by filmmaker Harry Sinclair, the Maori's dreamtime and old-fashioned fairy tales collide. In the lush-green, rolling hills of New Zealand an unusual love story between a man, a woman, and 117 cows unfolds and tests the boundaries of our imagination. Sinclair's *The Price of Milk* possesses that fragile fey quality often found in dreams and in this story, the characters believe in little elves they call Jacksons. They also believe that love can survive any circumstance, including a golden-haired fiancee swapping 117 cows for a stolen quilt. But then again, those princesses found in Western fairy tales always possess a naïve quality and no matter what their hair color, they're all high maintenance and out to cause some trauma. Sinclair's character Lucinda (Danielle Cormack) is not an exception to the rule, even going as far as allowing pots and teacups to tangle in her golden tresses while washing dishes. She's completely hapless.

Sinclair happens to be obsessed with fairy tales and in a press kit interview spoke of 20th-century Russian composers and their obsession with enchanted entities: "It was all about fairies and goblins with such titles as *Enchanted Lake*." So along with a soundtrack provided by the Moscow Symphony Orchestra, Sinclair brings to us a magical world that literally leaps from the screen. In Sinclair's world characters appear victims to the powers that surround them. A Maori woman known as Auntie (Rangi Motu)—who may represent an evil witch—suddenly appears in the middle of the road and is hit by Lucinda, who at that particular moment found herself questioning her love for her boyfriend Rob (Karl Urban). Lucinda, in a sense, represents a dim-witted princess who doesn't know a good thing when it stares her in the face, and she can't leave well enough alone. Similar to many women not sure about their relationships with their lovers, Lucinda engages her best friend in analyzing her relationship to death. The friend, Drosophilia (Willa O'Neill), complicates matters by telling Lucinda that upsetting the unflappable Rob will ignite romantic sparks into the relationship.

So Lucinda goes swimming in a vat of milk worth $1500, which does upset Rob, but only until he decides to join Lucinda on her sensual adventure. However, after Lucinda swaps Rob's beloved dairy cows for the quilt that Auntie has had stolen from their bed, Rob not only loses his voice (he can only utter squeaks of frustration), he also loses his affection for Lucinda. Lucinda tries to make up the loss to Rob by posing as a Jackson and supplying Rob with food, bedding, and furniture while he lives out of his pickup truck near a friend's farm. Lucinda is clearly heartbroken, realizing too late her love for Rob. Auntie tells Lucinda to sacrifice the thing she loves the most so that Rob's cows will be returned to him. Lucinda, much wiser, chooses to return the cows to Rob and suffer the consequences, which involve watching her best friend marry Rob. However, like all fairy tales, the truth is revealed and the princess ends up married to the prince as they live happily ever after.

The most memorable aspects of *The Price of Milk* are the surreal photography and Cushla Dillon's seamless editing. While a warm on-screen chemistry flows between Urban and Cormack, it is not so much their performances as the scene set-ups and cinematographer Leon Narby's handy work that supply the film's absurd moments. We see rolling hills of a lush farmland melt into a quilt in which two lovers perform a sort of tug of war as they sleep. We see Lucinda almost drown in milk that has flooded her home to the brim. And we see Lucinda dressed in a red sari with a long train chasing a dog-powered cardboard box (the dog is agoraphobic) across a field.

*The Price of Milk*, although never short on eye-popping visuals, often feels incongruent and relies too heavily on improvisation from its cast and crew. Even traditional fairy tales follow some form of logic. Still with all of its faults, *The Price of Milk* has its quirky down under humor to save it from completely sinking from its own sweetness.

—*Patty-Lynne Herlevi*

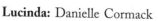
## CREDITS

**Lucinda:** Danielle Cormack
**Rob:** Karl Urban
**Drosophilia:** Willa O'Neill
**Bernie:** Michael Lawrence
**Auntie:** Rangi Motu

**Origin:** New Zealand
**Released:** 2000
**Production:** Fiona Copland; New Zealand Film Commission; released by Lot 47 Films
**Directed by:** Harry Sinclair
**Written by:** Harry Sinclair
**Cinematography by:** Leon Narby
**Sound:** David Madigan
**Editing:** Cushla Dillon
**Costumes:** Kristy Cameron
**Production Design:** Kristy Cameron
**MPAA rating:** PG-13
**Running time:** 87 minutes

## REVIEWS

*Chicago Sun-Times Online.* April 27, 2001.
*Los Angeles Times Online.* March 23, 2001.
*New York Times Online.* February 14, 2001.
*Seattle Weekly.* April 5, 2001, p. 99.
*Variety.* June 5, 2000, p. 21.
*Washington Post Online.* March 23, 2001.

## QUOTES

Lucinda (Danielle Cormack) about testing Rob's (Karl Urban) love: "I might have pushed it a bit too far."

# The Princess and the Warrior (Der Krieger und die Kaiserin)

 **Box Office:** $.7 million

Viewers will either applaud or bash German director Tom Tykwer's 2000 release *The Princess and The Warrior*. Not only does the German film lack the adrenaline drive of Tykwer's film *Run Lola Run*, but the poorly written screenplay with its forced happy ending proves to be overly bleak. After all, the film is sounds like it's suppose to be a fairy tale—only the princess appears to be on quaaludes, the warrior's emotionally deranged, and the story takes place in a mental hospital. Tykwer's fans and film critics have praised the director's innovative approach to fate's machinations and the director's ability to take risks. And while no one would argue those points, Tykwer is capable of writing stronger material and creating more assertive female characters.

The film proves problematic for several reasons. First, the character Sissi (Franka Potente) lacks any sort of drive and she passively accepts her destructive fate. She's hit by a truck, beaten by a mental patient, humiliated by the criminal who rescued her from the truck accident, and never defends herself. She's too nice and rather dull. Second, there are too many coincidences and miracles in the film's plot. For example, a Mack truck runs over Sissi but she survives the accident and within 53 days she's up and running again.

Finally, although this is a fairy tale, no one would actually believe that the two dysfunctional characters that Tykwer created could live happily ever after. Either they'll eventually be arrested for the crimes they committed or the emotionally deranged Bodo (Benno Furmann) would kill Sissi during one of his violent rages. Which brings up the question is the concept of fate so romantic that we would sit for two hours watching two humans suffer through a dysfunctional love affair and have we grown too cynical towards love?

However, fate proves to be an intriguing topic and we are all hooked on the idea of destiny, synchronicity, and how people's live intertwine with one another. For instance, a casting agent discovers Franka Potente at a bar one night and casts her in *It's a Jungle Out There*, which Tykwer saw. Then he casts Potente in *Run Lola Run*. and Tykwer and Potente have since become romantic partners. In an interview with Potente, which appeared in *RANT*, the actresses spoke of fate: "If it was raining that night, six years ago, I would have not gone to the bar. I wouldn't have met the casting agent. Sometimes you find out years later what this or that did or didn't do for you." One might even say that *Run Lola Run*'s smashing success was do in part to Tykwer's obsession with fate. However, characters that live by fate prove rather complacent and such is the case with Sissi and Bodo. At least in *Run Lola Run*, Lola took charge of her destiny by racing against time and acting in a heroic fashion.

As the film opens we see a woman write, then mail, a letter. Similar to Krzysztof Kieslowski's *Three Colors: Red*, we watch the letter travel through a network, then landing at its final destination, implying the beginning of a fateful encounter. The letter leads us to shy nurse Sissi who works at a psychiatric hospital. Later we learn that she was born at the hospital where her schizophrenic father is still a patient. The writer of the letter (Sissi's mother?) asks Sissi to retrieve a family heirloom from a bank. Meanwhile, brothers Walter (Joachim Krol) and Bodo plan a bank robbery at the same bank where Sissi's heirloom awaits.

One fateful day, Sissi makes a trip to the bank, but is hit by a truck. Bodo ducks under the truck to escape from security guards in pursuit of him and notices Sissi's distress, so he rescues her. A month and a half later, Sissi returns to the bank to retrieve the heirloom on the same day that the brothers decide to rob the bank and Sissi gets caught up in Bodo's criminal activity simply because she loves him. They escape, then hide out in the mental hospital, but a patient rats on them, so they escape again—this time to the seaside, where they live happily ever after despite their human frailties.

Tykwer's loyal followers will forgive *The Princess and The Warrior*'s flaws and go beyond suspending belief. While the rest of us will await another gem like *Run Lola Run* to manifest.

—*Patty-Lynne Herlevi*

## CREDITS

**Sissi:** Franka Potente
**Bodo:** Benno Furmann
**Walter:** Joachim Krol
**Sissi's Mother:** Marita Breuer
**Steini:** Lars Rudolph
**Schmatt:** Jurgen Tarrach
**Otto:** Melchior Beslon
**Werner Durr:** Ludger Pistor

**Origin:** Germany
**Language:** German
**Released:** 2000
**Production:** Stefan Arndt, Maria Kopf; X-Films Creative Pool; released by Sony Pictures Classics
**Directed by:** Tom Tykwer
**Written by:** Tom Tykwer
**Cinematography by:** Frank Griebe
**Music by:** Tom Tykwer, Johnny Klimek, Reinhold Heil
**Sound:** Arno Wilms, Elmar Wilms
**Editing:** Mathilde Bonnefoy
**Costumes:** Monika Jacobs
**Production Design:** Uli Hanisch
**MPAA rating:** R
**Running time:** 130 minutes

## REVIEWS

*Boxoffice.* November, 2000, p. 163.
*Chicago Sun-Times Online.* July 6, 2001.
*Entertainment Weekly.* July 20, 2001, p. 45.
*Hollywood Reporter.* September 19, 2000, p. 20.
*New York Times Online.* June 22, 2001.
*New York Times Online.* June 22, 2001.
*Sight and Sound.* July, 2001, p. 49.
*USA Today Online.* June 21, 2001.
*Variety.* September 18, 2000, p. 34.
*Washington Post.* July 13, 2001, p. WE37.

# The Princess Diaries

*She rocks. She rules. She reigns.*
—**Movie tagline**

**Box Office:** $108.2 million

One of the great joys of Meg Cabot's novel *The Princess Diaries* is the way it juxtaposes a teenage girl's everyday anxieties, like failing algebra class, with the surprising discovery that she is a princess and the heir to the throne of a small European country, the fictional Genovia. Told through the diary entries of Mia Thermopolis in an honest teenage voice tinged with just enough sarcasm and self-awareness to be believable, the novel is a fresh story that miraculously balances fairy tale whimsy with teenage angst.

Garry Marshall's film version, which was adapted to the screen by Gina Wendkos, lacks the edgy point of view that makes the novel a fresh coming-of-age story. Softened considerably, for example, are the heroine's concerns about her slowly developing breasts and her mother's sex life with one of her teachers. In the novel, Mia's father is a womanizer—in the film, he is recently deceased but imparts uplifting wisdom to his daughter through a letter at the film's climax. In the novel, Mia's grandmother, the queen, is an often shrewish, scary figure—in the film, she is played by the regal yet kind Julie Andrews with a humanity and inner glow befitting the screen legend she is. In short, one could rightly accuse the filmmakers of effacing the more mature aspects of the novel as well as the protagonist's wry point of view in favor of a wholesome, G-rated Cinderella tale. And yet, while the film lacks the quirkiness of the novel, it does succeed, on its own terms, as a sweet fairy tale of self-discovery for a 15-year-old girl who feels out of place in the world.

Mia (Anne Hathaway) lives with her single mother, Helen (Caroline Goodall), in a converted firehouse in San Francisco (transplanted from the New York of the novel). Helen is a bohemian artist, and Mia's best friend, Lilly (Heather Matarazzo), is a politically active teenager with her own talk show on cable TV. Poor Mia, with her frizzy, unmanageable hair and big glasses, is an awkward teen who is, at best, ignored by her classmates, and, at worst, viciously ridiculed. During debate class, she freezes at the podium and runs out of the room sick, which makes her an object of fun to all the pretty girls, especially popular cheerleader Lana (Mandy Moore).

When the grandmother she has never met, Clarisse Renaldi (Andrews), comes to visit Mia, her life changes instantly. She learns that she is the sole heir to the throne of Genovia (her long-absent father, the prince, has recently died, leaving no other children). Mia is, of course, startled and resists the notion of her being a princess since her only goal in life is to be invisible to everyone around her and avoid the scorn of her classmates. At first, she refuses to be taken under Clarisse's wing to learn the ways of royalty but finally relents when her mother persuades her to go along with her grandmother's instruction until the night of the royal ball. She can then decide if she wants to be presented to the public as the Genovian princess.

Mia is given lessons in posture, table manners, dance, literature, the royal wave—basically everything a young princess would need to know. Many of the scenes are funny, albeit in a predictable sort of way, and one cannot help but be reminded of Julia Roberts's transformation from hooker to society girl in Marshall's *Pretty Woman*. For Mia not only receives lessons in etiquette, as Roberts's Vivian did, but she is also physically transformed from the dorky, bespectacled teen to a graceful, young lady with plucked eyebrows, straightened hair, and contact lenses. Even the casting of Hector Elizondo as Joe, the head of security, who gives Mia dancing lessons and becomes a mentor of sorts, and Larry Miller as Paolo, the stylist who transforms her into a stunning knockout, hearkens back to Marshall's earlier take on the Pygmalion myth. *The Princess Diaries*, in short, veers close to feeling like a family-friendly version of *Pretty Woman* but never quite captures that film's spontaneous magic.

Mia's new look causes some problems, however. It sparks jealousy from Lilly and draws admiration from Lilly's brother, Michael (Robert Schwartzman), who clearly pines for her. Mia's true identity is soon revealed to the public, and hordes of press ambush Mia outside of school. It turns out that Paolo, so proud of the work he had done on Mia, alerted the press because he wanted public acclaim. (In the novel, the grandmother, who is not nearly as sympathetic as she is in the film, is the one responsible for the public revelation of Mia's royal lineage.)

Much of the fun of the early parts of *Diaries* revolves around an insecure teen coping with the idea that she is royalty. The situation may be farfetched, but the actors make the most of this comic dilemma, and Hathaway is both quite appealing and very funny in her awkward stage, when she has spunk and a certain sassy playfulness. Once the big physical transformation happens, however, Mia becomes a typical glamorous girl—virtually a fashion model whose struggles are simply not as compelling. Moreover, the film loses some of its energy and devolves into a series of clichéd episodes dealing with Mia's new life as a beauty. Interestingly enough, the novel does not contain a big transformation scene, which is obviously a Hollywood device, but instead focuses on a girl juggling family obligations, schoolwork, and cliques at school with her newfound identity while maintaining a wry, even sometimes acerbic voice, which is lacking in the film.

Marshall has clearly opted for a more conventional Hollywood story full of amusing but familiar comic setups, and they largely work because of Hathaway's deft comedic skills. There is a state dinner, for example, in which the clumsy Mia accidentally sets a man's sleeve on fire, breaks a champagne glass when tinkling the glass to call for a toast, and sets off a chain reaction of slapstick pratfalls. Then Mia and Clarisse spend a day seeing the sights in San Francisco, and Clarisse, in a cute scene, uses her royal influence to avert trouble with the police when Mia crashes her beloved Mustang into a cable car.

Mia's education, it seems, also extends to learning some tough lessons about being true to one's real friends. She accepts an invitation from Josh (Erik von Detten), the cutest boy in school, to go to a beach party on the same night she said she would watch Michael's band perform. She casually breaks her engagement with Michael, not even thinking that it may hurt his feelings. She also does not keep her word to appear on Lilly's talk show, which also happens to be taping on the same night. Mia is ultimately embarrassed at the party when Josh sets her up for a kiss in front of photographers, which, for some odd reason, is seen as a big scandal, and is further humiliated when Lana sets her up for another photo when she is getting dressed. The whole situation, however, seems contrived. Since Mia is not a callous person to begin with, it feels completely out of character for her to abandon her friends in the first place.

Similar episodes are handled with more nuance in the novel, mainly because we receive everything through Mia's diary entries and can better understand her inner struggles. There is, nonetheless, something oddly appealing about the situation in the film—the idea that a mere kiss on the lips could cause a huge scandal in today's seen-it-all world is quaint and even refreshing, although totally unbelievable. Because the beach party photos are splashed across the front page of the local newspaper, Clarisse does not feel that Mia is fit to rule, but Joe puts in a good word for her and thus serves as a kind of mediator for Clarisse and Mia, just as Elizondo's hotel manager did for Edward and Vivian in *Pretty Woman*.

All of Mia's little problems are gradually resolved in fairly conventional ways. Mia makes up with Lilly and passes gym by hitting a line drive that knocks Josh down in a softball game (thus getting even with him). She apologizes to Michael and invites him to the Genovian ball. She also gets even with Lana by shoving an ice cream cone on her when she is making fun of one of the unpopular students in school—a silly prank that is more fun in the novel.

The big climax of the story is the Genovian Ball, where Mia, still unconfident in her ability to rule, plans to renounce her title to the throne, which will, in effect, leave the small country without an heir and put it in the hands of foreigners. However, Clarisse gives Mia a gift from her late father for her 16th birthday. It is a diary, which includes a letter from him encouraging Mia to be brave. Inspired by his words, Mia races to the ball, where she accepts the title of princess and makes a speech in which she embraces her new role, which she feels will allow her to do good for others. The queen's assistants get Mia out of her regular clothes and dress her in a beautiful gown, and Michael shows up as her date. The story concludes with Mia flying to Genovia to assume her place on the throne.

Garry Marshall's film version of *The Princess Diaries* is not as rich or as smart as the novel, but it still has enough easygoing humor and fairy tale charm to win over audiences that are willing to accept some clichés and a few creaky plot turns. The film's gentle tone and good heart go a long way in turning a fairly formulaic enterprise into a pleasant summer diversion.

*—Peter N. Chumo II*

## CREDITS

**Mia Thermopolis:** Anne Hathaway
**Queen Clarisse Renaldi:** Julie Andrews
**Joe:** Hector Elizondo
**Lily Moscovitz:** Heather Matarazzo
**Josh Bryant:** Erik von Detten
**Lana Thomas:** Mandy Moore
**Michael Moscovitz:** Robert Schwartzman
**Helen:** Caroline Goodall
**Paolo:** Larry Miller
**Vice Principal Gupta:** Sandra Oh
**Mr. O'Connell:** Sean O'Bryan

**Origin:** USA
**Released:** 2001
**Production:** Whitney Houston, Debra Martin Chase, Mario Iscovich; Walt Disney Pictures, Brownhouse Productions; released by Buena Vista
**Directed by:** Garry Marshall
**Written by:** Gina Wendkos
**Cinematography by:** Karl Walter Lindenlaub
**Music by:** John Debney
**Sound:** Keith Wester
**Music Supervisor:** Dawn Soler
**Editing:** Bruce Green
**Art Direction:** Caty Maxey
**Costumes:** Gary Jones
**Production Design:** Mayne Berke
**MPAA rating:** G
**Running time:** 114 minutes

## REVIEWS

*Boxoffice.* September, 2001, p. 147.
*Chicago Sun-Times Online.* August 3, 2001.
*Entertainment Weekly.* August 10, 2001, p. 49.
*Los Angeles Times Online.* August 3, 2001.
*New York Times Online.* August 3, 2001.
*People.* August 13, 2001, p. 33.
*USA Today Online.* August 3, 2001.
*Variety.* July 30, 2001, p. 18.
*Washington Post.* August 3, 2001, p. WE37.

Mia (Anne Hathaway): "Most kids hope for a car for their 16th birthday, not a country."

Author Patricia Cabot uses the pen name Meg Cabot for her Princess series; she also writes under the name of Jenny Carroll.

# Rat Race

**Box Office:** $56.6 million

The opening credits of *Rat Race* feature all of the movie's principal characters represented as animated figures jostling each other for position on the screen. It is a cute, silly opening that sets the tone for this lark of a move, for *Rat Race* plays as a kind of human cartoon—full of zany chases, pratfalls, and slapstick. Director Jerry Zucker is known for wacky, fast-paced comedies like *Airplane!* and *Ruthless People,* and *Rat Race* carries on this tradition. The script by Andy Breckman is broad, and the execution is cheerfully over-the-top.

John Cleese plays a Las Vegas casino magnate, Donald Sinclair, a pure eccentric who engineers an outrageous contest in which a group of strangers race each other to claim two million dollars stashed in a locker 563 miles away in Silver City, New Mexico. At Sinclair's casino, six lucky guests who find a special gold coin in their slot machine winnings are summoned to a special penthouse meeting, where the contest is announced.

They make up an odd cross section of vacationers. Nick Shaffer (Breckin Meyer), the most straitlaced of the bunch, is leaving a wild bachelor party early when he wins his coin. Owen Templeton (Cuba Gooding, Jr.) is a football referee whose bad call on a coin toss at a big game has made him an outcast among sports fans. The Cody brothers, Duane (Seth Green) and Blaine (Vince Vieluf), are two schemers whose attempt at the beginning to fake an accident in the hotel lobby so that they can make some quick money results instead in a passerby getting injured. Vera Baker (Whoopi Goldberg) has just met her grownup daughter, Merrill Jennings (Lanai Chapman), for the first time since giving her up for adoption. Randy Pear (Jon Lovitz) is checking in for a family vacation with his wife, Bev (Kathy Najimy), and two kids. He seems to be a bit of a ne'er-do-well—his wife does not want him gambling, and he is currently out of work. Rounding out the ragtag group is Enrico Pollini (Rowan Atkinson), an Italian whose running shtick is that he is narcoleptic and keeps butchering the English language.

Once Sinclair gets the race going, the players are off on a mad dash to get to the locker first. At the same time, the players are, unbeknownst to them, part of another game—Sinclair and his wealthy friends, an international group of tycoons, are tracking the players' progress and placing bets among themselves on who will be victorious in the quest.

When the Cody brothers cannot get an airplane, they disable the airport's radar tracking system, and the contestants are left to find other means of transportation out of Las Vegas. Owen takes a taxi, but the driver, Gus (Paul Rodriguez), turns out to be a football fan who lost $20,000 on the game Owen botched, and he leaves Owen stranded in the desert and stripped of most of his clothes. Owen later tricks a bus driver out of his uniform and ends up driving a busload of Lucille Ball impersonators on their way to an *I Love Lucy* convention. Nick meets Tracy Faucet (Amy Smart), a helicopter pilot, and persuades her to take him to Silver City. At first, he was not even going to compete, but, when he realizes that he will be the only one who can fly out, he decides to take a chance. It does not hurt that he is starting to fall for the cute Tracy. Meanwhile, Randy, telling his wife that he has a job interview, whisks his family away on such a mad car trip that they can barely catch their breath.

The fun of *Rat Race* lies in its sheer goofiness. It is a madcap romp in which one outlandish event after another conspires to stymie the participants in their goal. Vera and Merrill, for example, meet a crazy lady (Kathy Bates) on the side of the road who desperately wants to sell them a squirrel. When they turn her down and ask for directions, she gets revenge by leading them down a steep cliff, where their rental car crashes. Randy faces similarly outrageous events when his wife and kids beg him to stop at a Barbie museum advertised on the road. It turns out, however, that the museum honors not the beloved doll but rather an infamous Nazi and is run by skinheads. The joke does not stop there but keeps getting bigger—the Jewish family flee by driving off in Hitler's Mercedes and nearly get killed when they crash the infamous car, decked out in swastikas, into a World War II veterans' rally.

Other episodes rely more on twisting the characters in surprising ways. Nick and Tracy make a short detour over to her boyfriend's house, but, when she finds him in his swimming pool with his ex-girlfriend, the mild-mannered Tracy is transformed into a madwoman who bears down on him and chases him, finally crashing her helicopter and then stealing his truck. Nick is reluctant to join her but finally goes along, which suggests that the straight arrow is finally loosening up and willing to do something loony.

Pollini, whose narcolepsy keeps him in the hotel lobby sleeping standing up, gets off to a slow start but gets hit by an ambulance as soon as he leaves the casino. So the driver, Zack (Wayne Knight), offers him a ride because he fears a lawsuit when famed attorney Gloria Allred (playing herself in a funny cameo), suddenly appears. Pollini's antics revolve around a human heart that the ambulance is transporting for an operation. The heart falls out of the speeding ambulance and ultimately ends up in the mouth of a dog. Figuring that he needs a fresh heart to replace the damaged one, Zack contemplates killing Pollini, who ultimately flees and, like a cartoon character defying the laws of physics, leaps onto a speeding train.

The Cody brothers have the wildest adventure. They decide to make a copy of the locker key and split up, thus doubling their chances of getting to the money first. But the key maker hears them talking about the two-million-dollar prize and steals the original key, leaving them with two blanks. They chase the thief to a field full of hot air balloons, where he tries to make his getaway but ends up, improbably enough, with a cow attached to a rope dangling from his balloon as the brothers finally wrest the key from him. Later, the Codys drive their car into a monster truck gathering and narrowly escape their car before it is crushed.

While some of these situations are funnier than others, *Rat Race* is quite clever in the way it deftly interweaves several story lines and has them intersect in surprising, unbelievable ways. Owen, for example, drives into the cow hanging from the hot air balloon and runs the bus of Lucys off the road. He finally confesses that he is not a real bus driver, and the angered Lucys gang up on him, forcing him to run for his life. Meanwhile, rounding out the general nuttiness, Sinclair and his rich cronies are making odd side bets. For example, Sinclair has his deadpan lawyer, Mr. Grisham (Dave Thomas), make a bizarre request from a prostitute named Vicky (Brandy Ledford), so that the group can wager on what her fee will be.

*Rat Race* seeks nothing more than to entertain its audience with the silliest gags, each one seeming to compound the outlandish dilemmas of each story, and, fortunately, enough of these jokes pay off, no matter how farfetched the situations. Vera and her daughter, for example, no sooner leave their crashed car than they stumble into an area where a rocket-shaped car is about to attempt to break the land-speed record. The women steal the car and race off with it, but the speed is so great that, when they come to a stop, they are disoriented, stagger out, and get hauled onto a bus carrying a group of retarded people. The jokes may be obvious and totally unbelievable, but most are funny nonetheless.

Eventually, everyone makes it to Silver City at about the same time. Pollini gets to the locker first, but, just when the money seems to be his, he falls asleep with his key in the lock. When everyone else arrives, madness ensues, and a struggle breaks out to open the locker, which turns out to be empty. Mr. Grisham and Vicky, now seemingly a team, have

somehow gotten hold of the bag of money and drive off with it but are ambushed when the cow, appearing one last time, falls on them and the key maker is able to fasten the bag to his balloon. When all the players finally catch up with the balloon and are ready to split the prize, they suddenly find themselves in the middle of a rock concert to feed the hungry of the world. Because everyone at the show thinks that the players are making a huge donation to the charity, they are, in effect, forced to give the money away. However, Sinclair and his friends arrive, and the last laugh is on them when Nick gives them credit for the contribution and promises that they will match all donations to the cause. Because it would be a big embarrassment not to go along with such a public display of generosity, Sinclair and his cohorts are going to have to pay over 20 million dollars as the tote board goes crazy.

The success of *Rat Race* is all the sweeter when one considers that it triumphs with a fairly thin premise and a roster of B-list actors that may not seem especially promising. Admittedly, Zucker's laughfest is not without its problems, including a running time that may be a bit long and a wobbly climax that feels like a copout, but *Rat Race* is still one of the most consistently satisfying and good-hearted comedies in an otherwise dreary summer.

—*Peter N. Chumo II*

## CREDITS

**Donald Sinclair:** John Cleese
**Vera Baker:** Whoopi Goldberg
**Owen Templeton:** Cuba Gooding Jr.
**Randy Pear:** Jon Lovitz
**Nick Schaffer:** Breckin Meyer
**Tracy Faucet:** Amy Smart
**Duane Cody:** Seth Green
**Bev Pear:** Kathy Najimy
**Enrico Pollini:** Rowan Atkinson
**Zack:** Wayne Knight
**Blaine Cody:** Vince Vieluf
**Merrill Jennings:** Lanei Chapman
**Gus:** Paul Rodriguez

**Origin:** USA
**Released:** 2001
**Production:** Jerry Zucker, Sean Daniel, Janet Zucker; Fireworks Pictures, Alphaville; released by Paramount Pictures
**Directed by:** Jerry Zucker
**Written by:** Andy Breckman
**Cinematography by:** Thomas Ackerman

**Music by:** John Powell
**Sound:** Jeff Wexler, David Ronne, Doug Johnston
**Music Supervisor:** Bonnie Greenberg-Goldman
**Editing:** Tom Lewis
**Art Direction:** Doug Byggdin, Seth Reed
**Costumes:** Ellen Mirojnick
**Production Design:** Gary Frutkoff
**MPAA rating:** PG-13
**Running time:** 92 minutes

## REVIEWS

*Boxoffice.* October, 2001, p. 62.
*Entertainment Weekly.* August 24, 2001, p. 97.
*Los Angeles Times Online.* August 17, 2001.
*New York Times Online.* August 17, 2001.
*People.* August 27, 2001, p. 36.
*Time.* August 20, 2001, p. 70.
*USA Today Online.* August 17, 2001.
*Variety.* August 13, 2001, p. 44.
*Washington Post.* August 17, 2001, p. WE34.

## QUOTES

Donald Sinclair (John Cleese) on the race: "The only rule is that there are no rules."

# Riding in Cars with Boys

*The story of a girl who did everything wrong, but got everything right.*
—Movie tagline

**Box Office:** $29.8 million

Beverly Donofrio (Drew Barrymore) is a young woman with a dream—to go to college and become a writer. Beverly, however, is also a young woman prone to all the emotional entanglements and hormones that plague the lives of those in high school. Beverly has not only set her professional sights high, she's also has a crush on one of the school's most popular boys. So, combining her two goals, she writes the big man on campus a poem and musters up the courage to give it to him at a party she and her pals Tina (Sara Gilbert) and Fay (Brittany Murphy) have crashed.

What follows is a lot of ridicule and tears and ends with Beverly locking herself in the bathroom that is already occupied by Raymond (Steve Zahn).

Raymond is the stereotypical high school slacker. He takes drugs and drinks but he's also a bit slow and the drugs he ends up stealing from the bathroom cabinet are birth control pills, which he washes down with swigs of water from a bidet. Nonetheless, Ray is also a basically nice guy and he becomes very concerned about the weeping Beverly who has just invaded his party sanctuary. He talks to her, calms her, and eventually becomes her white knight by returning to the party and slugging out the inconsiderate jock who was the source of her sobbing.

Well, one thing leads to another and the next thing you know, Beverly is riding around in a car with Raymond and making out with him as not only the car windows but also her future become fogged up because, you see, Beverly becomes pregnant. This throws an incredible monkey wrench into her plans, especially since this is the 1960s, and very reluctantly she agrees to marry Ray even though, in her words, "You are not the guy I'm supposed to end up with." But then how can she refuse Ray, who responds with, "Please marry me because I'm shit without you." Now there's a proposal no 15-year-old pregnant girl could possibly refuse.

Of course telling her traditional, Italian, Catholic parents (Lorraine Bracco and James Woods) is not going to be easy, especially since her father is the chief of police. So, resorting to her writing talents, she writes them a note. Her father's reaction is typical: "You were special and you ruined your life and you broke my heart." So Beverly and Ray marry primarily to please her father, but nobody is happy, except for maybe the oblivious Ray who can't believe his good luck at landing Bev.

The wedding that follows is seen as a trial by Bev's father, who toasts the friends who are standing by him in his time of trouble but never toasts his daughter's happiness or future. And so the screw-up and the over-achiever set out on life together and await the arrival of their baby in a run-down shack of a house on a dead-end cul-de-sac. Luckily for Bev, but maybe not so lucky for Fay, Fay is also pregnant. Now the two teenagers can go through the experience together. Bev eventually gives birth to a baby boy, Jason, while Fay gives birth to a girl, Amelia, and both try to get on with their lives. Considering Beverly's original plans, however, that is almost impossible while saddled with a needy baby and an even needier and irresponsible husband.

Believe it or not, it will get worse. Ray will become a heroin addict and a once pimply-faced classmate (now handsome and a Berkeley graduate) shows up on Bev's doorstep to tempt Bev with visions of freedom in California. Could it get any worse? Yep. Bev and Fay are arrested by Bev's own father after he is tipped off by Bev's own young son that the two are in the kitchen drying and bagging marijuana. The question becomes who is to blame for Beverly's life going off track? Is it Ray? Is it Jason? Or should Bev accept responsibility herself for what her life has become? These are intriguing questions with no easy answer.

The story of *Riding in Cars With Boys* is told through a frame. The 35-year-old Bev is picked up by a young man who will be driving her somewhere. We don't know where they're going or who the young man is. He's just another boy in whose car Beverly will be riding. It is a coy device, because we will eventually learn that the young man is really Bev's grown son, Jason. It is also a device that is not in the original 1990 memoir written by Donofrio. It is not the only detour the movie makes from the original.

Donofrio's book, which shares its title with the movie and chronicles her life from 1961 to 1986, is funny and sometimes painful, but Donofrio's writing style is entertaining, casual and witty. Somehow, this is all diluted when the job of writing the screenplay was given to Morgan Upton Ward (*A Pyromaniac's Love Story*). Perhaps the problem is that he is a man and seems more interested in Ray (a wonderfully well-written character) and Jason (who inexplicably gets to do the film's voiceover) than in Beverly, whose story it actually is. Be that as it may, Donofrio was included in the making of the movie and she has indicated that she is happy with the final product. And as for that fictional framing device, which has Jason and his mother going to see his father to get a release for her book, it actually did happen, but the release was for the movie makers not the publishers.

Producer James L. Brooks must have loved this story right from the start, because he optioned the rights in 1989 when it was still a manuscript. Interestingly enough, the production was put on hold for a while, which was good for Barrymore because she was only 14 at the time. The role of Beverly Donofrio is well served by Drew Barrymore. In fact, Barrymore's intrinsic likableness was a characteristic the real Beverly Donofrio latched on to for the actress who would portray her on the screen. Why? Because Beverly is basically a flawed character, which may make her more interesting, but can also make her hard to like or identify with. Even on screen, she comes off as annoying and selfish, as rebellious and resentful, as smart but also stupid. Barrymore deserves credit for taking on this basically unlikable character and helping to convey her complexities as she goes from headstrong teenager to seemingly indifferent 35-year-old. Barrymore helps us to see that underlying all the yelling and whining, beneath all the self-centeredness and bad mothering is a woman who has a dream and the determination to obtain it.

Barrymore also proves herself to be adept at both the dramatic scenes and the comic ones. Especially funny are her attempts to end her pregnancy by "falling" down the stairs. (FYI: Donofrio did finally make it to college, attending Wesleyan University, then going on to receive a masters in

creative writing from Columbia. She is currently working on a historical novel and is engaged with a wedding planned for 2002.)

Adam Garcia, who plays Bev's grown son Jason, does a good job of hiding his natural Australian accent, but he seems too old for the part once we realize who he is. (In fact, Garcia is only two years older than Barrymore.) His role in the film is minimal and he looks thoroughly uncomfortable in all his scenes. Maybe that's because he only has two plot lines: driving his mother to see his estranged father and trying to hook up with Amelia. Neither plot point is in the original book and the romance is purely fictional. (FYI: it must be in the genes, because Jason is currently working on his own memoir.)

If there is one actor who absolutely shines in *Riding*, it is Steve Zahn. Zahn has made a career playing lovable goofballs and it would have been easy for him to play Ray as just one more endearing loser. Zahn, however gives Ray real depth. In his capable portrayal, Ray becomes a man with a good heart but no brain to rudder his life. He, too, is a victim of what life has thrown his way. In fact, Zahn's Ray helps us to realize the incredibly sad fact that Beverly probably IS the best thing that ever happened to him, and he hasn't a clue how to hold on to her. Ray could have been an immensely unlikable character, an unreliable, drug and alcohol-addicted loser, but in Zahn's hands we also see his vulnerability. Ray does love his son and wife, he knows when he screws up, but he is clueless as to how to change his life. When we see him at the end of the film, living in a seedy trailer with a shrewish second wife (an unbilled Rosie Perez), a mere shell of his former self, our hearts break. For this man who could never cope, nothing has changed, and for that reason, we never see his final redemption coming. (The real Ray died several years ago.)

It's odd that the most endearing and touching character in this chick flick is a man, especially since not only was the story written by a woman about her own life, but also because it was directed by a woman who lived through similar experiences. Director Penny Marshall should have found a resonant chord in Beverley Donofrio's experiences since Marshall herself was married and became pregnant at the early age of 18. So why is Ray the character we remember? Marshall's movies always have heart, and this one does too, but it's symbolized in Ray not Beverly.

*Riding in Cars With Boys* ends up being a bittersweet comedy that vacillates between energy and too much riding in cars. (Beverly also rides with her father in several scenes.) Thankfully it doesn't try to sweeten up Beverly's character and opts for the humor of the human condition over Hollywood treacle. It, undoubtedly, will not be to everyone's taste, chick flicks rarely are, but in the end it tells an interesting story and the characters, especially Ray, are worth the time one spends with them. 🎞

*—Beverley Bare Buehrer*

## CREDITS

**Beverly Donofrio:** Drew Barrymore
**Ray Hasek:** Steve Zahn
**Fay Forrester:** Brittany Murphy
**Jason Donofrio:** Adam Garcia
**Mrs. Donofrio:** Lorraine Bracco
**Mr. Donofrio:** James Woods
**Tina:** Sara Gilbert
**Bobby:** Desmond Harrington
**Lizard:** David Moscow
**Amelia:** Maggie Gyllenhaal
**Tommy Butcher:** Peter Facinelli
**Janet Donofrio:** Marisa Ryan
**Beverly (age 11):** Mika Boorem
**Amelia (age 8):** Skye McCole Bartusiak
**Jason (age 8):** Logan Lerman

**Origin:** USA
**Released:** 2001
**Production:** James L. Brooks, Julie Ansell, Richard Sadai; Gracie Films; released by Columbia Pictures
**Directed by:** Penny Marshall
**Written by:** Morgan Ward
**Cinematography by:** Miroslav Ondricek
**Music by:** Hans Zimmer
**Sound:** T.J. O'Mara
**Editing:** Lawrence Jordan, Richard Marks
**Art Direction:** Teresa Carriker-Thayer
**Costumes:** Cynthia Flynt
**Production Design:** Bill Groom
**MPAA rating:** PG-13
**Running time:** 132 minutes

## REVIEWS

*Boxoffice.* November, 2001, p. 61.
*Chicago Sun-Times Online.* October 19, 2001.
*Chicago Tribune Online.* October 19, 2001.
*Entertainment Weekly.* October 26, 2001, p. 91.
*Hollywood Reporter Online.* October 12, 2001.
*Los Angeles Times Online.* October 19, 2001.
*New York Post Online.* October 19, 2001.
*New York Times Online.* October 19, 2001.
*People.* October 29, 2001, p. 39.
*USA Today Online.* October 18, 2001.
*Variety.* October 15, 2001, p. 33.
*Village Voice Online.* October 17, 2001.
*Washington Post.* October 19, 2001, p. C5.

## QUOTES

Beverly (Drew Barrymore): "One day can make your life; one day can ruin your life. All life is is four or five big days that change everything."

## TRIVIA

The real Beverly and Jason Donofrio appear as weddings guests sitting behind Drew Barrymore.

# The River (He Liu)

In its own quiet way, *The River* makes a bold statement about the devastating effects of repressed behavior. Ming-liang Tsai's film deserves patience and undivided attention from audiences. In his other films Tsai explored similar issues. Here, his plot centers around a highly dysfunctional family of three living in Tawain. The grown son, Kang-Sheng (Kang-sheng Lee), feels adrift and tries to find work as an extra in the movies. The mother (Hsiao-Lin Lu) seeks the attention of an inattentive lover (Shiao-Lin Lu), and the father (Tien Miao) turns to anonymous sex in gay bathhouses.

After Kang-Sheng finds work as the body double for a corpse in a movie production, he starts getting severe headaches. Kang-Sheng is forced to stop working and start finding a solution to his physical pain. He even visits a mystical monk, but can't seem to shake his misery. At least, however, the young man is finally feeling something in life, unlike his father, who works obsessively on a leaky roof in his bedroom, and his mother, who doesn't seem to care that her lover is a pornographer.

Finally in a twist on the *Oedipus* legend, both father and son end up in the same bathhouse, looking for the same sort of escape from life. Their encounter is a devastating one. Simple as the plot sounds, Tsai makes it contemplative. Like his other films, *Viva L'Amour* and *What Time Is It There?*, *The River* says a lot without a lot of words (or, for that matter music, close-ups, or a moving camera). It is almost as though Tsai has adopted the Dogma 95 rules, and *The River* does contain some of the same sort of understated humor in the face of social tragedy.

Don't confuse this *River* with earlier films by the same title (directed by Pare Lorentz, Jean Renoir, and Mark Rydell), or the recent Chinese film that remade *Vertigo.*

With its spare but rigorously controlled production, and worthwhile topics regarding sexual identity, social alienation, and the role of the environment in everyday life, *The River* deserves its own place as a important piece of work.

—*Eric Monder*

## CREDITS

**Xiao-Kang:** Kang-sheng Lee
**Mother:** Hsiao-Ling Lu
**Father:** Tien Miao
**Mother's lover:** Shiao-Lin Lu
**Girl:** Shiang-chyi Chen
**Director:** Ann Hui

**Origin:** Taiwan
**Language:** Chinese
**Released:** 1997
**Production:** Li-Kong Hsu, Shun-Ching Chiu; released by Leisure Time Features
**Directed by:** Ming-liang Tsai
**Written by:** Ming-liang Tsai, Yi-chun Tsai, Bi-ying Yang
**Cinematography by:** Pen-jung Liao
**Editing:** Sheng-Chang Chen, Chen-Ching Lei
**Art Direction:** Pao-lin Lee
**Costumes:** Wang Yu
**Production Design:** Tony Lan
**MPAA rating:** Unrated
**Running time:** 115 minutes

## REVIEWS

*New York Times Online.* July 27, 2001.
*San Francisco Chronicle.* October 26, 2001, p. C3.
*San Francisco Examiner Online.* April 27, 2001.

# The Road Home (Wo De Fu Qin Mu Qin)

**Box Office:** $1.2 million

Timing is everything in the movie business and determines whether or not an international film will break into the American boxoffice. Marry timing to star power and a strong story and success is (almost) insured. Take for instance the release of *The Road Home*, directed by Zhang Yimou. The film was produced in 1999 and stars Zhang Ziyi in her debut cinematic role; Ziyi then went on to star in Ang Lee's smash hit *Crouching Tiger, Hidden Dragon*, sending the young actress into the stellar heights of international stardom. Because of this newly acquired fame, Ziyi had become the star power that pulls audiences into Yimou's *The Road Home*.

Of course, Yimou has already made a name for himself—at least in the arthouse circuit—with such Chinese classics as *Raise the Red Lantern*, *Red Sorghum*, *Shanghai Triad*, and *Not One Less*. In a press kit interview Yimou reflected on his interest in Iranian cinema as well as his use of non-professional actors. Yimou cites Iranian director Abbas Kiarostami as a key influence, especially with the production of *Not One Less*, in which Yimou also employed non-professional performers; he notes that *The Road Home* is "closer to another Chinese tradition, that of the poetic narrative." Unlike Iranian cinema, Yimou chose to shoot his contemporary footage in black and white, while shooting the characters' memories or past events in color. The funeral sequence was shot in black and white while the courtship of Luo Yusheng's (Sun Honglei) parents appears in warm amber tones even in the midst of winter. This psychological approach pulls on viewers' heartstrings by presenting the past as a last bastion of happiness and presenting the future as bleak and stark.

As the film opens, Luo Yusheng drives to his birthplace in Northern China. He meets with the village's elderly mayor (Chang Guifa), who reveals the details of Yusheng's father's recent death. The mayor also confides to the young man about his mother's wish to perform an ancient funeral service in which her husband's body would be carried from the morgue for several miles by foot to his final resting place, so that he will know his way home. Although the mother (Zhao Yuelin) takes an adamant stance regarding this special ceremony for her loved one, the mayor fears that the elderly men of the village wouldn't be able to carry out the arduous task. So Yusheng visits his mother in hopes of convincing her to forgo the ceremony. Only she's persistent in not only providing her husband this last rite but also in weaving his funeral shroud through the night. Yusheng finds a photograph of his mother and father during their courtship and the film's narrative travels back in time to when Yusheng's parents first met.

While the opening black and white sequence recalls arthouse films of a bygone era, the nostalgic color section that follows recalls both the simple composition of an Iranian film and a majestic love story of a Hollywood classic. The middle portion of the film provides viewers with poetic narrative, epic-style photography in which the landscape's beauty is carefully rendered, and a heart-wrenching performance by a leading lady. And to further emphasize Zhao Di's girlish sweetness, cinematographer Hou Yong's camera gazes on Ziyi's face in the same compassionate fashion as it shoots the surrounding landscape. The fateful day in which 20-year-old teacher Luo Changyu (Zheng Hao) arrives in town, we see Zhao running through a field, framed by amber grain, as she sneaks a peek at her first and only love. Further into the story, on another fateful and dire occasion, we see Zhao running across a golden field as she frantically tries to catch up with the teacher who has been summoned back to the city.

Zhao, who happens to be the prettiest girl in the village, is also an illiterate peasant living with her blind grandmother. Changyu, on the other hand, is sophisticated and out of her league. However, that doesn't stop Zhao from winning his heart. After all, her cooking talents and sweetness certainly make up for her lowly birth. She lovingly cooks special dishes, hoping that the teacher will choose her dishes from the many awaiting him during the construction process of the new school. When it is her turn to invite the teacher to her home for dinner, she spends all day cooking a special meal hoping that he'll return her love.

But then the teacher is suddenly called back to the city. He's forced to turn down a second dinner invitation, but gives a small token, a hair clip, to Zhao. In one of the most heartbreaking scenes in the film, Zhao chases after Changyu's wagon while carrying a bowl of mushroom dumplings. Not only does she fall and drop the contents of the bowl, she loses her precious hair clip in her flight. Changyu promised Zhao that he would return on a specific day in the middle of winter. So on that day Zhao stands in a field waiting for his arrival, despite the freezing temperature. She develops pneumonia and the teacher never does arrive. Later, she sets out to the city where she hopes to bring Changyu back. Again, she lands in the sick bed.

When Luo Changyu hears of Zhao's condition he returns to the village. But because he broke the law, he's again summoned back to the city. After two year's detainment, he returns to the village and never leaves Zhao until his death. The story returns to the present and Yusheng decides to honor his mother's wishes. He hires men from surrounding villages to carry his father's coffin, but the men refuse payment as they honor the teacher. Scene by scene Yimou carefully builds to a tear-stained conclusion, making *The Road Home* a top 10 heartbreaker for 2001.

—*Patty-Lynne Herlevi*

**Zhao Di:** Zhang Ziyi

**Luo Yusheng:** Sun Honglei
**Luo Changyu:** Zheng Hao
**Elderly Zhao Di:** Zhao Yuelin
**Grandmother:** Li Bin

**Origin:** China
**Language:** Chinese
**Released:** 1999
**Production:** Zhao Yu; Guangxi Film Studio, Columbia Film Production Asia, Beijing New Picture Distribution Company; released by Sony Pictures Classics
**Directed by:** Zhang Yimou
**Written by:** Bao Shi
**Cinematography by:** Hou Yong
**Music by:** San Bao
**Sound:** Wu Lala
**Editing:** Zhai Ru
**Art Direction:** Cao Jiuping
**Costumes:** Dong Huamiao
**MPAA rating:** G
**Running time:** 100 minutes

**REVIEWS**

*Boxoffice.* April, 2001, p. 219.
*Entertainment Weekly.* June 8, 2001, p. 47.
*Los Angeles Times Online.* May 25, 2001.
*New York Times Online.* May 25, 2001.
*RANT.* November/December, 2000, p. 28.
*San Francisco Chronicle Online.* June 8, 2001.
*Seattle Weekly Online.* June 21, 2001.
*USA Today Online.* May 24, 2001.
*Washington Post Online.* June 8, 2001.

# Rock Star

*The story of a wannabe who got to be.*
—Movie tagline

 **Box Office:** $17 million

Mark Wahlberg is an incredibly winsome actor, projecting a childlike innocence that engages audiences and engenders sympathy even for characters who are venal or selfish. These qualities elevate *Rock Star* above the middling level of its pedestrian plot. Since *A Star Is Born*—and even before that—Hollywood has been making movies about ordinary people who get their big shot at entertainment fame, succeed beyond their wildest dreams, and inevitably suffer disillusionment. *Rock Star* is just one more such picture, differing from the rest only in that it is the first (and presumably also the last) to apply the formula to the genre of 1980s heavy-metal rock-and-roll.

Wahlberg is ideally suited to play the role of a formulaic dinosaur rock star wanna-be— both because of his winning personality and because he started his career as a hip-hop singer known as Marky Mark. Wahlberg proved he could handle similar territory in the acclaimed *Boogie Nights.* In that film, he plays Dirk, an ordinary guy who becomes a porn star. Here, he plays Chris Cole, an ordinary guy who becomes a rock star. In both films, he projects the bemused air of an adulated stranger in a strange land. In *Boogie Nights,* however, Wahlberg's character is corrupted by his experiences as an on-camera stud. In *Rock Star,* despite sexual escapades and ego trips that are potentially just as damaging to the psyche, Walhberg's character inexplicably emerges unscathed. It's that kind of movie—not at all deep and not at all apologetic for being shallow.

And why should it be? Director Steve Herek isn't exactly a heavy hitter (his roster of previous movies includes *Bill & Ted's Excellent Adventures, The Mighty Ducks,* and *101 Dalmatians*). Working from an intermittently clever script by John Stockwell, it's clear that Herek is out to enjoy himself, and let audiences enjoy themselves, and his explorations of the rock star scene are closer to a travelogue than an exegesis. *Almost Famous,* another recent film about a young man's eye-opening journey into the hyperbolic celebrity music world, explores how fame and its temptations twist and distort souls, emotions and relationships. *Rock Star* doesn't even attempt such introspection, and when it tries to deal with emotional fallout, it confines its scope to predictable, soap-opera-like scenes about how unlimited access to groupies damages Chris's relationship with longtime girlfriend and manager, Emily (Jennifer Aniston).

Despite its self-imposed limitations, however, *Rock Star* is fairly observant, piling up telling iconic moments that paint a fairly believable, if pedestrian, picture of the heavy metal scene. In Pittsburgh, Chris is a copy machine repairman and the lead singer for Blood Pollution, a "tribute band" for the popular British metal group Steel Dragon. Chris repeatedly insists it is not a "cover band," even though Blood Pollution performs only Steel Dragon songs and imitates the band's dress, mannerisms, and stage moves. Chris is obsessed with becoming a clone of Steel Dragon's lead singer, Bobby Beers (Jason Flemyng), and he does not tolerate any band members who deviate, even by a single chord, from the canon of his heroes. Chris demonstrates his encyclopedic knowledge of Steel Dragon trivia in several scenes, including one in which he dresses down a member of a rival band who has purchased a Steel Dragon jacket he thinks is authentic but Chris knows to be fake.

Herek takes paints to portray Chris as a regular guy who just happens to be obsessed with a rock star. He still lives at home with his supportive and tolerant parents (his mother (Beth Grant) runs a child care center in the house and his dad (Michael Shamus Wiles), presumably, works in a steel mill). His brother, a policeman, makes fun of him for being juvenile and unable to live on his own. Being a heavy metal clone can cause problems on the job, it seems—as in one laughably lame scene where a client spies a speck of stray mascara on Chris's eyelid. And that's about all *Rock Star* has to say about Chris's ambition. We never get a sense of why Chris is so driven, and, more importantly, how this kind of music has taken hold of his soul. Strip away the clothes and the makeup and the music, and this could be the story of an overgrown adolescent enthralled with any celebrity. That's one of the problems with *Rock Star:* for all its attention to the scenery of arena concerts and long-haired men striking phallic poses with screeching guitars, it has nothing to say about the meaning of rock music in general or heavy metal in particular.

The plot unfolds with stunning predictability: Band members who want to do their own music revolt against Chris's straightjacket "tribute band" approach and replace him with a more pliable lead singer. There is an angry band break-up scene followed by a tearful coming-to-terms-with-self-and-dreams scene with Emily in a parked car in the rain. Then, one day, out of the blue, the big phone call comes: Steel Dragon invites Chris to audition for the band. In one of the low points of the film, Chris and Emily arrive at one of the band member's mansions, which doubles as a recording studio, to find their heroes feuding. Just as his band forced Chris out, Steel Dragon is forcing Bobby Beers to leave, but the main reason, it appears, is not so much artistic differences as the fact that Bobby is gay. Why that would matter in a world of rampant and ubiquitous sexual license is left unexplained. This scene is not nearly as stilted as what happens when Chris (renamed Izzy) makes his stage debut, falls down a set of stairs during his big entrance, and ends up playing the rest of the night with blood streaming down his face.

At times, the makers of *Rock Star* seem to be toying with the notion of exploring something deeper. The after-concert club party to which Chris and Emily repair after his electrifying debut with the band turns into a strobe-lit multiple seduction dance, with a laughably oversexed vixen named Tania (Dagmara Dominczyk) coming on to both of them. There's a cruel revelation about Tania awaiting them when the newcomers to Oz wake up in a hotel room of naked bodies. These scenes capture well the disorientation of the ingenues as they enter a world that seems both exhilaratingly free and threatening. Unfortunately, the tantalizing possibilities of moral deterioration are left largely unexplored as the plot descends into the cliched rapid-fire montage of the endless road tour. Emily finds herself stuck with the wives and girlfriends in the van that follows the band's bus, where the groupies entertain their men, and the film moves quickly to the inevitable scene in which Emily leaves the tour, unable to compete with the seductions of fame.

By the time they next meet, Chris is lost in a fog of drugs and sex and Emily finds herself in a line of groupies awaiting their turns at the celebrity meat market. But these dark clouds miraculously part. With little explanation, Chris eventually walks out on the scene that was once his dream and turns up in a Seattle coffeehouse singing gentle angst-ridden songs of his own composing in an acoustic folk-rock group. The 1980s have become the 1990s, and Chris has suddenly grown up. It's not the kind of transformation many heavy metal singers actually have made, but it makes a convenient cultural shorthand for audiences of a certain age.

Throughout his odyssey, Chris undergoes only temporary and superficial changes, and he emerges as the same nice guy he was before he entered the world of stardom—just a little older and wiser. Wahlberg's charms help obscure this lack of development in Chris's character. Herek doesn't seem interested in—or capable of—exploring what happens to an obsessive personality when he gets to live his ultimate dream and finds it lacking. In *Rock Star,* both the music and the celebrity scene are surprisingly devoid of any emotional potency, and watching the film is like watching an entire set of actors going through the motions. There is no danger and little discovery in the music, and no notion of what it might represent to its followers. Herek takes a light, happy-go-lucky approach, and the movie ends up being as mainstream as heavy metal itself has become, despite all its poses.

Besides Wahlberg, who is always a pleasure to watch, the movie's greatest diversions come not from Aniston (who doesn't look or act the part of a heavy metal girlfriend, but more like a cast member of *Friends* lost on a strange set) but from the British character actor Timothy Spall. Spall, best known as a reliable member of director Mike Leigh's casts, plays Steel Dragon's manager, Mats, a paunchy, seen-it-all, philosophical type. Spall gives the character far more nuance and appeal than the script bestows; he's a standout. The rest of the supporting cast can't break out of the cardboard cut-out molds that screenwriter Stockwell has constructed for them.

*Rock Star* is enjoyable brain candy, but breaks no new ground, even as middling entertainment. Wahlberg is more or less reprising his role in *Boogie Nights,* but with far weaker material. He deserves—and should select—more challenging roles, rather than more beauty parts.

—*Michael Betzold*

## CREDITS

**Chris Cole:** Mark Wahlberg

**Emily Poule:** Jennifer Aniston
**Rob:** Timothy Olyphant
**Mats:** Timothy Spall
**Bobby Beers:** Jason Flemyng
**Kirk Cuddy:** Dominic West
**Joe Jr.:** Matthew Glave
**Mrs. Cole:** Beth Grant
**Bradley:** Stephan Jenkins
**A.C.:** Jason Bonham
**Kirk's wife:** Heidi Mark
**Mr. Cole:** Michael Shamus Wiles
**Tania Asher:** Dagmara Dominczyk
**A.C.'s wife:** Rachel Hunter

**Origin:** USA
**Released:** 2001
**Production:** Robert Lawrence, Toby Jaffe; Bel-Air Entertainment, Maysville Pictures; released by Warner Bros.
**Directed by:** Stephen Herek
**Written by:** John Stockwell
**Cinematography by:** Ueli Steiger
**Music by:** Trevor Rabin
**Sound:** Petur Hliddal
**Music Supervisor:** Budd Carr
**Editing:** Trudy Ship
**Art Direction:** Caty Maxey
**Costumes:** Aggie Guerard Rodgers
**Production Design:** Mayne Berke
**MPAA rating:** R
**Running time:** 106 minutes

## REVIEWS

*Chicago Sun-Times Online.* September 7, 2001.
*Entertainment Weekly.* September 14, 2001, p. 61.
*Hollywood Reporter.* September 4, 2001, p. 19.
*Los Angeles Times Online.* September 7, 2001.
*New York Times Online.* September 7, 2001.
*USA Today Online.* September 7, 2001.
*Variety.* September 3, 2001, p. 38.
*Washington Post.* September 7, 2001, p. WE41.

## QUOTES

Road manager Mats (Timothy Spall) to Chris (Mark Wahlberg): "Dream big. Live the life."

# The Royal Tenenbaums

*Family isn't a word, it's a sentence.*
—Movie tagline

**Box Office:** $50.1 million

Most people believe that if they consider a film good, it is good, and if they think it is bad, it is bad, not realizing that their subjective reaction to a film or any work of art or entertainment depends upon what they bring to it. Unsophisticated viewers are unlikely to appreciate demanding films, and sophisticated viewers are often snobbish toward popular entertainments. Evaluations of films also depend upon expectations, mood, the quality of the sound and picture in the theater, etc. These considerations are applicable to *The Royal Tenenbaums* because it is one of those films that people will either love or hate, though they may change their views entirely upon subsequent viewings.

Writer-director Wes Anderson and his co-writer Owen Wilson showed considerable promise with their first feature film, *Bottle Rocket* (1996), an offbeat, low-budget heist comedy with plenty of style and originality. Their second film, *Rushmore* (1998), is even better. *Rushmore* is one of the best films ever about the ridiculous pains of adolescence, especially for the sensitive, artistically inclined. *The Royal Tenenbaums* presents three sensitive, artistically inclined children and shows what happens when they grow up—or fail to grow up.

To call any Anderson-Wilson film offbeat, stylish, and original is to be redundant. If Alfred Hitchcock is the master of suspense, Anderson is the master of the quirky. As many reviewers observed, with *Tenenbaums*, Anderson and Wilson push the too-sensitive quirkiness of their characters much further than in the earlier films. As a result, the film walks a very thin line between the charming and the insufferable.

Royal Tenenbaum (Gene Hackman), a completely selfish disbarred attorney, decides to become reunited with his estranged family. Wife Etheline (Anjelica Huston), an archaeologist from whom he has long been separated, wants to marry her accountant, Henry Sherman (Danny Glover). Oldest son Chas (Ben Stiller), an entrepreneur, is unsuccessfully recovering from the recent death of his wife while raising their two young sons (Grant Rosenmeyer and Jonah Meyerson). The other Tenenbaum son, Richie (Luke Wilson), is literally drifting aimlessly on a cruise ship after the collapse of his tennis career. Likewise, adopted daughter Margot (Gwyneth Paltrow) can no longer write plays, spending her days locked in her bathroom away from husband Raleigh St. Clair (Bill Murray), a neurologist and writer.

All three young Tenenbaums were child prodigies who have failed to live up to their promise. Chas is haunted by irrational fears and resentment of his father who stole much of the money he earned as a precocious investor. Richie and Margot are frozen in ennui with Richie's plight intensified by his unspoken love for his foster sister. Even Eli Cash (Owen Wilson), their childhood neighbor and honorary family member, has caught the Tenenbaum disease. A successful novelist and former lover of Margot, he has developed a self-destructive drug habit.

Despite all these melodramatic touches, which eventually include a suicide attempt and the death of a beloved family pet, *The Royal Tenenbaums* is a comedy with one wacky incident after another. These include Royal's rather pathetic attempt to convince the family that he is dying of cancer while hiding in a closet eating cheeseburgers and his zany efforts to win the affections of his grandsons whom Chas is trying to turn into copies of his morose self. Richie camps out in a tent inside the family townhouse surrounded by his tennis trophies. Raleigh devotes himself to the rather obvious mysteries of a nerdy adolescent who follows him everywhere. The townhouse is filled by monotonously repetitive childhood art, mostly by Richie, that underscores the children's arrested development. The finger Margot loses in an ill-fated visit to her real family in Indiana is a constant reminder of her incompleteness. Chas and his boys always wear matching red Adidas warm-up suits, so when required to attend a funeral, Chas simply switches to black sweats. Family factotum Pagoda (Kumar Pallana) wears hot pink trousers. (Most of the characters are badly dressed most of the time.) And the Dalmatian mice which started young Chas on the road to success still inhabit the townhouse.

The Tenenbaums clearly owe a debt to the Glass family of eccentric, precocious New Yorkers depicted in J. D. Salinger's *Franny and Zooey* (1961) and *Raise High the Roofbeam; and Seymour: An Introduction* (1963), though Anderson and Wilson, to their credit, take their characters far less seriously than does Salinger. The filmmakers want their audience to like the characters but also to be a bit exasperated by them. There is always a barrier of ironic distance between the viewers and the characters, aided by Alec Baldwin's tongue-in-cheek narration. At Royal's lowest point, Anderson punctures the possibility of unearned sympathy for the old rascal by having Pagoda become so exasperated that he plunges a pocket knife into his friend's stomach.

Anderson has said in interviews that in addition to Salinger, he was heavily influenced by stories and articles in old issues of *The New Yorker*. (Some might say the film resembles a live-action version of *New Yorker* cartoons.) The setting, though never officially identified as Manhattan, is a grubby fantasy version of the city with imaginary locations like Archer Avenue and the 375th Street Y and the constant appearance of the rusted vehicles of the Gypsy Cab Company. All this is far removed from Woody Allen's romantic, pristine view of New York. The film was shot on more than 100 Manhattan locations, including Harlem, the setting of the Tenenbaum townhouse, with the sites chosen for their oddness or decay.

Anderson and Wilson are making fun of the characters' self-absorption, but the three young Tenenbaums and Eli do take themselves a bit seriously and are perhaps, especially Margot, too glum. Chas's red warm-ups, Richie's headband, Eli's cowboy outfits, and the dark makeup around Margot's eyes—all of which accent their cartoonishness—grow tiresome. It is easy to see why some reviewers wanted to slap them around.

Anderson can be criticized for giving his younger performers only one note to play. Stiller is a gifted comic actor but is merely constipated here. Paltrow is a lovely, charming, potentially great actress, but her Margot is an unattractive drip. It is hard to imagine how Margot and Raleigh could ever have had a relationship. Luckily, the older performers fare better. Anderson and Wilson do not seem to know how to develop their female characters, so Huston has little to do. Yet she has considerable presence as the one sane Tenenbaum. Huston has not been this commanding on the screen since *The Dead* (1987).

Hackman, one of the greatest of screen actors, has not been this good since *Get Shorty* (1995). He manages to look ridiculous and dignified at the same time. Hackman's delight in Royal's behavior is infectious. When Eli says he always wanted to be a Tenenbaum and Royal says, "So did I," Hackman's perfect delivery conveys not just a joke but the character's sudden realization that he has always been an outsider within his own family. In one of Hackman's best scenes, Royal confronts Etheline on the street to tell her he's dying. When she responds with great pain, he takes back the lie, only to lie again when she begins stalking away. Hackman's expression is priceless as he looks around to see if anyone is witnessing his foolishness. Royal realizes he is no good but continues charging through life nonetheless. The inventive energy of Hackman's performance is the main element keeping *Tenenbaums* on track. Without him, it could easily be too irritating.

An unusually literary film, *The Royal Tenenbaums* opens with a book of the same title being checked out of a library. Most of the characters have published books, and their dust jackets, done primarily in the style of the 1950's, are displayed. Careful attention is paid to such details. The townhouse, a character in itself, looks lived in, with artifacts of the family's life scattered throughout. These include murals of significant events in the family's life by Eric Anderson, the director's brother. Production designer David Wasco has designed all of Anderson's films as well as all of Quentin Tarantino's. He is an excellent example of the designer serving the distinctive vision of the director.

In addition to Mark Mothersbaugh's lively score, the soundtrack features songs by the Beatles, the Clash, Nick Drake, Nico, the Rolling Stones, the Ramones, Elliot Smith, and the Velvet Undergound. Some of the folk rock tunes, however, are a tad sincere and self-conscious and distract from the film's ironic tone. The use of this pop music can be said to owe a debt to Mike Nichols' *The Graduate* (1967), which features songs by Simon and Garfunkel. The highlight of *Tenenbaums* comes when Royal takes his grandsons on an outing to introduce them to the joys of jaywalking, shoplifting, riding on the sides of fire trucks, and other acts sure to horrify their uptight father, and this wonderfully delightful montage, also featuring Hackman's best moments, is accompanied by Paul Simon's "Me and Julio." While too many recent films have included songs in their closing credits that violate the mood of the film's ending, Anderson concludes *The Royal Tenenbaums* with the great Van Morrison's "Everyone," a song recalling the joyful aspects of what has come before.

—*Michael Adams*

## CREDITS

**Royal Tenenbaum:** Gene Hackman
**Etheline Tenenbaum:** Anjelica Huston
**Margot Tenenbaum:** Gwyneth Paltrow
**Chas Tenenbaum:** Ben Stiller
**Richie Tenenbaum:** Luke Wilson
**Eli Cash:** Owen C. Wilson
**Raleigh St. Clair:** Bill Murray
**Henry Sherman:** Danny Glover
**Dusty:** Seymour Cassel
**Pagoda:** Kumar Pallana
**Ari Tenenbaum:** Grant Rosenmeyer
**Uzi Tenenbaum:** Jonah Meyerson
**Dudley Heinsbergen:** Stephen Lea Sheppard
**Narrator:** Alec Baldwin

**Origin:** USA
**Released:** 2001
**Production:** Barry Mendel, Scott Rudin, Wes Anderson; American Empirical Pictures; released by Touchstone Pictures
**Directed by:** Wes Anderson
**Written by:** Owen C. Wilson, Wes Anderson

**Cinematography by:** Robert Yeoman
**Music by:** Mark Mothersbaugh
**Sound:** Pavel Wdowczak
**Music Supervisor:** Randall Poster
**Editing:** Dylan Tichenor
**Art Direction:** Carl Sprague
**Costumes:** Karen Patch
**Production Design:** David Wasco
**MPAA rating:** R
**Running time:** 108 minutes

## REVIEWS

*Boston Globe.* December 21, 2001, p. F1.
*Chicago Sun-Times Online.* December 21, 2001.
*Entertainment Weekly.* January 11, 2002, p. 46.
*Film Comment.* November-December, 2001, p. 24.
*Los Angeles Times Online.* December 14, 2001.
*New Republic.* December 31, 2001, p. 24.
*New York.* December 17, 2001, p. 60.
*New York Times.* October 5, 2001, p. D14.
*New Yorker.* December 17, 2001, p. 97.
*Newsweek.* December 24, 2001, p. 41.
*People.* December 17, 2001, p. 33.
*Premiere.* January, 2002, p. 18.
*San Francisco Chronicle.* December 21, 2001, p. D3.
*Time.* December 31, 2001, p. 146.
*USA Today.* December 14, 2001, p. E5.
*Village Voice.* December 18, 2001, p. 38.
*Washington Post.* December 21, 2001, p. C1.

## QUOTES

Royal (Gene Hackman) to his estranged wife: "I want my family back." Etheline (Anjelica Huston) replies: "Well, you can't have it. It's too late."

## TRIVIA

Eldest Wilson brother Andrew plays Margot Tenenbaum's biological father; the Tenenbaum name is borrowed from a childhood friend.

## AWARDS AND NOMINATIONS

**Golden Globes 2002:** Actor—Mus./Comedy (Hackman)
**Natl. Soc. Film Critics 2001:** Actor (Hackman)
**Nomination:**
**British Acad. 2001:** Orig. Screenplay
**Writers Guild 2001:** Orig. Screenplay
**Broadcast Film Critics 2001:** Cast.

# Rush Hour 2

*Get ready for a second rush!*
—Movie tagline
*The Mouth of the West and the Hands of the East are back!*
—Movie tagline

 **Box Office:** $226.2 million

Rush Hour 2 had a hard time coming into being. You'd think that after the studio saw the boxoffice receipts for the original *Rush Hour*, a surprise hit making $250 million worldwide, they would have been rushing to put out its sequel. And that was indeed the original plan. But Chris Tucker, who co-starred in the original with Chinese martial arts legend Jackie Chan, was a hold-out. He didn't like the first script he saw and told producers he wasn't interested in making the film. The desperation on the part of the studio to dip into that *Rush Hour* money pot again won out and not only did Tucker get himself a new script, but he also boosted his salary by several million dollars. It wasn't a bad deal for someone who worked on exactly zero films in between the two *Rush Hour*s. (His previous film credits were meager, too—just a part in *The Fifth Element* and a co-starring role in *Money Talks.*)

It is difficult to imagine just how bad that first script must have been because it's not like the second one is any kind of comic masterpiece. The jokes in the film are weak enough that all of the better ones fit neatly into the film's trailer, with room to spare. And the story certainly isn't a contender for any 2001 screenwriting awards. But it does have Chan and Tucker together again, which is something. Mismatched crime fighting teams are one of the hoariest conventions in movies, but when one works, it's still fun to watch. The team of Chan and Tucker has a loopy charm and anything that's good about the sequel is because of that chemistry.

In this installment (yes, the whole team has already unofficially agreed that there will be a *Rush Hour 3*), Detective James Carter (Tucker) is in Hong Kong visiting his old buddy Inspector Lee (Chan). Carter just wants to party and get some "moo shu," his slang for women, but the hardworking and conscientious Lee can't seem to stop taking calls from the office. Carter is merely annoyed by this until he hears about one particular case where Americans have been killed. His philosophy, apparently, is that it's fine if Chinese people are killed but if it's Americans, then well, sign him up for the case.

Lee and Carter figure out that the motive for the crime is to get some printing plates from the U.S. mint that make perfect "super bills," counterfeit bills that are only detectable by lighting them on fire. But they're having a little more trouble figuring out who they should arrest. It seems that local crime lord Ricky Tan (John Lone) might have something to do with the crime. Or is he the victim of a power play by a young upstart in his gang, Hu Li (Zhang Ziyi of *Crouching Tiger, Hidden Dragon*)? Or is the whole Chinese gang being set up by Rich White Guy (Alan King)? To confuse matters further, there's also a woman, Isabella Molina (Roselyn Sanchez), who claims to be with the United States Secret Service. But is she just using Carter and Lee so that they will find the plates and she can steal them? If you're concerned about such plot points, you're watching the wrong film because *Rush Hour 2* is not about any of that. It's about Tucker riffing and Chan fighting, and then to mix matters up a bit, Tucker trying to fight and Chan trying to riff.

There's also some great scenery during the sequences filmed in Hong Kong. Reportedly this was the American film to make the most use of that setting ever and it's a treat. The shots of the city are gorgeous and the peeks into another society are intriguing. But then, for no other reason than the director of the film, Brett Ratner, liked to gamble, the film has the dynamic duo rush off to Las Vegas to follow the action. The second half of the movie takes place in a brand-new Chinese-themed casino run by the aforementioned Rich White Guy.

It's an unfortunate move because what little humor in the movie works is because Carter is a fish out of water in Hong Kong. Once they get to Vegas, his comedy (or, mostly, comedy attempts) lose their steam. Seeing Carter in Hong Kong asking for directions from a street vendor and being handed a live chicken has a lot more potential than Carter playing dice in a same old/same old casino back in the U.S.

That's not to say that Tucker's comedy is great during the Hong Kong segments. There are some good moments, like when he does a dead-on Michael Jackson impersonation in a karaoke bar as a bewildered Chinese audience looks on, but these inspired moments are far outnumbered by jokes that don't work or jokes that are plain old offensive. At one point, Carter and Lee are at a massage parlor where a group of women are lined up before them for the men to select. Lee says something to Carter and Carter admonishes him, "Never step in front of a black man at a buffet line." Most of the jokes in the movie involve Lee and Carter making supposedly insightful jibes at the other person's race or ethnicity. "I will slap you so hard you'll end up in the Ming dynasty," says Carter to Lee, in a typically unfunny example.

The jokes go only as deep as the most surface stereotypes about the Chinese eating dogs, looking alike, etc. At one point, Lee warns Carter that they are on his turf and that

Carter should behave. "Here I am Michael Jackson, you are Toto." Carter answers, "You mean Tito. Toto is what we ate last night." During one of the fight sequences, where the duo is battling a group of baddies, Carter accidentally punches his buddy Lee. "All y'all look alike," he explains, looking like the typical ugly American (as he does through most of his visit to Hong Kong). To be fair, the jibes are about equal for each of the guys. When Carter is walking down a hall in Hong Kong, a woman comes up to him and says, "Move it, Kobe."

That leaves us with the fighting, which is surprisingly limited and subdued. Chan is famous for the fighting in his martial arts movies, but he tries to make sure that his films are not gory or very violent. Instead, he focuses on intricate choreography and funny situations. Instead of disarming an opponent by, say, gouging his eyes out, Chan would throw a pie in his face. Reportedly Chan wanted more time in this film to map out his lavish fight sequences, but wasn't allowed to so the film could be rushed out. The skimping shows. Now in his 40's, Chan is as agile and inventive as always but with the exception of a scene where he must fight with his mouth and hands taped, none of the fight sequences are particularly memorable.

Besides the lack of great humor and creative fighting, there are also a lot of bad movie touches, like the Chinese characters who speak in English to each other when they're alone, despite having only the most tenuous grasp on the language. There are also jokes about gay people, women objectified, blah blah blah.

Critics weren't too enthralled with the film. Kenneth Turan at the *Los Angeles Times* said, "*Rush Hour 2* has an anemic, haphazard feeling to its plotting." *Entertainment Weekly*'s Lisa Schwarzbaum called the film a "coarser, more hectic, more cheaply written sequel." Roger Ebert at the *Chicago Sun-Times* signaled out Tucker's performance for special ridicule and said, "his endless rants are like an anchor around the ankles of the humor." Many critics made the point that the outtakes shown over the closing credits—a Chan tradition—were by far the best part of the movie. Of course in the end, none of this mattered because *Rush Hour 2* was a big old hit. It made almost $67 million in its opening weekend and along with *Planet of the Apes* and *The Princess Diaries* helped form one of the biggest non-holiday weekend takes in history.

*—Jill Hamilton*

## CREDITS

**Carter:** Chris Tucker
**Lee:** Jackie Chan
**Agent Sterling:** Harris Yulin
**Hu Li:** Zhang Ziyi

**Ricky Tan:** John Lone
**Steven Reign:** Alan King
**Isabella:** Roselyn Sanchez
**Capt. Chin:** Kenneth Tsang
**Zing:** Ernie Reyes Jr.
**Verace salesman:** Jeremy Piven
**Red Dragon Box Man:** Saul Rubinek
**Kenny:** Don Cheadle

**Origin:** USA
**Released:** 2001
**Production:** Arthur Sarkissian, Roger Birnbaum, Jay Stern, Jonathan Glickman; released by New Line Cinema
**Directed by:** Brett Ratner
**Written by:** Jeff Nathanson
**Cinematography by:** Matthew F. Leonetti
**Music by:** Lalo Schifrin, Kathy Nelson
**Sound:** Kim Harris Ornitz
**Editing:** Mark Helfrich
**Art Direction:** Andrew Max Cahn, James E. Tocci
**Costumes:** Rita Ryack
**Production Design:** Terence Marsh
**MPAA rating:** PG-13
**Running time:** 91 minutes

## REVIEWS

*Boxoffice.* July, 2001, p. 37.
*Boxoffice.* September, 2001, p. 148.
*Chicago Sun-Times Online.* August 3, 2001.
*Entertainment Weekly.* August 10, 2001, p. 46.
*Los Angeles Times Online.* August 3, 2001.
*New York Times Online.* August 3, 2001.
*People.* August 13, 2001, p. 36.
*USA Today Online.* August 3, 2001.
*Variety.* July 30, 2001, p. 17.
*Washington Post.* August 3, 2001, p. WE37.

## QUOTES

Lee (Jackie Chan): "Do you understand the words that are coming out of my mouth?!" Carter (Chris Tucker): "Man, nobody understands the words that come out of your mouth."

# Saltwater

I rish award-winning playwright Conor McPherson's directorial debut *Saltwater* might as well be called *Backwater* because the film lacks any cinematic qualities with its poorly composed shots, ill-constructed narrative, and flat characters. Although the film is an adaptation of McPherson's play *The Lime Tree Bower*, one would have to be drunk to enjoy the humor in his film or completely obsessed with Irish culture. Even though the film does present us with some raucous comedic scenes and some dramatic turn of events, it's still not worth the price of admission.

*Saltwater*'s cast consists of several emerging actors such as Peter McDonald, who recently starred in the screwball comedy *When Brendan Met Trudy,* Pat Shortt, Glendan Gleeson, and young actor Laurence Kinlan, whose face might seem familiar since he appeared in *Angela's Ashes* and it was his face staring up at us from the film's promotional poster. While most of the cast seem well suited for their roles, McDonald seems miscast in the role of Frank. It's not that the actor can't portray a gawky young man who feels responsible for his father's misfortunes, it's just that after seeing McDonald play a sexy lead role in *When Brendan Met Trudy,* his talents are wasted in this transparent role.

The story revolves around widower George Beneventi (Brian Cox), a chip-shop owner who has fallen into debt with loan shark Simple Simon (Brendan Gleeson), and George's children: Frank (McDonald), who is Mr. Responsible, teenager Joe (Kinlan), and daughter Carmel (Valerie Spelman). Frank despises Simple Simon and wants to help his father free himself from debt, so with a set of blackened pipes (posing as a rifle) and dressed in army fatigues and a black stocking cap, Frank robs Simon's bookie establishment of 40 grand. Meanwhile, Joe hangs out with a juvenile delinquent from his school, Damien (David O'Rourke). Damien injures two of the school's teachers but loyal Joe refuses to turn in his friend. However, one night after the boys sneak into a nightclub, Joe sees Tara (Caroline O'Boyle), a girl that he has a crush on. Tara and Joe drink too much, are beaten up by a gang of older boys, and later, when Damien hooks up with the couple, he rapes Tara in front of Joe.

Meanwhile, Carmel is involved with two-timing, middle-aged university lecturer Ray (Conor Mullen), who can't keep his hands off his students. Against his better judgment, Ray seeks out an affair with Deborah (Eva Birthistle), a sexy 21-year-old. On one fateful night, after having been threatened by a colleague to give up his illicit affair, Ray gets wasted and laid. The next day, Ray wakes up with a hangover, downs a couple of aspirins and a carton of orange juice, then attends an important lecture by a visiting philosopher. In the film's only climatic moment, Ray spews vomit ala *The Exorcist* all over his colleagues and students. The vomit literally drips from attendees' eyeglasses.

The problem with *Saltwater* isn't the scenes' set ups, but that McPherson fails to deliver the goods and the narrative lacks believability for the most part. Frank's sequence lacks tension and a payoff. The character manages to successfully steal the money needed to pay off his father's debt, but nothing comes of it. The sequence would have been better had a conflict between the overwrought father and responsible Frank transpired. Another problem is that McPherson forgot that cinema is a visual medium. He employs static shots in the drab settings of the chip shop and a local pub, occasionally showing the nearby ocean or the cobblestone street where Joe rides his bike to school. It's as if McPherson lacks the visual skills to show us his story even if BBC Online journalist Neil Smith felt that *Saltwater* was "a gentle piece that combines laugh-out-loud comedy with poignant heart-felt drama."

—*Patty-Lynne Herlevi*

## CREDITS

**George Beneventi:** Brian Cox
**Frank Beneventi:** Peter McDonald
**Dr. Raymond Sullivan:** Conor Mullen
**Joe Beneventi:** Laurence Kinlan
**Simple Simon:** Brendan Gleeson
**Deborah McCeever:** Eva Birthistle
**Carmel Beneventi:** Valerie Spelman
**Damien Fitzgibbon:** David O'Rourke
**Tara:** Caroline O'Boyle
**Sgt. Duggan:** Gina Moxley

**Origin:** Ireland, Great Britain
**Released:** 1999
**Production:** Robert Walpole; Treasure Film Production
**Directed by:** Conor McPherson
**Written by:** Conor McPherson
**Cinematography by:** Oliver Curtis
**Sound:** Michael Crouch
**Editing:** Emer Reynolds
**Art Direction:** Sara Hauldren
**Costumes:** Kathy Strachan
**Production Design:** Luana Hanson
**MPAA rating:** Unrated
**Running time:** 97 minutes

## REVIEWS

*Sight and Sound.* January, 2001, p. 58.
*Variety.* March 6, 2000, p. 40.

# Save the Last Dance

*One life. One love.*
—Movie tagline
*The only person you need to be is yourself.*
—Movie tagline

 **Box Office:** $91.2 million

It's difficult to believe that anyone expected much of *Save the Last Dance.* For one thing, it didn't have the kind of big stars that bring in audiences. Julia Stiles was the biggest name in the film and her co-star was an unknown, Sean Patrick Thomas. It certainly didn't have any stunning special effects or dramatic computerized monsters. And its plot was nothing spectacular. The young-dancer-escapes-dreary-life-with-amazing-dance-routine story line was familiar from similar films like *Flashdance, Footloose,* or *Dirty Dancing* The only thing that gave it a new twist was that the love story was interracial.

Maybe people in 2001 were hungering for an interracial love story because *Save the Last Dance* was the number one film the first two weeks it came out. The film's success could have also been due to the timing of its release. The film came out in January, which is generally not a time when the studios—still hoping to be raking in big bucks from their holiday blockbusters—release any of their big films. Another factor in the film's favor was that it's a movie truism that every decade must have at least one lightweight dance movie that becomes a box office success. Perhaps *Save the Last Dance* was the lucky film that scored that slot for the early 2000s.

When the film begins, Sara Johnson (Stiles) is riding on a train. As she stares sadly out the window (why is everyone on trains in films always wistful? Are there no happy train travelers?), she flashes back to the source of her misery. Sara was a promising ballet student who was getting ready to audition for Julliard. Her mother, a florist, thinks she will be too busy to make the audition but Sara pouts and insists that she come. The mother rushes to attend the audition but is killed in a car crash. Sara deals with her grief and self-blame by deciding to give up ballet. After her mother's death, Sara is forced to move in with her estranged father, Roy (Terry Kinney). Roy, who has not been a part of Sara's life, is a jazz musician who still lives like a 20-year-old. His idea of nurturing his daughter is to offer to cook her one of the many Swanson dinners he has in his refrigerator. During one of Roy and Sara's first encounters, he says, "Sorry I couldn't hang around at the funeral longer. If I could have gotten out of the gig in South Bend, I would have."

Besides dealing with her grief and having to live with a father who is a virtual stranger, Sara also has to contend with an entirely new environment. Her father lives in a poor, almost entirely African-American neighborhood on Chicago's South Side. Her new high school is completely different from her old one. One of her first experiences there is having to be searched for weapons as she arrives. Sara finds herself between two worlds. Her friends from her old neighborhood don't understand her new circumstance and say boorish things like, "Did you see anyone get shot yet?" And as one of the few white students, Sara feels isolated and alone. Finally, she is taken under the wing by Chenille (Kerry Washington), a popular girl and aspiring fashion designer who shows Sara how to dress and be cool. (Tip #1: don't be like the white wannabe girl who tries to blend in by using hip-hop jargon like, "You know whad I'm sayin'?") Chenille, who has a child by her errant boyfriend, introduces Sara to the local hangout, the Steppes Club, where the kids try out their latest hip-hop (and pickup) moves.

At school, Sara takes an immediate dislike to Derek (Thomas), after they argue in class over a Truman Capote book. Derek also happens to be Chenille's brother. This instant hate, of course, is a sure sign of impending romance. Sara and Derek start a friendship after Derek offers to help Sara learn some hip-hop moves. (Sara, though trained in ballet, is for some reason completely cloddish at hip-hop. It would be one thing to be a little off—after all, it's a different style of dance—but Sara is strangely bad.)

All that training and dancing together soon leads to l-o-v-e and soon Derek and Sara are a couple. This is the signal that the complications must begin. Derek's former girlfriend (Bianca Lawson), who took an instant dislike to Sara (though in this case it did not lead to love) tries to win Derek back. Other kids at Steppes look down upon the relationship because it is interracial. And even Chenille starts to disapprove. In one scene, she tells Sara that she is being unfair by dating Derek since he is one of the few good men in the neighborhood. Derek, who is smart, ambitious and plans to go to med school, is a prime catch and Sara shouldn't just waltz in and take him away from the sistahs.

Though Derek seems to be able to deal with the peer pressure regarding the relationship better than Sara can, he has problems of his own. His gangster past has been coming back to haunt him. His best friend from childhood, Malakai (Fredro Starr of the hip-hop group Onyx), is pressuring him to take part in a gang hit. Derek would refuse his loose cannon friend but feels that he owes him since Malakai once took the blame for a crime they had both committed.

Will Derek throw his future away to help his friend out? Will Derek and Sara stay together? Will Sara ever go back to ballet? These are the questions that Save the Last Dance asks. But perhaps the question they should have asked is why they didn't cast someone with more dancing skills that Stiles. Stiles, while a perfectly fine actress, does not look like a dancer and she certainly doesn't move like a dancer. In the dancing-as-life-savior genre of movies, there has to be a climatic dance where the freedom of dance liberates the dancer. An example of this is the audition scene in Flashdance where Jennifer Beals' (or, really, her double's) wild dancing impresses even the stuffy judges. Poor Stiles doesn't have enough skill to be able to convey this joy of dance.

Besides that major casting mistake, the rest of the cast is good. Especially good is Starr as Derek's friend who cannot escape the gang life. There is a poignant scene where Derek tries to get Malakai to give up his violent lifestyle. "You could be so much more," he says. But Malakai sees no future for himself. With no marketable skills, he feels that the only way he can be a man is to stay with the violence. At least he can be successful at that. Also good is Kinney as Sara's dad, Roy. There's a certain sweetness to his performance as a man who wants to do right by his daughter but doesn't know how. The two need each other but constantly say exactly the wrong things to each other.

In 2001, an interracial love story was still a big deal. Because of what some studios thought of as a touchy subject matter, the film took five years to come about. Producer Robert Cort, who also produced Mr. Holland's Opus admitted that the film included the dancing theme to make it more palatable to a wide audience. "Because race is a heavy issue, you want to be able to do it in a form that is entertaining," he said in an interview with the Los Angeles Times. "If it's a dance movie, then you deliver your message through that. Ultimately, this is a commercial medium, and you have to make it look entertaining."

Though audiences liked the film, critics were divided. Entertainment Weekly gave it a C-, saying, "This wan, formulaic teen movie from Metro director Thomas Carter is afraid to pump up the volume on its own interracial, hip-hop Romeo and Juliet story, lest it challenge even one sedated viewer or disturb the peace." The reviewer for the Kansas City Star took issue with the poorly edited dance sequences and said, "The routines have been so chopped up— apparently to disguise Stiles' only limited dance ability— that they're incomprehensible." The Los Angeles Times reviewer was a fan of the film and said, "Melodrama, wishful thinking, and grit strike just the right balance to make it work." The reviewer for the Philadelphia Daily News also liked Save the Last Dance, saying, "The movie looks at interracial relationships from a fresh perspective and gives the audience something real to think about. Definitely worth seeing."

—Jill Hamilton

## CREDITS

**Sara:** Julia Stiles
**Derek:** Sean Patrick Thomas
**Malakai:** Fredro Starr
**Chenille:** Kerry Washington
**Roy:** Terry Kinney
**Nikki:** Bianca Lawson
**Kenny:** Garland Whitt
**Snookie:** Vince Green

**Origin:** USA
**Released:** 2001
**Production:** Robert W. Cort, David Madden; MTV; released by Paramount Pictures
**Directed by:** Thomas Carter
**Written by:** Duane Adler, Cheryl Edwards
**Cinematography by:** Robbie Greenberg
**Music by:** Mark Isham
**Sound:** David Obermeyer
**Music Supervisor:** Michael McQuarn
**Editing:** Peter E. Berger
**Art Direction:** Diane Hughes
**Costumes:** Sandra Hernandez
**Production Design:** Paul Eads
**MPAA rating:** PG-13
**Running time:** 112 minutes

## REVIEWS

*Chicago Sun-Times Online.* January 12, 2001.
*Hollywood Reporter.* January 8, 2001, p. 20.
*New York Times Online.* January 12, 2001.
*Sight and Sound.* April, 2001, p. 57.
*USA Today Online.* January 11, 2001.
*Variety.* January 8, 2001, p. 40.
*Washington Post Online.* January 12, 2001.

# Saving Silverman (Evil Woman)

*They swore nothing could come between them. Then she came along.*
—Movie tagline

   **Box Office:** $19.4 million

*S*aving Silverman sounded like it would be a lot better than it actually turned out to be. Not to be misleading here, it was never the type of movie that sounded like it would be the subject of "for your consideration" Oscar® hype ads, but it did seem like it could have been a nice little comedy. The most promising thing about the film was its casting, specifically Jack Black. For Black, who played the surly record store clerk in *High Fidelity* to perfection, this was a chance for a role with more screen time. That sounded good because Black, the bigger-than-life singer of cult band Tenacious D, is the type of guy who could shine in a big showy role. Also promising was the casting of Steve Zahn as his best buddy. Zahn was notably good in *Happy, Texas* and this role was a good opportunity for him, too. Amanda Peet was hot off a fresh turn in *The Whole Nine Yards*, a comedy with Matthew Perry and Bruce Willis. Casting Jason Biggs, whose movies get worse each time out (starting high with *American Pie* and reaching the depths with *Loser*), was not so promising, but it was perhaps unavoidable in the early 2000s to make a teen comedy that did not have Biggs in it. The casting (plus the fact that Neil Diamond was to show up in the film playing himself) sounded like a good bet.

What good there is in the film does end up coming from the casting of these actors, but it's never enough to carry the whole movie. These folks, especially Black, try their darndest in each scene. Black and Zahn have a ton of energy and they seemed more than willing to use it in every scene, but the script was just not meaty enough to give them enough to work with.

Wayne Le Fessier (Zahn), J.D. McNugent (Black) and Darren Silverman (Biggs) are three buddies who have been friends since grade school. As all young men must be in recent teen flicks, they are not the brightest guys around. They all live together in a house donated by Wayne's grandmother and spend their time in man heaven—watching TV, sitting in reclining chairs and eating junk food. Wayne is a rodent control guy who loves his work. J.D. works at a fast food restaurant, and Darren works at a retirement home where his typical work banter is, "Sir, if you don't pull your pants up, no more *Matlock*." Their common bond is that they all worship Neil Diamond. They periodically don long black wigs and tight pants and play together in their Neil Diamond tribute band called Diamonds in the Rough.

Their other common bond, which they would be less quick to admit, is that they all also have really bad luck with women. But Wayne, using a bit of projection, thinks that it is Darren who has the problem. So when they first see the beautiful Judith Snodgrass-Fessbeggler (Peet) at a bar, Wayne rushes over to her and tries to talk Darren up to her. She coldly brushes him off, but Wayne returns to Darren's table and says that she is dying to meet him. When Darren approaches her, Judith is initially cruel to Darren, too, but uses him as a buffer when a pushy magician tries to put the moves on her.

Judith and Darren, somewhat unbelievably, start dating. The meek Darren is way out of his league, but Judith seems to like the fact that she can control him. "I am the puppet master and he is my puppet," she explains smugly to Wayne and J.D. Judith is very cruel to Darren, but he is so happy to be with such a beautiful woman that he puts up with all of it. For example, she doesn't allow him any sexual contact with her but does allow him "masturbation privileges." She also allows him to wax her legs. Top on her list of things to rework about Darren's life is Wayne and J.D. She insists that he stop hanging out with them and, worse, decides that he can no longer play in Diamonds in the Rough. Darren, who seems to be in some sort of love daze, reluctantly agrees to ditch his longtime friends.

For Wayne and J.D., this is the last straw. They take it upon themselves to save Darren from Judith and the horrible relationship. Their tiny minds try to think of good plans. One such plan is to take pictures of themselves cavorting with prostitutes, then put Darren's head on the photos and send them anonymously to Judith. Judith, who is a high powered psychotherapist and no match for them, immediately sees that the man in the photo has tattoos . . . hmmm, just like Wayne's tattoos. Their stupid ideas reach a pinnacle when they get the idea that they should kidnap Judith. After she's out of the picture, they theorize, they can reunite Darren with an old girlfriend, Sandy Perkus (Amanda Detmer). Sandy, who had been Darren's true love, broke his heart after she moved away from town with her circus freak family. Now she's back in town, but, uh-oh, just a week away from taking her chastity vows to become a nun.

It's testament to the silliness of the script for *Saving Silverman* that Wayne and J.D.'s cockamamie plan has a high likelihood of working. It's also testament to the heartlessness of the film that kidnapping someone and holding them for days tied up in a basement is treated so casually. Still, the film is not without its funny moments. If you put these guys on screen for an hour and a half, something funny is bound to come up, and it does. In one flashback scene, we see why there is a restraining order issued by Diamond against the guys. We see Diamond walking on the red carpet to attend some event and J.D. leans over the velvet rope and grabs Diamond in a giant bear hug. "Neil, I love you!" he cries desperately. "I want to party with you!" With the same kind of large-man-with-grace quality that John Belushi had, Black gives it his all as the crazed, lovestruck fan.

But most of the humor is pretty tired. There have been so many films about two doofy guys that try to succeed in some sort of plan. To stand out, a movie would have to go beyond that, either by expanding the basic premise or having a sharper, wittier script. Two guys who do dumb things isn't enough to hold a movie together. And despite the build-up the film's PR people gave Diamond's appearance, it is a letdown. The only funny thing about Diamond's performance is that it's Neil Diamond; other than that, there's

nothing notable. It didn't have to be that way. *Wayne's World*, for example, made wonderful use of its Alice Cooper cameo. And in this film, Diamond certainly seemed up for the challenge. Too bad screenwriters Greg DePaul and Hank Nelken couldn't come up with some good lines for him to say.

The acting is as good as it could have been, given the vehicle. Black is nicely frenetic as J.D. His very presence in the film is a good thing, but it's too bad he's stuck playing the stupid fat guy role. It's especially disappointing after seeing how fully he embodied his character in *High Fidelity*. Still, he certainly tries his hardest in this role and he squeezes out some funny moments. Zahn is energetic as Wayne, who by default ends up being the brains of the group. He plays his character eager and guileless, like a frisky puppy. Peet is gamely evil as Judith, although her character is so unredeemingly evil, it's more of a character sketch than a recognizable human. R. Lee Ermey is suitably strange as the guy's very odd, gung-ho high school football coach. Biggs plays his loser, unlucky-in-love character yet again. He's certainly perfected the role, but it's time for him to branch out and try something new.

In general, critics hated the film, though they seemed to give it more guff than it deserved. Although the film wasn't brilliant, it wasn't void of humor and it wasn't overly offensive either (compared to its peers, that is). *Entertainment Weekly* gave it an F and said "all involved have managed to create the most unlikable, man-hating, woman-hating, unfunny idiots since *Whipped* ended up on worst-movie lists last year." The *Miami Herald* said, "Does it all represent Hollywood slipping down another evolutionary rung from Pauly Shore movies?" Roger Ebert of the *Chicago Sun-Times* said, "As for Neil Diamond . . . one can only marvel that he waited 20 years to appear in a second film, and found one even worse than his first one."

—*Jill Hamilton*

## CREDITS

**Darren Silverman:** Jason Biggs
**Wayne:** Steve Zahn
**J.D.:** Jack Black
**Judith:** Amanda Peet
**Coach:** R. Lee Ermey
**Sandy:** Amanda Detmer
**Himself:** Neil Diamond

**Origin:** USA
**Released:** 2001
**Production:** Neal H. Moritz; Village Roadshow Pictures, NPV Entertainment, Original Film; released by Columbia Pictures

**Directed by:** Dennis Dugan
**Written by:** Hank Nelken, Greg DePaul
**Cinematography by:** Arthur Albert
**Music by:** Mike Simpson
**Sound:** Martin Fossum
**Music Supervisor:** Mary Ramos, Michelle Silverman
**Editing:** Debra Neil-Fisher
**Art Direction:** James Steuart
**Costumes:** Melissa Toth
**Production Design:** Michael Bolton
**MPAA rating:** PG-13
**Running time:** 90 minutes

## REVIEWS

*Chicago Sun-Times Online.* February 9, 2001.
*Entertainment Weekly.* February 16, 2001, p. 70.
*New York Times Online.* February 9, 2001.
*USA Today Online.* February 9, 2001.
*Variety.* February 5, 2001, p. 38.
*Washington Post Online.* February 9, 2001.

## QUOTES

Judith (Amanda Peet) about Darren: "He's my puppet and I'm his puppet master!"

# Say It Isn't So

**Box Office:** $5.5 million

The ads for *Say It Isn't So* trumpeted "from the guys that brought you *Something About Mary*." The first movie advertised in that manner was the underwhelming Jim Carrey/Renee Zellwegger vehicle *Me, Myself and Irene*. Bleating that a new product is from "the guys"—Peter and Bobby Farrelly—is starting to become more of a liability than an asset. Judging by this most recent output, maybe it's true that the high point of their career were the *Something About Mary, Kingpin, Dumb and Dumber* years. Let's hope not. There's something sad about having *Dumb and Dumber* be some of your top work.

Actually, despite the ads, this isn't the next "real" Farrelly brother film. (Or maybe we should refer to it as a "movie." The term film seems a little highfalutin' for *Say It Isn't So*.) The Farrellys are, with Bradley Thomas, merely producers of the movie. The real creative forces, if that term

would be correct, are screenwriters Peter Gaulke and Gerry Swallow and director J.B. Rogers. All are first-timers in their roles, though Rogers was an apprentice to the Farrellys on their earlier films. The trio clearly seem to be going for a Farrelly-like project, but that's all they come up with—Farrelly-like. It resembles a Farrelly project, but only in the most obvious ways. It's gross—boy is it gross—but never is cleverly gross. It's tasteless, but more offensive tasteless than funny tasteless. As Roger Ebert put it in his review for the *Chicago Sun-Times,* "They know the words but not the music."

The aforementioned doofus is Gilly Nobel (Chris Klein). Gilly is a sensitive soul who works at an animal shelter in the tiny town of Shelbyville, Indiana. So sensitive is he that he reads a poem he wrote to each animal before they are put to sleep. Despite his kind personality and well-scrubbed good looks, Gilly is a lonely man. He was given up by his family when he was an infant and still searches for his missing mother and father. He is also searching for that special girl to make his life complete but has so far been unlucky in love.

That all changes when he catches a glimpse of Jo Wingfield (Heather Graham). Jo is a local girl who has just returned to town after dumping her rich Oregon boyfriend. She is working as a haircutter in a local shop. She is possibly the worst haircutter ever to appear on celluloid but no one seems to care because she's just so darned hot. After taking a seat in line with all of the other lovelorn schmucks in town, Gilly gets his chance to sit in her barber's chair. She starts hacking away at his hair haphazardly and ends up cutting off a big chunk of his ear. This, by the way, is all shown in graphic detail. We see the ear, the slice, the missing chunk—all in living color. This is an example of the gross out humor in the film. It's gross, that's for sure, but is it funny? Maybe if there were some interesting circumstances surrounding the ear cutting, it could—maybe, possibly—be funny, but alas, there are no interesting circumstances. It's just the ear being cut off and that is the extent of the joke. An unfortunate side effect of this is that everyone who sees the movie will forever have the image of that severed ear stuck in their brains. And that's not something that's pleasant to waste brains cells on.

Despite Jo's violence to his ear, Gilly is smitten. The two start dating and are soon fully ensconced in a romantic montage that involves scenes of them doing things like playing with a litter of roly-poly puppies and smooching near attractive backdrops. Gilly's life couldn't get any better but it seems like it might when he gets the news that a local detective has found his natural parents. There's one catch though, and it's a big one. His mother is Valdine (Sally Field), who also happens to be Jo's mother. This means, yuck, some incest has happened.

Gilly is stricken, especially when Jo decides to move back to Oregon without even saying good-bye. Gilly moves in with his newfound parents, Valdine and Walter (Richard Jenkins), and starts going to seed. The town turns against him and the locals taunt him with nasty remarks about his sister. And Valdine and Walter aren't exactly the nurturing types who can help him get over his pain. Valdine is a spiritual relation of *Married . . . With Children*'s Peg Bundy and spends most of her time mincing around in overly tight capri pants. Walter is recovering from one of his many strokes and is immobile. He is forced to speak through a voice box. The voice box provides another instance for the film writers to make what they think are snappy jokes. They seem to think that the voice box itself is inherently hilarious. They would be wrong about that, but still they press on. They've also made Walter a foul-mouthed character. This allows them to have Walter swearing in his robotic voice box voice. This doesn't happen just once or even twice. It happens all through the movie, countless times, becoming less funny each time.

Gilly is resigned to his new bad life, complete with a new bad beard, until he gets some surprise news. Walter and Valdine's real long lost son shows up, meaning that Gilly and Jo are not related. He immediately sets off to Oregon to tell her the big news. His plans are foiled by Valdine, who calls ahead to Oregon authorities and tells them that Gilly is a sex offender. She has nothing against Gilly, really, but she wants Jo to marry her Oregon boyfriend, Jack Mitchell (Eddie Cibrian) because he is a multi-millionaire. Jack is Valdine's ticket out of poverty and she is not about to let him slip away.

At this point, the film deteriorates into what could be called a "frustration comedy." It seems like it should be easy for Gilly to convey the we're-not-brother-and-sister news to Jo with a minimum of fuss (like, say, getting her number from information and calling her on the phone) but all kinds of frustrating factors come into play to thwart him. Gilly gets beaten up repeatedly by thugs, committed to a mental institution and sent on a plane to Mexico. (Naturally, the Mexican sitting next to him on the plane wants Gilly's food because Mexicans are all beggars, right?)

His problems reach their high point, or perhaps low point is more accurate, when he is dragged into town by a herd of cows. You see, his hand and arm are caught up the cow's nether regions. This is another one of those things that is supposed to be funny, but again it falls short. Humor should be rooted in truth and this joke forgets that rule. The reason Gilly's hand is up the cow's patootie is because Gilly becomes so frustrated trying to get to Jo that he starts punching cows, trying to get them out of his way. If it had not been so well established early on that Gilly was a big animal lover, this might be somewhat believable, but what little we do know about him shows that he would never do such a thing. But who cares about consistency when there's a lame joke to be had?

In his role, Klein is exactly like he's been in all his other roles. His main asset is that he seems to be a clean-cut, nice guy and that's about as far as he generally goes. Graham mainly stands around looking pretty. Field is over-the-top as the gold-digging mother. The most amazing aspect of her performance is that she manages to fit in all those leopard print tight pants. She seems to be having fun playing such an unsympathetic character but it's hard not to feel sorry for her that she's wasting so much energy in such a bad film. One of the most enjoyable performances in the film is Orlando Jones who plays a legless pilot Dig McCaffey who helps Gilly get his girl. Jones makes his character lively and entertaining despite being given such schtick as losing his prosthetic legs not once, not twice, but three times.

Critics hated the film. The *Kansas City Star* said it was "a scattershot shock comedy that bounces between romantic cliche and new-millenium risque to the point of irritation and, all too quickly, boredom." *Entertainment Weekly* gave it an F and called it "so unfunny it hurts."

—*Jill Hamilton*

## CREDITS

**Gilly Noble:** Chris Klein
**Jo Wingfield:** Heather Graham
**Dig McCaffey:** Orlando Jones
**Valdine Wingfield:** Sally Field
**Walter Wingfield:** Richard Jenkins
**Larry Falwell:** John Rothman
**Leon Pitofsky:** Jack Plotnick
**Jack Mtichelson:** Eddie Cibrian
**Jimmy Mitchelson:** Mark Pellegrino
**Sheriff Merle Hobbs:** Richard Riehle
**Det. Vic Bloomfield:** Brent Briscoe
**Freddy:** Henry Cho
**Herself:** Suzanne Somers
**Streak:** Brent Hinkley

**Origin:** USA
**Released:** 2001
**Production:** Bobby Farrelly, Peter Farrelly, Bradley Thomas; Conundrum Entertainment; released by 20th Century-Fox
**Directed by:** James B. Rogers
**Written by:** Peter Gaulke, Gerry Swallow
**Cinematography by:** Mark Irwin
**Music by:** Mason Daring
**Sound:** Jonathan Stein, Darren Brisker
**Music Supervisor:** Tom Wolfe, Manish Raval
**Editing:** Larry Madaras
**Art Direction:** Arlan Jay Vetter, Andrew Deskin
**Costumes:** Lisa Jensen

**Production Design:** Sidney J. Bartholomew Jr.
**MPAA rating:** R
**Running time:** 95 minutes

## REVIEWS

*Boxoffice.* May, 2001, p. 59.
*Entertainment Weekly.* March 30, 2001, p. 47.
*Los Angeles Times Online.* March 23, 2001.
*New York Times Online.* March 23, 2001.
*People.* April 2, 2001, p. 34.
*Sight and Sound.* July, 2001, p. 53.
*Variety.* March 26, 2001, p. 42.
*Washington Post Online.* March 23, 2001.

# Scary Movie 2

*More merciless. More shameless.*
—Movie tagline

 **Box Office:** $71.3 million

The Wayans brothers swore they would not make a sequel to their surprise big summer hit, *Scary Movie.* But it was not that big of a shock when it was announced that there would indeed be a *Scary Movie 2.* After all, the first film made over $260 million worldwide. And, after seeing this film, it becomes pretty obvious that the reasons for making the sequel were a lot more motivated by that $260 million figure than any sudden flash of creative inspiration. Of course, choosing greed over art is almost a necessity when making a sequel. It just wouldn't be right, somehow, if sequel makers had a fresh, exciting new twist on their original idea.

In a way, the Wayans—director Keenen Ivory Wayans, plus actors and co-writers Shawn and Marlon Wayans and co-writer Craig Wayans (there are also five non-Wayans writers)—could have saved themselves some trouble by just re-releasing the first movie because the second one treads over the same familiar ground. It was probably a good idea since the formula is a near perfect mix to attract teens. It's as though it was formulated in secret European laboratories to be of maximum attractiveness to boys aged 12–18. The Wayans mix together a little sex (i.e. characters going to "third base," a new busty character), a little bit of frightening stuff (though not enough to really scare anyone), some pop culture references, a wee bit of gore, and lots and lots of jokes about bodily functions. Here the Wayans comedy philosophy seems to be: when in doubt, have a character fart or throw up or otherwise eject something from some sort of bodily orifice.

*Scary Movie 2* is loosely a parody of the 1999 film *The Haunting.* It's a strange choice since that film didn't have nearly the popular culture impact as *Scream* and *I Know What You Did Last Summer*—the two films that the first *Scary Movie* focused on. Like its predecessor, the sequel parodies a lot of different movies, whether they're horror movies or not. So me of the jokes are based on the audience having a knowledge of films as diverse as *Charlie's Angels, Dude, Where's My Car?* and *Poltergeist.*

The movie starts off with a mini-parody that's unrelated to the rest of the film. It's a short goof on *The Exorcist* with Father McFeely (ha ha) who is an overly randy priest (James Woods), his sidekick, a sincere younger priest (Andy Richter, late of Conan O'Brien's talk show) and the possessed young woman (Natasha Lyonne). The sequence very much sets the tone for the rest of the film. The low level of the humor in the film is established when the possessed girl stands in the living room of her parents' house and interrupts a wholesome evening of singing around the piano to pee on the floor. But it's not enough that the girl urinates on the floor—she goes for what must be two minutes. If going to the bathroom on the floor is funny, the writers must have reasoned, then going for a really really long time must be funnier. Other gross-out highlights include McFeely trying to have sex with the possessed girl, McFeely in a bathroom scene that outdoes even Jeff Daniels' one in *Dumb and Dumber* and a sequence of characters throwing up huge volumes of vomit on each other. With the vomit, it's another case of the more vomit = funnier scene philosophy. They must have had their prop people busy for hours mixing up so much fake barf.

The story has characters from the first film, and some new people, who go to a haunted house for the weekend. They are supposed to be participating in some sort of psychological experiment, but really they are being studied by an evil professor (Tim Curry) and his prize student Dwight (David Cross), who is brilliant, wheelchair-bound and kind of weird. What science they are trying to do is fairly nebulous in the script, but the professor, at least, just seems to want to see some coeds getting it on.

When the kids get to the house, they meet creepy caretaker Hanson (Chris Elliot), who speaks in a Southern accent and has a tiny deformed hand that's the focus of way, way too many jokes. There is a scene where the caretaker has prepared a fancy banquet for all the students. They look hungrily at the food until they see the caretaker rake his hand through the mashed potatoes, the turkey and the pie. Elliot hams it up by licking his hand before serving each thing. The scene in itself would be overkill, but it's only one of many instances where Elliot and the presumed ickiness of his hand are the sole source of humor.

As the kids spend time in the house, they quickly realize that it is haunted. The house was haunted because, as movie haunted houses are invariably created, someone was killed there. In this case, it's a wealthy husband who was killed by his lovely young wife. The "plot" is that the students are trying to defeat this poltergeist couple and get out alive. There is no drama in this though, since the ghosts are more cartoony than scary and the students never seem in any kind of true danger.

Each of the character is sketched out only enough to hang some jokes on. Cindy (Anna Faris) is the not-so smart girl, Shorty (Marlon Wayans) is the resident pothead, Ray (Shawn Wayans) just wants to get in bed with everyone, and Brenda (Regina Hall) is the brash one who worries that she will be killed first since she's black. Tori Spelling plays a girl who has a nighttime erotic encounter with the ghost, then becomes fatally attracted to him. Buddy (Chris Masterson) pretends to be interested in Cindy's personality so that he can get in bed with her. And Kathleen Robertson, formerly of *Beverly Hills 90210*, is the busty sexpot—the Ginger, if you will.

*Scary Movie 2* has an *Airplane*-like rapid fire delivery of gags. Everything that can have a joke attached to it, does. (And with so many writers involved, there should be a lot of jokes.) The invitation for the weekend, for example, reads "If you had any brains you would take your $#$ home." Some of the jokes are bound to hit and a few do. A scene where Cindy faces an evil cat turns into a drawn-out, slo mo boxing match that's good for a few laughs. And after Cindy tells Buddy that she thinks they should just be friends, Buddy takes it to mean that he should treat her like one of the guys. "Think fast!" he says, pummeling her with a ball. And when the three black characters have to be separated from the others, they—who are well versed in the way horror movies work—look at each other in terror and say "We gonna die, y'all!"

But for every mildly funny joke, there are about ten instances of really disgusting things. Disgusting is not necessarily bad, but the writers seem to forget that something disgusting, on its own, does not constitute a joke. Among cringe-inducing moments are a segment with a guy who can perform oral sex on himself, a bird poop scene, and, well, other stuff that there's not really a nice way to explain. The Wayans also seem obsessed with deformity and, besides Elliot's hand, there is a man's strangely large nipple and several jokes about being in a wheelchair.

Critics, who had sat through a whole summer of gross out fare, were pretty cranky about the whole *Scary Movie 2* business. "By the time *Scary Movie 3* inevitably arrives to slime us, exhibitors might want to consider handing out moist towelettes to the audience. It's important to feel fresh, even if what you're watching no longer is," wrote Peter Howell at the *Toronto Star*. *Entertainment Weekly* gave the film a "C" and said, "*Scary Movie 2* is a desperate act of nose

thumbing that never quite figures out how, or even where, to position its thumb." Steven Rea at the *Philadelphia Inquirer* wrote, "Where, a year ago, audiences laughed at the unalloyed audacity of the filmmakers and their lewd, phallocentric brand of comedy, the second time around, it just seems boring. Boring, and decidedly misogynistic."

—*Jill Hamilton*

## CREDITS

**Cindy:** Anna Faris
**The Professor:** Tim Curry
**Ray:** Shawn Wayans
**Shorty:** Marlon Wayans
**Hanson:** Chris Elliott
**Alex:** Tori Spelling
**Buddy:** Christopher K. Masterson
**Theo:** Kathleen Robertson
**Brenda:** Regina Hall
**Father McFeely:** James Woods
**Dwight:** David Cross
**Father Harris:** Andy Richter
**Megan Voorhees:** Natasha Lyonne
**Mrs. Voorhees:** Veronica Cartwright
**Huey Cain:** Richard Moll

**Origin:** USA
**Released:** 2001
**Production:** Eric Gold; Wayans Bros. Entertainment; released by Dimension Films
**Directed by:** Keenen Ivory Wayans
**Written by:** Shawn Wayans, Marlon Wayans, Alyson Fouse, Greg Grabianski, Dave Polsky, Michael Anthony Snowden, Craig Wayans
**Cinematography by:** Steven Bernstein
**Sound:** David Kirschner
**Music Supervisor:** Randy Spendlove
**Editing:** Peter Teschner, Tom Nordberg, Richard Pearson
**Art Direction:** Cat Smith
**Costumes:** Mary Jane Fort, Valari Adams
**Production Design:** Cynthia Charette
**MPAA rating:** R
**Running time:** 82 minutes

## REVIEWS

*Boxoffice.* September, 2001, p. 151.
*Entertainment Weekly.* July 20, 2001, p. 42.
*Los Angeles Times Online.* July 4, 2001.
*New York Times Online.* July 4, 2001.

*TV Guide*. June 30, 2001, p. 8.
*USA Today Online*. July 6, 2001.
*Variety*. July 9, 2001, p. 21.
*Washington Post Online*. July 6, 2001.

# The Score

*There are no partners in crime.*
—Movie tagline

 **Box Office:** $71.1 million

Heist or caper films are hard to botch, probably much harder than the real crimes. There's something about seeing skilled criminals stealing money or jewels or art or whatever that's fascinating to many viewers who would like to pull off the perfect crime themselves but lack the courage, skills, or brains. Even when the Hollywood Production Code deemed that the thieves could not get away with it, the process of the robberies unveiled in films such as John Huston's *The Asphalt Jungle* (1950) or Stanley Kubrick's *The Killing* (1956) is highly watchable. The best heist films, such as Jules Dassin's *Rififi* (1955) or Wes Anderson's *Bottle Rocket* (1996), offer more than the process, making the character of the criminals and their milieu equally important to the job at hand. While *The Score* is entertaining, it disappoints in offering too few extras beyond the crime itself. All its elements, including the two ironic twists at the end, are woefully predictable. The main thing it has going for it is seeing three generations of vastly different Method actors working together.

Nick (Robert De Niro) is an aging safecracker who uses his ill gains to support NYC, the jazz club he runs in Montreal. (Singers Mose Allison and Cassandra Wilson make cameo appearances performing at the club.) Nick has a relationship with Diane (Angela Bassett), a flight attendant who jokes about his dangerous work. Nick tells her he will quit, but then Max (Marlon Brando), who brokers Nick's crimes, asks him to pull one more job. The catch is not just Nick's promise to Diane but the fact that the robbery is to take place in Montreal. Nick has made a rule not to steal on his home turf.

After hemming and hawing, Nick, of course, gives in, angering Diane, because Max is his friend and Max is being threatened by some big-time gangster. (Warning: the clichés don't stop there.) The object to be stolen is a 17th-century French scepter worth $30 million, heavily guarded in the basement of Montreal's Customs House. How it ended up there, hidden in a piano leg, is one of the film's more clever plot points. Nick is to carry out the theft with the aid of Jack

Teller (Edward Norton), the inside man, disguised as the retarded Brian, working as an assistant janitor at the Customs House. Another problem is Nick's instant distrust of Jack.

The one last job, unforgiving girlfriend, old friend in a spot, breaking an unbreakable rule, and tensions between veteran and young upstart are beyond hoary clichés. Then there are the last-minute improvements in the security guarding the scepter. The predictable aspects of *The Score* are even more disappointing given that one of its screenwriters is Lem Dobbs who wrote the masterful crime film *The Limey* (1999). The only slightly offbeat touch is making Nick's computer expert (Jamie Harrold) a housebound geek nagged constantly by his unseen mother, but even that could be seen as a stereotype. There are also a few holes in the plot as with the magical reappearance of a supposed burned piano leg.

The robbery itself, however, works as Nick makes his way slowly to the safe holding the scepter while Jack disables the security. Director Frank Oz has a feel for exposition, and *The Score* is one of the few heist films in which the robbery is relatively easy to follow. The viewer knows, for the most part, exactly what is going on and why.

Many reviewers questioned Oz's being hired to direct a crime film given that he has specialized almost exclusively in comedy with such films as *Dirty Rotten Scoundrels* (1988), *What About Bob?* (1991), *In & Out* (1997), and *Bowfinger* (1999). The latter has an action element superficially similar to *The Score*, but the main problem with these films is their being rather impersonal and emotionless. Oz is a craftsman, not an artist, and while he is competent at moving the narrative from point to point, there are no interesting detours, no quirky touches, no directorial signatures along the way.

Oz's impersonal style may have led to the well-reported conflict on the set between the director and his most venerable star. Early false reports had Brando being naked from the waist down to force Oz to shoot him in close-up. The real problem, as reported by Jess Cagle in *Time*, was the actor's refusal to tone down his campy interpretation of Max and his ultimate refusal to be on the set at the same time as Oz. As a result, the director watched the action on an off-site monitor while relaying instructions to De Niro who directed the great man's scenes. Brando ridiculed the filmmaker by calling him Miss Piggy, the beloved Muppet whose voice Oz originated.

Brando himself has been taken to task for his sloppy, self-indulgent work since *Last Tango in Paris* (1972), in which he gave one of the truly great performances in film history. Since then, except for *Apocalypse Now* (1979) and *The Freshman* (1990), Brando has chosen his work unwisely and has been known to misbehave on location, most notoriously on the *Island of Dr. Moreau* (1996). Nevertheless, he is a great actor who retains considerable screen presence despite the bulk that makes him look more like Sidney

Greenstreet than the Brando audiences and critics once adored. (In his rumpled linen, he also dresses like Greenstreet.) Brando gives Max an effeminate voice somewhat like that of Truman Capote, who once wrote a famous unflattering profile of the actor, though this voice comes and goes. Still, whenever he is on screen, he dominates it. His best moment—and one of Oz's—comes when Max watches a television report about the robbery. It's a medium shot with Brando filling the frame. He stares impassively, displaying no emotion until a brief flutter of his lips when he hears of Nick's fate. Few actors could convey so much with so little effort. It's a great moment.

De Niro, who in his prime has been Brando's equal, has also been criticized for not being choosy enough about his projects, resulting in *The Fan* (1996), *Flawless* (1999), *Men of Honor* (2000), and *15 Minutes* (2001). With the notable exceptions of *Wag the Dog* (1997), *Analyze This* (1999), and *Meet the Parents* (2000), in too many of his recent films, De Niro has too little to do and coasts through his parts. (He is rumored to spend all his off-camera time on sets on the phone dealing with his restaurants, the films his company is producing, or other business interests.)

De Niro doesn't need the flamboyance of roles such as *Raging Bull* (1980) to showcase his considerable skills. He is adept at finding the nuances in subtle parts, particularly with *True Confessions* (1981) and *Wag the Dog*, but the script for *The Score*, rather than his own indifference, seems to have let him down. Perhaps he decided that Nick is too much of a cliché to make much of an effort. Still, there are a few moments of note, as when he displays Nick's conflicting emotion when he tells Diane about one more job. Though she has even less to do, Bassett commands the screen through sheer presence.

Norton's acting style resembles De Niro's with his being equally at ease in both colorful and more subdued roles. Norton's potential for greatness is unusual because the best film actors are, at least when young, almost always handsome—Brando, Laurence Olivier, Paul Newman—or distinctive looking—Humphrey Bogart, Lee Marvin, Dustin Hoffman. Very few—Alec Guinness, Gene Hackman, Jack Nicholson—are ordinary, like Norton. Such bland looks are helpful in such parts as Jack because those he encounters underestimate him.

Norton can be accused of plagiarism since his retarded Brian is almost identical vocally with Hoffman's savant character in *Rain Man* (1988). As Jack, he more than holds his on with Brando and De Niro. Norton is equally compelling when Jack is talkative, as with a showdown in a public park with a nervous blackmailer, and in quieter moments, as when Jack adopts a mysterious façade while letting Nick literally dangle in the middle of the heist.

*The Score* is watchable but no more than that. The viewer's frustration comes from expecting explosions from this cast while Oz and the screenwriters provide mere puffs of smoke.

—*Michael Adams*

### CREDITS

**Nick:** Robert De Niro
**Jack/Brian:** Edward Norton
**Max:** Marlon Brando
**Diane:** Angela Bassett
**Burt:** Gary Farmer
**Danny:** Paul Soles
**Steven:** Jamie Harold

**Origin:** USA
**Released:** 2001
**Production:** Gary Foster, Lee Rich; Mandalay Pictures, Horseshoe Bay; released by Paramount Pictures
**Directed by:** Frank Oz
**Written by:** Kario Salem, Scott Marshall Smith, Lem Dobbs
**Cinematography by:** Rob Hahn
**Music by:** Howard Shore
**Sound:** Glen Gauthier
**Editing:** Richard Pearson
**Art Direction:** Tom Reta, Claude Pare
**Costumes:** Aude Bronson-Howard
**Production Design:** Jackson De Govia
**MPAA rating:** R
**Running time:** 124 minutes

### REVIEWS

*Boston Globe.* July 13, 2001, p. D1.
*Boxoffice.* September, 2001, p. 150.
*Chicago Sun-Times Online.* July 13, 2001.
*Entertainment Weekly.* July 20, 2001, p. 40.
*Hollywood Reporter.* July 11, 2001, p. 2.
*Los Angeles Times Online.* July 13, 2001.
*Maclean's.* July 16, 2001, p. 53.
*New York Times.* July 13, 2001, p. E12.
*People.* July 23, 2001, p. 33.
*Rolling Stone.* August 2, 2001, p. 70.
*San Francisco Chronicle.* July 13, 2001, p. C1.
*USA Today.* July 13, 2001, p. E6.
*Variety.* July 16, 2001, p. 18.
*Washington Post.* July 13, 2001, p. C1.

## QUOTES

Nick (Robert De Niro): "After this, no more jobs. This is the last one I'm doing." Max (Marlon Brando): "How many times have you told me that in 25 years?"

# See Spot Run

*The smart one isn't wearing any pants.*
—Movie tagline

**Box Office:** $33.4 million

*See Spot Run* is meant as family viewing fun, but this dog movie is itself a dog of a movie. David Arquette plays Gordon, a slacker letter carrier who agrees to babysit for the little boy next door, James (Angus T. Jones), as a means to impress James's pretty mother, Stephanie (Leslie Bibb). But Stephanie becomes detained on an overnight business trip, and asks Gordon to take care of James much longer than he wanted or anticipated.

Coincidentally, Gordon is forced to look after a dog he finds one morning in his post office truck. What neither Gordon nor James know is that the dog is a special agent for the FBI. Apparently, this canine "Agent 11" is the target of a mafia boss, Sonny Talia (Paul Sorvino), because he has kept Sonny from stealing $22 million. Just as Agent 11's partner, Agent Murdoch (Michael Clarke Duncan), prepared to ship the dog to safe haven in Alaska, Agent 11 escaped from his kennel and found Gordon's vehicle. While both the Mafia don's thugs and several FBI agents search for Agent 11, the boy bonds with the pooch and names him Spot. Inevitably, the FBI agents capture the mafiosi and demand to have the dog back. But Spot prefers to stay with James, so Agent Murdoch reluctantly gives away his prized pet and partner. Stephanie, who finally returns from her trip, sees the good influences on her son while she was away, and expresses her wish to form an instant family with Gordon, James, and Spot.

Sadly, for some reason, contemporary filmmakers feel it necessary to add low bathroom humor to nearly every kind of comedy, even when it is inappropriate and more unpleasant than funny. For "family" movies, it's more than inappropriate . . . it's unseemly. But some children like scenes of people smeared in feces, so who are the adult critics to say anything?

"Keep it on cartoons—don't try to get smart!," Gordon informs James regarding his television viewing habits, and in an instant, Gordon sums up the viewpoint of Warner Bros.' *See Spot Run*. The screenplay by George Gallo, Dan Baron and Chris Faber offers a primer to preteens on how they, too, can be slacker dudes like Gordon. Chasing down Fruit Loops with a liter of Pepsi is just the first step. Along the way, this *K-9* redux (or is it *Turner & Hooch* redux?) proudly shills for lots of other products, including Warner Bros. movies (e.g. *The Godfather* series, *The Matrix*, *Pokémon*), Blockbuster, Petcetera, and more junk food—Pringles, Oreos, Cheetos, Miller Beer and Hawaiian Punch.

But the product plugs are no more brazen than the fact that this "children's film" is rated PG and includes (as the MPAA warning states) "Crude Humor, Language And Comic Violence." David Arquette's biggest comic set-piece has him sloshing and tumbling about in dog excrement. Paul Sorvino's key scenes have Spot chewing off his testicles. And Leslie Bibb's most memorable moment has her splashed by mud so that we can see her breasts through her clothes. Of course, all of this is played for laughs, leading Roger Ebert to say, "There seems to be some kind of desperate downward trend in American taste, so that when we see a dog movie like this we think back nostalgically to the *Beethoven* dog pictures, which now represent a cultural high-water mark."

Typically, Warner Bros. marketed *See Spot Run* to African-American youths, yet it humiliates them just the same. In just the first reel, black FBI agent Murdoch is mistaken for being the dog agent; our "hero" (Arquette) dubs a chained dog "Tyson" (after Mike Tyson); and a Black mail carrier (Anthony Anderson) lusts after a woman and barks like a dog. A fight scene involving two deaf women isn't any more politically correct or funny. The lone actor to emerge unharmed by the cynical crumminess of the enterprise is little Angus T. Jones, a sincerely likable child performer. Jones' responses to Arquette's foolish antics are the only reasons to get anywhere near *See Spot Run*. "That's it. It's over," says one of the FBI agents—but not at the end of the film. Sadly, you can't trust the FBI—or the American film industry—anymore.

—*Eric Monder*

## CREDITS

**Gordon Smith:** David Arquette
**Agent Murdoch:** Michael Clarke Duncan
**Stephanie:** Leslie Bibb
**James:** Angus T. Jones
**Gino Valente:** Joe Viterelli
**Sonny Talia:** Paul Sorvino
**Benny:** Anthony Anderson

**Origin:** USA
**Released:** 2001

**Production:** Robert Simonds, Tracey Trench, Andrew Deane; Village Roadshow Pictures, NPV Entertainment; released by Warner Bros.
**Directed by:** John Whitesell
**Written by:** George Gallo, Dan Baron, Chris Faber
**Cinematography by:** John Bartley
**Music by:** John Debney
**Sound:** Patrick Ramsay
**Music Supervisor:** Michele Wernick
**Editing:** Cara Silverman
**Art Direction:** Catherine Ircha
**Costumes:** Diane M. Widas
**Production Design:** Mark Freeborn
**MPAA rating:** PG
**Running time:** 94 minutes

## REVIEWS

*Boxoffice.* May, 2001, p. 61.
*Chicago Sun-Times Online.* March 2, 2001.
*Entertainment Weekly.* March 9, 2001, p. 57.
*New York Times Online.* March 2, 2001.
*San Francisco Chronicle Online.* March 2, 2001.
*Sight and Sound.* June, 2001, p. 52.
*USA Today Online.* March 2, 2001.
*Variety.* February 26, 2001, p. 40.
*Washington Post Online.* March 2, 2001.

## TRIVIA

Canine Agent 11 is played by a Bull Mastiff named Bob.

# Sentimental Destiny (Destinees Sentimentales)

In France, filmmaker Olivier Assayas has become known for his films revolving around relationships such as *Cold Water* and *Late August, Early September*. But American audiences will most likely recall Assayas' stylized vampire flick *Irma Vep*, which starred the Hong Kong actress Maggie Cheung (who later married Assayas). Viewers expecting to view Assayas' signature film etchings, street reflections on café windows and quick edits, will be disappointed with his latest release *Sentimental Destiny*, a three-hour long epic drama (spanning 1900–1930). However, those viewers who cherish Assayas' depiction of relationship tensions will embrace the director's latest work.

For true Francophiles *Sentimental Destiny* will be a treat. The film stars Emmanuel Bèart, Charles Berling, and Isabelle Huppert, the screenplay was adapted from Jacques Chardon's famous novel, and renowned cinematographer Eric Gautier shot the sumptuous French and Swiss landscapes. However, *Sentimental Destiny* isn't without faults. First, the film's narrative proves confusing since it becomes increasingly difficult to keep track of the various members of this family dynasty; second, Assayas himself seems confused as he attempts to mesh a little bit of history with social politics, religion, and universal themes revolving around loyalty and commitment; finally, the film's narrative plods along while only providing a thimble full of tension and is almost absent of humor.

As the film opens, we are introduced to Protestant minister Jean Barnery (Charles Berling). Controversy has risen about his wife Nathalie's (Isabelle Huppert) possible infidelity, so Nathalie and their daughter Aline are sent away to Limoges. Meanwhile, Pauline (Emmanuel Beart), the niece of a brandy maker, arrives in town to stay with her uncle after her father's death. She makes eye contact with Barnery at a church service and is immediately captivated by the minister. When Pauline and Jean meet at a ball, they seem to hit it off. However, Jean decides to reunite with his wife and child, so Pauline leaves the small town of Charante.

Eventually, Jean divorces his wife, leaves the church, and gives his money to his daughter Aline. Pauline visits the penniless and seriously ill Jean in his sparse hotel room in Paris and demands that Jean stay in Switzerland until he recovers. Pauline and Jean set up house in Switzerland, marry, and have a son, Max. However, their enchanted stay is interrupted by the dire future of the Barnery family business, a porcelain factory in Limoges. Once again Jean faces conflicts with regard to his lack of commitment and loyalty to his family and Pauline doesn't want to have to deal with the failing family business. Soon World War I breaks out, causing Jean to leave his helm at the factory, and also causing another rift in his marriage.

Meanwhile, Nathalie has passed on her bitterness towards men to a grown-up Aline (Mia Hansen-Love), causing her to mingle with the wrong crowd in a seedy Parisian district. Eventually, Aline runs into childhood friend Dominique (Sophie Aubry) and it is suggested that a lesbian relationship develops between the two women. As this subplot unfolds, Aline becomes a deacon in the church after Dominique dies a painful death, and her father sees her take her vows.

After the war ends, Jean embraces capitalism and becomes a leader of industry while ignoring his family's needs. He becomes obsessed with outbidding the German and Japanese porcelain factories and with a particular design he'd like to manufacture. However, in order to build a new factory that can accommodate his needs, he is forced to make tough choices that result in a worker's strike. Eventually age catches up with Jean and he admits defeat just as he and his wife grow closer. However, with Pauline's help Jean's dream porcelain becomes a reality even if the family dynasty will die with him.

Assayas has matured artistically during the past two years and stretched his cinematic wings with *Sentimental Destiny*. However, some viewers will be disappointed with the uninvolving film. But the on-screen chemistry between Bèart and Berling will provide much needed respite.

—*Patty-Lynne Herlevi*

## CREDITS

**Jean Barnery:** Charles Berling
**Pauline:** Emmanuelle Beart
**Nathalie:** Isabelle Huppert
**Philippe Pommerel:** Olivier Perrier
**Julie Desca:** Dominique Reymond
**Paul Desca:** Andre Marcon
**Louise Desca:** Alexandra London
**Marcelle:** Julie Depardieu

**Origin:** France, Switzerland
**Language:** French
**Released:** 2000
**Production:** Bruno Pesery; Arena Films, TF-1 Films, CAB Productions
**Directed by:** Olivier Assayas
**Written by:** Olivier Assayas, Jacques Fieschi
**Cinematography by:** Eric Gautier
**Music by:** Guillaume Lekeu
**Sound:** Jean-Claude Laureaux
**Editing:** Luc Barnier
**Costumes:** Anais Romand
**Production Design:** Katia Wyszkop
**MPAA rating:** Unrated
**Running time:** 180 minutes

## REVIEWS

*Boxoffice*. November, 2000, p. 164.
*Sight and Sound*. January, 2001, p. 46.

# Serendipity

*The comedy that proves destiny has a sense of humor.*
—Movie tagline
*Can Once In A Lifetime Happen Twice?*
—Movie tagline
*No name. No address. Just fate.*
—Movie tagline

**Box Office:** $50.2 million

The charming romantic comedy *Serendipity* was released at exactly the right time last year. After the tragic events of September 11, moviegoers were in the mood for lighthearted, escapist fare and this delightful fairy tale provided the perfect break from reality. Like *Sleepless in Seattle* or *An Affair to Remember*, this love story's premise is that boy and girl meet and are meant to be together, yet they must overcome several obstacles before destiny plays out.

New Yorkers Jonathan (John Cusack) and Sara (Kate Beckinsale) meet cute at Bloomingdale's while both are reaching for a pair of cashmere gloves during a pre-Christmas rush. They feel a strong attraction at first sight and end up spending a few magical, unexpected hours together—ice skating in Central Park and sharing hot chocolate at Serendipity, a real-life Manhattan dessert shop. The title of the sweets shop gives the film a nice touch, as well as an appropriate title. "A fortunate accident," says Sara on the meaning of the word.

While on their dream date, Sara and Jon learn that each is involved with someone else. They part, but end up running into each other again when Jon returns for a scarf and Sara for a package. At this point, Jon asks for Sara's phone number, but she decides that it's best if they leave everything up to Fate. Instead she writes her name and phone number in a copy of Gabriel Garcia Marquez's *Love in the Time of Cholera*, which she plans to sell to a used bookstore. Then she makes Jon, who is clearly frustrated by all of this, put his phone number on a $5 bill, which she promptly spends. Sara firmly believes if the universe wants them to be together, these objects will come back into their lives.

The movie then jumps ahead "a few years later," and Jon, who is still living in New York, is about to marry the pretty and unsuspecting Halley (Bridget Moynahan). Although his wedding date is quickly approaching, Jon can't get Sara out of his mind. Meanwhile, Sara, who now lives in San Francisco, is also engaged to a nice, but clueless New Age pop star named Lars (John Corbett). Of course, Sara can't stop thinking about Jon either. Jon starts searching for

Kate with the help of his best friend, Dean (Jeremy Piven), while Sara begins looking for Jon with the assistance of her girlfriend, Eve (Molly Shannon). Comical situations ensue as Jon and Sara fly to opposite coasts at the same time and engage in a series of farfetched coincidences, forcing the audience to suspend disbelief more than once.

Although the outcome is highly contrived in this light-weight fluff, the predictable climax doesn't in any way diminish one's enjoyment of the film. Both Cusack and Beckinsale are likeable and believable as the would-be sweet-hearts. From the very beginning of the story, it's apparent that they have a real chemistry onscreen. The solid work of the supporting cast also adds to the pic's overall charm. Piven (a longtime friend and colleague of Cusack's) and Shannon are pitch perfect in their roles as the wisecracking best friends of the leads, and Eugene Levy does a hilarious turn as the officious Bloomie's salesclerk. Corbett also deserves special mention as the laughable, New Age musician. His longhaired hippie character exists mainly for comic relief and he doesn't disappoint.

But perhaps the real star of *Serendipity* is the city itself. Manhattan has never looked as glamorous or as magically romantic as it does in this film. As Charles Taylor wrote in his review for *Salon*, "*Serendipity* works overtime to sprinkle moonlight and stardust over itself. If you've ever been lucky enough to chance upon the spectacular view of the New York skyline at dusk, when the lights of the city come on and everything looks shiny and promising, you know the romantic wistfulness the movie is striving to conjure up." In *Variety*, Todd McCarthy shared a similar view, "*Serendipity* does deliver an ultra-romanticized vision of a New York aglow with glorious urban spaces, beautiful people, and the warm potential of eternal love."

This romantic fantasy served as director Peter Chelsom's (*Hear My Song, Funny Bones*) rebound from *Town & Country*, which flopped with critics and audiences alike. Although *Serendipity* fared much better at the box-office, critical reaction was decidedly mixed. Desson Howe, of the *Washington Post*, called the film an "insipid, by-the-numbers romance." *People* magazine commented that the film was a "cloying dust-mite of a romantic comedy." *Los Angeles Times* critic Kenneth Turan saw the film for what it was, "a blithe and unapologetic fairy tale about affairs of the heart, it's a spun-sugar confection that's so light and airy it threatens to simply float away."

On the other hand, Lisa Schwarzbaum, writing for *Entertainment Weekly*, gave the film and cast high praise in her review, "Every pairing is a pleasure: Cusack's spicy wry charm is refreshed by Beckinsale's forthright intelligence. Beckinsale's British delicacy is challenged by Shannon's generous, madcap enthusiasm. As for Cusack and Piven, those old Chicago pals, I can't say enough about the fun the boys communicate so palpably . . . every scene between them is a delight." Claudia Puig of *USA Today* called *Serendipity* "a

satisfying date movie. The always-intelligent Cusack projects a winsome blend of affability, wit, and sexiness." This reviewer has to agree with the comments of the latter critics. As far as romantic comedies go, this winning film works and is a real treat for fans not only of the genre, but Cusack too.

—*Beth Fhaner*

## CREDITS

**Jonathan Trager:** John Cusack
**Sara Thomas:** Kate Beckinsale
**Eve:** Molly Shannon
**Lars Hammond:** John Corbett
**Dean Kansky:** Jeremy Piven
**Halley Buchanan:** Bridget Moynahan
**Bloomingdale's Salesman:** Eugene Levy

**Origin:** USA
**Released:** 2001
**Production:** Simon Fields, Peter Abrams, Robert Levy; Tapestry Films; released by Miramax Films
**Directed by:** Peter Chelsom
**Written by:** Marc Klein
**Cinematography by:** John de Borman
**Music by:** Alan Silvestri
**Sound:** Tod A. Maitland
**Music Supervisor:** Laura Ziffren
**Editing:** Christopher Greenbury
**Art Direction:** Tom Warren, Andrew Stearn
**Costumes:** Marie-Sylvie Deveau, Mary Claire Hannon
**Production Design:** Caroline Hanania
**MPAA rating:** PG-13
**Running time:** 87 minutes

## REVIEWS

*Chicago Sun-Times Online.* October 5, 2001.
*Entertainment Weekly.* October 12, 2001, p. 60.
*Hollywood Reporter.* September 17, 2001, p. 7.
*Los Angeles Times Online.* October 5, 2001.
*New York Times Online.* October 5, 2001.
*People.* October 15, 2001, p. 42.
*USA Today Online.* October 5, 2001.
*Variety.* September 24, 2001, p. 25.
*Washington Post.* October 5, 2001, p. WE38.

Sara (Kate Beckinsale) while they're ice skating: "Favorite New York moment?" Jonathan (John Cusack) replies: "This one is climbing the charts."

# Series 7: The Contenders

*Are You Game?*
—Movie tagline
*No lifelines. No free spins. No bonus rounds. In this game, if you can stay alive, you survive.*
—Movie tagline
*Real People In Real Danger.*
—Movie tagline
*6 contestants, 6 guns, no rules!*
—Movie tagline

 **Box Office:** $.1 million

A satire of reality TV that owes as much to Richard Connell's classic short story "The Most Dangerous Game" as it does to hit shows like *The Real World* and *Cops*, writer-director Daniel Minahan's *Series 7: The Contenders* probably looked like a clever, timely idea on paper. With the reality genre a major force on TV, the time seems right for a film that can have fun with the formulas and conventions with which many of us have become familiar. Unfortunately, this sometimes biting and funny film fails to live up to its full potential and explore this recent cultural phenomenon in a fresh, exciting way.

The movie plays out as a marathon of episodes from a popular TV game show called *The Contenders,* which is currently in its seventh season. There is no framing device or back story to remind us that we are watching a movie, and Minahan even shot *Series 7* on digital videotape and employed a film crew with experience in television to achieve the look of a cheesy TV show. The setup is simple—contestants are chosen at random in a government lottery, given a gun, and assigned a cameraman to follow them around. Their objective, however, is outrageous—kill the other contestants and be the last person standing. The winner then goes on to face five new challengers in the show's next season. While *Series 7* is commonly seen as a parody of *Survivor,* Minahan reportedly conceived his movie before *Survivor* became a television phenomenon in the summer of 2000.

Brooke Smith gives an intense, nuanced, strangely sympathetic performance as Dawn, the show's reigning champion, who is set to face a new group of challengers. She has triumphed for two seasons, and, if she can survive this round of play, she can retire from the show. The stakes are especially high for Dawn because this season the game is being played in the Connecticut town where she grew up and she is eight months pregnant. Unmarried and seemingly alone in the world, Dawn is a fierce, determined hard-luck case who has probably never succeeded at anything until *The Contenders.*

Right from the start, however, the film runs into some problems. Unlike reality game shows or dramas, where thousands of people audition for the chance to be on the show, the players on *The Contenders* are forced to participate, and yet the social context is never explained. Are we in a quasi-fascist future where common people are drafted to murder each other for the sake of entertainment? Does law enforcement just blindly accept armed citizens running around shooting each other, even in public places where innocent nonparticipants could stumble into the line of fire? These may seem like nitpicky questions, but they are crucial since social satire, in order to be effective and relevant, has to have a foundation in reality. *Series 7,* however, in its very premise, remains vague and feels severed from the genre it is trying to satirize.

Dawn's competition composes a variety of character types, most of them thinly drawn. Tony (Michael Kaycheck) is a 39-year-old, laid-off asbestos-removal worker with a wife and three children. Connie (Marylouise Burke), 57-years-old, is an emergency-room nurse whose seemingly devout religious faith masks an extreme ruthlessness. The least developed character is Franklin (Richard Venture), a 72-year-old retiree who resists playing and practically has to have a gun forced into his hand. Lindsay (Merritt Wever), on the other hand, seems ready for action. She is an 18-year-old who proudly displays the bulletproof vest her boyfriend chipped in to buy her. "I think it shows how much he cares about me," she cheerfully declares. Finally, Jeff (Glenn Fitzgerald) is a 33-year-old artist and Dawn's old boyfriend from high school. He has cancer, and his wife, Doria (Angelina Phillips), who has stood by him through the removal of his testicles, is jealous that Dawn is now reentering his life, even if she is doing so as a potential assassin.

Minahan has perfectly nailed a certain TV style of storytelling. From the authoritative voice of the omniscient narrator to the confessional moments of characters addressing the camera to the constant barrage of teasers foreshadowing upcoming plot twists and montages recapping past events, *Series 7* expertly employs the conventions of reality TV. And yet these familiar gimmicks soon become tiresome and obvious.

While the overall social context and even the game's rules are fuzzy, occasional satiric jabs feel right on target.

Lindsay's parents are so supportive of their daughter that they ask her if she has all her weaponry as they drive her to the site of her first attempted hit and then pump her up psychologically for the battle. It is a sly comment on the competitive American ethos as well as the on the way violence is easily accepted in our everyday lives, as if sending one's daughter out to kill were a normal part of family life.

The film also taps into the way troubled families are exploited by tabloid TV. When Dawn, the black sheep of her family, returns to her hometown, she has a painful yet funny reunion with her mother and sister in which all the old conflicts are dredged up and Dawn finally commandeers her sister's SUV at gunpoint. Tony may be the most outwardly disturbed and desperate player. When Dawn goes after him, he kidnaps one of his children and flees, injuring himself in the process. He is eventually apprehended by the show's SWAT team and put in the hospital, where Connie's background as a nurse helps her dispose of him with a lethal injection. Connie is a frightening character who sees herself as a humane killer and whose sense of moral superiority makes her feel completely justified in hunting the other contestants.

The emotional heart of the film is the strange yet oddly poignant relationship between Dawn and Jeff, which dates back to their days as outcasts in high school. She visits him just to talk, not to kill him, and, in the midst of the crazy circumstances in which they find themselves, they evoke a genuine tenderness that makes us believe that they were once a couple. Since Jeff is sick anyway, he agrees to let Dawn kill him—he would rather that she do it than someone else—but she first has to get the medication that will painlessly end his life. His wife, Doria, meanwhile, grows increasingly jealous of the intimacy they share and thinks that Dawn still loves him.

The killings themselves, supposedly the main interest of the show, are not very clever. In one of the film's big set pieces, the contestants are summoned to a busy mall in what turns out to be an ambush planned by Connie. Franklin beats Lindsay to death with a cane when the safety on her gun jams (as her parents helplessly watch). Connie then shoots and kills Franklin, but Dawn is able to escape.

In *Series 7*'s most outrageous, darkly humorous segment, Dawn confronts Connie in her home, but the killing goes awry, and Dawn goes into labor, which elicits the hard-hearted Connie's instincts as a nurse. Connie tries to deliver the baby of the very woman she intends to kill, but, because Dawn is having a breech birth, she is rushed to the hospital to deliver the child (and then is forced to give up the baby so that the game can continue). Meanwhile, Jeff, who has tried to kill himself with Doria's help instead of waiting for Dawn, has coincidentally ended up in the same hospital. (He was pronounced dead but was revived.) When Connie arrives to kill Jeff, he actually summons the strength to fight back and kills her instead, and then Dawn appears almost immedi-

ately and confronts Jeff with the realization that they are the last two contestants. But Jeff has changed his mind about wanting to die, and Dawn, who could kill him on the spot, instead lets him flee.

Through some behind-the-scenes machinations, Dawn and Jeff agree to have a showdown on a football field, but, when they meet, they decide not to kill each other. Instead, they turn their guns on the cameramen and hit the road together, hoping to escape the game and eventually be reunited with her baby. We are then treated to glimpses of the fugitives filmed by security cameras as they go on a little crime spree, and, in the style of *America's Most Wanted*, viewers help track the fleeing couple. The idea of contestants turning against the show could be provocative and address the moral questions at the heart of the program, but Minahan does not pursue this angle. Instead, the film takes a conventional turn when Dawn enters a crowded movie theater and takes a whole auditorium of moviegoers hostage, vowing to kill them if her demands for the return of her newborn baby and passage across the border are not met. (In a funny aside, the moronic theater patrons, probably thrilled to be on TV, cheer her, not realizing that they are her intended victims.)

At this point, the screenplay makes a huge miscalculation from which the already tedious film never recovers. The show's narrator tells us that the original footage from the show's final moments was accidentally destroyed and that the producers have enlisted actors to portray the real Jeff and Dawn in a re-enactment of the conclusion. This ending is a complete failure. No so-called reality show whose tagline is "Real people in real danger in a fight for their lives" would substitute actors for real-life contestants, especially in a climactic situation. If Minahan's point is that reality TV is not so real after all and that the producers of *The Contenders* actually manipulate the scenario to get the results they want (a point worth satirizing since this is a common charge against reality TV), then this is the laziest, most unrealistic way to explore such fraud.

With actors filling in for the contestants, the host offers Dawn her baby if she will shoot Jeff, and Jeff goes along with the proposal. As Dawn is about to comply, however, an actress playing Doria bursts into the theater and shoots Dawn. Jeff then shoots himself, and it appears that the lovers will be united in death. In the film's final joke, however, it turns out that the seemingly indestructible Jeff has once again survived his own suicide attempt and is recovering in the hospital. The sole survivor, he will be forced to play again in *Series 8*.

*Series 7* takes the reality-TV genre to the limit by creating an extreme, absurd version of a game show in which life and death are the stakes but fails to make many provocative points about this national obsession. If the film had been either a riotously funny, over-the-top farce or a chilling cautionary tale of media run amuck, *Series 7* could have captured the zeitgeist. But Minahan seems to have tried a combination of both approaches and ended up with a mediocre concoction that offers few fresh insights into our media-obsessed culture.

—*Peter N. Chumo II*

## CREDITS

**Dawn:** Brooke Smith
**Jeff:** Glenn Fitzgerald
**Lindsay:** Merritt Wever
**Tony:** Michael Kaycheck
**Franklin:** Richard Venture
**Sheila:** Donna Hanover
**Connie:** Marylouise Burke
**Michelle:** Nada Despotovich
**Bob:** Danton Stone
**Laura:** Jennifer Van Dyck
**Doria:** Angelina Phillips
**Dawn's mother:** Tanny McDonald
**Narrator:** Will Arnett

**Origin:** USA
**Released:** 2001
**Production:** Jason Kliot, Joana Vicente, Christine Vachon, Katie Roumel; Killer Films, Open City Films, Blow Up Pictures; released by USA Films
**Directed by:** Daniel Minahan
**Written by:** Daniel Minahan
**Cinematography by:** Randy Drummond
**Music by:** Girls Against Boys
**Sound:** Mark Maloof, Eddie O'Conner, Giles Kahn, Jason Blackburn
**Music Supervisor:** Julie Panebianco
**Editing:** Malcolm Jamieson
**Art Direction:** Ann McKinnon
**Costumes:** Christine Biselin
**Production Design:** Gideon Ponte
**MPAA rating:** R
**Running time:** 86 minutes

## REVIEWS

*Chicago Sun-Times Online.* March 16, 2001.
*Entertainment Weekly.* March 9, 2001, p. 54.
*Entertainment Weekly.* March 16, 2001, p. 45.
*New York Times Online.* March 2, 2001.
*Newsweek.* March 5, 2001, p. 58.
*Rolling Stone.* February 15, 2001, p. 83.
*Sight and Sound.* June, 2001, p. 53.
*USA Today Online.* March 2, 2001.
*Variety.* January 29, 2001, p. 48.

*Washington Post Online.* March 16, 2001.

# Session 9

*Fear is a place.*
—Movie tagline

**Box Office:** $.2 million

The imposing, almost sinister, Danvers State Mental Hospital was built in 1871 and closed in 1985, a victim of the de-institutionalization program and budget cuts. When it closed, many of its patients were just thrown out onto the street. Its rooms and halls and tunnels are strewn with abandoned medical paraphernalia, its walls covered in graffiti and patient artwork, and its pipes insulated with asbestos.

The hospital sits on valuable land, but it cannot be torn down because it is listed with the National Historic Register. Consequently it is going to be turned into the town hall complete with visitor center and historic library. However, before remodeling can begin it must have its hazardous materials removed. Bids are being taken for the job, and time is a factor, so Gordon Fleming (Peter Mullan) promises his company can get the job done in one week. To be done safely, it should take about three weeks, but Gordon has a brand new baby and desperately needs the job. If sacrificing safety for speed is what it will take, that's what he'll do. Plus there's a $10,000 bonus for finishing by the 13th.

Gordon's crew consists of his close friend, Phil (David Caruso); Hank Romero (Josh Lucas), a gambling ladies man who maliciously needles Phil about the fact that he has stolen Phil's girlfriend; Mike King (Stephen Gevedon), a law-school drop-out who has worked for Gordon for more than five years and who has a more than casual interest in the hospital's past patients; and Jeff Fleming (Brendan Sexton III) Gordon's inexperienced, young nephew who, conveniently for the story, has a severe fear of the dark.

Not long after starting the job, Mike discovers boxes of sealed evidence in the basement. He opens them up only to find audio tapes, beginning with session 1, for patient Mary Hobbes which Mike begins to play on a tape player. Mary suffered from multiple personalities, and as we listen in on the tapes with Mike we find them uncovered one by one. The tape label tells us we will meet "the Princess," "Billy," and "Simon," and as we listen in and we gradually come to realize that something terrible happened in Mary's past and that one of these personalities will be more than a bit harmful.

Mike, however, is not the only one to find a "treasure" in the hospital. While working in the basement, Hank follows a trail of very old quarters and finds a jackpot of not only quarters but keys and teeth and other assorted items hidden in a brick wall on the other side of which is an incinerator and the morgue. To ensure that he won't have to share his prize, Hank re-hides his prize and comes back in the middle of the night to reclaim it, but either the hospital claims him first . . . or he has hit it big in the lottery and run off to Miami, at least that's what Phil tells us. But isn't that Hank looking very lost on the stairway?

And doesn't Phil seem to be growing a little more malevolent every time we see him? Why he even starts undermining the leadership of his friend and boss Gordon. Eventually Phil tells Mike that Gordon is coming unhinged. That he hit his wife and they are in danger of not only losing the bonus but also losing the job. But if anyone's wasting time on the job it's Mike who keeps sneaking off to listen to the session tapes or Phil who sneaks a little reefer on the side and seems to becoming more and more unhinged himself.

Director Brad Anderson who also directed *The Darien Gap* (1995) and *Next Stop Wonderland* (1998) seems right in his element in working class New England. Here both his characters and the dialogue ring true but some of the credit is to be shared with Stephen Gevedon who not only co-wrote the screenplay with director Anderson but also stars in the film as Mike.

Audiences who are used to hit-'em-over-the-head frenzy and gore which is the norm for most contemporary horror films, may be a little put off by the leisurely pace of *Session 9*, but if that prejudice can be overcome, the movie is a rare treat. Anderson slowly builds his tension which means there is none of the usual sense of urgency which the genre normally has but instead offers a more thoughtful mystery which can be no less scary.

For some, however, the film may leave a feeling that while trying to solve this mystery one instead stumbles into narrative holes. Yes, the story seems underwritten compared to other films which feel they must explain everything, but in the end—and perhaps especially after a second viewing—one realizes that many of the film's seeming ambiguities are not really so and even if they are, the are a part of the film's appeal.

Anderson doesn't need to rely on scary special effects to tell his tale because by concentrating on the shadows in the corners of the hospital and the characters' minds the result is much more intellectually satisfying. We don't need the usual jumping-out-of-the-screen phony scares, the atmosphere does it all for us in the corners of our own imaginations. When the Hospital seems to call out "welcome Gordon," we're not sure if it's the hospital or if it's Gordon or if it's just the director playing with us. And that's OK.

Shot on HD video with the new Sony CineAlta 24 HD cameras, *Session 9* also has the advantage of looking great.

Alternating between the brightly lit, exterior day scenes of the crew getting ready to work or eating lunch and the dark, dirty and confusing interior scenes where the men work, the film keeps us off balance. Also working in the film's favor is the atmospheric setting of the Danvers Hospital. It is a natural setting for a horror film and several critics have compared it to the Overlook Hotel in *The Shining* or the hospital in the Danish film *The Kingdom*. It seems intrinsically evil, inhabited by its past occupants in much the same way as the house is in *The Haunting*.

*Session 9* is also blessed with a great ensemble cast and solid performances especially by Peter Mullan, the wonderful Scottish actor from *My Name Is Joe* and *Miss Julie*. He always has this distant look on his face and we're again kept off balance. Is it a sign of his listening to his inner voices, listening to the hospital or just gradually disconnect himself from reality? Again, the unknown is a benefit because the characters are intriguing in their enigmaticness. All of them seem to have their secrets—but they also seem to come up with rational explanations for their suspicious behavior, and we're once again kept off balance.

*Session 9* is not a typical horror film. It is not obvious nor is it aimed at teenagers. It is thoughtful, innovative and creative. Yes, it leaves a lot of questions as it goes along, but it's never a dull trip. It certainly deserved to be treated better than it was by its distributer, USA Films, which didn't even bother to open it in many major cities let alone smaller venues. One wonders if the film is just another victim of what has been called the David Caruso curse. Since leaving his successful television career for the glamour of films, he hasn't had a hit. *Session 9* didn't deserve to fall into this pit since even Caruso does a good job in the film.

*—Beverley Bare Buehrer*

## CREDITS

**Gordon Fleming:** Peter Mullan
**Phil:** David Caruso
**Hank:** Joshua Lucas
**Jeff:** Brendan Sexton III
**Bill Griggs:** Paul Guilfoyle
**Mike:** Stephen Gevedon

**Origin:** USA
**Released:** 2001
**Production:** David Collins, Dorothy Aufeiro, Michael Williams; Scout Productions; released by USA Films
**Directed by:** Brad Anderson
**Written by:** Brad Anderson, Stephen Gevedon
**Cinematography by:** Uta Briesewitz
**Music by:** Climax Gold Twins
**Sound:** Tom Williams

**Music Supervisor:** Barry Cole, Christopher Covert
**Editing:** Brad Anderson
**Art Direction:** Roger Danchik
**Costumes:** Aimee E. McCue
**Production Design:** Sophie Carlhian
**MPAA rating:** R
**Running time:** 99 minutes

## REVIEWS

*Boxoffice.* August, 2001, p. 57.
*Entertainment Weekly.* August 17, 2001, p. 44.
*Hollywood Reporter.* August 8, 2001, p. 18.
*Los Angeles Times Online.* August 10, 2001.
*New York Times Online.* August 5, 2001.
*New York Times Online.* August 10, 2001.
*USA Today Online.* August 10, 2001.
*Variety.* August 13, 2001, p. 45.

## TRIVIA

The film was shot in 22 days.

# Sexy Beast

*Sometimes it's hard to say no.*
—Movie tagline
*There's a bit of the beast in all of us.*
—Movie tagline

**Box Office:** $6.7 million

Don Logan (Ben Kingsley) is the very devil. Not only does the British gangster intimidate everyone comes into contact with, but director Jonathan Glazer surrounds him with devilish images. Glazer's stylish touches, the highly original screenplay by Louis Mellis and David Scinto, and Kingsley's overwhelming performance make *Sexy Beast* much more than yet another British imitation of the American film noir crime genre.

Gal Dove (Ray Winstone), a retired criminal, lives in peaceful, uneventful retirement in Spain with his lover, DeeDee (Amanda Redman), a former pornographic film star. Gal is content to lie beside his pool, bark good-humored orders at Enrique (Alvaro Monje), the young Spaniard who performs odd jobs around the villa, and dine out with DeeDee and fellow exiles Aitch (Cavan Kendall)

and Jackie (Julianne White). Gal is not that perturbed when a huge boulder comes tumbling down the hill above the villa, narrowly misses his head, and smashes into his pool, breaking the tiles at the bottom.

Unfortunately, the boulder is a sign of things to come. Don Logan, whose very name can make the four friends tremble, arrives from London to ask Gal to take part in a big heist. Crime kingpin Teddy Bass (Ian McShane), almost as ruthless as Don, plans to break into a supposedly impregnable bank run by the decadent Harry (James Fox) and steal the contents of the safety deposit boxes.

Gal's dilemma is how to refuse Don and get rid of him as soon as possible. Gal has enough money to live comfortably and doesn't want to risk losing his and DeeDee's life of ease. She wants nothing to do with their former life in England. And Aitch and Jackie seem even more terrified of Don than are their friends. When Gal politely, but highly nervously, turns down Don's offer, the visitor becomes more vindictive, saying Gal has gone soft, calling DeeDee disgusting because of her past, and revealing he has had an affair with Jackie. He even intimidates himself, talking to himself in a bathroom mirror while shaving, pumping himself up to strike and kick the sleeping Gal. But Don surprises them all by apparently giving up and heading for the airport. On the plane, however, he refuses to put out his cigarette, is removed from the flight, and returns to Gal's villa to increase his invective. The consequences are appropriately unexpected.

A director of music videos for such acts as Blur, Massive Attack, and Radiohead, and of television commercials, Glazer, making his first feature, does everything he can to intensify Don's menace, including bathing him in a red glow in a London bar. Kingsley, however, needs little help in being devilish. With his shaved head, prominent ears, and goatee, he is the personification of evil. Some reviewers of *Sexy Beast* criticized Glazer and the screenwriters for the fantasy/dream sequences in which a hairy demon with large, pointed ears threatens Gal. The final shot, in which this demon meets Don, can be said to undercut the film's intense tone with unnecessary levity. *Sexy Beast* is about the inescapable hold of the past, the impossibility of avoiding responsibility for one's acts, the inevitability of evil. This last shot, though it intends to reinforce these themes, almost turns them into a joke, much like the ending to Neil Jordan's *Interview with the Vampire* (1994).

This misstep is one of few in *Sexy Beast*. The film opens with an overhead shot of Gal, tanned and slightly bloated, floating in his pool, telling himself how content he is, with "Peaches" by the Stranglers roaring suggestively in the background. The striking images, Gal's working-class mumble, and the music assert the director's intention of controlling the audience's mood. Then the boulder comes crashing down to signal that anything may happen at any time. It's not just the serenity of Gal's world that's at risk: chaos is forever lurking around every corner.

Glazer, Mellis, and Scinto provide numerous indelible touches. At a London orgy, with sex, booze, and drugs all around, on a sofa with a half-nude woman, the equally undressed Teddy calmly sips a cup of tea. When the robbery finally occurs, the thieves enter a pool at a Turkish bath and attack the bottom of the vault from underwater. (With their swimming trunks, diving goggles, and drills, the men resemble gladiators.) The screenwriters also know when less can be more: nothing is said about Gal's prior relationship with Don, about how Gal and DeeDee got together, about what Don's criminal specialty is. Such details would distract from the emotional impact the filmmakers are aiming for.

*Sexy Beast* succeeds so well to a great extent because of the casting. Kingsley may seem at first an odd choice for such a despicable creature as Don Logan. Best known for playing saintly characters in such films as *Gandhi* (1982), *Turtle Diary* (1985), and *Schindler's List* (1993), Kingsley has played bad guys a few times, as with *Bugsy* (1991), *Sneakers* (1992), and *Death and the Maiden* (1994), but nothing like Don Logan. The Kingsley role and performance most comparable is the 1983 film of Harold Pinter's *Betrayal* in which his cuckolded publisher delivers every line and gesture with a poisoned sense of menace. The quality of his work in *Sexy Beast*, comparable to Terence Stamp's great performance in *The Limey* (1999), is less surprising than the insight of the filmmakers for giving him this opportunity.

An ability too few actors possess is knowing when to be subtle, when to go all out, and when to use the shadings in between. Kingsley realizes there is nothing subtle about Don, not even his homoerotic feelings for the suggestively named Gal, so he pours it on, shouting all his threats, trembling in anger at not having his way, acting like a spoiled child grown into a brutal bully. Kingsley does not show Don thinking: the man is completely instinctive. The scenes in which Don insists and Gal declines are like duels, with Don heavily armed and Gal barely dancing out of the way of his weaponry. The highlight of Kingsley's performance is Don's confrontation with himself in the bathroom mirror as he expresses not just anger but despair at the possibility of showing any weakness, at the remotest chance of failure. Don is clearly his own worst enemy, the most memorable villain since Dennis Hopper's Frank in *Blue Velvet* (1986).

Glazer observes in an interview with *The Financial Times* that the film's dialogue has a Pinteresque rhythm. Mellis and Scinto, who originally conceived this material as a stage play, have clearly studied Pinter's threatening poetry. With the repetitions, excessive profanity, and verbless sentences, the dialogue resembles a merging of the styles of Pinter and David Mamet, both also adept at portraying the criminal milieu. One distinct problem with the dialogue is its being presented in thick working-class accents in which

"something" becomes "sommink." As a result, for American viewers anyway, at least ten percent of the dialogue is unintelligible.

Kingsley could not give such a masterful performance without having actors like Winstone to play off. Best known as the abusive husband in *Nil by Mouth* (1997) and the sexually abusive father in *The War Zone* (1999), Winstone has a more difficult role because half the film is devoted to staring at his misshapen face. He is called upon to display a wide range of emotions, from contentment to abject fear, with little dialogue. While Kingsley, who makes his distinctive eyes as dead as possible, acts with a rigid body and hysterical voice, Winstone conveys Gal's confused emotions mostly with his eyes. His best moment, however, comes when Gal calls the angry DeeDee from London and begs her to say his name. Winstone perfectly captures Gal's anxiety and his genuine love for DeeDee.

Glazer's style, aided considerably by Ivan Bird's cinematography, emphasizes close-ups to call attention to the characters' vulnerability. (The first shot of Don is of the back of his head, suggesting he lives in a totally different moral universe.) Redman, resembling a shopworn Catherine Zeta-Jones, has very few lines and must convey DeeDee's emotions with her face, sometimes firm and proud, then collapsed into despair. McShane's best work has been on television in such series as *Disraeli* (1979) and *Lovejoy* (1986–1994), and Teddy is the best film role he's had since *The Last of Sheila* (1973). With black, slicked-back hair and black clothing, the loquacious Teddy is a different type of devil than Don but just as dangerous. Shot mostly in shadows, McShane's heavily lined face is a portrait of evil.

*Sexy Beast*, whose title is the British expression for someone dangerously attractive, is much more than a depiction of fear and evil. There are many darkly comic moments, as when Don leaves the plane by telling his fellow passengers he hopes it crashes. Except for the final shot, the film keeps its serious and humorous moments well balanced. *Sexy Beast* is a remarkable debut for Glazer and finally puts to rest the mistaken belief that Kingsley is just that guy from *Gandhi*.

*—Michael Adams*

## CREDITS

**Gal Dove:** Ray Winstone
**Don Logan:** Ben Kingsley
**Teddy Bass:** Ian McShane
**DeeDee:** Amanda Redman
**Harry:** James Fox
**Andy:** Robert Atiko
**Jackie:** Julianne White
**Aitch:** Cavan Kendall

**Enrique:** Alvaro Monje

**Origin:** Great Britain
**Released:** 2000
**Production:** Jeremy Thomas; Recorded Pictures Company, FilmFour, Kanzaman; released by Fox Searchlight
**Directed by:** Jonathan Glazer
**Written by:** Louis Mellis, David Scinto
**Cinematography by:** Ivan Bird
**Music by:** Roque Banos
**Sound:** Antonio Bloch
**Editing:** John Scott, Sam Sneade
**Art Direction:** Steve Simmonds
**Costumes:** Louise Stjernsward
**Production Design:** Jan Houllerigue
**MPAA rating:** R
**Running time:** 88 minutes

## REVIEWS

*Boston Globe.* June 22, 2001, p. D1.
*Boxoffice.* November, 2000, p. 160.
*Chicago Sun-Times Online.* June 22, 2001.
*Entertainment Weekly.* June 22, 2001, p. 60.
*Film Comment.* March/April, 2001, p. 16.
*Hollywood Reporter.* November 29, 2000, p. 17.
*Los Angeles Times Online.* June 13, 2001.
*Maclean's.* June 25, 2001, p. 48.
*New Statesman.* January 15, 2001, p. E1.
*New York.* June 25, 2001, p. 140.
*New York Times.* June 13, 2001, p. E1.
*New York Times Online.* July 22, 2001.
*Newsweek.* June 18, 2001, p. 53.
*People.* June 25, 2001, p. 35.
*Sight and Sound.* January, 2001, p. 19.
*Sight and Sound.* February, 2001, p. 49.
*USA Today.* June 13, 2001, p. D4.
*Variety.* September 25, 2001, p. 63.
*Washington Post.* June 22, 2001, p. C5.

## QUOTES

Don (Ben Kingsley) to Gal (Ray Winstone): "I won't let you be happy. Why should I?"

## AWARDS AND NOMINATIONS

**Broadcast Film Critics 2002:** Support. Actor (Kingsley) **Nomination:**
**Oscars 2001:** Support. Actor (Kingsley)
**Golden Globes 2002:** Support. Actor (Kingsley)
**Screen Actors Guild 2001:** Support. Actor (Kingsley).

# Shadow Magic

*Peking, 1902. East meets West and a new technology is born.*
—Movie tagline

During the final years of the Qing Dynasty, Westerners brought modern inventions to China, including the invention of moving pictures. One hundred years later, the Chinese film industry has become a formidable force of cinema especially within the last decade. Chinese filmmaker and NYU Film School graduate Ann Hu reflects on the birth of Chinese cinema in her sumptuous debut *Shadow Magic.* And like Guiseppe Tornatore's *Cinema Paradiso,* Hu's film portrays a valentine to the alluring cinematic craft, as well as serving as a love story between a working-class dreamer and an upper-class beauty.

*Shadow Magic* proves to be more than a marriage between Bernardo Bertolucci's *The Last Emperor* and Tornatore's *Cinema Paradiso* in that the film relies heavily on what a person can achieve when he or she decides to live out their biggest dream. *Shadow Magic* reflects on what Brazilian alchemist/author Paulo Coelho calls "fighting the good fight" and it asks viewers to fight against the apathy of their everyday life while mustering the courage to follow their passion. Englishman Raymond Wallace (Jared Harris) ambitiously pedals his motion picture technology to both simple Chinese folk and royalty. He claims "motion pictures are the future" and he hopes that future also includes a reunion with his estranged wife, who left him for a wealthier man.

Similar to the storyline of *Cinema Paradiso* projectionist Wallace befriends a young man, Liu Jinglun (Xia Yu), who is enamored by the magic of motion pictures. Liu barely makes a living working as a photographer's apprentice, but appears to be fertile ground to plant the seed of a dream. Liu, who has never kissed a woman and lives under his aging father's roof, exudes a boyish innocence as he pines for Lord Tan's (Li Yusheng) gorgeous daughter Ling (Xing Yufei) and worships Wallace's movie technology. However, conflict arises when Liu's father decides to marry his son off to the Widow Jiang (Fang Qing Zhuo) because this marriage would destroy Liu's relationship with Wallace and his dream of marrying Ling. Soon Lui is forced to choose between fighting the good fight or proving his loyalty to his father and his employer Master Ren (Liu Peiqi).

The larger theme that emerges revolves around tradition verses the new technology brought about by Western inventions. Lord Tan and his ancient Chinese operatic performances represent the old way, whereas Wallace's "shadow magic" represents a threat to the ancient Chinese art form and familiarity. However, this doesn't stop the Chinese from packing Wallace's makeshift cinema house where they witness people from other cultures dancing across the screen or a locomotive coming straight at them via the screen. And for awhile, Wallace's life moves along a smooth course as he collects revenues for his show and shoots new footage of the Chinese along with Liu. However, a fire breaks out when Wallace's technology breaks down while showing the Empress (Ci Xi Li Bin) a bit of motion picture magic and Wallace is deported back to the West. However, we all know the progression of this story, which culminated 98 years later with the success of the Chinese sensation *Crouching Tiger, Hidden Dragon,* a wonderful blend of Western technology and Chinese entertainment.

Jack Matthews of the *New York Daily News* called *Shadow Magic* "A story of triumph and a beautiful love story to boot." While Jay Carr of the *Boston Globe* labeled the film "Magically beguiling!" Six years in the making (most of that time was spent seeking financing for the film), Hu's film, with its story about magic, romance, and dreams—not to mention cinema—failed to attract a sizable audience partly do to Sony Pictures Classics poor promotional campaign. Although the distributor has brought us many Chinese features including *Crouching Tiger, Hidden Dragon, Shower,* and *The Road Home, Shadow Magic* received little promotion outside of a handful reviews and a trailer. Perhaps the film couldn't compete with *Crouching Tiger, Hidden Dragon,* which was playing in theatres at the same time when *Shadow Magic* was released.

Hu, though, created a film full of magic and nostalgia for a time when society appeared to be giving birth to itself. By blending the sepia tones of the old world with modern colored film, Hu shows us how far cinema has evolved in the last 100 years. And women filmmakers such as Hu and her cinematographer Nancy Schreiber have been given the canvas to express their artistry.

—*Patty-Lynne Herlevi*

### CREDITS

**Raymond Wallace:** Jared Harris
**Liu Jing Lun:** Xia Yu
**Master Ren:** Liu Peiqi
**Madame Ren:** Lu Liping
**Tan Xialing:** Xing Yufei
**Lao Liu:** Wang Jingming
**Lord Tan:** Li Yusheng

**Origin:** China
**Language:** Chinese
**Released:** 2000
**Production:** Ann Hu; Beijing Film Studio, China Film, Road Movies; released by Sony Pictures Classics
**Directed by:** Ann Hu

**Written by:** Ann Hu, Huang Dan, Tang Louyi, Kate Raisz, Bob McAndrew
**Cinematography by:** Nancy Schreiber
**Music by:** Zhang Lida
**Editing:** John Gilroy, Keith Reamer
**Costumes:** Huang Bao Rong
**Production Design:** Wang Jixian
**MPAA rating:** PG
**Running time:** 115 minutes

### REVIEWS

*Boxoffice.* November, 2000, p. 167.
*Chicago Sun-Times Online.* May 18, 2001.
*Los Angeles Times Online.* April 6, 2001.
*New York Times Online.* April 6, 2001.
*People.* April 16, 2001, p. 37.
*Variety.* February 28, 2000, p. 52.
*Washington Post Online.* April 20, 2001.

### QUOTES

Liu Jinglun (Xia Yu) after taking Ling's (Xing Yu Fei) picture: "You are captured forever."

### TRIVIA

The first Chinese narrative film, which has been lost, was an adaptation of the opera *Ding Jung Mountain* in 1905.

# Shallow Hal

*The Biggest Love Story Ever Told.*
—Movie tagline
*Are You a Shallow Guy?*
—Movie tagline

 **Box Office:** $68.4 million

Peter and Bobby Farrelly never met a bodily fluid or function they did not like. Semen, vomit, mucus, bowel movements—they are all putty in the hands of the brothers who have enthusiastically used them as comedic tools in fashioning such films as *Dumb & Dumber* (1994), *Kingpin* (1996), *There's Something About Mary* (1998) and last year's *Me, Myself & Irene*. Their latest, *Shallow Hal*, is even more of a departure than *Outside Providence* (1999), the nostalgic coming of age film they co-wrote with director Michael Corrente, as the bodily function in their newest offering is the beating of hearts in love.

The title character is Jack Larsen (Jack Black), a slightly tubby, average guy who lusts after above-average women. His sole focus on looks can be traced back to the age of nine, when his father's dying breaths instructed him in the crudest of terms that happiness in life comes not through finding love but through getting your hands on the most mouth-watering examples of the female form possible. Vowing to make his father proud of him, Hal grows up to be sublimely superficial, his eyes practically popping out of his head whenever a stunner comes into view. While he is clearly not in their league, he is constantly striving for a chance to play. He longs for the kind of women he has surely drooled over while watching *Baywatch*, but the beauties he encounters in real life are content to let him drown. Now thirty-some-thing, his latest failure is with his ravishing neighbor Jill (Susan Ward), who informs him of her lack of attraction to him and suggests that he consider moving if he cannot bear to continue living across the hall from her.

Things are not going so well for his equally superficial pal, Mauricio (Jason Alexander), who could simply no longer stomach his last girlfriend's "freakishly-long" second toes. Together, Hal and Mauricio head to dance clubs in what amounts to an enthusiastic, pathetic hunt for certain key female body parts. Hal is actually a nice guy, just acutely misguided. Hampered by his "high standards," things do not look especially promising for Hal until getting stuck in an elevator gets his life unstuck. Luckily for Hal, he is trapped with motivational speaker Tony Robbins (playing himself), who recognizes Hal's problem and ends up hypnotizing him so that he sees what is inside a woman instead of merely their outward appearance.

Soon after, Hal shares a cab with good-looking Katrina (Brooke Burns, who actually appeared on *Baywatch*) and is amazed that she is flattered by, and receptive to, his interest. When he insists that she must be a model and the cabbie chortles, we realize that perhaps Hal is, indeed, now seeing things differently. Later, we are sure of it when Hal dances with a group of babes while, from Mauricio's point of view, we see that they are in actuality less than classically beautiful. One is Rosemary Shanahan (Gwyneth Paltrow), who is actually morbidly obese but who appears to Hal as a reedy, lovely woman. (A heavyset body double portrays the larger Rosemary when we are not seeing the character from Hal's perspective as the fair Gwyneth.) That Hal would more than politely acknowledge her or her friends absolutely baffles Mauricio and Jill.

Things do not start out smoothly for Hal and Rosemary when he makes snide remarks about the plus-size underwear she selects in a store, unaware, of course, that they are for her. She is angry and hurt, which is understandable to us but is mystifying to Hal. When he compliments her on her svelte appearance, she thinks that he is being a sarcastic jerk. Hal is incredulous and thinks that she has the world's worst self-image. Mauricio comes to the park to meet Rosemary, and as she comes into view, he inquires "Is she behind the rhino?," certain that Rosemary cannot be the hot thing he has been hearing so much about. (We react by thinking to ourselves that he is no prize himself, with his ridiculous, painted-on hair.)

Whatever her outsides look like, she has a big heart, volunteering at a childrens' hospital where Hal sees firsthand that everyone adores her. The film does have numerous moments which admittedly poke fun at Rosemary's weight and appetite. When the two go out to eat, she puts in a hefty order, and even before eating it snaps her steel seat and tumbles to the ground. She states that this is a regular occurrence for her (Hal apparently chalks this up to wide-spread shoddy workmanship), and we actually see it happen more than once. When Rosemary and Hal share a huge milkshake, most of it is sucked up through her straw rather than his. When she is offered a piece of cake, her idea of what that means would make Richard Simmons gasp.

The two lovers go canoeing, and she weighs down her end to such a degree that Hal rides high out of the water. When they go swimming, her belly-flop into the pool cata-pults a small child into nearby trees. Some could see this as mean, but the way Rosemary's character is written, and as a result of Paltrow's fine performance, we somehow laugh at the jokes but not at Rosemary herself. She is an endearing, sweet character with whom we sympathize. When she falls off the stool, for example, we sense her embarrassment, and we feel for her. When she tells Hal that she has had few boyfriends, knows full well how people look at her, and therefore would Hal please stop insisting she is beautiful because "it isn't nice," her words are sad and touching. Whatever Rosemary actually looks like, she is someone we find ourselves caring about.

Rosemary turns out to be the daughter of Hal's boss (Joe Viterelli), and when Hal goes to the family's home for dinner and Mr. Shanahan merely refers to his daughter in realistic terms, Hal is shocked and outraged, sticking up for her and declaring the man to be the source of Rosemary's horribly inaccurate self-image. Hal's gutsiness shows us that he truly values her, but will he continue to care when the spell he is under inevitably wears off? We know that we are about to find out when Mauricio, apparently feeling left behind, goes to Robbins and demands that he "take the whammy off" Hal and get things back to the way they were. Hal and Rosemary are out on a date (she destroys another booth), and after Hal complains to the manager and returns to the dining room, he cannot understand where Rosemary is and why some rotund lady is now sitting at their table. He

agill's Cinema Annual 2002

also meets Katrina again, and searches her face in bewilderment, unable to believe that it is the same woman.

When Mauricio explains to Hal what has been happening, Hal is angry, because regardless of what anyone else saw or thought when they looked at Rosemary, what he had seen was beautiful. The two decide to get a hold of Robbins again to reverse his reversal, and Hal avoids Rosemary until the motivational speaker can recreate their previous blissful circumstances. Of course Rosemary thinks she is being dumped, and when we see her from behind, nervously playing with the telephone chord while trying to understand what has gone wrong, Paltrow's voice imbues the scene with an affecting poignancy. Rosemary is devastated when she sees Hal out to dinner with Jill and he, not recognizing her, barely acknowledges her as she passes by. (At this point, the plus-sized Rosemary is played by Paltrow in a specially-designed fat suit and make up which took three hours to don.)

As Hal finally sizes up his situation with Rosemary, he realizes that the things which he was most taken with about her—what made her different from all the other pretty girls—still exists, and he rushes off to tell her how he feels before she leaves the country to work for the Peace Corps. All is forgiven, and we learn that Hal has enlisted in the Corps to go with her. Amidst cheers and congratulations from friends and family, he tries unsuccessfully to carry off his beloved behemoth, and so she does the favor instead. It is also a happy ending for Mauricio, who we learn has a vestigial, puppy-like tail that wags when he is excited, and it does so as he walks away with a woman who adores anything canine. (Remember, this still is a Farrelly brothers' film.)

*Shallow Hal*, which received mixed reviews, was filmed on a budget of $40 million, and grossed almost $69 million in domestic boxoffice. The film succeeds to a large extent because of Paltrow's Rosemary, but Black also strikes a pleasing note as average Joe Hal. Especially memorable is a moving scene in which Hal, no longer hypnotized, receives a jolt when he realizes that the cute little girl he had played with at the hospital days before is actually a patient in the burn unit, and he reaches out tenderly to her scarred face with a soft "Hi, beautiful." The film has a nice mix of these touching moments and those which are humorous, although people looking for gags that make you gag from the Farrellys will be disappointed. (It does have its own degree of strangeness, such as the presence of a character with spina bifida who crawls around on all fours and checks out his reflection in hubcaps.) However, like Black's character at the end, there is a welcome depth to *Shallow Hal*.

—*David L. Boxerbaum*

## CREDITS

**Hal:** Jack Black
**Rosemary:** Gwyneth Paltrow
**Mauricio:** Jason Alexander
**Steve Shanahan:** Joe Viterelli
**Reverend Larson:** Bruce McGill
**Jill:** Susan Ward
**Walt:** Rene Kirby
**Himself:** Tony Robbins
**Ralph:** Zen Gesner
**Katrina:** Brooke Burns
**Other Hostess:** Rob Moran
**Nurse Tyler Peeler:** Nan Martin

**Origin:** USA
**Released:** 2001
**Production:** Bradley Thomas, Charles B. Wessler, Bobby Farrelly, Peter Farrelly; Conundrum Entertainment; released by 20th Century-Fox
**Directed by:** Bobby Farrelly, Peter Farrelly
**Written by:** Bobby Farrelly, Peter Farrelly, Sean Moynihan
**Cinematography by:** Russell Carpenter
**Sound:** Jonathan Earl Stein
**Music Supervisor:** Tom Wolfe, Manish Raval
**Editing:** Christopher Greenbury
**Art Direction:** Arlan Jay Vetter
**Costumes:** Pamela Ball Withers
**Production Design:** Sidney J. Bartholomew Jr.
**MPAA rating:** PG-13
**Running time:** 114 minutes

## REVIEWS

*Boxoffice.* February, 2002, p. 60.
*Chicago Sun-Times Online.* November 9, 2001.
*Entertainment Weekly.* November 16, 2001, p. 141.
*Los Angeles Times Online.* November 9, 2001.
*New York Times.* November 9, 2001, p. E13.
*People.* November 19, 2001, p. 43.
*Premiere.* November, 2001, p. 92.
*Rolling Stone.* December 6, 2001, p. 156.
*USA Today Online.* November 8, 2001.
*Variety.* November 5, 2001, p. 23.
*Wall Street Journal.* November 9, 2001, p. W1.
*Washington Post.* November 9, 2001, p. WE39.

# The Shipping News

*Dive beneath the surface.*
—Movie tagline
*You'll never guess what you'll find inside . . .*
—Movie tagline

 **Box Office:** $11.3 million

E. Annie Proulx's Pulitzer Prize–winning novel *The Shipping News,* an alternately funny and poignant work with a wide range of odd and quirky characters and a loose, rambling structure, would seem to be a daunting adaptation for the screen. Composed of a lot of little incidents in the life of a sad sack named Quoyle, who attempts to rebuild his life in Newfoundland after a series of tragedies, the novel paints a broad portrait of life in a small community and touches on everything from everyday work life to dark ancestral secrets. Quoyle is not the typical hero who undergoes huge changes, but he gradually begins to put his life together and, by the end, takes steps to see his way to a better future.

Screenwriter Robert Nelson Jacobs and director Lasse Hallström achieve generally satisfying if mixed results in bringing this difficult, idiosyncratic material and introverted protagonist to the screen. They have created an adaptation true to the essence of the novel but one that tends to plod through a wide range of episodes without developing a strong narrative line.

In the film's opening, Quoyle's father pushes him off a pier to teach him how to swim—a traumatic childhood event that seems to shape his whole life. The little boy's face underwater morphs into the adult Quoyle (Kevin Spacey), thus establishing a motif for the film—he is scared to death of water, and his feeling of drowning, both literally and metaphorically, hangs over his sad life. He has a low-level job as an ink setter at a Poughkeepsie newspaper when the sexy Petal (Cate Blanchett) comes on to him like a sexual fireball. They are married and have a daughter named Bunny (played by triplets Alyssa, Kaitlyn, and Lauren Gainer), although this does not stop Petal from sleeping around with other men. (A second daughter in the novel, Sunshine, does not appear in the film.)

Years pass, and Quoyle is hit with back-to-back tragedies, his parents' double suicide and Petal's death in a car accident. Fortunately, Bunny is retrieved from the black-market adoption agency where Petal sold her for $6,000. Blanchett's role is brief, an extended cameo, really, but her cruel floozy casts a spell over the whole film, constantly dragging the hapless Quoyle into the past. Despite the way she treated him, Quoyle truly loved Petal, probably because

he could not believe that such a sexy gal would fall for him in the first place.

Quoyle's aunt, Agnis Hamm (Judi Dench), has appeared at his door, and soon Quoyle is moving with her and six-year-old Bunny, who has not fully accepted her mother's death, to the Quoyles' deserted home in Newfoundland. Despite Quoyle's lack of experience, he inadvertently lands a job as a reporter at the local newspaper, *The Gammy Bird.* He also begins a tender friendship with a local woman named Wavey Prowse (Julianne Moore), who runs the town's daycare canter and is herself an emotionally wounded woman raising a slightly retarded son on her own.

Spacey is a controversial choice for the part of Quoyle. First of all, he looks nothing like the lumbering giant of an oaf that Proulx describes in her novel. More important, the role requires him to play against his natural intelligence and sardonic wit. It is not a signature Spacey role, and yet, while other actors may have better fit the introverted Quoyle, he does a credible job of expressing his awkwardness and fear of the world at large. From his soft-spoken, halting voice to his shuffling gait, Spacey creates a character ill at ease in almost every social situation. Moore is capable of much more challenging roles than the underwritten Wavey, but she complements Spacey quite nicely as a steadfast beacon of hope for the future.

Unfortunately, some of the delightful, eccentric edges of the novel have been flattened out a bit in the film, especially at the newspaper, which is more of a simmering hubbub of conflicting personalities in the novel. Still, they are a fun assortment of oddballs in the film: crusty editor Jack Buggit (Scott Glenn), who trusts Quoyle immediately; managing editor Tert Card (Pete Postlethwaite), who becomes Quoyle's nemesis; the mentor-like Billy Pretty (Gordon Pinsent), who teaches Quoyle how to be a reporter; and Nutbeem (Rhys Ifans), who was shipwrecked on the Newfoundland shore and is getting ready to sail away.

Quoyle is assigned to cover auto wrecks (one of the quirks of the paper is that a car wreck has to be featured in every edition), which is particularly painful when he goes on his first assignment and envisions Petal's leg dangling out of the wrecked car. In his coverage of the shipping news, however, Quoyle begins to distinguish himself, first in a piece he writes about a yacht once owned by Hitler and then in a surprisingly eloquent attack on oil tankers that earns him the enmity of Tert, who rewrites and prints the piece with a pro-tanker slant. Jack ultimately sides with Quoyle in his rivalry with Tert and agrees to run the original article. Quoyle tastes success for the first time in his life and seems to have found his niche as a reporter.

Other aspects of his life do not go as smoothly. His undying devotion to Petal stands in his way of moving forward in his new relationship with Wavey, and he does not know how to relate to his troubled daughter. He also nearly drowns sailing in an old boat he has purchased, which highlights his discomfort in his new environment.

Aside from Quoyle's growing confidence as a newspaperman, he does not undergo much character development. Instead, he merely learns deep, dark secrets about his family, which are meant to help him move on with his life. Billy, for example, tells him about the viciousness of the old Quoyles. Long ago, Quoyle's ancestors were pirates who lured ships to the coast so that they could loot and plunder them. When the Quoyles went too far by torturing one of their victims, they were driven from their home and forced to move their house to where it stands today. Quoyle also meets an old family recluse who lives in a shack, Cousin Nolan (Marc Lawrence), who reveals that Quoyle's father raped his half-sister, Agnis, when they were young. (This explains why, early in the film, Agnis stole her brother's ashes and surreptitiously poured them down an outhouse toilet.)

Quoyle tells Agnis that he knows her secret, but her traumatic past is largely glossed over so that Quoyle can learn yet another secret—Agnis's late lover was a woman. This episode teaches Quoyle the lesson that a person can move on after tragedy and even love again after being hurt, but the overall effect is that Agnis's incestuous rape and resulting abortion are downplayed. (Hallström, unfortunately, has a penchant for raising complex, disturbing issues—incest and abortion in *The Cider House Rules,* spousal abuse in *Chocolat*—and then not really dealing with their full import.) In the novel, Agnis does not reveal her lesbianism to Quoyle because she is unsure how he would react, but, in the film, this secret is reduced to a device meant to catalyze Quoyle's own healing process. While it would be difficult to fault Dench's workmanlike performance, she has played a version of the wise yet crotchety old woman so many times now that it can hardly be considered a stretch for her.

More revelations designed to enlighten Quoyle soon follow. At a farewell party for Nutbeem, the rowdy, drunken partygoers destroy his boat so that he cannot leave. In a change from the novel, Quoyle joins in the mayhem, and his participation is heavy-handedly linked to his ancestors' violence to show that the dark family past is in his blood. He then staggers to Wavey's house, where he rages to her about being a Quoyle—apparently he is shocked by his own violent tendencies—and he also confronts her about the unhappy marriage she endured to the town philanderer.

The next morning she reveals her big secret—her husband was not lost at sea as everyone believes but rather ran off with a younger woman. Wavey had destroyed his boat to make it look like he had died and was planning to run away when the townspeople's love persuaded her to stay. This complicated back story is another departure from the novel, where Quoyle and Wavey simply take solace in knowing that each endured a bad marriage to someone who cheated on

them and realize that they may be able to start anew with each other. Jacobs thus punches up the revelations for dramatic effect, but herein lies the film's major flaw—instead of traveling a dramatic arc and developing through his own actions, Quoyle largely learns through everyone else's stories, which creates a somewhat stilted narrative.

Like the novel, the movie ends with a fierce storm that appears to take Jack's life, but, at his wake, he literally and shockingly wakes up—a farcical "resurrection" of sorts that portends Quoyle's own rebirth. It also gives Quoyle the chance to level with Bunny about the real nature of death, and, by the end, she seems finally to have accepted that her mother is gone. The old Quoyle house is destroyed in the storm, which suggests that Quoyle may really get a chance to make a fresh start.

The great triumph of *The Shipping News* is its evocation of a particular place, not just in the life of the town but in the environment as well. The cold and harsh rain, the craggy coastline, and the gray landscape are beautifully rendered in Oliver Stapleton's cinematography so that Newfoundland itself becomes a supporting character—austerely beautiful yet hostile and full of secrets.

The rich assortment of story lines and often poetic prose of Proulx's novel do not lend themselves naturally to film, but the essential story remains intact (if simplified), and at least some of the humor and much of the local color have survived. Nonetheless, instead of trying to cover so much of the novel, it may have been better if Hallström and Jacobs had taken Billy Pretty's journalistic advice to Quoyle about the importance of "finding the center of your story, the beating heart of it," and applied it to their film. If *The Shipping News* contained such a core, it might have been a great adaptation instead of merely a good one. 🎬

*—Peter N. Chumo II*

## CREDITS

**Quoyle:** Kevin Spacey
**Agnis Hamm:** Judi Dench
**Petal:** Cate Blanchett
**Wavey Prowse:** Julianne Moore
**Tert Card:** Pete Postlethwaite
**Jack Buggit:** Scott Glenn
**Beaufield Nutbeem:** Rhys Ifans
**Billy Pretty:** Gordon Pinsent
**Dennis Bugit:** Jason Behr
**Bayonet Melville:** Larry Pine
**Silver Melville:** Jeanetta Arnette
**EMS Officer:** Robert Joy
**Bunny:** Alyssa Gainer
**Bunny:** Kaitlyn Gainer
**Bunny:** Lauren Gainer

**Origin:** USA
**Released:** 2001
**Production:** Irwin Winkler, Linda Goldstein Knowlton, Leslie Holleran; released by Miramax Films
**Directed by:** Lasse Hallstrom
**Written by:** Robert Nelson Jacobs
**Cinematography by:** Oliver Stapleton
**Music by:** Christopher Young
**Sound:** Glen Gauthier
**Music Supervisor:** Randy Spendlove
**Editing:** Andrew Mondshein
**Art Direction:** Karen Schulz Gropman, Peter Rogness
**Costumes:** Renee Ehrlich Kalfus
**Production Design:** David Gropman
**MPAA rating:** R
**Running time:** 120 minutes

## REVIEWS

*Boxoffice.* February, 2002, p. 56.
*Chicago Sun-Times Online.* December 25, 2001.
*Entertainment Weekly.* January 11, 2002, p. 48.
*Los Angeles Times Online.* December 25, 2001.
*New York Times Online.* December 25, 2001.
*People.* January 14, 2002, p. 30.
*USA Today Online.* December 24, 2001.
*Variety.* December 24, 2001, p. 20.
*Washington Post.* December 25, 2001, p. C1.

## TRIVIA

"Quoyle" is the old English spelling for a coil of rope; author E. Annie Proulx was inspired by a book of knots.

## AWARDS AND NOMINATIONS

**Natl. Bd. of Review 2001:** Support. Actress (Blanchett)
**Nomination:**
**British Acad. 2001:** Actor (Spacey), Support. Actress (Dench)
**Golden Globes 2002:** Actor—Drama (Spacey), Score
**Screen Actors Guild 2001:** Support. Actress (Dench)
**Broadcast Film Critics 2001:** Film, Score.

# Shrek

*The greatest fairy tale never told.*
—Movie tagline

**Box Office:** $267.7 million

There's something about Shrek lighting up an earwax candle and digging into a plate of slime on a dinner table decorated with a jar of eyeballs that's awfully appealing to an animation audience sick to death of sanitized, politically correct characters and egregious displays of high-tech cartoon trickery. That must be why this purposefully contrary and technically groundbreaking cartoon feature hauled in $42.3 million at the boxoffice the weekend it opened and became one of the biggest hits of 2001.

It's true that this oddball film about a stubborn green ogre with a Scottish accent (courtesy of Mike Myers) has something to appeal to all ages—fantasy for the little ones, flatulence humor for the pre-adolescents, cool music for older jaded youth, and lots of in-jokes and movie references for the adult audience. But it doesn't play like a slickly marketed package; in fact, it's a way-out-on-the-limb, almost misanthropic twist on fairy tales, and it sports a mean, devilish though sometimes optimistic attitude.

As this film's producer and driving force, DreamWorks executive Jeffrey Katzenberg's purpose can be summed up in one word: desanitization. That is a subversive mission, but one that has deep roots in cartoon films, dating back to when Warner Bros.' Looney Tune characters first ran amok, deflating the pretensions of animators who aimed at moralizing. Then and recently, it was one overly successful studio that dominated in its pretentious mission of edifying youngsters—and profited richly in so doing. And it's quite clear that Katzenberg takes great delight in pulling the tail of his former employer, Disney Studios. With reckless abandon, Katzenberg reappropriates fairy tale characters that Disney previously had filched from the public domain and all but trademarked, including Cinderella, Snow White, Pinocchio, and the Three Little Pigs. This alone is an almost revolutionary act, given that generations of moviegoers have been conditioned into thinking of these fairy tale folk as Disney property.

If that isn't enough to send Mickey Mouse into a tizzy, consider that the villain of *Shrek* is a megalomaniacal, very *short* prince, Lord Farquaad (John Lithgow), who resembles Katzenberg's former Disney boss Michael Eisner in stature (and perhaps demeanor) and who presides over a "perfect"—and perfectly soulless—fantasy kingdom. Farquaad's realm, named Duloc, has lots of lovely facades and manicured lawns and streetscapes, those familiar rope lines and wait signs, and a decidedly unfriendly attitude toward the fairy tale creatures it has exploited. As the movie opens, Farquaad is inexplicably banishing them all to Shrek's swamp.

All this is both pointed and funny for those who enjoy a few digs at the Mouse Kingdom, but *Shrek*'s against-the-grain sensibility goes much deeper than vengeful satire.

Ambitiously, the film aims not merely to lampoon, but to harpoon, the pretensions and conventions of fairy tales (at least the modern, popularized versions of them), and to call into question the messages they aim at the young and impressionable.

Shrek, the hero of the piece, is an ogre, and the villain is the prince who wants to rescue a fair maiden. Shrek is ugly and ornery, but he's not a very convincing ogre. He's got the necessary me-against-the-world attitude, but doesn't seem to have his heart in his terrorizing. The horror he inspires in neighbors and townspeople is somewhat perfunctory. "This is the part where you run away," he explains after unleashing his much-advertised scream on a group of citizens. His comment establishes this story as a riff on a fairy tale, an examination of the roles these stock characters play in such dramas.

Later on, when Shrek does conquer considerable obstacles (a molt of flaming lava, a fire-breathing dragon) to rescue the lovely Princess Fiona (Cameron Diaz) from the tower where she has been imprisoned, Fiona anxiously jumps back into bed and lies lifelessly on her back, clutching a bouquet and awaiting the kiss from her true love which will awaken her from her enchantment. When instead Shrek merely drags her away without a kiss, she complains that he is not following romantic protocol. After she insists on his taking off his helmet, she is befuddled by his horns and fat green face. "You're not supposed to be an ogre," she complains. "You were expecting Prince Charming?" Shrek asks rhetorically. Quite simply and neatly, these few scenes lay waste to an entire realm of socialization that is rooted in these fairy-tale views of gender behavior.

Not that *Shrek* is one of those pseudo-feminist revisionist fables. Far from it. After all, it features a dragon who wears lipstick and acts like a vixen, and it sports a contrary attitude that lays waste to most civilizing impulses. But the film does offer quite a refreshing twist on the *Beauty and the Beast* fable. Unfortunately it gets there by indulging in at least one hackneyed plot device: the partially overheard conversation that results in a massive and mutual misunderstanding between the would-be lovers. True, it's something even Shakespeare occasionally stooped to, but it's part of a long stretch where *Shrek*'s rather rude demeanor goes inexplicably soft and flabby.

Fortunately, Eddie Murphy is around to keep audiences laughing when the material goes a little gooey. As a sidekick donkey for Shrek, named simply Donkey, Murphy is in top form. He's a jive-talking, ingratiating, cowardly second banana who steals many of this witty film's wittiest lines. Running off at the mouth and breaking into corny songs, Murphy is unrestrained in animated form, as if he has finally achieved his long-hoped-for goal and transcended his body. He makes a perfect ass of himself—and it's one of Murphy's best roles.

Myers also does surprisingly well with the Scottish accent and the proud-loner personality. For once, Myers doesn't overplay his part, keeping Shrek agreeably low-key and gloomy. And once again, Diaz displays a deft comic sensibility. As in the live-action *Charlie's Angels*, she is expert at both inhabiting and satirizing a traditionally feminine role, and her character fits her voice perfectly. Lithgow competently rounds out what is essentially a four-character cast of wacky characters.

But the real stars of *Shrek* are the animators who take computer graphics (CG) animation into a new realm. Just as *Toy Story* was a landmark in showing that CG could carry a film, *Shrek* demonstrates how sophisticated computer imagery has become since then in displaying emotion. It's one thing to use computers to animate toys, but it's quite another trick to make human faces, such as Princess Fiona's, look and behave realistically. Although there are some technically dazzling sequences, especially during the fights between Shrek and the dragon, most of the animation wizardry is quietly placed in service to the story line. Like all good cartooning, the animation in *Shrek* doesn't intrude or grandstand.

In years to come, as CG continues to advance, some of the scenes in the film will look laughably crude. In a few big crowd scenes, some of the figures look stiff and awkward. Not every movement is seamless. But the overall effect is quite pleasing, something of a cross between puppets and drawn figures, and *Shrek* will be remembered as a huge leap forward in realism. Directors Andrew Adamson and Vicky Jenson make the most of the material by eschewing every temptation to show off the technology.

What really makes *Shrek* work is an attitude that is agreeably off-kilter without being in-your-face rude or offensive. Even in the musical numbers, there is a sly irreverence, as when the Donkey is seen urinating to put out a campfire. The film is filled with wacky, nonsensical moments, such as the appearance of a French Robin Hood and his merry men, and a sequence (which might be parodying a certain type of early 1960s movie) in which Shrek and Fiona use a snake and a frog as inflatable balloons. During a romantic scene around a campfire, Fiona munches on rotisseried rat.

Probably the funniest scene in this very humorous film involves Prince Farquaad's merciless interrogation of the nursery rhyme Gingerbread Man, who is impaled on a cookie sheet as he is tortured by the pompous dictator. For anyone who's ever thought sweet fairy tales had an element of the ridiculous, *Shrek* is a dream come true.

"I don't care what everyone likes," Shrek tells the Donkey at one point as he stomps off in a tizzy. That could be the motto for this unusually headstrong fractured fairy tale. There's little pretension and zero tolerance for the kind of slick, smooth storytelling and animation that comes off as calculated. In other words, the film is thoroughly antithetical to Disney. Yet it is just whimsical enough to appeal to the child in all of us and just rebellious enough to appeal to a more grown-up sense of indignation at packaged merchandise. Its very disdain for likeability ends up, ironically, making this one of the most appealing animated features in a long time. And the ending of the film is a pleasant and wicked surprise that stands fairy tales on their heads and, despite its somewhat trite message, is genuinely moving.

As an animated feature film, *Shrek* is nearly revolutionary, both in its attitude and in its inventive use of computer graphics. It is much more than a mean-spirited jab at Disney; it almost single-handedly redeems the fairy-tale genre by spurning the standard moralizing and substituting its own daring statement on what is good, right and beautiful. The "perfect" cartoon it's not, but after all, the real world isn't perfect, is it? And that's the point of *Shrek:* to hell with all this pretense about a fairy-tale world in which every princess and prince are transformed by love into fashion models. For once, it's nice to see a family-friendly film poking holes in the idea that perfection, beauty and truth can be manufactured and marketed—and that dares to give a new meaning to the phrase "happily ever after."

—*Michael Betzold*

## CREDITS

**Shrek:** Mike Myers (Voice)
**Princess Fiona:** Cameron Diaz (Voice)
**Donkey:** Eddie Murphy (Voice)
**Lord Farquaad:** John Lithgow (Voice)
**Monsieur Hood:** Vincent Cassel (Voice)
**Old Woman:** Kathleen Freeman (Voice)
**Gingerbread Man:** Conrad Vernon (Voice)

**Origin:** USA
**Released:** 2001
**Production:** Aron Warner, John H. Williams, Jeffrey Katzenberg; PDI; released by Dreamworks Pictures
**Directed by:** Andrew Adamson, Victoria Jenson
**Written by:** Ted Elliott, Terry Rossio, Roger S.H. Schulman, Joe Stillman
**Music by:** Harry Gregson-Williams, John Powell
**Editing:** Sim Evan-Jones
**Art Direction:** Guillaume Aretos, Douglas Rogers
**Production Design:** James Hegedus
**Visual Effects:** Ken Bielenberg
**MPAA rating:** PG
**Running time:** 89 minutes

## REVIEWS

*Boxoffice.* July, 2001, p. 101.
*Chicago Sun-Times Online.* May 18, 2001.
*Entertainment Weekly.* May 25, 2001, p. 50.
*Los Angeles Times Online.* May 16, 2001.
*New York Times Online.* May 13, 2001.
*New York Times Online.* May 16, 2001.
*Newsweek.* May 7, 2001, p. 62.
*People.* May 21, 2001, p. 41.
*Sight and Sound.* July, 2001, p. 54.
*Variety.* May 7, 2001, p. 49.
*Washington Post Online.* May 18, 2001.

## QUOTES

Donkey (Eddie Murphy): "Ooh, this is gonna be so much fun! We can stay up late, swappin' manly stories, and in the mornin', I'm makin' waffles!"

## AWARDS AND NOMINATIONS

**Oscars 2001:** Animated Film
**British Acad. 2001:** Adapt. Screenplay
**L.A. Film Critics 2001:** Animated Film
**Broadcast Film Critics 2001:** Animated Film
**Nomination:**
**British Acad. 2001:** Film, Sound, Support. Actor (Murphy), Visual FX, Score
**Golden Globes 2002:** Film—Mus./Comedy
**Broadcast Film Critics 2001:** Film.

# Sidewalks of New York

*In a city of 8 million people, what are the odds the perfect two will meet?*
—**Movie tagline**

 **Box Office:** $2.3 million

Aimless meanderings on love, lust, sex, fidelity and heartbreak by an eclectic cast of New York characters in a pseudo-documentary are the shaky bonds that hold this aimless and meandering comedy together. A thin and shadowy redo of a host of Woody Allen films, namely *Husbands and Wives,* Edward Burns' reflections on Sex and the City are easily forgettable and ring false. Like the twin towers of the World Trade Center briefly glanced over the *Brothers McMullen* writer/director/star's shoulder, one feels the loss of them as much as the genuine authenticity of Burns' earlier successes, which include *Brothers* and *She's the One.* After a long stint as a mere movie star, Burns' return to moviemaking, although laced with moments of humor and heart, breezes by airily and forgettably in a film as obsessed with sex as it's characters seem to be.

The films opens with the six main characters addressing the camera directly after being questioned by an unknown interviewer about their respective sexual "first times." The unseen documentarist then follows the everyday comings and goings of the characters, who ultimately and too coincidently, intersect at various points throughout the film.

Casting himself as the film's only truly eligible bachelor, Burns is a hunk with a heart of gold, who's tossed out of the love nest by his witchy girlfriend Sue (Callie Thorne) who, naturally, fears commitment and family and craves independence. Limning his own early days in entertainment as an Irish New Yorker working as an underling on the celebrity news show, *Entertainment Tonight,* Burns plays Tommy, an Irish celebrity-news show producer from Queens. In a nutshell, the love connections with characters culled from each of New York's boroughs play as follows: Tommy meets Maria (Rosario Dawson), a teacher, in a video store, whose ex-husband Benny (David Krumholtz) is simultaneously trying to woo Maria back and chase after teenage waitress Ashley (Brittany Murphy), who begins an affair with a cheating dentist (Stanley Tucci)—married to Annie (Heather Graham)—who becomes Tommy's real estate agent/new love interest.

Rounding out the cast and providing comic relief is Tommy's libidinous and cynical boss Carpo (Dennis Farina) who provides crass and funny dating advice to his on-the-rebound employee. His expertise in matters of amore, after claiming some 500 conquests in one year alone, range from the practical—where to spray cologne on your body for the best results—to the philosophical—"A wife and children will drive you to any early grave."

Tommy, who is now forced to bunk with his boss in an *Odd Couple* type scenario, takes his advice and upon spotting the gorgeous Maria plucking a video that he wanted to rent for himself (*Breakfast at Tiffany's* it is later revealed), decides to seize on the coincidence and ask her out. Complicating matters, however, is Benny, the pushy ex-husband who verges on stalker-ish by hanging out outside Maria's door, guitar in hand. Benny is a classic New York "character," annoying and mostly harmless who's persistence passes as charm. Crushed by Maria's insistence to get on with his life, the young doorman and aspiring musician picks himself up, dusts himself off, and finds someone new to obsess over in the form of 19-year-old Ashley, a canny but sympathetic waitress from Iowa. A clueless suitor, Benny's idea of romance is throwing himself on the girl after leaving her a 50

cent tip. The fact that she may be falling for him, however, must be attributed to his unstudied "style."

Tucci's shameless infidel Griffin is the most interesting of the lovelorn bunch, his unapologetic drives fueling pick-up lines such as the cliche uttered to an unsuspecting Ashley, "Are you a model?" Although an amazing creep, Ashley falls for the middle-aged pursuer's continued flattery ("I think you have the look of the new millennium.") and begins a hopeless affair with the degenerate dentist who tells her though technically married, he and his wife have an "understanding."

Griffin's wife Annie (another thinly veiled Allen reference), however, not aware that their relationship was an open one, begins to suspect him of a dalliance. On cue, the beautiful but rigid and repressed real estate agent takes on a new client—Tommy, who's looking for a new apartment and perhaps, a new girlfriend as Maria conveniently begins to back off from the affair. With Tommy's wholesome charm working its magic and her marriage on the rocks, Annie begins to soften.

The merry-go-round of lovers and disfunction continue in this fashion interspersed with some shaky-passing-for-insightful theories about love, life, and New York delivered via the main characters. Despite these disjointed and rambling monologues, the film's many snippets of a variety of takes on love, the numerous romantic and sexual entanglements, and a lively cast make the film easy to watch and more than occasionally likeable. Its cliched documentary style and dearth of freshness in the writing, however, prevent it from being a truly good and interesting film.

As palatable as Burns' tries to make Tommy, it comes off as simply egotistic. He's just a great-looking guy, with a great job and great sense of humor and style who just wants to settle down and have a family. There's nothing else working inside this guy—no inner demons to fight—just a hopeless romantic on a cosmic search for love in the big city. Mostly, the other characters are written to either come off as unsympathetic (Griffin and Ashley) or simply pathetic (Ben and Annie) in comparison to the godlike Tommy.

Although a somewhat unlikable character, Burns turns his usual solid performance. Dawson's turn makes her the most relatable character, showing a genuine humanity lacking elsewhere in the film. Graham shows her range with a canny portrayal of the uptight agent stuck in a loveless marriage. Murphy is appealing and avoids all cliche, showing a vulnerability mixed with insight. As aforementioned, Tucci is highly watchable and injects his character with a watchability that many actors would find hard to pull off. Despite playing a walking cliche, Krumholtz finds his niche and runs with it. Farina's cartoonish, oily Lothario is an over-the-top character that viewers will either find either very amusing or totally abhorrent. Either way, his refreshing lack of urbanity is a nice change of pace after the neurotic, unhappy, and windy lovers get done with their endless soul-searching.

Stylistically, the film suffers from the pseudo-sophisticated presentation that never lives up to it's imitator. The dramatics seems tinny and forced as if based on a "concept" of a movie instead of delivered from the moviemaker to the heart. The documentary going on inside the film essentially comes from nowhere and goes the same way, leaving the viewer with a more interesting problem to consider than those within the actual plot itself. Who was doing this documentary and why? What is the point of it, however, is probably the better question to consider as nothing is particularly gained with use of this technique, except for the sake of using it. Persistent use of jump cuts, quirky pacing of the dialogue and scenes, and overall disjointedness seeks to imitate the pacing and quirkiness of city life but comes off as studied and merely disconcerting.

For all the talking the characters do, not much is very insightful and in fact, runs toward the trivial. The married participants do little more than argue about the size, frequency, quantity, and quality of their sexual experiences. One of the film's messages, truthfully enough, is that very little of what the characters say have anything to do with how they act. However, raising the mundane to an art form, the film's revelations on sex are not poignant enough to put on a pedestal and examine from every angle, as it constantly seeks to do. By focusing so narrowly on one topic, Burns, in fact, has found a way to take all the joy out of sex. The cleverness of the dialogue and the fact that it is delivered so well only underscores the fact that there is very little being said about love and angst in the big city.

Burns' regular cinematographer (Frank Prinzi) makes New York look its best even while shot completely on location and without a production designer. The film's release was postponed because of the September 11th tragedies (due to its location and airy nature) but was quickly pulled from theaters after its late year release, signifying that there wasn't much fear of triggering any kind of strong emotion.

—*Hilary White*

## CREDITS

**Tommy:** Edward Burns
**Annie:** Heather Graham
**Maria:** Rosario Dawson
**Carpo:** Dennis Farina
**Ben:** David Krumholtz
**Ashley:** Brittany Murphy
**Griffin:** Stanley Tucci
**Sue:** Callie (Calliope) Thorne
**Shari:** Aida Turturro
**Hilary:** Nadia Dajani

**Gio/Harry:** Michael Leydon Campbell

**Origin:** USA
**Released:** 2001
**Production:** Margot Bridger, Edward Burns, Cathy Schulman, Rick Yorn; Marlboro Road Gang Productions, Newmarket Capital Group, Artists Production Group; released by Paramount Classics
**Directed by:** Edward Burns
**Written by:** Edward Burns
**Cinematography by:** Frank Prinzi
**Sound:** Matthew Price
**Editing:** David Greenwald
**Costumes:** Catherine Thomas
**MPAA rating:** R
**Running time:** 107 minutes

## REVIEWS

*Boxoffice.* May, 2001, p. 57.
*Chicago Sun-Times Online.* November 21, 2001.
*Entertainment Weekly.* November 30, 2001, p. 62.
*Los Angeles Times Online.* November 21, 2001.
*New York Times Online.* November 21, 2001.
*People.* December 10, 2001, p. 38.
*San Francisco Chronicle.* November 21, 2001, p. D5.
*Sight and Sound.* January, 2002, p. 56.
*USA Today Online.* November 21, 2001.
*Variety.* April 30, 2001, p. 31.
*Washington Post.* November 23, 2001, p. WE41.

## QUOTES

Griffin (Stanley Tucci) uses a line on Ashley (Brittany Murphy): "I think you have the look of the new millennium."

# Signs & Wonders

Jonathan Nossiter's *Signs & Wonders* proves the point that not all intriguing ideas evolve into interesting films and despite stylized camcorder photography and an outstanding cast *Signs & Wonders* might just be a cure for insomnia. First, the writer and director team of James Lasdun and Nossiter allow too much improvisation from the actors, not realizing that even the best performers need direction, and the camcorder lens seems a bit hyperactive. Second, Stellan Skarsgard delivers a flat performance, playing a Swedish-born American residing in Greece who's unwilling to give up his American patriotism or entitlement to happiness. And, well, the end result is a film that is more confusing than its bemused characters.

In an interview that appeared in *Filmmaker,* American director Nossiter spoke about his desire to direct a film about world domination: "The politics of the film, I think, have more to do with anti-globalization, and America is certainly in the forefront, but is this a peculiarly American problem? No, Charlotte Rampling said she feels that the film is about domination." Yet, American products dominate the film's environment, which is set in Athens, Greece. McDonalds and 7-11 stores appear on every corner, the characters munch on American junk food, and political activist Andreas (Dimitris Katalifos) claims that he was tortured with boxes of Tide when the former dictator imprisoned him. While a slight clash between Greek and American culture presents itself, viewers might find themselves laughing uncomfortably at Americans who import their cultural identity to Europe.

Perhaps Alec (Stellan Skarsgard) took his American citizenship a bit too far by portraying himself as someone straight out of the television show *Father Knows Best.* In any case, he appears to be more like a television character than a human being. Liz Braun of the *Toronto Sun* wrote, "Skarsgard's role, for example, is so badly written that his performance rings false throughout." While Elvis Mitchell of the *New York Times* noted that Skarsgard's performance was a high point of the film, but cited another weakness: "*Signs & Wonders* fails because Mr. Nossiter doesn't bother to define the women as characters; he seems as deluded as Alec."

Aside from a weak plot and flat characters, Nossiter tosses in discordant music at every turn while teasing viewers into thinking something intriguing will take place. He throws in violent images here and there as we witness Katherine (Deborah Kara Unger) undergoing an abortion or Andreas accidentally bite into a piece of glass. We also witness a metal skewer being plunged into a goat's carcass, leaving some viewers to consider vegetarianism. It's as if the director had decided to shock his viewers in order to keep them awake.

However, *Signs & Wonders* isn't a complete loss. The plot eddies around misunderstandings, deception, and betrayal, then shows us the consequences of clinging to premonitions. Alec confesses an affair that he's having with his colleague Katherine to his wife Marjorie (Charlotte Rampling), who instantly forgives her husband. But after Alec follows various signs, he divorces Marjorie, then heads to the U.S. with Katherine—only to learn that she has betrayed his trust. Alec returns to Greece hoping to win back Marjorie's affections, but discovers that Marjorie has fallen in love with political activist Andreas and plans on marrying him.

Meanwhile, Katherine, now pregnant with Alec's child, returns to Greece hoping to reunite with him. But Alec has become obsessed with Marjorie as he tries to eliminate Andreas from Marjorie's life. Through a series of misunderstandings, Katherine thinks that Marjorie has taken Alec back, so she has an abortion. Alec sabotages Andreas' apartment—almost killing him—and is arrested and thrown in prison, while Andreas, Marjorie, and her two children relocate to the Greek mountains. Then Alec and Marjorie's daughter baits and kills Andreas.

The signs and premonitions presented in the film appear to have been written in a code that only the characters understand. For instance, what do the adventures of *Alice in Wonderland* have to do with the film's plot? And the plot device of replaying a taped conversation between Alec and Marjorie in several climatic scenes seems overwrought. Charlotte Rampling offers respite, not only does she present a nice contrast to the shifty-eyed Skarsgard but her outbursts towards Alec add fire to the film. Deborah Kara Unger is luminescent while trying to flesh out an underwritten role.

—*Patty-Lynne Herlevi*

## CREDITS

**Alec:** Stellan Skarsgard
**Marjorie:** Charlotte Rampling
**Katherine:** Deborah Kara Unger
**Andreas:** Dimitris Katalifos
**Siri:** Ashley Remy
**Marcus:** Michael Cook

**Origin:** France
**Released:** 2000
**Production:** Marin Karmitz; Goatworks Films, IdeeFixe Productions, Industry Entertainment, Sunshine Amalgamedia; released by Strand Releasing
**Directed by:** Jonathan Nossiter
**Written by:** Jonathan Nossiter, James Lasdun
**Cinematography by:** Yorgos Arvanitis
**Music by:** Adrian Utley
**Sound:** Neil Riha, Thierry Lebon, Jean-Piere Halbwachs
**Editing:** Madeleine Gavin
**Costumes:** Kathryn Nixon
**MPAA rating:** Unrated
**Running time:** 108 minutes

## REVIEWS

*Entertainment Weekly.* March 2, 2001, p. 44.
*eye Weekly Online.* March 8, 2001.
*Filmmaker.* Fall, 2000, p. 86.
*Los Angeles Times Online.* April 6, 2001.

*New York Times Online.* February 9, 2001.
*People.* February 26, 2001, p. 31.
*Toronto Sun Online.* March 9, 2001.
*Village Voice Online.* February 7, 2001.

## QUOTES

Andreas (Dimitris Katalifos): "When Americans offer you money, it means they're ashamed of something."

## TRIVIA

Jonathan Nossiter and James Lasdun also worked together on the director's first film, *Sunday* (1997).

# Simon Magnus

**S**imon Magus presents a folk tale from the old school. The story of a young man whose visions change the history of a medieval Jewish village is pleasant but flawed. In his debut as writer and director, Ben Hopkins revives the kind of narrative employed in the Yiddish cinema of the 1930s and 1940s. Simon Magus (Noah Taylor) is the young outcast in the 19th-century Polish village, who claims to see the Devil and have mystical powers. Though the townspeople shun him, Simon's preternatural abilities help bring his village into modernity.

Due to his trusting nature, Simon becomes a pawn in the love triangle involving Dovid (Stuart Townsend), a poor, hard-working Jewish scholar, Leah (Embeth Davidtz), a proud young widow, and Hase (Sean McGinley), a selfish aristocratic gentile. Both men also fight over the property owned by the poet Count Albrect (Rutger Hauer), which promises to be the key to the town's future fortunes. In the end, Simon is looked to for resolution and closure.

In the grand tradition of *Tevye, Green Fields,* and other Yiddish film classics, *Simon Magus* begins in an Old World, mittle-European-style sepia tone. After the title sequence, more traditional, albeit soft-focus, color photography takes over. Though the film looks good throughout, this opening shift becomes a metaphor for the story's theme of personal and cultural transformation. Unfortunately, it also becomes symbolic of how the film itself does not quite fulfill its promise as a modern-day Yiddish fable.

Certainly for a first film, Ben Hopkins (a Tim Burton disciple) deserves plaudits for trying something unusual. But instead of turning old film genres into modernist flights of fancy (as in the work of Guy Maddin), Hopkins plays it safe.

In fact, many of the scenes in *Simon Magus* resemble those from the film version of *Fiddler on the Roof,* a rather pedestrian "remake" of those Yiddish films.

Still, *Simon Magus* features a large, talented ensemble of players, most of whom fit nicely into the misty landscape A few of the actors sound a bit more modern than probably intended, but at least they look right. Likewise, the production has a clean elegance to it (The charming set decorations are by Rebecca Gilles, the production design by Angela Davies).

Incidentally, this *Simon Magus* is unrelated to another 1999 release, an Hungarian film with the same title and the same mysticism theme. You won't be overwhelmed by Ben Hopkins' *Simon Magus*, but at least it lingers inoffensively in the memory.

*—Eric Monder*

## CREDITS

**Simon:** Noah Taylor
**Dovid:** Stuart Townsend
**Maximillian Hase:** Sean McGinley
**Leah:** Embeth Davidtz
**Count Albrect:** Rutger Hauer
**Sirius/Boris:** Ian Holm
**Sarah:** Amanda Ryan
**Bratislav:** Terence Rigby

**Origin:** Great Britain
**Released:** 1999
**Production:** Robert Jones; Channel Four Film; released by Fireworks Pictures
**Directed by:** Ben Hopkins
**Written by:** Ben Hopkins
**Cinematography by:** Nicholas D. Knowland
**Music by:** Deborah Mollison
**Editing:** Alan Levy
**Costumes:** Michele Clapton
**Production Design:** Angela Davies
**MPAA rating:** Unrated
**Running time:** 106 minutes

## REVIEWS

*Boxoffice.* December, 2000, p. 56.
*Chicago Sun-Times Online.* April 27, 2001.
*Los Angeles Times Calendar.* February 25, 2001, p. 24.
*New York Times Online.* March 30, 2001.
*San Francisco Chronicle Online.* June 1, 2001.

# Skipped Parts

Being able to do anything especially well takes a great deal of practice. We had to work at it before we could walk, or ride a bike, or learn to read, or master any of the other significant skills we acquired as we were growing up. The same goes, of course, for learning how to some day be a mind-blowing lover. No sense in leaving it to chance: before that monumental and memorable day when a wave of romantic passion leads to your first time, why not find a friend you can practice with? That is the bright idea that a pair of 14-year-olds have in *Skipped Parts,*, based upon the 1991 novel of the same name by Tim Sandlin, which the *Los Angeles Times Book Review* called "funny, shocking, downright revolting, and occasionally sad."

The film includes a recurring narration by Sam Callahan (Bug Hall), the male half of the aforementioned duo engaged in undressed rehearsals. He promises us that he will include the risque but nevertheless illuminating and instructive parts most stories maddeningly skip over. In early 1960's North Carolina, Sam, amiable, bright and imaginative, is emerging from childhood with his naivete intact, which is somewhat hard to believe when his mother Lydia (Jennifer Jason Leigh) is anything but naive. Having conceived Sam out of wedlock with an unidentified man at age 15, she remains determinedly wild and loose, and considers the term "mother" to be an insult. She revels in sex, but steers clear of real intimacy. Her flower has attracted far too much attention from far too many bees, and alcohol has only accentuated her licentious ways.

Lydia's father, Caspar (R. Lee Ermey), is running for governor, and he is worried that Lydia's acting up could bring him down. So he ships her and Sam off to Wyoming, out of sight and where, he figures, there is little trouble to be had. Most of the time, Lydia and Sam have an unusual but breezy, close relationship, with Sam acting more as a levelheaded pal and even a caretaker. (He has, for example, been writing their checks since he was six.) When they get to Wyoming, Lydia announces that she has vowed to be "emotionally catatonic" in order to prevent dear old daddy from cutting her off entirely. Sam's emotions, on the other hand, are in turmoil when he starts his new school: he stinks at sports, and the kids all seem mean or ignorant or both, as if they result from the "mating of first cousins." He seeks refuge in his love of books, as well as in his fertile and sometimes hormone-driven fantasies (which include brief appearances by Drew Barrymore)

One girl who strikes his fancy despite initial friction is Maurey Pierce (Mischa Barton), a pretty, intelligent and popular girl who shares Sam's love of reading. If Sam feels that there is an amazing contrast between himself and most of the other kids, there is an even greater one between Lydia

and Maurey's mother (Peggy Lipton), a cross between Betty Crocker and a Stepford wife, who comes with Maurey to the Callahans' door representing the Welcome Wagon. The woman is dressed in her Sunday best, including coat, hat, gloves, and pearls, and exhibits unflinchingly impeccable manners. Mrs. Pierce comes face to face with her polar opposite when Lydia, stretched against the door frame like a hooker looking for business, nearly bursting out of a little hot pink top and enjoying a cigarette, announces that she and Sam do not expect to be in town for long, and slams the door in the woman's face.

When the assassination of President Kennedy occurs, Maurey's peculiarly placid mother keeps her feelings wrapped up tight, baking cookies and making hot cocoa ("It's always time for cocoa!" she asserts brightly.) In contrast, much looser Lydia throws her nearly empty liquor bottle at the TV, goes into town to watch in a store window, and hooks up with a Blackfoot Indian named Hank Elkrunner (Michael Greyeyes), a decision which she is gleefully sure would infuriate her father. It has been said that the country suffered a loss of innocence when the young, vibrant president was killed, and the event is used here to signal that these babes in the virgin Wyoming woods will soon be less virginal. "All the rules are off today, Sam," says Maurey with a new seriousness.

As their friendship develops, Maurey asserts that she does not want to "come off ignorant" when she loses her virginity, and decides the two should explore what the big deal is about this "sex thing." Sam is not opposed to looking into the matter, especially because he is painfully aware of his lack of knowledge in this department. (His first wet dream absolutely baffles and bewilders him until he takes a sock with the semen on it to Lydia, who proceeds to determine the nature of the liquid by not only smelling and feeling it but, in a revolting act which mars the scene, also tasting it.) Not surprisingly, Sam and Maurey's first awkward attempts are none too successful, so the girl feels that, unlike her own mother, Lydia would be open to discussing how to vault over their sexual hurdles. Lydia not only offers advice, but uses a taco shell as a visual aid in showing how a woman is best pleased. She does insist, however, that this honing of their skills stop immediately upon Maurey's first period. ("What's a period?" Sam asks)

So the two keep on experimenting, and while Sam starts to actually fall for his friend, she continues to date Dothan Talbot (Brad Renfro), a rough, older jock, and pressures Sam into unwillingly accepting the attentions of ultra-conservative Chuckette Morris (Alison Pill), who lets Sam know in no uncertain terms that French kissing is something Nazarenes just will not do. Things continue on this way until the inevitable announcement that stops everyone short: even though she has not yet had her first period, Maurey is almost certain that she is pregnant. She turns down Sam's chivalrous offer to marry her because, as she forlornly points out,

"I'm 14 years old!" Director Davis lingers on the two, framed in a mirror, to emphasize that what we are looking at are very scared kids. Lydia lends a much-needed shoulder to Maurey, whose own mother, the girl is sure, would swoon at the mere mention of sex.

Lydia, Sam, and Maurey take a trip to the nearest abortion clinic where the film loses some credibility, as it turns out that not only has Maurey's mother strayed from her hard-working but often-absent husband and gotten pregnant by the school's football coach/English teacher (Gerald Lenton-Young), but she has also sought an abortion at that clinic on the very same day as her daughter. Shocked and in tears, Maurey runs out and heads back home, still pregnant. When she tells her father about her pregnancy and is temporarily rejected, she goes to live with the Callahans. It is Hank who looks at the unfortunate situation Lydia has helped Sam and Maurey get themselves into and calls her on her heedless irresponsibility. Although she reacts angrily to his judgmental attitude and breaks up with him, he has jolted her into a new awareness. Also jolting is a scene in which Maurey's distraught mother has a nervous breakdown at a rodeo. Afterward, Lydia reconciles with Hank, realizing that life is too short for her to waste anymore of it.

Everyone gathers for an unusual 15th birthday party for a clearly pregnant Maury, which includes Lydia (still licentious but determined to be more conscientious) and Maurey's equally-bawdy Aunt Delores (Angela Featherstone) chatting about fake orgasms. It is definitely a bad time for Caspar Callahan to show up to check on how his daughter and grandson are faring. When he sees that things have been pretty wild out West, he declares that he is sending Sam to a military academy. Lydia and Sam like the life they have now—their own newfangled version of the modern American family—and so as Maurey gives birth to a baby girl, Sam proudly stays on to care for little Shannon, dreaming of a romantic future with the mother of his child, and tapping out stories about his experiences with hopes of success as a writer. Lydia succeeds for the first time in her life at earning her own way, working as a waitress in the local coffee shop.

*Skipped Parts* was skipped over for theatrical release when Lion's Gate Entertainment acquired the completed production in a merger with Trimark Pictures and released it to video. Most films which receive that treatment are without merit, but *Skipped Parts* is not without its modest charms. With a screenplay adapted by the author and directed by Tamra Davis, the film weaves together humorous and touching moments, innocence and raunchiness, into a pleasing if somewhat impotent and inconsequential effort. The success it has is thanks largely to the likeability of young Hall and the usual good work of Leigh, who at times is rather affecting as a woman whose heart is the only body part she refuses to let a man touch. Not only is this a coming of age tale for Sam and Maurey, who, while still very much

children, take a premature sexual leap into adulthood, but also for Lydia, who took a similar leap forward years before, and who has finally begun to develop another kind of maturity to go with the one she has reveled (and hidden) in for so long.

—*David L. Boxerbaum*

## CREDITS

**Lydia Callahan:** Jennifer Jason Leigh
**Sam Callahan:** Bug Hall
**Hank Elkrunner:** Michael Greyeyes
**Maurey Pierce:** Mischa Barton
**Laurabel Pierce:** Peggy Lipton
**Dothan Talbot:** Brad Renfro
**Caspar Callahan:** R. Lee Ermey
**Aunt Delores:** Angela Featherstone
**Chuckette Morris:** Alison Pill
**Coach Howard Stebbins:** Gerald Lenton-Young
**Fantasy Girl:** Drew Barrymore (Cameo)

**Origin:** USA
**Released:** 2000
**Production:** Shelby Stone, Alison Dickey, Sharon Oreck; released by Lion's Gate Films
**Directed by:** Tamra Davis
**Written by:** Tim Sandlin
**Cinematography by:** Claudio Rocha
**Music by:** Stewart Copeland
**Editing:** Luis Colina
**Costumes:** Wendy Schalper
**Production Design:** Ian D. Thomas
**MPAA rating:** R
**Running time:** 93 minutes

## REVIEWS

*Boxoffice.* July, 2001, p. 90.

# The Sleepy Time Gal

American independent filmmaker Christopher Munch creates a cinematic puzzle with his fifth outing, *The Sleepy Time Gal*. Beautifully shot by Rob Sweeney, against music by J. S. Bach, Munch's film possesses the same wandering soul as its central character, Frances (Jacqueline Bisset). Munch explores subtle and not-so-subtle human connections with family members and a past lover. The director doesn't dole out information through obvious exposition nor does he allow his characters to overtly confess to viewers their thoughts or feelings. Instead, Munch forces viewers to dig for clues and put the puzzle together even if the final piece remains missing.

*The Sleepy Time Gal* portrays Americana and acts as a bit of a travelogue since the story takes place in several cities, including New York, Boston, Daytona Beach, and San Francisco. The film possesses a story about belonging, home and family, as well as death. The pacing is slow and dreamy, yet melancholic. Frances learns that she has cancer and as she faces her impending death, she attempts to patch up her relationship with her son Morgan (Nick Stahl), a gay photographer, and she searches for the daughter that she gave up for adoption. She also reunites with a past lover, Bob (Seymour Cassel), now married to a Pennsylvania Dutch woman, Betty (Peggy Gormley), and living on a farm.

Meanwhile, the adopted daughter, lawyer Rebecca (Martha Plimpton), finds herself in the midst of a corporate takeover of a small radio station in Daytona Beach. While at the station, Rebecca is seduced by the aging station manager Jimmy Dupree (Frankie Faison). Rebecca also discovers an old photograph of Frances, "The Sleepy Time Gal," a sexy radio announcer who broke men's hearts. Later, Rebecca learns the true identity of Frances as she searches for her birth parents.

As time passes, Frances' health deteriorates and she makes a decision to take her own life. Only Morgan and her nurse Maggie (Amy Madigan) protest this decision. Frances chooses not to hurt those who love her so she suffers in silence. After her death, Betty writes a book about her husband's love affair with The Sleepy Time Gal. Even though Rebecca never meets her mother, she reads Betty's book about Frances and is able to piece together the mysterious woman who gave birth to her.

Kent Jones of *Film Comment* described the film as "a lovingly crafted patchwork quilt, sewn by hand, billowing as it falls over the bed." Jones certainly picked up on the film's poetic qualities. Both the spoken and visual language of the film carries with it a timeless quality inherent in poetry; even the film's characters possess a fey and elusive quality. Though we learn of the characters' past and can piece together their lives, we can never quite grasp the inner workings that make these characters tick. Munch chooses not to solve their mysteries or to deliver closure at the end of his film. Jones comments on this uneasiness: "As he does throughout the movie, Munch drops us into a moment without a setup. One moment is linked to the next without an immediately clear reason . . ." This results in hypersurrealism, leaving the film's viewers to feel a bit disoriented, as if they had just woken from an intense dream.

Although the film's performances appear subtle on the surface, the actors deliver outstanding performances. Thankfully, Bisset doesn't play the cliched woman dying of cancer, but instead acts in a dignified fashion. Jones states: "If there's one actor that holds this dangerously delicate movie together, it's Bisset. In many ways, the film hinges on her character's peculiar discomfort, her rethink of her image as a bewitching, intelligent and adventuress, her wanderlust vying for supremacy with her pride and fierce sense of conviction." Plimpton transforms her character from a no-nonsense attorney to that of a fragile child in search of her real mother, Cassel plays the abandoned lover with aplomb, and Stahl plays up the brooding qualities of his lost character. Although fractured, this film portrays a character-driven story in which one piece remains missing, but its humanity remains fully intact.

*—Patty-Lynne Herlevi*

## CREDITS

**Frances:** Jacqueline Bisset
**Rebecca:** Martha Plimpton
**Morgan:** Nick Stahl
**Maggie:** Amy Madigan
**Jimmy Dupree:** Frankie Faison
**Anna:** Carmen Zapata
**Bob:** Seymour Cassel
**Betty:** Peggy Gormley

**Origin:** USA
**Released:** 2001
**Production:** Ruth Charny, Christopher Munch; C-Hundred Film Corporation
**Directed by:** Christopher Munch
**Written by:** Christopher Munch
**Cinematography by:** Rob Sweeney
**Sound:** Fredrick Helm, Fernando Muga, Aaron Saddler
**Music Supervisor:** S.A. Lipton
**Editing:** Christopher Munch, Annette Davey
**Art Direction:** Jody Asnes, Melissa Frankel, Bryan Hedge
**Costumes:** Kristen Anacker
**MPAA rating:** Unrated
**Running time:** 94 minutes

## REVIEWS

*Boxoffice*. April, 2001, p. 225.
*Film Comment*. November/December, 2000, p. 14.
*Variety*. February 12, 2001, p. 39.

# Snatch

*Now you see it, now you don't!*
—Movie tagline
*Stealin' Stones and Breakin' Bones.*
—Movie tagline

 **Box Office:** $30.2 million

When most writer-directors make a promising, small-scale first film, they try something more adventurous the second time out. With *Snatch*, however, Guy Ritchie seems to be trying to duplicate the characters and plot of *Lock, Stock, and Two Smoking Barrels* (1998), but the result offers grating shifts in tone. Although many reviewers, while noting the strong similarities between the two, praised *Snatch* as an improvement over the earlier film, its frequent jumps from the light-hearted to the deadly violent, the shallowness of the development of its characters, and occasional gaps in logic make it appear to be something a talented filmmaker threw together perhaps too hastily.

*Snatch* opens with one of its high points as Franky Four Fingers (Benicio Del Toro) leads a gang disguised as Hasidim into the vaults of an Antwerp jeweler to steal an 84-carat diamond. Franky takes the diamond to London to await transferring it to his cousin Avi (Dennis Farina), a New York criminal. Meanwhile, Russian gangster Boris the Blade (Rade Sherbedgia) learns about the jewel and hires three bumbling small-timers to steal it. These three, Sol (Lennie James), Vincent (Robbie Gee), and Tyrone (Ade), provide comic relief with much humor derived from the massive Tyrone's bulk and Vincent's devotion to his recently acquired dog, a rather temperamental mongrel.

All of this is secondary, however, to the main storyline of *Snatch*. Turkish (Jason Statham), a small-time promoter of illegal boxing matches, wants to replace the dilapidated caravan (trailer to us Yanks) that serves as his office. He sends his associate Tommy (Stephen Graham) to the camp of some Irish Gypsies to negotiate a deal for a caravan. The inept Tommy not only manages to lose their money but their best fighter, the ironically named Gorgeous George (Adam Fogerty), as well when Mickey O'Neil (Brad Pitt), the pugnacious leader of the Gypsies, lays out the much larger man with one crushing punch. The illegal fight game is controlled by Brick Top (Alan Ford), a particularly nasty bit of baggage. Mickey agrees to substitute for George, but when he does not go down in the fourth round, as demanded by Brick Top, mayhem ensues.

Ritchie's gift as a screenwriter comes with his ability to create divergent strands of a story and then bring them together unexpectedly. The charm of *Lock* comes primarily from how the characters merge as their plots begin to overlap. What Alfred Hitchcock called the Maguffin (arbitrary plot mechanism) was, in *Lock,* a pair of antique shotguns which accidentally unify all the warring sides. In *Snatch,* there is the diamond, of course, but keep an eye on that dog.

In Ritchie's first film, soccer star Vinnie Jones plays a stylish enforcer central to bringing everything into focus. In *Snatch,* he plays a slightly darker version of the same character performing the same function. In both films, the worst of the bad guys are punished more severely, with the most sympathetic ones coming out mostly all right at the end. Many of the same actors appear in both films: not just Jones but Statham, Ford (narrator of the earlier film), and Jason Flemyng, who goes from playing one of the leads to an almost-wordless role as Mickey's mate.

But while Ritchie's first film is mostly comedic, despite considerable gunplay, his second constantly undercuts its laughs with unpleasantness, most centering around Brick Top. A relatively innocent remark sets off this thug who cuts the speaker's hand, and Ritchie's camera lingers on the victim's pain. Brick Top has someone killed, and Ritchie shows the anguish of the victim's loved one at great length—and then returns to it later. In addition to letting humans batter each other, Brick Top also arranges dog fights, and he disposes of his enemies by having them cut up and fed to pigs. Ritchie never actually shows any of this grusomeness, but the threat is always there, making the audience more than a bit uncomfortable. The possibility that Vincent's dog may meet a bad end also undercuts some of the humor provided by the animal.

Ritchie has clearly studied the dialogue of Harold Pinter, David Mamet, and, particularly, Quentin Tarantino. While reviewers have pointed out obvious parallels between Ritchie's films and Tarantino's, there is an even closer similarity to Martin Scorsese's *Mean Streets* (1973), though Scorsese manages the contrasts between humor and violence much more skillfully. The most Tarantinoesque moment in *Snatch* comes when Brick Top describes in detail how to feed humans to pigs. The speech is so over the top that viewers are supposed to be amused by its excess, but Brick Top has been so evil to this point that his words never achieve the desired effect.

Then there is the sloppiness in Ritchie's plotting. It is hard to believe that Boris would hire such a trio to find the diamond for him. As he proves repeatedly, Boris is the type to take matters into his own bloody hands. It is even harder to believe that Brick Top would give Turkish a second chance after Mickey's stunt. Too many things happen just to get the story from one point to another with little attention to the logical motivations of the characters.

The major complaint reviewers have against Ritchie is that he is a case of style over content. The director does call attention to himself by using slow motion, fast motion, flashbacks, flashforwards, a jittery camera, and quick cuts. Occasionally, it seems as if editor Jon Harris has been hitting the caffeine a tad hard. But the reviewers of both Ritchie films give the impression that there is more of this sort of thing than actually occurs. A strong case can be made that Ritchie underplays his rococo visuals, especially when compared to similar directors such as Oliver Stone. Parts of the film aggressively assault the viewers, keeping them constantly off-balance, but most of it is fairly standard medium-shot, let's-watch-the-lads-chat-for-awhile filmmaking. As with failing to strike the right balance between the comic and violent tones of the film, Ritchie's visual styles also conflict with each other, making his pyrotechnics seem to be jarring.

Nevertheless, some of Ritchie's flourishes sparkle. Avi goes back and forth between New York and London in a comically effective sped-up process as the director, again like Tarantino, plays with time. Ritchie cuts from a group of characters in a room in London to Avi in New York to Avi in London and back to the room where only minutes have passed. The best scene in *Snatch* occurs when several of the factions merge into the same location, the violent actions bringing them together seen from the perspectives of each group as the narrative jumps forward and back in time several times within seconds. Another unusual narrative element is Ritchie's suddenly killing off one of the main characters halfway through the film. It is not as shocking as Janet Leigh's demise in *Psycho* (1960) but still surprising.

Even though Tim Maurice-Jones photographed both films, they have different looks. *Lock* has a brownish tinge, an almost sepia glow, accenting the film's unrealistic approach to comedy and creating counterpoint between the lovely visuals and the crude behavior of the protagonists. There is nothing, however, beautiful about *Snatch*. To express Ritchie's darker vision, Maurice-Jones gives the film a grungier, greenish palette. Even the sunlight at the Gypsies' camp is disturbingly unrealistic. The cinematographer's work is complemented by that of production designer Hugo Luczyc-Wyhowski who gives every locale the appropriately died-in look. With films such as *My Beautiful Laundrette* (1985), *Prick Up Your Ears* (1987), and *Nil By Mouth* (1997) to his credit, Luczyc-Wyhow is the master of the London-as-working-class-hell look.

Del Toro, Pitt, and Farina are all good, but they have played these characters before. Pitt does add the nuance of an almost impenetrable Irish accent. While it is difficult to tell if Mickey does this deliberately to keep outsiders off-balance or this is simply the actor having fun, the befuddlement of the listeners is amusing. Grimy and covered in tattoos, with a reproduction of "The Last Supper" on his back, Pitt continues in the great tradition of attractive actors such as Laurence Olivier and Marlon Brando who like to hide behind accents and makeup.

Ford, who has a small role in *The Long Good Friday* (1980), perhaps the greatest British crime film, is truly frightening as Brick Top. Ritchie again demonstrates his sense of style by casting a rather ordinary-looking actor as such a monster. Statham is solid as the film's lone voice of reason, doing his best to keep chaos from overwhelming him and his mates. As in *Lock*, Jones has considerable screen presence. *Snatch* brightens when he appears midway through. Sherbedgia, who normally plays rather solemn types, is a comic revelation as the seemingly indestructible Boris.

While its warring parts coalesce even less well than its embattled criminals, *Snatch* continues to show that Ritchie has a good ear for dialogue and a strong visual sense. If only he could make his characters more than types and create a more coherent narrative.

*—Michael Adams*

## CREDITS

**Franky Four Fingers:** Benicio Del Toro
**Avi:** Dennis Farina
**Mickey O'Neil:** Brad Pitt
**Bullet Tooth Tony:** Vinnie Jones
**Boris the Blade:** Rade Serbedzija
**Turkish:** Jason Statham
**Sol:** Lennie James
**Mullet:** Ewen Bremner
**Brick Top:** Alan Ford
**Doug the Head:** Mike Reid
**Vincent:** Robbie Gee
**Darren:** Jason Flemyng
**Mrs. O'Neil:** Sorcha Cusack
**Tommy:** Stephen Graham

**Origin:** Great Britain
**Released:** 2000
**Production:** Matthew Vaughn; Screen Gems, SKA Films; released by Columbia Pictures
**Directed by:** Guy Ritchie
**Written by:** Guy Ritchie
**Cinematography by:** Tim Maurice-Jones
**Music by:** John Murphy
**Sound:** Simon Hayes
**Editing:** Les Healey, John Harris
**Art Direction:** Julie Philpott
**Costumes:** Verity Hawkes
**Production Design:** Hugo Luczyc-Wyhowski
**MPAA rating:** R
**Running time:** 104 minutes

## REVIEWS

*Boxoffice.* January, 2001, p. 28.
*Boxoffice.* January, 2001, p. 62.
*Chicago Sun-Times Online.* January 19, 2001.
*Entertainment Weekly.* January 26, 2001, p. 73.
*Film Comment.* January/February, 2001, p. 37.
*Hollywood Reporter.* September 5, 2000, p. 23.
*Maclean's.* January 24, 2001, p. 44.
*New Republic.* February 5, 2001, p. 24.
*New York Times.* January 19, 2001, p. E18.
*Newsweek.* January 22, 2001, p. 61.
*People.* January 29, 2001, p. 34.
*Sight and Sound.* October, 2000, p. 59.
*Time.* January 22, 2001, p. 77.
*USA Today.* January 19, 2001, p. E6.
*Variety.* September 25, 2000, p. 59.
*Washington Post Online.* January 19, 2001.

## QUOTES

Bullet Tooth Tony (Vinnie Jones): "You should never underestimate the predictability of stupidity."

# Sobibor, October 14, 1943, 4 p.m.

The master French film documentarist Claude Lanzmann's latest offering, *Sobibor, October 14, 1943, 4 p.m.*, is nothing more than a survivor's account of an uprising at a Nazi extermination camp in Poland. Yet Lanzmann's approach to the documentary form is so stark and simple that what he has to say about the film becomes as important as the film itself. Lanzmann, from the podium of the 2001 New York Film Festival, claimed that he had initially planned the interview that comprises *Sobibor* to be a part of his monumental nine-hour *Shoah*, which assaults the viewer's conscience by allowing both the victims and perpetrators of the Nazi Holocaust to relate their experiences in their own words. Lanzmann then felt that this one interview deserved a film of its own, since it was thematically in a world apart, focussing as it did on, what he calls, "the reappropriation of power and violence by the Jews."

Even so, *Sobibor* cannot stand on its own as a documentary feature. Quite apart from the background needed to place the interview against a historical context, it lacks the filmic overlay of the work it was originally intended to be a part of. *Shoah*, with its prolonged takes of the most insignificant bits of contemporary physical reality, such as those of train tracks and the Siemens logo fluttering over truck tires

in motion, seems to hint that the institutions and technologies of the time were as much responsible for the Holocaust as the will of the Nazis. *Sobibor* contains no such discursive depth. While Lanzmann does show us brief shots of today's Warsaw and Minsk, as well as the forest around Sobibor, for the most part the film consists of one interview.

In fact, the interview mode seems to have taken over Lanzmann's artistic intentions in *Sobibor*. In allowing Yehuda Lerner, the film's sole focus, to recount in his own words the steps leading to the uprising at the Nazi extermination facility, Lanzmann risks the viewer finding it all very tedious. Yehuda speaks in Hebrew, which is then translated by the voice of a female interpreter into French, which then is retranslated into English subtitles. What this no doubt original technique in film interviewing achieves is that the viewer's attention is not distracted while Yehuda is speaking to the camera. It is Yehuda's congenial personality, not Lanzmann's rigorous insistence on form, that makes it all work.

Lanzmann's intentions, some of which are explained in the lengthy introductory titles that introduce the film, were to basically dispel two myths that have continued to linger over accounts of the Nazi Holocaust. One, that the Jews, except for the Warsaw Ghetto Uprising, offered no resistance to their Nazi oppressors and two, that the Jews allowed themselves to be led into the gas chambers without suspecting the fate that was in store for them.

Yehuida Lerner in 1979, the year the interview was filmed, describes his travails under the Nazis, from the time he is taken prisoner in Warsaw at the age of 16, until his break for freedom at Sobibor the following year. Lanzmann intercuts medium shots and extreme close-ups of Lerner talking at the camera with footage of the places he is talking about, as they look today. Even so, the film remains incomplete for someone who hasn't seen *Shoah*, which provides the background to how the camp was constructed and the precise manner in which the exterminations were carried out. Furthermore, we never get to see the kind of life the extraordinary Lerner, who happens to be alive today, is living at the time of the film's release, or the kind of life he was living at the time he was being interviewed by Lanzmann. Thus, a viewer cannot help but feel that Lanzmann has exploited Lerner to suit his own aims as a documentary filmmaker, just as the Nazis exploited Lerner and other skilled Jews, keeping them alive so as to reap their services. Alas, poor Yehuda, whose superhuman bravery led him out of the vicious clutches of an unimaginably brutal regime, appears ironically trapped within the confines of Lanzmann's camera and the filmmaker's agenda.

When Lerner starts speaking about the uprising itself, of which he was an integral part, the film manages to hold its own against the whole gamut of absurdist concentration camp film fiction, from Andrej Munk's Polish masterwork *Eroica* (1957) to Billy Wilder's *Stalag 17* (1953), not to mention the avowedly serious *Schindler's List* (1993) by Steven Spielberg. Yet it is different from them, and not just owing to its being comprised of actual fact. Even as a documentary filmmaker, Lanzmann, by his own admission, does not want to use the film medium to illustrate any fact. This is why he shuns newsreel footage, and suchlike. His cutaways to how the cities of Poland Yehuda speaks about look like today are not meant to illustrate Yehuda's words, but to add another layer of filmic discourse to what Yehuda is saying.

A case in point is when Yehuda recounts how the Germans maintained a huge flock of over 800 geese for the express purpose of using their loud crying to drown out the screams of the men being forced into the gas chambers. This became necessary so that the men at the back of the line, who were being unloaded from the rail cars, wouldn't suspect what lay ahead. The geese would cry for an hour, and after that they would be silent. Lanzmann punctuates this account with shots of a flock of geese, so that we actually get to hear the kind of din they must have made. Simple as this may appear, when Lanzmann speaks of his artistic decision to insert the shot of a flock of geese, it brings to light the complex issues involved in cinematic representation that only a film documentarian of Lanzmann's stature would be aware of. Just as the screams of the geese reared by the Nazis were meant to cover human screams, Lanzmann wanted Yehuda's voice to "fight" the sound of his geese crying in unison. When Lanzmann shot his flock of white geese, he did not manipulate them. What we see on screen is the geese turning by themselves and forming, what Lanzmann describes as, "a white immaculate circle." He then decided to cut the sound, so that what resulted was "the real terrifying silence of death."

As a feisty prisoner, Lerner had tried to escape from camps before Sobibor but was caught. Surprisingly, owing to nothing more than his luck, according to him, he was not shot by the Germans but merely reassigned to another camp. At Sobibor, Lerner and the Soviet Jews he came to know got word that the camp was going to be dismantled soon, and so it would be just a matter of time before they too would be put to death. To hear him tell it, they had nothing to lose in trying to escape. Earlier attempts by prisoners had failed, so Lerner and his group of 20 others decided that the only way had to be to kill the Germans, and then flee.

The plan, as hatched by their committee of carpenters, tailors and other skilled workers, sought to capitalize on the element of surprise. Lerner explains that, as Jewish prisoners, they were "already nothing" and that their courage came from the fact that they "wanted to die like men." Consequently, the German officers at Sobibor, who had already killed hundreds of thousands like them, wouldn't even have dreamt of, much less been prepared for, an insurrection. The power structure at Sobibor, we come to know, consisted of only 30 Germans, half of whom were usually away, and a support structure of a 1,000 Ukrainian lackeys. The film gets its title from the punctual visit the Nazi commander, Greischutz, was scheduled to make to the tailor's shop for a fitting. Lerner recalls it all with a smile, no doubt owing to the pride that hindsight has brought him in "avenging all those who died" at Sobibor.

Never having killed anyone before, Lerner felt petrified as the appointed time drew near. Greischutz was a huge man, over six feet and broad-shouldered. Simply put, Greischutz had to remove his gun belt for the fitting, whereupon as the tailor was mearuing him from the front, Lerner struck the commander from behind, "splitting his skull in two halves." Others then leapt in, needing to clean up the mess in less than five minutes, since 4:05 was the time set for the second German to walk in. True enough, he did.

"Without German punctuality, we could not have achieved anything," Lerner chuckles. With all other phases of the plan proceeding apace, suspense crept in when Lerner saw that Greischutz's lifeless hand was sticking out from under a pile of coats. Moreover, the second German even stepped on the hand, without realizing what it was, but before he could investigate, he too was fatally struck. All in all, 11 Germans were killed, soon resulting in a stamped to freedom by the prisoners even as the Ukrainians were firing upon them. Lerner himself managed to escape into the dense forest nearby, where he fell asleep from exhaustion.

Lanzmann, however, saves his own wallop for the end of the film. As he explains it, if the film had ended with Lerner's escape, it would have been a happy ending. Instead, the viewer's conscience is bombarded by an endless series of titles, the names of towns and the numbers from each, which comprised the 250,000 exterminated at Sobibor. We watch transfixed, realizing the correlation between the objectivity of the film medium and the empiricism of numbers, both proving closed doors between us and the horror of our time.

Critical opinion seems to have accepted *Sobibor* as a documentary feature capable of standing by itself. A.O. Scott in the *New York Times* finds a moral justification for Lanzmann's style of filmic discourse. He notes that the Warsaw and Minsk that we see in the film are "bustling modern cities where the past is visible in the shape of monuments." He then quotes Lanzmann from the film's introductory titles: "Museums and monuments institute oblivion as much as remembrance." As for Lerner's personality, Scott argues that the emotion he demonstrates while recounting the momentous but horrendous deed he was forced to perform could easily be mistaken for joy, "but which seems like something unspeakably more complex." He concludes that this extends to the film as well, as it evokes "feelings that . . . are as hard to name as they are to dispel."

—*Vivek Adarkar*

## CREDITS

**Origin:** France
**Language:** French, Hebrew
**Released:** 2001
**Production:** France 2 Cinema, Les Films Aleph; released by New Yorker Films
**Directed by:** Claude Lanzmann
**Written by:** Claude Lanzmann
**Cinematography by:** Caroline Champetier, Dominique Chapuis
**Sound:** Bernard Aubouy
**Editing:** Chantal Hymans, Sabine Marnou
**MPAA rating:** Unrated
**Running time:** 95 minutes

## REVIEWS

*Entertainment Weekly.* November 2, 2001, p. 51.
*New York Times Online.* October 10, 2001.
*New York Times Online.* October 11, 2001.
*Variety.* May 21, 2001.

# Someone Like You

*A story about the one that got away and the one she never saw coming.*
—Movie tagline

**Box Office:** $27.3 million

Someone Like You is a predictable romantic comedy, not without its own charm thanks to its attractive cast. It's your basic story: girl meets boy, falls madly in love, gets dumped, tries to figure out what when wrong, and finally realizes she was in love with the wrong guy all along. Only when she's trying to figure things out, the girl—Jane Goodale (yes, there is a joke about getting her confused with the primatologist)—comes up with her new cow/old cow theory. The film is based on Laura Zigman's 1998 novel *Animal Husbandry* and begins with a display of Jane's new cow journal, but, as Jane herself remarks in the constant voice-overs: "I'm getting ahead of myself."

Jane (Ashley Judd) is an attractive, personable woman who works as the talent booker for the Diane Roberts talk show—a local New York show that has just been syndicated and gone national, which means the hyperactive Diane (Ellen Barkin) is even more impossible than usual. The viewer is then introduced to the two men who will become so important in Jane's life. First there's writer, producer, and "pathological womanizer" Eddie Alden (Hugh Jackman). Eddie's a good-looking, "hey, babe" kind of guy who primarily resembles a prowling tomcat. Then there's Ray Brown (Greg Kinnear). He's the new executive producer—clean-cut, charming, seemingly sensitive and romantic. Naturally Jane is attracted to him at first glance. In fact, the film has intertitles to its various chapters and "Attraction" is the first one.

But Jane tells her seen-it-all best friend Liz (Marisa Tomei) that Ray has a girlfriend and, even though they're having problems, she's going to leave him alone. Only Ray has other ideas and Jane is oh-so-easy to convince. He and Jane have lunch in the park, go for walks—they are now at the "Establishment of Intimacy" point and Jane is suffering joy, rapture, and ecstasy. Then comes the "Vocalization of Emotions" and both admit they love each other. In fact, Ray thinks they should get their own apartment together since he's finally told his old girlfriend it's over between them and Jane gives her landlord notice. This, of course, is just asking for trouble.

Ray now has more than cold feet and starts to slide out of their relationship. Jane's been watching a nature program about an animal's escape behavior from predators and realizes the similarities (no, the movie's not subtle). Jane's apartment has been re-rented and she needs a place to live. Eddie needs a roommate for his two-bedroom loft and has told Jane if she's ever looking that it would be a strictly financial arrangement since "I've got no interest in you that way, whatsoever." Hey, it's a romantic comedy—that situation will change. Especially when Jane decides to become Eddie's new roommate.

Eddie, even though he has a bathroom cabinet full of boxes of condoms, isn't the casual sex fiend he seems. He got the loft with a girlfriend who dumped him and he's hiding (well) his own bruised heart. But Jane's heart just won't mend; she doesn't understand why Ray left. Then she reads the science section of the newspaper and the headline suddenly strikes her: "Polygamy Preferred by Male Bovine." This is the "Birth of a Theory." A male will only mate once with any female cow. He knows when he's previously serviced a female cow. He wants new cow and rejects old cow. Jane is now an "old cow" to Ray and he no longer has any interest in her. She reads voraciously to find factoids supporting her new theory.

Liz works for a men's magazine and tells Jane that there is to be a new column about men's behavior. She thinks that Jane should use her new cow/old cow theory and write the column under a pen name. The women have "A Call to Arms" and come up with a background for their nonexistent scientist: an elderly PhD. named Dr. Marie Charles. The column is a big hit. Still, it doesn't seem to be doing

Jane much good since she's still pining for Ray. They talk at the office Christmas party and he winsomely makes a move on her, asking Jane out for New Year's Eve. Jane agrees to go while Eddie just shakes his head in dismay and wonders what she's doing to herself. Jane gets stood up. Back at work, Jane sees Diane wearing a familiar man's shirt—one, in fact, that Jane bought for Ray. As it turns out, the old girlfriend of Ray's was actually Diane and they've gotten back together, thus proving Jane's "old cow" theory wrong. Jane has an emotional meltdown in the office and must listen to Diane tell her she understands because her boyfriend once left her and she felt lost without him.

After a bar trip with Liz, Jane and Eddie continue a heated discussion about male/female relationships back at their loft. Jane is wallowing in self-pity and Eddie thinks she should get a grip. Jane finally breaks down and admits she can't let go because she was happy with Ray and she fears that she will never find that feeling with anyone again. As she cries on Eddie's shoulder, he softly reassures her that: "Ray is not the last man you're ever going to love." When Jane wakes to find Eddie in her bed (they fell chastely asleep), she panics and lashes out that all men are basically pond scum. A fed-up Eddie tells her that the problem isn't with all men—that something is going on with Jane herself that she has to figure out.

It takes a crisis to bring a resolution to Jane's romantic dilemma. Her sister miscarries a long-desired pregnancy and, while visiting the hospital, Jane witnesses a tender moment between her sister and brother-in-law that demonstrates what true love is all about. Jane then calls Diane to say that elusive cow theorist Dr. Charles will appear on her talk show. When Jane walks out, Eddie leaves in disgust while Jane explains herself to the audience. She was heartbroken, lost, and looking to blame someone but she's had an epiphany about love. What she's realized is that Eddie was right and Ray was not the last man she would ever love, in fact, Jane finally figures out that she loves Eddie. She chases him down and they kiss on the street while Van Morrison sings "Someone Like You" in the background. (It's a good soundtrack.)

Sometimes predictable is okay. Sometimes you want to know that everything is going to turn out the way you expect it to. And *Someone Like You* is exactly that kind of movie. Since Ray is seemingly so right for Jane, he will turn out to be a two-timing, moist-eyed wuss. Since Eddie, who's "whoring his way through Manhattan," is seemingly so wrong for Jane, he will turn out to be Mr. Right. Jane will have to come to grips with all her emotional baggage (although you wish it had been in some other fashion than her sister's miscarriage, which seems a cheap ploy). The cast plays the material as if it matters. Ashley Judd is pretty and bright and has a mildly amusing and gratuitous underwear scene with hunky Hugh Jackman (also in his skivvies) in their loft kitchen. Everyone talks about sex but you never see

anything graphic (the PG-13 rating is primarily for language). Kinnear has patented the cad role and Tomei is a fine cynical, unlucky in love best friend. Barkin displays lots of energy and her great legs. New York looks picturesque. Sometimes predictable is just what you need.

—*Christine Tomassini*

## CREDITS

**Jane Goodale:** Ashley Judd
**Eddie Alden:** Hugh Jackman
**Ray Brown:** Greg Kinnear
**Liz:** Marisa Tomei
**Diane Roberts:** Ellen Barkin
**Stephen:** Peter Friedman
**Alice:** Catherine Dent
**Evelyn:** Laura Regan

**Origin:** USA
**Released:** 2001
**Production:** Lynda Obst; Fox 2000 Pictures; released by 20th Century-Fox
**Directed by:** Tony Goldwyn
**Written by:** Elizabeth Chandler
**Cinematography by:** Anthony B. Richmond
**Music by:** Rolfe Kent
**Sound:** James J. Sabat Sr.
**Music Supervisor:** Dana Millman-DuFine
**Editing:** Dana Congdon
**Art Direction:** Fredda Slavin
**Costumes:** Ann Roth, Michelle Maitlin
**Production Design:** Dan Leigh
**MPAA rating:** PG-13
**Running time:** 97 minutes

## REVIEWS

*Boxoffice.* June, 2001, p. 60.
*Chicago Sun-Times Online.* March 30, 2001.
*Entertainment Weekly.* April 6, 2001, p. 88.
*Los Angeles Times Online.* March 30, 2001.
*New York Times Online.* March 30, 2001.
*People.* April 9, 2001, p. 47.
*Rolling Stone.* April 12, 2001, p. 146.
*Sight and Sound.* September, 2001, p. 36.
*USA Today Online.* March 30, 2001.
*Variety.* March 26, 2001, p. 42.
*Washington Post Online.* March 30, 2001.

# The Son's Room (La Stanza del Figlio)

 **Box Office:** $.6 million

Within the arena of contemporary world cinema, the influence of foreign films on Hollywood, through their stars and filmic styles, becomes readily evident. Not so apparent is Hollywood's impact on the imaginations of filmmakers overseas. Nanni Moretti's *The Son's Room* not only sports a protagonist who looks like a dead ringer for a kinder, gentler Robert De Niro, but the very narrative contours of the film make it appear an attempt to transpose James L. Brooks' 1983 weepie, *Terms of Endearment* onto an Italian setting, right down to the recurrent, lyrical piano theme music. What redeems Moretti's effort at tackling the subgenre of family melodrama Hollywood-style is his own complex performance, which leaves the film looking ideologically constrained, in the light of politically committed Italian cinema, but yet not commercial.

As in more conventional film melodramas, *The Son's Room* is built around that one moment that changes everything for one family living in an unidentified Northern Italian city. Before that moment strikes at the core of their middle class existence, the film takes its time setting up their lives, making them appear typical as only film can, with its affinity for the untouched surfaces of urban existence.

Moretti himself plays Giovanni, a psychotherapist and a loving husband and father. The welding of his personal and professional life becomes evident in the fact that his office is just across the hall from the family apartment. His patients reveal their everyday problems and neuroses to him, and he in turn offers them simple solutions, or no solutions at all.

But the simplest thing in life, the film seems to say, is death. As such, it undermines all the other simplicity

Giovanni is trying to cultivate, from his daily jogging to his devotion to his family and patients. His beautiful wife, Paola (Laura Morante), works as an editor of art books. Irene (Jasmine Trinca), their teenage daughter, is a plain-looking dumpy basketball player in high school. Andrea (Giuseppe Sanfelice), the son a few years younger than her, is a keen part-time scuba diver.

The film begins with Giovanni being told by the school principal that Andrea has been accused of stealing a fossil of ammonite. Giovanni cannot imagine his son stealing anything, and neither can Paola. Eventually, Andrea does admit to the theft, but Giovanni merely shrugs it off. What does bother Giovanni though is Andrea giving up during a tennis match. The generation gap between them manifests itself in Giovanni unable to instill in his son any competitive values. "Don't you want to play to win?" Giovanni pleads. "No," Andrea simply answers. Even so, Giovanni does not give up on his son. We see them together in the city, in a bookshop, and on a football field. As Giovanni demonstrates a kick, the piano theme on the soundtrack alludes to the fleeting aspect of these all too precious moments in relation to the divergent lifestyles of father and son.

True enough, Giovanni has to excuse himself from a Sunday family outing, so he can visit a patient throwing a fit over the phone. That night, Giovanni learns that Andrea has had a fatal diving accident. He, Paola, and Irene clutch each other in paroxysmal sorrow. The film does not gloss over the gritty duties that follow such a tragic event. Giovanni has to recall facts for the coroner, and then choose a coffin. At the wake, we see the steel lid of the mahogany coffin welded shut in extreme close-ups, then the whirring of the screws as they are driven in with a mechanical persistence, a noise that resounds even after Giovanni returns to his apartment.

But it is on Paola that her son's violent death takes its most crippling toll. She screams in agony when she's by herself, and does not want to even stir out of bed. Giovanni, as we come to see, becomes racked by guilt. He imagines going on the five-mile run with Andrea that he had planned for that fateful Sunday. Unlike his wife, however, he doesn't feel a total helplessness. He decides to investigate the possibility that Andrea's diving gear may have been defective. When he tells Paola, over dinner at a restaurant, that Andrea's pressure guage could have failed, she reminds him that their son was trapped inside a cave when he died, and that they found torn hands and nails. She then breaks down weeping, and Giovanni joins her.

Even religion appears to offer no consolation to the couple. At a church service, as a pastor declaims that the answer to the "why" of death is that it is God who "makes the appointment" and that it is meant to "surpass our understanding," Giovanni gazes unmoved while Paola shows the first glimmering of being able to reflect upon what has befallen her. The spiritual dimension of their loss takes a violent turn that night as Giovanni trashes the prized objects that they have collected over the years. As Paola sits clutching her forehead at the dinner table, he breaks a teapot he had fixed, so as to demonstrate that it is really broken.

Increasingly, Giovanni finds himself in the same boat as his patients, unable to make sense of any of it. When Oscar (Silvio Orlando), who fears he may be dying of cancer, wants to know if Giovanni believes in the power of the mind to cure any illness, he retorts that often in the case of serious illnesses, the patient is cured even if he doesn't want to live. Clearly, Giovanni feels that no pat New Age thinking can offer him or Oscar any solace. Worse, he finds he has become alienated from his daughter as well. In a moment of frankness, she accuses him and Paola of "acting" for her benefit, by which she means, putting on a face of normalcy.

The catalyst that turns the tide for Giovanni and Paola comes from an unexpected direction. One morning in the mail, Paola finds a letter addressed to Andrea from a girl named Arianna, who claims to be secretly in love with him. For Paola, this has the effect of revivifying the memory of her son. She rushes into his room, which has been immaculately preserved, then into his closet, and breaks down as she clutches his red coat. She then tells Giovanni that she has to meet this Arianna.

When Giovanni starts to write a letter to the girl, in order to inform her of Andrea's death, he ends up doodling all over the page. This action is symptomatic of his inability to connect. He now begins to break down when he is with his patients, and confesses that he has lost his clinical objectivity. When he tells a patient that he intends to retire from his profession, the patient throws a fit and starts to trash his office. Giovanni has to physically overpower him to hold him in check. Closer to his heart, a rift now develops between him and Paola, stemming from his inability to write the letter.

When Paola takes matters into her own hands and rings the girl herself, she breaks down as she tells her the news. Then when she invites Arianna over, she finds the girl is not at all keen on seeing her. The generation gap proves stronger than any bond that could have been forged out of their common tragedy. Or so it seems. Days later, Arianna (Sofia Vigliar) does spring a surprise when she arrives at their doorstep.

What she brings with her are snapshots taken by Andrea of his room. Though these are nothing more than moments of horsing around, for Paola they become slices of a lost time. It is as if, in its own insignificant manner, life has offered her closure. She begins to smile again. Giovanni uses the occasion to take the family to Genoa, planning to drop Arianna and her hitchhiker friend off along the way. The new extended family sets off in their old car, almost recreating the domestic togetherness we saw Giovanni and Paola experience at the start of the film.

The film's final scene takes place at dawn on the beach of a seaside resort. To the simple guitar strains accompanying the English lyrics of Brian Eno's "By This River," Giovanni, Paola and Irene walk beside the water's edge, each alone with their thoughts. What has brought them together again, the film seems to be pointing out, has also made them come to terms with their loss in their own solitary manner. "He we are," the lyrics of the song point out, "underneath a sky that is ever falling down."

For all its generic aspects, the film does strike an universal note of poignancy. If this is what it has taken from Hollywood, then it has drawn upon the best that Hollywood has offered through the years, and even transmuted it. We take leave of Moretti's fictional family realizing that his camera has been turned upon us, our lives and our world, animated by a flow of undercurrents similar to the flow of life Moretti has portrayed in his "ordinary" unassuming manner.

With the Golden Palm from the Cannes Film Festival, art cinema's highest honor, under its belt, the film will probably be forgiven its minor lapses by American critics. In fact, Stephen Holden argues, in a *New York Times* review published at the time of the film's showcasing at the 2001 New York Film Festival, that the film possesses "a special integrity," the result of its "rejection of even a tinge of melodrama." Holden even goes on to note its timeliness in relation to the monumental World Trade Center tragedy suffered by New York City a month before the film's Festival screening. "As most of us know too well," Holden writes, "tragedy has a way of striking out of nowhere, leaving the survivors stunned, grief-stricken, angry and desperately groping for answers and some stability."

*—Vivek Adarkar*

## CREDITS

**Giovanni:** Nanni Moretti
**Paola:** Laura Morante
**Andrea:** Giuseppe Sanfelice
**Irene:** Jasmine Trinca
**Tommaso:** Stefano Accorsi
**Arianna:** Sofia Vigliar
**Oscar:** Silvio Orlanda
**Raffaella:** Claudia Della Seta

**Origin:** Italy, France
**Language:** Italian
**Released:** 2000
**Production:** Nanni Moretti, Angelo Barbagallo; BAC Films Ltd., Studio Canal Plus, Sacher Film; released by Miramax Films
**Directed by:** Nanni Moretti
**Written by:** Nanni Moretti, Linda Ferri, Heidrun Schleef

**Cinematography by:** Giuseppe Lanci
**Music by:** Nicola Piovani
**Sound:** Alessandro Zanon
**Editing:** Esmeralda Calabria
**Art Direction:** Giancarlo Basili
**Costumes:** Maria Rita Barbera
**MPAA rating:** Unrated
**Running time:** 99 minutes

## REVIEWS

*Boxoffice.* August, 2001, p. 55.
*Film Comment Online.* May/June, 2001.
*New York Times Online.* October 12, 2001.
*Sight and Sound.* January, 2002, p. 28.
*Variety.* March 19, 2001, p. 30.

## QUOTES

Shrink Giovanni (Nanni Moretti) to his patients: "We can't control our lives completely. We do what we can. Just take a more relaxed approach to life and the world."

## TRIVIA

The film was awarded Best Picture, Best Actress (Laura Morante), and Best Composer (Nicola Piovani) at Italy's Donatello Awards.

## AWARDS AND NOMINATIONS

**Cannes 2001:** Film.

# Soul Survivors

*The world of the dead and the world of the living . . . are about to collide.*
—Movie tagline

**Box Office:** $3.1 million

*S*oul Survivors was one of those films that was supposed to come out, then was pulled for reworking. It took some time before it was eventually readied for the screen and, during its time off, had two post-production makeovers. Writer and director Steve Carpenter would probably argue that the powers that be that took over the film ruined it (he wasn't a part of some of the reworking), but after seeing the final product, it's difficult to believe that there was ever anything worthy in there in the first place. Obviously, the studio, Artisan Entertainment, wasn't feeling too confident about the film's quality because they pulled the film from pre-screenings for critics. Although the film has a "trick" ending, it wasn't pulled because of that. More likely, it was just because the film is embarrassing.

Soul Survivors is what happens when a bad script idea is made, then tinkered with, then subjected to test audiences and cut and re-grafted together. The result is like a Frankenstein's monster—all disjointed, cobbled together, and spewing an incoherent message. It moves forward, but with a lurching gracelessness. If it were at its very best, the film would have been a teen rip-off of the film *Jacob's Ladder.* It takes so much of the earlier film's plot that at least one critic thought Carpenter could be considered a plagiarist.

In *Soul Survivors,* Cassie (Melissa Sagemiller) leaves her loving family and heads off to college. She goes to a fraternity party with her boyfriend Sean (Casey Affleck, Ben's brother), wild child friend Annabel (Eliza Dushku) and ex-boyfriend Matt (Wes Bentley). She and Sean are not going to the same school so they mutually mope about this and awkwardly try to declare their feelings for each other. The party happy Annabel decides that they should go to a party off-campus. The fact that the party is in a creepy abandoned church and has a lot of weirdos lurking about signals to us that something scary should be happening soon. And it's certainly about time for it. The movie drags on for about 30 minutes without anything scary (or even anything of interest) happening.

While Sean is in the church fetching Annabel, Matt confesses to Cassie that he has never gotten over her. She rebuffs him, but he says that they should end their relationship with a final kiss. She demurs, but he finally convinces her that, over the years, one kiss isn't going to make that much difference in her life. Overwhelmed by this masterful argument, she starts smooching with him, at which time Sean walks up and spots them. Cassie drives the gang home while she and Sean argue in the front seat. She turns her head away from the road, as actors in films are wont to do in driving scenes, and ends up driving off a cliff in order to miss a car in the road. Sean dies and Cassie gets a head injury.

Cassie goes back to college with her friend Annabel and eventually Matt joins them, giving up his spot at Harvard. But the help of her friends isn't doing much for Cassie. She's failing tests and having all sorts of weird hallucinations. Blood spews from a shower drain, she's chased by various scary types and she has a brain hemorrhage in class. She keeps having visions of her beloved Sean and, at one point, even goes on a woodland stroll with him. A creepy friend of Annabel tells Cassie that some bad people are going to kill her. Is all this stuff real or is it just her imagination?

Additionally, Matt and Annabel are acting really creepy. Are they somehow in on a plot to kill her? She meets a kindly priest, Father Jude (Luke Wilson), who listens to her woes and assures her that everything is going to be all right. But even he has something creepy going on. When she goes to the church to try to find him later, the priest there explains that Father Jude died in 1981. Oh no!

The scary quotient could have been several times higher than it is. Carpenter (or whoever) fills the screen with all kinds of fake-out false jolts, like a shot of some scary people in the mirror that turn out to be nothing. That sudden gun shot? Oh, it's just the gun that fires at the beginning of a swimming race. There are so many things that turn out to be fake-outs or just something that Cassie imagined that it's difficult to work up a good scare about any of the stuff that happens. The film is also interspersed with chase scenes that are equally hard to care about. Cassie sees someone scary, she runs, and they almost get her. In the meantime, she fumbles with locks that don't work—until just the last second!—and the like.

To make up for the lack of real thrills, Carpenter tries to lay on the atmosphere. The whole movie seems to lack daylight. Every setting is dark, murky and dreamlike. Even the college campus seems to be filled with narrow dark alleys, small dank dorm rooms, and empty cavernous libraries. It's difficult to imagine the photos the college must put in recruitment brochures. Even hospitals, which tend to be among the most well-lit places around, are dim and foreboding in this film. (Carpenter could probably even make a fluorescent-lit Blockbuster video outlet look somehow dark and scary.) But instead of adding artistic atmosphere, all the darkness is just claustrophobic. Someone needs to crack a window or something. Even when Matt tries to cheer Cassie up by helping her paint her dorm room, he picks a dark orange color. It's surprising he didn't also suggest that she add on a narrow alleyway to her room.

The final indignity in the film is that there's a sudden turn of events and then a strangely happy ending. The ending is so abrupt and different from the rest of the film that it seems like it's not actually true. But the credits do indeed roll and audience slinks away, feeling gypped.

The performances of the leads don't do anything to make the film more palatable. Particularly bad is Affleck who reads his lines like . . . he's reading lines. It's hard to picture him as the perfect boyfriend who got away. Sagemiller is like a low-rent version of Gwyneth Paltrow, with an extra dose of perkiness. She looks like she might break into a cheer at any given time and appears too vapid to be experiencing any sort of deep emotions. Even though Bentley did

this film before he played the kid with the video camera in *American Beauty*, it's disappointing to see him in such a movie. He brings an off-kilter quality to his role, but it's pretty much for naught.

*Soul Survivors* was meant to be a teen horror exploitation film but it's strangely void of horror (or even anything racy, for that matter). For a few minutes, it seems like the film might go somewhere, but as time and the film wear on, it becomes apparent that nothing much of interest or consequence is going to happen. Teens hoping for a bit of that horror movie thrill will be sorely disappointed.

It was difficult, if not impossible to find a positive review of *Soul Survivors*. "The film is a dog. It's tepid and clumsy, and entirely derivative," wrote Norman Wilner of the *Toronto Star*. "In *Soul Survivors* a relatively inventive horror movie concept is used as a launching pad for a pathetic parade of standard-issue jumps and frights that can't raise a single goosebump," wrote Rob Blackwelder of *Spliced Wire*. "*Soul Survivors*, a completely mudded and moronic teen horror film, has been languishing on the shelf for the past couple of years. I'll give you a hint: It's not because it was ripening like a fine wine," wrote the *Globe and Mail*'s Kevin Courrier. And Kevin Thomas of the *Los Angeles Times* wrote that the film is "a glum would-be thriller of the supernatural that loses interest early on, never to regain it."

—*Jill Hamilton*

---

## CREDITS

**Cassie:** Melissa Sagemiller
**Matt:** Wes Bentley
**Sean:** Casey Affleck
**Annabel:** Eliza Dushku
**Father Jude:** Luke Wilson

**Origin:** USA
**Released:** 2001
**Production:** Neal H. Moritz, Stokely Chaffin; released by Artisan Entertainment
**Directed by:** Steve Carpenter
**Written by:** Steve Carpenter
**Cinematography by:** Fred Murphy
**Music by:** Daniel Licht
**Sound:** Ray Cymoszinski
**Music Supervisor:** Jennifer Pyken, Madonna Wade-Reed
**Editing:** Janice Hampton, Todd C. Ramsay
**Art Direction:** Keith Cunningham
**Costumes:** Denise Wingate
**Production Design:** Larry Fulton
**MPAA rating:** R
**Running time:** 85 minutes

## REVIEWS

*Boxoffice.* August, 2001, p. 20.
*Entertainment Weekly.* September 21, 2001, p. 60.
*Los Angeles Times Online.* September 10, 2001.
*New York Times Online.* September 8, 2001.
*San Francisco Chronicle.* September 8, 2001, p. D2.
*Variety.* September 17, 2001, p. 20.

# Spy Game

*It's not how you play the game . . . it's how the game plays you.*
—Movie tagline

 **Box Office:** $61 million

"Tony Scott has never made a smarter movie," in the opinion of Terry Lawson of the *Detroit Free Press,* but that would seem to be a left-handed compliment. Rita Kempley of the *Washington Post,* agreed, however, that *Spy Game* was "uncommonly smart," a "taut, timely and intelligent thriller." Joel Siegel of ABC television's *Good Morning America* was impressed by the film's "heart-pounding suspense." Thus the movie floated on air-bubbles of hyperbole, but one might wonder whether this "terrific, superbly produced CIA tale" was really the most cerebral film of the year, or merely one that made greater demands for an attention-deficit disorder audience than most of the films produced in what was a dismal swamp of a movie season. On the other hand, the film does comment intelligently on the role of the Central Intelligence Agency in a changing world, during and after the Cold War.

Certainly, *Spy Game* was far more complicated and challenging than the weekly plots of the CBS television series *The Agency,* produced with the cooperation of the Central Intelligence Agency and no doubt intended to make the "Agency" look invincible, wise, maybe even compassionate and humane. If *Spy Game* resembles the CBS television series, the reason is that Tony Scott's screenwriter Michael Frost Beckner is the creator of *The Agency,* in association with Wolfgang Petersen's Radiant Television. As Owen Gleiberman wrote in *Entertainment Weekly,* "the film's version of the CIA—what's right with it, and what's wrong with if—has a spark of genuine dramatic interest that overlaps, however unintentionally, with the urgency of our own current global concerns." The film appears to have a more authentic edge than the television series, though in the opinion of *Variety* it is "not fundamentally anti-CIA per se."

On the other hand, Bard Pitt was quoted by *Entertainment Weekly,* as saying "There's a term in the CIA called 'blowback,' the unintentional repercussions of our actions." According to Pitt the "movie is about how we may have been causing more damage than good—all in the name of democracy."

The CIA's operation in the film is nastier than what *The Agency* television series suggests, however, as the Agency intends to hang a rogue agent named Tom Bishop (Brad Pitt) out to dry. When the film begins in 1991 Bishop has been imprisoned on an espionage charge in a Chinese prison, and has been sentenced to be executed in 24 hours. Afraid of causing an international incident because of sensitive trade negotiations in progress with China, the CIA has decided against a rescue mission. The only person interested in saving Bishop's life is Nathan Muir (Robert Redford), the agent who originally recruited him out of Vietnam. But Muir, who is about to retire, is no longer an insider at the CIA and is out of touch with those who are making the decision. It's Muir's last day at work in Washington before he retires, and the clock it ticking. Tony Scott certainly knows how to make the clock tick.

British director Tony Scott is known primarily for his flashy and flamboyant filmmaking. His debut film, *The Hunger* (1983), was a vampire picture starring Catherine Deneuve, Susan Sarandon, and David Bowie, but the younger Scott really hit his stride in Hollywood with action-adventure pictures, notably two Tom Cruise movies, *Top Gun* (1986) and *Days of Thunder* (1990), which were popular but not very thoughtful, followed by more sophisticated thrillers such as *Crimson Tide* (1995) and *Enemy of the State* (1998), both starring Gene Hackman, the latter espionage thriller produced by Jerry Bruckheimer. Though always wedded to action-adventure as his specialty, Scott's pictures have matured over the past decade. Scott was certainly inventive in manipulating his locations for the film. The prison sequences were filmed in a 16th-century prison in Oxford, for example, not in China; the Berlin sequences were filmed in Budapest, Hungary, since the Hungarian capital still had the gritty, threadbare appearance that Berlin might have had in 1975. The Beirut and Vietnam sequences were shot in Morocco, with Casablanca standing in for Beirut. The CIA set was filmed at Shepperton Studios in England. In fact, *Spy Game* could well be the smartest movie Tony Scott has made. At least it is in the running.

Having set up the central dilemma, the film then has to rewind to explain how Bishop ended up in such a fix. Scott tells Bishop's backstory in flashback about how Muir recruited Bishop as a sharp-shooter to assassinate a Viet Cong officer and then later became his Agency mentor. A series of flashbacks shows Muir working with Bishop, training him to be an assassin in Berlin in 1976, then later working with him in Beirut in 1985 in a plot to assassinate a sheik. On this mission Bishop becomes romantically involved with one of his "assets," a foreign-aid worker who is also apparently a double agent named Elizabeth Hadley (Catherine McCormack). After she is later incarcerated in China, Bishop's personal mission is to rescue her because of an emotional attachment. The only reason Muir is made aware of Bishop's current fate was his earlier history of working with Bishop. Top-level CIA officers want more information about Bishop and his attachment to Hadley, but Muir knows he has been given an incomplete briefing.

And so, in Langley, Virginia, Muir, a relic of Cold War operations and now an outsider in what Gleiberman described as a "paranoid bureaucracy" that has become "a glorified tool of capitalism," launches his own special operation in a nail-biting attempt to save Bishop. Muir understands Agency procedure and calls in favors to set up the rescue mission, using his retirement account to finance the operation. The problem is that he is no longer trusted and he has to use his wits to maneuver his way around security checkpoints and safeguards that would impede his progress.

*Variety* reviewer Todd McCarthy considered *Spy Game* Robert Redford's "most engaging performance in years" and predicted boxoffice success because of the picture's "snazzy filmmaking, topical relevance of CIA and Middle Eastern issues, and star pairing." Pitt's Bishop appears to be a younger incarnation of Redford's Muir, but, even though he is a trained assassin, he never "loses touch with his inner Boy Scout," in the words of *Washington Post* reviewer Rita Kempley, who believed Redford gave his "best performance" in recent memory for this picture. Certainly there is considerable satisfaction in watching Redford's Muir outsmart the Agency's heartless bureaucratic careerists. His main adversary is Charles Harker, played by the award-winning British actor Stephen Dillane, who is gifted enough to pass for an American, though he has also played a defining Hamlet for the Royal National Theatre in London.

The plot effectively plays Bishop's idealism against Muir's realism, and, as one reviewer noted, Pitt is somehow able to suggest that his character, a trained killer, after all, "is innocent but not innocent, managing to keep the boy alive within the man." Sean Macaulay of the *London Times* applauded the film's "shrewd casting." Redford had himself directed Brad Pitt in *A River Runs Through It* (1992). In his role as Redford's CIA protégé, Pitt now seems to have become Redford's "natural successor," Macaulay wrote. *Spy Game* allows Redford at the age of 64 "to segue into the mentor roles which most suit the one thing he has to be in his later roles. Namely, the smartest guy in the room." Since the Redford character in the film is tied to his desk in Langley, the challenge for Tony Scott is to build dramatic suspense in that bureaucratic setting. This was not Redford's first role involving the CIA, however. At least two of the film's reviewers were reminded of Redford's CIA analyst in *Three Days of the Condor* (1975), though, as Todd McCarthy

noted, *Spy Game* does not evoke the earlier film's "fashionable anti-establishment paranoia."

Not all of the reviews were so positive, however. *New York Times* reviewer A.O. Scott has reservations about the film's "calculating pretentiousness of using human misery to make shallow entertainment seem serious," and believed that director John Boorman did a much better job with *The Tailor of Panama* earlier in the year, a film that had the advantage of being adapted from a novel by espionage master John le Carré. Scott described the film as having "the pointless, thrilling kineticism of a sports car commercial," though he conceded that it was "seamlessly and crisply edited." Stanley Kauffmann of *The New Republic* also praised Christian Wagner's editing that "Makes us feel that the film itself is responding to the time pressures of its story." Kauffmann added that Dan Mindel's camera work seemed to suggest "OK, we can now show you mankind's messes in Panavision and gorgeous color," but, he added, wryly, "how does that help human blunders?"

In London, Barbara Ellen wrote for *The Times* that *Spy Game* "makes the old-fashioned espionage thriller look better, leaner, wittier, [and] more relevant than it has done for many years." She wondered why "neither lead seems to age much (in either direction) during their odyssey" and grumbled about Tony Scott's "gratuitously tiring visuals," concluding that "stylistically" the film "is as ripe as a month-old fruit bowl." Overall, however, *Spy Game* was essentially a well-made popcorn movie about loyalty, friendship, and betrayal, but it tells a well-plotted story involving complicated characters, one that seems to be timely and one that was graced with appealing star power. And that's more than one usually gets these days.

*—James M. Welsh*

## CREDITS

**Nathan Muir:** Robert Redford
**Tom Bishop:** Brad Pitt
**Elizabeth Hadley:** Catherine McCormack
**Charles Harker:** Stephen (Dillon) Dillane
**Troy Folger:** Larry Bryggman
**Vincent Vy Ngo:** Michael Paul Chan
**Gladys Jennip:** Marianne Jean-Baptiste
**Harry Duncan:** David Hemmings
**Dr. Byars:** Matthew Marsh
**Robert Aiken:** Todd Boyce
**Anne Cathcart:** Charlotte Rampling

**Origin:** USA
**Released:** 2001
**Production:** Douglas Wick, Marc Abraham; Beacon Pictures; released by Universal Pictures

**Directed by:** Tony Scott
**Written by:** Michael Frost Beckner, David Arata
**Cinematography by:** Dan Mindel
**Music by:** Harry Gregson-Williams
**Sound:** Simon Kaye
**Editing:** Christian Wagner
**Art Direction:** Kevin Phipps
**Costumes:** Louise Frogley
**Production Design:** Chris Seagers, Norris Spencer
**MPAA rating:** R
**Running time:** 127 minutes

## REVIEWS

*Chicago Sun-Times Online.* November 27, 2001.
*Entertainment Weekly.* November 30, 2001, p. 55.
*London Times.* November 22, 2001, p. 10.
*Los Angeles Times Online.* November 21, 2001.
*New Republic.* December 24, 2001, p. 24.
*New York Times.* November 21, 2001, p. E1.
*USA Today Online.* November 21, 2001.
*Variety.* November 19, 2001, p. 39.
*Washington Post.* November 21, 2001, p. C1.

# Spy Kids

*Real spies . . . only smaller.*
—Movie tagline

**Box Office:** $112.7 million

Like all good children's story, *Spy Kids* also begins with a "Once upon a time . . ." In this case it's a bedtime story told by Ingrid Cortez (Carla Gugino) to her two children, Carmen (Alexa Vega) and Juni (Daryl Sabara). In this case, the fairy tale begins with two spies working on opposite sides. Each has as their mission to terminate the other. But the beautiful lady spy on one side and the handsome gentleman spy on the other end up subverting their original mission and creating one of their own. They have fallen in love. After a few clandestine lunch dates and a romantic, but distant, dinner date in Paris, the two become engaged and get married. But as Ingrid points out to her children, "together they made a tempting target." So even on their wedding day, they have to make an emergency getaway using heart-shaped parachutes and an escape boat proclaiming "just married." As a result, the two spies from opposite sides exchanged missions again, retired, settled down, had a few kids, and lived happily ever after.

Well, that's a nice fantasy, but Ingrid and Gregorio's kids have their own problems. Juni is plagued by warts on his hands, has no friends and is picked on by bullies, so, like most kids, he lives life vicariously through the characters on his favorite television show hosted by Fegan Floop (Alan Cumming). The older Carmen, on the other hand, seems more mature, but she has been regularly skipping classes and like most older siblings, hates being around her pesky brother. Carmen and Juni's lives are hardly as romantic as made-up spy stories. Or are those stories made up?

After Juni and Carmen are tucked into bed, we discover that Ingrid and Gregorio really are the spies in the fairy tale as make-up jars become secret buttons and mirrors reveal spy information. It seems that Ingrid and Gregorio are now consultant spies and are facing an important assignment, a fellow spy, Donnagon (Mike Judge), is the latest of several spies who have gone missing. So while the children sleep and Uncle Felix (Cheech Marin) babysits, Ingrid and Gregorio set out to find Donnagon. Unfortunately, they too disappear. Now who will save them?

That job falls to Juni and Carmen who are absolutely incredulous to discover their parents' other lives. "My parents can't be spies, they're not cool enough," Carmen blurts out in a typical kid's analysis of their parents. But before this information can sink in, their house is attacked by Thumb Thumbs, soldiers that literally are all thumbs. Luckily, Uncle Felix is there to help and the kids quickly escape via a submarine that takes them on a long journey to a secret spy hideaway where the children can begin to come up with a plan to save their parents.

Then, into their secret location, comes Ms. Gradenko (Teri Hatcher), a fellow spy from Ingrid and Gregorio's past. The kids initially trust her, but in reality she is working for the other side. The other side, it turns out, is Fegan Floop who has been trying to put together a world-conquering army for Mr. Lisp (Robert Patrick). Fegan, along with his sidekick, appropriately called Minion (Tony Shalhoub), has tried inventing several types of soldiers. The clumsy Thumb Thumbs failed for obvious reasons, and the seven abducted spies he has mutated into cartoon characters for his television show ended up with mush for brains and speaking backwards. His latest invention is also imperfect. He has created robot children who look exactly like the children of important world leaders. The can go where no other spy can go, but Fegan's creations have a problem. They have no brains and therefore no language ability. This is a problem that can be solved, however, by an invention created by Gregorio's team back in his spy days, an artificial intelligence called "the third brain," and Ms. Gradenko has just taken it from Juni and Carmen.

So now Juni and Carmen must not only save their parents but also save the world. The first thing they do is head to Machete's Spy Shop where all the great spy gadgets are made. Machete (Danny Trejo), a kind of Acme version of James Bond's Q, begrudgingly helps the kids get to Floop's by supplying them with jet-propelled backpacks, crayons that eat through steel, electro-shock gumballs and a tiny high-speed plane. But the real question may not be will Carmen and Juni be able to save the world and their parents, but will their typical sibling rivalry sabotage their mission.

Writer/director/producer Roberto Rodriguez is usually known for more adult fare like *El Mariachi, Desperado,* and *From Dusk Till Dawn* but he "stooped" to teen fare with *The Faculty* and now has gone the kiddie route with *Spy Kids,* the second of five films in Rodriguez's deal with Miramax. And although violence may be the better known of the Rodriguez film styles, he claims he has always wanted to make family films. One of his earliest and shortest works was a little comedy called *Bedhead,* the story of a psychic little girl which starred his four younger siblings.

The idea for *Spy Kids,* however, came to him while working on another film. In *Four Rooms,* a compilation film in which Rodriguez directed a segment with Antonio Banderas, there is a scene in which Banderas' character's children appear in tuxedos. Rodriguez is supposed to have taken one look at those kids and thought how much they looked like mini-James Bondses. What a great angle for a movie! The result: *Spy Kids.*

While dropping the ferocity of his previous films, *Spy Kids* does retain Rodriguez's trademark high spirits and frenetic pacing. This film has action aplenty, but no gore. Juni and Carmen must perform their mission using ingenuity, bravery and brains, not violence. Which means Rodriguez has worked hard to provide a film in which dialogue, characters, action, and sets all carry weight in the film instead of being nothing more than backdrops to fist fights and explosions.

Thankfully his efforts have paid off. His characters come to life in the hands of the expert cast. Antonio Banderas and Carla Gugino easily slip from normal Mom and Dad to sophisticated and sexy spies with their tongues firmly planted in their cheeks. Alexa Vega and Daryl Sabara are convincingly normal as 8 and 11 year olds, quibbling and fighting, but also coming together when needed. Danny Trejo does a wonderful about-face playing an inventor instead of his usual menacing character and Alan Cumming keeps us guessing as to whether he is evil or not. Many of these actors have worked with Rodriguez before, but watch for a special repeat-performance cameo at the end that is far too much fun to give away.

Complementing the superb job done by the actors is that done by the set designers and decorators. The colors run the gamut from the cartoonish to the vivid reds, yellows and oranges of Latin decor. The later of which is just one of the many bows Rodriguez makes to his Latino roots, incorporating them seamlessly into this "All American" film. *Spy Kids'* sets and gadgets wonderfully remain within the realm of the childish without ever making us doubt that they'd

work. They perform their job, but never feel threatening. From the Super Guppy underwater escape vehicle that looks like a huge goldfish to a smashingly funny jigsaw puzzle floor in Floop's Castle, everything is deliberately cartoonish but believable. This, of course makes several aspects of the movie perfect for commercialization, and indeed this is Miramax/Dimension's first try at marketing promotion with McDonald's.

The end product provided by Rodriguez is imaginative and exuberant. It is surreally quirky, colorful and downright enjoyable. It is *Home Alone* meets *Willy Wonka.* It is a perfect family film stressing values like belief in one's self, facing one's fears, and sticking together as a family. And it does all this without being saccharine, and with no curse words, double entendres, sexual innuendo, or fart jokes anywhere to be found. Less than a week after the film's highly successful theatrical release, news stories began touting the sequel. And that may not be a bad thing. If it's anything like its big brother, families will win big.

—*Beverley Bare Buehrer*

## CREDITS

**Carmen Cortez:** Alexa Vega
**Juni Cortez:** Daryl Sabara
**Gregorio Cortez:** Antonio Banderas
**Ingrid Cortez:** Carla Gugino
**Fegan Floop:** Alan Cumming
**Alexander Minion:** Tony Shalhoub
**Ms. Gradenko:** Teri Hatcher
**Felix Gumm:** Richard "Cheech" Marin
**Mr. Lisp:** Robert Patrick
**Machete:** Danny Trejo
**Devlin:** George Clooney

**Origin:** USA
**Released:** 2001
**Production:** Robert Rodriguez, Elizabeth Avellan; released by Dimension Films
**Directed by:** Robert Rodriguez
**Written by:** Robert Rodriguez
**Cinematography by:** Guillermo Navarro
**Music by:** Robert Rodriguez, Danny Elfman, John Debney
**Sound:** Mark Ulano
**Editing:** Robert Rodriguez
**Art Direction:** Ed Vega
**Costumes:** Deborah Everton
**Production Design:** Cary White
**MPAA rating:** PG
**Running time:** 88 minutes

## REVIEWS

*Boxoffice.* May, 2001, p. 58.
*Chicago Sun-Times Online.* March 30, 2001.
*Chicago Tribune Online.* March 31, 2000.
*Entertainment Weekly.* April 6, 2001, p. 90.
*Los Angeles Times Online.* March 30, 2001.
*New York Post Online.* March 30, 2001.
*New York Times Online.* March 30, 2001.
*People.* April 9, 2001, p. 49.
*Sight and Sound.* June, 2001, p. 54.
*USA Today Online.* March 29, 2001.
*Variety.* March 26, 2001, p. 41.
*Washington Post Online.* March 30, 2001.

## QUOTES

Carmen (Alexa Vega): "My parents can't be spies, they're not cool enough."

## TRIVIA

Antonio Banderas' character was named for Robert Rodriguez's uncle who was an FBI agent.

# Stanley Kubrick: A Life in Pictures

Jan Harlan's documentary *Stanley Kubrick: A Life in Pictures* chronicles the life of the American director, beginning with his childhood and ending with clips and anecdotes from his final release, *Eyes Wide Shut*. However, unlike Kubrick's much-touted films, Harlan merely combines interviews with other filmmakers who had worked with Kubrick along with footage from all of the director's films. The only viewers that would benefit from Harlan's documentary would be students of cinema or hard-core Kubrick fans. However, the aficionados would have already seen Kubrick's oeuvre and they would be knowledgeable about the facts presented in this film. In other words, Harlan's tribute to his brother-in-law comments mainly on Kubrick's professional life within a documentary of mostly talking heads espousing the director's virtues. While the documentary proves to be educational, it's hardly enthralling. Most viewers will walk away knowing little about the director with a few exceptions, such as Kubrick was a perfectionist, he suffered many setbacks, but was

allowed to make art films through the Hollywood studio system. Viewers of the film should go out and become reacquainted with Kubrick's films instead.

Narrated by Tom Cruise (who starred in *Eyes Wide Shut*) and running at 142 minutes, *A Life in Pictures* played to packed houses and appreciative audiences at its Seattle International Film Festival. But of course, it was the subject matter that drew audiences to the documentary and not the documentary itself. This old-fashioned style documentary wears thin because of its predictability. One expects a host of celebrities and family members to chat on camera about the subject of the film and, because the film is a bio-pic, one expects to see a series of film clips of the subject's work. However, why not create a more engaging documentary structure? Filmmakers Chris Hegedus and Jehane Noujaim created a compelling documentary about the rise and fall of a startup company with *Startup.com* by presenting the subjects as characters and their lives as a drama. What if Harlan had created a dramatic arc for the subject of his documentary?

According to the Seattle International Film Festival program: "Harlan paints a vivid portrait of the screen's ultimate iconoclast." But if viewers of Kubrick's films need anecdotes and fascinating facts about the director's professional life, why not watch Kubrick's films and read cinematic essays of the director's oeuvre? That's not to say that a master of cinema doesn't deserve a cinematic tribute, but that Kubrick deserves to be the subject of a more inspired documentary. After all, Kubrick himself was the iconoclastic master who directed such controversial films as *A Clockwork Orange*, *Dr. Strangelove*, and *Lolita*.

Format aside, Harlan's well-researched documentary does provide viewers with an inside look to Kubrick's childhood, his early career as a photojournalist, and his relationship with his wife and children. As it turns out, Kubrick worked close to home but this also caused him to treat his family in the same manner that a director treats his crew and performers. At times Kubrick's professional life threatened his personal life. Such was the case with the release of the ultra-violent film *A Clockwork Orange*, which provoked death threats for Kubrick. The director was forced to remove the film from British cinemas despite its popularity.

Kubrick was known for pushing the envelope artistically and otherwise. In the cult classic *Dr. Strangelove*, Kubrick's biting humor about a psychotic American commander who snaps and orders his pilots to bomb Russian missile sites is set amidst a backdrop of the idiocy of the U.S. military and nuclear holocaust paranoia. *Lolita* focused on a sexual relationship between an adult male and a precocious sexy teen who, it turns out, has been having an affair with another adult. Harlan suggests that cinema's wonder boy was an astonishing filmmaker surely missed by critics and fans. According to Jack Nicholson, "everyone says he's the man, but to this day I find this underrates him." After Shelley Duvall underwent a harrowing experience with Kubrick for

*The Shining,* she commented, "I wouldn't change the experience for anything." Neither would Harlan.

—*Patty-Lynne Herlevi*

## CREDITS

**Narrator:** Tom Cruise

**Origin:** Great Britain, USA
**Released:** 2001
**Production:** Jan Harlan; released by Warner Bros.
**Directed by:** Jan Harlan
**Cinematography by:** Manuel Harlan
**Sound:** Manuel Harlan
**Editing:** Melanie Viner-Cuneo
**MPAA rating:** Unrated
**Running time:** 142 minutes

## REVIEWS

*New York Times Online.* June 12, 2001.
*USA Today Online.* June 12, 2001.

## QUOTES

Shelley Duvall on her role in Kubrick's *The Shining:* "He could do cruel things because the end justifies the means."

## TRIVIA

Stanley Kubrick directed 13 feature films over a 44-year period.

# Startup.com

*The rise and fall of the American dream.*
—Movie tagline

 **Box Office:** $1.2 million

When filmmakers Chris Hegedus and Jehane Noujaim began making *Startup.com,* a documentary chronicling the life of a Web business called govWorks.com, they could not have imagined where their journey would take them. Nor could they have foreseen the odd, often poignant turns the story would take or the way the site's fate would become a kind of microcosm for the promise and failure of so many dot-coms that, just a few years ago, seemed to herald a new and exciting economic order. And yet *Startup.com,* while tracing the heady days of the Internet boom and the subsequent bust, is just as effective as a personal story delving into the contentious relationship of two friends at the center of a new business. Surprisingly enough, in the candid, sometimes painful moments of young hotshots on the rise, the film finds its richest moments.

The film introduces Kaleil Isaza Tuzman and Tom Herman, friends from childhood who are starting an Internet venture together. As the story begins in 1999, Kaleil is leaving his job at Goldman Sachs to dedicate himself full-time to his new company. He is the stereotype of the brash and workaholic dot-com entrepreneur as well as a gifted leader and the driving force behind his company. When we meet Tom, he is braiding his little girl's hair, as if such commonplace domestic duties were closer to his heart than running a business. From the very beginning, then, in the way each man is introduced, the filmmakers set up a contrast that will reverberate throughout the film. Kaleil is the quintessential go-getter, the charismatic, young upstart determined to make a name for himself in the new economy. Tom is more laid-back, the slightly nerdy techie who may be smart and dedicated to the company but does not let it rule his life and who does not have the competitive brio and cocky swagger of his friend.

Their idea for a Web business is one that can better facilitate the average citizen's interaction with local government by cutting through bureaucratic red tape—enabling people to pay their parking tickets or renew their driver's licenses online are prime examples of how the site would help people. From the outset, the company is marked by internal squabbling. For example, Kaleil cannot abide the times when Tom makes them look unprofessional in front of potential investors by deviating from the plan and sending an unfocused message.

Some of the most compelling scenes are those depicting the formation of the company. Watching two twenty-something pals pitching their idea to venture capitalists to raise funding and then securing millions of dollars is unbelievable. They seem to have little more than a simple, somewhat sketchy idea and yet end up raising 60 million dollars. One tense but entertaining scene shows them on the verge of obtaining 17 million dollars but having difficulty contacting their lawyer by phone to get advice before signing the papers.

Noujaim was Kaleil's roommate and a fellow Harvard alum, and their friendship clearly guaranteed her nearly unlimited access to her subjects. She and Hegedus film these entrepreneurs everywhere that business is conducted—in cars, in meetings with investors, in the gym. At times, however, we may feel a bit lost, as if we have not been given all of the pertinent details. At one point, for example, there is a mini-drama over buying out a man named Chieh, referred to as the third founder of the company. He and Kaleil haggle over a price until Chieh walks away with $700,000 and the usually shrewd and hard-nosed Kaleil, in an emotional climax to the ordeal, needs a hug from Tom because he feels bad that a personal relationship has been reduced to money. The problem with this segment is that the film suddenly introduces Chieh only to dismiss him from the story. Since we have barely met him, the drama means far less to us than it does to the principals.

Other details are skimmed over as well. When Kaleil appears on a TV news program and says that the company is presently worth approximately 50 million dollars, it is a surprising revelation. After all, we have only the most rudimentary understanding of what govWorks.com plans to do, and the goal itself seems rather limited. How did it acquire so much capital in a matter of mere months, and where is the money going? Perhaps, however, this slipperiness is a key lesson of the Internet frenzy—fortunes were made quickly on paper and ultimately lost just as fast.

Interspersed with the scenes of wheeling and dealing are the more personal moments, which are often the funniest and most human. During a company retreat, Tom takes the employees out to commune with nature, something that obviously means a lot to him but which comes across as awkward, possibly even New Age or cultish when done in a company setting. We also meet his parents, who have obviously given him a strong moral foundation that stresses people over material things. It is too bad we could not have met the mother of his daughter—a gap that leaves us wanting to know more about Tom's personal life.

Then there is Dora, Kaleil's girlfriend at the start of the film, perhaps the most honest and amusing person we meet. Obviously proud of her boyfriend, she is also frustrated that his Internet enterprise leaves little time for her. In one of her humorous speeches to the camera, she confides that she told Kaleil she wants a dog if she moves in with him. The quintessential supportive woman yearning in vain for time with a boyfriend who is always on the go, Dora is also very perceptive. Referring to Kaleil and Tom and their fancy businessman's attire, she observes, "They're such grownup gentlemen. But you know what? They're not," which beautifully and poignantly captures some weird truth about the dot-com world. These are boys trying to play a man's game and not really knowing all the rules or how the stress of a new business can test a friendship. Sure enough, in the next scene, Kaleil, in the role of a little boy, is talking to his mother on the phone and expressing his ambivalence over his attraction to Dora. He complains that she wants a puppy or a child, whereas he does not want either. When we later see him with a new girlfriend, it is clear that she is also struggling to make a claim on his time.

The actual product Kaleil and Tom are trying to launch is not discussed in great detail beyond its general goal, so when we learn that a competitor is using the same ideas and language, we do not know exactly what that means. We get one telling sequence in which Tom, Kaleil, and other employees are at their computers testing the site over one frenetic weekend and, for a while at least, nothing is working. While it is good that the film does not get bogged down in Internet minutiae, more information on the creation of the site and its problems would have been helpful, especially given the fact that an Internet business is a relatively new concept for many viewers.

Once the site starts working, however, the future seems bright, at least for a while. govWorks.com is the subject of numerous magazine and newspaper articles, and Kaleil emerges as the superstar he was always meant to be. He appears on TV in a roundtable discussion on the economy that includes President Bill Clinton and, in one of the film's most memorable moments, Kaleil brags about how he gave the president his business card and offered him a job when he leaves office.

Soon, however, the big Internet dream starts to sour. First, govWorks.com's offices are broken into, and crucial files are stolen. Was a seemingly friendly visit by a competitor a prelude to the break-in? The film hints that may be so, but the case is never solved, and we do not know the impact, if any, this incident had on the company's eventual failure. Then comes April 14, 2000—a disastrous day for the stock market. The business is in trouble, and Kaleil fears that the board will get rid of him and Tom, who, true to his more casual character, is not very worried.

To compound problems, they soon realize that their site is not doing what it needs to do—that their very product is not living up to expectations and is not as good as the competitors'. Kaleil and Tom certainly have an enormous amount of capital and a large staff, so why the site never fulfilled its potential is left a mystery. However, the specific details may not really matter since govWorks.com seems emblematic of the whole dot-com ethos, in which enormous amounts of money were thrown at a business but the product itself was not given the chance to develop before it was marketed.

The most heartbreaking scenes in the film chronicle the rift between Kaleil and Tom. As tensions mount over the company's troubles, Tom fears that he will be forced out. He knows that Kaleil has lost faith in him and that new talent is coming in. So he seeks the advice of his lawyer, who tells him not to leave the building, even though Kaleil would prefer that he take a leave of absence. It is obvious that neither trusts the other, and the pressures of the business have driven both men to act a bit irrationally. Kaleil finally sends Tom a letter of termination, and poor Tom is essentially escorted from the building as if he were a security threat. Kaleil in fact institutes new security measures after

Tom's departure. Both men seem to feel bad about what has happened, and we do see them slowly patching things up by film's end. By this time, however, the business has failed. Eventually, the offices are empty, and there are 50 employees left, down from a high of 233. We learn at the film's end that a multinational corporation bought the company on New Year's Day 2001, and Tom and Kaleil later started a company designed to help failing dot-coms.

It is an odd feeling to see an era that seemed to pass right before our eyes already documented on film, as if it were now part of the historical record. For even when *Startup.com* skims over certain details about govWorks.com, it successfully captures the energy and anxiety that fueled the dot-com phenomenon—from the relentless optimism of the govWorks.com founders to dot-com customs like the company cheer performed at meetings to the final fall that leaves Kaleil and Tom with nothing but perhaps a little wisdom. In the film's last scene, Kaleil brings a dog to yet another new girlfriend—perhaps he has finally learned a lesson from Dora that there is more to life than work.

Not only does *Startup.com* serve as a timely documentary that represents the plight of many dot-coms, but it also has a universal appeal: struggles like Kaleil and Tom's, after all, have happened in many other kinds of businesses throughout history. The time frame may be compressed in the fast-paced world of the Internet (govWorks.com existed from May 1999 to December 2000), but the age-old themes of friendship, loyalty, ambition, and greed remain the same.

—*Peter N. Chumo II*

## CREDITS

**Origin:** USA
**Released:** 2001
**Production:** D.A. Pennebaker; released by Artisan Entertainment
**Directed by:** Chris Hegedus, Jehane Noujaim
**Cinematography by:** Jehane Noujaim
**Sound:** Chris Hegedus
**Editing:** Chris Hegedus, Jehane Noujaim, Erez Laufer
**MPAA rating:** Unrated
**Running time:** 103 minutes

## REVIEWS

*Boxoffice.* May, 2001, p. 56.
*Chicago Sun-Times Online.* May 25, 2001.
*Entertainment Weekly.* May 18, 2001, p. 55.
*Entertainment Weekly.* May 25, 2001, p. 24.
*Los Angeles Times Online.* May 18, 2001.
*New York Times Online.* May 11, 2001.
*People.* May 21, 2001, p. 42.
*USA Today Online.* May 11, 2001.
*Variety.* January 29, 2001, p. 49.
*Washington Post Online.* May 25, 2001.

# Suddenly Naked

Beginning as a documentary filmmaker in the 1970s, director Anne Wheeler has, like other Canadian directors, ventured into the world of commercial features. In fact the director's last three theatrical releases, *Better Than Chocolate, Marine Life,* and *Suddenly Naked,* are all aimed at the commercial boxoffice. It's not that Wheeler has given up her interests in family issues, which she dealt with in *Better Than Chocolate* and *Marine Life,* but she has opted for a lighter approach with *Suddenly Naked,* which veers away from family life and focuses instead on a 39-year-old author's erotic machinations.

Similar to Susan Seidelman's *Gaudi Afternoon,* Wheeler and screenwriter Elyse Friedman's *Suddenly Naked* revolves around a jaded female author. The protagonists in both films suffer from writer's block but for different reasons. The character Cassandra (played by Judy Davis in Seidelman's film) has soured towards family and romance and finds herself caught up in a disturbing mystery that involves two lesbians' identity crises and a custody battle. *Suddenly Naked*'s Jackie York (Wendy Crewson) experiences writer's block because she seeks revenge on a former lover. Jackie takes her frustrations out on her male fans, who stand outside her door waiting for autographs, and she lies to keep up appearances. Her life is thrown into disarray after she falls for an aspiring author half her age.

Thankfully, Wheeler and Friedman do not emphasize the shock value of a romance between a 40-year-old and a 20-year-old. Instead, the team focuses on Jackie's transformation from a pretentious snob into a vulnerable woman who stops using sex as a weapon and worrying about what the public will think of her personal life. However, this transformation is painfully slow and only at the end of the movie does Jackie knock down the psychological walls that disallow her from living an authentic life.

In a sense, the author has fabricated her own life. Along with her agent, Jackie has covered up her damaged reputation (caused by a disastrous romantic relationship) by posing as lovers with her colleague Lionel Heathcote (Peter Coyote). To further stack the cards against Jackie, a television crew has decided to film a day in the life of the author even though the reality of Jackie's life consists of masturbation sessions, food binging, and erotic sex with young aspiring author Patrick McKeating (Joe Cobden). Jackie lies to the public and her agent by telling them that she is in the process of polishing a novel that she hasn't even written. She also lies about dating Patrick and, in public, condescends to Patrick to cover up their secret affair. That is until Patrick gives Jackie a piece of his mind and walks out on her. Jackie then tries to find sexual gratification with men her own age, but finds that she can't function without Patrick. Fortunately, the two lovers reunite and throw caution to the wind.

Wendy Crewson, who played a mother rediscovering her sexuality in *Better Than Chocolate,* shines as an author having a mid-life crisis; Peter Coyote adds warmth to his stick-in-the-mud character; and Joe Cobden blends eroticism with post-adolescence innocence. Wheeler's latest release might be dubbed "Canada lite" but producer Gavin Wilding summed it up in the press notes with "let's make Canadian movies that appeal to the whole world."

*—Patty-Lynne Herlevi*

## CREDITS

**Jackie York:** Wendy Crewson
**Lionel Heathcote:** Peter Coyote
**Patrick McKeating:** Joe Cobden
**Lupe Martinez:** Emmanuelle Vaugier

**Origin:** Canada
**Released:** 2001
**Production:** Gavin Wilding; Show and Tell Productions, Rampage Entertainment; released by Remstar
**Directed by:** Anne Wheeler
**Written by:** Elyse Friedman
**Cinematography by:** David Frazee
**Music by:** Chris Ainscough
**Sound:** Gord Anderson
**Editing:** Lara Mazur
**Art Direction:** Cheryl Marion
**Costumes:** Toni Rutter
**Production Design:** Cathy Robertson
**MPAA rating:** Unrated
**Running time:** 105 minutes

## REVIEWS

*Variety Online.* November 29, 2001.

# Sugar & Spice

*Get ready to cheer for the BAD girls.*
—Movie tagline

**Box Office:** $13.3 million

The name "Sugar & Spice" doesn't tell you much about what to expect from the movie. Is it about cooking? Is it about a nice twin and an evil twin? Is it something more appropriate for adult viewing? But in a way it's an appropriate name for the film because *Sugar & Spice* never figures out what it wants to be. The title is just vague and bland enough to suit it perfectly.

The "sugar" is the A-squad cheerleading team at Lincoln High School. These cheerleaders believe in their superiority and the power of togetherness and conformity. Their rallying cry is "Cheerleaders kick!," followed by a coy slap of their derrieres. They, of course, would never finish the sentence with any kind of vulgarity.

Each of the girls represents a stereotype, which they never go beyond. Diane (Marley Shelton) is the blonde captain. Diane is an innocent who believed all the up-with-people slogans she grew up with. When she gets in financial trouble, for example, she tells a bank loan officer cheerfully, "We want a hand up, not a handout." Kansas (Mena Suvari) is a tough girl whose mother (Sean Young in a dressed-down cameo) is in prison. Hannah (Rachel Blanchard) is a born-again girl who shuns all evil. Lucy (Sara Marsh) is the smart girl who wants to go to Harvard. That's it. She is never developed beyond that. (And oddly, screenwriter Mandy Nelson never even uses her like we'd expect such a stock character to be used. Shouldn't the girls be calling upon her smarts to help them out of jams?) Cleo (Melissa George) is, for some reason, obsessed with Conan O'Brien. The only facet of her character, if you could use such a strong word for the mere sketch that she is, is that she makes references to O'Brien every once in a while.

Diane is in her dreamy little cheerleading world until a new guy comes to school to be, natch, the captain of the football team. She and Jack (James Marsden) immediately become alpha couple of the school. (That their names are Jack and Diane like the couple in the John Cougar Mellancamp song is the kind of half-joke or almost joke that this movie is filled with.) Jack and Diane are the golden couple until Diane gets pregnant and their parents disown them. With their mutual pluck, they decide cheerily that they will just get jobs and live their happy lives together. They move to a hideous apartment run by a sleazy guy who seems to be into some illegal activities, though neither Jack

---

END

nor Diane appear to notice. Although she continues to keep her frown turned upside down, Diane starts realizing that Jack's salary as a video store clerk isn't going to be enough for she and the baby.

This is where the "spice" of the title comes in. One night while watching a crime film with her squad, the idea occurs to her. "Money makes dreams come true," she says perkily, then suggests that the way to earn extra money for her baby is to rob a bank. She convinces her friends by saying planning the robbery will be like "a craft project!" To these girls, that is the big convincer.

The girls plan to rob a bank in a grocery store. To prepare for their heist, they watch and study old movies like *Reservoir Dogs* and *Point Blank*. In one of the more funny jokes of the film, the religious Hannah is only allowed to watch G-rated movies, so she has to study *The Apple Dumpling Gang*. They further prepare by visiting Kansas' mother in jail to pick up tips from the inmates. They get some illegal guns from a dealer who will only sell to them if they let his mousy daughter Fern (Alexandra Holden) have—horrors!—a spot on the squad. And, most importantly, they decide what to wear—red, white and blue outfits topped with Betty doll masks.

All of this sounds better written down than it is when it's up there on the screen. *Sugar & Spice* probably sounded like a big winner in its pitch meeting, but it somehow never gels. One of the film's biggest problems is that writer Nelson and director Francine McDougall seem to think the contrast between these sweet innocent girls and their criminal intentions is inherently hilarious. So they dwell on the moments of this kind of contrast. Diane, for example, writes a note to herself on her girly pink stationary that reads, "Buy 'gats' (guns) from 'the terminator.'" Since the filmmakers are convinced that this kind of thing in itself is so funny, instead of making a wide variety of jokes, they tend to stick to varieties of the same one.

Not that there aren't good moments in the film. One of the best is the character of Lisa (Marla Sokoloff). Lisa, who is the embittered captain of the Lincoln High School B-squad serves as a narrator of the film. The story is told in flashback as she sits in the interrogation room telling police about the Betty doll crime. Unlike the rest of the inhabitants of the film, she actually has a dimension or two. As B-squad captain, she is eternally vigilant over the A-squad. She is certain that she should be on the A-squad and, with her encyclopedic knowledge of the cheerleading code, is constantly noticing minor infractions that the team makes in their routines. Ironically, she is actually never very good herself during the try-outs, but she chalks it up to being unfairly treated, or being teamed with the wrong person. etc. Lisa's huge self-delusion and biting wit are a welcome diversion in the film. As she watches the A-squad doing their "hey, ho" routine, she whispers bitterly to her loyal underling, "I don't know about the 'hey' but the 'ho' is right on."

After Diane beats her in winning Jack's heart, Lisa complains, "They were like frigging Barbie and Ken without the pink Corvette."

And the film isn't completely void of good jokes. After some particularly tense interactions with her cheerleading sisters, Diana wails, "I can't take this, the back stabbing, the fighting—we're acting like sorority sisters, not cheerleaders." But there are too many jokes that just aren't there or don't play out well enough. And the film, inexplicably, is also colored with gay jokes. Not that those jokes don't seem crass now, but it seems like in a few years, though kind of jokes will look even more boorish and offensive.

The filmmakers seem to be trying to parody the sweet innocent cheerleaders and the various "types" within the group, but they've made their characters too flat and unrealistic. For parody to work, the target must be recognizable. These cheerleaders are too fake to be worthy of parody. Does anyone really know anyone who's sole characteristic is that they lust after Conan O'Brien? Does anyone really believe that cheerleaders are so bizarrely innocent and peppy? Perhaps to make up for this, the filmmakers have the girls wearing their cheerleading costumes all the time. The exceptions would be the times they sit around together wearing skimpy lingerie. This particular touch is strange since most of the people behind this film are women.

The acting in the movie is uneven. Sokoloff is excellent in portraying the vanity and insecurity of the envious B-squad leader. The cheerleaders are generally fine, though all they have to do is exemplify their one characteristic. Surprisingly, one of the sour notes in the film is Suvari. Perhaps it is because she is accustomed to having a larger role, but whenever she is in the scene, she is always overacting. Her overreactions draw attention to herself even when she's supposed to be sitting in the frame just listening to another character.

Critics were divided on the film. *Entertainment Weekly* gave it a B and said, "*Sugar & Spice* isn't a well-shaped movie, but it's fun in its raunchy unwieldness." The *Chicago Sun-Times'* Roger Ebert, who often favors movies with scantily clad women, also liked the film and not only called it "sassy and satirical" but also "alive and risky and saucy." Other critics were not so enthralled. The *Toronto Star's* Peter Howell said, "Watching a teen flick as morally bankrupt as *Sugar & Spice*. . .you have to wonder if Hollywood is really getting the message about gratuitous film violence." The *Associated Press'* Christy Lemire was similarly unimpressed and wrote, "What *Sugar & Spice* tries to pass off as biting, sardonic wit is simply over-the-top, forced humor." By trying to be everything for everybody—an *Election*-like teen satire, a neo-*Bring It On* for cheerleading fans and a T & A flick for Roger Eberts—*Sugar & Spice* ended up not being enough of anything. 🎞

—*Jill Hamilton*

## CREDITS

**Diane Weston:** Marley Shelton
**Jack Bartlett:** James Marsden
**Kansas:** Mena Suvari
**Lisa:** Marla Sokoloff
**Hannah:** Rachel Blanchard
**Cleo:** Melissa George
**Fern:** Alexandra Holden
**Lucy:** Sara Marsh
**Mrs. Hill:** Sean Young

**Origin:** USA
**Released:** 2001
**Production:** Wendy Finerman; released by New Line Cinema
**Directed by:** Francine McDougall
**Written by:** Mandy Nelson
**Cinematography by:** Robert Brinkmann
**Music by:** Mark Mothersbaugh
**Editing:** Sloane Klevin
**Art Direction:** Maria Baker
**Costumes:** Wendy Chuck
**Production Design:** Jeff Knipp
**MPAA rating:** PG-13
**Running time:** 81 minutes

## REVIEWS

*Boxoffice.* April, 2001, p. 240.
*Chicago Sun-Times Online.* January 26, 2001.
*New York Times Online.* January 27, 2001.
*Rolling Stone.* February 15, 2001, p. 84.
*US Weekly.* February 12, 2001, p. 35.
*Variety.* January 29, 2001, p. 60.

## QUOTES

Kansas (Mena Suvari) instructs her friends: "It's *Point Break.* Just shut up and look at Keanu."

# Summer Catch

*Are you game?*
—Movie tagline

**Box Office:** $19.6 million

Baseball movies have been done and done and done. Freddie Prinze Jr. movies where he gets the girl have been done and done and done. Director Michael Tolin and screenplay writers Kevin Falls and John Gatins must have thought that combining the two overdone stories would somehow create something new and fresh. They were wrong. What they did come up with is a movie that feels like we've seen it before—several times, actually.

In this version, Ryan Dunne (Prinze Jr.) is a kid from the wrong side of the tracks. He's lives in a quaint Cape Cod town that is probably the reason why in about 15% of the scenes, Prinze seems to be attempting some sort of East Coast accent. (In other parts of the film the accent is mysteriously—and thankfully—missing.) The town is also host to a team on the hot Cape Cod Baseball League. This venerable league has been a training ground for such pro baseball players as Carlton Fisk, Thurman Munson, and Mo Vaughn. Each summer the league attracts an influx of college boys who play in it in hopes of being spotted by one of the many major league scouts lurking around at the games. Even though Ryan's not a college boy, he is a darned fine pitcher and this summer, the gruff yet kindly coach, John Schiffner (Brian Dennehy), has offered Ryan a spot on the team. The opportunity means everything to Ryan. It's his big chance to rise about his humble circumstances and live his dream. If he fails, he will end up in dead end jobs like his bartender brother and his father (Fred Ward) who's a gardener.

And there's a good chance Ryan will fail, too. Ever since his mother died, he's had a habit of choking during games just at the crucial moment. Getting his spot on the team doesn't mean Ryan is set. He has to deal with a hotshot competing pitcher, Eric (Corey Pearson), who's just in the league because he feels insulted that the Dodgers only offered him two million dollars to pitch for them. To show how "cool" Eric is, they have him sport rock and roll clothes and dyed hair that makes him look about as cool as a member of Motley Crue. And Ryan is quite a formidable enemy for himself, too. Whenever he gets the rare chance to pitch for his team, he starts repeating his old behavior of screwing up at the last minute. He's the type of player that can pitch a no-hitter, then give up a crucial grand slam home run to lose the game for his team.

Things are confusing off the field, too. In a particularly dumb sequence, he's mowing the lawn of town rich guy, Rand Parrish (Bruce Davison), when he spots the lovely Parrish daughter, Tenley (Jessica Biel from TV's *7th Heaven*). Tenley, who's home on summer break after graduating from Vassar, is walking around in a bathing suit in slow motion. Ryan responds by gawking and running his mover into a flower bed. Ryan's teammate, Billy Brubaker (Matthew Lillard), a jovial frat boy type who is pretty much all id, finds out about Ryan's crush. "So you mow her lawn and now you want to MOW HER LAWN," says Brubaker in an example of the film's typically clunky dialogue.

Despite the fact that Ryan acts like a big dolt around her, Tenley takes a liking to him and soon Ryan's tossed over his slutty hometown girlfriend Dede (Brittany Murphy) and is dating Tenley. They bond over their uncertainty about the future. Ryan's afraid of what's going to happen with his baseball career and Tenley is being pushed into a career she doesn't want by her overbearing father. The two have what they perceive to be meaningful conversations where Tenley gives Ryan yucky advice like "You just have to allow yourself to succeed" and "You want big rewards? Then you have to take big risks."

Tenley's father isn't just overbearing on career choices, he's also not too happy with his daughter hanging around with a landscaper's son. Instead of just having a talk with his daughter about this, he threatens Ryan by saying that if he continues to see Tenley, he will fire his father and tell all his rich friends to fire him, too. And just to make things more melodramatic, the writers threw in a few chunks of other movies, too. There's a character played by Beverly D'Angelo who likes to seduce young ball players and give them good luck that's quite a bit like Susan Sarandon's in *Bull Durham*. There's also a scene that's a lot like one in *Good Will Hunting* in which his hometown buddy (Jed Robert Rhein) begs Ryan to succeed—because the whole town's counting on him. In case the dead mom, the drunken father, and all the other traumas weren't enough, the writers also threw in a scene where Ryan must rescue some teammates from a burning building. Oh yeah, and to make sure they touch all the emotional bases, the writers included a cute precocious girl who wants to be the team's mascot and cutely tries out various costumes like dressing up like a crab.

Another big element of the film is Sam Adams beer, which is always prominently displayed in all of the bar scenes. It's quite unusual how all of the characters have such a dead-on ability to make sure that their beer label is always pointing toward the camera. The movie is held together by some of the tritest dialogue to hit the screen this year. With all the lame advice his friends give him, it's no wonder Ryan has problems with success. "Let yourself be great," says Tenley. "Bear down," offers his coach. The dialogue between Ryan and Tenley is particularly stiff. "I just pitched the game of my life," says Ryan at one point. "Let's be together," says Tenley. Do real humans really say things like, "Let's be together"? Perhaps the single worst dialogue moment comes when local dumb guy sees the team's mascot, a clam. "Didn't I get clams from Dee Dee Mulligan?" "Crabs, you got crabs from Dee Dee Mulligan," responds his friends.

Prinze is out of his league in this film. Besides his accent problems, he doesn't seem scrappy enough to have had such

a background. He looks like he'd be more comfortable in one of his other films where he plays a popular guy or an earnest college student. He also seems to lack any sort of natural pitching ability. Although he trained to look good pitching in the role, it doesn't work. He must have looked really bad because every time he pitches, the camera cuts away so that we can't see the full throw. It's hard to say whether Biel is good or not in her role because her role is so dumb. Could anyone sound good saying lines like "Why are you afraid of success?" Davison seems to be having fun as the evil rich father, but his character would be more suited to a 1980s evening soap opera like *Dynasty* than a modern big-screen offering. And Dennehy does his best with a role playing the gruff guy with the heart of gold, even though that role was nailed years ago with Ed's Asner's Lou Grant. The best of the bunch are Murphy, who is always reliably off-kilter and strange, and Lillard, who has the cockiness and light humor of a Will Smith.

Critics had seen it all before. "*Summer Catch*, a trite, bantamweight *Bull Durham*, hasn't a single line, gibe, gesture, or twist that hasn't already been chewed up and spat out in many a movie baseball dugout," wrote Rita Kempley of the *Washington Post*. "Prinze could beat out his bat for Most Wooden Performance. . . . The interplay of Ryan's professional and romantic challenges rings true, but unfortunately the writers pile on contrivances and needless distractions that seriously diminish the film's overall effect," wrote Kevin Thomas of the *Los Angeles Times*. "Prinze, with his puppy-dog frown and unconvincing athleticism, is about as lightweight as a leading man can get, and Biel's line-readings make a perfect match for his: the vacuity is frightening," wrote Steven Rea of the *Philadelphia Inquirer*. And the *Boston Globe*'s Jay Carr scoffed: "*Summer Catch* is *Bull Durham* for dummies."

—*Jill Hamilton*

## CREDITS

**Ryan Dunne:** Freddie Prinze Jr.
**Tenley Parrish:** Jessica Biel
**Billy Brubaker:** Matthew Lillard
**John Schiffner:** Brian Dennehy
**Sean Dunne:** Fred Ward
**Mike Dunne:** Jason Gedrick
**Dede Mulligan:** Brittany Murphy
**Miles Dalrymple:** Marc Blucas
**Rand Parrish:** Bruce Davison
**Mickey Dominguez:** Wilmer Valderrama
**Dale Robin:** Christian Kane
**Auggie:** Gabriel Mann
**Calvin Knight:** Cedric Pendleton
**Katie Parrish:** Zena Grey

**Eric Van Leemer:** Corey Pearson

**Origin:** USA
**Released:** 2001
**Production:** Mike Tollin, Brian Robbins, Sam Weisman;
released by Warner Bros.
**Directed by:** Mike Tollin
**Written by:** Kevin Falls, John Gatins
**Cinematography by:** Tim Suhrstedt
**Music by:** George Fenton
**Sound:** Jeffree Bloomer
**Editing:** Harvey Rosenstock
**Costumes:** Juliet Polsca
**Production Design:** John D. Kretschmer
**MPAA rating:** PG-13
**Running time:** 108 minutes

## REVIEWS

*Entertainment Weekly.* September 7, 2001, p. 135.
*Los Angeles Times Online.* August 24, 2001.
*New York Times Online.* August 24, 2001.
*People.* September 3, 2001, p. 38.
*USA Today Online.* August 24, 2001.
*Variety.* August 27, 2001, p. 32.
*Washington Post.* August 24, 2001, p. C5.

## QUOTES

Tenley (Jessica Biel) to Ryan (Freddie Prinze Jr.): "You want big
rewards? You've got to take big risks."

## TRIVIA

John C. McGinley and Beverly D'Angelo have unbilled cameos—
the former as a baseball scout and the latter as a baseball groupie.

# Suspicious River

*What you desperately want but dread being given.*
—Movie tagline

Anyone familiar with Luis Bunuel's body of cinematic
work would recall the placid expression on Catherine
Denueve's face when she played the high-class call girl,
Severine, in *Belle du Jour,* a compelling mystery that revolved
around the character's unusual need to coldly give pleasure to
men. Sure, her jet-set life left room for boredom, but we

were left wondering why a woman that was frigid towards
her handsome doctor husband would freely give her body to
other men. Canadian filmmaker Lynne Stopkewich delves
deeper into women's sexual psychology with her equally
compelling character Leila Murray, rendered to life by the
courageous actress Molly Parker.

Based on the novel *Suspicious River* by Laura Kasischke,
Stopkewich's brave new film journeys into blackness and
sheer terror. We learn very little about Leila Murray's childhood other than that her mother had an affair with a lover
who killed her out of rage. But this back story slowly comes
together throughout the film, while leading viewers through
a dark forest where no bread crumbs have been left for a safe
return. We see an innocent girl (Mary Kate Welsh) watching her parents fight or passively going along on a picnic
with her mother (Sarah Jane Redmond) and her lover
(Byron Lucas), whom the mother calls the child's uncle.
This little girl appears to Leila when Leila takes breaks from
her receptionist position at the Swan Motel.

One day, the girl tells Leila, "When I grow up, I'm
going to stay in motels all the time and have my boyfriends
pay for it." A look of pained shock crosses Leila's face and
her expression comes as a surprise since Leila kept a placid
expression while she endured rape and beatings by two self
righteous men who found her prostituting herself to be
revolting. Parallel stories emerge involving Leila and her
sexual exploits and the little girl dealing with her severely
dysfunctional home life. Despite the bleak life that surrounds both characters, a sense of sweetness and hope also
prevails, carrying them throughout their collective horrors to
a place of understanding and redemption.

As the film opens, we see Leila working behind the
counter at a small town motel. Although she shares many
things in common with her glamorous Parisian sister-by-
association Severine, Leila doesn't live in a chic city, but a
dismal town called Suspicious River. However, like Severine, Leila suffered some sort of mysterious childhood
trauma that has left her frigid in her marriage, but addicted
to sexually pleasing abusive men. These women experience
an odd sort of sexual hunger that leads them down an
extremely dangerous road yet, as Leila tells her coworker
Millie (Deanna Milligan), "I can't stop."

We get the feeling from her husband Rick's (Joel Bissonnette) reaction when Leila comes home late at night,
smelling like a bar and sporting red spike heels, that Leila
has traveled this road before. Her addiction resurfaces when
she begins giving men staying at the motel blow jobs for the
price of a room. Soon a moody drifter, Gary Jensen (Callum
Keith Rennie), shows up at the motel, sweet-talking Leila.
He turns out to be one of those deranged men that alternately beats women, then tells them later that they're sweet
and sexy. Gary rapes Leila, yet she seems just as intrigued by
his antics as she does indifferent to them. She appears to be

looking for some sort of demon to purge of her past and she seems to have found that devil in Gary.

On another night, a man sporting a ball cap (Michael Shanks) brutally beats and rapes Leila and, ironically, Gary becomes her protector. They pursue a sexual relationship in which Gary lures Leila away from her dead end job and marriage. However, Gary takes Leila to his home where she is gang raped by Gary's friends (including the baseball cap man) and others that were seen earlier at a bar where Gary took Leila to show her off. It turns out that Gary passionately hates women who prostitute themselves and planned on killing Leila. However, Leila escapes and lives to tell her tale.

Stopkewich suspends time in her film by showing parallel stories as opposed to flashbacks. Similar to Robert Lepage's *Possible Worlds* and Carlos Saura's *Goya at Bordeaux*, Stopkewich brings the past physically into the present. With Stopkewich's film we recall what psychoanalysts term talking to our inner child, but Leila actually manifests hers into the physical realm while showing a protective tenderness towards the innocent child. It takes an amazingly gifted screenwriter to pull this type of narrative off and Stopkewich has proven herself with both *Kissed* and *Suspicious River* to be a first-rate filmmaker. She takes on disturbing subjects that few people care to explore and then, with much restraint, employs a humanistic approach to her subjects. Her films prove challenging to watch, definitely heartbreaking, but also compelling as we grow to care deeply about the women protagonists. We wonder what makes them tick and we plead for their safety as they dive into the blackness of their subconscious desires.

Although reluctant at first, Parker, who played a necrophiliac in Stopkewich's *Kissed*, plunged into the emotionally dangerous role. Parker appears to be an alter ego for Stopkewich and the perfect actress to play the roles of women that society chooses to ignore, but which fascinate Stopkewich. Again, Parker brings an ironic blend of schoolgirl innocence and Anais Nin-style forbidden eroticism to her character. Callum Keith Rennie, who might be remembered as the comedic sex fiend in Don McKellar's *Last Night* or the drunken, womanizing punk musician in Bruce Mc-Donald's *Hard Core Logo,* here plays a character with a black heart. Easily the most challenging role of his cinematic career, it becomes extremely difficult to separate the actor from the devil that he plays in Stopkewich's film. Mary Kate Welsh, who plays the young girl, brings a sweetness to the film. Due to the film's violent content, Stopkewich gave Welsh only the bits of information that would allow her to perform her role in order to protect the child's innocence. According to the film's press kit, "Mary Kate sees her character in *Suspicious River* as being Leila's guardian angel." And through Leila's memory, the young girl ends up saving Leila from dire consequences.

*Belle du Jour* and *Suspicious River* both delve into the subconscious urges of women who suffered childhood trauma, but the two films have more in common than their women characters. The films blend reality with dreams of the past and one might call Stopkewich's adaptation an updated version of *Belle du Jour,* set in 1980's rural Canada in a haze of cigarette smoke and stone-washed denim. *Belle du Jour* once shocked audiences and even as unflappable as today's audiences pride themselves on being, *Suspicious River* will send shock waves through its viewers as they learn the truth about the fresh-face girl-next-door.

—*Patty-Lynne Herlevi*

## CREDITS

**Leila Murray:** Molly Parker
**Gary Jensen:** Callum Keith Rennie
**Rick Schmidt:** Joel Bissonnette
**Young girl:** Mary Kate Welsh
**Millie:** Deanna Milligan
**Bonnie (Mother):** Sarah Jane Redmond
**Jack (Father):** Norman Armour
**Uncle Andy:** Byron Lucas
**Ball Cap Man:** Michael Shanks
**Suitcase Man:** Jay Brazeau

**Origin:** Canada
**Released:** 2000
**Production:** Raymond Massey, Michael Okulitch; released by TVA International
**Directed by:** Lynne Stopkewich
**Written by:** Lynne Stopkewich
**Cinematography by:** Gregory Middleton
**Music by:** Don MacDonald
**Sound:** James Genn
**Editing:** Allan Lee
**Art Direction:** Ray Lai
**Costumes:** Sheila White
**Production Design:** Don MacAulay
**MPAA rating:** R
**Running time:** 98 minutes

## REVIEWS

*Boxoffice.* December, 2000, p. 55.
*Reel West.* August/September, 2000, p. 20.
*Sight and Sound.* September, 2001, p. 53.
*Variety.* October 9, 2000, p. 31.

Leila (Molly Parker): "What's to tell. I was born in Suspicious River, I grew up here, and now I live here."

# Sweet November

*She just needed a month to change his life forever.*
—Movie tagline

**Box Office:** $25.2 million

Nelson Moss (Keanu Reeves) is a high-powered ad agency executive who is consumed with landing the Dr. Diggity fast food account. His life is so busy that he doesn't have time to meet his girlfriend Angelica's (Lauren Graham) family or even go to the department of motor vehicles to take the test to renew his license. Of course, as his secretary informs him, if he doesn't renew his license, the next time he is pulled over by the police he'll have an expired license and go to jail and he doesn't have time for that either.

So Nelson begrudgingly goes off to the DMV where also taking the test is Sara Deever (Charlize Theron). Naturally they "meet cute:" She enters the test area dropping groceries the whole way, and he tries to cheat on the test by asking her for an answer. She gets caught talking, however, and is evicted from the test. Nelson never explains that it was his fault since expediency and not honor is Nelson's motto. Only when confronted by Sara in the parking lot does he begrudgingly offer to cover her expenses. She refuses but later tracks him down to his apartment to ask for a ride since he was the cause of her losing her license. Again Nelson begrudgingly gives in, but what he doesn't realize is that Sara is going to involve Nelson in a little breaking and entering in which Sara "steals" two dogs.

Practically blackmailing Nelson up to her apartment for a cup of coffee, Sara confronts Nelson with his workaholic nature and his emotionally unavailability but also offers to "cure" him. The cure involves his moving in with her for one month, which, according to Sara is "long enough to be meaningful and short enough to stay out of trouble." Having known her less than 24-hours and believing her to be quite nuts, Nelson not-so-politely refuses.

The next day at work, Nelson's cheap and tasteless presentation to Dr. Diggity's representatives goes terribly awry and he ends up snapping, yelling at the rep and losing the account. His boss (Robert Joy), faced with Nelson's arrogance, fires him. To make matters worse, when Nelson arrives back at his apartment, Angelica is packed and ready

to leave him. Later that night a package arrives containing one of Sara's "stolen" dogs and the key to her apartment. Nelson storms over to Sara's to return the dog, but the two end up making love. It is November 1st, and he will be her Mr. November.

Under Sara's tutelage, Nelson learns to relax. In an almost cliched montage, they walk dogs on the beach, they form the rooting section for a young neighbor boy Abner (Liam Aiken) who's racing his puny little sailboat against the rich kids', they visit the old house where Nelson grew up, they play hide and seek in her apartment, they go out for ice cream, they take PG-13 bubble baths together—you get the idea.

Charlize Theron plays Sara as suitably cute and kooky, what with all her hand-knit scarves and PETA animal saving. She is terminally perky but with an undercurrent of sadness. We know there's something wrong, and most of us can probably easily figure it out—especially since ads for the film gave away the ending—but what's even more puzzling is where the income to support her kooky lifestyle comes from. There are hints of a business, but it seems irrelevant to her life now. (What world do these people live in?)

Also puzzling is the way the filmmakers have the allegedly smart but in this case painfully obtuse Nelson never seeing Sara's secret coming. (How can he possibly miss the dark circles under her eyes?) Guess he's just too busy being jealous of Sara's downstairs neighbor, Chaz (Jason Isaacs), until he realizes that 1.) Chaz is a gay transvestite and 2.) he's another highly respected ad executive, and one of Nelson's prime competitors.

As Nelson, Keanu Reeves looks decidedly uncomfortable and is therefore anything but convincing in this role. It's hard to see him as anything other than a brooding anti-hero a la *The Matrix* or *Speed* unless one wants to harken back to his old *Bill and Ted* days, but few will buy his confrontational ad man or his quick transformation to caring lover. He looks especially discomfited in the scene where he plays Santa and lugs a bag of goodies into Sara's apartment. But then most viewers will be equally bothered by the scene. Reeves and Theron have very little on-screen sizzle, but as to who is to blame is anyone's guess. The two have played a couple before, in *The Devil's Advocate*, but if one remembers, their relationship in that film was less than romantic, too. Here it fares no better.

In 1968, a zany and Bohemian Sandy Dennis took on a new lover every month to help them gain confidence in themselves. Her Mr. November is an uptight Anthony Newley. Her downstairs neighbor is Theo Bikel, a political activist and sign painter. The setting is Greenwich Village. Sound vaguely familiar? It should. It was a hokey plot even back in the 1960's but it was a better fit then than the story, as adapted here, is today. Consequently one has to ask, "why bother to remake it, especially if you're not going to make it any better?"

The original *Sweet November* isn't the only movie that invites comparisons between itself and this version. One can't help thinking of 1970's *Love Story* (The *New York Times*' A.O. Scott headlined his review "love means not ever having to make a bit of sense"). And if those movies are before your time, then one need look no further back than *Autumn in New York.* (2000).

The 2001 *Sweet November* leaves a lot of room for yawns and even more room for questions about its assumptions. Why should we accept that Nelson's life is less happy, less fulfilling than Sara's? A temporary setback shouldn't nullify a whole lifestyle choice. Further, why should we believe this A-type personality would be seduced by Sara's lifestyle as easily as he was seduced into her bed? Similarly, Sara's motives are also unknown. Humanitarianism? Altruism? She's out to save workaholic men in the same way she saves animals? We are never given a clue so we end up wondering, what is she after? What does she want from these men? "You don't need to understand me. You just need to let it happen," Sara tells Nelson. Audiences may not be so willing to make that leap of faith.

Even the supporting players in the film don't come off well. Greg Germann, as Nelson's ad-business buddy, plays just another version of his Ally McBeal lawyer: sleazy, money-obsessed and heartless. Jason Isaacs as Sara's gay, downstairs neighbor provides peripheral support but is most amusing when seen wearing a green sequined dress, wig and makeup. That's when one may finally remember where one has seen him before—he was the villainous British officer to Mel Gibson's *Patriot*. Frank Langella, plays a very brief role as "god," Edgar Price, one of the top ad men in the business. His role exists, however, only to show Nelson how callous he will become if he doesn't change his life according to Sara's direction. Edgar Price is a cardboard character used only to move the plot in the direction the writers want to manipulate us.

And that's a big part of the problem with the lightweight, but heavy-handed *Sweet November*. It starts with a terribly contrived storyline and ends up having to manipulate us just so we'll buy the whole premise. Unfortunately, the writers' manipulation is inept and the whole project just ends up taking itself much too seriously. Critic Roger Ebert was much less kind to the movie. He said it was about "two sick and twisted people playing mind games and calling it love." Ouch.

*—Beverley Bare Buehrer*

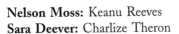

## CREDITS

**Nelson Moss:** Keanu Reeves
**Sara Deever:** Charlize Theron
**Chaz:** Jason Isaacs

**Vince:** Greg Germann
**Abner:** Liam Aiken
**Angelica:** Lauren Graham
**Brandon:** Michael Rosenbaum
**Raeford Dunne:** Robert Joy
**Manny:** Jason Kravits
**Edgar Price:** Frank Langella

**Origin:** USA
**Released:** 2001
**Production:** Elliot Kastner, Steven Reuther, Erwin Stoff, Deborah Aal; Bel-Air Entertainment, 3 Arts Productions; released by Warner Bros.
**Directed by:** Pat O'Connor
**Written by:** Kurt Voelker
**Cinematography by:** Edward Lachman
**Music by:** Christopher Young
**Sound:** Nelson Stoll
**Music Supervisor:** G. Marq Roswell
**Editing:** Anne Coates
**Art Direction:** Kevin Constant
**Costumes:** Shy Cunliffe
**Production Design:** Naomi Shohan
**MPAA rating:** PG-13
**Running time:** 114 minutes

## REVIEWS

*Boxoffice.* May, 2001, p. 62.
*Chicago Sun-Times Online.* February 16, 2001.
*Hollywood Reporter.* February 13, 2001, p. 25.
*Los Angeles Times Online.* February 16, 2001.
*New York Times Online.* February 16, 2001.
*People.* February 26, 2001, p. 29.
*Sight and Sound.* July, 2001, p. 56.
*USA Today Online.* February 16, 2001.
*Variety.* February 19, 2001, p. 37.
*Washington Post Online.* February 16, 2001.

## QUOTES

Nelson (Keanu Reeves) to Sara (Charlize Theron): "Why is doing something fundamentally trivial better than living a responsible life, as boring as it might seem? Who made you the expert, the doc, the guru? Why do you have all the answers?"

# Swordfish

*Log on. Hack in. Go anywhere. Steal everything.*
—Movie tagline
*Password accepted.*
—Movie tagline

 **Box Office:** $69.8 million

No one could accuse director Dominic Sena of lacking confidence. He opens his egregiously hyperactive John Travolta action movie *Swordfish* with close-ups of Travolta's latest suave-but-malicious hoodlum character, Gabriel Shear, talking about the putative deficiencies of *Dog Day Afternoon.* You don't know at first if Travolta is a director pitching a Hollywood screenplay; it's unclear who he's talking to as he argues that, for all its merits, Sidney Lumet's tense drama about a bank robber who takes hostages doesn't go far enough. What if the Al Pacino character started killing his captives one by one, asks the cigar-smoking, Armani-wearing Travolta. After a few minutes of this speculation, Travolta rises from the table, and Sena pulls his camera back to set the scene: Shear is actually in the middle of masterminding just such a ruthless robbery. But his hostages are strapped with explosives triggered to go off if they move beyond the perimeter of the bank. And when some of the security forces don't take him seriously enough, one hostage is blown to bits, along with a whole lot of cops, some bystanders, many cars, and huge chunks of buildings. Sena gleefully executes a circular pan filled with many crashing panes of glass (this is one director who simply loves windows shattering), exploding vehicles, and burning rubble.

*See?* Sena is fairly shouting. *I'm no namby-pamby Sidney Lumet. When I'm filming a bank robbery, my criminal is a totally immoral, bloodthirsty, brilliant jerk. I'm not afraid to show people getting killed.* And Sena is certainly unafraid of going way, way over the top with mindless violence and spectacular crashes. Unfortunately, for all his histrionics, he doesn't have a clue of how to build tension the way Lumet does. In Sena's movies—his last before this was the hyperactive *Gone in 60 Seconds*—psychological impact can only be measured in decibels and body counts. That would be tolerable if Sena's undertaking was simply to make a blood-and-guts action flick. But the prologue shows that Sena has more pretensions than that. He thinks he's a thinking man's action director, and this is a dangerous conception.

The opening scene and another near the beginning of the film tell you everything you need to know about the modus operandi of Sena. Shear, touted as a shadowy crimi-

nal genius, is putting together a crack team of hackers to pull off a big computer-assisted heist. He sends the kittenish vixen Ginger (Halle Berry) to recruit prison parolee and ex-hacker Stanley Jobson (Hugh Jackman) for the job. Jobson, formerly celebrated as the nation's top hacker, is trying to turn straight after being convicted of cracking a secret FBI computer surveillance operation. He's now working on an oil rig in the middle of the desert. Ginger's teasing, seductive come-on doesn't crack Stanley's resistance—he's determined to stay straight—but a suitcase full of cash does, especially when Ginger promises that Gabriel will come up with much more money to help Stanley hire a top lawyer to get his daughter back from his ex-wife, Melissa (Drea de Matteo). So, after drinking in many provocative poses by Ginger in a short, short dress, Stanley agrees to meet Gabriel, after Ginger has promised Stanley is under no obligation to continue.

At the meeting, Gabriel swiftly puts Stanley in a chair with a gun to his head and tells him he has a minute to crack into a super-secure government site. And just to make things even more fun, Stanley has to break the code while one of Gabriel's sultry female playthings administers fellatio to him. Sweat pouring off his brow, Stanley's fingers fly over the keyboard; of course, he beats the clock at the last second. This is Gabriel's idea of a performance test—and Sena's idea of entertainment. If this type of crudeness doesn't sicken you, you'll love the rest of the movie. Actually, it might have been better—at least from a gross entertainment standpoint—if the movie continued along these lines. At least you would know then that it was intended as a cartoon in the mode of the recent *Charlie's Angels.* But the long middle of this ridiculous movie is not only stupid but dull, filled with needless exposition and devoid of much action.

After passing his daunting "test," Stanley wants to walk away from the assignment, but Ginger keeps reminding him that Gabriel's offer of megabucks is his only hope of regaining his daughter, Holly (Camryn Grimes). The script's idea of upping the emotional ante is to have Holly's mother be a hopeless substance abuser whose new husband is a pornographer using their home as a shooting location. This plot device itself is a sort of pornography. But that's how Sena likes to operate.

The plot sputters along, with the wonderful Don Cheadle largely wasted as FBI honcho Roberts who sent Stanley to prison in the first place and is now trying to use Stanley to catch Gabriel; Sam Shepard totally wasted as a senator who is in cahoots with Gabriel; and Berry vamping shamelessly as Sena stages unsubtle scenes that make Stanley confused about whose side she is on. Along the way things are so becalmed that we get one hilarious scene in which Stanley flees from Roberts and his men by jumping down a beachfront hillside. They roll down the hill for several minutes, only to get on their feet at the beach and have the same conversation they might have had at the top.

The movie also tries to spin the usual sort of false bravado about computer hacking. Stanley does his best work while boozing, dancing and chain-smoking; like everything in Sena's movies, breaking code is depicted a reckless, macho undertaking. It's a desperate effort to cover up the obvious fact that there is no way to make computer work thrilling on screen. Sena tries every trick he can, even giving Gabriel's office a cool work station with seven flat monitors almost suspended in mid-air and displaying data simultaneously.

Travolta takes an easy walk to the bank by essentially reprising his overly ballyhooed persona of *Pulp Fiction*. By now this character is an awful caricature, esepcially in Travolta's hands—the refined, intelligent, cool-as-ice, and incredibly ruthless crime lord. Sporting ridiculous suits and haircuts, Travolta smirks and deadpans—a talented actor settling for another inexplicably ridiculous role. At one point, he helicopters to a trout stream and, sporting a beret and ultra-cool sunglasses, machine guns to death a former partner who betrayed him. Later on, we again see how ruthless Gabriel is as Sena reprises the same sort of ugly scene he milked earlier. This time, Stanley must crack a code not with a gun to his head, but as Ginger is strung up in a noose; he must do the job before she chokes to death. (Stanley somehow has developed a soft spot for Ginger despite her constant betrayals of him, but then everyone in this film is more than a little soft in the head.)

Screenwriter and co-producer Skip Woods must think audiences are brain-dead, too. In the last half of the film, there is much prattle about the ethics of what Gabriel is doing, after he is revealed as being the maverick head of some sort of freelance patriotic anti-terrorist operation. Gabriel is willing to rob banks, rack up high body counts, and use women like tools and toys because he has a higher mission—to blow up or assassinate those who would put America to shame around the world. He's kind of like an updated, cyber version of a Charlton Heston character. This still doesn't explain why Gabriel is portrayed—at least to Roberts and his law enforcement figures—as a shadowy, elusive figure who at the same time he is open and careless enough to be easily spotted and tracked by the sophisticated technology of binoculars.

Sena spends most of the movie laboriously working his way back to the scene he opened with—and then tacking on what may be filmdom's most laughable chase-and-escape sequence, involving Gabriel, Stanley, and the hostages on a bus that is being dangled all across Los Angeles by a helicopter. In the end, Gabriel becomes a Houdini, pulling off what has become a rather hackneyed escape by faking his own death. Sena doesn't even bother to give any plausible explanation for how this happens. We're supposed to believe it's magical moviemaking.

For all the flying glass and exploding bodies, this is fairly ho-hum stuff, derivative of a slew of movies including the much classier James Bond efforts. Sena rubs our faces in his crudities without any subtlety and without much humor, other than the crotch-grabbing variety. *Swordfish* looks like an emotionally stunted male adolescent's idea of what a Hollywood movie should feature—compliant females, cartoonish politics, and plenty of twists on hostage situations. In the end, it's the audience that is held hostage to what might be one of the most frenzied, furious and pretentious pieces of trash that a studio has foisted on the public in recent years. It's not so bad that *Swordfish* is offensive and brainless, but it's not much fun either—and that's a deadly combination.

—*Michael Betzold*

## CREDITS

**Gabriel Shear:** John Travolta
**Stanley Jobson:** Hugh Jackman
**Ginger:** Halle Berry
**Agent Roberts:** Don Cheadle
**Marco:** Vinnie Jones
**Senator Reisman:** Sam Shepard
**A.D. Joy:** Zach Grenier
**Holly:** Camryn Grimes
**Axl Torvalds:** Rudolf Martin
**Melissa:** Drea De Matteo

**Origin:** USA
**Released:** 2001
**Production:** Joel Silver, Jonathan D. Krane; Village Roadshow Pictures, NPV Entertainment; released by Warner Bros.
**Directed by:** Dominic Sena
**Written by:** Skip Woods
**Cinematography by:** Paul Cameron
**Music by:** Christopher Young
**Sound:** Edward Tise
**Music Supervisor:** Paul Oakenfold
**Editing:** Stephen E. Rivkin
**Art Direction:** Geoff Hubbard, Andrew Laws, Jeff Wallace
**Costumes:** Ha Nguyen
**Production Design:** Jeff Mann
**MPAA rating:** R
**Running time:** 99 minutes

 ## REVIEWS

*Boxoffice.* August, 2001, p. 61.
*Chicago Sun-Times Online.* June 8, 2001.
*Entertainment Weekly.* June 15, 2001, p. 56.
*Los Angeles Times Online.* June 8, 2001.

*New York Times Online.* June 8, 2001.
*People.* June 18, 2001, p. 32.
*Sight and Sound.* September, 2001, p. 54.
*USA Today Online.* June 8, 2001.
*Variety.* June 4, 2001, p. 16.
*Washington Post Online.* June 8, 2001.

## QUOTES

Gabriel (John Travolta): "Misdirection. What the eyes see and the ears hear, the mind believes."

# The Tailor of Panama

*In a place this treacherous, what a good spy needs is a good spy of his own.*
—Movie tagline

**Box Office:** $13.5 million

John le Carré (the pen-name of former British intelligence officer David Cornwell) was a prime architect of Cold War spy novels, particularly *The Spy Who Came In From the Cold* (1965), but, having outlived the Cold War, he has had to find other plots. His best espionage fiction almost came to rival that of Graham Greene, involving wonderfully intricate plots and interestingly conflicted characters. This latter talent was still evident in *The Tailor of Panama* (1996), which took the genre into satiric territory—well exploited by John Boorman's film adaptation, thanks to excellent casting and a deftly written screenplay (by Andrew Davis, Boorman, and the novelist himself). Several reviewers of the film mentioned Graham Greene's *Our Man In Havana* as an antecedent, but, as Stanley Kauffmann noted in the *New Republic,* the novelist forestalled any criticism by noting in his acknowledgments for the novel that "without Graham Greene this book would never have come about." The novelist added, "After Greene's *Our Man In Havana,* the notion of an intelligence fabricator would not leave me alone."

The "tailor" of the title, Harry Pendel (Geoffrey Rush) is an imposter who claims to be carrying on the Saville Row tradition brought to Panama by his conveniently deceased partner, Arthur Braithwaite. But the "tradition" and partnership are bogus, a complete fabrication made up by Harry when he immigrated to Panama, after having served hard time for arson in a British prison. Harry knows the trade, however, which he learned in prison and has been quite successful in reinventing himself in Central America. His

wife, Louisa (Jamie Lee Curtis), a "Zonian" (i.e., an American born and raised in the Panama Canal Zone), who works for Ernesto Delgado, one of the few honest bureaucrats in Panama, knows nothing of Harry's true background.

Harry has the gift of gab, and his clients include the wealthy members of the Panamanian ruling class. But he is not a good manager, and he has invested unwisely in an unsuccessful rice farm. His bank is threatening to call in a loan that Harry, head over heels in debt, cannot possibly cover. His prospects look bleak, until, one day, dapper Andrew Osnard (Pierce Brosnan), a secret service operative assigned to the British Embassy, happens into his shop to be measured for a suit. Or so it seems. In fact, Andrew wants to recruit Harry because of Harry's connections with the ruling class, and he is willing to reward Harry for any information Harry may be willing to tender. Thus, an unholy alliance is formed. Harry is desperate for money and is given to stretching the truth. He is not really an insider, but he wants to make himself seem important to Andrew.

Andrew is a cad and a bounder who disgraced himself on a previous assignment and has been assigned to Panama by M.I.6 as a sort of punishment. He acts like a pared-down version of James Bond, Bond's evil twin, with feet of clay—a humorous touch, since Brosnan, after all, played Bond in previous movie roles—but he is actually a greedy schemer, planning to con his handlers out of millions. He comes to Harry knowing everything about Harry's past, and, after a cruel but amusing cat-and-mouse game, blackmails Harry into cooperating by threatening to expose Harry to his wife. Problem is that Harry is an incorrigible liar, who enjoys tailoring fabrications that will eventually cause problems for his friends and family. Unfortunately, Harry cannot help himself as he "giddily" ascends "to hitherto unscaled heights of fantasy" as he concocts a completely untrue conspiracy theory involving Panama's "Silent Opposition" to the thoroughly corrupt ruling class.

The action is set in 1999. There are hawks in the American military who would like nothing more than an excuse to recapture the Panama Canal. Harry's false information about political unrest in Panama goes to London and is then passed along to Washington. Harry identifies his friend Mickie Abraxas (Brendan Gleeson) as the leader of the "Silent Opposition." Mickie is an alcoholic who had served time as a political prisoner under Panama's dictator, General Manuel Noreiga. Once a radical, Mickie has had his spirit broken by torture and prison abuse. He is so afraid of being sent back to prison that he commits suicide once Harry's lies begin to complicate his life, as well as the life of Harry's faithful assistant, Marta (Leonor Varela), whose face had been scarred by Noreiga's thugs.

Harry knows that he is responsible for Mickie's despair and rash behavior. Although Harry has a conscience, Andrew does not and is utterly ruthless. Harry becomes a perfect patsy for Andrew's schemes. Andrew merely intends to take the money and run. Harry knows himself to be a "Muddler," as le Carré writes: "Somewhere in his overworked mind was an idea that he could make a gift of love to Mickie, build him into something he could never be, a Mickie redux, dried out, shining bright, militant and courageous." The film's comic irony and its parody of a silly genre stumbles for those who might reflect on the awful past that has disfigured Marta's face and turned Mickie into a pathetic, terrified drunk. In the *New Yorker,* Anthony Lane protested that, although apparently headed for high comedy, the film makes a wrong turn "and winds up as dispiriting farce." Harsh, but true.

Harry's muddling has disastrous consequences for Mickie, and, also, potentially, for himself, since he stupidly betrays his wife by copying documents she brings home to work on. Louisa, however, knows that Harry is a good man at heart, a kind husband and father, and even after he tells her the truth about himself, she is willing to forgive his indiscretions. In the novel Louisa says "Whatever you've done wrong, I've done worse. Harry I do not mind what you are or who you are or what you've done or who to." But at that point in the novel, Harry is walking away from his wife and family and into the burning city. There is no calm and easy reconciliation in the novel, which has rather more magnitude. The ghost of Harry's Uncle Benny (played by Britain's foremost playwright, Harold Pinter) appears with some frequency to help Harry get his moral bearings after he has "lost his innocence." In general, the film is true to the letter and the spirit of the novel, though, as David Stratton noted in his *Variety* review, the ending of the novel "has been modified and is now far more upbeat," but, then, le Carré himself retailored the screenplay to make the film more humorous and agreeable to a mass audience. To take one of David Stratton's examples, Andrew takes Harry into a gay bar at one point and dances with him as they talk, in order to avoid being "bugged," with Irving Berlin's "Let's Face the Music, and Dance" playing over the scene.

One problem with doing an espionage spoof built around a James Bond look-alike is that viewers may expect the real thing instead of a comic spin-off. Satire will always be a hard sell at the multiplex, even when it is expertly done, as it is in this film. Brosnan plays the villainous and manipulative Andrew to perfection as a parody of an unworthy and conniving Agent 007, but the performance of Geoffrey Rush is what makes the picture work as what *Variety* called "a stylish, sardonic addition to the spy genre." *Variety* went on to offer a warning that Columbia Pictures would have to "position the film carefully in the marketplace," since it is "not an action-adventure but a film for adults who [might] appreciate the wry humor and irony." Stephen Farber of *Movieline* wrote that Brosnan gave "the loosest, most compelling performance of his career" in this picture.

The script is witty and polished, nicely ornamented with inside jokes, as when Harry tells Andrew about another client named "Mr. Connery," or when Harry describes Panama as "Casablanca without heroes." John Boorman was generally praised for his "masterful" direction, as was cinematographer Philippe Rousselot. Although Stanley Kauffmann had some reservations about Boorman's "thematically checkered career," the director earned Academy Award® nominations for two films, *Deliverance* (1972), adapted from James Dickey's Southern gothic novel, and *Hope and Glory* (1987), which was autobiographical and sweetly nostalgic. Most reviews were positive and respectful of this absorbing, "lively, and provocative" film. This is a well made, entertaining film, though somewhat disappointing as an adaptation.

*—James M. Welsh*

## CREDITS

**Andy Osnard:** Pierce Brosnan
**Harry Pendel:** Geoffrey Rush
**Louise Pendel:** Jamie Lee Curtis
**Mickie Abraxas:** Brendan Gleeson
**Francesca:** Catherine McCormack
**Marta:** Leonor Varela
**Uncle Benny:** Harold Pinter
**Mark Pendel:** Daniel Radcliffe
**Luxmore:** David Hayman
**Rafi Domingo:** Mark Margolis
**Teddy:** Martin Ferrero
**Ambassador Malty:** John Fortune

**Origin:** USA, Ireland
**Released:** 2000
**Production:** John Boorman; Merlin Films; released by Columbia Pictures
**Directed by:** John Boorman
**Written by:** John Boorman, Andrew Davies, John Le Carre
**Cinematography by:** Philippe Rousselot
**Music by:** Shaun Davey
**Sound:** Brendan Deasy
**Editing:** Ron Davis
**Costumes:** Maeve Patterson
**Production Design:** Derek Wallace
**MPAA rating:** R
**Running time:** 109 minutes

## REVIEWS

*Boxoffice.* June, 2001, p. 61.

*Chicago Sun-Times Online.* March 30, 2001.
*Entertainment Weekly.* April 6, 2001, p. 85.
*Los Angeles Times Online.* March 30, 2001.
*New Republic.* April 30, 2001, p. 30.
*New York Times.* March 30, 2001, p. B12.
*New Yorker.* April 2, 2001, p. 98.
*People.* April 9, 2001, p. 48.
*USA Today.* March 30, 2001, p. E4.
*Variety.* February 19, 2001, p. 41.
*Washington Post.* March 30, 2001, p. C1.
*Washington Post Weekend.* March 30, 2001, p. 41.

**QUOTES**

Andy Osnard (Pierce Brosnan) to Harry Pendel (Geoffrey Rush) about spying: "It's a game. Let's have some fun."

# Tape

*some things can't be erased*
—Movie tagline

**Box Office:** $.5 million

D irector Richard Linklater brought two films to the 2001 Sundance Festival—*Waking Life* and *Tape*—and both of them were released by the end of the year. Each is among the bravest, most probing, most honest, and most mesmerizing films in recent memory, and each deserved a place among the 10 best films of 2001. Linklater's willingness to look unflinchingly at usually undiscussed aspects of human behavior and existence is matched by his risk-taking in style and technique.

Each film was shot entirely with digital videotape, and then Linklater used the videos in almost opposite fashions. Using the labor-intensive technique of rotoscoping, *Waking Life*'s original video was painted over by 30 different animators and turned into a disconcerting, exhilarating and fantastic dream/philosophical journey, and the result was one of the most original, courageous, and groundbreaking films in recent years. *Tape* is less ambitious in style and topic and much more confined in scope. Instead of ranging over deep matters of life and death and transcending space and time as *Waking Life* does, *Tape* takes place entirely within a standard motel room, with only three characters, and it focuses on their differing views of a single incident from 10 years earlier. Its running time of 86 minutes encompasses the same amount of story time—and this non-stop interaction almost has the feel of a live stage performance.

In fact, *Tape* is based on a play by Stephen Belber, who adapted his own work into the screenplay. Yet despite its hothouse atmosphere, *Tape* is never claustrophobic, thanks to the deft camera work of Linklater and cinematographer Maryse Alberti, who together constituted the entire camera crew. Their shots are both telling and unobtrusive, except for a few unfortunate sequences in which the camera pans rapidly back and forth between two participants in a conversation as each speaks—a technique that seems to be gaining in popularity but that should be consigned to the scrap heap. The technique seems designed to make the audience blatantly aware that they are watching a filmed dialogue. But doing this breaks up the emotional tension and authenticity that permeate the rest of the film. It's Linklater's one serious misjudgment. But the strength of the acting and dialogue transcend this misstep.

*Tape* doesn't need camera tricks. Its plot and dialogue are dripping with verisimilitude. Vince (Ethan Hawke) and John (Robert Sean Leonard) are two old high school buddies who have kept in touch and seen each other on occasion in the 10 years since their graduation. Their latest encounter takes place in Vince's motel room in Lansing, Michigan. Before John arrives, we see Vince chugging beers and doing push-ups in his boxer shorts. He greets his old friend gleefully. John, who has gone on to a graduate degree in filmmaking from a prestigious California school, is showing a film at the mythical Lansing Film Festival, and Vince is in town at John's request to see the film.

John soon learns that Vince's longtime girlfriend has broken up with him. John quizzes Vince closely as to why and soon passes over into lecturing. John scolds Vince for being "a dick" with violent tendencies, too rough and crude with women, and it's clear that he doesn't blame Vince's girlfriend for breaking up with him. In fact, John self-righteously passes judgment on Vince's entire life—and not without reason. Vince, who portrays himself as a firefighter, is actually a dope dealer who fights fires as a volunteer. He's also fond of getting high himself, and over the course of the first hour of their conversation consumes considerable amounts of beer, marijuana, and cocaine.

Vince, tired of ceaseless criticisms from his old best friend, defends his lifestyle against what he sees as John's high-minded but vague and pointless life as embodied in his cinematic crusade. John says he's trying to make films that will examine society's flaws, and that his big break at this film festival may give him the means to go forward. Vince cynically says that John will either make it big and follow the money or continue to wallow in pretentious artistic inconsequence, and that, in any event, his films aren't all that interesting.

It's clear that these two old friends are also bitter rivals who play a deft and complicated game of comparing their own lives and trying to control each other's behavior. Although John at first appears to have the upper hand, being more articulate and socially smooth, Vince has a plan to turn the tables. He steers the conversation to a mutual high school girlfriend, Amy, revealing that she is living in Lansing and working as an assistant district attorney. Amy was Vince's girlfriend in high school but near the end of high school John and Amy had sex, and that has remained a sore point with Vince.

Vince is adept at exposing John's hypocrisy and his capacity for talking in circles rather than zeroing in on the truth. Vince insists that John tell him exactly what happened between him and Amy. Vince thinks it was rape, and John, after much resistance, finally admits it amounted to that. At that point, Vince triumphantly produces a tape recorder, extracts the tape, and plays back John's recorded "confession" to the rape. He says he wants John to apologize to Amy, and that he will use the tape as his evidence that John raped her.

The final act plays out as Vince summons Amy (Uma Thurman, Hawke's wife) to the motel room. She believes she is coming to go out to dinner with her old friend. And then things get really interesting, as each of the three friends confronts feelings from the past that have never been properly buried. As a law enforcement professional, Amy ends up holding the trump cards.

What makes *Tape* work so well are the taut camera work and editing, a marvelous script full of humor and sarcasm and cunning repartee, and three fine acting performances. Leonard, who made a big splash as a teenager in *Dead Poets Society* but hadn't done much of great film interest since then (he's had more success on the stage), is totally convincing as a young man who has learned to speak the language of respectability and who uses his linguistic skills to control relationships. Leonard inhabits the personality of a smooth, seemingly innocent manipulator, but his face reveals the fear and self-loathing behind John's adopted air of the sensitive man.

Hawke, one of the most underrated and underappreciated actors in Hollywood, gives a disarming performance as a young man who knows his weaknesses and refuses to apologize for them, especially not to his chief rival. Hawke, an extremely versatile actor, presents Vince as a not overly bright but cunning and adept emotional gamester, a man who has finally chosen to risk his friendship with John in order to gain a twisted sort of satisfaction. Hawke is alarming and hilarious, sweet and dangerous, crazy and self-controlled.

Thurman's role is relatively small but she commands attention once she enters the room. With a few lines and nervous laughter, she conveys youthfulness, charm, and a wary but seasoned worldliness, as her character Amy navigates some tricky emotional shoals she didn't expect to encounter. It is one of her most shaded and engaging performances.

Belber's dialogue at times verges on the hysterical, but for the most part it crackles with wit and knowingness. It's pitch-perfect culturally; these characters talk like real young people in their late 20s, adept at sarcasm and irony, self-assured yet self-abnegating. It's interesting that Linklater would make a film with a character who is a rather high-minded young director making pretentious films, since some critics have accused Linklater of doing just that. They're wrong, however; Linklater makes brutally honest films. Some may consider *Waking Life* pretentious, but it would be hard to label *Tape* as such. In fact, John's character—and what *Tape* does with him—reveals Linklater to be a thoughtful, probing, and risk-taking director.

Ingmar Bergman wouldn't write the dialogue this way—it would be much more ponderous and "deep"—but in other respects that master examiner of human frailties and contradictions would be quite comfortable with the daunting and cynical interpersonal dynamics of *Tape*. Like many Bergman films, it peels off layers of personality one by one until the main characters are left raw and revealed for what they are.

Bergman would also admire some of Linklater's wonderfully simple compositions. Hawke's Vince cowers in a corner; John looms sad and forlorn, one minute a monster and the next a clown; Amy's half-terrified, half-incredulous face is reflected in a mirror. The way these characters move and interact within the crowded confines of a single motel room, and the way the camera frames them, shows that Linklater is masterful at milking maximum emotions out of simple encounters. It's a wonderfully rich minimalism. There is no grandstanding in this film, just a confident self-assurance in the powerful, direct material.

*Tape* says much about friendship, authenticity, ethical behavior, posing, and male-female relationships. Its tiny canvas is surprisingly rich in detail; and it is, in its own way, a sort of *Who's Afraid of Virginia Woolf?* for the 21st Century. With *Tape* and *Waking Life*, Linklater has produced a pair of Oscar®-worthy directorial efforts in the same year—a remarkable achievement.

—*Michael Betzold*

## CREDITS

**Vince:** Ethan Hawke
**Johnny:** Robert Sean Leonard
**Amy:** Uma Thurman

**Origin:** USA
**Released:** 2001
**Production:** Anne Walker-McBay, Gary Winick, Alexis Alexanian; Detour Filmproduction, InDigEnt; released by Lion's Gate Films

**Directed by:** Richard Linklater
**Written by:** Stephen Belber
**Cinematography by:** Maryse Alberti
**Editing:** Sandra Adair
**Costumes:** Catherine Thomas
**Production Design:** Stephen Beatrice
**MPAA rating:** R
**Running time:** 86 minutes

## REVIEWS

*Boxoffice.* November, 2001, p. 38.
*Chicago Sun-Times Online.* November 16, 2001.
*Detroit News Online.* December 14, 2001.
*Entertainment Weekly.* November 9, 2001, p. 81.
*Los Angeles Times Online.* November 2, 2001.
*New York Times Online.* November 2, 2001.
*People.* November 12, 2001, p. 38.
*USA Today Online.* November 2, 2001.
*Variety.* February 5, 2001, p. 37.
*Washington Post.* November 16, 2001, p. WE43.

# The Taste of Others (Le Gout des Autres)

**Box Office:** $.9 million

Noted scenarist-cum-actress Agnes Jaoui's willfully naughty debut film from France, *The Taste of Others,* will hopefully get American audiences and filmmakers to hang loose as regards those two contemporary evils: illicit drug use and promiscuous sex. In her sprightly comedy-drama, as this subgenre has come to be known in France, both the above "scourges" are embodied in the character of Manie (played by the co-writer and director herself), an attractive, prescient barmaid in Rouen, in the north of France, who makes a play for any man she finds desirable, as if the realm of sex were free of transmittable diseases, fatal or otherwise. Manie also (shock, shock) has no compunctions about using and dealing varieties of hashish in her spare time. While Manie remains a subsidiary character, she functions as the film's liberal, and liberating, conscience, set apart from the ideological tug-of-war revolving around the antinomies of taste.

Castella (Jean-Pierre Bacri), the film's main concern, a seemingly guileless, mild-mannered oil magnate, represents a man so self-made as to be lacking even the basic cultural

wherewithal required for hobnobbing amongst the arty literati. In the film's opening scene, his domineering harridan of a wife, Angelique (Christiane Millet), has to remind him over lunch, in the presence of his right-hand man, Weber (Xavier De Guillebon), a French yuppie, that "those little cakes," as he calls them, are really "petit fours," a prompt that is followed by the admonition that he has surpassed his quota of rich food as it is. Castella would like to cast this clinical advice to the winds, but Angelique prevails.

Since Castella is in the process of signing an oil deal with the Iranians, an insurance company requires that he be accompanied by a bodyguard, Moreno (Gerard Lanvin), at all times. With nothing to do while their boss pursues his high-powered tasks, Deschamps (Alain Chabat), Castella's chauffeur, and Moreno exchange notes about their work and private life. Moreno relates how an airtight case against a politician had to be dropped because of pressures from the top. Deschamps, on his part, confides of how his sex life has been put on hold because of his girlfriend being away in the States.

From this basic situation of Castella's home and business affairs, the film's social realism expands outward to take in a range of sensibilities, and tastes, prevalent within its setting. Jaoui's perspective, as filmmaker, becomes that of a social butterfly, so that interesting scenes are repeatedly cut short, but not arbitrarily, as is so often the case in social comedies, but by the flow of life. It is that element of the unforeseeable that eventually asserts itself in its own unique way towards the end of the film.

For a start, Deschamps' path accidentally crosses that of Manie when he steps into her bar for a drink. She is someone with whom he has had sex, but now cannot remember. Manie attributes this lapse to his gender. "It happens mostly to guys," she muses. "Different plumbing. Different implications." When Deschamps relates his failing to Moreno, the latter puts him at ease by admitting that out of the 300 women he has slept with, he remembers only 20. Deschamps' naivete proves a perfect foil for Manie's worldliness when we see both of them in bed that evening. Confessing as to why he cannot have a relationship with her, Deschamps confesses, "I have a girlfriend." With a laugh, Manie intones, "You're so sweet!" We later come to know that Manie has her sights set elsewhere.

The vagaries of Cupid's arrow are, as would be expected, reserved for Castella. We see him in his office peremptorily dismissing Clara (Anne Alvaro), an unassuming part-time stage actress who has come to apply for the post of teaching him English. That night, however, when Angelieque drags him to the theater to see his niece, Virginie (Celine Arnaud), in Racine's *Berenice,* Castella is enraptured by Clara in the title role. The following night, he returns to see the play by himself. This time, he's visibly moved to tears. In her dressing room, he tells Clara that she's got the job. We are set up for Castella's extramarital dalliance through a scene between

Manie and Clara, in which the latter sees herself as nothing more than a "jobless 40-year-old actress." Life has also turned Clara into a cynic, so that she finds hope "pathetic," and now "cannot make the effort to find a guy." Even so, her relationship with Castella doesn't really get going, as we would expect it to. It is an English lesson, and nothing more.

Later, through a chance remark Clara makes to Antoine (Wladimir Yordanoff), her producer friend, we learn precisely why. It is Castella flaunting his wealth that Clara sees as an affront to her sensibility. "To impress me," Clara relates, "he added a hundred francs to the bill, then told the waiter to keep the change." This, combined with Castella's utter lack of schooling even in traditional culture, is enough for her to condemn him as a "jerk." At a café, in the presence of Antoine, Castella, with a good-natured smile, commits the blunder of identifying a piece of classical muzak as the theme from the "Juanita Banana" commercial, a blooper akin to referring to the "Peer Gynt" overture as the theme from "The Lone Ranger."

The parallel storylines range from Angelique helping Beatrice (Brigitte Catillon), Castella's divorced and perpetually morose sister, with designing her apartment, to Flucky, Angelique's poodle, whose urge to bite at strangers remains unchecked. The most interesting subplot, however, remains that of Manie boldly making a play for Moreno, leaving Deschamps alone with his idealism. This time, we actually see Manie and her new lover in the throes of sexual desire. Yet, here again, it is Manie's different lifestyle (read "taste," if you will) that comes in between. When she lights up a joint of hashish in bed, Moreno is not prepared to take even a puff. Furthermore, he becomes upset when he finds her dealing in order to support her meager income. With a skillful bit of framing, Jaoui has Manie conducting a drug transaction in the foreground of the shot, with an amoral swiftness, while Moreno sits, slumped, cheerless, in her kitchen in the background. "Cigarettes are ten times worse!" she screams, but Moreno storms out just the same.

Castella, as befitting his generous nature, uses his plastic in an attempt to fit in with Clara's crowd, even to the extent of picking up the drinking tab for as many as ten of her cohorts. Yet each attempt only makes things worse. While exploiting him, Clara's friends are cruel in their snobbery. After recounting an off-color joke at a café soiree, Castella suggests the troupe do comedies, which could get them a larger audience. "We're doing Ibsen next," says one. "He's a real Norwegian comic!" Castella nods, smiling. Then, another pipes up: "And what about Strindberg? He's even funnier!"

If that isn't enough to ostracize Castella in Clara's eyes, there's his total lack of tact. At an art opening, he calls the critics who haven't bothered to attend a bunch of "faggots," thereby bristling the feathers not only of Antoine, but of his artist-lover, Benoit (Raphael Defour). Subsequently, Castella apologizes for his political incorrectness by saying to

Antoine: "I meant 'faggot' as a figure of speech." "That's just the problem," Antoine shoots back. The kindly soul that he is, Castella bends over backwards to make amends by buying one of Benoit's paintings, and giving him the commission to redesign the front of his office building.

Castella's romantic infatuation with Clara finds expression when, with the innocence of a schoolboy, he reads out a poem he has composed for her in English. She however is quick to nip any personal sentiment in the bud. A crestfallen Castella merely accepts her decision. Eventually, Castella, who has been absorbing insults to his taste like a milquetoast, gets to let off steam. When Clara comes to warn him that Antoine and Benoit may be exploiting his kind nature, he defends his choices by claiming to possess an innate aesthetic sense. Similarly, when he finds that Angelique has removed the Benoit painting he had purchased from the wall of their living room, he uses the occasion to rant at her taste, saying that she has turned their house into a "candy box."

In keeping with the flow of life dictating the film's narrative, the accidental rears its ugly head. During a rare instance when Castella is left alone—as Deschamps goes to get Moreno from Manie's apartment—he is mugged, but loses only his wallet. As Manie nurses his head wound, she also helps in cementing his bond with Clara who, at the film's end, has had a change of heart, and is now ready to accept him.

Reviewers seem to have unanimously noted the film's true-to-life feel. Stephen Holden in the *New York Times* calls it "a witty, sociologically astute reflection on the attraction between opposites" that is "beautifully acted" and shows "a rich understanding of human quirks." Andrew Sarris in the *New York Observer* finds the film "goes beyond satire into Chekhovian irony as it traces a variety of socially awkward moments without condescension or exaggeration."

—*Vivek Adarkar*

## CREDITS

**Castella:** Jean-Pierre Bacri
**Angelique:** Christiane Millet
**Manie:** Agnes Jaoui
**Clara:** Anne Alvaro
**Moreno:** Gerard Lanvin
**Antoine:** Wladimir Yordanoff
**Beatrice:** Brigitte Catillon
**Weber:** Xavier De Guillebon
**Deschamps:** Alain Chabet
**Benoit:** Raphael Defour

**Origin:** France
**Language:** French

**Released:** 2000
**Production:** Charles Gassot, Christian Berard; released by Offline Releasing
**Directed by:** Agnes Jaoui
**Written by:** Jean-Pierre Bacri, Agnes Jaoui
**Cinematography by:** Laurent Dailland
**Music by:** Jean-Charles Jarrell
**Editing:** Herve De Luze
**Production Design:** Francois Emmanuelli
**MPAA rating:** Unrated
**Running time:** 112 minutes

## REVIEWS

*Boxoffice.* November, 2000, p. 172.
*Chicago Sun-Times Online.* March 9, 2001.
*Entertainment Weekly.* February 16, 2001, p. 73.
*Los Angeles Times Online.* March 2, 2001.
*New York Observer Online.* February 12, 2001.
*New York Times Online.* October 6, 2000.
*New York Times Online.* February 4, 2001.
*Newsweek.* February 26, 2001, p. 70.
*Wall Street Journal Online.* March 2, 2001.

## TRIVIA

Agnes Jaoui and Jean-Pierre Bacri also wrote and starred in *Un Air de Famille/Family Resemblances* and *On Connait la Chanson/Same Old Song.*

# Thomas in Love (Thomas Est Amoureux)

*Introducing the age of virtual romance.*
—Movie tagline

Belgian screenwriter Philippe Blasband and director Pierre-Paul Renders create a new definition for computer dating with their futuristic feature, *Thomas in Love.* Not only does this filmmaking team sterilize romantic encounters via cyberspace but they also place the viewer into the protagonist Thomas' (Benoit Verhaert) head as he struggles with his psychosis and sexual urges. Thomas sufferers from acute agoraphobia and hasn't left his apartment in over eight years nor has he had any physical contact with other human beings. It appears that Thomas has adapted to his situation. His mother (Micheline Hardy), psychologist (Frèdèric Topart), and insurance agent/manager (Alexandre von Sivers) all communicate with Thomas via a visaphone (in which the characters can see each other while they talk) and Thomas pursues a sexual relationship with an animated woman via his computer.

However, as anyone would imagine, Thomas has grown restless with his usual routine. His psychologist signs Thomas up for a computer dating service and his manager informs Thomas that the insurance company will cover the cost of prostitutes for handicapped persons such as Thomas. Soon various desperate woman, including a young mother with wailing children, invade Thomas' privacy. However, Thomas deflects the women by telling them that he will never leave his home and they would have to have a relationship with him via the visaphone. Eventually two women, Eva (Aylin Yay), a distraught, surly prostitute and a poet, Mèlodie (Magali Pinglault), enter Thomas' life. The lonely Mèlodie and Thomas hit it off until Mèlodie engages in cybersex with Thomas. Later, she confesses to Thomas that she found cybersex creepy and longed to visit Thomas at home so she could touch him. Thomas refuses to see anyone in person and so the short-lived relationship ends.

Feeling rejected Thomas stalks Eva over the phone and blackmails her into giving him her code. Eventually, Thomas falls in love and convinces the tough-as-nails Eva to date him. Eva tells Thomas that she will only pursue a relationship with him if he exits his apartment. But once Thomas exits his apartment, he suffers convulsions and lands in the hospital. Eva, who has been serving a prison sentence through an arrangement in which she acts as a prostitute for disabled men, is forced to disappear for breaking the rules that govern her imprisonment. As the film ends, we see Thomas for the first time (shot from behind), as he walks out of his sequestered apartment into a white light in which we hear the faint sound of a woman screaming.

Upon hearing the film's synopsis, a 32-year-old agoraphobic living in a computerized world stumbles onto love with a prostitute, one might compare *Thomas in Love* to the 2001 release *Center of the World.* The two films share many common denominators. Both films were shot on digital video, both feature a computer geek in search of love in the real world, and both comment on our involvement in the technological age, but the Belgian release focuses less on sex and more on human connections. We never see Thomas until the end of the film as he exits his sterile environment and throughout the film the viewer is forced to see the world through Thomas' eyes as his disembodied voice communicates to all of the people staring at us through Thomas' computer screen. We never see two people engaging in the sexual act and all the sex is computer-simulated, leading us to believe that even an erotic act could be completely sanitized.

The filmmakers had a lot to say about the current age in which we reside. Modern psychology, high tech devices, New Age philosophy, and tribal rituals such as face painting color this film. On first look, it appears that metaphysical elements are used as a counter force to the faceless technology that rules the characters' lives, but even the metaphysical elements lack deeper meaning. One woman brags about how she visits sweat tents similar to the Native American's sweat lodge ceremonies, but she's unaware of the reason for the Indian practice. The characters recall trendy rave devotees who treat shamanism like the latest fashion.

Renders and Blasband had a single goal in mind. Renders stated that he desired "to submerge the spectator in the claustrophobic universe of an agoraphobic, hoping that he/she would come out of it with pins and needles ... inside his/her head." The filmmakers succeeded in creating an unforgettable yet creepy film served best by seeking solace from the outside world.

—*Patty-Lynne Herlevi*

## CREDITS

**Thomas:** Benoit Verhaert
**Eva:** Aylin Yay
**Melodie:** Magali Pinglault
**Nathalie:** Micheline Hardy
**Insurance agent:** Alexandre von Sivers
**Psychologist:** Frederic Topart
**Receptionist:** Serge Lariviere

**Origin:** Belgium
**Language:** French
**Released:** 2001
**Production:** Diana Elbaum; Chien et Loup, JBA Production; released by IFC Films
**Directed by:** Pierre-Paul Renderss
**Written by:** Philippe Blasband
**Cinematography by:** Virginie Saint-Martin
**Music by:** Igor Sterpin
**Sound:** Olivier Hespel
**Editing:** Ewin Ryckaert
**Costumes:** Anne Fournier
**Production Design:** Pierre Gerbaux
**Animation:** Fred Beltran
**MPAA rating:** Unrated
**Running time:** 97 minutes

## REVIEWS

*Boxoffice.* July, 2001, p. 93.
*Chicago Sun-Times Online.* August 24, 2001.
*Entertainment Weekly.* August 17, 2001, p. 48.
*Los Angeles Times Online.* August 3, 2001.
*New York Times Online.* August 3, 2001.
*San Francisco Chronicle Online.* August 3, 2001.

# 3000 Miles to Graceland

*Crime Is King.*
—Movie tagline

 **Box Office:** $15.7 million

If Elvis Presley's memory had not already been tarnished for merchandising purposes more times than radio stations have played "Heartbreak Hotel," the feckless *3,000 Miles to Graceland* might be considered the most offensive celebrity homage in film history. But the ghost of Elvis must have become accustomed long ago to junk being perpetrated in his name, so this reprehensible film about a ruthless killer claiming to be Elvis's illegitimate child is merely more white trash.

From the title and the film's promotional campaign, one might expect this movie to be a bit of delicious brain candy about a group of thieves robbing a Las Vegas casino while posing as entrants in an Elvis impersonator contest. But brain candy has to have at least a minimal connection to the cerebellum, and this junkyard film is unabashedly visceral, from its grotesque, MTV-style imagery to its thumping, mindless soundtrack to its unsympathetic, cardboard characters. In style, *Graceland* most resembles Oliver Stone's *Natural Born Killers,* but it utterly lacks the daring, inventiveness, and satirical impact of that film.

The first-time screenwriter-director responsible for this mess announces *3,000 Miles to Graceland* as a "Demian Lichtenstein film," but to call this series of extended music videos, gunfight bloodbaths, and obscene vignettes a film is a stretch. This is a film in the same sense in which an Elvis impersonators show is a concert. There is absolutely nothing fresh or original in this two hours of dim-witted self-indulgence. And it is something of a fraud too. The title makes no sense—neither Las Vegas, nor any of the spots to its north where the criminals flee after the heist, is 3,000 miles from Memphis, the site of Presley's famous mansion. The advertising of the movie is misleading too. A story about a heist at an Elvis impersonators show holds the promise of comic criminal creativity. But the actual robbery is neither funny nor inventive, and takes place entirely in the first half-hour. It's just an excuse for a shootout, and the rest of the film has little to do with the Elvis plot line.

Lichtenstein, a veteran director of music videos, sees no stylistic distinctions between them and feature films. He revels in volleys of gunfire. When the gang gets the loot at the casino and tries to escape up an elevator to a rooftop, the outlaws spray security guards, blackjack tables, slot machines, and glass walls—*especially* glass walls—with hailstorms of bullets. The camera cuts back and forth to the floor show and its scantily clad dancers gyrating around a phony Elvis. In this and subsequent shootout scenes, the soundtrack pumps with high-energy rock or rap. Later, in a climactic warehouse shootout, a gunman suspends himself upside-down from a ceiling and whirls about firing madly. These are two of the least creative action scenes imaginable. There is nothing interesting about the gunfights, except a huge body count. And there is nothing novel about Lichtenstein's directorial techniques, which use stock music-video tricks such as speeded-up photography of zooming cars and clouds.

Kevin Costner looks ridiculous as the vile Thomas Murphy, the gang leader who believes himself to be Elvis's bastard child. His triangular sideburns nearly touch the corners of his mouth. In oversized tinted sunglasses and his Elvis impersonator suit, his face pinched with a sneer, Costner's Murphy strides through the casino looking exactly like an aging superstar trying out another ill-fitting macho part. Murphy's actions are consistently soulless—he kills people for sport and to get them out of his way—but Costner doesn't give this villain any particular zing or compelling motivation. He's flat and one-dimensional, not twisted or horrifying, and Costner is so low-key his character becomes a puzzle, but not a very intriguing one. The biographical back story about Murphy's relationship to Elvis makes little sense, because Costner does little that references the famed pop singer. The whole Elvis motif is a just a coat hanger on which to suspend a very ordinary story about the members of a criminal gang turning on one another.

Kurt Russell, who plays Murphy's partner Michael Zane, is the film's sole saving grace. He looks like a bloated, Vegas-era Elvis, with a fat face, a slow-moving brain and an easily bamboozled personality. Michael is supposed to be the criminal with a heart, though his heart is encased in icy distrust. He's not pure evil like Murphy; he's the stereotypical career criminal who really doesn't want to hurt anybody but just get enough money to retire and sail his boat. Russell makes the most out of a character who's been seen in films time and time again—the misunderstood, well-meaning bad guy.

Of course, Michael is a hard-ass just waiting to be melted by the love of a passionate woman who sees his sensitivity beneath his criminal armor. This thankless task falls to Courteney Cox, who plays Cybil Waingrow, a stunning piece of trailer trash with a son named Jesse James, who is a thief in the making. Cox is a long way from television's *Friends* here, and she struggles mightily to give her character some shred of believability or motivation. But Lichtenstein's script is the kind where women fall head over heels for gunmen, explaining that they have a jolt of electricity run

through them when they lay eyes on a latter-day cowboy. (Later, another young woman begs for a chance to ride with Costner's Murphy after he senselessly shoots up her old man and blows up their gas station.)

Cox's Cybil and Russell's Michael have about as much romantic chemistry between them as Costner's Murphy has an emotional nexus with Elvis. Lichtenstein's idea of a budding attraction is to have the pair go directly from suggestive conversation to the crudest sort of bang-the-bed lovemaking. Why does Cybil keep pursuing this guy? There is no answer. But then Lichtenstein's story is very short on logic. In one crucial plot twist, Cybil abandons her son to the care of Michael in order to steal Michael's car and his bag of loot and take off to get it laundered, hundreds of miles away. This is the film's idea of a loving mother. It's also a weak excuse to have Jesse (David Kaye) do a stretch of absurd male bonding scenes with Michael.

The chase-and-pursue plot rambles and roams northward, in fits and starts, never building up any real tension, and zigzagging across chasms of logic and believability. There's no explanation given or even sought for why the getaway helicopter arrives late to the casino heist, or why the police are helpless to pursue it. Into the unholy mix are thrown Jon Lovitz as the money-laundering antique dealer with a bad case of false bravado; Christian Slater, Bokeem Woodbine, and David Arquette as the gang's quickly-dispatched remaining members; and ex-football player Howie Long as Murphy's logistics expert. A couple of casual federal marshals, including one played for cheap laughs by Kevin Pollak, seem content to sit in their office and trace the criminals' routes on maps, until they finally strap on some weapons and move in to take down Murphy. The other marshal opines, leaning over a bloodied criminal corpse: "I'm glad he didn't give up. I wouldn't have." Right.

*Graceland* is full of gratuitous violence and other totally senseless bits of obscenity, and many such moments involve the young Jesse to add some crude puerile humor. The men revel in their insensitivity while the women chase them as if they were gods. There is not a shred of romance in the subplot involving Cox and Russell. As an action film, *Graceland* fails miserably, because Costner's character is not a compelling villain and the shootout scenes are both pedestrian and excessive. Lichtenstein's idea of pumping up the action is to have the combatants fire more shots. The director doesn't sustain any psychological tension because plot points are not allowed to build; almost every significant dramatic encounter takes place within the framework of a single scene. Nothing takes place that is hidden, mysterious or below the surface; nothing is demanded of the viewer. There is little or no irony to this cartoon, so, even with a generous dose of charity, there is no chance of interpreting it as a satire of the genre from which it so shamelessly pilfers material.

Regardless of the execution, studio executives know that if you get the right cast, you can get a boxoffice bang for your buck. But at what cost? Costner's presence in this film represents another, particularly shameful step in the long and inglorious decline of his once respectable career. Russell finds himself strapped into yet another silent-man role, after the promise of a breakout with his brilliant performance in *Breakdown*. Cox isn't likely to help her transition from television to film stardom with this rather muddled, unsympathetic portrayal. As for Lichtenstein, he should stick to music videos. If not the worst movie of the year 2001, *3,000 Miles to Graceland* certainly is a leading contender for the most tawdry.

—*Michael Betzold*

## CREDITS

**Murphy:** Kevin Costner
**Michael Zane:** Kurt Russell
**Hanson:** Christian Slater
**Franklin:** Bokeem Woodbine
**Gus:** David Arquette
**Cybil Waingrow:** Courteney Cox Arquette
**Damitry:** Kevin Pollak
**Jay Peterson:** Jon Lovitz
**Jack:** Howie Long
**Quigley:** Thomas Haden Church
**Hamilton:** Ice-T
**Jesse Waingrow:** David Kaye

**Origin:** USA
**Released:** 2001
**Production:** Elie Samaha, Andrew Stevens, Demian Lichtenstein, Richard Spero, Eric Manes; Morgan Creek Productions, Franchise Pictures, Lightstone Entertainment; released by Warner Bros.
**Directed by:** Demian Lichtenstein
**Written by:** Demian Lichtenstein, Richard Recco
**Cinematography by:** David Franco
**Music by:** George S. Clinton
**Sound:** Michael Williamson
**Editing:** Michael J. Duthie, Miklos Wright
**Art Direction:** Willie Heslup
**Costumes:** Mary McLeod
**Production Design:** Robert De Vico
**MPAA rating:** R
**Running time:** 125 minutes

## REVIEWS

*Boxoffice.* May, 2001, p. 61.
*Chicago Sun-Times Online.* February 23, 2001.
*Entertainment Weekly.* March 2, 2001, p. 40.
*New York Times Online.* February 23, 2001.
*People.* March 5, 2001, p. 37.
*Variety.* February 26, 2001, p. 39.
*Washington Post Online.* February 23, 2001.

## QUOTES

Jay (Jon Lovitz) after Murphy (Kevin Costner) fires an arrow at him: "You almost hit me! What are you?! Nuts?!" Murphy: "Probably."

# Tigerland

*The system wanted them to become soldiers. One soldier just wanted to be human.*
—Movie tagline

Set in 1971, *Tigerland* managed to be about the Vietnam war without ever taking viewers to Southeast Asia. The action begins in a military barracks in Fort Polk, Louisiana, where fresh recruits have been sent for eight weeks of basic training. After they have finished at Fort Polk, the next stop is "Tigerland," the last phase of combat boot camp training before the recruits are sent to Nam to become grunts and get their baptism of fire. But "Tigerland" approximates jungle conditions and provides its own baptism of fire. Structurally this picture refigures the action of almost any war film ever made. In particular, it resembles the first half of Stanley Kubrick's *Full Metal Jacket* (1987). The Private Joker character in *Tigerland* is a soldier named Roland Bazz (Colin Farrell), who is more than merely a cynical smart aleck. Like Kubrick's Joker, he is smart enough to realize he is in an absurd "world of shit," but unlike Joker, he becomes an antimilitary activist. He resists being trapped in the army.

A college dropout from Texas, Bozz has a single agenda—to get himself out of the army. The problem is that he is a natural leader whom the other recruits turn to for advice, and he has a conscience. "I heard that if you want out, you have to either pray to Jesus or talk to Roland Bozz," one recruit tells him. Early on Bozz befriends Jim Paxton (Matthew Davis), who wants to be a writer and has enlisted so that he can experience the war first-hand. Bozz sees to it that Paxton is wounded in a training skirmish and discharged. He also finds a way out of the army for two others, a young farmer named Cantwell (Thomas Guiry) with a wife and four kids to support who only has had a sixth-grade education and was tricked into the army by dishonest recruiters who did nothing to inform him of his hardship status, and a soldier named Miter (Clifton Collins, Jr.), who cracks under the pressure of boot camp. Bozz therefore alienates himself from the military leadership by helping these men. His nemesis is Sergeant Thomas (James McDonald), who is unable to control Bozz. Sergeant Landers (Afemo Omilami), an African-American, has better luck in dealing with Bozz and seems to understand him better than the others. But when Bozz needs their help and support later on, he finds himself essentially on his own.

The most scary recruit is a racist redneck named Wilson (Shea Whigham), who is a crazed psychopath intent on killing Bozz, whom he hates. Wilson turns his pistol on Bozz on the firing range and would have killed him had the weapon not jammed. Bozz understandably wants Wilson court-martialed, but the commanding officer, Captain Saunders (Nick Searcy) tells Bozz "I'll take care of Wilson." Wilson is not court-martialed, however, and turns up later to confront Bozz in Tigerland, firing on him with live ammunition. Wilson is a natural born killer, and the army is willing to send him to war, crazy or not.

In the Tigerland ordeal the recruits are under the supervision of Sergeant Cota (Cole Hauser), who had already served two tours of duty in Vietnam. Bozz survives his second encounter with Wilson, and the film ends with Bozz and his men being shipped out for Southeast Asia. Just before they leave, Paxton tells Bozz he is going to write a novel about him, but Bozz says at the end "No, you're not." As the convoy drives off, Bozz waves Paxton's journal out of the bus window and rips out the pages, destroying it.

While in Tigerland, Bozz had devised a plan to go AWOL and escape from Louisiana to Mexico. The only reason he does not follow through is that he realizes that Wilson is a real threat and needs to be taken care of, since this psychopath is sure to get someone killed in Vietnam. A final voice-over from Paxton, who apparently did write the story after all, tells us that Bozz "disappeared" missing in action in Vietnam. A friend later told Paxton that he thought he had seen Bozz in Mexico with a beautiful woman, but the "truth" about what happened to Bozz is finally wrapped in mystery. The film also begins with a voice-over that establishes the theme, again, enigmatically: "My father said that the army makes all men into one man, but you never know which one."

The plot, scripted by Ross Klaven and Michael McGruther, is simple, but tight and effective. Director Joel Schumacher shot the film on a shoestring budget with a cast of talented but unknown actors, led by the 24-year-old Irish stage actor Colin Farrell from Castleknock, Ireland, as Bozz, who rather steals the show. Mike Clark of USA Today saw Bozz as a "throwback to the hardheaded Prewitt character Montgomery Clift played in From Here to Eternity," director Fred Zinnemann's Academy Award®–winning Pearl Harbor epic made in 1953. Clark thought the film might have done better had it been made in 1971, but 30 years later, though "it has the feel of authenticity," it "also feels like a movie out of its time." In fact, it has been years since Hollywood produced its last Vietnam film.

In his Variety review Emanuel Levy praised Tigerland as "the most coherent and satisfying work" Joel Schumacher had done since Falling Down (1993), his film about a well-structured businessman (Michael Douglas) driven to madness of the urban chaos of Los Angeles. Levy was also the first reviewer to notice that in Tigerland, Schumacher had been influenced by the Dogma 95 style of filmmaking. Later reviewers also noticed the hand-held camera work and the grainy 16-millimeter stock that helped to enhance the apparent "reality" of the story. New Republic reviewer Stanley Kauffmann was impressed by the "open-pore realism" of this fiction film and singled out the "documentary grit" of Matthew Libatique's camerawork for special praise.

"Films about military training are not scarce," Stanley Kauffmann wrote, "but most of them are hard in manner and soft at the core, accounts of how seasoned commanders make tough soldiers out of civilian putty, with the men grateful and proud at the end." But Tigerland, he concludes, "shows us men more obedient than keen; yet, paradoxically, they share a growing awareness of group existence." Though effectively creating a sense of entrapment, the film also creates "the sense of the making of a unit."

New York Times reviewer A.O. Scott was less enthusiastic, however, claiming that "beneath the rough vérité exterior" of this film "beats the same slick, corny heart that has pumped blood (and money) through Mr. Schumacher's Batman" (in fact, Schumacher directed the sequel, Batman Forever, in1995) and "his revanchist provocation Falling Down." Scott also objected to the film's "secondhand sentimentality," its "stagy" speechmaking, and the way Bozz is "pushed unconvincingly toward sainthood" at the end. "as he heads off to [a] war from which he has saved so many of his friends, toward implicit martyrdom." Scott used the film as a springboard for an ad hominem attack on the director and his previous work. This was the sort of review that could send a film straight to video, and, perhaps, did just that.

In Tigerland, Joel Schumacher is attempting to make a low-budget, anti-war picture with a cast of relative unknowns and manages to create a credible picture that has something to say worth listening to. He is courageous enough to take chances by making a picture that goes against the grain of mainstream Hollywood features. He has discovered a potential new star of considerable talent and charisma. This picture was far better than dozens of others that were far more expensive to make. But Schumacher's work went unnoticed by the movie-going public, proving that not all independent features are destined for success.

Despite more enthusiastic reviews and a strong reception at the Toronto International Film Festival, Tigerland performed poorly in limited release. Emanuel

Levy's prediction in *Variety* was surely on target: "even under the best circumstances, critical support and effective marketing will be crucial for the positioning of this intimately scaled Fox picture." It got good critical support from Stanley Kauffmann and from Lisa Schwarzbaum in *Entertainment Weekly*, who wrote enthusiastically of the film as "a blast of fresh air in the Hollywood jungle, an inspiration." Effective marketing, however, was not forthcoming. The film, made on a modest budget of only $8 million, deserved much better than it got.

—*James M. Welsh*

## CREDITS

**Roland Bozz:** Colin Farrell
**Jim Paxton:** Matthew Davis
**Miter:** Clifton (Gonzalez) Collins Jr.
**Cantwell:** Tom Guiry
**Johnson:** Russell Richardson
**Sgt. Cota:** Cole Hauser
**Wilson:** Shea Whigham

**Origin:** USA
**Released:** 2000
**Production:** Arnon Milchan, Steven Haft, Beau Flynn; Regency Enterprises, New Regency Pictures, Haft Entertainment; released by 20th Century-Fox
**Directed by:** Joel Schumacher
**Written by:** Ross Klaven, Michael McGruther
**Cinematography by:** Matthew Libatique
**Music by:** Nathan Larsen
**Sound:** Jay Meager
**Editing:** Mark Stevens
**Art Direction:** Andrew Laws
**MPAA rating:** R
**Running time:** 101 minutes

## REVIEWS

*Boxoffice*. November, 2000, p. 178.
*Entertainment Weekly*. October 13, 2000, p. 43.
*Entertainment Weekly*. November 3, 2000, p. 23.
*New Republic*. October 16, 2000, p. 40.
*New York Times*. October 6, 2000, p. B14.
*People*. October 16, 2000, p. 43.
*Rolling Stone*. October 12, 2000, p. 100.
*USA Today*. October 6, 2000, p. E6.
*Variety*. September 18, 2000, p. 29.

## QUOTES

Roland Bozz (Colin Farrell): "Courage is when you're the only guy who knows how scared you are."

## AWARDS AND NOMINATIONS

**Nomination:**
**Ind. Spirit 2001:** Support. Actor (Hauser).

# Time and Tide (Seunlau Ngaklau)

*Trust is fatal.*
—Movie tagline
*No tigers, no dragons . . . just a hell of a lot of bullets.*
—Movie tagline

Time and Tide gives requisite flash to the Hong Kong action genre, but there's not much substance behind all the blood and glittery gore. In the story by Koan Hui and director Tsui Hark, Tyler (Nicholas Tse), dreams of a better life than his one in Hong Kong. Tyler's idea of scoring big and settling in a South American paradise is interrupted when he meets Jack (Wu Bai), a jungle combat mercenary who urges Tyler to join his father-in-law's bodyguard team.

At first, Tyler and Jack become close friends, but later they grow apart over their feelings toward drug trafficking. In addition, both men have complicated love lives: Tyler pursues Ah Jo, the policewoman (Cathy Chui) he impregnated one wild night, but she wants nothing to do with him; and Jack tries to spend time with his pregnant wife Ah Hui (Candy Lo), but his dangerous work keeps him away from home. Ultimately, a showdown determines who will live and who will die according to the laws of the lawless.

Tsui Hark's *Time and Tide* revives the Hong Kong martial arts film with stylish, imaginative direction. Scene after scene features dazzling stunts, great design, rapid montage, and dizzying camerawork. The story is secondary to the action, which is fierce and constant. The characters are not very well developed, but the actors play their roles with energy and zest.

Tsui Hark seems to get the formula just right, which is not surprising given his previous experience with such films (including *Peking Opera Blues*). But like the work of Jean-Pierre Jeunet and Marc Caro (*Delicatessen*, *Amelie*), Hark's new film is all surface razzle-dazzle, which eventually grows tiring to watch. At least John Woo paces his action flicks to make the "big" moments count. But Hark seems to think every moment ought to be "big"; though only 110 minutes long, *Time and Tide* feels at least three times that length.

More disturbingly, Hark reverses whatever gains were made ideologically in *Crouching Tiger, Hidden Dragon* by making the women silly caricatures (since both leading women characters are pregnant, it also keeps them out of the men's macho action). But fans of the genre won't be all that disappointed since *Time and Tide* isn't really worse than the old model—it's just a lot gaudier.

—*Eric Monder*

## CREDITS

**Tyler:** Nicholas Tse
**Jack:** Wu Bai
**Uncle Ji:** Anthony Wong
**Ah Hui:** Candy Lo
**Ah Jo:** Cathy Chui
**Miguel:** Joventino Couto Remotigue

**Origin:** Hong Kong
**Language:** Chinese
**Released:** 2000
**Production:** Tsui Hark; Film Workshop Co. Ltd.; released by TriStar Pictures
**Directed by:** Tsui Hark
**Written by:** Tsui Hark, Koan Hui
**Cinematography by:** Herman Yau, Ko Chiu-lam
**Music by:** Tommy Wai
**Sound:** Martin Richard
**Editing:** Marco Mak
**MPAA rating:** R
**Running time:** 113 minutes

## REVIEWS

*Chicago Sun-Times Online.* March 18, 2001.
*Los Angeles Times Online.* May 4, 2001.
*New York Times Online.* May 11, 2001.
*San Francisco Chronicle.* June 22, 2001, p. C3.
*Washington Post Online.* May 4, 2001.

# Time of Favor

Awarded six major Israeli Oscars, Joseph Cedar's debut feature, *Time of Favor*, unspools as a film meant for an Israeli audience. In this, it is honestly insular. Had it been aimed at a world market, it would have exploited the sensationalistic aspects of its subject matter. Cedar is clearly wary of the subversive potential of the plot elements he is handling, and so, remains content to approach them at a tangent.

Menachem (Aki Avni), his hero, a dark, handsome soldier with a congenial disposition, is the farthest thing from a religious militant. The film opens with him on leave from the army for two days. On a stretch of highway, in the early light of dawn, Menachem is waiting for a ride. The van that stops for him is packed with passengers, amongst whom is Michal (Tinkerbell), a plain-looking but kindly rabbi's daughter. She smiles at Menachem as he gets in. The film thus sets into motion its romantic trajectory, putting it across as one nurtured by providence. Yet it is a romance that is slow to develop. In the very next scene, as the two get down from the van at the same town, we can see that nothing of note has taken place between them, since they part with a smile.

In the film's scheme of things, the working of fate that we have seen transpire is pitted against the will of a male orthodoxy, both revolving around Michal. We soon learn that Menachem, on his way back to his home in Jerusalem, has broken his journey to reunite with his two closest friends, both of them religious students, Pini (Edan Alterman) and Itamar (Micha Selektar). He finds that Pini is in love with Michal and that Rabbi Meltzer (Assi Dayan) is actually fostering the romance between his best pupil and his daughter. We can see that Menachem, the noble soul that he is, would rather not allow his heart to disturb the institutional status quo.

When he calls on the Rabbi, we come to know just where Menachem fits into the scheme of things, or is intended to. The Rabbi has his heart set on forming a fighting unit which he calls "a religious company." This will comprise only Yeshiva scholars, some of them as young as 16. The Rabbi wants to bestow the privilege of leading such a company on Menachem. "Use it well," the Rabbi says, his face aglow with hope, "and make history." Menachem however remains diffident.

It is when we see the Rabbi's students, dressed in starched whites, singing and dancing with gusto, celebrating "a time of mercy and favor," that the film's ideological concerns become clear. These are young men on a quest for purity, united not just by religion, but by an underlying need to wage war in its name. As they surround Menachem, hailing him as their leader, he can only smile at their fervor.

The film's omniscient perspective then takes us to a meeting of the country's Secret Service, amongst whom the Rabbi is seen as a fanatic, a loose cannon, and no longer to be ignored since his students have begun to express their radical views in the media. As the worst fears of the Secret Service begin to materialize, the film shows the powerlessness of a country's intelligence system against internal religious zealotry.

On the Day of Shabbat, to a raptly attentive gathering of boys, the Rabbi asserts the right of every Jew to pray at the Temple Mount in Jerusalem, a right that has not only been sacrificed by the country's politicians, but by its people. The reason for this becomes clear to those acquainted with the history of the site. Cedar makes no effort to provide a historical background for those who aren't. The Temple Mount has also served as amongst the most sacred of Islamic holy sites. In fact, it is the very site where the Prophet Muhammad is supposed to have ascended to heaven.

Whatever its ideological merits, the Rabbi's rhetoric finds a rabid believer in Pini. The film shies away from showing his indoctrination to the point that he becomes ready to sacrifice his life for the Rabbi's lifetime project. Instead, the film takes up his insipid crush on Michal. As Pini catches up with her excitedly after the Rabbi's sermon, she punctures his hopes by telling him, "Stop marrying me!" She then adds that she doesn't want to hurt him. Pini of course is crushed, more so because his fellow scholars are looking on. Also a witness is the Rabbi, who glares at his daughter's behavior.

Menachem, at this stage, serves as a confidant for both Pini and Michal. First, he tries to pull Pini out of a bout of self-pity. Then, that night, as he is waiting for the bus to Jerusalem, he is accosted by Michal. He withdraws initially from her advances, but then allows her to take him to an abandoned construction site. There, he tells her how much she has hurt Pini. She answers that she doesn't want to be her father's trophy for the best student. The awkwardness between the two is resolved through what begins as an idle shadow play of their hands, then turns into an expression of intimacy as the shadows of their fingers unite while their hands remain apart.

While Menachem stays behind to train the company of Yeshiva scholars, the Rabbi's sermons become increasingly militant. Pini listens, captivated, as the Rabbi intones that he who does not know that a dead lion can be more alive than a living dog, will stay a dog.

Michal herself shares none of her father's religious fervor. At a power spot, overlooking a vista of bare hills, she tells Menachem of her disillusionment with life on the settlement, and how the Rabbi refused to move to the city, despite her late mother's deteriorating health. With a petulant frown, she mocks the dictum, "The land of Israel has been bought with pain!," then adds, "The more it hurts, the more my father enjoys it." Menachem agrees. "Idealists don't

really suffer," he remarks. To which, she replies, "But those around them do." Eventually, she asks Menachem flat out, "Do you love me?" He can only smile and blush. He does however kiss her on the lips for the first time, but makes no commitment.

From here, the film gravitates towards an action thriller plot that proves original only for its setting. Menachem undergoes a reversal when he meets the Rabbi again. "What you're doing to Pini is murder," the Rabbi tells him, and advises Menachem to return to the army. Menachem puts the interests of orthodoxy before his own, and agrees. Before walking away with his gear into the night, however, he confesses to Pini that he wants Michal. "I hope you understand," he adds. Pini replies, "I understand that you're weak."

What turns Menachem in his tracks is Michal running away from home to join an all-female kibbutz, and news of Pini stealing four cases of explosives for a suicide plot to bomb the Dome of the Rock on the Temple Mount. Menachem promptly realizes his mission must be to help the Secret Service who have gotten wind of Pini's plan. Menachem has thus to not only prevent the bombing, but save his best friend from being killed in the process.

The Secret Service haul up Menachem, Michal, and even the Rabbi for questioning. A helpless Chief of Intelligence accuses the Rabbi of instigating the plot. "For years you've been feeding them, Temple, Temple, Temple!" the Chief says. The Rabbi argues, "The Temple is an idea!" "You don't need explosives for an idea," the Chief retorts.

Menachem, who has been roughed up to no avail by the Secret Service, finally proves their only hope to foil the bombing plot. At the end of his tether, he screams at the officers holding him captive, "A military raid won't work here!" He then cites the problem of tunnels into which no one has ventured for two thousand years. Menachem is finally allowed to proceed into the quagmire and take Michal with him.

In a tame climax, as Menachem confronts Pini, and tries to talk him into giving up, he finds that his best friend is on the other side of a chasm of religious belief. However, before Pini can blow himself up, along with the Dome, he is shot dead. As a closing image, we see the Dome at dawn, as part of a Jerusalem blissfully ignorant of the bloodshed that has been averted.

Despite its routine action ending, the film leaves us with the disturbing thought that the most dangerous thing in today's world doesn't have to be a bomb or germ or virus, but a fanatical quest for purity. While we cannot help but wish that Cedar, as writer-director, had confronted this issue, an impact still lingers from his film having raised it in the first place.

Critical reception to the film has excused some of its staginess, and instead focussed on its depiction of how the personal cannot but intersect with the political, given the reality of Israel today. Kenneth Turan in the *Los Angeles Times* finds the film so "intensely contemporary . . . that to watch it is to feel the country having a passionate argument with itself." He also notes that "Cedar's script also allows for divergent philosophical viewpoints not often given screen time." J. Hoberman in the *Village Voice* calls the film "one of the few Israeli features made from a religious point of view" and one "relentlessly honest in representing . . . the potential civil war between uncomprehending idealists and grim pragmatists."

—*Vivek Adarkar*

## CREDITS

**Menachem:** Aki Avni
**Michal:** Tinkerbell
**Pini:** Edan Alterman
**Rabbi Meltzer:** Assi Dayan
**Itamar:** Micha Selektar
**Mookie:** Amnon Volf

**Origin:** Israel
**Language:** Hebrew
**Released:** 2000
**Production:** David Mandil, Eyal Shiray; Israel Film Fund, Yes, Cinema Factory; released by Kino International
**Directed by:** Joseph Cedar
**Written by:** Joseph Cedar
**Cinematography by:** Ofer Inov
**Music by:** Yonatan Bar-Girora
**Sound:** Israel David
**Editing:** Tova Asher
**Costumes:** Etiti Lugassi
**Production Design:** Yair Greenberg
**MPAA rating:** Unrated
**Running time:** 98 minutes

## REVIEWS

*Los Angeles Times Online.* February 1, 2002.
*New York Times Online.* January 18, 2002.
*Variety.* February 12, 2001, p. 36.
*Village Voice Online.* January 22, 2002.

## TRIVIA

Assi Dayan is the son of former Defense Minister Moshe Dayan.

# Together (Tillsammans)

*one house. one revolutionary. two open straight marriages. three gay people (maybe four). three children. two carnivores. and eight vegetarians. there's only one way they're going to make it . . .*
Together.
—Movie tagline

**Box Office:** $1 million

In the mid-70's when American youth were trading their peace signs for disco balls and cocaine, the hippie movement in Sweden gained momentum. While Swedish pop sensation ABBA sang "Money, Money, Money," Swedish youth were swapping sexual partners and turning their noses up anything they considered bourgeois. No TV or Coke, please. Swedish writer/director Lukas Moodysson (*Show Me Love*) focuses on a single commune and its vegetarian, socialist, fun-loving inhabitants, and its transformation after the arrival of a suburban housewife and her two reluctant children. Moodysson's *Together* allows viewers to laugh at the so-called bourgeoise and also the so-called radicals who live by their own rigid set of guidelines that include a lot of no to this, none of that.

Moodysson's *Together* is portrayed from a child's point of view so the film's narrative never loses its sense of fun even when the children suffer the anguish of changing times. After Rolf (Michael Nyqvist) beats his wife Elisabeth (Lisa Lindgren), she decides to leave him and takes her two children, 10-year-old Stefan (Sam Kessel) and the bespectacled 13-year-old Eva (Emma Samuelsson), to live at her brother's commune. As ABBA's song *S.O.S.* fades up on the soundtrack, Elisabeth and the kids are whisked away in a VW hippie bus to an over-crowded house filled with freaks of all stripes. When the group arrives at the house, which is led by Elisabeth's brother Goran (Gustaf Hammarstan), they encounter an argument between Anna (Jessica Liedberg), who insists on airing out her vagina in the kitchen, and her former husband Lasse (Ola Norell), who decides to expose his genitalia to prove an opposing point.

It's not exactly the heart-warming welcome Elisabeth and her children expected, but an eye-opening experience of future events.

Eva and Stefan suffer while Elisabeth blooms within the radical household. Anna, who decided to be a lesbian for political reasons, befriends Elisabeth hoping to pursue something romantic with her, but only manages to convince Elisabeth to stop shaving. Leftist Erik (Olle Sarri) preaches Marxist principles until he's blue in the face, then out of sheer frustration joins a leftist group. Meanwhile, homosexual Klas (Shanti Roney) develops a fancy for the recently divorced Lasse, even though Lasse finds the situation laughable. Goran's horny lover Lena (Anja Lundqvist) experiences her first orgasm after making love to Erik, while Mr. Nice Guy Goran makes light of the situation, then pukes in a toilet out of disgust. And finally the most radical couple in the group protest the addition of a television to the household by moving out.

Meanwhile, Elisabeth's husband Rolf drowns his sorrows with alcohol while creating a bigger mess of his life. A lonely divorced neighbor befriends Rolf and gives him advice on how to see his children and also how to get back together with his wife. However, it isn't until Rolf ends up in jail that he realizes the extent of his damaged life. He quits drinking and takes the advice of his new friend, hoping to win back his family.

Eva spends most of her time hiding out in Goran's VW van until she befriends the friendless Fredrik (Henrik Lundstrom), the son of busybody and conservative neighbors. Her passion for pop music and her friendship with Fredrik allow her to deal with her unbearable surroundings and anguish from her parent's separation. Stefan befriends Lasse and Anna's son Tet (Axel Zuber) and the two boys spend many fun-filled hours playing torture games in which they take turns playing Pinochet, watching the TV show *Baretta*, or playing war games. But soon these kids want more—with picket signs in hand, they protest, thus allowing the consuming of meat back into the household. By the film's end, a blending of radical and conservative values takes place and the household is transformed. Rolf, his lonely neighbor, and the bourgeois housewife neighbor who just left her misogynist husband, join the household for a game of football.

In an interview that appeared in the May/June 2001 issue of *RANT*, director Lukas Moodysson spoke of his inspiration for his film "I'm happy to say that kind of lifestyle is becoming popular again and I honestly think that it has a lot to offer. But I want people to learn from some of the past mistakes." However, even non-vegetarians can partake in the comic relief *Together* offers while escaping the usual bourgeois fare.

—*Patty-Lynne Herlevi*

## CREDITS

**Elisabeth:** Lisa Lindgren
**Rolf:** Michael Nyqvist
**Eva:** Emma Samuelsson
**Stefan:** Sam Kessell
**Goran:** Gustaf Hammarsten
**Lena:** Anja Lundqvist
**Anna:** Jessica Liedberg
**Lasse:** Ola Norell
**Tet:** Axel Zuber
**Klass:** Shanti Roney
**Erik:** Olle Sarri
**Fredrik:** Henrik Lindstrom
**Margit:** Therese Brunnander
**Ragnar:** Claes Hartelius
**Birger:** Sten Ljunggren
**Signe:** Cecilia Frode
**Sigvard:** Lars Frode
**Mane:** Emil Moodysson

**Origin:** Sweden, Denmark, Italy
**Language:** Swedish
**Released:** 2000
**Production:** Lars Jonsson; Memfis Film; released by IFC Films
**Directed by:** Lukas Moodysson
**Written by:** Lukas Moodysson
**Cinematography by:** Ulf Brantas
**Sound:** Niklas Merits, Ander Billing
**Editing:** Michael Leszcylowski, Fredrik Abrahamsen
**Art Direction:** Carl Johan De Geer
**Costumes:** Mette Moller
**MPAA rating:** R
**Running time:** 106 minutes

## REVIEWS

*Boxoffice.* August, 2001, p. 23.
*Chicago Sun-Times Online.* September 14, 2001.
*Entertainment Weekly.* September 4, 2001, p. 64.
*Los Angeles Times Online.* September 7, 2001.
*New York Times Online.* August 24, 2001.
*RANT.* May/June, 2001, p. 9.
*Sight and Sound.* July, 2001, p. 59.
*Variety.* September 4, 2000, p. 25.
*Washington Post.* October 26, 2001, p. WE40.

## QUOTES

Eva (Emma Samuelsson) describes the commune to Fredrik (Henrik Lundstom): "We have ugly clothes and we listen to terrible music. There's this one girl who's a homosexual. She won't like guys because everyone else does."

Shot in Trollhattan on the west coast of Sweden, which was also used by Moodysson for his first film.

# Tomcats

*The Last Man Standing Gets the Kitty.*
—Movie tagline

 **Box Office:** $13.5 million

**T**omcats was a movie that the critics and teenage boys could both agree on. Both thought it stank. Critics wrote scathing reviews of the film and the teen boy target audience stayed away. It probably wasn't a cause and effect situation. It wasn't like one high school freshman said to another, "I don't know about this *Tomcats*. The reviewer in the *New Yorker* had a tepid response to the film. Let's just rent *Porky's* again instead."

Besides the bad reviews and bad word of mouth (not to mention the badness of the movie itself), the movie was also hurt because it had an R rating. Anyone who was old enough to get in, was old enough not to be entertained or titillated by the film. And even though the R rating effectively kept a lot of kids out, it's hard to see what got the film the rating. There is no nudity, no violence and the sex is only implied. Teens who go to an R rated movie that's purportedly a raunchy teen sex comedy presumably want a little more raciness than this film provides. There is, of course, the requisite tastelessness, but that is so prevalent in films these days, it's barely worth mentioning. Before releasing the film, Columbia TriStar gave it a lot of hype, plastering TV and radio with ads for the picture, but even this big effort didn't brainwash enough randy teens to check the movie out.

The Tomcats of the title refer to a group of friends who pride themselves on their womanizing, love 'em and leave 'em ways. That they would give themselves such a corny name as Tomcats shows just how uncool these supposedly cool guys are. In a flashback, we see one of their friends, Steve (Horatio Sanz) succumbing to, uh-oh, matrimony. The other guys are shocked and appalled, even though Steve should be thanking his lucky stars since he looks like a lost Belushi brother and his future wife is played by way-out-of-

his-league Jaime Pressly. The Tomcats make a bet then and there: they will put some money in a pot each year, invest the money in mutual funds and whoever is the last guy to get married will get the money. They exclude their token gay friend from the bet.

After several years, the money has grown to be a considerable sum and Michael Delaney (Jerry O'Connell) and Kyle (Jake Busey, Gary Busey's equally toothy son) are the only two guys left. Michael doesn't give the bet much thought until an unfortunate night in Las Vegas. Egged on by a beautiful redhead (Amber Smith) who only likes high rollers, Michael quickly proceeds to lose $51,000 in short order. He is quickly whisked away to some secret room where he meets the casino owner (an unbilled Bill Maher, host of *Politically Incorrect*). The casino owner gives Michael one month to pay off the debt. In the meantime, Michael will get periodic visits from casino underlings who come to repossess his stuff, piece by piece.

Michael decides the smartest way to handle the situation is to betray his longtime friend, Kyle. Nice. Kyle doesn't elicit too much sympathy though because he's really quite a jerk. He's a rich guy who's completely dedicated to conquering any and all women. He seeks out new experiences, like bedding a stewardess, and entices his women by doing "sexy" things like wearing thong underwear and slapping his own behind. The women in the film, who tend to be a dumb lot, are unbelievably attracted to such antics. "I love the smell of bridesmaids in the morning," is a typical Kyle line. Or, if a friend exhibits any vaguely feminine quality: "You're not going fag on me, are you?" It is up to Michael to break Kyle's womanizing ways and get his friend to fall for someone and marry her so that Michael can get win the bet and pay off the casino owner.

Michael gets Kyle to admit that there was once a girl who touched his heart, Natalie (Shannon Elizabeth). At a friend's wedding years before, Kyle and Natalie had had a romantic encounter on the beach in Malibu. Afterwards, he ditched her with a roll of quarters to catch a cab home, but for Kyle, that was his idea of something close to love. Michael tracks down Natalie and gets her to agree to a deal: She will romance Kyle, they'll get married, then she and Michael will split the money.

Natalie is a policewoman who's as spunky as she is beautiful so naturally, as Michael and Natalie start working together, he starts falling for her. The fact that she is so willing to ruin another guy's life just to get some money doesn't speak very well for her character, but then Michael's the one who came up with the idea in the first place. It's not like he's a man of sterling character either. It's also difficult to see what Natalie sees in Michael. Compared to Kyle, he's a prince. But this is a guy who wears a t-shirt with one arrow pointing up with the words, "The Man," and one pointing down, with "The Legend." Bring this boy home to mother!

There are a lot of jokes in this movie that seem like they could have only been written by a guy and, indeed they were. Gregory Poirier was both writer and director on this project, and reportedly this was a labor of love for him. (One reviewer reported that Poirier was loathe to cut some of his precious material and that's the reason why the film kept the R rating.) It's hard to believe he would fight so hard for sequences like the one that takes place in a sperm bank. Kyle has to make a donation for medical reasons, and for some unexplained reason, Michael goes with him and decides to donate, too. When Michael goes in his cubicle, he fantasizes about Natalie and ends up with a several cups of output. When he turns them into the busty (of course) worker at the bank, she looks at him and coos, highly impressed. It seems very difficult to believe that a sperm bank worker would behave in any way even close to that.

Other male-oriented jokes include some pretty bad treatment of women. In one sequence when Kyle and Michael are having a talk during a golf game, they take the cart while Kyle's unnamed girlfriend has to run behind, dragging her heavy clubs. While the guys ignore her, she does such comical feats as falling into a water hazard or, even funnier, being run over by the cart. Dim as she is, she doesn't seem to notice she's being treated like an old washcloth and keeps smiling and waving at her man Kyle.

But the boorishness doesn't just apply to women. The one gay guy in the group repeatedly says, "Blow me," whenever one of his male friends tease him. But the movie reaches its pinnacle of tastelessness in an extended gag involving . . . testicular cancer. That's right, ha-ha. Kyle gets a case of it and has to have one of his orbs removed. He asks Michael to get it back for him so he can have it as a keepsake. So begins an overly long segment where Michael locates the object, then proceeds to drop it, as it rolls and bounces all over the hospital. Eventually it bounces onto the lunch plate of Kyle's surgeon, played by poor David Ogden Stiers, who ends up eating it. It's hard to believe that Poirier could take such a comedy killer as cancer and manage to make it even less funny.

No one but Poirier was laughing. Roger Ebert of the *Chicago Sun-Times* thought the characters behaved "outside the normal range of human response." "All sex comedies have scenes in which characters are embarrassed, but I can't remember one in which women are so consistently and venomously humiliated, as if they were some kind of hateful plague," he wrote. Bill Muller of the *Arizona Republic* wrote that the film "achieves the perfect balance of being as repellent as it is pointless, as dull as it is disgusting and as vapid as it is crass." Sunny Lee of *Entertainment Weekly* wrote, "All the comedy bits seem pilfered out of a joke-reject bin. And to think, a few short years ago, an apple pie was the limit of bad taste."

—*Jill Hamilton*

## CREDITS

**Michael Delancey:** Jerry O'Connell
**Natalie Parker:** Shannon Elizabeth
**Kyle Brenner:** Jake Busey
**Tricia:** Jaime Pressly
**Officer Hurley:** Bernie Casey
**Dr. Crawford:** David Ogden Stiers
**Jan:** Travis Fine
**Jill:** Heather Stephens
**Steve:** Horatio Sanz
**Shelby:** Julia Schultz

**Origin:** USA
**Released:** 2001
**Production:** Paul Kurta, Tony Ludwig, Alan Riche; Revolution Studios, Eagle Cove Entertainment; released by Columbia Pictures
**Directed by:** Gregory Poirier
**Written by:** Gregory Poirier
**Cinematography by:** Charles Minsky
**Music by:** David Kitay
**Sound:** Douglas Axtell
**Music Supervisor:** Spring Aspers
**Editing:** Harry Keramidas
**Costumes:** Alix Friedberg
**Production Design:** Robb Wilson King
**MPAA rating:** R
**Running time:** 92 minutes

## REVIEWS

*Chicago Sun-Times Online.* March 30, 2001.
*Los Angeles Times Online.* March 30, 2001.
*New York Times Online.* March 30, 2001.
*San Francisco Chronicle Online.* March 30, 2001.
*Variety Online.* March 26, 2001.

# Too Much Sleep

*A bus, a gun, a girl and a bad case of narcolepsy. A suburban folk story.*
—Movie tagline

*Too Much Sleep* benefitted from being part of the Shooting Gallery film series. The Shooting Gallery is both a development company and a film distributor. Each year they choose a selection of what they think are the top films on the indie circuit, then they exhibit the films in a special series. The idea is to help underappreciated or underviewed films get out to a wider audience. The Shooting Gallery series is quite helpful to the films. In the past the series helped give a higher profile to quality films like *A Time for Drunken Horses* and *Croupier*.

*Too Much Sleep* is the film major project of David Maquiling, who wrote and directed it. Maquiling is the son of a surgeon who was a Filipino immigrant, and he grew up in Holmdel, New Jersey. He attended the prestigious New York University film school and used some of his fellow alumni on *Too Much Sleep*, including cinematographer Robert Mowen, editor Jim Villone and composer Mitchell Toomey. Maquiling has said that he based the film on an old Filipino folk story. It's hard to see how that folk story would have made for a tale because it seems much more like a cinematic kind of story than something that would be a good oral tale. The charm of the plot is not the plot itself, but rather the interesting characters who populate it.

The center of the film is Jack Crawford (Marc Palmieri). Despite his action hero name, Jack is a man of little action. When we first see him, he is lying in his bed, a twin bed that looks like it came into the world in the 1970s. It's obvious from the decor—the old trophies, the pennants that have been there forever, the dated posters—that Jack still lives in his boyhood room. Like he probably does every day, Jack wakes up to the sound of his mother's (Joan Maquiling—note the last name) gently nagging voice. Today she is concerned because her son missed work the previous day and shows no signs of going to work today. "Do you want me to go down there and talk to them for you?" she asks, not realizing that her 20-year-old son is probably a wee bit old to have his mother making work excuses for him.

Jack finally manages to rouse himself enough to get on the city bus to ride to his job as a security guard. In what would probably normally be the highlight of his day, while on the bus, he makes sleepy eye contact with a young pretty girl, Kate (Nicol Zanzarella). So entranced is he by this girl that he doesn't notice until she gets off the bus that someone has stolen a paper bag that contained the gun he uses for his job. Jack needs that gun to keep his job but can't go to the police to report the crime because the gun was his father's and Jack never got around to registering it. Jack, with no where else to turn, enlists the help of Eddie DeLuca (stage veteran Pasquale Gaeta), a friend's father who is the indie film version of Joe Pesci. Eddie used to be a government official and brags that he has all his big time connections. Eddie promises to find a list of suspects so that he and Jack can go hunt the criminals themselves.

The rest of the plot is just that—the two men go on their quest to find the criminals. But it's not the twists and turns of their adventure that make up the movie, it's more the journey that they take to get there. The point of the film is not to show a tense, action-packed crime mystery but rather to indulge itself in showing off the wacky array of

characters that populate Jack's suburban New Jersey town. V.A. Musetto, a writer for the *New York Post* who seemed to think that Maquiling's portray of suburbia was a little too accurate, wrote that the film "perfectly captures the cultural and emotional wasteland that is suburban Jersey. *Too Much Sleep* reminds me why, many years ago, I fled that state for Manhattan." As Austin, Texas, was so much a part of Richard Linklater's seminal slacker flick, *Slacker*, suburban Jersey is also a palpable part of *Too Much Sleep*. The settings—a bowling alley, a manicure joint, a Chinese restaurant—are notable in how unnotable they are. It's only after Jack starts prying around and asking questions does he realize how these mundane settings are full of strange characters.

*Too Much Sleep* is also a lot like *Slacker* in the way it gives so much screentime to these odd characters. What the characters say may or may not advance the plot (usually not) but Maquiling is happy to give them their screentime to let them advance their theories of life. At a tedious suburban party filled with middle-aged people who look like they are stuck in a party from the early 1960s, Jack meets the seemingly normal bartender host (Jon Langione). The man first starts talking about making the perfect scotch, veers off into his love of racquetball and ends up with a plea for Jack to join his club where men like to give each other massages. "Massages at a spa are so expensive," explains the host. There's also a bouncer (R.G. Rader) at an exotic male dancing club who's really trying to be a musician. He's the kind of guy who worries about things like karma so after he beats Jack up, he apologizes and gives Jack some medical advice about treating his wounds. Eddie and Jack also meet Mrs. Bruner (Peggy Lord Chilton), who is the mother of a person they suspect of taking the gun. As Mrs. Bruner sits in her house that's remained unchanged since she decorated it in avocado green and yellow in 1974, her talk gradually turns from sunny chit-chat to rather dark tales about her husband's strange mental illness. In this film, the more normal a character appears, the stranger they usually are.

But the biggest character of all is Eddie DeLuca. In a way, he's really the star of the film. Jack ostensibly is the main character, but he's more of an observer than a forceful character. His job is to stand around and hear these others spout off. Eddie, on the other hand, has to command every situation that he's in. Though he's now an older and rather portly man, he prides himself on his way with the ladies and in fact he charms several ladies in the course of their detective work. He is an endless fountain of stories, including the time he won a ton of money in Vegas and ended up sleeping with Doris Day. Another time he gives a graphic description of some laser surgery he once had on his private parts.

*Too Much Sleep* is a subtle film; one that's content to take a leisurely pace. Its hero seems to barely be able to rouse himself through most of the film and is not really someone who the audience would be cheering for. The movie is funny, but in a dry, quiet way. For example, when Jack gets involved in a chase with a bad guy, the chase is through suburban backyards. When Jack catches the guy, he starts fighting with him by wielding the only weapon available—an oversized plastic wiffle ball bat. Other humor comes from characters saying funny things that they don't realize are funny. One older gentleman, who watches a neighbor change through her open curtains, says lasciviously, "She works at the Department of Motor Vehicles and she's got the body to prove it."

Maquiling also shows the kind of casual racism that sometimes permeates these kinds of towns. Characters pepper their speech with warnings like, "I can only trust the Jewish doctors, you know" or "He's Korean—they're industrious types." The racism is also the result of a lack of intelligence. One guy impersonates an Irishman by saying, "Look, I'm drunk. Want to fight?" He thinks he's being quite clever.

Critics liked the film, though they didn't get overly enthusiastic about it. It's the kind of film that is pleasant, but doesn't incite big passion. The *New York Post* called it "delightful." The *New Times Los Angeles* called it a "quirky, little" film. Roger Ebert of the *Chicago Sun-Times* said the film is "rich and droll, and yet slight—a film of modest virtues, content to be small, achieving what it intends."

—*Jill Hamilton*

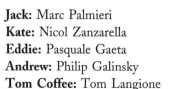

## CREDITS

**Jack:** Marc Palmieri
**Kate:** Nicol Zanzarella
**Eddie:** Pasquale Gaeta
**Andrew:** Philip Galinsky
**Tom Coffee:** Tom Langione
**Jonathan:** R.G. Rader
**Mrs. Bruner:** Peggy Lord Chilton
**Jack's Mother:** Joan Maquiling

**Origin:** USA
**Released:** 2001
**Production:** Jason Kliot, Joana Vicente; released by Shooting Gallery
**Directed by:** David Maquiling
**Written by:** David Maquiling
**Cinematography by:** Robert Mowen
**Music by:** Mitchell Toomey
**Editing:** Jim Villone
**MPAA rating:** Unrated
**Running time:** 86 minutes

## REVIEWS

*Boxoffice.* May, 2001, p. 59.
*Entertainment Weekly.* March 30, 2001, p. 47.
*Los Angeles Times Online.* March 23, 2001.
*Washington Post Online.* March 23, 2001.

# Top of the Food Chain (Invasion!)

*Something is eating the residents of Exceptional Vista!*
—Movie tagline

Imagine a marriage between American sci-fi B-flicks from the 1950's and the Canadian comedy series *This Hour Has 22 Minutes* and you've envisioned the Canadian sci-fi spoof *Top of the Food Chain*. Written by Phil Bedard and Larry Lalonde, who wrote scripts for *Royal Canadian Farce*, and directed by Winnipeg's John Paizs, who's best known for his work with *Kids In The Hall, Top of the Food Chain* lacks the outrageous humor one would expect. The film, which stars Campbell Scott and the alluring Fiona Loewi not only pokes fun at B-films of a long gone era but also pokes fun at American naïveté. Characters dress in '50s fashion and spout words like "gee" and "fruit of the womb of the Holy Mother" and some viewers might be reminded of the pilot for *Twin Peaks*.

The film's writers and director have researched 1950's B-flicks and have learned the sci-fi formula complete with stock characters, trite dialogue, and mistaken identities. (Traveling vacuum salesman Michael O'Shea [Nigel Bennett] lies about his true identity.) And the character Guy Fawkes (Tom Everett Scott) will humor Anglophiles since in England Guy Fawkes is considered horrific and his likeness is burned on Guy Fawkes Day. Of course, here, Guy Fawkes is Sandy Fawkes' (Fiona Loewi) younger brother who happens to be as ignorant as Sandy is intelligent. And the sexy virgin Sandy happens to be quite knowledgeable about atomic science.

The story begins with Jan Bathgate (Robert Bockstael) fishing at a local river when his TV loses reception. Next a sexy bombshell appears asking if Jan would like to procreate the species only the bombshell happens to be an alien and she devours Jan. Next the story moves to a local shop where town folk complain about the closure of the nut factory and how all of the town's TV sets have lost their reception. But the kittenish Sandy shows up to cheer the men in the store and to brag that the world famous atomic scientist Dr. Karel Lamonte (Campbell Scott) is staying at her hotel. Sandy runs into the scientist in the store and of course falls for his geek appeal because in B-flicks women fell for physics/science professors. However, Lamonte possesses a cautious demeanor and after viewing Sandy and Guy tongue-diving, he grows even more cautious.

Meanwhile, aliens begin feasting on the residents of Exceptional Vista and one-by-one the town folk's bodies end up mangled in the woods and the butcher shop. The aliens cut off all forms of communication, eat the man posing as the town cop and his deputy, all the while destroying the wiring system of the residents' cars. O'Shea abducts Sandy under false pretenses and it turns out he's not a salesman or a government agent, but an alien. He plans on eating Sandy for dinner, but not if the professor and Guy can save the day. It turns out that television waves kill aliens so, with a crucifix in hand, Guy blows up several aliens with good television reception. But Sandy saves humankind when she plunges the crucifix into the base of a satellite dish.

The women of the town resurrect all of the bodies that were devoured by the aliens as the town folk learn a lesson that spirituality is more important than sex or television. And once again the residents of Exceptional Vista have found meaning in their lives as they celebrate the marriage between the professor, Sandy, and Guy. End of story.

The actors handle their tongue-in-cheek performances to great effect. In the press kit Tom Everett Scott recalls how difficult it was keeping a straight face, "I think the funniest scene that was the hardest for me to keep a straight face is when Dr. Karel Lamonte and I have a near kiss." Campbell Scott describes the audience's reaction to the film "You can cry, you can laugh. Just don't ask for your money back!" Of course, some non-Canadians might not react with a sigh or a chuckle, but with confusion as to why an alleged comedy lacks hilarity. But viewers who enjoy Canadian spoofs on American culture can rent *Top of the Food Chain* and not be disappointed.

—*Patty-Lynne Herlevi*

## CREDITS

**Dr. Karel Lamonte:** Campbell Scott
**Sandy Fawkes:** Fiona Loewi
**Guy Fawkes:** Tom Everett Scott
**Officer Gayle:** Hardee T. Lineham
**Mayor Claire:** Bernard Behrens
**Michael O'Shea:** Nigel Bennett
**Jim Hickey:** Peter Donaldson
**Jan Bathgate:** Robert Bockstael
**Pat:** Lorry Ayers
**Leslie Binkley:** Ron Gabriel
**Deputy Dana:** James Allodi
**Shelley Bathgate:** Maggie Butterfield

**Abby:** Kathryn Kirkpatrick

**Origin:** Canada
**Released:** 1999
**Production:** Suzanne Berger, Jana Edelbaum; Upstart Pictures; released by Red Sky Entertainment
**Directed by:** John Paizs
**Written by:** Phil Bedard, Larry Lalonde
**Cinematography by:** Bill Wong
**Music by:** David Krystal
**Sound:** Cory Mandel
**Editing:** Bert Kish
**Art Direction:** Mark Kowalsky
**Costumes:** Lisa Martin
**Production Design:** Rupert Lazarus
**MPAA rating:** PG-13
**Running time:** 99 minutes

## REVIEWS

*eye Weekly Online.* September 9, 1999.

## QUOTES

Jim (Peter Donaldson) predicts the end of the world: "First TV, then people."

## TRIVIA

The film was retitled *Invasion!* upon its video release.

# Tortilla Soup

*A comedy to arouse your appetite.*
—Movie tagline

**Box Office:** $4.4 million

There's no doubt who the star of *Tortilla Soup* is. In this remake of Ang Lee's film *Eat Drink Man Woman*, actors Hector Elizondo and Elizabeth Pena may get top billing, but the main screen time, the best camera angles and the most sympathetic character is food. Besides *Eat Drink Man*

*Woman*, this kind of food-as-character film includes films like *Babette's Feast, Big Night, Soul Food*, and *Like Water For Chocolate*. At the end of the film, the first credit to roll by is: "Food and menus created and designed by Mary Sue Milliken and Susan Feniger." (Milliken and Feniger are chefs at the Los Angeles restaurants Border Grill and Ciudad). All of the delectable dishes made movie critics break out their food metaphors. It was difficult, if not impossible, to find a review that didn't have some cutesy reference to food like describing the film as "a movie that gently simmers as its flavors and pleasures deepen" or "a flavorful tale . . . bound to pique discerning appetites."

The first scene is, naturally, food-based. Martin (Elizondo) is preparing an elaborate feast for Sunday dinner with his daughters. It's a weekly ritual and Martin, who is a chef, goes all out. The camera lingers lovingly over shots of Martin slicing onions, dicing tomatoes and preparing pieces of cactus. As Tom Maurstad of the *Dallas Morning News* put it, "You may want to eat before seeing *Tortilla Soup*, because if you're at all hungry, you may find yourself lunging at the screen as all the delicious-looking food is served." Ironically, few of the characters in the film ever end up getting a chance to eat much of the food because these meals inevitably end up with some sort of drama. The daughters, who all still live with their father in his East Los Angeles home, like to use the time together to make "announcements," usually the kind that are going to shock their long-widowed dad.

The film's first announcement is from the middle daughter, Carmen (Jacqueline Obradors). Carmen is a beautiful woman who has pleased her father by pursuing her MBA and becoming a successful business woman instead of following her dream to become a chef like her father. She announces that she has bought a condo in Playa Vista and will be moving out of the family home. Martin, a strong, quiet man who has selflessly attended to his daughters' needs without the help of a wife, is upset that Carmen is leaving. But instead of being honest with his daughter and himself, he says that he is angry that she failed to ask him for advice on the purchase.

But Carmen's not the only one who's causing trouble. Youngest daughter Maribel (Tamara Mello) is a senior in high school and unsure of what to do with her life. When she meets a Brazilian boy, Andy (Nikolai Kinski, son of Klaus Kinski), she decides that she wants to put off college and travel around "finding herself," just like he is doing. Dad's answer to her finding herself is: "You're right there." Maribel shocks her father, as well as her new boyfriend, by saying at dinner that she's going to move into Andy's apartment.

The oldest daughter is Letitia (Elizabeth Pena) a witty but plain woman. Letitia doesn't have much of a personal life so she throws herself into church activities and her job teaching chemistry at the local school. She acts as though she likes her pious life, but there's a feistier spirit in her

wanting to break out. She's the kind of person who people give "helpful" advice to on hair styles, how to get rid of her tiny wrinkles, and what she should wear. Even when she meets the man who will be her great love, the school's chunky new basketball coach (Paul Rodriguez), he tells her that she could improve her triceps if only she would start working out.

The extended family includes Martin's business partner and best friend Gomez (Julio Oscar Mechoso) as well as a neighbor family, Hortensia (Raquel Welch), her daughter Yolanda (Constance Marie), and young granddaughter, April (Marisabel Garci). Hortensia, a flashy, aging sexpot who's had several husbands is making it her quest to get Martin to be her next husband.

Life is changing around Martin. Letitia runs off and marries her boyfriend in secret. Carmen gets offered a big job with a tech start-up company in Barcelona, Spain. (That particular opportunity probably sounded a lot more inviting when the film was made.) Maribel can't seem to decide what to do with her life. And Gomez is starting to suffer from some health problems. Will Martin be able to hold his family together? Even his beloved food is giving him problems. He is losing his sense of taste and smell and he worries that he will no longer be able to be a great chef.

The story makes a nice transition from its original Chinese incarnation. The plot is basically the same and some of the dialogue is the same, but the movie stands well on its own. Someone who had seen *Eat Drink Man Woman* could easily see *Tortilla Soup* without feeling like they were getting served leftovers. One of the strengths of *Tortilla Soup* is the quiet dignity that Elizondo gives to Martin. Elizondo has few lines, but he conveys a lot. He doesn't talk much to his daughters but they are never in any doubt as to what his feelings are. Elizondo is also good at portraying the passion of a person who is utterly involved with what he is doing. When Martin cooks, he does it with an intense focus and enjoyment that is obvious. Also good is Pena, who suffers being the "ugly" sister, but manages to keep her dignity and sense of self. She manages to be prim and proper, while hinting at her wilder self underneath. Kinski as the Brazilian love interest doesn't have the intense presence of his father, but he's exotic enough to seem worldly to young Maribel. Welch as the man-hunter does a good, if a little over-the-top job. She's a woman of a certain era, who believes and lives by the rules she learned as a girl, like "Men don't like a smartass." Despite her overacting, it's nice to see her on the screen again.

And, of course, the food has a fine screen presence. It's strangely fascinating to see Martin start with such simple ingredients as flour and egg and end up with such stunning results. (However, some vegetarians might not enjoy such sights as a whole fish cooking on a grill and an entire pig served on a platter for dinner.) Though a lot of things happen over the course of the film, it's a gentle film that takes time to explore its characters and situations. Just the fact that no one has to save the world—and they only have three days to do it!—is a refreshing change. The characters are allowed to be multi-dimensional and have faults as well as good points.

Critics, who perhaps are a hungry lot, liked the film—and their food metaphors—a lot. "*Tortilla Soup* is the ultimate comfort food, blending the heartiness of chicken and corn tortillas with the dulcet flavor of avocado, the heat of peppers, and the tang of cilantro and lime," wrote Reel.com. Marta Barber of the *Miami Herald* wrote, "The film is a charmer, filled with homey details that make you nostalgic for a warm and spicy tortilla soup." "Make no mistake," wrote Malcolm Ritter of the *Associated Press.* "This movie is as delectable as the gourmet food it features. You'll savor it." And Kevin Thomas of the *Los Angeles Times* wrote, "*Tortilla Soup* is worth sipping."

—*Jill Hamilton*

**CREDITS**

**Martin:** Hector Elizondo
**Carmen:** Jacqueline Obradors
**Letitia:** Elizabeth Pena
**Maribel:** Tamara Mello
**Andy:** Nikolai Kinski
**Hortensia:** Raquel Welch
**Orlando:** Paul Rodriguez
**Antonio:** Joel Joan
**Yolanda:** Constance Marie

**Origin:** USA
**Released:** 2001
**Production:** John Bard Manulis; released by Samuel Goldwyn Films
**Directed by:** Maria Ripoli
**Written by:** Tom Musca, Ramon Menendez, Vera Blasi
**Cinematography by:** Xavier Perez Grobet
**Music by:** Bill Conti
**Sound:** Billy Flick
**Editing:** Andy Blumenthal
**Art Direction:** John Mott
**Costumes:** Ileane Neltzer
**Production Design:** Alicia Maccarone
**MPAA rating:** PG-13
**Running time:** 102 minutes

**REVIEWS**

*Boxoffice.* July, 2001, p. 24.
*Boxoffice.* August, 2001, p. 57.
*Chicago Sun-Times Online.* August 24, 2001.
*Entertainment Weekly.* September 14, 2001, p. 66.
*Los Angeles Times Online.* August 24, 2001.
*New York Times Online.* August 31, 2001.
*People.* September 3, 2001, p. 40.
*Variety.* July 23, 2001, p. 19.

**QUOTES**

Carmen (Jacqueline Obradors) to her father (Hector Elizondo): "Don't treat me like a slut just because I've had sex in this decade."

# Town and Country

*A comedy about men who do stupid things . . . and the women who get even.*
—Movie tagline

 **Box Office:** $6.7 million

The very wealthy architect Porter (Warren Beatty) and his designer wife Ellie (Diane Keaton) have been married 25 years. They have an impeccable New York City apartment and a beautiful pastoral house in the Hamptons. So it makes sense that this beautiful couple would celebrate their anniversary by flying off to Paris in a private jet with their best friends antique dealer Griffin (Gary Shandling) and his wife Mona (Goldie Hawn). After 25 years of wedded bliss, however, Porter is quite belatedly feeling the seven-year itch and as a result he is having an affair with flaky cellist, Alex (Nastassja Kinski). Similarly, Porter's best friend Griffin is also having an affair, but his is with a cross-dressing man. When Mona catches Griffin in the act (although she, and everyone else think the man is a woman), divorce proceedings are started.

As if that weren't enough to effect the long-standing friendship between the two couples, when Porter accompanies Mona to Mississippi to see her new antebellum home, she seduces him. The next thing you know, Alex announces to Porter that she is pregnant and Ellie finds out about Porter's affair with Alex (although she doesn't find out about Porter and Mona). So what happens next? Porter and Griffin inexplicably go off to snowy Sun Valley, Idaho. There they meet Auburn (Jenna Elfman) who works at the fishing tackle store and a loopy, stuffed animal-obsessed heiress Eugenie (Andie MacDowell). Eugenie takes Porter to meet her parents, gun-obsessed Hemingway-obsessed

Dad (Charlton Heston) and wheel-chair klutz, drink-obsessed Mom (Marian Seldes).

After a frightening face-down with Dad, Porter sneaks off in the middle of the night only to have Auburn show up at his cabin dressed as Marilyn Monroe and bearing Halloween party costumes for Porter (a polar bear) and Griffin (Elvis). So, after this totally illogical interlude, how do we get back to the original story? Have Porter's son Tommy (Josh Hartnett) show up in Idaho totally out of the blue and immediately leave in disgust after seeing Marilyn Monroe Auburn and polar bear Dad sexually wrestling in the snow.

The story reaches its climax—such as it is—at the New York Design Institute's award banquet where Ellie, Mona, Alex, Eugenie and Auburn all meet up in the bathroom (but nothing happens!), Griffin disruptively yells out he's gay in the dinning room, and Eugenie's shot-gun totting Dad shows up loaded for polar bear. From here there is only one place for the story to go, the divorce lawyer's office, and one thing to say, a last-ditch declaration of love. Will it work? Well, nothing else in this movie does, so why should this? And considering the talent involved, that's incredible.

Beside some big-name actors who seem to play characters we've seen them play before, director Peter Chelsom is no amateur either. He previously helmed such gems as *Hear My Song* (1991) and *Funny Bones* (1995). But the magic he worked on those two whimsical movies is totally missing in *Town & Country*. It has been said that Chelsom constantly experimented while making the film, shooting lots of takes and retakes and just taking his time. This may be explained, though, by the fact that shooting began before the script was finished. And when it was finally done more scenes had to be shot to make sense out of the whole mess. (Rumor has it that in the end, New Line Cinema had two complete and different versions of the film.)

Writers Michael Laughlin and Buck Henry have attempted to capture the classic heyday of screwball romantic comedy, but there's little zip to the dialogue and only a clumsy, leaden plot. There's no complexity, only disjointedness accompanied by desperate plot meanderings like moving the action to Mississippi or Sun Valley. We never truly understand—or care about—the main characters, and the antics of infidelity are decidedly unfunny. Even the coupling of the two most opposite Hollywood ideologues—ultra liberal Beatty and ultra conservative Heston—doesn't make the movie any funnier or worth watching. The result is a story that seems very segmented, awkwardly wandering from location to location, from person to person, from story to story. We get disconnected, brief glimpses into the lives of the four main characters but then we have to weave them together into a coherent story. The result is a feeling of watching purposeless vignettes instead of a cohesive plot.

The film was a plagued production right from the start. All the A-list stars meant juggling shooting to fit schedules and when one adds the script problems the result is a movie

whose production started three years prior to the film's release. But then *Town & Country* also went through 11 release dates before finally hitting theaters. But maybe even that's an overstatement. The movie was given no premier party, and was in theaters only for a very limited run. When one considers the cost and the names involved, that's very unusual. The film has variously been reported as costing between $80 to 90 million, and at that price it gains the dubious title as one of the most expensive romantic comedies ever made. Unfortunately the studio has gotten very little bang for the Buck Henry: it's not romantic and it's barely a comedy.

*—Beverley Bare Buehrer*

## CREDITS

**Porter Stoddard:** Warren Beatty
**Ellie Sotddard:** Diane Keaton
**Mona:** Goldie Hawn
**Eugenie:** Andie MacDowell
**Auburn:** Jenna Elfman
**Griffin:** Garry Shandling
**Eugenie's father:** Charlton Heston
**Eugenie's mother:** Marian Seldes
**Alice:** Tricia Vessey
**Tom:** Josh Hartnett
**Alex:** Nastassia Kinski
**Holly:** Katharine Towne
**Suttler:** Buck Henry

**Origin:** USA
**Released:** 2001
**Production:** Andrew Karsch, Fred Roos, Simon Fields; Longfellow Pictures, Sidney Kimmell Entertainment, FR Productions; released by New Line Cinema
**Directed by:** Peter Chelsom
**Written by:** Buck Henry, Michael Laughlin
**Cinematography by:** William A. Fraker
**Music by:** Rolfe Kent
**Sound:** Charles Wilborn
**Editing:** David Moritz, Claire Simpson
**Art Direction:** Anthony Mark Worthington
**Costumes:** Molly Maginnis
**Production Design:** Caroline Hanania
**MPAA rating:** R
**Running time:** 104 minutes

## REVIEWS

*Chicago Tribune Online.* April 27, 2001.
*Entertainment Weekly.* May 11, 2001, p. 53.

*Los Angeles Times Online.* April 27, 2001.
*New York Times Online.* April 15, 2001.
*New York Times Online.* April 27, 2001.
*People.* May 14, 2001, p. 42.
*Sight and Sound.* April, 2001, p. 60.
*Variety.* April 30, 2001, p. 25.
*Washington Post Online.* April 27, 2001.

# The Town Is Quiet (La Ville Est Tranquille)

Robert Guediguian's kaleidoscopic political thriller from France, *The Town Is Quiet,* demonstrates that in order to convincingly render the randomness of violence in today's world, we need to shed outdated modes of drama centered on the nucleus of a central character into whose life the violence explodes. While true to contemporary experience, the cathartic event coming out of nowhere cannot help but feel contrived in dramatic terms. Guediguian shows that what is needed is for the very narrative fabric of the film to be woven around the nucleus of a substratum, as in Robert Altman's *Nashville* (1975). In this manner, when the violence does strike, it appears as endemic as the film's other events. With such an ambitious agenda in mind, Guediguian opens his film, and repeatedly gravitates towards, circular aerial pans of the port and city of Marseille in southern France, as if to feature the city itself as a character rather than to use it as mere background.

Amongst the panoply of the city's residents the film hovers over, the two closest to its heart are Michele (Ariane Ascaride), a gritty but attractive fishwife, who also has to serve as nurse to her recalcitrant teenage daughter and baby granddaughter with an unknown father, and Paul (Jean-Pierre Darroussin), a kindly, balding cabbie, devoted to his parents, who is romantically drawn to Michele. Despite the filmmaker's intentions, it is Michele's plight that elicits our sympathy the most, making the other goings-on appear dull in comparison.

When Michele returns from work one evening, she finds her daughter Fiona (Julie-Marie Parmentier) performing fellatio on a stranger who has hired her services. Michele threatens the man with a kitchen knife and chases him away. Paul, meanwhile, discovers that trusting the union bosses on the docks is a no-win situation. He purchases a brand-new cab instead, largely out of the pay owing to him. With pride, he shows off his acquisition to his father (Jacques Boudet) who, like his son, has been disillusioned by union politics. In the background is his loving mother (Pascale Roberts), who is prevented from voicing any opinion whatsoever by her husband. Paul's customers turn out to be Yves Froment (Jacques Pieller), a middle-aged leftist architect, and his wife, the beautiful Viviane (Christine Brucher). We have earlier witnessed Yves' open philandering with Ameline (Veronique Balme), the daughter of a right-wing senator, at an elite rooftop party comprised of the city's political bigwigs. Now in Paul's cab, Viviane says that she is leaving him.

With the precision of a graph, the film gets under way by charting the underbelly of tension and contradictions in the lives of the characters it has introduced, gradually expanding its narrative focus. Viviane, we learn, has an independent career as a music teacher to mentally challenged children. The quiet of her class is intruded upon by the return of an old student, a fiery black, Abderamane (Alexandre Ogou), out of jail and wanting to start a fruitful new life. To make amends, Michele treats her daughter to lunch at a rooftop restaurant. Their waiter is none other than Abderamane. The dysfunctional aspect of Michele's family is merely smoldering at this stage. Fiona's real grouse, we learn, is that she wants her mother to divorce her "jerk" of a dad. That very evening, Abderamane is confronted by a group of racist thugs, which introduces the xenophobic element into this complex mixture. At the end of the same working day, we see Paul retiring by himself, lonely and weary.

The next morning, when Michele has trouble starting her moped, Paul drives up and helps her siphon gas into the tank. From this brief chance encounter, we can see that Paul feels drawn to her independent, self-assured air. When Michele takes a breather to return home for lunch, she finds the unfed baby crying, Fiona shivering from the effects of drug withdrawal, and Claude (Pierre Banderet), her unemployed husband, drunk. Yet it is only her husband she curses. Soothing the baby with a milk bottle with one arm, while comforting her daughter with the other, Michele seems to accept her lot as today's working mother. When the tranquilizers prescribed for her daughter fail to work, Michele approaches Gerard (Gerard Meylan), a bartender friend, whom we later come to know was a teenage flame owing to whom Michele had to have an abortion. She now pleads for him to get her a drug fix at any cost as a means of saving Fiona.

Through Yves, we come to know the wider economic and political crisis, stemming from the closure of the port. A workers' city "for centuries," Marseille is now being prepared for globalisation, tourism and hi-tech industry. The Far Right, according to Yves, is merely capitalizing on the discontent of the excluded work force. That evening, as Yves reaches out to Viviane for understanding, she dismisses him as a '60s revolutionary-turned-reactionary now shorn of all ideals.

As if reflecting this degeneration on a microcosmic level, Michele is forced to prepare a drug dose for Fiona when her daughter cannot even do that for herself.

Guediguian, at this stage, reinforces the wider socio-political angle with three brief unrelated and undramatic scenes, at the risk of straining our interest. First, there is a rightist political meeting where a speaker argues for national preferences in immigration quotas. Then there is a child pianist, an émigré, who is playing on a public lawn to raise funds to purchase a piano so he can study at the conservatory. This is followed by Viviane approaching Abderamane while he's serving as a bartender.

When we next see Michele she is walking out of a café, tipsy in broad daylight. We see why. As she openly solicits cabbies, offering to sleep with them, they reject her with rude epithets. When she collapses on the concrete, Paul literally extends her a helping hand. He drops her off for free and gives her the amount she has been seeking, without making any demands. In her humiliation, Michele grabs the money and remains silent. Paul then tails her as she meets Gerard outside his bar and scores the drug fix. With its psychological and political crises in place, the film now builds on the tension that will eventually explode.

Gerard becomes involved in a political conspiracy, but we are kept at a distance about the details. All we know at this stage is that it requires him to cultivate a relationship with Ameline, sitting a few tables away in the same café. He follows her, then makes his move, pretending to be drawn by her physical charms. Paul gets around to telling his mother that he's serious about Michele, after which he drops by Michele's place to give her more money. Viviane sleeps with Abderamane in her own living room. We then see Abderamane attempting to talk sense into the head of his younger brother who is an anarchist rapper. Paul soon loses his cabbie license owing to his working double time. This does not however come in the way of his intimacy with Michele, which progresses with her having sex with him in his car, openly defying her husband.

Guediguian's scenes now become even more truncated, reinforcing the feel of an urban mosaic. Michele's flare-up with Claude leads to him storming out with the household savings. Paul's attempts to acquire the cash he needs for Michele has him approaching a friend of his father, but to no avail. Despite Michele administering the doses to her daughter, Fiona's desperate demands for fixes become more frequent, and harrowingly worse. Then the violence erupts. When Abderamane goes skinnydipping at night with his white friends, a racist seen earlier at the political meeting guns him down in cold blood. Gerard, who unbeknownst to him is being followed by Paul, takes aim using a riflescope at a liberal politician attending a rooftop dinner party, and shoots him dead. The following afternoon, Paul's father rages that the assassination is just another symptom of the lion lying down with the lamb, of the elitism in contemporary politics having obliterated the age-old divisions between Right and Left. "It's like DeGaulle drinking with Hitler," he

rants, then adds, "I'll never vote again!" Paul takes it all in, without saying a word.

Michele finally frees herself from her daughter's clutches by administering an overdose, thereby killing Fiona. Gerard comes over and plants the evidence to make it look like an unintentional suicide. "You didn't kill her," Gerard tells her. "She started killing herself long ago." When Paul drops by, and the two men are alone with each other, Gerard tells him of his past with Michele. Soon after, Gerard has a chance altercation with a long-haired youth at a traffic intersection. Gerard steps out of his car and threatens the youth with a revolver, but then his road rage takes a suicidal twist. After a brief flashback of him and Michele in their teens, he shoots himself instead. As an epilogue, a brand-new grand piano is delivered in front of a near slum building by none other than the racists responsible for killing Abderamane. His dream having come true, the child pianist, as innocent as the rest of the city, begins to play a lyrical medley of classical tunes.

Even critics sympathetic to Guediguian's omniscient stance have found the film "indulgent" and only "intermittently compelling" (Elizabeth Weitzman in the *Daily News*). Jan Stuart in *Newsday* finds the film captures "disparate lives at a moment when they are about to connect and combust." Except for Michele and Paul, whom she sees as "studies in well-meaning folk who make misguided decisions with calamitous results . . . (the) other characters fail to engage our sympathies on the same level, a weakness that blunts the film's overall impact." Stephen Holden in the *New York Times* compares Guediguian's effort favorably with *Nashville* and points out that American audiences have been cheated out of the longer version of *The Town Is Quiet* that was shown at the Toronto Film Festival.

*—Vivek Adarkar*

## CREDITS

**Michele:** Ariane Ascaride
**Gerard:** Gerard Meylan
**Fiona:** Julie-Marie Parmentier
**Claude:** Pierre Banderet
**Paul:** Jean-Pierre Darroussin
**Paul's father:** Jacques Boudet
**Paul's mother:** Pascale Roberts
**Yves:** Jacques Pieller
**Viviane:** Christine Brucher
**Abderamane:** Alexandre Ogou

**Origin:** France
**Language:** French
**Released:** 2000

**Production:** Robert Guediguian, Gilles Sandoz, Michel Saint-John; Agat Films, Cie-Diaphana; released by New Yorker Films
**Directed by:** Robert Guediguian
**Written by:** Robert Guediguian, Jean-Louis Milesi
**Cinematography by:** Bernard Cavalie
**Sound:** Laurent Lafran
**Editing:** Bernard Sasia
**Costumes:** Catherine Keller
**Production Design:** Michel Vandestein
**MPAA rating:** Unrated
**Running time:** 132 minutes

## REVIEWS

*Boxoffice.* October, 2001, p. 58.
*Entertainment Weekly.* November 9, 2001, p. 84.
*New York Daily News Online.* October 26, 2001.
*New York Post Online.* October 26, 2001.
*New York Times Online.* October 21, 2001.
*New York Times Online.* October 26, 2001.
*Newsday Online.* October 26, 2001.
*Sight and Sound.* November, 2001, p. 59.
*Variety.* September 25, 2000, p. 66.

## TRIVIA

The film was set and shot in director/writer Robert Guediguian's birthplace of Marseilles, France.

# Training Day

*The only thing more dangerous than the line being crossed, is the cop who will cross it.*
—Movie tagline

**Box Office:** $76.3 million

Denzel Washington plays bad—defiantly, unrepentantly, charismatically bad—as L.A.P.D. Detective Sergeant Alonzo Harris, a 13-year narcotics officer who sees himself as the King Kong of the streets. Maybe he should have remembered just how the big ape ended up. Washington's character wears black and leather and lots of very expensive, ostentatious jewelry. He struts and swaggers with a wide smile, a soft voice, and dead eyes. He can glad-hand with the best, play the paternal mentor, and then pull a gun

and turn rabid. He's so corrupt, he can't believe anyone else could be different.

Think of your worst day at the office and then try to imagine what young police officer Jake Hoyt (Ethan Hawke) is going to go through. Because *Training Day* takes Jake through one day in hell. Jake, who's married with an infant daughter, has only been with the department for 19 months but he's ambitious. He wants to move from a patrol car to become a detective but to do this he needs more experience and thinks he's found his path by working with Alonzo. Jake has only one day to show Alonzo he's worthy of joining his crew but doesn't know that Alonzo has his own plans in motion.

Alonzo starts by intimidation. He has a nervous Jake meet him in a coffee shop and proceeds to belittle his abilities. Then he takes him to his "office," a custom black 1978 Monte Carlo, and drives Jake around the mean L.A. streets. They make a small-time drug bust on some college kids when things first turn freaky. Alonzo forces Jake to smoke a pipe of PCP-laced pot before they have a friendly little drink with Roger (Scott Glenn). Now Roger and Alonzo seem to be old friends—Roger even warns Alonzo that his recent trouble in Vegas is well-known and the Russians still want Alonzo's head—a problem the narc dismisses.

Alonzo and Jake hit the streets again when Jake notices two crackheads about to rape a Hispanic schoolgirl in an alley. He forces Alonzo to stop the car and subdues the two but Alonzo doesn't want to bother arresting them. The girl goes home but Jake picks up her wallet in one of those throwaway moments that will turn out to be of great import later on. Alonzo then rousts Sammy (Snoop Dogg), a wheelchair-bound crack dealer who gives up the name of his supplier. Alonzo and Jake then go to the supplier's house where Alonzo steals the man's considerable money stash.

Alonzo, who's quite the ladies' man, next takes Jake to the home of one of his girlfriends, Lisa (Charlotte Ayanna), in a gangbanger neighborhood where Alonzo gets sullen respect for the favors and protection he offers the inhabitants. All the while they're journeying, Alonzo is offering Jake his wisdom, which consists of street justice, letting the animals take care of each other, and deciding just which animal Jake will be—a wolf or a sheep. If Jake expects to survive he needs to be a wolf. Especially with the trap Alonzo is laying.

At an upscale restaurant, Alonzo meets the "three wise men" (Harris Yulin, Tom Berenger, Raymond J. Barry), three top brass willing to give Alonzo a clear field in return for payoffs. He reassures them he can take care of his Vegas problem and gets a search warrant he needs. Then he calls the other members of his narcotics team to do a bust. They go back to Roger (who it turns out is a longtime dealer) and Alonzo takes the four million dollars Roger has buried beneath the floorboards and then executes him in front of the horrified rookie's eyes. Then Alonzo blackmails him with a murder rap if Jake doesn't go along—or he can just kill Jake as well and put out the usual story about an officer dying in the line of duty.

In one of the film's quietest and therefore most notable scenes, Alonzo has a paternal chat with Jake in the car. Washington excels here as he tries to reassure a shaken Jake that everything that has gone on is ugly but necessary, that Jake needs "a little dirt" on him to prove his loyalty. For a brief moment both Jake and the viewer are lulled by Alonzo's seemingly rational soothing speech. And then Jake sees just what a pawn he truly is. Alonzo goes to do business with some Hispanic homeboys and Jake finally learns that a hotheaded Alonzo beat a man to death during a Vegas weekend and the unfortunate turned out to be connected to the Russian mob. The Russians want a million in cash by midnight to call things even (or they kill Alonzo) and, after ripping Roger off, Alonzo can pay. Jake's just a loose end and Alonzo abandons him.

And here's where that far-fetched coincidence comes into play. One of the would-be killers finds the girl's wallet on Jake and—ta-da!—it so happens the girl is his cousin! So Jake tells how he stopped her from getting raped, his story is confirmed, and they let him go—one good deed deserving another. Now all Jake can think about is stopping Alonzo.

Jake finds him at Lisa's where they first have a shootout and then Jake gets the stuffing kicked out of him. But he's the Energizer bunny of cops and their beef winds up in the street where Alonzo learns that his homies are tired of him playing the big man and they refuse to back him up by killing Jake for him. Jake walks away with the cash that Alonzo needs to keep the Russians from killing him and Alonzo winds up resembling Swiss cheese when the mobsters stop firing their automatic weapons through him. It's all very Bonnie and Clyde but, by this time, the movie has become so implausible that why shouldn't Alonzo's end come in such a fashion. And Jake? Why he goes home as a voiceover explains that officer Alonzo Harris was killed in the line of duty (ah, the coverup). Just imagine what Jake can tell his wife when she asks about his day.

Ethan Hawke can't be said to hold his own against Washington's powerhouse performance of manipulation but he's not blown off the screen either. His weedy look and kid from the 'burbs naivete prove a good counterpoint to the arrogance of Washington's character. When Jake keeps showing up—still seeking justice—Alonzo is surprised. The street player has badly underestimated his opponent and it costs him everything.

*Training Day* is basically a two-character movie; though the film has several other "name" players, only Scott Glenn gets more than one scene to make any impression. As can also be expected the film is very violent and the language is continuously profane for a well-deserved "R" rating. Director Antoine Fuqua keeps the action moving so the viewer is

caught up even as the plot veers further and further off into impossibility. Imagine what would have happened if somehow Alonzo had gotten away with his schemes and Jake was left in even more of a moral quagmire (or been killed)? But no, the good guys win—for what it's worth.

—*Christine Tomassini*

## CREDITS

**Alonzo Harris:** Denzel Washington
**Jake Hoyt:** Ethan Hawke
**Roger:** Scott Glenn
**Smiley:** Clifford Curtis
**Paul:** Dr. Dre
**Sammy:** Snoop Dogg
**Stan Gursky:** Tom Berenger
**Doug Rosselli:** Harris Yulin
**Lou Jacobs:** Raymond J. Barry
**Lisa:** Charlotte Ayanna
**Sandman's wife:** Macy Gray
**Sara:** Eva Mendez
**Tim:** Nicholas Chinlund
**Mark:** Jaime Gomez
**Sniper:** Raymond Cruz

**Origin:** USA
**Released:** 2001
**Production:** Jeffrey Silver, Robert Newmyer; Village Roadshow Pictures, NPV Entertainment, Outlaw Productions; released by Warner Bros.
**Directed by:** Antoine Fuqua
**Written by:** David Ayer
**Cinematography by:** Mauro Fiore
**Music by:** Mark Mancina
**Sound:** Russell Williams II
**Music Supervisor:** John Houlihan
**Editing:** Conrad Buff
**Art Direction:** David Lazan
**Costumes:** Michele Michel
**Production Design:** Naomi Shohan
**MPAA rating:** R
**Running time:** 120 minutes

## REVIEWS

*Chicago Sun-Times Online.* October 5, 2001.
*Entertainment Weekly.* September 21, 2001, p. 52.
*Hollywood Reporter.* September 4, 2001, p. 19.
*Los Angeles Times Online.* October 5, 2001.
*New York Times Online.* October 5, 2001.
*Rolling Stone.* October 11, 2001, p. 98.
*US Weekly.* October 15, 2001, p. 56.

*USA Today Online.* October 5, 2001.
*Variety.* September 3, 2001, p. 38.
*Washington Post Online.* October 5, 2001.

## QUOTES

Alonzo (Denzel Washington) warns Jake (Ethan Hawke): "It's not what you know. It's what you can prove."

## TRIVIA

There were both police consultants and a technical advisor on gangs to help production maintain authenticity as director Antoine Fuqua filmed on street locations in Los Angeles.

## AWARDS AND NOMINATIONS

**Oscars 2001:** Actor (Washington)
**L.A. Film Critics 2001:** Actor (Washington)
**Nomination:**
**Oscars 2001:** Support. Actor (Hawke)
**Golden Globes 2002:** Actor—Drama (Washington)
**Screen Actors Guild 2001:** Actor (Washington), Support. Actor (Hawke).

# The Trumpet of the Swan

 **Box Office:** $.1 million

Many pint-sized filmgoers have been inspired to go the library in search of books by E.B. White after seeing the films of his works, *Charlotte's Web* and *Stuart Little.* But it's difficult to picture any child wanting to search out the *The Trumpet of the Swan* in book form after seeing this film version. As *Entertainment Weekly* put it, "This cartoon adaptation is a pox on the man's memory. The tale of a mute swan who finally finds voice via a trumpet, the film features charmless songs, junky animation, hambone voice talent, deeply square attempts to be hip, and a narrative tone that changes migratory direction every five minutes." Not to put too fine a point on it.

The star of the story is a Canadian trumpeter swan who is named Louie (voiced by Dee Baker), because, according to his father (Jason Alexander), "You were named in the tradition of my father Louie and his father Louie Louie." (See the

EW reference above to "deeply square attempts to be hip.") Louie is a really nice guy and all, but has one problem—he is mute. This is a problem since, in this story, trumpeter swans are big on their trumpeting skills. The problem is compounded by the fact that Louie's father—who is an obnoxious blowhard who could stand to become mute himself—but we digress—is very unaccepting of his son's inability to talk.

This is all very familiar territory to anyone who has ever seen the Rankin-Bass version of *Rudolph the Red-Nosed Reindeer* on TV. It's kid has flaw. Kid is shunned by tough guy father, babied by softie mother (Mary Steenburgen). Just like poor Rudolph, Louie isn't allowed to join in any reindeer, er, swan games. He does find a lovely girl swan, Serena (Reese Witherspoon), who, like Rudolph's Clarese, overlooks his "handicap" and sees the lovely soul within. "I bet it makes you a great listener," she says sweetly.

Louie is frustrated by his predicament and doesn't know what to do about it until he meets a friendly boy, Sam (Sam Gifaldi), who is staying at a nearby summer camp. Louie observes humans communicating through writing and he convinces Sam to take him to school so he, too, can learn to read and write. (Why it is so easy to communicate such a complex sentiment to Sam when he can't convey the simplest of ideas to members of his own species is a little plot problem that probably won't bother most kids—unless they are doomed to become film critics.) Louie leaves the village on a journey that he hopes will return him to his colony as a man, or a man swan, that is.

Louie is one smart swan and quickly learns how to read and write. (The school teacher is voiced by Carol Burnett but the film makes zero use of her ample comedic talents.) Armed with some chalk and a small chalkboard tied around his neck, Louie returns home, ready to communicate with his friends and loved ones. When he gets home, he victoriously scrawls a note on his chalkboard, along with a drawing of a heart. But, uh-oh, there's one big problem with his plan. He didn't factor in the rather important fact that swans can't read. His fellow swans stare at Louie and his cryptic message and decide that he is even weirder than they first thought.

In the meantime, his father has come up with another plan for Louie. The dad flies into the town of Billings, Montana, and creates a ruckus in a local music store. In the midst of the confusion, dad leaves with a trumpet for his son. The dejected Louie gets the trumpet and soon starts learning to play it, which, what with his beak and all, is pretty darned amazing. Would-be girlfriend Serena digs the music, and Louie starts playing well enough to get along in the swan community.

But Louie decides he must leave the pond again. This time his reason is that he has to earn some money to pay for the trumpet to regain his father's honor. His father, who is given to long-winded stories about his own heroics, is the kind of guy who would care deeply about his own honor. If

Louie thought things through, he would realize that maybe it is not the best time to leave since Serena's father is trying to match up his daughter with the local swan Casanova, Boyd (Seth Green).

Louie first gets a job as the bugler at Sam's summer camp but after seeing the meager pay, heads off to Boston to hit the big time. Louie is discovered by a sleazy con man, Monty (Joe Mantegna) who poses as a talent manager in order to exploit Louie's talents for his own gain. Monty may be practically a bum but he turns out to be a successful manager, at least as far as getting Louie big gigs. Louie soon turns into the toast of the town and starts staying in a swank hotel and earning some cash. But will he be able to break out of his restrictive contract with Monty? Will he even make it back to Montana before Serena marries the boorish Boyd? Eh, probably. At this point, only the youngest of children will care—that is, the youngest of children who have remained awake this long.

The film's pace drags so, when plot points like Louie's needing to leave for Boston comes up, instead of the watcher feeling excited about the new adventures yet to come, it's more like, "Oh no, that means the movie's going to last at least 20 more minutes." The jokes meant to ease the film along are simply lame. One such joke is that someone taunts a swan by saying, "Swans are foul." Yeesh. Screenwriter Judy Rothman Rofe throws nary a bone in there for any adults who might be in the audience. The fact that she also includes a goatee-sporting, jive-talking squirrel in the mix just makes matters worse.

In 2001, when *The Trumpet of the Swan* came out, the standards for animated kids' features had become high. It was no longer acceptable to slap a few drawings on film, tell a little morality tale and call it a kids' movie. Kids' movies also had to have artistic, realistic or interesting animation, perhaps a star or two voicing some parts (what kid cares about Jason Alexander?) and, most importantly, a witty and culturally-literate script. Films like the *Toy Story* series and *A Bug's Life* where the story, animation and jokes fairly leaped off the screen, had set the standard and *The Trumpet of the Swan* looked like it wasn't even trying. Audiences noticed too. During a matinee showing opening week in Southern California, there was also a sneak preview of *Shrek*. The line for *Shrek* was out the door. The crowd in the theater for *The Trumpet of the Swan* was so sparse that every person could have had their own row, plus another one to put their feet on.

Critics didn't like the film so much either. Or as the movie's corny screenwriter Rofe might have put it, they, ha-ha, did not "trumpet" their praise for the film. In the *Los Angeles Times,* Jan Stuart wrote, "Nothing quite works about *The Trumpet of the Swan,* one of those animated films that makes you realize just how hard it is to strike the right tone for a family film." Liz Braun of the *Toronto Sun* was not a fan

of the film. She wrote: "The real difficulties lie with a vocal cast inclined to overdo it, the absolute dullness of the story, the moral that (inadvertently or otherwise) suggests a handicap is a bad thing—but—surmountable by fame, and an anthropmorhic presentation of trumpet swans that does little to help conservation efforts on their behalf." Sean Axmaker of the *Seattle Post-Intelligencer* was particularly disappointed in the animation, and wrote, "Badly designed and executed with a perfunctory blandness and cheap bluntness that looks all the more impoverished in the unforgiving dimensions of the big screen, it suffers from sheer creative apathy. The leads flap their arms and mouths and blankly look off into the distance with a glassy stare, while background characters simply rock from side to side as if the animators just needed to get them moving."

—*Jill Hamilton*

## CREDITS

**Louie:** Dee Baker (Voice)
**Father:** Jason Alexander (Voice)
**Mother:** Mary Steenburgen (Voice)
**Serena:** Reese Witherspoon (Voice)
**Boyd:** Seth Green (Voice)
**Mrs. Hammberbotham:** Carol Burnett (Voice)
**Monty:** Joe Mantegna (Voice)
**Sam Beever:** Sam Gifaldi (Voice)

**Origin:** USA
**Released:** 2001
**Production:** Lin Oliver; released by TriStar Pictures
**Directed by:** Richard Rich, Terry L. Noss
**Written by:** Judy Rothman Rofe
**Music by:** Marcus Miller
**Editing:** Joseph L. Campana
**MPAA rating:** G
**Running time:** 75 minutes

## REVIEWS

*Boxoffice.* July, 2001, p. 102.
*Chicago Sun-Times Online.* May 11, 2001.
*Los Angeles Times Online.* May 11, 2001.
*New York Times Online.* May 11, 2001.
*Variety.* May 14, 2001, p. 22.

# The Turandot Project

In 1997 when Zubin Mehta decided to take his Florence production of Puccini's opera *Turandot* to Beijing, China, he wanted the young, "Fifth Generation" film director Zhang Yimou to direct the production, which both artists wanted to be "authentic" in a way no production of the opera had ever been. *The Turandot Projcet*, directed by Allan Miller, provides a fascinating record of that artistic collaboration. Miller is a gifted documentary filmmaker whose work includes the Academy Award®–winning *From Mao to Mozart: Isaac Stern in China* (1980). Though *The Turandot Project* will have special resonance for those who love opera, the political, artistic, and multi-cultural issues at work here are of equal importance. In fact, the plot of the opera is dismissed in one single line: That Princess Turandot will choose from her suitors only the one who answers three riddles. When Calaf succeeds, she accepts him. But even those unfamiliar with the plot of *Turandot* will be swept away by colorful and extravagant spectacle. This is not so much a documentary about a single opera as one about the problems of mounting an amazing production in a decidedly exotic setting.

The documentary begins in Florence, Italy, with rehearsals and costume designs for the *Turandot*. Zubin Mehta is conducting the production and Zhang Yimou is observing, since he has been selected to stage the opera a year later in Beijing, where the opera was set. Therefore, Yimou is there on site in Florence to witness the impact and the original spectacle of the Italian production, which he will later modify for a Chinese audience. The challenge for him is to mount an even larger and more "authentic" spectacle in the People's Republic. After extensive preparations in Italy, then, the Chinese production suffered many changes, not the least of which was the redesigning of 900 costumes to match the style of the Ming dynasty (the time period in which the opera was purportedly set). Coordinating that effort alone would have been demanding, expensive, and time-consuming, but there are other issues as well.

The young Zhang Yimou had been one of the most gifted students of the first "generation" (or class) to graduate from the Beijing Film Academy after the turmoil of China's Cultural Revolution. Because he was both contemporary and controversial, a film director who had broken with tradition in the way he made films about ordinary people in China, Mehta had to lobby with politicians in the People's Republic in order to get approval for the artistic director of his choice before the whole production could move on to Beijing.

At issue here, of course, is the question of what might constitute an "authentic" performance? In the first place, Puccini himself, as Mehta points out, was highly multi-cultural in that he set most of his operas in countries outside of Italy. Secondly, one senses that for Mehta, the performance is more of a stunt than a tribute to Chinese culture, but, if so, that could never be openly stated. Thirdly, if one lights the vast outdoor Beijing pavilion in the high-key way Yimou insists upon to exploit the raw colors and the vividness of the costumes and spectacle, then one sacrifices the subtleties of modulated lighting accents which lighting designer Guido Levi insists best suits Puccini. Often the artists are at odds. Which will win out—the contexts of Chinese theatre, or the drama of Puccini's opera? Both sides are obdurate. While Yimou wanted high-key lighting that would emphasize the colors of the spectacle, the Italian dismissed this rationale as simply "vulgar." Amusingly, Levi notes that the brevity of preparation time and the quirky weather will ultimately force a decision on this issue and prohibit his mounting of all the lights Yimou demands. The director and the lighting designer are constantly at odds, then, on the very nature of the spectacle and how it will appear. Oddly, the issues of the proper performance practice are not addressed. Riding above it all is the problem of directorship: Will this opera more properly be directed by a Chinese artist (Yimou, an opera neophyte) or by a Western artist (Mehta, a world-renowned conductor)? Artistic compromises will be mandatory.

Allan Miller's documentary approach includes interviews with Mehta, Yimou, Levi, cast members, and other talents involved in the production. The singers, most of whom are Italian and American (including Barbara Hendricks), are not used to the Chinese gesturing traditional with operatic performance, though the cast does include one Chinese baritone trained in the West, Zhang Yalun. The documentary demonstrates many other frustrations, such as the spectacular head-dresses that do not sit comfortably atop the requisite wigs.

Other telling details are obvious, such as the casting of 300 Red Army soldiers as drummers and warriors from another era, their commander ordering them not to pay attention to the beautiful women who surround them: "Ignore the ballet girls," he orders. "Violators will be severely punished." When the soldiers march onto the stage to announcement the arrival of the Emperor, they are beating authentic Ming drums. When the extras complain abut the music, which sounds to them like the "sounds of cows moaning," they are chastised: "An army without culture is a stupid army," says the officer in charge of this battalion of soldiers to be used as extras. The lovely, agile female acrobat who is cast as the Executioner is instructed to love her trade and pursue it with sensuous agility. "She's 4 feet 2 and made of rubber!" Mehta remarks in astonishment after seeing her perform.

Once the rehearsal gets underway in China, Miller effectively cross-cuts rehearsal footage with footage of the finished product and the crowds eager to see it, so that viewers have a sense of how the production was received in China. The production was performed out of doors on nine successive nights in the Forbidden City. The role of Turandot is considered so demanding that no one could be expected to sing the role two nights in a row. In China three different performers alternated in singing the lead, and the documentary devotes time to each one; but the primary interest here is in the behind-the-scenes disagreements that needed to be resolved. This documentary has been called a tribute to the creative process re-inventing itself. And so it is.

*—James M. Welsh and John C. Tibbetts*

## CREDITS

**Origin:** USA, Germany
**Language:** English, Chinese, Italian
**Released:** 2000
**Production:** Margaret Smilov; Alternate Current Inc., Four Oaks Foundation, EuroArts Entertainment; released by Zeitgeist Films
**Directed by:** Allan Miller
**Cinematography by:** Tom Hurwitz
**Sound:** Peter Miller
**Editing:** Allan Miller, Donald Klocek
**MPAA rating:** Unrated
**Running time:** 84 minutes

## REVIEWS

*Los Angeles Times Online.* September 14, 2001.
*New York Times Online.* August 10, 2001.
*San Francisco Chronicle.* December 21, 2001, p. D3.
*Village Voice Online.* August 8, 2001.

## QUOTES

Chinese officer to the soldier extras: "Ignore the ballet girls. Violators will be severely punished."

# Two Can Play That Game

*The rules are simple. There are no rules.*
—Movie tagline

**Box Office:** $22.2 million

Have we seen this movie before? It's the one with the successful Buppies and the guys who don't want to commit and the attractive cast. It starts out with a helicopter shot of Los Angeles set to a thumping R&B soundtrack. As we zoom in closer to the city, we hear a female voice saying to her unseen friend, "Oh, you know, he's just a dog!" It all sounds so familiar. Isn't that *The Best Man*? Or is it *The Brothers*? Or maybe even *Waiting to Exhale*? It's actually the latest in Buppie love comedies (BLCs), *Two Can Play That Game*. This film doesn't try to stray too far from the BLCs that have come before it. In fact, its male lead, Morris Chestnut, was also in *The Brothers* and *The Best Man*. How many times do we need to see this man tamed?

The way to tell this film apart from the others is its strong sassy female lead, Shante Smith (Vivica A. Fox). Shante is a woman who has it all together. She is impeccably groomed, gorgeous, and completely sure of herself. She is the youngest partner in a high powered advertising firm, lives in what anyone would describe as a mansion and has her man, Keith Fenton (Chestnut) suitably tamed. Keith is a good catch. He's a successful attorney who is cute, kind, and available for surprise midday romps in his office.

Because she is so smooth, Shante is sort of the mother hen and advice giver to her circle of friends, Karen (Wendy Raquel Robinson), Tracy (Tamala Jones another BLC regular) and Diedre (Mo'Nique), who are less fortunate in love. Their various subplots add a little spice to the story but are very much in the background of the central story of Keith and Shante. One friend, who declares herself "ghetto fabulous," is sticking with a guy who has no job and no charm just because she can't give up the sex. Another friend is mooning over Michael (singer Bobby Brown), a guy she found when he was an ugly mechanic with crooked buck teeth, bad Jheri-curls, and practically zero potential. She paid to fix up his teeth, bought him some new clothes and now Michael, who once begged daily to marry her, is saying that he might need some space.

Shante's world is rocked—just a little—one night when she's out with her friends and she sees Keith at a nightclub dancing with a woman from his office. Shante, who seemingly lives her life by the kind of philosophy laid out in the book *The Rules*, is upset, but she has a plan. After all, her whole worldview is shaped by such rules as "The best way to a man's heart is through his stomach and his sports," "Whoever breaks up with the person first, wins," and "Men want a lady in public and a freak in private." Even though she's secretly upset by Keith's semi-indiscretion, she has a whole 10-day plan mapped out just for such circumstances. After all, in her world, men must be appropriately punished for such minor infractions so that they will become even more malleable and obedient.

The film follows Shante's plan and is divided into segments detailing each day. Her plan involves such tactics as pretending not to be around when the guy calls and suggesting a little break-up so that they can explore other options. It escalates into letting your man see you with a more handsome, successful man and showing up at your man's house clad in your sexiest clothes (in this instance, you tease the man to arousal, then abruptly leave). What Shante doesn't expect is that Keith has a secret back-up strategy. His rotund buddy, Tony (Anthony Anderson), seems to be some sort of savant on relationships. When Keith wants to just give in and crawl back to Shante, Tony urges him to play some games of his own. "This is bigger than you," Tony says with the urgency of one swept away by a cause. "You have to do this for all men." Keith, mainly due to the help of Tony, turns out to be quite a player himself. (Actually the more interesting match-up would have been Shante and Tony, but the movie doesn't head in that direction.) Keith has some tricks up his sleeve, like dating Shante's arch-rival, the equally smooth Conny Spaulding (Gabrielle Union, also a BLC veteran).

Will Shante break Keith? Will Keith break Shante? Will Shante ever free herself of her rules and be able to respond as a human being? If she does, it will be an uphill battle. After all, this is a woman who has her image so tightly controlled that even after she sees Keith with the other women, she goes and cries in the bathroom so that her friends don't see her. Even in her upset state, she doesn't want to spoil her image of invincibility.

Shante's image and rule driven character doesn't sound very attractive on paper, but it's a credit to Fox that she makes Shante a likable and funny character. The whole film rests on Fox pulling it off because not only is Shante the central character, but she narrates most of the film. There are a lot of scenes where she's talking straight to the camera, even in the midst of a kissing scene, but Fox manages to make these seem less gimmicky and more clever than they really are. The same goes for the lines she's forced to say like, "Hmmmpf, what is it with men and booty?" It's a bad line, but Fox gives it every amount of humor it can possibly have. Fox shows a true movie star's skill in being able to carry a film.

Chestnut is less successful as Keith. Since he keeps showing up in these films, he must have something going for him, but it's difficult to tell what that might be. He is handsome, but there's not much going on beyond that. His lawyer is bland, and sort of a dolt as far as love games go. With his job, his looks, and his probable faithfulness, it's like he represents the ideal man, but Chestnut doesn't give him a soul. Anderson gives his all to playing Tony. He is utterly devoted to his friend Keith and takes on his cause with an unrelenting enthusiasm. Anderson brings his big energy to every scene he's in and that's a big plus for the movie. Union, who has a very sweet smile and is thus usually cast as a very sweet girl, plays against type here as an evil rival. She slips into the role well. Poor Mo'Nique is stuck with the stereo-

typical role of ghetto queen. She's funny, but we've seen this before.

In many ways, *Two Can Play That Game* has the feel of a classic battle of the sexes film. The banter and machinations that the characters go through to one up the other one more resembles films with Katherine Hepburn and Spencer Tracy than the usual bland fare that passes for romantic comedy today. If nothing else, it's a vast improvement for writer and director Mark Brown, who was a writer on *How To Be A Player*.

Critics had a wide range of reactions to the film. Generally, the ones who didn't like it, objected to Shante's reliance on playing games. Those who did like it saw it a light, saucy comedy. Gene Seymour in the *Los Angeles Times* wrote, "No one in this buppie fantasy, including its creative team, seems to have any interest in leaving the high school of the mind." The *Philadelphia Inquirer*'s Carrie Rickey said "*Two Can Play That Game*, a snappily fun Mantrap Movie, as films about husband-hunting gals are known, is that rare hybrid of romantic comedy and Super Bowl." Roger Ebert of the *Chicago Sun-Times* thought that "Among the movie's pleasures is the fact that everybody on the screen is very good-looking." Stephanie Zacharek of Salon.com commented that it was refreshing to see a movie not focused on white people: "For one thing, scenes that take place in restaurants and other public places are often only dotted with token whites. It makes you think differently about decades' worth of restaurant scenes with that one black guy seated over in the corner behind the potted palm."

—*Jill Hamilton*

## CREDITS

**Shante Smith:** Vivica A. Fox
**Keith Fenton:** Morris Chestnut
**Tony:** Anthony Anderson
**Conny:** Gabrielle Union
**Karen:** Wendy Raquel Robinson
**Trayce:** Tamala Jones
**Diedre:** Mo'Nique
**Bill:** Ray Wise
**Michael:** Bobby Brown
**Dwain:** Dondre T. Whitfield

**Origin:** USA
**Released:** 2001
**Production:** Doug McHenry, Mark Brown, Paddy Cullen; Screen Gems; released by Sony Pictures
**Directed by:** Mark Brown
**Written by:** Mark Brown
**Cinematography by:** Alexander Grusynski
**Music by:** Marcus Miller

**Sound:** C. Darin Knight
**Music Supervisor:** Rashad Liston
**Editing:** Earl Watson
**Art Direction:** Chase Harlin
**Costumes:** Debrae Little
**Production Design:** Amy Ancona
**MPAA rating:** R
**Running time:** 90 minutes

## REVIEWS

*Boxoffice.* September, 2001, p. 26.
*Boxoffice.* October, 2001, p. 61.
*Chicago Sun-Times Online.* September 7, 2001.
*Los Angeles Times Online.* September 7, 2001.
*New York Times Online.* September 7, 2001.
*Variety.* September 3, 2001, p. 40.
*Washington Post.* September 7, 2001, p. WE43.

# Two Ninas

*Every man's fantasy. This man's nightmare.*
—Movie tagline

Depending on the sophistication of the filmgoer, Neil Turitz's debut *Two Ninas* will either be welcomed by *Friends* or *Seinfeld* devotees or seen as a cliché-filled film by a more sophisticated cineaste. Critics also doled out mixed reviews. Peter Travers of *Rolling Stone* called the film a good date movie whereas, *New York Times* critic Stephen Holden labeled the film, "(a) far less intellectual offspring of Woody Allen's characters drenched in a whiny seinfeldian dyspepsia."

*Two Ninas* is the non-thinking guy's wet dream in that its character Marty (Ron Livingston), an aspiring novelist who happens to like baseball and vintage cars, also happens to be dating two beautiful woman at the same time. Women viewers, on the other hand, might be mildly entertained by Marty's dilemma. He's not such a bad fellow but an average fellow that feasts on the banquet presented before him. He's been in the proverbial desert for some time and hasn't been laid in a year. What's an All-American guy to do? The French would engage in a menage a trois, hearts would be broken, the women would sulk—end of story. We would cry.

However, *Two Ninas* happens to be another one of those tales about the perils of dating in Manhattan. Apparently, in New York the dating scene is either feast or famine. We have seen this with such recent films as *The Sidewalks of New York* and *Fast Food Fast Women*, as well as *Hit and Runway*. At best, it's a beer and buddy film and, at

worse, it's a canvas in which pop culture icons and iconographic images are slapped with references to Barry White and *Pulp Fiction*. And it's a good example of why Europeans find Americans lacking sophistication. However, to its credit, *Two Ninas* doesn't present any slacker characters and in that sense resembles Woody Allen's oeuvre with its relationship-obsessed characters.

Also similar to Allen, Turitz's film opens with the character Dave Trout (Bray Poor) sharing his friend Marty's story directly to the camera. Marty hasn't been laid in a year, he hates his job, and has become despondent over trying to find an agent for his novel. But of course his life changes for the better after he meets his soulmate at a party he didn't even wish to attend. In parallel scenes we see Marty lamenting about women to Dave, while Nina Cohen (Cara Buono) whines about men hitting on her to her friend Carrie (Linda Larkin). As you would expect, Nina and Marty meet at the same party and connect with each other. But when it rains, it pours, and a week or so later, Marty meets another woman named Nina (Amanda Peet) and even though they don't hit it off, he still dates her.

Three months pass by and Marty can't seem to choose between the two Ninas. He finds that he has many things in common with Nina #1, even if she does hold out sexually. He has nothing in common with Nina #2 but loves the sexual nature of their relationship and the fact that her parents are wealthy. Marty's a bit slow in the relationship department, even if he is a so-called genius where novel writing is concerned. He can't seem to figure out that sex isn't everything and that soulmates don't come around every day. As the story unfolds, Marty encounters many close calls. He confuses the two Ninas' numbers (which later culminates in the film's ugly climax), he shows up at the wrong apartment on the wrong night, and he can't keep straight what he's has confessed to each woman.

One close call involves Nina Cohen showing up at the bar where Marty is on a date with Nina Harris. Although Marty isn't caught in the act, it turns out that the two Ninas went to high school together. This scene foreshadows the climax in which Marty leaves a message on the wrong Nina's answering machine and tells her to show up at Dave's party. The two Ninas run into each other and learn that they have been dating the same man. Woe to the average man's fantasy because it leads to dire consequences in heartbreak city. However, Marty does learn from his mistakes. If nothing else, perhaps single men can learn a lesson from Marty and finally move past the whore/virgin dichotomy or the dating scene will improve in the city of Manhattan and filmgoers will be spared another Woody Allen clone.

—*Patty-Lynne Herlevi*

## CREDITS

**Marty Sachs:** Ron Livingston
**Nina Cohen:** Cara Buono
**Nina Harris:** Amanda Peet
**Dave Trout:** Bray Poor
**Mike the bartender:** Jill(ian) Hennessey

**Origin:** USA
**Released:** 2000
**Production:** Denise Doyle, E. Greg Scheinman; released by Castle Hill Productions
**Directed by:** Neil Turitz
**Written by:** Neil Turitz
**Cinematography by:** Joaquin Baca-Asay
**Music by:** Joseph Saba
**Editing:** Jay Chandrasekhar
**Costumes:** Stacey Lapidus
**Production Design:** Anthony Gasparro
**MPAA rating:** R
**Running time:** 90 minutes

## REVIEWS

*Hollywood Reporter.* January 30, 2001, p. 21.
*Los Angeles Times Online.* January 26, 2001.
*New York Times Online.* January 26, 2001.
*Village Voice Online.* January 24, 2001.

## QUOTES

Dave Trout (Bray Poor): "Chicks can smell fear like wolverines."

# Unconquering the Last Frontier

It might be news to non-residents of the Pacific Northwest that many species of salmon have made it on to the Endangered Species list or that much of the Northwest has been deforested in the name of progress. And viewers only now waking up to the nation's environmental disasters might find it inconceivable that the dams once built to provide cheap electricity are one cause for the loss of salmon in Washington State, as suggested by director Robert Lundahl with *Unconquering the Last Frontier.* Lundahl focuses the Klallam people of Port Angeles, Washington, and

their battle to remove two dams off of the Elwha River in order to save the salmon and their sacred way of life from extinction. Although the Klallam people won their battle, the dams still have not been removed and controversy ensues.

Lundahl spent seven years producing *Unconquering the Last Frontier,* a rebuttal to dam founder and developer Thomas Aldwell's biography *Conquering the Last Frontier.* Lundahl's film presents a carefully researched debate on the removal of the dams, along with archival photographs, and interviews with fishery workers, biologists, Klallam tribal elders, a historian, and Port Angeles' old timers. The downside of Lundahl's documentary is that it's a traditional PBS-style documentary filled with talking heads and mixed with archival footage and provocative sound bites. The documentary's structure tends to be run of the mill, whereas the documentary's message proves to be emotionally charged and timely. But despite the environmental-related subject matter, Lundahl's standard narrative structure could garner a large audience interested in protecting the planet's wildlife, salmon included.

At the opening of the film, a camera pans over a lit-up Port Angeles while a narrator recites Raymond Carver's poem "At Night the Salmon Move." The sequence recalls the Beat Poets in San Francisco in the 1950s, San Francisco acting as the bigger brother to Port Angeles, another city founded by the timber industry and the gold rush. While Port Angeles never grew to the size of San Francisco or Seattle, it's a city founded by aggressive entrepreneurs out to conquer the west in the name of progress. In the case of Port Angeles, Ontario-born Tom Aldwell made his fortune as a real estate developer and the founder of the first dam to be built illegally on the Elwha River in 1910. Depending on what side of the argument viewers fall, Aldwell might be seen as a villain or an upstanding citizen. However, the Elwha people, who lost their way of life and their land to the destructive forces of the Euro-American settlers, blame Aldwell and his progress manifesto for the loss of salmon.

Cut to tribal elders performing a salmon ceremony on a Port Angeles beach as they give thanks to their life sustainer. At one time in history, this ceremony would have been performed by a large gathering of tribal people but today only a handful gather at the beach as only a handful of salmon return to their spawning ground. It becomes increasingly clear as footage of deforested hillsides, empty rivers, and small tribal gatherings take place that the heritage of the Olympic Peninsula is also disappearing—creating an explosive situation for environmental activists, ecologists, politicians, and Native Americans. And the controversy that surrounds the dams on the Elwha River will not disappear after the dams have been removed.

Tribal fisherman Joe Luce claims, "It will be 20 years before the river will restore itself." At a county commissioner's meeting, a scientist argues, "fish restoration and dam removal are not compatible," as he also notes the negative environmental impact of removing the dams. Another attendee notes that given the history of how the European-Americans treated the Klallam people by building an illegal dam that destroyed their livelihood, no judge would deny the Klallam their request to remove the dams. And in February 2000, the federal government purchased the dams in the first step towards removal.

Lundahl provides viewers with an intriguing history lesson of the Pacific Northwest and also presents viewers with a microcosmic debate that has been played out across the U.S. As the title implies, tribal nations and environmentalists have united to reclaim land scarred by progress. Some day, someone will direct a feature about the Klallam people's victory, until then, Lundahl whets our appetite for underdogs who work to reclaim their land.

—*Patty-Lynne Herlevi*

## CREDITS

**Narrator:** Gary Farmer

**Origin:** USA
**Released:** 2000
**Production:** Robert Lundahl; Evolution Films
**Directed by:** Robert Lundahl
**Cinematography by:** Robert Lundahl, Hillary Morgan
**Sound:** Peter Bettendorf, Scot Charles
**Editing:** Robert Lundahl, Scott Cliffin
**MPAA rating:** Unrated
**Running time:** 100 minutes

## REVIEWS

*San Francisco Bay Guardian.* October 18, 2000, p. 82.

## QUOTES

Beatrice Charles, Klallam Elder: "We were told that the land was given to us by the maker."

# Under Hellgate Bridge

U*nder Hellgate Bridge* offers nothing original to the drugs-and-gangsters movie genre, but at least it is efficiently made. Michael Sergio writes, directs and produces the story of three brothers whose lives are destroyed by heroin addiction. Sergio keeps the subject and style basic, but the work is surprisingly accomplished for a first-time effort.

In Queens, New York, a young man dies from a drug overdose. At the funeral, the family's mourning is disrupted when Ryan (Michael Rodrick), the dead man's eldest brother, arrives late. Now back in the neighborhood, after serving time in prison, Ryan tries to help his surviving brother, Eddie (Brian Vincent), who is also addicted to drugs. Ryan restarts an old feud with the small-time druglord Vincent (Jonathan LaPaglia), who married Ryan's former flame, Carla (Jordan Bayne), while Ryan was in jail.

Eventually, Ryan tells Carla he still loves and cares for her, while Carla, in turn, surprises Ryan with the news that he, not Vincent, is the father of her young boy. When Vincent catches word of the renewed affair, he tortures Carla, which leads to a deadly confrontation between Ryan and Vincent in a neighborhood bar. The conflict ends with Vincent's death and Ryan, Carla, and their son fleeing the crime scene to start a new life.

Hellgate Bridge is a bridge in Queens, New York City, best known as a drug-trade location. It is also the place—in the story—where Ryan's brother dies, and it further stands as a metaphor for the bridge to a better place for the protagonists. Michael Sergio has called his film, "a modern-day western in present-day Astoria" and "*Shane* meets *Goodfellas.*" Yet, there is little irony or revisionism in the writer-director's "modern" riff—the film more resembles *Dead End* or *Angels With Dirty Faces*, from 1930's Hollywood, than any kind of recent gangster picture—e.g. *Pulp Fiction*, with Quentin Tarantino's Chinese Box storytelling, or *The Sopranos*, with its sardonic tone. Even *The Godfather* and *Goodfellas* display more innovation, stylistically and thematically.

But the classical throwback approach underscores the cautionary anti-drug message, and befits the serious, elemental storyline. No less than an old James Cagney-Warner Bros. film, *Under Hellgate Bridge* becomes emotionally involving. Sergio does a good job of creating a gritty world, pacing the lively action, and keeping focus on his functional narrative. Moreover, for a low-budget indie, Sergio mounts a exceptional production, thanks primarily to cinematographer Leland Krane, production designer Casey Benjamin, and composer Stephen Moccio.

Best of all, the actor-turned-director shows deft handling of his cast, including Michael Rodrick and Jonathan

LaPaglia (brother of Anthony) as the arch enemies (both actors reveal true star potential), and Dominic Chianese (from *The Sopranos*) as a sympathetic priest. Jordan Bayne, as Carla, has a little more problem portraying the heroine caught between husband and lover, because Carla's motivations are not so clearly defined and because her part, like the other women's roles, are more passive than active (one can't help wondering why Carla ever married the despicable Vincent, especially if she knew she was pregnant with Ryan's child).

There are a few other liabilities, including an unpleasantly graphic rape scene (representing Vincent's revenge on Carla), the overly pat ending, and the fact that there is so little comic relief (*Goodfellas* and *Sopranos* aficionados will find *Under Hellgate Bridge* just too earnest and downbeat). Still, the film meets the requirements of the traditional gangster movie genre, so if you don't expect too much, you might be perfectly satisfied.

—*Eric Monder*

# Under the Sand (Sous le Sable)

*Can love vanish without a trace?*
—Movie tagline

**Box Office:** $1.5 million

American viewers became acquainted with French auteur Francois Ozon's films in 1998 when his shorts *See the Sea* and *Summer Dress* hit the North American festival circuit. In 1999, the Seattle International Film Festival (SIFF) included Ozon in its Emerging Master series while introducing Ozon's debut feature *Sitcom*. In 2000, Ozon's *Criminal Lovers* and *Water Drops on Burning Rocks* played to a devoted SIFF audience, then in 2001, the director's release *Under The Sand* sold out at the festival. Ozon has become one of France's hottest young directors, ripe with imagination while recalling the genius of a Luis Buñuel.

Extremely prolific, Ozon's oeuvre runs the gamut from chilling to audacious, whimsical, dark, and amusing. Similar to Claude Chabrol, Ozon appears keenly interested in the psychological workings of human beings. However, despite the comparison, Ozon has thrown a curve ball with *Under the Sand*, a compassionate unsolved mystery and Ozon's most mature film to date.

*Under the Sand* stars the middle-aged Charlotte Rampling as a woman in denial over the loss of her husband. While the film revolves around the mystery of a disappearing husband (did he commit suicide, drown by accident, or just walk away?), Ozon focuses on how vibrant, devoted wife Marie (Rampling) grapples with her circumstances. According to Ozon: "I wanted to show a woman who was beautiful at 50, with an active sexual and social life." Rampling seemed at ease wearing a bathing suit while showing off her body and cinematographer Jeanne Lapoirie decided not to use filters in order to portray the beauty of age. The French have a saying that a woman's life begins at 50 and perhaps that is why French women age so well, whereas, in North America, women over 35 are expected to partake in anti-aging technology or hide in a closet. However, we only have to look at Rampling to realize that ageism is a powerful myth.

Ozon makes another bold move by creating an examination of a 50-year-old woman's sexuality along with his team of women screenwriters. If Federico Fellini had hired women to script the controversial *City of Women*, the compassionate sensibility for women present in Ozon's feature might have also been present in Fellini's film. Ozon takes it a few steps further by focusing on the two men that engage

## CREDITS

**Eddie:** Brian Vincent
**Doreen:** Careena Melia
**Ryan:** Michael Rodrick
**Vincent:** Jonathan LaPaglia
**Carla:** Jordan Bayne
**Big Sal:** Frank Vincent
**Mitch:** Vincent Pastore
**Father Nichols:** Dominic Chianese

**Origin:** USA
**Released:** 1999
**Production:** Isil Bagdadi; Fortune Films, D3 Films; released by CAVU Pictures
**Directed by:** Michael Sergio
**Written by:** Michael Sergio
**Cinematography by:** Leland Krane
**Music by:** Stephan Moccio
**Sound:** Joe Cunningham
**Editing:** Stan Warnow
**Costumes:** Melissa Bruning
**Production Design:** Casey Benjamin
**MPAA rating:** R
**Running time:** 87 minutes

## REVIEWS

*New York Times Online.* May 11, 2001.

Marie. First we meet Marie's husband Jean (Bruno Cremer), who is an equivalent to the macho Burt Lancaster, and his opposite, Maria's new lover, the ultra-sensitive Vincent (Jacques Nolot), who can't satisfy Marie in the sack. Jean appears as a ghost to Marie while Vincent grapples with Marie's inability to let go of her deceased husband.

Married for 25 years, Marie and Jean are vacationing at their summer cottage. One day at the beach, Marie takes a nap while Jean goes for a swim, only he vanishes. A frantic search, complete with helicopter, ensues, but eventually Marie must return to Paris and her busy teaching schedule while still grappling with Jean's disappearance. However, Marie doesn't appear to be grieving and she acts as if her husband is still alive. Her friend Amanda (Alexandra Stewart) fixes her up with Vincent but Marie just goes through the motions.

Marie receives a call from the authorities who claim they found the body of a man that fits Jean's description, but the man's body has deteriorated past the point of recognition. Meanwhile, Jean's recalcitrant mother (Andree Tainsy) predicts that Jean left Marie because he was depressed. Marie replies caustically that his mother should have been committed to a mental hospital instead of a nursing home. When Marie visits the coroners, she claims that the watch found on the corpse isn't Jean's watch, but is this denial or did Jean abandon Marie on purpose? Ozon isn't saying.

*Under the Sand* proves that filmmaking is a collaborative work and Ozon had the good sense to allow Rampling and his women co-writers to render a compelling character. Ozon goes boldly into dangerous cinematic territory by focusing on a grieving middle-aged woman and Rampling mesmerizes viewers daring enough to take the ride.

—*Patty-Lynne Herlevi*

## CREDITS

**Marie Drillon:** Charlotte Rampling
**Jean Drillon:** Bruno Cremer
**Vincent:** Jacques Nolot
**Amanda:** Alexandra Stewart
**Gerard:** Pierre Vernier
**Suzanne, Jean's mother:** Andree Tainsey

**Origin:** France
**Language:** French
**Released:** 2000
**Production:** Olivier Delbosc, Marc Missionier; Haut et Court, Arte France Cinema, Euro Space; released by Winstar Cinema
**Directed by:** Francois Ozon
**Written by:** Francois Ozon, Marina de Van, Emmanuele Bernheim, Marcia Romano

**Cinematography by:** Jeanne Lapoirie, Antoine Heberle
**Music by:** Philippe Rombi
**Sound:** Jean-Luc Audy, Benoit Hillebrant, Jean-Pierre Laforce
**Editing:** Lawrence Bawedin
**Art Direction:** Sandrine Canoux
**Costumes:** Pascaline Chavanne
**MPAA rating:** Unrated
**Running time:** 95 minutes

## REVIEWS

*Boxoffice.* May, 2001, p. 57.
*Entertainment Weekly.* May 11, 2001, p. 51.
*Los Angeles Times Online.* May 18, 2001.
*New York Times Online.* May 4, 2001.
*People.* May 14, 2001, p. 40.
*Sight and Sound.* April, 2001, p. 59.
*Variety.* September 25, 2000, p. 63.
*Washington Post Online.* July 20, 2001, p. WE30.

## TRIVIA

The first part of the film was shot on 25mm in September; the second part was shot 6 months later with Super 16.

# Under the Sun (Under Solen)

English-born director Colin Nutley, who has lived and worked in Sweden for many years, has, on one hand, been blessed with the generous Swedish film grant system that has allowed him to forge a career as a filmmaker. On the other hand, Nutley has suffered the same distribution woes as other international directors due to the subtitling of his films. Distribution politics aside, Nutley doesn't appear to be complaining and why would he? He married his leading lady, Helena Bergstrom. and has garnered several film awards including an Oscar® nomination for Best Foreign Language Film for his feature, *Under The Sun*, a subtle romantic gem with spectacular photography.

Although Nutley might be English by blood ties, he is Swedish at heart, capturing the Swedes love of nature and familial connections. Cinematographer Jens Fischer lovingly captures Olof's (Rolf Lassgard) dog emerging from a sun-drenched lake or close-ups of insects that have been integrated into the film. Later, the same lens captures the awkwardness between two lovers when the 40-year-old Olof finally loses his virginity to the beautiful woman who has captured his heart. To say that *Under The Sun* waxes poetic at every turn would be an understatement and it is as the press notes claim, "a lovely and sensuous film that is truly timeless" and recalls Bo Widerberg's classic *Elvira Madigan* with a happy ending. This film makes country life seem appealing to say the least, despite the lack of proper toilet facilities or barn roofs that leak during a heavy summer rainstorm. We forget those things as we watch a romance blossom between two unlikely lovers.

In 1956, Olof places an ad in a local newspaper that reads, "lonely farmer, 39, own car, seeks a young lady house-keeper. Photograph appreciated." Ironically, Olof never even reads the newspaper since he's illiterate. Two young women answer the ad, but only one, Ellen (Helena Bergstrom), a sophisticated and beautiful 34-year-old woman from the city, sends a photograph. Soon Ellen moves in and takes over Olof's household, to the protests of Olof's 27-year-old friend Erik (Johan Widerberg), a Don Juan who brags about bagging over 100 women. In an earlier scene, Erik asks Olof why he doesn't learn to read and Olof responds by telling Erik that he trusts him and therefore doesn't need to learn how to read. This scene foreshadows future complications that arise between the self-serving Erik and the innocent Olof.

As Ellen cooks and cleans for Olof, she develops an attraction for the naïve farmer and tries to protect him from the scheming Erik. Although Erik is involved with a young farm girl, Lena (Linda Ulvaeus), he finds Ellen to be irresist-ible even if she doesn't fall prey to his James Dean act. Ellen only sees Erik's insecurities, which are hidden behind macho bravado, and she finds his antics to be laughable at best and dangerous to Olof at worst. But as a romance develops between Olof and Ellen, we learn that Ellen harbors a secret that will render the demise of the budding romance. One day, after Olof practically proposes marriage to the dis-traught housekeeper, Ellen decides to leave Olof and return to her husband in the city. She leaves a note behind, but because Olof can't read, he enlists the help of duplicitous Erik. Erik lies and tells Olof that Ellen confessed that she stole the money that Erik paid back to Olof for a loan. When in fact, the letter confesses that Ellen was returning to her husband even though she will always love Olof.

Fortunately, Olof isn't a fool and he realizes that Erik has lied to him. Chagrined, Erik decides to board a mer-chant ship heading to the U.S. Ellen returns to Olof, leading to a sweet ending full of promise for the couple's future as they spend their days on the farm. Although Nutley's scen-ario takes place in rural Sweden during the 1950s, this story of innocence lost still reverberates through contemporary society. And in any case *Under The Sun*, with its luminous performances, pastoral photography, and soundtrack com-

pliments of The Chieftains' Paddy Maloney, allows us an alternative to the current trend of dark cinema that has dominated arthouse screens.

—*Patty-Lynne Herlevi*

## CREDITS

**Olof:** Rolf Lassgard
**Ellen:** Helena Bergstrom
**Erik:** Johan Widerberg
**Preacher:** Jonas Falk
**Lena:** Linda Ulvaeus

**Origin:** Sweden
**Language:** Swedish
**Released:** 1998
**Production:** Colin Nutley; Svensk Filmindustri, Sweetwater; released by Shadow Distribution
**Directed by:** Colin Nutley
**Written by:** Colin Nutley
**Cinematography by:** Jens Fischer
**Music by:** Paddy Maloney
**Sound:** Bo Persson, Lasse Liljeholm
**Editing:** Perry Schaffer
**Costumes:** Camilla Thulin
**Production Design:** Bengt Froderberg
**MPAA rating:** Unrated
**Running time:** 118 minutes

## REVIEWS

*Boxoffice.* May, 2001, p. 57.
*Chicago Sun-Times Online.* August 31, 2001.
*Hollywood Reporter.* August 8, 2001, p. 18.
*Los Angeles Times Online.* August 17, 2001.
*New York Times Online.* August 3, 2001.
*Variety.* January 18, 1998, p. 44.
*Washington Post.* October 12, 2001, p. WE45.

## AWARDS AND NOMINATIONS

**Nomination:**
**Oscars 1999:** Foreign Film.

# Va Savoir
# (Who Knows?)

*In matters of the heart, it's anyone's guess.*
—Movie tagline

 **Box Office:** $.7 million

Jacques Rivette, who provided much of the intellectual drive for the French New Wave right from its inception in the late '50s, is perhaps the most serious living filmmaker his country has produced. His latest opus, *Va Savoir (Who Knows?)* could easily be mistaken for a sophisticated comic soap opera if one didn't place it in the context of his last major work, *La Belle Noiseuse* (1991). Not that you couldn't enjoy *Va Savoir* all by itself, but you could very easily miss out on its ideological core.

In *La Belle Noiseuse,* we watch enthralled for nearly four hours as an once-famous artist paints a portrait in front of our eyes, inspired by his beautiful model. When he completes this work, we never get to see it. Instead, he buries it in the wall of his studio so that it will remain lost to the world as well. In *Va Savoir,* Ugo (Sergio Castellito), an Italian stage director in charge of a modest theater troupe performing in Italian in Paris, is driven to hunt out an apocryphal work by the late 18th-century Italian playwright, Goldoni, who is supposed to have written it while in Paris, and gifted it to Vernet, the friend he was staying with. The manuscript of the play, when Ugo does manage to get his hands on it at the end of the film, proves too valuable for Ugo to commit himself to a production. "To produce the play," he admits, "will only reduce its value." He means amongst that coterie who prize "lost" works. Like the painting buried in the wall, Rivette seems to hint, the world will never get to see this comic masterpiece.

*Va Savoir* is strewn with such dichotomies: theater versus life, philosophy versus academicism and most important, love versus jealousy. Beneath it all, of course, is the dichotomy of Rivette's cinematic vision versus the artifice of the theater he portrays. Like Ugo, Rivette's other characters too embody these contradictions.

Ugo's lover, the slinky Camille (Jeanne Balibar) is the leading light of his theater troupe and the only outsider amongst them. As a French expatriate, she is back in Paris after leaving it three years ago. The déjà vu she seems to be experiencing is making her highly-strung and, by all indications, schizoid. Her reason for exiling herself in the first place was to get away from Pierre (Jacques Bonaffe), a balding, amiable academic-cum-philosopher. Pierre resists her charms, but only at first. Soon his passion becomes too much for the one week fling Camille has in mind. He is ready not only to cast his philosophy to the winds but, along with it, his loving relationship with the beautiful and wily Sonia (Marianne Basler), a ballet teacher, with whom he is now living, and hopes to marry within a year.

This basic emotional triangle at the heart of the film extends itself through subplots until it becomes a mesh of of interweaving lives and sensibilities. Ugo, looking for the manuscript of the Goldoni play, enters the world of Madame Desprez (Catherine Rouvel), a kindly widow who is heir to the Vernet collection, which she has been unable to sell owing to her attachment to her first husband. Trouble is, none of it has been classified, so Pierre in effect has to look for a needle in a haystack. In the process, he meets the young, vivacious Dominique (Helene De Fougerolles), the daughter of the family and a graduate student in antiquities, who develops a crush on him. Her half-brother, Arthur (Bruno Todeschini), from Madame Desprez' second marriage, is wooing Sonia behind Pierre's back.

The Pirandello comedy, "As You Desire Me," which Ugo's troupe is performing provides the center of gravity to which the film keeps returning. As in his *Mad Love* (1968), Rivette shows how theater can influence life, but more important, how both are sustained by a substratum of artifice. Thus, the jealousy created by the husband's return from the dead in the Pirandello play is mirrored in the lives of the film's principals. Pierre even goes to the extent of proposing that Martin Heidegger, the famous German 20th-century existential philosopher preoccupied with radical notions of time and being, was really jealous of life itself. Furthermore, according to the treatise Pierre is working on, the history of man shows jealousy as the dominant force behind dictatorships, on all levels.

We see Camille jealous of Sonia, since Pierre admits to loving her. Ugo becomes jealous of Pierre, as he comes to realize that Camille is still emotionally attached to him. Pierre becomes jealous of Ugo, since Camille is not only living with him but shares the even tighter bond of theater. Sonia, on her part, is jealous of Camille when she realizes that Pierre is still in love with his old flame. Arthur, after seeing Camille perform, becomes smitten by her, and that makes him hostile to, and jealous of Ugo. Young Dominique, pure as sunshine, and buried in the work required for her thesis, finds her equanimity disturbed by her sudden urge for Ugo, which in turn makes her jealous of Camille.

Jealousy also seems to pervade the film's antinomies. The Pirandello play within the film, cursed to remain within the classical boundaries of the proscenium arch, would appear to be jealous of the emotional rhythms of contemporary life transpiring outside its pale. On a deeper level, both theater and life, as Rivette juxtaposes them, would appear to be jealous of the medium of film that, in Rivette's hands, can laugh at both. Lastly, on the deepest level of all, is the jealousy at the core of the film, which suggests that all the art that we will ever come to know would appear to be jealous of the art that is lost to us forever.

If *Va Savoir* can be said to be dramatically flawed in comparison with *La Belle Noiseuse*, it could lie in the fact that we never get to know what the "lost" play really means to Ugo. This detracts from our emotional involvement, though Rivette keeps his scenes moving at a sprightly pace. First come the scenes in which there is so much going on that a viewer couldn't possibly take it in at a first viewing, given the added task of having to read the subtitles. Such a scene is the intimate dinner at Pierre's. While Pierre speaks of Heidegger and Malaparte, Sonia, Camille and Ugo can be seen to interpret the philosophy, each according to their own preoccupations. Similarly, the scenes between Dominique and Ugo, where her sly astuteness shows that she knows that Ugo's real interest is not in the cause of theater. Also, after remaining supercilious to Camille's all too human admission of love for him, Pierre's resolve seems to be crumbling from within even as he speaks to her about the intellectual conflict in his life between teaching and writing philosophy. Also, the scenes between Sonia and Camille where, behind the surface congeniality, Sonia tries to gauge Camille's feelings for Pierre and then, enlists her help to get back at Arthur.

Then come the scenes of a quixotic nature that veer off in unexpected directions. After Pierre finally admits his mad love for Camille, it is her turn to play the rational one, whereupon he locks her up in a back room in his apartment. Since she's required to be at the theater to perform, she manages to open a skylight and climb her way out. Similarly, Ugo decides to challenge Pierre to an old-fashioned duel in which, as the offended party, Ugo gets to choose the weapons and the place. In this case, two full bottles of vodka, which the two will consume on a catwalk high above the stage, each one daring the other to keep his balance. The duel results in revealing Pierre himself to be jealous of Heidegger, before he falls off and, as planned by Ugo, is saved by a trampoline.

A similar irony surrounds the discovery of the lost Goldoni, which winds up amongst a stack of cookbooks. Though it is Madame Desprez who finds it, it is Dominique who recognizes it as the volume Ugo is after. What steers the film towards its denouement is the subplot involving Sonia's ring, an heirloom from the Second Empire embedded with two diamonds. While recounting to Camille the antisocial social life of her youth, she suddenly realises that Arthur has stolen her ring and substituted it with a fake. In desperation, she later pleads with Camille to steal the ring back from him. Camille, who already has had to fight off a love struck Arthur, agrees, presumably as a means of having Sonia under her thumb.

To this end, Camille strikes a deal with Arthur that she will sleep with him, but only for one night. Then at dawn, she slips out of bed and looks for the ring in his kitchen, of all places. She hunts in the salt and the sugar, and finally finds it in the flour. Sonia, after all that, admits to "feeling lighter" without the ring, and gifts it to Camille, who in turn presents it to Ugo, who plans to sell it and thereby save his ailing theater troupe. To the strains of Peggy Lee's "Senza Fine," the film strikes its closing note with the lyrics, "No end at all. No tears. No fears. No love that dies."

Critics have welcomed what they perceive as a departure for Rivette from the seriousness of his previous work. Even so, they have noticed the mastery of a chef trying his hand at a new dessert. Jay Carr in the *Boston Globe* calls the film a "seductively appealing comedy" that is "soufflé-light and airily playful." Edward Guthmann in the *San Francisco Chronicle* points out that as the film "develops new layers as the characters collide and intertwine, its pleasures increase with its complexity." Elvis Mitchell in the *New York Times,* while waxing eloquent on the film's guilty pleasures, sees it as Rivette proclaiming "the second half of his career at age 73."

*—Vivek Adarkar*

## CREDITS

**Camille:** Jeanne Balibar
**Ugo:** Sergio Castellitto
**Pierre:** Jacques Bonnaffe
**Sonia:** Marianne Basler
**Do:** Helene de Fougerolles
**Arthur:** Bruno Todeschini
**Mother:** Catherine Rouvel
**Librarian:** Claude Berri

**Origin:** France, Italy, Germany
**Language:** French
**Released:** 2001
**Production:** Martine Marignac; Pierre Grise Productions, France 2 Cinema, Mikado Films, Kinowelt, VM Productions; released by Sony Pictures Classics
**Directed by:** Jacques Rivette
**Written by:** Jacques Rivette, Christine Laurent, Pascal Bonitzer
**Cinematography by:** William Lubtchansky
**Sound:** Florian Eidenbenz
**Editing:** Nicole Lubtchansky
**Costumes:** Christine Laurent, Laurence Struz
**Production Design:** Manu de Chauvigny
**MPAA rating:** PG-13
**Running time:** 154 minutes

**REVIEWS**

*Boston Globe Online.* October 12, 2001.
*Boxoffice.* September, 2001, p. 144.
*Chicago Sun-Times Online.* November 16, 2001.
*Entertainment Weekly.* October 5, 2001, p. 109.
*Los Angeles Times Online.* October 5, 2001.
*New Republic Online.* October 15, 2001.
*New York Times Online.* Septembe 28, 2001.
*San Francisco Chronicle Online.* October 12, 2001.
*USA Today Online.* September 28, 2001.
*Variety.* May 28, 2001, p. 18.
*Washington Post.* October 26, 2001, p. C5.

# Valentine

*Love hurts.*
—Movie tagline

*Remember that kid everyone ignored on Valentine's Day? He remembers you.*
—Movie tagline

 **Box Office:** $20.4 million

1988 was a tough year for Jeremy Melton. An awkward, bespectacled, nerdy pre-teen, he had a crush on every cute girl in the sixth grade: Shelley, the smart one; Lily, the fun one; Kate, the nice one; and Paige, the sexy one. Can we begin to imagine the courage he had to muster just to ask each of them to dance at his school's Valentine's Day party? Can we imagine his pain as each one rejects him with lines as kind as "maybe later" to as cruel as "I'd rather be boiled alive."

Then, in the bleachers, he spied a lonely, overweight young girl. Her classmates call her Buffalo and she is obviously as much an outcast as is Jeremy. Together the two loners found solace in each other's prepubescent arms, kissing under the bleachers. When a group of the school's tough guys find them, their taunts are especially hurtful. To protect herself, Buffalo loudly claims that she wasn't making out with Jeremy, he was attacking her. With this further rejection, the stressed out Jeremy drips blood from his nose just before the boys jump on him, strip him down to his underwear, drag him out onto the dance floor and beat him up. One of the last images Jeremy must have seen were the faces of his classmates passively watching his complete humiliation, including one who is wearing a Cupid mask.

Fast forward 13 years later. Shelley (Katherine Heigl), the smart one, is now studying to be a doctor. As she prepares to dissect a corpse while studying for her anatomy exams the next day, she suddenly hears unusual sounds in the lab. Following them into the changing area, she finds a Valentine's Day card stuck to her locker. "The journey of love is an arduous trek. My love grows for you as you bleed from your neck," it reads. Shelley dismisses the gory rhyme and returns to her autopsy. Just as she is about to plunge in her scalpel, the corpse begins to breath. Of course it's not the corpse, it's the killer who is going to begin his spree by killing Shelly. It's a killer who dresses only in black. A killer who wears that same Cupid mask from the school party 13 years ago. A killer who bleeds from his nose after the emotional high of killing, just as Jeremy did after being caught under the bleachers.

At Shelley's funeral, all the cute girls from Robert F. Kennedy school are together again. The fun one, Lily (Jessica Cauffiel), the nice one, Kate (Marley Shelton), the sexy one, Paige (Denise Richards), and even the fat one, Dorothy (Jessica Capshaw), formerly known as the Buffalo but now slim and pretty and rich. As Detective Vaughn (Fulvio Cerce) tries to find the murderer, more Valentines arrive. Dorothy receives one that says, "roses are red, violets are blue, they'll need dental records to identify you." Signed "J.M." Dorothy is not the next victim, however, instead Lily is dispatched by the masked Cupid's bow and arrows at an art exhibit by an oversexed artist named Max (Johnny Whitworth).

Detective Vaughn—and the audience—has no shortage of suspects. Shelley's date from the night she was murdered is missing, Max is obviously short on morals, Dorothy has taken a nere-do-well named Campbell (Daniel Cosgrove) into her home, Kate has a neighbor everyone calls "scary Gary," and then there's Adam (David Boreanaz). Adam is Kate's ex-boyfriend. She broke up with him because he drank too much, but he's been on the wagon for three weeks and is begging Kate for a second chance. But he can't possibly be the murderer, he's such a nice guy . . . when he's sober. And besides, he's so cute . . . Jeremy was a grade A nerd.

As the body count rises, the remaining girls and Detective Vaughn begin to believe the murders are being done by Jeremy. (But one has to wonder why he's not taking his anger out on the boys who humiliated and beat him. Oh yeah, men in peril won't bring 'em in at the boxoffice the way beautiful, sexy women in peril will.) However, Jeremy's history since the sixth grade is a bit hazy. It seems that Dorothy's false accusations caused the young boy to be sent to a reform school and from there to Juvenile Hall and then on to a state mental hospital. After that is a blank. No records and no photos of an adult Jeremy exist . . . he could be anywhere . . . or anyone.

So, with all this mayhem going on around them, what's the next thing the girls do? Hold a huge Valentine's Day party. Nothing like rounding up all the victims and suspects in a hubbub of loud music, shadowy party lights, and a large mansion with lots of rooms, closets, crawlspaces, basements and hot tubs. Have they never seen a horror movie in their entire lives? How did they miss *Scream*? Could they do anything more stupid? Yep, they keep splitting up. That way they're easier pickings for the murderer.

*Valentine* is a movie that might have had potential but ends up falling flat. For those who don't want anything more from their horror films but a body count, they'll be satisfied with what's dished up here. For those of us who at least expect a degree of thoughtfulness, or ingenuity, or humor, they're all lost in the mail in *Valentine*. Perhaps its most fatal flaw is that it's just not scary. It begins by making the viewer feel sympathy for the character who will turn out to be the murderer and proceeds by making us feel very little sympathy for those getting killed. If we don't care about the victims, tension is hard to generate.

All the actresses play characters who are pretty, self-absorbed, self-assured, rich, and/or mean. We don't like these kind of people in real life, why should we like them on film? Even the actresses themselves are standard issue, pretty-faced, mix-and-match blondes who take a while to straighten out as characters. The only non-blonde is Denise Richards—seen previously in *Wild Things* and as possibly one of the worst ever Bond girls in *The World Is Not Enough*. Here she is so over the top on bitchiness that we hope she gets killed early in the film. No such luck.

Of course the actor who probably has the most recognizable face and name in *Valentine*, the actor with top billing, is David Boreanaz. Making his theatrical film debut after a highly successful run as the vampire Angel in TV's *Buffy the Vampire Slayer* and its equally successful spin-off *Angel*, Boreanaz is miscast and underused in the film. Boreanaz is not given much screen time and is basically delegated to being just another suspect. Even worse for the hunky actor, though is the fact that he seems too old to play a contemporary of the other actresses who, given the chronology of the film, are playing women in their early 20s. (Boreanaz turns 30 in May 2001). The only benefit to having Boreanaz in the film (besides his name value) are the weak jokes made in reference to his vampire character. When one woman confronts Kate that her boyfriend might really be the killer she replies with, "I know Adam. OK, he's no angel, but . . ." Unfortunately, the film is so inept one can't help but wonder if it was accidental humor.

Writers Donna and Wayne Powers and Gretchen J. Berg and Aaron Harberts make it fairly easy to figure out who the killer is despite some red herrings that stink to high heaven because they are so tired. We've seen all this before: *My Bloody Valentine* and *Prom Night* just to name a few. And in that passive, white Cupid's mask, the killer in *Valentine* looks like a Michael Meyers offspring. *Valentine* director Jamie Blanks also made *Urban Legends*, a movie with a great premise (people killed according to urban legends) weakly delivered on. In *Valentine* the same problem occurs. It has one interesting gimmick, the gory valentines, but then doesn't even deliver on the gruesome fate predicted in the grisly rhymes. In fact, except for the decorations at Dorothy's party, the movie doesn't even exploit the holiday very well. It is, however, the decorations that deliver one of the film's most annoying and illogical missteps. When all the power goes off at Dorothy's mansion during the final reel, all the decorations stay eerily lit—good for atmosphere and so we can see what's going on, but totally illogical. But then, is being illogical any worse than being just plain boring?

*—Beverley Bare Buehrer*

## CREDITS

**Adam Carr:** David Boreanaz
**Paige Prescott:** Denise Richards
**Kate Davies:** Marley Shelton
**Dorothy Wheeler:** Jessica Capshaw
**Shelley:** Katherine Heigl
**Max Ives:** Johnny Whitworth
**Ruthie:** Hedy Burress
**Lily:** Jessica Cauffiel
**Det. Vaughn:** Fulvio Cecere
**Campbell:** Daniel Cosgrove

**Origin:** USA
**Released:** 2001
**Production:** Dylan Sellers; NPV Entertainment, Village Roadshow Pictures; released by Warner Bros.
**Directed by:** Jamie Blanks
**Written by:** Donna Powers, Wayne Powers, Gretchen J. Berg, Aaron Harberts
**Cinematography by:** Rick Bota
**Music by:** Don Davis
**Sound:** William Butler
**Editing:** Steve Mirkovich
**Art Direction:** Sue Parker
**Costumes:** Kavin Nosella
**Production Design:** Stephen Geaghan
**MPAA rating:** R
**Running time:** 96 minutes

## REVIEWS

*Boxoffice.* April, 2001, p. 240.
*Entertainment Weekly.* February 16, 2001, p. 71.
*New York Post Online.* February 2, 2001.
*New York Times Online.* February 3, 2001.
*San Francisco Chronicle.* February 3, 2001, p. B3.
*Sight and Sound.* June, 2001, p. 55.
*Variety.* February 5, 2001, p. 39.

Kate (Marley Shelton): "So what do you think? Why am I surrounded by all this craziness?" Adam (David Boreanez): "It's Valentine's. People get lonely and they start acting strange."

# Vanilla Sky

*Looks can be deceiving.*
—Movie tagline
*LoveHateDreamsLifeWorkPlayFriendshipSex.*
—Movie tagline

 **Box Office:** $71.4 million

Tom Cruise in a way replicates the hedonistic character he played for Stanley Kubrick in *Eyes Wide Shut* (1999) in *Vanilla Sky,* directed by Cameron Crowe for Paramount, adapted from the 1997 Spanish film *Open Your Eyes (Abre Los Ojos),* written by Alejandro Amenabar and Mateo Gil, and starring Penelope Cruz, who is also featured in the remake, which, of course, changes the setting from Madrid to New York City. The problem is that the Cruise character is no more likable here than he was in Kubrick's final film, just more self-centered.

The fabulously wealthy David Aames (Cruise) heads a publishing empire he inherited from his father and controls 51 percent of the stock. He is pitted against a hostile board of directors, whom he contemptuously dismisses as the "seven dwarfs," a potentially dangerous group who may be organizing a conspiracy to lever David out of his controlling position. His sole advocate seems to be corporate lawyer Thomas Tipp, played by the incomparable Timothy Spall, memorable for his previous roles as Guildenstern in Kenneth Branagh's *Hamlet* (1996) and as the sleazy Eric Lyle in Bernardo Bertolucci's respectful but distorted adaptation of the Paul Bowles novel *The Sheltering Sky* (1990). Lawyer Tipp seems loyal to David, but the details of David's story are so ambiguous that it is difficult to know exactly what to believe. David is an unreliable narrator, unable to distinguish between his dreams and the reality that leads him to prison, where he attempts to remember what has happened for a psychologist whose job it is to make a decision about his sanity. In other words, the plot is potentially insane, perhaps a tale twice told by an idiot.

David is used to getting his way and enjoys an indulgent lifestyle, but, as the film suggests from the very opening, he is troubled by bad dreams that only get worse as the story unfolds. David is awakened one morning by a voice urging him to "open your eyes," after which he gets up, dresses, plucks a gray hair from his hairline, then goes for a drive through oddly deserted streets; he stops the car at Times Square, gets out, leaving the door open at an intersection, then starts running full tilt through the deserted streets, panicked, and looking for other people. But this is apparently only a dream, an isolating nightmare, one that is immediately corrected when his awakening is then repeated. This time, however, he drives undisturbed through streets that are populated. David therefore appears to exist in two worlds, one a disturbing and perhaps prefiguring dreamscape. All this occurs well before the later accident that will change his life and outlook. Thus the camera takes the viewer into David's disturbed mind.

David's femme of the moment is Julie Gianni (Cameron Diaz), who has a passion for multiple orgasms that David is at first happy to satisfy, until he meets Spanish beauty Sofia Serrano (Penelope Cruz), who is considerably less horny and plays harder to get. The film's odd title is explained only in a throwaway comment David makes to her, describing the "vanilla sky" that is a background in a Monet painting he owns. David's friend, Brian Shelby (Jason Lee), a writer, first introduces him to Sofia, who accompanies him to David's birthday party. When David promptly makes passes at her, Brian is disappointed, but hardly surprised. Possessed of a *Fatal Attraction*-level of insane obsession, Julie, who was not invited to the party but turns up there anyway, stalks David as he takes Sofia home after the party. As David leaves Sofia's apartment and is about to get into his Mustang, Julie drives up and wants to talk. Unwisely, he gets into her car, and the ride gets bumpy as soon as the rubber hits the road.

Julie is psychotic, as David is about to learn. Julie asks David to define happiness and then turns recklessly suicidal, driving 80 miles per hour through city streets until she crashes through a bridge railing and wrecks the car, as well as David's good looks. That should have taken Julie out of the picture, but she lingers on in David's subconscious. David is seriously injured and disfigured, meanwhile, and after some time in a coma, is operated upon. His face is so twisted and scarred, however, that he wears a prosthetic latex mask, and he walks with a limp. More significant is the damage done to his brain; after pins have been inserted as part of his reconstructive surgery, David suffers from headaches and delusions, as is gradually revealed. He becomes a delusional, paranoid psychopath, unable to distinguish between reality and his disturbed dreamworld.

The film is determined to play head games with the viewer. Just as sequences seem to make sense, the film pulls the rug out from under the viewer by taking several bizarre and unexpected, grotesque turns. In one narrative strand, for example, David appears to have recovered from his trauma, his face returned to its former attractiveness by skilled plastic surgeons; he appears to have resumed his romance with Sofia; he at first appears to be "normal," but later turns violent.

This episode is preceded by a prison interrogation involving David and a psychologist named McCabe (Kurt Russell), who is charged with determining whether David is sane. On this narrative plane David has been charged with murder. He thinks he has killed Julie, who somehow survived her accident, but, apparently, he has in fact murdered Sofia, thinking she was Julie. As the story continues David gets even more delusional. Was he killed by the accident or merely maimed? Either way, did he sign a contract with an agent from the "Life Extended" cryogenic corporation? Does he exist in fact, or is he living in a state of suspended animation? Towards the end the film takes a turn towards science fiction as the "Life Extended" agent urges David to "take charge" of his life. *Washington Post Weekend* reviewer Desson Howe complained that "the movie conceals its compass" from the viewers, and, consequently, "we don't know north from south, up from down." In other words, viewers are abandoned in "mega-weird territory," then left to their own devices.

Key events of David's disturbed life are repeated. An apparently healed David goes to bed with Sofia and wakes up to find himself with the apparently dead Julie. Portraits he has drawn of Sofia on one narrative level turn into portraits of Julie on another. When he is in bed with Sofia at her apartment, the wall is decorated with a poster of Jeanne Moreau from Truffaut's *Jules and Jim* (1961), but when Sofia turns into Julie, the poster changes to Godard's *Breathless* (1959), suggesting a split between romance and fatality. When Sofia turns into Julie, David snaps and smothers her, as if trying to escape from a nightmare. By this point the viewer may also be looking for an escape route from an irritatingly insane plot.

The last time actor Tom Cruise joined forces with writer-director Cameron Crowe they struck Oscar® gold with *Jerry Maguire* in 1996, so expectations might have been high for *Vanilla Sky*, but in this case a very confusing plot could not be saved by either top-ranked stars or Crowe's music track, or, for that matter, by a cameo appearance by Steven Spielberg at David's birthday party. The usually gentle Owen Gleiberman of *Entertainment Weekly* was more confused than dazzled by the convoluted plot: "The way that the film has been edited," he wrote, "none of the fake-outs and reversals have any weight; the more they pile up, the less we hold on to any of them." In a fit of petulance he gave the film a D+, which presumably means a thumbs down. Other reviewers were also put off by the manipulative plot, and the reviews were mixed, as *Variety* predicted they would be. *Washington Post* reviewer Stephen Hunter dismissed this "erotic thriller" which he found "neither erotic nor thrilling" as being "overblown and idiotic."

Joe Morgenstern of the *Wall Street Journal* was puzzled by *Vanilla Sky*, not so much by figuring out what is a dream and what is not, as determining why Tom Cruise would have acquired the rights to the picture and why Crowe chose to write and direct an "almost shot-for-shot rendering" of the Spanish original about "a handsome, shallow playboy who may or may not have murdered a young woman, and who may or may not have been disfigured by an accident." Hence Morgenstern took nothing suggested by the film as being real or true. Morgenstern criticized Crowe for taking "a clever little art film" and then turning it into a pretentious and "ponderous star vehicle with a pop-rock soundtrack."

*Variety* reviewer Todd McCarthy pointed out that although Crowe's adaptation follows the structure of the original, it also sanitizes the action to a degree, making David's disfiguring less grotesque and attempting to explain more fully what might have happened in the film's final moment, "so the audience won't go out totally flummoxed." The remake may be a little less confusing, but, like its title, it is "more bland and less provocative." Morgenstern was more demanding in his charge that *Vanilla Sky* "betrays its source by softening its selfish hero." The Cameron Diaz character is also softened into being an unbalanced kook rather than the apparently dangerous stalker she turns into.

*Variety* praised Cruise's portrayal of the superficial playboy who is at the center of this mystery and praised the picture for its "vitality, a fine cast, and excellent craft." The production design was also singled out as being "especially fine in its detail." *New York Times* reviewer Stephen Holden considered the film a "timely fable about male vanity" and described it as a "highly entertaining, erotic science-fiction thriller" that shifts from "a yuppie frolic to a morality tale, framed in a Hitchcockian riddle." In his *Washington Times* review Gary Arnold quoted an "elegant statement" by Alejandro Amenabar, who likened his original and the American remake to "two very special brothers. They have the same concerns, but their personalities are quite different. In other words, they sing the same song but with quite different voices: One likes opera, and the other likes rock 'n' roll." That seems quite appropriate, given the particular enthusiasms of Cameron Crowe. And, certainly, anyone could be charmed by the performance of Penelope Cruz, whose presence makes the puzzle a little less irritating and more watchable, though the picture is still out of joint.

—*James M. Welsh*

## CREDITS

**David Aames:** Tom Cruise
**Sofia Serrano:** Penelope Cruz
**Julie Gianni:** Cameron Diaz
**Brian Shelby:** Jason Lee

**McCabe:** Kurt Russell
**Edmund Ventura:** Noah Taylor
**Thomas Tipp:** Timothy Spall
**Rebecca Dearborn:** Tilda Swinton
**Libby:** Alicia Witt
**Peter Brown:** Johnny Galecki
**Aaron:** Michael Shannon

**Origin:** USA
**Released:** 2001
**Production:** Tom Cruise, Paula Wagner, Cameron Crowe; Cruise-Wagner Productions, Vinyl Films; released by Paramount Pictures
**Directed by:** Cameron Crowe
**Written by:** Cameron Crowe
**Cinematography by:** John Toll
**Music by:** Nancy Wilson
**Sound:** Jeff Wexler
**Music Supervisor:** Danny Bramson
**Editing:** Joe Hutshing, Mark Livolsi
**Art Direction:** Beat Frutiger
**Costumes:** Betsy Heimann
**Production Design:** Catherine Hardwicke
**MPAA rating:** R
**Running time:** 135 minutes

## REVIEWS

*Baltimore Sun.* December 14, 2001, p. E1.
*Chicago Sun-Times Online.* December 14, 2001.
*Entertainment Weekly.* January 4, 2002, p. 45.
*Los Angeles Times Online.* December 14, 2001.
*New York Times.* December 14, 2001, p. E28.
*People.* December 24, 2001, p. 32.
*USA Today Online.* December 13, 2001.
*Variety.* December 10, 2001, p. 32.
*Wall Street Journal.* December 14, 2001, p. W1.
*Washington Post.* December 14, 2001, p. C1.
*Washington Post Weekend.* December 14, 2001, p. 37.
*Washington Times.* December 7, 2001, p. B6.

## QUOTES

Julie (Cameron Diaz) to David (Tom Cruise): "When you sleep with someone, your body makes a promise whether you do or not."

## AWARDS AND NOMINATIONS

**Nomination:**
**Golden Globes 2002:** Song ("Vanilla Sky"), Support. Actress (Diaz)

**Screen Actors Guild 2001:** Support. Actress (Diaz)
**Broadcast Film Critics 2001:** Song ("Vanilla Sky"), Support. Actress (Diaz).

# The Vertical Ray of the Sun

 **Box Office:** $.1 million

The *Vertical Ray of the Sun* seems like an apology from director Tran Anh Hung for having shown Vietnam in such a harsh light in his last film, *Cyclo.* One can almost hear the chattering types influencing the filmmaker: "Why doesn't he make nice movies like his first?" (the stylish, sensual *Scent of Green Papaya*). Whatever the inspiration, *Vertical Ray* is a likable little movie, though nothing that revelatory.

The story seems like an update of Chekhov's *Three Sisters,* set in Hanoi, with three Vietnamese sisters, all cafe owners, still mourning the death of their mother after four years. The two older sisters are married to temperamental artists, while the youngest shares a house with the family's one brother. This latter relationship is considered odd by outsiders; many onlookers believe Lien (Tran Nu Yen Khe) and Hai (Ngo Quang Hai) are committing incest. Lien tries to find a husband who looks like Hai, but the one man she has any interest in (Le Vu Long) rejects her bossy ways.

Meanwhile, oldest sister Suong (Nguy Nhu Quynh) learns that her photographer husband, Quoc (Chu Hung), is a bigamist who has a family in other town; and middle sister Khanh (Le Khanh) tries to work things out with her husband, Kien (Tran Manh Cuong), who looks at other women instead of finishing his novel. Finally, the married sisters reconcile with their straying husbands, and Lien, after suggesting she might be pregnant, joins her siblings in commemorating their father's death.

*The Vertical Ray of the Sun* features all the stylish polish of Tran Anh Hung's impressive debut. It is magnificently shot by Mark Lee Ping-Bin, who helped Wong Kar-wai create the lovely, voluptuous *In the Mood for Love.* The leisurely pace and attention to detail is another trademark from Tran's first film (not his more boisterous second). But there is a stately sadness that permeates the narrative this time, making *Vertical Ray* potentially more adult, and less melodramatic, than *The Scent of Green Papaya.*

Unfortunately, there is no way getting around the fact that Tran sees modern Vietnam world through ethnocentric eyes of his other native country, France (the director was born in Asia but grew up in Europe). Thus, the very way the sisters accept the erring ways of their philandering husbands is more retro than even a Douglas Sirk scenario. What should have been revisionist and contemplative in the manner of Robert Altman's *Three Women* ends up pat and sexist. The shift in the women's mourning from their mother to their father symbolizes Tran's patriarchal attitude and message. So, for all its aesthetic riches, *Vertical Ray* has a barren soul.

—*Eric Monder*

## CREDITS

**Lien:** Tran Nu Yen-Khe
**Suong:** Nguyen Nhu Quynh
**Khanh:** Le Khanh
**Kien:** Tran Manh Cuong
**Quoc:** Chu Ngoc Hung
**Hai:** Ngo Quang Hai

**Origin:** Vietnam, France
**Language:** Vietnamese
**Released:** 2000
**Production:** Christophe Rossignon; Canal Plus, Arte France Cinema, Lazennec; released by Sony Pictures Classics
**Directed by:** Tran Anh Hung
**Written by:** Tran Anh Hung
**Cinematography by:** Mark Lee Ping-Bin
**Music by:** Ton That Tiet
**Editing:** Mario Battistel
**Art Direction:** Benoit Barouh
**Costumes:** Susan Lu
**MPAA rating:** PG-13
**Running time:** 112 minutes

## REVIEWS

*Entertainment Weekly.* July 27, 2001, p. 47.
*Los Angeles Times Online.* July 6, 2001.
*New York Times Online.* July 6, 2001.
*USA Today Online.* July 6, 2001.
*Washington Post.* August 17, 2001, p. WE34.

# The Visit

*Believe In Miracles.*
—Movie tagline

he Visit took the tortoise's "slow and steady wins the race" technique to getting out in theaters. The film, adapted from a play by Kosmond Russell (which in turn was inspired by a true story of Russell's brother), first came out in 2000. It played at several film festivals and was nominated for four Independent Spirit Awards. It got picked up for distribution by tiny Urbanworld Films, and was the first film for that company. Urbanworld's debut efforts paid off, the film made its premiere nationwide in theaters in mid-2001.

The film itself takes the same "slow and steady" tack in telling its story. Director Jordan Walker-Pearlman, a 33-year-old making his directorial debut, doesn't stray too far from the story's origins as a play. Most of the film takes place in a single place—the visiting room of a prison—and most of the action involves conversation.

The film is centered around Alex Waters (Hill Harper), a young, attractive African-American who's serving a 25-year sentence for a rape he says he didn't commit. Alex had a rough adolescence, filled with mischief, petty crime, and a drug addiction and even some of his family members aren't sure whether Alex is innocent. Alex hasn't been helping matters by the way he treats his family. He's prickly and combative. When his brother, Tony (Obba Babatunde), an upstanding citizen with a wife and kids, comes to visit, Alex reprimands him for not visiting in 10 months. Alex's hostility is not unmerited. Through his merciless questioning of his brother, it becomes apparent that Tony's excuses for not visiting—the wife, the kids, being busy—are covering up the real reason for his absence. He's ashamed of his brother and doesn't want his family exposed to him.

Relations are even more strained between Alex and his parents. His mother, Lois (1970s TV star Marla Gibbs), loves her son and thinks he's innocent but doesn't come to visit him because she is afraid to defy the wishes of her husband, Henry (Billy Dee Williams). Henry is a stern man who has earned everything in his life through hard work and self-discipline. He is bitterly disappointed in his son and thinks that the young man is probably guilty of rape. In a way, Henry's belief in his son's guilt is a coping mechanism. When Alex was first put on trial for rape, the boy was too proud to ask for his father's financial help to get a good lawyer. Henry was also too proud to offer his son any financial help. So, instead of facing his own responsibility for his son's incarceration, Henry has to tell himself that the boy is guilty. Despite the strain between Alex and his family, he's trying to connect with them. His quest for a closeness is made for urgent because he's dying of AIDS.

Because Alex often acts so surly to his family members, it's hard to see that he even wants their love but director Walker-Pearlman inserts some oddly effective and touching scenes into the film that make Alex more sympathetic. When Alex's mother finally comes to visit, it doesn't go well. Conversation is awkward and eventually Alex gets into a yelling match with his father. The strained encounter is highlighted by a group photo that the family poses for. The family could pretend that they are a normal family taking a normal family picture, but it's obvious they aren't, especially when photographer suggests that the group stands away from the prison sign that forbids the taking of hostages. The final picture shows the mother beaming, the father scowling, and the son looking defiant.

But later we see Alex in his cell. The photo has been lovingly pasted, alongside other cherished photos, on his wall. In a sepia-toned sequence, we see Alex's dream. He dances with his mother in his tiny cell. The mother holds him lovingly, laughing, and the son beams with love for his mama, as a jazz song plays on the soundtrack. In the sequence, Alex is not a surly criminal; he is a son who just wants to bask in some love. In another sequence, the father reads from *The Little Prince* to his attentive son. The director has some of the credit for the effectiveness of these scene. The music, the unreal lighting, and the giddy camera work are all Walker-Pearlman's doing. But Harper shares credit, too. Even though he's a grown man, he's able to convey the openness and joy of a young boy. With his subtle acting, he lets us see the happy boy that he once was.

The film shows Alex's slow progression from isolated criminal to a man who finds a sort of redemption through love. He's helped along the way by the prison psychologist, Dr. Coles (Phylicia Rashad), and a former childhood friend-turned crack addict-turned religious mother of a handicapped child, Felicia McDonald (Rae Dawn Chong). With its subject matters of AIDS, prison and family strain, *The Visit* covers some heavy territory and the film never lets the viewer forget this. There are some tear-jerking segments, but all of the moments grow organically from the subject matter and aren't overplayed just for effect, like in many Hollywood films. But despite the dark subject matter, the film doesn't seem oppressively gloomy. Or at least, not in a bad way.

Much of the film's charm comes from Walker-Pearlman's direction. His work has the freshness and energy of a debut from a young person. It's like he's been saving up ideas all his life and finally has a film to try them out on. Besides the dream sequences, which include scenes of Alex dancing or playing with Felicia, his brother and his father, Walker-Pearlman seems willing to try out unusual ideas. When Alex goes up against the parole board, for example, the board sits up high in their chairs behind an impenetra-ble-seeming desk. They are eerily lit, which reinforces the kind of ominous and mysterious power that they hold over Alex. The jazz soundtrack also adds a lot to the film, adding a touch of moodiness here and there (although moodiness is not something the film was lacking in the first place.)

The acting in the film is uniformly outstanding. Harper's Alex doesn't get to reveal very much of his character through what he says, so the actor has the tall order of letting the audience discover his feelings through his demeanor. Harper does just that and exceptionally well. Williams is also good as Alex's stern father. Williams, who's known as a sex symbol, is almost unrecognizable at first as a middle-aged man who's let life beat him down a bit. Gibbs is also good at portraying the difficult area of a woman who loves her child with all her heart but is simultaneously willing to turn away from the child in order to please her husband and keep her marriage running smoothly. Chong plays Felicia as a woman filled with the newfound power of one who feels they have been saved by Jesus. In flashback sequences of her life as a homeless crack addict, she releases all vanity to show the character as a crazed, toothless, desperate woman.

The majority of critics liked the film, although, of course, not everyone did. Filmcritic.com, which was in the latter category, said, "*The Visit* is a prime example of a movie that has clearly been agonized over and loved, but to virtually no ultimate effect. Pearlman is so obviously enamored with the material, he can't see the forest for the trees." But *The Visit* had more good reviews than bad. The *Philadelphia Inquirer* wrote that "the work of its exceptionally fine cast resonates in the viewer's consciousness long after the credits have rolled." The *Los Angeles Times* credited Walker-Pearlman's "acute sense of how to realize visually a work intended for the stage while respecting its text" and cinematographer John Ndiaga Demps' "fluid and expressive camera work."

The director saw the film and its setting as a metaphor. "I think we all go through periods in our lives where we feel that we're imprisoned by something," he said in an interview with the *Los Angeles Times*. "But wherever you are in life, if you find yourself isolated in an emotional prison or a spiritual prison or a physical prison, you always have an opportunity to break out. It's never too late."

—*Jill Hamilton*

## CREDITS

**Alex Waters:** Hill Harper
**Tony Waters:** Obba Babatunde
**Henry Waters:** Billy Dee Williams
**Lois Waters:** Marla Gibbs
**Felicia McDonald:** Rae Dawn Chong
**Dr. Coles:** Phylicia Rashad

**Marilyn Coffey:** Talia Shire
**Bill Brenner:** David Clennon
**Al Reingold:** Glynn Turman
**Max Cruz:** Efrain Figueroa
**Julie Bronsky:** Amy Stiller

**Origin:** USA
**Released:** 2000
**Production:** Jordan Walker-Pearlman; DaWa Films; released by Urbanworld Films
**Directed by:** Jordan Walker-Pearlman
**Written by:** Jordan Walker-Pearlman
**Cinematography by:** John Ndiaga Demps
**Music by:** Michael Bearden
**Sound:** Mike Hall
**Editing:** Jordan Walker-Pearlman, Alison Learned
**Art Direction:** Andy Brittan
**Costumes:** Carlos Rosario
**Production Design:** John Larena
**MPAA rating:** R
**Running time:** 107 minutes

## REVIEWS

*Chicago Sun-Times Online.* April 20, 2001.
*Entertainment Weekly.* May 4, 2001, p. 45.
*Hollywood Reporter.* December 15, 2000, p. 22.
*Los Angeles Times Online.* April 20, 2001.
*New York Times.* April 15, 2001, p. AR25.
*People.* May 7, 2001, p. 35.
*Variety.* June 26, 2000, p. 24.
*Washington Post Online.* April 20, 2001.

## TRIVIA

Kosmond Russell based his play *The Visit* on his experiences with his brother who was in prison.

# Voyages

I n Emmanuel Finkiel's debut feature *Voyages,* estranged Jewish exiles search for roots and identity while missing important familial connections. Imagine two buses, one with a long lost child and the other with a parental figure thought deceased, passing each other and neither the child nor the parent take notice. In an press kit interview, Finkiel described his inspiration: "I tried to recreate the feelings I had years ago when I first heard the incredible tales of these people scattered all over the world, but whose lives were intertwined."

Finkiel, who began his career working as an assistant director for Jean-Luc Godard and Krzysztof Kieslowski, paints with a similar palette. Leslie Camhi in the *New York Times* describes the Kieslowski's impact on Finkiel's work: "Kieslowski's influence may be felt in Mr. Finkiel's preoccupation with the themes of chance and destiny, and his way of filming characters from behind to preserve their essential mystery." And Godard's lack-of-structure and unresolved sequences can also be seen in Finkiel's *Voyages.*

Finkiel tells three stories about three different women in Poland, Paris, and Tel Aviv. All of the women have a connection to Paris and all three of the women lost relatives at Auschwitz, but only a thin thread connects the destiny of the women. It's plausible, even though it's not revealed, that the three women are related but, nevertheless, their lives intertwine, adding a unique tension to the film's narrative structure.

Rivka (Shulamit Adar), a 65-year-old Frenchwoman who found exile in Israel after the war, joins a group of Jews on a bus tour from Warsaw to Auschwitz. Rivka engages in an explosive argument with her husband that brings the couple to the verge of breaking up. The bus breaks down in the middle of rural Poland, adding to the mounting tension between the couple and also allowing various Jews to tell their personal stories regarding the Holocaust. As this takes place, cinematographer Hans Meier's lens loving lingers on the passengers' aging faces. Eventually, the passengers reach Auschwitz where a young filmmaker shoots footage of a Jewish ceremony. However, Rivka has fallen asleep on the bus so she doesn't appear in the documentary film that captured the Auschwitz visit.

Cut to a presentation of the same documentary for a Jewish club in Paris. Regine (Liliane Rovere), who resembles and is the same age as Rivka, watches the screening of the film. Later, Regine receives a call from a stranger who claims to be her deceased father. Although Regine wants to believe that the man actually is her father, he turns out to be someone who happens to share her maiden name. Regine takes him in just the same and introduces him to her daughter and grandchildren as if he were a long-lost relative. Regine joins her "father" in finding his real daughter, who might be in Israel.

Cut to another tour bus on route to Israel. Vera (Esther Gorintin), an 85-year-old Russian-Jew, immigrates to Israel with her Russian neighbors, hoping to reunite with her cousin. But after a long search through a city where no one speaks Yiddish anymore and after enduring blinding heat, Vera learns that her cousin has ended up in a retirement home. Vera then makes her way through the chaotic streets of Tel Aviv where she finally reunites with her cousin. But Vera takes the wrong bus back to her hotel and she encounters Rivka, leaving behind a question in viewers' minds as to the relationship between the two women. That evening Rivka receives a phone call from Paris from a stranger with the same last name as hers. Again, we are left wondering if Regine was the Paris caller.

Finkiel's unconventional and open-ended film might not interest viewers outside of the film festival circuit or Jewish communities. Although the director explores intriguing concepts revolving around identity and destiny, the film's slow pace requires that viewers possess extraordinary patience. The director complicates matters by presenting three languages (French, Yiddish, and Hebrew) within three stories that barely connect to one another. While *Voyages* boasts ambitious film making, the film will only be enjoyed by a select audience. It is not a film for the young and restless but for older folks who desire sustenance during their twilight years. It needs to simmer.

—*Patty-Lynne Herlevi*

## CREDITS

**Rivka:** Shulamit Adar
**Regine:** Liliane Rovere
**Vera:** Esther Gorintin
**Graneck:** Nathan Cogan
**Shimon:** Moscu Alcalay
**Mendelbaum:** Maurice Chevit

**Origin:** France
**Language:** French, Hebrew, Yiddish
**Released:** 1999
**Production:** Yael Fogiel; Studio Canal Plus, Arte France Cinema, Paradise Films; released by New Yorker Films
**Directed by:** Emmanuel Finkiel
**Written by:** Emmanuel Finkiel
**Cinematography by:** Hans Meier, Jean-Claude Larrieu
**Sound:** Pierre Gamet, Francois Waledisch, William Flageollet
**Editing:** Emmanuelle Castro
**Costumes:** Tzipi Anglisher, Jeannine Gonzalez
**Production Design:** Katia Wyszkop, Dorota Ignaczak
**MPAA rating:** Unrated
**Running time:** 115 minutes

## REVIEWS

*eye Weekly Online.* July 13, 2000.
*New York Times Online.* March 27, 2000.
*San Francisco Chronicle Online.* December 15, 2000.
*Toronto Sun Online.* July 14, 2000.
*Village Voice Online.* January 24, 2001.

## AWARDS AND NOMINATIONS

**Cesar 2000:** Director, Film Editing.

# Waking Life

**Box Office:** $2.5 million

For the first time since making a name for himself with the cult hit *Slacker* (1991), director Richard Linklater got the chance to direct his first big budget studio feature, *The Newton Boys*, in 1998. That western, about some bank robbers, did not even gross half of its budget. After that, mainstream Hollywood was unwilling to bank on him, which, to use the title of his 1993 effort, must have left him a little *Dazed and Confused*. So now Linklater has gone back to the drawing board—both figuratively and literally—with his latest indie offering *Waking Life,* which utilized over 30 artists and cutting-edge computer wizardry to make the first independent computer-animated feature.

Like the works which got him noticed, *Waking Life* is filled with people who have a lot they want to say, and has a nearly nonexistent storyline. It deals with a character who wanders from one chatty person to another, repeatedly waking up only to find that he is still dreaming. Having that happen would be a strange experience, which is exactly what it is to watch the highly novel *Waking Life*. Linklater had just such an unsettling incidence of being trapped in a dream state which did not seem to want to end. He also has had episodes of "lucid dreaming," which is basically when, while dreaming, you are able to recognize that what is occurring is, indeed, only a dream.

The idea to make a film exploring how our minds work when we dream stayed on the back burner for years because Linklater could not see how it could be successfully realized on the screen. He felt that live action would ground it inappropriately in reality, and that the styles of animation he saw simply did not come close enough to duplicating what he saw in his own head. Then he saw the work of animator Bob Sabiston, who created a technique called interpolated rotoscoping, which made Linklater's dream come true. Rotoscoping has been around since 1917, an animation technique invented by Max Fleischer (who brought us Popeye, Betty Boop, etc.), which paints over previously shot live action footage frame by frame. Sabiston created a computer program which could be used to do the same process, and also fills in brush strokes between frames, giving the end product a surrealistic, fluid, undulating quality.

It sometimes looks as if the film is being presented to you through water: objects wobble about, outlines wave, strands of hair twist and snap, different plains move independently of each other, shifting and swaying. (Viewers who suffer from motion sickness might want to have their Dramamine at the ready.) The film was shot in New York and Linklater's native Texas with a tiny crew using hand-held digital cameras and a script which was partly from the director and partly from a cast which includes stars from previous Linklater films like Wiley Wiggins, Ethan Hawke, and Julie Delpy, as well as "interesting people" from academia who have piqued his curiosity. It was then handed over to Sabiston and his team. For almost a year, different artists "painted" different characters and different scenes, giving the film a style which to a degree is constantly in flux.

We first see the main character (Wiggins) as he awakens on a train and looks dreamily out the window as he pulls into a station. After calling unsuccessfully for a ride, he goes out to the street and is offered one in a whimsical vehicle which is half car and half boat. He gets advice comparing life to crayons (it is what you do with the colors you get that counts) and to drawing (do not be afraid to go outside the lines). A character in the back seat (played by Linklater himself) tells the driver/captain where to let off the young man, and says that it is somewhere which will determine the rest of his life. After the young man gets out, he is hit by a car, at which point it appears that he had merely been dreaming, and proceeds to go about his daily life.

When he leaves his home, *Waking Life* begins its string of vociferous vignettes on the meaning of life, reality, identity, freedom, and a host of other deep topics. These are usually monologues the young man only passively listens to but which sometimes include conversations sharing thoughts and feelings. Some scenes he does not even appear in, and at least one he watches on a screen in a theater, a spectator along with us. Sometimes when the young man has one of his false awakenings, he knows he is still asleep because the numbers on his watch and clock are blurred and he then levitates through the ceiling and into the sky, drifting lazily over the city below. (To get the proper floating effect, Linklater shot these sequences from a hot air balloon.) After wandering for 90-some minutes of screen time, an eerie undertone creeps in as the character expresses a growing and unsettling feeling that perhaps he is not asleep but actually dead. The film's final image, in which he floats up into the sky and disappears, is rather haunting.

In his film, Linklater tries to stretch our minds in our waking lives to the way they are in the world of dreams, exploring thought-provoking ideas with limitless possibility. Linklater is clearly energized when immersing himself in the many and often contradictory ideas of the people around him. He does not feel the need to agree with or even understand all that is said, but finds it fascinating and liberating to ponder such things, and he hopes that we meet the material in the same way. His script includes ideas from philosophers like Plato, Sartre, Nietzsche, authors like Dostoevsky and D.H. Lawrence, and the film criticisms of Andre Bazin and Francois Truffaut. (There are some lighter moments mixed in with the heaviness.) It is like 90 minutes of snippets from college lectures and late-night mind-bending dorm room musings, as well as the ramblings and just plain weird pronouncements of some truly strange characters.

If you can follow what they are saying, they sometimes pique your interest and sometimes not, but the visuals almost always do. While a man drones on about a "new evolution," his eyes and then whole face swell as he makes his point, and a fish in the aquarium behind him sprouts a tiny foot. Another man speaks his piece before calmly dousing himself with gasoline and setting himself ablaze. A man in a dark prison cell rails against the people who put him there and vows revenge, literally turning red-hot with anger. Another character drives through the streets ranting about freedom through a bullhorn, and his face turns shades of purple and red as he bellows. As a man relates how we are made mostly of water, we see water bubble up inside him. Another's eyes keep popping as he talks. At the end of the "Holy Moment" segment, two men (one being indie director Caveh Zahedi) are transformed into puffy white clouds in a blue sky. Speed Levitch, the bizarre New York tour guide from the 1998 documentary *The Cruise*, walks with the young man across what appears to be the Brooklyn Bridge and says things like "On really romantic nights of self, I go salsa dancing with my own confusion." As he talks, his eyes dilate wildly, stars cascade from his mouth, and his surroundings in general are as kinetic as he is.

In *Waking Life*, the director Steven Soderbergh relates a conversation between film making giants Louis Malle and Billy Wilder, in which Malle commented that he had just spent $2 million on a film about a dream within a dream, and Wilder replied "Then you just lost $2 million." It is a significant comment, highly pertinent to the highly unusual *Waking Life*, its inclusion showing that Linklater realized his film might be too far from the mainstream to be accepted by a large audience. A film which might have been better as a short, *Waking Life* cost a few million dollars to shoot and grossed $2.7 million in limited release. It was a big hit at the Sundance Film Festival, and received many positive reviews, particularly for its innovative and fascinating visuals. Without them, many would find themselves falling asleep during the droning on of *Waking Life*. 🎞

—*David L. Boxerbaum*

CREDITS

Richard Linklater
Glover Gill
Julie Delpy
Wiley Wiggins
Ethan Hawke
Adam Goldberg
Nicky Katt
Steven Soderbergh

**Origin:** USA
**Released:** 2001
**Production:** Anne Walker-McBay, Tommy Pallotta, Palmer West, Jonah Smith; Detour Filmproduction, Independent Film Channel (IFC), Line Research, Thousand Words; released by Fox Searchlight
**Directed by:** Richard Linklater
**Written by:** Richard Linklater
**Cinematography by:** Richard Linklater, Tommy Pallotta
**Music by:** Glover Gill
**Sound:** Ethan Andrus
**Editing:** Sandra Adair
**Animation:** Bob Sabiston
**MPAA rating:** R
**Running time:** 99 minutes

 REVIEWS

*Chicago Sun-Times Online.* October 19, 2001.
*Entertainment Weekly.* October 26, 2001, p. 89.
*Film Comment.* March, 2001, p. 66.
*Los Angeles Times Online.* October 19, 2001.
*New York Times.* October 12, 2001, p. E15.
*New Yorker.* November 12, 2001, p. 138.
*People.* October 29, 2001, p. 42.
*Premiere.* November, 2001, p. 91.
*Rolling Stone.* November 8, 2001, p. 134.
*Sight and Sound.* February, 2002, p. 64.
*Variety.* January 29, 2001, p. 43.
*Washington Post.* October 26, 2001, p. C5.

AWARDS AND NOMINATIONS

**N.Y. Film Critics 2001:** Animated Film.

# Warm Water Under a Red Bridge (Akai Hashi no Shita no Nurui Mizu)

Veteran filmmaker Shohei Imamura's wackily erotic *Warm Water Under a Red Bridge* proves that when the fantastic is a part of the cultural tradition of a country, such as Japan, and when that sensibility is transposed onto contemporary filmic realism, the mixture can make the otherworldly appear seductively real. Combining the riddle of "is-ness" at the heart of Zen haiku ("The old pond./A frog jumps in./Plop!") with the gritty realism that today's cinema is capable of could have made for arduous viewing, more so for audiences not so spiritually attuned. Instead, Imamura spins a tale of surprising twists and turns as to hold the interest of any viewer anywhere. Its Zen subtext, that of the unsolvable riddle ("What is the sound of one hand clapping?") finds expression on the face of the film's protagonist, and the advice he keeps receiving from a dead sidewalk philosopher.

Yosuke, played by the ubiquitous Koji Yakusho, who has starred in a number of notable Japanese films of late from *Shall We Dance?* (1998) to *Eureka* (reviewed in this volume), is a refugee from Tokyo's corporate limbo. As someone whose wife and children have left him, Yakusho's deeply affecting performance shows the inability of such a character to make sense of the surprises that a small town has in store for him. In this, he is no different from his medieval counterpart, the unsuspecting peasant forced to flee from brigands in Kenji Mizoguchi's classic *Ugetsu Monogatari* (1953) or his more recent cousin, the entomologist searching on a remote island for an insect that can be named after him in Hiroshi Teshigahara's *Woman in the Dunes* (1964). All three stalwarts are lured by mysterious women to the point that they are made to question the nature of reality itself.

Our Yosuke, unable to find employment after the architect firm for which he worked as a salesman goes bust, recalls that the "blue tent philosopher" Taro (Kazuo Kitamura), whose funeral ceremony Yosuke attends, had once told him of a treasure locked inside a house by a red bridge in a town on the tip of the Noto peninsula. From what Yosuke can glean, it is a gold statue stolen from a Buddhist temple in Kyoto. Dismissing his wife's urgent pleas for money, which he keeps hearing on his cell phone, Yosuke sets off on his quest. True enough, there is a red bridge over a river that runs through the town, and there is a house as described. As

Yosuke whoops in joy, he sees the attractive young Saeko (Misa Shimizu) emerge out of the house wearing a red sweater over a black skirt. He follows her to a supermarket and finds her shoplifting a piece of cheese, as water collects around her feet. As she goes off, Yosuke picks up a locket in the water and sets off after her.

Saeko, it turns out, is a worker in a confectionary who lives with her quirky grandmother, Mitsu (Mitsuko Baisho) who, despite her infirmity, continues to fashion scrolls of Zen koans for tea ceremonies (where each koan is meant to be contemplated as part of the age-old ritual of drinking tea). Saeko, as the shy Yosuke has noticed already, has quirks of her own. With forthright candor, on their first meeting, she confesses that her shoplifting sprees are merely the tip of the iceberg: when water "fills up" inside her, she has to do "something wicked." Since Yosuke now knows her secret, she feels a bond has developed between them. She flings herself on him, kissing him passionately and riding him to the point of her gratification, while he remains fully clothed. Their love play takes a curious turn, however, as an unnatural amount of water gushes out of her. We see the water flow down the drain and into the river.

Realizing his project of getting at the treasure hidden inside the house is going to take longer than he expected, Yosuke finds employment on a fishing trawler run by the arrogant young Shintaro (Yukiya Kitamura). He also finds digs in the town. That evening, he has a waking dream of sorts where he sees himself as a kind of adult "star child" trapped within a womb in interstellar space. Along with this vision, he recalls Saeko moaning in ecstasy, "It's coming!," referring, of course, to the water.

The next day, Yosuke musters up the gall to admit to her that he found their strange bout of sexual intimacy exciting, and even suggests that he can "help out" so as to prevent her from stealing. We can see that their relationship, at this stage, is still based on Yosuke's hunt for the treasure rather than any genuine feeling for her. When she leaves him alone inside the house, he recalls Taro's instruction about a pot. As he stealthily slides a closet door open, Saeko catches him but he explains his action by saying he was looking for the toilet.

It now becomes clear to Yosuke that his materialistic goal will require him to be sexually adept as well. He recalls in a flashback looking through Taro's collection of erotic classics. "Man has always been a lecher throughout his history," we see Taro spouting. "Today, people are too learned to admit to their desires!" Taro's epigrammatic wisdom remains as vague for Yosuke as any of the Zen koans Granny keeps laboring over, and Saeko keeps reciting. Instead, his life becomes ruled by Saeko's seemingly unnatural urges to which he is forced to respond as to a call of nature, even at the risk of appearing a comic buffoon. Those who have seen Imamura's previous film, *Dr. Akagi* (1999), are bound to recall Yosuke's resemblance to the beleagured doctor who

has to scurry like a clown to whosoever is in need of him on his tiny island.

One morning, as Yosuke is returning on a fishing boat from a night's work, he spots Saeko on her balcony signalling to him with a mirror. Using binoculars, he sees that water has already begun to gather at her feet. This sends him leaping onto the dock and running at a furious pace to her house. To sprightly music, he reaches her just as she exclaims, "I'm full!," whereupon he spreads a plastic sheet over a mattress, removes his clothes, and gets right down to it. This time her water spurts upwards in a fountain-like spray. We then see the steamy liquid make its way down the pipe to the fish in the river, as if Saeko's inexplicable gift is part of the symbiotic wholeness of nature.

To affirm the notion of symbiosis, Saeko speaks of the water around the town as being special, since this is where the river meets the Sea of Japan. Moreover, it is this "good water" that is required for confectionery, and which attracts all manner of fish. Imamura then adds a third factor into the equation when he cuts to an immense hollow tunnel at a nearby scientific facility specializing in research into neutrinos, which are supposed to come from the farthest reaches of space. Here too, what is needed, a guide explains to Yosuke and Saeko, is "super pure water," unlike the water we drink which has calcium and magnesium.

In the very next scene, a drunk Saeko picnicking with Yosuke accuses him of not thinking out the "connections" that hold his life together. It is a charge intended to make the film's audience feel guilty as well. Taro too, in a flashback, calls Yosuke a victim of the corporate culture that doesn't want its employees to think. In its own ambivalent way, the film puts across a view of the history of man as a struggle not so much between the privileged and the exploited as between the thinking few and the non-thinking multitudes. As his life and quest soon begin to cave in, Yosuke recalls Taro's admonition that "you have to think till your brain cells rot!" It is this overriding perspective that transforms the film into an universal parable.

The catalytic rush of events in the final third of the film require Yosuke to do just that: to think his way out, something his life hasn't prepared him for. Gen (Manasaku Fuwa), a layabout and mutual friend of his and Taro's, arrives from Tokyo, and behind Yosuke's back, cultivates a momentary bond of frankness with Granny, through which we learn that Taro was actually her lover, and the father Saeko never knew. In return for the precious news of Taro's death that Gen has brought, Granny retrieves the treasure hidden under the floorboards and presents it to Gen in strictest confidence. It is priceless Noto silk meant to keep one cool in the summer. Gen quickly takes his leave of Yosuke, saying that he has given up on finding the treasure.

When Yosuke's wife calls him on his cell phone to tell him that she's divorcing him, it marks the beginning of his life falling apart. For one, it hampers his sexual proficiency.

Saeko ceases to spurt as copiously as before. "You're curing me!" she exclaims. As if all this weren't enough, Yosuke learns that Saeko has all along been waiting for a lover, Kojo, whom he resembles, and who is serving a 13 year stint in prison for murder. When Kojo's friend, a jailbird who is now a prosperous drug dealer, arrives on the scene and makes out with Saeko, Yosuke is thrown into a helpless rage. Even a violent confrontation, in which Yosuke triumphs with Shintaro's help, cannot heal Yosuke's hurt at being betrayed.

In the film's denouement, set within the hidden recesses of concrete girders along the sea front, Yosuke decides to come clean. He admits to Saeko his hunt for the treasure. She in turn places all that he has heard about her questionable past in the context of what she now feels for him. This leads to the two consummating their feelings. As a fitting tribute to their born again romance, we see water gushing up from under the rocks, but that is not all. An ethereal rainbow now forms over the pier as Taro's laughter can be heard on the soundtrack. His voiceover now becomes that of the narrator as he declaims, "You know yourself it's an impossible tale!"

Critics can be expected to find the film a little too eccentric to satisfy the demands of western realism. Elvis Mitchell in the *New York Times,* while referring admiringly to Imamura's previous work, finds that this time the master "doesn't come through," that the "silliness" of the water Saeko unleashes "washes away any attempt at narrative completion."

—*Vivek Adarkar*

## CREDITS

**Yosuke:** Koji Yakusho
**Saeko:** Misa Shimizu
**Mitsu:** Mitsuko Baisho
**Gen:** Mansaku Fuwa
**Taro:** Kazuo Kitamura
**Masayuki:** Isao Natsuyagi
**Shintaro:** Yukiya Kitamura
**Miki:** Hijiri Kojima

**Origin:** Japan
**Language:** Japanese
**Released:** 2001
**Production:** Hisa Iino; Imamura Productions; released by Cowboy Booking International
**Directed by:** Shohei Imamura
**Written by:** Shohei Imamura, Motofumi Tomikawa, Daisuke Tengan
**Cinematography by:** Shigeru Komatsubara
**Music by:** Shinichiro Ikebe
**Sound:** Kenichi Benitani

**Editing:** Hajime Okayasu
**Production Design:** Hisao Inagaki
**MPAA rating:** Unrated
**Running time:** 119 minutes

## REVIEWS

*New York Times Online.* September 29, 2001.
*Sight and Sound.* July, 2001, p. 15.

## QUOTES

Saeko (Misa Shiizu) explains her shoplifting: "I have to do something wicked."

# The Way We Laughed (Cosi Ridevano)

Perhaps no movement in the history of world cinema has globally inspired the low budget feature film as much as Italian neo-realism, that exuberant, raw spurt of on-the-street and in-your-face camera stylistics that burst upon an unsuspecting world as a logical aftermath of the devastation of the Second World War. If anything, it proved that good films could be made outside the studio system, and using actors who had never acted before. As in its present-day offspring, the Dogma 95 Movement, the narratives had to be stories of everyday life, and the filmmaker had to demonstrate a compassion for characters, other than the leads, who were caught up in the same economic plight.

Gianni Amelio's celebrated *the Way We Laughed,* winner of the Golden Lion at the Venice Film Festival of 1998, is the contemporary flagbearer of this filmic credo. Unlike its founding fathers though, such as DeSica and Visconti, who aspired to universal appeal, Amelio isn't hesitant to blazon forth with an assertion of national identity and societal values, almost as if his agenda was one to preserve what is traditionally Italian against the encroachment of the American behemoth of commercial populism.

When we place Amelio's effort against Visconti's classic *Rocco and His Brothers* (1960), a film with similar thematic concerns, we can see the change neo-realism has undergone. Visconti showed how a simple-minded, close-knit family from Southern Italy is destroyed by the rapacious urban blight of Milan. Amelio, on his part, harking back to the same historical period, depicts how the bond between the rustic, illiterate Giovanni (Enrico Lo Verso) and his much younger brother, the bookish Pietro (Francesco Guiffrida), both from Sicily, becomes strained, strengthened and finally torn apart through the tests it is put through in the urban wasteland of the North.

Visconti used the famous Greek actress Katina Paxinou who, as the domineering Mother, contributed an elemental intensity which functioned as the conscience that Rocco and his brothers were prepared to shed. Amelio does not shift his attention from his two principals, so that when his camera is not focused on them, it serves as an intermediary between them, taking in what each brother is saying to himself about the other. Thus, if we do not identify with the film's peculiarly Italian code of brotherly love, there is nothing universal on an emotional level to grip us, or even meet us halfway. Which is not to say that the film doesn't prove rewarding if taken on its own terms.

We first see Giovanni, dressed as an unkempt peasant full of cheer, as he arrives on a station platform in the Turin of 1958 to spend a few days with his kid brother, before returning to his much quieter life in Sicily. Pietro, immaculately attired as a student, sees him but hides from his view, as if ashamed of him. When Giovanni goes to his uncle, with whom Pietro is staying, he finds that his brother has been sharing a room in a congested slum, with only a cot and books to call his own. Worse, their aunt suspects Pietro of theft. This enrages Giovanni to the point where he gives the aunt a part of the missing amount, then gathers his brother's things. Before he storms out, he curses, "This is a pigsty! Not fit for people!"

Giovanni's decision to side with his brother becomes a vow to look after him in Turin, regardless of whatever sacrifice it may entail on his part. We come to know that the reason Pietro is in school in the first place is because Giovanni has been financing him towards getting a diploma and becoming a schoolteacher. A year later, Giovanni is working as a garbage collector at a refuse site, a milieu that is rendered with all its repugnant authenticity across the width of the anamorphic screen. What makes it worthwhile for Giovanni is that the two now have a clean, modest apartment to themselves, even though Pietro seems sunk in a melancholic drift that takes him away from his studies.

Two brief subplots ensue. Pietro tries to deceive Giovanni about his academic progress by hiring a janitor to impersonate a professor at the parent-teacher meeting. Meanwhile, Giovanni is too ashamed to show up at the event and thinks of hiring a dapper dance teacher to impersonate him. These drawn-out machinations are amusing but of little dramatic value. The deceptions however bring the brothers closer to each other. The second subplot gets under way when Giovanni treats Pietro to a fling with a prostitute in a classy bordello, but even here, we remain dramatically shortchanged. The girl in question, we later learn, is Lucia (Rosaria Danze), whom Pietro knew in his childhood as the

shoemaker's daughter. By cutting away from the scene the moment Pietro enters her room, the film denies us the drama resulting from this encounter, presumably in the interests of returning to the bond between the brothers.

The next year finds Giovanni running a shelter for workers from the South, while himself working at a construction site, just so he can afford to buy the expensive textbooks Pietro needs. One morning on a streetcar, Pietro witnesses a wallet being picked. As the victim cries out, the pickpocket panics and runs. In the ensuing fracas, Pietro is able to pick up the wallet and finds it is stashed with notes of high denominations. The money provides Pietro a means of paying back his debt to his brother, which he does surreptitiously by sneaking the notes into his bag, before he drops out of school and takes off.

A year passes, and Giovanni still has no news of his brother. In desperation, he even lands up at the school and creates a scene, for which he is taken into police custody. Here again, his rustic past comes to his rescue. An officer from his village intervenes on his behalf, and releases him. Clutching his brother's books to his heart, Giovanni composes a long imaginary letter to him through which it becomes clear that Pietro was in a sense living out the life that Giovanni never had.

We now realize that Giovanni's sacrifices were like those of a father for his son, hardships that couldn't be paid back in money or in kind, but by Pietro becoming a respectable member of society. The father motif becomes reinforced through Giovanni's nostalgic recollection of how during their father's funeral, little Pietro had been locked away in the kitchen so as to protect him from the sadness. The little boy had then got drunk on a bottle of wine, and laughed through the event, contributing the merriment referred to in the film's title.

Again the film skips a year, but this time switches viewpoints. Even though both brothers are still in Turin, their paths do not cross. There is even a scene in an empty streetcar at night in which we see both of them in the same shot, but they do not see each other. When Pietro passes his final exams, he becomes so overjoyed that he sets out to look for Giovanni. In the process he finds that Giovanni has moved in with Lucia, and now heads an employment cooperative for workers. When the brothers do meet, it is Pietro's turn to bare his soul and admit how much he loves his brother. However, that very night, sudden violence comes in between. As the two are strolling arm in arm, the sight of a worker draws Giovanni away. When Pietro gives chase, he is shocked to see Giovanni stabbing the worker to death. Pietro can only stare at his brother in disbelief and silence as the scene fades out.

The story then resumes on a Sunday three years later amidst the pastoral quiet of a village in the Po valley. Giovanni is now married to Ada (Simonetta Benozzo) and has a baby he dotes over. When we see Pietro, it is clear he has lost his boyish innocence. He is now long-haired, unshaven and sullen. We learn that he has taken the rap for the murder, and has been allowed three days off from the reformatory, under the supervision of a guard, so as to attend the christening of Giovanni's baby. Through the family feasting and festivity, the film affirms the purity and plenitude of the life Giovanni has carved out for himself, away from the downtrodden in the big city.

The sequence also functions as an epilogue to point out the sadness of Pietro's wasted youth. All of Giovanni's cheer and optimism feel hollow. When Pietro is back on the train to return to his incarceration, it becomes clear to him, and to us, that the tragedy of his life was not one of hopes he could not fulfill, but of a promise he never imagined would be betrayed. As a final twist, the pop song accompanying the end titles reminds us we've been watching a period piece. The high-pitched adolescent wailing of Neil Sedaka's "One Way Ticket to the Blues" bestows its own cheer on Pietro's dilemma, as if pointing out its transiency.

Understandably, the reaction of American critics to the film has been mixed. On the less favorable side of the spectrum, it has ranged from calling it "slow-starting but moving" (Jonathan Foreman in the *New York Post*) to "ponderously slow" at times, but possessing a "stately grandeur" (Jack Mathews in the *Daily News*). Both Stephen Holden and Stuart Klawans in the *New York Times* have raised the issue of the film requiring three years to find a distributor here. Holden describes the film as "gorgeously atmospheric," its narrative "closer to that of an experimental novel than that of a historical epic." He goes on to note that the film's ideological impact lies in pointing out "how an entire society can operate on an unspoken agreement not to look too deeply into the workings of its social and political machinery."

—*Vivek Adarkar*

## CREDITS

**Giovanni:** Enrico Lo Verso
**Pietro:** Francesco Giuffrida
**Lucia:** Rosaria Danze
**Ada:** Simonetta Benozzo

**Origin:** Italy
**Language:** Italian
**Released:** 1998
**Production:** Rita Cecchi Gori, Vittorio Cecchi Gori; Cecchi Gori Group, Pacific Pictures; released by New Yorker Films
**Directed by:** Gianni Amelio
**Written by:** Gianni Amelio, Daniele Gaglianone, Lillo Iacolino, Alberto Taraglio

**Cinematography by:** Luca Bigazzi
**Music by:** Franco Piersanti
**Sound:** Alessandro Zanon
**Editing:** Simona Paggi
**Costumes:** Gianna Gissi
**Production Design:** Giancarlo Basili
**MPAA rating:** Unrated
**Running time:** 124 minutes

## REVIEWS

*Nation Online.* October 19, 1998.
*New York Daily News.* November 21, 2001.
*New York Post Online.* November 21, 2001.
*New York Times Online.* November 18, 2001.
*New York Times Online.* November 21, 2001.
*Variety Online.* September 14, 1998.
*Village Voice Online.* November 21, 2001.

## AWARDS AND NOMINATIONS

**Venice Film Fest. 1998:** Film.

# The Wedding Planner

*A romantic comedy about love, destiny and other events you just can't plan for.*
—Movie tagline

 **Box Office:** $60.4 million

Jennifer Lopez stars as the title character in Adam Shankman's overdone screwball romantic comedy of mis-matched lovers coming together. Mary is a tightly pulled-together wedding coordinator who strides confidently through church after church and reception hall after reception hall confronting each problem, big or small, that is bound to disrupt the meticulously planned nuptials, with equal coolness and aplomb. Mary is singularly equipped to offer everything from sisterly comfort and sage advice to a nervous bride, to providing a more practical solution for a bridesmaid disappointed with her cleavage (she quickly ruches the top of the dress with a pin), to corralling a drunken father of the bride suddenly gone missing ("The F.O.B. is M.I.A.," she hisses into her ever-present headset). Carefully choreographing every detail of each blissful event is nothing new for Mary, who has prepared for her calling since childhood when she pulled off Barbie's big day. The first of many celebrity clients, it seems, and Mary is steadily climbing to the top of the company ladder but needs to land one more important client to make partner. No problem, for the focused and career-minded planner.

The scenes in the first half of the film are among the best and show an interesting and as yet unseen side of Lopez's abilities. She is surprisingly genuine and convincing as the Martha Stewart of matrimony who opens her coat, in an amusing scene, to reveal a wedding day emergency kit with everything in it from sedatives and mini bottles of booze to more traditional pain relievers and Evian mist spray.

Glamorous, well-dressed and successful Mary is also very lonely and it seems she has thrown herself into her work to compensate for lack of a relationship. Her well-meaning but unromantic father Salvatore (Alex Rocco), therefore feels it is time for her single life to come to an end and attempts to set her up with Massimo (Justin Chambers), a goofy and annoying young fellow Italian who Mary has known, and probably avoided, since childhood. Her father isn't the only one trying to play cupid—admittedly dateless for a full two years, everyone else seems to be chomping at the bit to set Mary up with anyone at all, never mind that they're complete losers.

Meanwhile, Mary is excitedly planning her wedding coup for the infamous Donolly family, which will make her the partner of her tough boss Geri (Kathy Najimy). Her prospective client wants to see her in action first and they are invited to see her do her thing at a current client's wedding. The young, blond, and rich Fran Donolly (Bridgette Wilson-Sampras) arrives just in time to see Mary feeding the best man his touching lines for the toast through an earpiece she's fitted him with. Thoroughly impressed, Fran and her parents (Joanna Gleason and Charles Kimbrough) hire the wedding whiz and preparations busily begin.

Practically a wedding savant, planning these events are all Mary ever thinks about. She can even predict how long a marriage will last by the color of the bridesmaid dresses and the couples' song. To save her from this empty life, Fate intervenes when her Gucci heel sticks in a sewer grate and a handsome stranger saves her from a runaway dumpster. He is a doctor, Mary learns, whose easy charm and demeanor is a perfect foil for her persnickety planner. A pediatrician, Dr. Steve (Matthew McConaughey) makes sure Mary has a clean bill of health at his clinic before releasing her to her assistant Penny (Judy Greer) who has rushed to the scene. Penny quickly seizes her chance to play cupid for her lovelorn boss and proposes that Steve meet them at the Golden Gate Park for a movie and a flimsy "medical discussion" premise. The trio indeed rendezvous at the aforementioned park, with Penny quickly excusing herself, allowing the Mary and Steve to watch the park's featured movie event: Janet Leigh and Tony Martin in *Two Tickets to*

*Broadway.* The couple share a dance but a would-be first kiss is spoiled by a sudden rainstorm.

The starry-eyed wedding planner gushes to her new client Fran about her new boyfriend until a horrified Mary realizes that Dr. Steve is really "Eddie" the fiancee (his full name is Steve Edison). The movie heats up with an artfully staged tango between Mary and Steve who bicker back and forth about the awkward situation he has created while expertly dipping and swaying around the dance floor. The momentum of the tango scene is matched in the following scene, cutting between two classic comedy exchanges where Penny convinces a rapidly unraveling Mary to stay on the Donolly job and remain professional while Steve's golfing buddy Dr. John (Kevin Pollak) talks Steve into dismissing his attraction to Mary as cold feet and to stay with Fran.

The plot decidedly thins after this point, with a flimsy sub-plot based on a seemingly inexplicable turn that has Massimo pop-up, literally from nowhere, and announce he and Mary are engaged. A tongue-tied Mary decides to go along with the ridiculous story to make Steve jealous, one must assume, as he is present during Massimo's declaration, which reeks of a last minute rewrite. Once being charming but twice a bit hokey, Steve saves Mary's life again (to cement their now shaky bond?) when the wedding party's horse-back ride goes awry. His knight in shining armor to her damsel in distress is heavily and clumsily underscored yet again.

Later, it becomes clear why Salvatore has pushed Massimo on his unwitting daughter in another overly melo-dramatic scene where he reveals the truth about the nature of his relationship with Mary's long-deceased mother. He ex-plains they were in an arranged marriage, met on their wedding day, and much later fell in love, and wonders couldn't she and Massimo have a similar scenario? Mary, touched by her father's revelation, starts to question her highly romantic standards of love.

Later scenes are predictable and disappointing. Fran, unaware of anything untoward taking place, leaves the two stars alone to plan the wedding as she has important business to attend to elsewhere, leaving Steve to lament that she always thinking of business. Hard-as-nails, business-whiz Fran started out as a bookie in college, Steve confides to the much more maternal Mary and though seemingly the per-fect couple, more flaws of Fran and Steve's relationship are then revealed. Mirroring these changes, we then see the reason for Mary's aversion to relationships after she runs into her ex-fiancee (she'd been jilted at the alter in favor of one of her best friends). The reason behind her obsessive planning of weddings becomes evident. She falls apart after the con-frontation and, predictably into the arms of Steve, willing to save her again, this time from herself. Especially because of her previous experience, Mary cannot bring herself to hurt Fran and nobly turns her engaged suitor away. Each are then resigned: Steve to wed Fran and Mary to wed Massimo, after he shows he's capable of losing his usual buffoonery for a moment and touchingly proposes. A hastily planned final act rights these wrongs, however, and things end up as they should.

The two leads are most compelling, especially Lopez, and they have decent chemistry that is wasted after a very good set-up during the first half of the film. It is clear they each have their share of burdens to carry, though. For example, Steve annoyingly refers to himself in the third person to give him nonexistent "character," while Mary is forced to gleefully enjoy a scene where they break a vital body part off a statue and later tenderly unglue it from Steve's hand after a quick-fix gone wrong. Supports are given very little to do, with the talented Greer given a chance to shine briefly, while the comically gifted Najimy is totally wasted. Wilson-Sampras' role is vaguely written, see-sawing from a well-defined character—a business whiz and determined fiancee totally in love with Steve—who then inexplicably changes into a confused person who suddenly is not in love with Steve and flounders in search of her true identity. Pollack's role is practically a cameo. Gleason and Kimbrough as the lush and stuffed shirt, respectively, read as thoroughly cartoonish but are somehow able to inject a mild amount of humor and humanity into their scenes in spite of that. Chambers, sporting a ridiculous Italian accent, is given the most thankless role, which is practically unsavable but for his one chance at drama in the proposal scene. Rocco is one-dimensional as Mary's Italian immigrant father. Willard, in a small role as the flamboyant dance instructor, is a bright spot among the supports.

*The Wedding Planner* is a visually pleasing production throughout due to the talent of cinematographer Julio Macat, which makes the film watchable even as it begins to sink plot-wise. The film's lifeless soundtrack is less successful.

—*Hilary White*

## CREDITS

**Mary Fiore:** Jennifer Lopez
**Steve Edison:** Matthew McConaughey
**Fran Donolly:** Bridgette Wilson
**Massimo:** Justin Chambers
**Salvatore:** Alex Rocco
**Penny:** Judy Greer
**Dr. John Dojny:** Kevin Pollak
**Mrs. Donolly:** Joanna Gleason
**Mr. Donolly:** Charles Kimbrough
**Basil St. Mosely:** Fred Willard
**Geri:** Kathy Najimy

**Origin:** USA

**Released:** 2001
**Production:** Peter Abrams, Robert Levy, Jennifer Gibgot, Gigi Pritzker, Deborah Del Prete; Intermedia Films, Prufrock Pictures, Tapestry Films, Dee Gee Entertainment; released by Columbia Pictures
**Directed by:** Adam Shankman
**Written by:** Michael Ellis, Pamela Falk
**Cinematography by:** Julio Macat
**Music by:** Mervyn Warren
**Sound:** Geoffrey Patterson
**Music Supervisor:** Mary Ramos, Michelle Kuznetsky
**Editing:** Lisa Zeno Churgin
**Art Direction:** Gregory Bolton
**Costumes:** Pamela Ball Withers
**Production Design:** Bob Ziembicki
**MPAA rating:** PG-13
**Running time:** 105 minutes

## REVIEWS

*Boxoffice.* April, 2001, p. 240.
*Chicago Sun-Times Online.* January 26, 2001.
*New York Times Online.* January 26, 2001.
*San Francisco Chronicle.* January 26, 2001, p. D1.
*Sight and Sound.* April, 2001, p. 60.
*USA Today Online.* January 26, 2001.
*Variety.* January 22, 2001, p. 52.
*Washington Post Online.* January 26, 2001.

# Wet Hot American Summer

*High times. Hard bodies. Soft rock.*
—Movie tagline

 **Box Office:** $.2 million

Wet Hot American Summer is the kind of movie that you are either the right age and have the right humor sensibility to enjoy it or you aren't. Which category you fall into will be apparent right from the opening frames of the film. It shows teens on the last day of camp in summer of the 1981 dancing around a campfire as "Jane" by Jefferson Starship blares on the soundtrack. Most people will see this scene as just a bunch of kids wearing 1970s clothes and dancing to a rock song. Only someone right age to have lived through just such a camp experience, or old enough to have watched the summer camp movies of that era, would realize that "Jane" is the perfect song to be playing and that the kids are wearing exactly what clothes they should be wearing. So much of the film is filled with these sort of "in" jokes, it's easy to see why a lot of critics didn't like (or get) the film at all.

The film is both parody and homage to the teen comedies of the late 1970s/early 1980s like *Meatballs* and *Porky's*. Owen Gleiberman of *Entertainment Weekly* describes the particular mini-genre as "brain-dead, teen-porn." The film takes place just as the 1970s were slowly morphing into the 1980s. Most of the kids are wearing tight cut-off jean shorts and the like, but a few are wearing the gothic look that Cure followers sport or the preppie look with pink Izod shirts and turned up collars. It's a hint of the impending cultural shift.

Not that any of that happens in this movie. The film takes place all in one day. The scenes are interspersed with title cards giving exceedingly accurate reports giving the time of day, like "2:37 p.m." One of the ongoing jokes of the film is that such an absurd amount of things would be happening in just one day. People fall in and out of love and back in again, lives are saved and nerds remake themselves into cool guys.

The story wanders back and forth between the stories of various campers and their counselors. Camp director Beth (Janeane Garafalo) develops a crush on a nerdy astrophysicist, Henry (David Hyde Pierce) who's vacationing nearby. In between awkward conversations with each other where they try to sound knowledgeable about the other's field of work, Henry gathers a group of the camp's nerdiest kids to help him make a machine that will deflect the pieces of Skylab that he believes will pummel the park. This quite resourceful geek brigade builds a fully operational machine with cans of Spam, doughnuts, and a box of Grapenuts.

Meanwhile skinny Coop (Michael Showalter, one of the co-writers of the film) gets a big crush on camp hottie Katie (Marguerite Moreau) after she speaks to him for the first time all summer. She thinks Coop is nice and might be in love with him but she's also quite taken with her lifeguard boyfriend, Andy (Paul Rudd), who's mean to Katie and pretty darn stupid, but really, really cute. Counselor Gail (Molly Shannon) is a recent divorcee who can't seem to pass out crayons to the campers without bursting into tears. One of her students, precocious nine-year-old Aaron (Gideon Jacobs) takes her through the steps to recovery, including role-playing, until Gail can become strong enough to face her ex. The camp chef and Vietnam vet, Gene (Christopher Meloni), yells at his hapless assistant Gary (A.D. Miles) because he can not accept his weird sexual impulses, like fondling his own sweater. Eventually he will get counseling from a can of talking mixed vegetables.

The fact that a can of vegetables is a character in the film is a hint of how strange and twisted *Wet Hot American Summer* can get. Writers Showalter and David Wain (who

also directed) are veterans of the sketch comedy show *The State*, and they throw all kinds of jokes into the film in the style of a movie like *Airplane!* Like any kind of film that uses that rapid-fire jokes-everywhere technique, some of it works and some of it doesn't. Wain and Showalter are happy to sacrifice logic for a good joke and are at their best when they let the movie drift off into absurd territory. In one sequence, there's a guy riding a motorcycle chasing his friend on foot. It's an even match. The motorcyclist is finally foiled when there's a small bale of hay in the road. It doesn't seem to occur to him to go around it. One montage is particularly inspired. The counselors head off into town to get some supplies and what starts as some minor misbehavior, like sneaking cigarettes, continues into ridiculously bad behavior. They increase their risky behavior until they are robbing old ladies and shooting drugs in a flop house, suffering from the shakes. When they get back to camp, they are perky and fine again. A camper asks Katie how the outing was. "Oh, it's great to get away, even though it was just an hour," she says.

The movie also makes jokes about itself and movies in general. In one scene, a motorcycle rider drives up. He's obviously a stunt man, because when they cut back to him, the character looks totally different and doesn't even have the same hairstyle. The movie also likes to play with time. In the latter part of the movie, Coop references the huge amount of stuff that's supposedly happened in one day when he tells Katie, "I've grown up a lot since before dinner when we first talked." They also make fun of "movie time." In a scene where a group of kids in a raft is about to go over a dangerous waterfall, a ridiculous amount of things happen while they are waiting to be rescued: Beth has to be located, she has to find another counselor and drive him out to the river, and all the while the campers in the raft are still hovering there at the precipice.

The characters in the film are very innocent. Two of the male counselors discuss that their friend has never been with a woman. It never dawns on them that he might be gay. They decide that what he needs is to be set up with a woman. "What a fag," one says, not realizing that that's exactly it.

Even when the jokes lag, it's fun to take note of all the period details crammed into the film. It's filled with products and styles that have now been abandoned like Pepsi Light, puka shell necklaces, and the name Debbie. "Let's get Debbie," one character says. "No, not that Debbie. How 'bout Debbie Debbie? Or how about tall Debbie?" Watching the film is like going through a time warp. At the talent show, which naturally is cast and presented in the space of one day, there is a sincere rendition of "Day by Day" from *Godspell*. Characters wear rainbow suspenders and say "Na-nu, na-nu." They work out in leg warmers and Jane Fonda inspired outfits. They organize their life with Trapper Keeper notebook systems. They decorate their room with Scott Baio posters. For a person who was a teen or pre-teen in that era, all of this is delicious detail. For someone who was working on paying off a mortgage or something during that time, the painstakingly accurate pop culture won't be that interesting.

Critics ranged wildly in their reactions to the film. Roger Ebert of the *Chicago Sun-Times*, who was not a kid at camp in the 1970s, hated the film and went to the trouble to compose his review in the style of the novelty hit "Hello Muddah, Hello Faddah:" "Wow I hate it/Something fierce/ Except the astrophysicist/David Hyde Pierce" is a sample verse. Charles Taylor of Salon.com wrote, "*Wet Hot American Summer* will have some lasting value to film schools as a model of how not to make a comedy." Owen Gleiberman gave the film a rare "A" grade and said, "The movie is so hilariously sly about something so trivial (as the teen flick genre) that at times it appears to take in an entire culture through a lens made of cheese." The *Village Voice*'s Michael Atkinson thought: "It will be loathed, but it might be ahead of its time."

—*Jill Hamilton*

## CREDITS

**Beth:** Janeane Garofalo
**Henry:** David Hyde Pierce
**Coop/Alan Shemper:** Michael Showalter
**Katie:** Marguerite Moreau
**Andy:** Paul Rudd
**J.J.:** Zak Orth
**Gene:** Christopher Meloni
**Gary:** A.D. Miles
**Gail:** Molly Shannon
**Victor:** Ken Marino
**McKinley:** Michael Ian Black
**Abby:** Marisa Ryan
**Ben:** Bradley Cooper

**Origin:** USA
**Released:** 2001
**Production:** Howard Bernstein; Eureka Pictures; released by USA Films
**Directed by:** David Wain
**Written by:** Michael Showalter, David Wain
**Cinematography by:** Ben Weinstein
**Music by:** Theodore Shapiro, Craig (Shudder to Think) Wedren
**Sound:** Dan Ferat
**Editing:** Meg Reticker
**Art Direction:** Brian Hodge
**Costumes:** Jill Kliber
**Production Design:** Mark White
**MPAA rating:** R

**Running time:** 97 minutes

## REVIEWS

*Boxoffice.* April, 2001, p. 221.
*Chicago Sun-Times Online.* August 31, 2001.
*Entertainment Weekly.* August 3, 2001, p. 41.
*Los Angeles Times Online.* August 31, 2001.
*Rolling Stone.* August 16, 2001, p. 113.
*USA Today Online.* July 27, 2001.
*Variety.* February 5, 2001, p. 43.
*Washington Post.* August 31, 2001, p. C8.

# What Time Is It There?

What emerged from young Taiwanese filmmaker Ming-liang Tsai's press conference, following the screening of his fifth feature, *What Time Is It There?*, at the 2001 New York Film Festival, was an unspoken conviction that if only American youth were exposed to his film, he was sure they would like it. It is a view that stems from a belief expounded by Hungarian film theorist Bela Balazs, writing in the '20's, that it is easier for a French worker to identify with an American worker than with a French aristocrat. Today, it remains a lamentable aspect of our global film culture that American teens are not exposed to films about their counterparts elsewhere in the world. Tsai's film would appear to be the latest victim of this state of affairs.

Accepting Tsai's argument, the film's mild boxoffice here, in relation to the success enjoyed by his previous release, *The River* (1997), could lie in the fact that U.S. arthouse cognoscenti belong to another generation from that portrayed in the film, and were thus unable to relate to Tsai's daring mix of youthful cynicism and metaphysical Oriental detachment, which of course a younger generation would have perceived as just plain cool.

The film's opening lays bare its unique blend of style and content. Out of the depths of a depth-of-field shot of a middle-class dining room and kitchen, the weary, middle-aged Father (Tien Miao) approaches with a plate full of food that he places on the dining table. We are forced into the real time of his life as he lights a cigarette, and sits smoking, without bothering to even look at the food. He then goes to the window and calls out his son's name, but there is no response. He returns to the table and continues smoking. Then he rises and goes to a balcony of sorts, where he lifts a plant out of his way, and stands looking out, still smoking. With nothing dramatic transpiring, Tsai cuts to the teenage son, Hsiao Kang (Kang-sheng Lee), a nondescript introvert, in the back seat of a car, holding the urn with his father's ashes. Hsiao actually speaks to the ashes, describing the journey in a matter-of-fact way, as if he were speaking into a cell phone and nothing more.

Whereas western film dramaturgy would require an explanation for such a catalytic event, Tsai seems to want us to adopt a sense of Buddhist detachment, so that Hsiao holding the urn with his father's ashes is intended to be perceived as a stage in the adolescent's life, a self-contained event in time and space, like the various worlds depicted on the mandala of The Wheel of Life, unrelated to each other but animated by the spinning of the Wheel itself.

From the car, Tsai cuts to the depths of a funeral vault, where a Buddhist priest is chanting, as part of a ritual requiring Hsiao to go through motions of veneration. Looming above Hsiao and his Mother (Yi-Ching Lu) is a wall, which resembles that of a safe deposit vault in a bank. The first part of the film then takes up the immediate aftereffects of the demise, specifically the presence/absence of the Father's spirit, and the counterpoint provided by the next important stage, or world, in Hsiao's life: romance.

We see that Hsiao is a street vendor of watches on a busy sidewalk. Romance comes in the form of Shiang-chyi (Shiang-chyi Chen), a pretty urban teen his age, who wants to buy a dual-time watch, since she is leaving for Paris. The only one Hsiao has is the one he's wearing, which belonged to his father. He does agree to look for one and gives her his card.

Shiang serves to provide the film with a narrative trajectory, independent of its main concern. Yet what happens to Shiang cannot be called a subplot, since here too, we are kept at a distance from her motivation, so that all that emerges from her axis is a vague unease, instead of the pangs of romance. We see Shiang in a pastry shop, then making a call to Hsiao from a pay phone. Eventually, Hsiao agrees to part with his father's watch for the fancy price of a thousand yuens, on which he gives her a 30 per cent discount. She in turn gifts him with a little cake.

It is from this point on that the film's detached stance works against conveying the melodramatic content of its teenage love story. What redeems the film though is its subplot, involving the mother's attempts to contact her husband's spirit through ways that range from the traditional to the bizarre. Here again, her plight is rendered in self-contained tableaus, with little or no dialogue.

The mother's dilemma, we soon realize, is that tradition and religion offer her no solace, so that she cannot blindly follow their dictates any longer. We thus see her shopping for the street food that her husband used to love, which she then lays dutifully on the dining table near the altar. Her obsessive urge to have her husband's spirit return to her also begins to drive a wedge between her and Hsiao. When he picks up a cockroach from the kitchen floor, she warns, in all seriousness, "It could be your father's reincarnation!" Hsiao, on his part, merely drops it into the fish tank, where we see it

float for a while, until the big fish swallows it up. Soon, Hsiao's incomprehension explodes into open hostility when he has to physically control his mother, after she starts covering up windows, so as not to let any light into the house. When Hsiao argues that turning off the power will kill the fish, she screams, "Your dad wants to come home! And you won't let him!"

Whenever the film leaves this emotional trajectory to take up the non-romance between Hsiao and Shiang, with half the world between them, it becomes arduous viewing. Hsiao first tries to keep up with the time in Paris, which he comes to know is seven hours behind. We then see him turning the clock in the living room to that time. He then visits a video store, looking for films about Paris. He is referred to Francois Truffaut's classic The 400 Blows in which Antoine Doinel (played by Jean-Pierre Leaud) plays truant from school and runs wild through the streets of Paris. We see Hsiao in bed, looking at Antoine on a roundabout that spins faster and faster. Hsiao watches unmoved, lured no doubt by the film's backgrounds rather than its characters.

Strangely, Hsiao doesn't gravitate towards Parisian websites at an Internet café. Instead, he embarks on an absurd course of action. He changes the time on the watches he's selling to Paris time, then sets about doing that to clocks in public places as well. These scenes are intercut with those of Shiang in the City of Lights, leading a lonely, urban existence. Not allowing us access to either her thoughts or motivation, Tsai's substitute for a subplot takes the form of prolonged takes of Shiang on a subway platform, eating cookies on a bed by herself in her hotel room, and suchlike. While the depth-of-field compositions show a meticulous placement of objects, they fail to hold our interest.

In this otherwise lugubrious section of the film, Tsai manages to pull off a serendipitous gem of a cinematic moment. While we see Hsiao returning to The 400 Blows video as a respite from troubled sleep, Shiang shares a public bench in a graveyard with Jean-Pierre Leaud, appearing as himself, now a man in late middle age. Here, the detached stance of Tsai's camera manages to lay bare the lines of maturity that time has chiseled on Leaud's face, an eventual victory over little Antoine's innocence and mischief.

The film's final section depicts its characters on the level of purely sexual passion. Hsiao has sex with a streetwalker. Shiang has a brief lesbian encounter with a woman from Hong Kong (Cecilia Yip), who offers her momentary solace. But here again, it is the mother's sexual craving that proves heart-wrenching. In what could well be the boldest depiction of female self-arousal in art cinema, we see her rubbing a cane hassock against her genitals, while a framed photograph of her husband illuminated by candles, looms over the foreground. Eventually, Hsiao is brought closer to his mother, though we don't see how, while Shiang remains isolated in Paris, her fate undecided.

Tsai's creative impulse to take arthouse filmic realism into a dimension of its own comes to the fore in his puzzling finish. A middle-aged, well-dressed Oriental gentleman, resembling Hsiao's father and played by the same actor, looks at Shiang asleep on a park bench, then walks across a bare, wintry expanse towards a ferris wheel that slowly begins to move, seemingly part of a metaphysical realm of its own, affirming the continuity of life in its own quixotic manner.

Writing at the time of the film's screening at the 2001 New York Film Festival, soon after the monumental tragedy of the World Trade Center, Elvis Mitchell in the *New York Times* finds that the film combines comic and tragic elements in a manner much needed for our time. For him, Tsai "sets loose shock waves of comedy" while keeping to his "deeply moving scenario," resulting in "a barely tapped genre, the absurdist melodrama . . ." Surprisingly, critics for the most part have excused the film's pace and its emotional vacuity. Desson Howe in the *Washington Post* even claims that "if you can acclimate yourself to the pace of this movie, some sort of mysterious transformation occurs. You're the eyes of nature itself, watching with an almost spiritual clarity."

—*Vivek Adarkar*

## CREDITS

**Hsiao Kang:** Kang-sheng Lee
**Shiang-chyi:** Shiang-chyi Chen
**Father:** Tien Miao
**Mother:** Yi-ching Lu
**Cameo:** Cecilia Yip
**Cameo:** Jean-Pierre Leaud

**Origin:** Taiwan
**Language:** Chinese, French
**Released:** 2001
**Production:** Bruno Pesery; released by Winstar Cinema
**Directed by:** Ming-liang Tsai
**Written by:** Ming-liang Tsai, Pi-Ying Yang
**Cinematography by:** Benoit Delhomme
**Editing:** Sheng-Chang Chen
**Production Design:** Kam Tim Yip
**MPAA rating:** Unrated
**Running time:** 116 minutes

## REVIEWS

*Boxoffice.* December, 2001, p. 38.
*Chicago Sun-Times Online.* March 1, 2002.
*Film Comment Online.* January/February, 2002.
*Los Angeles Times Online.* January 18, 2002.
*New York Times Online.* September 29, 2001.
*Variety Online.* May 28, 2001.
*Village Voice Online.* January 15, 2002.
*Washington Post.* February 1, 2002, p. WE37.

# What's the Worst That Could Happen?

*It takes a thief to nail a crook.*
—Movie tagline

 **Box Office:** $32 million

When you make a film entitled *What's the Worst That Could Happen?*, you are virtually going out on a limb and handing critics a saw. The film is admittedly based upon a Dortmunder novel by Donald E. Westlake of the same name, but there were published plans to re-christen the story on its way to the screen which never materialized. It shows that the filmmakers were either especially nervy or a little bit nutty, much like the film's lead characters played by Danny DeVito and Martin Lawrence. A title change would not have been enough to put over this meager comedy which tries awfully hard—but, for the most part, unsuccessfully—to convince us that there is fun to be had here.

Working particularly strenuously is Lawrence, whose comedy gets more over-the-top as the film goes on, far more kinetic than comedic. He plays Kevin Caffrey, a thief with an eye for high-end loot. When we first meet him, he is attending an auction in a posh section of Boston where expensive works of art are being sold. While there, he sees a classy work of art which is definitely to his liking: beautiful Amber Belhaven (Carmen Ejogo), who is there to sell a beloved painting that belonged to her father so she can pay mounting hotel bills. Kevin tries to appear as if he belongs in such tony company while gathering useful information for his "business," but Amber seems like the real deal, a classy young Englishwoman with a degree in anthropology. To impress and comfort her, he steals the painting and brings it to her hotel room, where things get as hot as the stolen artwork. Their coupling and profession of unusually deep feelings for each other seem all too quick and forced.

Also rather unconvincing is Kevin's early and casual admission about how he makes his living to someone who could wind up being a one night stand, as well as the fact that Amber does not seem a bit fazed or put off when she finds out that she has just slept with a criminal. Having just been sniffling at the auction earlier in the day because the loss of her father's painting was almost too much to bear, it strains credulity that she just pops a ring off her finger that she says he gave to her as a daily reminder of his love and gives it to this man she just met and only really knows in the Biblical sense. The film's plot dictates it, however, and so Kevin happily takes possession.

Across town, things are not looking as rosy for diminutive and dishonorable billionaire businessman Max Fairbanks (DeVito), who has filed for Chapter 11 protection for a division of his huge media empire. As part of the legal proceedings, he has been denied access to some of his many luxurious properties, and when this is pointed out to Kevin by his partner in crime Berger (John Leguizamo), the two head for Max's Marblehead beachfront mansion.

Unbeknownst to them, Max has gleefully ignored the court order and the oft-broken marriage vows he took to his upper-crust wife Letitia (Nora Dunn), and is upstairs leering at bubble-headed Miss September (Sascha Knopf) in a bubble bath. As Kevin pops a Faberge egg and other valuables into his sack, he is stunned to find himself looking down the barrel of Max's gun. When the police arrive, Max delights in a little revenge against the brazen burglar by claiming that Kevin's ring belongs to him, and the police make Kevin hand it over. On the way to the station, Kevin escapes from the police car in rather unbelievable fashion and, not to be outdone, heads back to Max's, getting $150,000 in valuables and a car but no ring. Max fumes when he finds out, but still enjoys the fact that he was able to steal from a thief, and becomes convinced that the ring will bring him good luck.

Now the battle lines are drawn, and the two begin an all-out ego-driven battle to outmaneuver the other and command possession of the ring. In Kevin's camp is Amber, Berger and his high-pitched wife (Anna Gasteyer), Kevin's uncle and fence Jack (Bernie Mac), hot-headed magician/escape artist Windham (Lenny Clarke) and his equally argumentative wife (Siobhan Fallon), and Shelley Nicks (Gregory Qaiyum), a computer hacker who has an annoyingly breezy disposition and who pops up repeatedly with just the right information to keep Kevin's quest moving forward and future skirmishes possible. (This includes things which one really questions that he could have found out through the computer, such as his assertion that the only person Max truly fears in his life is Letitia). Max is surrounded by his various women, including his tarot card-reading personal secretary and one-time lover Gloria (Glenne Headly), his company's loopy head of security Earl (comedian Larry Miller), and his increasingly chagrined attorney Walter (Richard Schiff).

As things escalate Amber tells Kevin to forget the stupid ring, and Walter tries to get Max to do the same, but neither man will stand for being bested. It all continues on tit for tat throughout the film. Kevin shows up at a glittering gala honoring Letitia, and after struggling with Max for the ring, only walks away with a red wine stain on his white suit. So Kevin and Berger rob another of Max's homes, taking time out to pour red wine on the white carpet. When Max goes to appear before a Senate subcommittee investigating his media monopoly with envelopes filled with graft money, Kevin and Berger take out the money and fill the envelopes with crude little notes before making another unproductive attempt to get the ring. Perhaps at this point it was realized that the film's attempts at humor had also been unproductive, and so they try harder still.

Max may lack morals and ethics but he clearly did not get where he is being a fool, and yet when Kevin calls his cell phone while the businessman is testifying before the senators and taunts him, Max (ridiculously) answers the phone and erupts into a televised tirade full of verbal and gestural profanities which the congressmen think are aimed at them. (The scene is even embellished with an interpreter for the deaf signing in an obscene manner.) A later scene in which the thief and his cohorts rig an auction to make off with more of Max's possessions is even more frantic and even less funny. By this time various characters in the film have also tired of these shenanigans—Walter and Gloria have quit, Amber and Letitia have banded together to put both out-of-control men in their place by stealing the ring from both—and in the preposterous end Kevin, spouting risque double-entendres and inane mumbo-jumbo, successfully represents Max before Congress, wiping away the tycoon's problems—and then triumphantly swiping his expensive watch.

*Worst* is the 11th film based on works by the prolific Westlake, the most recent major production being *Payback* (1999), starring Mel Gibson. Films from the Dortmunder series have included such films as *The Hot Rock* (1972), *Bank Shot* (1974), and *Why Me?* (1990). *Worst* was adapted by Matthew Chapman, whose last screenplay was the best-forgotten Bruce Willis film *Color of Night* (1994). Director Sam Weisman is best known for his work in television on numerous series and for 1997's *George of the Jungle*.

*What's the Worst That Could Happen?* caused more than a few critics to remark that its content answered the question posed by its title. Made on a budget of almost $50 million, it grossed just over $32 million, and along with fellow-flop *Josie and the Pussycats*, helped MGM to a second quarter loss of almost $61.5 million. It is one of those films where, as Roger Ebert put it, the actors are "trying to act funny instead of simply being funny." This is especially true of Lawrence, whose dancing around, hand gestures, face contortions and other overblown antics must have expended a lot of calories but generate few laughs. DeVito as Max comes off better in a character type he has expertly played before, a rich cousin perhaps of his Louie DePalma from TV's *Taxi*, who we also enjoyed despite the character's loathsome qualities. William Fichtner delivers a highly enjoyable, scene-stealing performance as swishy Detective Alex Tardio. The film wastes a lot of fine talent, and, while occasionally amusing, is unquestionably forgettable fare.

—David L. Boxerbaum

*Variety.* June 4, 2001, p. 17.
*Wall Street Journal.* June 1, 2001, p. W1.
*Washington Post Online.* June 1, 2001.

## CREDITS

**Kevin Caffery:** Martin Lawrence
**Max Fairbanks:** Danny DeVito
**Lutetia Fairbanks:** Nora Dunn
**Detective Alex Tardio:** William Fichtner
**Gloria:** Glenne Headly
**Berger:** John Leguizamo
**Uncle Jack:** Bernie Mac
**Amber Belhaven:** Carmen Ejogo
**Earl Radburn:** Larry Miller
**Walter Greenbaum:** Richard Schiff
**Ann Marie:** Ana Gasteyer
**Tracey Kimberly:** Sascha Knopf
**Edwina:** Siobhan Fallon
**Shelly Nix:** GQ
**Windham:** Lenny Clarke

**Origin:** USA
**Released:** 2001
**Production:** Lawrence Turman, David Hoberman, Ashok Amritraj, Wendy Dytman; Hyde Park Entertainment; released by MGM
**Directed by:** Sam Weisman
**Written by:** Matthew Chapman
**Cinematography by:** Anastas Michos
**Music by:** Tyler Bates
**Sound:** David M. Kelson
**Music Supervisor:** Anita Camarata
**Editing:** Garth Craven, Nick Moore
**Art Direction:** David Lazan
**Costumes:** Jeffrey Kurland
**Production Design:** Howard Cummings
**MPAA rating:** PG-13
**Running time:** 95 minutes

## REVIEWS

*Boxoffice.* August, 2001, p. 62.
*Chicago Sun-Times Online.* June 1, 2001.
*Entertainment Weekly.* June 8, 2001, p. 45.
*Los Angeles Times Online.* June 1, 2001.
*New York Times.* June 1, 2001, p. E14.
*People.* June 11, 2001, p. 33.
*Premiere.* July, 2001, p. 86.
*Rolling Stone.* July 5, 2001, p. 149.
*USA Today Online.* June 1, 2001.

## QUOTES

Max Fairbanks (Danny DeVito): "I don't have coronaries—I *give* coronaries!"

# When Brendan Met Trudy

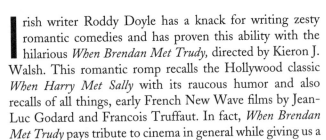

**Box Office:** $.1 million

Irish writer Roddy Doyle has a knack for writing zesty romantic comedies and has proven this ability with the hilarious *When Brendan Met Trudy,* directed by Kieron J. Walsh. This romantic romp recalls the Hollywood classic *When Harry Met Sally* with its raucous humor and also recalls of all things, early French New Wave films by Jean-Luc Godard and Francois Truffaut. In fact, *When Brendan Met Trudy* pays tribute to cinema in general while giving us a sneak peek at an odd couple's amorous adventures.

Doyle's screenplay portrays dynamic characters, refreshing dialogue mixed with classic movie quotes, and a flawless screenplay that twists its plot at just the right moments. What makes the film so remarkable are the characters. Brendan (Peter McDonald) teaches at a private boys school by day and the rest of his time is spent watching classic and arthouse cinema or singing in a church choir. Brendan possesses a wholesome quality that others want to sully and he's, as they say, ripe for the picking.

One fateful night Brendan meets the vivacious Trudy (Flora Montgomery) at a local pub where he visits after choir practice. Trudy lies to Brendan, telling him that she's a Montessori teacher when we learn later that she's a house burglar and in her opinion, quite good at her job. As we follow the relationship, we watch Brendan grow more rebellious and we watch his goody-two-shoes attitude transform into a bit of an outlaw ala Michel of the New Wave classic *Breathless.* In fact, when Brendan begins dressing like Michel by wearing a fedora, he possesses a striking resemblance to actor Jean-Paul Belmondo, who played the character. But as much as Doyle admires Francois Truffaut's screenplay, Doyle has a few twists of his own. This time nobody dies in the street and the girl turns herself into the police.

There are plenty of nods towards French New Wave in this film. Brendan gives his mother a biography of Godard and a biography of Truffaut to one of his nephews for

Christmas. And, judging from his mother's comments, Brendan's probably already given her a library of French New Wave biographies. In a scene where Brendan is teaching his class, the camera pans over a wall where a poster of you guess it, *Breathless,* hangs. Later in the film, Brendan and Trudy dress up like Michel and Patricia (Jean Seberg), pretending that the Dublin streets are Parisian boulevards. However, *When Brendan Met Trudy* is not an Irish *Breathless* but an original screenplay that just happens to be as much fun as watching the Godard film. *When Brendan Met Trudy* also bounces along with its quick edits and roving camera eye.

McDonald brings plenty of sex appeal to his straight-laced character turned-outlaw. At times he resembles Belmondo and also Jean-Pierre Leaud (Truffaut's Antoine Doinel) and at other times, he resembles a gawky choirboy. McDonald has immaculate comic timing and he can shift from a sullen mood to a passionate one in a blink of an eye. He also brings physicality to his role, especially in scenes when he's dragged off and beaten by cops. Brendan proves to be a complicated character that will do anything, even steal for love and McDonald renders those qualities on the big screen.

Montgomery is a delightful actress and fun to watch as she teases the conservative Brendan. She brings out the sassy passionate side of Trudy with ease and we forgive the fact that she's a thief because after all, she's good at her job. She is what Meg Ryan was to the character Sally and we will also be quoting the character Trudy for years to come.

Director Walsh, along with Doyle, have created an Irish romantic comedy that will soon become a classic. With all of the elements in place, two strong leads, memorable characters, quotable dialogue, and familiar scenes with universal themes, *When Brendan Met Trudy* deserves multiple viewings. Similar to the cineaste Brendan, many of us will quote the films characters', wondering why our love relationships do not compare to the characters in the film. Brendan committed crimes because he loves Trudy. Trudy went to prison because she loved Brendan. And Doyle wrote *When Brendan Met Trudy* as a love letter to cinema.

—*Patty-Lynne Herlevi*

## CREDITS

**Brendan:** Peter McDonald
**Trudy:** Flora Montgomery
**Mother:** Marie Mullen
**Nuala:** Pauline McLynn
**Niall:** Don Wycherley

**Origin:** Ireland, Great Britain
**Released:** 2000

**Production:** Lynda Myles; Collins Avenue, Deadly Films 2; released by Shooting Gallery
**Directed by:** Kieron J. Walsh
**Written by:** Roddy Doyle
**Cinematography by:** Ashley Rowe
**Music by:** Richard Hartley
**Sound:** Gerard Roche
**Editing:** Scott Thomas
**Art Direction:** Susan Cullen
**Costumes:** Consolata Boyle
**Production Design:** Fiona Daly
**MPAA rating:** Unrated
**Running time:** 95 minutes

 REVIEWS

*Boxoffice.* May, 2001, p. 60.
*Chicago Sun-Times Online.* March 9, 2001.
*Entertainment Weekly.* March 16, 2001, p. 44.
*Sight and Sound.* May, 2001, p. 60.
*Variety.* September 25, 2000, p. 65.
*Washington Post Online.* March 9, 2001.

## QUOTES

Brendan (Peter McDonald) says he's going to choir practice and Trudy (Flora Montgomery) replies: "I'll never come between you and your hymns."

 TRIVIA

Roddy Doyle has adapted three of his three novels (*The Commitments, The Snapper,* and *The Van*) for the screen. This is his first original screenplay.

# The Widow of Saint-Pierre (La Veuve de Saint-Pierre)

*A true story of revenge and redemption, fear and forgiveness, and the true meaning of love.*
—Movie tagline

**Box Office:** $3.2 million

In *The Widow of Saint-Pierre,* "widow" is French slang for the guillotine, but also could refer to the many sailors' widows who live in Saint-Pierre, a French territory off the coast of Newfoundland. But more than likely, the widow of Saint-Pierre refers to the women whose husbands were sacrificed so that French law was upheld in the colonies. The first man, Neel Auguste, is a condemned criminal; the second, an army captain who refused to execute him. In any case, Patrice Leconte's adapted (from a real life event) feature claims that the man who is sentenced and the man that is executed are seldom the same man. People change.

Set in 1850, remorseful killer Neel Auguste (Yugoslav director Emir Kusturica) is to be executed by guillotine, only he can't be executed until a guillotine from France arrives and an executioner is chosen. In the meantime, Jean (Daniel Auteuil), the garrison's captain, takes custody of the prisoner and his compassionate wife Pauline (Juliette Binoche), known as "Madame La," turns the killer into her protégé. She believes that a person can change and she's right. Auguste helps his fellow villagers out with various chores, saves a café owner's life, and even volunteers to haul the ship that contains the guillotine to shore so that the villagers won't refuse badly needed employment because they don't want to see him die.

By attempting to save Auguste's life, Madame La sacrifices her husband since he sides with his wife. He refuses to take part in the execution and the governor punishes him for blocking justice from being carried out. And of course, the question arises is the death penalty a form of justice? After all, the governor is the true murderer here and when he tries to save face with the French government, he wastes the lives of an executioner, a captain, and a condemned man-turned-humanitarian. While this story takes place during the 19$^{th}$ century, we still engage in debates over the death penalty in the 21st.

*The Widow of Saint-Pierre* proves to be a noteworthy film because Leconte chose to direct the actors from behind a camera claiming that "Being my own [camera] operator has helped me in my relationship with actors because there is no intermediary." Couple that with director Emir Kusturica's debut performance in a major role and one might be reminded of Lars von Trier's directing Bjork in her debut acting performance in *Dancer in the Dark.* And other comparisons can be made between the two films—not only did non-professionals render these meaty lead roles but both characters inched their way to the gallows while sacrificing their lives for those they loved.

Of course, other international directors have acted in films, including Fritz Lang in Jean-Luc Godard's *Contempt* and Francois Truffaut in *Day for Night* and *The Green Room.*

But the difference here is that Kusturica plays a lead role in another director's film opposite two of France's most esteemed actors, Binoche and Autueil, and his performance matches the performances of the seasoned actors. In one scene, we see Auguste's trembling hands reach out to his lover's face while he waits behind bars for his execution. After his lover leaves, Madame La peers into Auguste's eyes through the bars and their exchange of glances reveals the love the characters have for each other and also their anguish of not being able to stop the inevitable.

Binoche, who has proven her range in such films as Kryysztof Kieslowski's *Blue* and Leo Carax's *Lovers on a Bridge,* delivers a courageous yet restrained performance. One might be reminded of Carole Bouquet's performance as the real-life heroine Lucie, who saved her Jewish husband from the Nazis in Claude Berri's *Lucie Aubrac.* Autueil, who played Lucie's husband in the Berri film, here plays a virtuous lover willing to die for his principles.

*The Widow of Saint-Pierre* shows a woman who involuntarily sacrifices her beloved husband's life while trying to save the life of a condemned man. And, similar to tragedies involving canonized saints such as St. Joan, we are left to decide the meaning of justice, corruption, and the ultimate betrayal of others.

—*Patty-Lynne Herlevi*

## CREDITS

**Pauline, Madame La:** Juliette Binoche
**Jean, Le Capitaine:** Daniel Auteuil
**Neel Auguste:** Emir Kusturica
**Le Gouverneur:** Michael Duchaussoy
**Adrienne:** Sylvie Moreau
**Emilie:** Sarah McKenna
**Louis Ollivier:** Reynald Bouchard
**President Venot:** Philippe Magnan

**Origin:** France
**Language:** French
**Released:** 2000
**Production:** Gilles Legrand, Frederic Brillon; Cinemaginaire Inc., France 2 Cinema, France 3 Cinema, Epitheta Films; released by Lion's Gate Films
**Directed by:** Patrice Leconte
**Written by:** Claude Faraldo
**Cinematography by:** Eduardo Serra
**Music by:** Pascal Esteve
**Sound:** Paul Laine, Jean Goudier
**Editing:** Joelle Hache
**Art Direction:** Ivan Maussion
**Costumes:** Christian Gasc
**MPAA rating:** R

**Running time:** 112 minutes

## REVIEWS

*Boxoffice.* July, 2000, p. 92.
*Chicago Sun-Times Online.* March 30, 2001.
*Entertainment Weekly.* March 2, 2001, p. 43.
*New York Times Online.* March 2, 2001.
*People.* March 5, 2001, p. 40.
*Sight and Sound.* September, 2000, p. 56.
*Variety.* April 24, 2000, p. 31.

## TRIVIA

Daniel Auteuil also worked with director Patrice Leconte in *The Girl on the Bridge* (1999).

## AWARDS AND NOMINATIONS

**Nomination:**
**Cesar 2001:** Actress (Binoche), Support. Actor (Kusturica)
**Golden Globes 2001:** Foreign Film.

# With a Friend Like Harry (Harry, He's Here to Help) (Harry, un Ami Qui Vous Veut du Bien) (Harry, A Friend Who Wishes You Well)

With a Friend Like Harry . . . *who needs enemies?*
—Movie tagline

**Box Office:** $3.8 million

The trouble with Harry in Dominik Moll's *With a Friend Like Harry* is that he's a man who needs solutions to other people's problems. He's a spooky charmer and sociopath who quickly eliminates anyone who deters him from his tranquil life. However, the root of Harry's irrational behavior never surfaces and Moll leaves viewers to do the dirty detective work despite the absence of hints of childhood traumas. At least Moll's psychological thriller guru, Alfred Hitchcock, planted seeds of childhood traumas in his characters (*Psycho, Vertigo*) or gave us the perfect set-up for crimes to take place (*Rear Window*). Trouble arises because Moll, like other filmmakers, can't duplicate Hitchcock's genius (Claude Chabrol comes close). But even though Moll's psychological thriller isn't ingenious, it possesses entertainment value.

As the film opens a tranquil piano sonata is quickly replaced by the sound of a screaming baby. Next we see a young family stuffed in an overheated car as they make their way to their summer cottage. With no hope for family bliss, Michel (Laurent Lucas) attempts to drive while one of his daughters repeatedly kicks the back of his seat, a baby screams, and his wife Claire (Mathilde Siegner) protests an impending visit to Michel's parents home. The family pulls into a rest stop and while Michel takes a breather from familial tension, an old classmate, Harry (Sergi Lopez), introduces himself while the two men cool off in the men's room. Disheveled and suffering from exhaustion, Michel doesn't remember Harry from their school days, but Harry persists and obsesses about a poem that Michel once wrote for a school publication.

Soon Harry and his starlet fiancé Plum (Sophie Guillemin) weasel their way into Michel's life. The couple sleep over at the Michel's modest cottage even though Claire doesn't appear too happy about Harry's intrusion. Harry recites Michel's adolescent poem at a group dinner. Everyone but Harry brushes off the badly-written poem and soon Harry decides to eliminate anyone or anything that stands in Michel's way of becoming a published author. When the family car breaks down, Harry buys Michel a 4X4 against everyone's wishes, and when Michel's relatives upset Harry, he quietly eliminates them. Soon Harry loses complete control, eventually leading to his own demise, and all seemingly over a poem about a murderer that stalks the night.

Lucas resembles Jimmy Stewart while portraying the wholesome quality of a family man who feels something might be missing from his life. While not exactly Grace Kelly, Seigner plays a sexy mother with fierce maternal instincts and impeccable intuition. Together they portray a married couple slowly unraveling while family tensions eat away at them, and yet, we still get that they love each other. Newcomer Guillemin recalls sex symbols Marilyn Monroe and Brigette Bardot—wearing skin-tight clothing or lying cherub-like on a hotel bed. The character Plum might appear superficial until she discusses the benefits of homeopathic medicine with Claire. Finally, rounding off the foursome, Lopez confuses viewers with his I-am-doing-this-out-of-friendship sentiment. But, he's not quite the Gary Cooper type, so Lopez does give off a whiff of cynicism to his role that leads us to think something is not right with him too early in the film.

Hitchcock emerged as a filmmaker during an era when Jungian psychology spoke through artists and symbolism was mainstreaming in society. Moll also employs symbolism in his film with a dozen eggs that, when filmed from the right angle, resemble a voluptuous woman's cleavage. These eggs represent sex and fertility but also contrast with Harry's dislike of children. Harry eats raw eggs for sexual potency and soon family man Michel portrays the eggs as sexual images and so he writes an erotic short story. However, unlike Hitchcock's characters' connection to symbols, the symbolic eggs do not lead us to understanding Harry's odd behavior.

Moll does employ Hitchcock's black humor: in one sequence, one of Michel's daughters drops a lollipop on the floor of the car so Claire throws it out the window. The child throws a tantrum and, just when you think that Michel and Claire will experience nervous breakdowns, the film cuts to a calm scene in which Claire and her infant ride in the back seat of Harry's air-conditioned Mercedes. Again, we see a stark contrast between calm bachelorhood and chaotic family life. Moll isn't Hitchcock, but Moll could redefine the psychological thriller on his own terms if he so chooses.

—Patty-Lynne Herlevi

## CREDITS

**Harry:** Sergei Lopez
**Michel:** Laurent Lucas
**Claire:** Mathilde Seigner
**Plum:** Sophie Guillemin

**Origin:** France
**Language:** French
**Released:** 2000
**Production:** Michel Saint-Jean; Diaphana Films; released by Miramax Films
**Directed by:** Dominik Moll
**Written by:** Dominik Moll, Gilles Marchand
**Cinematography by:** Mathieu Poirot-Delpech
**Music by:** David Whitaker
**Sound:** Francois Maurel, Gerard Hardy
**Editing:** Yannick Kergoat
**Costumes:** Virginie Montel
**Production Design:** Michel Barthelemy
**MPAA rating:** R

**Running time:** 117 minutes

## REVIEWS

*Chicago Sun-Times Online.* April 27, 2001.
*Entertainment Weekly.* April 27, 2001, p. 90.
*Los Angeles Times Online.* April 27, 2001.
*New York Times Online.* April 15, 2001.
*New York Times Online.* April 20, 2001.
*Seattle Weekly.* April 26, 2001, p. 71.
*USA Today Online.* April 20, 2001.
*Variety.* May 15, 2000, p. 28.
*Washington Post Online.* April 27, 2001.

## QUOTES

Harry (Sergi Lopez) speaks to Michel (Laurent Lucas) about his girlfriend: "How do you like Plum? She's not brainy like Claire, but she has an animal intelligence that I like. Know what I mean?"

## AWARDS AND NOMINATIONS

**Cesar 2001:** Actor (Lopez), Director (Moll), Film Editing, Sound
**Nomination:**
**Cesar 2001:** Film, Screenplay, Support. Actress (Seigner).

# Zoolander

*3% body fat. 1% brain activity.*
—Movie tagline

 **Box Office:** $45.1 million

It was almost as though two versions of *Zoolander* were released because reactions to the film differed so greatly. Some critics thought the film was a hilarious, subversive romp, akin to Ben Stiller's glory days on his acclaimed TV sketch comedy, *The Ben Stiller Show.* Others thought that the jokes were tired, the targets too obvious and the subject matter passe. *Zoolander* was also a test case of sorts. It was the first major comedy to come out in the wake of the World Trade Center bombings. Studios were unsure whether Americans would be in the mood to see a light-hearted film or if they'd think comedies to be too frivolous. As it turned out, Americans were ready for a comedy. The film debuted as the second biggest film of the week.

The film was also a test for Stiller himself. Although *The Ben Stiller Show* was a critical favorite, it didn't have a very wide audience and did little to get Stiller into the public consciousness. *Reality Bites* helped make him popular among the twenty-something set but it wasn't until films like *There's Something About Mary* and *Meet the Parents* that Stiller became a bankable box office star. In those films, Stiller played a certain type of character—a nerdy, hapless, anxiety prone guy. When he veered from that persona, as he did by portraying his ex-junkie friend Jerry Stahl in the drama *Permanent Midnight* or as a director in the much maligned Jim Carrey film *The Cable Guy,* audiences stayed away. Stiller had said in interviews that he didn't want to be pigeon-holed as "Mr. Anxiety Guy" and *Zoolander* was a chance to see if audiences would accept him in a role that was more like a sketch comedy character.

Stiller first unveiled his character Derek Zoolander at the VH1 Fashion Awards. The vapid awards show was the perfect setting for the preening, vapid Zoolander to debut. Out of that setting, the Zoolander character doesn't seem nearly as subversive and funny. The central joke of *Zoolander* is that male models are dense. Zoolander is exhibit A. He talks in a breathy Marilyn Monroe-type voice and is confused by big words like "eulogy" and "bulimic." He prides himself on being the top male model and is known for his patented facial expressions like "Blue Steel" and "The Magnum." Part of the joke is that all of the expressions are the same. Zoolander purses his lips, sucks in his cheekbones and glares moodily at the camera. He's friends with equally clueless fellow male models who think it's the height of witty banter to preface their statements with "Earth to . . ."

Zoolander has three problems in his life. First is up-and-coming model Hansel (Owen Wilson of *Shanghai Noon*). Hansel is a too-cool, laid-back surfer dude who is always having great adventures like repelling down Mount Vesuvius or going to the islands for the weekend to hang out with the spider monkeys and who has an entourage that includes a Sherpa and an Aztec tea brewer named Ennui. Hansel wins the top male model award at a fashion awards show, breaking Zoolander's three-year winning streak. Zoolander's second problem is that he's just been interviewed by a pretty journalist from *Time* magazine, Matilda Jeffries (Christine Taylor, Stiller's real life wife), and is the subject of an unflattering cover story. Zoolander's pain is dulled though because he reads the cover blurb, "A Model Idiot" as "A Model, Idiot." The story is just one more blow to a career that seems to be suddenly and quickly disappeared.

Zoolander's third and most absurd problem is that designer Mugatu (*Saturday Night Live*'s Will Ferrell, who is always in these sorts of movies) has targeted Zoolander to be

a unwitting part of an evil scheme. Mugatu is getting pressure from his superiors in the fashion industry because the prime minister of Malaysia has raised child labor standards in his country. This will hurt the fashion industry so the fashionistas decide that the prime minister must be assassinated. They choose Zoolander for the job because they need a "beautiful self-absorbed simpleton who can be molded like Jell-O." They enlist Zoolander's help by telling him he's going to be the star of Mugatu's new campaign "Derelicte," a fashion show based on derelicts' clothing. As part of the training, they send Zoolander to a fake day spa where Mugatu's evil assistant Katinka (real life model Milla Jovovich) subjects Zoolander to hypnosis. When Zoolander hears the song "Relax" by Frankie Goes To Hollywood, he will go into a killing rage and attack the prime minister.

*Zoolander* has its moments, but they're more the type that seem clever than laugh out loud hilarious. Stiller parodies the meaninglessness of ad campaigns with one that features the tag line "Moisture . . . the essence of wetness." And Zoolander falls in love with his former foe, the magazine reporter, after she participates in a strange orgy with a cast that includes Hansel, two Finish midgets, and the Sherpa. (Apparently there was originally a goat too, but the MPAA nixed that idea.)

The film is populated by recognizable faces. Zoolander's old-timey manager, Maury Ballstein, who betrays him, is played by Stiller's dad Jerry Stiller. Stiller's mother, comedian Anne Meara, makes a cameo as a workers' rights demonstrator. When Zoolander's career begins to falter, he decides he needs a dose of reality and heads back to the coal mines of New Jersey to work with his family, including his dad (Jon Voight) and his brothers (one of whom is played by an uncredited and silent Vince Vaughn). David Duchovny shows up as J.P. Prewitt, a Deep Throat-type character, who once was a famous hand model and who has information about Mugatu's nefarious doings.

The whole movie is filled with cameos. Winona Ryder, N' Sync's Lance Bass, Sandra Bernhard, Billy Zane, Fabio, Lenny Kravitz, and Donald Trump are just a few of the recognizable faces. But with the exception of an appearance by David Bowie playing a mediator at a "walk off" modeling competition between Zoolander and Hansel, the cameos are wasted. The famous faces aren't saying anything clever and the only thing they add to the film is the chance for audience members to think, "Hey, wasn't that . . ."

Overall, the performances are pretty one-dimensional, although in Stiller's case, maybe that's the whole point. Stiller's Zoolander seems like it might have been funny several years ago, but now seems out of date. Even his outfits, like a headband resembling something someone in Loverboy might have worn in the 1980s, seem dated. And, after years of comedies featuring dumb guys saying and doing dumb things, that kind of character has been done way too much. If any one could make a dumb guy seem funny again it would be Stiller, but even he is not up to the challenge. Hearing him pronounce "eulogy" as "u-googely" just isn't the sidesplitter the film imagines it to be. Also stuck in a rut is Stiller's father. The elder Stiller is playing a role he's played over and over again. He's an uncouth guy who gripes that his prostate is the size of a honeydew. He's George Costanza's dad all over again. The brightest spot in the film is Wilson's Hansel. Wilson gives the character the same kind of talky, new age goofiness that his character in *Shanghai Noon* had. A movie about Hansel would have been a lot more interesting and funny.

Lisa Schwarzbaum of *Entertainment Weekly* was on the side of the critics who didn't like the film. "The movie's an ill-fitting suit of gags, too long in the crotch even at 90 minutes," she wrote, giving the film a C-. Gary Thompson of the *Philadelphia Daily News* wrote, "There are plenty of moments when *Zoolander* feels like a sequel to an earlier, funnier movie." Carrie Rickey of the *Philadelphia Inquirer* wrote, "As a writer, actor and director, Stiller has good instincts. But he's working triple-time here and has spread himself too thin." Kenneth Turan of the *Los Angeles Times* was on the side of critics who enjoyed the film, calling it an "exuberant and insidiously funny satire." And Rob Blackwelder of Spliced Wire wrote, "The fashion world has never taken it on the chin harder than in this screamingly funny spoof of modeling and international intrigue, the likes of which Austin Powers can only dream about."

—*Jill Hamilton*

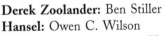

## CREDITS

**Derek Zoolander:** Ben Stiller
**Hansel:** Owen C. Wilson
**Matilda Jeffries:** Christine Taylor
**Mugatu:** Will Ferrell
**Katinka:** Milla Jovovich

**Maury Ballstein:** Jerry Stiller
**Larry Zoolander:** Jon Voight
**J.P. Prewitt:** David Duchovny

**Origin:** USA
**Released:** 2001
**Production:** Scott Rudin, Stuart Cornfeld, Ben Stiller; Village Roadshow Pictures, Red Hour; released by Paramount Pictures
**Directed by:** Ben Stiller
**Written by:** Ben Stiller, John Hamburg, Drake Sather
**Cinematography by:** Barry Peterson
**Music by:** David Arnold
**Sound:** Danny Michael
**Music Supervisor:** Randall Poster, George Drakoulias
**Editing:** Greg Hayden
**Art Direction:** Stephen Alesch
**Costumes:** David C. Robinson
**Production Design:** Robin Standefer
**MPAA rating:** PG-13
**Running time:** 89 minutes

## REVIEWS

*Boxoffice.* November, 2001, p. 150.
*Chicago Sun-Times Online.* September 28, 2001.
*Entertainment Weekly.* October 5, 2001, p. 107.
*Los Angeles Times Online.* September 28, 2001.
*New York Times Online.* September 28, 2001.
*USA Today Online.* September 28, 2001.
*Variety.* October 1, 2001, p. 35.
*Washington Post.* September 28, 2001, p. WE37.

## QUOTES

Derek Zoolander (Ben Stiller): "Is there more to life than being really, really, really ridiculously good-looking?"

# List of Awards

**Academy Awards**
Film: *A Beautiful Mind*
Animated Film: *Shrek*
Director: Ron Howard (*A Beautiful Mind*)
Actor: Denzel Washington (*Training day*)
Actress: Halle Berry (*Monster's Ball*)
Supporting Actor: Jim Broadbent (*Iris*)
Supporting Actress: Jennifer Connelly (*A Beautiful Mind*)
Original Screenplay: Julian Fellowes (*Gosford Park*)
Adapted Screenplay: Akvia Goldsman (*A Beautiful Mind*)
Cinematography: Andrew Lesnie (*The Lord of the Rings: The Fellowship of the Ring*)
Editing: Pietro Scalia (*Black Hawk Down*)
Art Direction: Catherine Martin (*Moulin Rouge*)
Visual Effects: Jim Rygiel, Randall William Cook, Richard Taylor (*The Lord of the Rings: The Fellowship of the Ring*)
Sound: Mike Minkler, Mysron Nettinga, Chris Munro (*Black Hawk Down*)
Makeup: Peter Owen, Richard Tayor (*The Lord of the Rings: The Fellowship of the Ring*)
Costume Design: Catherine Martin, Angus Strathie (*Moulin Rouge*)
Original Score: Howard Shore (*The Lord of the Ring: The Fellowship of the Ring*)
Original Song: "If I Didn't Have You" (Randy Newman; *Monster's Inc.*)
Foreign Language Film: *No Man's Land*
Documentary, Feature: *Murder on a Sunday Morning*

**Directors Guild of America Award**
Director: Ron Howard (*A Beautiful Mind*)

**Writers Guild of America Awards**
Original Screenplay: Julian Fellowes (*Gosford Park*)
Adapted Screenplay: Akiva Goldsman (*A Beautiful Mind*)

**Golden Globes**
Film, Drama: *A Beautiful Mind*
Film, Musical or Comedy: *Moulin Rouge*
Director: Robert Altman (*Gosford Park*)

Actor, Drama: Russell Crowe (*A Beautiful Mind*)
Actor, Musical or Comedy: Gene Hackman (*The Royal Tenenbaums*)
Actress, Drama: Sissy Spacek (*In the Bedroom*)
Actress, Musical or Comedy: Nicole Kidman (*Moulin Rouge*)
Supporting Actor: Jim Broadbent (*Iris*)
Supporting Actress: Jennifer Connelly (*A Beautiful Mind*)
Screenplay: Akiva Goldsman (*A Beautiful Mind*)
Score: Craig Armstrong (*Moulin Rouge*)
Song: "Until" (Sting; *Kate and Leopold*)
Foreign Language Film: *No Man's Land*

**Independent Spirit Awards**
Film: *Memento*
First Film: *In the Bedroom*
Director: Christopher Nolan (*Memento*)
Debut Performance: Paul Franklin Dano (*L.I.E.*)
Actor: Tom Wilkinson (*In the Bedroom*)
Actress: Sissy Spacek (*In the Bedroom*)
Supporting Actor: Steve Buscemi (*Ghost World*)
Supporting Actress: Carrie-Anne Moss (*Memento*)
Screenplay: Christopher Nolan (*Memento*)
First Screenplay: Daniel Clowes, Terry Zwigoff (*Ghost World*)
Cinematography: Peter Deming (*Mulholland Drive*)
Foreign Language Film: *Amelie*
Documentary: *Dogtown and Z-Boys*

**Los Angeles Film Critics Awards**
Film: *In the Bedroom*
Director: David Lynch (*Mulholland Drive*)
Actor: Denzel Washington (*Training Day*)
Actress: Sissy Spacek (*In the Bedroom*)
Supporting Actor: Jim Broadbent (*Iris, Moulin Rouge*)
Supporting Actress: Kate Winslet (*Iris*)
Screenplay: Christopher Nolan (*Memento*)
Cinematography: Roger Deakins (*The Man Who Wasn't There*)

Score: Howard Shore (*The Lord of the Rings: The Fellowship of the Ring*)

Animated Film: *Shrek*

Foreign Language Film: *No Man's Land*

Documentary: *The Gleaners and I*

### National Board of Review Awards

Film: *Moulin Rouge*

Director: Todd Field (*In the Bedroom*)

Actor: Billy Bob Thornton (*Bandits, The Man Who Wasn't There, Monster's Ball*)

Actress: Halle Berry (*Monster's Ball*)

Supporting Actor: Jim Broadbent (*Iris, Moulin Rouge*)

Supporting Actress: Cate Blanchett (*The Lord of the Rings: The Fellowship of the Ring, The Man Who Cried, The Shipping News*)

Screenplay: Todd Field, Rob Festinger (*In the Bedroom*)

Animated Feature: *Shrek*

Foreign Language Film: *Amores Perros*

### National Society of Film Critics Awards

Film: *Mulholland Drive*

Director: Robert Altman (*Gosford Park*)

Actor: Gene Hackman (*The Royal Tenenbaums*)

Actress: Naomi Watts (*Mulholland Drive*)

Supporting Actor: Steve Buscemi (*Ghost World*)

Supporting Actress: Helen Mirren (*Gosford Park*)

Screenplay: Julian Fellowes (*Gosford Park*)

Cinematography: Christopher Doyle, Mark Li Ping-bin (*In the Mood for Love*)

Foreign Language Film: *In the Mood for Love*

Documentary: *The Gleaners and I*

### New York Film Critics Awards

Film: *Mulholland drive*

Director: Robert Altman (*Gosford Park*)

Actor: Tom Wilkinson (*In the Bedroom*)

Actress: Sissy Spacek (*In the Bedroom*)

Supporting Actor: Steve Buscemi (*Ghost World*)

Supporting Actress: Helen Mirren (*Gosford Park*)

Screenplay: Julian Fellowes (*Gosford Park*)

Cinematography: Christopher Doyle, Mark Li Ping-bin (*In the Mood for Love*)

Foreign Language Film: *In the Mood for Love*

Documentary: *The Gleaners and I*

Animated Film: *Waking Life*

### Screen Actors Guild Awards

Actor: Russell Crowe (*A Beautiful Mind*)

Actress: Halle Berry (*Monster's Ball*)

Supporting Actor: Ian McKellen (*The Lord of the Rings: The Fellowship of the Ring*)

Supporting Actress: Helen Mirren (*Gosford Park*)

Ensemble Cast: *Gosford Park*

# Obituaries

**Aaliyah** (January 16, 1979–August 25, 2001). Born Aaliyah Haughton in Brooklyn, New York and best-known for her successful singing career, Aaliyah made her acting debut opposite Jet Li in *Romeo Must Die* (2000). She also had the lead role in *Queen of the Damned* (2002) and had signed for *The Matrix* sequels before being killed in a charter plane crash in the Bahamas. The singer was raised in Detroit, Michigan, and released her first album at the age of 15, 1994's platinum-selling "Age Ain't Nothing but a Number." This was followed by "One in a Million" (1996) and "Aaliyah" (2001).

**Henri Alekan** (February 10, 1909–June 15, 2001). Born in Paris, France, the cinematographer began work as an assistant cameraman in the late 1920s. He began working as a director of photography in the 1930s and had a 60-year career. Films included *The People of France* (1936), *Beauty and the Beast* (1946), *Anna Karenina* (1948), *Paris Is Always Paris* (1951), *Three Women* (1952), *Roman Holiday* (1953), *Zoe* (1954), *Casino de Paris* (1957), *Marriage of Figaro* (1959), *Topkapi* (1964), *Mayerling* (1968), *Red Sun* (1971), *The State of Things* (1982), *Wings of Desire* (1986), *Berlin-Jerusalem* (1989), and *Golem, the Ghost of Exile* (1992).

**John Alonzo** (June 12, 1934–March 13, 2001). Born in Dallas, Texas, cinematographer Alonzo's first jobs were in television and taking still photos of actors, which led to his moving to Hollywood. He played a number of bit parts before being admitted to the American Society of Cinematographers in the sixties and he worked as a director of photography for a number of *National Geographic* TV specials. Alonzo's first director of photography credit on a feature film was 1970's *Bloody Mama*. He received an Oscar nomination for shooting *Chinatown* (1974). His other credits included *Harold and Maude* (1971), *Lady Sings the Blues* (1972), *Sounder* (1972), *Conrack* (1974), *Farewell, My Lovely* (1975), *The Bad News Bears* (1976), *Black Sunday* (1977), *Norma Rae* (1979), *Back Roads* (1981), *Scarface* (1983), *Runaway* (1984), *Nothing in Common* (1986), *Overboard* (1987), *Steel Magnolias* (1989), *Internal Affairs* (1990), *Cool World* (1992), *Star Trek: Generations* (1994), *The Grass Harp* (1995), *The Prime Gig* (2000), and *Deuces Wild* (2001). In addition, Alonzo directed the 1978 feature *FM* and the tele-films *Champions: A Love Story* (1979), *Portrait of a Stripper* (1979), *Belle Starr* (1980), and *Blinded by the Light* (1980).

**Samuel Z. Arkoff** (June 12, 1918–September 16, 2001). Low-budget movie producer who, along with partner James H. Nicholson, formed American Releasing Corporation in 1954, which was later renamed American International Pictures (AIP) in 1956. The studio released more than 460 films, primarily to the drive-in market, and catered to the interests of teenagers with sci-fi, horror, beach, biker, and other genre films. AIP directors included Roger Corman, Martin Scorsese, John Milius, Woody Allen, David Cronenberg, and Francis Ford Coppola. Born in Fort Dodge, Iowa, Arkoff moved to Los Angeles after serving in WWII, graduated from Loyola University Law School, and began a practice in entertainment law before starting AIP. AIP went public in 1972 and was sold in 1979 to Filmways. Arkoff later formed Arkoff International Pictures. Arkoff's autobiography *Flying Through Hollywood by the Seat of My Pants* was published in 1992.

**Lewis Arquette** (December 14, 1935–February 10, 2001). The son of comic actor Cliff (Charley Weaver) Arquette, Lewis Arquette was born in Chicago, Illinois but grew up in Hollywood, graduating from Hollywood High. He studied with Lee Strasberg at the Actors Studio in New York and began to work on the stage before becoming a regular with Chicago's Second City company. He returned to Los Angeles in the seventies and became a versatile character actor. Arquette's credits included *Johnny Got His Gun* (1971), *The China Syndrome* (1979), *Nobody's Fool* (1986), *Tango & Cash* (1989), *Sleep With Me* (1994), *Waiting for Guffman* (1996), *Meet Wally Sparks* (1997), *Scream 2* (1997), *Twilight* (1998), *Best in Show* (2000), *Little Nicky* (2000), and *Ready to Rumble* (2000). He also had a recurring role as J.D. Pickett on the television series *The Waltons* (1978–81). Arquette was the father of actors Rosanna, Richmond, Patricia, Alexis, and David.

**Pat Ast** (1942?–October 2, 2001). Born in Brooklyn, New York, the actress was working as a clerk/receptionist in a box factory when she met Andy Warhol and appeared in his

1972 film *Heat.* Moving to Los Angeles in the mid-1970's, Ast appeared in such films as *The World's Greatest Lover* (1977), *Foul Play* (1978), *The Incredible Shrinking Woman* (1981), *The Pursuit of D.B. Cooper* (1981), *Reform School Girls* (1986), *Homer & Eddie* (1989), and *Loving Lulu* (1993).

**Jean-Pierre Aumont** (January 5, 1911–January 30, 2001). Born Jean-Pierre Salomons in Paris, France, the actor had a versatile 65-year career. He trained at the Paris Conservatory of Drama and made his film debut in 1932's *Jean de la Lune.* Aumont served with the Free French Army, leaving for the United States after France fell to German forces. His first appearance in the U.S. was in the Broadway play *Rose Burke* (1942) before coming to Hollywood for *Assignment in Brittany* (1943) and *The Cross of Lorraine* (1943). Aumont divided his time between Europe and America and between stage and film roles. His credits included *Hotel du Nord* (1938), *The Song of Scheherazade* (1947), *Wicked City* (1948), *Revenge of the Pirates* (1951), *Lili* (1953), *Napoleon* (1955), *The Devil at Four O'Clock* (1961), *The Seven Deadly Sins* (1962), *Five Miles to Midnight* (1963), *Cauldron of Blood* (1970), *Day for Night* (1973), *Cat and Mouse* (1978), *Becoming Colette* (1991), *Jefferson in Paris* (1994), and *The Proprietor* (1996). His last role was in the television miniseries *The Count of Monte Cristo* (1998). Aumont received an honorary Cesar award in 1991 for lifetime achievement. His autobiography *Sun and Shadow* was published in 1976.

**Sandy Baron** (May 5, 1937–January 21, 2001). Born Sanford Beresofsky in Brooklyn, New York, the nightclub performer also appeared in stage, television, and films. After graduating from Brooklyn College, Baron began his own stand-up act in New York, eventually moving to Hollywood in the mid-sixties, where he became a regular on the political satire show *That Was The Week That Was.* Film credits included *Sweet November* (1968), *The Out of Towners* (1970), *Straight Time* (1978), *Birdy* (1984), *Broadway Danny Rose* (1984), *Sid and Nancy* (1986), *Vamp* (1986), *The Grifters* (1990), *Leprechaun 2* (1994), and *Hi-Lo Country* (1998). Baron also had a recurring role on television's *Seinfeld* as retiree Jack Klompus.

**Ted Berman** (1920–July 15, 2001). Animator and director of cartoons for the Walt Disney studio where he worked for 45 years, beginning in 1940. Berman was born in Los Angeles, California, and studied at the Chouinard Art Institute; he worked on such films as *Bambi* (1942), *Alice in Wonderland* (1951), *Peter Pan* (1953), *Lady and the Tramp* (1955), *Paul Bunyan* (1958), *Mary Poppins* (1964), *Bedknobs and Broomsticks* (1972), *Winnie the Pooh and Tigger Too* (1974), *The Fox and the Hound* (1981), and *The Black Cauldron* (1985).

**James Bernard** (September 20, 1925–July 12, 2001). Born in India to a military family, the film composer was educated in England, graduating from the Royal College of Music in 1949 after wartime service. He was asked by screenwriter friend Paul Dehn to collaborate on the 1951 film *Seven Days to Noon,* which won them an Academy Award for best motion picture story. Dehn also found work for Bernard with the BBC in radio drama. In 1955, Bernard wrote his first score for Hammer Films, *The Quartermass Experiment,* becoming well-known for his work with the studio, including the scores for *The Curse of Frankenstein* (1957), *Dracula* (1958), *The Hound of the Baskervilles* (1959), *The Kiss of the Vampire* (1964), *She* (1965), *The Devil Rides Out* (1968), and *Frankenstein and the Monster from Hell* (1974). In 1997 Bernard wrote the score for the restored version of F.W. Murnau's 1921 classic *Nosferatu.* His last score was for the Kevin Brownlow documentary *Universal Horror* (1998).

**Ramon Bieri** (June 16, 1929–May 27, 2001). The character actor began his career on stage in the mid-1950s before appearing in supporting roles on television and in films. Credits included *R.P.M.* (1970), *The Andromeda Strain* (1971), *Brother John* (1971), *Badlands* (1973), *Sorcerer* (1977), *The Frisco Kid* (1979), *Reds* (1981), *The Zoo Gang* (1985), *Vibes* (1988), and *Ghosts of Mississippi* (1996).

**Julie Bishop** (August 30, 1914–August 30, 2001). Born Jacqueline Wells Brown in Denver, Colorado, the actress also appeared under the names Jacqueline Wells and Diane Duval, making more than 80 movies from the 1923 silent film *Children of Jazz* to *The Big Land* (1957) before retiring from the screen. Films as Jacqueline Wells included *Any Old Port* (1932), *Clancy of the Mounted* (1933), *Tarzan the Fearless* (1933), *Tillie and Gus* (1933), *The Black Cat* (1934), *Bohemian Girl* (1936), *The Frame Up* (1937), *Highway Patrol* (1938), *My Son Is A Criminal* (1938), *My Son Is Guilty* (1939), and *Torture Ship.* Warner Bros. placed her under contract in 1940 and changed her name to Julie Bishop. Additional credits included *Her First Romance* (1940), *Young Bill Hickok* (1940), *Will Bill Hickok Rides Again* (1941), *International Squadron* (1941), *The Hard Way* (1942), *Action in the North Atlantic* (1943), *Northern Pursuit* (1943), *Rhapsody in Blue* (1945), *Last of the Redmen* (1947), *Sands of Iwo Jima* (1949), *Westward the Women* (1951), and *The High and the Mighty* (1954) .

**Ralf D. Bode** (March 31, 1941–February 27, 2001). Born in Berlin, Germany, the cinematographer moved to the United States at 14 and graduated from the University of Vermont. Bode photographed more than 40 films, including *Saturday Night Fever* (1977), *Dressed to Kill* (1980), *Coal Miner's Daughter* (1980), for which he received an Oscar nomination, *Gorky Park* (1983), *The Accused* (1988), *Cousins* (1989), *Love Field* (1991), *Don Juan DeMarco* (1994), *Boys and Girls*

(2000), and the television movies *Gypsy* (1993), *A Streetcar Named Desire* (1995), and *Annie* (1999), for which Bode was nominated for an Emmy.

**Budd Boetticher** (July 29, 1916–November 29, 2001). Born Oscar Boetticher Jr. in Chicago, Illinois, the director was also a professional matador—a career he trained for after witnessing his first bullfight in Mexico City while on a break from Ohio State University in 1936. His mother considered his profession unacceptable and arranged for producer Hal Roach Jr., a family friend, to give Boetticher a job in Hollywood. He served as technical director on Rouben Mamoulian's *Blood and Sand* (1941) and began his own directorial career at Columbia Studios in 1944 with *The Missing Juror;* his first major success came with 1951's *Bullfighter and the Lady,* starring Robert Stack. Boetticher and Ray Nazzaro received an Oscar® nomination for best motion-picture story for that film. Boetticher made seven low-budget westerns with Randolph Scott in the 1950s that are considered genre classics: *Seven Men from Now* (1956), *Decision at Sundown* (1957), *The Tall T* (1957), *Buchanan Rides Alone* (1958), *Westbound* (1958), *Ride Lonesome* (1959), and *Comanche Station* (1960). Other films included *The Cimarron Kid (1951),* Horizons West *(1952),* Red Ball Express *(1952),* City Beneath the Sea *(1953),* The Man from the Alamo *(1953),* The Magnificent Matador *(1955),* and The Killer Is Loose *(1956). After the 1960 gangster film,* Rise and Fall of Legs Diamond, *the director left Hollywood to return to Mexico to make a documentary on bullfighter Carlos Azzura (who had trained Boetticher), which finally premiered in 1971. His last directorial effort was the western* A Time for Dying *(1971). He and wife Mary later moved to San Diego where Boetticher bred Portuguese bullfighting horses and put on demonstrations. The director published his memoirs,* When in Disgrace, *in 1989.*

**Mauro Bolognini** (June 28, 1922–May 14, 2001). Born in Pistoia, Italy, the director made some 42 films over a 40-year career. Films included *Wild Love* (1955), *Marisa* (1957), *Bad Girls Don't Cry* (1959), *Beautiful Anthony* (1960), *Careless* (1961), *Corruption* (1963), *The Dolls* (1965), *Mademoiselle de Maupin* (1966), *Arabella* (1967), *That Splendid November* (1968), *Drama of the Rich* (1974), *The Inheritance* (1976), *Lady of the Camelias* (1981), *The Venetian Woman* (1986), *Farewell Moscow* (1987), and *Husbands and Lovers* (1992).

**Roy Boulting** (November 21, 1913–November 5, 2001). The producer/director/writer and his twin brother John were born in Bray, Berkshire, England, and set up their production company, Charter Films, in 1937 and they worked together until John's death in 1985, varying the roles of producer, director, and screenwriter. The brothers first gained attention with *Pastor Hall* (1940). Among Boulting's other films were *Brighton Rock* (1947), *Seven Days to Noon* (1950),

*Lucky Jim* (1957), and *I'm All Right, Jack* (1959). Boulting also produced the WWII documentaries *Desert Victory: Battle of El Alamein* (1943), which won an Oscar®, and *Burma Victory* (1945).. Among Roy Boulting's five wives was Hayley Mills, 33 years his junior, whom he met while working on the film *The Family Way* (1966); they married in 1971 and divorced in 1977.

**Alfonso Brescia** (January 6, 1930–June 6, 2001). Born in Rome, Italy, the film director began his career in the early 1960s working on numerous science fiction, action, and western features, often credited as Al Bradley on the U.S. releases. Films included *Revolt of the Praetorains* (1964), *Conqueror of Atlantis* (1965), *The Colt Is My Law* (1966), *Hell in Normandy* (1967), *Cry of Death* (1968), *Kill Rommel!* (1969), *The Loves of Don Juan* (1971), *Battle of the Amazons* (1973), *White Fang and the Hunter* (1975), *War of the Robots* (1978), *Bloody Avenger* (1980), *Iron Warrior* (1987), *Getting Even* (1988), *Miami Cops* (1990), *Homicide in Blue Light* (1991), and *Deadly Chase* (1998).

**Owen Bush** (November 10, 1921–June 12, 2001). Born in Savannah, Missouri, the character actor appeared in films from the early sixties. Film credits included *Ma Barker's Killer Brood* (1960), *Roustabout* (1964), *Bonnie and Clyde* (1967), *Valley of the Dolls* (1967), *The Reivers* (1969), *Vanishing Point* (1971), *The Man Who Loved Cat Dancing* (1973), *The Apple Dumpling Gang* (1975), *Skateboard* (1978), *The Last Starfighter* (1984), *Prehysteria 2* (1994), *Best Laid Plans* (1999), and *Red Letters* (2000). He guest-starred in numerous television series, with his final appearance as Orville Perkins in the soap opera *Passions* (1999–2000).

**Corinne Calvet** (April 30,1925–June 23, 2001). Born Corinne Dibos in Paris, France, the actress appeared in radio and stage productions when she came to the attention of Paramount Studios at the end of WWII and came to Hollywood. Films included *Rope of Sand* (1949), *When Willie Came Marching Home* (1950), *On the Riviera* (1951), *Sailor Beware* (1951), *What Price Glory?* (1952), *So This Is Paris* (1954), *Far Country* (1955), *Apache Uprising* (1966), *Too Hot to Handle* (1976), and *Dr. Heckyl and Mr. Hype* (1980). Calvet's memoir *Has Corinne Been a Good Girl?* was published in 1983.

**John Chambers** (September 12, 1922–August 25, 2001). Born in Chicago, Illinois, was a pioneer in film and television makeup. He trained as a commercial artist before working as a medical technician in WWII, where he helped develop prosthetic devices for disfigured veterans. In 1953, Chambers began his Hollywood career with a job at NBC, where he worked on such series as *The Outer Limits, The Munsters, Lost in Space, Mission: Impossible,* and *Star Trek* (he made the Vulcan ears for Leonard Nimoy's Spock role).

Among his innovations was a new technique for making bald caps, a plastic-based material for making scars and wounds, and a technique for making veneer false teeth. While working for 20th Century Fox studio, Chambers devised new makeup, including a new type of foam rubber, for the 1968 film *Planet of the Apes*, and received an honorary Academy Award® for his outstanding achievement.

**Grigory Chukhrai** (May 23,1921–October 28, 2001). Born in the eastern Ukrainian city of Melitopol, the Soviet-era director was best-known for his war-themed films. He studied cinematography at the All-Union State Institute of Cinematography before serving in WWII and later graduated from the Soviet State Film School. His first feature film was *The Forty-First* (1956), which was awarded a jury prize at the Cannes Film Festival. His next film, *Ballad of a Soldier* (1959), won the 1960 Cannes award for best direction as well as the 1961 Lenin Prize and other awards. Chukhrai also directed, and wrote the screenplay for, *Clear Skies* (1961), as well as directing *People!* (1966) and *Life is Beautiful* (1982).

**Imogene Coca** (November 18, 1908–June 2, 2001). Diminutive comedian best-known for co-starring with Sid Caesar on *Your Show of Shows* from 1950–54. Born in Philadelphia, Pennsylvania, Coca was the daughter of a conductor and a vaudeville performer and began her own stage career at the age of 11. She went to New York at age 15 and worked in nightclubs, variety shows, and revues until beginning her television career in 1949. Film roles included *Under the Yum Yum Tree* (1963), *Rabbit Test* (1978), and as Aunt Edna in *National Lampoon's Vacation* (1983). Coca was nominated for a Tony award for her last stage appearance in *On the Twentieth Century* (1978).

**Charlotte Coleman** (April 3, 1968–November 14, 2001). Born in London, England, the actress was best-known for her comedic role of Scarlett in the 1994 hit, *Four Weddings and a Funeral*. She began her career at the age of 11 with the children's sitcom *Worzel Gummidge*. Other roles included "Oranges Are Not the Only Fruit *(1990)*, Map of the Human Heart *(1992)*, The Young Poisoner's Handbook *(1995)*, Different for Girls *(1996)*, The Revengers' Comedies *(1998)*, Beautiful People *(1999)*, and Bodywork *(1999)*. Coleman died from a massive asthma attack.*

**Peggy Converse** (April 3, 1905–March 2, 2001). Born in Oregon City, Oregon, Converse's family moved to Los Angeles and she began her career at 16 in the *Pilgrimage Play*. She graduated from Stanford University in 1927 and played a number of ingenue roles on Broadway during the 1920s and 30s, continuing her stage work throughout her career. Converse's films included *The Girl of the Limberlost* (1945), *Just Before Dawn* (1946), *Rusty Leads the Way* (1947),

*Father Is a Bachelor* (1950), *Miss Sadie Thompson* (1953), *They Rode West* (1954), *Day of the Bad Man* (1958), and *The Thing That Couldn't Die* (1958). She came out of retirement for *The Accidental Tourist* (1988).

**Fred de Cordova** (October 27, 1910–September 15, 2001). Born in New York City, the producer/director was active in Hollywood for more than 50 years. Upon graduation from Harvard in 1933, de Cordova went to work for Shubert theaters for 10 years before moving to Los Angeles in 1944 and working for Warner Bros. as a dialogue director. He made his directorial debut with *Too Young to Know* (1945) and later moved to Universal. Other directorial credits included *The Countess of Monte Cristo* (1948), *For the Love of Mary* (1948), *The Desert Hawk* (1950), *Peggy* (1950), *Bedtime for Bonzo* (1951), *Finders Keepers* (1951), *Little Egypt* (1951), *Bonzo Goes to College* (1952), *I'll Take Sweden* (1965), and *Frankie and Johnny* (1966). De Cordova then moved into television and was the producer/director of such series as *The Burns and Allen Show, December Bride, The Jack Benny Show,* and *My Three Sons*. De Cordova was also famous for producing *The Tonight Show Starring Johnny Carson* for 22 years, beginning in 1970. He was nominated for 17 Emmys and won a seven-time winner. De Cordova published his memoirs, *Johnny Came Lately* in 1988.

**Rosemary DeCamp** (November 14, 1910–February 20, 2001). Born in Prescott, Arizona, the actress attended Mills College in Oakland, California, where she appeared in a number of plays. Before beginning her film career, DeCamp worked in radio, playing Nurse Judy for 16 years on the drama *Dr. Christian*. DeCamp made her screen debut in *Cheers for Miss Bishop* (1941) but was frequently cast in mother roles in such films as *Yankee Doodle Dandy* (1942), *The Jungle Book* (1942), *This Is the Army* (1943), *Rhapsody in Blue* (1945), and *Night Unto Night* (1949). She played the wife in the film version of *The Life of Riley* (1948) and then played the same role in the television series (1949–50). DeCamp also played a widowed housewife on *The Bob Cummings Show* (1955–61) and played Marlo Thomas's mother on *That Girl* (1966–70).

**Anthony Dexter** (January 19, 1913–March 27, 2001). Born Walter Craig in Talmadge, Nebraska, the actor performed with the Army Special Services during WWII and acted on Broadway after the war. Because of his resemblance to silent screen star Rudolf Valentino, Dexter was chosen to star in the 1951 biopic *Valentino*, his screen debut. Other screen credits included *Captain John Smith and Pocahontas* (1953), *Captain Kidd and the Slave Girl* (1954), *The Black Pirates* (1954), *He Laughed Last* (1956), *The Story of Mankind* (1957), *Three Blondes in His Life* (1960), *Married Too Young* (1962), *Saturday Night in Apple Valley* (1965), and his last film before retirement, *Thoroughly Modern Millie* (1967).

**Troy Donahue** (January 27, 1936–September 2, 2001). A blond teen heartthrob of the sixties, the actor was born Merle Johnson Jr. in New York. He moved to Hollywood at the age of 19 and was signed by Warner Bros. His name was changed by film agent Henry Wilson, who was also responsible for naming Rock Hudson and Tab Hunter. Donahue first starring role was in *Summer Place* (1959), opposite Sandra Dee. He also starred in *Parrish* (1961), *Rome Adventure* (1962), *Palm Springs Weekend* (1963), and *Distant Trumpet* (1964). During this time, the actor also appeared in the ABC detective series *Surfside 6* (1960–62) and *Hawaiian Eye* (1962–63). His last notable role was a small part in 1974's *The Godfather, Part II* where his character was named Merle Johnson. Donahue had bit parts in other films and worked on direct-to-video releases and in the theater after his recovery from the drug and alcohol abuse that damaged his later career.

**Danilo Donati** (1926–December 1, 2001). Born in Suzzara, Italy, the costume designer began his career in 1954, doing costumes for a Luchino Visconti theater production. After moving to cinema work in the 60s, Donati won Oscars® for his costumes in *Romeo and Juliet* (1968) and *Casanova* (1976). Among his other films were *Gospel According to St. Matthew* (1964), *The Taming of the Shrew* (1967), *Fellini Satyricon* (1969), *Fellini's Roma* (1972), *Salo, or the 120 Days of Sodom* (1975), *Caligula* (1979), *Red Sonja* (1985), *Ginger and Fred* (1986), *Fellini's Intervista* (1987), *St. Francis of Assisi* (1989), *The Monster* (1996), and *Nostromo* (1996). Donati also designed the sets for the Roberto Benigni films *Life Is Beautiful* (1998) and *Pinocchio* (2002).

**Robert Enrico** (April 13, 1931–February 23, 2001). Born to Italian immigrant parents in Lievin, France, the director received the Palme d'Or at the 1962 Cannes Film Festival and the Oscar for best short film at the 1964 Academy Awards for his 24-minute film, *An Occurrence at Owl Creek Bridge*. Other films included *The Jailbird's Vacation* (1965), *Rum Runners* (1971), *The Old Gun* (1975), and *Winter Tale* (1999).

**Dale Evans** (October 31, 1912–February 7, 2001). Born Frances Octavia Smith in Uvalde, Texas, Evans changed her name after going into show business as a radio and club singer. She signed a contract in 1943 with Republic Pictures, the home of Western hero Roy Rogers with whom Evans was first paired in *The Cowboy and the Senorita* (1944). They married in 1947, with Evans becoming "Queen of the West" to Rogers's "King of the Cowboys." The duo co-starred in 35 movies and in the television series *The Roy Rogers Show* (1951–57); Evans also composed their theme song, "Happy Trails to You." Evans later became a speaker and volunteer with Christian groups and the author of some 17 books dealing primarily with her faith.

**Gloria Foster** (November 16, 1936–September 29, 2001). Born in Chicago, Illinois, the actress was best-known for her stage career. She studied at the Goodman Theater School of Drama and moved to New York in 1963 where she won a role in Martin B. Duberman's *In White America*. She played 27 characters and won her first (of three) Obie awards. Other notable stage productions included *Medea* (1965), *Agamemnon* (1977), *Trespassing* (1982), *Forbidden City* (1989), *Having Our Say* (1995), and her last stage role in a revival of *A Raisin in the Sun* (1999). Foster also worked in film and television, including *The Cool World* (1963), *Nothing but a Man* (1964), *Leonard Part 6* (1987), *Separate But Equal* (1991), and her role as Oracle in the 1999 blockbuster *The Matrix*. Foster had finished her scenes for the film's first sequel, *Matrix Reloaded*, before her death.

**Arlene Francis** (October 20, 1907–May 31, 2001). Born Arline Francis Kazanjian in Boston, Massachusetts, the actress was best-known as a panelist on the television quiz program *What's My Line?* (1950–75). Francis also had a daily radio interview program, *The Arlene Francis Show* from 1960 until 1984. Films included *Murders in the Rue Morgue* (1932), *Stage Door Canteen* (1943), *All My Sons* (1948), *One Two Three* (1961), and *The Thrill of It All* (1963).

**Kathleen Freeman** (February 17, 1919–September 23, 2001). Born in Chicago, Illinois, the comic character actress had a career on stage, screen, and television that spanned 50 years. Her parents were vaudevillians and she joined the act at age 2. The family moved to Los Angeles and Freeman studied music at UCLA, before beginning her acting career with a number of local theater groups in the 1940s. Freeman began her movie career with a one-line role in *The Naked City* (1948). Other credits included *Mr. Belvedere Goes to College* (1949), *Once a Thief* (1950), *A Place in the Sun* (1951), *The Greatest Show on Earth* (1952), *Singin' in the Rain* (1952), *The Affairs of Dobie Gillis* (1953), *Artists and Models* (1955), *The Fly* (1958), *North to Alaska* (1960), *The Errand Boy* (1961), *The Nutty Professor* (1963), *The Disorderly Orderly* (1964), *The Patsy* (1964), *The Rounders* (1965), *Support Your Local Sheriff* (1969), *Support Your Local Gunfighter* (1971), *The Blues Brothers* (1980), *Dragnet* (1987), *Gremlins 2* (1990), *At First Sight* (1995), *Blues Brothers 2000* (1998), and *Ready to Rumble* (2000), and as the voice of the old woman in *Shrek* (2001). Freeman played Katie the maid in the sitcom *Topper* (1953), appeared as Flo Schafter on *The Beverly Hillbillies* (1969–71), and as Mrs. Belmont on *Lotsa Luck* (1973–74). She received a Tony nomination for her last stage role in *The Full Monty* (2001).

**Giacomo Gentilomo** (April 5, 1909–April 16, 2001). Born in Trieste, Italy, Gentilomo was a movie critic, screenwriter, and assistant director before making his first feature film, *Rome Symphonies,* in 1937. He made his name with the sword-and-sandal genre, including *Goliath and the Vampires* (1961), *Last of the Vikings* (1961), *Battle of the Valiant* (1963), *Hercules Against the Moon Men* (1964), and *Slave Girls of Sheba* (1964). Among the director's other films were *The Brothers Karamazov* (1947), *The Accusation* (1951), *Young Caruso* (1951), *Immortal Melodies* (1953), and *Two Orphans* (1954). In 1964 Gentilomo quit directing for a career in art.

**Sy Gomberg** (1919–February 11, 2001). Born in New York, screenwriter Gomberg came to California to attend the University of Southern California. He spent WWII in the Air Force Motion Picture Unit, later contributing articles and short stories to popular magazines. A story for Collier's won Gomberg a screenwriting contract at Fox and an Oscar nomination for best story for 1951's *When Willie Comes Marching Home*. That same year Gomberg also received a nomination for best screenplay from the Writers Guild of America for *Summer Stock*. Other films included *The Toast of New Orleans* (1950), *Joe Butterfly* (1957), *The Wild and the Innocent* (1959), and *Three Warriors* (1977). Gomberg was also the creator, producer, and writer of the television series *The Law and Mr. Jones* (1960–62).

**David Graf** (April 16, 1950–April 7, 2001). Character actor best-known for his role as Officer Eugene Tackleberry in the seven *Police Academy* movies. Born in Lancaster, Ohio, Graf moved to Los Angeles in 1980 and began work in films and in numerous guest spots on television. Other films included *Four Friends* (1981), *Irreconcilable Differences* (1984), *Love at Stake* (1987), *Fatal Skies* (1990), *Guarding Tess* (1994), *The Brady Bunch Movie* (1995), *Citizen Ruth* (1996), and *Rules of Engagement* (2000). Graf also starred as Tom Arnold in the 1994 TV movie *Roseanne: An Unauthorized Biography* and had a recurring role as Col. Chase on *West Wing*.

**Jane Greer** (September 9, 1925–August 24, 2001). Born Bettejane Greer in Washington, D.C., the brunet beauty made 24 films and is best-remembered for her film noir roles. Onetime film producer Howard Hughes put Greer under contract but gave her no acting roles. She sued to end her contract and then signed with RKO studio, which Hughes eventually bought, once again derailing Greer's career. Her most memorable role was the bad girl in 1947's *Out of the Past*. Greer later played the mother of her original character in Taylor Hackford's remake *Against All Odds* (1984). Other films included *Two O'Clock Courage* (1945), *Dick Tracy, Detective* (1945), *George White's Scandals* (1945), *They Won't Believe Me* (1947), *You're in the Navy Now* (1951), *The Prisoner of Zenda* (1952), and *Man of a Thousand Faces* (1957). Greer also played Vivian Smythe in David Lynch's television series *Twin Peaks* (1991).

**Albert Hague** (October 13, 1920–November 12, 2001). Born Albert Macuse into a Jewish family in Berlin,

Germany, the composer and sometime actor was raised Lutheran to protect him from the Nazis. He fled to Italy in 1937, where he studied at a music conservatory in Rome, and immigrated to the U.S. after obtaining a scholarship to the University of Cincinnati. Hague then took the last name of his adopted father, Elliott B. Hague, and graduated in 1942. His first Broadway success was with the hit musical *Plain and Fancy* (1955) and he won a Tony award for his score for *Redhead* (1959). Hague also served as a music and acting coach, which led to his role as music teacher Benjamin Shorofsky in the film *Fame* (1980), a role he reprised for the NBC series. He appeared in several TV movies as well as the films *Space Jam* (1996) and *The Story of Us* (1999).

**Jack Haley Jr.** (October 25,1933–April 21, 2001). Director, producer, writer, and film executive, Haley was born in Los Angeles, California, the son of actor Jack Haley. He graduated from Loyola University and studied filmmaking at the University of Southern California and the University of California at Los Angeles. Haley was a producer/director for David L. Wolper Productions from 1959 to 1970 and became a senior vice president in 1967. He moved into films in 1970 and was named MGM's director of creative affairs in 1973, serving as producer, writer, and director for 1974's *That's Entertainment!* and *That's Dancin'!* (1985). Haley became the president of 20th Century Fox Television and directed the Academy Awards shows in 1970, 1974, and 1979. Haley also won a number of Emmy and Peabody awards for his television work.

**Anne Haney** (March 4,1934–May 26, 2001). Born in Memphis, Tennessee, Haney did not begin her career as a character actress until her mid-40s but then appeared in more than 50 motion pictures and television programs. Film roles included *Hopscotch* (1980), *Making Love* (1982), *The Osterman Weekend* (1983), *Mrs. Doubtfire* (1993), *The American President* (1995), *Mother* (1996), *Changing Habits* (1996), *Liar, Liar* (1996), *Midnight in the Garden of Good and Evil* (1997), *Psycho* (1998), and *The Out-of-Towners* (1999). Haney also had regular roles on the television series *Lime Street* (1985) and *George* (1993).

**William Hanna** (July 14, 1910–March 22, 2001). Born in Melrose, New Mexico, Hanna began his animation career in 1930, taking a position in the ink and paint department of Harman-Ising Studios. Hanna was the co-founder and co-chairman of Hanna-Barbera Studios, which he founded with Joseph Barbera in 1957. The partners met at MGM studios in 1937, where they created the "Tom and Jerry" cartoon series. The first cartoon in the series, *Puss Gets the Boot*, received an Academy Award nomination for best cartoon short in 1940 and Hanna-Barbera received 12 nominations and seven Oscars in the next 12 years. Hanna-Barbera developed more than 150 cartoon and live-action television series, including *Huckleberry Hound, The Flintstones, Scooby-Doo, Yogi Bear,* and *The Jetsons.* Hanna remained active even after the company was sold to Warner Bros. in 1996. William Hanna's autobiography *A Cast of Friends* was published in 1996.

**George Harrison** (February 25, 1943–November 29, 2001). Born in Liverpool, England, the lead guitarist for The Beatles also enjoyed a long solo career as a composer/singer/musician. In addition to appearing in the Beatles films, Harrison founded the movie production company HandMade films in 1979, which produced more than 20 films, including *Monty Python's Life of Brian* (1979), *The Long Good Friday* (1980), *Time Bandits* (1981), *The Missionary* (1982), *A Private Function* (1985), *Mona Lisa* (1986), *Withnail and I* (1987), and *Nuns on the Run* (1990). Harrison sold the company in 1994.

**Nigel Hawthorne** (April 5, 1929–December 26, 2001). Born in Coventry, England, the actor grew up in South Africa and made his debut in a Cape Town stage production of "The Shop at Sly Corner" in 1950. He moved to London in 1951 but a lack of success forced his return to Cape Town in 1957. He returned to England in 1963 and began working in repertory theater and on British television. His first notable success came with the satiric television series, *Yes, Minister* and its sequel *Yes, Prime Minister,* which ran between 1980 and 1987. Hawthorne also continued his stage career and won a 1991 Tony Award for *Shadowlands* and a 1992 Olivier Award for *The Madness of King George.* The actor repeated his portrayal as George III in the film adaptation, for which he received an Academy Award® nomination as best actor in 1994. Among his other films roles were *Richard III* (1995), *Twelfth Night* (1996), *Amistad* (1997), *The Winslow Boy* (1998), *The Object of My Affection* (1998), and *Madeline* (1998). Hawthorne was knighted in 1999.

**Eileen Heckart** (March 29, 1919–December 31, 2001). Born Anna Eileen Heckart in Columbus, Ohio, the husky voiced actress graduated from Ohio State University in 1942 and began her career in summer stock and on live television in New York. She made her Broadway debut in 1943 with *The Voice of the Turtle* but Heckart's big break came with her role as Rosemary Sidney in William Inge's *Picnic* in 1953. She played Mrs. Daigle in *The Bad Seed* (1954) and repeated her role for the 1956 film adaptation. She also played the mother in the Broadway version of *Butterflies Are Free* (1969) and reprised her role for the 1972 film, which earned her an Academy Award® for best supporting actress. Heckart's films included *Miracle in the Rain* (1956), *Somebody Up There Likes Me* (1956), *Bus Stop* (1956), *Up the Down Staircase* (1967), *No Way to Treat a Lady* (1968),

*Zandy's Bride* (1974), *Heartbreak Ridge* (1986), and *The First Wives Club* (1996). She was Emmy-nominated for her role as Aunt Flo Meredith on both *The Mary Tyler Moore Show* and *Lou Grant.* Heckart received a special lifetime achievement Tony Award for her theater work in 2000. Her last role was in Kenneth Longergan's play *The Waverly Gallery* (2000).

**Christopher Hewett** (April 5, 1922–August 3, 2001). Born in Worthing, Sussex, England, the character actor was best known for his role as television's *Mr. Belvedere* (1985–1990). He began acting at the age of seven and appeared in more than 100 plays as well as in several films in England, including *Pool of London* (1951) and *The Lavender Hill Mob* (1951), before coming to the U.S., where he played Zoltan Karpathy in the original stage version of *My Fair Lady* (1956). Hewett was also featured in Mel Brooks' *The Producers* (1968), before beginning his TV work.

**Faith Hubley** (1924?–December 7, 2001). Born Faith Elliott in New York City, Hubley and her husband John won three Academy Awards® for their animated films: *Moonbird* (1960), *The Hole* (1963), and *Tijuana Brass Double Feature* (1966) as well as seven nominations. Faith Hubley first worked in New York as a stage manager while she studied acting and directing as well as editing. She continued her editing career after moving to Hollywood in the 1940s and met her husband who worked for animation studio UPA (United Productions of America). They married in 1955 and their first collaboration was 1956's *The Adventure of an \**. Later returning to New York, the Hubleys established their own independent animation studio and made some 21 films together until John's death in 1977. Faith then directed and produced 25 more films, including *Step by Step* (1979), *Seers and Clowns* (1994), Witch Madness *(1999), and her last,* Northern Ice, Golden Sun *(2001).*

**Ken Hughes** (January 19, 1922–April 28, 2001). Born in Liverpool, England, screenwriter/director Hughes began his film career making documentaries and short features in 1941 but was probably best known for the children's film *Chitty Chitty Bang Bang* (1968). Other films included *Wide Boy* (1952), *Balck 13* (1953), *The Drayton Case* (1953), *Heat Wave* (1954), *Joe MacBeth* (1955), *Night Plane to Amsterdam* (1955), *The Atomic Man* (1956), *The Long Haul* (1957), *The Trials of Oscar Wilde* (1960), *The Small World of Sammy Lee* (1963), *Of Human Bondage* (1964), *Casino Royale* (1967), *Cromwell* (1970), *Oh, Alfie* (1975), *Sextette* (1978), and *Night School* (1981).

**Eugene Jackson** (December 25, 1916–October 26, 2001). Born in Buffalo, New York, the actor began his career at the age of six. He was introduced to Hal Roach, who signed him for the role of Pineapple in six of the *Our Gang* shorts: *The*

*The Mysterious Mystery, The Big Town, Circus Fever, Dog Days, The Love Bug,* and *Shootin' Injuns.* After his contract ended in 1926, Jackson worked for Mack Sennett in the Buster Brown comedies and with Mary Pickford in *Little Annie Rooney.* Jackson worked on a number of other silent films and made his talkie debut in *Hearts in Dixie.* He later went on the vaudeville circuit and later taught dance in studios he established while still working in small movie roles and on stage. The actor also appeared in several television series, including *Daktari, Julia,* and *Sanford and Son.* Jackson published his autobiography, *Eugene Pineapple Jackson: His Own Story,* in 1998.

**Pauline Kael** (June 19, 1919–September 3, 2001). Influential movie critic and writer who wrote for *The New Yorker,* beginning in 1967, until her retirement in 1991. Born in Petaluma, California, Kael's family moved to San Francisco when she was eight. She later majored in philosophy at the University of California at Berkeley. Kael reviewed movies for a Berkeley public radio station and also managed an arthouse theater before publishing her first film review in 1953 in the San Francisco magazine *City Lights.* After moving to New York in 1965, Kael wrote on film for national magazines until she was hired by *New Yorker* editor William Shawn. Kael wrote 13 books, including *I Lost It At the Movies* (1965), *Kiss Kiss Bang Bang* (1968), *Going Steady* (1970), *Deeper Into Movies* (1973), *Reeling* (1976), *When the Lights Go Down* (1980), *Hooked* (1989), *Movie Love* (1991), and *For Keeps* (1994).

**Burt Kennedy** (September 3, 1922–February 15, 2001). Screenwriter and director born in Muskegon, Michigan, he joined the family vaudeville act at the age of five. After serving in WWII, Kennedy moved to California and studied acting, later finding work writing for radio. He had a contract with John Wayne's film company, Batjac Productions, and his first produced screenplay was *Seven Men from Now* (1956). Kennedy also wrote *The Tall T* (1957), *Ride Lonesome* (1959), *Comanche Station* (1960), *The Rounders* (1965, also director), *Welcome to Hard Times* (1967, also director), *Dirty Dingus McGee* (1970, also director), *Hannie Caulder* (1972, also director), and *White Hunter, Black Heart* (1990). Burt Kennedy made his directorial debut with *The Canadians* in 1961; other films included *Mail-Order Bride* (1964), *The War Wagon* (1967), *Support Your Local Sheriff* (1969), *Support Your Local Gunfighter* (1971), and *Big Bad John* (1990).

**Howard W. Koch** (April 11, 1916–February 16, 2001). Born in New York City, the producer/director began his career as a film librarian at 20th Century Fox in 1935. In 1944, he began his directorial career as the first assistant director on *The Keys to the Kingdom.* He was the head of production at Paramount Pictures from 1964 to 1966, and was

still an independent producer at the studio at the time of his death. His directorial efforts included *The Girl in Black Stockings* (1957), *Andy Hardy Comes Home* (1958), *Born Reckless* (1959), and *Badge 373* (1973). Koch and partner Aubrey Schenck formed Bel Air Productions in 1953 and produced movies for Warner Bros. and such TV series as *Maverick, Cheyenne, The Untouchables* and *Hawaiian Eye.*

**Stanley Kramer** (September 29, 1913–February 19, 2001). Producer/director best known for his so-called "message" films. Born in New York City, Kramer produced 20 and directed 15 films, beginning with producing *So This is New York* in 1948; his films received 85 Academy Award nominations and won 15 Oscars. His directorial efforts included *Not as a Stranger* (1955), *The Defiant Ones* (1958, Oscar nomination), *On the Beach* (1959), *Inherit the Wind* (1960), *Judgment at Nuremberg* (1961, Oscar nomination), *It's a Mad, Mad, Mad, Mad World* (1962), *Ship of Fools* (1965), *Guess Who's Coming to Dinner* (1967, Oscar nomination), *The Secrets of Santa Vittoria* (1969), *Bless the Beasts and Children* (1971), *Oklahoma Crude* (1973), and *The Runner Stumbles* (1979). Kramer also produced such films as *Champion* (1949), *Home of the Brave* (1949), *The Men* (1950), *Cyrano de Bergerac* (1950), *Death of a Salesman* (1951), *High Noon* (1952), *A Member of the Wedding* (1952), *The Wild One* (1954), *The Caine Mutiny* (1954), and *Invitation to a Gunfighter* (1964).

**Lawrence M. "Larry" Lansburgh** (1912?–March 25, 2001). Producer/director who received Academy Awards for short subject *The Wetback Hound* (1958) and documentary *The Horse With the Flying Tail* (1961), as well as a nomination for short feature *Cow Dog* (1957). Lansburgh joined Walt Disney Co. in 1939 as a messenger and worked his way up, learning film editing, writing, sound, cinematography, directing, and producing before working on such animated features as *Fantasia* (1940), *The Three Caballeros* (1945), and *Cinderella* (1950) .

**Jack Lemmon** (Febrary 8, 1925–June 27, 2001). Born John Uhler Lemmon III in Boston, Massachusetts, Lemmon made some 60 pictures. A graduate of Harvard University, the actor moved to New York in 1947 after serving in the Navy and found regular work in radio and early television productions. He moved to Hollywood and signed with Columbia Pictures, making his debut in *It Should Happen to You* (1954). Lemmon won a best supporting actor Oscar for *Mister Roberts* (1955), a best actor Oscar for *Save the Tiger* (1973), and was nominated seven other times. He also won an Emmy for *Tuesdays with Morrie* (1999). Director Billy Wilder first teamed Lemmon with actor Walter Matthau in *The Fortune Cookie* (1966); Lemmon went onto make seven films with Wilder and eight with Matthau. Lemmon's other films included *Some Like It Hot* (1959), *The Apartment*

(1960), *Days of Wine and Roses* (1962), *Irma La Douce* (1963), *The Odd Couple* (1968), *The Out-of-Towners* (1970), *The Front Page* (1974), *The China Syndrome* (1979), *Buddy Buddy* (1981), *Missing* (1982), *Glengarry Glen Ross* (1992), *Grumpy Old Men* (1993), *Grumpier Old Men* (1995), *My Fellow Americans* (1996), *The Odd Couple 2* (1998), and *The Legend of Bagger Vance* (2000).

**Philippe Leotard** (August 28, 1940–August 25, 2001). Born in Nice, France, the actor made more than 70 films and won a Cesar Award for his role in *The Balance* (1983). Screen credits included *Bed and Board* (1970), *Anne and Muriel* (1971), *Camille* (1971), *The Day of the Jackal* (1973), *French Connection 2* (1975), *Cat and Mouse* (1975), *The Little Mermaid* (1980), *Hiver 60* (1982), *Tchao Pantin* (1983), *Dawn* (1985), *The Abyss* (1988), and *Les Miserables* (1995).

**Jay Livingston** (March 28, 1915–October 17, 2001). Composer and lyricist who collaborated with Ray Evans on three songs that won Academy Awards®: "Buttons and Bows" from *The Paleface* (1948), "Mona Lisa" from *Captain Carey, U.S.A.* (1950), and "Que Sera Sera" from *The Man Who Knew Too Much* (1956). The Livingston-Evans team also received Oscar nominations for "The Cat and the Canary" from *Why Girls Leave Home* (1945); "Tammy" from *Tammy and the Bachelor* (1957); "Almost in Your Arms" from *Houseboat* (1957); and "Dear Heart" from the 1964 movie of the same name. Livingston was born in McDonald, Pennsylvania, and became friendly with Evans when they played in a dance band at the University of Pennsylvania. The duo worked in New York and wrote specialty material before going to Hollywood in 1944. They contributed songs to more than 80 films, including writing the Christmas classic "Silver Bells," which was first sung by Bob Hope and Marilyn Maxwell in *The Lemon Drop Kid* (1951). They later worked for television, including composing the theme music for *Bonanza* and *Mr. Ed*, with Livingston singing that show's theme song.

**Lawrence B. Marcus** (1925–August 28, 2001). Born in Beaver, Utah, the screenwriter received an Oscar® nomination for *The Stunt Man* (1980). Born in Beaver, Utah, Marcus grew up in Chicago and began his writing career scripting radio shows for the Army Air Force during WWII. Other credits included *Petulia* (1968), *Justine* (1969), *Going Home* (1971), and *Alex and the Gypsy* (1976).

**Scott Marlowe** (1932–January 6, 2001). The actor started his career with roles in a number of popular juvenile delinquent dramas, including *The Restless Breed* (1957), *The Cool and the Crazy* (1958), *Young and Wild* (1958), and *Riot in Juvenile Prison* (1959). Other credits included *The Young Guns* (1956), *The Subterraneans* (1960), *Lonnie* (1963), *Journey into Fear* (1975), *Lightning in a Bottle* (1993), and

*Counter Measures* (1998). Marlowe also made appearances on numerous television shows.

**Gerald Mayer** (1919–September 21, 2001). Born in Montreal, Quebec, Canada, Mayer was the nephew of MGM studio chief Louis B. Mayer and grew up in Los Angeles. His father, Jerry G. Mayer, was the MGM studio manager and Mayer joined the studio in 1945 to direct screen tests and shorts. His feature film career began with *Mr. Whitney Had a Notion* (1949). Other credits included *Dial 1119* (1950), *Inside Straight* (1951), *Holiday for Sinners* (1952), *The Sellout* (1952), and *Bright Road* (1953). Mayer also directed episodes for numerous television series, including *Adventures in Paradise, Bonanza, The Fugitive, Gunsmoke, Mannix, Mission:Impossible, Quincy, Lou Grant,* and *Nero Wolfe.*

**Dorothy McGuire** (June 14, 1916–September 13, 2001). Born in Omaha, Nebraska, McGuire was known for a long career playing understanding girlfriends and wives. She made her stage debut in her hometown in 1930, opposite Henry Fonda, in the James Barrie play *A Kiss for Cinderella*. McGuire became a star with her first film *Claudia* (1943), in the role she had originated on Broadway. This led to a film contract with producer David O. Selznick. Her other films included *A Tree Grows in Brooklyn* (1945), *The Enchanted Cottage* (1945), *The Spiral Staircase* (1946), *Gentleman's Agreement* (1947), for which McGuire received a Best Actress Academy Award nomination, *Three Coins in the Fountain* (1954), *Friendly Persuasion* (1956), *Old Yeller* (1957), *A Summer Place* (1959), *The Swiss Family Robinson* (1960), and *The Greatest Story Ever Told* (1965) as the Virgin Mary. Later, the actress moved into character parts in films, television, and the theater.

**James Pinckney Miller** (December 18, 1919–November 1, 2001). Born in San Antonio, Texas, the screenwriter began his career writing for television in the 1950s for such shows as *Philco Television Playhouse* and *The Goodyear Television Playhouse*. He later wrote a number of telefilms, including *The Lindbergh Kidnapping Case* (1976), *Helter Skelter* (1976), *Gaugin the Savage* (1980), and *I Know My First Name Is Steven* (1989). Miller's film scripts included *The Rabbit Trap* (1959), *The Young Savages* (1961), *Days of Wine and Roses* (1962), *Behold a Pale Horse* (1964), and *The People Next Door* (1970).

**Jason Miller** (April 2, 1939–May 13, 2001). Born in Long Island City, New York, playwright/actor Miller grew up in Scranton, Pennsylvania and graduated from the Jesuit-run University of Scranton where he studied English and philosophy, later earning a master's degree from Catholic University. He worked a variety of odd jobs, while working on his plays, before his success with the *That Championship*

*Season,* which opened at Joseph Papp's Public Theater in 1972. Miller also adapted the play into a film, which he directed in 1982. The play won a Pulitzer Prize and a Tony Award in 1973. Also in 1973, Miller was nominated for a best supporting actor Oscar for his role as Father Damien Karras in the horror film *The Exorcist.* He repeated the role of Father Karras in *Exorcist 3: Legion* (1990). Among his other acting roles were *The Nickel Ride* (1973), *F. Scott Fitzgerald in Hollywood* (1976), *The Dain Curse* (1978), *Monsignor* (1982), *Light of Day* (1987), *The Best Little Girl in the World* (1988), *Rudy* (1993), *Slice* (2000), and *Finding Home* (2001).

**John Mitchum** (September 6, 1919–November 27, 2001). Born in Bridgeport, Connecticut, the character actor was the younger brother of actor Robert Mitchum. The brothers moved to California in 1933 and Mitchum graduated from Long Beach Polytechnic High School in 1936. He was drafted in 1944 and after his discharge, Mitchum was approached by an agent and asked if he wanted to be an actor, which lead to a role in *The Prairie* (1946). He worked under the name John Mallory in the 1950s and under his own name after 1962, including roles in a number of Clint Eastwood films such as *Paint Your Wagon* (1969), *Dirty Harry* (1971), *High Plains Drifter* (1973), *Magnum Force* (1973), *The Enforcer* (1976), and *The Outlaw Josey Wales* (1976). The Mitchum brothers worked together on several films, including *The Lusty Men* (1952) and *The Way West* (1967), as well as in the TV movie "Jake Spanner, Private Eye" (1989). John Mitchum was also a songwriter and poet and wrote or co-wrote the patriotic poems for the only album recorded by John Wayne: "America, Why I Love Her" (1973), for which Mitchum received a Grammy nomination in the spoken word category. Mitchum published his memoirs, *Them Onery Mitchum Boys,* in 1989.

**Pauline Moore** (June 14, 1914–December 8, 2001). Born in Harrisburg, Pennsylvania, the actress starred in some 25 B-movies between 1937 and 1941. Moore first toured with the Edna Preston theater company and then found success on the New York stage as well as modeling for magazine covers and advertising photos. She screen tested for Universal Studio and had an uncredited bit part in 1931's *Frankenstein.* Moore then signed to a contract at 20th Century Fox, appearing in *Heidi* (1937), and three Charlie Chan films— *Charlie Chan at the Olympics* (1937), *Charlie Chan in Reno* (1939), and *Charlie Chan at Treasure Island* (1939)—as well as a musical version of *The Three Musketeers* (1939) and briefly in *Young Mr. Lincoln* (1939). Moore then moved on to Republic Studios and appeared in five Roy Rogers westerns and the 1941 movie serial *King of the Texas Rangers.* In the early 1940s, the actress left Hollywood to raise her children but appeared on television in the 1950s.

**Alex Nicol** (January 20, 1919–July 28, 2001). Born in Ossining, New York, the character actor and director began his career working on the stage and, after serving in World War II, became a charter member of Lee Strasberg's Actors Studio. A film contract with Universal Studio had Nicol making his screen debut in *The Sleeping City* (1950). Other film roles included *Tomahawk* (1951), *Meet Danny Wilson* (1952), *Champ for a Day* (1953), *Face the Music* (1954), *The Man from Laramie* (1955), *Strategic Air Command* (1955), and *Stranger in Town* (1957). Nicol also acted in and directed *The Screaming Skull* (1958). He was also the director of *Then There Were Three* (1961) and *Point of Terror* (1971).

**Virginia O'Brien** (April 8, 1919–January 16, 2001). Born in Los Angeles, the actress was known as "Miss Frozen Face" for her deadpan delivery. She was discovered by Louis B. Mayer while making her stage debut in 1940 and was soon signed to a MGM contract. Films included: *Hullabaloo* (1940), *Lady Be Good* (1941), *Panama Hattie* (1942), *Thousands Cheer* (1943), *DuBarry Was a Lady* (1943), *Two Girls and a Sailor* (1944), *Till the Clouds Roll By* (1946), *The Harvey Girls* (1946), *Merton of the Movies* (1947), and *Francis in the Navy* (1955). O'Brien largely retired after her 1955 film, only making one last appearance in *Gus* (1976).

**Carroll O'Connor** (August 2, 1924–June 21, 2001). In a career spanning five decades, the actor was best known for his role as bigoted Archie Bunker in the television series *All in the Family* (1971–79), for which he won four Emmys. He later continued the role in *Archie Bunker's Place* (1979–83). O'Connor won a fifth Emmy for his role as Chief Bill Gillespie in the series *In the Heat of the Night* (1988–94). Born in New York, he worked as a journalist before leaving for Ireland in 1950 and enrolling in University College, Dublin, where he began acting under the stage name George Roberts. O'Connor returned to New York in 1954 and began a teaching career before winning a role in a stage production of James Joyce's *Ulysses.* He got further stage and television work before getting character roles in movies. Among his films were *A Fever in the Blood* (1961), *Lonely Are the Brave* (1962), *Cleopatra* (1963), *In Harm's Way* (1965), *Point Blank* (1967), *Kelly's Heroes* (1970), and *Return to Me* (2000). O'Connor's memoirs, *I Think I'm Outta Here* were published in 1998.

**Lester Persky** (July 6, 1925—December 16, 2001). Born in Brooklyn, New York, the film and television producer attended Brooklyn College and served as a reporter trainee at the *New York Times* after serving in World War II. He eventually went into advertising and opened his own agency. Perksy and his partner, Richard S. Bright, produced more than 28 films, including *The Last Detail* (1973), *The Man Who Would Be King* (1975), *Shampoo* (1975), *The Front*

(1976), *Missouri Breaks* (1976), and *Taxi Driver* (1976). On his own, Perksy produced *Equus* (1977), *Hair* (1979), *Yanks* (1979), and the television miniseries *Poor Little Rich Girl* (1988).

**Nyree Dawn Porter** (January 22, 1936–April 10, 2001). Born in Napier, New Zealand, the actress was awarded a scholarship and left for England in 1958. She was best known for her role as Irene Forsyte in the BBC adaptation of John Galsworthy's *The Forsyte Sage* (1967), which made her a television star, later re-creating the role for a 1991 stage production. Films included *Sentenced for Life* (1960), *Identity Unknown* (1960), *Part-time Wife* (1961), *The Cracksman* (1963), *The House That Dripped Blood* (1970), *From Beyond the Grave* (1973), *The Martian Chronicles* (1979), and *Hilary and Jackie* (1998). Porter also played the Contessa Caroline di Contini in the British television series, *The Protectors*.

**Anthony Quinn** (April 21, 1915–June 3, 2001). Born Anthony Rudolph Oaxaca Quinn in Chihuahua, Mexico, the actor made more than 100 films, winning best supporting actor Oscars for *Viva Zapata!* (1952) and *Lust for Life* (1956). His family worked as migrants in Texas and California before his father found various jobs in the movie industry. Quinn also tried a number of jobs before taking acting lessons, making his debut in Mae West's play *Clean Beds* (1936) and winning his first nonspeaking movie role in *Parole* that same year. He appeared in bits parts throughout the 1930s and 40s in roles of almost every ethnicity. His best known role was probably the exuberant title character *Zorba the Greek* (1964) for which he received a Best Actor Oscar® nomination; he even played the role in a revival of the stage musical in 1982. Other notable films included *La Strada* (1954), *The Hunchback of Notre Dame* (1957), *The Guns of Navarone* (1961), *Lawrence of Arabia* (1962), *Requiem for a Heavyweight* (1962), *The Shoes of the Fisherman* (1968), *The Greek Tycoon* (1978), *Jungle Fever* (1991), *Last Action Hero* (1993), and *A Walk in the Clouds* (1995). The actor also appeared on stage and on television, with his own series, *The Man and the City*, in 1971. In addition, Quinn became an artist with exhibitions of his paintings and sculpture. He had a complicated private life, fathering 13 children by five women, several of whom have followed him into acting. Quinn wrote two autobiographies: *The Original Sin* (1972) and *One Man Tango* (1995).

**Francisco "Paco" Rabal** (March 8, 1926–August 29, 2001). Born in Aguilas, Murcia, Spain, the stage and film actor appeared in over 200 roles. After playing supporting roles, Rabal became a star with his lead role in *Nazarin* (1958). He won the best actor award at the Cannes Film Festival for *The Holy Innocents* (1984). Other credits included *Tie Me Up! Tie Me Down!* (1989), *The Man Who Lost His Shadow* (1991), *A Hundred and One Nights* (1995), *Little Miracles*

(1997), *Goya in Bordeaux* (1999), *Divertimento* (2000), and *Dagon* (2001).

**Rockets Redglare** (1948–May 28, 2001). Born Michael Morra, the actor/comedian grew up in Brooklyn and on Long Island, working as a roadie and bodyguard for various bands. In the 1980s he began performing comedy in clubs on the Lower East Side of Manhattan and began appearing in films. Films included *Stranger Than Paradise* (1984), *After Hours* (1985), *Desperately Seeking Susan* (1985), *Down by Law* (1986), *Candy Mountain* (1987), *Big* (1988), *Mystery Train* (1989), *In the Soup* (1992), *Basquiat* (1996), *Trees Lounge* (1996), and *Animal Factory* (2000).

**Walter Reed** (1916–August 20, 2001). Born on Bainbridge Island, Washington, the character actor best known for his work in westerns. He began his movie career as an extra in *Redskin* (1929) and later did stand-in work for Joel McCrea. Reed got a contract with RKO in 1941, appearing in *Army Surgeon* (1942)as well as *Bombardier* (1943). After serving in WWII, Reed began his work in character parts, including *Return of the Bad Men* (1948), *Fighter Squadron* (1948), *The Lawless* (1950), *Desert Passage* (1952), *Seven Men from Now* (1956), *The Horse Soldiers* (1959), *Sergeant Rutledge* (1960), *and* Cheyenne Autumn *(1960), as well as starring in two Republic serials,* Government Agents vs. Phantom Legion *(1951) and* Flying Disc Man from Mars *(1951). Reed also appeared on such television series as* Annie Oakley, Cheyenne, Gunsmoke, Have Gun Will Travel, *and* The Lone Ranger.

**Michael Ritchie** (November 28, 1938–April 16, 2001). Born in Waukesha, Wisconsin, the director graduated from Harvard University where he made his debut with the original production of the Arthur Kopit play "Oh Dad, Poor Dad, Mamma's Hung You in the Closet and I'm Feelin' So Sad *(1960). Ritchie then turned to television work before making his feature film debut with* Downhill Racer *(1969), reteaming with actor Robert Redford for 1972's* The Candidate. *Other films included* Smile *(1975),* The Bad News Bears *(1976),* Semi-Tough *(1978),* Fletch *(1985),* The Golden Child *(1986),* Fletch Lives *(1989),* Diggstown *(1992),* The Scout *(1994),* The Fantasticks *(1995), and* A Simple Wish *(1997). Ritchie continued to direct for television and won a Directors Guild of America award for the TV movie* The Positively True Adventures of the Alleged Texas Cheerleader-Murdering Mom *in 1993.*

**Norman Rodway** (February 9,1929–March 13, 2001). Born in London, England, the actor grew up in Dublin, Ireland, where his family moved when he was a baby. He graduated from Trinity College and made his first stage appearance in *The Seventh Step* at the Cork Opera House in 1953. He made his London debut in 1959 and joined the Royal Shakespeare Company in 1966, acting with the company until the late 1990s when ill health forced him from the stage. Although primarily known for his stage work, Rodway made more than 300 radio broadcasts and also acted on television and in films, including *This Other Eden* (1959), *Murder in Eden* (1961), *The Quare Fellow* (1962), *Chimes at Midnight* (1967), *Coming Through* (1985), *Tai-Pan* (1986), *Mother Night* (1996), and *The Empty Mirror* (1999).

**Herbert Ross** (May 13, 1927–October 9, 2001). Born in Brooklyn, New York, the choreographer-turned-director's family moved to Miami after his mother's death when he was nine. Ross joined a touring theatrical troupe—without his father's knowledge—when he was 15 and then dropped out of high school to move to New York, taking dance classes and getting stage work as a chorus boy. He worked as a choreographer of short ballets for American Ballet Theater and also began work for television and on Broadway for such shows as *I Can Get It for You Wholesale* and *Anyone Can Whistle*. In 1965, Ross directed Natalie Wood's dance numbers in *Inside Daisy Clover* and the dance sequences in *Doctor Dolittle* (1967), among other films. He made his directorial debut with *Goodbye Mr. Chips* (1969). In 1977, Ross directed both *The Turning Point*, which received 11 Academy Award® nominations, including best director, and *The Goodbye Girl*, which received five nominations. Other films included *The Owl and the Pussycat* (1970), *Play It Again, Sam* (1972), *Funny Lady* (1975), *The Sunshine Boys* (1975), *The Seven Percent Solution* (1976), *California Suite* (1978), *Ninjinsky* (1980), *I Ought to Be in Pictures* (1982), *Max Dugan Returns* (1983), *Footloose* (1984), *Dancers* (1987), *Steel Magnolias* (1989), and *Boys on the Side* (1995).

**Polly Rowles** (January 10, 1914–October 7, 2001). Born Mary Elizabeth Rowles in Philadelphia, Pennsylvania, the character actress had a career that covered six decades, including her appearances as Inspector No. 12 in a series of television commercials for Hanes underwear in the 1980s. After graduating from Carnegie Institute of Technology, Rowles moved to Hollywood and signed a contract with Universal Studios. Films included *Love Letters of a Star* (1936), *Some Blondes Are Dangerous* (1937), *Wings Over Honolulu* (1937), *Westbound Limited* (1937), and *Springtime in the Rockies* (1937). She made her Broadway debut in 1938 in the Orson Welles production of *Julius Caesar* and began appearing on television in the late 1940s and in the 50s. Rowles returned to film for *Power* (1986) and *Sweet Liberty* (1986).

**Harry Secombe** (September 8, 1921–April 10, 2001). Born in Swansea, Wales, the comedian was particularly known for his antics on BBC Radio's *The Goon Show*, beginning in 1949. He made his film debut in 1948's *Hocus Pocus*. Other film roles included *Down Among the Z Men* (1952), *Svengali* (1955), *Jet Storm* (1959), *Oliver!* (1968), *Doctor in Trouble*

(1970), *Song of Norway* (1970), and *Sunstruck* (1972). He later became a presenter of the British television shows *Highway* and *Songs of Praise*. Secombe was knighted in 1981 and retired from show business in 1999.

**Pilar Seurat** (July 25, 1938–June 2, 2001). Born Rita Hernandez in Manila, The Phillippines, Seurat moved to Los Angeles as a child and began her career as a dancer. She played an exotic beauty, guest-starring in a number of television shows in the 1950s and 60s. Film roles included *Battle at Bloody Beach* (1961), *Seven Women from Hell* (1961), and *The Young Savages* (1961). Seurat's son is producer/writer Dean Devlin.

**Anthony Shaffer** (May 15, 1926–November 6, 2001). Born in Liverpool, England, Shaffer and his twin brother Peter both became successful playwrights. The family moved to London in 1955 and Anthony later went to Cambridge University where he studied law. He practiced law, wrote three novels with his brother, went into advertising, and then sent up his own television production company before turning to writing fulltime. Shaffer's best known work was the thriller *Sleuth*, which won a 1970 Tony award as best play and became a film (for which Shaffer did the adaptation) in 1972, starring Michael Caine and Laurence Olivier who were bother nominated for Oscars®. Shaffer also adapted his novel *Mr. Forbush and the Penguins* for the screen in 1971 and wrote the screenplays for *Frenzy* (1972), *The Wicker Man* (1973), *Murder on the Orient Express* (1974), *Death on the Nile* (1978), and *Evil Under the Sun* (1982). Shaffer's autobiography, *So What Did You Expect?* was published in 2001.

**Janet Shaw** (January 23, 1919–October 15, 2001). Born Ellen Martha Clancy Stuart in Beatrice, Nebraska, the actress began her career under the name Ellen Clancy. Her family moved to Los Angeles when Shaw was a teenager and she began her career in 1934 in a number of uncredited roles. In 1937, Jack L. Warner signed her to a contract and changed her name, as well as expanding her role as Molly Allen in the 1938 film *Jezebel*. Other film credits included *Arizona Trail* (1943), *Ladies Courageous* (1944), *I'll Tell the World* (1945), *Dark Alibi* (1946), *Time Out of Mind* (1947), and her last film, *Prehistoric Women* (1950).

**Joan Sims** (May 9, 1930–June 28, 2001). Born Irene Joan Marion Sims in Laindon, Essex, England, the actress played the flirtatious blonde in 24 of the 30 British *Comedy On* comedies from 1957's *Carry On Admiral* to 1978's *Carry On Emmannuelle*. After graduating from the Royal Academy of Dramatic Art in 1950, Sims got her first small film role in 1952's *Colonel March Investigates* and her first comedic role in *Will Any Gentleman?* (1953). She also acted in nearly 40 other films, including *Doctor in the House* (1954), *Doctor at*

Sea (1955), *Doctor in Love* (1960), and *Doctor in Clover* (1966), as well as on the stage, radio, and in such television productions as *Love Among the Ruins* (1975), *Martin Chuzzlewit* (1994), *The Canterville Ghost* (1996), and *The Last of the Blonde Bombshells* (2000). Sims published her autobiography *High Spirits* in 2000.

**Piotr Sobocinski** (February 3, 1958–March 26, 2001). Born in Lodz, Poland, the son of cinematographer Witold Sobocinski, he graduated from the city's film school and followed his father's profession. He was nominated for an Academy Award for director Kryzystof Kieslowski's *Red* (1994). Sobocinski also worked on the director's 10-part *Dekalog* (1988) as well as the films *Blue* (1993) and *White* (1994). Other films included *Ransom* (1996), *Marvin's Room* (1996), *Twilight* (1998), and *Angel Eyes* (2001). He died in his sleep while working on the film *24 Hours*.

**Ann Sothern** (January 22, 1909–March 15, 2001). Comedic actress and singer who was the star of a successful series of 10 movies at MGM about Brooklyn chorus girl Maisie Ravier, beginning with 1939's *Maisie*. Sothern was born Harriette Lake in Valley City, North Dakota. She was signed by Columbia Pictures in 1933, who renamed her and dyed Sothern's hair from red to blonde as well as giving her roles in numerous lightweight musicals, including *Let's Fall in Love* (1933), *Kid Millions* (1934), and *Folies-Bergere* (1935). Other film roles included *Trade Winds* (1939), *Brother Orchid* (1940), *Lady Be Good* (1941), *Panama Hattie* (1942), *Cry Havoc* (1943), *A Letter to Three Wives* (1949), *Shadow on the Wall* (1950), *The Best Man* (1964), and *Lady in a Cage* (1964). At the age of 79, Sothern received her only Academy Award nomination as best supporting actress for *The Whales of August* (1987). Sothern was also a shrewd businesswoman who had ownership of her two television series, *Private Secretary*(1953–57) and *The Ann Sothern Show* (1958–61). Sothern also lent her voice to the television series *My Mother the Car* (1965).

**Kim Stanley** (February 11, 1925–August 20, 2001). Born Patricia Reid in Tularosa, New Mexico, she was raised in Texas. Stanley acted in school plays and later at the Pasadena Playhouse before moving to New York in 1947. She eventually joined the Actors Studio and was best-known for her stage work, including lead roles in *Picnic, The Traveling Lady,* and *Bus Stop.* Her last appearance on the New York stage was in Chekov's *Three Sisters* in 1964; that same year Stanley received a best actress Oscar® nomination for her work in the thriller *Seance on a Wet Afternoon.* Her first film was *The Goddess* (1958) and Stanley served as the narrator for *To Kill a Mockingbird* (1962). After her role in *Seance*, Stanley did not return to the screen until 1982, when she played the ambitious mother of actress Frances Farmer in the film *Frances,* for which Stanley received a best sup-

porting actress Oscar® nomination. Her last film was a small role in *The Right Stuff* (1983). Stanley also won two Emmy's: in 1963 for an episode of *Ben Casey* and in 1984 for her role as Big Mama in the PBS production of *Cat on a Hot Tin Roof.*

**Anthony Steel** (May 20, 1920–March 21, 2001). Born in London, England, Anthony Maitland Steel was educated at Cambridge University and served with the Grenadier Guards during WWII. He starred in a series of adventures films for the J. Arthur Rank studio that included *The Wooden Horse* (1950), *Where No Vultures Fly* (1951), *Another Man's Poison* (1952), *Albert RN* (1953), *Malta Story* (1953), *The Master of Ballantrae* (1953), *The Sea Shall Not Have Them* (1954), *West of Zanzibar* (1955), *Storm Over the Nile* (1956), and *Checkpoint* (1957). Steel moved to Hollywood after marrying Swedish actress Anita Ekberg in 1956, which proved to be a professional disappointment; after his return to Europe in the early sixties, Steel found only sporadic acting work in films and on television and was largely retired by the 1980s.

**Beatrice Straight** (August 2, 1914–April 7, 2001). Born Beatrice Whitney Straight in Old Westbury, New York, the actress was educated at private schools in New York and England, where she studied acting. She received a best supporting actress Oscar for her role in *Network* (1976). Other films included *Phone Call From a Stranger* (1952), *The Nun's Story* (1959), *The Young Lovers* (1964), *The Promise* (1979), *Endless Love* (1980), *Poltergeist* (1982), *Two of a Kind* (1983), *Power* (1986), and *Deceived* (1991). Straight also had a long stage and television career. She debuted on Broadway in *Bitter Oleander* (1935) and received a Tony as best supporting actress for her role in *The Crucible* (1953). Straight also received an Emmy nomination for the miniseries *The Dain Curse* (1978).

**Hiroshi Teshigahara** (January 28, 1927–April 14, 2001). Born in Tokyo, Japan; Teshigahara's father founded the Sogetsu School of Ikebana, one of the country's most famous schools of flower arranging, which the director became master of in 1980. The avant-garde filmmaker gained international acclaim for *Suna no Onna/Woman in the Dunes* (1964), which received Academy Award nominations for best director and best picture. His first feature film was *Otoshiana/Pitfall* (1962); others included *Tanin no Kao/The Face of Another* (1966), *Moetsukita Chizu/The Ruined Map* (1968), *Natsu no Heitai/Summer Soldiers* (1972), *Rikyu* (1989), and *Goh-hime/Basara: The Princess Goh* (1992).

**Ralph Thomas** (August 10, 1915–March 17, 2001). British director best remembered for the seven *Doctor* film comedies from 1954–70. Born in Hull, England, Thomas worked a series of production jobs in the film industry before serving in WWII. He joined the Rank Organization in 1946 and directed his first film, *Once Upon a Dream,* in 1948. Thomas directed 39 films, 30 of them in partnership with producer Betty E. Box, beginning with 1951's *The Clouded Yellow.* Their fifth collaboration was *Doctor in the House* (1954), followed by *Doctor at Sea* (1955), *Doctor at Large* (1957), *Doctor in Love* (1960), *Doctor in Distress* (1963), *Doctor in Clover* (1965), and their last, *Doctor in Trouble* (1970). Thomas also directed *The Dog and the Diamonds* (1953), *Above Us the Waves* (1955), *The Iron Petticoat* (1956), *Campbell's Kingdom* (1957), *The Wind Cannot Read* (1958), *The 39 Steps* (1959), *Conspiracy of Hearts* (1960), *No Love for Johnnie* (1961), *The Wild and the Willing* (1962), *Hot Enough for June* (1964), *Quest for Love* (1971), *Percy* (1971), and *A Nightingale Sang in Berkeley Square* (1979).

**Harry Townes** (September 18, 1914–May 23, 2001). Born in Huntsville, Alabama, the character actor made his debut on stage in the mid-1930s. Films included *Operation Manhunt* (1954), *The Mountain* (1956), *The Brothers Karamazov* (1958), *Screaming Mimi* (1958), *Cry Tough* (1959), *Sanctuary* (1961), *Fitzwilly* (1967), *Strategy of Terror* (1969), *Heaven with a Gun* (1970), and *The Warrior and the Sorceress* (1984). Townes also made numerous television appearances.

**Dorothy Tutin** (April 8,1930–August 6, 2001). Born in London, England, Tutin, a graduate of the Royal Academy of Dramatic Arts, was primarily known for her long stage career. Film credits included *The Importance of Being Earnest* (1952), *The Beggar's Opera* (1953), *A Tale of Two Cities* (1958), *Cromwell* (1970), *Savage Messiah* (1972), *The Shooting Party* (1984), and *Indian Summer* (1996). Tutin also had memorable roles in the television dramas *The Six Wives of Henry VII* (1971), *Body and Soul* (1994), *Scarlett* (1994), *Jake's Progress* (1995), and *This Could Be the Last Time* (1998).

**Sachy Vierny** (August 10, 1919–May 15, 2001). French cinematographer who worked with such directors as Alain Resnais, Peter Greenaway, Chris Marker, Agnes Varda, and Luis Bunuel. Born at Bois-le-Roi, France, Vierny was the son of Russian immigrants and was educated in Paris. He entered the Institut des Hautes Etudes Cinematographiques, where he met Resnais, and worked on the director's first feature-length film *Hiroshima Mon Amour* (1959). He also photographed *Last Year at Marienbad* (1961), *Muriel* (1963), *La Guerre est Finie* (1966), *Stavisky* (1974), *Mon Oncle d'Amerique* (1980), and *L'Amour a Mort* (1984) with the director. Vierny made seven films with director Peter Greenaway: *Two Zeds and a Nought* (1985), *Drowning by Numbers* (1987), *The Cook, the Thief, His Wife and Her Lover* (1989), *The Belly of an Architect* (1991), *Prospero's Books* (1991), *The Baby of Macon* (1993), *8 and a Half Women* (1999), and *The Pillow Book* (1999). Other films included *L'Opera-Mouffe* (1958), *Lettres de Siberie* (1958), *Le*

*Bel Age* (1961), *La Musica* (1966), and *Belle du Jour* (1967). Vierny's last film was *The Man Who Cried* (2000).

**Joan Vohs** (July 30, 1931–June 4, 2001). Born in Queens, New York, Vohs began her career as a model and a Radio City Rockette. She moved to Hollywood and made her screen debut in 1949's *The Girl from Jones Beach.* Screen credits included *My Dream Is Yours* (1949), *Yes, Sir, That's My Baby* (1949), *County Fair* (1950), *Girls' School* (1950), *Royal Wedding* (1951), *Vice Squad* (1953), *Crazylegs* (1953), *Sabrina* (1954), *Cry Vengeance* (1954), *Fort Yuma* (1955), *Terror at Midnight* (1956), and *Lure of the Swamp* (1957). Vohs also had a recurring role as Miss Cummings in the *Family Affair* television series and then retired from acting.

**Deborah Walley** (August 12, 1943–May 10, 2001). Born in Bridgeport, Connecticut, Walley was the daughter of Ice Capades skaters and toured with her parents as a child before studying acting at New York's Academy of Dramatic Arts. The petite actress succeeded Sandra Dee in the first *Gidget* sequel, 1961's *Gidget Goes Hawaiian,* and made other lighthearted fare in the sixties, including *Bon Voyage!* (1962), *Summer Magic* (1963), *Beach Blanket Bingo* (1965), *Dr. Goldfoot and the Bikini Machine* (1966), and *Spinout* (1966), and later appeared in *Benji* (1974) and *The Severed Arm* (1975). Walley also worked on television, including the sitcom *The Mothers-in-Law* (1967–69). She moved to Sedona, Arizona and co-founded two children's theater companies and a theater company for Native American culture, where she was a writer and producer.

**Ray Walston** (December 2, 1914–January 1, 2001). Character actor best known for his television roles as the lovable alien in *My Favorite Martian* (1963–66) and cranky Judge Henry Bone in *Picket Fences* for which he won Emmy awards in 1995 and '96. Born in New Orleans, Louisiana, Walston's career began with a local stock company. By 1945, he had moved to New York and begun his stage career. Walston made his film debut in *Kiss Them for Me* (1957); other films included *South Pacific* (1958), *The Apartment* (1960), *Kiss Me, Stupid* (1964), *The Sting* (1973), *Silver Streak* (1976), *Popeye* (1980), *Fast Times at Ridgemont High* (1982), *The Player* (1992), and a cameo in the film version of *My Favorite Martian* in 1998. Walston won a Tony award in 1955 for his role as the devil in Broadway's *Damn Yankees,* reprising the role for the 1958 film version.

**Al Waxman** (March 2, 1935–January 17, 2001). Born Albert Samuel Waxman in Toronto, Ontario, the stage, film, and television actor was known for his leading role in the Canadian TV series *The King of Kensington* (1975–80) and as the boss of police detectives *Cagney & Lacey* (1982–88). Waxman studied at New York's Playhouse Theatre and made his film debut in *The War Lover* (1961). He also wrote, directed, and produced the feature film *The Crowd Inside* (1970). Other films included *Man in the Middle* (1964), *Isabel* (1968), *Vengeance Is Mine* (1974), *Wild Horse Hank* (1979), *Atlantic City* (1980), Meatballs 3 *(1987),* Switching Channels *(1988),* The Hitman *(1991),* Iron Eagle 4 *(1995),* Net Worth *(1997) and* Hurricane *(1999). His autobiography,* That's What I Am *was published in 1999.*

**Michael Williams** (July 9, 1935–January 11, 2001). Born in Manchester, England, Williams was a noted character and Shakespearean actor who frequently performed opposite his wife, actress Judi Dench, including the British TV comedy series *A Fine Romance* (1980–82). He grew up in Liverpool and was admitted on a scholarship to the Royal Academy of Dramatic Art. He joined the Royal Shakespeare Company in 1963 and spend 14 years with the RSC. Films included *Marat/Sade* (1966), *The Benefit of the Doubt* (1967), *Dead Cert* (1974), *Educating Rita* (1982), *Enigma* (1982), *Henry V* (1990), and *Tea with Mussolini* (1999).

**Toby Wing** (July 14, 1915–March 23, 2001). Born Martha Virginia Wing in Amelia Court House, Virginia, the vivacious blonde made more than 30 movies from 1931 to 1938 before retiring after her marriage to aviator, Dick Merrill. She was the original Goldwyn Girl, the first of Samuel Goldwyn's sex symbols, in 1931's *Palmy Days.* Wing also appeared in *Alaska Love* (1932), *Baby Face* (1933), *Blue of the Night* (1933), *42nd Street* (1933), *Torch Singer* (1933), *Murder at the Vanities* (1934), *School for Girls* (1934), *Rhythm on the Roof* (1935), *Mister Cinderella* (1936), *True Confessions* (1937), and *Mr. Boggs Steps Out* (1938). Wing made one final film in 1943, *The Marines Come Through.*

**Edward Winter** (June 3, 1937–March 8, 2001). Born in Ventura, California, the character actor began his career with the San Francisco Actors Workshop before moving to New York. Winters made his Broadway debut in *Cabaret* (1966) and was nominated for a best supporting actor Tony Award for his role as Ernst. He also appeared as the paranoid Colonel Flagg in the television series *M\*A\*SH.* Film credits included *A Change of Seasons* (1980), *Porky's 2* (1983), *The Buddy System* (1984), and *From the Hip* (1987).

**Victor Wong** (July 30, 1927–September 12, 2001). Born in San Francisco, California, the character actor landed his first film role at the age of 57 in *Dim Sum: A Little Bit of Heart* (1984). After attending the University of Chicago, Wong became a founding member of Chicago's Second City comedy troupe; he later obtained a master's degree from the Art Institute of San Francisco and had his first art exhibit at Lawrence Ferlinghetti's City Lights Bookstore. He became a reporter on San Francisco's public television station, KQED, from 1968–74 before refocusing on acting. He appeared in some 28 films before retiring in 1998. Films included *Big Trouble in Little China* (1986), *The Golden Child* (1986), *The Last Emperor* (1987), *Eat a Bowl of Tea* (1989), *3 Ninjas* (1992), *The Joy Luck Club* (1993), *3 Ninjas Kick Back* (1994), *3 Ninjas Knuckle Up* (1995), *3 Ninjas: High Noon at Mega Mountain* (1997), and *Seven Years in Tibet* (1997).

**Otis Young** (1932–October 12, 2001). Born in Providence, Rhode Island, Young became the first black actor to star on a television Western series, co-starring with Don Murray in *The Outcasts* (1968–69). His best known film role was *The Last Detail* (1973). Other films included *Murder in Mississippi* (1965), *Don't Just Stand There!* (1968), *The Clones* (1974), *The Hollywood Knights* (1980), and *Blood Beach* (1981). Young later became a minister and community college professor.

# Selected Film Books of 2001

**Adams, Max.** *The Screenwriter's Survival Guide: Or, Guerilla Meeting Tactics and Other Acts of War.*
New York: Warner, 2001.

Sixty-four chapters on pitching and selling your screenplay. Includes lists of screenwriters' directories and organizations, cover and query letters, and other resources.

**Affron, Charles.** *Lillian Gish: Her Legend, Her Life.*
New York: Scribner, 2001.

Biography of the actress, known for her silent screen roles for D.W. Griffith, which also examines her later career in both films and on the stage.

**Badal, Robert.** *Romance in Film, Volume 1: From the Silent Era to 1950.*
Carson: Jalmar Press, 2001.

Looks at romance and romanticism in the movies, including romantic scenes, romantic pairings, trends and changes towards sex and love, off-screen love stories, and recommended romantic films.

**Beck, Nicholas.** *Budd Schulberg: A Bio-Bibliography.*
Lanham: Scarecrow Press, Inc., 2001.

Overview of the Oscar-winning screenwriter's career from 1937–2000.

**Behlmer, Rudy.** *Henry Hathaway: A Director's Guild of America Oral History.*
Lanham: Scarecrow Press, Inc., 2001.

Collection of interviews with the filmmaker from his days as a child actor in 1911 through his directorial career.

**Bernstein, Arnie, editor.** *'The Movies Are': Carl Sandburg's Film Reviews and Essays, 1920–1928*
Chicago: Lake Claremont Press, 2001.

A collection of the film criticism the Pulitzer Prize-winning author wrote for the *Chicago Daily News.*

**Bowser, Pearl, Jane Gaines and Charles Musser, editors.**
*Oscar Micheaux and His Circle: African-American Filmmaking and Race Cinema of the Silent Era.*
Bloomington: Indiana University Press, 2001.

Focuses on the African-American director by examining his surviving films, his contemporaries, and cultural attitudes of the silent era.

**Buhle, Paul and Dave Wagner.** *A Very Dangerous Citizen: Abraham Lincoln Polonsky and the Hollywood Left.*
Berkeley: University of California Press, 2001.

Critical and cultural biography of Polonsky, a screenwriter and director who was blacklisted in1951 and could only resume his career under a pseudonym.

**Buskin, Richard.** *Blonde Heat: The Sizzling Screen Career of Marilyn Monroe.*
New York: Watson-Guptill, 2001.

Covers film and screen tests as well as television and ad appearances by the screen icon.

**Campbell, Bruce.** *If Chins Could Kill: Confessions of a B Movie Actor.*
New York: St. Martin's, 2001.

Humorous acting memoir covers independent filmmaking and becoming a cult hero.

**Carney, Ray, editor.** *Cassavetes on Cassavetes.*
New York: Faber & Faber, 2001.

Interviews, conducted in a question-and-answer format, over the last 10 years of the director's life.

**Carr, Steven A.** *Hollywood and Anti-Semitism: A Cultural History up to World War II.*
New York: Cambridge University Press, 2001.

Examines the role of American Jews in the entertainment industry from the beginning of the 20th century to the onset of the World War II.

**Carroll, Willard.** *I Toto: The Autobiography of Terry, the Dog Who Was Toto.*
New York: Stewart, Tabori & Chang, 2001.

Fanciful diary of Terry and her work on the 1939 classic as well as her career on some 14 other films and that of her manager and trainer, Carl Spitz.

**Celli, Carlo.** *The Divine Comic: The Cinema of Roberto Benigni.*
Lanham: Scarecrow Press, Inc., 2001.

Introduces the film, stage, and television performance of the Italian comedian, actor, director, and writer.

**Chadwick, Bruce.** *The Reel Civil War: Mythmaking in American Film.*
New York: Knopf, 2001.

Chadwick posits that depictions of the Civil War in film present the conflict as a national tragedy while obscuring its origins and marginalizing blacks and the question of slavery.

**Childers, Michael.** *Hollywood Voyeur.*
Berlin: Janssen Publishers, 2001.

The Los Angeles photographer offers a black-and-white collection of his male nudes.

**Conrad, Peter.** *The Hitchcock Murders.*
New York: Faber and Faber, 2001.

Subjective essay on the author's preoccupation with the director, including his theories on Hitchcock's life and work.

**Cornes, Judy.** *Stuart Erwin: The Invisible Actor.*
Lanham: Scarecrow Press, Inc., 2001.

Analyzes the work of the actor and his film work during the 1930s and 40s.

**Cowie, Peter.** *The Apocalypse Now Book.*
Cambridge: Da Capo Press, 2001.

Gives a detailed account of the filming of the 1979 epic, including interviews with director Francis Ford Coppola, cinematographer Vittorio Storaro, and others in the production.

**Dale, Alan.** *Comedy Is a Man in Trouble: Slapstick in American Movies.*
Minneapolis: University of Minnesota Press, 2001.

A personal and philosophical observation of film slapstick.

**DeAngelis, Michael.** *Gay Fandom and Crossover Stardom: James Dean, Mel Gibson, and Keanu Reeves.*
Durham: Duke University, 2001.

DeAngelis explores how male film icons help shape gay male style and are also influenced by gay culture.

**Dendle, Peter.** *The Zombie Movie Encyclopedia.*
Jefferson: McFarland & Company, Inc., 2001

Evaluations of more than 200 movies from 16 countries made from the 1930s to the present, including production credits, plot summary, and alternate titles.

**DeNeut, Richard.** *Inside Hollywood: 60 Years of Globe Photos.*
New York: Konemann, 2001.

Offers 1, 500 images of celebrity photojournalism, covering 1942–2000, from one of the world's largest photo agencies.

**DeRosa, Steven.** *Writing With Hitchcock: The Collaboration of Alfred Hitchcock and John Michael Hayes.*
New York: Faber and Faber, 2001.

Biographical sketches, anecdotes, and a detailed explanation of how screenwriter Hayes and director Hitchcock work together on *Rear Window, To Catch a Thief, The Trouble with Harry,* and *The Man Who Knew Too Much.*

**DiBattista, Maria.** *Fast-Talking Dames.*
New Haven: Yale University Press, 2001.

Looks at the screwball and romantic comedies of the 1930s and '40s and the actresses who brought the lead roles to life through dialogue.

**Dick, Bernard F.** *Engulfed: The Death of Paramount Pictures and the Birth of Corporate Hollywood.*
Lexington: University Press of Kentucky, 2001.

A corporate biography of the film studio from its beginnings under Adolph Zukor to the studio becoming a subsidiary of Gulf+Western in 1966 and its subsequent fate.

**Dixon, Wheeler Winston, editor.** *Collected Interviews: Voices from Twentieth-Century Cinema.*
Carbondale: Southern Illinois University Press, 2001.

Fifteen interviews spanning two decades are collected, covering both major and marginalized figures from a range of cinematic professions, including directors, animators, actors, writers, and producers.

**Earnshaw, Tony.** *An Actor and a Rare One: Peter Cushing as Sherlock Holmes.*
Lanham: Scarecrow Press, Inc., 2001.

Details the British actor's career as Holmes.

**Engelmeier, Peter W., editor.** *Icons of Film: The 20th Century.*
New York: Prestel Publishing, 2001.

The film historian selects 84 films representing the best of cinema from the 1920's to the '90s. Includes more than 300 photographs.

**Fawell, John.** *Hitchcock's* Rear Window: *The Well-Made Film.*
Carbondale: Southern Illinois University Press, 2001.

Offers an extensive analysis of the film as well as a look at the myths and clichés that surround the director.

**Field, Syd.** *Going to the Movies: A Personal Journal Through Four Decades of Modern Film.*
New York: Dell, 2001.

Field offers technical and practical insight into the film-making process from his personal knowledge of the industry and his love of film.

**Finstad, Suzanne.** *Natasha: The Biography of Natalie Wood.*
New York: Harmony Books, 2001.

In-depth study of the actress's life from her traumatic childhood to her drowning death in 1981.

**Gale, Steven H.** *The Films of Harold Pinter.*
Albany: State University of New York, 2001.

Ten essays cover the processes of Pinter's screenplays for such films as *Lolita, The French Lieutenant's Woman, The Remains of the Day,* and others.

**Giroux, Henry A.** *Breaking in to the Movies: Film and the Culture of Politics.*
Boston: Blackwell Publishers, 2001.

Offers 20 years of essays and film analysis of Hollywood pop culture.

**Glassy, Mark C.** *The Biology of Science Fiction Cinema.*
Jefferson: McFarland & Company, Inc., 2001.

Criticism relates 71 science fiction films to the biological sciences and includes plot summary, biological principles, and correct and incorrect biological information.

**Goodrich, David L.** *The Real Nick and Nora: Frances Goodrich and Albert Hackett, Writers of Stage and Screen Classics.*
Carbondale: Southern Illinois University Press, 2001.

Dual biography of the married screenwriters, who wrote such films as *The Thin Man, It's a Wonderful Life,* and *Father of the Bride.* The author is the nephew of Frances Goodrich.

**Greene, Ray.** *Hollywood Migraine: The Inside Story of a Decade In Film.*
Dublin: Merlin Publishing, 2001.

A collection of articles and interviews from the entertainment journalist.

**Greiff, Louis K.** *D. H. Lawrence: Fifty Years on Film.*
Carbondale: Southern Illinois University Press, 2001.

Examines ten feature films based on the life and works of D. H. Lawrence as adaptations, cultural or historical documents, and works of art.

**Griffin, Susan M., editor.** *Henry James Goes to the Movies.*
Lexington: University Press of Kentucky, 2001.

Sixteen academics examine the novelist's works and their cinematic counterparts in this anthology of essays. Includes a filmography of 113 film and television adaptations.

**Gutner, Howard.** *Gowns by Adrian: The MGM Years, 1928–1941.*
New York: Abrams, 2001.

A tribute to Hollywood costume designer and couturier Gilbert Adrian. The author focuses in particular on three actresses whose images Adrian helped to create: Greta Garbo, Norma Shearer, and Joan Crawford.

**Haberski Jr., Raymond Jr.** *It's Only a Movie: Films and Critics in American Culture.*
Lexington: University Press of Kentucky, 2001.

Traces the shifting role of movies in American entertainment and American culture.

**Hanfling, Barrie.** *Westerns and the Trail of Tradition: A Year-by-Year History, 1929–1962.*
Jefferson: McFarland & Company, Inc., 2001.

Discusses the cultural and industry trends, directors, producers, studios, and performers in the western genre beginning in 1929.

**Hanson, Peter.** *Dalton Trumbo, Hollywood Rebel.*
Jefferson: McFarland & Company, Inc., 2001.

Critical survey of the life of the screenwriter, novelist, and political activist.

**Harvey, James.** *Movie Love in the Fifties.*
New York: Knopf, 2001.

Title refers to the author's love for the movies as he dissects the era and its stars, from thrillers to message movies, sex to politics.

**Hill, Lee.** *A Grand Guy: The Art and Life of Terry Southern.*
New York: HarperCollins, 2001.

Biography of the satiric writer who received two Oscar® nominations for his screenplays for *Dr. Strangelove* and *Easy Rider,* as well as being the author of *Candy* and *The Magic Christian.*

**Hirschhorn, Clive.** *The Columbia Story.*
New York: Sterling, 2001.

A year-by-year examination of the motion picture studio, showing the movies produced and reviews of the year's major films. Includes a timeline of films that were nominated for or earned awards.

**Hirschhorn, Clive.** *The Universal Story.*
New York: Sterling, 2001.

Follows the same format as the preceding title, examining the motion picture studio through each year of its existence.

**Hoffman, Carol Stein.** *The Barrymores: Hollywood's First Family.*
Lexington: University Press of Kentucky, 2001.

Collective biography of the theatrical and screen dynasty from silent movie idol John Barrymore to present-day actress Drew Barrymore.

**Horne, Gerald.** *Class Struggle in Hollywood 1930–1950: Moguls, Mobsters, Stars, Reds & Trade Unionists.*
Austin: University of Texas Press, 2001.

Labor-oriented view of the film industry, including the lengthy 1945 strike by the Conference of Studio Unions.

**Izod, John.** *Myth, Mind and the Screen: Understanding the Heroes of Our Time.*
New York: Cambridge University Press, 2001.

Applies Jungian theory to the analysis of films and cultural icons.

**Jarecki, Nicholas.** *Breaking In: How 20 Film Directors Got Their Start.*
New York: Broadway, 2001.

Interviews with three generations of directors on how films are begun, shot, and distributed. Interviewees include John Schlesinger, Amy Heckerling, Ben Younger, Edward Zwick, Peter Farrelly, John Dahl, Brett Ratner, and others.

**Javier, Frank and Garcia Berumen.** *Ramon Navarro: The Life and Films of the First Latino Hollywood Superstar.*
New York: Vantage Press, 2001.

Examines the life and career of the matinee idol of the silent screen, his work in talkies, his comeback, and his murder in 1968.

**Johnson, Brian D.** *Brave Films, Wild Nights: 25 Years of Festival Fever.*
Plattsburgh: McClelland & Stewart, 2001.

A retrospective look at the Toronto International Film Festival.

**Jurow, Martin** as told to Philip Wuntch. *Marty Jurow Seein' Stars.*
Dallas: Southern Methodist University Press, 2001.

The producer talks about his career at Warner Bros. studio, working with such stars as Burt Lancaster, Katharine Hepburn, Frank Sinatra, Natalie Wood, and many more.

**Keaton, Eleanor and Jeffrey Vance.** *Buster Keaton Remembered.*
New York: Abrams, 2001.

Keaton, the comedian's third wife, and film historian Vance have compiled more than 225 photographs and film stills depicting Buster Keaton's entire career.

**Keil, Charlie.** *Early American Cinema in Transition: Story, Style, and Filmmaking, 1907–1913.*
Madison: University of Wisconsin Press, 2001.

Examines the development of narrative techniques suitable to the 15 minute, one-reel format.

**Kelly, Richard.** *The Name of This Book is Dogme 95.*
New York: Faber and Faber, 2001.

Examines the so-called Dogme 95 Manifesto of Danish directors Lars von Trier, Thomas Vinterberg, Soren Kragh-Jacobsen, and Kristian Levring to simplify modern filmmaking and the Dogme film movement.

**King, Geoff.** *Spectacular Narratives: Hollywood in the Age of the Blockbuster.*
New York: Palgrave, 2001.

A series of essays detailing movies that feature big-budgets and special effects, including *Star Wars, Twister, Jurassic Park,* and *The Matrix.*

**Konstantarakos, Myrto.** *Spaces in European Cinema.*
Exeter: Intellect, 2001.

Essays on the function of setting within European film narrative and their political, social, and cultural contexts.

**Krantz, Les.** *Their First Time in the Movies.*
New York: Overlook Press, 2001.

Showcases some 100 stars from Cary Grant to Tom Cruise and their first film roles. Packaged with a 60-minute documentary on DVD or VHS.

**Lardner Jr., Ring.** *I'd Hate Myself in the Morning: A Memoir.*
New York: Thunder's Mouth Press, 2001.

The Oscar®-winning screenwriter offers a look at his life, including being a member of the Hollywood Ten, the filmmakers jailed by HUAC for refusing to disclose their political affiliations, and his career after being blacklisted in Hollywood.

**Lean, Lady Sandra and Barry Chattington.** *David Lean: An Intimate Portrait.*
New York: Universe, 2001.

A personal account by Lady Lean of her late husband's film career, which spanned six decades.

**Lehman, Peter, editor.** *Masculinity: Bodies, Movies, Culture.*
New York: Routledge, 2001.

Examines issues of masculinity as depicted in film.

**Levy, Emmanuel.** *Oscar Fever: The History and Politics of the Academy Awards.*
New York: Continuum, 2001.

Comprehensive look at the Hollywood history and lore that surrounds the awards.

**Long, Robert Emmet, editor.** *John Huston: Interviews.*
Jackson: University Press of Mississippi, 2001.

A collection of 21 interviews with the screenwriter/director/actor spanning 1952–1985. Includes a chronology and a filmography.

**Lowenstein, Stephen.** *My First Movie: Twenty Celebrated Directors Talk About Their First Film.*
New York: Pantheon, 2001.

Collection of interviews that offer a behind the scenes look at the directors' first professional experience. Includes Anthony Minghella, Steve Buscemi, Barry Levinson, James Mangold, Tom DiCillo, Mike Figgis, Ang Lee, Pedro Almodovar, Neil Jordan, Joel and Ethan Coen, and others.

**Loy, R. Philip.** *Westerns and American Culture 1930–1955.*
Jefferson: McFarland & Company, Inc., 2001.

Focuses on how Western movies reflected American life and culture, including representing racial minorities, women, and Native Americans.

**Mann, William J.** *Behind the Screen: How Gays and Lesbians Shaped Hollywood, 1910–1969.*
New York: Viking, 2001.

Looks at the gay subculture and how the gay experience influenced studio-era Hollywood behind the scenes from directors to designers and other industry personnel.

**McBride, Joseph.** *Searching for John Ford: A Biography.*
New York: St. Martin's, 2001.

First full-length critical examination of the director whose work helped define the western.

**McCaughey, Martha and Neal King, editors.** *Reel Knockouts: Violent Women in the Movies.*
Austin: University of Texas Press, 2001.

A study of violent women in the history of films from Hollywood to foreign films, including blockbusters, direct-to-video, and skin flicks.

**McGee, Marty.** *Encyclopedia of Motion Picture Sound.*
Jefferson: McFarland & Company, Inc., 2001.

Includes the people, processes, innovations, facilities, formats, and films that played an integral role in the development of motion picture sound.

**McMurtry, Larry.** *Film Flam: Essays on Hollywood.*
New York: Touchstone, 2001.

Series of essays covers a 20-year period of his film collaborations, including *Hud* and *The Last Picture Show.*

**Mesce Jr., Bill.** *Peckinpah's Women: A Reappraisal of the Portrayal of Women in the Period Westerns of Sam Peckinpah.*
Lanham: Scarecrow Press, Inc., 2001.

A reevaluation of the role of women in the director's Western films.

**Muller, Eddie.** *Dark City Dames: The Wicked Women of Film Noir.*
New York: HarperCollins, 2001.

Documents the role of women as characters and performers in the genre, including interviews with actresses Marie Windsor, Audrey Totter, Jane Greer, Ann Savage, Evelyn Keyes, and Coleen Gray.

**Muller, Jurgen, editor.** *Movies of the 90s: A Story in Celluloid.*
New York: Taschen America, 2001.

Discusses key commercial and artistic films of the decade in a year-by-year layout.

**Nelson, Al P. and Mel R. Jones.** *A Silent Siren Song: The Aitken Brothers' Hollywood Odyssey, 1905–1926*
New York: Cooper Square Press, 2001.

The rise and fall of the Aitken brothers from successful nickelodeon salesmen to overly ambitious producers and industry entrepreneurs.

**Osterberg, Bertil O.** *Colonial America on Film and Television.*
Jefferson: McFarland & Company, Inc., 2001.

Alphabetical arrangement of films depicting the early history of American settlement and independence.

**Parrish, James Robert.** *The Hollywood Book of Death.*
New York: McGraw-Hill, 2001.

Compilation that looks at the deaths of some 127 actors. Appendices include a necrology, a list of dead actors and directors, and a list of notable actors' and directors' gravesites.

**Perella, Marco.** *Adventures of a No-Name Actor.* New York: St. Martin's, 2001.

Wry account of the actor's showbiz career in minor film and television roles.

**Pettigrew, Terence.** *Trevor Howard: A Personal Biography.* London: Peter Owen Ltd., 2001.

Biography of the British actor, who was best known for his military roles, which the author completed some 20 years after his first research and interviews. (Howard died in 1988.)

**Pratt, Ray.** *Projecting Paranoia: Conspiratorial Visions in American Film.* Lawrence: University Press of Kansas, 2001.

Examines images of conspiracy in films from blockbusters to cult favorites and how they reflect the public's distrust of government and corporate entities since the Cold War.

**Rashkin, Elissa J.** *Women Filmmakers in Mexico: The Country of Which We Dream.* Austin: University of Texas Press, 2001.

Examines the history and themes of films by Mexican women in the 1980s and '90s.

**Rees, Nigel, editor.** *Cassell's Movie Quotations.* New York: Sterling Publishing Co., 2001.

A compendium of more than 4,000 quotations covering all areas of the movie industry.

**Reeves, Tony.** *The Worldwide Guide to Movie Locations.* Chicago: A Capella, 2001.

Offers information on key locations for some 1,500 blockbuster, cult, and arthouse films.

**Rigby, Jonathan.** *English Gothic: A Century of Horror Cinema.* North Pomfret: Trafalgar Square, 2001.

Details the history of British horror films from the silent era through 1975. Includes more than 150 film stills and photographs.

**Ringler, Stephen M.** *A Dictionary of Cinema Quotations from Filmmakers and Critics: Over 3400 Axioms, Criticisms, Opinions and Witticisms from 100 Years of the Cinema.* Jefferson: McFarland & Company, Inc., 2001.

Includes quotes from some 1,850 film people in a topical arrangement.

**Robert-Frenzel, Caren.** *Rita Hayworth: A Photographic Retrospective.* New York: Abrams, 2001.

Offers nearly 300 images of Hayworth from her early years to her death.

**Roeper, Richard.** *Hollywood Urban Legends: The Truth Behind All Those Delightfuly Persistent Myths of Films, Television, and Music.* Franklin Lakes: Career Press, 2001.

Roeper explores the false stories that follow favorite stars, films, and TV shows.

**Rosenthal, Daniel.** *Shakespeare on Screen.* New York: Sterling, 2001.

Commentary, criticism, and profiles on the films made from the works of William Shakespeare, both traditional productions and modern reinterpretations.

**Russo, Joe and Larry Landsman with Edward Gross.** *Planet of the Apes Revisited: The Behind-the-Scenes Story of the Classic Science Fiction Saga.* New York: St. Martin's, 2001.

Entertaining guide to late producer Arthur P. Jacob's ape saga covers the 1968 film, its four sequels, and two TV shows.

**Sanders, James.** *Celluloid Skyline: New York and the Movies.* New York: Knopf, 2001.

Sanders, a practicing architect, looks at the many movies that have depicted New York in both location scenes and Hollywood sets. Includes numerous photographs, notes, a bibliography, and a filmography.

**Schreck, Nikolas.** *The Satanic Screen: An Illustrated History of the Devil in Cinema.* New York: Creation Books, 2001.

Comprehensive study of some 300 films from the mainstream to the marginal that depict the devil.

**Server, Lee.** *Robert Mitchum: 'Baby, I Don't Care'.* New York: St. Martin's Press, 2001.

Biography of the actor who personified cynical cool with a dangerous edge.

**Shapiro, Jerome F.** *Atomic Bomb Cinema: The Apocalyptic Imagination on Film.* New York: Routledge, 2001.

An examination of the hundreds of movies that dealt with survival in the face of destruction.

**Silverman, Stephen M.** *Movie Mutts: Hollywood Goes to the Dogs.* New York: Abrams, 2001.

A scrapbook-like overview of canine performers, including Rin Tin Tin and Lassie, and their human co-stars.

**Siodmak, Curt.** *Wolf Man's Maker: Memoir of a Hollywood Writer.*
Lanham: Scarecrow Press, Inc., 2001.

Autobiography of the German-born writer best know for his science fiction and horror movies.

**Sova, Dawn B.** *Forbidden Films: Censorship Histories of 125 Motion Pictures.*
New York: Facts on File, 2001.

Outlines each film's troubles with censorship as well as providing plot summaries, production details, and suggestions for further reading.

**Spignesi, Stephen J.** *The Hollywood Book of Lists: From Great Performances and Romantic Epics to Bad Remakes and Miscasting Debacles.*
New York: Citadel, 2001.

Provides more than 100 lists of trivia and factoids.

**Starr, Jimmy.** *Barefoot on Barbed Wire.*
Lanham: Scarecrow Press, Inc., 2001.

Autobiography covers the 40-year Hollywood career of the screenwriter, publicist, press agent, and gossip columnist.

**Telotte J. P.** *Science Fiction Film.*
New York: Cambridge University Press, 2001.

Examines one of the most popular Hollywood genres and how American attitudes towards science, technology, and reason have evolved in the culture over the course of the 20th century.

**Vieth, Errol.** *Screening Science: Contexts, Texts, and Science in Fifties Science Fiction Film.*
Lanham: Scarecrow Press, Inc., 2001.

Examines the genre of the science fiction film and the nature of science and its cultural representation.

**Waldman, Harry.** *Maurice Tourneur: The Life and Films.*
Jefferson: McFarland & Company, Inc., 2001.

Focuses on the life and work of the French-born director, actor, and theatrical manager.

**Wallace, Pamela.** *You Can Write a Movie.*
Cincinnati: Writer's Digest Books, 2001.

Provides the essentials for developing and writing an original screenplay or an adaptation.

**Waller, Gregory.** *Moviegoing in America: A Sourcebook in the History of Film Exhibition.*
Boston: Blackwell Publishers, 2001.

Catalogs the social and cultural changes in moviegoing from the nickelodeon to the multiplex.

**Watson Jr., Coy.** *The Keystone Kid: Tales of Early Hollywood.*
Santa Monica: Santa Monica Press, 2001.

As a child actor from 1912–1930, Watson Jr. appeared in more than 60 movies, including the Keystone Cops comedies.

**Watts, Jill.** *Mae West: An Icon in Black and White.*
New York: Oxford University Press, 2001.

Detailed biography of the tough-talking sexual icon of both stage and screen.

**Weaver, Tom.** *I Was a Monster Movie Maker.*
Jefferson: McFarland & Company, Inc., 2001.

Collects 22 interviews with filmmakers and performers who worked in the science fiction and horror genres.

**Willoquet-Maricondi, Paula and Mary Alemany-Galway, editors.** *Peter Greenaway's Postmodern/Poststructuralist Cinema.*
Lanham, Scarecrow Press, Inc., 2001.

Essays cover the career of British multi-media artist, Peter Greenaway, including his films, paintings, and art installations.

**Wilson, John Morgan.** *Inside Hollywood: A Writer's Guide to Researching the World of Movies and TV.*
Cincinnati: Writer's Digest Books, 2001.

A detailed look at Hollywood for people who are writing about Hollywood or using the film/TV industry as a backdrop, including its history and geography. Includes appendices on the language of Hollywood, trade organizations, research resources, and other lists.

**Wooley, Peter.** *What! And Give Up Show Business?—A View from the Hollywood Trenches.*
Santa Barbara: Fithian Press, 2001.

The production designer recounts his experiences scouting and creating sets for feature films and TV movies and his encounters with directors and stars.

**Wurtzel Semenov, Lillian and Carla Winter, editors.** *William Fox, Sol M. Wurtzel and the Early Fox Film Corporation: Letters, 1917–1923.*
Jefferson: McFarland & Company, Inc., 2001.

Collection of correspondence between personal secretary Sol Wurtzel and his boss, Fox Film Corporation founder William Fox, after Wurtzel was sent to California to supervise West Coast operations.

# Magill's Cinema Annual 2002
# Indexes

# Director Index

ANDREW ADAMSON
Shrek  *437*

JASON ALEXANDER
(1959-)
Just Looking  *250*

WOODY ALLEN (1935-)
The Curse of the Jade
Scorpion  *107*

ROBERT ALTMAN (1925-)
Gosford Park  *182*

GIANNI AMELIO (1945-)
The Way We
Laughed  *528*

ALEJANDRO AMENABAR
(1972-)
The Others  *373*

BRAD ANDERSON
Happy Accidents  *191*
Session 9  *427*

WES ANDERSON
The Royal
Tenenbaums  *406*

JEAN-JACQUES ANNAUD
(1943-)
Enemy at the Gates  *134*

SHINJI AOYAMA (1964-)
Eureka  *138*

DUDI APPLETON
The Most Fertile Man in
Ireland  *334*

PETER ASKIN
Company Man  *99*

OLIVIER ASSAYAS (1955-)
Sentimental Destiny  *422*

DAVID ATKINS
Novocaine  *354*

AMIR BAR-LEV
Fighter  *157*

ANDRZEJ BARTKOWIAK
(1950-)
Exit Wounds  *146*

MICHAEL BAY (1965-)
Pearl Harbor  *379*

HAROLD BECKER (1950-)
Domestic Disturbance  *125*

BRUCE BERESFORD
(1940-)
Bride of the Wind  *71*

JAMIE BLANKS
Valentine  *516*

JOHN BOORMAN (1933-)
The Tailor of Panama  *475*

PADDY BREATHNACH
Blow Dry  *64*

CATHERINE BREILLAT
Fat Girl  *154*

ADAM BROOKS (1956-)
Invisible Circus  *225*

ERIC BROSS
On the Line  *361*

MARK BROWN
Two Can Play That
Game  *506*

EDWARD BURNS (1968-)
Sidewalks of New
York  *439*

TIM BURTON (1960-)
Planet of the Apes  *384*

LAURENT CANTET
Human Resources  *216*

J.S. CARDONE
The Forsaken  *160*

JOHN CARPENTER (1948-)
John Carpenter's Ghosts of
Mars  *240*

STEVE CARPENTER
Soul Survivors  *455*

STEVE CARR
Dr. Dolittle 2  *123*

THOMAS CARTER (1953-)
Save the Last Dance  *411*

JOSEPH CEDAR
Time of Favor  *487*

PETER CHELSOM (1956-)
Serendipity  *423*
Town and Country  *497*

PATRICE CHEREAU
(1944-)
Intimacy  *224*

LOUIS CK
Pootie Tang  *390*

LARRY CLARK (1943-)
Bully  *78*

JOEL COEN (1954-)
The Man Who Wasn't
There  *312*

ROB COHEN (1949-)
The Fast and the
Furious  *150*

CHRIS COLUMBUS (1958-)
Harry Potter and the
Sorcerer's Stone  *195*

FRANCIS FORD COPPOLA
(1939-)
Apocalypse Now
Redux  *35*

GERARD CORBIAU
The King Is Dancing  *266*

MICHAEL CRISTOFER
(1945-)
Original Sin  *367*

CAMERON CROWE (1957-)
Vanilla Sky  *518*

MICHAEL CUESTA
L.I.E.  *273*

ALAN CUMMING (1965-)
The Anniversary Party  *31*

VONDIE CURTIS-HALL
(1956-)
Glitter  *178*

JOHN DAHL (1956-)
Joy Ride  *244*

JEFF DANIELS (1955-)
Escanaba in da
Moonlight  *136*

FRANK DARABONT (1959-)
The Majestic  *307*

TERENCE DAVIES (1945-)
House of Mirth  *213*

DEMANE DAVIS
Lift  *293*

JOHN A. DAVIS
Jimmy Neutron: Boy
Genius  *234*

TAMRA DAVIS
Skipped Parts  *444*

GUILLERMO DEL TORO
The Devil's Backbone  *115*

TED (EDWARD) DEMME
(1964-2002)
Blow  *62*

DOMINIQUE
DERUDDERE
Everybody's Famous!  *142*

DANTE DESARTHE
Dad on the Run  *110*

PETE DOCTER
Monsters, Inc.  *332*

ANDREW DOMINIK
Chopper  *91*

OLIVIER DUCASTEL
The Adventures of Felix  *7*

DENNIS DUGAN (1946-)
Saving Silverman  *413*

BILL EAGLES
Beautiful Creatures  *47*

HARRY ELFONT
Josie and the
Pussycats  *242*

BEN ELTON
Maybe Baby  *318*

RICHARD EYRE (1943-)
Iris  *226*

PHILIPPE FALARDEAU
The Left Hand Side of the
Fridge  *283*

LEONARD FARLINGER
The Perfect Son  *382*

BOBBY FARRELLY (1958-)
Osmosis Jones  *371*
Shallow Hal  *432*

PETER FARRELLY (1957-)
Osmosis Jones *371*
Shallow Hal *432*

JON FAVREAU (1966-)
Made *305*

ROBERT FAVREAU
The Orphan Muses *369*

JOHN FAWCETT
Ginger Snaps *172*

TODD FIELD (1964-)
In the Bedroom *220*

EMMANUEL FINKIEL
Voyages *523*

LAURENT FIRODE
Happenstance *190*

GARY FLEDER
Don't Say a Word *126*

MARC FORSTER
Monster's Ball *330*

STEPHEN FREARS (1941-)
Liam *289*

ANTOINE FUQUA
Training Day *501*

JOEL GALLEN
Not Another Teen
Movie *352*

GEORGE GALLO (1956-)
Double Take *129*

EVA GARDOS
An American
Rhapsody *22*

CESC GAY
Nico and Dani *348*

BOB GIRALDI
Dinner Rush *116*

JONATHAN GLAZER
Sexy Beast *429*

FRIGYES GODROS
Glamour *174*

TONY GOLDWYN (1960-)
Someone Like You *451*

DENNIE GORDON
Joe Dirt *236*

MARLEEN GORRIS (1948-)
The Luzhin Defence *303*

TOM GREEN
Freddy Got Fingered *162*

LUKE GREENFIELD
The Animal *29*

JOHN GREYSON (1960-)
The Law of
Enclosures *282*

ROBERT GUEDIGUIAN
(1953-)
The Town Is Quiet *499*

LAWRENCE (LARRY)
GUTERMAN
Cats & Dogs *85*

LASSE HALLSTROM
(1946-)
The Shipping News *435*

GARY HARDWICK
The Brothers *74*

TSUI HARK (1951-)
Time and Tide *486*

JAN HARLAN
Stanley Kubrick: A Life in
Pictures *461*

RENNY HARLIN (1959-)
Driven *133*

BLAIR HAYES
Bubble Boy *76*

CHRIS HEGEDUS
Startup.com *462*

BRIAN HELGELAND
A Knight's Tale *271*

STEPHEN HEREK (1958-)
Rock Star *403*

JOEL HERSHMAN
Greenfingers *185*

JOHN HERZFELD
15 Minutes *155*

SCOTT HICKS (1953-)
Hearts in Atlantis *202*

TIMOTHY HILL
Max Keeble's Big
Move *316*

BEN HOPKINS
Simon Magnus *443*

JOEL HOPKINS
Jump Tomorrow *246*

RON HOWARD (1954-)
A Beautiful Mind *49*

PETER HOWITT
Antitrust *33*

JAN HREBEJK
Divided We Fall *120*

ANN HU
Shadow Magic *431*

ALBERT HUGHES (1972-)
From Hell *164*

ALLEN HUGHES (1972-)
From Hell *164*

TRAN ANH HUNG (1963-)
The Vertical Ray of the
Sun *520*

PETER HYAMS (1943-)
The Musketeer *343*

LEON ICHASO
Pinero *383*

SHOHEI IMAMURA (1926-)
Warm Water Under a Red
Bridge *526*

ALEJANDRO GONZALEZ
INARRITA
Amores Perros *26*

JAMES IVORY (1928-)
The Golden Bowl *180*

PETER JACKSON (1961-)
Lord of the Rings 1: The
Fellowship of the
Rings *295*

LANE JANGER
Just One Time *252*

AGNES JAOUI
The Taste of Others *479*

VICTORIA JENSON
Shrek *437*

JEAN-PIERRE JEUNET
(1955-)
Amelie *14*

JOE JOHNSTON
Jurassic Park 3 *247*

GIL JUNGER
Black Knight *60*

DAVID KANE
Born Romantic *67*

DEBORAH KAPLAN
Josie and the
Pussycats *242*

WONG KAR-WAI (1958-)
In the Mood for Love *223*

AMOS KOLLEK
Fast Food, Fast
Women *152*

BALTASAR KORMAKUR
101 Reykjavik *364*

PIET KROON
Osmosis Jones *371*

ZACHARIAS KUNUK
Atanarjuat, the Fast
Runner *38*

CHRISTINE LAHTI (1950-)
My First Mister *346*

CLAUDE LANZMANN
Sobibor, October 14, 1943,
4 p.m. *449*

RAY LAWRENCE
Lantana *274*

PATRICE LECONTE
(1947-)
The Widow of Saint-
Pierre *539*

JENNIFER JASON LEIGH
(1963-)
The Anniversary Party *31*

KASI LEMMONS (1961-)
The Caveman's
Valentine *87*

BARRY LEVINSON (1942-)
Bandits *43*
An Everlasting Piece *140*

KRISTIAN LEVRING
The King Is Alive *265*

DEMIAN LICHTENSTEIN
3000 Miles to
Graceland *482*

SABASTIAN LIFSHITZ
Come Undone *98*

RICHARD LINKLATER
(1961-)
Tape *477*
Waking Life *524*

CHRISTOPHER
LIVINGSTON
Hit and Runway *211*

KEN LOACH (1936-)
Bread and Roses *68*

BAZ LUHRMANN (1962-)
Moulin Rouge *335*

ROBERT LUKETIC
Legally Blonde *284*

ROBERT LUNDAHL
Unconquering the Last
Frontier *509*

ROD LURIE
The Last Castle *278*

DANA LUSTIG
Kill Me Later *263*

DAVID LYNCH (1946-)
Mulholland Drive *338*

JOHN MADDEN (1949-)
Captain Corelli's
Mandolin *83*

SHARON MAGUIRE
Bridget Jones's Diary *72*

MAJID MAJIDI
Baran *45*

MOHSEN MAKHMALBAF
Kandahar *257*

DAVID MAMET (1947-)
The Heist *206*

LUIS MANDOKI
Angel Eyes *27*

JAMES MANGOLD
Kate & Leopold *260*

MICHAEL MANN (1943-)
Ali *10*

DAVID MAQUILING
Too Much Sleep *492*

DAVOR MARJANOVIC
My Father's Angel *345*

GARRY MARSHALL (1934-)
The Princess Diaries *394*

PENNY MARSHALL (1947-)
Riding in Cars with
Boys *399*

LUCRETIA MARTEL
La Cienaga *92*

JACQUES MARTINEAU
The Adventures of Felix *7*

LES MAYFIELD
American Outlaws *18*

CARLO MAZZACURATI
The Holy Tongue *212*

JONAS MCCORD
The Body *66*

FRANCINE MCDOUGALL
Sugar & Spice *465*

SCOTT MCGEHEE
The Deep End *114*

DOUGLAS MCGRATH
Company Man *99*

DOUG MCHENRY
Kingdom Come *267*

JIM MCKAY
Our Song *376*

CONOR MCPHERSON
Saltwater *410*

MARZIEH MESHKINI
(1969-)
The Day I Became a
Woman *112*

ALLAN MILLER
The Turandot Project *505*

DANIEL MINAHAN
Series 7: The
Contenders *425*

DAVID MIRKIN
Heartbreakers *200*

JOHN CAMERON
MITCHELL
Hedwig and the Angry
Inch *204*

DOMINIK MOLL
With a Friend Like
Harry *541*

LUKAS MOODYSSON
Together *489*

JOHN MOORE
Behind Enemy Lines *51*

NANNI MORETTI (1953-)
The Son's Room *453*

CHRISTOPHER MUNCH
The Sleepy Time Gal *445*

PAT MURPHY
Nora *351*

CHRIS NAHON
Kiss of the Dragon *269*

JESSIE NELSON
I Am Sam *217*

TIM BLAKE NELSON
(1965-)
O *356*

CHRISTOPHER NOLAN
(1970-)
Memento *321*

TERRY L. NOSS
Trumpet of the Swan *503*

JONATHAN NOSSITER
Signs & Wonders *441*

JEHANE NOUJAIM
Startup.com *462*

COLIN NUTLEY (1944-)
Under the Sun *512*

PAT O'CONNOR (1943-)
Sweet November *471*

TOMMY O'HAVER
Get Over It! *167*

ARNE OLSEN
Here's to Life *208*

FRANK OZ (1944-)
The Score *419*

FRANCOIS OZON
Under the Sand *511*

FERZAN OZPETEK
Ignorant Fairies *219*

JOHN PAIZS
Top of the Food
Chain *494*

JAFAR PANAHI
The Circle *93*

PIYUSH DINKER PANDYA
American Desi *17*

JOHN PASQUIN
Joe Somebody *238*

KRUTIN PATEL (1966-)
ABCD *4*

PAWEL PAWLIKOWSKI
Last Resort *281*

RAOUL PECK
Lumumba *302*

GABRIEL PELLETIER
Life After Love *290*

SEAN PENN (1960-)
The Pledge *387*

JEAN-MARIE POIRE
(1945-)
Just Visiting *253*

GREGORY POIRIER
Tomcats *491*

MICHAEL POLISH
Jackpot *230*

LEA POOL
Lost and Delirious *297*

SALLY POTTER (1947-)
The Man Who Cried *310*

ROB PRITTS
Corky Romano *101*

BARNARD RAPP
A Matter of Taste *315*

BRETT RATNER
Rush Hour 2 *408*

IVAN REITMAN (1946-)
Evolution *144*

PIERRE-PAUL RENDERSS
Thomas in Love *481*

RICHARD RICH
Trumpet of the Swan *503*

MARIA RIPOLI
Tortilla Soup *495*

GUY RITCHIE
Snatch *447*

JACQUES RIVETTE (1928-)
Va Savoir *514*

BRIAN ROBBINS (1964-)
Hardball *193*

ROBERT RODRIGUEZ
(1968-)
Spy Kids *459*

JAMES B. ROGERS
American Pie 2 *20*
Say It Isn't So *415*

JOE ROTH (1948-)
America's Sweethearts *24*

DANIEL SACKHEIM
The Glass House *175*

HIRONOBU SAKAGUCHI
Final Fantasy: The Spirits
Within *158*

WALTER SALLES
Behind the Sun *54*

VICTOR SALVA (1958-)
Jeepers Creepers *233*

LONE SCHERFIG
Italian for Beginners *229*

VOLKER SCHLONDORFF
(1939-)
The Legend of Rita *287*

BARBET SCHROEDER
(1941-)
Our Lady of the
Assassins *375*

JOEL SCHUMACHER
(1942-)
Tigerland *484*

RIDLEY SCOTT (1939-)
Black Hawk Down *57*
Hannibal *187*

TONY SCOTT (1944-)
Spy Game *457*

SUSAN SEIDELMAN
(1952-)
Gaudi Afternoon *166*

HENRY SELICK
Monkeybone *327*

DOMINIC SENA
Swordfish *473*

MICHAEL SERGIO
Under Hellgate
Bridge *510*

ADAM SHANKMAN
The Wedding Planner *530*

DAVID SHAPIRO
Keep the River On Your
Right: A Modern
Cannibal Tale *262*

LAURIE GWEN SHAPIRO
Keep the River On Your
Right: A Modern
Cannibal Tale *262*

CHARLES SHYER (1941-)
The Affair of the
Necklace *8*

DAVID SIEGEL
The Deep End *114*

HARRY SINCLAIR
The Price of Milk *392*

JOHN SINGLETON (1968-)
Baby Boy *41*

ROB SITCH
The Dish *118*

TOM SITO
Osmosis Jones *371*

KEVIN SMITH (1970-)
Jay and Silent Bob Strike
Back *231*

MEL SMITH (1952-)
High Heels and Low
Lifes *209*

STEVEN SODERBERGH
(1963-)
Ocean's Eleven *359*

IAIN SOFTLEY
K-PAX *255*

SILVIO SOLDINI
Bread and Tulips *70*

STEPHEN SOMMERS
The Mummy Returns *341*

STEVEN SPIELBERG
(1947-)
A. I.: Artificial
Intelligence *1*

GERARD STEMBRIDGE
About Adam *5*

PATRICK STETTNER
The Business of
Strangers *80*

BEN STILLER (1965-)
Zoolander *542*

JOHN STOCKWELL (1961-)
crazy/beautiful *103*

LYNNE STOPKEWICH
Suspicious River *469*

KHARI STREETER
Lift *293*

JAN SVERAK (1965-)
Dark Blue World *111*

LEE TAMAHORI (1950-)
Along Came a Spider *12*

DANIS TANOVIC
No Man's Land *349*

JONATHAN TEPLITZKY
Better Than Sex *56*

JAMIE THRAVES
The Low Down *301*

RICKY TOGNAZZI
Making Love *309*

MIKE TOLLIN
Summer Catch *467*

GARY TROUSDALE
Atlantis: The Lost
Empire *39*

FERNANDO TRUEBA
(1955-)
Calle 54 *82*

MING-LIANG TSAI
The River *401*
What Time Is It
There? *534*

NEIL TURITZ
Two Ninas *508*

TOM TYKWER (1965-)
The Princess and the
Warrior *393*

LIV ULLMANN (1939-)
Faithless *148*

AGNES VARDA (1928-)
The Gleaners and I *177*

FRANCIS VEBER (1937-)
The Closet *96*

GORE VERBINSKI
The Mexican *323*

CLEMENT VIRGO
Love Come Down *299*

ANDRUCHA
WADDINGTON
Me You Them *320*

DAVID WAIN
Wet Hot American
Summer *532*

JORDAN WALKER-
PEARLMAN
The Visit *521*

KIERON J. WALSH
When Brendan Met
Trudy *538*

WAYNE WANG (1949-)
The Center of the
World *89*

MARK WATERS
Head Over Heels *198*

KEENEN IVORY WAYANS
(1958-)
Scary Movie 2 *417*

SAM WEISMAN
What's the Worst That
Could Happen? *536*

CHRIS WEITZ (1970-)
Down to Earth *131*

PAUL WEITZ (1966-)
Down to Earth *131*

WIM WENDERS (1945-)
The Million Dollar
Hotel *325*

SIMON WEST (1961-)
Lara Croft: Tomb
Raider *276*

ANNE WHEELER (1946-)
Suddenly Naked *464*

JOHN WHITESELL
See Spot Run *421*

SIMON WINCER
Crocodile Dundee in Los
Angeles *105*

IRWIN WINKLER (1934-)
Life as a House *291*

MICHAEL
WINTERBOTTOM
(1961-)
The Claim *94*

KIRK WISE
Atlantis: The Lost
Empire *39*

JAMES WONG
The One *363*

HASSAN YEKTAPNAH
Djomeh *121*

ZHANG YIMOU (1951-)
The Road Home *402*

JERRY ZUCKER (1950-)
Rat Race *397*

HARALD ZWART
One Night at
McCool's *365*

TERRY ZWIGOFF
Ghost World *170*

# Screenwriter Index

JOEL COEN (1954-)
The Man Who Wasn't
There *312*

JAFFE COHEN
Hit and Runway *211*

LEWIS COLICK
Domestic Disturbance *125*

PAUL R. COLLINS
Pavilion of Women *378*

UMBERTO CONTARELLO
The Holy Tongue *212*

FRANCIS FORD COPPOLA
(1939-)
Apocalypse Now
Redux *35*

ANDREE CORBIAU
The King Is Dancing *266*

GERARD CORBIAU
The King Is Dancing *266*

FRANK COTTRELL-
BOYCE
The Claim *94*

MICHAEL CRISTOFER
(1945-)
Original Sin *367*

LANCE CROUTHER
Down to Earth *131*

CAMERON CROWE (1957-)
Vanilla Sky *518*

BILLY CRYSTAL (1947-)
America's Sweethearts *24*

GERALD CUESTA
L.I.E. *273*

MICHAEL CUESTA
L.I.E. *273*

ALAN CUMMING (1965-)
The Anniversary Party *31*

RICHARD CURTIS
Bridget Jones's Diary *72*

HUANG DAN
Shadow Magic *431*

JEFF DANIELS (1955-)
Escanaba in da
Moonlight *136*

KEN DAURIO
Bubble Boy *76*

ANDREW DAVIES
Bridget Jones's Diary *72*
The Tailor of Panama *475*

TERENCE DAVIES (1945-)
House of Mirth *213*

DEMANE DAVIS
Lift *293*

JOHN A. DAVIS
Jimmy Neutron: Boy
Genius *234*

EVE DE CASTRO
The King Is Dancing *266*

MARINA DE VAN
Under the Sand *511*

DIDIER DECOIN
The King Is Dancing *266*

GUILLERMO DEL TORO
The Devil's Backbone *115*

GREG DEPAUL
Saving Silverman *413*

DOMINIQUE
DERUDDERE
Everybody's Famous! *142*

AGNES DESARTHE
Dad on the Run *110*

DANTE DESARTHE
Dad on the Run *110*

GILLES DESJARDINS
The Orphan Muses *369*

GERALD DI PEGO
Angel Eyes *27*

DAVID DIAMOND
Evolution *144*

GRAZIANO DIANA
Making Love *309*

LEM DOBBS
The Score *419*

ANDREW DOMINIK
Chopper *91*

SIMON DONALD
Beautiful Creatures *47*

RICHARD D'OVIDIO
Exit Wounds *146*

RODDY DOYLE
When Brendan Met
Trudy *538*

OLIVIER DUCASTEL
The Adventures of Felix *7*

ROBERT DUNN
Heartbreakers *200*

CHERYL EDWARDS
Save the Last Dance *411*

HARRY ELFONT
Josie and the
Pussycats *242*

TED ELLIOTT
Shrek *437*

MICHAEL ELLIS
The Wedding Planner *530*

BEN ELTON
Maybe Baby *318*

ADAM JAY EPSTEIN
Not Another Teen
Movie *352*

RICHARD EYRE (1943-)
Iris *226*

CHRIS FABER
See Spot Run *421*

PHILIPPE FALARDEAU
The Left Hand Side of the
Fridge *283*

PAMELA FALK
The Wedding Planner *530*

KEVIN FALLS
Summer Catch *467*

CLAUDE FARALDO
The Widow of Saint-
Pierre *539*

LEONARD FARLINGER
The Perfect Son *382*

BOBBY FARRELLY (1958-)
Shallow Hal *432*

PETER FARRELLY (1957-)
Shallow Hal *432*

JON FAVREAU (1966-)
Made *305*

JULIAN FELLOWES
Gosford Park *182*

LINDA FERRI
The Son's Room *453*

ROB FESTINGER
In the Bedroom *220*

GLENN FICARRA
Cats & Dogs *85*

TODD FIELD (1964-)
In the Bedroom *220*

HELEN FIELDING
Bridget Jones's Diary *72*

JACQUES FIESCHI
Sentimental Destiny *422*

EMMANUEL FINKIEL
Voyages *523*

LAURENT FIRODE
Happenstance *190*

R. LEE FLEMING, JR.
Get Over It! *167*

ALYSON FOUSE
Scary Movie 2 *417*

HOWARD FRANKLIN
Antitrust *33*

JILL FRANKLYN
My First Mister *346*

ELYSE FRIEDMAN
Suddenly Naked *464*

KIM FULLER
High Heels and Low
Lifes *209*

DANIELE GAGLIANONE
The Way We
Laughed *528*

GEORGE GALLO (1956-)
Double Take *129*
See Spot Run *421*

EVA GARDOS
An American
Rhapsody *22*

DAVID GARRETT
Corky Romano *101*

JOHN GATINS
Hardball *193*
Summer Catch *467*

PETER GAULKE
Black Knight *60*
Say It Isn't So *415*

CESC GAY
Nico and Dani *348*

DANIEL GERSON
Monsters, Inc. *332*

STEPHEN GEVEDON
Session 9 *427*

TOM GLEISNER
The Dish *118*

ALAIN GODARD
Enemy at the Gates *134*

FRIGYES GODROS
Glamour *174*

WILLIAM GOLDMAN
(1931-)
Hearts in Atlantis *202*

AKIVA GOLDSMAN
A Beautiful Mind *49*

GREG GRABIANSKI
Scary Movie 2 *417*

GEORGE DAWES GREEN
The Caveman's
Valentine *87*

TOM GREEN
Freddy Got Fingered *162*

JAMES GREER
Max Keeble's Big
Move *316*

JOHN GREYSON (1960-)
The Law of
Enclosures *282*

TED GRIFFIN
Ocean's Eleven *359*

PAUL GUAY
Heartbreakers *200*

ROBERT GUEDIGUIAN
(1953-)
The Town Is Quiet *499*

FABRICE GUEZ
Dad on the Run *110*

PATRICK MASSETT
Lara Croft: Tomb
Raider *276*

STEVE MAZUR
Heartbreakers *200*

CARLO MAZZACURATI
The Holy Tongue *212*

BOB MCANDREW
Shadow Magic *431*

JONAS MCCORD
The Body *66*

BARRY MCEVOY
An Everlasting Piece *140*

SCOTT MCGEHEE
The Deep End *114*

JIMMY MCGOVERN
Liam *289*

DOUGLAS MCGRATH
Company Man *99*

MICHAEL MCGRUTHER
Tigerland *484*

JIM MCKAY
Our Song *376*

DAVID MCKENNA
Blow *62*

JAMES MCMANUS
ABCD *4*

CONOR MCPHERSON
Saltwater *410*

LOUIS MELLIS
Sexy Beast *429*

RAMON MENENDEZ
Tortilla Soup *495*

JAMES MHYRE
Gaudi Afternoon *166*

JEAN-LOUIS MILESI
The Town Is Quiet *499*

JOHN MILIUS (1944-)
Apocalypse Now
Redux *35*

DANIEL MINAHAN
Series 7: The
Contenders *425*

JOHN CAMERON
MITCHELL
Hedwig and the Angry
Inch *204*

DOMINIK MOLL
With a Friend Like
Harry *541*

LUKAS MOODYSSON
Together *489*

NANNI MORETTI (1953-)
The Son's Room *453*

GLEN MORGAN
The One *363*

MARC MOSS
Along Came a Spider *12*

SEAN MOYNIHAN
Shallow Hal *432*

CHRISTOPHER MUNCH
The Sleepy Time Gal *445*

DAVID MUNOZ
The Devil's Backbone *115*

PAT MURPHY
Nora *351*

TAB MURPHY
Atlantis: The Lost
Empire *39*

TOM MUSCA
Tortilla Soup *495*

JEFF NATHANSON
Rush Hour 2 *408*

HANK NELKEN
Saving Silverman *413*

JESSIE NELSON
I Am Sam *217*

MANDY NELSON
Sugar & Spice *465*

CHRISTOPHER NOLAN
(1970-)
Memento *321*

KEN NOLAN
Black Hawk Down *57*

JONATHAN NOSSITER
Signs & Wonders *441*

COLIN NUTLEY (1944-)
Under the Sun *512*

STEVE OEDEKERK (1961-)
Jimmy Neutron: Boy
Genius *234*

ARNE OLSEN
Here's to Life *208*

MARY OLSON-
KROMOLOWSKI
The Pledge *387*

FRANCOIS OZON
Under the Sand *511*

FERZAN OZPETEK
Ignorant Fairies *219*

PIYUSH DINKER PANDYA
American Desi *17*

KAMBOZIA PARTOVI
The Circle *93*

KRUTIN PATEL (1966-)
ABCD *4*

CINCO PAUL
Bubble Boy *76*

PAWEL PAWLIKOWSKI
Last Resort *281*

ALEXANDER PAYNE
(1961-)
Jurassic Park 3 *247*

CRAIG PEARCE
Moulin Rouge *335*

RAOUL PECK
Lumumba *302*

ANTHONY PECKHAM
Don't Say a Word *126*

ZAK PENN
Behind Enemy Lines *51*

MARCO PETTENELLO
The Holy Tongue *212*

HARLEY PEYTON
Bandits *43*

JEAN-MARIE POIRE
(1945-)
Just Visiting *253*

GREGORY POIRIER
Tomcats *491*

MARK POLISH
Jackpot *230*

MICHAEL POLISH
Jackpot *230*

DAVE POLSKY
Scary Movie 2 *417*

SALLY POTTER (1947-)
The Man Who Cried *310*

DONNA POWERS
Valentine *516*

WAYNE POWERS
Valentine *516*

ROGER PULLIS
Bully *78*

DARRYL QUARLES
Black Knight *60*

GENE QUINTANO (1946-)
The Musketeer *343*

KATE RAISZ
Shadow Magic *431*

BARNARD RAPP
A Matter of Taste *315*

RICHARD RECCO
3000 Miles to
Graceland *482*

AL REINERT
Final Fantasy: The Spirits
Within *158*

JOHN REQUA
Cats & Dogs *85*

GUY RITCHIE
Snatch *447*

STEPHEN J. RIVELE
Ali *10*

JACQUES RIVETTE (1928-)
Va Savoir *514*

CHRIS ROCK (1966-)
Down to Earth *131*

ROBERT RODRIGUEZ
(1968-)
Spy Kids *459*

JUDY ROTHMAN ROFE
Trumpet of the Swan *503*

JOHN ROGERS
American Outlaws *18*

STEVEN ROGERS
Kate & Leopold *260*

WILL ROKOS
Monster's Ball *330*

MARCIA ROMANO
Under the Sand *511*

GIANNI ROMOLI
Ignorant Fairies *219*

MARK ROSENTHAL
Planet of the Apes *384*

TERRY ROSSIO
Shrek *437*

ERIC ROTH
Ali *10*

STEPHEN M. RYDER
L.I.E. *273*

KARIO SALEM
The Score *419*

WALTER SALLES
Behind the Sun *54*

VICTOR SALVA (1958-)
Jeepers Creepers *233*

TIM SANDLIN
Skipped Parts *444*

DRAKE SATHER
Zoolander *542*

DAVID SCARPA
The Last Castle *278*

LONE SCHERFIG
Italian for Beginners *229*

HEIDRUN SCHLEEF
The Son's Room *453*

VOLKER SCHLONDORFF
(1939-)
The Legend of Rita *287*

ROB SCHNEIDER (1963-)
The Animal *29*

ROGER S.H. SCHULMAN
Shrek *437*

DAVID SCINTO
Sexy Beast *429*

KEN SCOTT
Life After Love *290*

STAN SEIDEL
One Night at
McCool's *365*

MICHAEL SERGIO
Under Hellgate
Bridge *510*

RICK SHAUGHNESSY
Dinner Rush *116*

JOHN SCOTT SHEPHERD
Joe Somebody *238*

BAO SHI
The Road Home *402*

MICHAEL SHOWALTER
Wet Hot American
Summer *532*

DAVID SIEGEL
The Deep End *114*

HARRY SINCLAIR
The Price of Milk *392*

JOHN SINGLETON (1968-)
Baby Boy *41*

ROB SITCH
The Dish *118*

MICHAEL SLOANE
The Majestic *307*

SHAWN SLOVO
Captain Corelli's
Mandolin *83*

KEVIN SMITH (1970-)
Jay and Silent Bob Strike
Back *231*

KIRSTEN SMITH
Legally Blonde *284*

SCOTT MARSHALL
SMITH
The Score *419*

MICHAEL ANTHONY
SNOWDEN
Scary Movie 2 *417*

ELENA SOAREZ
Me You Them *320*

SILVIO SOLDINI
Bread and Tulips *70*

STEPHEN SOMMERS
The Mummy Returns *341*

DAVID SPADE (1964-)
Joe Dirt *236*

STEVEN SPIELBERG
(1947-)
A. I.: Artificial
Intelligence *1*

SYLVESTER STALLONE
(1946-)
Driven *133*

ANDREW STANTON
Monsters, Inc. *332*

PAUL STANTON (1884-
1955)
On the Line *361*

J. DAVID STEM
Jimmy Neutron: Boy
Genius *234*

GERARD STEMBRIDGE
About Adam *5*
Nora *351*

PATRICK STETTNER
The Business of
Strangers *80*

BEN STILLER (1965-)
Zoolander *542*

JOE STILLMAN
Shrek *437*

JOHN STOCKWELL (1961-)
Rock Star *403*

LYNNE STOPKEWICH
Suspicious River *469*

WESLEY STRICK (1954-)
The Glass House *175*

LARRY SULKIS
John Carpenter's Ghosts of
Mars *240*

ZDENEK SVERAK
Dark Blue World *111*

GERRY SWALLOW
Black Knight *60*
Say It Isn't So *415*

JOHN SWEET
The Affair of the
Necklace *8*

DANIS TANOVIC
No Man's Land *349*

ALBERTO TARAGLIO
The Way We
Laughed *528*

CLAY TARVER
Joy Ride *244*

GILLES TAURAND
A Matter of Taste *315*

JIM TAYLOR
Jurassic Park 3 *247*

RODERICK TAYLOR
American Outlaws *18*

DAISUKE TENGAN
Warm Water Under a Red
Bridge *526*

JONATHAN TEPLITZKY
Better Than Sex *56*

GARY SCOTT
THOMPSON
The Fast and the
Furious *150*

JUDITH THOMPSON
Lost and Delirious *297*

JAMIE THRAVES
The Low Down *301*

RICKY TOGNAZZI
Making Love *309*

PETER TOLAN
America's Sweethearts *24*

MOTOFUMI TOMIKAWA
Warm Water Under a Red
Bridge *526*

ANTONIO TRASHORROS
The Devil's Backbone *115*

ANNE-LOUISE TRIVIDIC
Intimacy *224*

FERNANDO TRUEBA
(1955-)
Calle 54 *82*

MING-LIANG TSAI
The River *401*
What Time Is It
There? *534*

YI-CHUN TSAI
The River *401*

NEIL TURITZ
Two Ninas *508*

TOM TYKWER (1965-)
The Princess and the
Warrior *393*

FERNANDO VALLEJO
Our Lady of the
Assassins *375*

JENNIFER VANDEVER
Just One Time *252*

AGNES VARDA (1928-)
The Gleaners and I *177*

FRANCIS VEBER (1937-)
The Closet *96*

DAVID VELOZ
Behind Enemy Lines *51*

JEFF VINTAR
Final Fantasy: The Spirits
Within *158*

CLEMENT VIRGO
Love Come Down *299*

KURT VOELKER
Sweet November *471*

DAVID WAIN
Wet Hot American
Summer *532*

JORDAN WALKER-
PEARLMAN
The Visit *521*

RANDALL WALLACE
Pearl Harbor *379*

FRAN WALSH
Lord of the Rings 1: The
Fellowship of the
Rings *295*

KAREN WALTON
Ginger Snaps *172*

WAYNE WANG (1949-)
The Center of the
World *89*

JASON WARD
Corky Romano *101*

MORGAN WARD
Riding in Cars with
Boys *399*

CRAIG WAYANS
Scary Movie 2 *417*

MARLON WAYANS (1972-)
Scary Movie 2 *417*

SHAWN WAYANS (1971-)
Scary Movie 2 *417*

DAVID N. WEISS
Jimmy Neutron: Boy
Genius *234*

DAVID WEISSMAN
Evolution *144*

GINA WENDKOS
The Princess Diaries *394*

CHRISTOPHER
WILKINSON
Ali *10*

OWEN C. WILSON (1968-)
The Royal
Tenenbaums *406*

FRED WOLF
Joe Dirt *236*

JAMES WONG
The One *363*

CHARLES WOOD
Iris *226*

SKIP WOODS
Swordfish *473*

J.H. WYMAN
The Mexican *323*

LUO YAN
Pavilion of Women *378*

PI-YING YANG
The River *401*
What Time Is It
There? *534*

HASSAN YEKTAPNAH
Djomeh *121*

**RAFAEL YGLESIAS**
From Hell  *164*

**GRAHAM YOST**
The Last Castle  *278*

**STEVEN ZAILLIAN (1951-)**
Hannibal  *187*

**JOHN ZINMAN**
Lara Croft: Tomb
Raider  *276*

**TERRY ZWIGOFF**
Ghost World  *170*

# Cinematographer Index

Made  *305*

**RANDY DRUMMOND**
Series 7: The
Contenders  *425*

**STUART DRYBURGH**
Bridget Jones's Diary  *72*
Kate & Leopold  *260*

**ANDREW DUNN**
Gosford Park  *182*
Liam  *289*
Monkeybone  *327*

**JEAN-RENE DUVEAU**
Happenstance  *190*

**ROBERT ELSWIT**
The Heist  *206*

**JEAN-YVES ESCOFFIER**
15 Minutes  *155*

**JEAN-MARC FABRE**
Fast Food, Fast
Women  *152*

**RENATO FALCAO**
American Desi  *17*

**DON E. FAUNTLEROY**
Jeepers Creepers  *233*

**ZHAO FEI**
The Curse of the Jade
Scorpion  *107*

**DAVID FERRARA**
Kill Me Later  *263*

**VILKO FILAC**
Novocaine  *354*

**RUSSELL FINE**
O  *356*

**MAURO FIORE**
The Center of the
World  *89*
Driven  *133*
Training Day  *501*

**JENS FISCHER**
Under the Sun  *512*

**RONAN FOX**
The Most Fertile Man in
Ireland  *334*

**ROBERT FRAISSE**
Enemy at the Gates  *134*

**WILLIAM A. FRAKER**
(1923-)
Town and Country  *497*

**DAVID FRANCO**
3000 Miles to
Graceland  *482*

**DAVID FRAZEE**
Suddenly Naked  *464*

**STEVE GAINER**
Bully  *78*

**BRENDAN GALVIN**
Behind Enemy Lines  *51*

**ERIC GAUTIER**
Intimacy  *224*
Sentimental Destiny  *422*

**DAVID GEDDES**
Here's to Life  *208*

**EBRAHEEM GHAFOURI**
The Day I Became a
Woman  *112*
Kandahar  *257*

**PIERRE GILL**
Lost and Delirious  *297*

**RICHARD GREATREX**
A Knight's Tale  *271*

**ROBBIE GREENBERG**
Save the Last Dance  *411*

**FRANK GRIEBE**
The Princess and the
Warrior  *393*

**GARY GRIFFIN**
Fighter  *157*

**XAVIER PEREZ GROBET**
Tortilla Soup  *495*

**ALEXANDER GRUSYNSKI**
The Brothers  *74*
Two Can Play That
Game  *506*

**ROB HAHN**
The Score  *419*

**GEOFFREY HALL**
Chopper  *91*

**POON HANG-SENG**
Pavilion of Women  *378*

**MANUEL HARLAN**
Stanley Kubrick: A Life in
Pictures  *461*

**ANTOINE HEBERLE**
Under the Sand  *511*

**ANDREAS HOFER**
The Legend of Rita  *287*

**SHANE HURLBUT**
crazy/beautiful  *103*

**TOM HURWITZ**
The Turandot Project  *505*

**PETER HYAMS** (1943-)
The Musketeer  *343*

**SLAWOMIR IDZIAK**
Black Hawk Down  *57*

**OFER INOV**
Time of Favor  *487*

**MARK IRWIN**
American Pie 2  *20*
Freddy Got Fingered  *162*
Osmosis Jones  *371*
Say It Isn't So  *415*

**TIM IVES**
Dinner Rush  *116*

**IGOR JADUE-LILLO**
The Low Down  *301*

**PETER JAMES**
Bride of the Wind  *71*

**JORGEN JOHANSSON**
Italian for Beginners  *229*

**SHELLY JOHNSON**
Jurassic Park 3  *247*
The Last Castle  *278*

**JEFFREY JUR**
Joy Ride  *244*
My First Mister  *346*

**MILTON KAM**
ABCD  .*4*

**JANUSZ KAMINSKI** (1959-)
A. I.: Artificial
Intelligence  *1*

**SANDOR KARDOS**
Glamour  *174*

**FRANCIS KENNY**
Kingdom Come  *267*

**GARY B. KIBBE**
John Carpenter's Ghosts of
Mars  *240*

**ALAR KIVILO**
The Glass House  *175*

**NICHOLAS D.
KNOWLAND**
Simon Magnus  *443*

**SHIGERU KOMATSUBARA**
Warm Water Under a Red
Bridge  *526*

**JONATHAN KOVEL**
Keep the River On Your
Right: A Modern
Cannibal Tale  *262*

**LELAND KRANE**
Under Hellgate
Bridge  *510*

**STEPHANE KRAUSZ**
The Gleaners and I  *177*

**ALWIN KUCHLER**
The Claim  *94*

**WILLY KURANT**
Pootie Tang  *390*

**ELLEN KURAS**
Blow  *62*

**EDWARD LACHMAN**
(1948-)
Sweet November  *471*

**RODRIGO LALINDE**
Our Lady of the
Assassins  *375*

**GIUSEPPE LANCI**
The Son's Room  *453*

**ROGER LANSER**
Maybe Baby  *318*

**JEANNE LAPOIRIE**
Under the Sand  *511*

**JEAN-CLAUDE LARRIEU**
Voyages  *523*

**RYSZARD LENCZEWSKI**
Last Resort  *281*

**JOHN R. LEONETTI**
Joe Dirt  *236*

**MATTHEW F. LEONETTI**
Along Came a Spider  *12*
Rush Hour 2  *408*

**ANDREW LESNIE**
Lord of the Rings 1: The
Fellowship of the
Rings  *295*

**PEN-JUNG LIAO**
The River  *401*

**MATTHEW LIBATIQUE**
Josie and the
Pussycats  *242*
Tigerland  *484*

**KARL WALTER
LINDENLAUB**
One Night at
McCool's  *365*
The Princess Diaries  *394*

**RICHARD LINKLATER**
(1961-)
Waking Life  *524*

**ALI LONGHMANI**
Djomeh  *121*

**JOSE LUIS LOPEZ-
LINARES**
Calle 54  *82*

**EMMANUEL LUBEZKI**
Ali  *10*

**WILLIAM LUBTCHANSKY**
Va Savoir  *514*

**ROBERT LUNDAHL**
Unconquering the Last
Frontier  *509*

**BERNARD LUTIC**
Lumumba  *302*
The Luzhin Defence  *303*

**JULIO MACAT**
Cats & Dogs  *85*
The Wedding Planner  *530*

THEO VAN DE SANDE
Double Take *129*

WALTHER VANDEN
ENDE
No Man's Land *349*

SACHA VIERNY (1919-2001)
The Man Who Cried *310*

REYNALDO VILLALOBOS
Not Another Teen
Movie *352*

AMELIA VINCENT
The Caveman's
Valentine *87*

MANDY WALKER
Lantana *274*

BEN WEINSTEIN
Wet Hot American
Summer *532*

JAMES WELLAND
Beautiful Creatures *47*

DARIUS WOLSKI
The Mexican *323*

BILL WONG
Top of the Food
Chain *494*

GRAEME WOOD
The Dish *118*

BRUCE WORRALL
My Father's Angel *345*

HERMAN YAU
Time and Tide *486*

ROBERT YEOMAN
The Royal
Tenenbaums *406*

HOU YONG
The Road Home *402*

JERZY ZIELINSKI
Bubble Boy *76*

VILMOS ZSIGMOND
The Body *66*
Life as a House *291*

# Editor Index

ROBERT DALVA
Jurassic Park 3  *247*

ANNETTE DAVEY
The Sleepy Time Gal  *445*

RON DAVIS
The Tailor of Panama  *475*

LUIS DE LA MADRID
The Devil's Backbone  *115*

HERVE DE LUZE
The Taste of Others  *479*

YANN DEDET
Come Undone  *98*

KEIKO DEGUCHI
The Business of
Strangers  *80*

PIA DI CIAULA
Nora  *351*

CUSHLA DILLON
The Price of Milk  *392*

HUMPHREY DIXON
Enemy at the Gates  *134*

DODY DORN (1955-)
Memento  *321*

BOB DUCSAY
The Mummy Returns  *341*

MICHAEL J. DUTHIE
3000 Miles to
Graceland  *482*

SKULE ERIKSEN
101 Reykjavik  *364*

SIM EVAN-JONES
Shrek  *437*

DAVID FINFER
Joe Somebody  *238*

CLAUDIA FINKLE
Pavilion of Women  *378*

MARY FINLAY
About Adam  *5*

RICK W. FINNEY
Cats & Dogs  *85*

ALOIS FISAREK
Dark Blue World  *111*

RICHARD FRANCIS-
BRUCE
Harry Potter and the
Sorcerer's Stone  *195*

JEFF FREEMAN
Glitter  *178*

LOIS FREEMAN-FOX
Osmosis Jones  *371*

CARMEN FRIAS
Calle 54  *82*

MADELEINE GAVIN
Signs & Wonders  *441*

FRANCOIS GEDIGIER
Intimacy  *224*

JOHN GILBERT
Lord of the Rings 1: The
Fellowship of the
Rings  *295*

JOHN GILROY
Shadow Magic  *431*

STEVE GILSON
Driven  *133*

HELENE GIRARD
The Orphan Muses  *369*

TULA GOENKA
Keep the River On Your
Right: A Modern
Cannibal Tale  *262*

MARK GOLDBLATT
Pearl Harbor  *379*

WILLIAM GOLDENBERG
Ali  *10*

MARGARET GOODSPEED
An American
Rhapsody  *22*

JEFF GOURSON
The Animal  *29*

BRUCE GREEN
The Princess Diaries  *394*

JERRY GREENBERG
Angel Eyes  *27*

CHRISTOPHER
GREENBURY
Serendipity  *423*
Shallow Hal  *432*

DAVID GREENWALD
Sidewalks of New
York  *439*

JON GREGORY
Beautiful Creatures  *47*

FRANK GUTIERREZ
Nico and Dani  *348*

JOELLE HACHE
The Widow of Saint-
Pierre  *539*

ANDREW HAFITZ
Bully  *78*

ALEX HALL
Our Song  *376*

RICHARD HALSEY
Kingdom Come  *267*

JANICE HAMPTON
Soul Survivors  *455*

DAN HANLEY
A Beautiful Mind  *49*

JOHN HARRIS
Snatch  *447*

HASSAN HASSANDUST
Baran  *45*

GREG HAYDEN
Zoolander  *542*

LES HEALEY
Snatch  *447*

CHRIS HEGEDUS
Startup.com  *462*

MARK HELFRICH
Rush Hour 2  *408*

CRAIG P. HERRING
Dr. Dolittle 2  *123*

KRISTINA
HETHERINGTON
Liam  *289*

MIKE HILL
A Beautiful Mind  *49*

NORMAN HOLLYN
Just Looking  *250*

PETER HOLLYWOOD
Maybe Baby  *318*

PETER HONESS
Domestic Disturbance  *125*
The Fast and the
Furious  *150*

GAETAN HUOT
Lost and Delirious  *297*

JOE HUTSHING
Vanilla Sky  *518*

CHANTAL HYMANS
Sobibor, October 14, 1943,
4 p.m.  *449*

ALEJANDRO GONZALEZ
INARRITA
Amores Perros  *26*

SYLVIA INGEMARSSON
Faithless  *148*

MICHAEL JABLOW
The Last Castle  *278*

ALAIN JAKUBOWICZ
The Body  *66*

MALCOLM JAMIESON
Series 7: The
Contenders  *425*

ALLYSON C. JOHNSON
Dinner Rush  *116*

LAWRENCE JORDAN
Riding in Cars with
Boys  *399*

MICHAEL KAHN
A. I.: Artificial
Intelligence  *1*

SHELDON KAHN
Evolution  *144*

SIJVALDI J. KARASON
101 Reykjavik  *364*

PIP KARMEL
Hearts in Atlantis  *202*

ELLEN KENESHEA
Atlantis: The Lost
Empire  *39*

MELISSA KENT
crazy/beautiful  *103*

HARRY KERAMIDAS
Tomcats  *491*

YANNICK KERGOAT
With a Friend Like
Harry  *541*

BERT KISH
Top of the Food
Chain  *494*

SLOANE KLEVIN
Sugar & Spice  *465*

ELIZABETH KLING
Invisible Circus  *225*

LYNZEE KLINGMAN
Ali  *10*

DONALD KLOCEK
The Turandot Project  *505*

GEORGES KLOTZ
The Closet  *96*

CAROLE KRAVETZ
Ghost World  *170*

JUSTIN KRISH
Greenfingers  *185*

VICENTE KUBRUSLY
Me You Them  *320*

ZACHARIAS KUNUK
Atanarjuat, the Fast
Runner  *38*

EREZ LAUFER
Startup.com  *462*

TONY LAWSON
Blow Dry  *64*

ALISON LEARNED
The Visit  *521*

DAN LEBENTAL
From Hell  *164*

CHRIS LEBENZON
Pearl Harbor  *379*
Planet of the Apes  *384*

SOPHIE LEBLOND
The Left Hand Side of the
Fridge  *283*

ALLAN LEE
Suspicious River  *469*

EWIN RYCKAERT
Thomas in Love  *481*

KEN SALLOWS
Chopper  *91*

KATE SANFORD
O  *356*

MARIE-CHRISTINE
SARDA
Atanarjuat, the Fast
Runner  *38*

BERNARD SASIA
The Town Is Quiet  *499*

PIETRO SCALIA
Black Hawk Down  *57*
Hannibal  *187*

GLEN SCANTLEBURY
Joy Ride  *244*
Lara Croft: Tomb
Raider  *276*

PERRY SCHAFFER
Under the Sun  *512*

STEPHEN R. SCHAFFER
Osmosis Jones  *371*

HERVE SCHNEID
Amelie  *14*
The Man Who Cried  *310*

JOHN SCOTT
Sexy Beast  *429*

ERIC A. SEARS
On the Line  *361*
Original Sin  *367*

SHAWN SEET
Better Than Sex  *56*

SAM SEIG
Osmosis Jones  *371*

TRUDY SHIP
Rock Star  *403*

TERILYN SHROPSHIRE
The Caveman's
Valentine  *87*

CARA SILVERMAN
Head Over Heels  *198*
See Spot Run  *421*

CARLA SIMONCELLI
Making Love  *309*

CLAIRE SIMPSON
Town and Country  *497*

DEIDRE SLEVIN
Gaudi Afternoon  *166*

DAVID LEWIS SMITH
Pootie Tang  *390*

HOWARD E. SMITH
The Glass House  *175*

KEVIN SMITH (1970-)
Jay and Silent Bob Strike
Back  *231*

NICHOLAS C. SMITH
Monkeybone  *327*

PAUL MARTIN SMITH
Behind Enemy Lines  *51*

SAM SNEADE
Sexy Beast  *429*

KARL SODERSTEIN
Lantana  *274*

SUZANNE SPANGLER
The Anniversary Party  *31*

TIM SQUYRES
Gosford Park  *182*

ZACH STAENBERG
Antitrust  *33*

MICHAEL STANLEY
Just One Time  *252*

WILLIAM STEINKAMP
Don't Say a Word  *126*
Heartbreakers  *200*

MARK STEVENS
Tigerland  *484*

MICHAEL A. STEVENSON
Cats & Dogs  *85*
Just Visiting  *253*

JIM STEWART
Monsters, Inc.  *332*

KEVIN STITT
A Knight's Tale  *271*
The Last Castle  *278*

RAVI SUBRAMANIAN
ABCD  *4*

WILLIAM CHANG SUK-
PING
In the Mood for Love  *223*

BRETT SULLIVAN
Ginger Snaps  *172*

LENKA SVAB
My Father's Angel  *345*

MARY SWEENEY
Mulholland Drive  *338*

ROBERT TATE
American Desi  *17*

DAVID TEDESCHI
Pinero  *383*

KEVIN TENT
Blow  *62*

PETER TESCHNER
Josie and the
Pussycats  *242*
Scary Movie 2  *417*

SCOTT THOMAS
When Brendan Met
Trudy  *538*

DYLAN TICHENOR
The Royal
Tenenbaums  *406*

GERD TJUR
Italian for Beginners  *229*

ROBERT L. TOMLINSON
Escanaba in da
Moonlight  *136*

CAMILLA TONIOLO
Company Man  *99*

NEIL TRAVIS
Along Came a Spider  *12*

LUDO TROCH
Everybody's Famous!  *142*
The King Is Dancing  *266*

MICHAEL TRONICK
American Outlaws  *18*

BARBARA TULLIVER
The Heist  *206*

AGNES VARDA (1928-)
The Gleaners and I  *177*

ELSA VASQUEZ
Our Lady of the
Assassins  *375*

JIM VILLONE
Too Much Sleep  *492*

MELANIE VINER-CUNEO
Stanley Kubrick: A Life in
Pictures  *461*

CHRISTIAN WAGNER
Spy Game  *457*

TREVOR WAITE
The Claim  *94*

JORDAN WALKER-
PEARLMAN
The Visit  *521*

MARTIN WALSH
Bridget Jones's Diary  *72*
Iris  *226*

MARK WARNER
Monkeybone  *327*

STAN WARNOW
Under Hellgate
Bridge  *510*

PAUL WARSCHILKA
John Carpenter's Ghosts of
Mars  *240*

EARL WATSON
The Brothers  *74*
Two Can Play That
Game  *506*

NICHOLAS WAYMAN-
HARRIS
The King Is Alive  *265*

STEVEN WELCH
Not Another Teen
Movie  *352*

JULIETTE WELFING
A Matter of Taste  *315*

TIM WELLBURN
Bride of the Wind  *71*

CRAIG WOOD
The Mexican  *323*

MIKLOS WRIGHT
3000 Miles to
Graceland  *482*

GABRIEL WYRE
Kill Me Later  *263*

HASSAN YEKTAPNAH
Djomeh  *121*

LUCIA ZUCCHETTI
The Low Down  *301*

LAUREN ZUCKERMAN
The Deep End  *114*

# Art Director Index

**STEPHEN ALESCH**
Invisible Circus  *225*
Zoolander  *542*

**GUILLAUME ARETOS**
Shrek  *437*

**JODY ASNES**
The Sleepy Time Gal  *445*

**MICHAEL ATWELL**
The Mexican  *323*

**ALAN AU**
Joe Dirt  *236*

**MARIA BAKER**
Sugar & Spice  *465*

**JACK BALLANCE**
O  *356*

**BENOIT BAROUH**
The Vertical Ray of the
Sun  *520*

**GIANCARLO BASILI**
The Son's Room  *453*

**BEN BAUER**
Crocodile Dundee in Los
Angeles  *105*

**ANN MARIE BEAUCHAMP**
Moulin Rouge  *335*

**JAMES BEIHOLD**
Jimmy Neutron: Boy
Genius  *234*

**JON BILLINGTON**
Pearl Harbor  *379*

**ANDY BISCONTINI**
Just One Time  *252*

**(PETER) JOE BLEAKLEY**
Lord of the Rings 1: The
Fellowship of the
Rings  *295*

**GREGORY BOLTON**
The Wedding Planner  *530*

**BILL BOOTH**
Crocodile Dundee in Los
Angeles  *105*

**ROGER A. BOWLES**
High Heels and Low
Lifes  *209*

**DANIEL BRADFORD**
Legally Blonde  *284*

**ANDY BRITTAN**
The Visit  *521*

**RICHARD BURGESS**
The Business of
Strangers  *80*

**MILAN BYCEK**
Divided We Fall  *120*

**DOUG BYGGDIN**
Antitrust  *33*
Rat Race  *397*

**ANDREW MAX CAHN**
Rush Hour 2  *408*

**TONY CAMPBELL**
Lantana  *274*

**DAVID CANNIZZARRO**
Jackpot  *230*

**SANDRINE CANOUX**
Under the Sand  *511*

**TERESA CARRIKER-
THAYER**
Riding in Cars with
Boys  *399*

**JOHN CHICHESTER**
Monkeybone  *327*

**BARRY CHUSID**
Domestic Disturbance  *125*

**ERIN COCHRAN**
I Am Sam  *217*

**SANDY COCHRANE**
Along Came a Spider  *12*

**CHRIS COMWELL**
Driven  *133*

**FRANCES CONNELL**
Beautiful Creatures  *47*

**KEVIN CONSTANT**
Sweet November  *471*

**CARLOS CONTI**
The Man Who Cried  *310*

**STEPHEN COOPER**
Just Visiting  *253*

**GONZALO CORDOBA**
Jump Tomorrow  *246*

**DAVID CRANK**
Hannibal  *187*

**SUSAN CULLEN**
About Adam  *5*
When Brendan Met
Trudy  *538*

**KEITH CUNNINGHAM**
Ocean's Eleven  *359*
Soul Survivors  *455*

**ROGER DANCHIK**
Session 9  *427*

**DENNIS DAVENPORT**
Angel Eyes  *27*
Don't Say a Word  *126*
Down to Earth  *131*

**CARL JOHAN DE GEER**
Together  *489*

**ROMAIN DENIS**
Human Resources  *216*

**ANDREW DESKIN**
Say It Isn't So  *415*

**KITTY DORIS-BATES**
American Pie 2  *20*

**DENISE L. DUGALLY**
America's Sweethearts  *24*

**KEVIN EGELAND**
Jeepers Creepers  *233*

**DAVID ENSLE**
Blow  *62*

**BENJAMIN FERNANDEZ**
The Others  *373*

**LAURENT FIRODE**
Happenstance  *190*

**MELISSA FRANKEL**
The Sleepy Time Gal  *445*

**JOHN FRANKISH**
Gosford Park  *182*

**GARY FREEMAN**
Captain Corelli's
Mandolin  *83*

**JOHN FRICK**
American Outlaws  *18*

**BEAT FRUTIGER**
Vanilla Sky  *518*

**JENNIFER GALVELIS**
ABCD  *4*

**GIANNI GIOVAGNONI**
The Golden Bowl  *180*

**DAVID GOETZ**
Atlantis: The Lost
Empire  *39*

**JESS GONCHOR**
15 Minutes  *155*
Kate & Leopold  *260*

**CHRIS GORAK**
The Man Who Wasn't
There  *312*

**BRANDT GORDON**
On the Line  *361*

**AUSTIN GORG**
The Brothers  *74*

**ANGELO GRAHAM**
Apocalypse Now
Redux  *35*

**T. ARV GREWAL**
Exit Wounds  *146*

**KAREN SCHULZ
GROPMAN**
The Shipping News  *435*

**PETER GRUNDY**
Glitter  *178*

**ISABELLE GUAY**
The Heist  *206*

**ROBERT GUERRA**
A Beautiful Mind  *49*

**RODRIGO GUERRERO**
ABCD  *4*

**ALEXANDER HAMMOND**
K-PAX  *255*

**ROSWELL HAMRICK**
Made  *305*

KELLY HANNAFIN
Max Keeble's Big
Move  *316*

CHASE HARLIN
Two Can Play That
Game  *506*

LAURA HARPER
Bully  *78*

SHANNON HART
In the Bedroom  *220*

CLAYTON HARTLEY
Double Take  *129*

ALISON HARVEY
Born Romantic  *67*

SARA HAULDREN
Blow Dry  *64*
Saltwater  *410*

SEAN HAWORTH
Planet of the Apes  *384*

BRYAN HEDGE
The Sleepy Time Gal  *445*

WILLIE HESLUP
3000 Miles to
Graceland  *482*

BRUCE ROBERT HILL
Monkeybone  *327*

JOHN HILL
A Knight's Tale  *271*

WILLIAM HINEY
John Carpenter's Ghosts of
Mars  *240*

BRIAN HODGE
Wet Hot American
Summer  *532*

SUSANNE HOPF
The Legend of Rita  *287*

GEOFF HUBBARD
Swordfish  *473*

LAWRENCE A. HUBBS
The Last Castle  *278*

DIANE HUGHES
Save the Last Dance  *411*

JEAN-MICHEL HUGON
The Affair of the
Necklace  *8*

ANDREW HULL
Get Over It!  *167*

KEVIN HUMENNY
Josie and the
Pussycats  *242*

CATHERINE IRCHA
See Spot Run  *421*

PHIL IVEY
Lord of the Rings 1: The
Fellowship of the
Rings  *295*

CRAIG JACKSON
Novocaine  *354*

PETER JAMISON
Mulholland Drive  *338*

HELEN JARVIS
The Pledge  *387*

KIM JENNINGS
Don't Say a Word  *126*

CAO JIUPING
The Road Home  *402*

LOUISE JOBIN
The Orphan Muses  *369*

RICHARD JOHNSON
A. I.: Artificial
Intelligence  *1*

BURTON E. JONES, JR.
Kingdom Come  *267*

JOHN J. KASARDA
Down to Earth  *131*

KEVIN KAVANAUGH
The Fast and the
Furious  *150*

BEHZAD KAZZAZI
Baran  *45*

KATTERINA KEITH-
SZALAY
Freddy Got Fingered  *162*

JOHN KING
Harry Potter and the
Sorcerer's Stone  *195*

LANCE KING
Head Over Heels  *198*

SARAH KNOWLES
The Glass House  *175*

GARY KOSKO
My First Mister  *346*

MARK KOWALSKY
Top of the Food
Chain  *494*

DIANA KUNCE
The Center of the
World  *89*

RAY LAI
Here's to Life  *208*
Suspicious River  *469*

NEIL LAMONT
Harry Potter and the
Sorcerer's Stone  *195*

MARK LANE-DAVIES
Lift  *293*

STEVEN LAWRENCE
Enemy at the Gates  *134*

ANDREW LAWS
Swordfish  *473*
Tigerland  *484*

DAVID LAZAN
One Night at
McCool's  *365*
Training Day  *501*
What's the Worst That
Could Happen?  *536*

PAO-LIN LEE
The River  *401*

MAN LIM-CHUNG
In the Mood for Love  *223*

MARK LOWRY
An Everlasting Piece  *140*

PATRICK LUMB
Behind Enemy Lines  *51*

CESAR MACARRON
The Devil's Backbone  *115*

CHRISTIAN MANN
Bride of the Wind  *71*

MARK MANSBRIDGE
John Carpenter's Ghosts of
Mars  *240*

CHERYL MARION
Suddenly Naked  *464*

ADELE MAROLF
The Musketeer  *343*

DOMINIC MASTER
Enemy at the Gates  *134*

GILES MASTERS
The Mummy Returns  *341*

IVAN MAUSSION
The Widow of Saint-
Pierre  *539*

CATY MAXEY
The Princess Diaries  *394*
Rock Star  *403*

RICHARD F. MAYS
Evolution  *144*

ANN MCKINNON
Series 7: The
Contenders  *425*

DOUG MEERDINK
Jurassic Park 3  *247*

TOM MEYER
crazy/beautiful  *103*

LLORENCE MIGUEL
Nico and Dani  *348*

BEN MORIESON
The Dish  *118*

HANNAH MOSELEY
Liam  *289*

JOHN MOTT
Tortilla Soup  *495*

CHRISTA MUNRO
Bubble Boy  *76*

ALAN E. MURAOKA
Ghost World  *170*

VACLAV NOVAK
Dark Blue World  *111*

LESLEY OAKLEY
The Most Fertile Man in
Ireland  *334*

GRACIELA ODERIGO
La Cienaga  *92*

PADRAIG O'NEILL
An Everlasting Piece  *140*

ROB OTTERSIDE
Lord of the Rings 1: The
Fellowship of the
Rings  *295*

NANCY PANKIW
Hedwig and the Angry
Inch  *204*

CLAUDE PARE
The Score  *419*

SUE PARKER
Valentine  *516*

NENAD PECUR
The Body  *66*

JAY PELISSIER
Not Another Teen
Movie  *352*

JULIE PHILPOTT
Snatch  *447*

KEVIN PHIPPS
Spy Game  *457*

GIORA PORTER
The Body  *66*

MARK RAGGET
From Hell  *164*

IRAJ RAMINFAR
The Circle  *93*

VIRGINIA RANDOLPH-
WEAVER
Double Take  *129*

BILL REA
Ali  *10*

ANTHONY READING
The Mummy Returns  *341*

SETH REED
Rat Race  *397*

TOM RETA
The Score  *419*

LUCY RICHARDSON
The Golden Bowl  *180*

BRADFORD RICKER
Dr. Dolittle 2  *123*

MARK RICKER
Just Looking  *250*

# Music Index

Osmosis Jones  *371*

**CLIFF EIDELMAN**
An American
Rhapsody  *22*

**DANNY ELFMAN (1953-)**
Planet of the Apes  *384*
Spy Kids  *459*

**STEPHEN ENDELMAN**
Bride of the Wind  *71*

**BRIAN ENO**
The Million Dollar
Hotel  *325*

**PASCAL ESTEVE**
The Widow of Saint-
Pierre  *539*

**GEORGE FENTON**
Bread and Roses  *68*
Summer Catch  *467*

**PIERRE FOLDES**
L.I.E.  *273*

**IVANO FOSSATI**
The Holy Tongue  *212*

**JOHN (GIANNI) FRIZZELL**
**(1966-)**
Josie and the
Pussycats  *242*

**MICHAEL GALASSO**
In the Mood for Love  *223*

**JAMES GELFAND**
The Orphan Muses  *369*

**LISA GERRARD**
Ali  *10*

**GILBERTO GIL**
Me You Them  *320*

**GLOVER GILL**
Waking Life  *524*

**GIRLS AGAINST BOYS**
Series 7: The
Contenders  *425*

**MURRAY GOLD**
Beautiful Creatures  *47*

**ELLIOT GOLDENTHAL**
Final Fantasy: The Spirits
Within  *158*

**JERRY GOLDSMITH**
**(1929-)**
Along Came a Spider  *12*
The Last Castle  *278*

**OSVALDO GOLIJOY**
The Man Who Cried  *310*

**JEAN-PHILIPPE GOUDE**
A Matter of Taste  *315*

**HARRY GREGSON-**
**WILLIAMS**
Shrek  *437*
Spy Game  *457*

**ANDREA GUERRA**
Ignorant Fairies  *219*

**RICHARD HARTLEY**
When Brendan Met
Trudy  *538*

**MICK HARVEY**
Chopper  *91*

**PAUL HASLINGER**
crazy/beautiful  *103*

**JOHN HASSELL**
The Million Dollar
Hotel  *325*

**REINHOLD HEIL**
The Princess and the
Warrior  *393*

**DAVID HIRSCHFELDER**
Better Than Sex  *56*

**DAVID HOLMES**
Ocean's Eleven  *359*

**JAMES HORNER (1953-)**
A Beautiful Mind  *49*
Enemy at the Gates  *134*
Iris  *226*

**JAMES NEWTON**
**HOWARD (1951-)**
America's Sweethearts  *24*
Atlantis: The Lost
Empire  *39*

**SHINICHIRO IKEBE**
Warm Water Under a Red
Bridge  *526*

**MARK ISHAM (1951-)**
Don't Say a Word  *126*
Hardball  *193*
Life as a House  *291*
The Majestic  *307*
Save the Last Dance  *411*

**JEAN-CHARLES JARRELL**
The Taste of Others  *479*

**ADRIAN JOHNSTON**
About Adam  *5*

**JAMES JOHNSTON**
The Most Fertile Man in
Ireland  *334*

**TIM JONES**
The Forsaken  *160*

**TREVOR JONES (1949-)**
From Hell  *164*

**DAVID JULYAN**
Memento  *321*

**PAUL KELLY**
Lantana  *274*

**ROLFE KENT (1963-)**
Kate & Leopold  *260*

Legally Blonde  *284*
Someone Like You  *451*
Town and Country  *497*

**JOHN KIMBOUGH**
Jump Tomorrow  *246*

**DAVID KITAY**
Ghost World  *170*
Tomcats  *491*

**JOHNNY KLIMEK**
The Princess and the
Warrior  *393*

**DAVID KRYSTAL**
Top of the Food
Chain  *494*

**NICK LAIRD-CLOWES**
Invisible Circus  *225*

**JOHN LANG**
Love Come Down  *299*

**DANIEL LANOIS**
The Million Dollar
Hotel  *325*

**NATHAN LARSEN**
Tigerland  *484*

**ALEXANDER LASARENKO**
The Business of
Strangers  *80*
Dinner Rush  *116*

**DAVID LAWRENCE**
American Pie 2  *20*
Company Man  *99*

**GUILLAUME LEKEU**
Sentimental Destiny  *422*

**KRISHNA LEVY**
Dad on the Run  *110*

**DANIEL LICHT**
Soul Survivors  *455*

**ZHANG LIDA**
Shadow Magic  *431*

**EVAN LURIE**
Happy Accidents  *191*

**DON MACDONALD**
Suspicious River  *469*

**PADDY MALONEY**
Under the Sun  *512*

**MARK MANCINA**
Domestic Disturbance  *125*
Training Day  *501*

**ANTHONY MARINELLI**
15 Minutes  *155*

**STUART MATTHEWMAN**
Jackpot  *230*

**LASZLO MELIS**
Glamour  *174*

**MARCUS MILLER**
Trumpet of the Swan  *503*

Two Can Play That
Game  *506*

**STEPHAN MOCCIO**
Under Hellgate
Bridge  *510*

**CHARLIE MOLE**
High Heels and Low
Lifes  *209*

**DEBORAH MOLLISON**
Simon Magnus  *443*

**ENNIO MORRICONE**
**(1928-)**
Making Love  *309*

**MARK MOTHERSBAUGH**
The Royal
Tenenbaums  *406*
Sugar & Spice  *465*

**JOHN MURPHY**
Liam  *289*
Snatch  *447*

**PETER NASHEL**
The Deep End  *114*

**JAVIER NAVARRETE**
The Devil's Backbone  *115*

**KATHY NELSON**
Rush Hour 2  *408*

**RENATO NERO**
Kill Me Later  *263*

**ERIC NEVEUX**
Intimacy  *224*

**DAVID NEWMAN (1954-)**
The Affair of the
Necklace  *8*
Dr. Dolittle 2  *123*

**RANDY NEWMAN (1943-)**
Monsters, Inc.  *332*

**THOMAS NEWMAN**
In the Bedroom  *220*

**MICHAEL NYMAN**
The Claim  *94*

**JOHN O'BRIEN**
Made  *305*

**PAUL O'LEARY**
Keep the River On Your
Right: A Modern
Cannibal Tale  *262*

**ROWAN OLIVER**
Last Resort  *281*

**JOHN OTTMAN**
Bubble Boy  *76*

**AHMAD PEJMAN**
Baran  *45*

**MICHAEL PENN**
The Anniversary Party  *31*

# Performer Index

CAROLINE AARON (1952-)
Joe Dirt *236*

HOSSEIN ABEDINI
Baran *45*

ABIOLA WENDY ABRAMS
Jump Tomorrow *246*

VICTORIA ABRIL (1959-)
101 Reykjavik *364*

STEFANO ACCORSI
Ignorant Fairies *219*
The Son's Room *453*

KIRK ACEVEDO
Dinner Rush *116*

JANE ADAMS (1965-)
The Anniversary Party *31*

JOEY LAUREN ADAMS
(1971-)
Dr. Dolittle 2 (V) *123*
Jay and Silent Bob Strike
Back *231*

SHULAMIT ADAR
Voyages *523*

MILO ADDICA
Monster's Ball *330*

MARK ADDY (1963-)
Down to Earth *131*
A Knight's Tale *271*

TUNDE ADEBIMPE
Jump Tomorrow *246*

MARTIN ADJEMIAN
La Cienaga *92*

BEN AFFLECK (1972-)
Jay and Silent Bob Strike
Back *231*
Pearl Harbor *379*

CASEY AFFLECK (1975-)
American Pie 2 *20*
Ocean's Eleven *359*
Soul Survivors *455*

ALEXANDRINE AGOSTINI
The Left Hand Side of the
Fridge *283*

PAUL AHMARANI
The Left Hand Side of the
Fridge *283*

DANNY AIELLO (1933-)
Dinner Rush *116*

LIAM AIKEN
Sweet November *471*

RASHID AKBARI
Djomeh *121*

FATEMEH CHERAGH
AKHTAR
The Day I Became a
Woman *112*

ADEWALE AKINNUOYE-
AGBAJE
The Mummy Returns *341*

ANTONIO ALBANESE
The Holy Tongue *212*

JOEY ALBRIGHT
Escanaba in da
Moonlight *136*

MOSCU ALCALAY
Voyages *523*

JASON ALEXANDER
(1959-)
Shallow Hal *432*
Trumpet of the Swan
(V) *503*

SUSAN ALGER
Lift *293*

TATYANA ALI
The Brothers *74*

NAHEEM ALLAH
Lift *293*

KAREN ALLEN (1951-)
In the Bedroom *220*

TIM ALLEN (1953-)
Joe Somebody *238*

WOODY ALLEN (1935-)
Company Man *99*
The Curse of the Jade
Scorpion *107*

JAMES ALLODI
Top of the Food
Chain *494*

MARIAM PALVIN
ALMANI
The Circle *93*

EDAN ALTERMAN
Time of Favor *487*

BRUCE ALTMAN
L.I.E. *273*

ANNE ALVARO
The Taste of Others *479*

CHISCO AMADO
Nico and Dani *348*

ANTHONY ANDERSON
(1970-)
Exit Wounds *146*
Kingdom Come *267*
See Spot Run *421*
Two Can Play That
Game *506*

GILLIAN ANDERSON
(1968-)
House of Mirth *213*

MICHAEL J. ANDERSON
Mulholland Drive *338*

MILES ANDERSON
The King Is Alive *265*

VITALBA ANDREA
Bread and Tulips *70*

FELICE ANDREASI
Bread and Tulips *70*

DAVID ANDREWS (1952-)
Hannibal *187*

JULIE ANDREWS (1935-)
The Princess Diaries *394*

JACK ANGEL
A. I.: Artificial Intelligence
(V) *1*

JENNIFER ANISTON
(1969-)
Rock Star *403*

FLAVIA MARCO
ANTONIO (1978-)
Behind the Sun *54*

CHRISTINA APPLEGATE
(1971-)
Just Visiting *253*

ANNABELLE APSION
From Hell *164*

MONIR ARAB
The Circle *93*

TOMAS ARANA (1959-)
Pearl Harbor *379*

MICHAEL ARANOV
Hedwig and the Angry
Inch *204*

NATHANIEL ARCAND
American Outlaws *18*

VICTOR ARGO (1934-)
Angel Eyes *27*
Don't Say a Word *126*
Fast Food, Fast
Women *152*

PEDRO ARMENDARIZ, JR.
(1930-)
Original Sin *367*

NORMAN ARMOUR
Suspicious River *469*

ALUN ARMSTRONG
(1946-)
The Mummy Returns *341*

KERRY ARMSTRONG
Lantana *274*

PETER HENRY
ARNATSIAQ
Atanarjuat, the Fast
Runner *38*

WILL ARNETT
Series 7: The Contenders
(N) *425*

JEANETTA ARNETTE
The Shipping News *435*

TOM ARNOLD (1959-)
Exit Wounds *146*

DAVID ARQUETTE (1971-)
See Spot Run *421*
3000 Miles to
Graceland *482*

ARIANE ASCARIDE
The Adventures of Felix *7*
The Town Is Quiet *499*

RENEE ASHERSON (1920-)
The Others *373*

KATE ASHFIELD
The Low Down *301*

ED ASNER (1929-)
The Animal *29*

RITA ASSEMANY
Behind the Sun *54*

HANS-JORG ASSMANN
Dark Blue World *111*

SEAN ASTIN (1971-)
Lord of the Rings 1: The
Fellowship of the
Rings *295*

ROBERT ATIKO
Sexy Beast *429*

EILEEN ATKINS (1934-)
Gosford Park *182*

ROWAN ATKINSON
(1955-)
Maybe Baby *318*
Rat Race *397*

DAVE ATTELL
Pootie Tang *390*

JULIET AUBREY
Iris *226*

MICHEL AUMONT (1936-)
The Closet *96*

DANIEL AUTEUIL (1950-)
The Closet *96*
The Widow of Saint-
Pierre *539*

ERIK AVARI
Planet of the Apes *384*

AKI AVNI
Time of Favor *487*

ERIC AXEN
American Desi *17*

CHARLOTTE AYANNA
Training Day *501*

LORRY AYERS
Top of the Food
Chain *494*

DAN AYKROYD (1952-)
The Curse of the Jade
Scorpion *107*
Evolution *144*
House of Mirth *213*
Pearl Harbor *379*

JOHN AYLWARD
Just Visiting *253*

FRASER AYRES
Intimacy *224*

HANK AZARIA (1964-)
America's Sweethearts *24*

OBBA BABATUNDE
The Visit *521*

KEVIN BACON (1958-)
Novocaine *354*

JEAN-PIERRE BACRI
(1951-)
The Taste of Others *479*

ANGELO BADALAMENTI
(1937-)
Mulholland Drive *338*

MICHAEL BADALUCCO
(1954-)
The Man Who Wasn't
There *312*

SARAH BADEL (1943-)
Just Visiting *253*

DIEDRICH BADER (1966-)
Jay and Silent Bob Strike
Back *231*

MINA (BADIYI) BADIE
The Anniversary Party *31*

DIEGO BAENAS
La Cienaga *92*

ZAHRA BAHRAMI
Baran *45*

WU BAI
Time and Tide *486*

MITSUKO BAISHO
Warm Water Under a Red
Bridge *526*

DEE BAKER
Trumpet of the Swan
(V) *503*

DYLAN BAKER (1958-)
Along Came a Spider *12*

KATHY BAKER (1950-)
The Glass House *175*

SIMON BAKER (1969-)
The Affair of the
Necklace *8*

SCOTT BAKULA (1955-)
Life as a House *291*

BOB BALABAN (1945-)
Ghost World *170*
Gosford Park *182*
The Majestic *307*
The Mexican *323*

LEONORA BALCARCE
La Cienaga *92*

ADAM BALDWIN (1962-)
Jackpot *230*

ALEC BALDWIN (1958-)
Cats & Dogs (V) *85*
Final Fantasy: The Spirits
Within (V) *158*
Pearl Harbor *379*
The Royal Tenenbaums
(N) *406*

CHRISTIAN BALE (1974-)
Captain Corelli's
Mandolin *83*

JEANNE BALIBAR
Va Savoir *514*

SAMUEL BALL
The Last Castle *278*

EDOARDO BALLERINI
Dinner Rush *116*

ANDERSON
BALLESTEROS
Our Lady of the
Assassins *375*

ERIC BANA (1968-)
Black Hawk Down *57*
Chopper *91*

ANNE BANCROFT (1931-)
Heartbreakers *200*

ANTONIO BANDERAS
(1960-)
The Body *66*
Original Sin *367*
Spy Kids *459*

PIERRE BANDERET
The Town Is Quiet *499*

AGNES BANFALVY
An American
Rhapsody *22*

JONATHAN BANKS (1947-)
Crocodile Dundee in Los
Angeles *105*

ELLEN BARKIN (1955-)
Someone Like You *451*

GYORGY BARKO
Glamour *174*

MARIA BARRANCO (1961-)
Gaudi Afternoon *166*

ADRIANA BARRAZA
Amores Perros *26*

CHANTAL BARRE
Human Resources *216*

CHRIS (CHRISTOPHER)
BARRIE (1960-)
Lara Croft: Tomb
Raider *276*

RAYMOND J. BARRY
(1939-)
The Deep End *114*
Training Day *501*

THOM BARRY
The Fast and the
Furious *150*

DREW BARRYMORE
(1975-)
Riding in Cars with
Boys *399*
Skipped Parts *444*

MISCHA BARTON (1986-)
Lost and Delirious *297*
Skipped Parts *444*

SKYE MCCOLE
BARTUSIAK
Don't Say a Word *126*
Riding in Cars with
Boys *399*

GIULIO BASE
The Holy Tongue *212*

MARIANNE BASLER
Va Savoir *514*

LANCE BASS
On the Line *361*

TAMARA LA SEON BASS
Baby Boy *41*

ANGELA BASSETT (1958-)
The Score *419*

OTHON BASTOS (1933-)
Behind the Sun *54*

ALAN BATES (1934-)
Gosford Park *182*

KATHY BATES (1948-)
American Outlaws *18*
Rat Race *397*

GUISEPPE BATTISTON
Bread and Tulips *70*

PATRICK BAUCHAU
(1938-)
Jackpot (V) *230*

VANESSA BAUCHE
Amores Perros *26*

SILVIA BAYLE
La Cienaga *92*

JORDAN BAYNE
Under Hellgate
Bridge *510*

ADAM BEACH (1972-)
Joe Dirt *236*

KATE BEAHAN
Chopper *91*

JENNIFER BEALS (1963-)
The Anniversary Party *31*

SEAN BEAN (1959-)
Don't Say a Word *126*
Lord of the Rings 1: The
Fellowship of the
Rings *295*

EMMANUELLE BEART
(1965-)
Sentimental Destiny *422*

WARREN BEATTY (1937-)
Town and Country *497*

GARCELLE BEAUVAIS
(1966-)
Double Take *129*

GRAHAM BECKEL (1955-)
Hardball *193*
Pearl Harbor *379*

KATE BECKINSALE (1974-)
The Golden Bowl *180*
Pearl Harbor *379*
Serendipity *423*

PURVA BEDI
American Desi *17*

MAX BEESLEY (1971-)
Glitter *178*
Kill Me Later *263*

JACQUES BOUDET
The Town Is Quiet *499*

LILY BOULOGNE
Happenstance *190*

FREDERIQUE BOURALY
Happenstance *190*

JOHN BOURGEOIS
Ginger Snaps *172*

CHRISTOPHER BOWEN
Gaudi Afternoon *166*

JULIE BOWEN (1970-)
Joe Somebody *238*

MICHAEL RAY BOWER
Evolution *144*

TOM BOWER
Hearts in Atlantis *202*
The Million Dollar
Hotel *325*

JESSICA BOWMAN
Joy Ride *244*

TODD BOYCE
Spy Game *457*

BILLY BOYD
Lord of the Rings 1: The
Fellowship of the
Rings *295*

DARREN BOYD
High Heels and Low
Lifes *209*

LYNDA BOYD
My Father's Angel *345*

PETER BOYLE (1933-)
Monster's Ball *330*

LORRAINE BRACCO
(1954-)
Riding in Cars with
Boys *399*

CATHLEEN BRADLEY
About Adam *5*

CHARLOTTE BRADLEY
About Adam *5*

DAVID BRADLEY
Harry Potter and the
Sorcerer's Stone *195*
The King Is Alive *265*

ORLA BRADY
The Luzhin Defence *303*

SONIA BRAGA (1951-)
Angel Eyes *27*

MARLON BRANDO (1924-)
Apocalypse Now
Redux *35*
The Score *419*

BENJAMIN BRATT (1963-)
Pinero *383*

TONI BRAXTON (1968-)
Kingdom Come *267*

JAY BRAZEAU (1945-)
Head Over Heels *198*
Suspicious River *469*

JONATHAN BRECK
Jeepers Creepers *233*

RICHARD BREMMER
Just Visiting *253*

EWEN BREMNER
Black Hawk Down *57*
Pearl Harbor *379*
Snatch *447*

EILEEN BRENNAN (1935-)
Jeepers Creepers *233*

MARITA BREUER
The Princess and the
Warrior *393*

JORDANA BREWSTER
(1980-)
The Fast and the
Furious *150*
Invisible Circus *225*

JEFF BRIDGES (1949-)
K-PAX *255*

BRENT BRISCOE (1961-)
Double Take *129*
Driven *133*
The Majestic *307*
Mulholland Drive *338*
Say It Isn't So *415*

JIM BROADBENT (1949-)
Bridget Jones's Diary *72*
Iris *226*
Moulin Rouge *335*

ADRIEN BRODY (1976-)
The Affair of the
Necklace *8*
Bread and Roses *68*

ELEANOR BRON (1940-)
Iris *226*
House of Mirth *213*

PAUL BROOKE
The Affair of the
Necklace *8*

ALBERT BROOKS (1947-)
My First Mister *346*

ANGELLE BROOKS
The Brothers *74*

AVERY BROOKS (1948-)
15 Minutes *155*

PIERCE BROSNAN (1953-)
The Tailor of Panama *475*

BILLE BROWN
The Dish *118*

BOBBY BROWN
Two Can Play That
Game *506*

ORLANDO BROWN
Max Keeble's Big
Move *316*

SAMANTHA BROWN
Lift *293*

CHRISTINE BRUCHER
The Town Is Quiet *499*

THERESE BRUNNANDER
Faithless *148*
Together *489*

DYLAN BRUNO (1972-)
The One *363*

LARRY BRYGGMAN
Spy Game *457*

MAURICE BULLARD
The Last Castle *278*

CARA BUONO (1974-)
Happy Accidents *191*
Two Ninas *508*

MICHAEL BURGESS
Black Knight *60*

BILLY BURKE
Along Came a Spider *12*

MARYLOUISE BURKE
Series 7: The
Contenders *425*

CAROL BURNETT (1933-)
Trumpet of the Swan
(V) *503*

BROOKE BURNS
Shallow Hal *432*

EDWARD BURNS (1968-)
15 Minutes *155*
Sidewalks of New
York *439*

JERE BURNS (1954-)
Crocodile Dundee in Los
Angeles *105*

MEGAN BURNS
Liam *289*

TY BURRELL (1967-)
Black Hawk Down *57*
Evolution *144*

HEDY BURRESS
Valentine *516*

JACKIE BURROUGHS
(1938-)
Lost and Delirious *297*

COREY BURTON
Atlantis: The Lost Empire
(V) *39*

LEVAR BURTON (1957-)
Ali *10*

STEVE (STEPHEN)
BURTON (1970-)
The Last Castle *278*

STEVE BUSCEMI (1957-)
Domestic Disturbance *125*
Final Fantasy: The Spirits
Within (V) *158*
Ghost World *170*

Monsters, Inc. (V) *332*

JAKE BUSEY (1972-)
Tomcats *491*

MANUEL BUSQUETS
Our Lady of the
Assassins *375*

HUMBERTO BUSTO
Amores Perros *26*

TOM BUTLER
Josie and the
Pussycats *242*

MAGGIE BUTTERFIELD
Top of the Food
Chain *494*

MARGHERITA BUY
Ignorant Fairies *219*

EUGENE BYRD
Lift *293*

GABRIEL BYRNE (1950-)
Making Love *309*

MICHAEL BYRNE
The Musketeer *343*


SCOTT CAAN (1976-)
American Outlaws *18*
Novocaine *354*
Ocean's Eleven *359*

NICOLAS CAGE (1964-)
Captain Corelli's
Mandolin *83*

DEAN CAIN (1966-)
Rat Race *397*

DAVID CALDER
The King Is Alive *265*

PAUL CALDERON
The Last Castle *278*

CORONJI CALHOUN
Monster's Ball *330*

JAMES CALLIS
Bridget Jones's Diary *72*

SIMON CALLOW (1949-)
No Man's Land *349*

PHILIPPE CALVARIO
Intimacy *224*

COLLEEN CAMP (1953-)
Apocalypse Now
Redux *35*

BRUCE CAMPBELL (1958-)
The Majestic *307*

GERARDO CAMPBELL
Amores Perros *26*

MICHAEL LEYDON
CAMPBELL
Sidewalks of New
York *439*

SERGE COCKBURN
Crocodile Dundee in Los
Angeles *105*

SCOTT COFFEY (1967-)
Mulholland Drive *338*

NATHAN COGAN
Voyages *523*

ENRICO COLANTONI
(1963-)
A. I.: Artificial
Intelligence *1*

ROSALYN COLEMAN
Our Song *376*

LEN COLLIN
High Heels and Low
Lifes *209*

CLIFTON (GONZALEZ)
COLLINS, JR.
The Last Castle *278*
Tigerland *484*

VINCE COLOSIMO
Chopper *91*
Lantana *274*

ROBBIE COLTRANE
(1950-)
From Hell *164*
Harry Potter and the
Sorcerer's Stone *195*

HOLLY MARIE COMBS
(1973-)
Ocean's Eleven *359*

SEAN (PUFFY, PUFF
DADDY, P. DIDDY)
COMBS (1969-)
Made *305*
Monster's Ball *330*

O'NEAL COMPTON (1951-)
Kill Me Later *263*

JENNIFER CONNELLY
(1970-)
A Beautiful Mind *49*

BILLY CONNOLLY (1942-)
An Everlasting Piece *140*

PADDY CONSIDINE
Born Romantic *67*
Last Resort *281*

WILLIAM CONVERSE-
ROBERTS
Bandits *43*

KEVIN CONWAY (1942-)
Black Knight *60*

MICHAEL COOK
Signs & Wonders *441*

RACHAEL LEIGH COOK
(1979-)
Antitrust *33*
Blow Dry *64*
Josie and the
Pussycats *242*

JENNIFER COOLIDGE
American Pie 2 *20*
Down to Earth *131*
Legally Blonde *284*
Pootie Tang *390*

COOLIO (1963-)
Get Over It! *167*

BRADLEY COOPER
Wet Hot American
Summer *532*

ZANE R. (LIL' ZANE)
COPELAND, JR.
(1982-)
Dr. Dolittle 2 *123*

JOHN CORBETT (1962-)
Dinner Rush *116*
Serendipity *423*

IMELDA CORCORAN
Better Than Sex *56*

DAVID COREY
Liam *289*

PROF. IRWIN COREY
(1912-)
The Curse of the Jade
Scorpion *107*

DANIELLE CORMACK
The Price of Milk *392*

MARIE-ANDREE
CORNEILLE
The Left Hand Side of the
Fridge *283*

ALEX CORRADO
Dinner Rush *116*

BUD CORT (1950-)
The Million Dollar
Hotel *325*

DANIEL COSGROVE
Valentine *516*

JAMES COSTA
L.I.E. *273*

PAULO COSTANZO
Josie and the
Pussycats *242*

BOB COSTAS (1951-)
Pootie Tang *390*

NIKOLAJ COSTER-
WALDAU (1970-)
Black Hawk Down *57*

KEVIN COSTNER (1955-)
3000 Miles to
Graceland *482*

MICHEL COTE
Life After Love *290*

MARISA COUGHLAN
(1973-)
Freddy Got Fingered *162*

VICTOR COWIE
The Law of
Enclosures *282*

BRIAN COX (1946-)
The Affair of the
Necklace *8*
L.I.E. *273*
Saltwater *410*

DEBORAH COX
Love Come Down *299*

RONNY COX (1938-)
American Outlaws *18*

COURTENEY COX
ARQUETTE (1964-)
3000 Miles to
Graceland *482*

PETER COYOTE (1942-)
Suddenly Naked *464*

DANIEL CRAIG (1968-)
Lara Croft: Tomb
Raider *276*

KENNETH CRANHAM
(1944-)
Born Romantic *67*
The Most Fertile Man in
Ireland *334*

PATRICK CRANSHAW
Bubble Boy *76*

WES CRAVEN (1939-)
Jay and Silent Bob Strike
Back *231*

BRUNO CREMER (1929-)
Under the Sand *511*

WENDY CREWSON (1956-)
Suddenly Naked *464*

MISSY (MELISSA) CRIDER
(1974-)
Mulholland Drive *338*

DAVID CROSS (1964-)
Scary Movie 2 *417*

LANCE CROUTHER
Pootie Tang *390*

RUSSELL CROWE (1964-)
A Beautiful Mind *49*

TOM CRUISE (1962-)
Stanley Kubrick: A Life in
Pictures (N) *461*
Vanilla Sky *518*

PENELOPE CRUZ (1974-)
Blow *62*
Captain Corelli's
Mandolin *83*
Vanilla Sky *518*

RAYMOND CRUZ
Training Day *501*

BILLY CRYSTAL (1947-)
America's Sweethearts *24*
Monsters, Inc. (V) *332*

MARTON CSOKAS
Lord of the Rings 1: The
Fellowship of the
Rings *295*

DAVID CUBITT (1965-)
Ali *10*
The Perfect Son *382*

ALAN CUMMING (1965-)
The Anniversary Party *31*
Josie and the
Pussycats *242*
Spy Kids *459*
Company Man *99*

MARTIN CUMMINS (1969-)
Love Come Down *299*

TRAN MANH CUONG
The Vertical Ray of the
Sun *520*

TONY CURRAN
Pearl Harbor *379*

TIM CURRY (1946-)
Scary Movie 2 *417*

CLIFFORD CURTIS (1968-)
Blow *62*
The Majestic *307*
Training Day *501*

JAMIE LEE CURTIS (1958-)
The Tailor of Panama *475*

JOHN CUSACK (1966-)
America's Sweethearts *24*
Serendipity *423*

SORCHA CUSACK
Snatch *447*

BILLY RAY CYRUS
Mulholland Drive *338*

ZSUZSI CZINKOCZI
An American
Rhapsody *22*

DA BRAT (1974-)
Glitter *178*

WILLEM DAFOE (1955-)
Pavilion of Women *378*

JUNI DAHR
Faithless *148*

NADIA DAJANI
Sidewalks of New
York *439*
Happy Accidents *191*

JENNIFER DALE (1955-)
Love Come Down *299*

SUSAN DALIAN
The Brothers *74*

TIMOTHY DALTON
(1944-)
American Outlaws *18*

CARSON DALY
Josie and the
Pussycats *242*

MATT DAMON (1970-)
Jay and Silent Bob Strike
Back *231*
Ocean's Eleven *359*

JORDAN DORRANCE
The Deep End  *114*

ILLEANA DOUGLAS
(1965-)
Ghost World  *170*

MICHAEL DOUGLAS
(1944-)
Don't Say a Word  *126*
One Night at
McCool's  *365*

SHIRLEY DOUGLAS
The Law of
Enclosures  *282*

SHAWN DOYLE
Don't Say a Word  *126*
The Majestic  *307*

POLLY DRAPER (1957-)
Dinner Rush  *116*

DR. DRE (1965-)
Training Day  *501*

KATIE DRINKWATER
Last Resort  *281*

MINNIE DRIVER (1971-)
High Heels and Low
Lifes  *209*

LIMA DUARTE
Me You Them  *320*

MICHAEL DUCHAUSSOY
(1938-)
The Widow of Saint-
Pierre  *539*

DAVID DUCHOVNY
(1960-)
Evolution  *144*
Zoolander  *542*

VERONICA DUFFY
Nora  *351*

BILL DUKE (1943-)
Exit Wounds  *146*

JOSE DUMONT
Behind the Sun  *54*

MICHAEL CLARKE
DUNCAN (1957-)
Cats & Dogs (V)  *85*
Planet of the Apes  *384*
See Spot Run  *421*

NORA DUNN (1952-)
Heartbreakers  *200*
Max Keeble's Big
Move  *316*
What's the Worst That
Could Happen?  *536*

KIRSTEN DUNST (1982-)
crazy/beautiful  *103*
Get Over It!  *167*

JAROSLAV DUSEK
Divided We Fall  *120*

ELIZA DUSHKU (1980-)
Jay and Silent Bob Strike
Back  *231*

Soul Survivors  *455*

ANDRE DUSSOLLIER
(1946-)
Amelie (N)  *14*

CLEA DUVALL (1977-)
John Carpenter's Ghosts of
Mars  *240*

ROBERT DUVALL (1931-)
Apocalypse Now
Redux  *35*

DANNY DYER
Greenfingers  *185*
High Heels and Low
Lifes  *209*

RODNEY EASTMAN
The Caveman's
Valentine  *87*

LUKE EBERL (1986-)
Planet of the Apes  *384*

ERIQ EBOUANEY
Lumumba  *302*

CHRISTOPHER
ECCLESTON (1964-)
Invisible Circus  *225*
The Others  *373*

EMILIO ECHEVERRIA
Amores Perros  *26*

AARON ECKHART (1968-)
The Pledge  *387*

RICHARD EDSON (1954-)
The Million Dollar
Hotel  *325*

ANTHONY EDWARDS
(1962-)
Jackpot  *230*

STACY EDWARDS (1965-)
Driven  *133*

CARMEN EJOGO (1975-)
What's the Worst That
Could Happen?  *536*

RON ELDARD (1965-)
Black Hawk Down  *57*

KEVIN ELDON
High Heels and Low
Lifes  *209*

CARMEN ELECTRA (1972-)
Get Over It!  *167*

JENNA ELFMAN (1971-)
Town and Country  *497*

SHANNON ELIZABETH
(1973-)
American Pie 2  *20*
Jay and Silent Bob Strike
Back  *231*
Tomcats  *491*

HECTOR ELIZONDO
(1936-)
The Princess Diaries  *394*

Tortilla Soup  *495*

JEREMIE ELKAIM
Come Undone  *98*

CHRIS ELLIOTT (1960-)
Osmosis Jones  *371*
Scary Movie 2  *417*

DAVID ELLIOTT
Ali  *10*

SHAWN ELLIOTT
Double Take  *129*

A. DELON ELLIS, JR.
Hardball  *193*

AUNJANUE ELLIS
The Caveman's
Valentine  *87*

DIDIER EMILE-
WOLDERMARD
Human Resources  *216*

COLETTE EMMANUELLE
The King Is Dancing  *266*

LENA ENDRE (1955-)
Faithless  *148*

KELLY ENDRESZ-
BANLAKI
An American
Rhapsody  *22*

KAROLY EPERIES
Glamour  *174*

MIKE EPPS
Dr. Dolittle 2 (V)  *123*

ADRIANE FORLANA
ERDOS
ABCD  *4*

R. LEE ERMEY (1944-)
Saving Silverman  *413*
Skipped Parts  *444*

GIANCARLO ESPOSITO
(1958-)
Ali  *10*
Monkeybone  *327*
Pinero  *383*

JENNIFER ESPOSITO
(1973-)
Don't Say a Word  *126*
Just One Time  *252*

TREVA ETIENNE
Black Hawk Down  *57*

CHRIS EVANS
Not Another Teen
Movie  *352*

CHAD EVERETT (1936-)
Mulholland Drive  *338*

PETER EYRE (1942-)
The Affair of the
Necklace  *8*
The Golden Bowl  *180*

FABIO (1961-)
Bubble Boy  *76*

PETER FACINELLI (1973-)
Riding in Cars with
Boys  *399*

DONALD ADEOSUN
FAISON (1974-)
Josie and the
Pussycats  *242*

FRANKIE FAISON (1949-)
Down to Earth  *131*
Hannibal  *187*
The Sleepy Time Gal  *445*

MARIANNE FAITHFULL
(1946-)
Intimacy  *224*

JONAS FALK
Under the Sun  *512*

PETER FALK (1927-)
Corky Romano  *101*
Made  *305*

SIOBHAN FALLON
What's the Worst That
Could Happen?  *536*

ROGER FAN
Corky Romano  *101*

DAKOTA FANNING
I Am Sam  *217*

MOJHAN FARAMARZI
The Circle  *93*

DENNIS FARINA (1944-)
Sidewalks of New
York  *439*
Snatch  *447*

DANIELA FARINACCI
Lantana  *274*

ANNA FARIS
Scary Movie 2  *417*

GARY FARMER (1953-)
The Score  *419*
Unconquering the Last
Frontier (N)  *509*

VERA FARMIGA
15 Minutes  *155*

COLIN FARRELL (1976-)
American Outlaws  *18*
Tigerland  *484*

JOEY FATONE
On the Line  *361*

FAUDEL
Happenstance  *190*

JON FAVREAU (1966-)
Made  *305*

DENISE FAYE
American Pie 2  *20*

ANGELA FEATHERSTONE
Skipped Parts  *444*

BRENDAN FEHR (1977-)
The Forsaken *160*
Kill Me Later *263*

ODED FEHR (1970-)
The Mummy Returns *341*

ERIC FELDMAN
Happenstance *190*

TOVAH FELDSHUH (1952-)
Happy Accidents *191*

TOM FELTON
Harry Potter and the
Sorcerer's Stone *195*

COLM FEORE
The Caveman's
Valentine *87*
Pearl Harbor *379*
The Perfect Son *382*

CRAIG FERGUSON
Born Romantic *67*

ISABELLA FERRARI
The Holy Tongue *212*

WILL FERRELL (1968-)
Jay and Silent Bob Strike
Back *231*
Zoolander *542*

MARTIN FERRERO
The Tailor of Panama *475*

DAN FERRO
Blow *62*

GLENN FICARRA
Cats & Dogs (V) *85*

WILLIAM FICHTNER
(1956-)
Black Hawk Down *57*
Pearl Harbor *379*
What's the Worst That
Could Happen? *536*

DAVID FIELD
Chopper *91*

SALLY FIELD (1946-)
Say It Isn't So *415*

JOSEPH FIENNES (1970-)
Enemy at the Gates *134*

EFRAIN FIGUEROA
The Visit *521*

TRAVIS FINE
Tomcats *491*

STICKY FINGAZ
Lift *293*

JOHN FIORE
Hit and Runway *211*
Ocean's Eleven *359*

COLIN FIRTH (1961-)
Bridget Jones's Diary *72*

PETER FIRTH (1953-)
Pearl Harbor *379*

LAURENCE "LARRY"
FISHBURNE (1963-)
Apocalypse Now
Redux *35*
Osmosis Jones (V) *371*

CARRIE FISHER (1956-)
Jay and Silent Bob Strike
Back *231*

NOEL FISHER
Max Keeble's Big
Move *316*

GLENN FITZGERALD
Series 7: The
Contenders *425*

TAC FITZGERALD (1981-)
Black Hawk Down *57*

TARA FITZGERALD
(1968-)
Dark Blue World *111*

COLLEEN (ANN)
(VITAMIN C)
FITZPATRICK (1972-)
Get Over It! *167*

LEO FITZPATRICK
Bully *78*

FIONNULA FLANAGAN
(1941-)
The Others *373*

JASON FLEMYNG (1966-)
The Body *66*
From Hell *164*
Rock Star *403*
Snatch *447*

BRENDAN FLETCHER
The Law of
Enclosures *282*
My Father's Angel *345*

SUSAN FLOYD
Domestic Disturbance *125*

ADAM FOGERTY
Greenfingers *185*

DAVE FOLEY (1963-)
Monkeybone *327*
On the Line *361*

BRIDGET FONDA (1964-)
Kiss of the Dragon *269*
Monkeybone *327*

ALAN FORD
Snatch *447*

HARRISON FORD (1942-)
Apocalypse Now
Redux *35*

STEVEN FORD (1956-)
Black Hawk Down *57*

CLAIRE FORLANI (1972-)
Antitrust *33*

FREDERIC FORREST
(1938-)
Apocalypse Now
Redux *35*

KATHRINE (KATE)
FORSTER (1969-)
Mulholland Drive *338*

ROBERT FORSTER (1941-)
Mulholland Drive *338*

ROSEMARY FORSYTH
(1945-)
John Carpenter's Ghosts of
Mars *240*

MARLENE FORTE
Our Song *376*

JOHN FORTUNE
The Tailor of Panama *475*

BEN FOSTER (1980-)
Get Over It! *167*

JAMES FOX (1939-)
The Golden Bowl *180*
Sexy Beast *429*

JORJA FOX (1968-)
Memento *321*

KERRY FOX (1966-)
Intimacy *224*

MICHAEL J. FOX (1961-)
Atlantis: The Lost Empire
(V) *39*

VIVICA A. FOX (1964-)
Kingdom Come *267*
Two Can Play That
Game *506*

JAMIE FOXX (1967-)
Ali *10*

RAINBOW SUN FRANCKS
Love Come Down *299*

JIM FRANGIONE
The Heist *206*

ELENA FRANKLIN
Osmosis Jones *371*

JOEY FRANQUINHA
Just Looking *250*

DANIEL FRANZESE
Bully *78*

BRENDAN FRASER (1968-)
Monkeybone *327*
The Mummy Returns *341*

LAURA FRASER (1976-)
A Knight's Tale *271*

TOMIKO FRASER
Head Over Heels *198*

KATHLEEN FREEMAN
(1919-2001)
Shrek (V) *437*

MORGAN FREEMAN
(1937-)
Along Came a Spider *12*

DAWN FRENCH
Maybe Baby *318*

PETER FRIEDMAN
Someone Like You *451*

ANNA FRIEL (1976-)
An Everlasting Piece *140*

CECILIA FRODE
Together *489*

LARS FRODE
Together *489*

STEPHEN FRY (1957-)
Gosford Park *182*

JOHN FUJIOKA
Pearl Harbor *379*

BENNO FURMANN
The Princess and the
Warrior *393*

MANSAKU FUWA
Warm Water Under a Red
Bridge *526*

RON GABRIEL
Top of the Food
Chain *494*

PASQUALE GAETA
Too Much Sleep *492*

KEVIN GAGE
Blow *62*

ALYSSA GAINER
The Shipping News *435*

KAITLYN GAINER
The Shipping News *435*

LAUREN GAINER
The Shipping News *435*

ALASTAIR GALBRAITH
Intimacy *224*

JOHNNY GALECKI (1975-)
Vanilla Sky *518*

PHILIP GALINSKY
Too Much Sleep *492*

BALAZS GALKO
An American
Rhapsody *22*

BRONAGH GALLAGHER
The Most Fertile Man in
Ireland *334*

MICHAEL GAMBON
(1940-)
Gosford Park *182*
High Heels and Low
Lifes *209*

JAMES GANDOLFINI
(1961-)
The Last Castle *278*
The Man Who Wasn't
There *312*
The Mexican *323*

RICHARD GANT
Kingdom Come *267*

PETER GANTZLER
Italian for Beginners *229*

BRUNO GANZ (1941-)
Bread and Tulips *70*

VICTOR GARBER (1949-)
Legally Blonde *284*

INIGO GARCES
The Devil's Backbone *115*

ADAM GARCIA (1973-)
Riding in Cars with
Boys *399*

ANDY GARCIA (1956-)
Ocean's Eleven *359*

JEFF GARCIA
Jimmy Neutron: Boy Genius
(V) *234*

JOANNA GARCIA
Not Another Teen
Movie *352*

STENIO GARCIA
Me You Them *320*

ALLEN (GOORWITZ)
GARFIELD (1939-)
The Majestic *307*

TROY GARITY
Bandits *43*

GABRIEL GARKO
Ignorant Fairies *219*

JAMES GARNER (1928-)
Atlantis: The Lost Empire
(V) *39*

JENNIFER GARNER (1972-)
Pearl Harbor *379*

KELLI GARNER
Bully *78*

JANEANE GAROFALO
(1964-)
Wet Hot American
Summer *532*

TERI GARR (1949-)
Ghost World *170*

NAOMI GASKIN
Love Come Down *299*

ANA GASTEYER
What's the Worst That
Could Happen? *536*

NONA GAYE
Ali *10*

JASON GEDRICK (1965-)
Summer Catch *467*

ROBBIE GEE
Snatch *447*

VALERIE GEFFNER
Fast Food, Fast
Women *152*

BRIAN GEORGE
Bubble Boy *76*

Ghost World *170*

MELISSA GEORGE
Mulholland Drive *338*
Sugar & Spice *465*

PETER GERETY
The Curse of the Jade
Scorpion *107*
K-PAX *255*

GREG GERMANN (1962-)
Down to Earth *131*
Joe Somebody *238*
Sweet November *471*

GINA GERSHON (1962-)
Driven *133*

ZEN GESNER (1970-)
Shallow Hal *432*

BALTHAZAR GETTY
(1975-)
The Center of the
World *89*

STEPHEN GEVEDON
Session 9 *427*

MARCUS GIAMATTI
The Business of
Strangers *80*

PAUL GIAMATTI (1967-)
Planet of the Apes *384*

GIANCARLO GIANNINI
(1942-)
Hannibal *187*

MARLA GIBBS (1946-)
The Brothers *74*
The Visit *521*

MARY GIBBS
Monsters, Inc. (V) *332*

MEL GIBSON (1956-)
The Million Dollar
Hotel *325*

TYRESE GIBSON
Baby Boy *41*

SAM GIFALDI
Trumpet of the Swan
(V) *503*

SARA GILBERT (1975-)
Riding in Cars with
Boys *399*

GLOVER GILL
Waking Life *524*

AIDAN GILLEN
The Low Down *301*

PERI GILPIN
Final Fantasy: The Spirits
Within (V) *158*

CARMINE D.
GIOVINAZZO
Black Hawk Down *57*

HIPPOLYTE GIRARDOT
(1955-)
Jump Tomorrow *246*

BERNARD GIRAUDEAU
(1947-)
A Matter of Taste *315*

FRANCESCO GIUFFRIDA
The Way We
Laughed *528*

MATTHEW GLAVE
Corky Romano *101*
Rock Star *403*

JOANNA GLEASON (1950-)
The Wedding Planner *530*

PAUL GLEASON (1944-)
Not Another Teen
Movie *352*

BRENDAN GLEESON
(1954-)
A. I.: Artificial
Intelligence *1*
Saltwater *410*
The Tailor of Panama *475*

IAIN GLEN (1961-)
Beautiful Creatures *47*
Lara Croft: Tomb
Raider *276*

ROBERT GLENISTER
Just Visiting *253*

SCOTT GLENN (1942-)
Apocalypse Now
Redux *35*
The Shipping News *435*
Training Day *501*

DANNY GLOVER (1947-)
The Royal
Tenenbaums *406*

ADAM GOLDBERG (1970-)
A Beautiful Mind *49*
Waking Life *524*

WHOOPI GOLDBERG
(1949-)
Kingdom Come *267*
Monkeybone *327*
Rat Race *397*

JEFF GOLDBLUM (1952-)
Cats & Dogs *85*

BOB(CAT) GOLDTHWAIT
(1962-)
Blow *62*

TONY GOLDWYN (1960-)
An American
Rhapsody *22*

ISABEL GOMES
Glitter *178*

JAIME GOMEZ
Training Day *501*

CAROLINE GOODALL
(1959-)
The Princess Diaries *394*

CONRAD GOODE
Don't Say a Word *126*

CUBA GOODING, JR.
(1968-)
Pearl Harbor *379*
Rat Race *397*

OMAR GOODING
Baby Boy *41*

BRIAN GOODMAN
The Last Castle *278*

HAZELLE GOODMAN
Hannibal *187*

JOHN GOODMAN (1952-)
Monsters, Inc. (V) *332*
My First Mister *346*
One Night at
McCool's *365*

RANDALL GOODWIN
Escanaba in da
Moonlight *136*

MEL GORHAM (1959-)
The Center of the
World *89*

ESTHER GORINTIN
Voyages *523*

EYDIE GORME
Ocean's Eleven *359*

PEGGY GORMLEY
The Sleepy Time Gal *445*

ELLIOTT GOULD (1938-)
Ocean's Eleven *359*

ROMAIN GOUPIL
Fat Girl *154*

GQ
On the Line *361*
What's the Worst That
Could Happen? *536*

TOPHER GRACE (1978-)
Ocean's Eleven *359*

ANA GRACIA
Nico and Dani *348*

HEATHER GRAHAM
(1970-)
From Hell *164*
Say It Isn't So *415*
Sidewalks of New
York *439*

KENNY GRAHAM
Chopper *91*

LAUREN GRAHAM
Sweet November *471*

MARCUS GRAHAM (1963-)
Mulholland Drive *338*

STEPHEN GRAHAM
Snatch *447*

KELSEY GRAMMER (1954-)
15 Minutes *155*

BETH GRANT (1949-)
Rock Star *403*

HUGH GRANT (1960-)
Bridget Jones's Diary *72*

LEE GRANT (1927-)
Mulholland Drive *338*

RICHARD E. GRANT
(1957-)
Gosford Park *182*

MACY GRAY
Training Day *501*

SPALDING GRAY (1941-)
Kate & Leopold *260*

AL GREEN
On the Line *361*

SETH GREEN (1974-)
America's Sweethearts *24*
Josie and the
Pussycats *242*
Rat Race *397*
Trumpet of the Swan
(V) *503*

TOM GREEN
Freddy Got Fingered *162*

VINCE GREEN
Save the Last Dance *411*

GRAHAM GREENE (1952-)
Lost and Delirious *297*

JUDY GREER (1971-)
The Wedding Planner *530*

ADRIAN GRENIER (1976-)
A. I.: Artificial
Intelligence *1*

ZACH GRENIER
Swordfish *473*

ZENA GREY
Max Keeble's Big
Move *316*
Summer Catch *467*

MICHAEL GREYEYES
(1967-)
Skipped Parts *444*

DAVID ALAN GRIER
(1955-)
15 Minutes *155*

PAM GRIER (1949-)
John Carpenter's Ghosts of
Mars *240*

JONATHAN (JON
FRANCIS) GRIES
Jackpot *230*

EDDIE GRIFFIN (1968-)
Double Take *129*

JULIAN GRIFFITH
Hardball *193*

RACHEL GRIFFITHS
(1968-)
Blow *62*

Blow Dry *64*

RICHARD GRIFFITHS
(1947-)
Harry Potter and the
Sorcerer's Stone *195*

CAMRYN GRIMES
Swordfish *473*

RUPERT GRINT
Harry Potter and the
Sorcerer's Stone *195*

GARY GRUBBS
Double Take *129*

IOAN GRUFFUDD (1974-)
Black Hawk Down *57*

ALVARO GUERRERO
Amores Perros *26*

KIMBERLY NORRIS
GUERRERO
Escanaba in da
Moonlight *136*

CARLA GUGINO (1971-)
The Center of the
World *89*
The One *363*
Spy Kids *459*

FLORA GUIET
Amelie *14*

PAUL GUILFOYLE (1955-)
Session 9 *427*

SOPHIE GUILLEMIN
With a Friend Like
Harry *541*

FRANCIS GUINAN
Hannibal *187*

TOM GUIRY (1981-)
Black Hawk Down *57*
Tigerland *484*

SEAN GULLETTE
Happy Accidents *191*

HILMIR SNAER
GUONASON
101 Reykjavik *364*

MICHELLE GYLEMO
Faithless *148*

JAKE GYLLENHAAL
(1980-)
Bubble Boy *76*

MAGGIE GYLLENHAAL
(1977-)
Riding in Cars with
Boys *399*

MATTHIAS HABICH
(1940-)
Enemy at the Gates *134*

CLAIRE HACKETT
Liam *289*

GENE HACKMAN (1930-)
Behind Enemy Lines *51*
Heartbreakers *200*
The Heist *206*
The Mexican *323*
The Royal
Tenenbaums *406*

KRYSTOF HADEK
Dark Blue World *111*

JULIE HAGERTY (1955-)
Freddy Got Fingered *162*

NGO QUANG HAI
The Vertical Ray of the
Sun *520*

BRIAN HALEY (1963-)
Pearl Harbor *379*

ALBERT HALL (1937-)
Ali *10*
Apocalypse Now
Redux *35*

ANTHONY MICHAEL
HALL (1968-)
The Caveman's
Valentine *87*
Freddy Got Fingered *162*
Happy Accidents *191*

BUG HALL (1985-)
Skipped Parts *444*

REGINA HALL
Scary Movie 2 *417*

MARK HAMILL (1952-)
Jay and Silent Bob Strike
Back *231*

GUSTAF HAMMARSTEN
Together *489*

DANIELLE HAMPTON
Ginger Snaps *172*

JAMES HANDY
15 Minutes *155*

COLIN HANKS (1977-)
Get Over It! *167*

DARYL HANNAH (1960-)
Jackpot *230*

JOHN HANNAH (1962-)
The Mummy Returns *341*

ALYSON HANNIGAN
(1974-)
American Pie 2 *20*

DONNA HANOVER
Series 7: The
Contenders *425*

THOMAS HANZON
Faithless *148*

ZHENG HAO
The Road Home *402*

MARCIA GAY HARDEN
(1959-)
Gaudi Afternoon *166*

MICHELINE HARDY
Thomas in Love *481*

THOMAS (TOM) HARDY
Black Hawk Down *57*

MARK HARELIK
Jurassic Park 3 *247*

DORIAN HAREWOOD
(1950-)
Glitter *178*

SUSANNAH HARKER
(1965-)
Intimacy *224*

SHALOM HARLOW (1973-)
Head Over Heels *198*

JAMIE HAROLD
The Score *419*

HILL HARPER (1973-)
The Visit *521*

LAURA HARRING
Mulholland Drive *338*

DESMOND HARRINGTON
(1976-)
My First Mister *346*
Riding in Cars with
Boys *399*

KEVIN HARRINGTON
The Dish *118*

ED HARRIS (1949-)
A Beautiful Mind *49*
Enemy at the Gates *134*

GEORGE HARRIS
Black Hawk Down *57*

HARRIET HARRIS
Memento *321*

JAMIE HARRIS
Fast Food, Fast
Women *152*

JARED HARRIS (1961-)
Shadow Magic *431*

RICHARD HARRIS (1932-)
Harry Potter and the
Sorcerer's Stone *195*

ROSEMARY HARRIS
(1930-)
Blow Dry *64*

DAVID HART
Liam *289*

IAN HART (1964-)
Born Romantic *67*
Harry Potter and the
Sorcerer's Stone *195*
Liam *289*

CLAES HARTELIUS
Together *489*

RONA HARTNER
Dad on the Run *110*

JOSH HARTNETT (1978-)
Black Hawk Down *57*

Blow Dry *64*
O *356*
Pearl Harbor *379*
Town and Country *497*

MEGAN TAYLOR
  HARVEY
Joe Dirt *236*

TERENCE HARVEY
From Hell *164*

COLLEEN HASKELL
The Animal *29*

TERI HATCHER (1964-)
Spy Kids *459*

ANNE HATHAWAY
The Princess Diaries *394*

RUTGER HAUER (1944-)
Simon Magnus *443*

COLE HAUSER (1975-)
Tigerland *484*

ETHAN HAWKE (1971-)
Tape *477*
Training Day *501*
Waking Life *524*

JOHN HAWKES
Hardball *193*

GOLDIE HAWN (1945-)
Town and Country *497*

KIM HAWTHORNE
Along Came a Spider *12*

ISAAC HAYES (1942-)
Dr. Dolittle 2 (V) *123*

SEAN P. HAYES
Cats & Dogs (V) *85*

DAVID HAYMAN (1950-)
The Tailor of Panama *475*

GLENNE HEADLY (1955-)
What's the Worst That
  Could Happen? *536*

JOHN HEARD (1946-)
O *356*

BRYAN C. HEARNE
Hardball *193*

DAN HEDAYA (1940-)
Mulholland Drive *338*

KATHERINE HEIGL
  (1978-)
Valentine *516*

NORMAN HELMS
Life After Love *290*

DAVID HEMMINGS (1941-)
Spy Game *457*

SHIRLEY HENDERSON
  (1966-)
Bridget Jones's Diary *72*

BARRY (SHABAKA)
  HENLEY
Ali *10*

JILL(IAN) HENNESSEY
  (1969-)
Exit Wounds *146*
Two Ninas *508*

KRISTER HENRIKSSON
Faithless *148*

BUCK HENRY (1930-)
Town and Country *497*

ELDEN (RATLIFF)
  HENSON (1977-)
O *356*

TARAJI P. HENSON
Baby Boy *41*

NATASHA HENSTRIDGE
  (1974-)
John Carpenter's Ghosts of
  Mars *240*

JAY HERNANDEZ
crazy/beautiful *103*

MICHAEL HERR
Apocalypse Now Redux
  (N) *35*

EDWARD HERRMANN
  (1943-)
Double Take *129*

BARBARA HERSHEY
  (1948-)
Lantana *274*

CHARLTON HESTON
  (1924-)
Cats & Dogs (V) *85*
Planet of the Apes *384*
Town and Country *497*

JENNIFER LOVE HEWITT
  (1979-)
Heartbreakers *200*

JOHN BENJAMIN HICKEY
The Anniversary Party *31*

AMY HILL
Max Keeble's Big
  Move *316*
Pavilion of Women *378*

BRENT HINKLEY
Say It Isn't So *415*

JUDD HIRSCH (1935-)
A Beautiful Mind *49*

DANNY HOCH
Black Hawk Down *57*

CHARLIE HOFHEIMER
Black Hawk Down *57*

PAUL HOGAN (1939-)
Crocodile Dundee in Los
  Angeles *105*

HAL HOLBROOK (1925-)
The Majestic *307*

ALEXANDRA HOLDEN
Sugar & Spice *465*

LAURIE HOLDEN (1972-)
The Majestic *307*

TOM HOLLANDER (1969-)
Gosford Park *182*
Maybe Baby *318*

IAN HOLM (1931-)
From Hell *164*
Lord of the Rings 1: The
  Fellowship of the
  Rings *295*
Simon Magnus *443*

LINDSEY HONEY
Last Resort *281*

SUN HONGLEI
The Road Home *402*

TAMARA HOPE
The Deep End *114*

ANTHONY HOPKINS
  (1937-)
Hannibal *187*
Hearts in Atlantis *202*

KAITLIN HOPKINS
Crocodile Dundee in Los
  Angeles *105*

DENNIS HOPPER (1936-)
Apocalypse Now
  Redux *35*

JANE HORROCKS (1964-)
Born Romantic *67*

BOB HOSKINS (1942-)
Enemy at the Gates *134*

GUY HOUSSIER
Come Undone *98*

KIM HOWARD
Our Song *376*

RON HOWARD (1954-)
Osmosis Jones (V) *371*

TERRENCE DASHON
  HOWARD
Angel Eyes *27*
Glitter *178*

PATRICK HUARD
Life After Love *290*

MARIN HUBA
Divided We Fall *120*

WOLFGANG HUBSCH
Bride of the Wind *71*

KATE HUDSON (1979-)
About Adam *5*

D.L. HUGHLEY (1964-)
The Brothers *74*

ANN HUI (1947-)
The River *401*

RENEE HUMPHREY
Jay and Silent Bob Strike
  Back *231*

CHU NGOC HUNG
The Vertical Ray of the
  Sun *520*

BONNIE HUNT (1964-)
Monsters, Inc. (V) *332*

HELEN HUNT (1963-)
The Curse of the Jade
  Scorpion *107*

KIM HUNTER (1922-)
Here's to Life *208*

RACHEL HUNTER
Rock Star *403*

SAM HUNTINGTON
Not Another Teen
  Movie *352*

ISABELLE HUPPERT
  (1955-)
Sentimental Destiny *422*

JOHN HURT (1940-)
Captain Corelli's
  Mandolin *83*
Harry Potter and the
  Sorcerer's Stone *195*

WILLIAM HURT (1950-)
A. I.: Artificial
  Intelligence *1*

ANJELICA HUSTON (1951-)
The Golden Bowl *180*
The Royal
  Tenenbaums *406*

DOUG HUTCHISON
I Am Sam *217*

ICE CUBE (1969-)
John Carpenter's Ghosts of
  Mars *240*

ICE-T (1958-)
3000 Miles to
  Graceland *482*

RHYS IFANS (1968-)
The Shipping News *435*

PALAK INNUKSUK
Atanarjuat, the Fast
  Runner *38*

MICHAEL IRBY
The Last Castle *278*
Pinero *383*

JASON ISAACS (1963-)
Black Hawk Down *57*
Sweet November *471*

KATHARINE ISABELLE
Ginger Snaps *172*

IRENE ISMAILOFF
Happenstance *190*

GREGORY ITZIN
Evolution *144*
Original Sin *367*

JAMIE KENNEDY (1970-)
Max Keeble's Big
Move *316*

REJANE KERDAFFREC
Come Undone *98*

SAM KESSELL
Together *489*

BOYD KESTNER (1964-)
Black Hawk Down *57*

LE KHANH
The Vertical Ray of the
Sun *520*

ARSINEE KHANJIAN
Fat Girl *154*

MAKRAM KHOURY
The Body *66*

NICOLE KIDMAN (1966-)
Moulin Rouge *335*
The Others *373*

CHARLES KIMBROUGH
(1936-)
The Wedding Planner *530*

ALAN KING (1927-)
Rush Hour 2 *408*

JAMES KING (1979-)
Blow *62*
Pearl Harbor *379*

LARRY KING (1933-)
America's Sweethearts *24*

REGINA KING (1971-)
Down to Earth *131*

VANESSA KING
My Father's Angel *345*

BEN KINGSLEY (1943-)
A. I.: Artificial Intelligence
(N) *1*
Sexy Beast *429*

LAURENCE KINLAN
An Everlasting Piece *140*
Saltwater *410*

GREG KINNEAR (1963-)
Someone Like You *451*

TERRY KINNEY (1954-)
House of Mirth *213*
Save the Last Dance *411*

NASTASSIA KINSKI (1959-)
An American
Rhapsody *22*
The Claim *94*
Town and Country *497*

NIKOLAI KINSKI
Tortilla Soup *495*

LUKE KIRBY
Lost and Delirious *297*

RENE KIRBY
Shallow Hal *432*

KATHRYN KIRKPATRICK
Top of the Food
Chain *494*

MIA KIRSHNER (1976-)
Not Another Teen
Movie *352*

KAZUO KITAMURA
Warm Water Under a Red
Bridge *526*

YUKIYA KITAMURA
Warm Water Under a Red
Bridge *526*

CHRIS KLEIN (1979-)
American Pie 2 *20*
Say It Isn't So *415*

KEVIN KLINE (1947-)
The Anniversary Party *31*
Life as a House *291*

HEIDI KLUM
Blow Dry *64*

SHIRLEY KNIGHT (1937-)
Angel Eyes *27*

WAYNE KNIGHT (1955-)
Rat Race *397*

SASCHA KNOPF
What's the Worst That
Could Happen? *536*

JIRI KODET
Divided We Fall *120*

HIJIRI KOJIMA
Warm Water Under a Red
Bridge *526*

BALTASAR KORMAKUR
101 Reykjavik *364*

DINA KORZUN
Last Resort *281*

ELIAS KOTEAS (1961-)
Novocaine *354*

MAKA KOTTO
Lumumba *302*

LINDA KOZLOWSKI
(1958-)
Crocodile Dundee in Los
Angeles *105*

JASON KRAVITS
Sweet November *471*

JAN GREGOR KREMP
The Musketeer *343*

KRIS KRISTOFFERSON
(1936-)
Planet of the Apes *384*

JOACHIM KROL
The Princess and the
Warrior *393*

DAVID KRUMHOLTZ
(1978-)
The Mexican *323*

Sidewalks of New
York *439*

OLEK KRUPA
Behind Enemy Lines *51*

PETER KUBHEKA
The King Is Alive *265*

LISA KUDROW (1963-)
Dr. Dolittle 2 (V) *123*

ANIL KUMAR
American Desi *17*

VUSI KUNENE
The King Is Alive *265*

MILA KUNIS
Get Over It! *167*

SIMON KUNZ
The Affair of the
Necklace *8*

SWOOSIE KURTZ (1944-)
Bubble Boy *76*
Get Over It! *167*

EMIR KUSTURICA (1954-)
The Widow of Saint-
Pierre *539*

MIMI KUZYK
Lost and Delirious *297*

BURT KWOUK (1930-)
Kiss of the Dragon *269*

PATRICK LABBE
The Orphan Muses *369*

RAVI RAMOS LACERDA
Behind the Sun *54*

DIANE LADD (1939-)
The Law of
Enclosures *282*

RONOBIR LAHRI
American Desi *17*

PADMA LAKSHMI
Glitter *178*

MARTIN LANDAU (1931-)
The Majestic *307*

DIANE LANE (1965-)
The Glass House *175*
Hardball *193*

MIKLOS LANG
Glamour *174*

FRANK LANGELLA (1940-)
Sweet November *471*

TOM LANGIONE
Too Much Sleep *492*

GERARD LANVIN
The Taste of Others *479*

ANTHONY LAPAGLIA
(1959-)
Company Man *99*
House of Mirth *213*
Lantana *274*

JONATHAN LAPAGLIA
(1967-)
Under Hellgate
Bridge *510*

VINCENT LARESCA
Just One Time *252*

SERGE LARIVIERE
Thomas in Love *481*

MICHELE LAROQUE
(1960-)
The Closet *96*

ALI LARTER (1976-)
American Outlaws *18*
Jay and Silent Bob Strike
Back *231*
Legally Blonde *284*

LOUISE LASSER (1939-)
Fast Food, Fast
Women *152*

ROLF LASSGARD
Under the Sun *512*

HUGH LAURIE (1959-)
Maybe Baby *318*

ED LAUTER (1940-)
Not Another Teen
Movie *352*

JUDE LAW (1972-)
A. I.: Artificial
Intelligence *1*
Enemy at the Gates *134*

CAROLYN LAWRENCE
Jimmy Neutron: Boy Genius
(V) *234*

MARTIN LAWRENCE
(1965-)
Black Knight *60*
What's the Worst That
Could Happen? *536*

MICHAEL LAWRENCE
The Price of Milk *392*

STEVE LAWRENCE (1935-)
Ocean's Eleven *359*

BIANCA LAWSON
Save the Last Dance *411*

JAKE LE DOUX
Love Come Down *299*

DENIS LEARY (1957-)
Company Man *99*

JEAN-PIERRE LEAUD
(1944-)
What Time Is It
There? *534*
A Matter of Taste *315*

SCOTTY LEAVENWORTH
Life as a House *291*

BRIAN LECKNER
Joy Ride *244*

HEATH LEDGER (1979-)
A Knight's Tale *271*

Monster's Ball  *330*

**CHRISTOPHER LEE
(1922-)**
Lord of the Rings 1: The
Fellowship of the
Rings  *295*

**JASON LEE (1970-)**
Heartbreakers  *200*
Jay and Silent Bob Strike
Back  *231*
Vanilla Sky  *518*

**KANG-SHENG LEE**
The River  *401*
What Time Is It
There?  *534*

**ADAM LEFEVRE**
Hearts in Atlantis  *202*
L.I.E.  *273*

**LAETITIA LEGRIX**
Come Undone  *98*

**JOHN LEGUIZAMO (1964-)**
Moulin Rouge  *335*
What's the Worst That
Could Happen?  *536*

**CHYLER LEIGH**
Not Another Teen
Movie  *352*

**JENNIFER JASON LEIGH
(1963-)**
The Anniversary Party  *31*
The King Is Alive  *265*
Skipped Parts  *444*

**KRIS LEMCHE**
Ginger Snaps  *172*

**GERALD LENTON-
YOUNG**
Skipped Parts  *444*

**ROBERT SEAN LEONARD
(1969-)**
Driven  *133*
Tape  *477*

**SYLVIE LEONARD**
Life After Love  *290*

**TEA LEONI (1966-)**
Jurassic Park 3  *247*

**LOGAN LERMAN**
Riding in Cars with
Boys  *399*

**JALIL LESPERT**
Human Resources  *216*

**ADRIAN LESTER**
Born Romantic  *67*
Maybe Baby  *318*

**RON LESTER**
Not Another Teen
Movie  *352*

**TONY LEUNG CHIU-WAI
(1962-)**
In the Mood for Love  *223*

**DOMINIQUE LEVESQUE**
Life After Love  *290*

**ILANA LEVINE**
Just Looking  *250*

**SAMM LEVINE**
Not Another Teen
Movie  *352*

**TED LEVINE (1958-)**
Ali  *10*
Evolution  *144*
The Fast and the
Furious  *150*
Joy Ride (V)  *244*

**EUGENE LEVY (1946-)**
American Pie 2  *20*
Down to Earth  *131*
Serendipity  *423*

**GILBERT LEVY**
Dad on the Run  *110*

**JENIFER LEWIS (1957-)**
The Brothers  *74*

**JULIETTE LEWIS (1973-)**
Gaudi Afternoon  *166*

**MATTHEW LEWIS**
Harry Potter and the
Sorcerer's Stone  *195*

**JOHAN LEYSEN (1950-)**
The King Is Dancing  *266*

**THIERRY LHERMITTE
(1957-)**
The Closet  *96*

**JET LI (1963-)**
Kiss of the Dragon  *269*
The One  *363*

**RICHARD V. LICATA**
Just Looking  *250*

**JESSICA LIEDBERG**
Together  *489*

**MATTHEW LILLARD
(1970-)**
Summer Catch  *467*

**PETER LINARI**
The Curse of the Jade
Scorpion  *107*

**CHAD LINDBERG**
The Fast and the
Furious  *150*

**LISA LINDGREN**
Together  *489*

**DELROY LINDO (1952-)**
The Heist  *206*
The Last Castle  *278*
The One  *363*

**HENRIK LINDSTROM**
Together  *489*

**HARDEE T. LINEHAM**
Top of the Food
Chain  *494*

**ROSALEEN LINEHAN
(1937-)**
About Adam  *5*

**RICHARD LINKLATER
(1961-)**
Waking Life  *524*

**LAURA LINNEY (1964-)**
House of Mirth  *213*

**KENT LINVILLE**
Black Hawk Down  *57*

**ALEX D. LINZ (1989-)**
Max Keeble's Big
Move  *316*

**RAY LIOTTA (1955-)**
Blow  *62*
Hannibal  *187*
Heartbreakers  *200*

**LU LIPING**
Shadow Magic  *431*

**PEGGY LIPTON (1947-)**
Jackpot  *230*
Skipped Parts  *444*

**THEODORE LISCINSKI**
Hedwig and the Angry
Inch  *204*

**JOHN LITHGOW (1945-)**
Shrek (V)  *437*

**NATASHA LITTLE**
Greenfingers  *185*

**RON LIVINGSTON**
Two Ninas  *508*

**STEN LJUNGGREN**
Together  *489*

**L.L. COOL J. (1968-)**
Kingdom Come  *267*

**CANDY LO**
Time and Tide  *486*

**ENRICO LO VERSO (1964-)**
Hannibal  *187*
The Way We
Laughed  *528*

**FIONA LOEWI**
Top of the Food
Chain  *494*

**DONAL LOGUE (1966-)**
The Million Dollar
Hotel  *325*

**LOUIS LOMBARDI**
The Animal  *29*

**DOMENICK
LOMBARDOZZI**
Just One Time  *252*

**ALEXANDRA LONDON**
Sentimental Destiny  *422*

**JOHN LONE (1952-)**
Rush Hour 2  *408*

**HOWIE LONG (1960-)**
3000 Miles to
Graceland  *482*

**JUSTIN LONG**
Jeepers Creepers  *233*

**TOM LONG**
The Dish  *118*

**LUCIEN LONGUEVILLE**
Human Resources  *216*

**ANITA LOO**
Pavilion of Women  *378*

**CARMEN LOPEZ**
Our Song  *376*

**GEORGE LOPEZ**
Bread and Roses  *68*

**JENNIFER LOPEZ (1970-)**
Angel Eyes  *27*
The Wedding Planner  *530*

**SERGEI LOPEZ**
With a Friend Like
Harry  *541*

**JEAN-PIERRE LORIT**
A Matter of Taste  *315*

**FAIZON LOVE**
Made  *305*

**JON LOVITZ (1957-)**
Cats & Dogs (V)  *85*
Rat Race  *397*
3000 Miles to
Graceland  *482*

**VICTOR LOW**
Everybody's Famous!  *142*

**HSIAO-LING LU**
The River  *401*

**SHIAO-LIN LU**
The River  *401*

**YI-CHING LU**
What Time Is It
There?  *534*

**BYRON LUCAS**
Suspicious River  *469*

**JOSHUA LUCAS**
A Beautiful Mind  *49*
The Deep End  *114*
Session 9  *427*

**LAURENT LUCAS**
With a Friend Like
Harry  *541*

**WILLIAM LUCKING**
K-PAX  *255*

**JOANNA LUMLEY (1946-)**
Maybe Baby  *318*

**ANJA LUNDQVIST**
Together  *489*

**PATTI LUPONE (1949-)**
The Heist  *206*
Just Looking  *250*

FEDERICO LUPPI (1934-)
The Devil's Backbone *115*

JOHN CARROLL LYNCH
Bubble Boy *76*

KELLY LYNCH (1959-)
Joe Somebody *238*

SUSAN LYNCH (1971-)
Beautiful Creatures *47*
From Hell *164*
Nora *351*

SIMON LYNDON
Chopper *91*

MEREDITH SCOTT LYNN
Legally Blonde *284*

NATASHA LYONNE (1979-)
American Pie 2 *20*
Kate & Leopold *260*
Scary Movie 2 *417*

BERNIE MAC (1958-)
Ocean's Eleven *359*
What's the Worst That
Could Happen? *536*

KELLY MACDONALD
(1977-)
Gosford Park *182*

NORM MACDONALD
(1963-)
Dr. Dolittle 2 (V) *123*

ANDIE MACDOWELL
(1958-)
Town and Country *497*

STERLING MACER
Double Take *129*

GABRIEL MACHT (1972-)
American Outlaws *18*
Behind Enemy Lines *51*

ALLISON MACKIE
Original Sin *367*

PETER MACNEILL
Angel Eyes *27*

WILLIAM H. MACY (1950-)
Jurassic Park 3 *247*

AMY MADIGAN (1957-)
The Sleepy Time Gal *445*

BENOIT MAGIMEL (1974-)
The King Is Dancing *266*

LICIA MAGLIETTA
Bread and Tulips *70*

PHILIPPE MAGNAN
The Widow of Saint-
Pierre *539*

ANN MAGNUSON (1956-)
The Caveman's
Valentine *87*
Glitter *178*

TOBEY MAGUIRE (1975-)
Cats & Dogs (V) *85*

ALAN MAHER
About Adam *5*

JOHN MAHONEY (1940-)
Atlantis: The Lost Empire
(V) *39*

MAKO (1933-)
Pearl Harbor *379*

PATRICK MALAHIDE
(1945-)
Captain Corelli's
Mandolin *83*

FANNY MALLETTE
The Orphan Muses *369*

JENA MALONE (1984-)
Life as a House *291*

NARGESS MAMIZADEH
The Circle *93*

AASIF MANDRI
ABCD *4*

COSTAS MANDYLOR
(1965-)
The Pledge *387*

RIZWAN MANJI
American Desi *17*

ALAKINA MANN
The Others *373*

GABRIEL MANN
Josie and the
Pussycats *242*
Summer Catch *467*

TARYN MANNING (1978-)
crazy/beautiful *103*

TOM MANNION
Beautiful Creatures *47*

JOE MANTEGNA (1947-)
Trumpet of the Swan
(V) *503*

WILLIAM MAPOTHER
In the Bedroom *220*

JOAN MAQUILING
Too Much Sleep *492*

MARY MARA
K-PAX *255*

ANDRE MARCON
Sentimental Destiny *422*

VLADIMIR MAREK
Divided We Fall *120*

IVANO MARESCOTTI
The Holy Tongue *212*

MARK MARGOLIS (1939-)
Dinner Rush *116*
Fast Food, Fast
Women *152*
Hardball *193*
The Tailor of Panama *475*

MIRIAM MARGOLYES
(1941-)
Cats & Dogs *85*

CONSTANCE MARIE
Tortilla Soup *495*

ELI MARIENTHAL (1986-)
American Pie 2 *20*

RICHARD "CHEECH"
MARIN (1946-)
Spy Kids *459*

KEN MARINO
Joe Somebody *238*
Wet Hot American
Summer *532*

HEIDI MARK
Rock Star *403*

BRIAN MARKINSON
The Curse of the Jade
Scorpion *107*

CHRISTIAN MARQUAND
(1927-2000)
Apocalypse Now
Redux *35*

JAMES MARSDEN (1973-)
Sugar & Spice *465*

MATTHEW MARSDEN
(1972-)
Black Hawk Down *57*

MATTHEW MARSH
Spy Game *457*

SARA MARSH
Sugar & Spice *465*

KRIS MARSHALL
The Most Fertile Man in
Ireland *334*

GABRIEL MARSHALL-
THOMSON
Enemy at the Gates *134*

ANDREA MARTIN (1947-)
Hedwig and the Angry
Inch *204*
Jimmy Neutron: Boy Genius
(V) *234*

NAN MARTIN (1927-)
Shallow Hal *432*

RUDOLF MARTIN
Swordfish *473*

STEVE MARTIN (1945-)
Novocaine *354*

MELISSA MARTINEZ
Our Song *376*

MASASA
Kingdom Come *267*

VLADIMIR MASHKOV
Behind Enemy Lines *51*

LAURENCE MASON
Ali *10*

ANNA MASSEY (1937-)
Dark Blue World *111*

MARINA MASSIRONI
Bread and Tulips *70*

CHRISTOPHER K.
MASTERSON
Scary Movie 2 *417*

WALTER MASTERSON
L.I.E. *273*

HEATHER MATARAZZO
(1982-)
Company Man *99*
The Princess Diaries *394*

MARIE MATHERON
Come Undone *98*

HANS MATHESON (1975-)
Making Love *309*

EVA MATTES (1954-)
Enemy at the Gates *134*

PATRICIA MAUCERI
Jump Tomorrow *246*

CLAIRE MAURIER (1929-)
Amelie *14*

JODHI MAY (1975-)
House of Mirth *213*

MONET MAZUR
Angel Eyes *27*

RUTH MCCABE
An Everlasting Piece *140*

VINCENT MCCABE
Nora *351*

SEAN MCCANN
The Law of
Enclosures *282*

CATHERINE
MCCLEMENTS
Better Than Sex *56*

MATTHEW
MCCONAUGHEY
(1969-)
The Wedding Planner *530*

CATHERINE
MCCORMACK (1972-)
Born Romantic *67*
Spy Game *457*
The Tailor of Panama *475*

ERIC MCCORMACK
(1963-)
Here's to Life *208*

MARY MCCORMACK
(1969-)
High Heels and Low
Lifes *209*
K-PAX *255*

WILL MCCORMACK
American Outlaws *18*

DARIUS MCCRARY
15 Minutes *155*
Kingdom Come *267*

GARRY MCDONALD
(1948-)
Moulin Rouge *335*

MO'NIQUE
Two Can Play That
Game *506*

ALVARO MONJE
Sexy Beast *429*

ISABELL MONK
Black Knight *60*

SEBASTIAN MONTAGNA
La Cienaga *92*

BARBARA
MONTGOMERY
Lift *293*

DAN MONTGOMERY, JR.
On the Line *361*

FLORA MONTGOMERY
When Brendan Met
Trudy *538*

LAFAYETTE
MONTGOMERY
Mulholland Drive *338*

EMIL MOODYSSON
Together *489*

JULIANNE MOORE (1961-)
Evolution *144*
Hannibal *187*
The Shipping News *435*

MANDY MOORE (1984-)
The Princess Diaries *394*

SHEMAR MOORE
The Brothers *74*

MERCEDES MORAN
La Cienaga *92*

NICK MORAN
The Musketeer *343*

ROB MORAN
Shallow Hal *432*

LAURA MORANTE
The Son's Room *453*

MARGUERITE MOREAU
Wet Hot American
Summer *532*

SYLVIE MOREAU
The Widow of Saint-
Pierre *539*

YOLANDA MOREAU
Amelie *14*

RITA MORENO (1931-)
Pinero *383*

NANNI MORETTI (1953-)
The Son's Room *453*

TREVOR MORGAN (1986-)
The Glass House *175*
Jurassic Park 3 *247*

MICHAEL MORIARTY
(1941-)
Along Came a Spider *12*

ALANIS MORISSETTE
Jay and Silent Bob Strike
Back *231*

GARRETT MORRIS (1944-)
Jackpot *230*

PHIL MORRIS (1958-)
Atlantis: The Lost Empire
(V) *39*

JAMES MORRISON
The One *363*

DAVID MORRISSEY (1963-)
Born Romantic *67*
Captain Corelli's
Mandolin *83*

DAVID MORSE (1953-)
Hearts in Atlantis *202*

GLENN MORSHOWER
(1959-)
Black Hawk Down *57*
Pearl Harbor *379*

VIGGO MORTENSEN
(1958-)
Lord of the Rings 1: The
Fellowship of the
Rings *295*

JOE MORTON (1947-)
Ali *10*

DAVID MOSCOW (1974-)
Riding in Cars with
Boys *399*

CARRIE-ANNE MOSS
(1970-)
Memento *321*

JESSE MOSS
Ginger Snaps *172*

RANGI MOTU
The Price of Milk *392*

THEOPHILE MOUSSA
SOWIE
Lumumba *302*

GINA MOXLEY
Saltwater *410*

BRIDGET MOYNAHAN
(1972-)
Serendipity *423*

MICHAEL MULHEREN
The Curse of the Jade
Scorpion *107*

MEGAN MULLALLY
(1958-)
Monkeybone *327*

PETER MULLAN
Session 9 *427*
The Claim *94*

CONOR MULLEN
Saltwater *410*

MARIE MULLEN
When Brendan Met
Trudy *538*

LOCHLYN MUNRO
Kill Me Later *263*

ENRIQUE MURCIANO
(1973-)
Black Hawk Down *57*

BRITTANY MURPHY
(1977-)
Don't Say a Word *126*
Riding in Cars with
Boys *399*
Sidewalks of New
York *439*
Summer Catch *467*

EDDIE MURPHY (1961-)
Dr. Dolittle 2 *123*
Shrek (V) *437*

BILL MURRAY (1950-)
Osmosis Jones *371*
The Royal
Tenenbaums *406*

RODRIGO MURRAY
Amores Perros *26*

MIKE MYERS (1963-)
Shrek (V) *437*

HASSAN NABEHAN
The Day I Became a
Woman *112*

FATEMEH NAGHAVI
The Circle *93*

AJAY NAIDU
K-PAX *255*

MOHAMMAD REZA NAJI
Baran *45*

KATHY NAJIMY (1957-)
Rat Race *397*
The Wedding Planner *530*

ISABELLE NANTY
Amelie *14*

TONY NARDI (1958-)
My Father's Angel *345*

OLIVIA NASH
The Most Fertile Man in
Ireland *334*

ISAO NATSUYAGI
Warm Water Under a Red
Bridge *526*

JALIL NAZARI
Djomeh *121*

ROME NEAL
Pinero *383*

SAM NEILL (1948-)
The Dish *118*
Jurassic Park 3 *247*

BADR IROUNI NEJAD
The Day I Became a
Woman *112*

CYRUS KAHOURI NEJAD
The Day I Became a
Woman *112*

JUDD NELSON (1959-)
Jay and Silent Bob Strike
Back *231*

SANDRA NELSON
Life as a House *291*

FRANCESCA NERI (1964-)
Hannibal *187*

GENEVIEVE NERON
The Left Hand Side of the
Fridge *283*

JAMES NESBITT (1966-)
The Most Fertile Man in
Ireland *334*

WAYNE NEWTON (1942-)
Ocean's Eleven *359*

THOMAS IAN NICHOLAS
(1980-)
American Pie 2 *20*

TAYLOR NICHOLS
Jurassic Park 3 *247*

JACK NICHOLSON (1937-)
The Pledge *387*

GRANT NICKALLS
Glitter *178*

BENNY NIEVES
Double Take *129*

BILL NIGHY (1949-)
Blow Dry *64*

LEONARD NIMOY (1931-)
Atlantis: The Lost Empire
(V) *39*

ALESSANDRO NIVOLA
(1972-)
Jurassic Park 3 *247*

JACQUES NOLOT
Under the Sand *511*

NICK NOLTE (1941-)
The Golden Bowl *180*

TOM NOONAN (1951-)
The Pledge *387*

OLA NORELL
Together *489*

EDUARDO NORIEGA
(1973-)
The Devil's Backbone *115*

HERMIONE NORRIS
Born Romantic *67*

JEREMY NORTHAM
(1961-)
The Golden Bowl *180*
Gosford Park *182*

ALEX NORTON
Beautiful Creatures *47*

CEDRIC PENDLETON
Summer Catch  *467*

ARTUS PENGUERN
Amelie  *14*

CHRISTOPHER PENN
(1967-)
American Pie 2  *20*
Corky Romano  *101*

KAL PENN
American Desi  *17*

SEAN PENN (1960-)
I Am Sam  *217*

PIPER PERABO (1977-)
Lost and Delirious  *297*

MARCO PEREZ
Amores Perros  *26*

VINCENT PEREZ (1964-)
Bride of the Wind  *71*

ELIZABETH PERKINS
(1960-)
Cats & Dogs  *85*

EMILY PERKINS
Ginger Snaps  *172*

OSGOOD PERKINS, II
(1974-)
Legally Blonde  *284*

MAX PERLICH (1968-)
Blow  *62*

RON PERLMAN (1950-)
Enemy at the Gates  *134*

OLIVIER PERRIER
Sentimental Destiny  *422*

CLAUDE PERRON
Amelie  *14*

LISA JANE PERSKY (1955-)
An American
Rhapsody  *22*
My First Mister  *346*

BOB PETERSON
Monsters, Inc. (V)  *332*

VALARIE PETTIFORD
Glitter  *178*

MICHELLE PFEIFFER
(1957-)
I Am Sam  *217*

PETER PHELPS (1960-)
Lantana  *274*

MEKHI PHIFER (1975-)
O  *356*

BRAUN PHILIP
Lift  *293*

ANNE-MARIE PHILIPE
A Matter of Taste  *315*

JULES PHILIPPE
The Left Hand Side of the
Fridge  *283*

RYAN PHILLIPPE (1974-)
Antitrust  *33*
Company Man  *99*
Gosford Park  *182*

ANGELINA PHILLIPS
Series 7: The
Contenders  *425*

BIJOU PHILLIPS (1980-)
Bully  *78*

GINA PHILLIPS
Jeepers Creepers  *233*

LESLIE PHILLIPS (1924-)
Lara Croft: Tomb
Raider  *276*

SALLY PHILLIPS
Bridget Jones's Diary  *72*

RAIN PHOENIX (1973-)
O  *356*

SUMMER PHOENIX
Dinner Rush  *116*

REBECCA PIDGEON
(1963-)
The Heist  *206*

JACQUES PIELLER
The Town Is Quiet  *499*

DAVID HYDE PIERCE
(1959-)
Osmosis Jones (V)  *371*
Wet Hot American
Summer  *532*

ALISON PILL
Skipped Parts  *444*

LARRY PINE
The Shipping News  *435*

SIU PING-LAM
In the Mood for Love  *223*

MAGALI PINGLAULT
Thomas in Love  *481*

JADA PINKETT SMITH
(1971-)
Ali  *10*
Kingdom Come  *267*

DOMINIQUE PINON
(1955-)
Amelie  *14*

GORDON PINSENT (1930-)
The Shipping News  *435*

HAROLD PINTER (1930-)
The Tailor of Panama  *475*

LUDGER PISTOR
The Princess and the
Warrior  *393*

BRAD PITT (1963-)
The Mexican  *323*
Ocean's Eleven  *359*
Snatch  *447*
Spy Game  *457*

MICHAEL PITT
Bully  *78*
Hedwig and the Angry
Inch  *204*

JEREMY PIVEN (1965-)
Black Hawk Down  *57*
Rush Hour 2  *408*
Serendipity  *423*

MARY KAY PLACE (1947-)
My First Mister  *346*

OLIVER PLATT (1960-)
Don't Say a Word  *126*

GEORGE PLIMPTON
(1927-)
Just Visiting  *253*

MARTHA PLIMPTON
(1970-)
The Sleepy Time Gal  *445*

JACK PLOTNICK
Say It Isn't So  *415*

AMANDA PLUMMER
(1957-)
The Million Dollar
Hotel  *325*

CHRISTOPHER PLUMMER
(1927-)
A Beautiful Mind  *49*

BEVERLY POLCYN
Not Another Teen
Movie  *352*

JON POLITO (1950-)
The Man Who Wasn't
There  *312*

BOLESLAV POLIVKA
Divided We Fall  *120*

KEVIN POLLAK (1958-)
Dr. Dolittle 2  *123*
3000 Miles to
Graceland  *482*
The Wedding Planner  *530*

SARAH POLLEY (1979-)
The Claim  *94*
The Law of
Enclosures  *282*
Love Come Down  *299*

ALEXANDER POLLOCK
Cats & Dogs  *85*

TERI POLO (1969-)
Domestic Disturbance  *125*

BRAY POOR
Two Ninas  *508*

GERT PORTAEL
Everybody's Famous!  *142*

LOUISE PORTAL (1951-)
The Orphan Muses  *369*

SUSIE PORTER
Better Than Sex  *56*

RICHARD PORTNOW
(1950-)
Happy Accidents  *191*

PARKER POSEY (1968-)
The Anniversary Party  *31*
Josie and the
Pussycats  *242*

PETE POSTLETHWAITE
(1945-)
The Shipping News  *435*

FRANKA POTENTE
Blow  *62*
The Princess and the
Warrior  *393*

MADELEINE POTTER
(1963-)
The Golden Bowl  *180*

MONICA POTTER (1971-)
Along Came a Spider  *12*
Head Over Heels  *198*

CLIFTON POWELL
The Brothers  *74*

SAMANTHA POWERS
The Low Down  *301*

KYLA PRATT (1988-)
Dr. Dolittle 2  *123*

JUDY PRESCOTT
Hit and Runway  *211*

HARVE PRESNELL (1933-)
Escanaba in da
Moonlight  *136*

JAIME PRESSLY
Joe Dirt  *236*
Not Another Teen
Movie  *352*
Tomcats  *491*

JOAN PRINGLE
Original Sin  *367*

FREDDIE PRINZE, JR.
(1976-)
Head Over Heels  *198*
Summer Catch  *467*

RUPERT PROCTOR
The Low Down  *301*

JONATHAN PRYCE (1947-)
The Affair of the
Necklace  *8*
Bride of the Wind  *71*

LEAH PURCELL
Lantana  *274*

JAMES PUREFOY (1964-)
A Knight's Tale  *271*
Maybe Baby  *318*

MISSI PYLE (1973-)
Josie and the
Pussycats  *242*

SHAOBO QIN
Ocean's Eleven  *359*

KAREL RODEN
15 Minutes  *155*

MICHAEL RODRICK
Under Hellgate
Bridge  *510*

MICHELLE RODRIGUEZ
(1978-)
The Fast and the
Furious  *150*

PAUL RODRIGUEZ (1955-)
Ali  *10*
Crocodile Dundee in Los
Angeles  *105*
Rat Race  *397*
Tortilla Soup  *495*

DANIEL ROEBUCK (1963-)
Double Take  *129*

MAURICE ROEVES (1937-)
Beautiful Creatures  *47*

MIMI ROGERS (1956-)
Ginger Snaps  *172*

WILL ROKOS
Monster's Ball  *330*

SHANTI RONEY
Together  *489*

MICHAEL ROOF
Black Hawk Down  *57*

MICHAEL ROSENBAUM
(1972-)
Sweet November  *471*

JOSEPH ROSENBERG
I Am Sam  *217*

GRANT ROSENMEYER
The Royal
Tenenbaums  *406*

CHELCIE ROSS (1942-)
The Majestic  *307*

MATT ROSS
Just Visiting  *253*

LEO ROSSI
One Night at
McCool's  *365*

EMMY ROSSUM
An American
Rhapsody  *22*

TIM ROTH (1961-)
The Million Dollar
Hotel  *325*
The Musketeer  *343*
Planet of the Apes  *384*

WILL ROTHHAAR
Hearts in Atlantis  *202*

JOHN ROTHMAN (1949-)
Say It Isn't So  *415*

RICHARD ROUNDTREE
(1942-)
Antitrust  *33*
Corky Romano  *101*

MICKEY ROURKE (1955-)
The Pledge  *387*

CATHERINE ROUVEL
(1939-)
Va Savoir  *514*

LILIANE ROVERE
Voyages  *523*

RICHARD ROXBURGH
(1962-)
Moulin Rouge  *335*

SAUL RUBINEK (1949-)
Rush Hour 2  *408*

PAUL RUDD (1969-)
Wet Hot American
Summer  *532*

LARS RUDOLPH
The Princess and the
Warrior  *393*

MARK RUFFALO (1967-)
The Last Castle  *278*

GENE RUFFINI
Jump Tomorrow  *246*

RUFUS (1942-)
Amelie  *14*

VYTO RUGINIS
The Fast and the
Furious  *150*
The Glass House  *175*

TYGH RUNYAN
Antitrust  *33*
My Father's Angel  *345*

GEOFFREY RUSH (1951-)
Lantana  *274*
The Tailor of Panama  *475*

DAVID LEE RUSSEK
Just One Time  *252*

KURT RUSSELL (1951-)
3000 Miles to
Graceland  *482*
Vanilla Sky  *518*

CAMILLA RUTHERFORD
Gosford Park  *182*

AMANDA RYAN
Simon Magnus  *443*

MARISA RYAN
Riding in Cars with
Boys  *399*
Wet Hot American
Summer  *532*

MEG RYAN (1961-)
Kate & Leopold  *260*

LINDA RYBOVA
Dark Blue World  *111*

MARK RYLANCE (1960-)
Intimacy  *224*

DARYL SABARA (1992-)
Spy Kids  *459*

ELHAM SABOKTAKIN
The Circle  *93*

ROBIN SACHS
Ocean's Eleven  *359*

MELISSA SAGEMILLER
Get Over It!  *167*
Soul Survivors  *455*

SOLEDAD ST. HILAIRE
crazy/beautiful  *103*

IRMA ST. PAUL
Fast Food, Fast
Women  *152*

YOHICHIROH SAITOH
(1972-)
Eureka  *138*

ZOE SALDANA
Get Over It!  *167*

DUNIA SALDIVAR
Amores Perros  *26*

JORGE SALINAS
Amores Perros  *26*

EMMA SAMUELSSON
Together  *489*

JAIME SANCHEZ
Pinero  *383*

ROSELYN SANCHEZ
Rush Hour 2  *408*

JAY O. SANDERS (1953-)
Along Came a Spider  *12*

MIGUEL (MICHAEL)
SANDOVAL (1951-)
Blow  *62*

JULIAN SANDS (1958-)
The Million Dollar
Hotel  *325*

GIUSEPPE SANFELICE
The Son's Room  *453*

RUBEN SANTIAGO-
HUDSON
Domestic Disturbance  *125*

RODRIGO SANTORO
Behind the Sun  *54*

HORATIO SANZ
Tomcats  *491*

RICHARD SARAFIAN
(1935-)
Dr. Dolittle 2 (V)  *123*

SUSAN SARANDON (1946-)
Cats & Dogs (V)  *85*

OLLE SARRI
Together  *489*

PETER SARSGAARD
The Center of the
World  *89*

FABIO SARTOR
The Luzhin Defence  *303*

SHEK SAU
Pavilion of Women  *378*

ERIC SAVIN
Happenstance  *190*

RAPHAEL SBARGE (1964-)
Pearl Harbor  *379*

JOHNATHON SCHAECH
(1969-)
The Forsaken  *160*

ERIC SCHAEFFER (1962-)
One Night at
McCool's  *365*

RICHARD SCHIFF (1959-)
I Am Sam  *217*
What's the Worst That
Could Happen?  *536*

JENNY SCHILY
The Legend of Rita  *287*

AUGUST SCHMOLZER
Bride of the Wind  *71*

ROB SCHNEIDER (1963-)
The Animal  *29*

ANDREW SCHOFIELD
Liam  *289*

DAVID SCHOFIELD
The Musketeer  *343*

LIEV SCHREIBER (1967-)
Kate & Leopold  *260*

HARALD SCHROTT
The Legend of Rita  *287*

JOHN SCHUCK (1940-)
The Curse of the Jade
Scorpion  *107*

JULIA SCHULTZ
Tomcats  *491*

MATT SCHULZE
The Fast and the
Furious  *150*

PAUL SCHULZE
Don't Say a Word  *126*

JENNIFER SCHWALBACH
Jay and Silent Bob Strike
Back  *231*

ROBERT SCHWARTZMAN
(1982-)
The Princess Diaries  *394*

DAGMAR SCHWARZ
Bride of the Wind  *71*

TIL SCHWEIGER (1963-)
Driven  *133*

ANDREW SCOTT
Nora  *351*

CAMPBELL SCOTT (1962-)
Top of the Food
Chain  *494*

GEORGE W. SCOTT
The Last Castle  *278*

SUZANNE SOMERS (1946-)
Say It Isn't So  *415*

GERALDINE
     SOMERVILLE
Gosford Park  *182*

PAUL SORVINO (1939-)
See Spot Run  *421*

SHANNYN SOSSAMON
A Knight's Tale  *271*

TALISA SOTO (1967-)
Pinero  *383*

FILIP SOVAGOVIC
No Man's Land  *349*

SISSY SPACEK (1949-)
In the Bedroom  *220*

KEVIN SPACEY (1959-)
K-PAX  *255*
The Shipping News  *435*

DAVID SPADE (1964-)
Joe Dirt  *236*

TIMOTHY SPALL (1957-)
Intimacy  *224*
Rock Star  *403*
Vanilla Sky  *518*

TORI SPELLING (1973-)
Scary Movie 2  *417*

VALERIE SPELMAN
Saltwater  *410*

NILDA SPENCER
Me You Them  *320*

LAURENT SPIELVOGEL
A Matter of Taste  *315*

STEVE SPIERS
The Musketeer  *343*

STEPHEN SPINELLA
Bubble Boy  *76*

GREGORY SPORLEDER
Black Hawk Down  *57*

G.D. SPRADLIN (1920-)
Apocalypse Now
     Redux  *35*

NICK STAHL (1979-)
Bully  *78*
In the Bedroom  *220*
The Sleepy Time Gal  *445*

SYLVESTER STALLONE
     (1946-)
Driven  *133*

FLORENCE STANLEY
Atlantis: The Lost Empire
     (V)  *39*

HARRY DEAN STANTON
     (1926-)
The Man Who Cried  *310*
The Pledge  *387*

FREDRO STARR
Save the Last Dance  *411*

SIMONA STASOVA
Divided We Fall  *120*

JASON STATHAM (1972-)
John Carpenter's Ghosts of
     Mars  *240*
The One  *363*
Snatch  *447*

MARY STEENBURGEN
     (1952-)
I Am Sam  *217*
Life as a House  *291*
Trumpet of the Swan
     (V)  *503*

ROB STEFANIUK
The Law of
     Enclosures  *282*

RICHARD STEINMETZ
The One  *363*

IDWIG STEPHANE
The King Is Dancing  *266*

HEATHER STEPHENS
Tomcats  *491*

JOE STEVENS
American Outlaws  *18*

ALEXANDRA STEWART
     (1939-)
Under the Sand  *511*

JON STEWART (1962-)
Jay and Silent Bob Strike
     Back  *231*

PATRICK STEWART
     (1940-)
Jimmy Neutron: Boy Genius
     (V)  *234*

DAVID OGDEN STIERS
     (1942-)
Atlantis: The Lost Empire
     (V)  *39*
The Curse of the Jade
     Scorpion  *107*
The Majestic  *307*
Tomcats  *491*

JULIA STILES (1981-)
The Business of
     Strangers  *80*
O  *356*
Save the Last Dance  *411*

AMY STILLER
The Visit  *521*

BEN STILLER (1965-)
The Royal
     Tenenbaums  *406*
Zoolander  *542*

JERRY STILLER (1927-)
On the Line  *361*
Zoolander  *542*

RACHAEL STIRLING
Maybe Baby  *318*

ERIC STOLTZ (1961-)
House of Mirth  *213*

DANTON STONE
Series 7: The
     Contenders  *425*

STUART STONE
Joy Ride  *244*

PETER STORMARE (1953-)
The Million Dollar
     Hotel  *325*

ANETTE STOVELBAEK
Italian for Beginners  *229*

MERYL STREEP (1949-)
A. I.: Artificial Intelligence
     (V)  *1*

ARTIOM STRELNIKOV
Last Resort  *281*

JOHNNY STRONG
Black Hawk Down  *57*
The Fast and the
     Furious  *150*

GLORIA STUART (1910-)
The Million Dollar
     Hotel  *325*

ERIK PER SULLIVAN
     (1991-)
Joe Dirt  *236*

CREE SUMMER
Atlantis: The Lost Empire
     (V)  *39*

ETHAN SUPLEE
Blow  *62*
Evolution  *144*

DONALD SUTHERLAND
     (1934-)
Final Fantasy: The Spirits
     Within (V)  *158*

MENA SUVARI (1979-)
American Pie 2  *20*
The Musketeer  *343*
Sugar & Spice  *465*

HILARY SWANK (1974-)
The Affair of the
     Necklace  *8*

D.B. SWEENEY (1961-)
Hardball  *193*

JEREMY SWIFT
Gosford Park  *182*

TILDA SWINTON (1961-)
The Deep End  *114*
Vanilla Sky  *518*

ERIC SYKES
The Others  *373*

WANDA SYKES
Pootie Tang  *390*

ELIZA SZONERT
The Dish  *118*

CARY-HIROYUKI
     TAGAWA (1950-)
Planet of the Apes  *384*

FARAN TAHIR
ABCD  *4*

ANDREE TAINSEY
Under the Sand  *511*

OLEG TAKTAROV
15 Minutes  *155*

HASSAN TANTAI
Kandahar  *257*

EMIL TARDING
The King Is Dancing  *266*

JURGEN TARRACH
The Princess and the
     Warrior  *393*

LARENZ TATE (1975-)
Love Come Down  *299*

AUDREY TAUTOU
Amelie  *14*
Happenstance  *190*

CHRISTINE TAYLOR
     (1971-)
Zoolander  *542*

HOLLAND TAYLOR
     (1943-)
Happy Accidents  *191*
Legally Blonde  *284*

LILI TAYLOR (1967-)
Gaudi Afternoon  *166*

NOAH TAYLOR (1969-)
Lara Croft: Tomb
     Raider  *276*
Simon Magnus  *443*
Vanilla Sky  *518*

BORIS TERRAL
The King Is Dancing  *266*

RICHARD TESARIK
Divided We Fall  *120*

TIA TEXADA
Glitter  *178*

SADOU TEYMOURI
Kandahar  *257*

CHARLIZE THERON
     (1975-)
The Curse of the Jade
     Scorpion  *107*
15 Minutes  *155*
Sweet November  *471*

JUSTIN THEROUX
Mulholland Drive  *338*

MELANIE THIERRY
Making Love  *309*

LYNNE THIGPEN (1948-)
Novocaine  *354*

EDDIE KAYE THOMAS
     (1980-)
American Pie 2  *20*
Freddy Got Fingered  *162*

PETER VAUGHN
Making Love *309*

ROBERT VAUGHN (1932-)
Pootie Tang *390*

VINCE VAUGHN (1970-)
Domestic Disturbance *125*
Made *305*

EMMANUELLE VAUGIER
Suddenly Naked *464*

ALEXA VEGA (1988-)
Spy Kids *459*

PATRICIA VELASQUEZ
The Mummy Returns *341*

RICHARD VENTURE
(1923-)
Series 7: The
Contenders *425*

NATALIA VERBEKE
Jump Tomorrow *246*

BENOIT VERHAERT
Thomas in Love *481*

SIMON VERHOEVEN
Bride of the Wind *71*

PIERRE VERNIER
Under the Sand *511*

KAILI VERNOFF
Jump Tomorrow *246*

CONRAD VERNON
Shrek (V) *437*

TRICIA VESSEY (1972-)
Town and Country *497*

ONDREJ VETCHY
Dark Blue World *111*

VINCE VIELUF
Rat Race *397*

SOFIA VIGLIAR
The Son's Room *453*

JORDI VILCHES
Nico and Dani *348*

PRUOUR
VILHJALMSDOTTIR
101 Reykjavik *364*

BRIAN VINCENT
Under Hellgate
Bridge *510*

CERINA VINCENT
Not Another Teen
Movie *352*

FRANK VINCENT (1940-)
Under Hellgate
Bridge *510*

IAN VIRGO (1981-)
Black Hawk Down *57*

IRENE VISEDO
The Devil's Backbone *115*

GORAN VISNJIC (1972-)
The Deep End *114*

JOE (JOHNNY) VITERELLI
(1941-)
See Spot Run *421*
Shallow Hal *432*

JON VOIGHT (1938-)
Ali *10*
Lara Croft: Tomb
Raider *276*
Pearl Harbor *379*
Zoolander *542*

AMNON VOLF
Time of Favor *487*

DANIEL VON BARGEN
(1950-)
The Majestic *307*

ERIK VON DETTEN (1982-)
The Princess Diaries *394*

ALEXANDRE VON SIVERS
Thomas in Love *481*

ARNOLD VOSLOO (1962-)
The Mummy Returns *341*

GARY WADDELL
Chopper *91*

JULIAN WADHAM (1958-)
High Heels and Low
Lifes *209*

MARK WAHLBERG (1971-)
Planet of the Apes *384*
Rock Star *403*

LIAM WAITE
John Carpenter's Ghosts of
Mars *240*

CHRISTOPHER WALKEN
(1943-)
The Affair of the
Necklace *8*
America's Sweethearts *24*
Joe Dirt *236*

CHRIS WALKER
The King Is Alive *265*

PAUL WALKER (1973-)
The Fast and the
Furious *150*
Joy Ride *244*

BASIL WALLACE
Joy Ride *244*

JULIE WALTERS (1950-)
Harry Potter and the
Sorcerer's Stone *195*

ZOE WANAMAKER (1949-)
Harry Potter and the
Sorcerer's Stone *195*

PATRICK WARBURTON
(1964-)
The Dish *118*
Joe Somebody *238*

FRED WARD (1943-)
Corky Romano *101*
Joe Dirt *236*
Summer Catch *467*

SUSAN WARD (1976-)
Shallow Hal *432*

DAVID WARNER (1941-)
Planet of the Apes *384*

DEWAYNE WARREN
Hardball *193*

ESTELLA WARREN (1978-)
Driven *133*
Planet of the Apes *384*

DENZEL WASHINGTON
(1954-)
Training Day *501*

ISAIAH WASHINGTON, IV
(1963-)
Exit Wounds *146*

KERRY WASHINGTON
Lift *293*
Our Song *376*
Save the Last Dance *411*

ALBERTA WATSON (1955-)
Hedwig and the Angry
Inch *204*

EMILY WATSON (1967-)
Gosford Park *182*
The Luzhin Defence *303*

EMMA WATSON
Harry Potter and the
Sorcerer's Stone *195*

NAOMI WATTS (1968-)
Mulholland Drive *338*

MARLON WAYANS (1972-)
Scary Movie 2 *417*

SHAWN WAYANS (1971-)
Scary Movie 2 *417*

SIGOURNEY WEAVER
(1949-)
Company Man *99*
Heartbreakers *200*

HUGO WEAVING (1959-)
Lord of the Rings 1: The
Fellowship of the
Rings *295*

TIMOTHY WEBBER
My Father's Angel *345*

RON WEBSTER
Gosford Park *182*

JEANNETTE WEEGAR
Black Knight *60*

MIKE WEINBERG
Life as a House *291*

RACHEL WEISZ (1971-)
Beautiful Creatures *47*
Enemy at the Gates *134*
The Mummy Returns *341*

RAQUEL WELCH (1940-)
Legally Blonde *284*
Tortilla Soup *495*

FREDERICK WELLER
The Business of
Strangers *80*

KENNETH WELSH
Love Come Down *299*

MARY KATE WELSH
Suspicious River *469*

DAVID WENHAM (1965-)
Better Than Sex *56*
Moulin Rouge *335*

DOMINIC WEST
Rock Star *403*

SAMUEL WEST (1966-)
Iris *226*

SHANE WEST (1978-)
Get Over It! *167*

TIMOTHY WEST (1934-)
Iris *226*

CELIA WESTON
Hearts in Atlantis *202*
In the Bedroom *220*
K-PAX *255*

MERRITT WEVER
Series 7: The
Contenders *425*

SHEA WHIGHAM
Tigerland *484*

JULIANNE WHITE
Sexy Beast *429*

MICHAEL JAI WHITE
Exit Wounds *146*

PAXTON WHITEHEAD
(1937-)
Kate & Leopold *260*

CHARLES MALIK
WHITFIELD
Behind Enemy Lines *51*

DONDRE T. WHITFIELD
Two Can Play That
Game *506*

BRADLEY WHITFORD
(1959-)
Kate & Leopold *260*

ISIAH WHITLOCK, JR.
Jump Tomorrow *246*

MAE WHITMAN (1988-)
An American
Rhapsody *22*

JAMES WHITMORE (1921-)
Here's to Life *208*
The Majestic *307*

GARLAND WHITT
Save the Last Dance *411*

**JOHNNY WHITWORTH
(1975-)**
Valentine *516*

**JOHAN WIDERBERG**
Under the Sun *512*

**DIANNE WIEST (1948-)**
I Am Sam *217*

**WILEY WIGGINS**
Waking Life *524*

**JAMES WILBY (1958-)**
Gosford Park *182*
Jump Tomorrow *246*

**TOYAH WILCOX**
The Most Fertile Man in
Ireland *334*

**MICHAEL SHAMUS
WILES**
Rock Star *403*

**TOM WILKINSON (1948-)**
Black Knight *60*
In the Bedroom *220*

**FRED WILLARD (1939-)**
The Wedding Planner *530*

**BARBARA WILLIAMS**
Love Come Down *299*

**BILLY DEE WILLIAMS
(1937-)**
The Visit *521*

**HARLAND WILLIAMS
(1967-)**
Freddy Got Fingered *162*

**LEE WILLIAMS**
Making Love *309*

**LIA WILLIAMS**
The King Is Alive *265*

**MARK WILLIAMS (1959-)**
High Heels and Low
Lifes *209*

**OLIVIA WILLIAMS (1969-)**
The Body *66*
Born Romantic *67*

**PETER WILLIAMS (1933-)**
Love Come Down *299*

**ROBIN WILLIAMS (1952-)**
A. I.: Artificial Intelligence
(V) *1*

**SAUL WILLIAMS**
K-PAX *255*

**TODD WILLIAMS**
Lift *293*

**MYKELTI WILLIAMSON
(1960-)**
Ali *10*

**BRUCE WILLIS (1955-)**
Bandits *43*

**SUSAN WILLIS**
The Majestic *307*

**ALEC WILSON**
Crocodile Dundee in Los
Angeles *105*

**BRIDGETTE WILSON
(1973-)**
Just Visiting *253*
The Wedding Planner *530*

**KRISTEN WILSON (1969-)**
Dr. Dolittle 2 *123*

**LUKE WILSON (1971-)**
Legally Blonde *284*
The Royal
Tenenbaums *406*
Soul Survivors *455*

**OWEN C. WILSON (1968-)**
Behind Enemy Lines *51*
The Royal
Tenenbaums *406*
Zoolander *542*

**RITA WILSON (1958-)**
The Glass House *175*

**SCOTT WILSON (1942-)**
Pearl Harbor *379*

**STUART WILSON (1934-)**
The Luzhin Defence *303*

**PENELOPE WILTON
(1946-)**
Iris *226*

**MICHAEL WINCOTT
(1959-)**
Along Came a Spider *12*

**KATE WINSLET (1975-)**
Iris *226*

**RAY WINSTONE (1957-)**
Sexy Beast *429*

**MAURICE DEAN WINT**
Hedwig and the Angry
Inch *204*

**RAY WISE (1947-)**
Two Can Play That
Game *506*

**WILLIAM WISE**
In the Bedroom *220*

**REESE WITHERSPOON
(1976-)**
Legally Blonde *284*
Trumpet of the Swan
(V) *503*

**ALICIA WITT (1975-)**
Vanilla Sky *518*

**ANTHONY WONG (1961-)**
Time and Tide *486*

**CYNTHIA WOOD**
Apocalypse Now
Redux *35*

**ELIJAH WOOD (1981-)**
Lord of the Rings 1: The
Fellowship of the
Rings *295*

**JOHN WOOD (1937-)**
The Body *66*

**ALFRE WOODARD (1953-)**
K-PAX *255*

**CHARLAINE WOODARD**
The Million Dollar
Hotel *325*

**BOKEEM WOODBINE
(1970-)**
3000 Miles to
Graceland *482*

**JAMES WOODS (1947-)**
Final Fantasy: The Spirits
Within (V) *158*
Riding in Cars with
Boys *399*
Scary Movie 2 *417*

**JEFFREY WRIGHT (1965-)**
Ali *10*

**MICHAEL WRIGHT**
Pinero *383*

**ROBIN WRIGHT PENN
(1966-)**
The Pledge *387*

**NATASHA WRIGHTMAN**
Gosford Park *182*

**VIVIAN WU (1966-)**
Dinner Rush *116*

**MARTIN WUTTKE**
The Legend of Rita *287*

**DON WYCHERLEY**
When Brendan Met
Trudy *538*

**DANIEL WYLLIE**
Chopper *91*

**SARAH WYNTER**
Bride of the Wind *71*

**KOJI YAKUSHO (1956-)**
Warm Water Under a Red
Bridge *526*
Eureka *138*

**LUO YAN**
Pavilion of Women *378*

**OLEG YANKOVSKY**
The Man Who Cried *310*

**AYLIN YAY**
Thomas in Love *481*

**ANTON YELCHIN**
Along Came a Spider *12*
Hearts in Atlantis *202*

**TRAN NU YEN-KHE**
The Vertical Ray of the
Sun *520*

**SERRA YILMAZ**
Ignorant Fairies *219*

**CECILIA YIP**
What Time Is It
There? *534*

**WLADIMIR YORDANOFF**
The Taste of Others *479*

**BILL YOUNG**
Chopper *91*

**BRUCE A. YOUNG**
Jurassic Park 3 *247*

**REX YOUNG**
ABCD *4*

**SEAN YOUNG (1959-)**
Sugar & Spice *465*

**XIA YU**
Shadow Magic *431*

**ZHAO YUELIN**
The Road Home *402*

**XING YUFEI**
Shadow Magic *431*

**HARRIS YULIN (1937-)**
American Outlaws *18*
The Million Dollar
Hotel *325*
Rush Hour 2 *408*
Training Day *501*

**RICK YUNE**
The Fast and the
Furious *150*

**LI YUSHENG**
Shadow Magic *431*

**MAHRAM ZEINAL
ZADEH**
The Day I Became a
Woman *112*

**STEVE ZAHN (1968-)**
Dr. Dolittle 2 (V) *123*
Joy Ride *244*
Riding in Cars with
Boys *399*
Saving Silverman *413*

**PHILIP ZANDEN (1954-)**
Faithless *148*

**LISA ZANE (1967-)**
Monkeybone *327*

**NICOL ZANZARELLA**
Too Much Sleep *492*

**CARMEN ZAPATA (1927-)**
The Sleepy Time Gal *445*

**RENEE ZELLWEGER
(1969-)**
Bridget Jones's Diary *72*

**CATHERINE ZETA-JONES
(1969-)**
America's Sweethearts *24*

**ZHANG ZIYI**
The Road Home *402*
Rush Hour 2 *408*

**AXEL ZUBER**
  Together  *489*

**JOSE ZUNIGA**
  Happy Accidents  *191*

# Subject Index

Don't Say a Word  *126*
Hannibal  *187*
Happy Accidents  *191*
K-PAX  *255*
A Matter of Taste  *315*
The Orphan Muses  *369*
The Others  *373*
Session 9  *427*
Simon Magnus  *443*
Soul Survivors  *455*
Thomas in Love  *481*
Under the Sand  *511*

MENTAL RETARDATION
I Am Sam  *217*

MEXICO OR MEXICANS
Amores Perros  *26*
Double Take  *129*
The Mexican  *323*

MIDDLE AGES
Black Knight  *60*
Just Visiting  *253*
A Knight's Tale  *271*

MILITARY LIFE OR
    SERVICE
Apocalypse Now
    Redux  *35*
Behind Enemy Lines  *51*
Black Hawk Down  *57*
Captain Corelli's
    Mandolin  *83*
Enemy at the Gates  *134*
Evolution  *144*
The Last Castle  *278*
No Man's Land  *349*
Pearl Harbor  *379*
Tigerland  *484*
Time of Favor  *487*
The Widow of Saint-
    Pierre  *539*

MINING OR MINERS
The Claim  *94*

MISTAKEN OR SECRET
    IDENTITY
Baran  *45*
The Claim  *94*
The Closet  *96*
Company Man  *99*
Corky Romano  *101*
Double Take  *129*
Exit Wounds  *146*
Gosford Park  *182*
Head Over Heels  *198*
A Knight's Tale  *271*
The Legend of Rita  *287*
Memento  *321*
Mulholland Drive  *338*
Say It Isn't So  *415*
Shallow Hal  *432*
The Sleepy Time Gal  *445*
The Tailor of Panama  *475*

MONKEYS
Jay and Silent Bob Strike
    Back  *231*
Monkeybone  *327*
Planet of the Apes  *384*

MOTHERS AND
    CHILDREN
ABCD  *4*
The Circle  *93*
Come Undone  *98*
The Deep End  *114*
Heartbreakers  *200*
Last Resort  *281*
Lift  *293*
Love Come Down  *299*
Monster's Ball  *330*
101 Reykjavik  *364*
Pavilion of Women  *378*
The Road Home  *402*
Say It Isn't So  *415*
Skipped Parts  *444*
The Visit  *521*
What Time Is It
    There?  *534*

MUSEUMS
The Mummy Returns  *341*

MUSIC OR MUSICIANS
Calle 54  *82*
Hedwig and the Angry
    Inch  *204*
Jackpot  *230*
Josie and the
    Pussycats  *242*
Moulin Rouge  *335*
Rock Star  *403*

NATIVE AMERICA
Skipped Parts  *444*
Unconquering the Last
    Frontier  *509*

NAZIS OR NAZISM
Divided We Fall  *120*
Enemy at the Gates  *134*
Fighter  *157*
Glamour  *174*
Sobibor, October 14, 1943,
    4 p.m.  *449*

NEW YORK CITY
ABCD  *4*
Calle 54  *82*
The Caveman's
    Valentine  *87*
The Curse of the Jade
    Scorpion  *107*
Dinner Rush  *116*
Don't Say a Word  *126*
Down to Earth  *131*
Fast Food, Fast
    Women  *152*
15 Minutes  *155*
Glitter  *178*
Happy Accidents  *191*
Head Over Heels  *198*
Hit and Runway  *211*
House of Mirth  *213*
Just One Time  *252*
K-PAX  *255*
Kate & Leopold  *260*
Made  *305*
Our Song  *376*
Pinero  *383*
The Royal
    Tenenbaums  *406*
Serendipity  *423*

Sidewalks of New
    York  *439*
Someone Like You  *451*
Town and Country  *497*
Two Ninas  *508*
Under Hellgate
    Bridge  *510*
Vanilla Sky  *518*

NIGHTCLUBS
Born Romantic  *67*
Love Come Down  *299*
Moulin Rouge  *335*
The Score  *419*

NUNS AND PRIESTS
The Body  *66*
Liam  *289*
Scary Movie 2  *417*
Soul Survivors  *455*

OPERA
The Man Who Cried  *310*
The Turandot Project  *505*

ORGANIZED CRIME
Corky Romano  *101*
Dinner Rush  *116*
High Heels and Low
    Lifes  *209*
Made  *305*
Snatch  *447*
Under Hellgate
    Bridge  *510*

PARENTING
Baby Boy  *41*
Blow  *62*
Dad on the Run  *110*
In the Bedroom  *220*
Jurassic Park 3  *247*
Life as a House  *291*
The Others  *373*
Riding in Cars with
    Boys  *399*
Together  *489*

PERIOD PIECE: 17TH
    CENTURY
The King Is Dancing  *266*
The Musketeer  *343*

PERIOD PIECE: 18TH
    CENTURY
The Affair of the
    Necklace  *8*

PERIOD PIECE: 19TH
    CENTURY
American Outlaws  *18*
The Claim  *94*
From Hell  *164*
Kate & Leopold  *260*
Moulin Rouge  *335*
Original Sin  *367*
Simon Magnus  *443*
The Widow of Saint-
    Pierre  *539*

PERIOD PIECE: 20TH
    CENTURY
Bride of the Wind  *71*
Iris  *226*

PETS
Amores Perros  *26*
Beautiful Creatures  *47*
Cats & Dogs  *85*
The Mexican  *323*
Sweet November  *471*

PHOTOGRAPHY OR
    PHOTOGRAPHERS
Amelie  *14*
The Caveman's
    Valentine  *87*
Memento  *321*
Shadow Magic  *431*

PHYSICAL PROBLEMS
Don't Say a Word  *126*
Freddy Got Fingered  *162*
Shallow Hal  *432*

POLITICS OR
    POLITICIANS
crazy/beautiful  *103*
An Everlasting Piece  *140*
Lumumba  *302*

PORNOGRAPHY
Last Resort  *281*

POVERTY OR POOR
    PEOPLE
La Cienaga  *92*
The Gleaners and I  *177*
Joe Dirt  *236*
Last Resort  *281*
Liam  *289*
Me You Them  *320*
Monster's Ball  *330*
The Road Home  *402*
The Way We
    Laughed  *528*

PREGNANCY
The Circle  *93*
Divided We Fall  *120*
Lift  *293*
Maybe Baby  *318*
Me You Them  *320*
The Most Fertile Man in
    Ireland  *334*
101 Reykjavik  *364*
Our Song  *376*
Riding in Cars with
    Boys  *399*
Series 7: The
    Contenders  *425*
Skipped Parts  *444*
Sugar & Spice  *465*
Time and Tide  *486*

PRISON OR PRISONERS
Blow  *62*
Chopper  *91*
Dark Blue World  *111*
Greenfingers  *185*
John Carpenter's Ghosts of
    Mars  *240*
The Last Castle  *278*
Monster's Ball  *330*
Ocean's Eleven  *359*
Spy Game  *457*
The Visit  *521*

# Title Index

This cumulative index is an alphabetical list of all films covered in the volumes of the *Magill's Cinema Annual*. Film titles are indexed on a word-by-word basis, including articles and prepositions. English and foreign leading articles are ignored. Films reviewed in this volume are cited in bold with an arabic number indicating the page number on which the review begins; films reviewed in past volumes are cited with the year in which the film was originally released. Film sequels are indicated with a roman numeral following the film title. Original and alternate titles are cross-referenced to the American release title. Titles of retrospective films are followed by the year, in brackets, of their original release.

A corps perdu. *See* Straight for
    the Heart.
**A. I.: Artificial Intelligence,**
    pg. 1
Á la Mode (Fausto) (In
    Fashion) 1994
A Ma Soeur *See* Fat Girl.
A nos amours 1984
**ABCD,** pg. 4
Abgeschminkt! *See* Making Up!.
**About Adam,** pg. 5
About Last Night . . . 1986
Above the Law 1988
Above the Rim 1994
Abre Los Ojos. *See* Open Your
    Eyes.
Abril Despedacado *See* Behind
    the Sun.
Absence of Malice 1981
Absolute Beginners 1986
Absolute Power 1997
Absolution 1988
Abyss, The 1989
Accidental Tourist, The 1988
Accompanist, The 1993
Accused, The 1988
Ace in the Hole [1951] 1991,
    1986
Ace Ventura: Pet Detective
    1994
Ace Ventura: When Nature
    Calls 1995
Aces: Iron Eagle III 1992
Acid House, The 1999
Acqua e sapone. *See* Water and
    Soap.
Across the Tracks 1991
Acting on Impulse 1994
Action Jackson 1988
Actress 1988
Adam's Rib [1950] 1992
Addams Family, The 1991
Addams Family Values 1993
Addicted to Love 1998
Addiction, The 1995
Addition, L'. *See* Patsy, The.
Adjo, Solidaritet. *See* Farewell
    Illusion.
Adjuster, The 1992
Adolescente, L' 1982
Adventure of Huck Finn, The
    1993
Adventures in Babysitting 1987
Adventures of Baron
    Munchausen, The 1989

Adventures of Buckaroo Banzai,
    The 1984
Adventures of Elmo in
    Grouchland, The 1999
**Adventures of Felix, The,** pg. 7
Adventures of Ford Fairlane,
    The 1990
Adventures of Mark Twain,
    The 1986
Adventures of Milo and Otis,
    The 1989
Adventures of Pinocchio, The
    1996
Adventures of Priscilla, Queen
    of the Desert, The 1994
Adventures of Rocky and
    Bullwinkle, The 2000
Adventures of Sebastian Cole,
    The, 1999
Adventures of the American
    Rabbit, The 1986
Advocate 1994
Aelita 1994
Affair of Love, An [1999] 2000
**Affair of the Necklace, The,**
    pg. 8
Affaire de Femmes, Une. *See*
    Story of Women.
Affaire de Gout, Un *See* Matter
    of Taste, A.
Affengeil 1992
Affliction 1998
Afraid of the Dark 1992
Africa the Serengeti 1994
After Dark, My Sweet 1990
After Hours 1985
After Life 1999
After Midnight 1989
After the Rehearsal 1984
Afterglow 1998
Against All Odds 1983
Age Isn't Everything (Life in
    the Food Chain) 1994
Age of Innocence, The 1993
Agent on Ice 1986
Agnes Browne [1999] 2000
Agnes of God 1985
Aid 1988
Aileen Wuornos: The Selling of
    a Serial Killer 1994
Air America 1990
Air Bud 1997
Air Bud: Golden Receiver 1998
Air Force One 1997
Air Up There, The 1994

Airborne 1993
Airheads 1994
Airplane II: The Sequel 1982
Akai Hashi no Shita no Nurui
    Mizo *See* Warm Water
    Under a Red Bridge.
Akira Kurosawa's Dreams 1990
Aladdin (Corbucci) 1987
Aladdin (Musker & Clements)
    1992
Alamo Bay 1985
Alan and Naomi 1992
Alan Smithee Film, An 1998
Alarmist, The 1998
Alaska 1996
Alberto Express 1992
Albino Alligator 1997
Alchemist, The 1986
Alfred Hitchcock's Bon Voyage
    & Aventure Malgache. *See*
    Aventure Malgache.
**Ali,** pg. 10
Alice (Allen) 1990
Alice (Svankmajer) 1988
Alice et Martin [1998] 2000
Alien Nation 1988
Alien Predator 1987
Alien Resurrection 1997
Alien³ 1992
Aliens 1986
Alive 1993
Alive and Kicking 1997
All About My Mother 1999
All Dogs Go to Heaven 1989
All Dogs Go to Heaven II,
    1996
All I Desire [1953] 1987
All I Want for Christmas 1991
All of Me 1984
All Over Me 1997
All Quiet on the Western Front
    [1930] 1985
All the Little Animals 1999
All the Pretty Horses 2000
All the Rage. *See* It's the Rage.
All the Right Moves 1983
All the Vermeers in New York
    1992
All's Fair 1989
All-American High 1987
Allan Quatermain and the Lost
    City of Gold 1987
Alley Cat 1984
Alligator Eyes 1990
Allnighter, The 1987

Almost an Angel 1990
Almost Famous 2000
Almost Heroes 1998
Almost You 1985
Aloha Summer 1988
Alone. *See* Solas.
**Along Came a Spider,** pg. 12
Alphabet City 1983
Alpine Fire 1987
Altars of the World [1976]
    1985
Always (Jaglom) 1985
Always (Spielberg) 1989
Amadeus 1984, 1985
Amanda 1989
Amantes. *See* Lovers.
Amants du Pont Neuf, Les
    1994
Amateur 1995
Amateur, The 1982
Amazing Grace and Chuck
    1987
Amazing Panda Adventure, The
    1995
Amazon Women on the Moon
    1987
Ambition 1991
**Amelie,** pg. 14
America 1986
American Anthem 1986
American Beauty 1999
American Blue Note 1991
American Buffalo 1996
American Cyborg: Steel Warrior
    1994
**American Desi,** pg. 17
American Dream 1992
American Dreamer 1984
American Fabulous 1992
American Flyers 1985
American Friends 1993
American Gothic 1988
American Heart 1993
American History X 1998
American in Paris, An [1951]
    1985
American Justice 1986
American Me 1992
American Movie 1999
American Ninja 1985
American Ninja II 1987
American Ninja III 1989
American Ninja 1984, 1991
**American Outlaws,** pg. 18
American Pie 1999

Can't Buy Me Love 1987
Can't Hardly Wait 1998
Candy Mountain 1988
Candyman 1992
Candyman II: Farewell to the Flesh 1995
Cannery Row 1982
Cannonball Run II 1984
Canone Inverso *See* Making Love.
Cape Fear 1991
Capitano, Il 1994
**Captain Corelli's Mandolin,** pg. 83
Captain Ron 1992
Captive Hearts 1987
Captive in the Land, A 1994
Captives 1996
Car 54, Where Are You? 1994
Caravaggio 1986
Cardinal, The [1963] 1986
Care Bears Adventure in Wonderland, The 1987
Care Bears Movie, The 1985
Care Bears Movie II 1986
Career Girls 1997
Career Opportunities 1991
Careful He Might Hear You 1984
Carlito's Way 1993
Carmen 1983
Carnal Knowledge [1971], 680
Carne, La (The Flesh) 1994
Caro Diario (Dear Diary) 1994
Carpenter, The 1988
Carpool 1996
Carried Away 1996
Carriers Are Waiting, The [1999] 2000
Carrington 1995
Casa in bilico, Una. *See* Tottering Lives.
Casino 1995
Casper 1995
Cast Away 2000
Castle, The 1999
Casual Sex? 1988
Casualties of War 1989
Cat on a Hot Tin Roof [1958] 1993
Cat People [1942] 1981, 1982
Catacombs 1988
Catch Me If You Can 1989
Catfish in Black Bean Sauce 2000
**Cats & Dogs,** pg. 85
Cats Don't Dance 1997
Cattle Annie and Little Britches 1981
Caught 1996
Caught Up 1998
Cave Girl 1985
**Caveman's Valentine, The** pg. 87
CB4 1993
Cease Fire 1985
Cecil B. Demented 2000
Celebrity 1998
Céleste 1982
Celestial Clockwork 1996
Cell, The 2000
Celluloid Closet, The 1996

Celtic Pride 1996
Cement Garden , The 1994
Cemetery Club, The 1993
Cemetery Man 1996
Center of the Web 1992
**Center of the World, The** pg. 89
Center Stage 2000
Central do Brasil. *See* Central Station.
Central Station 1998
Century 1994
Ceravani tanto Amati. *See* We All Loved Each Other So Much.
Ceremonie, La 1996
Certain Fury 1985
Certain Regard, Un. *See* Hotel Terminus.
C'est la vie 1990
Ceux qui m'aiment predont le train. *See* Those Who Love Me Can Take the Train.
Chac 2000
Chain of Desire 1993
Chain Reaction 1996
Chaindance. *See* Common Bonds.
Chained Heat 1983
Chairman of the Board 1998
Challenge, The 1982
Chamber, The 1996
Chambermaid of the Titanic, The 1998
Chameleon Street 1991
Champion [1949] 1991
Champions 1984
Chan Is Missing 1982
Chances Are 1989
Chantilly Lace 1994
Chaos. *See* Ran.
Chaplin 1992
Character 1998
Chariots of Fire 1981
Charlie's Angels 2000
Charm Discret de la Bourgeoisie, Le. *See* The Discreet Charm of the Bourgeoisie.
Chase, The 1994
Chasers 1994
Chasing Amy 1988
Château de ma mère, Le. *See* My Mother's Castle.
Chattahoochee 1990
Chattanooga Choo Choo 1984
Cheap Shots 1991
Cheatin' Hearts 1993
Check Is in the Mail, The 1986
Checking Out 1989
Cheech & Chong Still Smokin' 1983
Cheech & Chong's The Corsican Brothers 1984
Cheetah 1989
Chef in Love, A 1997
Chère Inconnue. *See* I Sent a Letter to My Love.
Chèvre, La. *See* Goat, The.
Chicago Joe and the Showgirl 1990

Chicken Hawk: Men Who Love Boys 1994
Chicken Run 2000
Chief Zabu 1988
Child's Play 1988
Child's Play II 1990
Child's Play III 1991
Children of a Lesser God 1986
Children of Heaven, The 1999
Children of Nature 1994
Children of the Corn II 1993
Children of the Revolution 1997
Chile, la Memoria Obstinada. *See* Chile, Obstinate Memory.
Chile, Obstinate Memory 1998
Chill Factor 1999
Chimes at Midnight. *See* Falstaff.
China Cry 1990
China Girl 1987
China Moon 1994
China, My Sorrow 1994
China Syndrome, The [1979] 1988
Chinatown [1974] 680
Chinese Box 1998
Chinese Ghost Story II, A 1990
Chinese Ghost Story III, A 1991
Chipmunk Adventure, The 1987
Chocolat (Denis) 1989
Chocolat (Hallstrom) 2000
Chocolate War, The 1988
Choke Canyon 1986
Choose Me 1984, 1985
**Chopper,** pg. 91
Chopper Chicks in Zombie Town 1991
Chopping Mall 1986
Chorus Line, A 1985
Chorus of Disapproval, A 1989
Chosen, The 1982
Christine 1983
Christine F. 1982
Christmas Story, A 1983
Christopher Columbus: The Discovery 1992
Chronos 1985
Chuck & Buck 2000
Chuck Berry: Hail! Hail! Rock 'n' Roll 1987
C.H.U.D. 1984
Chungking Express 1996
Chunhyang 2000
Chutney Popcorn 2000
Ciao, Professore! 1994
Cider House Rules, The 1999
**Cienaga, La,** pg. 92
Cinema Paradiso 1989
Cinema Verite: Defining the Moment [1999] 2000
**Circle, The,** pg. 93
Circle of Deceit 1982
Circle of Friends 1995
Circuitry Man 1990
Citizen Ruth 1996
Città della donne, La. *See* City of Women.
City Girl, The 1984

City Hall 1996
City Heat 1984
City Limits 1985
City of Angels 1998
City of Hope 1991
City of Industry 1997
City of Joy 1992
City of Lost Children 1996
City of Women 1981
City Slickers 1991
City Slickers II: The Legend of Curly's Gold 1994
City Zero 1994
Civil Action, A, 1998
**Claim, The,** pg. 94
Claire of the Moon 1993
Clan of the Cave Bear, The 1986
Clara's Heart 1988
Clash of the Titans 1981
Class 1982
Class Act 1992
Class Action 1991
Class of 1984 1982
Class of 1999 1990
Class of Nuke 'em High 1986
Class of Nuke 'em High Part II 1991
Clay Pigeons 1998
Clean and Sober 1988
Clean Slate 1994
Clean Slate. *See* Coup de torchon.
Clear and Present Danger 1994
Clearcut 1992
Cleopatra [1963] 1993
Clerks 1994
Client, The 1994
Cliffhanger 1993
Clifford 1994
Climate for Killing, A (A Row of Crows) 1994
Cloak and Dagger 1984
Clock, The 1981
Clockers 1995
Clockwatchers 1998
Clockwise 1986
Close My Eyes 1991
Close to Eden 1992
Closer You Get, The 2000
**Closet, The,** pg. 96
Closet Land 1991
Club Earth. *See* Galactic Gigolo.
Club Paradise 1986
Clue 1985
Clueless 1995
Cobb 1994
Cobra Verde 1988
Cobra 1986
Coca-Cola Kid, The 1985
Cocaine Wars 1986
Cocktail 1988
Cocoon 1985
Cocoon: The Return 1988
Code of Silence 1985
Coeur en hiver, Un 1993
Coeur qui bat, Un. *See* Beating Heart, A.
Coldblooded 1995
Cold Comfort 1989
Cold Comfor Farm 1995

For Roseanna 1997
For Sasha 1992
For the Boys 1991
For the Moment 1996
For Your Eyes Only 1981
Forbidden Choices. *See* Beans of Egypt, Maine, The.
Forbidden Dance, The 1990
Forbidden Quest 1994
Forbidden World 1982
Forced Vengeance 1982
Forces of Nature 1999
Foreign Affair, A [1948] 1986
Foreign Body 1986
Foreign Student 211
Forever 1994
Forever, Lulu 1987
Forever Mary 1991
Forever Young 1992
Forget Paris 1995
Forrest Gump 1994
**Forsaken, The,** pg. 160
Fort Apache [1948] 1983
Fort Apache, the Bronx 1981
Fortress 1993
Fortune Cookie, The [1966] 1986
48 Hrs. 1982
Foster Daddy, Tora! 1981
Four Adventures of Reinette and Mirabelle 1989
Four Days in September 1998
Four Friends 1981
4 Little Girls 1997
Four Rooms 1995
Four Seasons, The 1981
Four Weddings and a Funeral 1994
1492: Conquest of Paradise 1992
4th Man, The 1984
Fourth Protocol, The 1987
Fourth War, The 1990
Fox and the Hound, The 1981
Foxfire 1996
Foxtrap 1986
Frances 1982
Frank and Ollie 1995
Frankenhooker 1990
Frankenstein Unbound. *See* Roger Corman's Frankenstein Unbound.
Frankenstein. *See* Mary Shelley's Frankenstein.
Frankie and Johnny 1991
Frankie Starlight 1995
Frantic 1988
Fraternity Vacation 1985
Frauds 1994
Freaked 1993
Freddie as F.R.O.7 1992
**Freddy Got Fingered,** pg. 162
Freddy's Dead 1991
Free and Easy 1989
Free Enterprise 1999
Free Ride 1986
Free Willy 1993
Free Willy II: The Adventure Home 1995
Free Willy III: The Rescue 1997
Freedom On My Mind 1994

Freejack 1992
Freeway 1988
Freeway 1996
Freeze-Die-Come to Life 1994
French Connection, The [1971] 1982
French Kiss 1995
French Lesson 1986
French Lieutenant's Woman, The 1981
French Twist 1996
Frequency 2000
Fresh 1994
Fresh Horses 1988
Freshman, The 1990
Freud [1962] 1983
Friday 1995
Friday the 13th, Part III 1982
Friday the 13th, Part IV 1984
Friday the 13th, Part VI 1986
Friday the 13th Part VII 1988
Friday the 13th Part VIII 1989
Fried Green Tomatoes 1991
Friend of the Deceased, A 1998
Friends & Lovers 1999
Fright Night 1985
Frighteners, The 1996
Fringe Dwellers, The 1987
From Beyond 1986
From Dusk Till Dawn 1996
From Hollywood to Deadwood 1988
From Swastikas to Jim Crow [1999] 2000
From the Hip 1987
Front, The [1976] 1985
Frosh: Nine Months in a Freshman Dorm 1994
Frozen Assets 1992
Frühlingssinfonie. *See* Spring Symphony.
Fruit Machine, The 1988
Fu-zung cen. *See* Hibiscus Town.
Fucking Åmål. *See* Show Me Love.
Fugitive, The 1993
Full Blast [1999] 2000
Full Metal Jacket 1987
Full Monty, The 1997
Full Moon in Paris 1984
Full Moon in the Blue Water 1988
Fun Down There 1989
Funeral, The 1987
Funeral, The 1996
Funny About Love 1990
Funny Bones 1995
Funny Farm (Clark) 1983
Funny Farm (Hill) 1988
Further Adventures of Tennessee Buck, The 1988

Gabbeh 1997
Gabriela 1984
Gaby-A True Story 1987
Gadjo Dilo 1998
Galactic Gigolo 1988
Galaxy Quest 1999
Gallipoli 1981

Gambler, The 1999
Game, The 1997
Game, The 1989
Gandhi 1982
Gang-Related 1997
Garbage Pail Kids Movie, The 1987
Garbo Talks 1984
Garde à vue 1982
Garden, The 1994
Gardens of Stone 1987
Gas Food Lodging 1992
Gate, The 1987
Gate II 1992
Gattaca 1997
**Gaudi Afternoon,** pg. 166
Gay Divorcée, The [1934] 1981
Genealogies D' Un Crime. *See* Genealogies of a Crime.
Genealogies of a Crime 1998
General, The 1998
General's Daughter, The 1999
Genghis Blues 1999
Gentilezza del tocco, La. *See* Gentle Touch, The.
Gentle Touch, The 1988
Gentlemen Don't Eat Poets 1997
Gentlemen's Agreement [1947] 1989
Genuine Risk 1990
George Balanchine's The Nutcracker 1993
George of the Jungle 1997
George's Island 1991
Georgia 1988
Georgia 1995
Germinal 1993
Geronimo 1993
Get Back 1991
Get Bruce! 1999
Get Carter 2000
Get Crazy 1983
Get on the Bus 1996
**Get Over It!,** pg. 167
Get Real 1999
Get Shorty 1995
Getaway, The 1994
Geteilte Liebe. *See* Maneuvers.
Getting Away with Murder 1996
Getting Even 1986
Getting Even With Dad 1994
Getting It Right 1989
Getting to Know You [1999] 2000
Gettysburg 1993
Ghare Bhaire. *See* Home and the World, The.
Ghost 1990
Ghost and the Darkness, The 1996
Ghost Dad 1990
Ghost Dog: The Way of the Samurai 1999
Ghosts Can't Do It 1990
Ghosts . . . of the Civil Dead 1988
Ghosts of Mississippi 1996
Ghost Story 1981
Ghost Town 1988
**Ghost World,** pg. 170

Ghosts of Mars *See* John Carpenter's Ghosts of Mars.
Ghostbusters 1984
Ghostbusters II 1989
G.I. Jane 1997
Giant [1956] 1993, 1996
Gift, The (Lang) 1983
Gift, The (Raimi) 2000
Gift From Heaven, A 1994
Gig, The 1986
Ginger Ale Afternoon 1989
Ginger and Fred 1986
**Ginger Snaps,** pg. 172
Gingerbread Man, The 1998
Giornata speciale, Una. *See* Special Day, A.
Giovane Toscanini, II. *See* Young Toscanini.
Girl in a Swing, The 1988
Girl, Interrupted 1999
Girl in the Picture, The 1986
Girl Next Door, The 2000
Girl 6 1996
Girl Talk 1988
Girl with the Hungry Eyes, The 1995
Girl with the Red Hair, The 1983
Girlfight 2000
Girls School Screamers 1986
Girls Town 1996
Give My Regards to Broad Street 1984
Giving, The 1992
Gladiator (Herrington) 1992
Gladiator (Scott) 2000
Glamazon: A Different Kind of Girl 1994
**Glamour,** pg. 174
Glaneurs et la Glaneuse, Les *See* Gleaners and I, The.
**Glass House, The,** pg. 175
Glass Menagerie, The 1987
Glass Shield, The 1995
Gleaming the Cube 1989
**Gleaners and I, The,** pg. 177
Glengarry Glen Ross 1992
Glimmer Man, The 1996
**Glitter,** pg. 178
Gloire de mon père, La. *See* My Father's Glory.
Gloria [1980] 1987
Gloria 1999
Glory 1989
Go 1999
Go Fish 1994
Go Now 1998
Goat, The 1985
Gobots 1986
God Doesn't Believe in Us Anymore 1988
God Is My Witness 1993
God Said "Ha"! 1999
God's Will 1989
Godfather, Part III, The 1990
Gods and Monsters 1998
Gods Must Be Crazy, The 1984
Gods Must Be Crazy II, The 1990
Godzilla 1985 1985
Godzilla 1997
Godzilla 2000 [1999] 2000

Heartaches 1982
Heartbreak Hotel 1988
Heartbreak Kid, The [1972] 1986
Heartbreak Ridge 1986
Heartbreaker 1983
**Heartbreakers,** pg. 200
Heartburn 1986
Heartland 1981
**Hearts in Atlantis,** pg. 202
Hearts of Darkness: A Filmmaker's Apocalypse 1992
Hearts of Fire 1987
Heat 1987
Heat 1995
Heat and Dust 1983, 1984
Heat of Desire 1984
Heathcliff 1986
Heathers 1989
Heatwave 1983
Heaven 1987
Heaven and Earth (Kadokawa) 1991
Heaven and Earth (Stone) 1993
Heaven Help Us 1985
Heaven's Gate 1981
Heaven's Prisoners 1996
Heavenly Bodies 1984
Heavenly Creatures 1994
Heavenly Kid, The 1985
Heavy 1996
Heavyweights 1995
Hecate 1984
**Hedwig and the Angry Inch,** pg. 204
Heidi Fleiss: Hollywood Madame 1996
**Heist, The,** pg. 206
Helas Pour Moi 1994
Held Up 2000
Hell High 1989
Hellbent 1989
Hellbound 1988
Heller Wahn. See Sheer Madness.
Hello Again 1987
Hello, Dolly! [1969] 1986
Hello Mary Lou 1987
Hellraiser 1987
Hellraiser III: Hell on Earth 1992
Hellraiser IV: Bloodline 1996
Hell's Angels on Wheels [1967] 679
Henna 1991
Henry 1990
Henry and June 1990
Henry IV 1985
Henry V 1989
Henry Fool 1998
Her Alibi 1989
Her Name Is Lisa 1987
Hercules, 245
Hercules 1983
Hercules II 1985
Herdsmen of the Sun 1994
Here Come the Littles 1985
Here On Earth 2000
**Here's to Life,** pg. 208
Hero 1992
Hero and the Terror 1988
Hexed 1993

Hibiscus Town 1988
Hidden Agenda 1990
Hidden, The 1987
Hidden Hawaii 1994
Hideaway 1995
Hideous Kinky 1999
Hiding Out 1987
Hifazaat. See In Custody.
High Art 1998
High Fidelity 2000
High Heels 1991
**High Heels and Low Lifes,** pg. 209
High Hopes 1988, 1989
High Lonesome: The Story of Bluegrass Music 258
High Risk 1995
High Road to China 1983
High School High 1996
High Season 1988
High Spirits 1988
High Tide 1987
Higher Learning 1995
Highlander 1986
Highlander 2: The Quickening 1991
Highlander 3: The Final Dimension 1995
Highlander: Endgame 2000
Highway 61 1992
Highway Patrolman 1994
Highway to Hell 1992
Hijacking Hollywood
Hi-Lo Country, The 1999
Hilary and Jackie 1998
Himmel über Berlin, Der. See Wings of Desire.
Histoires d'amerique. See American Stories.
History Is Made at Night [1937] 1983
Hit, The 1985
**Hit and Runway,** pg. 211
Hit List 1989
Hit the Dutchman 1994
Hitcher, The 1986
Hitman, The 1991
Hocus Pocus 1993
Hoffa 1992
Holcroft Covenant, The 1985
Hold Back the Dawn [1941] 1986
Hold Me, Thrill Me, Kiss Me 1993
Holiday [1938] 1985
Holiday Inn [1942] 1981
Hollow Man 2000
Hollow Reed 1997
Hollywood in Trouble 1986
Hollywood Mavericks 1990
Hollywood Shuffle 1987
Hollywood Vice Squad 1986
Holy Blood. See Santa Sangre.
Holy Innocents, The 1985
Holy Man 1998
Holy Smoke 1999
**Holy Tongue, The,** pg. 212
Hombre [1967] 1983
Home Alone 1990
Home Alone II: Lost in New York 1992
Home Alone III 1997

Home and the World, The 1985
Home for the Holidays 1995
Home Free All 1984
Home Fries 1998
Home Is Where the Heart Is 1987
Home of Our Own, A 1993
Home of the Brave 1986
Home Remedy 1987
Homeboy 1988
Homegrown 1998
Homer and Eddie 1990
Homeward Bound 1993
Homeward Bound II: Lost in San Francisco 1996
Homework 1982
Homicide 1991
Homme et une femme, Un. See Man and a Woman, A.
Hondo [1953] 1982
Honey, I Blew Up the Kid 1992
Honey, I Shrunk the Kids 1989
Honeybunch 1988
Honeymoon Academy 1990
Honeymoon in Vegas 1992
Hong Gaoliang. See Red Sorghum.
Honky Tonk Freeway 1981
Honkytonk Man 1982
Honneponnetge. See Honeybunch.
Honor Betrayed. See Fear.
Honorable Mr. Wong, The. See Hatchet Man, The.
Honour of the House [1999] 2000
Hoodlum 1997
Hook 1991
Hoop Dreams 1994
Hoosiers 1986
Hope and Glory 1987
Hope and Pain 1988
Hope Floats 1998
Horror Show, The 1989
Hors la Vie (Out of Life) 1994
Horse of Pride, The 1985
Horse Whisperer, The 1998
Horseman on the Roof, The 1996
Hot Dog . . . The Movie 1984
Hot Pursuit 1987
Hot Shots! 1991
Hot Shots! Part Deux 1993
Hot Spot, The 1990
Hot to Trot 1988
Hotel Colonial 1987
Hotel De Love 1997
Hotel New Hampshire, The 1984
Hotel Terminus 1988
Hotshot 1987
Hound of the Baskervilles, The 1981
Hours and Times, The 1992
House 1986
House II 1987
House Arrest 1996
House of Cards 1993
House of Games 1987
House of Luk 2000

**House of Mirth,** pg. 213
House of the Spirits, The 1994
House of Yes, The 1997
House on Carroll Street, The 1988
House on Haunted Hill 1999
House on Limb, A. See Tottering Lives.
House Party 1990
House Party II 1991
House Party III 1994
House Where Evil Dwells, The 1982
Houseboat [1958] 1986
Houseguest 1995
Household Saints 1993
Householder, The 1984
Housekeeper, The 1987
Housekeeping 1987
Housesitter 1992
How I Got into College 1989
How Stella Got Her Groove Back 1998
How to Get Ahead in Advertising 1989
How to Make an American Quilt 1995
How to Make Love to a Negro Without Getting Tired 1990
Howard the Duck 1986
Howard's End 1992
Howling, The 1981
Howling III, The. See Marsupials, The.
Hsi Yen. See Wedding Banquet, The.
Hsimeng Jensheng. See Puppetmaster, The.
Hudson Hawk 1991
Hudsucker Proxy, The 1994
Hugh Hefner: Once Upon a Time 1992
Hugo Pool 1997
**Human Resources,** pg. 216
Human Shield, The 1992
Humongous 1982
Hunchback of Notre Dame, The 1996
Hungarian Fairy Tale, A 1989
Hunger, The 1983
Hungry Feeling, A 1988
Hunk 1987
Hunt for Red October, The 1990
Hunted, The 1995
Hunters of the Golden Cobra, The 1984
Hurlyburly 1998
Hurricane, The 1999
Hurricane Streets 1998
Husbands and Wives 1992
Hush 1998
Hyenas (Hyenes) 1994
Hyenes See Hyenas 1994


I Am My Own Woman 1994
**I Am Sam,** pg. 217
I Can't Sleep 1995
I Come in Peace 1990
I Demoni. See Demons.

Loser 2000
Losin' It 1983
Losing Isaiah 1995
Loss of Sexual Innocence 1999
**Lost and Delirious**, pg. 297
Lost and Found 1999
Lost Angels 1989
Lost Boys, The 1987
Lost Highway 1997
Lost in America 1985
Lost in Siberia 1991
Lost in Space 1998
Lost in Yonkers. *See* Neil
  Simon's Lost in Yonkers.
Lost Moment, The [1947] 1982
Lost Prophet 1994
Lost Souls 2000
Lost Weekend, The [1945]
  1986
Lost Words, The 1994
Lost World, The 1997
Lou, Pat, and Joe D 1988
Louis Bluie 1985
Louis Prima: The Wildest
  [1999] 2000
Loulou 1981
Love Affair 1994
Love After Love (Apres
  l'amour) 1994
Love Always 1997
Love and a .45 1994
Love and Basketball 2000
Love and Death in Long Island
  1998
Love and Human Remains
  1995
Love and Murder 1991
Love and Other Catastrophes,
  342
Love & Sex 2000
Love at Large 1990
Love Child, The 1988
Love Child: A True Story 1982
**Love Come Down**, pg. 299
Love Crimes 1992
Love Field 1992
Love in Germany, A 1984
Love in the Afternoon [1957]
  1986
Love Is a Dog from Hell 1988
Love is the Devil 1998
love jones 1997
Love/Juice 2000
Love Letter, The 1999
Love Letters 1984
Love Potion #9 1992
Love Serenade 1997
Love Stinks 1999
Love Story, A. *See* Bound and
  Gagged.
Love Streams 1984
Love, the Magician. *See* Amor
  brujo, El.
Love! Valour! Compassion!
  1997
Love Walked In 1998
Love Without Pity 1991
Loveless, The 1984, 1986
Lovelines 1984
Lover, The 1992
Loverboy 1989
Lovers 1992

Lovers of the Arctic Circle 1999
Lovers on the Bridge 1999
Love's a Bitch *See* Amores
  Perros.
Love's Labour's Lost 2000
Loves of a Blonde [1965] 1985
Lovesick 1983
Loving Jezebel 2000
Low Blow 1986
**Low Down, The**, pg. 301
Low Down Dirty Shame, A
  1994
Low Life, The 1996
Lucas 1986
Lucie Aubrac 1999
Luckiest Man in the World,
  The 1989
Lucky Numbers 2000
Luminous Motion 2000
**Lumumba**, pg. 302
Lumumba: Death of a Prophet
  1994
Luna Park 1994
Lunatic, The 1992
Lunatics: A Love Story 1992
Lune Froide. *See* Cold Moon.
Lunga vita alla signora! *See*
  Long Live the Lady!
Lurkers 1988
Lush Life 371
Lust for Life [1956] 1991
Lust in the Dust 1985
**Luzhin Defence, The**, pg. 303

M. Butterfly 1993
Ma Vie en Rose 1997
Mac 1993
Mac and Me 1988
Macaroni V, 1988
MacArthur's Children 1985
Maccheroni. *See* Macaroni.
Macht der Bilder, Die. *See* The
  Wonderful, Horrible Life of
  Leni Riefenstahl.
Mack the Knife 1990
Macomber Affair, The [1947]
  1982
Mad City 1997
Mad Dog and Glory 1993
Mad Dog Coll. *See* Killer
  Instinct.
Mad Dog Time 1996
Mad Love 1995
Mad Max Beyond
  Thunderdome 1985
Madagascar Landing. *See*
  Aventure Malgache.
Madagascar Skin 1996
Madame Bovary 1991
Madame Sousatzka 1988
**Made**, pg. 305
Made in America 1993
Made in Heaven 1987
Madeline 1998
Madhouse 1990
Madman 1983
Madness of King George, The
  1994
Maelstrom 2000
Mafia! 1998
Magic Hunter 1996

Magic in the Water 1995
Magnolia 1999
Magyar Stories 1988
Mahabharata, The 1990
Maid to Order 1987
**Majestic, The**, pg. 307
Major and the Minor, The
  [1942] 1986
Major League 1989
Major League: Back to the
  Minors 1998
Major League II 1994
Major League III. *See* Major
  League: Back to the Minors.
Major Payne 1995
Make Way for Tomorrow
  [1937] 1981
Making Love 1982
**Making Love**, pg. 309
Making Mr. Right 1987
Making the Grade 1984
Making Up! (Abgeschminkt!)
  1994
Makioka Sisters, The 1985
Mal d'aimer, Le. *See* Malady of
  Love, The.
Malady of Love, The 1987
Malcolm 1986
Malcolm X 1992
Malena 2000
Malibu Bikini Shop, The 1987
Malice 1993
Mallrats 1995
Malone 1987
Maltese Falcon, The [1941]
  1983
Mama, There's a Man in Your
  Bed 1990
Mamba 1988
Mambo Kings, The 1992
Man and a Woman, A 1986
Man Bites Dog 1993
Man Called Sarge, A 1990
Man from Snowy River, The
  1982
Man Hunt [1941] 1984
Man I Love, The [1946] 1986
Man in Love, A 1987
Man in the Iron Mask, The
  1998
Man in the Moon, The 1991
Man in Uniform, A 1994
Man Inside, The 1990
Man of Iron 1981
Man of Marble [1977] 1981
Man of No Importance, A 1994
Man of the Century 1999
Man of the House 1995
Man of the Year 1996
Man on the Moon 1999
Man Outside 1988
Man Trouble 1992
**Man Who Cried, The**, pg. 310
Man Who Fell to Earth, The
  [1975] 1982
Man Who Knew Too Little,
  The 1997
Man Who Loved Women, The
  1983
Man Who Wasn't There, The
  1983

**Man Who Wasn't There, The**,
  pg. 312
Man Who Would Be King,
  The [1975] 1983
Man with One Red Shoe, The
  1985
Man with Three Coffins, The
  1988
Man with Two Brains, The
  1983
Man Without a Face, The 1993
Man Without a World, The
  1992
Man, Woman and Child 1983
Man's Best Friend 1993
Maneuvers 1988
Mangler, The 1995
Manhattan by Numbers 1994
Manhattan Murder Mystery
  1993
Manhattan Project, The 1986
Manhunter 1986
Maniac Cop 1988
Manifesto 1989
Mannequin 1987
Mannequin Two 1991
Manny & Lo 1996
Manon des sources. *See* Manon
  of the Spring.
Manon of the Spring 1987
Mansfield Park 1999
Map of the Human Heart 1993
Mapantsula 1988
Margaret's Museum
Maria's Lovers 1985
Mariachi, El 1993
Marie 1985
Marie Baie des Anges. *See*
  Marie from the Bay Angels.
Marie from the Bay Angels
  1998
Marilyn Monroe 1987
Marine Life 2000
Marius and Jeannette 1998
Marius et Jeannette: Un Conte
  de L'Estaque. *See* Marius and
  Jeannette.
Marked for Death 1990
Marlene 1986
Marquis 1994
Married to It 1993
Married to the Mob 1988
Marrying Man, The 1991
Mars Attacks! 1996
Marsupials, The 1987
Martha and Ethel 1995
Martha and I 1995
Martha, Ruth, and Edie 1988
Martians Go Home 1990
Marusa No Onna. *See* Taxing
  Woman, A.
Marvin & Tige 1983
Marvin's Room 1996
Mary Reilly 1996
Mary Shelley's Frankenstein
  1994
Masala 1993
Mask 1985
Mask, The 1994
Mask of the Phantasm. *See*
  Batman.
Mask of Zorro, The 1998

Masque of the Red Death 1989
Masquerade 1988
Mass Appeal 1984, 1988
Masterminds 1997
Masters of the Universe 1987
Matchmaker, The 1997
Matewan 1987
Matilda 1996
Matinee 1993
Matrix, The 1999
Matter of Struggle, A 1985
**Matter of Taste, A,** pg. 315
Maurice 1987
Maverick 1994
Max Dugan Returns 1983
**Max Keeble's Big Move,**
pg. 316
Maxie 1985
Maximum Overdrive 1986
Maximum Risk 1996
May Fools 1990
**Maybe Baby,** pg. 318
Maybe . . . Maybe Not 1996
McBain 1991
McHale's Navy 1997
Me and Isaac Newton 2000
Me and My Gal [1932] 1982
Me and the Kid 1993
Me and Veronica 1994
Me, Myself & Irene 2000
Me Myself I [1999] 2000
**Me You Them,** pg. 320
Mean Season, The 1985
Meatballs II 1984
Meatballs III 1987
Meatballs IV 1992
Medicine Man 1992
Mediterraneo 1992
Meet Joe Black 1998
Meet John Doe [1941] 1982
Meet the Applegates 1991
Meet the Deedles 1998
Meet the Hollowheads 1989
Meet the Parents 2000
Meet Wally Sparks 1997
Meeting Venus 1991
Megaforce 1982
Mein Liebster Feind. See My
Best Fiend.
Melvin and Howard 1981
**Memento,** pg. 321
Memoirs of a Madman 1994
Memoirs of a River 1992
Memoirs of an Invisible Man
1992
Memories of Me 1988
Memphis Belle 1990
Men 1986
Men 1998
Men at Work 1990
Men Don't Leave 1990
Men in Black 1997
Men in Tights. See Robin
Hood.
Men of Honor 2000
Men of Respect 1991
Men With Guns 1998
Menace II Society 1993
Ménage 1986
Men's Club, The 1986
Mephisto 1981
Mercenary Fighters 1988

Mercury Rising 1998
Mermaids 1990
Merry Christmas, Mr. Lawrence
1983
Merry War, A 1998
Message in a Bottle 1999
Messenger, The 1987
The Messenger: Joan of Arc
1999
Messenger of Death 1988
Metalstorm: The Destruction of
Jarred-Syn 1983
Metamorphosis: The Alien
Factor 1994
Meteor Man, The 1993
Metro, 368
Metroland 1999
Metropolitan 1990
**Mexican, The,** pg. 323
Mi Vida Loca (My Crazy Life)
1994
Mia Eoniotita ke Mia Mers. See
Eternity and a Day.
Miami Blues 1990
Miami Rhapsody 1995
Michael 1996
Michael Collins 1996
Mickey Blue Eyes 1999
Micki & Maude 1984
Microcosmos 1996
Midnight (Leisen) 1986
Midnight (Vane) 1989
Midnight Clear, A 1992
Midnight Crossing 1988
Midnight in the Garden of
Good and Evil
Midnight Run 1988
Midsummer Night's Sex
Comedy, A 1982
Midwinter's Tale, A 1996
Mifune [1999] 2000
Mighty, The 1998
Mighty Aphrodite 1995
Mighty Ducks, The 1992
Mighty Joe Young 1998
Mighty Morphin Power
Rangers: The Movie 1995
Mighty Quinn, The 1989
Mike's Murder 1984
Mikey and Nicky 1984
Milagro Beanfield War, The
1988
Mildred Pierce [1945] 1986
Miles from Home 1988
Milk and Honey 1989
Milk Money 1994
Millennium 1989
Miller's Crossing 1990
**Million Dollar Hotel, The,**
pg. 325
Million Dollar Mystery 1987
Million to Juan, A 1994
Mimic 1997
Mina Tannenbaum 1995
Mindwalk 1991
Ministry of Vengeance 1989
Minner. See Men.
Minotaur 1994
Minus Man, The 1999
Miracle, The 1991
Miracle Mile 1988, 1989
Miracle on 34th Street 1994

Miracle Woman, The (1931)
1982
Mirror, The 1999
Mirror Has Two Faces, The
1996
Misadventures of Mr. Wilt, The
1990
Mischief 1985
Misery 1990
Misfits, The [1961] 1983
Mishima 1985
Misplaced 1994
Misplaced 1989
Miss Congeniality 2000
Miss Firecracker 1989
Miss Mary 1986
Miss Mona 1987
Miss . . . or Myth? 1987
Missing 1982, 1988
Missing in Action, 1984
Missing in Action II 1985
Mission, The (Joffé) 1986
Mission, The (Sayyad) 1983
Mission: Impossible 1996
Mission: Impossible 2 2000
Mission to Mars 2000
Missionary, The 1982
Mississippi Burning 1988
Mississippi Masala 1992
Missouri Breaks, The [1976]
680
Mrs. Brown 1997
Mrs. Dalloway 1998
Mrs. Doubtfire 1993
Mrs. Parker and the Vicious
Circle 1994
Mrs. Soffel 1984
Mrs. Winterbourne 1996
Mr. and Mrs. Bridge 1990
Mr. Baseball 1992
Mr. Death: The Rise and Fall
of Fred A. Leuchter, Jr. 1999
Mr. Deeds Goes to Town
[1936] 1982
Mr. Destiny 1990
Mr. Frost 1990
Mr. Holland's Opus 1995
Mr. Jealousy 1998
Mister Johnson 1991
Mr. Jones 1993
Mr. Love 1986
Mr. Magoo 1997
Mr. Mom 1983
Mr. Nanny 1993
Mr. Nice Guy 1998
Mr. North 1988
Mr. Payback 1995
Mister Roberts [1955] 1988
Mr. Saturday Night 1992
Mr. Smith Goes to Washington
[1939] 1982
Mr. Wonderful 1993
Mr. Write 1994
Mr. Wrong 1996
Mistress 1992
Misunderstood 1984
Mit Liv som Hund. See My
Life as a Dog.
Mitad del cielo, La. See Half of
Heaven.
Mixed Blood 1985
Mixed Nuts 1994

Mo' Better Blues 1990
Mo' Money 1992
Mobsters 1991
Mod Squad, The 1999
Modern Girls 1986
Modern Romance 1981
Moderns, the 1988
Mois d'avril sont meurtriers, Les
See April Is a Deadly Month.
Moitie Gauche du Frigo, La See
Left Hand Side of the
Fridge, The.
Moll Flanders 1996
Molly 1999
Mom and Dad Save the World
1992
Mommie Dearest 1981
Mon bel Amour, ma dechirure.
See My True Love, My
Wound.
Mona Lisa 1986
Mondo New York 1988
Money for Nothing 1993
Money Man 1994
Money Pit, The 1986
Money Talks 1997
Money Train 1995
Money Tree, The 1992
Mongolian Tale, A 1997
Monkey Shines 1988
Monkey Trouble 1994
**Monkeybone,** pg. 327
Monsieur Hire 1990
Monsignor 1982
Monster, The 1996
Monster in a Box 1992
Monster in the Closet 1987
Monster Squad, The 1987
**Monster's Ball,** pg. 330
**Monsters, Inc.,** pg. 332
Montana Run 1992
Montenegro 1981
Month by the Lake, A 1995
Month in the Country, A 1987
Monty Python's The Meaning
of Life 1983
Monument Ave. 1998
Moon in the Gutter 1983
Moon Over Broadway 1998
Moon over Parador 1988
Moon Shadow [1995] 2000
Moonlight and Valentino 1995
Moonlighting 1982
Moonstruck 1987
Morgan Stewart's Coming
Home 1987
Moriarty. See Sherlock Holmes.
Morning After, The 1986
Morning Glory 1993
Morons from Outer Space 1985
Mort de Mario Ricci, La. See
Death of Mario Ricci, The.
Mortal Kombat 1995
Mortal Kombat II: Annihilation
1997
Mortal Thoughts 1991
Mortuary Academy 1988
Mosca addio. See Moscow
Farewell.
Moscow Farewell. 1987
Moscow on the Hudson 1984
Mosquito Coast, The 1986

Most Dangerous Game, The
[1932] 1985
**Most Fertile Man in Ireland,
The,** pg. 334
Most Wanted 1997
Mother 1996
Mother Lode 1983
Mother Night 1996
Mother Teresa 1986
Mother's Boys 1994
Mothering Heart, The [1913]
1984
Motorama 1993
**Moulin Rouge,** pg. 335
Mountain Gorillas 1994
Mountains of Moon 1990
Mountaintop Motel Massacre
1986
Mouse Hunt 1997
Mouth to Mouth 1997
Movers and Shakers 1985
Moving 1988
Moving the Mountain 1995
Moving Violations 1985
Much Ado About Nothing
1993
Mui du du Xanh. *See* The Scent
of Green Papaya.
Mujeres al borde de un ataque
de nervios. *See* Women on
the Verge of a Nervous
Breakdown.
Mulan 1998
**Mulholland Drive,** pg. 338
Mulholland Falls 1996
Multiplicity 1996
Mumford 1999
Mummy, The 1999
**Mummy Returns, The,** pg. 341
Munchie 1994
Munchies 1987
Muppet Christmas Carol, The
1992
Muppets from Space 1999
Muppet Treasure Island 1996
Muppets Take Manhattan, The
1984
Mur, Le. *See* Wall, The.
Murder at 1600 1997
Murder in the First 1995
Murder One 1988
Muriel's Wedding 1995
Murphy's Law 1986
Murphy's Romance 1985
Muse, The 1999
Muses Orphelines, Les, *See*
Orphan Muses, The.
Music Box 1989
Music for the Movies: Bernard
Herrmann 1994
Music From Another Room
1998
Music of Chance, The 1993
Music of the Heart 1999
Music Tells You , The 1994
Musime si Pomahat *See* Divided
We Fall.
**Musketeer, The,** pg. 343
Mustang: The Hidden
Kingdom 1994
Musuko. *See* My Sons.
Mutant on the Bounty 1989

Mute Witness 1995
Mutiny on the Bounty [1962]
1984
My African Adventure 1987
My American Cousin 1986
My Apprenticeship. *See* Among
People.
My Beautiful Laundrette 1986
My Best Fiend 1999
My Best Friend Is a Vampire
1988
My Best Friend's Girl 1984
My Best Friend's Wedding
1997
My Blue Heaven 1990
My Boyfriend's Back 1993
My Chauffeur 1986
My Cousin Rachel [1952] 1981
My Cousin Vinny 1992
My Crazy Life. *See* Mi Vida
Loca.
My Dark Lady 1987
My Demon Lover 1987
My Dinner with André 1981
My Family (Mi Familia) 1995
My Father Is Coming 1992
My Father, the Hero 1994
**My Father's Angel,** pg. 345
My Father's Glory 1991
My Favorite Martian 1999
My Favorite Season 1996
My Favorite Year 1982
My Fellow Americans 1996
**My First Mister,** pg. 346
My First Wife 1985
My Foolish Heart (1949) 1983
My Giant 1998
My Girl 1991
My Girl II 1994
My Heroes Have Always Been
Cowboys 1991
My Left Foot 1989
My Life 1993
My Life and Times with
Antonin Artaud 1996
My Life as a Dog [1985] 1987
My Life in Pink. *See* Ma Vie en
Rose.
My Life So Far 1999
My Life's in Turnaround 1994
My Little Pony 1986
My Mom's a Werewolf 1989
My Mother's Castle 1991
My Mother's Courage
My Name is Joe 1999
My Neighbor Totoro 1993
My New Gun 1992
My New Partner 1985
My Other Husband 1985
My Own Private Idaho 1991
My Reputation [1946] 1984,
1986
My Science Project 1985
My Son the Fanatic 1999
My Sons (Musuko) 1994
My Stepmother Is an Alien
1988
My Sweet Little Village 1986
My True Love, My Wound
1987
My Tutor 1983
My Twentieth Century 1990

My Uncle's Legacy 1990
Mystery, Alaska 1999
Mystery Date 1991
Mystery of Alexina, The 1986
Mystery of Rampo 1995
Mystery of the Wax Museum
[1933] 1986
Mystery Men 1999
Mystery Science Theater 3000:
The Movie 1996
Mystery Train 1989
Mystic Pizza 1988
Myth of Fingerprints, The

Nadine 1987
Nadja 1995
Naked 1993
Naked Cage, The 1986
Naked Gun, The 1988
Naked Gun 2 1/2, The 1991
Naked Gun 33 1/3: The Final
Insult 1994
Naked in New York 1994
Naked Lunch 1991
Name of the Rose, The 1986
Nanou 1988
Napoleon [1927] 1981
Napoleon 1997
Narrow Margin 1990
Nasty Girl, The 1990
Nate and Hayes 1983
National Lampoon's Christmas
Vacation 1989
National Lampoon's Class
Reunion 1982
National Lampoon's European
Vacation 1985
National Lampoon's Loaded
Weapon I 1993
National Lampoon's Senior Trip
1995
National Lampoon's Vacation
1983
National Velvet [1944] 1993
Native Son 1986
Natural, The 1984
Natural Born Killers 1994
Navigator, The 1989
Navy SEALs 1990
Near Dark 1987
Nebo nashevo detstva. *See* Sky
of Our Childhood, The.
Necessary Roughness 1991
Needful Things 1993
Negotiator, The 1998
Neil Simon's Lost in Yonkers
1993
Neil Simon's The Odd Couple
2 1998
Neil Simon's The Slugger's
Wife 1985
Nell 1994
Nell Gwyn [1934] 1983
Nelly & Mr. Arnaud 1996
Nemesis 1993
Nenette et Boni 1997
Neon Bible, The 1995
Nervous Ticks 1994
Net, The 1995
Nettoyoge a Sec. *See* Dry
Cleaning.

Never Been Kissed 1999
Never Cry Wolf 1983
Never Say Never Again 1983
Never Talk to Strangers 1995
Never too Young to Die 1986
Neverending Story, The 1984
Neverending Story II, The 1991
New Adventures of Pippi
Longstocking, The 1988
New Age, The 1994
New Babylon, The [1929] 1983
New Eve, The [1998] 2000
New Jack City 1991
New Jersey Drive 1995
New Kids, The 1985
New Life, A 1988
New Nightmare. *See* Wes
Craven's New Nightmare.
New Rose Hotel 1999
New Year's Day 1989
New York in Short: The Shvitz
and Let's Fall in Love 1994
New York, New York [1977]
1983
New York Stories 1989
Newsies 1992
Newton Boys, The 1998
Next Best Thing, The 2000
Next Friday 2000
Next Karate Kid, The 1994
Next of Kin 1989
Next Stop Greenwich Village
[1976] 1984
Next Stop Wonderland 1998
Next Summer 1986
Next Year if All Goes Well
1983
Niagara Falls 1987
Niagara, Niagara 1998
Nice Girls Don't Explode 1987
Nick and Jane 1997
Nick of Time 1995
**Nico and Dani,** pg. 348
Nico Icon 1996
Niezwykla podroz Balthazara
Kobera. *See* Tribulations of
Balthasar Kober, The.
Night and Day 1994
Night and the City 1992
Night at the Roxbury, A 1998
Night Crossing 1982
Night Falls on Manhattan 1997
Night Friend 1988
Night Game 1989
Night in Heaven, A 1983
Night in the Life of Jimmy
Reardon, A 1988
'night, Mother 1986
Night of the Comet 1984
Night of the Creeps 1986
Night of the Demons II 1994
Night of the Hunter, The
[1955] 1982
Night of the Iguana, The
[1964] 1983
Night of the Living Dead 1990
Night of the Pencils, The 1987
Night of the Shooting Stars,
The 1983
Night on Earth 1992
Night Patrol 1985
Night Shift 1982

Telephone, The 1988
Telling Lies in America 1997
Temp, The 1993
Tempest 1982
Temps Retrouve. *See* Time Regained.
Temptress Moon 1997
Ten Things I Hate About You 1999
10 to Midnight 1983
Tender Mercies 1983
Tenebrae. *See* Unsane.
Tenue de soirée. *See* Ménage.
Tequila Sunrise 1988
Terminal Bliss 1992
Terminal Velocity 1994
Terminator, The 1984
Terminator II 1991
Termini Station 1991
Terminus. *See* End of the Line.
Terms of Endearment 1983
Terror Within, The 1989
Terrorvision 1986
Tess 1981
Test of Love 1985
Testament 1983
Testimony 1987
Tetsuo: The Iron Man 1992
Tex 1982, 1987
Texas Chainsaw Massacre, Part II, The 1986
Texas Comedy Massacre, The 1988
Texas Tenor: The Illinois Jacquet Story 1994
Texasville 1990
Thank You and Good Night 1992
That Championship Season 1982
That Darn Cat 1997
That Night 1993
That Old Feeling 1997
That Sinking Feeling 1984
That Thing You Do! 1996
That Was Then . . . This Is Now 1985
That's Entertainment! III 1994
That's Life! 1986, 1988
Thé au harem d'Archi Ahmed, Le. *See* Tea in the Harem.
Thelma and Louise 1991
Thelonious Monk 1988
Theory of Flight, The 1998
There Goes My Baby 1994
There Goes the Neighborhood 1994
There's Nothing Out There 1992
There's Something About Mary 1998
Theremin: An Electronic Odyssey 1995
They All Laughed 1981
They Call Me Bruce 1982
They Drive by Night [1940] 1982
They Live 1988
They Live by Night [1949] 1981
They Might Be Giants [1971] 1982

They Still Call Me Bruce 1987
They Won't Believe Me [1947] 1987
They're Playing with Fire 1984
Thiassos, O. *See* Traveling Players, The.
Thief 1981
Thief, The 1998
Thief of Hearts 1984
Thieves (Les Voleurs) 1996
Thin Blue Line, The 1988
Thin Line Between Love and Hate, A 1996
Thin Red Line, The 1998
Thing, The 1982
Thing Called Love, The 1994
Things Are Tough All Over 1982
Things Change 1988
Things to Do in Denver When You're Dead 1995
Think Big 1990
Third World Cop [1999] 2000
Thirteen Days 2000
Thirtieth Floor, The 1999
Thirtieth Warrior, The 1999
Thirty Two Short Films About Glenn Gould 1994
Thirty-five Up 1992
Thirty-six Fillette 1988
37, 2 le Matin. *See* Betty Blue.
This Boy's Life 1993
This is My Life 1992
This Is Elvis 1981
This is My Father 1999
This Is Spinal Tap 1984
This World, Then the Fireworks 1997
Thomas and the Magic Railroad 2000
Thomas Crown Affair, The 1999
**Thomas in Love,** pg. 481
Those Who Love Me Can Take the Train 1999
Thou Shalt Not Kill 1988
Thousand Acres, A 1997
Thousand Pieces of Gold 1991
Thrashin' 1986
Three Amigos 1986
Three Brothers 1982
3:15 1986
Three for the Road 1987
Three Fugitives 1989
Three Kinds of Heat 1987
Three Kings 1999
Three Lives & Only One Death 1996
Three Madeleines, The 2000
Three Men and a Baby 1987
Three Men and a Cradle 1986
Three Men and a Little Lady 1990
Three Musketeers, The 1993
Three Ninjas Kick Back 606
Three Ninjas 1992
Three O'Clock High 1987
Three of Hearts 1993
Three Seasons 1999
Three Sisters 1988
3 Strikes 2000

**3000 Miles to Graceland,** pg. 482
Three to Get Ready 1988
Three to Tango 1999
Three Wishes 1995
Threesome 1994
Threshold 1983
Through the Eyes of the Children. *See* 112th and Central.
Through the Olive Trees 1995
Through the Wire 1990
Through the Window 2000
Throw Momma from the Train 1987
Thumbelina. *See* Hans Christian Andersen's Thumbelina.
Thunder Alley 1986
Thunder Island [1963] 680
Thunderheart 1992
THX 1138 [1971] 1984
Thy Kingdom Come . . . Thy Will Be Done 1988
Tian Yu. *See* Xiu Xiu: The Sent Down Girl.
Tie Me Up! Tie Me Down! 1990
Tie That Binds, The 1995
Tieta of Agreste 1999
Tiger Warsaw 1988
**Tigerland,** pg. 484
Tiger's Tale, A 1987
Tigger Movie, The 2000
Tightrope 1984
Til' There Was You 1997
Tillsammans *See* Together.
Time After Time 1983
Time Bandits 1981
Time Code 2000
Time for Drunken Horses, A 2000
Time Indefinite 1994
Time Machine, The [1960] 1983
Time of Destiny, A 1988
**Time of Favor,** pg. 487
Time of the Gypsies 1990
Time Regained [1999] 2000
Time to Die, A 1991
Time to Kill, A 1996
Time Will Tell 1992
Timebomb 1992
Timecop 1994
Timerider 1983
Timothy Leary's Dead 1997
Tin Cup 1996
Tin Men 1987
Titan A.E. 2000
Titanic 1997
Tito and Me 1993
Titus 1999
To Be or Not to Be 1983
To Begin Again. *See* Volver a empezar.
To Die For 1989
To Die For 1995
To Die Standing (Crackdown) 1994
To Gillian on Her 37th Birthday 1996

To Kill a Mockingbird [1962] 1989
To Kill a Priest 1988
To Live 1994
To Live and Die in L.A. 1985, 1986
To Protect Mother Earth 1990
To Render a Life 1994
To Sir with Love [1967] 1992
To Sleep with Anger 1990
To Wong Foo, Thanks for Everything! Julie Newmar 1995
Todo Sobre Mi Madre. *See* All About My Mother.
**Together,** pg. 489
Tokyo Pop 1988
Tokyo-Ga 1985
Tom and Huck 1995
Tom and Jerry 1993
Tom & Viv 1994
Tomb Raider *See* Lara Croft: Tomb Raider.
Tomboy 1985
Tombstone 1993
**Tomcats,** pg. 491
Tommy Boy 1995
Tomorrow [1972] 1983
Tomorrow Never Dies 1997
Tomorrow's a Killer. *See* Prettykill.
Too Beautiful for You 1990
Too Hot to Handle [1938] 1983
Too Much Sun 1991
Too Much 1987
**Too Much Sleep,** pg. 492
Too Outrageous! 1987
Too Scared to Scream 1985
Too Soon to Love [1960] 679
Tootsie 1982
Top Dog 1995
Top Gun 1986
**Top of the Food Chain,** pg. 494
Top Secret 1984
Topio stin omichi. *See* Landscape in the Mist.
Topsy-Turvy 1999
Tora-San Goes to Viena 1989
Torajiro Kamone Uta. *See* Foster Daddy, Tora!
Torch Song Trilogy 1988
Torment 1986
Torn Apart 1990
Torn Curtain [1966] 1984
Torrents of Spring 1990
**Tortilla Soup,** pg. 495
Total Eclipse 1995
Total Recall 1990
Totally F***ed Up 1994
Toto le héros. *See* Toto the Hero.
Toto the Hero 1992
Tottering Lives 1988
Touch 1997
Touch and Go 1986
Touch of a Stranger 1990
Touch of Evil [1958], 1998
Touch of Larceny, A [1959] 1986
Tough Enough 1983